HIPPOCRENE PRACTICAL DICTIONARY

FRENCH-ENGLISH
ENGLISH-FRENCH

Rosalind Williams

D0190796

HIPPOCRENE BOOKS
New York

First Hippocrene Edition, 1983.
© Laurence Urdang Associates, 1982.

Revised Hippocrene Edition with larger type, 1993.

Glossary of Menu Terms and special American usage entries
© Hippocrene Books, 1983

ISBN 0-7818-0178-8

For information, address:
Hippocrene Books, Inc.
171 Madison Avenue
New York, NY 10016

Printed in the United States of America.

Abbreviations/Abréviations

adj adjective, adjectif
admin administration
adv adverb, adverbe
aero aeronautics
aéro aéronautique
anat anatomy, anatomie
arch architecture
art article
astrol astrology, astrologie
astron astronomy, astronomie
auto automobile
aux auxiliary, auxiliaire
bot botany, botanique
chem chemistry
chim chimie
coll colloquial
comm commerce
conj conjunction, conjonction
derog derogatory
econ economics
écon économie
elec electricity
élec électricité
f feminine, féminin
fam familiar, familier
geog geography
géog géographie
geol geology

géol géologie
gramm grammar, grammaire
impol impolite, impoli
interj interjection
invar invariable
m masculine, masculin
math mathematics,
    mathématiques
med medicine
méd médicine
mil military, militaire
n noun, nom
naut nautical, nautique
péj péjoratif
phone telephone
phot photography, photographie
pl plural, pluriel
pol politics, politique
prep preposition, préposition
pron pronoun, pronom
psych psychology, psychologie
rail railways
rel religion
sing singular, singulier
tech technical, technique
v verb, verbe
V vide (see, voir)
zool zoology, zoologie

French pronunciation

ɑ pate [pɑt]

a rame [ram]

ɛ baie [bɛ]

e pré [pre]

i fiche [fiʃ]

ɔ col [kɔl]

o pot [po]

u route [rut]

y vue [vy]

ə me [mə]

ø deux [dø]

œ jeune [ʒœn]

ɑ̃ vent [vɑ̃]

ɛ̃ fin [fɛ̃]

ɔ̃ ton [tɔ̃]

œ̃ brun [brœ̃]

' hibou ['ibu] (no liaison)

b bière [bjɛr]

d dame [dam]

f faîte [fɛt]

g gant [gɑ̃]

h hola [hɔla]

j pierre [pjɛr]

k conte [kɔ̃t]

l lieu [ljø]

m mon [mɔ̃]

n nid [ni]

p poli [pɔli]

r rage [raʒ]

s sein [sɛ̃]

t tube [tyb]

v vite [vit]

w oui [wi]

z zone [zon]

ɥ lui [lɥi]

ʃ chou [ʃu]

ʒ neige [nɛʒ]

ɲ ligne [liɲ]

ŋ parking [parkiŋ]

In French, the stress always falls on the final syllable of a word or group of words.

Prononciation de l'anglais

a hat [hat]
e bell [bel]
i big [big]
o dot [dot]
ʌ bun [bʌn]
u book [buk]
ə alone [ə'loun]
a: card [ka:d]
ə: word [wə:d]
i: team [ti:m]
o: torn [to:n]
u: spoon [spu:n]
ai die [dai]
ei ray [rei]
oi toy [toi]
au how [hau]
ou road [roud]
eə lair [leə]
iə fear [fiə]
uə poor [puə]
b back [bak]
d dull [dʌl]
f find [faind]

g gaze [geiz]
h hop [hop]
j yell [jel]
k cat [kat]
l life [laif]
m mouse [maus]
n night [nait]
p pick [pik]
r rose [rouz]
s sit [sit]
t toe [tou]
v vest [vest]
w week [wi:k]
z zoo [zu:]
θ think [θiŋk]
ð those [ðouz]
ʃ shoe [ʃu:]
ʒ treasure ['treʒə]
tʃ chalk [tʃo:k]
dʒ jump [dʒʌmp]
ŋ sing [siŋ]

Le signe ' est placé devant la syllabe qui porte l'accent tonique.
Le signe ˌ est placé devant la syllabe qui porte l'accent secondaire.

Guide to the dictionary

Irregular plural forms are shown at the headword and in the text. The following categories of French plural forms are considered regular:

main	mains
prix	prix
cheval	chevaux
feu	feux
seau	seaux

Irregular feminine forms of adjectives are shown at the headword and in the text. The following categories are considered regular:

brun	brune
digne	digne
précieux	précieuse
vif	vive
artificiel	artificielle
ancien	ancienne
premier	première

Irregular verbs marked with an asterisk in the headword list are listed in the verb tables, with the following exceptions:

For verbs ending in -aindre, -eindre, or -oindre see atteindre.
For verbs ending in -aître (except naître) see connaître.
For verbs ending in -cevoir see apercevoir.
For verbs ending in -clure see conclure.
For verbs ending in -crire see écrire.
For verbs ending in -entir (also dormir, partir, servir, sortir) see mentir.
For verbs ending in -quérir see acquérir.
For verbs ending in -uire (except luire, nuire) see conduire.

Adverbs are shown only if their formation is irregular. English adverbs are considered regular if they are formed by adding -ly to the adjective. French adverbs are considered regular if they are formed by adding -ment to the feminine form of the adjective.

Guide au dictionnaire

Les formes irrégulières au pluriel sont indiquées après le mot cherché et dans le texte. Les catégories suivantes des formes plurielles sont considérées régulières en anglais:

cat	cats
glass	glasses
fly	flies
half	halves
wife	wives

Les formes irrégulières des adjectifs au féminin sont indiquées après le mot cherché et dans le texte. Les catégories suivantes des formes féminines sont considérées régulières:

brun	brune
digne	digne
precieux	précieuse
vif	vive
artificiel	artificielle
ancien	ancienne
premier	première

Les verbes irréguliers se trouvant dans la liste des verbes sont marqués d'un astérisque dans la liste des mots du dictionnaire.

Les adverbes se construisant régulièrement ne sont pas indiqués. Les adverbes anglais sont considérés réguliers s'ils sont construits en ajoutant -*ly* à l'adjectif. Les adverbes français sont considérés réguliers s'ils sont construits en ajoutant -*ment* à la forme féminine de l'adjectif.

French irregular verbs

Infinitive	Present	Imperfect	Past Participle	Future
absoudre	absous	absolvais	absous	absoudrai
acquérir	acquiers	acquérais	acquis	acquerrai
aller	vais	allais	allé	irai
apercevoir	aperçois	apercevais	aperçu	apercevrai
assaillir	assaille	assaillais	assailli	assaillirai
asseoir	assieds	asseyais	assis	assiérai
atteindre	atteins	atteignais	atteint	atteindrai
avoir	ai	avais	eu	aurai
battre	bats	battais	battu	battrai
boire	bois	buvais	bu	boirai
bouillir	bous	bouillais	bouilli	bouillirai
braire	brais	brayais	brait	brairai
circoncire	circoncis	circoncisais	circoncis	circoncirai
clore	clos		clos	clorai
conclure	conclus	concluais	conclu	conclurai
conduire	conduis	conduisais	conduit	conduirai
confire	confis	confisais	confit	confirai
connaître	connais	connaissais	connu	connaîtrai
coudre	couds	cousais	cousu	coudrai
courir	cours	courais	couru	courrai
couvrir	couvre	couvrais	couvert	couvrirai
croire	crois	croyais	cru	croirai
croître	croîs	croissais	crû	croîtrai
cueillir	cueille	cueillais	cueilli	cueillerai
devoir	dois	devais	dû	devrai
dire	dis	disais	dit	dirai
dissoudre	dissous	dissolvais	dissous	dissoudrai
échoir	il échoit		échu	il échoira
écrire	écris	écrivais	écrit	écrirai
envoyer	envoie	envoyais	envoyé	enverrai
être	suis	étais	été	serai
faillir			failli	faillirai
faire	fais	faisais	fait	ferai
falloir	il faut	il fallait	fallu	il faudra
foutre	fous	foutais	foutu	foutrai
frire	fris		frit	frirai
fuir	fuis	fuyais	fui	fuirai

Infinitive	Present	Imperfect	Past Participle	Future
gésir	gis	gisais		
haïr	hais	haïssais	haï	haïrai
importer	il importe			
lire	lis	lisais	lu	lirai
luire	luis	luisais	lui	luirai
maudire	maudis	maudissais	maudit	maudirai
mentir	mens	mentais	menti	mentirai
mettre	mets	mettais	mis	mettrai
moudre	mouds	moulais	moulu	moudrai
mourir	meurs	mourais	mort	mourrai
mouvoir	meus	mouvais	mû	mouvrai
naître	nais	naissais	né	naîtrai
nuire	nuis	nuisais	nui	nuirai
offrir	offre	offrais	offert	offrirai
ouïr	ois	oyais	ouï	oirrai
ouvrir	ouvre	ouvrais	ouvert	ouvrirai
plaire	plais	plaisais	plu	plairai
pleuvoir	il pleut	il pleuvait	plu	il pleuvra
pouvoir	peux *or* puis	pouvais	pu	pourrai
prendre	prends	prenais	pris	prendrai
résoudre	résous	résolvais	résolu	résoudrai
rire	ris	riais	ri	rirai
savoir	sais	savais	su	saurai
seoir	il sied	il seyait		
souffrir	souffre	souffrais	souffert	souffrirai
suffire	suffis	suffisais	suffi	suffirai
suivre	suis	suivais	suivi	suivrai
surseoir	sursois	sursoyais	sursis	surseoirai
taire	tais	taisais	tu	tairai
tenir	tiens	tenais	tenu	tiendrai
traire	trais	trayais	trait	trairai
tressaillir	tressaille	tressaillais	tressailli	tressaillirai
vaincre	vaincs	vainquais	vaincu	vaincrai
valoir	vaux	valais	valu	vaudrai
venir	viens	venais	venu	viendrai
vêtir	vêts	vêtais	vêtu	vêtirai
vivre	vis	vivais	vécu	vivrai
voir	vois	voyais	vu	verrai
vouloir	veux	voulais	voulu	voudrai

Verbes irréguliers anglais

Infinitif	Prétérit	Participe Passé	Infinitif	Prétérit	Participe Passé
abide	abode	abode	**deal**	dealt	dealt
arise	arose	arisen	**dig**	dug	dug
awake	awoke	awoken	**do**	did	done
be	was	been	**draw**	drew	drawn
bear	bore	borne	**dream**	dreamed	dreamed
		or born		*or* dreamt	*or* dreamt
beat	beat	beaten	**drink**	drank	drunk
become	became	become	**drive**	drove	driven
begin	began	begun	**dwell**	dwelt	dwelt
behold	beheld	beheld	**eat**	ate	eaten
bend	bent	bent	**fall**	fell	fallen
bet	bet	bet	**feed**	fed	fed
beware			**feel**	felt	felt
bid	bid	bidden	**fight**	fought	fought
		or bid	**find**	found	found
bind	bound	bound	**flee**	fled	fled
bite	bit	bitten	**fling**	flung	flung
bleed	bled	bled	**fly**	flew	flown
blow	blew	blown	**forbid**	forbade	forbidden
break	broke	broken	**forget**	forgot	forgotten
breed	bred	bred	**forgive**	forgave	forgiven
bring	brought	brought	**forsake**	forsook	forsaken
build	built	built	**freeze**	froze	frozen
burn	burnt	burnt	**get**	got	got
	or burned	*or* burned	**give**	gave	given
burst	burst	burst	**go**	went	gone
buy	bought	bought	**grind**	ground	ground
can	could		**grow**	grew	grown
cast	cast	cast	**hang**	hung	hung
catch	caught	caught		*or* hanged	*or* hanged
choose	chose	chosen	**have**	had	had
cling	clung	clung	**hear**	heard	heard
come	came	come	**hide**	hid	hidden
cost	cost	cost	**hit**	hit	hit
creep	crept	crept	**hold**	held	held
cut	cut	cut	**hurt**	hurt	hurt

Infinitif	Prétérit	Participe Passé	Infinitif	Prétérit	Participe Passé
keep	kept	kept	say	said	said
kneel	knelt	knelt	see	saw	seen
knit	knitted	knitted	seek	sought	sought
	or knit	or knit	sell	sold	sold
know	knew	known	send	sent	sent
lay	laid	laid	set	set	set
lead	led	led	sew	sewed	sewn
lean	leant	leant			or sewed
	or leaned	or leaned	shake	shook	shaken
leap	leapt	leapt	shear	sheared	sheared
	or leaped	or leaped			or shorn
learn	learnt	learnt	shed	shed	shed
	or learned	or learned	shine	shone	shone
leave	left	left	shoe	shod	shod
lend	lent	lent	shoot	shot	shot
let	let	let	show	showed	shown
lie	lay	lain	shrink	shrank	shrunk
light	lit	lit	shut	shut	shut
	or lighted	or lighted	sing	sang	sung
lose	lost	lost	sink	sank	sunk
make	made	made	sit	sat	sat
may	might		sleep	slept	slept
mean	meant	meant	slide	slid	slid
meet	met	met	sling	slung	slung
mow	mowed	mown	slink	slunk	slunk
must			slit	slit	slit
ought			smell	smelt	smelt
pay	paid	paid		or smelled	or smelled
put	put	put	sow	sowed	sown
quit	quitted	quitted			or sowed
	or quit	or quit	speak	spoke	spoken
read	read	read	speed	sped	sped
rid	rid	rid		or speeded	or speeded
ride	rode	ridden	spell	spelt	spelt
ring	rang	rung		or spelled	or spelled
rise	rose	risen	spend	spent	spent
run	ran	run	spill	spilt	spilt
saw	sawed	sawn		or spilled	or spilled
		or sawed	spin	spun	spun

Infinitif	Prétérit	Participe Passé	Infinitif	Prétérit	Participe Passé
spit	spat	spat	**swim**	swam	swum
spilt	split	split	**swing**	swung	swung
spread	spread	spread	**take**	took	taken
spring	sprang	sprung	**teach**	taught	taught
stand	stood	stood	**tear**	tore	torn
steal	stole	stolen	**tell**	told	told
stick	stuck	stuck	**think**	thought	thought
sting	stung	stung	**throw**	threw	thrown
stink	stank	stunk	**thrust**	thrust	thrust
	or stunk		**tread**	trod	trodden
stride	strode	stridden	**wake**	woke	woken
strike	struck	struck	**wear**	wore	worn
string	strung	strung	**weave**	wove	woven
strive	strove	striven	**weep**	wept	wept
swear	swore	sworn	**win**	won	won
sweep	swept	swept	**wind**	wound	wound
swell	swelled	swollen	**wring**	wrung	wrung
		or swelled	**write**	wrote	written

Glossary of menu terms

France is the home of the most elegant cooking in the world. French-speaking people take eating seriously, and visitors can find a great variety of good food in many different kinds of eating establishments. **Cafés, restaurants, bistros, charcuteries** (delicatessens), and that popular import from the United States, **le drugstore,** can provide nourishment almost around the clock. French meals are **petit déjeuner** (breakfast), **déjeuner** (lunch), and **diner** (dinner). Breakfast is usually only coffee and a roll; if you need more sustenance, stock up on fruit and cheese from a food store the night before. Lunch and dinner are both large meals. If you aren't up to both, eat from a delicatessen or market for one of them.

Menus will list **hors d'oeuvre** (appetizers); **potages** or **soupes** (soups); **entrées** (main courses) including **poissons** (fish), **volailles** (poultry), **oeufs** (eggs), and **viandes** (meats); **légumes** (vegetables); and **entremets** (desserts). **Volailles** usually means chicken (**poulet**) but may include duck (**canard**), or quail (**cailles**) or one of many other birds; if you're fussy, ask. Desserts may also include cheeses (**fromages**) and fruits and so on (**fruits et les autres**).

A complete meal (not including drinks and tip) at a set price is **prix fixe.** A tip is called **service** and is either **compris** (included on the check) or **pas compris** (not included). Look at the menu or the sign on the café wall to see which way the establishment works. In a restaurant serving both ways, you must pay extra for drinks on the **à la carte** menu, but the **service** is usually **compris.**

Hors d'Oeuvre (Appetizers, but sometimes served as main courses as well)

artichaut entier whole artichoke

assiette de charcuterie cold cuts that most Americans will recognize in the Italian version as antipasto, but meat only in France

assiette de crudités raw sliced vegetables, often served with an oil and vinegar sauce or dip

caviar sturgeon caviar; expensive

céleri remoulade celery with a mayonnaise sauce (anything *remoulade* is in a mayonnaise sauce)

champignons à la greque mushrooms with an oil, vinegar, and herb dressing

coeur de palmier hearts of palm

coquilles au crabe, or **colin,** or **langouste,** or **saumon** medallions of crab, or hake, or spiny lobster, or salmon garnished with mayonnaise

coquilles St. Jacques bay scallops in creamy sauce served in large scallop shells

escargots snails, usually dressed in herb or butter or cognac sauce and served in their shells

feuilles de vigne vine leaves stuffed with rice

filets de hareng de la baltique crème herring in sour cream

moules remoulade mussels in mayonnaise sauce

oeufs de lumps lumpfish caviar; less expensive than **caviar**

pâté finely chopped meat cooked with a variety of other ingredients and spices

pâté imperial egg roll in the Vietnamese style (Vietnamese food is to French as Chinese is to American)

quiche non-sweet custard in a pastry shell with any of many ingredients: spinach, bacon, onion

salade niçoise anchovies, eggs, black and green olives, peppers, tomatoes, green beans, and usually tuna; a very

popular dish, ubiquitous in **charcuteries**
salade piemontaine like salade niçoise except with radishes instead of anchovies
salade verte green salad; also served as a side dish with the main course or, more rarely, as a last course
sardines à l'huile sardines in oil (**huile** is oil)
saucissons sausages: **à l'ail,** with garlic; **sec,** dry (actually rather moist and tender)
saucissons chaud lyonnais hot sausages Lyonnais style, which means they are usually white
saumon fumé smoked salmon or lox, very popular and expensive
terrine de canard sauvage wild smoked duck pâté
le thon mayonnaise tuna with mayonnaise, or, tunafish salad

Potages or Soupes (Soups)

bisque shellfish soup
bouillabaisse fish and shellfish stew
bouillon any clear soup stock
consommé de volaille chicken soup (clear)
consommé madrilène chicken stock flavored with tomato juice, lemon rind, and spices
petite marmite hearty soup of chicken, beef, and vegetables
potage crème Saint-Germain cream of pea soup
sorbet tomate gazpacho-type soup
soup à l'oignon onion soup
vichyssoise cream of leek and potato soup, usually served cold; pronounce the last "s"

Entrées (Main Courses)

Poissons (Fish)

bar bass
crevettes shrimp
daurade gilthead bream, a popular fish with white flesh and a delicate taste

filet de maquerreaux mackerel filet
filet de sole the one and only
grenouilles frogs' legs
homard lobster
limande meunière lemon sole or flounder sautéed in oil and butter
poire d'avocat au crabe avocado stuffed with crab meat
raie skatefish: **au beurre noir** (browned butter and vinegar sauce); **au beurre blanc** (butter sauce with shallots and spices)
truite au bleu de meunière trout in oil and butter
turbot also called turbot in English, but not usually available in the U.S.; light, white-fleshed salt-water fish

Volailles (Poultry)

cailles aux raisins quail with raisins, a popular recipe for these tiny birds, usually served two to an order
caneton aux cerises duckling with cherries
coq au vin chicken with vegetables in red wine sauce
coquelet sauté sautéed baby rooster
fricassé de volailles aux cepes wings and backs of a bird cooked with mushrooms
pardix partridge
poulet à la Kiev chicken Kiev
poulet imperial Vietnamese chicken
poulet rôti au froid chicken roasted on a rotisserie and served cold

Oeufs (Eggs)

oeufs à la coque boiled eggs; **brouillé** (scrambled); **en gelée** (in aspic, often a first course); **sur le plat** (fried)

Viandes (Meats)

bifteck steak: **entrecôte** (usually a good cut); **pavé** (a thick steak often served **au poivre,** with pepper and very spicy);

filet mignon (same as in English); **à l'échalote** (with shallots); **chateau briant frite** (chateaubriand with French-fried potatoes — most steaks are served with French-fried potatoes automatically in France); **steak tartare** or **cru** (raw chopped steak); **steak frites** (fried) is the national dish; **bleu** means meat is still almost raw, just heated up; **saignant** is rare; **au point** is medium; **bien cuit** is well done; French restaurants have difficulty cooking **au point** steaks

boeuf burguignonne stew of beef chunks, vegetables and burgundy wine sauce

boeuf en gelée sliced beef in a jelled sauce

boeuf Stroganoff same as in English
boudin blood sausage

brochette de mouton shish kebab: mutton on a skewer, broiled

carre de porc florentine ribs of pork in the Italian style with spinach and cheese

jambon ham: **Parme** (red and uncooked); **de Prague** (Polish); other varieties are named for the place they were made, such as Virginia, York, and various French provinces

jarret de veau veal knuckles, sometimes **au citron** (with lemon)

l'andouillette intestines of pork, often mixed with other parts of the animal — liver, heart — and chopped and wrapped into a sausage

l'escalope panne spaghetti filet, rib, or leg of an animal with spaghetti

lapin en papilotte rabbit cooked wrapped in paper or foil

osso bucco Italian dish of braised chucks of meat

pieds de porc pigs' feet

tournedos de veau medallions of veal, usually broiled or sautéed

les tripes au vin blanc tripe (usually pork) in white wine

vol au vent de ris de veau veal sweetbreads served in pastry shell

Légumes (Vegetables)

asperges fraiches fresh asparagus
choux blanc; choux rouge white or red cabbage
concombres cucumbers
girolles one of many varieties of mushrooms
haricots rouges; haricots verts kidney beans and string beans
maïs corn
petits pois tiny green peas
poireaux leeks, often served **vinaigrette** as an appetizer
pommes mayonnaise potato salad
radis beurre radishes with butter and salt
vapeur riz steamed or boiled rice

Entremets (Desserts)

crème caramel caramel custard
crème chantilly whipped cream lightly sweetened
crème fraiche slightly soured sweet cream
crème de marrons pureed chestnuts in cream
gâteau cake
glaces ice creams
meringue glaces chantilly meringue filled with chocolate ice cream and topped with whipped cream
omelette norvegienne baked Alaska
pêche ou banane melba poached peach or banana with vanilla ice cream, raspberry puree, and kirsch
poire belle Hélène pear with ice cream, a cookie, and hot chocolate sauce
profiterolles au chocolate cream puffs filled with ice cream and covered with chocolate sauce; supposedly Napoleon's favorite dessert
salade au citron green salad dressed with sliced lemon dressing; refreshing after a big meal
sorbets sherbets
tarte aux fruits fruit tarts: small pastries filled with custard and topped with glazed fruits

Fromages (Cheeses)

Cheeses are almost always offered as dessert in cafés and restaurants. Among the great varieties of cheeses commonly offered are: Camembert, Cantal, Gruyère, St. Paulin, Pont l'Eveque, Gorgonzola, Munster, Brie de Meaux, and a special favorite with the French, goat cheese under the blanket name of Chèvre. **Fromage aux herbes** is mild white cheese with various herbs.

Fruits

ananas pineapple; **l'ananas au sirop** (pineapple in syrup)
fraises strawberries
framboises raspberries
melon nature plain melon in season

pamplemousse grapefruit
plum au rhum plum in rum sauce
poire au vin rouge pear poached in red wine
prunneaux au sirop prunes in syrup

Boissons (Drinks)

Restaurants have a variety of **vin** (wine), usually including house liters and demi-liters of Beaujolais, côte de Rhone, and others. After-dinner **liqueurs** are also called **digestifs** and **plus cafés.** Ask for **de l'eau** for a glass or carafe of water. **De l'eau mineral** is mineral water, a popular alternative to wine with dinner. Common French brands include Perrier, Vittel, Vichy, and Evian.

Note: Sometimes you will see a cooking style noted on a menu that puzzles even the French. Some regions of France are used to connote a style known primarily to the chef. Or there are simply esoteric designations, such as **Limousin** (done with onions, shallots, mushrooms, and seasonings). If you know some of the basic words for French foods, you will be able to understand an explanation by restaurant employees.

English—Français

A

a [ə], an art un, une.
aback [ə'bak] adv be taken aback être déconcerté.
abandon [ə'bandən] v abandonner; (hope, etc.) renoncer à.
abashed [ə'baʃt] adj décontenancé, confus.
abate [ə'beit] v (storm) s'apaiser; (fever) baisser; (courage) diminuer. abatement n suppression f; réduction f.
abattoir ['abətwɑ] n abattoir m.
abbey ['abi] n abbaye f. abbess n abbesse f. abbot n abbé m.
abbreviate [ə'briːvieit] v abréger. abbreviation n abréviation f.
abdicate ['abdikeit] v (king, etc.) abdiquer; (give up) renoncer à. abdication n abdication f; renonciation f.
abdomen ['abdəmən] n abdomen m. abdominal adj abdominal.
abduct [əb'dʌkt] v enlever. abduction n enlèvement m.
aberration [abə'reiʃən] n aberration f. aberrant adj aberrant.
abet [ə'bet] v encourager. abettor n complice m, f.
abeyance [ə'beiəns] n be in abeyance rester en suspens. fall into abeyance tomber en désuétude.
abhor [əb'hɔː] v abhorrer. abhorrence n horreur f. abhorrent adj odieux.
*abide [ə'baid] v (tolerate) supporter. abide by (rule) se conformer à; (promise) rester fidèle à.
ability [ə'biləti] n capacité f; talent m. to the best of one's ability de son mieux.
abject [,abdʒekt] adj abject; misérable; (apology) servile. in abject poverty dans la misère noire.

ablaze [ə'bleiz] adv, adj en feu.
able ['eibl] adj capable. be able pouvoir; (know how to) savoir. able-bodied adj robuste.
abnormal [ab'nɔːml] adj anormal. abnormality n anomalie f; malformation f.
aboard [ə'bɔːd] adv à bord. prep à bord de. go aboard s'embarquer.
abode [ə'boud] V abide. n demeure f; (law) domicile m.
abolish [ə'boliʃ] v abolir; supprimer. abolition n abolition f; suppression f.
abominable [ə'bominəbl] adj abominable. abomination n abomination f.
Aborigine [abə'ridʒini] n aborigène m, f.
abort [ə'bɔːt] v avorter. abortion n avortement m. have an abortion se faire avorter. abortive adj manqué.
abound [ə'baund] v abonder.
about [ə'baut] adv (approximately) vers, environ; (here and there) çà et là; (around) autour. prep (concerning) au sujet de; (around) autour de. about to sur le point de. what is it about? de quoi s'agit-il?
above [ə'bʌv] adv, prep au-dessus (de). above all surtout. above-mentioned adj ci-dessus.
abrasion [ə'breiʒən] n frottement m; (med) écorchure f. abrasive nm, adj abrasif.
abreast [ə'brest] adv de front. keep abreast of se tenir au courant de.
abridge [ə'bridʒ] v abréger. abridgment n résumé m.
abroad [ə'brɔːd] adv à l'étranger.
abrupt [ə'brʌpt] adj soudain; brusque; (slope) abrupt.
abscess ['abses] n abscès m.
abscond [əb'skond] v s'enfuir.
absent ['absənt] adj absent. absent-minded adj distrait. absent-mindedness n distraction f. absence n absence f. in the

absence of faute de. **absentee** n absent,
-e m, f.
absolute ['absəluɪt] adj absolu; complet,
-ète. **absolutely** adv absolument, tout à
fait.
absolve [əb'zolv] v absoudre; (law)
acquitter. **absolution** n absolution f.
absorb [əb'zoɪb] v absorber. **absorbent** adj
absorbant. **absorbing** adj (book, etc.)
passionnant. **absorption** n absorption f.
abstain [əb'stein] v s'abstenir. **abstention**
n abstention f. **abstinence** n abstinence f.
abstract ['abstrakt; v ab'strakt] adj
abstrait. n abstrait m; résumé m. v isoler.
abstraction n (removal) extraction f;
(absent-mindedness) distraction f; (concept) abstraction f.
absurd [əb'səɪd] adj absurde.
abundance [ə'bʌndəns] n abondance f.
abundant adj abondant. **abundantly** adv
abondamment; (grow) à foison; (completely) tout à fait.
abuse [ə'bjuɪz; n ə'bjuɪs] v (misuse) abuser
de; (insult) injurier, insulter. n abus m;
insultes f pl. **abusive** adj abusif;
injurieux.
abyss [ə'bis] n abîme m.
academy [ə'kadəmi] n académie f. **academic** adj académique; théorique; (studies) scolaire, universitaire.
accede [ak'siɪd] v **accede to** agréer.
accelerate [ak'seləreit] v accélérer. **acceleration** n accélération f. **accelerator** n
accélérateur m.
accent ['aksənt] n accent m. v also **accentuate** accentuer.
accept [ak'sept] v accepter. **acceptable** adj
acceptable. **acceptance** n acceptation f;
approbation f.
access ['akses] n accès m. **accessible** adj
accessible. **accession** n accession f; (to
throne) avènement m.
accessory [ak'sesəri] nm, adj accessoire.
accident ['aksidənt] n accident m. **by accident** par hasard. **accidental** adj
accidentel.
acclaim [ə'kleim] v acclamer. n also **acclamation** acclamation f.
acclimatize [ə'klaimətaiz] v acclimater;
habituer.
accolade ['akəleid] n accolade f.
accommodate [ə'komədeit] v loger;
(adapt) accommoder. **accommodating** adj
obligeant. **accommodation** n logement m,
chambres f pl.

accompany [ə'kʌmpəni] v accompagner.
accompaniment n accompagnement m.
accompanist n accompagnateur, -trice m,
f.
accomplice [ə'kʌmplis] n complice m, f.
accomplish [ə'kʌmpliʃ] v accomplir; réaliser. **accomplished** adj (skilled) doué;
accompli. **accomplishment** n accomplissement m; talent m.
accord [ə'koɪd] v (s')accorder. n accord m.
of one's own accord de son plein gré.
accordance n conformité f. **in accordance
with** conformément à. **according to** selon.
accordion [ə'koɪdiən] n accordéon m.
accost [ə'kost] v accoster.
account [ə'kaunt] n compte m; (report)
exposé m. **on account of** à cause de. **on
no account** en aucun cas. **take into
account** tenir compte de. v **account for**
justifier; expliquer. **accountant** n comptable m, f.
accrue [ə'kruɪ] v revenir; s'accumuler.
accrued interest intérêt couru m.
accumulate [ə'kjuɪmjuleit] v
(s')accumuler. **accumulation** n accumulation f.
accurate ['akjurət] adj exact, précis. **accuracy** n exactitude f, précision f.
accuse [ə'kjuɪz] v accuser. **accusation** n
accusation f. **accusing** adj accusateur,
-trice.
accustom [ə'kʌstəm] v habituer.
ace [eis] n as m.
ache [eik] v faire mal. n douleur f.
achieve [ə'tʃiɪv] v (task) accomplir; (aim)
atteindre. **achievement** n (feat) exploit
m; (completion) exécution f.
acid ['asid] nm, adj acide.
acknowledge [ak'nolidʒ] v reconnaître;
(letter, etc.) accuser réception de, répondre à. **acknowledgment** n reconnaissance
f; (of error) aveu m; (receipt) reçu m.
acne ['akni] n acné f.
acorn ['eikoɪn] n gland m.
acoustic [ə'kuɪstik] adj acoustique. **acoustics** pl n acoustique f sing.
acquaint [ə'kweint] v (inform) aviser.
acquaint with mettre au courant de. **be
acquainted with** (a fact) savoir; (a place
or person) connaître. **become acquainted
with** faire la connaissance de. **acquaintance** n connaissance f, relation f.
acquiesce [akwi'es] v acquiescer. **acquiescence** n consentement m.

acquire [ə'kwaɪə] v acquérir; prendre. **acquired taste** goût qui s'acquiert m. **acquisition** n acquisition f. **acquisitive** adj âpre au gain.

acquit [ə'kwit] v acquitter. **acquittal** n acquittement m.

acrid ['akrid] adj âcre; (biting) acerbe. **acrimony** ['akrɪmənɪ] n acrimonie f. **acrimonious** adj acrimonieux.

acrobat ['akrəbat] n acrobate m, f. **acrobatic** adj acrobatique. **acrobatics** pl n acrobatie f sing.

across [ə'kros] prep en travers de, à travers; de l'autre côté. adv (width) de large. **go across** traverser.

acrylic [ə'krilik] adj acrylique.

act [akt] n acte m, action f; (law) loi f; (theatre) acte m. **in the act of** en train de. v agir; (theatre) jouer. **act the fool** faire l'idiot. **acting** adj (temporary) suppléant, par intérim. **actor** n acteur m. **actress** n actrice f.

action ['akʃən] n action f; (law) procès m; (mil) combat m. **out of action** hors d'usage.

active ['aktiv] adj actif. **activate** v activer. **activity** n activité f.

actual ['aktʃuəl] adj réel; (factual) positif. **actually** adv effectivement; à vrai dire.

actuary ['aktjuərɪ] n actuaire m.

acumen [ə'kjuːmen] n perspicacité f.

acupuncture ['akjupʌŋktʃə] n acupuncture f.

acute [ə'kjuːt] adj aigu, -guë; (mind) pénétrant; (pain, etc.) vif.

adamant ['adəmənt] adj inflexible.

Adam's apple [adəm'zapl] n pomme d'Adam f.

adapt [ə'dapt] v (s')adapter. **adaptable** adj adaptable. **adaptation** n adaptation f. **adaptor** n (elec) prise multiple f.

add [ad] v ajouter; (numbers) additionner. **addition** n addition f. **in addition** de plus. **in addition to** en plus de. **additional** adj additionnel; supplémentaire.

addendum [ə'dendəm] n addendum m invar.

adder ['adə] n vipère f.

addict ['adikt; v ə'dikt] n (drugs) toxicomane m, f; fanatique m, f. v **become addicted to** s'adonner à. **addiction** n (med) dépendance f.

additive ['aditiv] nm, adj additif.

address [ə'dres] n adresse f; (talk) discours m. v (s')adresser (à).

adenoids ['adənoidz] pl n végétations adénoïdes f pl.

adept [ə'dept] adj expert, versé.

adequate ['adikwət] adj suffisant.

adhere [əd'hiə] v adhérer. **adherent** n adhérent, -e m, f. **adhesion** n adhérence f. **adhesive** nm, adj adhésif.

adjacent [ə'dʒeisənt] adj adjacent, contigu, -guë.

adjective ['adʒiktiv] n adjectif m.

adjoin [ə'dʒoin] v être contigu à. **adjoining** adj voisin.

adjourn [ə'dʒəɪn] v ajourner; (meeting) suspendre la séance; (move) se retirer.

adjudicate [ə'dʒuːdikeit] v juger. **adjudication** n jugement m. **adjudicator** n juge m.

adjust [ə'dʒʌst] v ajuster; (s')adapter; (correct) régler. **adjustment** n réglage m.

ad-lib ['ad'lib] adv à volonté. v improviser.

administer [əd'ministə] v administrer; (business, etc.) gérer. **administration** n administration f; gestion f. **administrative** adj administratif. **administrator** n administrateur, -trice m, f.

admiral ['admərəl] n amiral m. **Admiralty** n ministère de la Marine m.

admire [əd'maiə] v admirer. **admirable** adj admirable. **admiration** n admiration f. **admiring** adj admiratif.

admit [əd'mit] v (let in) laisser entrer; (acknowledge) admettre. **admission** n admission f.

adolescence [adə'lesns] n adolescence f. **adolescent** n, adj adolescent, -e.

adopt [ə'dopt] v adopter. **adopted** adj (child) adoptif. **adoption** n adoption f.

adore [ə'doɪ] v adorer. **adorable** adj adorable. **adoration** n adoration f.

adorn [ə'doin] v orner, parer.

adrenalin [ə'drenəlin] n adrénaline f.

adrift [ə'drift] adv à la dérive. **come adrift** (wire, etc.) se détacher.

adroit [ə'droit] adj adroit.

adulation [adju'leiʃən] n adulation f.

adult ['adʌlt] n(m + f), adj adulte.

adulterate [ə'dʌltəreit] v adultérer, falsifier.

adultery [ə'dʌltərɪ] n adultère m. **adulterer** n adultère m, f.

advance [əd'vaɪns] v (s')avancer. n avance f. **advance booking office** location f. **book in advance** retenir à l'avance. **luggage in advance** bagages enregistrés m pl.

advantage [əd'vɑːntidʒ] *n* avantage *m*. take advantage of profiter de. **advantageous** *adj* avantageux.

advent ['advənt] *n* venue *f*. Advent *n* (*rel*) Avent *m*.

adventure [əd'ventʃə] *n* aventure *f*. **adventurer** *n* aventurier, -ère *m, f*. **adventurous** *adj* aventureux.

adverb ['advɜːb] *n* adverbe *m*.

adversary ['advəsəri] *n* adversaire *m, f*.

adverse ['advɜːs] *adj* défavorable, hostile.

adversity *n* adversité *f*.

advertise ['advətaiz] *v* (*comm*) faire de la publicité (pour); (*newspaper, etc.*) insérer une annonce. **advertisement** *n* (*comm*) réclame *f*, publicité *f*; (*newspaper*) annonce *f*. **advertising** *n* publicité *f*.

advise [əd'vaiz] *v* conseiller; recommander; (*inform*) aviser. **advice** *n* conseils *m pl*; avis *m*. **advisable** *adj* recommandable. **adviser** *n* conseiller, -ère *m, f*. **advisory** *adj* consultatif.

advocate ['advəkeit] *v* recommander.

aerial ['eəriəl] *adj* aérien. *n* antenne *f*.

aerodynamics [eərədai'namiks] *n* aérodynamique *f*.

aeronautics [eərə'nɔːtiks] *n* aéronautique *f*.

aeroplane ['eərəplein] *n* avion *m*.

aerosol ['eərəsɒl] *n* bombe *f*; (*perfume*) atomiseur *m*.

aesthetic [iːs'θetik] *adj* esthétique.

affair [ə'feə] *n* affaire *f*. have an affair with avoir une liaison avec.

affect[1] [ə'fekt] *v* (*influence*) affecter, toucher.

affect[2] [ə'fekt] *v* (*feign*) affecter, feindre. **affected** *adj* affecté, maniéré.

affection [ə'fekʃən] *n* affection *f*. **affectionate** *adj* affectueux.

affiliate [ə'filieit] *v* affilier. **affiliated company** filiale *f*. **affiliation** *n* affiliation *f*.

affinity [ə'finəti] *n* affinité *f*.

affirm [ə'fɜːm] *v* affirmer. **affirmative** *nm, adj* affirmatif.

affix [ə'fiks; *n* 'afiks] *v* apposer; (*stick*) coller. *n* (*gramm*) affixe *m*.

afflict [ə'flikt] *v* affliger. **affliction** *n* affliction *f*; infirmité *f*.

affluent ['afluənt] *adj* abondant; riche. **affluence** *n* abondance *f*; richesse *f*.

afford [ə'fɔːd] *v* avoir les moyens d'acheter; (*provide*) fournir.

affront [ə'frʌnt] *v* insulter. *n* affront *m*.

afield [ə'fiːld] *adv* far afield très loin. farther afield plus loin.

afloat [ə'flout] *adv* à flot.

afoot [ə'fut] *adv* there's something afoot il se prépare quelque chose.

aforesaid [ə'fɔːsed] *adj* susdit.

afraid [ə'freid] *adj* effrayé. be afraid avoir peur; (*polite regret*) regretter.

afresh [ə'freʃ] *adv* de nouveau. start afresh recommencer.

Africa ['afrikə] *n* Afrique *f*. **African** *adj* africain; *n* Africain, -e *m, f*.

aft [ɑːft] *adv* sur *or* à l'arrière.

after ['ɑːftə] *prep, conj* après. *adv* après; ensuite. **after all** après tout.

after-effect *n* suite *f*.

aftermath ['ɑːftəmæθ] *n* conséquences *f pl*.

afternoon [ˌɑːftə'nuːn] *n* après-midi *m*.

afterthought ['ɑːftəθɔːt] *n* pensée après coup *f*.

afterwards ['ɑːftəwədz] *adv* ensuite.

again [ə'gen] *adv* de nouveau, encore. again and again à plusieurs reprises.

against [ə'genst] *prep* contre. **against the law** contraire à la loi.

age [eidʒ] *n* âge *m*; (*historical*) époque *f*. for ages pendant une éternité. of age majeur, -e. under age mineur, -e. *v* vieillir. **aged** *adj* âgé.

agency ['eidʒənsi] *n* agence *f*, bureau *m*.

agenda [ə'dʒendə] *n* ordre du jour *m*.

agent ['eidʒənt] *n* agent, -e *m, f*; représentant, -e *m, f*.

aggravate ['agrəveit] *v* aggraver; (*increase*) augmenter; (*annoy*) agacer. **aggravation** *n* aggravation *f*; agacement *m*.

aggregate ['agrigət] *n* ensemble *m*. *adj* collectif.

aggression [ə'greʃən] *n* agression *f*. **aggressive** *adj* agressif.

aghast [ə'gɑːst] *adj* atterré.

agile ['adʒail] *adj* agile. **agility** *n* agilité *f*.

agitate ['adʒiteit] *v* (*shake*) agiter; (*worry*) troubler. **agitated** *adj* inquiet, -ète. **agitation** *n* agitation *f*; émotion *f*. **agitator** *n* agitateur, -trice *m, f*.

agnostic [ag'nostik] *n(m+f)*, *adj* agnostique.

ago [ə'gou] *adv* il y a: *il y a deux mois*.

agog [ə'gog] *adj, adv* en émoi. be all agog être impatient.

agony ['agəni] *n* (*mental*) angoisse *f*; (*med*) agonie *f*. be in agony souffrir le martyre. **agonizing** *adj* angoissant.

agree [əˈgriː] v être d'accord; consentir; (concur) convenir, s'accorder. **agreeable** adj agréable. **agreement** n accord m.
agriculture [ˈagrikʌltʃə] n agriculture f. **agricultural** adj agricole.
aground [əˈgraund] adv échoué. **run aground** s'échouer.
ahead [əˈhed] adv en avant; (time) en avance.
aid [eid] v aider. **aid and abet** être complice de. n aide f. **in aid of** au profit de.
aim [eim] v viser; aspirer. n (purpose) but m. **take aim (at)** viser. **aimless** adj (person) sans but; (action) futile.
air [eə] n air m. **by air** par avion. v aérer; (opinion) faire connaître. **airy** adj bien aéré.
airbed [ˈeəbed] n matelas pneumatique m.
airborne [ˈeəbɔin] adj aéroporté. **become airborne** (aircraft) décoller.
air-conditioned adj climatisé. **air-conditioning** n climatisation f.
aircraft [ˈeəkraift] n avion m. **aircraft-carrier** n porte-avions m invar.
airfield [ˈeəfiːld] n terrain d'aviation m.
air force n armée de l'air f.
air-hostess n hôtesse de l'air f.
airing cupboard n placard-séchoir m.
air lift n pont aérien m.
airline [ˈeəlain] n ligne aérienne f.
airmail [ˈeəmeil] n poste aérienne f. **airmail letter** lettre par avion f. **by airmail** par avion.
airport [ˈeəpɔit] n aéroport m.
air-raid n attaque aérienne f. **air-raid shelter** abri antiaérien m.
airtight [ˈeətait] adj hermétique.
aisle [ail] n (church) allée centrale f, bas-côté m; (theatre) passage m; (train, etc.) couloir central m.
ajar [əˈdʒai] adj, adv entrouvert.
akin [əˈkin] adj **be akin to** (resemble) tenir de, ressembler à; (family) être parent de.
alabaster [ˈaləbaistə] n albâtre m.
alarm [əˈlaim] n alarme f. **alarm clock** n réveil m. v alarmer. **alarmist** n alarmiste m, f.
alas [əˈlas] interj hélas!
Albania [alˈbeinjə] n Albanie f. **Albanian** nm, adj albanais; n (people) Albanais, -e m, f.
albatross [ˈalbətros] n albatros m.
albino [alˈbiinou] n albinos m, f.
album [ˈalbəm] n album m.

alchemy [ˈalkəmi] n alchimie f. **alchemist** n alchimiste m.
alcohol [ˈalkəhol] n alcool m. **alcoholic** n(m+f), adj alcoolique. **alcoholism** n alcoolisme m.
alcove [ˈalkouv] n (room) alcôve f; (wall) niche f.
alderman [ˈoildəmən] n conseiller municipal m.
ale [eil] n bière f.
alert [əˈloit] adj alerte; vigilant. n alerte f. **on the alert** sur le qui-vive. v alerter, éveiller l'attention de.
algebra [ˈaldʒibrə] n algèbre f. **algebraic** adj algébrique.
Algeria [alˈdʒiəriə] n Algérie f. **Algerian** n Algérien, -enne m, f; adj algérien.
Algiers [alˈdʒiəz] n Alger.
alias [ˈeiliəs] adv alias. n faux nom m.
alibi [ˈalibai] n alibi m.
alien [ˈeiliən] n, adj étranger, -ère. **alien to** contraire à. **alienate** v aliéner. **alienation** n aliénation f; éloignement m.
alight¹ [əˈlait] v descendre; (bird) se poser.
alight² [əˈlait] adj allumé; en feu. **set alight** mettre le feu à.
align [əˈlain] v (s')aligner. **alignment** n alignement m.
alike [əˈlaik] adj semblable. adv pareillement, de la même façon. **be alike** se ressembler.
alimentary canal [aliˈmentəri] n tube digestif m.
alimony [ˈaliməni] n pension alimentaire f.
alive [əˈlaiv] adj vivant.
alkali [ˈalkəlai] n alcali m. **alkaline** adj alcaline.
all [oil] pron, adj tout, toute (pl tous, toutes). adv tout, complètement. **all right** ça va. **All Saints' Day** le Toussaint. **all the same** tout de même. **not at all** pas du tout.
allay [əˈlei] v apaiser; (suspicion) dissiper.
allege [əˈledʒ] v alléguer. **allegation** n allégation f. **alleged** adj prétendu, allégué; présumé.
allegiance [əˈliidʒəns] n fidélité f.
allegory [ˈaligəri] n allégorie f. **allegorical** adj allégorique.
allergy [ˈalədʒi] n allergie f. **allergic** adj allergique.
alleviate [əˈliivieit] v soulager.
alley [ˈali] n ruelle f.

alliance [ə'laiəns] *n* alliance *f.*

alligator ['aligeitə] *n* alligator *m.*

alliteration [əlitə'reiʃən] *n* allitération *f.*

allocate ['aləkeit] *v* (*allot*) allouer; (*share*) répartir. **allocation** *n* allocation *f;* (*share*) part *f.*

allot [ə'lot] *v* assigner. **allotment** *n* (*land*) parcelle de terre *f.*

allow [ə'lau] *v* permettre; (*give*) accorder. **allow for** tenir compte de. **allowance** *n* allocation *f;* (*subsistence*) indemnité *f,* pension *f;* (*comm*) rabais *m.*

alloy ['aloi; *v* ə'loi] *n* alliage *m. v* allier; faire un alliage de.

allude [ə'luːd] *v* faire allusion. **allusion** *n* allusion *f.*

allure [ə'ljuə] *v* attirer. *n* charme *m.* **alluring** *adj* séduisant.

ally ['alai; *v* ə'lai] *n* allié, -ée *m, f. v* allier. **allied** *adj* allié; (*connected*) apparenté.

almanac ['oːlmənak] *n* almanach *m.*

almighty [oːl'maiti] *adj* tout-puissant; (*coll*) fameux.

almond ['aːmənd] *n* (*nut*) amande *f;* (*tree*) amandier *m.*

almost ['oːlmoust] *adv* presque, à peu près.

alms [aːmz] *n* aumône *f.* **almshouse** *n* hospice *m.*

aloft [ə'loft] *adv* en haut.

alone [ə'loun] *adj, adv* seul. **leave alone** laisser tranquille. **let alone** sans parler de.

along [ə'loŋ] *prep* le long de. **alongside** *prep* à côté de.

aloof [ə'luːf] *adj* distant. *adv* à l'écart.

aloud [ə'laud] *adv* (*reading*) à voix haute; (*think*) tout haut.

alphabet ['alfəbit] *n* alphabet *m.* **alphabetical** *adj* alphabétique. **in alphabetical order** par ordre alphabétique.

already [oːl'redi] *adv* déjà.

Alsatian [al'seiʃən] *n* (*dog*) chien-loup *m.*

also ['oːlsou] *adv* aussi.

altar ['oːltə] *n* autel *m.*

alter ['oːltə] *v* changer; (*dress, etc.*) retoucher. **alteration** *n* changement *m;* retouchage *m.*

alternate [oːl'təːnət; *v* 'oːltəneit] *adj* alternatif, alterné; (*every other*) tous les deux. *v* alterner. **alternating current** courant alternatif *m.* **alternator** *n* alternateur *m.*

alternative [oːl'təːnətiv] *n* (*of two*) alternative *f;* (*of several*) choix *m;* autre solution *f. adj* autre, alternatif.

although [oːl'ðou] *conj* bien que, quoique.

altitude ['altitjuːd] *n* altitude *f.*

alto ['altou] *n* (*male*) haute-contre *f;* (*female*) contralto *m;* (*instrument*) alto *m.*

altogether [oːltə'geðə] *adv* (*completely*) entièrement; (*including everything*) en tout.

altruistic [altru'istik] *adj* altruiste.

aluminium [alju'miniəm] *n* aluminium *m.*

always ['oːlweiz] *adv* toujours.

am [am] *V* be.

amalgamate [ə'malgəmeit] *v* (*companies*) fusionner; (*metals*) amalgamer. **amalgamation** *n* fusionnement *m;* amalgamation *f.*

amass [ə'mas] *v* amasser.

amateur ['amətə] *n* amateur *m.*

amaze [ə'meiz] *v* stupéfier. **amazed** *adj* stupéfait. **amazement** *n* stupéfaction *f.* **amazing** *adj* stupéfiant, ahurissant.

ambassador [am'basədə] *n* ambassadeur *m.*

amber ['ambə] *n* ambre; (*traffic lights*) feu orange *m.*

ambidextrous [ambi'dekstrəs] *adj* ambidextre.

ambiguous [am'bigjuəs] *adj* ambigu, -guë. **ambiguity** *n* ambiguïté *f.*

ambition [am'biʃən] *n* ambition *f.* **ambitious** *adj* ambitieux.

ambivalent [am'bivələnt] *adj* ambivalent. **ambivalence** *n* ambivalence *f.*

amble ['ambl] *v* marcher d'un pas tranquille; (*horse*) ambler. *n* pas tranquille *m;* (*horse*) amble *m.*

ambulance ['ambjuləns] *n* ambulance *f.*

ambush ['ambuʃ] *n* embuscade *f.* **in ambush** en embuscade. *v* attirer dans une embuscade.

ameliorate [ə'miːliəreit] *v* (s')améliorer. **amelioration** *n* amélioration *f.*

amenable [ə'miːnəbl] *adj* (*cooperative*) maniable; (*answerable*) responsable.

amend [ə'mend] *v* (s')amender; (*revise*) modifier; (*correct*) corriger. **amendment** *n* amendement *m;* modification *f.*

amenity [ə'miːnəti] *n* agrément *m.* **amenities** *pl n* commodités *f pl.*

America [ə'merikə] *n* Amérique *f;* (*United States*) Etats-Unis *m pl.* **American** *n* Américain, -e *m, f; adj* américain.

amethyst ['aməθist] *n* améthyste *f.*
amiable ['eimiəbl] *adj* aimable.
amicable ['amikəbl] *adj* amical; *(law)* à l'amiable.
amid [ə'mid] *prep* au milieu de.
amiss [ə'mis] *adv* de travers. *adj* mal à propos. **something is amiss** quelque chose ne va pas.
ammonia [ə'mouniə] *n (gas)* ammoniac *m*; *(liquid)* ammoniaque *f.*
ammunition [amju'niʃən] *n* munitions *f pl.*
amnesia [am'niːziə] *n* amnésie *f.*
amnesty ['amnəsti] *n* amnistie *f.*
amoeba [ə'miːbə] *n* amibe *f.*
among [ə'mʌŋ] *prep* entre, parmi.
amoral [ei'morəl] *adj* amorale.
amorous ['amərəs] *adj* amoureux.
amorphous [ə'moːfəs] *adj* amorphe; *(ideas, etc.)* sans forme.
amount [ə'maunt] *n* quantité *f*; *(total)* montant *m. v* **amount to** s'élever à; *(be equivalent to)* revenir à, équivaloir à.
ampere ['ampeə] *n* ampère *m.*
amphetamine [am'fetəmiːn] *n* amphétamine *f.*
amphibian [am'fibiən] *nm, adj* amphibie. **amphibious** *adj* amphibie.
amphitheatre ['amfiθiətə] *n* amphithéâtre *m.*
ample ['ampl] *adj (plenty)* bien assez de; *(large)* ample.
amplify ['amplifai] *v* amplifier; développer. **amplifier** *n* amplificateur *m.*
amputate ['ampjuteit] *v* amputer. **amputation** *n* amputation *f.*
Amsterdam [amstə'dam] *n* Amsterdam.
amuse [ə'mjuːz] *v (cause laughter)* faire rire; *(entertain)* distraire. **amuse oneself** s'amuser. **amused** *adj* amusé. **amusement** *n* amusement *m*; distraction *f.*
an [ən] *V* a.
anachronism [ə'nakrənizəm] *n* anachronisme *m.* **anachronistic** *adj* anachronique.
anaemia [ə'niːmiə] *n* anémie *f.* **anaemic** *adj* anémique.
anaesthetic [anəs'θetik] *nm, adj* anesthésique. **under anaesthetic** sous anesthésie. **anaesthetist** *n* anesthésiste *m, f.* **anaesthetize** *v* anesthésier.
anagram ['anəgram] *n* anagramme *f.*
anal ['einl] *adj* anal.
analogy [ə'nalədʒi] *n* analogie *f.*
analysis [ən'aləsis] *n* analyse *f.* **analyse** *v*

analyser, faire l'analyse de, **analytical** *adj* analytique.
anarchy ['anəki] *n* anarchie *f.* **anarchist** *n* anarchiste *m, f.*
anathema [ə'naθəmə] *n* anathème *m.* **it is anathema to me** je l'ai en abomination.
anatomy [ə'natəmi] *n (med)* anatomie *f*; structure *f.*
ancestor ['ansestə] *n* ancêtre *m,* aïeul, -e *m, f.* **ancestral** *adj* ancestral. **ancestry** *n* ascendance *f*; ancêtres *m pl,* aïeux *m pl.*
anchor ['aŋkə] *n* ancre *f. v (naut)* (se) mettre à l'ancre; *(fasten)* ancrer.
anchovy ['antʃəvi] *n* anchois *m.*
ancient ['einʃənt] *adj* antique; ancien.
ancillary [an'siləri] *adj* auxiliaire.
and [and] *conj* et.
Andorra [an'dorə] *n* Andorre *f.*
anecdote ['anikdout] *n* anecdote *f.*
anemone [ə'nemoni] *n* anémone *f.*
anew [ə'njuː] *adv* de nouveau.
angel ['eindʒəl] *n* ange *m.* **angelic** *adj* angélique.
angelica [an'dʒelikə] *n* angélique *f.*
anger ['aŋgə] *n* colère *f. v* mettre en colère.
angina [an'dʒainə] *n* angine de poitrine *f.*
angle ['aŋgl] *n* angle *m*; aspect *m.*
angling ['aŋgliŋ] *n* pêche à la ligne *f.* **angler** *n* pêcheur, -euse *m, f.*
angry ['aŋgri] *adj* en colère; furieux. **become angry** se fâcher.
anguish ['aŋgwiʃ] *n* angoisse *f.*
angular ['aŋgjulə] *adj* anguleux.
animal ['animəl] *nm, adj* animal.
animate ['animət; *v* 'animeit] *adj* animé. *v* animer. **animation** *n* animation *f.*
animosity [ani'mosəti] *n* animosité *f.*
aniseed ['anisiːd] *n* graine d'anis *f*; *(as modifier)* à l'anis.
ankle ['aŋkl] *n* cheville *f.*
annals ['anlz] *pl n* annales *f pl.*
annex [ə'neks; *n* 'aneks] *v* annexer. **annexe** *n* annexe *f.*
annihilate [ə'naiəleit] *v (mil)* anéantir; annihiler. **annihilation** *n* anéantissement *m.*
anniversary [ˌani'vəːsəri] *n* anniversaire *m.*
annotate ['anəteit] *v* annoter. **annotation** *n* annotation *f.*
announce [ə'nauns] *v* annoncer. **announcement** *n* annonce *f*; *(official)* avis *m*; *(of birth, etc.)* faire-part *m.* **announcer** *n (radio, TV)* speaker, -erine *m, f.*

annoy [ə'noi] *v* ennuyer, agacer. **annoyance** *n* mécontentement *m*; (*nuisance*) tracas *m*. **annoyed** *adj* mécontent. **annoying** *adj* agaçant, ennuyeux.

annual ['anjuəl] *adj* annuel. *n* (*bot*) plante annuelle *f*; (*children's book*) album *m*.

annul [ə'nʌl] *v* (*marriage*) annuler; (*law*) abroger. **annulment** *n* annulation *f*; abrogation *f*.

anode ['anoud] *n* anode *f*.

anomaly [ə'noməli] *n* anomalie *f*. **anomalous** *adj* anormal.

anonymous [ə'noniməs] *adj* anonyme. **anonymity** *n* anonymat *m*.

anorak ['anərak] *n* anorak *m*.

another [ə'nʌðə] *pron, adj* (*different*) un autre; (*extra*) encore un. **one another** l'un l'autre, les uns les autres.

answer ['aɪnsə] *n* réponse *f*; solution *f*. *v* répondre (à). **answerable** *adj* responsable.

ant [ant] *n* fourmi *f*. **anthill** *n* fourmilière *f*.

antagonize [an'tagənaiz] *v* contrarier. **antagonism** *n* antagonisme *m*. **antagonist** *n* antagoniste *m*, *f*. **antagonistic** *adj* opposé.

antecedent [anti'siːdənt] *adj* antérieur, -e. *n* antécédent *m*.

antelope ['antəloup] *n* antilope *f*.

antenna [an'tenə] *n* antenne *f*.

anthem ['anθəm] *n* (*national*) hymne *m*; motet *m*.

anthology [an'θolədʒi] *n* anthologie *f*.

anthropology [anθrə'polədʒi] *n* anthropologie *f*. **anthropological** *adj* anthropologique. **anthropologist** *n* anthropologiste *m*, *f*.

anti-aircraft [anti'eəkraɪft] *adj* antiaérien.

antibiotic [antibai'otik] *nm, adj* antibiotique.

antibody ['anti,bodi] *n* anticorps *m*.

anticipate [an'tisipeit] *v* (*foresee*) prévoir; (*act in advance*) prévenir, anticiper. **anticipation** *n* attente *f*; appréhension *f*. **in anticipation** par anticipation, d'avance.

anticlimax [anti'klaimaks] *n* chute *f*.

anticlockwise [anti'klokwaiz] *adj* dans le sens inverse des aiguilles d'une montre.

antics ['antiks] *pl n* singeries *f pl*, cirque *m sing*.

anticyclone [anti'saikloun] *n* anticyclone *m*.

antidote ['antidout] *n* antidote *m*.

antifreeze ['antifriɪz] *n* antigel *m*.

antihistamine [anti'histəmin] *n* antihistaminique *m*.

antipathy [an'tipəθi] *n* antipathie *f*. **antipathetic** *adj* antipathique.

antique [an'tiɪk] *adj* ancien; antique. *n* (*ornament*) objet d'art ancien *m*; (*furniture*) meuble ancien *m*. **antique dealer** *n* antiquaire *m*, *f*. **antique shop** *n* magasin d'antiquités *m*. **antiquated** *adj* vieilli. **antiquity** *n* antiquité *f*.

anti-Semitic [antisə'mitik] *adj* antisémite. **anti-Semite** *n* antisémite *m*, *f*. **anti-Semitism** *n* antisémitisme *m*.

antiseptic [anti'septik] *nm, adj* antiseptique.

antisocial [anti'souʃəl] *adj* antisocial.

antithesis [an'tiθəsis] *n* antithèse *f*.

antlers ['antləz] *pl n* bois *m pl*, ramure *f sing*.

antonym ['antənim] *n* antonyme *m*.

anus ['einəs] *n* anus *m*.

anvil ['anvil] *n* enclume *f*.

anxious ['aŋkʃəs] *adj* (*worry*) anxieux; (*desire*) impatient. **anxiety** *n* anxiété *f*; grand désir *m*. **anxiously** *adv* avec inquiétude; avec impatience.

any ['eni] *adj* (*interrogative*) du, de la, des; (*negative*) de; (*whichever*) n'importe quel. *pron* en: *je n'en ai pas*; aucun; n'importe lequel. **anybody** *or* **anyone** *pron* n'importe qui; (*somebody*) quelqu'un; (*negative*) personne. **anyhow** *or* **anyway** *adv* en tout cas; quand même. **any more** encore (de); (*negative*) plus. **anything** *pron* n'importe quoi; (*something*) quelque chose; (*negative*) rien. **anywhere** *adv* n'importe où; (*somewhere*) quelque part; (*negative*) nulle part. **at any rate** en tout cas. **in any case** de toute façon.

apart [ə'paɪt] *adv* à part; à distance; séparément; en pièces. **apart from** en dehors de. **come apart** se défaire. **take apart** démonter. **tell apart** distinguer l'un de l'autre.

apartment [ə'paɪtmənt] *n* (*room*) pièce *f*; (*flat*) appartement *m*.

apathy ['apəθi] *n* apathie *f*, indifférence *f*. **apathetic** *adj* apathique.

ape [eip] *n* singe *m*, *f*. *v* singer, imiter.

aperture ['apətjuə] *n* (*phot*) ouverture *f*; orifice *m*.

apex ['eipeks] *n* sommet *m*.
aphid ['eifid] *n* aphidé *m*.
aphrodisiac [afrə'diziak] *nm, adj* aphrodisiaque.
apiece [ə'piːs] *adv* chacun; par personne; la pièce.
apology [ə'polədʒi] *n* excuses *f pl*; (*defence*) apologie *f*. **apologize** *v* s'excuser. **be apologetic** se répandre en excuses.
apoplexy ['apəpleksi] *n* apoplexie *f*. **fit of apoplexy** coup de sang *m*.
apostle [ə'posl] *n* apôtre *m*.
apostrophe [ə'postrəfi] *n* apostrophe *f*.
appal [ə'poɪl] *v* (*shock*) consterner; (*frighten*) épouvanter. **appalling** *adj* consternant; épouvantable.
apparatus [apə'reitəs] *n* appareil *m*, dispositif *m*.
apparent [ə'parənt] *adj* (*not real*) apparent; (*obvious*) évident, manifeste. **apparently** *adv* apparemment; paraît-il.
apparition [apə'riʃən] *n* apparition *f*.
appeal [ə'piːl] *v* faire (un) appel. **appeal to** (*please*) plaire à; (*request*) s'adresser à. **appealing** *adj* (*moving*) attendrissant; (*attractive*) attirant.
appear [ə'piə] *v* (*be seen*) apparaître, se montrer; (*seem*) paraître. **appearance** *n* apparition *f*; (*aspect*) apparence *f*.
appease [ə'piːz] *v* apaiser. **appeasement** *n* apaisement *m*.
appendix [ə'pendiks] *n* appendice *m*. **appendicitis** *n* appendicite *f*.
appetite ['apitait] *n* appétit *m*. **appetizer** *n* apéritif *m*. **appetizing** *adj* appétissant.
applaud [ə'ploɪd] *v* applaudir. **applause** *n* applaudissements *m pl*.
apple ['apl] *n* (*fruit*) pomme *f*; (*tree*) pommier *m*.
apply [ə'plai] *v* appliquer; (*paint, etc.*) mettre; (*ask*) s'adresser; (*refer*) s'appliquer. **appliance** *n* appareil *m*. **applicable** *adj* applicable. **applicant** *n* candidat, -e *m, f*. **application** *n* application *f*; (*job*) demande *f*.
appoint [ə'point] *v* désigner, nommer. **at the appointed time** à l'heure convenue. **appointment** *n* (*meeting*) rendez-vous *m*; (*job*) poste.
apportion [ə'poːʃən] *v* partager, répartir; assigner.
appraise [ə'preiz] *v* estimer, évaluer. **appraisal** *n* évaluation *f*; appréciation *f*.
appreciate [ə'priːʃieit] *v* (*value*) apprécier;

(*be aware of*) se rendre compte de; (*be grateful for*) être reconnaissant de; (*rise in value*) prendre de la valeur. **appreciation** *n* appréciation *f*; reconnaissance *f*.
apprehend [apri'hend] *v* (*arrest*) arrêter, appréhender; (*understand*) comprendre. **apprehension** *n* (*fear*) appréhension *f*; arrestation *f*. **apprehensive** *adj* inquiet, -ète; appréhensif.
apprentice [ə'prentis] *v* placer *or* mettre en apprentissage (chez). *n* apprenti, -e *m, f*. **apprenticeship** *n* apprentissage *m*.
approach [ə'proutʃ] *v* (s')approcher (de). *n* approche *f*, accès *m*.
appropriate [ə'prouprieit; *adj* ə'proupriət] *v* s'approprier. *adj* (*name, etc.*) juste, bien choisi; (*correct*) approprié.
approve [ə'pruːv] *v* approuver. **approval** *n* approbation *f*. **on approval** à l'essai.
approximate [ə'proksimeit; *adj* ə'proksimət] *v* se rapprocher (de). *adj* approximatif.
apricot ['eiprikot] *n* (*fruit*) abricot *m*; (*tree*) abricotier *m*.
April ['eiprəl] *n* avril *m*. **April fool** *n* poisson d'avril *m*.
apron ['eiprən] *n* tablier *m*; (*aero*) aire de manœuvre *f*.
apt [apt] *adj* (*fitting*) juste, convenable; (*inclined*) enclin, porté. **aptly** *adv* à propos.
aptitude ['aptitjuːd] *n* aptitude *f*.
aqualung ['akwəlʌŋ] *n* scaphandre autonome *m*.
aquarium [ə'kweəriəm] *n* aquarium *m*.
Aquarius [ə'kweəriəs] *n* Verseau *m*.
aquatic [ə'kwatik] *adj* aquatique.
aqueduct ['akwidʌkt] *n* aqueduc *m*.
Arab ['arəb] *n* Arabe *m, f*. *adj* arabe. **Arabia** *n* Arabie *f*. **Arabian** *or* **Arabic** *adj* arabe.
arable ['arəbl] *adj* arable.
arbitrary ['aɪbitrəri] *adj* arbitraire.
arbitrate ['aɪbitreit] *v* arbitrer, juger. **arbitration** *n* arbitrage *m*. **arbiter** *n* arbitre *m*.
arc [aɪk] *n* arc *m*. **arc lamp** lampe à arc *f*. **arc light** arc voltaïque *m*.
arcade [aɪ'keid] *n* arcade *m*; (*shopping*) passage *m*.
arch [aɪtʃ] *v* (s')arquer. *n* (*church, etc.*) voûte *f*, cintre *m*; (*bridge*) arche *f*.
archaeology [aɪki'olədʒi] *n* archéologie *f*. **archaeological** *adj* archéologique. **archaeologist** *n* archéologue *m, f*.

archaic [aɪˈkeiik] *adj* archaïque. **archaism** *n* archaïsme *m*.

archbishop [aɪtʃˈbiʃəp] *n* archevêque *m*.

archduke [aɪtʃˈdjuɪk] *n* archiduc *m*. **archduchess** *n* archiduchesse *f*.

archery [ˈaɪtʃəri] *n* tir à l'arc *m*. **archer** *n* archer *m*.

archetype [ˈaɪkitaip] *n* archétype *m*.

archipelago [aɪkiˈpeləgou] *n* archipel *m*.

architect [ˈaɪkitekt] *n* architecte *m*. **architecture** *n* architecture *f*.

archives [ˈaɪkaivz] *pl n* archives *f pl*. **archivist** *n* archiviste *m*, *f*.

ardent [ˈaɪdənt] *adj* ardent.

ardour [ˈaɪdə] *n* ardeur *f*.

arduous [ˈaɪdjuəs] *adj* ardu.

are [aɪ] *V* be.

area [ˈeəriə] *n* aire *f*; (*region*) étendue *f*, région *f*.

arena [əˈriɪnə] *n* arène *f*.

argue [ˈaɪgjuɪ] *v* se disputer, discuter. **argument** *n* dispute *f*; (*debate*) discussion *f*; (*reasons*) argument *m*.

arid [ˈarid] *adj* aride. **aridity** *n* aridité *f*.

Aries [ˈeəriɪz] *n* Bélier *m*.

*arise [əˈraiz] *v* s'élever; (*question*) se présenter; resulter.

arisen [əˈrizn] *V* arise.

aristocracy [ariˈstokrəsi] *n* aristocratie *f*. **aristocrat** *n* aristocrate *m*, *f*. **aristocratic** *adj* aristocratique.

arithmetic [əˈriθmətik] *n* arithmétique *f*, calcul *m*.

arm[1] [aɪm] *n* bras *m*. **armchair** *n* fauteuil *m*. **arm in arm** bras dessus bras dessous. **armpit** *n* aisselle *f*.

arm[2] [aɪm] *n* arme *f*. **be up in arms against** s'élever contre. *v* armer.

armistice [ˈaɪmistis] *n* armistice *m*.

armour [ˈaɪmə] *n* armure *f*. **suit of armour** armure complète *f*. **armoured** *adj* cuirassé, blindé. **armoury** *n* arsenal *m*.

army [ˈaɪmi] *n* armée *f*.

aroma [əˈroumə] *n* arome *m*; (*wine*) bouquet.

arose [əˈrouz] *V* arise.

around [əˈraund] *prep* autour de; (*approximately*) à peu près. *adv* autour, à l'entour.

arrange [əˈreindʒ] *v* arranger; (*meeting, etc.*) fixer; (*make plans*) s'arranger. **arrangement** *n* arrangement *m*. **make arrangements** faire des préparatifs, prendre des mesures.

array [əˈrei] *v* (*adorn*) orner; (*mil*) ranger. *n* (*display*) étalage *m*; (*mil*) ordre *m*.

arrears [əˈriəz] *pl n* arriéré *m sing*. **in arrears** arriéré; en retard.

arrest [əˈrest] *v* arrêter. *n* arrestation *f*. **under arrest** en état d'arrestation.

arrive [əˈraiv] *v* arriver. **arrival** *n* arrivée *f*; (*person*) arrivant, -e *m*, *f*.

arrogant [ˈarəgənt] *adj* arrogant. **arrogance** *n* arrogance *f*.

arrow [ˈarou] *n* flèche *f*.

arse [aɪs] *n* (*vulgar*) cul *m*.

arsenal [ˈaɪsənl] *n* arsenal *m*.

arsenic [ˈaɪsnik] *n* arsenic *m*.

arson [ˈaɪsn] *n* incendie criminel *m*.

art [aɪt] *n* art *m*; (*painting, etc.*) beaux-arts *m pl*; (*cunning*) artifice *m*. **art gallery** musée d'art *m*. **arts and crafts** artisanat *m sing*. **art school** école des beaux-arts *f*. **Arts degree** licence ès lettres *f*. **artful** *adj* rusé.

artefact [ˈaɪtifakt] *n* objet fabriqué *m*.

artery [ˈaɪtəri] *n* artère *f*.

arthritis [aɪˈθraitis] *n* arthrite *f*.

artichoke [ˈaɪtitʃouk] *n* artichaut *m*.

article [ˈaɪtikl] *n* article *m*; objet *m*.

articulate [aɪˈtikjuleit; *adj* aɪˈtikjulət] *v* articuler. **articulated lorry** semi-remorque *m*. *adj* bien articulé; net, nette. **be articulate** s'exprimer bien. **articulation** *n* articulation *f*.

artifice [ˈaɪtifis] *n* artifice *f*, stratagème *m*.

artificial [aɪtiˈfiʃəl] *adj* artificiel; synthétique; (*affected*) factice, forcé. **artificial respiration** respiration artificielle *f*.

artillery [aɪˈtiləri] *n* artillerie *f*.

artisan [aɪtiˈzan] *n* artisan *m*.

artist [ˈaɪtist] *n* artiste *m*, *f*. **artistic** *adj* artistique.

as [az] *conj* (*while*) comme, tandis que, à mesure que; (*because*) puisque; (*like*) comme, en. *adv* aussi. **as ... as ...** aussi ... que .... **as for** quant à. **as if** comme si. **as it were** pour ainsi dire. **as usual** comme d'habitude. **as well** aussi.

asbestos [azˈbestos] *n* amiante *f*.

ascend [əˈsend] *v* monter. **ascension** *n* ascension *f*. **Ascension Day** jour de l'Ascension *m*. **ascent** *n* ascension *f*; montée *f*.

ascertain [asəˈtein] *v* établir; vérifier.

ascetic [əˈsetik] *adj* ascétique. *n* ascète *m*, *f*.

ash[1] [aʃ] *n* cendre *f*. **ashtray** *n* cendrier *m*. **Ash Wednesday** mercredi des cendres *m*.

ash² [aʃ] *n* (*tree*) frêne *m*.
ashamed [ə'ʃeimd] *adj* honteux. **be ashamed** avoir honte.
ashore [ə'ʃɔɪ] *adv* à terre. **go ashore** débarquer.
Asia ['eiʃə] *n* Asie *f*. **Asian** *n* Asiatique *m*, *f*; *adj* asiatique.
aside [ə'said] *adv* de côté, à part. *n* aparté *m*.
ask [aɪsk] *v* demander; inviter. **ask about** s'informer de. **ask after** demander des nouvelles de. **ask a question** poser une question. **ask for** demander.
askew [ə'skjuɪ] *adv* de travers.
asleep [ə'sliːp] *adj* endormi. **be asleep** dormir. **fall asleep** s'endormir.
asparagus [ə'spærəgəs] *n* asperge *f*.
aspect ['aspekt] *n* aspect *m*; (*of house*) orientation *f*.
asphalt ['asfalt] *n* asphalte *m*. *v* asphalter.
asphyxiate [əs'fiksieit] *v* (s')asphyxier. **asphyxia** *or* **asphyxiation** *n* asphyxie *f*.
aspire [ə'spaiə] *v* aspirer, ambitionner. **aspirate** *adj* aspiré. **aspiration** *n* aspiration *f*. **aspiring** *adj* ambitieux.
aspirin ['aspərin] *n* aspirine *f*.
ass [as] *n* âne, -esse *m*, *f*; (*coll*) imbécile *m*.
assail [ə'seil] *v* assaillir. **assailant** *n* agresseur *m*.
assassinate [ə'sasineit] *v* assassiner. **assassin** *n* assassin *m*. **assassination** *n* assassinat *m*.
assault [ə'sɔɪlt] *n* attaque *f*; (*mil*) assaut *m*; (*law*) voies de fait *f pl*. *v* attaquer.
assemble [ə'sembl] *v* (*things*) (s')assembler; (*people*) (se) rassembler; (*put together*) monter. **assembly** *n* assemblée *f*; rassemblement *m*; montage *m*. **assembly line** chaîne de montage *f*.
assent [ə'sent] *n* assentiment *m*. *v* consentir.
assert [ə'sɔɪt] *v* (*declare*) affirmer; (*rights, etc.*) revendiquer. **assertion** *n* affirmation *f*; revendication *f*.
assess [ə'ses] *v* évaluer; (*payment, etc.*) fixer le montant de; (*property*) calculer la valeur imposable de. **assessment** *n* évaluation *f*; calcul *m*.
asset ['aset] *n* avantage *m*. **assets** *pl n* biens *m pl*; (*comm*) actif *m sing*.
assiduous [ə'sidjuəs] *adj* assidu. **assiduity** *n* assiduité *f*.
assign [ə'sain] *v* (*job, etc.*) assigner;

(*meaning*) attribuer; (*person*) nommer.
assignation *n* (*meeting*) rendez-vous *m*.
assignment mission *f*; (*school*) devoir *m*.
assimilate [ə'simileit] *v* (s')assimiler. **assimilation** *n* assimilation *f*.
assist [ə'sist] *v* aider. **assistance** *n* aide *f*, secours *m*. **assistant** *n* auxiliaire *m*, *f*; (*school*) assistant, -e *m*, *f*; (*shop*) vendeur, -euse *m*, *f*; (*as modifier*) adjoint, sous-.
associate [ə'sousiət; *v* ə'sousieit] *n* associé, -e *m*, *f*, collègue *m*, *f*. *v* associer. **be associated with** (*things*) être associé à; (*people*) s'associer avec. **association** *n* association *f*.
assorted [ə'sɔɪtid] *adj* assorti. **assortment** *n* assortiment *m*; mélange *m*.
assume [ə'sjuɪm] *v* supposer, présumer; (*take on*) assumer, adopter. **assumption** *n* supposition *f*.
assure [ə'ʃuə] *v* assurer. **assurance** *n* assurance *f*.
asterisk ['astərisk] *n* astérisque *m*. *v* marquer d'un astérisque.
asthma ['asmə] *n* asthme *m*. **asthmatic** *n*(*m*+*f*), *adj* asthmatique.
astonish [ə'stoniʃ] *v* étonner. **astonishment** *n* étonnement *m*.
astound [ə'staund] *v* stupéfier, abasourdir.
astray [ə'strei] *adv* **go astray** s'égarer.
astride [ə'straid] *adv* à califourchon. *prep* à califourchon sur.
astringent [ə'strindʒənt] *nm*, *adj* astringent.
astrology [ə'strolədʒi] *n* astrologie *f*. **astrologer** *n* astrologue *m*. **astrological** *adj* astrologique.
astronaut ['astrənɔɪt] *n* astronaute *m*, *f*.
astronomy [ə'stronəmi] *n* astronomie *f*. **astronomer** *n* astronome *m*. **astronomical** *adj* astronomique.
astute [ə'stjuɪt] *adj* fin, astucieux. **astuteness** *n* finesse *f*, astuce *f*.
asunder [ə'sʌndə] *adv* (*in two*) en deux; (*in pieces*) en morceaux.
asylum [ə'sailəm] *n* asile *m*.
at [at] *prep* à; chez: *chez le docteur*; (*towards*) vers. **at first** d'abord. **at last** enfin. **at least** au moins. **at once** tout de suite.
ate [et] *V* eat.
atheism ['eiθiizəm] *n* athéisme *m*. **atheist** *n* athée *m*, *f*. **atheistic** *adj* athée.
Athens ['aθinz] *n* Athènes. **Athenian** *adj* athénien; *n* Athénien, -enne *m*, *f*.

athlete ['aθliːt] *n* athlète *m, f.* **athlete's foot** *n* mycose *f.* **athletic** *adj* sportif, athlétique. **athletics** *n* athlétisme *m.*
Atlantic [ət'lantik] *adj* atlantique. **the Atlantic (Ocean)** l'(océan) Atlantique *m.*
atlas ['atləs] *n* atlas *m.*
atmosphere ['atməsfiə] *n* atmosphère *f*; ambiance *f.* **atmospheric** *adj* atmosphérique.
atom ['atəm] *n* atome *m*; (*tiny part*) grain *m.* **atom bomb** bombe atomique *f.* **atomic** *adj* atomique. **atomizer** *n* atomiseur *m.*
atone [ə'toun] *v* **atone for** expier; réparer. **atonement** *n* expiation *f*; réparation *f.*
atrocious [ə'trouʃəs] *adj* atroce. **atrocity** *n* atrocité *f.*
attach [ə'tatʃ] *v* attacher, joindre. **attached** *adj* (*letter, etc.*) ci-joint; (*fond*) attaché. **attachment** *n* accessoire *m*; affection *f.*
attaché [ə'taʃei] *n* attaché, -e *m, f.* **attaché case** mallette *f.*
attack [ə'tak] *n* attaque *f*; (*med*) accès *m*, crise *f.* *v* attaquer, combattre. **attacker** *n* attaquant *m.*
attain [ə'tein] *v* atteindre (à). **attainments** *pl n* résultats *m pl.*
attempt [ə'tempt] *v* tenter (de), essayer (de). *n* tentative *f*, essai *m.*
attend [ə'tend] *v* (*meeting*) assister à; (*school*) aller à; servir; faire attention. **attend to** s'occuper de. **attendance** *n* présence *f*; (*number present*) assistance *f*; service *m.* **attendant** *n* gardien, -enne *m, f.* **attendants** *pl n* suite *f sing.*
attention [ə'tenʃən] *n* attention *f*; (*mil*) garde-à-vous *m.* **pay attention** faire attention. **attentive** *adj* (*caring*) prévenant; (*listening*) attentif.
attic ['atik] *n* grenier *m.* **attic room** mansarde *f.*
attire [ə'taiə] *v* parer (de). *n* habits *m pl*; (*ceremonial*) tenue *f.*
attitude ['atitjuːd] *n* attitude *f.*
attorney [ə'təːni] *n* mandataire *m*; (*US*) avoué, *m.* **Attorney General** Procureur Général *m.*
attract [ə'trakt] *v* attirer. **attract attention** éveiller l'intérêt. **attraction** *n* attraction *f*; (*charm*) attrait *m.* **attractive** *adj* attrayant; (*price, etc.*) intéressant.
attribute [ə'tribjuːt; *n* 'atribjuːt] *v* attribuer; (*crime, etc.*) imputer. *n* attribut *m.* **attribution** *n* attribution *f*; imputation *f.*
attrition [ə'triʃən] *n* usure *f.*
atypical [ei'tipikl] *adj* atypique.

aubergine ['oubəʒiːn] *n* aubergine *f.*
auburn ['oibən] *adj* auburn *invar*; roux, rousse.
auction ['oikʃən] *n* vente aux enchères *f. v* vendre aux enchères. **auctioneer** *n* commissaire-priseur *m.*
audacious [oi'deiʃəs] *adj* (*brave*) audacieux; (*impudent*) effronté. **audacity** *n* audace *f*; effronterie *f.*
audible ['oidəbl] *adj* audible, distinct.
audience ['oidjəns] *n* spectateurs *m pl*, auditeurs *m pl*; (*interview*) audience *f.*
audiovisual [oidiou'viʒuəl] *adj* audiovisuel. **audiovisual aids** support audiovisuel *m sing.*
audit ['oidit] *v* vérifier. *n* vérification *f.* **auditor** *n* expert-comptable *m.*
audition [oi'diʃən] *n* audition *f. v* auditionner.
auditorium [oidi'toiriəm] *n* salle *f.*
augment [oig'ment] *v* (s')augmenter.
August ['oigəst] *n* août *m.*
aunt [aint] *n* tante *f.*
au pair [ou 'peə] *adv* au pair. *n* jeune fille au pair *f.*
aura ['oirə] *n* aura *f*; ambiance *f.*
auspicious [oi'spiʃəs] *adj* favorable, de bon augure.
austere [oi'stiə] *adj* austère. **austerity** *n* austérité *f.*
Australia [o'streiljə] *n* Australie *f.* **Australian** *n* Australien, -enne *m, f*; *adj* australien.
Austria ['ostriə] *n* Autriche *f.* **Austrian** *n* Autrichien, -enne *m, f*; *adj* autrichien.
authentic [oi'θentik] *adj* authentique. **authenticity** *n* authenticité *f.*
author ['oiθə] *n* auteur *m.*
authority [oi'θorəti] *n* (*power*) autorité *f*; (*permission*) autorisation *f.* **authoritative** *adj* (*source, etc.*) autorisé; (*person*) autoritaire.
authorize ['oiθəraiz] *v* autoriser. **authorization** *n* autorisation *f*; (*legal*) mandat *m.*
autobiography [oitoubai'ografi] *n* autobiographie *f.* **autobiographical** *adj* autobiographique.
autocratic [oitou'kratik] *adj* autocratique. **autocracy** *n* autocratie *f.* **autocrat** *n* autocrate *m.*
autograph ['oitəgraif] *v* dédicacer, signer. *n* autographe *m.*
automatic [oitə'matik] *adj* automatique. *n* (*car*) voiture automatique *f.* **automation** *n* automatisation *f.*

automobile ['ɔɪtəməbiːl] *n* automobile *f.*
autonomous [ɔɪ'tonəməs] *adj* autonome.
autonomy *n* autonomie *f.*
autopsy ['ɔɪtopsi] *n* autopsie *f.*
autumn ['ɔɪtəm] *n* automne *m.*
auxiliary [ɔɪg'ziljəri] *n(m+f), adj* auxiliaire.
avail [ə'veil] *v* **avail oneself of** utiliser; profiter de. *n* **to no avail** sans résultat.
available [ə'veiləbl] *adj* disponible. **availability** *n* disponibilité *f.*
avalanche ['avəlɑɪnʃ] *n* avalanche *f.*
avarice ['avəris] *n* avarice *f.* **avaricious** *adj* avare.
avenge [ə'vendʒ] *v* venger. **avenge oneself** prendre sa revanche.
avenue ['avinjuɪ] *n* avenue *f.*
average ['avəridʒ] *n* moyenne *f. adj* moyen.
aversion [ə'vɔɪʃən] *n* aversion *f.* **averse** *adj* adversaire (de). **be averse to** avoir horreur de.
avert [ə'vɔɪt] *v* (*avoid*) prévenir; (*turn away*) écarter; (*eyes, etc.*) détourner.
aviary ['eiviəri] *n* volière *f.*
aviation [eivi'eiʃən] *n* aviation *f.*
avid ['avid] *adv* avide. **avidity** *n* avidité *f.*
avocado [avə'kɑɪdou] *n* (*pear*) avocat *m*; (*tree*) avocatier *m.*
avoid [ə'void] *v* éviter. **avoidable** *adj* évitable.
await [ə'weit] *v* attendre.
***awake** [ə'weik] *v* (s')éveiller. *adj* éveillé. **awake to** conscient de.
award [ə'wɔɪd] *v* décerner; (*damages*) accorder. *n* récompense *f*, prix *m.*
aware [ə'weə] *adj* conscient; au courant. **be aware of** savoir. **awareness** *n* conscience *f.*
away [ə'wei] *adv* au loin, à une distance de; absent. *adj* (*sport*) à l'extérieur.
awe [ɔɪ] *n* crainte révérentielle *f.* **aweinspiring** *adj* impressionnant. **awe-struck** *adj* stupéfait. **be in awe of** être intimidé par.
awful ['ɔɪful] *adj* affreux, épouvantable. **awfully** *adv* (*very*) vraiment.
awkward ['ɔɪkwəd] *adj* (*difficult*) peu commode; (*situation*) délicat; (*inconvenient*) inopportun; (*clumsy*) maladroit. **awkwardness** *n* maladresse *f*; embarras *m.*
awning ['ɔɪniŋ] *n* (*shop*) banne *f*; (*tent*) auvent *m*; (*naut*) taud *m.*
awoke [ə'wouk] *V* awake.

awoken [ə'woukn] *V* awake.
axe [aks] *n* hache *f.*
axiom ['aksiəm] *n* axiome *m.*
axis ['aksis] *n* axe *m.*
axle ['aksl] *n* axe *m*; (*mot*) essieu *m.*

B

babble ['babl] *v* bredouiller; (*baby*) babiller; (*stream*) gazouiller. *n* babil *m*; (*noise*) rumeur *f.*
baboon [bə'buɪn] *n* babouin *m.*
baby ['beibi] *n* bébé *m.* **babyish** *adj* enfantin.
bachelor ['batʃələ] *n* célibataire *m.* **Bachelor of Arts/Science** licencié, -e ès lettres/sciences *m, f.*
back [bak] *n* dos, derrière *m*; (*reverse side*) revers *m*, verso *m*; (*furthest part*) fond *m. adj* arrière. *adv* en arrière. *v* renforcer; financer; (*bet on*) parier sur. **back away** se reculer. **back out** (*car, etc.*) sortir en marche arrière; (*duty, etc.*) se dérober (à).
backache ['bakeik] *n* mal aux reins *m.*
backdate [bak'deit] *v* (*cheque*) antidater. **backdated to** avec rappel à.
backfire [bak'faiə] *v* (*mot*) pétarader; (*plan, etc.*) échouer.
backgammon ['bak,gamən] *n* trictrac *m.*
background ['bakgraund] *n* fond *m*, arrière-plan *m*; (*social*) milieu *m.* **background music** musique de fond *f.*
backhand ['bakhand] *adj, adv* (*sport*) en revers. *n* revers *m.*
backlog ['baklog] *n* arriéré *m.*
backside ['baksaid] *n* arrière *m*; (*coll*) derrière *m.*
backstage ['baksteidʒ] *adv* derrière la scène. **go backstage** aller dans la coulisse.
backstroke ['bakstrouk] *n* dos crawlé *m.*
backward ['bakwəd] *adj* en arrière; (*retarded*) arriéré. **backwardness** *n* arriération mentale *f.*
backwards ['bakwədz] *adv* en arrière; (*back first*) à rebours, à reculons; (*in reverse order*) à l'envers.
backwater ['bakwɔɪtə] *n* (*place*) trou perdu *m*; (*pool*) eau stagnante *f.*

bacon ['beikən] *n* bacon *m*. **bacon and eggs** œufs au jambon *m pl*.

bacteria [bak'tiəriə] *pl n* bactéries *f pl*.

bad [bad] *adj* mauvais; (*naughty*) méchant; (*serious*) grave; (*decayed*) gâté, carié. **bad-mannered** *adj* mal élevé. **bad-tempered** *adj* acariâtre. **badly** *adv* mal; (*seriously*) grièvement; (*very much*) absolument.

badge [badʒ] *n* insigne *m*; (*scouting*) badge *m*; (*police, etc*.) plaque *f*.

badger ['badʒə] *n* blaireau *m*. *v* harceler.

badminton ['badmintən] *n* badminton *m*.

baffle ['bafl] *v* déconcerter.

bag [bag] *n* sac *m*. **baggage** *n* bagages *m pl*. **baggy** *adj* bouffant; trop ample.

bagpipes ['bagpaips] *pl n* cornemuse *f sing*.

bail[1] [beil] *n* (*law*) caution *f*. **on bail** sous caution. **stand bail for** se rendre garant de. *v* **bail out** faire mettre en liberté provisoire sous caution.

bail[2] *or* **bale** [beil] *v* **bail out** (*flooded boat*) écoper; (*from aircraft*) sauter en parachute.

bailiff ['beilif] *n* (*law*) huissier *m*; (*of estate*) régisseur *m*.

bait [beit] *n* (*fishing*) amorce *f*; (*lure*) appât *m*. *v* amorcer; (*annoy*) tourmenter.

bake [beik] *v* (faire) cuire au four. **baked beans** haricots blancs à la sauce tomate *m pl*. **baker** *n* boulanger, -ère *m, f*. **bakery** *n* boulangerie *f*.

balance ['baləns] *n* equilibre *m*; (*scales*) balance *f*; (*comm*) solde *m*. **balance of payments** balance des paiements *f*. *v* (se) tenir en équilibre; (*equal*) équilibrer; (*comm*) balancer, solder. **balance the books** dresser le bilan.

balcony ['balkəni] *n* balcon *m*; (*theatre*) fauteils de deuxième balcon *m pl*.

bald [bɔild] *adj* chauve; (*tyre*) lisse; (*style*) plat.

bale[1] [beil] *n* ballot *m*; (*hay*) balle *f*. *v* emballotter.

bale[2] *V* **bail**[2].

ball[1] [bɔil] *n* balle *f*, boule *f*; (*football*) ballon *m*; (*wool, etc*.) pelote *f*; (*of foot*) plante *f*. **ball bearings** roulement à billes *m sing*. **ball-point pen** stylo bille *m*.

ball[2] [bɔil] *n* (*dance*) bal *m*. **ballroom** *n* salle de danse *f*.

ballad ['baləd] *n* ballade *f*; (*music*) romance *f*.

ballast ['baləst] *n* (*naut*) lest *m*; (*rail*) ballast *m*. *v* lester; ballaster.

ballet ['balei] *n* ballet *m*. **ballerina** *n* ballerine *f*.

ballistic [bə'listik] *adj* balistique. **ballistic missile** engin balistique *m*.

balloon [bə'luin] *n* ballon *m*. **balloonist** *n* aéronaute *m, f*.

ballot ['balət] *n* scrutin *m*; (*paper*) bulletin de vote *m*. **ballot box** urne électorale *f*. *v* voter au scrutin secret.

bamboo [bam'bui] *n* bambou *m*.

ban [ban] *v* interdire. *n* interdit *m*. **put a ban on** interdire.

banal [bə'nail] *adj* banal. **banality** *n* banalité *f*.

banana [bə'nainə] *n* (*fruit*) banane *f*; (*tree*) bananier *m*.

band[1] [band] (*group*) bande *f*; (*music*) orchestre *m*; (*mil*) fanfare *f*. **bandstand** *n* kiosque à musique *m*. **jump on the bandwagon** prendre le train en marche.

band[2] [band] *n* (*strip*) bande *f*.

bandage ['bandidʒ] *n* pansement *m*, bandage *m*. *v* mettre un pansement sur.

bandit ['bandit] *n* bandit *m*.

bandy ['bandi] *adj* *also* **bandy-legged** bancal, arqué. *v* échanger. **bandy about** faire circuler. **bandy words** discuter.

bang [baŋ] *n* (*noise*) claquement *m*, détonation *f*; (*blow*) coup *m*. *interj* pan! *v* (*hit*) frapper, cogner; (*door*) claquer; (*gun, etc*.) détoner.

bangle ['baŋgl] *n* bracelet *m*, jonc *m*.

banish ['baniʃ] *v* bannir; exiler. **banishment** *n* bannissement *m*, exil *m*.

banister ['banistə] *n* rampe *f*.

banjo ['bandʒou] *n* banjo *m*.

bank[1] [baŋk] *n* (*edge*) bord *m*; (*river*) rive *f*; (*sand*) banc *m*; (*earth, etc*.) talus *m*.

bank[2] [baŋk] *n* banque *f*. **bank account** compte en banque *m*. **bank holiday** jour férié *m*. **bank statement** relevé de compte *m*. *v* mettre en banque. **bank on** compter sur. **bank with** avoir un compte à. **banker** *n* banquier *m*. **banker's order** ordre de virement bancaire *m*.

bankrupt ['baŋkrʌpt] *adj* failli, en faillite. **go bankrupt** faire faillite. *n* failli, -e *m, f*. *v* mettre en faillite. **bankruptcy** *n* faillite *f*.

banner ['banə] *n* bannière *f*.

banquet ['baŋkwit] *n* banquet *m*.

banter ['bantə] *v* plaisanter. *n* badinage *m*.

baptize [bap'taiz] *v* baptiser. **baptism** *n* baptême *m*. **Baptist** *n*(*m*+*f*), *adj* baptiste.

bar [baɪ] *n* (*rod*) barreau *f*, barre *f*; obstacle *m*; (*law*) barreau *m*; (*chocolate*) tablette *f*; (*for drinks*) bar *m*, comptoir *m*; (*music*) mesure *f*. *v* barrer; défendre. *prep* sauf.

barbarian [baɪ'beəriən] *n*(*m*+*f*), *adj* barbare. **barbaric** *or* **barbarous** *adj* barbare. **barbarism** *or* **barbarity** *n* barbarie *f*.

barbecue ['baɪbikjuɪ] *n* barbecue *m*. *v* griller au charbon de bois.

barbed wire [baɪbd] *n* fil de fer barbelé *m*.

barber ['baɪbə] *n* coiffeur pour hommes *m*.

barbiturate [baɪ'bitjurət] *n* barbiturique *m*.

bare [beə] *v* mettre à nu. **bare one's teeth** montrer les dents. *adj* nu; dénudé. **barefaced** *adj* éhonté. **barefoot** *adv* nu-pieds. **the bare necessities** le strict nécessaire *m*. **barely** *adv* à peine.

bargain ['baɪgin] *n* (*transaction*) marché; (*offer*) occasion. **into the bargain** par-dessus le marché. *v* négocier. **bargain for** (*expect*) s'attendre à. **bargain with** marchander avec.

barge [baɪdʒ] *n* chaland *m*, péniche *f*. *v* **barge in** faire irruption, entrer sans façons. **barge through** traverser comme un ouragan.

baritone ['baritoun] *n* baryton *m*.

bark¹ [baɪk] *v* (*dog*) aboyer. *n* aboiement *m*.

bark² [baɪk] *n* (*tree*) écorce *f*.

barley ['baɪli] *n* orge *f*. **barley sugar** sucre d'orge *m*. **barley water** orgeat *m*.

barn [baɪn] *n* grange *f*.

barometer [bə'romitə] *n* baromètre *m*.

baron ['barən] *n* baron *m*. **baroness** *n* baronne *f*. **baronet** *n* baronnet *m*.

barracks ['barəks] *n* (*mil*) caserne *f*, quartier *m*.

barrage ['baraɪʒ] *n* barrage *m*; (*of questions*) pluie *f*; (*of words*) flot *m*.

barrel ['barəl] *n* (*cask*) tonneau *m*; (*gun, etc.*) canon *m*.

barren ['barən] *adj* stérile; aride. **barrenness** *n* stérilité *f*; aridité *f*.

barricade [bari'keid] *n* barricade *f*. *v* barricader.

barrier ['bariə] *n* barrière *f*; (*rail*) portillon *m*.

barrister ['baristə] *n* avocat *m*.

barrow ['barou] *n* voiture de quatre saisons *f*.

barter ['baɪtə] *v* troquer, faire un troc. *n* troc *m*.

base¹ [beis] *n* base *f*. *v* baser. **baseless** *adj* sans fondement.

base² [beis] *adj* bas, basse; ignoble. **baseness** *n* bassesse *f*.

baseball ['beisbɔɪl] *n* base-ball *m*.

basement ['beismənt] *n* sous-sol *m*.

bash [baʃ] *v* cogner. *n* coup *m*. **have a bash** (*try*) essayer un coup.

bashful ['baʃful] *adj* timide.

basic ['beisik] *adj* fondamental; (*salary, etc.*) de base; (*chem*) basique.

basil ['bazl] *n* basilic *m*.

basin ['beisin] *n* cuvette *f*; (*bowl*) bol *m*; (*bathroom*) lavabo *m*; (*geog*) bassin *m*.

basis ['beisis] *n* base *f*.

bask [bask] *v* (*in the sun*) se dorer; (*in glory, etc.*) jouir (de).

basket ['baɪskit] *n* (*shopping*) panier *m*; (*linen, etc.*) corbeille *f*. **basketball** *n* basket *m*.

bass¹ [beis] *n* (*voice*) basse *f*.

bass² [bas] *n* (*freshwater*) perche *f*; (*sea*) bar *m*.

bassoon [bə'suɪn] *n* basson *m*.

bastard ['baɪstəd] *n* bâtard, -e *m*, *f*; (*derog*) salaud *m*; (*coll*) type *m*.

baste [beist] *v* (*cookery*) arroser.

bastion ['bastjən] *n* bastion *m*.

bat¹ [bat] *n* (*sport*) batte *f*. **off one's own bat** de sa propre initiative. *v* frapper; manier la batte. **bat an eyelid** sourciller.

bat² [bat] *n* chauve-souris *f*.

batch [batʃ] *n* (*loaves*) fournée *f*; (*letters*) paquet *m*; (*goods*) lot *m*.

bath [baɪθ] *n* bain *m*; (*tub*) baignoire *f*. **bathchair** *n* fauteuil roulant *m*. **bathroom** *n* salle de bains *f*. **baths** *pl n* (*swimming*) piscine *f* *sing*. *v* baigner; prendre un bain.

bathe [beið] *v* (se) baigner; (*wound*) laver. **bather** *n* baigneur, -euse *m*, *f*. **bathing** *n* baignade *f*. **bathing costume** maillot *m*. **bathing trunks** slip de bain *m*.

baton ['batn] *n* bâton *m*; (*police*) matraque *f*; (*race*) témoin *m*.

battalion [bə'taljən] *n* bataillon *m*.

batter¹ ['batə] *v* battre. **battered** *adj* délabré.

batter² ['batə] n pâte à frire f; (pancakes) pâte à crêpes f.

battery ['batəri] n (elec) pile f; (mot) batterie f; (mil) batterie f.

battle ['batl] n bataille f. **battlefield** n champ de bataille m. **battlements** pl n remparts m pl. **battleship** n cuirassé m. v se battre, lutter.

bawl [bɔːl] v brailler.

bay¹ [bei] n (geog) baie f.

bay² [bei] v aboyer. n aboi m. **at bay** à distance.

bay³ [bei] n laurier m. **bay leaf** feuille de laurier f.

bayonet ['beiənit] n baïonnette f.

bay window n fenêtre en saillie f.

bazaar [bə'zɑː] n (charity sale) vente de charité f; (eastern) bazar m.

***be** [biː] v être.

beach [biːtʃ] n plage f. v échouer.

beacon ['biːkən] n phare m; (naut) balise f.

bead [biːd] n perle f; (rosary) grain m.

beak [biːk] n bec m.

beaker ['biːkə] n gobelet m.

beam [biːm] n (arch) poutre f; (light) rayon m, faisceau m; (smile) sourire épanoui m. v rayonner.

bean [biːn] n haricot m; (coffee) grain m. **full of beans** en pleine forme.

***bear¹** [beə] v (carry) porter; (support) soutenir; (tolerate) supporter; (give birth) donner naissance à. **bear right/left** prendre à droit/gauche. **bearable** adj supportable. **bearing** n (behaviour) maintien m; (relation) rapport m; (direction) relèvement m. **lose one's bearings** être désorienté.

bear² [beə] n ours m.

beard [biəd] n barbe f. **bearded** adj barbu.

beast [biːst] n bête f; (person) brute f. **beastly** adj abominable; (unkind) sale.

***beat** [biːt] v battre. n battement m; rythme m; (police) ronde f. **beating** n (as punishment) rossée f; (defeat) défaite f.

beaten ['biːtn] V beat.

beauty ['bjuːti] n beauté f. **beautician** n esthéticien, -enne m, f. **beautiful** adj beau, belle; magnifique. **beautify** v embellir.

beaver ['biːvə] n castor m.

became [bi'keim] V become.

because [bi'kɔz] conj parce que. **because of** à cause de.

beckon ['bekən] v faire signe (à).

***become** [bi'kʌm] v devenir; (suit) aller à. **becoming** adj convenable; (clothes) seyant.

bed [bed] n lit m; (coal, etc.) couche f; (flowers) parterre m. **bedclothes** pl n literie f sing. **bedridden** adj alité. **bedroom** n chambre f. **bedside** n chevet m. **bed-sitter** n studio m. **bedspread** n couvre-lit m. **go to bed** se coucher.

bedraggled [bi'dragld] adj débraillé.

bee [biː] n abeille f. **beehive** n ruche f. **have a bee in one's bonnet** avoir une marotte. **make a beeline for** filer droit sur.

beech [biːtʃ] n hêtre m.

beef [biːf] n bœuf m.

been [biːn] V be.

beer [biə] n bière f.

beetle ['biːtl] n coléoptère m.

beetroot ['biːtruːt] n betterave f.

before [bi'fɔː] prep avant; (in front of) devant. adv auparavant, avant. conj avant de, avant que. **beforehand** adv à l'avance.

befriend [bi'frend] v traiter en ami; (help) venir en aide à.

beg [beg] v mendier; (entreat) supplier, demander. **beggar** n mendiant, -e m, f.

began [bi'gan] V begin.

***begin** [bi'gin] v commencer. **to begin with** pour commencer. **beginner** n novice m, f. **beginning** n commencement m, début m; origine f.

begrudge [bi'grʌdʒ] v envier. **begrudge doing** faire à contre-cœur.

begun [bi'gʌn] V begin.

behalf [bi'hɑːf] n part f. **on behalf of** de la part de; en faveur de.

behave [bi'heiv] v se conduire. **behave yourself!** sois sage! **behaviour** n conduite f.

behead [bi'hed] v décapiter.

behind [bi'haind] adv, prep derrière, en arrière (de); (late) en retard. n (coll) postérieur m. **behindhand** adv, adj en retard.

***behold** [bi'hould] v voir.

beige [beiʒ] nm, adj beige.

being ['biːiŋ] n existence f; être m. **for the time being** pour le moment.

belated [bi'leitid] adj tardif.

belch [beltʃ] v roter; (smoke, etc.) vomir. n renvoi m.

belfry ['belfri] *n* beffroi *m*; (*church*) clocher *m*.
Belgium ['beldʒəm] *n* Belgique *f*. **Belgian** *n* Belge *m*, *f*; *adj* belge.
Belgrade ['belgreid] *n* Belgrade.
believe [bi'liːv] *v* croire. **believe in** (*God*) croire en; (*ghosts, etc.*) croire à; (*approve of*) être partisan de. **belief** *n* croyance *f*; (*rel*) credo *m*, foi *f*; opinion *f*. **believable** *adj* croyable. **believer** *n* partisan, -e *m*, *f*; (*rel*) croyant, -e *m*, *f*.
bell [bel] *n* cloche *f*, clochette *f*; (*door*) sonnette *f*; (*telephone*) sonnerie *f*; (*bicycle*) timbre *m*.
belligerent [bi'lidʒərənt] *n*, *adj* belligérant, -e. **belligerence** *n* belligérance *f*.
bellow ['belou] *v* mugir; (*cow*) beugler; (*person*) brailler. *n* mugissement *m*; beuglement *m*; (*person*) hurlement *m*.
bellows ['belouz] *pl n* (*organ*) soufflerie *f* *sing*; (*fire*) soufflet *m* *sing*.
belly ['beli] *n* ventre *m*.
belong [bi'loŋ] *v* appartenir; (*club*) être membre (de). **belongings** *pl n* affaires *f* *pl*.
beloved [bi'lʌvid] *adj* bien aimé. *n* bien-aimé, -e *m*, *f*.
below [bi'lou] *prep* sous, au-dessous de. *adv* en bas, en dessous; (*letters, etc.*) ci-dessous. **hit below the belt** porter un coup bas (à).
belt [belt] *n* ceinture *f*; (*land*) zone *f*, région *f*; (*tech*) courroie *f*. *v* (*slang: hit*) flanquer un gnon à; (*slang: rush*) se carapater.
bench [bentʃ] *n* banc *m*; (*workshop*) établi *m*; (*law*) tribunal *m*.
*****bend** [bend] *n* coude *m*; (*road*) virage *m*; (*arm, knee*) pli *m*. *v* (se) courber; plier. **bend over** se pencher. **bend over backwards** se mettre en quatre.
beneath [bi'niːθ] *prep* sous, au-dessous de; (*unworthy*) indigne de. *adv* au-dessous, en bas.
benefactor ['benəfaktə] *n* bienfaiteur *m*. **benefactress** *n* bienfaitrice *f*.
benefit ['benəfit] *n* avantage *m*; (*money*) allocation *f*. **for the benefit of** dans l'intérêt de. **the benefit of the doubt** le bénéfice du doute. *v* faire du bien à; gagner (à). **beneficial** *adj* salutaire.
benevolent [bi'nevələnt] *adj* (*kindly*) bienveillant; (*charitable*) bienfaisant. **benevolence** *n* bienveillance *f*; bienfaisance *f*.

benign [bi'nain] *adj* (*med*) bénin, -igne; (*kindly*) bienveillant.
bent [bent] *V* **bend**. *adj* courbé; (*slang: dishonest*) véreux; (*slang: homosexual*) homosexuel. **be bent on** vouloir absolument. *n* aptitude *f*, disposition *f*.
bequeath [bi'kwiːð] *v* léguer. **bequest** *n* legs *m*.
bereaved [bi'riːvd] *adj* endeuillé. **bereavement** *n* deuil *m*.
beret ['berei] *n* béret *m*.
Berlin [bəːˈlin] *n* Berlin.
Bern [bəːn] *n* Berne.
berry ['beri] *n* baie *f*.
berserk [bəˈsəːk] *adj* fou furieux, folle furieuse. **go berserk** devenir fou furieux; (*with anger*) se mettre en rage.
berth [bəːθ] *n* couchette *f*; (*naut*) mouillage *m*. **give a wide berth to** éviter. *v* (*naut*) mouiller, amarrer.
beside [bi'said] *prep* à côté de. **beside oneself** (*with anger*) hors de soi. **besides** *adv* (*as well*) de plus; (*moreover*) d'ailleurs.
besiege [bi'siːdʒ] *v* (*town*) assiéger; (*pester*) assaillir.
best [best] *adj* le meilleur, la meilleure. **best man** garçon d'honneur *m*. *adv* le mieux. *n* mieux *m*. **at best** au mieux. **do one's best** faire de son mieux. **make the best of** s'accommoder de; profiter de.
bestow [bi'stou] *v* accorder; (*title*) conférer.
bet [bet] *v* parier. *n* pari *m*. **betting shop** bureau de paris *m*.
betray [bi'trei] *v* trahir. **betrayal** *n* trahison *f*.
better ['betə] *adj* meilleur. *nm*, *adv* mieux. **be better** (*after illness*) aller mieux. **get the better of** triompher de. *v* améliorer, dépasser.
between [bi'twiːn] *prep* entre.
beverage ['bevəridʒ] *n* boisson *f*.
*****beware** [bi'weə] *v* prendre garde. *interj* attention (à)!
bewilder [bi'wildə] *v* dérouter, abasourdir. **bewilderment** *n* confusion *f*; abasourdissement *m*.
beyond [bi'jond] *prep* au delà de; (*exceeding*) au-dessus de. *adv* au delà. **be beyond** dépasser.
bias ['baiəs] *n* tendance *f*; préjugé *m*; (*sewing*) biais *m*. *v* influencer; (*prejudice*) prévenir. **biased** *adj* partial. **be biased** avoir un préjugé.

bib [bib] *n* bavoir *m*; (*of apron*) bavette *f*.

Bible ['baibl] *n* Bible *f*. **biblical** *adj* biblique.

bibliography [bibli'ogrəfi] *n* bibliographie *f*. **bibliographer** *n* bibliographe *m, f*. **bibliographical** *adj* bibliographique.

biceps ['baiseps] *n* biceps *m*.

bicker ['bikə] *v* se chamailler. **bickering** *n* chamailleries *f pl*.

bicycle ['baisikl] *n* bicyclette *f*, vélo *m*.

***bid** [bid] *n* offre *f*; (*auction*) enchère *f*; (*cards*) demande *f*; (*attempt*) tentative *f*. *v* faire une offre *or* enchère (de); (*cards*) demander; (*command*) ordonner; (*greeting*) dire, souhaiter. **bidder** *n* offrant *m*. **bidding** *n* enchères *f pl*; ordre *m*.

bidet ['biːdei] *n* bidet *m*.

biennial [bai'eniəl] *adj* biennal.

bifocals [bai'foukəlz] *pl n* lunettes bifocales *f pl*.

big [big] *adj* grand; gros, grosse.

bigamy ['bigəmi] *n* bigamie. **bigamist** *n* bigame *m, f*. **bigamous** *adj* bigame.

bigot ['bigət] *n* fanatique *m, f*. **bigoted** *adj* fanatique.

bikini [bi'kiːni] *n* bikini *m*.

bilingual [bai'lingwəl] *adj* bilingue.

bilious ['biljəs] *adj* bilieux. **bilious attack** crise de foie *f*. **biliousness** *n* affection hépatique *f*.

bill¹ [bil] (*hotel, shop*) note *f*; (*restaurant*) addition *f*; (*fuel, etc.*) facture *f*; (*pol*) projet de loi *m*; (*poster*) affiche *f*.

bill² [bil] *n* bec *m*.

billiards ['biljədz] *n* billard *m*.

billion ['biljən] *n* (*10¹²*) billion *m*; (*10⁹*) milliard *m*.

billow ['bilou] *n* flot *m*; (*sail*) gonflement *m*. *v* (*sail*) se gonfler; (*smoke*) tournoyer.

bin [bin] *n* (*rubbish*) poubelle *f*; (*coal*) coffre *m*; (*wine*) casier *m*.

binary ['bainəri] *adj* binaire.

***bind** [baind] *v* lier; (*book*) relier; (*neaten edge*) border; (*force*) obliger. *n* (*coll*) barbe *f*.

binding ['baindin] *n* (*book*) reliure *f*; (*tape*) extra-fort *m*; (*skis*) fixation *f*. *adj* obligatoire.

binoculars [bi'nokjuləz] *pl n* jumelles *f pl*.

biography [bai'ogrəfi] *n* biographie *f*. **biographer** *n* biographe *m, f*. **biographical** *adj* biographique.

biology [bai'olədʒi] *n* biologie *f*. **biological** *adj* biologique. **biologist** *n* biologiste *m, f*.

birch [bəːtʃ] *n* bouleau *m*; (*punishment*) verge *f*.

bird [bəːd] *n* oiseau *m*.

birth [bəːθ] *n* naissance *f*; (*confinement*) accouchement *m*. **birth certificate** acte de naissance *m*. **birth control** contrôle des naissances *m*. **birthday** *n* anniversaire *m*. **birthmark** *n* tache de vin *f*. **birthplace** *n* lieu de naissance *m*. **birth rate** natalité *f*. **give birth to** donner naissance à.

biscuit ['biskit] *n* petit gâteau sec *m*; biscuit *m*.

bishop ['biʃəp] *n* évêque *m*.

bison ['baisən] *n* bison *m*.

bit¹ [bit] *V* **bite**. *n* (*horse*) mors *m*; (*drill*) mèche *f*.

bit² [bit] *n* morceau *m*, bout *m*, brin *m*. **a bit** *adv* un peu. **bit by bit** petit à petit. **do one's bit** fournir sa part d'effort.

bitch [bitʃ] *n* (*dog*) chienne *f*; (*slang*) garce *f*.

***bite** [bait] *v* mordre; (*insect*) piquer. *n* morsure *f*; piqûre *f*; (*mouthful*) bouchée *f*. **biting** *adj* (*remark, etc.*) mordant; (*wind*) cinglant; (*cold*) âpre.

bitten ['bitn] *V* **bite**.

bitter ['bitə] *adj* amer; (*cold*) glacial. **to the bitter end** jusqu'au bout. **bitterness** *n* amertume *f*.

bizarre [bi'zaː] *adj* bizarre.

black ['blak] *adj* noir. *n* noir *m*; (*person*) Noir, -e *m, f*. *v* (*comm*) boycotter. **blacken** *v* noircir. **blackness** *n* noirceur *f*; (*darkness*) obscurité *f*.

blackberry ['blakbəri] *n* (*fruit*) mûre *f*; (*bush*) mûrier *m*.

blackbird ['blakbəːd] *n* merle *m*.

blackboard ['blakbɔːd] *n* tableau (noir) *m*.

blackcurrant [,blak'kʌrənt] *n* cassis *m*.

black eye *n* œil poché *m*.

blackhead ['blakhed] *n* point noir *m*.

black ice *n* verglas *m*.

blackleg ['blakleg] *n* jaune *m*.

blackmail ['blakmeil] *n* chantage *m*. *v* faire chanter. **blackmailer** *n* maître-chanteur *m*.

black market *n* marché noir *m*.

blackout ['blakaut] *n* (*med*) étourdissement *m*; (*war*) black-out *m*; (*power cut*) panne d'électricité *f*.

blacksmith ['blaksmiθ] *n* (*iron*) forgeron *m*; (*horses*) maréchal-ferrant *m*.

bladder ['bladə] *n* vessie *f*.

blade [bleid] *n* lame *f*; (*oar*) plat *m*; (*grass*) brin *m*; (*propeller*) pale *f*.

blame [bleim] *v* attribuer (à), rejeter la responsabilité (sur); (*censure*) blâmer. *n* responsabilité *f*; blâme *m*.

blank [blaŋk] *adj* blanc, blanche; (*cheque*) en blanc; (*empty*) vide; (*puzzled*) déconcerté. *n* blanc *m*, vide *m*; (*gun*) cartouche à blanc *f*.

blanket ['blaŋkit] *n* couverture *f*. *v* recouvrir; (*muffle*) étouffer.

blare [bleə] *n* vacarme *m*; (*trumpet*) sonnerie *f*. *v* retentir; (*radio, etc.*) beugler.

blaspheme [blas'fiːm] *v* blasphémer. **blasphemous** *adj* blasphématoire. **blasphemy** *n* blasphème *m*.

blast [blaːst] *n* explosion *f*; (*noise, wind*) coup *m*; (*trumpet*) fanfare *f*; (*steam*) jet *m*. *v* (*rocks*) faire sauter; (*hopes, etc.*) détruire. *interj* la barbe!

blatant ['bleitənt] *adj* (*obvious*) flagrant; (*shameless*) éhonté.

blaze [bleiz] *n* (*flare*) flambée *f*; (*large fire*) incendie *m*; (*sun*) flamboiement *m*; (*anger*) explosion *f*. *v* flamber; flamboyer; (*light*) resplendir. **blazing** *adj* en flammes; (*sun*) éclatant; (*coll*) furibond.

bleach [bliːtʃ] *n* blanchir; (*hair*) décolorer. *n* décolorant *m*; (*household*) eau de Javel *f*.

bleak [bliːk] *adj* (*landscape*) morne, désolé; (*bare*) austère; (*prospect*) triste; (*weather*) froid.

bleat [bliːt] *v* bêler. *n* bêlement *m*.

bled [bled] *V* **bleed**.

***bleed** [bliːd] *v* saigner. **bleeding** *n* saignement *m*, hémorragie *f*.

blemish ['blemiʃ] *n* défaut *m*; (*reputation*) souillure *f*; (*fruit*) tache *f*. *v* gâter; (*reputation*) ternir.

blend [blend] *v* (se) mélanger; (*ideas*) fusionner; (*colours*) (se) fondre, aller bien ensemble. *n* mélange *m*.

bless [bles] *v* bénir. **bless you!** à vos souhaits! **blessed** (*rel*) béni, bienheureux; (*coll*) sacré. **blessing** *n* bénédiction *f*; (*at meal*) bénédicité; (*benefit*) bien *m*. **what a blessing!** quelle chance!

blew [bluː] *V* **blow²**.

blind [blaind] *adj* aveugle. **blind spot** (*mot*) angle mort *m*. *v* aveugler. *n* (*window*) store *m*; (*mask*) feinte *f*. **the blind** les aveugles *m pl*. **blindness** cécité *f*.

blindfold ['blaindfould] *v* bander les yeux à. *n* bandeau *m*. *adv* les yeux bandés.

blink [bliŋk] *v* cligner des yeux. *n* clignotement *m*. **blinkers** *pl n* œillères *f pl*.

bliss [blis] *n* bonheur suprême *m*. **blissful** *adj* merveilleux, divin.

blister ['blistə] *n* ampoule *f*; (*paint*) boursouflure *f*. *v* se couvrir d'ampoules; se boursoufler.

blizzard ['blizəd] *n* tempête de neige *f*.

blob [blob] *n* goutte *f*.

bloc [blok] *n* (*pol*) bloc *m*.

block [blok] *n* bloc *m*; (*wood*) billot *m*; (*flats*) immeuble *m*; (*houses*) pâté *m*; obstruction *f*. **block letters** majuscules *f pl*. *v* (*obstruct*) bloquer, boucher; (*hinder*) gêner. **blockage** *n* obstruction *f*.

bloke [blouk] *n* (*coll*) type *m*.

blond [blond] *adj* blond. **blonde** *nf, adj* blonde.

blood [blʌd] *n* sang *m*. **bloody** *adj* sanglant, ensanglanté; (*slang*) foutu.

bloodcurdling ['blʌdkəːdliŋ] *adj* à figer le sang.

blood donor *n* donneur, -euse de sang *m, f*.

blood group *n* groupe sanguin *m*.

bloodhound ['blʌdhaund] *n* limier *m*.

blood poisoning *n* empoisonnement du sang *m*.

blood pressure *n* tension *f*. **have high/low blood pressure** faire de l'hypertension/hypotension.

bloodshed ['blʌdʃəd] *n* effusion de sang *f*.

bloodshot ['blʌdʃot] *adj* injecté de sang.

bloodstream ['blʌdstriːm] *n* système sanguin *m*.

bloodthirsty ['blʌdθəːsti] *adj* sanguinaire.

bloom [bluːm] *v* fleurir. *n* floraison *f*; (*single flower*) fleur *f*. **in full bloom** en pleine floraison.

blot [blot] *n* tache *f*; (*ink*) pâté *m*. *v* tacher; (*dry*) sécher. **blot out** effacer. **blotting paper** papier buvard *m*.

blouse [blauz] *n* chemisier *m*.

blow¹ [blou] *n* (*hit*) coup. **come to blows** en venir aux mains.

***blow²** [blou] *v* souffler; (*trumpet*) sonner; (*whistle*) siffler. **blow away** chasser. **blow off** (faire) s'envoler. **blow one's nose** se moucher. **blow out** (s')éteindre. **blow up** (*explode*) (faire) sauter; (*inflate*) gonfler.

blown [bloun] *V* **blow²**.

blubber ['blʌbə] *n* blanc de baleine *m. v* pleurer comme un veau.

blue [bluɪ] *adj* bleu; (*coarse*) grivois. *n* bleu *m*. **bluebell** *n* jacinthe des bois *f*. **blueprint** *n* bleu *m*; plan *m*.

bluff [blʌf] *n* bluff *m. v* bluffer.

blunder [blʌndə] *n* bévue *f*; (*coll*) gaffe *f*; (*social*) impair *m. v* faire une bévue.

blunt [blʌnt] *adj* (*blade*) émoussé; (*point*) épointé; (*frank*) carré, brusque. *v* émousser; épointer.

blur [blɜɪ] *n* tache floue *f. v* estomper. **blurred** *adj* flou.

blush [blʌʃ] *v* rougir. *n* rougeur *f*.

boar [bɔɪ] *n* sanglier *m*.

board [bɔɪd] *v* (*ship, plane*) monter à bord de; (*train, bus*) monter dans; (*lodge*) prendre en pension. *n* (*wood*) planche *f*; (*meals*) pension *f*; (*officials*) conseil *m*; (*naut*) bord *m*. **above board** régulier. **across the board** de portée générale. **boardroom** *n* salle du conseil *f*. **go on board** (s')embarquer. **on board** à bord. **boarder** *n* pensionnaire *m, f*. **boarding card** carte d'embarquement *f*. **boarding house** pension *f*. **boarding school** pensionnat *m*.

boast [bəust] *v* se vanter. *n* fanfaronnade *f*. **boastful** *adj* vantard.

boat [bəut] *n* bateau *m*. **all in the same boat** tous logés à la même enseigne. **boater** *n* (*hat*) canotier *m*. **boating** *n* canotage *m*.

bob¹ [bob] *v* (*up and down*) sautiller; (*curtsy*) faire une révérence. *n* révérence *f*.

bob² [bob] *v* (*hair*) couper court; (*tail*) écourter. *n* (*hairstyle*) coiffure à la Jeanne d'Arc *f*.

bobbin ['bobin] *n* bobine *f*.

bodice ['bodis] *n* corsage *m*.

body ['bodi] *n* corps *m*; (*corpse*) cadavre *m*. **bodyguard** *n* garde du corps *m*. **bodywork** *n* (*mot*) carrosserie *f*.

bog [bog] *n* marais *m*. **get bogged down** s'embourber. **boggy** *adj* marécageux.

bogus ['bougəs] *adj* faux, fausse.

bohemian [bə'hiːmiən] *n*(*m*+*f*), *adj* (*artist*) bohème; (*gipsy*) bohémien, -enne.

boil¹ [boil] *v* (faire) bouillir; (*vegetables, etc.*) cuire à l'eau. **boil down to** revenir à. **boil over** déborder. **boiled egg** œuf à la coque *m*. **boiler** *n* chaudière *f*. **boiler suit** bleus *m pl*. **boiling point** point d'ébullition *m*.

boil² [boil] *n* furoncle *m*.

boisterous ['boistərəs] *adj* (*person*) turbulent; (*sea*) tumultueux.

bold [bould] *adj* hardi. **boldness** *n* hardiesse *f*.

bolster ['boulstə] *n* (*pillow*) traversin *m. v* **bolster up** soutenir.

bolt [boult] *n* (*door*) verrou *m*; (*for nut*) boulon *m*; (*dash*) bond *m. v* verrouiller; (*food*) engouffrer; (*run away*) se sauver.

bomb [bom] *v* bombarder. *n* bombe *f*. **bomber** *n* (*aircraft*) bombardier *m*.

bombard [bəm'baɪd] *v* bombarder. **bombardier** *n* (*mil*) caporal d'artillerie *m*. **bombardment** *n* bombardement *m*.

bond [bond] *n* (*agreement*) engagement *m*; (*tie*) lien *m*; (*comm*) bon *m*; (*glue*) adhérence *f*. **bondage** *n* esclavage *m*.

bone [boun] *n* os *m*; (*fish*) arête *f*. **bone china** porcelaine tendre *f*. **bone-dry** *adj* absolument sec, absolument sèche. **have a bone to pick with** avoir un compte à régler avec. **boned** or **boneless** *adj* désossé. **bony** *adj* osseux; (*person*) anguleux.

bonfire ['bonfaiə] *n* feu de joie *m*.

Bonn [bon] *n* Bonn.

bonnet ['bonit] *n* (*hat*) capote *f*; (*mot*) capot *m*.

bonus ['bounəs] *n* prime *f*.

booby trap ['buɪbi] *n* traquenard *m*; (*mil*) object piégé *m*.

book [buk] *n* livre *m*; (*writing*) cahier *m*; (*tickets*) carnet *m. v* retenir, réserver. **booked up** complet, -ète.

bookcase ['bukkeis] *n* bibliothèque *f*.

booking ['bukiŋ] *n* réservation *f*. **booking office** location *f*.

book-keeper ['buk,kiɪpə] *n* comptable *m, f*. **book-keeping** *n* comptabilité *f*.

booklet ['buklit] *n* brochure *f*.

bookmaker ['bukmeikə] *n* bookmaker *m*.

bookmark ['bukmaɪk] *n* marque *f*.

bookseller ['buksɛlə] *n* libraire *m, f*.

bookshop ['bukʃop] *n* librairie *f*.

bookstall ['bukstoɪl] *n* kiosque à livres *m*.

boom [buɪm] *v* (*noise*) gronder; (*comm*) prospérer. *n* grondement *m*; (*comm*) forte hausse *f*; (*econ*) boom *m*.

boost [buɪst] *v* (*confidence*) renforcer; (*comm*) faire monter; (*publicize*) faire de la réclame pour.

boot [buɪt] *n* (*shoe*) botte *f*; (*mot*) coffre *m*.

booth [buɪð] *n* cabine *f*; (*voting*) isoloir *m*.

booze [buɪz] (*coll*) *n* boissons alcoolisées *f pl*. *v* biberonner. **booze-up** *n* beuverie *f*.

border ['bɔɪdə] *n* (*edge*) bord *m*; (*boundary*) frontière *f*; (*garden*) bordure *f*. **borderline** *n* ligne de démarcation *f*. **borderline case** cas limite *m*. *v* border. **border on** (*be adjacent*) avoisiner; (*be almost*) frôler.

bore¹ [bɔɪ] *v* (*hole*) percer; (*well*) creuser; (*rock*) forer. *n* (*gun*) calibre *m*.

bore² [bɔɪ] *n* (*person*) raseur, -euse *m, f*; (*situation*) corvée *f*. *v* ennuyer. **be bored** s'ennuyer (à). **boredom** *n* ennui *m*. **boring** *adj* ennuyeux.

bore³ [bɔɪ] *V* **bear¹**.

born [bɔɪn] *adj* né. **be born** naître.

borne [bɔɪn] *V* **bear¹**.

borough ['bʌrə] *n* circonscription électorale *f*; (*London*) arrondissement *m*.

borrow ['bɔrou] *v* emprunter (à).

bosom ['buzəm] *n* (*woman*) seins *m pl*; (*of family, etc.*) sein *m*. **bosom friend** ami, -e intime *m, f*.

boss [bos] *n* chef *m*; patron, -onne *m, f*. *v* régenter. **bossy** *adj* tyrannique.

botany ['botəni] *n* botanique *f*. **botanical** *adj* botanique. **botanist** *n* botaniste *m, f*.

both [bouθ] *adj* les deux. *pron* tous les deux.

bother ['boðə] *v* (*annoy*) ennuyer; (*make effort*) se donner la peine (de). *n* ennui *m*. *interj* zut!

bottle ['botl] *n* bouteille *f*; (*beer*) canette *f*; (*perfume*) flacon *m*; (*baby's*) biberon *m*. **bottle-neck** *n* (*road*) rétrécissement de la chaussée *m*; (*traffic*) embouteillage *m*. **bottle-opener** *n* ouvre-bouteilles *m*. *v* (*fruit*) mettre en bocal; (*wine*) mettre en bouteilles. **bottle up** contenir.

bottom ['botəm] *n* fond *m*, bas *m*; (*buttocks*) derrière *m*. **bottomless** *adj* sans fond.

bough [bau] *n* rameau *m*.

bought [bɔɪt] *V* **buy**.

boulder ['bouldə] *n* rocher *m*.

bounce [bauns] *v* (faire) rebondir; (*cheque*) être sans provision. *n* bond *m*.

bound¹ [baund] *v* (*leap*) bondir. *n* bond *m*.

bound² [baund] *v* (*limit*) borner. **bounds** *pl n* limites *f pl*, bornes *f pl*.

bound³ [baund] *V* **bind**. *adj* obligé; sûr; (*tied*) lié.

bound⁴ [baund] *adj* **bound for** en route pour; à destination de.

boundary ['baundəri] *n* limite *f*, frontière *f*.

bouquet [buɪkei] *n* bouquet *m*.

bourgeois ['buəʒwaɪ] *n, adj* bourgeois, -e.

bout [baut] *n* (*illness*) accès *m*; (*fight*) combat *m*; (*period*) période *f*.

bow¹ [bau] *v* (*bend*) (se) courber; (*greeting*) saluer. *n* salut *m*.

bow² [bou] *n* (*archery*) arc *m*; (*music*) archet *m*; (*ribbon*) nœud *m*. **bow-legged** *adj* aux jambes arquées. **bow tie** nœud papillon *m*. **bow window** fenêtre en saillie *f*.

bow³ [bau] *n* (*naut*) avant *m*.

bowels ['bauəlz] *pl n* (*anat*) intestins *m pl*; (*of earth, etc.*) entrailles *f pl*.

bowl¹ [boul] *n* bol *m*; (*for water*) cuvette *f*.

bowl² [boul] *v* (*cricket, etc.*) lancer; (*bowls*) faire rouler. **bowls** *n* jeu de boules *m*. **bowler** *n* (*cricket*) lanceur *m*; (*hat*) chapeau melon *m*. **bowling alley** bowling *m*. **bowling green** terrain de boules *m*.

box¹ [boks] *n* boîte *f*; (*theatre*) loge *f*. **box number** boîte postale *f*. **box office** guichet *m*.

box² [boks] *v* (*sport*) boxer. **boxer** *n* boxeur *m*. **boxing** *n* boxe *f*.

Boxing Day *n* le lendemain de Noël *m*.

boy [boi] *n* garçon *m*; (*son*) fils *m*; (*pupil*) élève *m*. **boyfriend** *n* petit ami *m*. **boyhood** *n* enfance *f*.

boycott ['boikot] *v* boycotter. *n* boycottage *m*.

bra [braɪ] *n* soutien-gorge *m*.

brace [breis] *n* (*dental*) appareil *m*; (*tool*) vilebrequin *m*; (*pair*) paire *f*. **braces** *pl n* bretelles *f pl*. *v* soutenir. **brace oneself** se préparer. **bracing** *adj* fortifiant.

bracelet ['breislit] *n* bracelet *m*.

bracken ['brakən] *n* fougère *f*.

bracket ['brakit] *n* support *m*; (*writing*) parenthèse *f*. *v* mettre entre parenthèses; (*group together*) accoler.

brag [brag] *v* se vanter.

braille [breil] *nm, adj* braille.

brain [brein] *n* cerveau *m*. **brains** *pl* intelligence *f sing*; (*cookery*) cervelle *f sing*. *adj* cérébral. **brain-child** *n* invention personnelle *f*. **brainwashing** *n* lavage de cerveau *m*; (*coll*) bourrage de crâne *m*.

brainwave n inspiration f. **brainy** adj intelligent.

braise [breiz] v braiser.

brake [breik] n frein m. v freiner.

bramble ['brambl] n roncier m; (blackberry bush) ronce des haies f.

branch [braɪntʃ] n branche f; (road) embranchement m, bifurcation f; (comm) succursale f. v (road) bifurquer.

brand [brand] v marquer. n marque f. **brand-new** adj tout neuf, toute neuve.

brandish ['brandiʃ] v brandir.

brandy ['brandi] n cognac m.

brass [braɪs] n cuivre jaune m. **brass band** fanfare f.

brassière ['brasiə] V **bra.**

brave [breiv] adj courageux. v braver. **bravery** n courage m.

brawl [broɪl] n rixe f. v se quereller.

brawn [broɪn] n (cookery) fromage de tête m; (strength) muscle m.

brazen ['breizn] adj effronté.

breach [briːtʃ] n (gap) brèche f; (violation) infraction f; (promise) violation f; (contract) rupture f. **breach of the peace** attentat à l'ordre public m.

bread [bred] n pain m; (slang: money) fric m. **breadcrumbs** pl n chapelure f sing. **bread-winner** n soutien de famille m.

breadth [bredθ] n largeur m.

***break** [breik] v (se) casser; (promise, law, etc.) violer. **break down** (cease functioning) tomber en panne; (cry) fondre en larmes. **breakdown** n panne f; (mental) depression nerveuse f; analyse f. **break into** (house) entrer par effraction; (safe, etc.) forcer. **breakthrough** n découverte sensationnelle f. **break up** (se) briser; (school) entrer en vacances. n pause f; rupture f; interruption f. **breakable** adj cassable, fragile. **breakage** n casse f. **breaker** n (wave) brisant m.

breakfast ['brekfəst] n petit déjeuner m.

breast [brest] n (chest) poitrine f; (woman's) sein m; (chicken) blanc m. **breast-feed** v allaiter. **breast-stroke** n brasse f.

breath [breθ] n haleine f, souffle m. **breathtaking** adj stupéfiant. **out of breath** à bout de souffle.

breathalyser ['breθəlaizə] n alcootest m.

breathe [briːð] v respirer; (sigh) pousser. **breather** n moment de répit m. **breathing** n respiration f.

bred [bred] V **breed.**

***breed** [briːd] n espèce f. v (rear) élever; (reproduce) se multiplier; (give rise to) engendrer. **breeding** n élevage m; (manners) savoir-vivre m.

breeze [briːz] n brise f.

brew [bruɪ] v (beer) brasser; (tea) (faire) infuser; (storm) (se) préparer. n brassage m; infusion f. **brewery** n brasserie f.

bribe [braib] n pot-de-vin m. v suborner, soudoyer. **bribery** n corruption f.

brick [brik] n brique f. **bricklayer** n maçon m. v **brick up** murer.

bride [braid] n mariée f. **bridegroom** n marié m. **bridesmaid** n demoiselle d'honneur f. **bridal** adj nuptial; de mariée.

bridge[1] [bridʒ] n pont m; (naut) passerelle m.

bridge[2] [bridʒ] n (cards) bridge m.

bridle ['braidl] n bride f. **bridle path** sentier m. v (horse) brider; (anger) regimber.

brief [briːf] adj bref, brève. v donner des instructions à. n (law) dossier m. **briefcase** n serviette f. **briefly** adv brièvement.

brigade [bri'geid] n brigade f.

bright [brait] adj (shining) brillant; (welllit) clair; (colour) vif; (clever) intelligent. **brighten** v faire briller; s'éclairer; (cheer) (s')égayer. **brightness** n éclat m; (of light) intensité f.

brilliant ['briljənt] adj (clever) brillant; (sun) éclatant. **brilliance** n éclat m.

brim [brim] n bord m. **brimful** adj plein à déborder.

brine [brain] n eau salée f; (cookery) saumure f.

***bring** [briŋ] v (person) amener; (object) apporter. **bring about** causer, provoquer. **bring in** faire entrer; introduire; (comm) rapporter. **bring off** (succeed) réussir. **bring out** sortir; (colour, etc.) faire ressortir; (publish) publier. **bring up** (rear) élever; (question) soulever; (vomit) vomir.

brink [briŋk] n bord m. **on the brink of** à deux doigts de.

brisk [brisk] adj vif; (trade) actif.

bristle ['brisl] n poil m. v se hérisser. **bristly** adj aux poils durs.

Britain ['britn] n Grande-Bretagne f. **British** adj britannique. **the British** les Britanniques m pl.

Brittany ['britəni] n Bretagne f.

brittle ['britl] adj fragile.

broad [brɔɪd] *adj* (*wide*) large; vaste; général; (*accent*) prononcé. **broad bean** fève *f*. **broad-minded** *adj* tolérant. **broaden** *v* (s')élargir. **broadly** *adv* en gros.
broadcast ['brɔɪdkaɪst] *v* *émettre; (*rumour, etc.*) répandre. *n* émission *f*. *adj* radiodiffusé; télévisé. **broadcasting** *n* radiodiffusion *f*; télévision *f*.
broccoli ['brɔkəli] *n* brocoli *m*.
brochure ['brouʃuə] *n* brochure *f*.
broke [brouk] *V* **break**. *adj* (*coll*) à sec.
broken ['broukn] *V* **break**.
broker ['broukə] *n* courtier *m*.
bronchitis [brɔŋ'kaitis] *n* bronchite *f*.
bronze [brɔnz] *n* bronze *m*. *v* brunir; (se) bronzer.
brooch [broutʃ] *n* broche *f*.
brood [bruɪd] *v* couver; (*think*) ruminer. *n* nichée *f*.
brook [bruk] *n* ruisseau *m*.
broom [bruɪm] *n* (*brush*) balai *m*; (*bush*) genêt *m*.
broth [brɔθ] *n* bouillon *m*.
brothel ['brɔθl] *n* bordel *m*.
brother ['brʌðə] *n* frère *m*. **brother-in-law** *n* beau-frère *m*. **brotherhood** *n* fraternité *f*. **brotherly** *adj* fraternel.
brought [brɔɪt] *V* **bring**.
brow [brau] *n* (*forehead*) front *m*; (*hill*) sommet *m*.
brown [braun] *n* brun, marron; (*tanned*) bronzé. *n* brun *m*. *v* (*skin*) brunir; (*cookery*) (faire) dorer. **be browned off** (*coll*) en avoir marre.
browse [brauz] *v* (*book*) feuilleter; (*animal*) brouter.
bruise [bruɪz] *n* bleu *m*, meurtrissure *f*. *v* faire un bleu à, (se) meurtrir; (*fruit*) (s')abîmer.
brunette [bruɪ'net] *n* brunette *f*.
brush [brʌʃ] *n* brosse *f*; (*broom*) balai *m*; (*undergrowth*) taillis *m*; (*skirmish*) accrochage *m*. *v* brosser; balayer. **brush against** effleurer. **brush up on** se remettre à.
brusque [bruʂk] *adj* brusque.
Brussels ['brʌsəlz] *n* Bruxelles. **Brussels sprouts** choux de Bruxelles *m pl*.
brute [bruɪt] *n* brute *f*. **brutal** *adj* brutal; de brute. **brutality** *n* brutalité *f*.
bubble ['bʌbl] *n* bulle *f*; (*in liquid*) bouillon *m*. *v* bouillonner; (*champagne*) pétiller.
Bucharest [buɪkə'rest] *n* Bucharest.
buck [bʌk] *n* mâle *m*. **buck-teeth** *pl n*

dents de lapin *f pl*. *v* lancer une ruade. **buck up** (*coll: hurry up*) se remuer; (*coll: cheer up*) ravigoter.
bucket ['bʌkit] *n* seau *m*.
buckle ['bʌkl] *n* (*fastening*) boucle *f*; (*distortion*) gauchissement *m*, voilure *f*. *v* (se) boucler; gauchir, (se) voiler.
bud [bʌd] *n* bourgeon *m*; (*flower*) bouton *m*. *v* bourgeonner. **budding** *adj* (*plant*) bourgeonnant; (*talent*) en herbe.
Budapest [buɪdə'pest] *n* Budapest.
budge [bʌdʒ] *v* (faire) bouger.
budgerigar ['bʌdʒərigaɪ] *n* perruche *f*.
budget ['bʌdʒit] *n* budget *m*. *v* budgétiser. **budget for** prévoir des frais de.
buffalo ['bʌfəlou] *n* buffle, -esse *m*, *f*.
buffer ['bʌfə] *n* tampon *m*.
buffet[1] ['bʌfit] *n* (*blow*) coup *m*. *v* frapper, battre; (*waves*) ballotter.
buffet[2] ['bufei] *n* buffet *m*. **buffet car** voiture-buffet *f*. **buffet lunch** lunch *m*.
bug [bʌg] *n* punaise *f*; (*germ*) microbe *m*; (*microphone*) micro *m*. *v* (*room*) poser des micros dans; (*annoy*) embêter.
bugger ['bʌgə] (*vulgar*) *n* con *m*. *interj* merde alors! **bugger off!** fous-moi la paix!
bugle ['bjuɪgl] *n* clairon *m*.
*build [bild] *v* bâtir, construire. **build up** (*land*) urbaniser; (*tension*) monter; (*develop*) se développer. *n* carrure *f*. **builder** *n* entrepreneur *m*; ouvrier du bâtiment *m*. **building** *n* construction *f*; (*thing built*) bâtiment *m*; (*offices, etc.*) immeuble *m*. **building site** chantier de construction *m*. **building society** société immobilière *f*.
built [bilt] *V* **build**.
bulb [bʌlb] *n* (*plant*) bulbe *m*; (*elec*) ampoule *f*; (*thermometer*) cuvette *f*.
Bulgaria [bʌl'geəriə] *n* Bulgarie *f*. **Bulgarian** *n* (*people*) Bulgare *m*, *f*; *nm*, *adj* bulgare.
bulge [bʌldʒ] *v* bomber; (*pocket, etc.*) être gonflé (de). *n* bombement *m*, gonflement *m*; (*increase*) poussée *f*, augmentation *f*. **bulging** *adj* (*eyes*) protubérant; (*pockets*) bourru.
bulk [bʌlk] *n* grosseur *f*; volume *m*. **in bulk** en gros. **the bulk of** la plus grande partie de. **bulky** *adj* encombrant.
bull [bul] *n* taureau *m*. **bulldog** *n* bouledogue *m*. **bulldozer** *n* bulldozer *m*. **bullfight** *n* corrida *f*. **bull's eye** (*target*) noir *m*, mille *m*.

bullet ['bulit] *n* balle *f*. **bullet-proof** *adj* pare-balles; (*car*) blindé.

bulletin ['bulətin] *n* bulletin *m*.

bullion ['buliən] *n* (*gold*) or en barre *m*; (*silver*) argent en lingot *m*.

bully ['buli] *n* tyran *m*; (*school*) brute *m*. *v* tyranniser; intimider; brutaliser.

bum [bʌm] (*coll*) *n* arrière-train *m*. *adj* moche. *v* **bum around** fainéanter.

bump [bʌmp] *n* (*blow*) heurt *m*, choc *m*; (*on road*) bosse *f*. *v* heurter; (*head, etc.*) cogner. **bump into** (*car*) tamponner; (*meet*) rencontrer par hasard. **bumpy** *adj* (*road*) bosselé; (*ride*) cahoteux.

bumper ['bʌmpə] *n* (*mot*) pare-chocs *m invar*. *adj* sensationnel.

bun [bʌn] *n* (*hair*) chignon *m*.

bunch [bʌntʃ] *n* (*flowers*) bouquet *m*; (*grapes*) grappe *f*; (*tuft*) touffe *f*; (*people*) bande *f*.

bundle ['bʌndl] *n* paquet *m*, ballot *m*. *v* empaqueter, faire un ballot de.

bungalow ['bʌŋgəlou] *n* bungalow *m*.

bungle ['bʌŋgl] *v* (*coll*) bâcler. **bungling** *adj* maladroit.

bunion ['bʌnjən] *n* oignon *m*.

bunk [bʌŋk] *n* couchette *f*.

bunker ['bʌŋkə] *n* (*coal*) coffre *m*; (*naut*) soute *f*; (*golf*) bunker *m*; (*mil*) blockhaus *m*.

buoy [boi] *n* bouée *f*. **buoyancy** *n* (*ship*) flottabilité *f*; (*liquid*) poussée *f*. **buoyant** *adj* flottable; (*mood*) gai.

burden ['bəidn] *n* fardeau *m*. *v* charger.

bureau ['bjuərou] *n* (*desk*) secrétaire *m*; (*office*) bureau *m*.

bureaucracy [bju'rokrəsi] *n* bureaucratie *f*. **bureaucrat** *n* bureaucrate *m, f*. **bureaucratic** *adj* bureaucratique.

burglar ['bəiglə] *n* cambrioleur, -euse *m, f*. **burglar alarm** sonnerie antivol *f*. **burglary** *n* cambriolage *m*. **burgle** *v* cambrioler.

Burgundy ['bəigəndi] *n* (*wine*) bourgogne *m*.

*** burn** [bəin] *v* brûler; (*building*) incendier. *n* brûlure *f*. **burning** *adj* brûlant; (*passion*) ardent; (*lit*) allumé.

burnt [bəint] *V* **burn**.

burrow ['bʌrou] *n* terrier *m*. *v* creuser.

*** burst** [bəist] *v* éclater; (*balloon, etc.*) crever. **burst in** faire irruption. *n* explosion *f*; éclat *m*.

bury ['beri] *v* enterrer. **burial** *n* enterrement *m*.

bus [bʌs] *n* autobus *m*. **bus shelter** abribus *m*. **bus station** gare routière *f*. **bus stop** arrêt d'autobus *m*.

bush [buʃ] *n* buisson *m*; (*thicket*) taillis *m*. **the bush** (*Australia*) la brousse *f*. **bushy** *adj* touffu.

business ['biznis] *n* affaires *f pl*; (*enterprise*) commerce *f*; (*matter*) affaire *f*. **businessman** *n* homme d'affaires *m*. **mind one's own business** se mêler de ses affaires. **businesslike** *adj* pratique; sérieux.

bust[1] [bʌst] *n* (*anat*) buste *m*; (*measurement*) tour de poitrine *m*.

bust[2] [bʌst] *adj* (*coll: broken*) fichu. **go bust** faire faillite.

bustle ['bʌsl] *v* s'affairer. *n* remue-ménage *m*.

busy ['bizi] *adj* occupé. **busybody** *n* mouche du coche *f*.

but [bʌt] *conj* mais. *adv* (*only*) seulement. *prep* (*except*) sauf. **but for** sans.

butane ['bjuitein] *n* butane *m*.

butcher ['butʃə] *n* boucher *m*. **butcher's shop** boucherie *f*. *v* massacrer; (*animal*) abattre.

butler ['bʌtlə] *n* maître d'hôtel *m*.

butt[1] [bʌt] *n* (*cigarette*) mégot *m*, bout *m*; (*gun*) crosse *f*.

butt[2] [bʌt] *n* victime *f*.

butt[3] [bʌt] *v* (*goat*) donner un coup de corne à. **butt in** s'immiscer dans la conversation, intervenir. *n* coup de corne *m*.

butter ['bʌtə] *n* beurre *m*. *v* beurrer.

buttercup ['bʌtəkʌp] *n* bouton d'or *m*.

butterfly ['bʌtəflai] *n* papillon *m*; (*swimming*) brasse papillon *f*. **have butterflies** (*coll*) avoir le trac.

buttocks ['bʌtəks] *pl n* (*person*) fesses *f pl*; (*animal*) croupe *f sing*.

button ['bʌtn] *n* bouton *m*. **buttonhole** *n* boutonnière *f*; (*flower*) fleur *f*. *v* (se) boutonner.

buttress ['bʌtris] *n* (*arch*) arc-boutant *m*; (*support*) soutien *m*. *v* soutenir.

*** buy** [bai] *v* acheter. *n* **a good/bad buy** une bonne/mauvaise affaire. **buyer** acheteur, -euse *m, f*.

buzz [bʌz] *v* bourdonner. *n* bourdonnement *m*.

by [bai] *prep* par; (*near*) près de; (*before*) avant; (*per*) à. *adv* près. **by and by** bientôt. **by the way** à propos. **go by** passer.

bye-law ['bailɔɪ] *n* arrêté municipal *m*.

by-election ['baiɪˌlekʃən] *n* election partielle *f*.

bypass ['baiˌpɑɪs] *n* route de contournement *f*. *v* contourner.

bystander ['baiˌstandə] *n* spectateur, -trice *m*, *f*.

C

cab [kab] *n* taxi *m*; (*lorry*) cabine *f*.

cabaret ['kabərei] *n* cabaret *m*; (*show*) spectacle *m*.

cabbage ['kabidʒ] *n* chou (*pl* choux) *m*.

cabin ['kabin] *n* cabine *f*; (*hut*) cabane *f*.

cabinet ['kabinit] *n* cabinet *m*; (*filing*) classeur *m*; (*pol*) cabinet *m*. **cabinet-maker** *n* ébéniste *m*. **cabinet minister** membre du cabinet *m*.

cable ['keibl] *n* câble *m*. **cablecar** *n* téléphérique *m*. *v* câbler.

cackle ['kakl] *v* caqueter; (*laugh*) glousser. *n* caquet *m*; gloussement *m*.

cactus ['kaktəs] *n* cactus *m*.

caddie ['kadi] *n* caddie *m*.

cadence ['keidəns] *n* cadence *f*; (*voice*) modulation *f*.

cadet [kə'det] *n* élève officier *m*.

café ['kafei] *n* café *m*.

cafeteria [kafə'tiəriə] *n* cafétéria *f*.

caffeine ['kafiɪn] *n* caféine *f*.

cage [keidʒ] *n* cage *f*.

cake [keik] *n* gâteau *m*; (*soap*, *etc*) pain *m*. **cake shop** pâtisserie *f*. **it's a piece of cake** c'est du gâteau. **like hot cakes** comme des petits pains. **caked** *adj* coagulé. **caked with** raidi par.

calamine ['kaləmain] *n* calamine *f*. **calamine lotion** lotion calmante à la calamine *f*.

calamity [kə'laməti] *n* calamité *f*.

calcium ['kalsiəm] *n* calcium *m*.

calculate ['kalkjuleit] *v* calculer; (*reckon*) évaluer. **calculable** *adj* calculable. **calculated** *adj* délibéré. **calculating** *adj* (*scheming*) calculateur, -trice. **calculation** *n* calcul *m*. **calculator** *n* machine à calculer *f*, calculatrice *f*.

calendar ['kaləndə] *n* calendrier *m*. **calendar month** mois de calendrier *m*.

calf¹ [kɑɪf] *n* (*animal*) veau *m*.

calf² [kɑɪf] *n* (*anat*) mollet *m*.

calibre ['kalibə] *n* calibre *m*.

call [kɔɪl] *n* appel *m*; cri *m*; visite *f*. **callbox** *n* cabine téléphonique *f*. *v* appeler; (*waken*) réveiller; (*visit*) passer. **be called** s'appeler. **call for** (*need*) demander; (*person*) passer prendre. **call off** (*cancel*) annuler. **call on** (*visit*) passer voir. **call up** (*mil*) mobiliser. **caller** *n* visiteur, -euse *m*, *f*; (*phone*) demandeur, -euse *m*, *f*. **calling** *n* vocation *f*; (*job*) métier *m*.

callous ['kaləs] *adj* dur, sans pitié.

calm [kɑɪm] *adj* calme. *n* calme *m*; période de tranquillité *f*. *v* calmer. **calm down** (se) calmer. **calmness** *n* calme *m*; sang-froid *m*.

calorie ['kaləri] *n* calorie *f*.

came [keim] *V* **come**.

camel ['kaməl] *n* chameau, -elle *m*, *f*. **camel-hair** *n* poil de chameau *m*.

camera ['kamərə] *n* appareil-photo *m*; (*cine*) caméra *f*.

Cameroon [kamə'ruɪn] *n* Cameroun *m*.

camouflage ['kaməflɑɪʒ] *n* camouflage *m*. *v* camoufler.

camp¹ [kamp] *v* camper. **go camping** faire du camping. *n* camp *m*. **camp-bed** *n* lit de camp *m*. **campsite** *n* camping *m*.

camp² [kamp] *adj* affecté; efféminé; (*slang: homosexual*) pédé.

campaign [kam'pein] *n* campagne *f*. *v* faire campagne.

campus ['kampəs] *n* campus *m*.

camshaft ['kamʃɑɪft] *n* (*mot*) arbre à cames *m*.

*can¹ [kan] *v* (*be able*) pouvoir; (*know how to*) savoir.

can² [kan] *n* (*oil*) bidon *m*; (*beer*, *fruit*) boîte *f*. **can-opener** *n* ouvre-boîtes *m* *invar*. *v* mettre en boîte.

Canada ['kanədə] *n* Canada *m*. **Canadian** *n* Canadien, -enne *m*, *f*; *adj* canadien.

canal [kə'nal] *n* canal *m*.

canary [kə'neəri] *n* serin *m*.

Canberra ['kanbərə] *n* Canberra.

cancel ['kansəl] *v* annuler; (*order*) décommander; (*contract*) résilier; (*train*) supprimer; (*cheque*) faire opposition à. **cancellation** *n* annulation *f*; suppression *f*.

cancer ['kansə] *n* cancer *m*. **Cancer** *n* Cancer *m*.

candid ['kandid] *adj* franc, franche.

candidate ['kandidət] *n* candidat *m*.

candle ['kandl] n (*wax*) bougie *f*; (*tallow*) chandelle *f*. candle-light n lumière de bougie *f*. candlestick n bougeoir *m*; chandelier *m*. candlewick n chenille de coton *f*.

candour ['kandə] n franchise *f*.

candy ['kandi] n (*US*) bonbons *m pl*. candied adj glacé, confit.

cane [kein] n canne *f*; (*school*) verge *f*. v fouetter.

canine ['keinain] adj canin. n (*tooth*) canine *f*.

canister ['kanistə] n boîte *f*.

cannabis ['kanəbis] n (*drug*) cannabis *m*; (*plant*) chanvre indien *m*.

cannibal ['kanibəl] n(*m+f*). adj cannibale. cannibalism n cannibalisme *m*.

cannon ['kanən] n canon *m*. cannonball n boulet de canon *m*.

canoe [kə'nuː] n canoë *m*; (*sport*) kayac *m*. v faire du canoë; faire du kayac.

canon ['kanən] n canon *m*. canonical adj canonique. canonize v canoniser.

canopy ['kanəpi] n baldaquin *m*, dais *m*.

canteen [kan'tiːn] n (*dining place*) cantine *f*; (*flask*) bidon *m*; (*cutlery*) ménagère *f*.

canter ['kantə] n petit galop *m*. v aller au petit galop.

canton ['kantən] n canton *m*.

canvas ['kanvəs] n toile *f*.

canvass ['kanvəs] v (*pol*) faire du démarchage électoral; (*for orders, votes*) solliciter. canvasser n (*pol*) agent électoral *m*; (*comm*) démarcheur *m*. canvassing n démarchage *m*.

canyon ['kanjən] n cañon *m*.

cap [kap] n (*hat*) casquette *f*; (*bottle*) capsule *f*; (*pen*) capuchon *m*. v capsuler; surpasser.

capable ['keipəbl] adj capable; (*situation*) susceptible. capability n capacité *f*; aptitude *f*.

capacity [kə'pasəti] n capacité *f*; (*status*) qualité *f*.

cape[1] [keip] n (*cloak*) pèlerine *f*.

cape[2] [keip] n (*geog*) cap *m*.

caper ['keipə] n (*cookery*) câpre *f*.

capital ['kapitl] n (*city*) capitale *f*; (*letter*) majuscule *f*; (*money*) capital *m*. adj capital. capitalism n capitalisme *m*. capitalist n capitaliste *m*, *f*. capitalize v capitaliser; (*word*) mettre une majuscule à. capitalize on tirer parti de.

capitulate [kə'pitjuleit] v capituler. capitulation n capitulation *f*.

capricious [kə'priʃəs] adj capricieux.

Capricorn ['kaprikoin] n Capricorne *m*.

capsicum ['kapsikəm] n piment *m*.

capsize [kap'saiz] v (*naut*) (faire) chavirer.

capsule ['kapsjuːl] n capsule *f*.

captain ['kaptin] n capitaine *m*.

caption ['kapʃən] n légende *f*; (*title*) sous-titre *m*.

captive ['kaptiv] n captif, -ive *m*, *f*. adj captif. captivate v captiver. captivity n captivité *f*.

capture ['kaptʃə] v prendre, capturer; (*attention*) capter. n capture *f*. captor n ravisseur *m*.

car [kaɪ] n voiture *f*; (*rail*) wagon *m*. car park parking *m*. car wash lave-auto *m*.

caramel ['karəmel] n caramel *m*.

carat ['karət] n carat *m*.

caravan ['karəvan] n caravane *f*; (*gipsy*) roulotte *f*.

caraway ['karəwei] n cumin *m*, carvi *m*.

carbohydrates [kaɪbə'haidreits] pl n farineux *m pl*, féculents *m pl*.

carbon ['kaɪbən] n carbone *m*. carbon copy (*typing*) carbone *m*; (*identical thing*) réplique *f*. carbon dioxide gaz carbonique *m*. carbon paper papier carbone *m*.

carburettor ['kaɪbjuretə] n carburateur *m*.

carcass ['kaɪkəs] n carcasse *f*.

card [kaɪd] n carte *f*; (*index*) fiche *f*. cardboard n carton *m*. card trick tour de cartes. it's on the cards il y a de grandes chances. play one's cards right bien mener son jeu.

cardiac ['kaɪdiak] adj cardiaque. cardiac arrest arrêt du cœur *m*.

cardigan ['kaɪdigən] n cardigan *m*.

cardinal ['kaɪdənl] nm, adj cardinal.

care [keə] v se soucier (de). care for (*like*) aimer; (*tend*) soigner; (*look after*) s'occuper de. n soin *m*, attention *f*; (*worry*) souci *m*. care of chez. take care faire attention. take care of s'occuper de. carefree adj sans souci, insouciant. careful adj prudent; conscientieux. be careful! faites attention! careless adj négligent; (*work*) peu soigné.

career [kə'riə] n carrière *f*.

caress [kə'res] v caresser. n caresse *f*.

caretaker ['keəteikə] n gardien, -enne *m*, *f*; concierge *m*, *f*.

cargo ['kaɪgou] n cargaison *m*.

caricature ['karıkətjuə] *n* caricature *f. v* caricaturer. **caricaturist** *n* caricaturiste *m, f.*

carnage ['kaınıdʒ] *n* carnage *m.*

carnal ['kaınl] *adj* charnel. **carnal knowledge** (*law*) relations sexuelles *f pl.*

carnation [kaı'neıʃən] *n* œillet *m.*

carnival ['kaınıvəl] *n* carnaval *m.*

carnivorous [kaı'nıvərəs] *adj* carnivore. **carnivore** *n* carnivore *m.*

carol ['karəl] *n* chant joyeux *m.* **Christmas carol** chant de Noël *m.*

carpenter ['kaıpəntə] *n* charpentier *m.* **carpentry** *n* charpenterie *f.*

carpet ['kaıpıt] *n* tapis *m.* **carpet-sweeper** *n* balai mécanique *m. v* moquetter.

carriage ['karıdʒ] *n* (*horse-drawn*) voiture *f*; (*rail*) wagon *m*; (*comm*) transport *m*; (*person*) maintien *m.* **carriageway** *n* chaussée *f.* **dual carriageway** route à chaussées séparées *f.*

carrier ['karıə] *n* (*comm*) entreprise de transports *f*; (*med*) porteur, -euse *m, f.* **carrier-bag** *n* sac en plastique *m.*

carrot ['karət] *n* carotte *f.*

carry ['karı] *v* porter; transporter. **carry away** emporter. **carrycot** *n* porte-bébé *m.* **carry on** continuer. **carry out** exécuter. **get carried away** (*coll*) s'emballer.

cart [kaıt] *n* (*horse-drawn*) charrette *f.* **cart-horse** *n* cheval de trait *m.* **turn a cart-wheel** faire la roue. *v* transporter; (*coll*) trimballer.

cartilage ['kaıtəlıdʒ] *n* cartilage *m.*

cartography [kaı'togrəfı] *n* cartographie *f.* **cartographer** *n* cartographe *m, f.*

carton ['kaıtən] *n* (*cream, etc.*) pot *m*; (*milk*) carton *m.*

cartoon [kaı'tuın] *n* dessin *m*; (*film*) dessin animé *m.* **cartoonist** *n* dessinateur, -trice *m, f*; animateur, -trice *m, f.*

cartridge ['kaıtrıdʒ] *n* cartouche *f*; (*camera*) chargeur *m.* **cartridge paper** papier à cartouche *m.*

carve [kaıv] *v* (*meat*) découper; (*wood, etc.*) tailler; sculpter; (*initials*) graver. **carving** *n* sculpture *f.* **carving knife** couteau à découper *m.*

cascade [kas'keıd] *n* cascade *f. v* tomber en cascade.

case¹ [keıs] *n* cas *m*; (*law*) affaire *f*; arguments *m pl.* **in any case** en tout cas. **in case** à tout hasard. **in case of** en cas de. **in that case** dans ce cas-là.

case² [keıs] *n* (*luggage*) valise *f*; (*crate*) caisse *f*; (*violin, camera, etc.*) étui *m.*

cash [kaʃ] *n* (*money*) argent *m*; (*not cheque*) espèces *f pl*; (*immediate payment*) argent comptant *m.* **cash desk** caisse *f.* **cash register** caisse enregistreuse *f. v* encaisser.

cashier¹ [ka'ʃıə] *n* caissier *m.*

cashier² [ka'ʃıə] *v* renvoyer; (*mil*) casser.

cashmere [kaʃ'mıə] *n* cachemire *m.*

casino [kə'sıınou] *n* casino *m.*

cask [kaısk] *n* fût *m.*

casket ['kaıskıt] *n* coffret *m.*

casserole ['kasəroul] *n* (*dish*) cocotte *f*; (*food*) ragoût en cocotte *m. v* cuire en cocotte.

cassette [kə'set] *n* cassette *f.*

cassock ['kasək] *n* soutane *f.*

*cast [kaıst] *n* (*mould*) moulage *m*; (*theatre*) distribution *f*; (*throw*) coup *m. v* (*throw*) jeter, lancer; (*plaster, etc.*) couler; (*theatre*) distribuer les rôles (de). **cast away** rejeter. **castaway** *n* naufragé, -e *m, f.* **casting vote** voix prépondérante *f.* **cast-iron** *adj* en fonte; (*excuse, etc.*) inattaquable.

caste [kaıst] *n* caste *f.*

castle ['kaısl] *n* château fort *m.*

castor oil ['kaıstə] *n* huile de ricin *f.*

castrate [kə'streıt] *v* châtrer; émasculer. **castration** *n* castration *f.*

casual ['kaʒuəl] *adj* (*chance*) fortuit, fait par hasard; (*informal*) sans-gêne, désinvolte. **casually** *adv* par hasard; avec désinvolture.

casualty ['kaʒuəltı] *n* (*injured*) blessé, -e *m, f*; (*dead*) mort, -e *m, f*; (*of accident*) victime *f*; (*hospital ward*) salle des accidentés *f.*

cat [kat] *n* chat, chatte *m, f.* **cat's eyes** (*road*) cataphotes *m pl.* **catsuit** *n* combinaison-pantalon *f.* **let the cat out of the bag** vendre la mèche.

catalogue ['katəlog] *n* catalogue *m. v* cataloguer.

catalyst ['katəlıst] *n* catalyse *f.*

catamaran [katəmə'ran] *n* catamaran *m.*

catapult ['katəpʌlt] *n* lance-pierres *m invar*; (*aero, mil*) catapulte *f. v* catapulter.

cataract ['katərakt] *n* cataracte *f.*

catarrh [kə'taı] *n* catarrhe *m.*

catastrophe [kə'tastrəfı] *n* catastrophe *f.* **catastrophic** *adj* catastrophique.

*catch [katʃ] v attraper; (by surprise) prendre; (train, etc.) ne pas manquer; (on nail) (s')accrocher; (hear) saisir. **catch fire** prendre feu. **catch on** devenir populaire; (understand) comprendre. **catch up** (se) rattraper. n prise f; (drawback) attrape f; (window) loqueteau m. **catching** adj contagieux.

category ['katəgəri] n catégorie f. **categorical** adj catégorique. **categorize** v classer par catégories.

cater ['keitə] v **cater for** (needs) pourvoir à. **caterer** n fournisseur m, traiteur m. **catering** n restauration f.

caterpillar ['katəpilə] n chenille f.

cathedral [kə'θiːdrəl] n cathédrale f.

cathode ['kaθoud] n cathode f. **cathode ray tube** tube cathodique m.

catholic ['kaθəlik] adj (rel) catholique; (tastes, etc.) éclectique. n catholique m, f. **catholicism** n catholicisme m.

catkin ['katkin] n chaton m.

cattle ['katl] pl n bétail m sing.

catty ['kati] adj (slang) vache.

caught [kɔit] V **catch**.

cauliflower ['koliflauə] n chou-fleur (pl choux-fleurs) m.

cause [cɔiz] v causer. n cause f.

causeway ['kɔizwei] n chaussée f.

caustic ['kɔistik] adj caustique.

caution ['kɔiʃən] n prudence f; (warning) avertissement m; réprimande f. v avertir. **cautious** adj prudent.

cavalry ['kavəlri] n cavalerie f.

cave [keiv] n caverne f, grotte f. v **cave in** s'effondrer; (wall) céder.

caviar ['kaviaı] n caviar m.

cavity ['kavəti] n cavité f. **cavity wall** mur creux m.

cayenne [kei'en] n cayenne m.

cease [siːs] v cesser. **cease-fire** n cessez-le-feu m invar. **ceaseless** adj incessant. **ceaselessly** adv sans cesse.

cedar ['siːdə] n cèdre m.

cedilla [si'dilə] n cédille f.

ceiling ['siːliŋ] n plafond m.

celebrate ['seləbreit] v célébrer. **celebrated** adj célèbre. **celebration** n célébration f; (occasion) festivités f pl. **celebrity** n célébrité f.

celery ['seləri] n céleri m. **stick of celery** côte de céleri f.

celestial [sə'lestiəl] adj céleste.

celibate ['selibət] n(m+f), adj célibataire. **celibacy** n célibat m.

cell [sel] n cellule f; (elec) élément m.

cellar ['selə] n cave f.

cello ['tʃelou] n violoncelle m. **cellist** n violoncelliste m, f.

cellular ['seljulə] adj cellulaire; (blanket) en cellular.

cement [sə'ment] n ciment m. **cement-mixer** n bétonnière f. v cimenter.

cemetery ['semətri] n cimetière m.

cenotaph ['senətaif] n cénotaphe m.

censor ['sensə] n censeur m. v censurer. **censorship** n censure f.

censure ['senʃə] v blâmer. n critique f.

census ['sensəs] n recensement m.

cent [sent] n cent m. **per cent** pour cent.

centenary [sen'tiːnəri] nm, adj centenaire.

centigrade ['sentigreid] adj centigrade.

centimetre ['sentimiitə] n centimètre m.

centipede ['sentipiid] n mille-pattes m invar.

central ['sentrəl] adj central. **central heating** chauffage central m. **centralization** n centralisation f. **centralize** v (se) centraliser.

centre ['sentə] n centre m. v centrer. **centre on** (thoughts) se concentrer sur; (problem) tourner autour de.

centrifugal [sen'trifjugəl] adj centrifuge.

century ['sentʃuri] n siècle m.

ceramic [sə'ramik] adj (en) céramique. **ceramics** n céramique f.

cereal ['siəriəl] n céréale f.

ceremonial [,serə'mouniəl] n cérémonial m. adj cérémoniel; de cérémonie.

ceremony ['serəməni] n (event) cérémonie f; (formality) cérémonies f pl. **stand on ceremony** faire des façons. **ceremonious** adj solennel; (over-polite) cérémonieux.

certain ['səitn] adj certain. **certainly** adv certainement; (willingly) volontiers. **certainty** n certitude f.

certificate [sə'tifikət] n certificat m; diplôme m. **certify** v certifier.

cervix ['səiviks] n col de l'utérus m.

cesspool ['sespuil] n fosse d'aisances f.

chafe [tʃeif] v (rub) frotter; (make sore) gratter.

chaffinch ['tʃafintʃ] n pinson m.

chain [tʃein] n chaîne f. **chain smoke** fumer cigarette sur cigarette. **chain store** magasin à succursales multiples m.

chair [tʃeə] n chaise f; (university) chaire f; (meeting) présidence f. **chairlift** n télésiège m. **chairman** n président. v présider.

chalet ['ʃalei] *n* chalet *m*; (*motel*) bungalow *m*.

chalk [tʃɔɪk] *n* craie *f*. **chalky** *adj* crayeux.

challenge ['tʃalɪndʒ] *n* défi *m*. *n* défier; (*sport*) inviter; (*question*) contester.

chamber ['tʃeimbə] *n* chambre *f*. **chambermaid** *n* femme de chambre *f*. **chamber music** musique de chambre *f*. **chamberpot** *n* pot de chambre *m*.

chameleon [kəmiːliən] *n* caméléon *m*.

chamois ['ʃamwaɪ] *n* chamois *m*. **chamois leather** peau de chamois *m*.

champagne [ʃam'pein] *n* champagne *m*.

champion ['tʃampiən] *n* champion, -onne *m*, *f*. *v* défendre. **championship** *n* championnat *m*.

chance [tʃɑːns] *n* (*luck*) hasard *m*; (*possibility*) chance *f*; (*opportunity*) occasion *f*. **by chance** par hasard. *adj* fortuit. *v* prendre le risque de.

chancellor [tʃɑːnsələ] *n* chancelier *m*.

chandelier [ʃandə'liə] *n* lustre *m*.

change [tʃeindʒ] *n* changement *m*; (*money*) monnaie *f*. *v* changer; échanger; (*clothes*) se changer. **changeable** *adj* changeant; (*weather*) variable. **changing-room** *n* vestiaire *m*.

channel ['tʃanl] *n* chenal *m*; (*duct*) conduit *m*; (*TV*) chaîne *f*. **the Channel Islands** les îles anglo-normandes *f pl*. **the English Channel** la Manche. *v* (*efforts, etc.*) canaliser.

chant [tʃɑːnt] *v* (*rel*) psalmodier; (*crowd*) scander. *n* psalmodie *f*; chant scandé *m*.

chaos ['keios] *n* chaos *m*. *adj* chaotique.

chap[1] [tʃap] *v* (*skin*) (se) gercer. *n* gerçure *f*.

chap[2] [tʃap] *n* (*coll*) type *m*.

chapel ['tʃapəl] *n* chapelle *f*.

chaperon ['ʃapəroun] *n* chaperon *m*. *v* chaperonner.

chaplain ['tʃaplin] *n* aumônier *m*.

chapter ['tʃaptə] *n* chapitre *m*.

char[1] [tʃaɪ] *v* (*burn*) carboniser.

char[2] [tʃaɪ] *v* faire des ménages. **charwoman** *n* femme de ménage *f*.

character ['karəktə] *n* caractère *m*; (*theatre, etc.*) personnage *m*. **characteristic** *nf*, *adj* caractéristique. **caracterize** *v* caractériser.

charcoal ['tʃaɪkoul] *n* charbon de bois *m*.

charge [tʃaɪdʒ] *n* (*law*) accusation *f*; (*mil*) charge *f*; (*cost*) prix *m*; responsabilité *f*; (*battery*) charge *f*. **in charge** responsable. **take charge of** se charger de. *v* (*law*)

accuser (de); (*mil*) charger; (*person*) faire payer; (*amount*) demander; (*battery*) (se) charger. **charge in/out** entrer/sortir en coup de vent.

chariot ['tʃariət] *n* char *m*.

charity ['tʃarəti] *n* charité *f*; (*society*) œuvre charitable *f*. **charitable** *adj* charitable.

charm [tʃaɪm] *n* charme *m*; (*on bracelet*) breloque *f*. *v* charmer. **charming** *adj* charmant.

chart [tʃaɪt] *n* (*map*) carte *f*; (*graph, etc.*) graphique *m*, diagramme *m*. *v* (*journey*) porter sur la carte; (*sales, etc.*) faire le graphique de.

charter ['tʃaɪtə] *v* (*boat, etc.*) affréter. **chartered accountant** expert-comptable *m*. *n* affrètement *m*; (*document*) charte *f*. **charter flight** charter *m*.

chase [tʃeis] *v* chasser, poursuivre. *n* chasse *f*, poursuite *f*.

chasm ['kazəm] *n* gouffre *m*.

chassis ['ʃasi] *n* (*mot*) châssis *m*.

chaste [tʃeist] *adj* chaste, pur. **chastity** *n* chasteté *f*.

chastise [tʃas'taiz] *v* châtier. **chastisement** *n* châtiment *m*.

chat [tʃat] *n* causette *f*. *v* bavarder.

chatter ['tʃatə] *v* jacasser; (*teeth*) claquer. *n* jacassement *m*; bavardage *m*. **chatterbox** *n* bavard, -e *m*, *f*.

chauffeur ['ʃoufə] *n* chauffeur *m*.

chauvinism ['ʃouvinizəm] *n* chauvinisme *m*. **chauvinist** *n*, *adj* chauvin, -e. **male chauvinist** (*slang*) phallocrate *m*.

cheap [tʃiːp] *adj* bon marché *invar*; (*reduced*) réduit. **cheapen** *v* baisser le prix de; (*degrade*) déprécier. **cheaply** *adv* à bon marché.

cheat [tʃiːt] *v* (*deceive*) tromper; (*at games*) tricher; frauder. *n* tricheur, -euse *m*, *f*; fraude *f*.

check [tʃek] *n* contrôle *m*, vérification *f*; (*restraint*) arrêt *m*; (*chess*) échec *m*; (*US: cheque*) chèque *m*; (*US: bill*) addition *f*. **checkmate** *n* échec et mat. **checkpoint** *n* contrôle *m*. **checks** *pl n* (*pattern*) carreaux *m pl*. *v* vérifier; contrôler; (*restrain*) maîtriser. **check-in** *n* (*aero*) enregistrement *m*. **check-out** *n* (*supermarket*) caisse *f*. **check out** (*hotel*) régler sa note. **check-up** *n* (*med*) bilan de santé *m*. **check up on** (*thing*) vérifier; (*person*) se renseigner sur. **checked** *adj* (*pattern*) à carreaux.

cheek [tʃiːk] *n* (*anat*) joue *f*; (*coll: impudence*) toupet *m*. **cheekbone** *n* pommette *f*. **cheeky** *adj* effronté.

cheer [tʃiə] *v* (*shout*) acclamer, pousser des hourras. **cheer up** (s')égayer; prendre courage; (*comfort*) consoler. *n* gaieté *f*; (*shout*) acclamation *f*. **cheerio!** *interj* salut! **cheers!** *interj* à la vôtre! **cheerful** *adj* gai; (*news*) réconfortant. **cheerless** *adj* morne. **cheery** *adj* joyeux.

cheese [tʃiːz] *n* fromage *m*. **cheesecake** *n* tarte au fromage blanc *f*. **cheesecloth** *n* (*for clothes*) toile à beurre *f*.

cheetah ['tʃiːtə] *n* guépard *m*.

chef [ʃef] *n* chef (de cuisine) *m*.

chemistry ['kemistri] *n* chimie *f*. **chemist** *n* chimiste *m*, *f*; pharmacien, -enne *m*, *f*. **chemist's shop** pharmacie *f*.

cheque *or US* **check** [tʃek] *n* chèque *m*. **chequebook** *n* chéquier *m*. **cheque card** carte d'identité bancaire *f*.

cherish ['tʃeriʃ] *v* chérir; (*hope, etc.*) nourrir.

cherry ['tʃeri] *n* (*fruit*) cerise *f*; (*tree*) cerisier *m*.

chess [tʃes] *n* échecs *m pl*. **chessboard** *n* échiquier *m*. **chessman** *n* pièce *f*.

chest [tʃest] *n* (*anat*) poitrine *f*; (*box*) caisse *f*. **chest of drawers** commode *f*. **chesty** *adj* (*cough*) de poitrine.

chestnut ['tʃesnʌt] *n* (*fruit*) châtaigne *f*. marron *m*; (*tree*) châtaigner *m*, marronnier *m*. *adj* (*hair*) châtain.

chew [tʃuː] *v* mâcher. **chewing gum** chewing-gum *m*. **chew over** ruminer. **chew the cud** ruminer. **chew up** mâchonner.

chicken ['tʃikin] *n* poulet *m*, (*very young*) poussin *m*. **chicken pox** *n* varicelle *f*. *v* **chicken out** (*slang*) se dégonfler.

chicory ['tʃikəri] *n* chicorée *f*.

chief [tʃiːf] *n* chef *m*. *adj* principal; en chef. **chiefly** *adv* principalement; surtout.

chilblain ['tʃilblein] *n* engelure *f*.

child [tʃaild] *n pl* **children** enfant. **childbirth** *n* accouchement *m*. **childhood** *n* enfance *f*. **childish** *adj* puéril. **childless** *adj* sans enfants.

chill [tʃil] *n* fraîcheur *f*, froid *m*; (*fear*) frisson *m*; (*med*) refroidissement *m*. *v* (*wine*) rafraîchir; (*champagne*) frapper. **chilled to the bone** transi jusqu'aux os. **chilly** *adj* froid.

chilli ['tʃili] *n* piment *m*.

chime [tʃaim] *v* carillonner; (*hours*) sonner. *n* carillon *m*.

chimney ['tʃimni] *n* cheminée *f*. **chimney pot** tuyau de cheminée *m*. **chimney sweep** ramoneur *m*.

chimpanzee [tʃimpən'ziː] *n* chimpanzé *m*.

chin [tʃin] *n* menton *m*.

china ['tʃainə] *n* porcelaine *f*.

China ['tʃainə] *n* Chine *f*. **Chinese** *nm*, *adj* chinois. **the Chinese** les Chinois *m pl*.

chink[1] [tʃiŋk] *n* (*slit*) fente *f*; (*door*) entrebâillement *m*.

chink[2] [tʃiŋk] *n* (*sound*) tintement *m*. *v* (*faire*) tinter.

chip [tʃip] *n* (*fragment*) éclat *m*; (*in cup, etc.*) ébréchure *f*; (*poker, etc.*) jeton *m*. **chipboard** *n* bois aggloméré *m*. **chips** *pl n* (*cookery*) frites *f pl*. *v* (s')ébrécher. **chip in** (*interrupt*) dire son mot; (*money*) contribuer.

chiropody [ki'ropədi] *n* soins du pied *m pl*. **chiropodist** *n* pédicure *m*, *f*.

chirp [tʃəːp] *v* pépier. *n* pépiement *m*. **chirpy** *adj* gai.

chisel ['tʃizl] *n* ciseau *m*. *v* ciseler.

chivalry ['ʃivəlri] *n* chevalerie *f*. **chivalrous** *adj* chevaleresque.

chive [tʃaiv] *n* ciboulette *f*.

chlorine ['klɔːriːn] *n* chlore *m*. **chlorinate** *v* javelliser.

chloroform ['klɔrəfɔːm] *n* chloroforme *m*. *v* chloroformer.

chlorophyll ['klɔrəfil] *n* chlorophylle *f*.

chocolate ['tʃokələt] *n* chocolat *m*.

choice [tʃois] *n* choix *m*. *adj* (*fruit*) de choix *invar*; (*word*) bien choisi.

choir ['kwaiə] *n* chœur *m*; chorale *f*. **choirboy** *n* jeune choriste *m*. **choir-stall** *n* stalle *f*.

choke [tʃouk] *v* (s')étrangler, étouffer; (*block*) boucher. *n* (*mot*) starter *m*.

cholera ['kɔlərə] *n* choléra *m*.

***choose** [tʃuːz] *v* choisir.

chop[1] [tʃop] *n* (*meat*) côtelette *f*; (*blow*) coup *m*. *v* trancher; (*wood*) couper à la hache; (*vegetables, etc.*) hacher. **chop down** (*tree*) abattre. **chopper** *n* hachoir *m*.

chop[2] [tʃop] *v* **chop and change** changer constamment. **chop logic** ergoter. **choppy** *adj* (*sea*) un peu agité.

chops [tʃops] *pl n* (*jaws*) mâchoires *f pl*. **lick one's chops** se lécher les babines.

chopstick ['tʃopstik] *n* baguette *f*.

chord [kɔːd] *n* (*anat*) corde *f*; (*music*) accord *m*.

chore [tʃɔː] n (*unpleasant*) corvée f.
chores pl n (*household*) travaux du ménage m pl.
choreography [kɔri'ɔgrəfi] n chorégraphie f. **choreographer** n chorégraphe m, f.
chorus ['kɔːrəs] n refrain m; (*singers*) chœur m; (*dancers*) troupe f. **choral** adj choral.
chose [tʃouz] V **choose.**
chosen ['tʃouzn] V **choose.**
christen ['krisn] v baptiser; (*nickname*) surnommer. **christening** n baptême m.
Christian ['kristʃən] n, adj chrétien, -enne. **Christian name** prénom m. **Christianity** n christianisme m.
Christmas ['krisməs] n Noël m. **Christmas Day** le jour de Noël m. **Christmas Eve** la veille de Noël f.
chromatic [krə'matik] adj chromatique.
chrome [kroum] n chrome m.
chromium ['kroumiəm] n chrome m. **chromium-plated** adj chromé. **chromium-plating** n chromage m.
chromosome ['krouməsoum] n chromosome m.
chronic ['kronik] adj chronique; (*coll*) atroce.
chronicle ['kronikl] n chronique f.
chronological [kronə'lodʒikəl] adj chronologique. **in chronological order** par ordre chronologique.
chrysalis ['krisəlis] n chrysalide f.
chrysanthemum [kri'sanθəməm] n chrysanthème m.
chubby ['tʃʌbi] adj potelé.
chuck [tʃʌk] (*coll*) v (*throw*) lancer; (*give up*) laisser tomber. **chuck out** (*thing*) balancer; (*person*) vider.
chuckle ['tʃʌkl] v glousser. n petit rire m.
chunk [tʃʌŋk] n gros morceau m; (*bread*) quignon m.
church [tʃəːtʃ] n église f. **churchgoer** n pratiquant, -e m, f. **church hall** salle paroissiale f. **churchyard** n cimetière m.
churn [tʃəːn] n baratte f. v baratter; (*water*) (faire) bouillonner. **churn out** (*coll: books, etc.*) pondre en série.
chute [ʃuːt] n glissière f.
cider ['saidə] n cidre m.
cigar [si'gɑː] n cigare m.
cigarette [sigə'ret] n cigarette f. **cigarette lighter** briquet m.
cinder ['sində] n cendre f. **burnt to a cinder** réduit en cendres.
cine camera ['sini] n caméra f.

cinema ['sinəmə] n cinéma m.
cinnamon ['sinəmən] n cannelle f.
circle ['səːkl] n cercle m; (*theatre*) balcon m. v (*surround*) encercler; (*move round*) tourner autour de; (*aircraft*) tourner. **circular** nf, adj circulaire.
circuit ['səːkit] n tour m; (*law*) tournée f; (*elec, sport*) circuit m. **circuitous** adj indirect.
circulate ['səːkjuleit] v (faire) circuler. **circulation** n circulation f; (*newspaper*) tirage m.
circumcise ['səːkəmsaiz] v circoncire. **circumcision** n circoncision f.
circumference [sər'kʌmfərəns] n circonférence f.
circumflex ['səːkəmfleks] adj circonflexe. n accent circonflexe m.
circumscribe ['səːkəmskraib] v circonscrire.
circumspect ['səːkəmspekt] adj circonspect.
circumstance ['səːkəmstans] n circonstance f. **circumstances** pl n (*financial*) moyens m pl. **under no circumstances** en aucun cas. **under the circumstances** vu l'état des choses.
circus ['səːkəs] n cirque m.
cistern ['sistən] n citerne f; (*toilet*) chasse d'eau f.
cite [sait] v citer. **citation** n citation f.
citizen ['sitizn] n (*town*) habitant, -e m, f; (*state*) citoyen, -enne m, f. **citizenship** n citoyenneté f.
citrus ['sitrəs] n citrus m pl. **citrus fruits** agrumes m pl. **citric acid** acide citrique m.
city ['siti] n ville f, cité f. **city centre** centre ville m.
civic ['sivik] adj (*authorities*) municipal; (*rights*) civique. **civic centre** centre administratif m.
civil ['sivl] adj civil; poli. **civil engineering** travaux publics m pl. **civil rights** droits civiques m pl. **civil servant** fonctionnaire m, f. **civil service** administration f. **civil war** guerre civile f.
civilian [sə'viljən] n, adj civil, -e.
civilization [ˌsivilai'zeiʃən] n civilisation f. **civilize** v civiliser.
clad [klad] adj habillé.
claim [kleim] v (*right, prize, etc.*) revendiquer; (*damages*) réclamer; (*profess*) déclarer. n revendication f; réclamation

f; (*insurance*) déclaration de sinistre *f*; (*right*) droit *m*.

clairvoyant [klɛə'vɔiənt] *n* voyant, -e *m, f*.

clam [klam] *n* praire *f*.

clamber ['klambə] *v* grimper en rampant.

clammy ['klami] *adj* moite.

clamour ['klamə] *n* clameur *f. v* vociférer.

clamp [klamp] *n* pince *f*, crampon *m. v* serrer, cramponner. **clamp down on** supprimer; restreindre.

clan [klan] *n* clan *m*.

clandestine [klan'destin] *adj* clandestin.

clang [klaŋ] *n* bruit métallique *m. v* résonner. **clanger** *n* (*coll*) gaffe *f*.

clap [klap] *v* applaudir. **clap one's hands** battre des mains. *n* (*noise*) claquement *m*; (*thunder*) coup *m*; (*applause*) applaudissements *m pl*.

claret ['klarət] *n* bordeaux *m*.

clarify ['klarəfai] *v* (se) clarifier; (*situation*) s')éclaircir.

clarinet [klarə'net] *n* clarinette *f*.

clarity ['klarəti] *n* clarté *f*.

clash [klaʃ] *n* (*bang*) s'entrechoquer; (*conflict*) se heurter; (*colours*) jurer. *n* (*dispute*) accrochage *m*; (*personalities*) incompatibilité *f*; (*noise*) choc *m*.

clasp [klaːsp] *v* serrer. *n* (*fastening*) fermoir *m*; (*grip*) étreinte *f*.

class [klaːs] *n* classe *f*; catégorie *f*; (*school*) cours *m*. **class-room** *n* salle de classe *f. v* classer.

classic ['klasik] *nm, adj* classique. **classical** *adj* classique. **classics** *n* humanités *f pl*.

classify ['klasifai] *v* classifier. **classification** *n* classification *f*. **classified** *adj* classifié; secret, -ète. **classified advertisement** petite annonce *f*.

clatter ['klatə] *n* cliquetis *m. v* cliqueter.

clause [klɔːz] *n* (*law*) clause *f*; (*gramm*) proposition *f*.

claustrophobia [klɔːstrə'foubiə] *n* claustrophobie *f*. **claustrophobe** *n* claustrophobe *m, f*. **claustrophobic** *adj* claustrophobique.

claw [klɔː] *n* griffe *f*; (*lobster*) pince *f. v* griffer.

clay [klei] *n* argile *f*.

clean [kliːn] *adj* propre; net, nette. *adv* entièrement. **clean-shaven** *adj* glabre. *v* nettoyer. **cleaner** *n* (*charwoman*) femme de ménage *f*. **cleaner's** *n* teinturerie *f*. **cleaning** *n* nettoyage *m*; (*housework*)

ménage. **cleanliness** *or* **cleanness** *n* propreté *f*.

cleanse [klenz] *v* nettoyer; purifier. **cleanser** *n* (*cosmetic*) démaquillant *m*.

clear [kliə] *adj* clair; transparent; distinct; (*without obstacles*) libre. *v* (s')éclaircir; clarifier; (*remove obstacles*) débarrasser; (*law*) disculper; (*jump*) franchir. **clearance** *n* (*space*) espace (*m*) libre; (*customs*) dédouanement *m*; (*aero*) autorisation *f*. **clearing** *n* clairière *f*. **clearness** *n* clarté *f*.

clef [klef] *n* clef *f*.

clench [klentʃ] *v* empoigner. **clench one's fists/teeth** serrer les poings/dents.

clergy ['klɔːdʒi] *n* clergé *m*. **clergyman** *n* (*Protestant*) pasteur *m*; (*Catholic*) prêtre *m*.

clerical ['klerikəl] *adj* (*office*) d'employé, de bureau; (*rel*) clérical.

clerk [klaːk] *n* employé, -e *m, f*.

clever ['klevə] *adj* intelligent; (*skilful*) habile; (*smart*) astucieux. **cleverness** *n* intelligence *f*; habileté *f*; astuce *f*.

cliché ['kliːʃei] *n* cliché *m*.

click [klik] *n* déclic *m. v* claquer, faire un déclic.

client ['klaiənt] *n* client, -e *m, f*. **clientele** *n* clientèle *f*.

cliff [klif] *n* falaise *f*.

climate ['klaimət] *n* climat *m*. **climatic** *adj* climatique.

climax ['klaimaks] *n* apogée *m*, point culminant *m*.

climb [klaim] *v* grimper, monter; (*mountain*) gravir. *n* montée *f*. **climbing** *n* (*sport*) alpinisme *m*.

***cling** [kliŋ] *v* se cramponner; (*stick*) (se) coller.

clinic ['klinik] *n* clinique *f*. **clinical** *adj* (*med*) clinique; (*attitude*) objectif.

clink [kliŋk] *v* (faire) tinter. *n* tintement *m*.

clip[1] [klip] *v* (*hedge*) tailler; (*hair*) couper; (*dog*) tondre. *n* (*coll: blow*) taloche *f*; (*cinema*) extrait *m*. **clipping** *n* (*newspaper*) coupure de presse *f*.

clip[2] [klip] *n* attache *f. v* attacher.

clitoris ['klitəris] *n* clitoris *m*.

cloak [klouk] *n* (*clothing*) cape *f*; (*mask*) manteau *m*. **cloakroom** *n* vestiaire *m. v* masquer.

clock [klok] *n* (*large*) horloge *f*; (*small*) pendule *f*. **against the clock** contre la montre. **clock-tower** *n* clocher *m*. **clock-**

wise *adj, adv* dans le sens des aiguilles d'une montre. **clockwork** *adj* mécanique. **like clockwork** comme sur des roulettes.
clog [klog] *n* sabot *m*. *v* boucher.
cloister ['kloistə] *n* cloître *m*. *v* cloîtrer.
close[1] [klous] *adj* (*near*) proche; (*friend*) intime; (*contest, etc.*) serré; (*atmosphere*) étouffant. *adv* de près. **close by** tout près. **close-fitting** *adj* ajusté. **close-up** *n* gros plan *m*. *n* cul-de-sac *m*. **closely** *adv* de près; attentivement.
close[2] [klouz] *n* (*end*) fin *f*. *v* (se) fermer; (*block*) boucher; (*finish*) (se) terminer. **close in** approcher; (*enclose*) clôturer. **close up** se rapprocher. **closing** *or* **closure** *n* fermeture *f*.
closet ['klozit] *n* placard *m*; (*room*) cabinet *m*. *v* enfermer.
clot [klot] *n* caillot *m*. *v* (se) coaguler.
cloth [kloθ] *n* (*fabric*) tissu *m*; (*linen*) toile *f*; (*cleaning*) chiffon *m*.
clothe [klouð] *v* vêtir, habiller. **clothes** *pl n* vêtements *m pl*. **clothes brush** brosse à habits *f*. **clothes horse** séchoir *m*. **clothes line** corde à linge *f*. **clothes peg** pince à linge *f*. **clothing** *n* vêtements *m pl*.
cloud [klaud] *n* nuage *m*. **cloudburst** *n* déluge de pluie *m*. *v* (*mind*) (s')obscurcir; (*face*) (s')assombrir. **cloud over** se couvrir de nuages. **cloudless** *adj* sans nuages. **cloudy** *adj* nuageux, couvert; (*liquid*) trouble.
clove[1] [klouv] *n* (*spice*) clou de girofle *m*. **oil of cloves** essence de girofle *f*.
clove[2] [klouv] *n* (*of garlic*) gousse *f*.
clover ['klouvə] *n* trèfle *m*.
clown [klaun] *n* clown *m*.
club [klʌb] *n* (*weapon*) massue *f*; (*cards*) trèfle; (*society*) club *m*. **club-foot** *n* pied-bot *m*. **clubhouse** *n* pavillon *m*. *v* matraquer. **club together** se cotiser.
clue [kluː] *n* indice *m*; (*crosswords*) définition *f*.
clump [klʌmp] *n* massif *m*; (*trees*) bouquet *m*; (*grass, flowers*) touffe *f*.
clumsy ['klʌmzi] *adj* maladroit, gauche. **clumsiness** *n* maladresse *f*, gaucherie *f*.
clung [klʌŋ] *V* **cling**.
cluster ['klʌstə] *n* (*flowers, fruit*) grappe *f*; groupe *m*. *v* se grouper.
clutch [klʌtʃ] *n* (*grip*) étreinte *f*; (*mot*) embrayage *m*. *v* empoigner, se cramponner à.
clutter ['klʌtə] *n* désordre *m*. *v* encombrer.

coach [koutʃ] *n* (*bus*) car *m*; (*rail*) voiture *f*; (*sport*) entraîneur *m*; (*school*) répétiteur, -trice *m, f*. *v* entraîner; (*for exam*) préparer. **coaching** *n* répétitions *f pl*; entraînement *m*.
coagulate [kou'agjuleit] *v* (se) coaguler. **coagulation** *n* coagulation *f*.
coal [koul] *n* charbon *m*, houille *f*. **coalman** *n* charbonnier *m*. **coalmine** *n* houillère *f*. **coalminer** *n* mineur *m*. **coalmining** *n* charbonnage *m*.
coalition [kouə'liʃən] *n* coalition *f*.
coarse [kɔːs] *adj* grossier; (*salt, etc.*) gros, grosse. **coarseness** *n* rudesse *f*.
coast [koust] *n* côte *f*. **coastguard** *n* garde maritime *m*. **coastline** *n* littoral *m*. **the coast is clear** la voie est libre. *v* (*mot*) descendre en roue libre. **coastal** *adj* côtier. **coaster** *n* (*mat*) dessous de verre *m*.
coat [kout] *n* manteau *m*; (*animal*) pelage *m*, poil *m*; (*horse*) robe *f*; (*paint, etc.*) couche *f*. **coat hanger** cintre *m*. *v* couvrir; (*cookery*) enrober. **coating** *n* couche *f*.
coax [kouks] *v* cajoler.
cobbler ['koblə] *n* cordonnier *m*.
cobra ['koubrə] *n* cobra *m*.
cobweb ['kobweb] *n* toile d'araignée *f*.
cocaine [kə'kein] *n* cocaïne *f*.
cock [kok] *n* coq *m*; mâle *m*; (*vulgar: penis*) bitte *f*. *v* (*gun*) armer; (*ears*) dresser.
cockle ['kokl] *n* coque *f*.
cockpit ['kokpit] *n* poste de pilotage *m*.
cockroach ['kokroutʃ] *n* blatte *f*.
cocktail ['kokteil] *n* cocktail *m*.
cocky ['koki] *adj* suffisant.
cocoa ['koukou] *n* cacao *m*.
coconut ['koukənʌt] *n* noix de coco *f*. **coconut palm** cocotier *m*.
cocoon [kə'kuːn] *n* cocon *m*.
cod [kod] *n* morue *f*. **cod-liver oil** huile de foie de morue *f*.
code [koud] *n* code *m*. *v* chiffrer.
codeine ['koudiːn] *n* codéine *f*.
coeducation [kouedju'keiʃən] *n* éducation mixte *f*. **coeducational** *adj* mixte.
coerce [kou'əːs] *v* contraindre. **coercion** *n* contrainte *f*. **coercive** *adj* coercitif.
coexist [kouig'zist] *v* coexister.
coffee ['kofi] *n* café *m*. **black/white coffee** café noir/au lait *m*. **coffee bar** café *m*. **coffee bean** grain de café *m*. **coffee pot** cafetière *f*. **coffee table** table basse *f*.

coffin ['kofin] *n* cercueil *m*.
cog [kog] *n* dent *f*.
cognac ['konjak] *n* cognac *m*.
cohabit [kou'habit] *v* cohabiter. **cohabitation** *n* cohabitation *f*.
coherent [kou'hiərənt] *adj* cohérent; (*account*, *etc*.) facile à suivre. **coherence** *n* cohérence *f*. **coherently** *adj* avec cohérence.
coil [koil] *n* rouleau *m*; (*elec*) bobine *f*; (*med*) stérilet *m*. *v* (s')enrouler; (*snake*) se lover.
coin [koin] *n* pièce (de monnaie) *f*. *v* (*money*) frapper; (*word*, *etc*.) inventer.
coincide [kouin'said] *v* coïncider. **coincidence** *n* coïncidence *f*. **coincidental** *adj* de coïncidence.
colander ['koləndə] *n* passoire *f*.
cold [kould] *adj* froid. **be cold** (*person*) avoir froid; (*weather*) faire froid. **cold-blooded** *adj* (*animal*) à sang froid; (*person*) insensible. **cold-hearted** *adj* impitoyable. **cold sore** *n* herpès *m*. *n* froid *m*; (*med*) rhume *m*. **have a cold** être enrhumé.
colic ['kolik] *n* colique *f*.
collaborate [kə'labəreit] *v* collaborer. **collaboration** *n* collaboration *f*. **collaborator** *n* collaborateur, -trice *m*, *f*.
collapse [ke'laps] *v* s'écrouler, s'éffondrer. *n* éffondrement *m*, écroulement *m*. **collapsible** *adj* pliant.
collar ['kolə] *n* (*on garment*) col *m*; (*dog*, *etc*.) collier *m*. **collarbone** *n* clavicule *f*.
collate [ko'leit] *v* collationner. **collation** *n* collation *f*.
colleague ['koliːg] *n* collègue *m*, *f*.
collect [kə'lekt] *v* (s')amasser; (se) rassembler; (*as hobby*) collectionner; (*pick up*) ramasser; (*gather*) recueillir; (*call for*) passer prendre. *adj*, *adv* (*US: phone*) en P.C.V. **collection** *n* rassemblement *m*; (*money*) quête *f*; (*stamps*, *etc*.) collection *f*; (*mail*) levée *f*. **collective** *adj* collectif. **collector** *n* (*stamps*, *etc*.) collectionneur, -euse *m*, *f*.
college ['kolidʒ] *n* collège *m*; (*professional*) école *f*.
collide [kə'laid] *v* se heurter. **collision** *n* collision *f*.
colloquial [kə'loukwiəl] *adj* familier. **colloquialism** *n* expression familière *f*.
colon ['koulon] *n* (*punctuation*) deux points *m invar*.

colonel ['kəːnl] *n* colonel *m*.
colony ['koləni] *n* colonie *f*. **colonial** *adj* colonial. **colonization** *n* colonisation *f*. **colonize** *v* coloniser.
colossal [kə'losəl] *adj* colossal.
colour ['kʌlə] *n* couleur *f*. **colour bar** discrimination raciale *f*. **colour-blind** *adj* daltonien. **colour scheme** combinaison de couleurs *f*. **colour television** (*set*) téléviseur couleur *m*. *v* colorer; (*picture*) colorier. **coloured** *adj* coloré; (*picture*) en couleur; (*person*) de couleur. **colourful** *adj* coloré. **colouring** *n* (*complexion*) teint *m*; coloration *f*. **colourless** *adj* incolore.
colt [koult] *n* poulain *m*.
column ['koləm] *n* colonne *f*. **columnist** *n* journaliste *m*, *f*.
coma ['koumə] *n* coma *m*. **in a coma** dans le coma.
comb [koum] *n* peigne *m*; (*bird*) crête *f*. *v* (*hair*) peigner; (*search*) fouiller.
combat ['kombat] *n* combat *m*. *v* combattre. **combatant** *n* combattant, -e *m*, *f*.
combine [kəm'bain; *n* 'kombain] *v* combiner; s'unir; en association *f*. **combination** *n* combinaison *f*. **combination lock** serrure à combinaison *f*.
combustion [kəm'bʌstʃən] *n* combustion *f*. **combustible** *adj* combustible.
*__come__ [kʌm] *n* venir; arriver. **come across** (*find*) tomber sur. **come back** revenir. **come-back** *n* rentrée *f*. **come down** descendre. **come-down** *n* déchéance *f*. **come in** entrer. **come off** se détacher; (*succeed*) réussir. **come out** sortir. **come to** (*from faint*) revenir à soi; (*total*) se monter à.
comedy ['komədi] *n* comédie *f*. **comedian** *n* comique *m*.
comet ['komit] *n* comète *f*.
comfort ['kʌmfət] *n* confort *m*; consolation *f*. *v* consoler; (*soothe*) soulager. **comfortable** *adj* confortable; (*person*) à l'aise.
comic ['komik] *adj* comique. *n* (*person*) comique *m*; (*magazine*) comic *m*. **comical** *adj* drôle.
comma ['komə] *n* virgule *f*.
command [kə'maind] *v* commander; ordonner; (*respect*) exiger. *n* commandement *m*; ordre *m*; (*mastery*) maîtrise *f*. **commander** *n* chef *m*; (*mil*) commandant *m*. **commandment** *n* commandement *m*. **commandeer** [komən'diə] *v* réquisitionner.

commando [kə'mɑɪndou] *n* commando *m*.
commemorate [kə'meməreit] *v* commémorer. **commemoration** *n* commémoration *f*. **commemorative** *adj* commémoratif.
commence [kə'mens] *v* commencer. **commencement** *n* commencement *m*.
commend [kə'mend] *v* (*praise*) louer; recommander; (*entrust*) confier. **commendable** *adj* louable; recommandable. **commendation** *n* louange *f*; recommandation *f*.
comment ['koment] *n* observation *f*, commentaire *m*. *v* remarquer. **comment on** commenter, faire des remarques sur. **commentary** *n* commentaire *m*; (*sport*) reportage *m*. **commentator** *n* reporter *m*.
commerce ['komɜɪs] *n* commerce *m*. **commercial** *adj* commercial; de commerce. **commercialize** *v* commercialiser.
commiserate [kə'mizəreit] *v* (*illness*) témoigner de la sympathie (à); (*bad luck*) s'apitoyer sur le sort (de). **commiseration** *n* commisération *f*.
commission [kə'miʃən] *n* commission *f*; ordres *m pl*; (*mil*) brevet *m*. *v* (*order*) commander; déléguer; (*mil*) nommer à un commandement. **commissioner** *n* commissaire *m*; (*police*) préfet *m*.
commit [kə'mit] *v* commettre; (*entrust*) confier. **commit oneself** s'engager. **commit suicide** se suicider. **commitment** *n* responsabilité *f*; (*comm*) engagement *m*.
committee [kə'miti] *n* commission *f*, comité *m*.
commodity [kə'modəti] *n* produit *m*, marchandise *f*.
common ['komən] *adj* commun; ordinaire; vulgaire. **Common Market** Marché Commun *m*. **commonplace** *adj* banal. **common-room** *n* salle commune *f*. **common sense** bon sens. **commonwealth** *n* république *f*; confédération *f*; (*British*) Commonwealth *m*.
commotion [kə'mouʃən] *n* commotion *f*; (*noise*) agitation *f*.
communal ['komjunəl] *adj* (*shared*) commun; (*of community*) communautaire.
commune[1] [kə'mjuɪn] *v* communier; converser intimement.
commune[2] ['komjuɪn] *n* communauté *f*; (*admin*) commune *f*.
communicate [kə'mjuɪnikeit] *v* communiquer. **communication** *n* communication *f*.

communication cord sonnette d'alarme *f*.
communicative *adj* communicatif, bavard.
communion [kə'mjuɪnjən] *n* communion *f*.
communism ['komjunizəm] *n* communisme *m*. **communist** *n*(*m*+*f*), *adj* communiste.
community [kə'mjuɪnəti] *n* communauté *f*; colonie *f*. **community centre** foyer socio-éducatif *m*.
commute [kə'mjuɪt] *n* (*travel*) faire la navette; échanger; (*law*) commuer. **commuter** *n* banlieusard, -e *m, f*.
compact[1] [kəm'pakt; *n* 'kompakt] *adj* compact; concis. *v* condenser. *n* (*powder*) poudrier *m*.
compact[2] ['kompakt] *n* (*agreement*) contrat *m*.
companion [kəm'panjən] *n* compagnon *m*, compagne *f*. **companionship** *n* camaraderie *f*.
company ['kʌmpəni] *n* compagnie *f*; (*theatre*) troupe *f*.
compare [kəm'peə] *v* (se) comparer. **comparable** *adj* comparable. **comparative** *adj* comparatif; relatif. **comparison** *n* comparaison *f*.
compartment [kəm'pɑɪtmənt] *n* compartiment *m*.
compass ['kʌmpəs] *n* boussole *f*; (*naut*) compas *m*; (*extent*) étendue *f*. **compasses** *pl n* (*math*) compas *m sing*.
compassion [kəm'paʃən] *n* compassion *f*. **compassionate** *adj* compatissant; (*leave, etc.*) pour raisons de famille.
compatible [kəm'patəbl] *adj* compatible. **compatibility** *n* compatibilité *f*.
compel [kəm'pel] *v* contraindre, forcer. **compelling** *adj* irrésistible.
compensate ['kompənseit] *v* compenser; (*money*) dédommager. **compensation** *n* compensation *f*.
compete [kəm'piɪt] *v* concourir; (*comm*) faire concurrence. **competition** *n* compétition *f*; (*contest*) concours *m*; (*rivalry*) concurrence *f*. **competitive** *adj* (*price*) compétitif; (*selection*) par concours. **competitor** *n* concurrent, -e *m, f*.
competent ['kompətənt] *adj* compétent; suffisant. **competence** *n* compétence *f*.
compile [kəm'pail] *v* compiler; (*dictionary*) composer; (*list*) dresser. **compilation** *n* compilation *f*.

complacent [kəm'pleisnt] *adj* content de soi. **complacency** *n* contentement de soi *m*.

complain [kəm'plein] *v* se plaindre. **complaint** *n* plainte *f*; (*comm*) réclamation *f*; (*med*) maladie *f*.

complement ['kompləmənt] *n* complément *m*. *v* compléter. **complementary** *adj* complémentaire.

complete [kəm'pliːt] *adj* complet, -ète; (*finished*) achevé. *v* compléter; achever. **completion** *n* achèvement *m*.

complex ['kompleks] *nm, adj* complexe. **complexity** *n* complexité *f*.

complexion [kəm'plekʃən] *n* teint *m*; aspect *m*.

complicate ['komplikeit] *v* compliquer. **complication** *n* complication *f*.

complicity [kəm'plisəti] *n* complicité *f*.

compliment ['kompləmənt] *n* compliment *m*. *v* complimenter (de). **complimentary** *adj* flatteur, -euse; (*free*) gracieux. **complimentary copy** exemplaire offert en hommage *m*. **complimentary ticket** billet de faveur *m*.

comply [kəm'plai] *n* se soumettre (à); (*wishes*) se conformer (à); (*request*) accéder (à). **compliant** *adj* accommodant. **in compliance with** conformément à.

component [kəm'pounənt] *n* (*tech*) pièce *f*; (*chem*) composant *m*. *adj* constituent.

compose [kəm'pouz] *v* composer. **composed** *adj* calme. **composer** *n* compositeur, -trice *m, f*. **composition** *n* composition *f*; (*essay*) rédaction *f*.

compost ['kompost] *n* compost *m*. **compost heap** tas de compost *m*.

composure [kəm'pouʒə] *n* sang-froid *m*.

compound[1] ['kompaund; *v* kəm'paund] *n* composé *m*. *adj* composé; (*number*) complexe; (*fracture*) compliqué. *v* composer; (*make worse*) aggraver.

compound[2] ['kompaund] *n* enclos *m*.

comprehend [kompri'hend] *v* comprendre. **comprehensible** *adj* compréhensible. **comprehension** *n* compréhension *f*. **comprehensive** *adj* compréhensif; détaillé; (*insurance*) tous-risques. **comprehensive school** centre d'études secondaires *m*.

compress [kəm'pres; *n* 'kompres] *v* (se) comprimer; (se) condenser. *n* compresse *f*. **compression** *n* compression *f*; concentration *f*.

comprise [kəm'praiz] *v* comprendre.

compromise ['komprəmaiz] *v* transiger; (*risk*) compromettre. *n* compromis *m*.

compulsion [kəm'pʌlʃən] *n* contrainte *f*. **compulsive** *adj* (*gambler, etc.*) invétéré; (*psych*) compulsif; (*demand*) coercitif. **compulsory** *adj* obligatoire.

compunction [kəm'pʌŋkʃən] *n* remords *m*.

computer [kəm'pjuːtə] *n* ordinateur *m*. **computer science** informatique *f*. **computerization** *n* automatisation électronique *f*. **computerize** *v* informatiser.

comrade ['komrid] *n* camarade *m, f*. **comradeship** *n* camaraderie *f*.

concave [kon'keiv] *adj* concave.

conceal [kən'siːl] *v* dissimuler, cacher. **concealment** *n* dissimulation *f*.

concede [kən'siːd] *v* concéder.

conceit [kən'siːt] *n* vanité *f*. **conceited** *adj* vaniteux.

conceive [kən'siːv] *v* concevoir; (*understand*) comprendre. **conceivable** *adj* concevable.

concentrate ['konsəntreit] *v* (se) concentrer. *n* (*chem*) concentré *m*. **concentration** *n* concentration *f*. **concentration camp** camp de concentration *m*.

concentric [kən'sentrik] *adj* concentrique.

concept ['konsept] *n* concept *m*. **conception** [kən'sepʃən] *n* conception *f*.

concern [kən'səin] *v* concerner; regarder. *n* (*business*) affaire *f*; (*comm*) entreprise *f*; (*anxiety*) inquiétude *f*. **concerned** *adj* inquiet, -ète; affecté; en question. **concerning** *prep* en ce qui concerne.

concert ['konsət; *v* kən'səit] *n* concert *m*. *v* concerter.

concertina [konsə'tiːna] *n* concertina *m*.

concerto [kən'tʃəitou] *n* concerto *m*.

concession [kən'seʃən] *n* concession *f*; (*comm*) réduction *f*. **concessionary** *adj* concessionnaire; (*cheap*) à prix réduit.

conciliate [kən'silieit] *v* (se) concilier; apaiser. **conciliation** *n* conciliation *f*; apaisement *m*. **conciliatory** *adj* conciliant.

concise [kən'sais] *adj* concis.

conclude [kən'kluːd] *v* conclure. **concluding** *adj* final. **conclusion** *n* conclusion *f*. **conclusive** *adj* définitif.

concoct [kən'kokt] *v* (*cookery*) confectionner; (*excuse*) fabriquer. **concoction** *n* confection *f*; (*excuse*) combinaison *f*.

concrete ['konkriːt] *adj* (*real*) concret,

-ète. *n* béton *m*. **concrete mixer** bétonnière *f*. *v* bétonner.

concur [kən'kəː] *v* (*agree*) être d'accord; coïncider. **concurrent** *adj* simultané.

concussion [kən'kʌʃən] *n* (*med*) commotion cérébrale *f*. *v* **be concussed** être commotionné.

condemn [kən'dem] *v* condamner. **condemnation** *n* condamnation *f*.

condense [kən'dens] *v* (se) condenser. **condensation** *n* condensation *f*. **condenser** *n* (*elec*) condensateur *m*.

condescend [kondi'send] *v* condescendre, daigner. **condescension** *n* condescendance *f*.

condition [kən'diʃən] *n* condition *f*; (*state*) état *m*. *v* conditionner. **conditional** *nm, adj* conditionnel. **be conditional on** dépendre de.

condolences [kən'doulənsiz] *pl n* condoléances *f pl*.

condom ['kondəm] *n* préservatif *m*.

condone [kən'doun] *v* pardonner; fermer les yeux sur.

conducive [kən'djuːsiv] *adj* contribuant. **be conducive to** conduire à.

conduct ['kondʌkt; *v* kən'dʌkt] *n* conduite *f*. *v* diriger; (*phys*) conduire. **conduct oneself** se conduire. **conducted tour** excursion accompagnée *f*; visite guidée *f*. **conduction** *n* conduction *f*.

conductor [kən'dʌktə] *n* (*music*) chef d'orchestre *m*; (*bus*) receveur *m*; (*phys*) conducteur *m*. **conductress** *n* (*bus*) receveuse *f*.

cone [koun] *n* cône *m*; (*ice cream*) cornet *m*.

confectioner [kən'fekʃənə] *n* (*cakes*) pâtissier, -ère *m, f*; (*sweets*) confiseur, -euse *m, f*. **confectionery** *n* confiserie *f*; pâtisserie *f*.

confederate [kən'fedərət] *n, adj* confédéré, -e. *v* (se) confédérer. **confederation** *n* confédération *f*.

confer [kən'fəː] *v* conférer. **conference** *n* conférence *f*.

confess [kən'fes] *v* confesser, avouer. **confession** *n* confession *f*; aveu *m*.

confetti [kən'feti] *n* confettis *m pl*.

confide [kən'faid] *v* confier; avouer en confidence. **confide in** (*tell*) se confier à; (*trust*) se fier à. **confidence** *n* (*trust*) confiance *f*; (*self-assurance*) assurance *f*; (*secret*) confidence *f*. **confident** *adj* assuré. **confidential** *adj* confidentiel. **confidently** *adv* avec confiance.

confine [kən'fain] *v* (*imprison*) enfermer; limiter. **be confined** (*childbirth*) accoucher. **confinement** *n* (*childbirth*) couches *f pl*; emprisonnement *m*.

confirm [kən'fəːm] *v* confirmer. **confirmation** *n* confirmation *f*. **confirmed** *adj* (*liar, etc.*) invétéré; (*bachelor*) endurci.

confiscate ['konfiskeit] *v* confisquer. **confiscation** *n* confiscation *f*.

conflict ['konflikt; *v* kən'flikt] *n* conflit *m*. *v* être en conflit; s'opposer. **conflicting** *adj* incompatible; contradictoire.

conform [kən'fɔːm] *v* (se) conformer. **conformity** *n* conformité *f*.

confound [kən'faund] *v* confondre.

confront [kən'frʌnt] *v* (*present*) confronter; (*face*) affronter. **confrontation** *n* confrontation *f*.

confuse [kən'fjuːz] *v* confondre; (*mix up*) embrouiller. **confused** *adj* confus; embrouillé. **confusing** *adj* déroutant. **confusion** *n* confusion *f*; désordre *m*.

congeal [kən'dʒiːl] *v* (se) figer; (*blood*) (se) coaguler; (*freeze*) (se) congeler.

congenial [kən'dʒiːniəl] *adj* sympathique.

congenital [kən'dʒenitl] *adj* congénital.

congested [kən'dʒestid] *adj* encombré; (*med*) congestionné. **congestion** *n* encombrement *m*; (*med*) congestion *f*.

conglomeration [kən,glomə'reiʃən] *n* agglomération *f*.

congratulate [kən'gratjuleit] *v* féliciter. **congratulations** *pl n* félicitations *f pl*.

congregate ['kongrigeit] *v* (se) rassembler. **congregation** *n* assemblée *f*.

congress ['kongres] *n* congrès *m*.

conical ['konikəl] *adj* conique.

conifer ['konifə] *n* conifère *m*. **coniferous** *adj* conifère.

conjecture [kən'dʒektʃə] *v* conjecturer. *n* conjecture *f*. **conjectural** *adj* conjectural.

conjugal ['kondʒugəl] *adj* conjugal.

conjugate ['kondʒugeit] *v* (se) conjuguer. **conjugation** *n* conjugaison *f*.

conjunction [kən'dʒʌŋkʃən] *n* conjonction *f*.

conjunctivitis [kən,dʒʌŋkti'vaitis] *n* conjonctivite *f*.

conjure ['kʌndʒə; (*appeal to*) kən'dʒuə] *v* (*magic*) faire apparaître; (*appeal to*) conjurer. **conjurer** *n* prestidigitateur, -trice *m, f*. **conjuring** *n* prestidigitation *f*. **conjuring trick** tour de passe-passe *m*.

connect [kə'nekt] v (se) relier. **be connected with** avoir des rapports avec. **connection** n jonction f; (elec) connexion f; relation f; (rail) correspondance f.

connoisseur [konə'səɪ] n connaisseur, -euse m, f.

connotation [konə'teiʃən] n connotation f.

conquer ['koŋkə] v conquérir; vaincre. **conqueror** n conquérant m. **conquest** n conquête f.

conscience ['konʃəns] n conscience f.

conscientious [konʃi'enʃəs] adj consciencieux. **conscientious objector** objecteur de conscience m.

conscious ['konʃəs] adj conscient. **consciousness** n (med) connaissance f; (awareness) conscience f.

conscript ['konskript] nm conscrit. **conscription** n conscription f.

consecrate ['konsikreit] v consacrer. **consecration** n consécration f.

consecutive [kən'sekjutiv] adj consécutif.

consensus [kən'sensəs] n consensus m.

consent [kən'sent] v consentir. n consentement m.

consequence ['konsikwəns] n conséquence f; importance f. **consequent** adj résultant. **consequently** adv par conséquent.

conservative [kən'sərvətiv] adj (pol) conservateur, -trice; modeste; traditionnel. n (pol) conservateur, -trice m, f.

conserve [kən'səɪv] v conserver. **conservation** n préservation f; défense de l'environnement f. **conservatoire** n (music) conservatoire m. **conservatory** n (greenhouse) serre f.

consider [kən'sidə] v considérer. **considerable** adj considérable. **considerate** adj prévenant. **consideration** n considération f. **considering** prep étant donné.

consign [kən'sain] v (goods) expédier; (entrust) confier. **consignment** n envoi m.

consist [kən'sist] v consister (en). **consistency** n (of substance) consistance f; (of behaviour, etc.) cohérence f. **consistent** adj logique; compatible.

console [kən'soul] v consoler. **consolation** n consolation f.

consolidate [kən'solideit] v (se) consolider. **consolidation** n consolidation f.

consommé [kən'somei] n consommé m.

consonant ['konsənənt] n consonne f. adj en accord.

conspicuous [kən'spikjuəs] adj remarquable; en vue. **be conspicuous** attirer les regards; se faire remarquer.

conspire [kən'spaiə] v conspirer. **conspiracy** n conspiration f. **conspirator** n conspirateur, -trice m, f.

constable ['kʌnstəbl] n agent de police m. **constabulary** n police f.

constant ['konstənt] adj (unchanging) constant; incessant. n constante f. **constancy** n constance f.

constellation [konstə'leiʃən] n constellation f.

consternation [konstə'neiʃən] n consternation f.

constipation [konsti'peiʃən] n constipation f. **constipated** adj constipé.

constituent [kən'stitjuənt] adj constituant. n élément constitutif m; (pol) electeur, -trice m, f. **constituency** n (pol) circonscription électorale f.

constitute ['konstitjuːt] v constituer. **constitution** n constitution f. **constitutional** adj constitutionnel.

constraint [kən'streint] n contrainte f.

constrict [kən'strikt] v resserrer. **constriction** n resserrement m.

construct [kən'strʌkt] v construire. **construction** n construction f; interprétation f. **constructive** adj constructif.

consul ['konsəl] n consul m. **consular** adj consulaire. **consulate** n consulat m.

consult [kən'sʌlt] v consulter. **consultant** n consultant m; (med) spécialiste m. **consultation** n consultation f.

consume [kən'sjuːm] v consommer; (fire) consumer. **consumer** n consommateur, -trice m, f. **consumer goods** biens de consommation m pl. **consumption** n consommation f.

contact ['kontakt] n contact m; (acquaintance) connaissance f. **contact lenses** verres de contact m pl. v se mettre en contact avec.

contagious [kən'teidʒəs] adj contagieux.

contain [kən'tein] v contenir. **container** n (box, etc.) récipient m; (transport) conteneur m.

contaminate [kən'taməneit] v contaminer. **contamination** n contamination f.

contemplate ['kontəmpleit] v (consider) envisager; (look at) contempler. **contemplation** n contemplation f. **contemplative** adj contemplatif.

contemporary [kən'tempərəri] *n, adj* contemporain, -e.
contempt [kən'tempt] *n* mépris *m*. **contempt of court** outrage à la Cour *m*. **contemptible** *adj* méprisable. **contemptuous** *adj* dédaigneux.
contend [kən'tend] *v* (*fight*) combattre (contre), faire face à; (*claim*) soutenir. **contention** *n* dispute *f*.
content[1] ['kontent] *n* contenu *m*. **contents** *pl n* contenu *m* *sing*; (*book*) table des matières *f*.
content[2] [kən'tent] *adj also* **contented** content, satisfait. **be content with** se contenter de. **contentment** *n* contentement *m*, satisfaction *f*.
contest [kən'test; *n* 'kontest] *v* contester; (se) disputer. *n* (*fight*) combat *m*; (*sport*) lutte *f*; (*competition*) concours *m*. **contestant** *n* concurrent, -e *m, f*.
context ['kontekst] *n* contexte *m*.
continent ['kontinənt] *n* continent *m*. **continental** *adj* continental. **continental breakfast** petit déjeuner à la française *m*. **continental quilt** couette *f*.
contingency [kən'tindʒənsi] *n* éventualité *f*. **contingent** *adj* contingent.
continue [kən'tinjuɪ] *v* continuer; (*after pause*) reprendre. **continual** *adj* continuel. **continuation** *n* continuation *f*; reprise *f*; (*serial*) suite *f*. **continuity** *n* continuité *f*. **continuous** *adj* continu.
contort [kən'toɪt] *v* tordre. **contortion** *n* (*acrobat*) contorsion *f*; (*twisting*) torsion *f*.
contour ['kontuə] *n* contour *m*. **contour line** courbe de niveau *f*.
contraband ['kontrəband] *n* contrebande *f*.
contraception [kontrə'sepʃən] *n* contraception *f*. **contraceptive** *nm, adj* contraceptif.
contract ['kontrakt; *v* kən'trakt] *n* contrat *m*. *v* (se) contracter. **contraction** *n* contraction *f*. **contractor** *n* entrepreneur *m*.
contradict [kontrə'dikt] *v* contredire. **contradiction** *n* contradiction *f*. **contradictory** *adj* contradictoire.
contralto [kən'traltou] *n* contralto *m*.
contraption [kən'trapʃən] *n* (*coll*) machin *m*.
contrary ['kontrəri; (*perverse*) kən'treəri] *adj* contraire; (*perverse*) contrariant. *adv* contrairement. *n* contraire *m*. **on the contrary** au contraire.

contrast [kən'traɪst; *n* 'kontraɪst] *v* contraster. *n* contraste *m*. **contrasting** *adj* contrasté.
contravene [kontrə'viɪn] *v* enfreindre. **contravention** *n* violation *f*.
contribute [kən'tribjut] *v* contribuer. **contribution** *n* contribution *f*. **contributor** *n* (*magazine, etc.*) collaborateur, -trice *m, f*; (*money*) donateur, -trice *m, f*.
contrive [kən'traiv] *v* (*invent*) combiner; (*manage*) s'arranger (pour). **contrived** *adj* artificiel.
control [kən'troul] *n* contrôle *m*; autorité *f*. **controls** *n* commandes *f pl*. *v* (*restrain*) maîtriser; (*prices, etc.*) contrôler; (*business*) diriger. **controller** *n* contrôleur *m*.
controversy [kən'trovəsi] *n* controverse *f*. **controversial** *adj* discuté; discutable.
convalesce [konvə'les] *v* se remettre. **convalescence** *n* convalescence *f*. **convalescent** *n, adj* convalescent, -e.
convector [kən'vektə] *n* radiateur à convection *m*.
convenience [kən'viɪnjəns] *n* commodité *f*, convenance *f*. **convenient** *adj* commode, convenable. **be convenient** convenir (à).
convent ['konvənt] *n* couvent *m*.
convention [kən'venʃən] *n* (*meeting*) convention *f*; (*tradition*) usage *m*. **conventional** *adj* conventionnel, classique.
converge [kən'vɔɪdʒ] *v* converger. **convergence** *n* convergence *f*. **convergent** *adj* convergent.
converse[1] [kən'vɔɪs] *v* causer. **conversation** *n* conversation *f*.
converse[2] ['konvɔɪs] *nm, adj* contraire, inverse.
convert [kən'vɔɪt; *n* 'konvɔɪt] *v* convertir; (*house*) aménager. *n* converti, -e *m, f*. **conversion** *n* conversion *f*; aménagement *m*.
convertible [kən'vɔɪtəbl] *n* (*car*) voiture décapotable *f*.
convex ['konveks] *adj* convexe.
convey [kən'vei] *v* transmettre; transporter; communiquer. **conveyance** *n* transport *m*. **conveyor belt** tapis roulant *m*.
convict ['konvikt; *v* kən'vikt] *n* forçat *m*. *v* déclarer coupable.
conviction [kən'vikʃən] *n* (*law*) condamnation *f*; (*belief*) conviction *f*.
convince [kən'vins] *v* convaincre.

convoy ['konvoi] *n* convoi *m*.
convulsion [kən'vʌlʃən] *n* (*med*) convulsion *f*. **convulsive** *adj* convulsif.
cook [kuk] *n* cuisinier, -ère *m, f*. *v* (faire) cuire; faire la cuisine. **cooker** *n* cuisinière *f*. **cookery** *or* **cooking** *n* cuisine *f*. **cookie** *n* (*US*) petit gâteau sec *m*.
cool [kuil] *adj* (*temperature*) frais, fraîche; calme; (*unfriendly*) froid. *v* (se) rafraîchir, (se) refroidir. **cooler** *n* glacière *f*. **coolness** *n* fraîcheur *f*; froideur *f*; (*calmness*) sang-froid *m*.
coop [kuip] *n* poulailler *m*. *v* **coop up** cloîtrer.
cooperate [kou'opəreit] *v* coopérer. **cooperation** *n* coopération *f*. **cooperative** *adj* coopératif.
coordinate [kou'oidineit] *v* coordonner. *adj* coordonné. *n* coordonnée *f*.
cope[1] [koup] *v* se débrouiller. **cope with** s'occuper de; (*solve*) venir à bout de.
cope[2] [koup] *n* chape *f*.
Copenhagen [koupən'heigən] *n* Copenhague.
copious ['koupiəs] *adj* copieux; abondant.
copper[1] ['kopə] *n* (*metal*) cuivre *m*. **coppers** *pl n* (*money*) petite monnaie *f sing*.
copper[2] ['kopə] *n also* **cop** (*slang*) flic *m*.
copulate ['kopjuileit] *v* copuler. **copulation** *n* copulation *f*.
copy ['kopi] *n* copie *f*; (*phot*) épreuve *f*; (*of book, etc.*) exemplaire *m*. *v* copier. **copyright** *n* copyright *m*.
coral ['korəl] *n* corail (*pl* -aux) *m*. **coral reef** récif de corail *m*.
cord [koid] *n* cordon *m*; (*windows*) corde *f*.
cordial ['koidiəl] *nm, adj* cordial. **cordiality** *n* cordialité *f*.
cordon ['koidn] *n* cordon *m*. *v* **cordon off** interdire l'accès à.
corduroy ['koidəroi] *n* velours côtelé *m*.
core [koi] *n* (*fruit*) trognon *m*; (*earth*) noyau *m*; (*problem, etc*) essential *m*. *v* enlever le trognon de.
cork [koik] *n* liège *m*; (*of bottle*) bouchon *m*. **corkscrew** *n* tire-bouchon *m*. *v* boucher.
corn[1] [koin] *n* blé *m*; (*US*) maïs *m*. **cornflour** *n* farine de maïs *f*. **cornflower** *n* bleuet *m*. **corn on the cob** épi de maïs *m*.
corn[2] [koin] *n* (*med*) cor *m*.
corner ['koinə] *n* coin *m*; (*mot*) tournant *m*. *v* (*coll*) coincer; (*comm*) accaparer.

cornet ['koinit] *n* cornet *m*.
Cornwall ['koinwoil] *n* Cornouailles *f*.
coronary ['korənəri] *adj* coronaire. **coronary thrombosis** infarctus (du myocarde) *m*.
coronation [korə'neiʃən] *n* couronnement *m*.
corporal[1] ['koipərəl] *adj* corporel.
corporal[2] ['koipərəl] *n* caporal-chef *m*.
corporation [koipə'reiʃən] *n* (*town*) conseil municipal *m*; (*comm*) société commerciale *f*.
corps [koi] *n* corps *m*.
corpse [koips] *n* cadavre *m*.
correct [kə'rekt] *adj* correct. *v* corriger. **correction** *n* correction *f*.
correlate ['korəleit] *v* correspondre; mettre en corrélation. **correlation** *n* corrélation *f*.
correspond [korə'spond] *v* correspondre. **correspondence** *n* correspondance *f*. **correspondent** *n* correspondant, -e *m, f*.
corridor ['koridoi] *n* couloir *m*.
corroborate [kə'robəreit] *v* corroborer. **corroboration** *n* confirmation *f*.
corrode [kə'roud] *v* (se) corroder. **corrosion** *n* corrosion *f*. **corrosive** *adj* corrosif.
corrugated ['korəgeitid] *adj* ondulé. **corrugated iron** tôle ondulée *f*.
corrupt [kə'rʌpt] *v* corrompre. *adj* corrompu. **corruption** *n* corruption *f*.
corset ['koiset] *n* corset *m*.
Corsica ['koisikə] *n* Corse *f*. **Corsican** *n* Corse *m, f*; *adj* corse.
cosmetic [koz'metik] *adj* cosmétique; (*surgery*) plastique. **cosmetics** *pl n* produits de beauté *m pl*.
cosmic ['kozmik] *adj* cosmique.
cosmopolitan [kozmə'politən] *n*(*m* + *f*), *adj* cosmopolite.
***cost** [kost] *v* coûter. *n* coût *m*; frais *m pl*. **cost of living** coût de la vie *m*. **costly** *adj* coûteux.
costume ['kostjuim] *n* costume *m*.
cosy ['kouzi] *adj* douillet, -ette.
cot [kot] *n* lit d'enfant *m*.
cottage ['kotidʒ] *n* cottage *m*; petite maison *f*; (*thatched*) chaumière *f*. **cottage cheese** fromage maigre *m*.
cotton ['kotn] *n* coton *m*; (*thread*) fil *m*. **cotton-wool** *n* ouate *f*.
couch [kautʃ] *n* canapé *m*. *v* exprimer.
cough [kof] *n* toux *f*. *v* tousser.
could [kud] *V* **can**[1].

council ['kaunsəl] *n* conseil *m*; (*of town*) conseil municipal *m*. **councillor** *n* conseiller, -ère *m*, *f*.

counsel ['kaunsəl] *n* conseil *m*; (*law*) avocat, -e *m*, *f*. *v* conseiller. **counsellor** *n* conseiller, -ère *m*, *f*; (*social*) orienteur *m*.

count¹ [kaunt] *v* compter; (*consider*) estimer. *n* compte *m*. **countdown** *n* compte à rebours *m*. **countless** *adj* innombrable.

count² [kaunt] *n* comte *m*. **countess** *n* comtesse *f*.

counter¹ ['kauntə] *n* (*shop, etc.*) comptoir *m*; (*bank*) guichet *m*; (*disc*) jeton *m*.

counter² ['kauntə] *adj* contraire. *v* (*blow*) parer; (*boxing, etc.*) riposter. **counter to** à l'encontre de.

counteract [kauntə'rakt] *v* neutraliser.

counterattack ['kauntərə͵tak] *v* contre-attaquer. *n* contre-attaque *f*.

counterfeit ['kauntəfit] *adj* faux, fausse. *v* contrefaire. *n* faux *m*.

counterfoil ['kauntə͵foil] *n* talon *m*.

counterpart ['kauntə͵paıt] *n* contrepartie *f*; équivalent *m*; (*person*) homologue *m*, *f*.

country ['kʌntri] *n* pays *m*; (*not town*) campagne *f*; (*native land*) patrie *f*. **the countryside** la campagne *f*.

county ['kaunti] *n* comté *m*. **county town** chef-lieu *m*.

coup [kuı] *n* (*pol*) coup d'Etat *m*.

couple ['kʌpl] *n* couple *m*. *v* accoupler; (*animals*) s'accoupler.

coupon ['kuıpon] *n* (*comm*) bon *m*; (*advertisements, etc.*) coupon *m*.

courage ['kʌridʒ] *n* courage *m*. **courageous** *adj* courageux.

courgette [kuə'ʒet] *n* courgette *f*.

courier ['kuriə] *n* guide *m*; (*messenger*) courrier *m*.

course [koıs] *n* cours *m*; (*naut*) route *f*; (*meal*) plat *m*. **of course** bien entendu.

court [koıt] *v* (*woman*) courtiser; (*favour*) solliciter; (*danger*) s'exposer à. *n* cour *m*; (*tennis*) court *m*; (*other sports*) terrain *m*. **court-martial** *n* conseil de guerre *m*. **court-room** *n* salle de tribunal *f*. **courtyard** *n* cour *f*.

courteous ['kəıtiəs] *adj* courtois. **courtesy** *n* courtoisie *f*, politesse *f*.

cousin ['kʌzn] *n* cousin, -e *m*, *f*.

cove [kouv] *n* anse *f*.

cover ['kʌvə] *n* couverture *f*; (*lid*) couver-

cle *m*; (*protective*) housse *f*; (*shelter*) abri *m*. *v* couvrir. **coverage** *n* reportage *m*. **covering** *n* (*wrapping*) couverture *f*; (*layer*) couche *f*.

cow [kau] *n* vache *f*. **cowboy** *n* cow-boy *m*. **cowslip** *n* primevère *f*.

coward ['kauəd] *n* lâche *m*, *f*. **cowardice** *n* lâcheté *f*. **cowardly** *adj* lâche.

cower ['kauə] *v* trembler; se blottir.

coy [koi] *adj* timide.

crab [krab] *n* crabe *m*. **crab-apple** pomme sauvage *f*. **crabby** *adj* revêche.

crack [krak] *n* (*split*) fente *f*; (*glass, china, etc.*) fêlure *f*; (*noise*) craquement *m*. *v* (se) fêler; (*ground*) (se) crevasser; (*ice*) (se) craqueler; (*nut*) casser; (*noise*) (faire) craquer.

cracker ['krakə] *n* (*biscuit*) craquelin *m*; (*firework*) pétard *m*; (*Christmas*) diablotin *m*.

crackle ['krakl] *v* crépiter. *n* crépitement *m*.

cradle ['kreidl] *n* berceau *m*. *v* bercer.

craft [kraıft] *n* (*skill*) art *m*; (*job*) métier *m*; (*boat*) barque *f*; (*cunning*) astuce *f*. **craftsman** *n* artisan *m*. **crafty** astucieux.

cram [kram] *v* fourrer, bourrer; (*people*) (s')entasser; (*for exam*) (faire) bachoter.

cramp [kramp] *n* (*med*) crampe *f*. **cramped** *adj* à l'étroit.

cranberry ['kranbəri] *n* canneberge *f*.

crane [krein] *n* grue *f*. **cranefly** *n* tipule *f*. *v* **crane one's neck** tendre le cou.

crank [kraŋk] *n* (*tech*) manivelle *f*. **crankshaft** *n* vilebrequin *m*.

crap [krap] (*vulgar*) *n* merde *f*; (*nonsense*) conneries *f pl*. **crappy** *adj* merdique.

crash [kraʃ] *n* fracas *m*; (*car, etc.*) accident *m*, collision *f*. *v* (*car, etc.*) s'écraser; (*collide*) se percuter; (*smash*) (se) fracasser. **crash course** cours intensif *m*. **crash helmet** casque *m*. **crash landing** atterrissage forcé *m*.

crate [kreit] *n* cageot *m*.

crater ['kreitə] *n* cratère *m*; (*bomb*) entonnoir *m*.

cravat [krə'vat] *n* foulard *m*.

crave [kreiv] *v* avoir grand besoin de; (*beg*) solliciter. **craving** *n* besoin maladif *m*; désir insatiable *m*.

crawl [kroıl] *v* ramper; (*cars*) avancer au pas; (*babies*) aller à quatre pattes; (*with lice, etc.*) grouiller. *n* (*swimming*) crawl *m*.

crayfish ['kreifiʃ] *n* écrevisse *f.*
crayon ['kreiən] *n* crayon de couleur *m.* *v* colorier au crayon.
craze [kreiz] *n* engouement *m.*
crazy ['kreizi] *adj* fou, folle. **crazy paving** dallage irrégulier *m.*
creak [kriːk] *v* grincer. *n* grincement *m.*
cream [kriːm] *nf, adj* crème. **cream cheese** fromage blanc *m.* *v also* **cream off** écrémer. **creamy** *adj* crémeux.
crease [kriːs] *n* pli *m.* **crease-resistant** *adj* infroissable. *v* (se) froisser.
create [kri'eit] *v* créer. **creation** *n* création *f.* **creative** *adj* créatif.
creature ['kriːtʃə] *n* créature *f;* bête *f.*
credentials [kri'denʃəlz] *pl n* références *f pl;* pièce d'identité *f sing.*
credible ['kredəbl] *adj* croyable; plausible. **credibility** *n* crédibilité *f.*
credit ['kredit] *n* crédit *m;* honneur *m.* **credit card** carte de crédit *f.* **credits** *pl n* (cinema) générique *m sing.* *v* croire; attribuer; (banking) créditer. **creditable** *adj* honorable. **creditor** *n* créancier, -ère *m, f.*
credulous ['kredjuləs] *adj* crédule. **credulity** *n* crédulité *f.*
creed [kriːd] *n* credo *m.*
*creep [kriːp] *v* se glisser. **creeper** *n* plante grimpante *f.* **creepy** *adj* qui fait frissonner.
cremate [kri'meit] *v* incinérer. **cremation** *n* crémation *f.* **crematorium** *n* crématorium *m.*
crêpe [kreip] *n* crêpe *m.* **crêpe paper** papier crêpon *m.*
crept [krept] *V* **creep.**
crescent ['kresnt] *n* croissant *m.*
cress [kres] *n* cresson *m.*
crest [krest] *n* crête *f;* (mark) timbre *m.* **crestfallen** *adj* découragé.
crevice ['krevis] *n* fissure *f.*
crew [kruː] *n* (naut) équipage *m;* (group) équipe *f.* *v* (sailing) être équipier. **crewcut** *n* cheveux en brosse *m pl.* **crew-neck** *n* col ras *m.*
crib [krib] *n* (baby's) berceau *m;* (manger) mangeoire *f;* (rel) crèche *f.* *v* copier.
cricket[1] ['krikit] *n* (insect) grillon *m.*
cricket[2] ['krikit] *n* (sport) cricket *m.*
crime [kraim] *n* crime *m.* **criminal** *n, adj* criminel, -elle.
crimson ['krimzn] *nm, adj* cramoisi.
cringe [krindʒ] *v* reculer; s'humilier.
crinkle ['krinkl] *v* (se) froisser. *n* fronce *f.*

cripple ['kripl] *v* estropier; (industry, etc.) paralyser. *n* estropié, -e *m, f.*
crisis ['kraisis] *n* crise *f.*
crisp [krisp] *adj* (biscuit) croquant; (snow) craquant; (weather, style) vif. **crisps** *pl n* chips *f pl.*
criterion [krai'tiəriən] *n, pl* **-ria** critère *m.*
criticize ['kritiˌsaiz] *v* critiquer. **critic** *n* critique *m.* **critical** *adj* critique. **criticism** *n* critique *f.*
croak [krouk] *v* (frog) coasser; (crow) croasser. *n* coassement *m;* croassement *m.*
crochet ['krouʃei] *n* travail au crochet *m.* *v* (activity) faire du crochet; (make) faire au crochet. **crochet hook** crochet *m.*
crockery ['krokəri] *n* vaisselle *f.*
crocodile ['krokəˌdail] *n* crocodile *m.*
crocus ['kroukəs] *n* crocus *m.*
crook [kruk] *n* (shepherd's) houlette *f;* (bend) angle *m;* (coll) escroc *m.*
crooked ['krukid] *adj* (bent) courbé; (path) tortueux; (askew) de travers; (dishonest) malhonnête.
crop [krop] *n* culture *f;* (harvest) récolte *f;* (cereals) moisson *f;* (riding) cravache *f.* *v* écourter, tondre; (graze) brouter; (hair) couper ras. **crop up** survenir.
croquet ['kroukei] *n* croquet *m.*
cross [kros] *n* croix *f;* hybride *m;* biais *m.* *adj* (angry) fâché; diagonal. *v* (se) croiser; (go across) traverser; (cheque) barrer.
cross-examine [ˌkrosig'zamin] *v* interroger. **cross-examination** *n* contre-interrogatoire *m.*
cross-eyed [ˌkros'aid] *adj* louche.
crossfire ['krosˌfaiə] *n* feux croisés *m pl.*
crossing ['krosin] *n* (junction) croisement *m;* (for pedestrians) passage clouté *m;* (journey) traversée *f.*
cross-legged [ˌkros'legid] *adj* les jambes croisées.
cross-reference [ˌkros'refərəns] *n* renvoi *m.* **cross-refer** *v* renvoyer.
crossroads ['krosˌroudz] *n* carrefour *m.*
cross section *n* coupe transversale *f;* (sample) échantillon *m.*
crosswind ['krosˌwind] *n* vent de travers *m.*
crossword ['krosˌwəːd] *n* mots croisés *m pl.*
crotchet ['krotʃit] *n* noire *f.* **crotchety** *adj* grognon, -onne.

crouch [krautʃ] *v* s'accroupir. *n* accroupissement *m*.

crow[1] [krou] *n* corneille *f.* **as the crow flies** à vol d'oiseau. **crowbar** *n* levier *m*.

crow[2] [krou] *v* (*cock*) chanter; (*baby*) gazouiller. *n* chant du coq *m*.

crowd [kraud] *n* foule *f.* *v* (*gather round*) s'attrouper; (*fill up*) (s')entasser. **crowded** *adj* plein (de monde).

crown [kraun] *n* couronne *f*; (*road*) milieu *m*; (*hat*) fond *m*. *v* couronner. **crown jewels** joyaux de la couronne *m pl*. **crown prince** prince héritier *m*.

crucial ['kruːʃəl] *adj* crucial.

crucify ['kruːsiˌfai] *v* crucifier. **crucifix** *n* crucifix *m*. **crucifixion** *n* crucifixion *f*, crucifiement *m*.

crude [kruːd] *adj* (*materials*) brut; rudimentaire; (*behaviour*) grossier. **crudely** *adv* crûment; imparfaitement.

cruel ['kruːəl] *adv* cruel. **cruelty** *n* cruauté *f*.

cruise [kruːz] *n* croisière *f*. *v* (*ship*) croiser; (*mot*) rouler. **cruising speed** vitesse de croisière *f*. **cruiser** *n* (*ship*) croiseur *m*.

crumb [krʌm] *n* miette *f*.

crumble ['krʌmbl] *v* (*to crumbs*) (s')émietter; (*to dust*) (s')effriter; (*collapse*) s'écrouler.

crumple ['krʌmpl] *v* (se) chiffonner.

crunch [krʌntʃ] *v* (*food*) croquer; (*snow, etc.*) faire craquer. *n* craquement *m*. **the crunch** (*coll*) l'instant critique. **crunchy** *adj* croquant.

crusade [kruːˈseid] *n* croisade *f*. *v* faire une croisade.

crush [krʌʃ] *v* (s')écraser; (*clothes*) (se) froisser. *n* cohue *f*. **crushing** *adj* (*defeat*) écrasant; (*remark*) percutant.

crust [krʌst] *n* croûte *f*. **crusty** *adj* (*bread*) croustillant; (*coll*) hargneux.

crutch [krʌtʃ] *n* béquille *f*; (*support*) soutien *m*.

cry [krai] *n* cri *m*. *v* (*shout*) crier; (*weep*) pleurer. **cry out** s'écrier, pousser un cri.

crypt [kript] *n* crypte *f*.

crystal ['kristl] *n* cristal *m*. **crystal-clear** *adj* clair comme le jour. **crystallize** *v* (se) cristalliser.

cub [kʌb] *n* petit, -e *m, f*; (*bear*) ourson *m*; (*fox*) renardeau *m*; (*lion*) lionceau *m*. **cub scout** louveteau *m*.

cube [kjuːb] *n* cube *m*. *v* (*maths*) cuber;

(*cookery*) couper en cubes. **cubic** *adj* cubique; (*in units*) cube.

cubicle ['kjuːbikl] *n* (*for changing*) cabine *f*; (*for sleeping*) alcôve *f*.

cuckoo ['kukuː] *n* coucou *m*.

cucumber [kjuˈkʌmbə] *n* concombre *m*.

cuddle ['kʌdl] *n* étreinte *f*. *v* serrer dans les bras; (*child*) câliner. **cuddle up** se pelotonner.

cue[1] [kjuː] *n* signal *m*; (*theatre*) réplique *f*.

cue[2] [kjuː] *n* (*billiards*) queue de billard *f*.

cuff[1] [kʌf] *n* (*shirt*) manchette *f*. **cuff-link** *n* bouton de manchette *m*. **off the cuff** à l'improviste.

cuff[2] [kʌf] *v* gifler. *n* gifle *f*.

culinary ['kʌlinəri] *adj* culinaire.

culminate ['kʌlmiˌneit] *v* culminer. **culminate in** se terminer par. **culmination** *n* point culminant *m*; (*success*) apogée *m*.

culprit ['kʌlprit] *n* coupable *m, f*; (*law*) accusé, -e *m, f*.

cult [kʌlt] *n* culte *m*.

cultivate ['kʌltiˌveit] *v* cultiver. **cultivation** *n* culture *f*.

culture ['kʌltʃə] *n* culture *f*. **cultural** *adj* culturel. **cultured** *adj* cultivé.

cumbersome ['kʌmbəsəm] *adj* encombrant.

cunning ['kʌniŋ] *adj* astucieux; rusé. *n* astuce *f*; ruse *f*.

cup [kʌp] *n* tasse *f*; (*prize*) coupe *f*.

cupboard ['kʌbəd] *n* placard *m*.

curate ['kjuərət] *n* vicaire *m*.

curator [kjuəˈreitə] *n* conservateur *m*.

curb [kəːb] *v* refréner; restreindre. *n* frein *m*.

curdle ['kəːdl] *v* (*milk*) (se) cailler; (*blood*) (se) figer.

cure [kjuə] *v* guérir; (*salt*) saler; (*smoke*) fumer. *n* remède *m*; (*recovery*) guérison *f*. **curable** *adj* guérissable.

curfew ['kəːfjuː] *n* couvre-feu *m*.

curious ['kjuəriəs] *adj* curieux. **curiosity** *n* curiosité *f*.

curl [kəːl] *v* (*hair*) friser, boucler. **curl up** (s')enrouler; (*person, animal*) se pelotonner. *n* boucle *f*; spirale *f*. **curler** *n* (*hair*) rouleau *m*. **curly** *adj* bouclé, frisé.

currant ['kʌrənt] *n* (*dried fruit*) raisin de Corinthe *m*; (*berry*) groseille *f*; (*bush*) groseillier *m*.

currency ['kʌrənsi] *n* monnaie *f*; (*foreign*) devise *f*; circulation *f*.

current ['kʌrənt] *adj* courant; (*fashion, etc.*) actuel. **current affairs** questions

d'actualité *f pl. n* courant *m*; tendance *f*.
currently *adv* en ce moment.
curry ['kʌri] *n* curry *m*. **curry powder** poudre de curry *f*. **curried** *adj* au curry.
curse [kəːs] *v* maudire; (*swear*) jurer. *n* malédiction *f*; juron *m*; (*bane*) fléau *m*.
curt [kəːt] *adj* brusque.
curtail [kəˈteil] *v* écourter; (*expenses*) réduire. **curtailment** *n* raccourcissement *m*; réduction *f*.
curtain ['kəːtn] *n* rideau *m*. **curtain call** rappel *m*. *v* garnir de rideaux.
curtsy ['kəːtsi] *n* révérence *f*. *v* faire une révérence.
curve [kəːv] *n* courbe *f*. *v* (se) courber.
cushion ['kuʃən] *n* coussin *m*. *v* amortir.
custard ['kʌstəd] *n* (*pouring*) crème anglaise *f*; (*with eggs*) flan *m*.
custody ['kʌstədi] *n* garde *f*; emprisonnement *m*.
custom ['kʌstəm] *n* coutume *f*; (*comm*) clientèle *f*. **customs** *n* douane *f*. **customs officer** douanier *m*. **customary** *adj* habituel. **customer** *n* client, -e *m*, *f*.
***cut** [kʌt] *n* (*slit*) coupure *f*; (*stroke*) coup *m*; réduction *f*; (*of clothes*) coupe *f*; (*of meat*) morceau *m*. *v* couper; (*slice*) découper; (*shape*, trim) tailler; réduire. **cutback** *n* réduction *f*. **cut down** (*tree*, *etc*.) abattre; réduire. **cut glass** cristal taillé *m*. **cut off** couper; isoler. **cut out** (*engine*) caler; (*picture*) découper; (*give up*) supprimer. **cut-price** *adv* à prix réduit.
cute [kjuːt] *adj* (*sweet*) mignon, -onne; (*clever*) rusé.
cutlery ['kʌtləri] *n* couverts *m pl*.
cutlet ['kʌtlit] *n* côtelette *f*.
cutting ['kʌtiŋ] *n* (*rail*) tranchée *f*; (*newspaper*) coupure *f*; (*plant*) bouture *f*. *adj* (*edge*) tranchant; (*wind*) cinglant; (*remark*) mordant.
cycle ['saikl] *n* cycle *m*; bicyclette *f*, vélo *m*. *v* faire de la bicyclette; aller à bicyclette. **cycling** *n* cyclisme *m*. **cyclist** *n* cycliste *m*, *f*.
cyclone ['saikloun] *n* cyclone *m*.
cylinder ['silində] *n* cylindre *m*. **cylinder head** (*mot*) culasse *f*. **cylindrical** *adj* cylindrique.
cymbal ['simbəl] *n* cymbale *f*.
cynic ['sinik] *n* cynique *m*, *f*. **cynical** *adj* cynique. **cynicism** *n* cynisme *m*.
cypress ['saiprəs] *n* cyprès *m*.

Cyprus ['saiprəs] *n* Chypre *f*. **Cypriot** *n* Cypriote *m*, *f*; *adj* cypriote.
cyst [sist] *n* (*med*) kyste *m*.
Czechoslovakia [ˌtʃekəsləˈvakiə] *n* Tchécoslovaquie *f*. **Czech** *n* (*people*) Tchèque *m*, *f*; *nm*, *adj* tchèque. **Czechoslovak** *n* (*people*) Tchécoslovaque *m*, *f*; *nm*, *adj* tchécoslovaque.

D

dab [dab] *n* goutte *f*, petite touche *f*. *v* tamponner; appliquer à petits coups.
dabble ['dabl] *v* (*in water*) barboter; (*politics*, *etc*.) se mêler un peu (de).
dad [dad] *n* (*coll*) papa *m*.
daffodil ['dafədil] *n* jonquille *f*.
daft [daːft] *adj* idiot.
dagger ['dagə] *n* poignard *m*.
daily ['deili] *adj* quotidien. *n* (*newspaper*) quotidien *m*; (*cleaner*) femme de ménage *f*. *adv* tous les jours.
dainty ['deinti] *adj* délicat; (*small*) menu.
dairy ['deəri] *n* laiterie *f*; crémerie *f*. **dairy farming** industrie laitière *f*. **dairy produce** produits laitiers *m pl*.
daisy ['deizi] *n* marguerite *f*; (*wild*) pâquerette *f*.
dam [dam] *n* barrage *m*. *v* endiguer; construire un barrage (sur).
damage ['damidʒ] *n* dommage *m*. **damages** *pl n* (*law*) dommages-intérêts *m pl*. *v* endommager; (*health*, *etc*.) abîmer; (*reputation*) nuire à. **damaging** *adj* préjudiciable.
damn [dam] *v* (*rel*) damner; condamner. *interj* (*coll*) zut! *adj also* **damned** (*slang*) fichu. *adv* (*slang*) sacrément. **damn all** (*slang*) zéro. **I don't give a damn** (*slang*) je m'en fiche pas mal. **damnable** *adj* odieux. **damnation** *n* (*rel*) damnation *f*.
damp [damp] *adj* humide; (*skin*) moite. *n also* **dampness** humidité *f*. *v also* **dampen** (*moisten*) humecter; (*noise*) étouffer; (*courage*) refroidir. **damp-course** *n* couche isolante *f*. **put a damper on** jeter un froid sur.
damson ['damzən] *n* (*fruit*) prune de Damas *f*; (*tree*) prunier de Damas *m*.
dance [daːns] *v* danser. *n* danse *f*; bal *m*.

dance floor piste de danse *f.* **dancer** *n* danseur, -euse *m, f.* **dancing** *n* danse *f.*

dandelion ['dandɪˌlaɪən] *n* pissenlit *m.*

dandruff ['dandrəf] *n* pellicules *f pl.*

danger ['deɪndʒə] *n* danger *m.* **be in danger of** risquer de. **danger money** prime de risque *f.* **on the danger list** dans un état critique. **dangerous** *adj* dangereux.

dangle ['daŋgl] *v* (*be hanging*) pendre; (*let hang*) balancer.

Danish ['deɪnɪʃ] *nm, adj* danois. **Dane** *n* Danois, -e *m, f.*

dare [deə] *v* oser; (*challenge*) défier. **I dare say** sans doute. *n* défi *m.*

daring ['deərɪŋ] *n* audace *f. adj* audacieux.

dark [dɑːk] *adj* obscur; (*colour*) foncé; (*hair*) brun. **be dark** (*night*) faire nuit. **dark horse** quantité inconnue *f.* **darkroom** *n* (*phot*) chambre noire *f. n* obscurité *f*; nuit *f.* **in the dark** (*ignorant*) dans le noir. **darken** *v* (s')obscurcir; (*sky*) (s')assombrir; foncer. **darkness** *n* obscurité *f*, ténèbres *f pl.*

darling ['dɑːlɪŋ] *n, adj* chéri, -e.

darn [dɑːn] *v* (*socks*) repriser; (*clothes*) raccommoder. *n* reprise *f.* **darning** *n* raccommodage *m.*

dart [dɑːt] *n* (*game*) fléchette *f*; (*sewing*) pince *f.* **dartboard** *n* cible *f. v* s'élancer; (*rays*) darder.

dash [daʃ] *n* (*drop*) goutte *f*; (*writing*) tiret *m*; (*rush*) élan *m. v* (*rush*) se précipiter; (*throw*) (se) jeter; (*hopes*) anéantir. **dashboard** *n* (*mot*) tableau de bord *m.* **dashing** *adj* plein de panache.

data ['deɪtə] *n* données *f pl.* **data processing** informatique *f.*

date[1] [deɪt] *n* date *f*; (*meeting*) rendez-vous *m.* **out of date** (*invalid*) périmé; (*old-fashioned*) démodé. **up to date** moderne; (*books, etc.*) à jour. *v* dater; fixer la date de; (*boyfriend, etc.*) sortir avec. **dated** *adj* démodé.

date[2] [deɪt] *n* (*fruit*) datte *f*; (*tree*) dattier *m.*

daub [dɔːb] *v* barbouiller.

daughter ['dɔːtə] *n* fille *f.* **daughter-in-law** *n* belle-fille *f.*

daunt [dɔːnt] *v* décourager. **dauntless** *adj* intrépide.

dawdle ['dɔːdl] *v* traîner.

dawn [dɔːn] *n* aube *f*; point du jour *m. v* (*day*) poindre; (*hope*) naître. **dawn on** venir à.

day [deɪ] *n* jour *m*, journée *f.* **day after** lendemain *m.* **day before** veille *f.* **daylight** *n* jour *m.* **day-to-day** *adj* journalier.

daydream ['deɪdriːm] *v* rêvasser. *n* rêvasserie *f.*

daze [deɪz] *v* hébéter; (*from blow*) étourdir; (*shock*) abasourdir. *n* hébétement *m*; étourdissement *m*; stupéfaction *f.*

dazzle ['dazl] *v* éblouir. *n* lumière aveuglante *f.*

dead [ded] *adj* mort. *adv* absolument. **dead-beat** *adj* (*coll*) claqué. **dead end** impasse *f.* **deadline** *n* date limite *f*; heure limite *f.* **deadlock** *n* impasse *f.* **deadpan** *adj, adv* sans expression. **deaden** *v* amortir; (*pain*) calmer. **deadly** *adj* mortel.

deaf [def] *adj* sourd. **deaf-mute** *n* sourd-muet, sourde-muette *m, f.* **deafen** *v* rendre sourd; (*noise*) assourdir. **deafness** *n* surdité *f.*

****deal** [diːl] *n* quantité *f*; (*bargain*) marché *m*; (*cards*) donne *f.* **a good deal** beaucoup. *v* (*cards*) distribuer. **deal in** être dans le commerce de. **deal with** (*comm*) négocier avec; (*handle*) se charger de; (*book, report, etc.*) traiter de. **dealer** *n* négociant *m*; (*cards*) donneur *m.* **dealings** *pl n* (*comm*) opérations *f pl*; (*people*) relations *f pl.*

dealt [delt] *V* deal.

dean [diːn] *n* doyen *m.*

dear [dɪə] *n, adj* cher, chère. **oh dear!** oh là là! **dearly** *adv* cher, chèrement.

death [deθ] *n* mort *f.* **death certificate** acte de décès *m.* **death duties** droits de succession *m pl.* **death penalty** peine de mort *f.* **death toll** chiffre des morts *m.* **deathly** *adj* cadavérique; mortel.

debase [dɪ'beɪs] *v* avilir; (*lower quality*) rabaisser. **debasement** *n* avilissement *m*; baisse *f.*

debate [dɪ'beɪt] *v* discuter. *n* débat *m*; discussion *f.* **debatable** *adj* contestable.

debit ['debɪt] *n* débit *m. v* débiter; porter au débit.

debris ['deɪbriː] *n* débris *m pl.*

debt [det] *n* dette *f.* **get into debt** s'endetter. **debtor** *n* débiteur, -trice *m, f.*

decade ['dekeɪd] *n* décade *f.*

decadent ['dekədənt] *adj* décadent. **decadence** *n* décadence *f.*

decant [dɪ'kant] *v* décanter. **decanter** *n* carafe *f.*

decapitate [di'kapi‚teit] *v* décapiter.
decapitation *n* décapitation *f.*
decay [di'kei] *v* (*rot*) pourrir; décliner;
tomber en ruines; (*tooth*) se carier. *n*
pourrissement *m*; décadence *f*, carie *f.*
decaying *adj* en pourriture; en décadence.
decease [di'siːs] *n* décès *m. v* décéder.
deceased *n*, *adj* défunt, -e.
deceit [di'siːt] *n* tromperie *f.* **deceitful** *adj*
trompeur, -euse. **deceitfully** *adv* fausse-
ment. **deceitfulness** *n* fausseté *f.*
deceive [di'siːv] *v* tromper.
December [di'sembə] *n* décembre *m.*
decent ['diːsənt] *adj* (*dress*) décent;
(*respectable*) convenable; (*coll: nice*) chic.
decency *n* décence *f*; convenances *f pl*;
(*kindness*) gentillesse *f.*
deceptive [di'septiv] *adj* trompeur. **deception** *n* tromperie *f*; illusion *f.*
decibel ['desi‚bel] *n* décibel *m.*
decide [di'said] *v* (se) décider. **decided** *adj*
résolu; incontestable; marqué. **deciding**
adj décisif.
deciduous [di'sidjuəs] *adj* à feuilles cad-
uques.
decimal ['desiməl] *adj* décimal. *n*
décimale *f.* **decimal point** virgule *f.*
decimalization *n* décimalisation *f.* **deci-
malize** *v* décimaliser.
decipher [di'saifə] *v* déchiffrer.
decision [di'siʒən] *n* décision *f.* **decisive**
adj décisif; (*manner*) décidé.
deck [dek] *n* (*naut*) pont *m*; (*records*)
table de lecture *f.* **deck-chair** *n* transat *m.*
v orner.
declare [di'kleə] *v* déclarer. **declaration** *n*
déclaration *f.*
decline [di'klain] *n* déclin *m*; (*prices*)
baisse *f. v* décliner; baisser. **declension** *n*
déclinaison *f.*
decompose [‚diːkəm'pouz] *v* (se) décomposer. **decomposition** *n* décomposition *f.*
decorate ['dekə‚reit] *v* décorer; orner;
(*room, house*) peindre et tapisser. **deco-
rating** *n* décoration intérieure *f.* **decoration** *n* décoration *f*; ornement *m*; (*room*)
décor *m.* **decorative** *adj* décoratif. **decorator** *n* décorateur *m.*
decoy ['diːkoi; *v* di'koi] *n* leurre *m*; (*person*) compère *m. v* leurrer.
decrease [di'kriːs] *v* diminuer, décroître. *n*
diminution *f*, décroissance *f.*
decree [di'kriː] *n* décret *m. v* décréter.
decrepit [di'krepit] *adj* décrépit; (*building*)

délabré. **decrepitude** *n* décrépitude *f*;
délabrement *m.*
dedicate ['dedi‚keit] *v* dédier; consacrer.
dedication dédicace *f*; consécration *f*;
dévouement *m.*
deduce [di'djuːs] *v* déduire. **deduction** *n*
déduction *f.*
deduct [di'dʌkt] *v* déduire; (*numbers*)
soustraire; (*from wage*) prélever (sur).
deductible *adj* déductible. **deduction** *n*
déduction *f*; prélèvement *m.*
deed [diːd] *n* action *f*; (*law*) contrat *m.*
deed poll acte unilatéral *m.*
deep [diːp] *adj* profond; (*broad*) large;
(*sound*) grave. *adv* profondément. **deep-
freeze** *n* congélateur *m.* **deep-seated** *adj*
profondément enraciné. **deepen** *v*
(s')approfondir.
deer [diə] *n* cerf *m*, biche *f.*
deface [di'feis] *v* mutiler; (*poster, etc.*)
barbouiller.
default [di'foːlt] *n* défaut *m.* **in default of**
faute de. *v* faire défaut; être en défaut.
defeat [di'fiːt] *v* vaincre, battre. *n* défaite
f. **defeatist** *n*(*m+f*), *adj* défaitiste.
defect ['diːfekt; *v* di'fekt] *n* défaut *m. v*
faire défection. **defection** *n* défection *f.*
defective *adj* défectueux. **defector** *n*
transfuge *m, f.*
defend [di'fend] *v* défendre. **defence** *n*
défense *f.* **defenceless** *adj* sans défense.
defendant *n* défendeur, -eresse *m, f.*
defending *adj* (*champion*) en titre; (*law*)
de la défense.
defensive [di'fensiv] *n* défensive *f.* *adj*
défensif.
defer [di'fəː] *v* (*put off*) différer. **deferment**
n ajournement *m*; suspension *f.*
defiant [di'faiənt] *adj* rebelle; provocant.
defiance *n* défi *m.* **in defiance of** au
mépris de. **defiantly** *adv* d'un air *or* ton
de défi.
deficient [di'fiʃənt] *adj* insuffisant. **be
deficient in** manquer de. **deficiency** *n*
manque *f*; (*med*) carence *f.*
deficit ['defisit] *n* déficit *m.*
define [di'fain] *v* définir. **definition** *n* définition *f*; délimitation *f*; (*clearness*) netteté *f.* **definitive** *adj* définitif.
definite ['definit] *adj* certain; déterminé;
manifeste; (*gramm*) défini. **definitely** *adv*
sans aucun doute; catégoriquement.
deflate [di'fleit] *v* (*tyre, etc.*) dégonfler;
(*person*) démonter. **deflation** *n* (*econ*)
déflation *f*; dégonflement *m.*

deform [di'fɔːm] *v* déformer. **deformation** *n* déformation *f.* **deformed** *adj* difforme. **deformity** *n* difformité *f.*

defraud [di'frɔːd] *v* (*state*) frauder; (*person*) escroquer.

defrost [diː'frost] *v* (*refrigerator*, etc.) dégivrer; (*frozen food*) décongeler.

deft [deft] *adj* habile. **deftness** *n* habileté *f.*

defunct [di'fʌŋkt] *adj* défunt.

defy [di'fai] *v* défier.

degenerate [di'dʒenəˌreit; *n*, *adj* di'dʒenərit] *v* dégénérer. *n*, *adj* dégénéré, -e. **degeneracy** *or* **degeneration** *n* dégénérescence *f.*

degrade [di'greid] *v* dégrader. **degradation** *n* (*person*) avilissement *m*; dégradation *f.*

degree [di'griː] *n* degré *m*; (*university*) licence *f.* **by degrees** petit à petit.

dehydrate [diː'haidreit] *v* déshydrater. **dehydration** *n* déshydratation *f.*

de-icer [diː'aisə] *n* dégivreur *m.* **de-ice** *v* dégivrer.

deity [''diːəti] *n* divinité *f*, déité *f.*

dejected [di'dʒektid] *adj* abattu. **dejection** *n* abattement *m.*

delay [di'lei] *v* (*make late*) retarder; (*put off*) différer. *n* délai *m*; retardement *m*; (*rail*) retard *m.* **delaying** *adj* dilatoire.

delegate [''deləgeit; *n*, *adj* 'deləgit] *v* déléguer. *n*, *adj* délégué, -e. **delegation** *n* délégation *f*; nomination *f.*

delete [di'liːt] *v* rayer. **deletion** *n* (*act*) suppression *f*; (*word*, *phrase*, etc.) rature *f.*

deliberate [di'libərət; *v* di'libəreit] *adj* (*intentional*) délibéré; réfléchi; mesuré. *v* délibérer (sur). **deliberately** *adv* exprès; avec mesure. **deliberation** *n* délibération *f.*

delicate [''delikət] *adj* délicat; (*health*) fragile. **delicacy** *n* délicatesse *f*; (*food*) friandise *f.*

delicious [di'liʃəs] *adj* délicieux.

delight [di'lait] *n* grand plaisir *m*, joie *f.* *v* enchanter; se délecter (à). **delighted** *adj* ravi. **delightful** *adj* charmant, ravissant.

delinquency [di'liŋkwənsi] *n* délinquance *f.* **delinquent** *n*, *adj* délinquant, -e.

delirious [di'liriəs] *adj* délirant. **be delirious** (*med*) avoir le délire; (*crowd*, etc.) être en délire. **delirium** *n* délire *m.*

deliver [di'livə] *v* (*message*) remettre; (*goods*) livrer; (*letters*) distribuer; (*save*) délivrer; (*speech*) prononcer; (*woman*) accoucher. **deliverance** *n* délivrance *f.* **delivery** *n* livraison *f*; distribution *f*; (*speech*) débit *m*; accouchement *m.*

delta [''deltə] *n* delta *m.*

delude [di'luːd] *v* tromper. **delude oneself** se faire des illusions. **deluded** *adj* induit en erreur. **delusion** *n* illusion *f*; (*psych*) fantasme *m.*

deluge [''deljuːdʒ] *n* déluge *n.* *v* inonder.

delve [delv] *v* creuser, fouiller.

demand [di'maːnd] *v* exiger, réclamer. *n* exigence *f*; (*claim*) réclamation *f*; (*comm*) demande *f.* **be in demand** être demandé.

democracy [di'mokrəsi] *n* démocratie *f.* **democrat** *n* démocrate *m*, *f.* **democratic** *adj* démocratique.

demolish [di'moliʃ] *v* démolir. **demolition** *n* démolition *f.*

demon [''diːmən] *n* démon *m.* **demoniacal** *adj* démoniaque.

demonstrate [''demənˌstreit] *v* démontrer; (*machine*, etc.) faire une démonstration de; (*pol*) manifester. **demonstration** *n* démonstration *f*; manifestation *f.* **demonstrative** *adj* démonstratif.

demoralize [di'morəˌlaiz] *v* démoraliser. **become demoralized** perdre courage. **demoralization** *n* démoralisation *f.*

demure [di'mjuə] *adj* modeste, sage.

den [den] *n* tanière *f*, repaire *m.*

denim [''denim] *n* toile de jean *f.* **denims** *pl n* (*jeans*) blue-jean *m sing.*

Denmark [''denmaːk] *n* Danemark *m.*

denomination [diˌnomi'neiʃən] *n* dénomination *f*; (*money*) valeur *f*; (*rel*) secte *f.* **denominator** *n* dénominateur *m.*

denote [di'nout] *v* dénoter.

denounce [di'nauns] *v* dénoncer.

dense [dens] *adj* dense; (*coll: stupid*) bouché. **density** *n* densité *f.*

dent [dent] *n* bosselure *f.* *v* bosseler, cabosser.

dental [''dentl] *adj* dentaire. **dental surgeon** chirurgien dentiste *m.*

dentist [''dentist] *n* dentiste *m*, *f.* **dentistry** *n* art dentaire *m.*

denture [''dentʃə] *n* dentier *m.*

denude [di'njuːd] *v* dénuder.

denunciation [dinʌnsi'eiʃən] *n* dénonciation *f.*

deny [di'nai] *v* nier; refuser. **denial** *n* dénégation *f*; (*accusation*, etc.) démenti *m.*

deodorant [diː'oudərənt] *nm*, *adj* déodorant, désodorisant.

depart [di'pɑɪt] *v* partir. **depart from** (*leave*) quitter; (*deviate*) s'écarter de. **departure** *n* départ *m*. **departure lounge** salle de départ *f*.

department [di'pɑɪtmənt] *n* département *m*; (*shop*) rayon *m*; (*school, university*) section *f*; domaine *m*; (*comm*) service *m*. **department store** grand magasin *m*.

depend [di'pend] *v* dépendre. **depend on** dépendre de; (*rely*) compter sur. **dependant** *n* personne à charge *f*. **dependence** *n* dépendance *f*. **dependent** *adj* dépendant.

depict [di'pikt] *v* (*words*) peindre; (*picture*) représenter. **depiction** *n* peinture *f*; représentation *f*.

deplete [di'pliɪt] *v* réduire. **depletion** *n* réduction *f*.

deplore [di'ploɪ] *v* déplorer. **deplorable** *adj* déplorable.

deport [di'poɪt] *v* déporter; expulser. **deportation** *n* déportation *f*; expulsion *f*. **deportment** *n* maintien *m*.

depose [di'pouz] *v* déposer. **deposition** *n* déposition *f*.

deposit [di'pozit] *v* déposer. *n* dépôt *m*; (*against damage*) caution *f*; (*token payment*) acompte *m*. **deposit account** compte de dépôt *m*. **depositor** *n* déposant, -e *m, f*.

depot ['depou] *n* dépôt *m*.

deprave [di'preiv] *v* dépraver. **depravity** *n* dépravation *f*.

depreciate [di'priɪʃi,eit] *v* (se) déprécier. **depreciation** *n* dépréciation *f*.

depress [di'pres] *v* déprimer; (*press down*) appuyer sur. **depression** *n* dépression *f*; découragement *m*; (*econ*) crise *f*.

deprive [di'praiv] *v* priver. **deprivation** *n* privation *f*.

depth [depθ] *n* profondeur *f*; (*breadth*) largeur *f*; intensité *f*.

deputy ['depjuti] *n* adjoint, -e *m, f*. **deputation** *n* délégation *f*. **deputize for** assurer l'intérim de.

derail [di'reil] *v* (faire) dérailler. **derailment** *n* déraillement *m*.

derelict ['derilikt] *adj* abandonné, délaissé.

deride [di'raid] *v* railler. **derision** *n* dérision *f*. **derisive** *adj* moqueur. **derisory** *adj* (*offer, etc.*) dérisoire.

derive [di'raiv] *v* (*gain*) trouver, tirer. **be derived from** dériver de, provenir de. **derivation** *n* dérivation *f*.

derogatory [di'rogətəri] *adj* dénigrant, désobligeant.

descend [di'send] *v* descendre. **descend to** (*crime, etc.*) s'abaisser à. **descendant** *n* descendant, -e *m, f*. **descent** *n* descente *f*; origine *f*.

describe [di'skraib] *v* décrire. **description** *n* description *f*. **descriptive** *adj* descriptif.

desert[1] ['dezət] *n* désert *m*.

desert[2] [di'zəɪt] *v* déserter, abandonner. **deserted** *adj* désert. **deserter** *n* déserteur *m*. **desertion** *n* désertion *f*; abandon *m*.

desert[3] [di'zəɪt] *n* dû *m*. **get one's just deserts** avoir ce que l'on mérite.

deserve [di'zəɪv] *v* mériter.

design [di'zain] *n* modèle *m*, plan *m*; (*pattern*) dessin *m*; (*comm*) design *m*; (*machine, etc.*) conception *f*; (*intention*) dessein *m*. *v* dessiner; projeter; concevoir. **designer** *n* (*comm*) concepteur-projeteur *m*; (*art*) dessinateur, -trice *m, f*.

designate ['dezig,neit] *v* désigner. **designation** *n* désignation *f*.

desire [di'zaiə] *n* désir *m*. *v* désirer. **desirable** *adj* désirable.

desk [desk] *n* bureau *m*; (*school*) pupitre *m*.

desolate ['desələt] *adj* désert; sombre; (*person*) affligé. **desolation** *n* désolation *f*.

despair [di'speə] *n* désespoir *m*. *v* désespérer.

desperate ['despərət] *adj* désespéré. **desperation** *n* désespoir *m*.

despise [di'spaiz] *v* mépriser.

despite [di'spait] *prep* malgré.

despondent [di'spondənt] *adj* découragé. **despondency** *n* découragement *m*.

despot ['despot] *n* despote *m*. **despotic** *adj* despotique.

dessert [di'zəɪt] *n* dessert *m*. **dessertspoon** *n* cuiller à dessert *f*.

destination [desti'neiʃən] *n* destination *f*.

destine ['destin] *v* destiner. **destiny** *n* destin *m*.

destitute ['destitjuɪt] *adj* indigent. **destitution** *n* dénuement *m*.

destroy [di'stroi] *v* détruire. **destroyer** *n* (*ship*) contre-torpilleur *m*. **destruction** *n* destruction *f*. **destructive** *adj* destructeur, -trice; destructif.

detach [di'tatʃ] *v* détacher. **detachable** *adj* détachable. **detached** *adj* détaché; (*unbiased*) objectif; indifférent. **detached house** maison individuelle *f*. **detachment** *n* détachement *m*; séparation *f*.

detail ['diɪteil] *n* détail *m*. *v* détailler; (*mil*) affecter.

detain [di'tein] *v* retenir; (*law*) détenir.

detect [di'tekt] *v* découvrir; distinguer. **detective** *n* agent de la sûreté *m*. **detective story** roman policier *m*. **detector** *n* detecteur *m*.

detention [di'tenʃən] *n* détention *f*; (*school*) retenue *f*.

deter [di'tɜɪ] *v* décourager; dissuader; (*prevent*) détourner. **deterrent** *n* force de dissuasion *f*.

detergent [di'tɜɪdʒənt] *nm*, *adj* détersif.

deteriorate [di'tiəriəˌreit] *v* (se) détériorer. **deterioration** *n* détérioration *f*.

determine [di'tɜɪmin] *v* déterminer; fixer; décider. **determination** *n* détermination *f*. **determined** *adj* déterminé; résolu.

detest [di'test] *v* détester.

detonate ['detəˌneit] *v* (faire) détoner. **detonation** *n* détonation *f*. **detonator** *n* détonateur *m*.

detour ['diɪtuə] *n* détour *m*. *v* faire un détour.

detract [di'trakt] *v* **detract from** diminuer.

detriment ['detrimənt] *n* détriment *m*. **detrimental** *adj* nuisible.

devalue [diɪ'valjuɪ] *v* dévaluer. **devaluation** *n* dévaluation *f*.

devastate ['devəˌsteit] *v* (*town*, *etc.*) dévaster; (*person*) terrasser. **devastating** *adj* (*power*) dévastateur, -trice; (*effect*) accablant. **devastation** *n* dévastation *f*.

develop [di'veləp] *v* (se) développer; contracter. **development** *n* développement *m*; exploitation *f*.

deviate ['diɪviˌeit] *v* dévier. **deviation** *n* déviation *f*.

device [di'vais] *n* appareil *m*; (*scheme*) formule *f*.

devil ['devl] *n* diable *m*. **talk of the devil!** quand on parle du loup! **devilish** *adj* diabolique.

devise [di'vaiz] *v* inventer; (*plan*) combiner.

devious ['diɪviəs] *adj* détourné, tortueux.

devoid [di'void] *adj* dénué.

devolution [ˌdiɪvə'luɪʃən] *n* (*pol*) décentralisation *f*.

devote [di'vout] *v* consacrer. **devoted** *adj* dévoué. **devotion** *n* dévouement *m*.

devour [di'vauə] *v* dévorer.

devout [di'vaut] *adj* (*person*) pieux; (*earnest*) fervent.

dew [djuɪ] *n* rosée *f*.

dexterous ['dekstrəs] *adj* adroit. **dexterity** *n* adresse *f*.

diabetes [ˌdiaə'biɪtiɪz] *n* diabète *m*. **diabetic** *n*(*m*+*f*), *adj* diabétique.

diagnose [ˌdiaəg'nouz] *v* diagnostiquer. **diagnosis** *n* diagnostic *m*. **diagnostic** *adj* diagnostique.

diagonal [dai'agənəl] *adj* diagonal. *n* diagonale *f*.

diagram ['daiəˌgram] *n* diagramme *m*; (*math*) figure *f*. **diagrammatic** *adj* schématique.

dial ['daiəl] *n* cadran *m*. *v* (*number*) faire. **dial direct** appeler par l'automatique. **dial 999** appeler Police Secours. **dialling code** indicatif *m*. **dialling tone** tonalité *f*.

dialect ['diaəlekt] *n* dialecte *m*; (*rural*) patois *m*.

dialogue ['daiəlog] *n* dialogue *m*.

diameter [dai'amitə] *n* diamètre *m*. **diametrically opposed** diamétralement opposé.

diamond ['daiəmənd] *n* (*gem*) diamant *m*; (*cards*) carreau *m*; (*shape*) losange *m*.

diaper ['daiəpə] *n* (*US*) couche *f*.

diaphragm ['daiəˌfram] *n* diaphragme *m*.

diarrhoea [ˌdaiə'riə] *n* diarrhée *f*.

diary ['daiəri] *n* (*record*) journal *m*; (*appointments*) agenda *m*.

dice [dais] *n* dé *m*. *v* couper en dés. **dice with death** jouer avec la mort.

dictate [dik'teit] *v* dicter. **dictation** *n* dictée *f*. **dictator** *n* dictateur *m*. **dictatorship** *n* dictature *f*.

dictionary ['dikʃənəri] *n* dictionnaire *m*.

did [did] *V* do.

die [dai] *v* mourir. **be dying** se mourir. **be dying to** mourir d'envie de. **be dying for** avoir une envie folle de. **die down** s'apaiser. **die out** disparaître.

diesel ['diɪzəl] *n* diesel *m*. **diesel oil** gas-oil *m*. **diesel train** autorail *m*.

diet ['daiət] *n* (*restricted*) régime *m*; (*normal food*) nourriture *f*. *v* suivre un régime.

differ ['difə] *v* différer; ne pas être d'accord. **difference** *n* différence *f*. **different** *adj* différent; (*another*) autre. **differential** *adj* différentiel. **differentials** *pl n* (*salary*) écarts salariaux *m pl*. **differentiate** *v* distinguer.

difficult ['difikəlt] *adj* difficile. **difficulty** *n* difficulté *f*.

dig [dig] *v* creuser; (*dog*) fouiller. **dig up** déterrer. *n* (*archaeol*) fouille *f*; (*coll*: *remark*) coup de patte *m*; (*with elbow*) coup de coude *m*.

digest [dai'dʒest] *v* digérer. **digestion** *n* digestion *f*.

digit ['didʒit] *n* (*math*) chiffre *m*; (*finger*) doigt *m*. **digital** *adj* (*clock*, *etc*.) à affichage numérique.

dignified ['digni,faid] *adj* digne.

dignity ['dignəti] *n* dignité *f*.

digress [dai'gres] *v* s'éloigner. **digression** *n* digression *f*.

digs [digz] *pl n* chambre *f sing*, logement *m sing*.

dilapidated [di'lapi,deitid] *adj* délabré.

dilate [dai'leit] *v* (se) dilater. **dilation** *n* dilatation *f*.

dilemma [di'lemə] *n* dilemme *m*.

diligent ['dilidʒent] *adj* assidu; laborieux. **diligence** *n* assiduité *f*, zèle *m*.

dilute [dai'luɪt] *v* diluer. *adj* dilué.

dim [dim] *adj* (*light*) faible; (*sound*) vague; (*coll: stupid*) bouché. **take a dim view of** voir d'un mauvais œil. *v* (*light*) baisser; (*sound*) affaiblir. **dimness** *n* faiblesse *f*; obscurité *f*.

dimension [di'menʃən] *n* dimension *f*. **two-/three-dimensional** à deux/trois dimensions.

diminish [di'miniʃ] *v* diminuer.

diminutive [di'minjutiv] *adj* (*small*) tout petit; (*gramm*) diminutif. *n* diminutif *m*.

dimple ['dimpl] *n* fossette *f*.

din [din] *n* vacarme *m*.

dine [dain] *v* dîner. **diner** *n* (*person*) dîneur, -euse *m*, *f*. **dining car** wagon-restaurant *m*. **dining room** salle à manger *f*.

dinghy ['diŋgi] *n* youyou *m*; (*with sail*) dériveur *m*.

dingy ['dindʒi] *adj* miteux.

dinner ['dinə] *n* dîner *m*; (*midday meal*) déjeuner *m*. **dinner jacket** smoking *m*.

dinosaur ['dainə,sɔɪ] *n* dinosaure *m*.

diocese ['daiəsis] *n* diocèse *f*.

dip [dip] *v* (*into water*, *etc*.) plonger; (*go down*) baisser. *n* (*coll: bathe*) baignade *f*; (*in ground*) déclivité *f*. **dip-stick** *n* jauge *f*.

diphthong ['difθoŋ] *n* diphtongue *f*.

diploma [di'ploumə] *n* diplôme *m*.

diplomacy [di'plouməsi] *n* diplomatie *f*. **diplomat** *n* diplomate *m*. **diplomatic** *adj* diplomatique; (*person*) diplomate.

dire [daiə] *adj* terrible; extrême. **in dire straits** dans une situation désespérée.

direct [di'rekt] *adj* direct. **direct object** complément direct *m*. *v* diriger; adresser; (*instruct*) charger. *adv* directement. **direction** *n* direction *f*; instruction *f*. **directly** *adv* directement; (*immediately*) tout de suite. **director** *n* directeur, -trice *m*, *f*; (*theatre*) metteur en scène *m*; (*film*, *TV*, *etc*.) réalisateur, -trice *m*, *f*. **directory** *n* (*phone*) annuaire *m*; (*addresses*) répertoire *m*. **directory enquiries** renseignements *m pl*.

dirt [dəɪt] *n* saleté *f*, crasse *f*.

dirty ['dəɪti] *adj* sale; (*vulgar*) grossier. *v* salir.

disability [disə'biləti] *n* incapacité *f*; infirmité *f*. **disabled** *adj* infirme, handicapé.

disadvantage [,disəd'vaɪntidʒ] *n* désavantage *m*. **at a disadvantage** dans une position désavantageuse.

disagree [,disə'griɪ] *v* ne pas être d'accord; (*be different*) ne pas concorder; (*food*, *etc*.) ne pas convenir (à). **disagreeable** *adj* désagréable. **disagreement** *n* désaccord *m*.

disappear [,disə'piə] *v* disparaître. **disappearance** *n* disparition *f*.

disappoint [,disə'point] *v* decevoir. **disappointment** *n* déception *f*.

disapprove [,disə'pruɪv] *v* désapprouver. **disapproval** *n* désapprobation *f*. **disapproving** *adj* désapprobateur, -trice *m*, *f*.

disarm [dis'aɪm] *v* désarmer. **disarmament** *n* désarmement *m*. **disarming** *adj* (*smile*) désarmant.

disaster [di'zaɪstə] *n* désastre *m*, catastrophe *f*. **disastrous** *adj* désastreux.

disband [dis'band] *v* (se) disperser.

disbelief [disbi'liɪf] *n* incrédulité *f*.

disc or US **disk** [disk] *n* disque *m*.

discard [dis'kaɪd; *n* 'diskaɪd] *v* se débarrasser de; abandonner; (*cards*) se défausser de. *n* défausse *f*.

discern [di'səɪn] *v* discerner. **discernible** *adj* perceptible. **discerning** *adj* judicieux. **discernment** *n* discernement *m*.

discharge [dis'tʃaɪdʒ] *v* (*patient*, *employee*) renvoyer; (*gun*) tirer; (*cargo*) décharger; (*duty*) remplir; (*law*, *mil*) libérer. *n* renvoi *m*; (*elec*) décharge *f*; (*med*) pertes *f pl*.

disciple [di'saipl] *n* disciple *m*.

discipline ['disiplin] *n* discipline *f*. *v* discipliner; punir. **disciplinary** *adj* disciplinaire.

disclaim [dis'kleim] v désavouer.

disclose [dis'klouz] v divulguer, révéler.

disclosure n divulgation f, révélation f.

discolour [dis'kʌlə] v (se) décolorer; (from white) jaunir. **discolouration** n décoloration f; jaunissement m.

discomfort [dis'kʌmfət] n malaise m, gêne f.

disconcert [diskən'sɔit] v déconcerter.

disconnect [diskə'nekt] v disjoindre; (gas, phone, etc.) couper; (television, etc.) débrancher. **disconnected** adj (thoughts, etc.) décousu.

disconsolate [dis'konsələt] adj adj inconsolable.

discontented [diskən'tentid] adj mécontent. **discontent** or **discontentment** n mécontentement m.

discontinue [diskən'tinjui] v cesser; interrompre.

discord ['diskoid] n discorde f; (music) dissonance f. **discordant** adj discordant; dissonant.

discotheque ['diskətek] n discothèque f.

discount ['diskaunt] n remise f, escompte m. **at a discount** au rabais. **discount store** magasin de demi-gros m. v ne pas tenir compte de.

discourage [dis'kʌridʒ] v décourager. **become discouraged** se laisser décourager. **discouragement** n désapprobation f.

discover [dis'kʌvə] v découvrir. **discovery** n découverte f.

discredit [dis'kredit] v discréditer. n discrédit m.

discreet [di'skriit] adj discret, -ète. **discretion** n discrétion f. **use your own discretion** c'est à vous de juger. **discretionary** adj discrétionnaire.

discrepancy [di'skrepənsi] n divergence f, désaccord m.

discrete [di'skriit] adj discret, -ète.

discriminate [di'skrimi‚neit] v distinguer; (unfairly) établir une discrimination. **discrimination** n distinction f; discrimination f; discernement m.

discus ['diskəs] n disque m.

discuss [di'skʌs] v discuter. **discussion** n discussion f.

disdain [dis'dein] n dédain m. **disdainful** adj dédaigneux. **disdainfully** adv avec dédain.

disease [di'ziiz] n maladie f. **diseased** adj malade.

disembark [disim'baik] v débarquer. **disembarkation** n débarquement m.

disengage [disin'geidʒ] v dégager; (tech) débrayer. **disengaged** adj libre; débrayé.

disentangle [disin'taŋgl] v débrouiller.

disfigure [dis'figə] v défigurer. **disfigurement** n défigurement m.

disgrace [dis'greis] n honte f; (disfavour) disgrâce f. **in disgrace** (child, etc.) en pénitence. v faire honte à; déshonorer. **disgraceful** adj honteux, scandaleux.

disgruntled [dis'grʌntld] adj mécontent.

disguise [dis'gaiz] v déguiser. n déguisement m; masque m. **in disguise** déguisé.

disgust [dis'gʌust] n dégoûter. **disgusting** adj dégoûtant, écœurant.

dish [diʃ] n plat m. **do the dishes** faire la vaisselle. **dishcloth** n lavette f. **dishwasher** n lave-vaisselle m invar. v **dish up** servir.

dishearten [dis'haitn] v décourager.

dishevelled [di'ʃevəld] adj échevelé.

dishonest [dis'onist] adj malhonnête. **dishonesty** malhonnêteté f.

dishonour [dis'onə] n déshonneur m. v déshonorer. **dishonourable** adj déshonorant.

disillusion [disi'luiʒən] v désillusionner. n désillusion f.

disinfect [disin'fekt] v désinfecter. **disinfectant** nm, adj désinfectant. **disinfection** n désinfection f.

disinherit [disin'herit] v déshériter.

disintegrate [dis'inti‚greit] v (se) désintégrer. **disintegration** n désintégration f.

disinterested [dis'intristid] adj désintéressé.

disjointed [dis'dʒointid] adj décousu.

disk V **disc.**

dislike [dis'laik] v ne pas aimer. n aversion f. **take a dislike to** prendre en grippe.

dislocate ['dislə‚keit] v disloquer. **dislocation** n dislocation f.

dislodge [dis'lodʒ] v faire bouger.

disloyal [dis'loiəl] adj déloyal. **disloyalty** déloyauté f.

dismal ['dizməl] adj morne, lugubre.

dismantle [dis'mantl] v démonter.

dismay [dis'mei] n consternation f. v consterner.

dismiss [dis'mis] v (send away) renvoyer, congédier; (meeting) dissoudre; (reject) écarter. **dismissal** n renvoi m, congédiement m.

dismount [dis'maunt] *v* descendre.

disobey [disə'bei] *v* désobeir à. **disobedience** *n* désobéissance *f*. **disobedient** *adj* désobéissant.

disorder [dis'ɔɪdə] *n* désordre *m*; (*med*) trouble *m*. **disorderly** *adj* désordonné.

disorganized [dis'ɔɪgənaizd] *adj* désorganisé.

disown [dis'oun] *v* renier.

disparage [di'sparidʒ] *v* dénigrer. **disparagement** *n* dénigrement *m*. **disparaging** *adj* désobligeant.

disparity [dis'pariti] *n* disparité *f*.

dispassionate [dis'paʃənit] *adj* calme; impartial. **dispassionately** *adv* sans émotion; impartialement.

dispatch [di'spatʃ] *v* expédier. *n* expédition *f*; (*report*) dépêche *f*.

dispel [di'spel] *v* dissiper.

dispense [di'spens] *v* distribuer, administrer; (*medicine*) préparer. **dispense with** se passer de. **dispensary** *n* pharmacie *f*. **dispensation** *n* (*decree*) décret *m*; (*rel*) dispense *f*.

disperse [di'spɔɪs] *v* (se) disperser; (se) dissiper. **dispersal** *n* dispersion *f*.

displace [dis'pleis] *v* déplacer. **displacement** *n* déplacement *m*.

display [dis'plei] *v* étaler; (*courage, etc.*) faire preuve de. *n* exposition *f*; (*comm*) étalage; (*courage, etc.*) manifestation *f*.

displease [dis'pliɪz] *v* déplaire à. **displeasure** *n* mécontentement *m*.

dispose [di'spouz] *v* disposer. **dispose of** se débarrasser de. **disposable** *adj* à jeter. **disposal** *n* disposition *f*; (*rubbish*) enlèvement *m*; (*bomb*) désamorçage *m*. **disposition** *n* tempérament *m*; inclination *f*.

disproportion [disprə'pɔɪʃən] *n* disproportion *f*. **disproportionate** *adj* disproportionné.

disprove [dis'pruɪv] *v* réfuter.

dispute [di'spjuɪt] *n* dispute *f*, (*argument*) discussion *f*; (*industrial*) conflit *m*. **beyond dispute** incontestable. *v* contester; discuter. **disputable** *adj* discutable.

disqualify [dis'kwoli,fai] *v* disqualifier. **disqualification** *n* disqualification *f*.

disregard [disrə'gaɪd] *v* (*ignore*) mépriser; négliger. *n* indifférence *f*; mépris.

disreputable [dis'repjutəbl] *adj* louche; (*clothes*) miteux.

disrespect [disrə'spekt] *n* manque de respect *m*. **disrespectful** *adj* irrespectueux. **be disrespectful to** manquer de respect envers.

disrupt [dis'rʌpt] *v* perturber, interrompre. **disruption** *n* perturbation *f*; interruption *f*. **disruptive** *adj* perturbateur, -trice.

dissatisfied [di'satis,faid] *adj* mécontent. **dissatisfaction** *n* mécontentement *m*.

dissect [di'sekt] *v* disséquer. **dissection** *n* dissection *f*.

dissent [di'sent] *v* différer. *n* dissentiment *m*. **dissension** *n* dissension *f*.

dissident ['disidənt] *n, adj* dissident, -e. **dissidence** *n* dissidence *f*.

dissimilar [di'similə] *adj* dissemblable. **dissimilarity** *n* dissemblance *f*.

dissociate [di'sousieit] *v* dissocier. **dissociation** *n* dissociation *f*.

dissolve [di'zolv] *v* (se) dissoudre.

dissuade [di'sweid] *v* dissuader. **dissuasion** *n* dissuasion *f*.

distance ['distəns] *n* distance *f*. **in the distance** au loin. **distant** *adj* lointain, éloigné; (*reserved*) distant.

distaste [dis'teist] *n* dégoût *m*. **distasteful** *adj* déplaisant.

distemper [di'stempə] *n* (*paint*) détrempe *f*. *v* peindre en détrempe.

distended [di'stendid] *adj* (*med*) dilaté; distendu. **distension** *n* dilatation *f*; distension *f*.

distil [di'stil] *v* (se) distiller. **distillery** *n* distillerie *f*.

distinct [di'stiŋkt] *adj* distinct; net, nette. **distinction** *n* distinction *f*. **distinctive** *adj* distinctif.

distinguish [di'stiŋgwiʃ] *v* distinguer; caractériser.

distort [di'stɔɪt] *v* déformer. **distortion** *n* distorsion *f*; déformation *f*.

distract [di'strakt] *v* distraire. **distracting** *adj* gênant. **distraction** *n* distraction *f*; interruption *f*.

distraught [di'strɔɪt] *adj* éperdu.

distress [di'stres] *n* douleur *f*, affliction *f*; (*poverty, danger*) détresse *f*. *v* affliger. **distressing** *adj* pénible.

distribute [di'stribjut] *v* distribuer; (*share*) répartir. **distribution** *n* distribution *f*; répartition *f*. **distributor** *n* (*mot*) distributeur *m*.

district ['distrikt] *n* (*of town*) quartier *m*; (*admin*) arrondissement *m*; (*of country*) région *f*. **district nurse** infirmière visiteuse *f*.

distrust [dis'trʌst] v se méfier de. n méfiance f. **distrustful** adj méfiant.

disturb [di'stɜːb] v déranger; troubler. **disturbance** n dérangement m; (noise) tapage m. **disturbing** adj inquiétant.

disuse [dis'juːs] n désuétude f. **fall into disuse** tomber en désuétude. **disused** adj désaffecté.

ditch [ditʃ] n fossé m.

ditto ['ditou] adv idem.

divan [di'van] n divan m.

dive [daiv] v plonger. n plongeon m; (submarine) plongée f. **diver** n plongeur m. **diving board** plongeoir m.

diverge [dai'vɜːdʒ] v diverger. **divergence** n divergence f. **divergent** adj divergent.

diverse [dai'vɜːs] adj divers. **diversity** n diversité f.

divert [dai'vɜːt] v détourner; (traffic) dévier; (amuse) divertir. **diversion** n déviation f; divertissement m. **create a diversion** faire une diversion.

divide [di'vaid] v (se) diviser; (se) séparer. **divided** adj (country) désuni. **dividers** pl n compas à pointes sèches m sing. **dividing** adj (wall, etc.) mitoyen. **divisible** adj divisible. **division** n division f; séparation f.

dividend ['dividend] n dividende m.

divine [di'vain] adj divin. **divinity** n divinité f; théologie f.

divorce [di'vɔːs] n divorce m. v divorcer (avec). **divorcee** n divorcé, -e m, f.

divulge [dai'vʌldʒ] v divulguer.

dizzy ['dizi] adj pris de vertige; (height) vertigineux. **dizziness** n vertige m.

*****do** [duː] v faire; (suffice) suffire (à); (coll: cheat) refaire. **do away with** supprimer. **do up** (clothes) (se) fermer; (parcel) emballer; (house) remettre à neuf. **do without** se passer de. **how do you do?** (on introduction) enchanté. **that will do!** ça suffit!

docile ['dousail] adj docile.

dock[1] [dok] n (ships) dock m, bassin m. **dockyard** n chantier naval m. v mettre à quai; (space) s'arrimer. **docker** n docker m.

dock[2] [dok] n (law) banc des accusés m.

dock[3] [dok] v écourter; (wages) rogner.

doctor ['doktə] n docteur m, médecin m; (university) docteur m. **doctorate** n doctorat m.

doctrine ['doktrin] n doctrine f.

document ['dokjumənt] n document m. v documenter. **documentary** nm, adj documentaire. **documentation** n documentation f.

dodge [dodʒ] v (s')esquiver; (tax) éviter de payer. n détour m; (sport) esquive f; (coll: trick) truc m. **dodgy** adj délicat; douteux.

dog [dog] n chien m. **dog-eared** adj écorné. **dogfish** n chien de mer m. **dog rose** églantine f. v (follow) suivre de près; (plague) harceler.

dogged ['dogid] adj tenace. **doggedly** adv avec ténacité.

dogma ['dogmə] n dogme m. **dogmatic** adj dogmatique.

do-it-yourself [,duːitjɔː'self] n bricolage m.

dole [doul] n allocation de chômage f. **on the dole** au chômage. v **dole out** distribuer.

doll [dol] n poupée f. v **doll up** bichonner.

dollar ['dolə] n dollar m.

dolphin ['dolfin] n dauphin m.

domain [də'mein] n domaine m.

dome [doum] n dôme m.

domestic [də'mestik] adj domestique; (not foreign) intérieur. **domestic science** arts ménagers m pl. n domestique.

dominate ['domineit] v dominer. **dominance** n dominance f. **dominant** adj dominant. **domination** n domination f.

domineering [domi'niəriŋ] adj dominateur, -trice.

dominion [də'minjən] n dominion m, territoire m.

domino ['dominou] n domino m.

don [don] v revêtir.

donate [də'neit] v faire don de; (blood) donner. **donation** n don m.

done [dʌn] V do.

donkey ['doŋki] n âne, -esse m, f.

donor ['dounə] n (med) donneur, -euse m, f; (charity) donateur, -euse m, f.

doom [duːm] v condamner. n destin m. **doomed** adj voué à l'échec.

door [dɔː] n porte f; (car, train) portière f. **doorbell** n sonnette f. **doorknob** n poignée de porte f. **door-knocker** n heurtoir m. **doormat** n essuie-pieds m invar. **doorstep** n pas de porte m. **door-to-door** adj, adv à domicile. **doorway** n embrasure de porte f.

dope [doup] v doper. n dopant m; (slang: drugs) drogue f; (slang: person) andouille f.

dormant ['dɔːmənt] *adj* en sommeil.

dormitory ['dɔːmitəri] *n* dortoir *m*. **dormitory town** ville dortoir *f*.

dormouse ['dɔːˌmaus] *n, pl* -**mice** loir *m*.

dose [dous] *n* dose *f*. *v* administrer un médicament à. **dosage** *n* dosage *m*; (*on bottle*) posologie *f*.

dot [dot] *n* point *m*. *v* pointiller. **dotted line** pointillé *m*.

dote [dout] *v* **dote on** raffoler de. **dotage** *n* (*senility*) gâtisme *m*.

double ['dʌbl] *adj, adv* double; deux fois. *n* double *m*. *v* doubler; plier en deux.

double-barrelled [ˌdʌbl'barəld] *adj* (*coll: name*) à rallonges; (*gun*) à deux coups.

double bass [beis] *n* contrebasse *f*.

double bed *n* grand lit *m*.

double cream *n* crème à fouetter *f*.

double-cross [ˌdʌbl'kros] *v* (*coll*) doubler.

double-decker [ˌdʌbl'dekə] *n* autobus à impériale *m*.

double dutch *n* baragouin *m*. **talk double dutch** baragouiner.

double-glazing [ˌdʌbl'gleiziŋ] *n* doubles fenêtres *f pl*.

double-jointed [ˌdʌbl'dʒointid] *adj* désarticulé.

double room *n* chambre à deux personnes *f*.

doubt [daut] *n* doute *m*. **no doubt** sans doute. *v* douter (de). **doubtful** *adj* douteux; incertain. **doubtless** *adv* sans aucun doute.

dough [dou] *n* pâte *f*; (*slang: money*) fric *m*. **doughnut** *n* beignet *m*.

dove [dʌv] *n* colombe *f*. **dovecote** *n* colombier *m*.

Dover ['douvə] *n* Douvres.

dowdy ['daudi] *adj* sans élégance; démodé.

down¹ [daun] *adv* en bas; (*to ground*) par terre. *prep* en bas de; (*along*) le long de. *v* (*coll: drink*) s'envoyer. **down tools** cesser le travail.

down² [daun] *n* duvet *m*. **downy** *adj* duveté.

downcast ['daunˌkaist] *adj* abattu.

downfall ['daunˌfoil] *n* chute *f*.

downhearted [ˌdaun'haitid] *adj* abattu.

downhill [ˌdaun'hil] *adj* en pente. **go downhill** descendre la pente; (*deteriorate*) être sur le déclin; (*business*) péricliter.

down payment *n* acompte *m*.

downpour ['daunˌpoi] *n* averse *f*.

downright ['daunˌrait] *adj* catégorique. *adv* carrément; purement et simplement.

downstairs ['daunˌsteəz; *adv* ˌdaun'steəz] *adj* (*ground floor*) du rez-de-chaussée; (*below*) d'en bas. *adv* au rez-de-chaussée; en bas. **go downstairs** descendre.

downstream [ˌdaun'striim] *adv* en aval. **go downstream** descendre le courant.

down-to-earth [ˌdauntə'əiθ] *adj* terre à terre.

downtrodden ['daunˌtrodn] *adj* opprimé.

downward ['daunwəd] *adj* vers le bas; (*glance*) baissé.

downwards ['daunwədz] *adv* vers le bas, en bas.

dowry ['dauəri] *n* dot *f*.

doze [douz] *v* sommeiller. *n* somme *m*.

dozen ['dʌzn] *n* douzaine *f*.

drab [drab] *adj* terne.

draft¹ [draift] *n* (*letter*) brouillon *m*; (*sketch*) ébauche *f*; (*money*) retrait *m*; (*mil*) détachement *m*. *v* faire le brouillon de; (*plan*) esquisser; (*comm*) rédiger; (*mil*) détacher.

draft² *V* **draught**.

drag [drag] *v* traîner; (*river*) draguer. *n* résistance; (*coll: bore*) corvée *f*; (*coll: smoke*) bouffée *f*. **in drag** en travesti.

dragon ['dragən] *n* dragon *m*. **dragonfly** *n* libellule *f*.

drain [drein] *n* (*pipe*) égout *m*; (*grid*) bouche d'égout *f*. *v* drainer, vider. **draining board** égouttoir *m*. **drainpipe** *n* tuyau d'écoulement *m*. **drainage** *n* drainage *m*; (*in town*) système d'égouts *m*.

drama ['draimə] *n* drame *m*; art dramatique *m*. **dramatic** *adj* dramatique; (*effect*) théâtral. **dramatist** *n* dramaturge *m*. **dramatize** *v* adapter pour la scène; (*exaggerate*) dramatiser.

drank [draŋk] *V* **drink**.

drape [dreip] *v* draper. **drapes** *pl n* (*US*) rideaux *m pl*.

draper ['dreipə] *n* marchand de nouveautés *m*. **draper's shop** magasin de nouveautés *m*. **drapery** *n* draperie *f*.

drastic ['drastik] *adj* énergique, radical.

draught *or US* **draft** [draift] *n* courant d'air *m*; (*drink*) coup *m*. **draughts** *pl n* dames *f pl*. **draught beer** bière à la pression *f*. **draughtboard** *n* damier *m*. **draught excluder** bourrelet *m*. **draughtsman** *n* dessinateur *m*.

*****draw** [droi] *v* (*art*) dessiner; (*pull*) tirer; (*attract*) attirer; (*be equal*) être ex aequo.

draw back reculer. **draw near** s'approcher (de). **draw out** prolonger. **draw up** (*plan*) dresser. *n* (*sport*) match nul *m*; (*lottery*) tirage au sort *m*.

drawback ['drɔːbak] *n* inconvénient *m*.

drawbridge ['drɔːbrɪdʒ] *n* pont-levis *m*.

drawer ['drɔːə] *n* tiroir *m*.

drawing ['drɔːɪŋ] *n* dessin *m*. **drawing board** planche à dessin *f*. **drawing pin** punaise *f*. **drawing room** salon *m*.

drawl [drɔːl] *n* voix traînante *f*. *v* parler d'une voix traînante.

drawn [drɔːn] *V* **draw.**

dread [dred] *v* redouter. *n* terreur *f*. **dreadful** *adj* épouvantable, atroce. **dreadfully** *adv* terriblement.

***dream** [driːm] *n* rêve *m*. *v* rêver; (*imagine*) songer. **dreamy** *adj* rêveur, -euse.

dreamt [dremt] *V* **dream.**

dreary ['drɪəri] *adj* morne; monotone.

dredge [dredʒ] *v* draguer. *n* drague *f*.

dregs [dregz] *pl n* lie *f sing*.

drench [drentʃ] *v* tremper.

dress [dres] *n* robe; (*clothing*) tenue *f*. **dress circle** premier balcon *m*. **dressmaker** *n* couturière *f*. **dressmaking** *n* couture *f*. **dress rehearsal** répétition générale *f*. *v* (s')habiller; (*salad*) assaisonner; (*wound*) panser. **dress up as** se déguiser en. **dressy** *adj* élégant.

dresser¹ ['dresə] *n* (*furniture*) buffet *m*.

dresser² ['dresə] *n* (*theatre*) habilleur, -euse *m*, *f*.

dressing ['dresɪŋ] *n* (*wound*) pansement *m*; (*cookery*) assaisonnement *m*. **dressing gown** robe de chambre *f*. **dressing room** (*theatre*) loge *f*; (*in house*) dressing-room *m*. **dressing table** coiffeuse *f*.

drew [druː] *V* **draw.**

dribble ['drɪbl] *v* (*child*) baver; (*liquid*) couler lentement; (*sport*) dribbler. *n* bave *f*; petite goutte *f*; dribble *m*.

dried [draid] *adj* séché; déshydraté; (*milk*) en poudre. **dried fruit** fruits secs *m pl*.

drier ['draiə] *n* séchoir *m*.

drift [drift] *v* dériver, aller à la dérive. *n* (*heap*) amoncellement *m*; (*deviation*) dérive *f*; (*gist*) but *m*. **driftwood** *n* bois flotté *m*.

drill [dril] *v* (*hole*) forer; (*tooth*) fraiser. *n* foret *m*; fraise *f*; (*mil*) exercice *m*.

***drink** [drɪŋk] *v* boire. *n* boisson *f*. **drinkable** *adj* potable. **drinking water** eau potable *f*.

drip [drip] *v* dégoutter. *n* (*drop*) goutte *f*; (*coll: person*) nouille *f*; (*med*) goutte-à-goutte *m invar*. **drip-dry** *adj* (*on label*) ne pas repasser. **dripping** *n* (*fat*) graisse *f*.

***drive** [draiv] *v* conduire; (*push*) chasser; (*nail*) enfoncer. *n* (*trip*) promenade en voiture *f*; (*to house*) allée *f*; (*energy*) dynamisme *m*. **driver** *n* conducteur, -trice *m*, *f*. **driving** *n* conduite *f*. **driving licence** permis de conduire *m*. **driving school** auto-école *f*. **driving test** examen du permis de conduire *m*.

drivel ['drɪvl] *v* radoter. *n* radotage *m*.

driven ['drɪvn] *V* **drive.**

drizzle ['drɪzl] *v* bruiner. *n* bruine *f*.

drone [droun] *v* ronronner, vrombir; (*bee*) bourdonner. *n* ronronnement *m*, vrombissement *m*; bourdonnement *m*.

droop [druːp] *v* s'affaisser, retomber.

drop [drop] *n* (*liquid*) goutte *f*; (*fall*) baisse *f*. *v* (*fall*) tomber; (*let fall*) laisser tomber; (*price*) baisser. **drop off** (*sleep*) s'endormir. **dropper** *n* compte-gouttes *m invar*. **droppings** *pl n* crottes *f pl*; (*bird*) fiente *f sing*.

drought [draut] *n* sécheresse *f*.

drove [drouv] *V* **drive.**

drown [draun] *v* (se) noyer.

drowsy ['drauzi] *adj* somnolent. **grow drowsy** s'assoupir. **drowsiness** *n* somnolence *f*.

drudgery ['drʌdʒəri] *n* corvée *f*.

drug [drʌg] *n* drogue *f*. **be on drugs** se droguer. **drug addict** drogué, -e *m*, *f*. *v* droguer.

drum [drʌm] *n* tambour *m*; (*oil*) tonnelet *m*. **drumstick** *n* baguette de tambour *f*; (*chicken*) pilon *m*. *v* tambouriner. **drummer** *n* tambour *m*.

drunk [drʌŋk] *V* **drink.** *adj* ivre. **get drunk** s'enivrer. *n also* **drunkard** ivrogne, -esse *m*, *f*. **drunkenness** *n* ivresse *f*.

dry [drai] *adj* sec, sèche; (*wit*) caustique; (*dull*) aride. **dry-clean** *v* nettoyer à sec. **dry cleaner's** teinturerie *f*. **dry rot** pourriture sèche *f*. **dry ski slope** piste artificielle *f*. *v* sécher. **dry up** se dessécher, se tarir; (*dishes*) essuyer la vaisselle.

dual ['djuəl] *adj* double.

dubbed ['dʌbd] *adj* (*film*) doublé. **dubbing** *n* doublage *m*.

dubious ['djuːbiəs] *adj* douteux.

Dublin ['dʌblin] *n* Dublin.

duchess ['dʌtʃis] n duchesse f.
duck¹ [dʌk] n canard m. **duckling** n caneton, canette m, f. **duckpond** n mare aux canards f.
duck² [dʌk] v (dodge) se baisser subitement; (submerge) plonger.
duct [dʌkt] n conduite f; (anat) conduit m.
dud [dʌd] adj raté; faux, fausse.
due [djuː] adj dû, due; (suitable) qui convient. **be due** devoir arriver. adv droit. **dues** pl n droits m pl.
duel ['djuəl] n duel m. v se battre en duel. **duellist** n duelliste m.
duet [dju'et] n duo m.
dug [dʌg] V **dig**.
duke [djuːk] n duc m.
dull [dʌl] adj terne; (sound) sourd; (weather) gris. (se) ternir; (s')assourdir; (blunt) (s')émousser.
dumb [dʌm] adj muet, muette; (slang: stupid) bêta, -asse. **dumbbell** n haltère m. **dumbfound** v confondre. **dumbness** n mutisme m.
dummy ['dʌmi] n (comm) factice m; (dressmaker's) mannequin m; (ventriloquist's) pantin m; (baby's) sucette f. **dummy run** coup d'essai m.
dump [dʌmp] n (tip) décharge f; (coll: place) trou. **be down in the dumps** avoir le cafard. v déposer.
dumpling ['dʌmpliŋ] n (savoury) boulette de pâte f; (fruit) chausson m.
dunce [dʌns] n âne m. **dunce's cap** bonnet d'âne m.
dune [djuːn] n dune f.
dung [dʌŋ] n crotte f; (manure) fumier m.
dungarees [ˌdʌŋgə'riːz] pl n salopette f sing.
dungeon ['dʌndʒən] n cachot m.
Dunkirk ['dʌnkəːk] n Dunkerque.
duplicate ['djuːplikeit; n, adj 'djuːplikət] v faire un double de; (photocopy) polycopier. n double m. adj en double; (comm) en duplicata.
durable ['djuərəbl] adj solide; durable.
duration [dju'reifən] n durée f.
during ['djuəriŋ] prep pendant.
dusk [dʌsk] n crépuscule m. **dusky** adj sombre.
dust [dʌst] n poussière f. **dustbin** n poubelle f. **dustman** n éboueur m. **dustpan** n pelle à poussière f. **dust sheet** housse f. v épousseter. **duster** n chiffon m. **dusty** adj poussiéreux.

Dutch [dʌtʃ] nm, adj hollandais, néerlandais. **the Dutch** les Hollandais m pl, les Néerlandais m pl.
duty ['djuːti] n devoir m; (job) fonction f; (tax) droit m. **duty-free** exempté de douane. **duty-free shop** magasin horstaxe m. **off duty** libre. **on duty** de service. **dutiful** adj respectueux; consciencieux.
duvet ['duːvei] n couette f.
dwarf [dwoːf] n, adj nain, -e m, f. v écraser.
***dwell** [dwel] v habiter. **dwell on** s'arrêter sur. **dwelling** n habitation f.
dwelt [dwelt] V **dwell**.
dwindle ['dwindl] v diminuer.
dye [dai] n teinture f. v teindre.
dyke [daik] n (ditch) fossé m; (barrier) digue f.
dynamic [dai'namik] adj dynamique. **dynamism** n dynamisme m.
dynamite ['dainəmait] n dynamite f.
dynamo ['dainəˌmou] n dynamo f.
dynasty ['dinəsti] n dynastie f.
dysentery ['disəntri] n dysenterie f.
dyslexia [dis'leksiə] n dyslexie f. **dyslexic** n(m+f), adj dyslexique.
dyspepsia [dis'pepsiə] n dyspepsie f.

E

each [iːtʃ] adj chaque. pron chacun, -e. **each other** l'un l'autre, les uns les autres.
eager ['iːgə] adj avide; ardent; impatient. **eagerness** n désir ardent m; impatience f.
eagle ['iːgl] n aigle m.
ear¹ [iə] n oreille f. **earache** n mal d'oreille m. **eardrum** n tympan m. **earmark** v réserver; (money) assigner. **earphones** pl n casque m sing. **earring** n boucle d'oreille f. **earshot** n portée de voix f.
ear² [iə] n (grain) épi m.
earl [əːl] n comte m.
early ['əːli] adv de bonne heure, tôt. adj tôt; prématuré; précoce.
earn [əːn] v gagner; mériter. **earnings** pl n salaire m sing; profits m pl.
earnest ['əːnist] adj sérieux; ardent; sincère. **in earnest** sérieusement.

earth [ɜːθ] *n* terre *f*; (*of fox*) terrier *m*.
earthenware *n* faïence *f*. **earthquake** *n* tremblement de terre *m*. *v* (*elec*) mettre à la terre.
earwig ['iəwig] *n* perce-oreille *m*.
ease [iːz] *n* aise *f*; (*easiness*) aisance *f*. **at ease** à l'aise; (*mil*) repos. **with ease** facilement. *v* (*pain*) soulager; calmer; diminuer; (*relax*) se détendre.
easel ['iːzl] *n* chevalet *m*.
east [iːst] *n* est *m*. *adj also* **easterly**, **eastern** oriental; d'est; à l'est. *adv* à *or* vers l'est. **eastbound** *adj* est *invar*.
Easter ['iːstə] *n* Pâques *f pl*. **Easter egg** œuf de Pâques *m*.
easy ['iːzi] *adj* facile. **easy chair** fauteuil *m*. **easy-going** *adj* accommodant. **take it easy** ne pas se fatiguer. **easily** *adv* sans difficulté; sans aucun doute. **easiness** *n* facilité *f*.
***eat** [iːt] *v* manger. **eat out** aller au restaurant. **eat up** finir. **eatable** *adj* mangeable.
eaten ['iːtn] *V* **eat**.
eavesdrop ['iːvzdrop] *v* écouter de façon indiscrète. **eavesdropper** *n* oreille indiscrète *f*.
ebb [eb] *n* reflux *m*. *v* refluer; (*courage, etc*.) décliner.
ebony ['ebəni] *n* ébène *f*.
eccentric [ik'sentrik] *n(m+f)*, *adj* excentrique. **eccentricity** *n* excentricité *f*.
ecclesiastical [iklɪːziː'astikl] *adj* ecclésiastique.
echo ['ekou] *n* écho *m*. *v* répercuter; répéter; résonner.
eclair [ei'kleə] *n* éclair *m*.
eclipse [i'klips] *n* éclipse *f*. *v* éclipser.
ecology [i'kolədʒi] *n* écologie *f*. **ecological** *adj* écologique. **ecologist** *n* écologiste *m*, *f*.
economy [i'konəmi] *n* économie *f*. **economic** *adj* économique; (*profitable*) rentable. **economical** *adj* économe, économique. **economics** *n* économique *f*. **economist** *n* économiste *m*, *f*. **economize** *v* économiser.
ecstasy ['ekstəsi] *n* extase *f*. **ecstatic** *adj* extasié. **be ecstatic about** s'extasier sur.
eczema ['eksimə] *n* eczéma *m*.
edge [edʒ] *n* bord *m*; (*of blade*) tranchant *m*. **on edge** énervé. *v* border; (*move*) se glisser. **edging** *n* bordure *f*. **edgy** *adj* énervé.
edible ['edəbl] *adj* comestible.

Edinburgh ['edinbərə] *n* Edimbourg.
edit ['edit] *v* (*text*) éditer; (*film*) monter; (*magazine*) diriger. **editor** *n* rédacteur, -trice *m*, *f*, éditeur, -trice *m*, *f*; (*newspaper*) rédacteur, -trice en chef *m*, *f*. **editorial** *n* éditorial *m*. **editorial staff** rédaction *f*.
edition [i'diʃən] *n* édition *f*.
educate ['edjuˌkeit] *v* instruire. **educated** *adj* instruit; cultivé. **education** *n* éducation *f*; (*teaching*) enseignement *m*; (*studies*) études *f pl*. **educational** *adj* (*methods*) pédagogique; (*game, etc*.) éducatif.
eel [iːl] *n* anguille *f*.
eerie ['iəri] *adj* étrange; sinistre.
effect [i'fekt] *n* effet *m*. **take effect** (*drug*) faire son effet; (*rule, etc*.) entrer en vigueur. *v* effectuer. **effective** *adj* efficace. **effectiveness** *n* efficacité *f*.
effeminate [i'feminət] *adj* efféminé.
effervescent [ˌefə'vesənt] *adj* effervescent; (*drink*) gazeux. **effervescence** *n* effervescence *f*; (*drink*) pétillement *m*.
efficient [i'fiʃənt] *adj* efficace; compétent. **efficiency** *n* efficacité *f*; compétence *f*.
effigy ['efidʒi] *n* effigie *f*.
effort ['efət] *n* effort *m*. **effortless** *adj* facile.
egg [eg] *n* œuf *m*. **egg-cup** *n* coquetier *m*. **egg-shaped** *adj* ovoïde. **eggshell** *n* coquille d'œuf *f*.
egotism ['egətizm] *n* égotisme *m*. **egotist** *n* égotiste *m*, *f*.
Egypt ['iːdʒipt] *n* Egypte *f*. **Egyptian** *n* Egyptien, -enne *m*, *f*; *adj* égyptien.
eiderdown ['aidədaun] *n* édredon *m*.
eight [eit] *nm*, *adj* huit. **eighth** *n(m+f)*, *adj* huitième.
eighteen [ei'tiːn] *nm*, *adj* dix-huit. **eighteenth** *n(m+f)*, *adj* dix-huitième.
eighty ['eiti] *nm*, *adj* quatre-vingts. **eightieth** *n(m+f)*, *adj* quatre-vingtième.
either ['aiðə] *adj* l'un ou l'autre; (*each*) chaque. *pron* l'un ou l'autre. *adv* non plus. *conj* ou. **either... or...** ou... ou
. . . .
ejaculate [i'dʒakjuleit] *v* éjaculer; (*shout*) s'exclamer. **ejaculation** *n* éjaculation *f*; exclamation *f*.
eject [i'dʒekt] *v* éjecter; expulser. **ejection** *n* éjection *f*; expulsion *f*. **ejector seat** siège éjectable *m*.
eke [iːk] *v* **eke out** (*add to*) augmenter; (*make last*) faire durer.

elaborate [i'labərət; v i'labəreit] adj compliqué, minutieux. v élaborer; donner des détails. **elaborately** adv en détail.

elapse [i'laps] v s'écouler.

elastic [i'lastik] nm, adj élastique. **elastic band** n élastique m. **elasticity** n élasticité f.

elated [i'leitid] adj transporté. **elation** n exultation f.

elbow ['elbou] n coude m. **elbow grease** (coll) huile de coude f.

elder[1] ['eldə] n, adj aîné, -e.

elder[2] ['eldə] n sureau m. **elderberry** n baie de sureau f.

elderly ['eldəli] adj âgé.

eldest ['eldist] adj aîné.

elect [i'lekt] v élire; choisir. adj futur. **election** n élection f. **electoral** adj électoral. **electorate** n électorat m.

electric [ə'lektrik] adj électrique. **electric blanket** couverture chauffante f. **electric fire** radiateur électrique m. **electric shock** décharge électrique f. **electrical** adj électrique. **electrician** n électricien m. **electricity** n électricité f. **electrify** v électriser; (rail) électrifier.

electrocute [i'lektrəkjuːt] v électrocuter. **electrocution** n électrocution f.

electrode [i'lektroud] n électrode f.

electronic [elək'tronik] adj électronique. **electronics** n électronique f.

elegant ['eligənt] adj élégant. **elegance** n élégance f.

elegy ['elidʒi] n élégie f.

element ['eləmənt] n élément m; (elec) résistance f. **elementary** adj élémentaire.

elephant ['elifənt] n éléphant m.

elevate ['eliveit] v élever. **elevation** n élévation f; altitude f. **elevator** n (US) ascenseur m.

eleven [i'levn] nm, adj onze. **eleventh** n(m+f), adj onzième.

elf [elf] n elfe m. **elfin** adj d'elfe.

eligible ['elidʒəbl] adj éligible.

eliminate [i'limineit] v éliminer. **elimination** n élimination f.

elite [ei'liːt] n élite f.

ellipse [i'lips] n ellipse f. **elliptical** adj elliptique.

elm [elm] n orme m.

elocution [elə'kjuːʃən] n élocution f.

elope [i'loup] v s'enfuir.

eloquent ['eləkwənt] adj éloquent. **eloquence** n éloquence f.

else [els] adv autre, d'autre. **or else** autrement, ou bien. **elsewhere** adv ailleurs.

elude [i'luːd] v éluder, échapper à. **elusive** adj insaisissable.

emaciated [i'meisieitid] adj émacié. **emaciation** n émaciation f.

emanate ['eməneit] v émaner. **emanation** n émanation f.

emancipate [i'mansipeit] v émanciper. **emancipation** n émancipation f.

embalm [im'baːm] v embaumer.

embankment [im'baŋkmənt] n (rail) talus m; (river) quai m; (canal) digue f.

embargo [im'baːgou] n embargo m.

embark [im'baːk] v (s')embarquer. **embark on** commencer; s'engager dans. **embarkation** n embarquement m.

embarrass [im'barəs] v embarrasser, gêner. **embarrassment** n embarras m, gêne f.

embassy ['embəsi] n ambassade f.

embellish [im'beliʃ] v embellir. **embellishment** n embellissement m.

ember ['embə] n charbon ardent m. **embers** pl n braise f sing.

embezzle [im'bezl] v détourner. **embezzlement** n détournement de fonds m. **embezzler** n escroc m.

embitter [im'bitə] v (person) aigrir; (relationship) envenimer.

emblem ['embləm] n emblème m.

embody [im'bodi] v exprimer; réunir. **embodiment** n incarnation f, personnification f.

emboss [im'bos] v (metal) repousser; (paper, etc.) gaufrer. **embossed** adj (letterhead, etc.) en relief.

embrace [im'breis] v (s')embrasser. n enlacement m.

embroider [im'broidə] v broder; (truth) broder sur. **embroidery** n broderie f. **embroidery silk** soie à broder f.

embryo ['embriou] n embryon m. **in embryo** (project, etc.) en germe.

emerald ['emərəld] n émeraude f.

emerge [i'məːdʒ] v émerger, surgir.

emergency [i'məːdʒənsi] n cas urgent m; (med) urgence f. **emergency exit** sortie de secours f. **emergency landing** atterrissage forcé m. **in case of emergency** en cas d'urgence.

emigrate ['emigreit] v émigrer. **emigration** n émigration f.

eminent ['eminənt] adj éminent. **eminence** n distinction f.

emit [i'mit] *v* émettre.

emotion [i'mouʃən] *n* émotion *f.* **emotional** *adj* (*state*) émotionnel; (*shock*) émotif. **emotionally** *adv* avec émotion.

empathy ['empəθi] *n* communion d'idées *f.*

emperor ['empərə] *n* empereur *m.* **empress** *n* impératrice *f.*

emphasis ['emfəsis] *n* accent *m*; importance *f.* **emphasize** *v* appuyer sur; accentuer. **emphatic** *adj* énergique.

empire ['empaiə] *n* empire *m.*

empirical [im'pirikəl] *adj* empirique.

employ [im'ploi] *v* employer. **employee** *n* employé, -e *m, f.* **employer** *n* patron, -onne *m, f.* **employment** *n* emploi *m.* **employment agency** agence de placement *f.*

empower [im'pauə] *v* autoriser.

empty ['empti] *adj* vide; vacant. **empty-handed** *adj* bredouille. *v* vider. **emptiness** *n* vide *m.*

emu ['iːmjuː] *n* émeu *m.*

emulate ['emjuːleit] *v* imiter. **emulation** *n* émulation *f.*

emulsion [i'mʌlʃən] *n* émulsion *f.*

enable [i'neibl] *v* permettre à.

enact [i'nakt] *v* (*play*) jouer; (*decree*) décréter.

enamel [i'naməl] *n* émail (*pl* -aux) *m. v* émailler.

enamour [i'namə] *v* enchanter. **be enamoured of** être épris de.

encase [in'keis] *v* recouvrir (de).

enchant [in'tʃaint] *v* enchanter. **enchanting** *adj* ravissant. **enchantment** *n* enchantement *m.*

encircle [in'səikl] *v* entourer.

enclose [in'klouz] *v* enclore; (*surround*) entourer; (*in letter*) joindre. **enclosed** *adj* ci-joint. **enclosure** *n* enceinte *f*; (*document*) pièce jointe *f.*

encore ['oŋkoi] *nm, interj* bis. *v* bisser.

encounter [in'kauntə] *v* affronter, rencontrer. *n* rencontre *f.*

encourage [in'kʌridʒ] *v* encourager. **encouragement** *n* encouragement *m.*

encroach [in'kroutʃ] *v* empiéter. **encroachment** *n* empiètement *m.*

encumber [in'kʌmbə] *v* encombrer. **encumbrance** *n* embarras *m.*

encyclopedia [insaiklə'piːdiə] *n* encyclopédie *f.*

end [end] *n* (*tip*) bout *m*; (*finish*) fin *f.*

end product (*comm*) produit fini *m*; (*result*) résultat *m.* **make ends meet** joindre les deux bouts. *v* finir; (se) terminer.

ending *n* fin *f*; (*of word*) terminaison *f.* **endless** *adj* interminable; incessant.

endanger [in'deindʒə] *v* mettre en danger; compromettre.

endeavour [in'devə] *n* effort *m. v* s'efforcer (de).

endemic [en'demik] *adj* endémique. *n* endémie *f.*

endive ['endiv] *n* endive *f*; (*curly*) chicorée *f.*

endorse [in'dois] *v* (*cheque, etc.*) endosser; approuver. **endorsement** *n* endossement *m*; sanction *f*; (*mot*) contravention *f.*

endow [in'dau] *v* doter (de); (*prize, etc*) fonder. **endowment** *n* dotation *f*; fondation *f.*

endure [in'djuə] *v* supporter; (*last*) durer. **endurance** *n* endurance *f*, résistance *f.*

enemy ['enəmi] *n* ennemi, -e *m, f.*

energy ['enədʒi] *n* énergie *f.* **energetic** *adj* énergique.

enfold [in'fould] *v* envelopper.

enforce [in'fois] *v* (*law*) faire obéir; (*discipline*) imposer.

engage [in'geidʒ] *v* (s')engager; (*employee*) embaucher; (*clutch*) s'embrayer. **engaged** *adj* fiancé; occupé. **get engaged** se fiancer. **engagement** *n* rendez-vous *m invar*; fiançailles *f pl*; (*actor*) engagement *m.*

engine ['endʒin] *n* machine *f*; moteur *m.* **engine driver** mécanicien *m.* **engine room** (*on ship*) salle des machines *f.*

engineer [endʒi'niə] *n* ingénieur *m*; (*mechanic*) technicien *m. v* machiner. **engineering** *n* ingénierie *f.*

England ['iŋglənd] *n* Angleterre *f.* **English** *nm, adj* anglais. **the English** les Anglais.

engrave [in'greiv] *v* graver. **engraver** *n* graveur *m.* **engraving** *n* gravure *f.*

engrossed [in'groust] *adj* absorbé.

engulf [in'gʌlf] *v* engouffrer.

enhance [in'hains] *v* mettre en valeur, rehausser.

enigma [i'nigmə] *n* énigme *f.* **enigmatic** *adj* énigmatique.

enjoy [in'dʒoi] *v* aimer; (*good health, etc.*) jouir de. **enjoy oneself** s'amuser. **enjoyable** *adj* agréable. **enjoyment** *n* plaisir *m.*

enlarge [in'laidʒ] *v* (s')agrandir. **enlargement** *n* agrandissement *m.*

enlighten [in'laitn] *v* éclairer. **enlighten-ment** *n* éclaircissement *m*.

enlist [in'list] *v* (s')engager; recruter. **enlistment** *n* engagement *m*.

enmity ['enmǝti] *n* inimitié *f*.

enormous [i'nɔːmǝs] *adj* énorme. **enor-mously** *adv* énormément.

enough [i'nʌf] *adj, adv, n* assez. **be enough** suffire.

enquire [in'kwaiǝ] *V* inquire.

enrage [in'reidʒ] *v* mettre en rage.

enrich [in'ritʃ] *v* enrichir; (*soil*) fertiliser.

enrol [in'roul] *v* (s')inscrire; (*mil*) (s')enrôler. **enrolment** *n* inscription *f*; enrôlement *m*.

ensign ['ensain] *n* (*emblem*) insigne *m*; (*flag*) drapeau *m*; (*naut*) pavillon *m*.

enslave [in'sleiv] *v* asservir. **enslavement** *n* asservissement *m*.

ensue [in'sjuː] *v* s'ensuivre.

ensure [in'ʃuǝ] *v* assurer.

entail [in'teil] *v* occasionner, comporter.

entangle [in'taŋgl] *v* empêtrer, emmêler.

enter ['entǝ] *v* entrer (dans); (*register*) inscrire. **enter for** (*exam*) (se) présenter à.

enterprise ['entǝpraiz] *n* entreprise *f*; initiative *f*. **enterprising** *adj* entreprenant.

entertain [entǝ'tein] *v* (*amuse*) divertir; (*guests*) recevoir; (*idea*) considérer. **entertainer** *n* artiste *m, f*. **entertainment** *n* divertissement *m*.

enthral [in'θrɔːl] *v* captiver.

enthusiasm [in'θuːziˌazǝm] *n* enthou-siasme *m*. **enthusiast** *n* enthousiaste *m, f*. **enthusiastic** *adj* enthousiaste, passionné.

entice [in'tais] *v* attirer, entraîner. **entic-ing** *adj* attrayant; (*food*) alléchant.

entire [in'taiǝ] *adj* entier. **in its entirety** en entier.

entitle [in'taitl] *v* autoriser, donner droit à; (*book*) intituler.

entity ['entǝti] *n* entité *f*.

entrails ['entreilz] *pl n* entrailles *f pl*.

entrance[1] ['entrǝns] *n* entrée *f*.

entrance[2] [in'trɑːns] *v* ravir.

entrant ['entrǝnt] *n* (*competition, exam*) candidat, -e *m, f*; (*race*) concurrent, -e *m, f*; (*profession*) débutant, -e *m, f*.

entreat [in'triːt] *v* supplier. **entreaty** *n* supplication *f*.

entrench [in'trentʃ] *v* (*mil*) retrencher. **entrenched** *adj* (*custom*) implanté; indé-logeable.

entrepreneur [ˌontrǝprǝ'nɔː] *n* entrepre-neur *m*.

entrust [in'trʌst] *v* confier; (*with task*) charger.

entry ['entri] *n* entrée *f*; (*on list*) inscrip-tion *f*. **entry form** feuille d'inscription *f*. **no entry** (*road*) sens interdit; (*gate, etc.*) défense d'entrer.

entwine [in'twain] *v* (s')entrelacer.

enunciate [i'nʌnsiˌeit] *v* articuler; (*theory*) énoncer. **enunciation** *n* articulation *f*; énonciation *f*.

envelop [in'velǝp] *v* envelopper.

envelope ['envǝˌloup] *n* enveloppe *f*.

environment [in'vaiǝrǝnmǝnt] *n* milieu *m*, environnement *m*.

envisage [in'vizidʒ] *v* (*foresee*) prévoir; (*imagine*) envisager.

envoy ['envoi] *n* envoyé, -e *m, f*.

envy ['envi] *n* envie *f*. *v* envier. **enviable** *adj* enviable. **envious** *adj* envieux. **envi-ously** *adv* avec envie.

enzyme ['enzaim] *n* enzyme *f*.

ephemeral [i'femǝrǝl] *adj* éphémère.

epic ['epik] *adj* épique. *n* épopée *f*.

epidemic [epi'demik] *n* épidémie *f*. *adj* épidémique.

epilepsy ['epilepsi] *n* épilepsie *f*. **epileptic** *n(m+f)*, *adj* épileptique. **epileptic fit** crise d'epilepsie *f*.

epilogue ['epilog] *n* épilogue *m*.

Epiphany [i'pifǝni] *n* Epiphanie *f*, fête des Rois *f*.

episcopal [i'piskǝpǝl] *adj* épiscopal.

episode ['episoud] *n* épisode *m*. **episodic** *adj* épisodique.

epitaph ['epiˌtɑːf] *n* épitaphe *f*.

epitome [i'pitǝmi] *n* modèle *m*; quintes-sence *f*. **epitomize** *v* incarner.

epoch ['iːpok] *n* époque *f*.

equable ['ekwǝbl] *adj* égal.

equal ['iːkwǝl] *adj* égal, -e. *v* égaler. **equal-ity** *n* égalité *f*. **equalize** *v* égaliser.

equanimity [ekwǝ'nimǝti] *n* sérénité *f*.

equate [i'kweit] *v* assimiler; (*make equal*) égaler. **equation** *n* équation *f*.

equator [i'kweitǝ] *n* équateur *m*. **equatori-al** *adj* équatorial.

equestrian [i'kwestriǝn] *adj* équestre. *n* cavalier, -ère *m, f*.

equilateral [ˌiːkwi'latǝrǝl] *adj* équilatéral.

equilibrium [ˌiːkwi'libriǝm] *n* équilibre *m*.

equinox ['ekwinoks] *n* équinoxe *m*. **equi-noctial** *adj* équinoxial.

equip [i'kwip] v équiper. **equipment** n équipement m; matériel m.

equity ['ekwəti] n équité f.

equivalent [i'kwivələnt] nm, adj équivalent.

era ['iərə] n ère f; époque f.

eradicate [i'radi‚keit] v extirper, supprimer.

erase [i'reiz] v effacer; (with rubber) gommer. **eraser** n gomme f.

erect [i'rekt] adj droit. v (statue, etc.) ériger; (build) bâtir; (tent, etc.) dresser. **erection** n érection f; construction f.

ermine ['əːmin] n hermine f.

erode [i'roud] v éroder, ronger. **erosion** n érosion f. **erosive** adj érosif.

erotic [i'rotik] adj érotique.

err [əː] v se tromper; (sin) pécher.

errand ['erənd] n course f. **errand boy** garçon de courses m.

erratic [i'ratik] adj irrégulier.

error ['erə] n erreur f.

erudite ['erudait] adj savant. **erudition** n érudition f.

erupt [i'rupt] v (volcano) entrer en éruption; (quarrel) éclater. **eruption** n éruption f.

escalate ['eskə‚leit] v (s')intensifier. **escalation** n escalade f. **escalator** n escalier roulant m.

escalope ['eskə‚lop] n escalope f.

escape [is'keip] v (s')échapper (à). n fuite f, évasion f.

escort ['eskoːt; v i'skoːt] n escorte f. v escorter.

esoteric [esə'terik] adj ésotérique.

especial [i'speʃəl] adj particulier. **especially** adv particulièrement, surtout.

espionage ['espiə‚naːʒ] n espionnage m.

esplanade [‚esplə'neid] n esplanade f.

essay ['esei] n essai m; (school) rédaction f, dissertation f. **essayist** n essayiste m, f.

essence ['esns] n essence f.

essential [i'senʃəl] adj essentiel. **essentials** pl n essentiel m sing.

establish [i'stabliʃ] v établir; fonder. **establishment** n établissement m; fondation f.

estate [i'steit] n propriété f; (houses) lotissement m; (law) biens m pl. **estate agent** agent immobilier m. **estate car** break m.

esteem [i'stiːm] v estimer. n estime f.

estimate ['estimət; v 'esti‚meit] n évaluation f; (comm) devis m. v estimer. **estimation** n jugement m; (esteem) estime f.

estuary ['estjuəri] n estuaire m.

eternal [i'təːnl] adj éternel. **eternity** n éternité f.

ether ['iːθə] n éther m.

ethereal [i'θiəriəl] adj éthéré.

ethical ['eθikl] adj moral. **ethics** pl n morale f sing.

ethnic ['eθnik] adj ethnique.

etiquette ['eti‚ket] n étiquette f.

etymology [‚eti'molədʒi] n étymologie f. **etymological** adj étymologique.

Eucharist ['juːkərist] n Eucharistie f.

eunuch ['juːnək] n eunuque m.

euphemism ['juːfə‚mizəm] n euphémisme m. **euphemistic** adj euphémique.

euphoria [ju'foːriə] n euphorie f. **euphoric** adj euphorique.

Europe ['juərəp] n Europe f. **European** n Européen, -enne m, f; adj européen. **European Economic Community (EEC)** Communauté Economique Européenne (CEE) f.

euthanasia [‚juːθə'neiziə] n euthanasie f.

evacuate [i'vakju‚eit] v évacuer. **evacuation** n évacuation f. **evacuee** n évacué, -e m, f.

evade [i'veid] v éviter. **evasion** n fuite f. **evasive** adj évasif.

evaluate [i'valju‚eit] v évaluer. **evaluation** n évaluation f.

evangelical [‚iːvan'dʒelikəl] adj évangélique. **evangelist** n évangéliste m.

evaporate [i'vapə‚reit] v s'évaporer; (fade away) se volatiliser. **evaporated milk** lait concentré m. **evaporation** n évaporation f.

eve [iːv] n veille f.

even ['iːvən] adj (surface) uni; régulier, égal; (number) pair. adv même; (more, etc.) encore. **even so** quand même. **even-tempered** adj placide. v égaliser.

evening ['iːvniŋ] n soir m, soirée f. **evening class** cours du soir m. **evening dress** (man) tenue de soirée f; (woman) robe du soir f.

evensong ['iːvən‚soŋ] n office du soir m.

event [i'vent] n évènement m; cas m; (race) course f. **in the event of** en cas de; au cas où. **eventful** adj mouvementé.

eventual [i'ventʃuəl] adj qui s'ensuit. **eventuality** n éventualité f. **eventually** adv finalement.

ever ['evə] adv jamais; (always) toujours.

evergreen ['evǝgriːn] *adj* vert, à feuilles persistantes. *n* arbre vert *m*.
everlasting [ˌevǝ'laːstiŋ] *adj* éternel.
every ['evri] *adj* (*all*) tous les, toutes les; (*each*) chaque, tout. **everybody** *or* **everyone** *pron* tout le monde. **everyday** *adj* banal; de tous les jours. **every other day** tous les deux jours, un jour sur deux. **everything** *pron* tout. **everywhere** *adv* partout.
evict [i'vikt] *v* expulser. **eviction** *n* expulsion *f*.
evidence ['evidǝns] *n* évidence *f*; (*testimony*) témoignage *m*; signe *m*. **give evidence** témoigner. **evident** *adj* évident. **evidently** *adv* évidemment; à ce qu'il paraît.
evil ['iːvl] *adj* mauvais. *n* mal *m*.
evoke [i'vouk] *v* évoquer. **evocation** *n* évocation *f*. **evocative** *adj* évocateur, -trice.
evolve [i'volv] *v* (se) développer. **evolution** *n* évolution *f*. **evolutionary** *adj* évolutionniste.
ewe [juː] *n* brebis *f*.
exacerbate [ig'zasǝˌbeit] *v* exacerber.
exact [ig'zakt] *adj* exact. *v* exiger. **exacting** *adj* exigeant; (*task*) astreignant. **exactly** *adv* précisément, exactement.
exaggerate [ig'zadʒǝˌreit] *v* exagérer; accentuer. **exaggeration** *n* exagération *f*.
exalt [ig'zolt] *v* élever; (*praise*) exalter.
examine [ig'zamin] *v* examiner; (*law*) interroger. **examination** *n* examen *m*. **examiner** *n* examinateur, -trice *m*, *f*.
example [ig'zaːmpl] *n* exemple *m*. **for example** par exemple. **set a good example** donner l'exemple.
exasperate [ig'zaːspǝˌreit] *v* exaspérer. **exasperation** *n* exaspération *f*.
excavate ['ekskǝˌveit] *v* excaver; (*dig*) creuser; (*archaeol*) fouiller, faire des fouilles. **excavation** *n* creusage *m*; fouille *f*.
exceed [ik'siːd] *v* dépasser. **exceedingly** *adv* extrêmement.
excel [ik'sel] *v* briller; surpasser. **excellence** *n* excellence *f*. **excellent** *adj* excellent.
Excellency ['eksǝlǝnsi] *n* Excellence *f*.
except [ik'sept] *prep* sauf, excepté; (*but*) sinon. *v* excepter. **exception** *n* exception *f*. **take exception to** s'offenser de. **exceptional** *adj* exceptionnel.
excerpt ['eksǝːpt] *n* extrait *m*.
excess [ik'ses] *n* excès *m*. **excess fare** sup-

plément *m*. **excess luggage** excédent de bagages *m*. **excessive** *adj* excessif.
exchange [iks'tʃeindʒ] *v* échanger; faire un échange (de). *n* échange *m*; (*phone*) central *m*; (*finance*) change *m*. **exchange rate** taux de change *m*.
exchequer [iks'tʃekǝ] *n* ministère des finances *m*.
excise ['eksaiz] *n* taxe *f*; (*department*) régie *f*. **excise duties** contributions indirectes *f pl*.
excite [ik'sait] *v* exciter. **excited** *adj* excité, agité. **get excited** s'exciter, s'agiter. **excitement** *n* excitation *f*. **exciting** *adj* passionnant.
exclaim [ik'skleim] *v* s'exclamer, s'écrier.
exclamation [ˌeksklǝ'meiʃǝn] *n* exclamation *f*. **exclamation mark** point d'exclamation *m*.
exclude [ik'skluːd] *v* exclure. **exclusion** *n* exclusion *f*. **exclusive** *adj* exclusif; select; (*dates, numbers, etc.*) exclusivement; (*price, charge*) non compris.
excommunicate [ekskǝ'mjuːniˌkeit] *v* excommunier. **excommunication** *n* excommunication *f*.
excrete [ik'skriːt] *v* excréter. **excrement** *n* excrément *m*. **excretion** *n* excrétion *f*.
excruciating [ik'skruːʃieitiŋ] *adj* (*pain*) atroce; (*noise*) infernal.
excursion [ik'skǝːʃǝn] *n* excursion *f*.
excuse [ik'skjuːz] *v* excuser. **excuse me!** excusez-moi! *n* excuse *f*. **excusable** *adj* excusable.
execute ['eksiˌkjuːt] *n* exécuter; accomplir. **execution** *n* exécution *f*; (*of duties*) exercice *m*. **executioner** *n* bourreau *m*.
executive [ig'zekjutiv] *adj* (*power*) exécutif; (*job*) administratif. *n* (*person*) cadre *m*; (*group*) bureau *m*.
exemplify [ig'zempliˌfai] *v* exemplifier.
exempt [ig'zempt] *adj* exempt. *v* exempter. **exemption** *n* exemption *f*.
exercise ['eksǝˌsaiz] *n* exercice *m*. **exercises** *pl n* (*physical*) gymnastique *f sing*. **exercise book** cahier *m*. *v* exercer.
exert [ig'zǝːt] *v* exercer; (*force*) employer. **exert oneself** se dépenser; s'appliquer. **exertion** *n* effort *m*; exercice *m*; emploi *m*.
exhale [eks'heil] *v* (*give off*) exhaler; (*breathe out*) expirer.
exhaust [ig'zoːst] *v* épuiser. *n* (*system*) échappement *m*; (*pipe*) tuyau d'échappement *m*. **exhaustion** *n* épuise-

ment *m*. **exhaustive** *adj* complet, -ète. **exhaustively** *adv* à fond.
exhibit [ig'zibit] *v* exposer; (*skill, etc*.) faire preuve de. *n* objet exposé *m*. **exhibition** *n* exposition *f*. **make an exhibition of oneself** se donner en spectacle. **exhibitionist** *n*(*m*+*f*), *adj* exhibitionniste. **exhibitor** *n* exposant, -e *m, f*.
exhilarate [ig'zilə,reit] *v* vivifier, stimuler. **exhilaration** *n* ivresse *f*.
exile ['eksail] *v* exiler. *n* exil *m*; (*person*) exilé, -e *m, f*. **go into exile** s'exiler.
exist [ig'zist] *v* exister; (*live*) vivre. **existence** *n* existence *f*. **existentialism** *n* existentialisme *m*. **existing** *adj* (*current*) actuel.
exit ['egzit] *n* sortie *f*.
exonerate [ig'zonə,reit] *v* (*from blame*) disculper; (*from obligation*) exempter. **exoneration** *n* disculpation *f*; exemption *f*.
exorbitant [ig'zorbitənt] *adj* exorbitant.
exorcise ['eksor,saiz] *v* exorciser. **exorcism** *n* exorcisme *m*. **exorcist** *n* exorciste *m*.
exotic [ig'zotik] *adj* exotique.
expand [ik'spand] *v* (se) dilater; (se) développer; (s')étendre. **expansion** *n* expansion *f*; développement *m*. **expansive** *adj* expansif.
expanse [ik'spans] *n* étendue *f*.
expatriate [eks'peitrieit; *n, adj* eks'peitriət] *v* expatrier. *n, adj* expatrié, -e.
expect [ik'spekt] *v* attendre; supposer; (*demand*) exiger. **expectancy** *or* **expectation** *n* attente *f*.
expedient [ik'spiːdiənt] *adj* (*convenient*) opportun; politique. *n* expédient *m*.
expedition [,ekspi'diʃən] *n* expédition *f*.
expel [ik'spel] *v* expulser; (*school*) renvoyer.
expenditure [ik'spenditʃə] *n* dépense *f*.
expense [ik'spens] *n* frais *m pl*. **at the expense of** aux dépens de. **expense account** frais de représentation *m pl*. **expensive** *adj* cher. **be expensive** coûter cher.
experience [ik'spiəriəns] *n* expérience *f*. *v* (*encounter*) rencontrer; (*feel*) éprouver. **experienced** *adj* expérimenté.
experiment [ik'sperimənt] *n* expérience *f*. *v* faire une expérience; expérimenter. **experimental** *adj* expérimental.
expert ['ekspəːt] *nm, adj* expert.

expertise [,ekspəː'tiːz] *n* adresse *f*.
expire [ik'spaiə] *v* expirer. **expiry** *n* expiration *f*.
explain [ik'splein] *v* expliquer. **explanation** *n* explication *f*. **explanatory** *adj* explicatif.
expletive [ek'spliːtiv] *n* (*oath*) juron *m*; exclamation *f*.
explicit [ik'splisit] *adj* explicite.
explode [ik'sploud] *v* (faire) exploser. **explosion** *n* explosion *f*. **explosive** *nm, adj* explosif.
exploit ['exploit; *v* ik'sploit] *n* exploit *m*. *v* exploiter. **exploitation** *n* exploitation *f*.
explore [ik'sploː] *v* explorer. **exploration** *n* exploration *f*. **explorer** *n* explorateur, -trice *m, f*.
exponent [ik'spounənt] *n* interprète *m*.
export [ik'spoːt; *n* 'ekspoːt] *v* exporter. *n* exportation *f*. **exporter** *n* (*person*) exportateur, -trice *m, f*; (*country*) pays exportateur *m*.
expose [ik'spouz] *v* exposer; révéler; (*uncover*) découvrir. **exposure** *n* exposition *f*; (*phot*) pose *f*. **die of exposure** mourir de froid.
express [ik'spres] *v* exprimer. *n* (*train*) rapide *m*. *adj, adv* exprès. **expression** *n* expression *f*. **expressive** *adj* expressif.
expulsion [ik'spʌlʃən] *n* expulsion *f*; (*school*) renvoi *m*.
exquisite ['ekswizit] *adj* exquis.
extend [ik'stend] *v* (s')étendre; (se) prolonger. **extension** *n* prolongation *f*; (*flex, etc.*) rallonge *f*; (*to house*) agrandissements *m pl*; (*phone*) poste *m*. **extensive** *adj* étendu; considérable.
extent [ik'stent] *n* étendue *f*. longueur *f*; (*range*) importance *f*; (*degree*) mesure *f*.
exterior [ik'stiəriə] *nm, adj* extérieur, -e.
exterminate [ik'stəːmi,neit] *v* exterminer. **extermination** *n* extermination *f*.
external [ik'stəːnl] *adj* externe, extérieur, -e. **for external use only** pour l'usage externe.
extinct [ik'stiŋkt] *adj* (*species*) disparu; (*volcano*) éteint. **extinction** *n* extinction *f*.
extinguish [ik'stiŋgwiʃ] *v* éteindre; (*hopes*) anéantir. **extinguisher** *n* extincteur *m*.
extort [ik'stoːt] *v* extorquer. **extortion** *n* extorsion *f*. **extortionate** *adj* exorbitant.
extra ['ekstrə] *adj* de plus; supplémentaire; de réserve. *n* supplément *m*; (*theatre, cinema*) figurant, -e *m, f*.

extract [ik'strakt; *n* 'ekstrakt] *v* extraire; (*tooth*) arracher. *n* extrait *m*. **extraction** *n* extraction *f*.

extradite ['ekstrə‚dait] *v* extrader. **extradition** *n* extradition *f*.

extramural [‚ekstrə'mjuərəl] *adj* (*course*) hors faculté; (*district*) extra-muros.

extraordinary [ik'strɔidənəri] *adj* extraordinaire.

extravagant [ik'stravəgənt] *adj* (*person*) dépensier; (*taste*) dispendieux; (*ideas, dress*) extravagant. **extravagance** *n* prodigalité *f*; (*expensive thing*) folie *f*; extravagance *f*.

extreme [ik'striim] *nm, adj* extrême. **extremist** *n*(*m + f*), *adj* extrémiste. **extremity** *n* extrémité *f*.

extricate ['ekstri‚keit] *v* dégager; tirer.

extrovert ['ekstrəvɔit] *n, adj* extraverti, -e.

exuberant [ig'zjuibərənt] *adj* exubérant. **exuberance** *n* exubérance *f*.

exude [ig'zjuid] *v* exsuder, suinter.

exult [ig'zʌlt] *v* se réjouir. **exultant** *adj* triomphant. **exultation** *n* exultation *f*.

eye [ai] *n* œil (*pl* yeux) *m*. **as far as the eye can see** à perte de vue. **keep an eye on** surveiller. *v* regarder.

eyeball ['aibɔil] *n* globe oculaire *m*.

eyebrow ['aibrau] *n* sourcil *m*.

eye-catching ['aikatʃiŋ] *adj* accrocheur, -euse.

eyelash ['ailaʃ] *n* cil *m*.

eyelid ['ailid] *n* paupière *f*.

eye shadow *n* fard à paupières *m*.

eyesight ['aisait] *n* vue *f*.

eyesore ['aisɔi] *n* horreur *f*.

eyewitness ['ai‚witnis] *n* témoin oculaire *m*.

F

fable ['feibl] *n* fable *f*.

fabric ['fabrik] *n* tissu *m*. **fabricate** *v* fabriquer. **fabrication** *n* fabrication *f*.

fabulous ['fabjuləs] *adj* fabuleux; (*coll: wonderful*) formidable.

façade [fə'said] *n* façade *f*.

face [feis] *n* visage *m*, figure *f*. **facecloth** *n* gant de toilette *m*. **facelift** *n* lifting *m*. **face pack** masque de beauté *m*. **face-to-face** *nm, adv* face à face. **face value** (*coin*) valeur nominale *f*. **at face value** au pied de la lettre. **in the face of** face à, devant. *v* faire face à; (*building*) donner sur. **face the facts** regarder les choses en face.

facet ['fasit] *n* facette *f*.

facetious [fə'siiʃəs] *adj* facétieux.

facial ['feiʃəl] *adj* facial. *n* soin de visage *m*.

facilitate [fə'sili‚teit] *v* faciliter.

facility [fə'siləti] *n* facilité *f*. **facilities** *pl n* installations *f pl*, équipements *m pl*.

facing ['feisiŋ] *n* (*sewing*) revers *m*; (*building*) revêtement *m*.

facsimile [fak'siməli] *n* fac-similé *m*.

fact [fakt] *n* fait *m*; réalité *f*. **as a matter of fact** à vrai dire. **in fact** en fait. **factual** *adj* basé sur les faits.

faction ['fakʃən] *n* faction *f*.

factor ['faktə] *n* facteur *m*.

factory ['faktəri] *n* usine *f*; (*smaller*) fabrique *f*.

faculty ['fakəlti] *n* faculté *f*; aptitude *f*.

fad [fad] *n* marotte *f*. **faddy** *adj* capricieux.

fade [feid] *v* (*light*) baisser; (*colour*) passer; (*flower*) se faner; (*sound*) s'affaiblir.

fag [fag] (*coll*) *n* (*cigarette*) sèche *f*; (*boring task*) barbe *f*. **fag end** (*of cigarette*) mégot *m*. **fagged out** claqué.

fail [feil] *v* (*not succeed*) échouer; (*grow weak*) faiblir, baisser; (*neglect*) manquer (de). *n* échec *m*. **without fail** à coup sûr; inévitablement. **failing** *n* défaut *m*. **failure** *n* échec *m*; (*person*) raté, -e *m, f*; (*breakdown*) panne *f*.

faint [feint] *adj* faible; (*colour*) pâle; (*idea*) vague. **I haven't the faintest idea** je n'en ai pas la moindre idée. *v* s'évanouir. *n* évanouissement *m*.

fair[1] [feə] *adj* juste, équitable; (*average*) passable; (*hair*) blond; (*skin*) clair; (*fine*) beau, belle. **by fair means or foul** par tous les moyens. **fair copy** copie au propre *f*. **fair-sized** *adj* assez grand. **play fair** jouer franc jeu. **fairly** *adv* avec justice; (*reasonably*) assez. **fairness** *n* justice *f*; blondeur *f*.

fair[2] [feə] *n* foire *f*. **fairground** *n* champ de foire *m*.

fairy ['feəri] *n* fée *f*. *adj* féerique. **fairy lights** guirlande électrique *f*. **fairy tale** conte de fées *m*.

faith [feiθ] *n* foi *f*. **have faith in** avoir confiance en. **faithful** *adj* fidèle. **faithfulness** *n* fidelité *f*.

fake [feik] *n* (*picture*) faux *m*; article truqué *m*; (*person*) imposteur *m*. *adj* faux, fausse; (*photo, interview, etc.*) truqué; falsifié. *v* faire un faux de; truquer; falsifier; (*illness*) faire semblant (de).

falcon ['fɔɪlkən] *n* faucon *m*.

*fall [fɔɪl] *v* tomber. **fall apart** tomber en morceaux; (*plans, life, etc.*) se désagréger. **fall back on** avoir recours à. **fall through** échouer. *n* chute *f*; (*US*) automne *m*; (*price, etc.*) baisse *f*.

fallacy ['faləsi] *n* erreur *f*.

fallen ['fɔɪlən] *V* **fall**.

fallible ['faləbl] *adj* faillible. **fallibility** *n* faillibilité *f*.

fallow ['falou] *adj* (*land*) en jachère; (*idea, etc.*) en friche.

false [fɔɪls] *adj* faux, fausse; artificiel. **false alarm** fausse alerte *f*. **false teeth** fausses dents *f pl*. **under false pretences** par des moyens frauduleux. **falsehood** *n* mensonge *m*. **falseness** *n* fausseté *f*. **falsify** *v* falsifier. **falsification** *n* falsification *f*.

falsetto [fɔɪl'setou] *n* fausset *m*.

falter ['fɔɪltə] *v* chanceler; (*voice*) hésiter.

fame [feim] *n* renommée *f*.

familiar [fə'miljə] *adj* familier. **be familiar with** bien connaître. **familiarity** *n* familiarité *f*. **familiarize** *v* familiariser.

family ['faməli] *n* famille *f*. **family allowance** allocations familiales *f pl*. **family planning** planning familial *m*. **family tree** arbre généalogique *m*.

famine ['famin] *n* famine *f*.

famished ['famiʃt] *adj* affamé. **be famished** (*coll*) avoir une faim de loup.

famous ['feiməs] *adj* célèbre; (*coll: excellent*) fameux.

fan¹ [fan] *n* ventilateur *m*; (*hand-held*) éventail *m*. **fan belt** courroie de ventilateur *f*. **fan heater** radiateur soufflant *m*. *v* éventer.

fan² [fan] *n* fan *m, f*, passionné, -e *m, f*, admirateur, -trice *m, f*. **fan club** club de fans *m*.

fanatic [fə'natik] *n* fanatique *m, f*. **fanatical** *adj* fanatique.

fancy ['fansi] *n* caprice *m*; (*desire*) envie *f*; imagination *f*. *v* (*imagine*) se figurer; croire; avoir envie de. **fancy oneself** se gober. *adj* de fantaisie. **fancy dress** travesti *m*. **fanciful** *adj* imaginaire; fantasque, bizarre.

fanfare ['fanfeə] *n* fanfare *f*.

fang [faŋ] *n* (*dog*) croc *m*; (*snake*) crochet *m*.

fantastic [fan'tastik] *adj* fantastique.

fantasy ['fantəsi] *n* fantaisie *f*.

far [fɑɪ] *adv* loin; (*much*) beaucoup. *adj* lointain; (*opposite*) autre. **as far as** jusqu'à, autant que. **far and wide** partout. **far away** *adv* au loin. **faraway** *adj* lointain. **Far East** Extrême Orient *m*. **far-fetched** *adj* tiré par les cheveux. **far-off** *adj* eloigné. **far-reaching** *adj* d'une grande portée. **so far so good** jusqu'ici ça va.

farce [fɑɪs] *n* farce *f*. **farcical** *adj* risible, grotesque.

fare [feə] *n* prix du billet *m*. **fare stage** section *f*.

farewell [feə'wel] *nm, interj* adieu.

farm [fɑɪm] *n* ferme *f*. **farmhouse** *n* ferme *f*. **farmland** *n* terres cultivées *f pl*. **farmyard** *n* cour de ferme *f*. *v* cultiver; être fermier. **farmer** *n* fermier *m*. **farmer's wife** fermière *f*. **farming** *n* agriculture *f*.

fart [fɑɪt] *n* (*vulgar*) pet *m*. *v* péter.

farther ['fɑɪðə] *adv* plus loin. *adj* plus lointain.

farthest ['fɑɪðist] *adv* le plus loin. *adj* le plus lointain.

farthing ['fɑɪðiŋ] *n* sou *m*.

fascinate ['fasi,neit] *v* fasciner. **fascination** *n* fascination *f*.

fascism ['faʃizəm] *n* fascisme *m*. **fascist** *n(m+f)*, *adj* fasciste.

fashion ['faʃən] *n* mode *f*; (*manner*) façon *f*. **after a fashion** tant bien que mal. **fashion show** présentation de collections *f*. **in fashion** à la mode. *v* façonner. **fashionable** *adj* à la mode.

fast¹ [fɑɪst] *adj* rapide; (*colour*) bon teint *invar*. **be fast** (*clock, etc.*) avancer. *adv* vite; (*securely*) ferme. **fast asleep** profondément endormi.

fast² [fɑɪst] *v* jeûner. *n* jeûne *m*.

fasten ['fɑɪsn] *v* (s')attacher; (*close*) (se) fermer. **fastener** or **fastening** *n* attache *f*; fermeture *f*.

fastidious [fa'stidiəs] *adj* méticuleux, exigeant.

fat [fat] *n* graisse *f*; (*on meat*) gras *m*. *adj* gros, grosse; gras, grasse. **get fat** grossir. **fatten** *v* engraisser. **fattening** *adj* (*food*) qui fait grossir.

fatal ['feitl] *adj* fatal, mortel. **fatality** *n* mort *m*; accident mortel *m*.

fate [feit] *n* sort *m.* **fated** *adj* destiné; (*condemned*) voué au malheur. **fateful** *adj* fatal.

father ['fɑːðə] *n* père *m.* **Father Christmas** le père Noël. **father-in-law** *n* beau-père *m.* **fatherland** *n* patrie *f. v* engendrer. **fatherhood** *n* paternité *f.* **fatherly** *adj* paternel.

fathom ['faðəm] *n* brasse *f. v* **fathom out** sonder.

fatigue [fə'tiːg] *n* fatigue *f. v* fatiguer.

fatuous ['fatjuəs] *adj* imbécile, stupide.

fault [fɔːlt] *n* (*failing*) défaut *m*; (*blame*) faute *f.* **at fault** fautif. **faultless** *adj* impeccable; irréprochable. **faulty** *adj* défectueux.

fauna ['fɔɪnə] *n* faune *f.*

favour ['feivə] *n* faveur *f*; service *m*; avantage *m.* **be in favour of** être partisan de. *v* favoriser; préférer. **favourable** *adj* favorable; (*wind, etc.*) propice. **favourite** *n, adj* favori, -ite.

fawn [fɔɪn] *n* faon *m. adj* fauve.

fear [fiə] *n* peur *f*, crainte *f. v* craindre. **fearful** *adj* (*terrible*) affreux; (*frightened*) peureux. **fearless** *adj* intrépide.

feasible ['fiːzəbl] *adj* faisable; plausible. **feasibility** *n* possibilité *f*; plausibilité *f.*

feast [fiːst] *n* festin *m*; (*rel*) fête *f.*

feat [fiːt] *n* exploit *m.*

feather ['feðə] *n* plume *f.* **feather bed** lit de plume *m.* **feathery** *adj* plumeux.

feature ['fiːtʃə] *n* trait *m*, caractéristique *f*; spécialité *f.* **feature film** grand film *m. v* (faire) figurer; (*make prominent*) mettre en vedette.

February ['februəri] *n* février *m.*

fed [fed] *V* **feed.**

federal ['fedərəl] *nm, adj* fédéral.

federate ['fedəˌreit] *v* (se) fédérer. *adj* fédéré. **federation** *n* fédération *f.*

fee [fiː] *n* droits *m pl*, frais *m pl*; (*doctor, etc.*) honoraires *m pl.*

feeble ['fiːbl] *adj* faible; (*excuse*) pauvre. **feebleness** *n* faiblesse *f.*

*feed [fiːd] *v* (se) nourrir; (*machine, fire*) alimenter. **be fed up** (*coll*) en avoir marre. *n* nourriture *f*; (*baby's*) tétée *f*, biberon *m.* **feedback** *n* feed-back *m.*

*feel [fiːl] *v* (se) sentir; (*touch*) palper; (*think*) avoir l'impression. *n* toucher *m*; sensation *f.* **feeler** *n* antenne *f.* **feeling** *n* sentiment *m*; sensation *f.*

feet [fiːt] *V* **foot.**

feign [fein] *v* feindre, simuler.

feline ['fiːlain] *n, adj* félin, -e.

fell¹ [fel] *V* **fall.**

fell² [fel] *v* abattre.

fellow ['felou] *n* compagnon *m*; (*coll*) type *m*; (*of society*) membre *m.* **fellowship** *n* amitié *f*; association *f.*

felony ['feləni] *n* crime *m.* **felon** *n* criminel, -elle *m, f.*

felt¹ [felt] *V* **feel.**

felt² [felt] *n* feutre *m.* **felt-tip pen** feutre *m.*

female ['fiːmeil] *adj* femelle, féminin. *n* femelle *f*; (*person*) femme *f.*

feminine ['feminin] *nm, adj* féminin. **femininity** *n* féminité *f.* **feminism** *n* féminisme *m.* **feminist** *n* féministe *m, f.*

fence [fens] *n* clôture *f*; (*horse-racing*) obstacle *m. v* clôturer; (*sport*) faire de l'escrime. **fencing** *n* (*sport*) escrime *f.*

fend [fend] *v* **fend for oneself** se débrouiller. **fend off** parer; (*attacker*) repousser.

fender ['fendə] *n* garde-feu *m invar*; (*US*) garde-boue *m invar.*

fennel ['fenl] *n* fenouil *m.*

ferment [fə'ment; *n* 'fɜɪment] *v* (faire) fermenter. *n* ferment *m*; agitation *f.* **fermentation** *n* fermentation *f.*

fern [fɜɪn] *n* fougère *f.*

ferocious [fə'rouʃəs] *adj* féroce. **ferocity** *n* férocité *f.*

ferret ['ferit] *n* furet *m. v* fureter. **ferret out** dénicher.

ferry ['feri] *n* ferry *m*; (*smaller*) bac *m. v* transporter.

fertile ['fɜɪtail] *adj* (*land*) fertile; (*person*) fécond. **fertility** *n* fertilité *f*; fécondité *f.* **fertilization** *n* fertilisation *f.* **fertilize** *v* fertiliser; féconder. **fertilizer** *n* engrais *m.*

fervent ['fɜɪvənt] *adj* fervent. **fervour** *n* ferveur *f.*

fester ['festə] *v* suppurer; (*anger, etc.*) couver.

festival ['festəvəl] *n* festival *m*; (*rel*) fête *f.*

festoon [fə'stuːn] *v* festonner. *n* feston *m.*

fetch [fetʃ] *v* aller chercher; (*person*) amener; (*thing*) apporter; (*sell for*) rapporter. **fetching** *adj* ravissant.

fête [feit] *n* fête *f.*

fetid ['fiːtid] *adj* fétide.

fetish ['fetiʃ] *n* fétiche *m.*

fetter ['fetə] *v* entraver. **fetters** *pl n* entraves *f pl*; (*irons*) fers *m pl.*

feud [fjuːd] *n* querelle *f. v* se quereller.

feudal ['fjuːdl] *adj* féodal.

fever ['fiːvə] *n* fièvre *f*. **feverish** *adj* fiévreux.

few [fjuː] *nm, adj* peu (de). **a few** quelques; quelques-uns, quelques-unes. **quite a few** pas mal (de). **fewer** *nm, adj* moins (de). **fewest** le moins (de).

fiancé [fi'onsei] *n* fiancé *m*. **fiancée** *n* fiancée *f*.

fiasco [fi'askou] *n* fiasco *m*.

fib [fib] *n* blague *f*. *v* raconter des blagues.

fibre ['faibə] *n* fibre *f*. **fibreglass** *n* fibre de verre *f*.

fickle ['fikl] *adj* inconstant.

fiction ['fikʃən] *n* (*stories*) romans *m pl*; (*invention*) fiction *f*. **fictional** *or* **fictitious** *adj* fictif.

fiddle ['fidl] *n* violon *m*; (*coll: fraud*) combine *f*. *v* jouer du violon; (*coll: cheat*) traficoter; (*coll: falsify*) truquer. **fiddle with** tripoter. **fiddly** *adj* minutieux.

fidelity [fi'deləti] *n* fidélité *f*.

fidget ['fidʒit] *v* se trémousser. **fidgety** *adj* remuant.

field [fiːld] *n* champ *m*; (*sport*) terrain *m*; (*of knowledge, etc.*) domaine *f*. **field glasses** jumelles *f pl*. **field marshal** maréchal *m*. **fieldwork** *n* recherches sur le terrain *f pl*.

fiend [fiːnd] *n* démon *m*; (*coll: enthusiast*) enragé, -e *m, f*. **fiendish** *adj* diabolique.

fierce [fiəs] *adj* féroce; violent; (*struggle*) acharné. **fierceness** *n* férocité *f*; violence *f*; acharnement *m*.

fiery ['faiəri] *adj* ardent, brûlant; (*temper*) violent.

fifteen [fif'tiːn] *nm, adj* quinze. **fifteenth** *n*(*m+f*), *adj* quinzième.

fifth [fifθ] *n*(*m+f*), *adj* cinquième.

fifty ['fifti] *nm, adj* cinquante. **fifty-fifty** *adj, adv* moitié-moitié, cinquante pour cent. **fiftieth** *n*(*m+f*), *adj* cinquantième.

fig [fig] *n* (*fruit*) figue *f*; (*tree*) figuier *m*.

*****fight** [fait] *v* se battre, combattre; (*argue*) se disputer. *n* combat *m*; (*struggle*) lutte *f*.

figment ['figmənt] *n* création *f*. **figment of the imagination** invention *f*.

figure ['figə] *n* figure *f*; (*number*) chiffre *m*; (*slimness*) ligne *f*; (*human*) forme *f*. **figurehead** *n* figure de proue *f*; (*derog*) prête-nom *m*. **figure skating** patinage artistique *m*. *v* (*appear*) figurer; (*think*) penser. **figure out** arriver à comprendre. **figurative** *adj* figuré.

filament ['filəmənt] *n* filament *m*.

file[1] [fail] *n* (*folder*) dossier *m*; (*card index*) fichier *m*; (*in office*) classeur *m*. **in single file** à la file. *v* classer; (*claim, etc.*) déposer, intenter. **file past** défiler; passer un à un. **filing** *n* classement *m*. **filing cabinet** classeur *m*. **filing clerk** documentaliste *m, f*.

file[2] [fail] *n* lime *f*. *v* limer. **filings** *pl n* limaille *f sing*.

filial ['filiəl] *adj* filial.

fill [fil] *v* (se) remplir; (*tooth*) plomber. **fill in** (*form*) remplir; (*hole*) boucher. **fill up** (*petrol tank*) faire le plein; (*cup, etc.*) remplir.

fillet ['filit] *n* filet *m*. **fillet steak** tournedos *m*. *v* désosser.

filling ['filiŋ] *n* plombage *m*; (*of pie, etc.*) garniture *f*. *adj* (*food*) substantiel. **filling station** poste d'essence *m*.

film [film] *n* film *m*; (*phot*) pellicule *f*; (*layer*) couche *f*. **film star** vedette *f*. **filmstrip** *n* film fixe *m*. *v* filmer.

filter ['filtə] *n* filtre *m*. **filter paper** papier filtre *m*. **filter-tipped** *adj* à bout filtre. *v* filtrer; purifier.

filth [filθ] *n* saleté *f*. **filthy** *adj* crasseux; (*language*) ordurier.

fin [fin] *n* nageoire *f*.

final ['fainl] *adj* (*last*) dernier; définitif. *n* finale *f*. **finalist** *n* finaliste *m, f*. **finalize** *v* mettre la dernière main à. **finally** *adv* enfin, finalement.

finance [fai'nans] *n* finance *f*. *v* financer. **financial** *adj* financier. **financial year** année budgétaire *f*. **financier** *n* financier *m*.

finch [fintʃ] *n* fringillidé *m*.

*****find** [faind] *v* trouver. **find out** se renseigner (sur); découvrir. *n* trouvaille *f*. **findings** *pl n* conclusions *f pl*.

fine[1] [fain] *adj* fin, délicat; (*sunny, excellent*) beau, belle. *adv* bien. **fine arts** beaux arts *m pl*. **finely** *adv* magnifiquement; (*small*) menu. **finery** *n* parure *f*.

fine[2] [fain] *n* amende *f*. *v* **be fined** avoir une amende.

finesse [fi'nes] *n* finesse *f*; (*cards*) impasse *f*.

finger ['fiŋgə] *n* doigt *m*. **finger bowl** rince-doigts *m invar*. **fingermark** *n* trace de doigt *f*. **fingernail** *n* ongle *m*. **finger-**

print *n* empreinte digitale *f*. **fingertip** *n* bout du doigt *m*. *v* toucher.
finish ['finiʃ] *v* finir, (se) terminer. **finishing line** ligne d'arrivée *f*. **finishing touch** touche finale *f*. *n* fin *f*; (*sport*) arrivée *f*; surface *f*.
finite ['fainait] *adj* fini.
Finland ['finlənd] *n* Finlande *f*. **Finn** *n* Finlandais, -e *m*, *f*; (*Finnish speaker*) Finnois, -e *m*, *f*. **Finnish** *adj* finlandais; *nm*, *adj* (*language*) finnois.
fir [fəɪ] *n* sapin *m*. **fir cone** pomme de pin *f*.
fire ['faiə] *n* feu *m*; (*uncontrolled*) incendie *m*. **set fire to** mettre le feu à. *v* (*enthusiasm, etc.*) enflammer; (*pottery*) cuire; (*gun*) tirer; (*coll: dismiss*) vider.
fire alarm *n* avertisseur d'incendie *m*.
firearm ['faiə,aɪm] *n* arme à feu *f*.
fire brigade *n* pompiers *m pl*.
fire door *n* porte anti-incendie *f*.
fire drill *n* exercice anti-incendie *m*.
fire engine *n* pompe à incendie *f*.
fire escape *n* (*stairs*) escalier de secours *m*; (*ladder*) échelle d'incendie *f*.
fire exit *n* sortie de secours *f*.
fire extinguisher *n* extincteur *m*.
fire-guard ['faiə,gaɪd] *n* garde-feu *m invar*.
firelight ['faiə,lait] *n* lueur du feu *f*.
fireman ['faiəmən] *n* pompier *m*.
fireplace ['faiə,pleis] *n* cheminée *f*.
fireproof ['faiə,pruːf] *v* ignifuger. *adj* ignifuge.
fireside ['faiə,said] *n* foyer *m*.
fire station *n* caserne de pompiers *f*.
firewood ['faiə,wud] *n* bois à brûler *m*.
firework ['faiə,wəːk] *n* feu d'artifice *m*.
firing squad *n* peloton d'exécution *m*.
firm[1] [fəɪm] *adj* ferme; solide. **firmness** *n* fermeté *f*; solidité *f*.
firm[2] [fəɪm] *n* (*comm*) compagnie *f*, firme *f*.
first [fəɪst] *n*, *adj* premier. *adv* d'abord; pour la première fois. **at first** d'abord. **first aid** premiers secours *m pl*. **first-class** *adj* (*ticket*) de première classe; (*mail*) tarif normal. **first floor** premier étage *m*. **first-hand** *adj* de première main. **first name** prénom *m*. **first-rate** *adj* excellent, de premier ordre. **in the first place** en premier lieu.
fiscal ['fiskəl] *adj* fiscal.
fish [fiʃ] *n* poisson *m*. *v* pêcher. **fish out** extirper. **fishy** *adj* (*coll*) louche.
fishbone ['fiʃ,boun] *n* arête *f*.

fish cake *n* croquette de poisson *f*.
fisherman ['fiʃəmən] *n* pêcheur *m*.
fish fingers *pl n* bâtonnets de poisson *m pl*.
fishing ['fiʃiŋ] *n* pêche *f*. **fishing boat** barque de pêche *f*. **fishing line** ligne de pêche *f*. **fishing rod** canne à pêche *f*. **fishing tackle** attirail de pêche *m*. **go fishing** aller à la pêche.
fishmonger ['fiʃ,mʌŋgə] *n* marchand de poisson *m*.
fishpond ['fiʃ,pond] *n* étang à poissons *m*.
fish shop *n* poissonnerie *f*.
fish slice *n* pelle à poisson *f*.
fish tank *n* aquarium *m*.
fission ['fiʃən] *n* fission *f*.
fissure ['fiʃə] *n* fissure *f*.
fist [fist] *n* poing *m*. **fistful** *n* poignée *f*.
fit[1] [fit] *adj* (*suitable*) convenable; (*competent*) capable; (*worthy*) digne; (*healthy*) en bonne santé. *v* (*clothes, etc.*) aller à; ajuster; (*match*) correspondre à; équiper; (*faire*) entrer. **fitness** *n* santé *f*, forme *f*; aptitudes *f pl*. **fitter** *n* (*tech*) monteur *m*; (*clothes*) essayeur, -euse *m*, *f*. **fitting** *adj* approprié. **fitting room** salon d'essayage *m*. **fittings** *pl n* installations *f pl*.
fit[2] [fit] *n* accès *m*, crise *f*. **fitful** *adj* intermittent; (*sleep*) troublé.
five [faiv] *nm*, *adj* cinq.
fix [fiks] *v* fixer; arranger; réparer. *n* (*coll*) embêtement *m*; (*slang: drugs*) piqûre *f*. **fixation** *n* fixation *f*. **fixed** *adj* fixe. **fixture** *n* installation *f*; (*sport*) épreuve *f*.
fizz [fiz] *v* pétiller. *n* pétillement *m*. **fizzy** *adj* pétillant.
flabbergasted ['flabə,gaɪstid] *adj* (*coll*) sidéré.
flabby ['flabi] *adj* mou, molle; (*person*) flasque.
flag[1] [flag] *n* drapeau *m*; (*naut*) pavillon *m*. **flagpole** *n* mât *m*. **flagship** *n* vaisseau amiral *m*. *v* **flag down** héler.
flag[2] [flag] *v* languir; (*tire*) s'alanguir; (*interest*) faiblir.
flagon ['flagən] *n* grande bouteille *f*; (*jug*) cruche *f*.
flagrant ['fleigrənt] *adj* flagrant.
flair [fleə] *n* flair *m*.
flake [fleik] *n* (*snow, etc.*) flocon *m*; (*paint, plaster, etc.*) écaille *f*. *v* s'écailler; (*skin*) peler. **flake out** (*coll*) tomber dans les pommes. **flaky** *adj* floconneux; (*pastry*) feuilleté.

flamboyant [flam,boiənt] *adj* flamboyant.
flame [fleim] *n* flamme *f.* **burst into flames** s'enflammer. *v* flamber. **flaming** *adj* ardent; (*slang*) foutu. **flammable** *adj* inflammable.
flamingo [flə'miŋgou] *n* flamant *m.*
flan [flan] *n* tarte *f.*
flank [flaŋk] *n* flanc *m. v* flanquer.
flannel ['flanl] *n* (*fabric*) flanelle *f*; (*facecloth*) gant de toilette *m.* **flannels** *pl n* pantalon de flanelle *m sing. v* (*slang*) baratiner.
flap [flap] *v* battre; (*sails*) claquer; (*coll*) paniquer. *n* (*envelope, etc.*) rabat *m*; battement *m*; claquement *m*; (*table*) abattant *m*; (*coll*) panique *f.*
flare [fleə] *n* signal lumineux *m*; (*clothes*) évasement *m. v* s'enflammer; (*clothes*) (s')évaser. **flare up** (*anger, etc.*) éclater; (*person*) s'emporter; (*fire*) s'embraser.
flash [flaʃ] *n* éclat *m,* éclair *m*; (*phot*) flash *m.* **flashback** *n* flashback *m invar.* **flash bulb** ampoule de flash *f.* **flash cube** cube-flash *m.* **flashlight** *n* (*torch*) lampe électrique *f. v* (*light*) projeter, (*intermittently*) clignoter; (*sparkle*) étinceler; (*show off*) étaler; (*mot*) faire un appel de phares. **flashy** *adj* tapageur, -euse; tape-à-l'œil *invar.*
flask [flaːsk] *n* flacon *m*; thermos ® *m.*
flat[1] [flat] *adj* plat; (*tyre, battery*) à plat; (*music*) faux, fausse; (*beer*) éventé. *n* (*music*) bémol *m.* **flat-fish** *n* poisson plat *m.* **flat-footed** *adj* aux pieds plats. **flat rate** taux fixe *m.* **go flat out** (*car*) être à sa vitesse de pointe. **work flat out** travailler d'arrache-pied. **flatly** *adv* carrément, catégoriquement. **flatten** *v* (s')aplatir; (*smooth*) (s')aplanir.
flat[2] [flat] *n* appartement *m.* **flatlet** *n* studio *m.*
flatter ['flatə] *v* flatter. **flatterer** *n* flatteur, -euse *m, f.* **flattering** *adj* flatteur, -euse. **flattery** *n* flatterie *f.*
flatulence ['flatjuləns] *n* flatulence *f.*
flaunt [flɔɪnt] *v* étaler, faire étalage de. **flaunt oneself** poser.
flautist ['flɔɪtist] *n* flûtiste *m, f.*
flavour ['fleivə] *n* goût *m*; (*ice-cream, etc.*) parfum *m. v* parfumer; assaisonner. **flavouring** *n* parfum *m*; assaisonnement *m.*
flaw [flɔɪ] *n* défaut *m.* **flawed** *adj* imparfait. **flawless** *adj* parfait.

flax [flaks] *n* lin *m.* **flaxen** *adj* de lin.
flea [fliɪ] *n* puce *f.*
fleck [flek] *n* (*colour*) moucheture *f*; particule *f. v* moucheter.
fled [fled] *V* flee.
***flee** [fliɪ] *v* fuir; s'enfuir (de).
fleece [fliɪs] *n* toison *f. v* (*coll*) tondre. **fleecy** *adj* (*cloud*) floconneux; (*woolly*) laineux.
fleet [fliɪt] *n* flotte *f.*
fleeting ['fliɪtiŋ] *adj* fugace, passager.
Flemish ['flemiʃ] *nm, adj* flamand. **the Flemish** les Flamands *m pl.*
flesh [fleʃ] *n* chair *f.* **flesh-coloured** *adj* couleur chair *invar.* **in the flesh** en chair et en os. **fleshy** *adj* charnu.
flew [fluɪ] *V* fly[1].
flex [fleks] *n* fil souple *m*; (*telephone*) cordon *m. v* fléchir; (*muscles*) tendre. **flexibility** *n* flexibilité *f.* **flexible** *adj* flexible, souple.
flick [flik] *v* donner un petit coup à. **flick through** (*book*) feuilleter. *n* petit coup *m*; (*with finger*) chiquenaude *f.* **the flicks** (*coll*) le ciné *m.*
flicker ['flikə] *v* danser, trembloter. *n* vacillement *m*; (*of hope, etc.*) lueur *f.*
flight[1] [flait] *n* (*of bird, etc.*) vol *m*; (*of stairs*) escalier *m.* **flight path** trajectoire *f.*
flight[2] [flait] *n* (*fleeing*) fuite *f.*
flimsy ['flimzi] *adj* peu solide; (*cloth, paper*) léger, mince; (*excuse*) piètre.
flinch [flintʃ] *v* broncher.
***fling** [fliŋ] *v* lancer, jeter. **have one's fling** se payer du bon temps.
flint [flint] *n* silex *m.*
flip [flip] *v* donner un petit coup à. **flip through** (*book*) feuilleter. *n* petit coup *m*; (*with finger*) chiquenaude *f.* **flipping** *adv* (*coll*) fichu.
flippant ['flipənt] *adj* désinvolte. **flippancy** *n* désinvolture *f.*
flipper ['flipə] *n* (*seal, etc.*) nageoire *f*; (*swimmer's*) palme *f.*
flirt [flɔɪt] *v* flirter. *n* flirteur, -euse *m, f.* **flirtation** *n* flirt *m.*
flit [flit] *v* voleter. **do a moonlight flit** déménager à la cloche de bois.
float [flout] *v* (faire) flotter; (*swimmer*) faire la planche. *n* (*fishing*) flotteur *m*; (*in procession*) char *m.*
flock[1] [flok] *n* (*animals*) troupeau *m*; (*birds*) volée *f*; (*people*) foule *f. v* s'attrouper.

flock² [flok] n (*wool*) bourre de laine f; (*cotton*) bourre de coton f.

flog [flog] v flageller. **flogging** n flagellation f; (*law*) fouet m.

flood [flʌd] n inondation f; (*sudden rush*) déluge m. **open the floodgates** ouvrir les vannes. v inonder; (*river*) (faire) déborder. **flooding** n inondation f.

*floodlight ['flʌd͵lait] v illuminer; (*sport*) éclairer. n projecteur m. **floodlighting** n illumination f; éclairage m.

floor [floɪ] n plancher m; (*ground*) sol m; (*storey*) étage m. **floorboard** n planche f. v terrasser; stupéfier.

flop [flop] n (*coll*) fiasco m. v s'effondrer; (*coll*) faire fiasco. **floppy** adj flottant; (*hat*) à bords flottants.

flora ['floɪrə] n flore f.

floral [floɪrəl] adj floral.

florist ['florist] n fleuriste m, f.

flounce¹ [flauns] v **flounce in/out** entrer/sortir dans un mouvement d'humeur. n geste impatient m.

flounce² [flauns] n (*of dress*) volant m.

flounder¹ ['flaundə] v patauger.

flounder² ['flaundə] n flet m.

flour ['flauə] n farine f. **floury** adj enfariné; (*potatoes*) farineux.

flourish ['flʌriʃ] v prospérer; (*wave*) brandir. n fioriture f; (*gesture*) moulinet m. **flourishing** adj florissant.

flout [flaut] v se moquer de.

flow [flou] v couler; circuler. n écoulement m; circulation f. **flow chart** organigramme m. **flowing** adj gracieux; (*hair, etc.*) flottant.

flower ['flauə] n fleur f. **flower arrangement** composition florale f. **flower bed** plate-bande f. **flowerpot** n pot à fleurs m. **flower show** floralies f pl. v fleurir. **flowery** adj fleuri.

flown [floun] V **fly¹**.

flu [fluɪ] n grippe f.

fluctuate ['flʌktju͵eit] v fluctuer, varier. **fluctuating** n fluctuation f, variation f.

flue [fluɪ] n tuyau m, conduit m.

fluent ['fluɔnt] adj coulant. **fluency** n aisance f. **fluently** adv couramment.

fluff [flʌf] n (*on animal, bird*) duvet m; (*from fabric*) peluche f. v (*coll: fail*) louper. **fluffy** adj duveteux; pelucheux.

fluid ['fluid] nm, adj fluide.

fluke [fluɪk] n coup de chance m, hasard extraordinaire m.

flung [flʌŋ] V **fling**.

fluorescent [fluɔ'resnt] adj fluorescent. **fluorescence** n fluorescence f.

fluoride ['fluɔraid] n fluor m.

flush¹ [flʌʃ] n (*blush*) rougeur f; (*burst*) éclat m. v rougir; (*wash out*) nettoyer à grande eau; (*toilet*) tirer la chasse. **flushed** adj rouge.

flush² [flʌʃ] adj à ras (de); (*slang: rich*) plein de fric.

fluster ['flʌstə] v énerver. **get flustered** s'énerver. n agitation f.

flute [fluɪt] n flûte f.

flutter ['flʌtə] v voleter; (*wings*) battre; (*heart*) palpiter. n battement m; palpitation f; agitation f.

flux [flʌks] n flux m. **be in a state of flux** changer sans arrêt.

*fly¹ [flai] v voler; (*aeroplane*) piloter; (*kite*) faire voler; (*time*) passer vite; (*flee*) fuir. **fly across** or **over** survoler. **fly away** s'envoler. **flyaway** adj (*hair*) difficile. **flyleaf** n page de garde f. **flyover** n (*mot*) autopont m. **flysheet** n feuille volante f. **flywheel** n (*tech*) volant m. n also **flies** (*on trousers*) braguette f.

fly² [flai] n mouche f.

foal [foul] n poulain m.

foam [foum] n mousse f; (*sea, animal*) écume f. **foam rubber** caoutchouc mousse m. v mousser; écumer. **foamy** adj mousseux; écumeux.

focal ['foukəl] adj focal. **focal point** foyer m; (*of attention*) point central m.

focus ['foukəs] n foyer m; (*of interest*) centre m. **in focus** au point. v (*phot, etc.*) mettre au point; (*rays*) (faire) converger; concentrer.

fodder ['fodə] n fourrage m.

foe [fou] n ennemi, -e m, f.

foetus ['fiɪtəs] n fœtus m. **foetal** adj fœtal.

fog [fog] n brouillard m. **fogbound** adj bloqué par le brouillard. **foghorn** n corne de brume f. **foglamp** n (*mot*) phare antibrouillard m. **foggy** adj brumeux. **it's foggy** il fait du brouillard.

foible ['foibl] n marotte f.

foil¹ [foil] v déjouer.

foil² [foil] n feuille de métal f; (*cooking*) papier d'aluminium m.

foil³ [foil] n (*fencing*) fleuret m.

foist [foist] v refiler.

fold¹ [fould] n pli m. v (se) plier. **fold one's arms** se croiser les bras. **fold up** plier; (*coll: collapse*) s'écrouler. **folder** n dossier *m*, chemise *f*. **folding** *adj* pliant. **folding door** porte en accordéon *f*.

fold² [fould] *n* (*sheep*) parc à moutons *m*.

foliage ['fouliidʒ] *n* feuillage *m*.

folk [fouk] *pl n* gens *f pl*. **folk dance** danse folklorique *f*. **folklore** *n* folklore *m*. **folk music** musique folk *f*. **folks** *pl n* (*coll*) famille *f sing*. **folk singer** chanteur, -euse de folk *m*, *f*.

follicle ['folikl] *n* follicule *m*.

follow ['folou] *v* suivre; (*result*) s'ensuivre. **follow up** exploiter; (faire) suivre. **follower** *n* disciple *m*.

folly ['foli] *n* folie *f*.

fond [fond] *adj* tendre, affectueux. **be fond of** aimer. **fondness** *n* (*for person*) affection *f*; (*for thing*) prédilection *f*.

fondant ['fondənt] *n* fondant *m*.

fondle ['fondl] *v* caresser.

font [font] *n* fonts baptismaux *m pl*.

food [fuːd] *n* nourriture *f*, aliments *m pl*. **food poisoning** intoxication alimentaire *f*. **foodstuffs** *pl n* aliments *m pl*.

fool [fuːl] *n* imbécile *m*, *f*. **foolproof** *adj* infaillible. *v* (*deceive*) duper. **fool around** faire l'imbécile. **foolhardy** *adj* téméraire. **foolish** *adj* idiot. **foolishly** *adv* bêtement. **foolishness** *n* bêtise *f*.

foolscap ['fuːlskap] *n* papier pot *m*.

foot [fut] *n*, *pl* **feet** pied *m*; (*bird, animal*) patte *f*; (*of page*) bas *m*. **get off on the right/wrong foot** être bien/mal parti. **on foot** à pied. **put one's foot in it** mettre les pieds dans le plat.

foot-and-mouth disease *n* fièvre aphteuse *f*.

football ['fut,boːl] *n* (*game*) football *m*; (*ball*) ballon *m*. **footballer** *n* footballeur *m*.

footbridge ['fut,bridʒ] *n* passerelle *f*.

foothold ['fut,hould] *n* prise de pied *f*.

footing ['futiŋ] *n* position *f*; relations *f pl*. **equal footing** pied d'égalité *f*.

footlights ['fut,laits] *pl n* rampe *f sing*.

footnote ['fut,nout] *n* note en bas de la page *f*.

footpath ['fut,paːθ] *n* sentier *m*.

footprint ['fut,print] *n* empreinte du pied *f*.

footstep ['fut,step] *n* pas *m*.

footwear ['fut,weə] *n* chaussures *f pl*.

for [foː] *prep* pour; (*exchange*) contre; (*distance*) pendant. *conj* car.

forage ['foridʒ] *v* fourrager. *n* fourrage *m*.

forbade [foː'bad] *V* **forbid**.

***forbear** [foː'beə] *v* s'abstenir. **forbearance** *n* patience *f*.

***forbid** [foː'bid] *v* défendre, interdire. **forbidding** *adj* menaçant; (*look*) rébarbatif.

forbidden [foː'bidn] *V* **forbid**.

force [foːs] *n* force *f*. **in force** en vigueur. *v* forcer; imposer; (*thrust*) pousser. **force-feed** *v* nourrir de force. **forceful** *adj* énergique, puissant. **forcibly** *adv* de force.

forceps ['foːseps] *pl n* forceps *m sing*.

ford [foːd] *n* gué *m*. *v* passer à gué.

fore [foː] *adj* antérieur, de devant. *n* (*naut*) avant *m*. **come to the fore** se faire remarquer. *adv* à l'avant.

forearm ['foːraːm] *n* avant-bras *m invar*.

forebears ['foːbeəz] *pl n* ancêtres *m pl*.

foreboding [foː'boudiŋ] *n* pressentiment *m*.

***forecast** ['foːkaːst] *n* prévision *f*. **weather forecast** bulletin météorologique *m*. *v* prévoir.

forecourt ['foːkoːt] *n* avant-cour *m*; (*of garage*) devant *m*.

forefathers ['foːfaːðəz] *pl n* ancêtres *m pl*.

forefinger ['foːfiŋgə] *n* index *m*.

forefront ['foːfrʌnt] *n* premier rang *m*.

foregone ['foːgon] *adj* **be a foregone conclusion** être à prévoir.

foreground ['foːgraund] *n* premier plan *m*.

forehand ['foːhand] *n* (*tennis*) coup droit *m*.

forehead ['forid] *n* front *m*.

foreign ['forən] *adj* étranger. **foreigner** *n* étranger, -ère *m*, *f*.

foreleg ['foːleg] *n* jambe antérieure *f*; patte de devant *f*.

foreman ['foːmən] *n* contremaître *m*.

foremost ['foːmoust] *adj* principal. **first and foremost** tout d'abord.

forename ['foːneim] *n* prénom *m*.

forensic [fə'rensik] *adj* (*medicine*) légal; (*evidence*) médico-légal.

forerunner ['foːrʌnə] *n* précurseur *m*.

***foresee** [foː'siː] *v* prévoir. **foreseeable** *adj* prévisible.

foreshadow [foː'ʃadou] *v* présager.

foresight ['foːsait] *n* prévoyance *f*.

foreskin ['foːskin] *n* prépuce *m*.

forest ['forist] *n* forêt *f*. **forester** *n* forestier *m*. **forestry** *n* sylviculture *f*. **Forestry Commission** Eaux et Forêts *f pl*.

forestall [fɔr'stɔɪl] v devancer, anticiper.
foretaste ['fɔɪteɪst] n avant-goût m.
***foretell** [fɔr'tel] v prédire.
forethought ['fɔɪθɔɪt] n prévoyance.
forever [fɔr'evə] adv toujours.
foreword ['fɔɪwɜɪd] n avant-propos m.
forfeit ['fɔɪfɪt] v perdre. n peine f; (game) gage m.
forgave [fə'geɪv] V **forgive**.
forge¹ [fɔɪdʒ] v (counterfeit) contrefaire; (metal) forger. n forge f. **forger** n faussaire m, f; (law) contrefacteur m. **forgery** n (act) contrefaçon f; (thing forged) faux m.
forge² [fɔɪdʒ] v **forge ahead** pousser de l'avant.
***forget** [fə'get] v oublier. **forget-me-not** n myosotis m. **forgetful** adj distrait.
***forgive** [fə'gɪv] v pardonner. **forgiveness** n pardon m; clémence f.
forgiven [fə'gɪvn] V **forgive**.
***forgo** [fɔr'gou] v renoncer à.
forgot [fə'got] V **forget**.
forgotten [fə'gotn] V **forget**.
fork [fɔɪk] n (cutlery) fourchette f; (branch) fourche f; (roads) embranchement m. v (road) bifurquer. **fork out** (slang: pay) allonger. **forked** adj fourchu.
forlorn [fə'lɔɪn] adj malheureux; abandonné.
form [fɔɪm] n forme f; (document) formulaire m; (bench) banc m; (school) classe f. v (se) former. **formation** n formation f. **formative** adj formateur, -trice.
formal ['fɔɪməl] adj (dress) de cérémonie; officiel; (person, manner) compassé; (in form only) formel. **formality** n formalité f.
format ['fɔɪmat] n format m.
former ['fɔɪmə] adj (previous) ancien; (first) premier. pron celui-là, celle-là. **formerly** adv autrefois.
formidable ['fɔɪmɪdəbl] adj redoutable.
formula ['fɔɪmjulə] n formule f.
formulate ['fɔɪmjuˌleɪt] v formuler. **formulation** n formulation f.
***forsake** [fə'seɪk] v abandonner.
forsaken [fə'seɪkn] V **forsake**.
forsook [fə'suk] V **forsake**.
fort [fɔɪt] n fort m.
forte ['fɔɪteɪ] n fort m.
forth [fɔɪθ] adv en avant. **and so forth** et ainsi de suite. **forthcoming** adj à venir, prochain; (person) ouvert. **forthright** adj franc, franche. **forthwith** adv sur-le-champ.

fortify ['fɔɪtɪˌfaɪ] v fortifier. **fortification** n fortification f.
fortitude ['fɔɪtɪˌtjuɪd] n courage m.
fortnight ['fɔɪtnaɪt] n quinzaine f. **fortnightly** adv tous les quinze jours.
fortress ['fɔɪtrɪs] n forteresse f.
fortuitous [fɔɪ'tjuɪɪtəs] adj fortuit.
fortunate ['fɔɪtjunət] adj heureux. **be fortunate** avoir de la chance. **fortunately** adv heureusement.
fortune ['fɔɪtʃən] n fortune f; (luck) chance f. **fortune-teller** n diseur, -euse de bonne aventure m, f.
forty ['fɔɪti] nm, adj quarante. **forty winks** un petit somme. **fortieth** n(m+f), adj quarantième.
forum ['fɔɪrəm] n forum m; (meeting) tribune f.
forward ['fɔɪwəd] adj en avant; (impudent) effronté. **come forward** se présenter. v expédier; (send on) faire suivre. **please forward** prière de faire suivre.
forwards ['fɔɪwədz] adv en avant.
fossil ['fosl] n fossile m. **fossilized** adj fossilisé.
foster ['fostə] v (child) élever; encourager; (idea) entretenir.
fought [fɔɪt] V **fight**.
foul [faul] adj infect; (language) ordurier; (weather) sale. **foul play** acte criminel m; (sport) jeu déloyal m. n (sport) coup défendu. v infecter; (entangle) (s')emmêler.
found¹ [faund] V **find**.
found² [faund] v fonder. **foundation** n fondation f; base f, fondement m. **founder** n fondateur, -trice m, f.
founder ['faundə] v (ship) sombrer; (collapse) s'effondrer.
foundry ['faundri] n fonderie f.
fountain ['fauntin] n fontaine f. **fountain pen** stylo à encre m.
four [fɔɪ] nm, adj quatre. **foursome** n (game) partie à quatre f; deux couples m pl. **on all fours** à quatre pattes. **fourth** n(m+f), adj quatrième.
fourteen [fɔɪ'tiɪn] nm, adj quatorze. **fourteenth** n(m+f), adj quatorzième.
fowl [faul] n volaille f.
fox [foks] n renard m. **foxglove** n digitale f. **foxhunting** n chasse au renard f. **foxtrot** n slow m. v (coll) mystifier.
foyer ['foiei] n foyer m.

fraction ['frakʃən] *n* fraction *f*. **fractionally** *adv* un tout petit peu.

fracture ['fraktʃə] *n* fracture *f*. *v* (se) fracturer.

fragile ['fradʒail] *adj* fragile. **fragility** *n* fragilité *f*.

fragment ['fragmənt] *n* fragment *m*. **fragmented** *adj* morcelé.

fragrant ['freigrənt] *adj* parfumé. **fragrance** *n* parfum *m*.

frail [freil] *adj* frêle, fragile. **frailty** *n* fragilité *f*; (*moral*) faiblesse *f*.

frame [freim] *n* cadre *m*; (*house*) charpente *f*; (*car*) châssis *m*; (*spectacles*) monture *f*; (*film*) image *f*. **frame of mind** humeur *f*. **framework** *n* charpente *f*; structure *f*. *v* encadrer.

franc [fraŋk] *n* franc *m*.

France [fraɪns] *n* France *f*.

franchise ['frantʃaiz] *n* droit de suffrage *m*.

frank [fraŋk] *adj* franc, franche. **frankness** *n* franchise *f*.

frantic ['frantik] *adj* frénétique; (*person*) hors de soi.

fraternal [frə'təɪnl] *adj* fraternel. **fraternity** *n* fraternité *f*; (*community*) confrérie *f*. **fraternize** *v* fraterniser.

fraud [froɪd] *n* (*law*) fraude *f*; (*deception*) supercherie *f*; (*financial*) escroquerie *f*; (*person*) imposteur *m*. **fraudulent** *adj* frauduleux.

fraught [froɪt] *adj* (*tense*) tendu. **fraught with** chargé de.

fray[1] [frei] *v* (s')effilocher; (*cuff, etc.*) (s')effranger.

fray[2] [frei] *n* rixe *f*.

freak [friɪk] *n* phénomène *m*; anomalie *f*. **freak of nature** accident de la nature *m*. *adj* insolite, inattendu.

freckle ['frekl] *n* tache de son *f*. **freckled** *adj* taché de son.

free [friɪ] *adj* libre; gratuit. **free-for-all** *n* mêlée générale *f*. **freehand** *adj, adv* à main levée. **freehold** *n* propriété foncière libre *f*. **freelance** *n, adj* indépendant, -e. **freemason** *n* francmaçon *m*. **freestyle** *n* nage libre *f*. **of one's own free will** de son propre gré. *v* libérer. **freedom** *n* liberté *f*.

freesia ['friɪziə] *n* freesia *m*.

***freeze** [friɪz] *v* geler; (*food*) congeler; (*prices, etc.*) bloquer. *n* gel *m*; blocage *m*. **freezer** *n* congélateur *m*. **freezing** *adj* glacial. **freezing point** point de congélation *m*.

freight [freit] *n* fret *m*; transport *m*; (*goods*) marchandises *f pl*. **freight train** train de marchandises *m*. *v* affréter; transporter. **freighter** *n* (*ship*) cargo *m*; (*aircraft*) avion-cargo *m*.

French [frentʃ] *nm, adj* français. **the French** les Français *m pl*. **French bean** haricot vert *m*. **French dressing** vinaigrette *f*. **French horn** cor d'harmonie *m*. **French-polish** *v* vernir à l'alcool. **french fries** *pl n* pommes frites *f pl*.

frenzy ['frenzi] *n* frénésie *f*. **frenzied** *adj* frénétique.

frequent ['friɪkwənt; *v* fri'kwent] *adj* fréquent. *v* fréquenter. **frequency** *n* fréquence *f*. **frequently** *adv* fréquemment.

fresco ['freskou] *n* fresque *f*.

fresh [freʃ] *adj* frais, fraîche; (*new*) nouveau, -elle. **freshwater** *adj* (*fish*) d'eau douce. **freshen up** faire un brin de toilette. **freshness** *n* fraîcheur *f*.

fret[1] [fret] *v* se tracasser. **fretful** *adj* agité; (*child*) pleurnicheur, -euse.

fret[2] [fret] *v* découper, chantourner. **fretsaw** *n* scie à découper *f*. **fretwork** *n* découpage *m*.

friar ['fraiə] *n* frère *m*, moine *m*.

friction ['frikʃən] *n* friction *f*; désaccord *m*.

Friday ['fraidei] *n* vendredi *m*.

fridge [fridʒ] *n* (*coll*) frigo *m*.

friend [frend] *n* ami, -e *m, f*. **make friends with** devenir ami avec. **friendliness** *n* bienveillance *f*. **friendly** *adj* amical; (*kind*) gentil, -ille. **friendship** *n* amitié *f*.

frieze [friɪz] *n* frise *f*.

frigate ['frigit] *n* frégate *f*.

fright [frait] *n* effroi *m*, peur *f*. **frighten** *v* effrayer. **be frightened** avoir peur. **frightening** *adj* effrayant. **frightful** *adj* affreux.

frigid ['fridʒid] *adj* glacial; (*manner*) froid; (*woman*) frigide. **frigidity** *n* froideur *f*; frigidité *f*.

frill [fril] *n* (*dress*) ruche *f*; (*shirt*) jabot *m*. **frilly** *adj* à fanfreluches.

fringe [frindʒ] *n* frange *f*; (*edge*) bord *m*. **fringe benefits** avantages supplémentaires *m pl*. *v* franger; border.

frisk [frisk] *v* gambader; (*search*) fouiller. **frisky** *adj* vif.

fritter[1] ['fritə] *v* **fritter away** gaspiller.

fritter[2] ['fritə] *n* (*cookery*) beignet *m*.

frivolity [fri'voliti] *n* frivolité *f*. **frivolous** *adj* frivole.

frizz [friz] v (*hair*) friser. **frizzy** adj crépu.
fro [frou] adv to and fro de long en large.
go to and fro between aller et venir entre.
frock [frok] n robe f.
frog [frog] n grenouille f. **frogman** n
homme-grenouille m. **frogs' legs** cuisses
de grenouille f pl.
frolic ['frolik] v folâtrer. n ébats m pl.
from [from] prep de; (*starting from*) à
partir de; (*extract*) dans, à.
front [frʌnt] n devant m, avant m; (*mil,
weather*) front m; (*promenade*) front de
mer m. in front of devant. adj de devant,
en avant; (*first*) premier. **front view** vue
de face f. **frontage** n façade f; (*shop*)
devanture f.
frontier ['frʌntiə] n frontière f.
frost [frost] n gelée f. **frostbite** n gelure f.
v geler. **frosted glass** verre dépoli m.
frosty adj glacial.
froth [froθ] n écume f, mousse f. v
écumer, mousser. **frothy** adj écumeux,
mousseux.
frown [fraun] n froncement de sourcils m.
v froncer les sourcils, se renfrogner.
frown on désapprouver.
froze [frouz] V **freeze**.
frozen ['frouzn] V **freeze**. adj gelé. **frozen
food** aliments congelés m pl.
frugal ['fruːgəl] adj (*meal, etc.*) frugal;
(*person*) économe. **frugality** n frugalité f.
fruit [fruːt] n fruit m. **fruit cake** cake m.
fruit machine machine à sous f. **fruit salad** salade de fruits f. **fruitful** adj fructueux. **fruition** n réalisation f. **fruitless**
adj stérile.
frustrate [frʌ'streit] v frustrer; (*plans, etc.*)
faire échouer. **frustration** n frustration f.
fry [frai] v (faire) frire. **fried** adj frit.
fried egg œuf sur le plat m. **frying** n friture f. **frying pan** poêle f.
fuchsia ['fjuːʃə] n fuchsia m.
fuck [fʌk] (*vulgar*) v baiser. **fuck off!** va te
faire foutre!
fudge [fʌdʒ] n fondant m.
fuel ['fjuəl] n combustible m; (*mot*)
carburant m. **fuel gauge** indicateur de
niveau de carburant m. **fuel pump** pompe
à essence f. v (*stove, etc.*) alimenter; (*aircraft*) (se) ravitailler en combustible.
fugitive ['fjuːdʒitiv] n, adj fugitif, -ive.
fulcrum ['fulkrəm] n pivot m.
fulfil [ful'fil] v accomplir; exécuter; satisfaire. **fulfilment** n accomplissement m;
exécution f; contentement m.

full [ful] adj plein; complet, -ète. **full blast**
adv (*radio, etc.*) à pleines tubes. **full-
length** adj (*picture*) en pied; (*film*) long
métrage. **full moon** pleine lune f. **full
name** nom et prénoms. **full-scale** adj de
grande envergure. **full stop** point m. **full-
time** adj, adv à plein temps. **fully** adv
entièrement.
fumble ['fʌmbl] v (*feel*) tâtonner; (*search*)
fouiller.
fume [fjuːm] v fumer; (*coll: rage*) être
furibond. **fumes** pl n vapeurs f pl.
fun [fʌn] n amusement m. **for fun** pour
rire. **funfair** n fête foraine f. **have fun**
bien s'amuser. **make fun of** se moquer
de.
function ['fʌŋkʃən] n fonction f; réception f. v fonctionner. **functional** adj fonctionnel.
fund [fʌnd] n fond m, caisse f. **funds** pl n
fonds m pl.
fundamental [fʌndə'mentl] adj fondamental.
funeral ['fjuːnərəl] n enterrement m;
(*state*) funérailles f pl. **funeral parlour**
dépôt mortuaire m. **funeral service** service funèbre m.
fungus ['fʌŋgəs] n, pl **fungi** champignon
m.
funnel ['fʌnl] n (*pouring*) entonnoir m;
(*ship*) cheminée f.
funny ['fʌni] adj drôle; bizarre.
fur [fəː] n fourrure f; (*kettle*) incrustation
f. v s'incruster. **furrier** n fourreur m. **furry**
adj à poil.
furious ['fjuəriəs] adj furieux.
furnace ['fəːnis] n fourneau m.
furnish ['fəːniʃ] v (*house, etc.*) meubler;
(*supply*) fournir. **furnishings** pl n mobilier
m sing.
furniture ['fəːnitʃə] n meubles m pl, mobilier m.
furrow ['fʌrou] n sillon m; (*brow*) ride f. v
sillonner; rider.
further ['fəːðə] adv (farther) plus loin;
(*more*) davantage. adj (farther) plus
lointain; additionnel. **further education**
enseignement post-scolaire m. **further-
more** en outre. **until further notice**
jusqu'à nouvel ordre. v avancer.
furthest ['fəːðist] adv le plus loin. adj le
plus lointain.
furtive ['fəːtiv] adj furtif.

fury ['fjuəri] *n* fureur *f.*
fuse¹ [fjuːz] *v* (*blend*) fusionner; (*melt*) fondre; (*elec*) faire sauter. **fused** *adj* (*plug*) avec fusible incorporé. *n* (*elec*) plomb *m.* **fuse box** boîte à fusibles *f.* **fuse wire** fusible *m.*
fuse² [fjuːz] *v* (*bomb*) amorcer. *n* amorce *f.*
fuselage ['fjuːzəlɑːʒ] *n* fuselage *m.*
fusion ['fjuːʒən] *n* fusion *f.*
fuss [fʌs] *n* façons *f pl*; agitation *f.* **make a fuss** faire des histoires. *v* s'affairer; (*worry*) se tracasser. **fussy** *adj* tatillon, -onne; (*overelaborate*) tarabiscoté.
futile ['fjuːtail] *adj* futile, vain. **futility** *n* futilité *f.*
future ['fjuːtʃə] *n* avenir *m*; (*gramm*) futur *m.* **in future** à l'avenir. *adj* futur, à venir.
futuristic *adj* futuriste.
fuzz [fʌz] *n* (*hair*) cheveux crépus *m pl*; (*on body*) duvet *m*; (*slang: police*) flicaille *f.* **fuzzy** *adj* crépu; (*photo*) flou.

G

gabble ['gabl] *v* brédouiller. *n* baragouin *m.*
gable ['geibl] *n* pignon *m.*
gadget ['gadʒit] *n* gadget *m.*
gag¹ [gag] *v* bâillonner. *n* bâillon *m.*
gag² [gag] (*coll*) *n* (*joke*) plaisanterie *f.* *v* plaisanter.
gaiety ['geiəti] *n* gaieté *f.*
gain [gein] *n* gain *m*, profit *m.* *v* gagner; (*speed, weight*) prendre; (*clock, watch*) avancer.
gait [geit] *n* démarche *f.*
gala ['gɑːlə] *n* gala *m.*
galaxy ['galəksi] *n* galaxie *f.*
gale [geil] *n* coup de vent *m.*
gallant ['galənt] *adj* courageux; noble; (*to women*) galant. **gallantry** *n* courage *m*; galanterie *f.*
gall-bladder ['gɔːl,bladə] *n* vésicule biliaire *f.*
galleon ['galiən] *n* galion *m.*
gallery ['galəri] *n* galerie *f*; (*spectators*) tribune *f*; (*theatre*) dernier balcon *m.*
galley ['gali] *n* (*ship*) galère *f*; (*kitchen*) cuisine *f.*
gallon ['galən] *n* gallon *m.*

gallop ['galəp] *n* galop *m.* *v* galoper.
gallows ['galouz] *n* gibet *m.*
gallstone ['gɔːlstoun] *n* calcul biliaire *m.*
galore [gə'lɔː] *adv* (*coll*) à gogo.
galvanize ['galvənaiz] *v* galvaniser. **galvanize into action** donner le coup de fouet à.
gamble ['gambl] *v* jouer. **gamble on** compter sur. *n* jeu (de hasard) *m*; entreprise risquée *f.* **gambler** *n* joueur, -euse *m, f.* **gambling** *n* jeu *m.*
game [geim] *n* jeu *m*; (*of cards, tennis, etc.*) partie *f*; (*hunting*) gibier *m.* **gamekeeper** *n* garde-chasse *m.* **games** *n* (*school*) sport *m. adj* courageux. **be game for** être prêt à.
gammon ['gamən] *n* jambon salé *m*; (*smoked*) jambon fumé *m.*
gang [gaŋ] *n* bande *f.* *v* **gang up on** se liguer contre. **gangster** *n* gangster *m.*
gangrene ['gaŋgriːn] *n* gangrène *f.*
gangway ['gaŋwei] *n* passage *m*; (*naut*) passerelle *f.*
gaol *V* **jail.**
gap [gap] *n* trou *m*, vide *m.*
gape [geip] *v* (*stare*) rester bouche bée; (*open wide*) bâiller. **gaping** *adj* béant.
garage ['garɑːʒ] *n* garage *m.*
garbage ['gɑːbidʒ] (*US*) *n* ordures *f pl.* **garbage can** poubelle *f.*
garble ['gɑːbl] *v* déformer, embrouiller. **garbled** *adj* confus; incompréhensible.
garden ['gɑːdn] *n* jardin *m.* **garden party** garden-party *f.* **gardens** *pl n* parc *m sing,* jardin public *m sing.* **gardener** *n* jardinier, -ère *m, f.* **gardening** *n* jardinage *m.*
gargle ['gɑːgl] *v* se gargariser. *n* gargarisme *m.*
gargoyle ['gɑːgoil] *n* gargouille *f.*
garland ['gɑːlənd] *n* guirlande *f.* *v* enguirlander.
garlic ['gɑːlik] *n* ail (*pl* aulx) *m.*
garment ['gɑːmənt] *n* vêtement *m.*
garnish ['gɑːniʃ] *v* garnir. *n* garniture *f.*
garrison ['garisn] *n* garnison *f.* *v* mettre en garnison.
garter ['gɑːtə] *n* jarretière *f*; (*for socks*) fixe-chaussette *m*; (*US*) jarretelle *f.* **garter belt** (*US*) porte-jarretelles *m invar.*
gas [gas] *n* gaz *m*; (*US: petrol*) essence *f.* **gasmask** *n* masque à gaz *m.* **gas ring** (*cooker*) brûleur *m.* **gasworks** *n* usine à gaz *f.* *v* asphyxier. **gaseous** *adj* gazeux. **gassy** *adj* gazeux.

gash [gaʃ] *n* entaille *f. v* entailler.
gasket ['gaskit] *n* joint (d'étanchéité) *m.*
gasoline ['gasə,liın] *n* (*US*) essence *f.*
gasp [gaısp] *v* haleter; (*from surprise*) avoir le souffle coupé. *n* halètement *m*; souffle *m.*
gastric ['gastrik] *adj* gastrique. **gastric ulcer** ulcère de l'estomac *m.* **gastroenteritis** *n* gastro-entérite *f.*
gastronomic [gastrə'nomik] *adj* gastronomique. **gastronomy** *n* gastronomie *f.*
gate [geit] *n* (*garden*) porte *f*; (*field*) barrière *f*; (*iron*) grille *f*; (*airport*) sortie *f.* **gatecrash** *v* s'introduire sans invitation. **gateway** *n* porte *f.*
gateau ['gatou] *n* gâteau *m.*
gather ['gaðə] *v* ramasser; (*people*) (se) rassembler; (*sewing*) froncer; (*infer*) déduire. **gathering** *n* rassemblement *m*, réunion *f.*
gaudy ['gɔıdi] *adj* criard.
gauge [geidʒ] *n* (*instrument*) jauge *f*; (*rail*) écartement *m*; (*measurement*) calibre *m. v* jauger, mesurer.
gaunt [gɔınt] *adj* décharné; (*face*) creux; (*grim*) lugubre.
gauze [gɔız] *n* gaze *f.*
gave [geiv] *V* **give**.
gay [gei] *adj* gai; (*slang*) homo. *n* (*slang*) homosexuel, -elle *m, f.*
gaze [geiz] *n* regard fixe *m. v* regarder.
gazelle [gə'zel] *n* gazelle *f.*
gazetteer [gazə'tiə] *n* index géographique *m.*
gear [giə] *n* (*equipment*) matériel *m*; (*belongings*) affaires *f pl*; (*mot*) vitesse *f.* **gearbox** *n* boîte de vitesses *f.* **gear lever** levier de vitesse *m.* **in gear** en prise. *v* adapter; préparer.
geese [giıs] *V* **goose**.
gelatine ['dʒelə,tiın] *n* gélatine *f.*
gelignite ['dʒelig,nait] *n* gélignite *f.*
gem [dʒem] *n* gemme *f*; (*delightful thing*) bijou (*pl* -oux) *m*, perle *f.*
Gemini ['dʒemini] *n* Gémeaux *m pl.*
gender ['dʒendə] *n* genre *m.*
gene [dʒiın] *n* gène *m.*
genealogy [dʒiıni,alədʒi] *n* généalogie *f.* **genealogical** *adj* généalogique.
general ['dʒenərəl] *nm, adj* général. **general election** elections législatives *f pl.* **general hospital** centre hospitalier *m.* **general knowledge** connaissances générales *f pl.* **general practitioner** généraliste

m. **in general** en général. **generalization** *n* généralisation *f.* **generalize** *v* généraliser.
generate ['dʒenəreit] *v* engendrer; produire. **generation** *n* génération *f*; production *f.* **generator** *n* (*elec*) génératrice *f*; (*steam*) générateur *m.*
generic [dʒi'nerik] *adj* générique.
generous ['dʒenərəs] *adj* généreux. **generosity** *n* générosité *f.*
genetic [dʒi'netik] *adj* génétique. **genetics** *n* génétique *f.*
Geneva [dʒi'niıvə] *n* Genève. **Lake Geneva** le lac Léman.
genial ['dʒiıniəl] *adj* cordial.
genital ['dʒenitl] *adj* génital. **genitals** *pl n* organes génitaux *m pl.*
genius ['dʒiınjəs] *n* génie *m.*
genteel [dʒen'tiıl] *adj* distingué.
gentle ['dʒentl] *adj* doux, douce; (*light*) léger. **gentleman** *n* monsieur (*pl* messieurs) *m*; (*courteous man*) gentleman *m.* **gentleness** *n* douceur *f.*
gentry ['dʒentri] *n* petite noblesse *f.*
gents [dʒents] *n* (*sign*) messieurs *m.*
genuine ['dʒenjuin] *adj* véritable, authentique; sincère.
genus ['dʒiınəs] *n* genre *m.*
geography [dʒi'ogrəfi] *n* géographie *f.* **geographer** *n* géographe *m, f.* **geographical** *adj* géographique.
geology [dʒi'olədʒi] *n* géologie *f.* **geological** *adj* géologique. **geologist** *n* géologue *m, f.*
geometry [dʒi'omətri] *n* géométrie *f.* **geometrical** *adj* géométrique.
geranium [dʒə'reiniəm] *n* géranium *m.*
geriatric [dʒeri'atrik] *adj* gériatrique. **geriatrics** *n* gériatrie *f.*
germ [dʒɜım] *n* (*med*) microbe *m*; germe *m.*
Germany ['dʒɜıməni] *n* Allemagne *f.* **German** *nm, adj* allemand; *n* (*people*) Allemand, -e *m, f.* **German measles** rubéole *f.* **Germanic** *adj* germanique.
germinate ['dʒɜımineit] *v* (faire) germer. **germination** *n* germination *f.*
gerund ['dʒerənd] *n* gérondif *m.*
gesticulate [dʒe'stikju,leit] *v* gesticuler. **gesticulation** *n* gesticulation *f.*
gesture ['dʒestʃə] *n* geste *m. v* faire signe.
***get** [get] *v* avoir; obtenir; recevoir; (*fetch*) aller chercher; (*go*) aller; (*become*) devenir. **get across** (*cross*) traverser; communiquer. **get at** (*reach*) atteindre; (*tease*) s'en prendre à. **getaway** *n* fuite *f.*

get back (*return*) revenir; (*recover*) retrouver. **get down** descendre. **get down to** se mettre à. **get off** descendre. **get on** continuer; (*horse, etc.*) monter (*sur*); (*agree*) s'accorder. **get out** sortir. **get up** se lever.

geyser ['giɪzə] *n* geyser *m*; (*water-heater*) chauffe-bain *m invar*.

ghastly ['gaɪstli] *adj* horrible; (*pale*) blême.

gherkin ['gəɪkin] *n* cornichon *m*.

ghetto ['getou] *n* ghetto *m*.

ghost [goust] *n* fantôme *m*. **ghostly** *adj* spectral.

giant ['dʒaiənt] *nm, adj* géant.

gibberish ['dʒibəriʃ] *n* baragouin *m*.

gibe [dʒaib] *n* raillerie *f*. *v* **gibe at** railler.

giblets ['dʒiblits] *pl n* abattis *m pl*.

giddy ['gidi] *adj* (*dizzy*) pris de vertige; (*height*) vertigineux; (*scatterbrained*) étourdi. **giddiness** *n* vertiges *m pl*.

gift [gift] *n* cadeau *m*; (*talent*) don *m*. **gift token** chèque-cadeau *m*. **gifted** *adj* doué.

gigantic [dʒai'gantik] *adj* gigantesque.

giggle ['gigl] *v* rire nerveusement, glousser. *n* gloussement *m*. **get the giggles** avoir le fou rire.

gill [gil] *n* (*fish*) branchie *f*; (*mushroom*) lamelle *f*.

gilt [gilt] *n* dorure *f*. *adj* doré.

gimmick ['gimik] *n* (*coll*) truc *m*.

gin [dʒin] *n* gin *m*.

ginger ['dʒindʒə] *n* gingembre *m*. **gingerbread** *n* pain d'épice *m*. *adj* (*hair*) roux, rousse.

gingerly ['dʒindʒəli] *adv* avec précaution.

gipsy ['dʒipsi] *n* bohémien, -enne *m, f*.

giraffe [dʒi'raɪf] *n* girafe *f*.

girder ['gəɪdə] *n* poutre *f*.

girdle ['gəɪdl] *n* ceinture *f*; (*corset*) gaine *f*. *v* ceindre.

girl [gəɪl] *n* fille *f*; (*pupil*) élève *f*. **girlfriend** *n* petite amie *f*. **girlhood** *n* enfance *f*.

girth [gəɪθ] *n* (*tree*) circonférence *f*; (*waist, etc.*) tour *m*; (*saddle*) sangle *m*.

gist [dʒist] *n* essentiel *m*.

***give** [giv] *v* donner; offrir; céder. **give-and-take** *n* concessions mutuelles *f pl*. **give away** faire cadeau de; révéler. **give back** rendre. **give in** se rendre. **give off** émettre. **give out** distribuer. **give up** abandonner. **give way** céder; (*collapse*) s'affaisser.

given ['givn] *V* **give**.

glacier ['glasiə] *n* glacier *m*. **glaciation** *n* glaciation *f*.

glad [glad] *adj* heureux. **gladden** *v* réjouir. **gladly** *adv* avec plaisir.

glamour [glamə] *n* prestige *m*; éclat *m*; (*person*) fascination *f*. **glamorous** *adj* (*life*) brillant; (*person*) séduisant; (*job*) prestigieux; (*dress*) splendide.

glance [glaɪns] *n* coup d'œil *m*. *v* jeter un coup d'œil.

gland [gland] *n* glande *f*. **glandular** *adj* glandulaire. **glandular fever** mononucléose infectieuse *f*.

glare [gleə] *v* lancer un regard furieux; (*light*) éblouir. *n* regard furieux *m*; éblouissement *m*.

glass [glaɪs] *n* verre *m*. **glasses** *pl n* lunettes *f pl*. **glassworks** *n* verrerie *f*. **glassy** *adj* vitreux.

glaze [gleiz] *v* (*window*) vitrer; (*pottery, etc.*) vernisser; (*cookery*) glacer. *n* vernis *m*; glaçage *m*. **glazier** *n* vitrier *m*.

gleam [gliɪm] *v* luire. *n* lueur *f*. **gleaming** *adj* brillant.

glean [gliɪn] *v* glaner.

glee [gliɪ] *n* joie *f*. **gleeful** *adj* joyeux.

glib [glib] *adj* désinvolte. **glibly** *adv* avec aisance, avec désinvolture.

glide [glaid] *v* (*aero*) planer; (*slide*) glisser. *n* vol plané *m*; glissement *m*. **glider** *n* planeur *m*.

glimmer ['glimə] *v* luire faiblement; miroiter. *n* faible lueur *f*; miroitement *m*.

glimpse [glimps] *v* entrevoir. *n* vision rapide *f*.

glint [glint] *v* étinceler. *n* reflet *m*.

glisten ['glisn] *v* briller.

glitter ['glitə] *v* scintiller. *n* scintillement *m*.

gloat [glout] *v* jubiler.

globe [gloub] *n* globe *m*. **globe artichoke** artichaut *m*. **globe-trotter** *n* globe-trotter *m*. **global** *adj* global; universel.

gloom [gluɪm] *n* obscurité *f*; mélancolie *f*. **gloomy** *adj* sombre, lugubre.

glory ['gloɪri] *n* gloire *f*; splendeur *f*. **glorify** *v* glorifier. **glorious** *adj* magnifique, glorieux.

gloss [glos] *n* lustre *m*; (*paint*) brillant *m*. **glossy** *adj* brillant, lustré.

glossary ['glosəri] *n* glossaire *m*.

glove [glʌv] *n* gant *m*. **glove compartment** vide-poches *m invar*.

glow [glou] *v* rougeoyer. *n* rougeoiement *m*. **glowing** *adj* rougeoyant; (*words*) chaleureux.

glucose ['gluːkous] *n* glucose *m*.

glue [gluː] *n* colle *f*. *v* coller.

glum [glʌm] *adj* triste.

glut [glʌt] *n* surplus *m*.

glutton ['glʌtən] *n* glouton, -onne *m*, *f*. **gluttonous** *adj* glouton. **gluttony** gloutonnerie *f*.

gnarled [naɪld] *adj* noueux.

gnash [naʃ] *v* **gnash one's teeth** grincer les dents.

gnat [nat] *n* moucheron *m*.

gnaw [nɔɪ] *v* ronger. **gnawing** *adj* tenaillant.

gnome [noum] *n* gnome *m*.

***go** [gou] *v* aller; (*leave*) partir; (*work*) marcher; (*become*) devenir; (*make sound*) faire. **go away** s'en aller. **go back** retourner. **go-between** *n* intermédiaire *m*, *f*. **go by** passer; (*judge by*) se fonder sur. **go down** descendre; (*temperature, etc.*) baisser. **go in** entrer. **go off** (*food*) se gâter; (*cease to like*) perdre le goût de. **go on** continuer. **go out** sortir. **go up** monter. **go with** (*match*) s'assortir avec. **go without** se passer de. *n* énergie *f*; (*try*) coup *m*. **it's your go** c'est à toi de jouer. **on the go** sur la brèche.

goad [goud] *v* aiguillonner. *n* aiguillon *m*.

goal [goul] *n* but *m*. **goalkeeper** *n* gardien de but *m*. **goal post** montant de but *m*.

goat [gout] *n* chèvre *f*. **act the goat** (*coll*) faire l'imbécile.

gobble ['gobl] *v* engloutir.

goblin ['goblin] *n* lutin *m*.

god [god] *n* dieu *m*. **goddaughter** *n* filleule *f*. **godfather** *n* parrain *m*. **godmother** *n* marraine *f*. **godsend** *n* aubaine *f*. **godson** *n* filleul *m*. **goddess** *n* déesse *f*.

goggles ['goglz] *pl n* lunettes protectrices *f pl*.

gold [gould] *n* or *m*. **goldfinch** *n* chardonneret *m*. **goldfish** *n* poisson rouge *m*. **goldfish bowl** bocal *m*. **gold mine** mine d'or *f*. **goldsmith** *n* orfèvre *m*. **golden** *adj* d'or, doré. **golden opportunity** occasion magnifique *f*. **golden rule** règle d'or *f*. **golden syrup** mélasse raffinée *f*.

golf [golf] *n* golf *m*. **golf course** terrain de golf *m*. **golfer** *n* golfeur, -euse *m*, *f*.

gondola ['gondələ] *n* gondole *f*. **gondolier** *n* gondolier *m*.

gone [gon] *V* **go**.

gong [goŋ] *n* gong *m*.

gonorrhoea [ˌgonə'riːə] *n* blennorragie *f*.

good [gud] *adj* bon, bonne; (*person*) brave; (*well-behaved*) sage. **good afternoon** bonjour; (*later*) bonsoir. **goodbye** *interj* au revoir. **good evening** bonsoir. **good-for-nothing** *nm*, *adj* propre à rien. **Good Friday** vendredi saint *m*. **good-looking** *adj* beau, belle. **good morning** bonjour. **goodnight** *interj* bonsoir; (*bedtime*) bonne nuit. **goodwill** *n* bonne volonté *f*; (*comm*) incorporels *m pl*. *n* bien *m*. **be no good** ne servir à rien. **for good** pour de bon. **goodness** *n* bonté *f*.

goods [gudz] *pl n* (*comm*) marchandises *f pl*, articles *m pl*; (*law*) biens *m pl*. **goods train** train de marchandises *m*.

goose [guːs] *n*, *pl* **geese** oie *f*.

gooseberry ['guzbəri] *n* (*fruit*) groseille à maquereau *f*; (*bush*) groseiller *m*. **play gooseberry** tenir la chandelle.

gore [gɔɪ] *v* encorner.

gorge [gɔɪdʒ] *n* gorge *f*. *v* se gorger.

gorgeous ['gɔɪdʒəs] *adj* magnifique.

gorilla [gə'rilə] *n* gorille *m*.

gorse [gɔɪs] *n* ajonc *m*.

gory [gɔɪri] *adj* sanglant.

gospel ['gospəl] *n* évangile *m*.

gossip ['gosip] *n* (*chat*) bavardage *m*; (*unkind*) commérage *m*; (*person*) commère *f*. *v* bavarder; (*unkindly*) potiner.

got [got] *V* **get**.

Gothic ['goθik] *adj* gothique.

goulash ['guːlaʃ] *n* goulache *f*.

gourd [guəd] *n* gourde *f*.

gourmet ['guəmei] *n* gourmet *m*.

gout [gaut] *n* goutte *f*.

govern ['gʌvən] *v* gouverner; administrer; déterminer. **governess** *n* gouvernante *f*. **government** *n* gouvernement *m*. **governor** *n* gouverneur *m*; (*school*) administrateur, -trice *m*, *f*; (*coll: boss*) patron *m*.

gown [gaun] *n* robe *f*; (*law, university*) toge *f*.

grab [grab] *v* saisir. *n* mouvement vif pour saisir *m*.

grace [greis] *n* grâce *f*; (*before meal*) bénédicité *m*. **graceful** *adj* gracieux, élégant. **gracious** *adj* gracieux; courtois.

grade [greid] *n* catégorie *f*; échelon *m*; qualité *f*; (*mark*) note *f*. *v* classer.

gradient ['greidiənt] *n* (*measurement*) inclinaison *f*; (*slope*) pente *f*.

gradual ['gradjuǝl] *adj* graduel.

graduate ['gradju,eit; *n, adj* 'gradjuǝt] *v* graduer; (*university*) obtenir sa licence. *n, adj* licencié, -e.

graffiti [grǝ'fiːtiː] *pl n* graffiti *m pl*.

graft [graːft] *n* greffe *f. v* greffer.

grain [grein] *n* grain *m*; (*wood*) fibre *f*.

gram [gram] *n* gramme *m*.

grammar ['gramǝ] *n* grammaire *f*. **grammar school** lycée *m*. **grammatical** *adj* grammatical.

gramophone ['gramǝfoun] *n* phonographe *f*.

granary ['granǝri] *n* grenier *m*.

grand [grand] *adj* magnifique; grandiose. **grandeur** *n* splendeur *f*.

grandchild ['grantʃaild] *n* petit-enfant, petite-enfant *m, f*.

grand-dad ['grandad] *n also* **grandpa** (*coll*) pépé.

granddaughter ['grandɔːtǝ] *n* petite-fille *f*.

grandfather ['gran,faːðǝ] *n* grand-père *m*.

grandma ['granmaː] *n also* **granny** (*coll*) mémé *f*.

grandmother ['gran,mʌðǝ] *n* grande-mère *f*.

grandparent ['gran,peǝrǝnt] *n* grand-parent *m*.

grand piano *n* piano à queue *m*.

grandson ['gransʌn] *n* petit-fils *m*.

grandstand ['granstand] *n* tribune *f*.

grand total *n* somme globale *f*.

granite ['granit] *n* granit *m*.

grant [graːnt] *v* accorder; admettre. *n* subvention *f*; (*student*) bourse *f*.

granule ['granjuːl] *n* granule *m*. **granulated sugar** sucre semoule *m*.

grape [greip] *n* raisin *m*. **grapevine** *n* vigne *f*; (*coll*) téléphone arabe *f*.

grapefruit ['greipfruːt] *n* pamplemousse *m*.

graph [graf] *n* graphique *f*. **graph paper** papier quadrillé *m*; papier millimétré *m*. **graphic** *adj* graphique; (*description*) vivant.

grapple ['grapl] *v* **grapple with** affronter résolument.

grasp [graːsp] *v* saisir. *n* prise *f*; compréhension *f*. **grasping** *adj* avare.

grass [graːs] *n* herbe *f*; (*lawn*) gazon *m*. **grasshopper** *n* sauterelle *f*. **grass snake** couleuvre *f*. **grassy** *adj* herbeux.

grate[1] [greit] *n* grille de foyer *f*. **grating** *n* grille *f*.

grate[2] [greit] *v* (*food*) râper; (*metal*) (faire) grincer. **grater** *n* râpe *f*.

grateful ['greitful] *adj* reconnaissant.

gratify ['grati,fai] *v* satisfaire; faire plaisir à. **gratifying** *adj* agréable.

gratitude ['gratitjuːd] *n* reconnaissance *f*.

gratuity [grǝ'tjuǝti] *n* pourboire *m*.

grave[1] [greiv] *n* tombe *f*. **gravedigger** *n* fossoyeur *m*. **gravestone** *n* pierre tombale *f*. **graveyard** *n* cimetière *m*.

grave[2] [greiv] *adj* grave.

gravel ['gravǝl] *n* gravier *m. v* couvrir de gravier.

gravity ['gravǝti] *n* (*physics*) pesanteur *f*; (*seriousness*) gravité *f*.

gravy ['greivi] *n* jus de viande *m*; sauce *f*.

graze[1] [greiz] *v* (*scrape*) écorcher; (*touch*) frôler. *n* écorchure *f*.

graze[2] [greiz] *v* (*animal*) brouter, paître.

grease [griːs] *n* graisse *f*. **grease-paint** *n* fard gras *m*. **greaseproof paper** papier parcheminé *m. v* graisser. **greasy** *adj* graisseux; (*hair, road*) gras, grasse.

great [greit] *adj* grand; magnifique. **Great Britain** Grande-Bretagne *f*. **greatly** *adv* fort, très. **greatness** *n* grandeur *f*.

Greece [griːs] *n* Grèce *f*. **Greek** *nm, adj* grec, grecque; *n* (*people*) Grec, Grecque *m, f*.

greed [griːd] *n* avidité *f*; (*for food*) gourmandise *f*. **greedy** *adj* avide; (*for food*) vorace.

green [griːn] *adj* vert; naïf, naïve; (*bacon*) non fumé. *n* vert *m*; (*grass*) gazon *m*. **greenfly** *n* puceron *m*. **greengage** *n* reine-claude *f*. **greengrocer's** *n* fruiterie *f*. **greenhouse** *n* serre *f*; **green light** feu vert *m*. **greens** *pl n* légumes verts *m pl*. **have green fingers** avoir le pouce vert. **greenery** *n* verdure *f*.

Greenland ['griːnlǝnd] *n* Groenland *m*. **Greenlander** *n* Groenlandais, -e *m, f*.

greet [griːt] *v* saluer, accueillir. **greeting** *n* salutation *f*. **greetings card** carte de vœux *f*.

gregarious [gri'geǝ,riǝs] *adj* grégaire.

grenade [grǝ'neid] *n* grenade *f*.

grew [gruː] *V* grow.

grey [grei] *nm, adj* gris. **greyhound** *n* lévrier, levrette *m, f*. **go grey** (*hair*) grisonner.

grid [grid] *n* grille *f*; (*elec*) réseau *m*.

grief [griːf] *n* chagrin *m*.

grieve [griːv] *v* (*upset*) peiner; (*sorrow*) s'affliger. **grieve for** pleurer. **grievance** *n* grief *m*; injustice *f*. **grievous** *adj* affreux; grave. **grievous bodily harm** coups et blessures *m pl*.

grill [gril] *v* (faire) griller. *n* gril *m*; (*meal*) grillade *f*. **grillroom** *n* rôtisserie *f*.

grille [gril] *n* grille *f*.

grim [grim] *adj* sinistre; (*coll*) désagréable. **grimly** *adv* d'un air mécontent.

grimace [gri'meis] *n* grimace *f*. *v* grimacer.

grime [graim] *n* crasse *f*. **grimy** *adj* crasseux.

grin [grin] *n* sourire *m*. *v* sourire.

***grind** [graind] *v* (*coffee*, *etc.*) moudre; (*crush*) écraser; (*knife*) aiguiser; (*teeth*) grincer. *n* grincement *m*; (*coll*) boulot *m*. **grinder** *n* broyeur *m*, moulin *m*.

grip [grip] *n* (*of hand*) poigne *f*; (*hold*) prise *f*; (*bag*) trousse *f*. *v* saisir; (*hold*) serrer; (*tyres*) adhérer. **gripping** *adj* passionnant.

gripe [graip] *n* colique *f*. *v* (*coll*) rouspéter.

grisly ['grizli] *adj* macabre; horrible.

gristle ['grisl] *n* cartilage *m*. **gristly** *adj* cartilagineux.

grit [grit] *n* sable *m*; gravillon *m*; (*coll: courage*) cran *m*. *v* (*teeth*) serrer; (*road*) répandre du gravillon sur.

groan [groun] *n* (*pain*) gémissement *m*; (*dismay*) grognement *m*. *v* gémir; grogner.

grocer ['grousə] *n* épicier, -ère *m, f*. **grocer's** *n* (*shop*) épicerie *f*. **groceries** *pl n* provisions *f pl*.

groin [groin] *n* aine *f*.

groom [gruːm] *n* (*for horse*) palefrenier *m*; (*of bride*) marié *m*. *v* (*horse*) panser; préparer.

groove [gruːv] *n* cannelure *f*, rainure *f*; (*record*) sillon *m*. *v* canneler.

grope [group] *v* tâtonner. **grope for** chercher à tâtons.

gross [grous] *adj* (*not net*) brut; flagrant; obèse; (*coarse*) grossier. *n* grosse *f*.

grotesque [grə'tesk] *nm, adj* grotesque.

grotto ['grotou] *n* grotte *f*.

ground¹ [graund] *V* **grind**.

ground² [graund] *n* terre *f*; (*area*) terrain *m*. **ground floor** rez-de-chaussée *m*. **ground frost** gelée blanche *f*. **grounds** *pl n* parc *m sing*; motifs *m pl*; (*coffee*) marc *m sing*. **groundsheet** *n* tapis de sol *m*. **groundwork** *n* base *f*. *v* (*aircraft*) retenir

au sol; fonder; (*ship*) s'échouer. **groundless** *adj* sans fond.

group [gruːp] *n* groupe *m*. *v* (se) grouper.

grouse¹ [graus] *n* grouse *f*.

grouse² [graus] (*coll*) *v* rouspéter. *n* grief *m*.

grove [grouv] *n* bocage *m*.

grovel ['grovl] *v* ramper.

***grow** [grou] *v* pousser; grandir; (*become*) devenir; cultiver. **grown-up** *n*(*m+f*), *adj* adulte. **growth** *n* croissance *f*; (*thing grown*) pousse *f*; (*med*) grosseur *f*.

growl [graul] *v* grogner. *n* grognement *m*.

grown [groun] *V* **grow**.

grub [grʌb] *n* larve *f*; (*slang: food*) bouffe *f*. **grubby** *adj* sale.

grudge [grʌdʒ] *v* donner à contre-cœur. *n* rancune *f*. **bear a grudge against** en vouloir à. **grudgingly** *adv* de mauvaise grâce.

gruelling ['gruəliŋ] *adj* exténuant.

gruesome ['gruːsəm] *adj* horrible.

gruff [grʌf] *adj* bourru.

grumble ['grʌmbl] *v* grommeler. *n* grognement *m*.

grumpy ['grʌmpi] *adj* maussade.

grunt [grʌnt] *v* grogner. *n* grognement *m*.

guarantee [garən'tiː] *n* garantie *f*. *n* garantir. **guarantor** *n* garant, -e *m, f*.

guard [gaːd] *n* garde *f*; (*rail*) chef de train *m*. **guard dog** chien de garde *m*. **guard's van** fourgon *m*. *v* garder; défendre. **guarded** *adj* (*remark*, *etc.*) prudent. **guardian** *n* gardien, -enne *m, f*; (*of child*) tuteur, -trice *m, f*. **guardian angel** ange gardien *m*.

Guernsey ['gəːnzi] *n* Guernesey *m*.

guerrilla [gə'rilə] *n* guérillero *m*. **guerrilla warfare** guérilla *f*.

guess [ges] *n* conjecture *f*. **at a guess** au jugé. **guesswork** *n* conjecture *f*. *v* deviner; estimer; supposer; (*believe*) croire.

guest [gest] *n* invité, -e *m, f*; (*hotel*) client, -e *m, f*. **guesthouse** *n* pension de famille *f*. **guest room** chambre d'ami *f*.

guide [gaid] *n* guide *m*; manuel *m*; (*girl*) éclaireuse *f*. **guidebook** *n* guide *m*. **guide dog** chien d'aveugle *m*. *v* guider. **guidance** *n* conseils *m pl*. **guided** *adj* (*missile*) téléguidé. **guided tour** visite guidée *f*.

guild [gild] *n* confrérie *f*; (*craftsmen*, *etc.*) guilde *f*.

guillotine ['gilətiːn] *n* (*beheading*) guillotine *f*; (*paper*) massicot *m*. *v* guillotiner; massicoter.

guilt [gilt] n culpabilité f. guilty adj coupable.

Guinea ['gini] n Guinée f.

guinea pig n cochon d'Inde m; (for experiment) cobaye m.

guitar [gi'taɪ] n guitare f. guitarist n guitariste m, f.

gulf [gʌlf] n golfe m; (abyss) gouffre m.

gull [gʌl] n mouette f.

gullet ['gʌlit] n œsophage m; (throat) gosier m.

gullible ['gʌləbl] adj crédule. gullibility n crédulité f.

gully ['gʌli] n ravine f.

gulp [gʌlp] v avaler; (food) engloutir; (drink) lamper. n (food) bouchée f; (drink) gorgée f; (action) coup (de gosier) m.

gum¹ [gʌm] n (glue) gomme f. gumboots pl n bottes de caoutchouc f pl. v gommer.

gum² [gʌm] n (mouth) gencive f.

gun [gʌn] n pistolet m; (rifle) fusil m. gunfire n fusillade f. gunman n bandit armé m. gunpowder n poudre à canon f. gunrunning n contrebande d'armes f. gunshot wound blessure de balle f.

gurgle ['gɔɪgl] n gargouillis m. v gargouiller.

gush [gʌʃ] v jaillir. n jaillissement m. gushing adj (person) trop exubérant.

gust [gʌst] n (wind) rafale f; (smoke) bouffée f; (laughter) éclat m. v souffler en bourrasque.

gut [gʌt] n (anat) boyau m. guts pl n (coll) cran m sing. v vider.

gutter ['gʌtə] n (roof) gouttière f; (street) caniveau m.

guy¹ [gai] n (coll) type m.

guy² [gai] n (rope) corde de tente f.

gymnasium [dʒim'neiziəm] n gymnase m. gymnast n gymnaste m, f. gymnastic adj gymnastique. gymnastics n gymnastique f.

gynaecology [gainə'kolədʒi] n gynécologie f. gynaecological adj gynécologique. gynaecologist n gynécologue m, f.

gypsum ['dʒipsəm] n gypse m.

gyrate [,dʒai'reit] v tournoyer. gyration n giration f.

gyroscope ['dʒairə,skoup] n gyroscope m.

H

haberdasher ['habədaʃə] n mercier, -ère m, f. haberdashery n mercerie f.

habit ['habit] n habitude f; (clothes) habit m. habitual adj habituel.

habitable ['habitəbl] adj habitable.

habitat ['habitat] n habitat m.

hack¹ [hak] v hacher, tailler. n entaille f. hacksaw n scie à métaux f.

hack² [hak] n (horse) cheval de selle m; (writer) nègre m.

hackneyed ['haknid] adj usé, rebattu.

had [had] V have.

haddock ['hadək] n églefin m.

haemorrhage ['heməridʒ] n hémorragie f.

haemorrhoids ['heməroidz] pl n hémorroïdes f pl.

hag [hag] n (coll) chameau m.

haggard ['hagəd] adj hagard.

haggle ['hagl] v marchander, chicaner. haggling n marchandage m.

Hague [heig] n The Hague La Haye.

hail¹ [heil] n grêle f. hailstone n grêlon m. v grêler.

hail² [heil] v saluer; (taxi) héler. hail from être originaire de.

hair [heə] n cheveux m pl; (single strand) cheveu m; (of body, animal) poil m; (animal coat) pelage m. hairy adj velu; (person) hirsute.

hairbrush ['heəbrʌʃ] n brosse à cheveux f.

haircut ['heəkʌt] n coupe f. have a haircut se faire couper les cheveux.

hairdresser ['heə,dresə] n coiffeur, -euse m, f. hairdresser's n salon de coiffure m. hairdressing n coiffure f.

hair-dryer ['heə,draiə] n sèche-cheveux m.

hairnet ['heənet] n filet à cheveux m.

hair-piece ['heə,piːs] n postiche m.

hairpin ['heəpin] n épingle à cheveux f. hairpin bend virage en épingle à cheveux m.

hair-raising ['heə,reiziŋ] adj horrifique.

hair spray n laque f.

hairstyle ['heəstail] n coiffure f.

Haiti ['heiti] n Haïti f.

hake [heik] n colin m.

half [haːf] n moitié f; demi, -e m, f. go halves se mettre de moitié. in half en deux. adj demi. adv à moitié, à demi.

half-and-half adv moitié-moitié.

half-baked [ˌhɑːfˈbeikt] (*coll*) *adj* (*idea*) à la noix; (*person*) mal dégrossi.

half-breed ['hɑːfbriːd] *n* (*person*) métis, -isse *m, f*; (*horse*) demi-sang *m invar*.

half-hearted [ˌhɑːfˈhɑːtid] *adj* (*person*) sans enthousiasme; (*attempt*) sans conviction.

half-hour [ˌhɑːfˈauə] *n* demi-heure *f*.

half-mast [ˌhɑːfˈmɑːst] *n* **at half-mast** en berne.

half-open [ˌhɑːfˈoupən] *adj* entrouvert.

half-price [ˌhɑːfˈprais] *adj, adv* demi-tarif; à moitié prix.

half-term [ˌhɑːfˈtɜːm] *n* congé de demi-trimestre *m*.

half-time [ˌhɑːfˈtaim] *adv, adj* à mi-temps.

halfway [ˌhɑːfˈwei] *adj* à mi-chemin. **meet halfway** (*compromise*) couper la poire en deux.

half-wit ['hɑːfwit] *n* idiot, -e *m, f*.

halibut ['halibət] *n* flétan *m*.

hall [hɔːl] *n* vestibule *m*; (*room*) salle *f*; (*corridor*) couloir *m*.

hallmark ['hɔːlmɑːk] *n* poinçon *m*; (*of genius, etc.*) sceau *m*. *v* poinçonner.

hallowed ['haloud] *adj* saint, sanctifié.

Halloween [halou'iːn] *n* veille de la Toussaint *f*.

hallucination [həˌluːsiˈneiʃən] *n* hallucination *f*.

halo ['heilou] *n* auréole *f*; (*astron*) halo *m*.

halt [hɔːlt] *n* halte *f*. *v* faire halte; (*car, etc.*) faire arrêter; interrompre.

halter ['hɔːltə] *n* licou *m*.

halve [hɑːv] *v* diviser en deux; réduire de moitié.

ham [ham] *n* jambon *m*.

hamburger ['hambɜːgə] *n* hamburger *m*.

hammer ['hamə] *n* marteau *m*. *v* marteler. **hammer in** enfoncer. **hammer out** (*disputes, etc.*) démêler.

hammock ['hamək] *n* hamac *m*.

hamper[1] ['hampə] *v* gêner.

hamper[2] ['hampə] *n* panier *m*.

hamster ['hamstə] *n* hamster *m*.

hand [hand] *n* main *f*; (*worker*) travailleur, -euse *m, f*; (*clock*) aiguille *f*; (*measure*) paume *f*; (*coll: assistance*) coup de main *m*. **by hand** à la main. **keep one's hand in** garder la main. **on the other hand** par contre. **to hand** sous la main. *v* passer. **hand down** transmettre. **hand in** remettre. **hand over** céder. **handful** *n* poignée *f*.

handbag ['handbag] *n* sac à main *m*.

handbook ['handbuk] *n* manuel *m*; guide *m*.

handbrake ['handbreik] *n* frein à main *m*.

handcuff ['handkʌf] *v* mettre les menottes à. **handcuffs** *pl n* menottes *f pl*.

handicap ['handikap] *n* handicap *m*. *v* handicaper.

handicraft ['handikrɑːft] *n* artisanat *m*.

handiwork ['handiwɜːk] *n* œuvre *f*, ouvrage *m*.

handkerchief ['haŋkətʃif] *n* mouchoir *m*.

handle ['handl] *n* (*broom, etc.*) manche *m*; (*door, drawer*) poignée *f*; (*basket*) anse *f*. *v* manier; (*control*) manœuvrer. **handlebars** *pl n* guidon *m sing*.

handmade [ˌhandˈmeid] *adj* fait main.

hand-out ['handaut] *n* (*leaflet*) prospectus *m*; charité *f*. *v* **hand out** distribuer.

hand-pick [handˈpik] *v* trier sur le volet.

handrail ['handreil] *n* rampe *f*.

handshake ['handʃeik] *n* poignée de main *f*.

handsome ['hansəm] *adj* beau, belle.

handstand ['handˌstand] *n* **do a handstand** faire l'arbre droit.

handwriting ['handˌraitiŋ] *n* écriture *f*. **handwritten** *adj* manuscrit.

handy ['handi] *adj* (*useful*) commode; accessible; (*to hand*) sous la main; adroit.

*****hang** [haŋ] *v* pendre; (*picture, etc.*) accrocher. **hang around** rôder. **hang fire** traîner en longueur. **hang-gliding** *n* vol libre *m*. **hangman** *n* bourreau *m*. **hang on** (*coll: wait*) attendre; (*hold out*) tenir bon; dépendre de. **hangover** *n* (*slang*) gueule de bois *f*. **hang up** accrocher; (*phone*) raccrocher. **hang-up** *n* (*coll*) complexe *m*.

hanger *n* cintre *m*.

hangar ['haŋə] *n* hangar *m*.

hanker ['haŋkə] *v* **hanker for** *or* **after** aspirer à. **hankering** *n* envie *f*.

haphazard [ˌhapˈhazəd] *adj* (*fait*) au petit bonheur.

happen ['hapən] *v* arriver, se passer. **happening** *n* événement *m*.

happy ['hapi] *adj* heureux. **happy birthday/Christmas!** joyeux anniversaire/Noël! **happy-go-lucky** *adj* insouciant. **happily** *adv* tranquillement; joyeusement. **happiness** *n* bonheur *m*.

harass ['harəs] *v* harceler.

harbour ['hɑːbə] *n* port *m*. *v* héberger; (*hope, suspicions, etc.*) entretenir.

hard [haɪd] *adj* dur; difficile. *adv* fort, ferme. **hard-and-fast** *adj* (*rule*) absolu; inflexible. **hardback** *n* livre relié *m*. **hardboiled** *adj* (*egg*) dur. **hard-hearted** *adj* impitoyable. **hard up** (*coll*) fauché. **hardware** *n* (*ironmongery*) quincaillerie *f*; (*computers*) hardware *m*. **try hard** faire un gros effort. **work hard** travailler dur. **harden** *v* durcir. **hardness** *n* dureté *f*; difficulté *f*. **hardship** *n* épreuves *f pl*; privation *f*.

hardly ['haɪdli] *adv* à peine.

hardy ['haɪdi] *adj* robuste; (*plant*) résistant au gel; (*bold*) hardi.

hare [heə] *n* lièvre *m*. **hare-brained** *adj* (*person*) écervelé; (*scheme*) insensé. **harelip** *n* bec-de-lièvre *m*.

haricot ['harikou] *n* haricot blanc *m*.

harm [haɪm] *n* mal *m*. *v* faire du mal à. **harmful** *adj* nuisible. **harmless** *adj* innocent; pas méchant.

harmonic [haɪ'monik] *nm*, *adj* harmonique.

harmonica [haɪ'monikə] *n* harmonica *m*.

harmonize ['haɪmənaiz] *v* (s')harmoniser.

harmony ['haɪməni] *n* harmonie *f*. **harmonious** *adj* harmonieux.

harness ['haɪnis] *n* harnais *m*. *v* harnacher; (*power, etc.*) exploiter.

harp [haɪp] *n* harpe *f*. **harpist** *n* harpiste *m, f*.

harpoon [haɪ'puɪn] *n* harpon *m*. *v* harponner.

harpsichord ['haɪpsi,koɪd] *n* clavecin *m*.

harrowing ['harouiŋ] *adj* poignant; (*cry*) déchirant.

harsh [haɪʃ] *adj* dur; (*texture*) rêche, rugueux; (*sound*) discordant, criard. **harshness** *n* dureté *f*; rugosité *f*; discordance *f*.

harvest ['haɪvist] *n* moisson *f*; (*fruit*) récolte *f*; (*grapes*) vendange *f*. *v* moissonner; récolter; vendanger.

has [haz] *V* have.

hash [haʃ] *n* (*food*) hachis *m*; (*coll: mess*) gâchis *m*.

hashish ['haʃi:ʃ] *n* haschisch *m*.

haste [heist] *n* hâte *f*. **hasten** *v* (se) hâter. **hastily** *adv* en hâte; sans réfléchir. **hasty** *adj* hâtif; rapide.

hat [hat] *n* chapeau *m*.

hatch[1] [hatʃ] *v* (faire) éclore; (*plot*) ourdir.

hatch[2] [hatʃ] *n* (*canteen*) passe-plats *m invar*; (*naut*) écoutille *f*. **hatchback** *adj* (*car*) avec hayon arrière *m*.

hatchet ['hatʃit] *n* hachette *f*.

hate [heit] *v* haïr, détester. *n also* **hatred** haine *f*. **pet hate** (*coll*) bête noire *f*. **hateful** *adj* haïssable, odieux.

haughty ['hoɪti] *adj* hautain. **haughtiness** *n* hauteur *f*.

haul [hoɪl] *v* traîner; (*naut*) haler. *n* (*fish*) prise *f*; (*stolen goods*) butin *m*. **haulage** *n* (*transport*) roulage *m*; (*naut*) halage *m*.

haunch [hoɪntʃ] *n* hanche *f*. **haunches** *pl n* derrière *m sing*.

haunt [hoɪnt] *v* hanter. *n* repaire *m*. **haunting** *adj* obsédant.

*have [hav] *v* avoir; (*meal*) prendre; (*cause to be*) faire. **have on** (*wear*) porter; (*coll: tease*) faire marcher. **have to** devoir, être obligé de.

haven ['heivn] *n* havre *m*.

haversack ['havəsak] *n* havresac *m*, sac à dos *m*.

havoc ['havək] *n* ravages *m pl*. **play havoc with** désorganiser complètement.

hawk [hoɪk] *n* faucon *m*.

hawthorn ['hoɪθoɪn] *n* aubépine *f*.

hay [hei] *n* foin *m*. **go haywire** (*plans*) mal tourner; (*machine*) se détraquer. **hay fever** rhume des foins *m*. **haystack** *n* meule de foin *f*.

hazard ['hazəd] *n* risque *m*; (*chance*) hasard *m*. *v* hasarder, risquer. **hazardous** *adj* hasardeux, risqué.

haze [heiz] *n* brume *f*. **hazy** *adj* brumeux; vague.

hazel ['heizl] *n* noisetier *m*. **hazel-nut** *n* noisette *f*. *adj* (*colour*) noisette *invar*.

he [hiɪ] *pron* il; (*emphatic*) lui. **he who** celui qui. *n* (*coll*) mâle *m*.

head [hed] *n* tête *f*; (*leader*) chef *m*; (*coin*) face *f*. *adj* principal. *v* se diriger; venir en tête de; intituler. **headed** *adj* (*paper*) à en-tête. **heading** *n* titre *m*. **heady** *adj* capiteux.

headache ['hedeik] *n* mal de tête *m*. **have a headache** avoir mal à la tête.

headfirst [,hed'fɔɪst] *adv* la tête la première.

headlamp ['hedlamp] *n also* **headlight** (*mot*) phare *m*.

headland ['hedlənd] *n* promontoire *m*.

headline ['hedlain] *n* (*newspaper*) manchette *f*; (*news*) grand titre *m*.

headlong ['hedloŋ] *adv* la tête la première; (*rush*) à toute allure.

headmaster [ˌhed'maɪstə] *n* directeur *m*.
headmistress *n* directrice *f*.
head-on *adj, adv* de plein fouet.
headphones ['hedfounz] *n* casque *m sing*.
headquarters [ˌhed'kwɔɪtəz] *n* bureau principal *m*.
headrest ['hedrest] *n* appui-tête *m*.
headscarf ['hedskaɪf] *n* foulard *m*.
headstrong ['hedstrɔŋ] *adj* têtu.
headway ['hedwei] *n* progrès *m*.
heal [hiːl] *v* guérir; (*wound*) (se) cicatriser.
health [helθ] *n* santé *f*. **health foods** aliments naturels *m pl*. **healthy** *adj* sain, en bonne santé; (*appetite*) robuste.
heap [hiːp] *n* tas *m*. *v* entasser, empiler.
*hear [hiə] *v* entendre. **hear from** avoir des nouvelles de. **hear of** entendre parler de. **hearing** *n* (*sense*) ouïe *f*; audition *f*. **hearing aid** appareil acoustique *m*. **hearsay** *n* ouï-dire *m invar*.
heard [hɔɪd] *V* **hear**.
hearse [hɔɪs] *n* corbillard *m*.
heart [haɪt] *n* cœur *m*. **by heart** par cœur. **set one's heart on** vouloir à tout prix. **to one's heart's content** tout son content. **hearten** *v* encourager. **heartless** *adj* cruel. **hearty** *adj* (*welcome, etc.*) chaleureux; (*meal*) copieux.
heart attack *n* crise cardiaque *f*.
heartbeat ['haɪtbiɪt] *n* battement de cœur *m*.
heart-breaking ['haɪtbreikiŋ] *adj* navrant. **heart-broken** *adj* navré.
heartburn ['haɪtbɜɪn] *n* brûlures d'estomac *f pl*.
heart failure *n* arrêt du cœur *m*.
heartfelt ['haɪtfelt] *adj* sincère.
hearth [haɪθ] *n* foyer *m*. **hearthrug** *n* devant de foyer *m*.
heart-throb ['haɪtθrob] *n* (*coll*) idole *f*.
heart-to-heart *adj, adv* à cœur ouvert. *n* **have a heart-to-heart** parler à cœur ouvert.
heartwarming ['haɪtwɔɪmiŋ] *adj* réconfortant.
heat [hiɪt] *n* chaleur *f*; (*sport*) épreuve éliminatoire *f*. **heatwave** *n* vague de chaleur *f*. *v* chauffer. **heated** *adj* chauffé; (*argument*) passionné. **heater** *n* appareil de chauffage *m*. **heating** *n* chauffage *m*.
heath [hiɪθ] *n* lande *f*.
heathen ['hiɪðn] *n, adj* païen, -enne.
heather ['heðə] *n* bruyère *f*.
heave [hiɪv] *v* (*lift*) lever avec effort; (*pull*)

tirer avec effort; (*sea*) se soulever; (*sigh*) pousser; (*retch*) avoir des haut-le-cœur. *n* (*sea*) houle *f*; haut-le-cœur *m invar*; effort *m*.
heaven ['hevn] *n* ciel *m*. **heavenly** *adj* céleste; (*excellent*) divin.
heavy ['hevi] *adj* lourd; (*rain*) fort; (*cold*) gros, grosse. **heavyweight** *nm, adj* poids lourd. **heaviness** *n* lourdeur *f*.
Hebrew ['hiɪbruɪ] *n* (*people*) Hébreu *m*, (*language*) hébreu *m*. *adj* hébreu, hébraïque.
heckle ['hekl] *v* chahuter; interrompre. **heckler** *n* interrupteur, -trice *m, f*. **heckling** *n* interpellations *f pl*.
hectare ['hektaɪ] *n* hectare *m*.
hectic ['hektik] *adj* mouvementé, très bousculé.
hedge [hedʒ] *n* haie *f*. *v* entourer d'une haie; (*be evasive*) répondre à côté; (*bet*) couvrir.
hedgehog ['hedʒhog] *n* hérisson *m*.
heed [hiɪd] *v* faire attention à. *n* attention *f*. **heedless** *adj* étourdi, insouciant.
heel [hiɪl] *n* talon *m*. *v* (*shoe*) remettre un talon à.
hefty ['hefti] *adj* (*person*) costaud; (*heavy*) lourd; (*large*) gros, grosse.
heifer ['hefə] *n* génisse *f*.
height [hait] *n* hauteur *f*; (*person*) taille *f*; (*aircraft*) altitude *f*; (*of success, etc.*) sommet *m*, point culminant *m*. **heighten** *v* augmenter; (*make higher*) relever.
heir [eə] *n* héritier *m*. **heiress** *n* héritière *f*.
heirloom *n* héritage *m*.
held [held] *V* **hold**.
helicopter ['helikoptə] *n* hélicoptère *m*.
hell [hel] *n* enfer *m*. **go to hell!** (*impol*) va te faire voir! **hell for leather** au triple galop. **hellish** *adj* infernal.
hello [hə'lou] *interj* bonjour! (*coll*) salut! (*phone*) allô!
helm [helm] *n* barre *f*. **be at the helm** tenir la barre.
helmet ['helmit] *n* casque *m*.
help [help] *n* aide *f*, secours *m*. *interj* au secours! *v* aider; (*at meal, etc.*) servir; (*prevent oneself from*) s'empêcher de. **can I help you?** (*in shop*) vous désirez? **help yourself!** servez-vous! **it can't be helped!** tant pis! **helper** *n* aide *m, f*. **helpful** *adj* utile, efficace. **helping** *n* portion *f*. **helpless** *adj* impuissant.
Helsinki [hel'siŋki] *n* Helsinki.

hem [hem] *n* ourlet *m*. *v* ourler.

hemisphere ['hemi,sfiə] *n* hémisphère *m*.

hemp [hemp] *n* (*plant*) chanvre *m*; (*drug*) haschish *m*.

hen [hen] *n* poule *f*; femelle *f*. **henhouse** *n* poulailler *m*. **hen party** réunion de femmes *f*. **henpecked** *adj* mené par le bout du nez.

hence [hens] *adv* (*therefore*) d'où; (*from now*) d'ici. **henceforth** *adv* désormais.

henna ['henə] *n* henné *m*.

her [həɪ] *pron* elle; (*direct object*) la; (*indirect object*) lui. *adj* son, sa; (*pl*) ses.

herald ['herəld] *n* héraut *m*. *v* annoncer. **heraldic** *adj* héraldique. **heraldry** *n* héraldique *f*.

herb [həɪb] *n* herbe *f*. **herbal** *adj* d'herbes.

herd [həɪd] *n* troupeau *m*. *v* mener. **herd together** s'attrouper.

here [hiə] *adv* ici. **hereafter** *adv* ci-après. **here and now** en ce moment même. **here and there** ça et là. **here goes!** allons-y! **here is/are** voici. **here, there, and everywhere** un peu partout.

hereditary [hi'redətəri] *adj* héréditaire.

heredity [hi'redəti] *n* hérédité *f*.

heresy ['herəsi] *n* hérésie *f*. **heretic** *n* hérétique *m*, *f*. **heretical** *adj* hérétique.

heritage ['heritidʒ] *n* héritage *m*.

hermit ['həɪmit] *n* ermite *m*.

hernia ['həɪniə] *n* hernie *f*.

hero ['hiərou] *n* héros *m*. **heroine** *n* héroïne *f*. **hero-worship** *n* culte du héros *m*. **heroic** *adj* héroïque. **heroism** *n* héroïsme *m*.

heroin ['herouin] *n* héroïne *f*.

heron ['herən] *n* héron *m*.

herring ['heriŋ] *n* hareng *m*.

hers [həɪz] *pron* le sien, la sienne.

herself [həɪ'self] *pron* se; (*emphatic*) elle-même. **by herself** toute seule.

hesitate ['heziteit] *v* hésiter. **hesitant** *adj* hésitant. **hesitation** *n* hésitation *f*.

heterosexual [hetərə'sekʃuəl] *n*, *adj* hétérosexuel, -elle.

hexagon ['heksəgən] *n* hexagone *m*. **hexagonal** *adj* hexagonal.

heyday ['heidei] *n* (*of person*) apogée *m*; (*of thing*) âge d'or *m*.

hiatus [hai'eitəs] *n* lacune *f*.

hibernate ['haibəneit] *v* hiberner. **hibernation** *n* hibernation *f*.

hiccup ['hikʌp] *n* hoquet *m*. **have hiccups** avoir le hoquet. *v* hoqueter.

hid [hid] *V* **hide**[1].

***hide**[1] [haid] *v* (se) cacher. **hide-and-seek** *n* cache-cache *m*. **hide-out** *n* cachette *f*.

hide[2] [haid] *n* peau *f*; (*leather*) cuir *m*.

hidden ['hidn] *V* **hide**[1].

hideous ['hidiəs] *adj* hideux.

hiding[1] ['haidiŋ] *n* **be in hiding** se tenir caché. **go into hiding** se cacher. **hiding place** cachette *f*.

hiding[2] ['haidiŋ] *n* (*beating*) correction *f*.

hierarchy ['haiəraɪki] *n* hiérarchie *f*. **hierarchical** *adj* hiérarchique.

hi-fi ['haifai] *n* hi-fi *f invar*; (*system*) chaîne hi-fi *f*.

high [hai] *adj* haut; (*speed*) grand; (*price, etc.*) élevé. *adv* (en) haut. **highly** *adv* (*very*) fort; (*recommend*) chaudement.

highbrow ['haibrau] *n*, *adj* intellectuel, -elle.

high chair *n* chaise haute *f*.

high-frequency [,hai'friːkwənsi] *adj* de haute fréquence.

high-heeled [,hai'hiːld] *adj* à hauts talons.

high jump *n* saut en hauteur *m*.

highland ['hailənd] *n* région montagneuse *f*. **the Highlands** (*Scotland*) les Highlands *m pl*.

highlight ['hailait] *v* mettre en lumière. *n* (*art*) rehaut *m*; (*hair*) reflet *m*; (*of evening, etc.*) clou *m*.

Highness ['hainis] *n* Altesse *f*.

high-pitched [,hai'pitʃd] *adj* aigu, -uë.

high-rise block *n* tour *f*.

high-speed [,hai'spiːd] *adj* ultra-rapide.

high-spirited [,hai'spiritid] *adj* plein d'entrain. **high spirits** entrain *m*.

high street *n* rue principale *f*.

highway ['haiwei] *n* grande route *f*; voie publique *f*. **highway code** code de la route *m*. **highwayman** *n* voleur de grand chemin *m*.

hijack ['haidʒak] *v* détourner. *n* détournement *m*.

hike [haik] *n* excursion à pied *f*. *v* excursionner à pied. **hiker** *n* excursionniste *n*, pied *m*, *f*. **hiking** *n* randonnées à pied *f pl*.

hilarious [hi'leəriəs] *adj* (*merry*) hilare; (*funny*) désopilant. **hilarity** *n* hilarité *f*.

hill [hil] *n* colline *f*; (*slope*) côte *f*. **hillside** *n* flanc de coteau *m*. **hilly** *adj* accidenté.

him [him] *pron* lui; (*direct object*) le.

himself [him'self] *pron* se; (*emphatic*) lui-même. **by himself** tout seul.

hind [haind] *adj* postérieur, -e; de derrière. **hindsight** *n* sagesse rétrospective *f*.
hinder ['hində] *v* gêner, entraver. **hindrance** *n* gêne *f*, entrave *f*.
Hindu [hin'duː] *n* Hindou, -e *m*, *f*. *adj* hindou. **Hinduism** *n* hindouisme *m*.
hinge [hindʒ] *n* charnière *f*; (*door*) gond *m*. *v* **hinge on** dépendre de.
hint [hint] *n* allusion *f*; (*tip*) conseil *m*; (*trace*) nuance *f*. *v* laisser entendre, insinuer.
hip [hip] *n* hanche *f*.
hippopotamus [hipə'potəməs] *n* hippopotame *m*.
hire [haiə] *v* louer; (*person*) engager. **hire out** louer. *n* location *f*; (*boat*) louage *m*. **for hire** à louer. **hire purchase** achat à crédit *m*.
his [hiz] *adj* son, sa; (*pl*) ses. *pron* le sien, la sienne.
hiss [his] *v* siffler. *n* sifflement *m*.
history ['histəri] *n* histoire *f*. **historian** *n* historien, -enne *m*, *f*. **historic** *adj* historique.
*hit [hit] *n* coup *m*; succès *m*, coup réussi *m*; (*slang: song*) tube *m*. *v* frapper; (*bump*) (se) heurter; (*reach*) atteindre. **hit-or-miss** *adv* au petit bonheur.
hitch [hitʃ] *n* (*obstacle*) anicroche *f*. *v* (*lift*) remonter; (*fasten*) accrocher. **hitch-hike** *v* faire du stop. **hitch-hiker** *n* auto-stoppeur, -euse *m*, *f*. **hitch-hiking** *n* auto-stop *m*.
hitherto [ˌhiðə'tuː] *adv* jusqu'ici.
hive [haiv] *n* ruche *f*.
hoard [hɔːd] *n* réserve *f*; trésor *m*. *v* amasser.
hoarding ['hɔːdiŋ] *n* (*advertising*) panneau d'affichage *m*; (*fence*) palissade *f*.
hoarse [hɔːs] *adj* enroué, rauque. **hoarsely** *adv* d'une voix rauque. **hoarseness** *n* enrouement *m*.
hoax [houks] *n* canular *m*.
hobble ['hobl] *v* clopiner; (*horse*) entraver.
hobby ['hobi] *n* passe-temps *m*.
hock[1] [hok] *n* jarret *m*.
hock[2] [hok] *n* vin du Rhin *m*.
hockey ['hoki] *n* hockey *m*. **hockey stick** crosse de hockey *f*.
hoe [hou] *n* houe *f*. *v* biner.
hog [hog] *n* porc *m*. *v* (*coll*) accaparer, monopoliser.
hoist [hoist] *v* hisser. *n* treuil *m*; (*for goods*) monte-charge *m invar*.

*hold[1] [hould] *n* prise *f*; influence *f*. **get hold of** saisir. *v* tenir; contenir; (*have*) avoir. **holdall** *n* fourre-tout *m invar*. **hold back** (se) retenir. **hold forth** pérorer. **hold on** (*wait*) attendre; maintenir en place; (*grip*) tenir bon. **hold out** tendre; (*resist*) tenir bon. **hold up** (*raise*) lever; (*support*) soutenir; (*delay*) retarder. **hold-up** *n* retard *m*; (*traffic*) bouchon *m*; (*robbery*) hold-up *m invar*. **holder** *n* (*person*) détenteur, -trice *m*, *f*; (*for object*) support *m*.
hold[2] [hould] *n* (*naut*) cale *f*.
hole [houl] *n* trou *m*; (*rabbit*) terrier *m*. *v* (se) trouer.
holiday ['holədi] *n* vacances *f pl*; (*day off*) jour de congé *m*. **holiday-maker** *n* vacancier, -ère *m*, *f*. **holiday resort** villégiature *f*.
Holland ['holənd] *n* Hollande *f*.
hollow ['holou] *adj*, *adv* creux. *n* creux *m*; (*in ground*) dépression *f*. *v* creuser.
holly ['holi] *n* houx *m*. **hollyhock** *n* rose trémière *f*.
holster ['houlstə] *n* étui de revolver *m*.
holy ['houli] *adj* saint. **holiness** *n* sainteté *f*.
homage ['homidʒ] *n* hommage *m*. **pay homage to** rendre hommage à.
home [houm] *n* maison *f*, foyer *m*. **at home** chez soi. **make oneself at home** faire comme chez soi. *adv* à la maison; (*right in*) à fond. **go home** rentrer. *adj* familial; domestique; (*not foreign*) intérieur, -e, national. **homeless** *adj* sans abri.
homely *adj* simple, confortable; (*US: ugly*) laid.
home address *n* domicile permanent *m*; adresse personnelle *f*.
homecoming ['houmˌkʌmiŋ] *n* retour *m*.
home-grown [houm'groun] *adj* du jardin.
home help *n* aide ménagère *f*.
homeland ['houmland] *n* patrie *f*.
home-made [houm'meid] *adj* fait à la maison.
Home Office *n* ministère de l'Intérieur *m*.
home rule *n* autonomie *f*.
homesick ['houmsik] *adj* nostalgique. **homesickness** *n* mal du pays *m*; nostalgie *f*.
homework ['houmwəːk] *n* devoirs *m pl*.
homicide ['homisaid] *n* homicide *m*. **homicidal** *adj* homicide.

homogeneous [homə'dʒiːniəs] *adj* homogène.

homosexual [homə'sekʃuəl] *n, adj* homosexuel, -elle. **homosexuality** *n* homosexualité *f*.

honest ['onist] *adj* honnête; sincère; franc, franche. **honesty** *n* honnêteté *f*; sincérité *f*.

honey ['hʌni] *n* miel *m*. **honeycomb** *n* rayon de miel *m*. **honeymoon** *n* lune de miel *f*. **honeysuckle** *n* chèvrefeuille *m*.

honour ['onə] *n* honneur *m*. *v* honorer. **honorary** *adj* honoraire. **honourable** *adj* honorable.

hood [hud] *n* capuchon *m*; (*car roof*) capote *f*; (*US: car bonnet*) capot *m*.

hoof [huːf] *n* sabot *m*.

hook [huk] *n* crochet *m*; (*on dress*) agrafe *f*; (*fishing*) hameçon *m*. *v* accrocher; agrafer; (*fishing*) prendre. **hooked** *adj* crochu.

hooligan ['huːligən] *n* voyou *m*. **hooliganism** *n* vandalisme *m*.

hoop [huːp] *n* cerceau *m*; (*for barrel*) cercle *m*.

hoot [huːt] *v* (*owl*) hululer; (*car*) klaxonner; (*boo*) huer. *n* hululement *m*; coup de klaxon *m*; huée *f*. **hooter** *n* klaxon *m*; (*factory*) sirène *f*.

hop¹ [hop] *v* sauter à cloche-pied; (*jump*) sauter, sautiller. *n* saut *m*, sautillement *m*; (*coll: dance*) sauterie *f*.

hop² [hop] *n* (*bot*) houblon *m*.

hope [houp] *n* espoir *m*. *v* espérer. **hopeful** *adj* plein d'espoir; encourageant. **hopeless** *adj* désespéré; (*coll: bad*) nul.

horde [hoːd] *n* horde *f*.

horizon [hə'raizn] *n* horizon *m*.

horizontal [hori'zontl] *adj* horizontal. *n* horizontale *f*.

hormone ['hoːmoun] *n* hormone *f*.

horn [hoːn] *n* corne *f*; (*music*) cor *m*; (*car, etc.*) klaxon *m*.

hornet ['hoːnit] *n* frelon *m*.

horoscope ['horəskoup] *n* horoscope *m*.

horrible ['horibl] *adj* horrible, affreux.

horrid ['horid] *adj* méchant, vilain.

horrify ['horifai] *v* horrifier. **horrific** *adj* horrifique.

horror ['horə] *n* horreur *f*. *adj* (*story, film, etc.*) d'épouvante.

horse [hoːs] *n* cheval *m*.

horseback ['hoːsbak] *n* **on horseback** à cheval.

horse-box ['hoːsboks] *n* fourgon à chevaux *m*.

horse chestnut *n* (*nut*) marron d'Inde *m*; (*tree*) marronnier d'Inde *m*.

horse-drawn ['hoːsdroːn] *adj* à chevaux.

horsefly ['hoːsflai] *n* taon *m*.

horsehair ['hoːsheə] *n* crin *m*.

horseman ['hoːsmən] *n* cavalier *m*.

horsepower ['hoːsˌpauə] *n* cheval-vapeur *m*.

horseradish ['hoːsˌradiʃ] *n* raifort *m*.

horseshoe ['hoːʃʃuː] *n* fer à cheval *m*.

horsewoman ['hoːsˌwumən] *n* cavalière *f*.

horticulture ['hoːtikʌltʃə] *n* horticulture *f*. **horticultural** *adj* horticole.

hose [houz] *n* tuyau *m*; (*mot*) durite *f*; (*stockings*) bas *m pl*. *v* arroser au jet.

hosiery ['houziəri] *n* bas *m pl*; (*business*) bonneterie *f*.

hospitable [ho'spitəbl] *adj* hospitalier.

hospital ['hospitl] *n* hôpital *m*. **hospitalize** *v* hospitaliser.

hospitality [ˌhospi'taliti] *n* hospitalité *f*.

host¹ [houst] *n* hôte *m*. **hostess** *n* hôtesse *f*.

host² [houst] *n* (*crowd*) foule *f*.

hostage ['hostidʒ] *n* otage *m*.

hostel ['hostəl] *n* foyer *m*. **youth hostel** auberge de jeunesse *f*.

hostile ['hostail] *adj* hostile. **hostility** *n* hostilité *f*.

hot [hot] *adj* chaud; (*curry, etc.*) fort; (*temper*) violent. **be hot** (*person*) avoir chaud; (*weather*) faire chaud. **hot dog** hot-dog *m*. **hot-house** *n* serre *f*. **hotplate** *n* chauffe-plats *m invar*. **hot-tempered** *adj* emporté. **hot-water bottle** bouillotte *f*.

hotel [hou'tel] *n* hôtel *m*.

hound [haund] *n* chien de meute *m*. *v* chasser, s'acharner sur.

hour ['auə] *n* heure *f*. **hourglass** *n* sablier *m*. **hourly** *adj, adv* toutes les heures.

house [haus; *v* hauz] *n* maison *f*; (*theatre*) salle *f*. *v* loger.

houseboat ['hausbout] *n* péniche aménagée *f*.

housebound ['hausbaund] *adj* confiné chez soi.

housecoat ['hauskout] *n* peignoir *m*.

household ['haushould] *n* maison *f*, ménage *m*.

housekeeper ['hausˌkiːpə] *n* gouvernante *f*. **housekeeping** *n* (*work*) ménage *m*; (*money*) argent du ménage *m*.

housemaid ['hausmeid] *n* bonne *f.*
house-to-house *adj, adv* porte à porte.
house-trained ['haustreind] *adj* propre.
house-warming ['haus,wɔːmiŋ] *n* have a house-warming (party) pendre la crémaillère.
housewife ['hauswaif] *n* ménagère *f.*
housework ['hauswəːk] *n* ménage *m.*
housing ['hauziŋ] *n* logement *m.* **housing estate** cité *f.*
hovel ['hovəl] *n* taudis *m.*
hover ['hovə] *v* planer; (*person*) rôder. **hovercraft** *n* aéroglisseur *m.*
how [hau] *adv* comment, comme. **how are you?** comment allez-vous? **how do you do?** bonjour; (*on introduction*) enchanté. **how much?** combien?
however [hau'evə] *conj* cependant. *adv* de quelque manière que.
howl [haul] *v* hurler. *n* hurlement *m.*
hub [hʌb] *n* moyeu *m;* pivot *m.* **hubcap** *n* (*mot*) enjoliveur *m.*
huddle ['hʌdl] *v* se blottir. *n* petit groupe *m.*
hue [hjuː] *n* teinte *f.*
huff [hʌf] *n* **in a huff** froissé.
hug [hʌg] *v* étreindre. *n* étreinte *f.*
huge [hjuːdʒ] *adj* énorme.
hulk [hʌlk] *n* épave *f,* carcasse *f;* (*derog: person*) mastodonte *m.* **hulking** *adj* balourd.
hull [hʌl] *n* (*naut*) coque *f.*
hum [hʌm] *v* bourdonner; (*tune*) fredonner; (*engine*) vrombir. *n* bourdonnement *m;* vrombissement *m.* **humming-bird** *n* oiseau-mouche *m.*
human ['hjuːmən] *nm, adj* humain. **human being** être humain *m.*
humane [hjuː'mein] *adj* humain.
humanity [hjuː'manəti] *n* humanité *f.* **humanitarian** *n(m+f), adj* humanitaire.
humble ['hʌmbl] *adj* humble. *v* humilier.
humdrum ['hʌmdrʌm] *adj* monotone.
humid ['hjuːmid] *adj* humide. **humidity** *n* humidité *f.*
humiliate [hjuː'milieit] *v* humilier. **humiliation** *n* humiliation *f.*
humility [hjuː'miləti] *n* humilité *f.*
humour ['hjuːmə] *n* humour *m;* (*mood*) humeur *f. v* ménager. **humorist** *n* humoriste *m, f.* **humorous** *adj* humoristique.
hump [hʌmp] *n* bosse *f.* **humpbacked** *adj* (*bridge*) en dos d'âne. *v* arrondir, voûter.

hunch [hʌntʃ] *v* arrondir, voûter. *n* pressentiment *m.* **hunchback** *n* bossu, -e *m, f.* **hunchbacked** *adj* bossu.
hundred ['hʌndrəd] *nm, adj* cent. **hundreds** *pl n* (*coll*) centaines *f pl.* **hundredth** *n(m+f), adj* centième.
hung [hʌŋ] *V* hang.
Hungary ['hʌŋgəri] *n* Hongrie *f.* **Hungarian** *nm, adj* hongrois; *n* (*people*) Hongrois, -e *m, f.*
hunger ['hʌŋgə] *n* faim *f. v* avoir faim. **be hungry** avoir faim. **hungrily** *adv* avidement.
hunt [hʌnt] *n* chasse *f;* (*search*) recherche *f. v* chasser; chercher. **hunting** *n* chasse *f.* **huntsman** *n* chasseur *m.*
hurdle ['həːdl] *n* obstacle *m;* (*sport*) haie *f.*
hurl [həːl] *v* jeter, précipiter. **hurl abuse** lancer des injures.
hurricane ['hʌrikən] *n* ouragan *m.*
hurry ['hʌri] *n* hâte *f.* **be in a hurry** être pressé. *v* (faire) se dépêcher, (se) presser. **hurried** *adj* précipité, pressé. **hurriedly** *adv* précipitamment.
*hurt [həːt] *v* faire mal (à), blesser. *n* mal *m. adj* blessé.
husband ['hʌzbənd] *n* mari *m.*
hush [hʌʃ] *n* silence *m. interj* chut! *v* faire taire. **hush up** (*news*) étouffer. **hushed** *adj* étouffé.
husk [hʌsk] *n* (*wheat*) balle *f;* (*rice, maize*) enveloppe *f;* (*nut*) écale *f. v* (*grain*) vanner; (*rice, maize*) décortiquer; écaler.
husky ['hʌski] *adj* enroué. **huskily** *adj* d'une voix rauque. **huskiness** *n* enrouement *m.*
hussar [hə'zaː] *n* hussard *m.*
hustle ['hʌsl] *v* (se) bousculer. *n* bousculade *f.* **hustle and bustle** tourbillon *m.*
hut [hʌt] *n* hutte *f.*
hutch [hʌtʃ] *n* clapier *m.*
hyacinth ['haiəsinθ] *n* jacinthe *f.*
hybrid ['haibrid] *nm, adj* hybride.
hydraulic [hai'drɔːlik] *adj* hydraulique.
hydrocarbon [,haidrou'kaːbən] *n* hydrocarbure *m.*
hydro-electric [,haidroui'lektrik] *adj* hydro-électrique.
hydrofoil ['haidroufoil] *n* hydrofoil *m.*
hydrogen ['haidrədʒən] *n* hydrogène *m.*
hyena [hai'iːnə] *n* hyène *f.*
hygiene ['haidʒiːn] *n* hygiène *f.* **hygienic** *adj* hygiénique.

hymn [him] *n* hymne *f*. **hymn-book** *n* livre de cantiques *m*.

hyphen ['haifən] *n* trait d'union *m*.

hypnosis [hip'nousis] *n* hypnose *f*. **under hypnosis** en état d'hypnose. **hypnotic** *adj* hypnotique. **hypnotism** *n* hypnotisme *m*. **hypnotist** *n* hypnotiseur, -euse *m, f*. **hypnotize** *v* hypnotiser.

hypochondria [haipə'kondriə] *n* hypochondrie *f*. **hypochondriac** *n(m+f)*, *adj* hypochondriaque.

hypocrisy [hi'pokrəsi] *n* hypocrisie *f*. **hypocrite** *n* hypocrite *m, f*. **hypocritical** *adj* hypocrite.

hypodermic [haipə'dəɪmik] *adj* hypodermique. *n* seringue hypodermique *f*.

hypothesis [hai'poθəsis] *n, pl* **-ses** hypothèse *f*. **hypothetical** *adj* hypothétique.

hysterectomy [histə'rektəmi] *n* hystérectomie *f*.

hysteria [his'tiəriə] *n* hystérie *f*. **hysterical** *adj* hystérique; *(laughter, crying)* convulsif. **hysterics** *pl n (crying)* crise de nerfs *f sing*; *(laughter)* crise de rire *f sing*.

I

I [ai] *pron* je; *(emphatic)* moi.

ice [ais] *n* glace *f*; *(on road)* verglas *m*. **iceberg** *n* iceberg *m*. **ice-cold** *adj* glacé. **ice cream** glace *f*. **ice cube** glaçon *m*. **ice rink** patinoire *f*. **ice-skate** *n* patin à glace *m*. **ice-skating** *n* patinage sur glace *m*. *v (chill)* rafraîchir; *(cake)* glacer. **ice over** or **up** *(lake)* geler; *(windscreen, etc.)* givrer. **iced** *adj* glacé; *(champagne)* frappé; *(melon)* rafraîchi. **icing** *n* glaçage *m*. **icing sugar** sucre glace *m*. **icy** *adj* glacial; *(road)* verglacé.

Iceland ['aislənd] *n* Islande *f*. **Icelander** *n* Islandais, -e *m, f*. **Icelandic** *nm, adj*. islandais.

icicle ['aisikl] *n* glaçon *m*.

icon ['aikon] *n* icône *f*.

idea [ai'diə] *n* idée *f*.

ideal [ai'diəl] *nm, adj* idéal. **idealist** *n* idéaliste *m, f*. **idealistic** *adj* idéaliste.

identical [ai'dentikəl] *adj* identique. **iden-tical twins** vrais jumeaux *m pl*, vraies jumelles *f pl*.

identify [ai'dentifai] *v* identifier. **identify with** s'identifier à or avec. **identification** *n* identification *f*; *(papers)* pièce d'identité *f*.

identity [ai'dentiti] *n* identité *f*. **identity card** carte d'identité *f*. **identity parade** séance d'identification *f*.

ideology [aidi'olədʒi] *n* idéologie *f*.

idiom ['idiəm] *n (expression)* idiotisme *m*; *(language)* idiome *m*. **idiomatic** *adj* idiomatique.

idiosyncrasy [ˌidiə'siŋkrəsi] *n* particularité *f*.

idiot ['idiət] *n* idiot, -e *m, f*. **idiotic** *adj* idiot.

idle ['aidl] *adj (doing nothing)* désœuvré; *(lazy)* oisif; *(machine)* en repos; *(talk, etc.)* oiseux. *v* fainéanter; *(engine)* tourner au ralenti. **idleness** *n* désœuvrement *m*; *(laziness)* paresse *f*.

idol ['aidl] *n* idole *f*. **idolatry** *n* idolâtrie *f*. **idolize** *v* idolâtrer.

idyllic [i'dilik] *adj* idyllique.

if [if] *conj* si. **as if** comme si. **if not** sinon. **if so** s'il en est ainsi.

ignite [ig'nait] *v (light)* mettre le feu à; *(catch fire)* prendre feu.

ignition [ig'niʃən] *n* ignition *f*; *(mot)* allumage *m*. **ignition key** clef de contact *f*. **ignition switch** contact *m*. **turn on the ignition** mettre le contact.

ignorant ['ignərənt] *adj* ignorant. **ignorance** *n* ignorance *f*.

ignore [ig'noɪ] *v (remark, etc.)* ne pas relever; *(person)* faire semblant de ne pas reconnaître; *(rule)* ne pas respecter.

ill [il] *adj (sick)* malade; *(bad)* mauvais. *nm, adv* mal. **ill-at-ease** *adj* mal à l'aise. **ill-bred** or **ill-mannered** *adj* mal élevé. **ill-gotten gains** biens mal acquis *m pl*. **ill-treat** *v* maltraiter. **illness** *n* maladie *f*.

illegal [i'liːgəl] *adj* illégal.

illegible [i'ledʒəbl] *adj* illisible.

illegitimate [ˌili'dʒitimit] *adj* illégitime. **illegitimacy** *n* illégitimité *f*.

illicit [i'lisit] *adj* illicite.

illiterate [i'litərit] *n, adj* illettré, -e. **illiteracy** *n* analphabétisme *m*.

illogical [i'lodʒikəl] *adj* illogique.

illuminate [i'luːmiˌneit] *v* éclairer; *(building)* illuminer. **illumination** *n* éclairage *m*; illumination *f*.

illusion [i'luːʒən] n illusion f.
illustrate ['iləˌstreit] v illustrer. **illustration** n illustration f. **illustrator** n illustrateur, -trice m, f.
illustrious [i'lʌstriəs] adj illustre.
image ['imidʒ] n image f; (public personality) image de marque f; (double) portrait vivant m. **imagery** n images f pl.
imagine [i'madʒin] v (s')imaginer. **imaginary** adj imaginaire. **imagination** n imagination f. **imaginative** adj plein d'imagination.
imbalance [im'baləns] n déséquilibre m.
imbecile ['imbəsiːl] n imbécile m, f.
imitate ['imiˌteit] v imiter. **imitation** n imitation f.
immaculate [i'makjulit] adj impeccable; (rel) immaculé.
immaterial [ˌimə'tiəriəl] adj insignifiant, indifférent.
immature [ˌimə'tjuə] adj pas mûr. **be immature** (person) manquer de maturité. **immaturity** n manque de maturité m.
immediate [i'miːdiət] adj immédiat. **immediately** adv tout de suite; directement.
immense [i'mens] adj immense.
immerse [i'məːs] v immerger, plonger. **immersion** n immersion f. **immersion heater** chauffe-eau électrique m invar.
immigrate ['imiˌgreit] v immigrer. **immigrant** n immigrant, -e m, f. **immigration** n immigration f.
imminent ['iminənt] adj imminent.
immobile [i'moubail] adj immobile. **immobilize** v immobiliser.
immoral [i'morəl] adj immoral. **immorality** n immoralité f.
immortal [i'moːtl] adj immortel. **immortality** n immortalité f. **immortalize** v immortaliser.
immovable [i'muːvəbl] adj fixe; inflexible.
immune [i'mjuːn] adj immunisé. **immunity** n immunité f. **immunization** n immunisation f. **immunize** v immuniser.
imp [imp] n diablotin m.
impact ['impakt] n impact m.
impair [im'peə] v détériorer, abîmer.
impale [im'peil] v empaler.
impart [im'paːt] v communiquer; (give) donner.
impartial [im'paːʃəl] adj impartial. **impartiality** n impartialité f.
impasse [am'paːs] n impasse f.

impassive [im'pasiv] adj impassible.
impatient [im'peiʃənt] adj impatient. **get impatient** s'impatienter. **impatience** n impatience f.
impeach [im'piːtʃ] v accuser; (question) mettre en doute. **impeachment** n accusation f; (US) procédure d'impeachment f.
impeccable [im'pekəbl] adj impeccable.
impede [im'piːd] v empêcher, gêner.
impediment [im'pedimənt] n obstacle m. **speech impediment** défaut d'élocution m.
impel [im'pel] v pousser, obliger.
impending [im'pendiŋ] adj imminent; menaçant.
imperative [im'perətiv] adj urgent, impérieux. n impératif m.
imperfect [im'pəːfikt] adj imparfait; défectueux. n imparfait m.
imperial [im'piəriəl] adj impérial; majestueux. **imperialism** n impérialisme m.
impersonal [im'pəːsənl] adj impersonnel.
impersonate [im'pəːsəˌneit] v se faire passer pour; (theatre) imiter. **impersonation** n imitation f.
impertinent [im'pəːtinənt] adj impertinent. **impertinence** n impertinence f.
impervious [im'pəːviəs] adj imperméable; (to criticism, etc.) fermé.
impetuous [im'petjuəs] adj impétueux.
impetus ['impətəs] n impulsion f, élan m.
impinge [im'pindʒ] v **impinge on** empiéter sur; affecter.
implement ['implimənt; v 'impliment] n instrument m. **implements** pl n matériel m sing. v exécuter.
implication [impli'keiʃən] n insinuation f, implication f.
implicit [im'plisit] adj implicite; absolu.
implore [im'ploː] v implorer. **imploring** adj suppliant.
imply [im'plai] v (laisser) supposer; suggérer; insinuer. **implied** adj implicite, tacite.
impolite [impə'lait] adj impoli.
import [im'poːt] n (comm) importation f; sens m; importance f. v (comm) importer; signifier.
importance [im'poːtəns] n importance f. **important** adj important.
impose [im'pouz] v imposer; (fine, etc.) infliger. **impose on** abuser de. **imposition** n imposition f.
impossible [im'posəbl] nm, adj impossible.

impostor [im'postə] *n* imposteur *m*.
impotent ['impətənt] *adj* impuissant.
impotence *n* impuissance *f*.
impound [im'paund] *v* confisquer.
impoverish [im'povəriʃ] *v* appauvrir.
impregnate ['impreg,neit] *v* imprégner.
impregnation *n* imprégnation *f*.
impress [im'pres] *v* impressionner; (*print*) imprimer. **impression** *n* impression *f*.
impressive *adj* impressionnant.
imprint [im'print; *n* 'imprint] *v* imprimer. *n* empreinte *f*.
imprison [im'prizn] *v* emprisonner. **imprisonment** *n* emprisonnement *m*.
improbable [im'probəbl] *adj* improbable; (*story, etc.*) invraisemblable.
impromptu [im'promptjuɪ] *adv, adj* impromptu.
improper [im'propə] *adj* indécent; malhonnête; incorrect.
improve [im'pruɪv] *v* (s')améliorer; perfectionner. **improvement** *n* amélioration *f*; progrès *m*.
improvise ['imprə,vaiz] *v* improviser. **improvisation** *n* improvisation *f*.
impudent ['impjudənt] *adj* impudent. **impudence** *n* impudence *f*.
impulse ['impʌls] *n* impulsion *f*. **impulsive** *adj* impulsif; irréfléchi.
impure [im'pjuə] *adj* impur. **impurity** *n* impureté *f*.
in [in] *prep* dans, en; (*town*) à. *adv* (*inside*) dedans; (*at home*) chez soi.
inability [,inə'biləti] *n* incapacité *f*.
inaccessible [,inak'sesəbl] *adj* inaccessible.
inaccurate [in'akjurit] *adj* inexact. **inaccuracy** *n* inexactitude *f*.
inactive [in'aktiv] *adj* inactif, peu actif. **inaction** *n* inaction *f*. **inactivity** *n* inactivité *f*.
inadequate [in'adikwit] *adj* insuffisant. **inadequacy** *n* insuffisance *f*.
inadvertent [,inəd'vəɪtənt] *adj* inattentif. **inadvertently** *adv* par inadvertance.
inane [in'ein] *adj* inepte. **inanity** *n* ineptie *f*.
inanimate [in'animit] *adj* inanimé.
inarticulate [,inaɪ'tikjulit] *adj* (*sound*) inarticulé; (*person*) incapable de s'exprimer.
inasmuch [,inəz'mʌtʃ] *adv* **inasmuch as** attendu que.
inaudible [in'oɪdəbl] *adj* inaudible.
inaugurate [i'noɪgju,reit] *v* inaugurer.

inaugural *adj* inaugural. **inauguration** *n* inauguration *f*.
inborn [,in'boɪn] *adj* inné; congénital.
incapable [in'keipəbl] *adj* incapable.
incendiary [in'sendiəri] *adj* incendiaire. **incendiary device** dispositif incendiaire *m*.
incense¹ ['insens] *n* encens *m*.
incense² [in'sens] *v* courroucer, exaspérer. **incensed** by outré de.
incentive [in'sentiv] *n* objectif *m*, stimulant *m*.
incessant [in'sesənt] *adj* incessant.
incest ['insest] *n* inceste *m*. **incestuous** *adj* incestueux.
inch [intʃ] *n* pouce *m*. **inch by inch** petit à petit. *v* **inch forward** avancer petit à petit.
incident ['insidənt] *n* incident *m*; épisode *m*. **incidental** *adj* accessoire; accidental. **incidental music** musique de fond *f*. **incidentally** *adv* (*by the way*) à propos.
incinerator [in'sinə,reitə] *n* incinérateur *m*. **incinerate** *v* incinérer. **incineration** *n* incinération *f*.
incite [in'sait] *v* pousser, inciter.
incline [in'klain] *v* (s')incliner. **be inclined to** incliner à. *n* pente *f*. **inclination** *n* inclination *f*; (*hill*) inclinaison *f*.
include [in'kluɪd] *v* inclure, comprendre. **including** *prep* y compris. **inclusion** *n* inclusion *f*. **inclusive** *adj* inclus.
incognito [,inkog'niɪtou] *adv* incognito.
incoherent [,inkə'hiərənt] *adj* incohérent. **incoherently** *adv* sans cohérence.
income ['inkʌm] *n* revenu *m*. **income tax** impôt sur le revenu *m*. **private income** rente *f*.
incompatible [inkəm'patəbl] *adj* incompatible. **incompatibility** *n* incompatibilité *f*.
incompetent [in'kompitənt] *adj* incompétent. **incompetence** *n* incompétence *f*.
incomplete [,inkəm'pliːt] *adj* incomplet, -ète.
incomprehensible [in,kompri'hensəbl] *adj* incompréhensible.
inconceivable [inkən'siːvəbl] *adj* inconcevable.
incongruous [in'koŋgruəs] *adj* incongru; peu approprié.
inconsiderate [,inkən'sidərit] *adj* inconsidéré; (*person*) sans égards.
inconsistent [,inkən'sistənt] *adj* inconsistant. **inconsistency** *n* inconsistance *f*.

incontinence [in'kontinəns] *n* incontinence *f*. **incontinent** *adj* incontinent.

inconvenience [inkən'viːnjəns] *n* inconvénient *m*; (*trouble*) dérangement *m*. *v* déranger. **inconvenient** *adj* inopportun,
incommode.

incorporate [in'koːpəˌreit] *v* incorporer,
contenir; (*comm*) fusionner.

incorrect [inkə'rekt] *adj* incorrect.

increase [in'kriːs] *v* augmenter;
(s')intensifier. *n* augmentation *f*. **increasing** *adj* croissant. **increasingly** *adv* de
plus en plus.

incredible [in'kredəbl] *adj* incroyable.

incredulous [in'kredjuləs] *adj* incrédule.
incredulity *n* incrédulité *f*.

increment ['iŋkrəmənt] *n* augmentation *f*.

incriminate [in'krimineit] *v* incriminer.
incriminating *adj* compromettant; (*evidence, etc.*) à conviction.

incubate ['iŋkjuˌbeit] *v* incuber, couver.
incubation *n* incubation *f*. **incubator** *n*
couveuse *f*.

incur [in'kəː] *v* encourir; contracter; (*risk*)
courir.

incurable [in'kjuərəbl] *adj* incurable.

indecent [in'diːsnt] *adj* indécent. **indecency** *n* indécence *f*.

indeed [in'diːd] *adv* en effet, vraiment.

indefinite [in'definit] *adj* indéfini,
indéterminé.

indelible [in'deləbl] *adj* indélébile; (*memory, etc.*) ineffaçable.

indemnity [in'demnəti] *n* indemnité *f*.

indent [in'dent] *v* denteler; (*printing*)
renfoncer. **indentation** *n* dentelure *f*;
renfoncement *m*.

independent [indi'pendənt] *adj*
indépendant. **independence** *n*
indépendance *f*.

index ['indeks] *n* index *m*, catalogue *m*;
(*ratio*) indice *m*. **index finger** index *m*.
index-linked *adj* indexé. *v* classer; (*book*)
mettre un index à.

India ['indjə] *n* Inde *f*. **Indian** *n* Indien,
-enne *m*, *f*; *adj* indien. **Indian ink** encre
de Chine *f*.

indicate ['indikeit] *v* indiquer. **indication** *n*
indication *f*, signe *m*. **indicative** *nm*, *adj*
indicatif. **indicator** *n* indicateur *m*; (*mot*)
clignotant *m*.

indict [in'dait] *v* accuser. **indictment** *n*
mise en accusation *f*.

indifferent [in'difrənt] *adj* indifférent;

(*derog*) médiocre. **indifference** *n* indifférence *f*.

indigenous [in'didʒinəs] *adj* indigène.

indigestion [indi'dʒestʃən] *n* dyspepsie *f*,
indigestion *f*.

indignant [in'dignənt] *adj* indigné. **get
indignant** s'indigner. **indignantly** *adv* avec
indignation. **indignation** *n* indignation *f*.

indignity [in'dignəti] *n* indignité *f*.

indirect [indi'rekt] *adj* indirect.

indiscreet [indi'skriːt] *adj* indiscret, -ète.
indiscretion *n* indiscrétion *f*.

indiscriminate [indi'skriminit] *adj* fait au
hasard; (*blind*) aveugle.

indispensable [indi'spensəbl] *adj* indispensable.

indisposed [indi'spouzd] *adj* (*ill*) indisposé; (*unwilling*) peu disposé. **indisposition** *n* indisposition *f*.

individual [indi'vidjuəl] *adj* individuel;
original. *n* individu *m*. **individuality** *n*
individualité *f*.

indoctrinate [in'doktriˌneit] *v* endoctriner.
indoctrination *n* endoctrination *f*.

indolent ['indələnt] *adj* indolent. **indolence** *n* indolence *f*.

indoor ['indoː] *adj* d'intérieur; (*swimming
pool, etc.*) couvert. **indoors** *adv* à
l'intérieur, à la maison.

induce [in'djuːs] *v* persuader; provoquer;
(*med: labour*) déclencher. **inducement** *n*
encouragement *m*; (*incentive*) motif *m*.

indulge [in'dʌldʒ] *v* satisfaire; (*give way
to*) céder à. **indulge in** se livrer à. **indulgence** *n* indulgence *f*; satisfaction *f*.
indulgent *adj* indulgent.

industry ['indəstri] *n* industrie *f*; zèle *m*.
industrial *adj* industriel. **industrial action**
action revendicative *f*. **industrialize** *v*
industrialiser. **industrious** *adj* indus-
trieux.

inebriated [i'niːbrieitid] *adj* ivre.

inedible [in'edibl] *adj* non comestible.

inefficient [ini'fiʃnt] *adj* inefficace;
incompétent. **inefficiency** *n* inefficacité *f*;
incompétence *f*.

inept [i'nept] *adj* inepte.

inequality [ini'kwoləti] *n* inégalité *f*.

inert [i'nəːt] *adj* inerte. **inertia** *n* inertie *f*.

inevitable [in'evitəbl] *adj* inévitable.

inexpensive [inik'spensiv] *adj* pas cher.

inexperienced [inik'spiəriənst] *adj*
inexpérimenté.

infallible [in'faləbl] *adj* infaillible.

infamous ['infəməs] *adj* infâme. **infamy** *n* infamie *f*.

infancy ['infənsi] *n* petite enfance *f*; (*of idea, etc.*) enfance *f*.

infant ['infənt] *n* bébé *m*; enfant en bas âge *m, f*. **infantile** *adj* enfantin, infantile.

infantry ['infəntri] *n* infanterie *f*.

infatuate [in'fatjueit] *v* **be infatuated with** (*person*) être entiché de; (*idea*) être engoué de. **infatuation** *n* engouement *m*.

infect [in'fekt] *v* infecter. **infection** *n* infection *f*. **infectious** *adj* infectieux, contagieux.

infer [in'fəɪ] *v* déduire. **inference** *n* déduction *f*.

inferior [in'fiəriə] *n(m+f)*, *adj* inférieur, -e. **inferiority** *n* infériorité *f*.

infernal [in'fəɪnl] *adj* infernal.

infest [in'fest] *v* infester. **infestation** *n* infestation *f*.

infidelity [,infi'deliti] *n* infidélité *f*.

infiltrate [in'fil,treit] *v* (s')infiltrer. **infiltration** *n* infiltration *f*; (*pol*) noyautage *m*.

infinite ['infinit] *nm, adj* infini. **infinity** *n* infinité *f*; (*maths*) infini *m*.

infinitive [in'finitiv] *nm, adj* infinitif.

infirm [in'fəɪm] *adj* infirme. **infirmity** *n* infirmité *f*.

inflame [in'fleim] *v* (s')enflammer. **inflammable** *adj* inflammable. **inflammation** *n* inflammation *f*.

inflate [in'fleit] *v* gonfler; (*prices*) faire monter. **inflation** *n* (*econ*) inflation *f*; (*of tyre, etc.*) gonflement *m*.

inflection [in'flekʃən] *n* inflexion *f*; (*word ending*) désinence *f*.

inflict [in'flikt] *v* infliger. **infliction** *n* infliction *f*.

influence ['influəns] *n* influence *f*. *v* influencer. **influential** *adj* influent.

influenza [,influ'enzə] *n* grippe *f*.

influx ['inflʌks] *n* flot *m*, afflux *m*.

inform [in'fɔɪm] *v* informer. **informative** *adj* instructif. **informer** *n* dénonciateur, -trice *m, f*.

informal [in'fɔɪml] *adj* familier; dénué de formalité; (*unofficial*) officieux.

information [,infə'meiʃən] *n* renseignements *m pl*.

infra-red [,infrə'red] *adj* infrarouge.

infringe [in'frindʒ] *v* enfreindre. **infringe on** empiéter sur. **infringement** *n* infraction *f*.

infuriate [in'fjuəri,eit] *v* rendre furieux. **infuriating** *adj* exaspérant.

ingenious [in'dʒiɪnjəs] *adj* ingénieux. **ingenuity** *n* ingéniosité *f*.

ingot ['iŋgət] *n* lingot *m*.

ingredient [in'griɪdjənt] *n* ingrédient *m*.

inhabit [in'habit] *v* habiter. **inhabitant** *n* habitant, -e *m, f*.

inhale [in'heil] *v* inhaler; (*smoke*) avaler; (*perfume*) aspirer.

inherent [in'hiərənt] *adj* inhérent.

inherit [in'herit] *v* hériter (de). **inheritance** *n* héritage *m*; succession *f*.

inhibit [in'hibit] *v* inhiber, gêner. **inhibition** *n* inhibition *f*.

inhuman [in'hjuɪmən] *adj* inhumain. **inhumanity** *n* inhumanité *f*.

iniquity [i'nikwəti] *n* iniquité *f*.

initial [i'niʃl] *adj* initial, premier. *n* initiale *f*. *v* parafer.

initiate [i'niʃi,eit] *v* initier; inaugurer; commencer. **initiation** *n* initiation *f*; commencement *m*; inauguration *f*.

initiative [i'niʃiətiv] *n* initiative *f*.

inject [in'dʒekt] *v* injecter. **injection** *n* injection *f*, piqûre *f*.

injure ['indʒə] *v* blesser. **injury** *n* blessure *f*.

injustice [in'dʒʌstis] *n* injustice *f*.

ink [iŋk] *n* encre *f*. **ink-well** *n* encrier *m*. *v* encrer.

inkling ['iŋkliŋ] *n* soupçon *m*.

inland ['inlənd; *adv* in'land] *adj* intérieur, -e. **Inland Revenue** fisc *m*. *adv* à l'intérieur.

in-laws ['in,lɔɪz] *pl n* (*coll*) beaux-parents *m pl*, belle-famille *f sing*.

inlay [,in'lei] *v* incruster; marqueter. *n* incrustation *f*; marqueterie *f*.

inlet ['inlet] *n* crique *f*.

inmate ['inmeit] *n* occupant, -e *m, f*; (*prison*) détenu, -e *m, f*; hospitalisé, -e *m, f*.

inn [in] *n* auberge *f*. **innkeeper** *n* aubergiste *m, f*.

innate [i'neit] *adj* inné.

inner ['inə] *adj* intérieur, -e; (*thoughts, etc.*) intime. **inner tube** chambre à air *f*.

innocent ['inəsnt] *adj* innocent. **innocence** *n* innocence *f*.

innocuous [i'nokjuəs] *adj* inoffensif.

innovation [inə'veiʃən] *n* innovation *f*.

innuendo [,inju'endou] *n* insinuation *f*.

innumerable [i'njuɪmərəbl] *adj* innombrable.

inoculate [i'nokjuˌleit] *v* inoculer. **inocula-tion** *n* inoculation *f*.
inorganic [ˌinɔɪ'ganik] *adj* inorganique.
input ['input] *n* (*elec*) énergie *f*; (*tech*) consommation *f*; (*computer*) input *m*.
inquest ['inkwest] *n* enquête *f*.
inquire [in'kwaiə] *v* s'informer (de), demander. **inquiring** *adj* (*mind*) curieux; (*look*) interrogateur, -trice. **inquiry** *n* (*official*) enquête *f*; (*individual*) demande de renseignements *f*. **inquiry desk** renseignements *m pl*.
inquisition [ˌinkwi'zifən] *n* investigation *f*. **the Inquisition** l'Inquisition *f*.
inquisitive [in'kwizətiv] *adj* curieux.
insane [in'sein] *adj* (*med*) aliéné; (*crazy*) fou, folle. **insanity** *n* aliénation *f*; folie *f*.
insatiable [in'seifəbl] *adj* insatiable.
inscribe [in'skraib] *v* inscrire, graver. **inscription** *n* inscription *f*.
insect ['insekt] *n* insecte *m*. **insecticide** *n* insecticide *m*.
insecure [ˌinsi'kjuə] *adj* (*future, etc.*) incertain; (*person*) anxieux; (*structure*) peu solide. **insecurity** *n* insécurité *f*.
inseminate [in'semineit] *v* inséminer. **insemination** *n* insémination *f*.
insensitive [in'sensətiv] *adj* insensible. **insensitivity** *n* insensibilité *f*.
inseparable [in'sepərəbl] *adj* inséparable.
insert [in'sə:t; *n* 'insə:t] *v* insérer. *n* inser-tion *f*; (*page*) encart *m*. **insertion** *n* inser-tion *f*.
inshore [ˌin'fɔː] *adj* côtier.
inside [ˌin'said] *adv* dedans. *prep* à l'intérieur de. *adj* intérieur, -e. *n* dedans *m*, intérieur *m*. **inside out** à l'envers.
insidious [in'sidiəs] *adj* insidieux.
insight ['insait] *n* perspicacité *f*.
insignificant [ˌinsig'nifikənt] *adj* insignifi-ant. **insignificance** *n* insignifiance *f*.
insincere [ˌinsin'siə] *adj* hypocrite; faux, fausse.
insinuate [in'sinjueit] *v* insinuer. **insinua-tion** *n* insinuation *f*.
insipid [in'sipid] *adj* insipide.
insist [in'sist] *v* insister; affirmer. **insis-tence** *n* insistance *f*. **insistent** *adj* insis-tant. **insistently** *adv* avec insistance.
insolent ['insələnt] *adj* insolent. **insolence** *n* insolence *f*.
insoluble [in'soljubl] *adj* insoluble.
insomnia [in'somniə] *n* insomnie *f*. **insom-niac** *n*(*m+f*), *adj* insomniaque.

inspect [in'spekt] *v* inspecter, examiner. **inspection** *n* inspection *f*; examen *m*. **inspector** *n* inspecteur, -trice *m, f*.
inspire [in'spaiə] *v* inspirer. **inspiration** *n* inspiration *f*.
instability [ˌinstə'biləti] *n* instabilité *f*.
install [in'stɔːl] *v* installer. **installation** *n* installation *f*.
instalment [in'stɔːlmənt] *n* (*comm*) acompte *m*; (*of serial*) épisode *m*.
instance ['instəns] *n* exemple *m*, cas *m*. **for instance** par exemple.
instant ['instənt] *adj* immédiat; (*comm*) courant; (*coffee*) soluble. *n* instant *m*. **instantaneous** *adj* instantané. **instantly** *adv* sur-le-champ.
instead [in'sted] *adv* à la place, plutôt. **instead of** au lieu de.
instep ['instep] *n* (*anat*) cou-de-pied *m*; (*shoe*) cambrure *f*.
instigate ['instigeit] *v* inciter; provoquer. **instigation** *n* instigation *f*. **instigator** *n* instigateur, -trice *m, f*.
instil [in'stil] *v* insuffler, inculquer.
instinct ['instiŋkt] *n* instinct *m*. **instinctive** *adj* instinctif.
institute ['institjuːt] *v* instituer, fonder. *n* institut *m*. **institution** *n* institution *f*; (*school, home*) établissement *m*.
instruct [in'strʌkt] *v* instruire; (*order*) charger. **instruction** *n* instruction *f*. **instructions** *pl n* directives *f pl*; (*comm*) indications *f pl*; (*for use*) mode d'emploi *m sing*. **instructive** *adj* instructif. **instruc-tor** *n* professeur *m*; (*skiing*) moniteur, -trice *m, f*.
instrument ['instrəmənt] *n* instrument *m*. **instrumental** *adj* (*music*) instrumental. **be instrumental in** contribuer à.
insubordinate [ˌinsə'bɔːdənət] *adj* insubordonné. **insubordination** *n* insub-ordination *f*.
insufficient [ˌinsə'fifənt] *adj* insuffisant.
insular ['insjulə] *adj* insulaire; (*outlook*) borné.
insulate ['insjuleit] *v* isoler. **insulation** *n* isolation *f*; (*against cold*) calorifugeage *m*; (*material*) isolant *m*.
insulin ['insjulin] *n* insuline *f*.
insult [in'sʌlt; *n* 'insʌlt] *v* insulter. *n* insulte *f*.
insure [in'fuə] *v* (faire) assurer. **insurance** *n* assurance *f*. **insurance certificate** (*mot*) carte d'assurance *f*.

intact [in'takt] *adj* intact.
intake ['inteik] *n* (*tech*) adduction *f*; (*school*) admission *f*; (*food*) consommation *f*.
intangible [in'tandʒəbl] *adj* intangible.
integral ['intigrəl] *adj* intégral; (*part*) intégrant. *n* intégrale *f*.
integrate ['intigreit] *v* intégrer. **integration** *n* intégration *f*.
integrity [in'tegrəti] *n* intégrité *f*.
intellect ['intilekt] *n* intellect *m*, intelligence *f*. **intellectual** *n*, *adj* intellectuel, -elle.
intelligent [in'telidʒənt] *adj* intelligent. **intelligence** *n* intelligence *f*; (*information*) renseignements *m pl*. **intelligence test** test d'aptitude intellectuelle *m*.
intelligible [in'telidʒəbl] *adj* intelligible.
intend [in'tend] *v* avoir l'intention (de). **intended** *adj* intentionnel; projeté.
intense [in'tens] *adj* intense; (*person*) véhément. **intensify** *v* (s')intensifier. **intensity** *n* intensité *f*; véhémence *f*. **intensive** *adj* intensif. **intensive care** service de réanimation *m*.
intent¹ [in'tent] *n* intention *f*.
intent² [in'tent] *adj* attentif; résolu; absorbé.
intention [in'tenʃən] *n* intention *f*. **intentional** *adj* intentionnel, voulu.
inter [in'tə:] *v* enterrer. **interment** *n* enterrement *m*.
interact [intər'akt] *v* agir réciproquement. **interaction** *n* interaction *f*.
intercede [intə'si:d] *v* intercéder.
intercept [intə'sept] *v* intercepter. **interception** *n* interception *f*.
interchange [intə'tʃeindʒ] *n* échange *m*; (*motorway*) échangeur *m*. *v* échanger. **interchangeable** *adj* interchangeable.
intercom ['intəkom] *n* interphone *m*.
intercourse ['intəkɔ:s] *n* relations *f pl*; (*sexual*) rapports *m pl*.
interest ['intrist] *n* intérêt *m*; (*comm*) intérêts *m pl*. *v* intéresser. **be interested in** s'intéresser à.
interfere [intə'fiə] *v* s'immiscer. **interfere with** (*plans*) contrecarrer; (*work*) empiéter sur; (*meddle*) tripoter. **interference** *n* intrusion *f*; (*radio*) parasites *m pl*. **interfering** *adj* importun.
interim ['intərim] *n* intérim *m*. *adj* provisoire, intérimaire.
interior [in'tiəriə] *adj* intérieur, -e. *n* intérieur *m*.

interjection [intə'dʒekʃən] *n* interjection *f*.
interlude ['intəlu:d] *n* intervalle *m*; (*theatre*) intermède *m*; (*musical*) interlude *m*.
intermediate [intə'mi:diət] *adj* intermédiaire.
interminable [in'tə:minəbl] *adj* interminable.
intermission [intə'miʃən] *n* interruption *f*; (*cinema*) entracte *m*.
intermittent [intə'mitənt] *adj* intermittent. **intermittently** *adv* par intermittence.
intern [in'tə:n] *v* interner. **internment** *n* internement *m*.
internal [in'tə:nl] *adj* interne, intérieur, -e. **internal combustion engine** moteur à explosion *m*.
international [intə'naʃənl] *adj* international.
interpose [intə'pouz] *v* intervenir; (*remark, etc.*) intercaler.
interpret [in'tə:prit] *v* interpréter. **interpretation** *n* interprétation *f*. **interpreter** *n* interprète *m*, *f*.
interrogate [in'terəgeit] *v* interroger. **interrogation** *n* interrogation *f*; (*police*) interrogatoire *m*. **interrogator** *n* interrogateur, -trice *m*, *f*.
interrogative [intə'rogətiv] *adj* interrogateur, -trice; (*gramm*) interrogatif. *n* interrogatif *m*.
interrupt [intə'rʌpt] *v* interrompre. **interruption** *n* interruption *f*.
intersect [intə'sekt] *v* (se) couper; (*math*) (s')intersecter. **intersection** *n* croisement *m*; intersection *f*.
intersperse [intə'spə:s] *v* parsemer.
interval ['intəvəl] *n* intervalle *m*; (*theatre*) entracte *m*.
intervene [intə'vi:n] *v* intervenir, survenir. **intervention** *n* intervention *f*.
interview ['intəvju:] *n* entrevue *f*; (*press, radio, etc.*) interview *f*. *v* interviewer.
intestine [in'testin] *n* intestin *m*. **intestinal** *adj* intestinal.
intimate¹ ['intimət] *adj* intime; (*detailed*) approfondi. **intimacy** *n* intimité *f*.
intimate² ['intimeit] *v* faire connaître; suggérer. **intimation** *n* annonce *f*; suggestion *f*.
intimidate [in'timideit] *v* intimider. **intimidation** *n* intimidation *f*.
into ['intu] *prep* dans, en.

intolerable [in'tolərəbl] *adj* intolérable.
intolerant [in'tolərənt] *adj* intolérant. **intolerance** *n* intolérance *f.*
intonation [,intə'neiʃən] *n* intonation *f.*
intoxicate [in'toksikeit] *v* enivrer. **intoxicated** *adj* ivre. **intoxication** *n* ivresse *f.*
intransitive [in'transitiv] *nm, adj* intransitif.
intravenous [,intrə'viːnəs] *adj* intraveineux.
intrepid [in'trepid] *adj* intrépide.
intricate ['intriket] *adj* complexe, compliqué. **intricacy** *n* complexité *f,* complication *f.*
intrigue ['intriːg; *v* in'triːg] *n* intrigue *f. v* intriguer.
intrinsic [in'trinsik] *adj* intrinsèque.
introduce [,intrə'djuːs] *v* présenter, introduire. **introduction** *n* introduction *f,* présentation *f.* **introductory** *adj* préliminaire.
introspective [,intrə'spektiv] *adj* introspectif. **introspection** *n* introspection *f.*
introvert ['intrə,vəːt] *n* introverti, -e *m, f.*
intrude [in'truːd] *v* s'imposer, s'immiscer. **intruder** *n* intrus, -e *m, f.* **intrusion** *n* intrusion *f.*
intuition [,intjuː'iʃən] *n* intuition *f.* **intuitive** *adj* intuitif.
inundate ['inʌndeit] *v* inonder. **inundation** *n* inondation *f.*
invade [in'veid] *v* envahir. **invader** *n* envahisseur, -euse *m, f.* **invasion** *n* invasion *f.*
invalid¹ ['invəlid] *n(m+f),* adj malade; (*disabled*) infirme, invalide.
invalid² [in'valid] *adj* non valide.
invaluable [in'valjuəbl] *adj* inestimable.
invariable [in'veəriəbl] *adj* invariable.
invective [in'vektiv] *n* invective *f.*
invent [in'vent] *v* inventer. **invention** *n* invention *f.* **inventor** *n* inventeur, -trice *m, f.*
inventory ['invəntri] *n* inventaire *m.*
invert [in'vəːt] *v* intervertir, renverser. **inverted commas** guillemets *m pl.* **inversion** *n* inversion *f,* renversement *m.*
invertebrate [in'vəːtibrət] *nm, adj* invertébré.
invest [in'vest] *v* investir, placer. **investment** *n* investissement *m,* placement *m.* **investor** *n* actionnaire *m, f.*
investigate [in'vestigeit] *v* examiner; (*crime*) enquêter sur. **investigation** *n* investigation *f.*

invigorating [in'vigəreitiŋ] *adj* vivifiant, tonifiant.
invincible [in'vinsəbl] *adj* invincible.
invisible [in'vizəbl] *adj* invisible.
invite [in'vait] *v* inviter. **invitation** *n* invitation *f.* **inviting** *adj* engageant, tentant.
invoice ['invois] *n* facture *f. v* facturer.
invoke [in'vouk] *v* invoquer. **invocation** *n* invocation *f.*
involuntary [in'voləntəri] *adj* involontaire.
involve [in'volv] *v* impliquer, mêler; (*entail*) entraîner. **involved** *adj* compliqué. **involvement** *n* rôle *m;* problème *m.*
inward ['inwəd] *adj* vers l'intérieur; (*thoughts*) intime. **inwardly** *adv* secrètement. **inwards** *adv* vers l'intérieur.
iodine ['aiədiːn] *n* iode *m.*
ion ['aiən] *n* ion *m.*
irate [ai'reit] *adj* furieux.
Ireland ['aiələnd] *n* Irlande *f.* **Irish** *nm, adj* irlandais. **Irish Sea** mer d'Irlande *f.* **the Irish** les Irlandais *m pl.*
iris ['aiəris] *n* iris *m.*
irk [əːk] *v* contrarier. **irksome** *adj* ennuyeux.
iron ['aiən] *n* fer *m.* **Iron Curtain** rideau de fer *m.* **ironmonger's** *n* quincaillerie *f. v* repasser. **iron out** faire disparaître. **ironing** *n* repassage *m.* **ironing board** planche à repasser *f.*
irony ['aiərəni] *n* ironie *f.* **ironic** *adj* ironique.
irrational [i'raʃənl] *adj* pas rationnel, déraisonnable; (*math*) irrationnel.
irregular [i'regjulə] *adj* irrégulier. **irregularity** *n* irrégularité *f.*
irrelevant [i'reləvənt] *adj* sans rapport, hors de propos.
irreparable [i'repərəbl] *adj* irréparable.
irresistible [,iri'zistəbl] *adj* irrésistible.
irrespective [,iri'spektiv] *adj* irrespective **of** sans tenir compte de.
irresponsible [,iri'sponsəbl] *adj* irréfléchi.
irrevocable [i'revəkəbl] *adj* irrévocable.
irrigate ['irigeit] *v* irriguer. **irrigation** *n* irrigation *f.*
irritate ['iriteit] *v* irriter. **irritable** *adj* irritable. **irritation** *n* irritation *f.*
is [iz] *V* be.
Islam ['izlaːm] *n* Islam *m.* **Islamic** *adj* islamique.

island ['ailənd] *n* île *f*; (*in road*) refuge *m*.

isolate ['aisəleit] *v* isoler. **isolation** *n* isolement *m*.

issue ['iʃuɪ] *n* question *f*; résultat *m*; (*copy*) numéro *m*; (*stamps, etc.*) émission *f*. *v* distribuer; émettre; (*writ, etc.*) lancer.

isthmus ['isməs] *n* isthme *m*.

it [it] *pron* (*subject*) il, elle; (*direct object*) le, la; (*indirect object*) lui. **it is** c'est, il est.

italic [i'talik] *adj* italique. **italics** *pl n* italique *m sing*.

Italy ['itəli] *n* Italie *f*. **Italian** *nm*, *adj* italien; (*people*) Italien, -enne *m, f*.

itch [itʃ] *n* démangeaison *f*. *v* démanger.

item ['aitəm] *n* article *m*; question *f*.

itinerary [ai'tinərəri] *n* itinéraire *m*.

its [its] *adj* son, sa; (*pl*) ses. *pron* le sien, la sienne.

itself [it'self] *pron* se; (*emphatic*) lui-même, elle-même. **by itself** en soi; (*alone*) tout seul.

ivory ['aivəri] *n* ivoire *m*. **Ivory Coast** Côte d'Ivoire *f*.

ivy ['aivi] *n* lierre *m*.

J

jab [dʒab] *v* enfoncer. *n* coup de pointe *m*; (*coll: injection*) piqûre *f*.

jack [dʒak] *n* (*mot*) cric *m*; (*cards*) valet *m*. *v* **jack up** soulever avec un cric.

jackal ['dʒakoɪl] *n* chacal *m*.

jackdaw ['dʒakdoɪ] *n* choucas *m*.

jacket ['dʒakit] *n* (*man's*) veston *m*; (*woman's*) jaquette *f*; (*of book*) couverture *f*. **jacket potato** pomme de terre au four *f*.

jackpot ['dʒakpot] *n* gros lot *m*.

jade [dʒeid] *nm* jade.

jaded ['dʒeidid] *adj* épuisé.

jagged ['dʒagid] *adj* déchiqueté.

jaguar ['dʒagjuə] *n* jaguar *m*.

jail *or* **gaol** [dʒeil] *n* prison *f*. *v* emprisonner. **jailer** *n* geôlier, -ère *m, f*.

jam¹ [dʒam] *v* (se) coincer; (*cram*) entasser; (*block*) encombrer. *n* embouteillage *m*.

jam² [dʒam] *n* confiture *f*.

janitor ['dʒanitə] *n* portier *m*.

January ['dʒanjuəri] *n* janvier *m*.

Japan [dʒə'pan] *n* Japon *m*. **Japanese** *nm*, *adj* japonais. **the Japanese** les Japonais *m pl*.

jar¹ [dʒaɪ] *n* pot *m*, bocal *m*.

jar² [dʒaɪ] *v* (*sound*) grincer; (*knock*) cogner; (*shake*) ébranler; (*irritate*) agacer.

jargon ['dʒaɪgən] *n* jargon *m*.

jasmine ['dʒazmin] *n* jasmin *m*.

jaundice ['dʒoɪndis] *n* jaunisse *f*.

jaunt [dʒoɪnt] *n* (*coll*) balade *f*.

jaunty ['dʒoɪnti] *adj* enjoué, vif.

javelin ['dʒavəlin] *n* javelot *m*.

jaw [dʒoɪ] *n* mâchoire *f*. **jawbone** *n* maxillaire *m*.

jay [dʒei] *n* geai *m*.

jazz [dʒaz] *n* jazz *m*.

jealous ['dʒeləs] *adj* jaloux, -ouse. **jealousy** *n* jalousie *f*.

jeans [dʒiɪns] *pl n* blue-jean *m sing*.

jeep [dʒiɪp] *n* jeep *f*.

jeer [dʒiə] *v* railler, huer. *n* raillerie *f*, huée *f*.

jelly ['dʒeli] *n* gelée *f*. **jellyfish** *n* méduse *f*.

jeopardize ['dʒepədaiz] *v* mettre en danger. **jeopardy** *n* danger *m*, péril *m*.

jerk [dʒəɪk] *n* saccade *f*, secousse *f*. *v* tirer brusquement; donner une secousse à. **jerky** *adj* saccadé. **jerkily** *adv* par saccades.

jersey ['dʒəɪzi] *n* tricot *m*. **Jersey** *n* Jersey *f*.

jest [dʒest] *n* plaisanterie *f*. *v* plaisanter. **jester** *n* bouffon *m*.

jet¹ [dʒet] *n* jet *m*. **jet lag** décalage horaire *m*. **jet-propelled** *adj* à réaction.

jet² [dʒet] *n* jais *m*.

jetty ['dʒeti] *n* jetée *f*.

Jew [dʒuɪ] *n* Juif, Juive *m, f*. **Jewish** *adj* juif.

jewel ['dʒuɪəl] *n* bijou (*pl* -oux) *m*. **jeweller** *n* bijoutier *m*. **jeweller's** *n* bijouterie *f*. **jewellery** *n* bijoux *m pl*.

jig [dʒig] *n* gigue *f*. *v* danser la gigue; sautiller.

jigsaw ['dʒigsoɪ] *n* (*puzzle*) puzzle *m*; (*saw*) scie à chantourner *f*.

jilt [dʒilt] *v* laisser tomber.

jingle ['dʒiŋgl] *n* tintement *m*; (*verse*) petit couplet *m*. *v* (faire) tinter.

jinx [dʒiŋks] *n* (*coll*) porte-guigne *m*. **jinxed** *adj* ensorcelé.

job [dʒɔb] *n* travail (*pl* -aux) *m*; poste *m*.
jobcentre *n* agence pour l'emploi *f*. **job lot** lot d'articles divers *m*.
jockey ['dʒɔki] *n* jockey *m*.
jocular ['dʒɔkjulə] *adj* jovial; facétieux.
jodhpurs ['dʒɔdpəz] *pl n* culotte de cheval *f sing*.
jog [dʒɔg] *n* (*jerk*) secousse *f*; (*with elbow*) coup de coude *m*. **jogtrot** *n* petit trot *m*. *v* secouer; (*elbow*) pousser; (*memory*) rafraîchir. **jogging** *n* footing *m*. **go jogging** faire du footing.
join [dʒɔin] *v* (se) joindre, (s')unir; devenir membre (de), s'inscrire (à); (*roads, rivers, etc.*) (se) rejoindre. **join in** participer (à). **join up** assembler; (*mil*) s'engager. **joiner** *n* menuisier *m*.
joint [dʒɔint] *n* jointure *f*; (*anat*) articulation *f*; (*of meat*) rôti *m*; (*slang: place*) boîte *f*. *adj* commun. **jointly** *adv* en commun.
joist [dʒɔist] *n* solive *f*.
joke [dʒouk] *n* plaisanterie *f*; (*trick*) farce *f*. *v* plaisanter. **joker** *n* blagueur, -euse *m*, *f*; (*cards*) joker *m*.
jolly ['dʒɔli] *adj* enjoué. *adv* (*coll*) drôlement. **jollity** *n* gaieté *f*.
jolt [dʒoult] *v* cahoter. *n* secousse *f*, cahot *m*; choc *m*.
jostle ['dʒɔsl] *v* (se) bousculer. *n* bousculade *f*.
jot [dʒɔt] *v* **jot down** noter. *n* iota *m*. **jotter** *n* bloc-notes *m*.
journal ['dʒəːnl] *n* revue *f*; (*comm*) livre de comptes *m*; (*diary*) journal *m*. **journalism** *n* journalisme *m*. **journalist** *n* journaliste *m*, *f*.
journey ['dʒəːni] *n* voyage *m*; (*distance*) trajet *m*. *v* voyager.
jovial ['dʒouviəl] *adj* jovial. **joviality** *n* jovialité *f*.
joy [dʒɔi] *n* joie *f*; plaisir *m*. **joyful** *or* **joyous** *adj* joyeux.
jubilant ['dʒuːbilənt] *adj* débordant de joie. **be jubilant** jubiler. **jubilation** *n* jubilation *f*.
jubilee ['dʒuːbiliː] *n* jubilé *m*.
Judaism ['dʒuːdeiˌizəm] *n* judaïsme *m*.
judge [dʒʌdʒ] *n* juge *m*. *v* juger. **judging by** à en juger par. **judgment** *n* jugement *m*; discernement *m*.
judicial [dʒuːˈdiʃəl] *adj* judiciaire.
judicious [dʒuːˈdiʃəs] *adj* judicieux.

judo ['dʒuːdou] *n* judo *m*.
jug [dʒʌg] *n* cruche *f*; (*for milk*) pot *m*; (*slang: prison*) taule *f*.
juggernaut ['dʒʌgənɔːt] *n* (*lorry*) mastodonte *m*.
juggle ['dʒʌgl] *v* jongler. **juggler** *n* jongleur, -euse *m*, *f*. **jugglery** *n* jonglerie *f*.
jugular ['dʒʌgjulə] *nf*, *adj* jugulaire.
juice [dʒuːs] *n* jus *m*. **juicy** *adj* juteux.
jukebox ['dʒuːkbɔks] *n* juke-box *m*.
July [dʒuːˈlai] *n* juillet *m*.
jumble ['dʒʌmbl] *v* brouiller. *n* mélange *m*, fouillis *m*. **jumble sale** vente de charité *f*.
jump [dʒʌmp] *n* saut *m*; (*start*) sursaut *m*. *v* sauter; sursauter. **jump at** (*offer, etc.*) sauter sur. **jumped-up** *adj* (*derog*) parvenu. **jumpy** *adj* (*coll*) nerveux.
jumper ['dʒʌmpə] *n* pull *m*.
junction ['dʒʌŋktʃən] *n* jonction *f*; (*roads*) bifurcation *f*; (*rail*) embranchement *m*.
juncture ['dʒʌŋkʃə] *n* conjoncture *f*. **at this juncture** à ce moment-là.
June [dʒuːn] *n* juin *m*.
jungle ['dʒʌŋgl] *n* jungle *f*.
junior ['dʒuːnjə] *adj* (*younger*) cadet, -ette; (*lower rank*) subalterne. *n* cadet, -ette *m*, *f*; (*clerk*) petit commis *m*; (*in names*) fils *m*.
juniper ['dʒuːnipə] *n* genévrier *m*. **juniper berry** baie de genièvre *f*.
junk[1] [dʒʌŋk] *n* bric-à-brac *m invar*; (*coll: rubbish*) camelote *f*. **junk-shop** *n* brocanteur *m*.
junk[2] [dʒʌŋk] *n* (*boat*) jonque *f*.
junta ['dʒʌntə] *n* junte *f*.
jurisdiction [dʒuərisˈdikʃən] *n* juridiction *f*.
jury ['dʒuəri] *n* jury *m*. **juror** *n* juré *m*, femme juré *m*, *f*.
just [dʒʌst] *adv* juste; simplement. **have just** venir de: *il vient de partir*. *adj* juste. **justice** ['dʒʌstis] *n* justice *f*. **Justice of the Peace** juge de paix *m*.
justify ['dʒʌstifai] *v* justifier. **justifiable** *adj* justifiable. **justification** *n* justification *f*.
jut [dʒʌt] *v* **jut out** saillir, dépasser.
jute [dʒuːt] *n* jute *m*.
juvenile ['dʒuːvənail] *n* adolescent, -e *m*, *f*. *adj* juvénile. **juvenile delinquent** mineur délinquant, mineure délinquante *m*, *f*.
juxtapose [ˌdʒʌkstəˈpouz] *v* juxtaposer. **juxtaposition** *n* juxtaposition *f*.

K

kaftan ['kaftan] n kaftan m.
kaleidoscope [kə'laidəskoup] n kaléidoscope m.
kangaroo [kaŋgə'ruː] n kangourou m.
karate [kə'raːti] n karaté m.
kayak ['kaiak] n kayak m.
kebab [ki'bab] n kébab m.
keel [kiːl] n quille f. v keel over (naut) chavirer; (coll: faint) tomber dans les pommes.
keen [kiːn] adj vif; enthousiaste; (sharp) aiguisé; (sight, judgment) pénétrant. **keenly** adv vivement, profondément; avec enthousiasme. **keenness** n finesse f; intensité f; enthousiasme m.
***keep** [kiːp] v garder; (observe, maintain) tenir; (support) entretenir; (remain) rester; (food, etc.) se garder. **keep-fit** n culture physique f. **keep on** continuer. **keep out!** (on notice) défense d'entrer! **keepsake** n souvenir m. **keep up with** suivre; aller aussi vite que. **keeper** n gardien, -enne m, f.
keg [keg] n tonnelet m.
kennel ['kenl] n niche f. **kennels** pl n chenil m sing.
kept [kept] V keep.
kerb [kəːb] n bordure du trottoir f.
kernel ['kəːnl] n (nut) amande f; (seed) graine m.
kerosene ['kerəsiːn] n kérosène m.
ketchup ['ketʃəp] n ketchup m.
kettle ['ketl] n bouilloire f. **kettledrum** n timbale f.
key [kiː] n clef f; (piano) touche f; (music) ton m. **keyboard** n clavier m. **keyhole** n trou de serrure m. **key-ring** n porte-clefs m invar. adj clef. v **key up** surexciter.
khaki ['kaːki] nm, adj kaki.
kick [kik] n coup de pied m; (gun) recul m. v donner un coup de pied (à). **kick off** (football) donner le coup d'envoi; (coll: party, etc.) démarrer. **kick-off** n coup d'envoi m; (coll) démarrage m. **kick out** (coll) flanquer dehors.
kid¹ [kid] n (goat, leather) chevreau m; (coll: child) gosse m, f.
kid² [kid] v (coll) faire marcher.
kidnap ['kidnap] v kidnapper. **kidnapper** n kidnappeur, -euse m, f. **kidnapping** n enlèvement m.

kidney ['kidni] n (anat) rein m; (as food) rognon m. **kidney bean** haricot rouge m. **kidney machine** rein artificiel m.
kill [kil] v tuer. **killjoy** n rabat-joie m invar. **killer** n tueur, -euse m, f; assassin m. **killing** n meutre m; massacre m.
kiln [kiln] n four m.
kilo ['kiːlou] n kilo m.
kilogram ['kiləgram] n kilogramme m.
kilometre ['kiləmiːtə] n kilomètre m.
kilt [kilt] n kilt m.
kin [kin] n parents m pl. **kinship** n parenté f.
kind¹ [kaind] adj aimable, gentil, -ille. **kind-hearted** adj bon, bonne. **kindness** n bonté f, gentillesse f.
kind² [kaind] n genre m; (brand) marque f. **in kind** en nature.
kindergarten ['kindəgaːtn] n jardin d'enfants m.
kindle ['kindl] v (s')allumer, (s')enflammer.
kindred ['kindrid] n parents m pl. adj (related) apparenté; similaire. **kindred spirit** âme sœur f.
kinetic [kin'etik] adj cinétique.
king [kiŋ] n roi m; (draughts) dame f. **kingfisher** n martin-pêcheur m. **kingdom** n royaume m; (plant, animal) règne m.
kink [kiŋk] n (rope) entortillement m; (hair) crêpelure f. v s'entortiller. **kinky** adj crêpelé; bizarre.
kiosk ['kiːosk] n kiosque m.
kipper ['kipə] n hareng fumé m.
kiss [kis] v (s')embrasser. n baiser m. **kiss of life** bouche à bouche m.
kit [kit] n (equipment) matériel m; (sport) affaires f pl; (tools, first-aid, etc.) trousse f; (do-it-yourself) kit m. v **kit out** équiper.
kitchen ['kitʃin] n cuisine f. **kitchen sink** évier m.
kite [kait] n cerf-volant m; (bird) milan m.
kitten ['kitn] n chaton m.
kitty ['kiti] n cagnotte f.
kleptomania [kleptə'meiniə] n kleptomanie f. **kleptomaniac** n(m + f), adj kleptomane.
knack [nak] n tour de main m, truc m. **get the knack of** attraper le tour de main pour.
knapsack ['napsak] n sac à dos m.
knead [niːd] v pétrir.

knee [niː] *n* genou (*pl* -oux) *m*. **kneecap** *n* rotule *f*.

***kneel** [niːl] *v* s'agenouiller.

knelt [nelt] *V* **kneel**.

knew [njuː] *V* **know**.

knickers ['nikəz] *pl n* culotte *f sing*; (*briefs*) slip *m sing*.

knife [naif] *n* couteau *m*. *v* donner un coup de couteau à.

knight [nait] *n* chevalier *m*. *v* faire chevalier. **knighthood** *n* titre de chevalier *m*. **get a knighthood** être fait chevalier.

knit [nit] *v* tricoter. **knit together** lier; (*bone*) se souder. **knitting** *n* tricot *m*. **knitting machine** tricoteuse *f*. **knitting needle** aiguille à tricoter *f*.

knob [nob] *n* bouton *m*; (*of butter*) noix *f*.

knobbly ['nobli] *adj* noueux.

knock [nok] *n* coup *m*. *v* frapper; (*bump*) heurter. **knock down** abattre; (*mot*) renverser. **knock knees** genoux cagneux *m pl*. **knock out** (*stun*) assommer; (*from contest*) éliminer. **knockout** *n* (*boxing*) knock-out *m*. **knock over** renverser. **knocker** *n* marteau de porte *m*.

knot [not] *n* nœud *m*. *v* nouer.

***know** [nou] *v* (*facts*) savoir; (*places, people*) connaître; (*recognize*) reconnaître. **know-all** *n* (*coll*) je-sais-tout *m, f*. **know-how** *n* (*coll*) technique *f*. **know how to** savoir. **knowing** *adj* fin; (*look*) entendu.

knowledge ['nolidʒ] *n* connaissance *f*, savoir *m*. **knowledgeable** *adj* bien informé.

known [noun] *V* **know**.

knuckle ['nʌkl] *n* articulation du doigt *f*.

L

label ['leibl] *n* étiquette *f*. *v* étiqueter.

laboratory [lə'borətəri] *n* laboratoire *m*.

labour ['leibə] *n* travail (*pl* -aux) *m*; (*workers*) main-d'œuvre *f*. **Labour** *nm, adj* (*pol*) travailliste. **labour pains** douleurs de l'accouchement *f pl*. **labour-saving device** appareil ménager *m*. *v* peiner. **laborious** *adj* laborieux. **labourer** *n* ouvrier *m*.

laburnum [lə'bəːnəm] *n* cytise *m*.

labyrinth ['labərinθ] *n* labyrinthe *m*.

lace [leis] *n* dentelle *f*; (*for shoe*) lacet *m*. *v* lacer; (*drink*) arroser.

lacerate ['lasəreit] *v* lacérer. **laceration** *n* (*act*) lacération *f*; (*tear*) déchirure *f*.

lack [lak] *n* manque *m*. **for lack of** faute de. *v* manquer (de).

lackadaisical [,lakə'deizikəl] *adj* apathique; indolent.

lacquer ['lakə] *n* laque *f*. *v* laquer.

lad [lad] *n* (*coll*) gars *m*.

ladder ['ladə] *n* échelle *f*. *v* (*stocking*) filer. **ladderproof** *adj* indémaillable.

laden ['leidn] *adj* chargé.

ladle ['leidl] *n* louche *f*.

lady ['leidi] *n* dame *f*. **ladies** *n* (*sign*) dames *f*. **ladies and gentlemen!** mesdames, messieurs! **ladybird** *n* coccinelle *f*. **lady-in-waiting** *n* dame d'honneur *f*.

lag¹ [lag] *v* traîner. *n* retard *m*; (*time difference*) décalage *m*.

lag² [lag] *v* calorifuger. **lagging** *n* calorifuge *m*.

lager ['laːgə] *n* bière blonde *f*.

lagoon [lə'guːn] *n* lagune *f*.

laid [leid] *V* **lay¹**.

lain [lein] *V* **lie¹**.

lair [leə] *n* tanière *f*.

laity ['leiəti] *n* laïcs *m pl*.

lake [leik] *n* lac *m*.

lamb [lam] *n* agneau *m*.

lame [leim] *adj* boîteux; (*excuse, etc.*) faible. **be lame** boîter. *v* estropier. **lamely** *adv* maladroitement. **lameness** *n* boîterie *f*; faiblesse *f*.

lament [lə'ment] *n* lamentation *f*. *v* se lamenter, pleurer. **lamentable** *adj* lamentable; regrettable.

laminate ['lamineit] *v* laminer. **laminated** *adj* laminé; (*glass*) feuilleté; (*windscreen*) en verre feuilleté.

lamp [lamp] *n* lampe *f*. **lamppost** *n* réverbère *m*. **lampshade** *n* abat-jour *m invar*.

lance [laːns] *n* lance *f*. *v* (*blister, etc.*) ouvrir.

land [land] *n* terre *f*; (*country*) pays *m*. **landlady** *n* propriétaire *f*; (*boarding house*) patronne *f*. **landlord** *n* propriétaire *m*; (*pub*) patron *m*. **landmark** *n* point de repère *m*. **landscape** *n* paysage *m*. *v* (*boat*) débarquer; (*aircraft*) atterrir; (*fall*) tomber. **landing** *n* débarquement *m*; atterrissage *m*; (*between floors*) palier *m*. **landing stage** débarcadère *m*.

lane [lein] *n* chemin *m*; (*on motorway, etc.*) voie *f*; (*line of traffic*) file *f*.
language ['laŋgwidʒ] *n* (*means of expression*) langage *m*; (*of a nation*) langue *f*.
languish ['laŋgwiʃ] *v* languir.
lanky ['laŋki] *adj* dégingandé.
lantern ['lantən] *n* lanterne *f*.
Laos ['laɪos] *n* Laos *m*.
lap[1] [lap] *n* (*sport*) tour de piste *m*. *v* (*wrap*) enrouler. **lap over** se chevaucher.
lap[2] [lap] *v* (*drink*) laper; (*waves*) clapoter.
lap[3] [lap] *n* genoux *m pl*.
lapel [lə'pel] *n* revers *m*.
Lapland ['lapland] *n* Laponie *f*. **Lapp** *nm, adj* lapon; *n* (*people*) Lapon, -e *m, f*.
lapse [laps] *n* (*fault*) défaillance *f*; (*time*) intervalle *m*; (*of custom*) disparition *f*. *v* (*expire*) se périmer; (*fall*) tomber; (*commit fault*) faire un écart.
larceny ['laɪsəni] *n* vol simple *m*.
larch [laɪtʃ] *n* mélèze *m*.
lard [laɪd] *n* saindoux *m*.
larder ['laɪdə] *n* garde-manger *m invar*.
large [laɪdʒ] *adj* grand; gros, grosse. **at large** en liberté; en général. **large-scale** *adj* à grande échelle; fait sur une grande échelle.
lark[1] [laɪk] *n* (*bird*) alouette *f*.
lark[2] [laɪk] (*coll*) *n* blague *f*. *v* **lark around** faire le petit fou, faire la petite folle.
larva ['laɪvə] *n, pl* **larvae** larve *f*.
larynx ['larɪŋks] *n* larynx *m*. **laryngitis** *n* laryngite *f*.
laser ['leizə] *n* laser *m*.
lash [laʃ] *n* coup de fouet *m*; (*thong*) mèche *f*; (*of eye*) cil *m*. *v* (*whip*) fouetter; (*rain, etc.*) cingler; attacher. **lash out** envoyer un coup; (*coll: money*) lâcher. **lashing** *n* flagellation *f*. **lashings of** (*coll*) des tas de.
lass [las] *n* jeune fille *f*.
lassitude ['lasitjuɪd] *n* lassitude *f*.
lasso [la'suɪ] *n* lasso *m*. *v* prendre au lasso.
last[1] [laɪst] *adj* dernier. **last-minute** *adj* de dernière minute. **last night** (*evening*) hier soir. *adv* en dernier; finalement; la dernière fois. *n* dernier, -ière *m, f*. **at last** enfin. **lastly** *adv* pour terminer.
last[2] [laɪst] *v* durer. **last out** *v* (*person*) tenir, (*money, food, etc.*) faire. **lasting** *adj* durable.
latch [latʃ] *n* loquet *m*. *v* fermer au loquet.

late [leit] *adj* en retard; récent; (*former*) ancien; (*dead*) feu. *adv* (*not on time*) en retard; (*not early*) tard. **lately** *adv* récemment. **lateness** *n* retard *m*. **later** *adj* plus tard. **see you later!** à tout à l'heure! **latest** *adj* (*most recent*) dernier. **at the latest** au plus tard.
latent ['leitənt] *adj* latent.
lateral ['latərəl] *adj* latéral.
lathe [leiδ] *n* tour *m*.
lather ['laɪδə] *n* mousse *f*. *v* (*apply soap*) savonner; (*foam*) mousser.
Latin ['latin] *nm, adj* latin.
latitude ['latitjuɪd] *n* latitude *f*.
latrine [lə'triɪn] *n* latrine *f*.
latter ['latə] *adj* dernier, deuxième. **the latter** celui-ci, celle-ci *m, f*.
lattice ['latis] *n* treillis *m*; (*frame*) treillage *m*.
laugh [laɪf] *v* rire. **laugh at** rire de; se moquer de. *n* rire *m*; éclat de rire *m*. **laughable** *adj* ridicule. **it's no laughing matter** il n'y a pas de quoi rire. **laughing-stock** *n* risée *f*. **laughter** *n* rires *m pl*.
launch[1] [loɪntʃ] *v* lancer. **launching** *n* lancement *m*.
launch[2] [loɪntʃ] *n* vedette *f*; (*of warship*) chaloupe *f*.
launder ['loɪndə] *v* blanchir. **launderette** *n* laverie automatique *f*. **laundry** *n* (*clothes, etc.*) linge *m*; (*place*) blanchisserie *f*.
laurel ['lorəl] *n* laurier *m*.
lava ['laɪvə] *n* lave *f*.
lavatory ['lavətəri] *n* toilettes *f pl*, cabinets *m pl*.
lavender ['lavində] *n* lavende *f*.
lavish ['laviʃ] *adj* prodigue; somptueux. *v* prodiguer.
law [loɪ] *n* loi *f*; (*profession*) droit *m*; justice *f*. **law-abiding** *adj* respectueux des lois. **lawsuit** *n* procès *m*. **lawful** *adj* légal, légitime. **lawyer** *n* avocat *m*.
lawn [loɪn] *n* pelouse *f*. **lawn-mower** *n* tondeuse *f*.
lax [laks] *adj* relâché. **laxity** *n* relâchement *m*.
laxative ['laksətiv] *nm, adj* laxatif.
*****lay**[1] [lei] *v* poser; (*eggs*) pondre. **layabout** *n* fainéant, -e *m, f*. **lay-by** *n* petite aire de stationnement *f*. **lay off** (*workers*) licencier. **lay on** (*provide*) fournir. **layout** *n* (*of house, etc.*) disposition *f*; (*of page*) mise en page *f*. **lay the table** mettre la table.

lay² [lei] *adj* laïque. **layman** *n* profane *m*.
lay³ [lei] *V* **lie¹**.
layer ['leiə] *n* couche *f*. *v* (*hair*) couper en dégradé.
lazy ['leizi] *adj* paresseux. **laze around** paresser. **laziness** *n* paresse *f*.
***lead¹** [liːd] *v* mener, conduire; être à la tête de; (*sport*) être en tête. **lead on** (*tease*) faire marcher; (*encourage*) amener. **lead up to** conduire à; précéder. *n* (*sport*) tête *f*; exemple *m*; (*clue*) piste *f*; (*for dog*) laisse *f*; rôle principal *m*; (*elec*) fil *m*. **leader** *n* chef *m*; guide *m*; (*newspaper*) éditorial *m*. **leadership** *n* direction *f*. **leading** *adj* principal; majeur, -e.
lead² [led] *n* plomb *m*; (*pencil*) mine *f*.
leaf [liːf] *n* feuille *f*; page *f*; (*of table*) rallonge *f*, rabat *m*. *v* **leaf through** feuilleter. **leaflet** *n* prospectus *m*.
league [liːg] *n* ligue *f*; (*sport*) championnat *m*.
leak [liːk] *n* fuite *f*. *v* fuir; (*information*) divulguer. **leakage** *n* fuite *f*.
***lean¹** [liːn] *v* (se) pencher; (*support*) (s')appuyer. *n* inclinaison *f*. **leaning** *n* penchant *m*.
lean² [liːn] *nm, adj* maigre. **leanness** *n* maigreur *f*.
leant [lent] *V* **lean¹**.
***leap** [liːp] *n* saut *m*, bond *m*. **by leaps and bounds** à pas de géant. *v* sauter, bondir. **leap-frog** *n* saute-mouton *m*. **leap year** année bissextile *f*.
leapt [lept] *V* **leap**.
***learn** [ləːn] *v* apprendre. **learned** *adj* savant. **learner** *n* débutant, -e *m, f*. **learning** *n* érudition *f*.
learnt [ləːnt] *V* **learn**.
lease [liːs] *n* bail *m*. *v* louer à bail. **leasehold** *adj* loué à bail.
leash [liːʃ] *n* laisse *f*.
least [liːst] *adj* (*amount*) le moins de; (*smallest*) le moindre, la moindre. *pron, adv* le moins. **at least** au moins.
leather ['leðə] *n* cuir *m*. **leathery** *adj* coriace; (*skin*) parcheminé.
***leave¹** [liːv] *v* laisser; (*go away from*) quitter; (*depart*) partir. **be left** rester. **leave out** omettre, exclure. **left-luggage office** consigne *f*. **left-overs** *pl n* restes *m pl*.
leave² [liːv] *n* permission *f*; (*holiday*) congé *m*.
lecherous ['letʃərəs] *adj* lubrique. **lecher** *n* débauché *m*. **lechery** *n* luxure *f*.

lectern ['lektən] *n* lutrin *m*.
lecture ['lektʃə] *n* conférence *f*; réprimande *f*. **lecture theatre** amphithéâtre *m*. *v* faire un cours; réprimander. **lecturer** *n* conférencier, -ère *m, f*; (*university*) maître assistant *m*.
led [led] *V* **lead¹**.
ledge [ledʒ] *n* rebord *m*, saillie *f*.
ledger ['ledʒə] *n* grand livre *m*.
lee [liː] *n* abri *m*; (*naut*) côté sous le vent *m*. **leeward** *adj, adv* sous le vent.
leech [liːtʃ] *n* sangsue *f*.
leek [liːk] *n* poireau *m*.
leer [liə] *v* lorgner. *n* regard mauvais *m*.
leeway ['liːwei] *n* (*naut*) dérive *f*; liberté d'action *f*.
left¹ [left] *V* **leave¹**.
left² [left] *nf, adj* gauche. *adv* à gauche. **left-hand** *adj* à gauche. **left-handed** *adj* gaucher. **left-wing** *adj* de gauche.
leg [leg] *n* (*person*) jambe *f*; (*animal*) patte *f*; (*pork, chicken*) cuisse *f*; (*lamb*) gigot *m*; (*furniture*) pied *m*.
legacy ['legəsi] *n* legs *m*.
legal ['liːgəl] *adj* légal; judiciaire. **legality** *n* légalité *f*. **legalize** *v* légaliser.
legend ['ledʒənd] *n* légende *f*. **legendary** *adj* légendaire.
legible ['ledʒəbl] *adj* lisible. **legibility** *n* lisibilité *f*.
legion ['liːdʒən] *n* légion *f*.
legislate ['ledʒisleit] *v* faire des lois, légiférer. **legislation** *n* législation *f*.
legitimate [lə'dʒitimət] *adj* légitime. **legitimacy** *n* légitimité *f*.
leisure ['leʒə] *n* loisir *m*.
lemon ['lemən] *n* (*fruit*) citron *m*; (*tree*) citronnier *m*. *adj* (*colour*) citron *invar*. **lemonade** *n* limonade *f*. **lemon sole** limande-sole *f*. **lemon tea** thé au citron *m*.
***lend** [lend] *v* prêter.
length [leŋθ] *n* longueur *f*; (*time*) durée *f*; (*piece*) morceau *m*. **lengthen** *v* (s')allonger, rallonger. **lengthy** *adj* long, longue.
lenient ['liːniənt] *adj* indulgent. **leniency** *n* indulgence *f*.
lens [lenz] *n* lentille *f*; (*camera*) objectif *m*; (*spectacles*) verre *m*; (*eye*) cristallin *m*. **lens hood** parasoleil *m*.
lent [lent] *V* **lend**.
Lent [lent] *n* Carême *m*.

lentil ['lentil] *n* lentille *f*.
Leo ['liːou] *n* Lion *m*.
leopard ['lepəd] *n* léopard *m*.
leotard ['liːətaɪd] *n* collant *m*.
leper ['lepə] *n* lépreux, -euse *m*, *f*. **leprosy** *n* lèpre *f*. **leprous** *adj* lépreux.
lesbian ['lezbiən] *n* lesbienne *f*. *adj* lesbien. **lesbianism** *n* lesbianisme *m*.
less [les] *nm*, *adv*, *prep* moins. *adj* moins de. **less and less** de moins en moins. **lessen** *v* diminuer. **lesser** *adj* moindre.
lesson ['lesn] *n* leçon *f*, cours *m*.
lest [lest] *conj* de peur que.
*let [let] *v* laisser; (*rent out*) louer. **let down** (*lower*) descendre; (*disappoint*) décevoir; (*dress*) rallonger. **let-down** *n* déception *f*. **let in** faire entrer. **let out** faire sortir; (*shout, cry*) laisser échapper; (*clothes*) élargir.
lethal ['liːθəl] *adj* mortel.
lethargy ['leθədʒi] *n* léthargie *f*. **lethargic** *adj* léthargique.
letter ['letə] *n* lettre *f*. **letter-box** *n* boîte aux lettres *f*.
lettuce ['letis] *n* laitue *f*.
leukaemia [luːˈkiːmiə] *n* leucémie *f*.
level ['levl] *n* niveau *m*; (*road, rail*) palier *m*. *adj* (*flat*) plat; horizontal; (*spoonful*) ras; (*equal*) à égalité. **be level with** être au niveau de; être à la hauteur de. **level crossing** passage à niveau *m*. **level-headed** *adj* équilibré. *v* niveler.
lever ['liːvə] *n* levier *m*.
levy ['levi] *n* taxation *f*, taxe *f*. *v* prélever, imposer.
lewd [luːd] *adj* obscène.
liable ['laiəbl] *adj* sujet, -ette; (*law*) responsable. **be liable to** risquer de. **liability** *n* responsabilité *f*; handicap *m*.
liaison [liˈeizon] *n* liaison *f*.
liar ['laiə] *n* menteur, -euse *m*, *f*.
libel ['laibəl] *n* (*act*) diffamation *f*; (*writing*) libelle *m*. *v* diffamer; (*insult*) calomnier. **libellous** *adj* diffamatoire.
liberal ['libərəl] *adj* libéral; généreux. **Liberal** *n*, *adj* (*pol*) libéral, -e.
liberate ['libəreit] *v* libérer. **liberation** *n* libération *f*.
liberty ['libəti] *n* liberté *f*. **at liberty** en liberté, libre.
Libra ['liːbrə] *n* Balance *f*.
library ['laibrəri] *n* bibliothèque *f*. **librarian** *n* bibliothécaire *m*, *f*.
libretto [liˈbretou] *n* livret *m*.
lice [lais] *V* **louse**.

licence ['laisəns] *n* permis *m*; (*comm*) licence *f*. **license** *v* donner une licence à; autoriser. **be licensed** (*shop, etc.*) détenir une licence. **licensee** *n* (*pub*) patron, -onne *m*, *f*.
lichen ['laikən] *n* lichen *m*.
lick [lik] *n* coup de langue *m*. *v* lécher.
lid [lid] *n* couvercle *m*.
lido ['liːdou] *n* complexe balnéaire *m*.
*lie¹ [lai] *v* s'allonger, se coucher; (*be lying*) être allongé, être couché; (*be*) être. **lie around** traîner. **lie down** s'allonger, se coucher. **lie in** faire la grasse matinée.
lie² [lai] *n* mensonge *m*. *v* mentir.
Liechtenstein ['liktən,stain] *n* Liechtenstein *m*.
lieutenant [ləfˈtenənt] *n* lieutenant *m*.
life [laif] *n* vie *f*. **lifeless** *adj* sans vie, inanimé.
lifebelt ['laifbelt] *n* bouée de sauvetage *f*.
lifeboat ['laifbout] *n* canot de sauvetage *m*; (*on ship*) chaloupe de sauvetage *f*.
lifeguard ['laifgaɪd] *n* surveillant de baignade *m*.
life insurance *n* assurance-vie *f*.
life-jacket *n* gilet de sauvetage *m*.
lifeline ['laiflain] *n* main courante *f*; (*diver's*) corde de sécurité *f*.
lifelong ['laiflon] *adj* de toujours.
life-saving *n* sauvetage *m*.
life story *n* biographie *f*.
lifetime ['laiftaim] *n* vie *f*; éternité *f*.
lift [lift] *n* ascenseur *m*. **give someone a lift** prendre quelqu'un en voiture. *v* (se) lever, soulever.
ligament ['ligəmənt] *n* ligament *m*.
*light¹ [lait] *n* lumière *f*; (*mot*) feu *m*. *adj* clair. **light bulb** ampoule *f*. **lighthouse** *n* phare *m*. **light meter** photomètre *m*. **light-year** année-lumineuse *f*. *v* (*set fire to*) allumer; (*room, etc.*) éclairer. **lighten** *v* (s')éclaircir. **lighter** *n* (*for cigarette*) briquet *m*. **lighting** *n* éclairage *m*.
light² [lait] *adj* léger. **light-headed** *adj* étourdi. **light-hearted** *adj* gai, joyeux. **lightweight** *adj* léger; (*boxing*) poids léger. **lighten** *v* alléger. **lightness** *n* légèreté *f*.
*light³ [lait] *v* **light upon** tomber sur.
lightning ['laitnin] *n* éclair *m*, foudre *f*. **lightning conductor** paratonnerre *m*.
like¹ [laik] *adj* semblable. *prep* comme. **be or look like** ressembler à. **liken** *v* comparer. **likeness** *n* ressemblance *f*; forme *f*; portrait *m*. **likewise** *adv* également.

like² [laik] v aimer; (want) vouloir. **likeable** adj sympathique. **liking** n goût m.
likely ['laikli] adj probable; plausible. **be likely to** risquer de. adv probablement.
likelihood n probabilité f.
lilac ['lailək] nm, adj lilas.
lily ['lili] n lis m. **lily-of-the-valley** n muguet m.
limb [lim] n membre m.
limbo ['limbou] n (rel) limbes m pl; oubli m.
lime¹ [laim] n chaux f. **limestone** n pierre à chaux f.
lime² [laim] n (fruit) lime f; (tree) limettier m; (linden) tilleul m. **lime green** nm, adj vert jaune. **lime juice** jus de citron vert m.
limelight ['laim,lait] n **in the limelight** en vedette.
limerick ['limərik] n poème humoristique m.
limit ['limit] n limite f. v limiter. **limitation** n limitation f. **limitless** adj illimité.
limousine ['limə,ziːn] n limousine f.
limp¹ [limp] v boîter.
limp² [limp] adj mou, molle. **limpness** n mollesse f.
limpet ['limpit] n patelle f.
line¹ [lain] n ligne f; corde f; (of poem) vers m; (row) rangée f, file f. v régler; (wrinkle) rider. **line up** (s')aligner. **linear** adj linéaire.
line² [lain] v (clothes) doubler; (brakes) garnir.
linen ['linin] n lin m; (sheets, etc.) linge m. **linen basket** panier à linge m.
liner ['lainə] n liner m.
linger ['lingə] v (person) s'attarder; (pain, memory, etc.) persister; (dawdle) traîner.
lingerie ['lãʒəriː] n lingerie f.
linguist ['lingwist] n linguiste m, f. **linguistic** adj linguistique. **linguistics** n linguistique f.
lining ['lainin] n (clothes) doublure f; (brakes) garniture f.
link [link] n lien m, liaison f; (of chain) maillon m. v lier.
linoleum [li'nouliəm] n linoléum m. **lino** n (coll) lino m.
linseed ['lin,siːd] n graines de lin f pl. **linseed oil** huile de lin f.
lint [lint] n tissu ouaté m.
lion ['laiən] n lion m. **lioness** n lionne f.
lip [lip] n lèvre f; (edge) bord m. **lip-read** v lire sur les lèvres. **lipstick** n rouge à lèvres m.
liqueur [li'kjuə] n liqueur f.
liquid ['likwid] nm, adj liquide. **liquidate** v liquider. **liquidation** n liquidation f. **liquidizer** n centrifugeuse f.
liquor ['likə] n spiritueux m.
liquorice ['likəris] n réglisse f.
lira ['liərə] n lire f.
Lisbon ['lizbən] n Lisbonne.
lisp [lisp] v zézayer.
list¹ [list] n liste f. v cataloguer, énumérer.
list² [list] v (naut) gîter. n inclinaison f.
listen ['lisn] v écouter. **listener** n auditeur, -trice m, f.
listless ['listlis] adj sans énergie; indolent, apathique.
lit [lit] V **light¹**, **light²**.
litany ['litəni] n litanie f.
literacy ['litərəsi] n degré d'alphabétisation m. **be literate** savoir lire et écrire.
literal ['litərəl] adj littéral.
literary ['litərəri] adj littéraire.
literature ['litrətʃə] n littérature f; (brochures) documentation f.
litigation [liti'geiʃən] n litige m.
litre ['liːtə] n litre m.
litter ['litə] n détritus m pl; (zool) portée f; (bedding) litière f. **litter-bin** n boîte à ordures f. v joncher; (make untidy) mettre en désordre.
little ['litl] adj (small) petit; (not much) peu de. nm, adv peu. **little by little** peu à peu.
liturgy ['litədʒi] n liturgie f. **liturgical** adj liturgique.
live¹ [liv] v vivre; habiter. **live down** faire oublier. **live on** vivre de.
live² [laiv] adj vivant; (broadcast) en direct; (coal) ardent; (wire) sous tension. adv en direct.
livelihood ['laivlihud] n gagne-pain m invar.
lively ['laivli] adj vif, plein d'entrain. **liveliness** n vivacité f, entrain m.
liven ['laivn] v **liven up** égayer, (s')animer.
liver ['livə] n foie m.
livestock ['laivstok] n bétail m.
livid ['livid] adj livide; furieux.
living ['livin] adj vivant, en vie. n vie f. **living room** salle de séjour f.
lizard ['lizəd] n lézard m.
load [loud] n charge f; (weight) poids m; (coll) tas m. v charger. **loaded** adj chargé;

(*dice*) pipé; (*question*) insidieux; (*slang: rich*) bourré de fric.

loaf¹ [ləuf] *n* pain *m*.

loaf² [ləuf] *v* **loaf around** fainéanter. **loafer** *n* (*coll*) flemmard, -e *m, f*.

loan [ləun] *n* prêt *m*. *v* prêter.

loathe [ləuð] *v* détester. **loathing** *n* dégoût *m*. **loathsome** *adj* détestable.

lob [lob] *v* lancer; (*tennis*) lober. *n* lob *m*.

lobby ['lobi] *n* vestibule *m*, foyer *m*; groupe de pression *m*. *v* faire pression (sur).

lobe [ləub] *n* lobe *m*.

lobster ['lobstə] *n* homard *m*.

local ['ləukəl] *adj* local; du pays. *n* (*coll: pub*) café du coin *m*. **the locals** (*coll: people*) les gens du coin. **locality** *n* (*region*) environs *m pl*; (*place*) lieu *m*. **localize** *v* localiser. **locally** *adv* localement; (*nearby*) dans les environs.

locate [lə'keit] *v* (*find*) repérer, localiser; situer. **location** *n* emplacement *m*; (*cinema*) extérieur *m*. **on location** en extérieur.

lock¹ [lok] *n* serrure *f*; (*canal*) écluse *f*. **locksmith** *n* serrurier *m*. **lock, stock, and barrel** en bloc. **under lock and key** sous clef. *v* fermer à clef; (*tech*) (se) bloquer. **lock away** mettre sous clef. **lock in** enfermer. **lock out** enfermer dehors. **lock up** tout fermer; (*jewels, etc.*) enfermer.

lock² [lok] *n* (*of hair*) mèche *f*; (*curl*) boucle *f*.

locker ['lokə] *n* casier *m*.

locket ['lokit] *n* médaillon *m*.

locomotive [,ləukə'məutiv] *n* locomotive *f*. *adj* locomotif. **locomotion** *n* locomotion *f*.

locust ['ləukəst] *n* locuste *f*.

lodge [lodʒ] *n* loge *f*; (*small house*) maison de gardien *f*. *v* (se) loger; (*report*) présenter. **lodge a complaint** porter plainte. **lodger** *n* locataire *m, f*; (*boarder*) pensionnaire *m, f*. **lodgings** *pl n* (*room*) chambre *f sing*; (*flatlet*) logement *m sing*.

loft [loft] *n* grenier *m*. **lofty** *adj* haut, élevé; (*haughty*) hautain.

log [log] *n* bûche *f*. **logbook** *n* registre *m*; (*naut*) livre de bord *m*; (*aero*) carnet de vol *m*; (*mot*) carnet de route *m*. **log cabin** cabane en rondins *f*. *v* noter.

logarithm ['logəriðəm] *n* logarithme *m*.

loggerheads ['logəhedz] *pl n* **at loggerheads** en désaccord.

logic ['lodʒik] *n* logique *f*. **logical** *adj* logique.

loins [loins] *pl n* reins *m pl*. **loin chop** côte première *f*. **loincloth** *n* pagne *m*.

loiter ['loitə] *v* traîner.

lollipop ['loli,pop] *n* sucette *f*.

London ['lʌndən] *n* Londres *m*.

lonely ['ləunli] *adj* seul, solitaire. **loneliness** *n* solitude *f*.

long¹ [loŋ] *adj* long, longue. *adv* longtemps. **as long as** pourvu que. **long-distance** *adj* (*race*) de fond; (*phone*) interurbain. **long-playing record** 33 tours *m invar*. **long-range** *adj* à longue portée; (*weather forecast*) à long terme. **long-sighted** *adj* hypermétrope; (*having foresight*) prévoyant. **long-sleeved** *adj* à manches longues. **long-standing** *adj* de longue date. **long-term** *adj* à long terme. **long-winded** *adj* (*person*) intarissable; (*speech*) interminable.

long² [loŋ] *v* avoir très envie. **long for** désirer ardemment. **longing** *n* désir *m*, envie *f*.

longevity [lon'dʒevəti] *n* longévité *f*.

longitude ['londʒitjuid] *n* longitude *f*. **longitudinal** *adj* longitudinal.

loo [luː] *n* (*coll*) cabinets *m pl*.

look [luk] *n* regard *m*; (*glance*) coup d'œil *m*; air *m*, allure *f*. *v* regarder; sembler, avoir l'air. **look after** s'occuper de; (*possessions*) prendre soin de. **look at** regarder. **look down on** mépriser. **look for** chercher. **look forward to** attendre avec impatience. **look out** faire attention. **look out of** regarder par. **look up** lever les yeux; (*word, etc.*) chercher; s'améliorer.

loom¹ [luːm] *v* apparaître indistinctement; menacer.

loom² [luːm] *n* métier à tisser *m*.

loop [luːp] *n* boucle *f*. *v* boucler; former une boucle. **loop the loop** (*aero*) faire un looping.

loophole ['luːphəul] *n* (*in law, etc.*) lacune *f*, échappatoire *f*.

loose [luːs] *adj* lâche; (*knot*) desserré; (*tooth*) branlant. **come loose** se desserrer; branler. **get loose** s'échapper. **let loose** lâcher. **loose change** petite monnaie *f*. **loose chippings** gravillons *m pl*. **loose covers** housses *f pl*. **loose-leaf** *adj* à feuilles volantes. *v* (*free*) lâcher; (*undo*) défaire. **loosely** *adv* lâchement; approximativement. **loosen** *v* relâcher; (se) desserrer; (se) défaire.

loot [luːt] *n* butin *m*. *v* piller. **looter** *n* pillard *m*. **looting** *n* pillage *m*.

lop [lop] *v* couper.

lopsided [ˌlopˈsaidid] *adj* de travers.

lord [loːd] *n* seigneur *m*; (*as title*) lord *m*.

lorry [ˈlori] *n* camion *m*. **lorry-driver** *n* camionneur *m*, routier *m*.

*lose [luːz] *v* perdre; (*watch, clock*) retarder. **loser** *n* perdant, -e *m, f*. **lost property** objets trouvés *m pl*.

loss [los] *n* perte *f*. **be at a loss** être embarrassé.

lost [lost] *V* **lose**.

lot [lot] *n* (*destiny*) sort *m*; (*auction*) lot *m*. **a lot** beaucoup. **lots of** beaucoup de. **quite a lot of** pas mal de. **the lot** tout *m*.

lotion [ˈloufən] *n* lotion *f*.

lottery [ˈlotəri] *n* loterie *f*.

lotus [ˈloutəs] *n* lotus *m*.

loud [laud] *adj* fort, sonore; (*gaudy*) voyant. *adv* fort. **loud hailer** porte-voix *m invar*. **loud-mouthed** *adj* braillard. **loud-speaker** *n* haut-parleur *m*. **loudly** *adv* fort. **loudness** *n* force *f*.

lounge [laundʒ] *n* salon *m*. **lounge suit** complet-veston *m*. *v* (*on bed*) se prélasser; (*idle*) paresser, flâner. **lounger** *n* (*bed*) lit de plage *m*.

louse [laus] *n*, *pl* **lice** pou (*pl* poux) *m*. **lousy** *adj* pouilleux; (*slang: bad*) moche, dégueulasse.

lout [laut] *n* rustre *m*.

love [lʌv] *n* amour *m*; (*tennis*) zéro *m*. **fall in love** tomber amoureux. **love affair** liaison *f*. **make love** faire l'amour. **with love from** (*in letter*) affectueusement. *v* aimer. **lovable** *adj* adorable. **lover** *n* amant *m*; (*enthusiast*) amateur *m*. **loving** *adj* affectueux.

lovely [ˈlʌvli] *adj* charmant, agréable.

low [lou] *adj* bas, basse; faible. *adv* bas. **low-cut** *adj* décolleté. **lowland** *n* plaine *f*. **low-lying** *adj* à basse altitude. **low-paid** *adj* mal payé. **lowly** *adj* humble, modeste.

lower [ˈlouə] *adj* inférieur, -e. *v* baisser; (*on rope*) descendre.

loyal [ˈloiəl] *adj* loyal, fidèle. **loyalty** *n* loyauté *f*; fidélité *f*.

lozenge [ˈlozindʒ] *n* pastille *f*.

lubricate [ˈluːbrikeit] *v* lubrifier; (*mot*) graisser. **lubricant** *nm*, *adj* lubrifiant. **lubrication** *n* lubrification *f*; graissage *m*.

lucid [ˈluːsid] *adj* lucide. **lucidity** *n* lucidité *f*.

luck [lʌk] *n* chance *f*, hasard *m*. **bad luck** malchance *f*, malheur *m*. **good luck** bonne chance *f*, bonheur *m*. **lucky** *adj* heureux; (*charm*) porte-bonheur *m invar*. **be lucky** avoir de la chance.

lucrative [ˈluːkrətiv] *adj* lucratif.

ludicrous [ˈluːdikrəs] *adj* ridicule.

lug [lʌg] *v* traîner.

luggage [ˈlʌgidʒ] *n* bagages *m pl*. **luggage label** étiquette à bagages *f*. **luggage rack** porte-bagages *m invar*.

lukewarm [ˈluːkwoːm] *adj* tiède.

lull [lʌl] *n* arrêt *m*; (*storm*) accalmie *f*. *v* apaiser.

lullaby [ˈlʌləˌbai] *n* berceuse *f*.

lumbago [lʌmˈbeigou] *n* lumbago *m*.

lumber[1] [ˈlʌmbə] *n* (*wood*) bois de charpente *m*; (*junk*) bric-à-brac *m invar*. **lumberjack** *n* bûcheron *m*. **lumber yard** chantier de scierie *m*. *v* **lumber with** (*coll*) coller à.

lumber[2] [ˈlʌmbə] *v* marcher pesamment.

luminous [ˈluːminəs] *adj* lumineux.

lump [lʌmp] *n* morceau *m*, masse *f*; (*med*) grosseur *f*. **lump sum** somme globale *f*. **lumpy** *adj* grumeleux.

lunacy [ˈluːnəsi] *n* folie *f*, démence *f*.

lunar [ˈluːnə] *adj* lunaire.

lunatic [ˈluːnətik] *n*, *adj* fou, folle; dément, -e. **lunatic asylum** asile d'aliénés *m*.

lunch [lʌntʃ] *n* déjeuner *m*. *v* déjeuner.

lung [lʌŋ] *n* poumon *m*.

lunge [lʌndʒ] *v* faire un mouvement brusque en avant. *n* coup en avant *m*.

lurch[1] [ləːtʃ] *v* (*person*) vaciller, tituber; (*car, ship*) faire une embardée. *n* vacillement *m*; embardée *f*.

lurch[2] [ləːtʃ] *n* **leave in the lurch** faire faux bond à.

lure [luə] *v* attirer par la ruse. *n* attrait *m*; (*decoy*) leurre *m*.

lurid [ˈluərid] *adj* affreux, horrible; à sensation.

lurk [ləːk] *v* (*person*) se tapir; (*danger*) menacer; (*doubt*) persister. **lurking** *adj* vague.

luscious [ˈlʌʃəs] *adj* succulent.

lush [lʌʃ] *adj* luxuriant, riche.

lust [lʌst] *n* (*sexual*) luxure *f*; (*for power, etc.*) soif *f*. *v* **lust after** convoiter; avoir soif de. **lusty** *adj* vigoureux.

lustre [ˈlʌstə] *n* lustre *m*.

lute [luːt] *n* luth *m*.

Luxembourg ['lʌksəm,bəɪg] *n* Luxembourg *m*.
luxury ['lʌkʃəri] *n* luxe *m*. **luxuriant** *adj* luxuriant. **luxurious** *adj* luxueux.
lynch [lintʃ] *v* lyncher.
lynx [links] *n* lynx *m invar*.
lyre [laiə] *n* lyre *f*.
lyrical ['lirikəl] *adj* lyrique.
lyrics ['liriks] *pl n* paroles *f pl*. **lyricist** *n* parolier, -ère *m, f*.

M

mac [mak] *n* (*coll*) imper *m*.
macabre [mə'kaːbr] *adj* macabre.
macaroni [makə'rouni] *n* macaroni *m*.
mace¹ [meis] *n* (*staff*) masse *f*; (*club*) massue *f*.
mace² [meis] *n* (*spice*) macis *m*.
machine [mə'ʃiːn] *n* machine *f*. **machine-gun** *n* mitrailleuse *f*. **machinery** *n* machinerie *f*; mécanisme *m*.
mackerel ['makrəl] *n* maquereau *m*.
mackintosh ['makin,tɔʃ] *n* imperméable *m*.
mad [mad] *adj* fou, folle; (*angry*) furieux. **madden** *v* rendre fou; exaspérer. **madly** *adv* follement, éperdument. **madness** *n* folie *f*.
madam ['madəm] *n* madame *f*.
Madrid [mə'drid] *n* Madrid.
made [meid] *V* **make**.
Madeira [mə'diərə] *n* (*place*) Madère *f*; (*wine*) madère *m*.
magazine [,magə'ziːn] *n* revue *f*, magazine *m*; (*mil*) magasin *m*.
maggot ['magət] *n* ver *m*.
magic ['madʒik] *n* magie *f*. *adj also* **magical** magique. **magician** *n* magicien, -enne *m, f*.
magistrate ['madʒistreit] *n* magistrat *m*.
magnanimous [mag'naniməs] *adj* magnanime. **magnanimity** *n* magnanimité *f*.
magnate ['magneit] *n* magnat *m*.
magnet ['magnət] *n* aimant *m*. **magnetic** *adj* magnétique. **magnetism** *n* magnétisme *m*. **magnetize** *v* magnétiser.
magnificent [mag'nifisnt] *adj* magnifique. **magnificence** *n* magnificence *f*.
magnify ['magnifai] *v* grossir. **magnifying**

glass loupe *f*. **magnification** *n* grossissement *m*.
magnitude ['magnitjuːd] *n* ampleur *f*.
magnolia [mag'nouliə] *n* magnolia *m*.
magpie ['magpai] *n* pie *f*.
mahogany [mə'hogəni] *n* acajou *m*.
maid [meid] *n* bonne *f*. **old maid** vieille fille *f*.
maiden ['meidən] *n* jeune fille *f*. *adj* (*first*) premier. **maiden aunt** tante célibataire *f*. **maiden name** nom de jeune fille *m*.
mail [meil] *n* (*letters*) courrier *m*; (*service*) poste *f*. **mail-bag** *n* sac postal *m*. **mailbox** *n* (*US*) boîte aux lettres *f*. **mailman** *n* (*US*) facteur *m*. **mail order** vente par correspondence *f*. *v* envoyer par la poste. **mailing list** liste d'adresses *f*.
maim [meim] *v* estropier.
main [mein] *adj* principal. **main course** plat principal *m*. **mainland** *n* continent *m*. **main-line station** gare de grande ligne *f*. **main road** grande route *f*. **mainstay** *n* soutien *m*. *n* (*gas, water*) conduite *f*. **in the main** en général. **mains** *n* (*elec*) secteur *m*.
maintain [mein'tein] *v* maintenir; (*car, family*) entretenir; continuer. **maintenance** *n* maintien *m*; entretien *m*; (*alimony*) pension alimentaire *f*.
maisonette [meizə'net] *n* duplex *m*.
maize [meiz] *n* maïs *m*.
majesty ['madʒəsti] *n* majesté *f*. **majestic** *adj* majestueux.
major ['meidʒə] *adj* majeur, -e. *n* (*mil*) commandant *m*.
majority [mə'dʒoriti] *n* majorité *f*. **be in the majority** être majoritaire.
*****make** [meik] *n* marque *f*. *v* faire; rendre; obliger; arriver à. **make believe** faire semblant. **make out** (*draw up*) dresser; discerner; prétendre. **makeshift** *adj* de fortune. **make up** inventer; (*face*) (se) maquiller; composer; assembler. **make-up** *n* maquillage *m*. **make up for** compenser. **maker** *n* fabricant *m*. **making** *n* fabrication *f*.
maladjusted [malə'dʒʌstid] *adj* inadapté.
malaria [mə'leəriə] *n* malaria *m*.
male [meil] *nm, adj* mâle.
malevolent [mə'levələnt] *adj* malveillant. **malevolence** *n* malveillance *f*. **malevolently** *adv* avec malveillance.
malfunction [mal'fʌŋkʃən] *n* mauvaise fonction *f*. *v* mal fonctionner.

Mali ['mɑːli] *n* Mali *m*.
malice ['malis] *n* malice *f*. **malicious** *adj* méchant, malveillant.
malignant [mə'lignənt] *adj* malfaisant; (*med*) malin, -igne. **malignancy** *n* malfaisance *f*; malignité *f*.
malinger [mə'lingə] *v* faire le malade. **malingerer** *n* faux malade, fausse malade *m*, *f*.
mallet ['malit] *n* maillet *m*.
malnutrition [malnjuˈtriʃən] *n* sous-alimentation *f*.
malt [mɔːlt] *n* malt *m*.
Malta ['mɔːltə] *n* Malte *f*. **Maltese** *nm*, *adj* maltais. **the Maltese** les Maltais.
maltreat [mal'triːt] *v* maltraiter. **maltreatment** *n* mauvais traitement *m*.
mammal ['maməl] *n* mammifère *m*.
mammoth ['maməθ] *n* mammouth *m*. *adj* géant.
man [man] *n*, *pl* **men** homme *m*. *v* armer. **manhood** *n* âge d'homme *m*. **manly** *adj* viril.
manage ['manidʒ] *v* (*business, etc.*) gérer, administrer; (*cope*) se débrouiller. **manage to** réussir à. **manageable** *adj* maniable. **management** *n* gestion *f*, administration *f*, direction *f*; (*not workers*) cadres *m pl*. **manager** *n* directeur *m*, gérant *m*. **manageress** *n* directrice *f*, gérante *f*. **managerial** *adj* directorial. **managing director** directeur général *m*.
mandarin ['mandərin] *n* mandarin *m*. **mandarin orange** (*fruit*) mandarine *f*; (*tree*) mandarinier *m*.
mandate ['mandeit] *n* mandat *m*. **mandatory** *adj* obligatoire; (*power, etc.*) mandataire.
mandolin ['mandəlin] *n* mandoline *f*.
mane [mein] *n* crinière *f*.
mange [meindʒ] *n* gale *f*. **mangy** *adj* galeux; (*coll*) minable, miteux.
manger ['meindʒə] *n* mangeoire *f*; (*rel*) crèche *f*.
mangle¹ ['mangl] *n* (*wringer*) essoreuse *f*. *v* essorer.
mangle² ['mangl] *v* mutiler, estropier.
mango ['mangou] *n* (*fruit*) mangue *f*; (*tree*) manguier *m*.
manhandle [man'handl] *v* maltraiter; (*goods*) manutentionner.
manhole ['manhoul] *n* trou d'homme *m*.
mania ['meiniə] *n* manie *f*. **maniac** *n* (*psych*) maniaque *m*, *f*; (*coll: madman*)

fou, folle *m*, *f*; (*coll: enthusiast*) mordu *m*.
manicure ['manikjuə] *n* soin des mains *m*. *v* (*nails*) faire. **manicurist** *n* manucure *m*, *f*.
manifest ['manifest] *adj* manifeste. *v* manifester. **manifestation** *n* manifestation *f*.
manifesto [mani'festou] *n* manifeste *m*.
manifold ['manifould] *adj* divers; multiple. *n* **exhaust manifold** (*mot*) collecteur d'échappement *m*.
manipulate [mə'nipjuleit] *v* manipuler; manœuvrer. **manipulation** *n* manipulation *f*; manœuvre *f*.
mankind [,man'kaind] *n* le genre humain *m*.
man-made [,man'meid] *adj* synthétique; artificiel.
manner ['manə] *n* manière *f*; attitude *f*; sorte *f*. **manners** *pl n* manières *f pl*.
mannerism ['manə,rizəm] *n* trait particulier *m*.
manoeuvre *or US* **maneuver** [mə'nuːvə] *n* manœuvre *f*. *v* manœuvrer.
manor ['manə] *n* manoir *m*.
manpower ['man,pauə] *n* main-d'œuvre *m*; force physique *f*.
mansion ['manʃən] *n* (*country*) château *m*; (*town*) hôtel particulier *m*.
manslaughter ,['man,slɔːtə] *n* homicide involontaire *m*.
mantelpiece ['mantlpiːs] *n* cheminée *f*.
mantle ['mantl] *n* (*of snow*) manteau *m*; (*cloak*) cape *f*; (*of gas lamp*) manchon *m*.
manual ['manjuəl] *nm, adj* manuel. **manually** *adv* à la main.
manufacture [manjuˈfaktʃə] *n* fabrication *f*; (*clothes*) confection *f*. *v* fabriquer; confectionner. **manufacturer** *n* fabricant *m*.
manure [mə'njuə] *n* fumier *m*; (*artificial*) engrais *m*. *v* fumer.
manuscript ['manjuskript] *nm, adj* manuscrit.
many ['meni] *adj* beaucoup de, un grand nombre de. *pron* beaucoup, un grand nombre. **as many** autant (de). **how many** combien (de). **so many** tant (de). **too many** trop (de).
map [map] *n* carte *f*; (*of town*) plan *m*. *v* faire la carte de. **map out** tracer.
maple ['meipl] *n* érable *m*.
mar [mɑː] *v* gâter.
marathon ['marəθən] *nm, adj* marathon.

marble ['mɑːbl] *n* marbre *m*; *(toy)* bille *f*.
v marbrer.

march [mɑːtʃ] *n* marche *f*. *v* marcher au
pas. **march-past** défilé *m*.

March [mɑːtʃ] *n* mars *m*.

marchioness [ˌmɑːʃəˈnes] *n* marquise *f*.

mare [meə] *n* jument *f*.

margarine [ˌmɑːdʒəˈriːn] *n* margarine *f*.

margin ['mɑːdʒin] *n* marge *f*. **marginal** *adj*
marginal. **marginally** *adv* de très peu.

marguerite [ˌmɑːgəˈriːt] *n* marguerite *f*.

marigold ['mɑːrigould] *n* souci *m*.

marijuana [mɑːriˈwɑːnə] *n* marihuana *f*.

marina [məˈriːnə] *n* marina *f*.

marinade [ˌmɑːriˈneid] *n* marinade *f*. *v*
mariner.

marine [məˈriːn] *adj* *(animal, plant)*
marin; *(products)* de mer; maritime. *n*
(naut) marine marchande *f*; *(mil)* fusilier
marin *m*.

marital ['mɑːritl] *adj* conjugal, matrimonial.

maritime ['mɑːritaim] *adj* maritime.

marjoram ['mɑːdʒərəm] *n* marjolaine *f*.

mark[1] [mɑːk] *n* marque *f*; *(school)* note *f*,
point *m*; *(model)* série *f*. **marksman** *n*
bon tireur *m*. *v* marquer; *(school)* corriger, noter. **marked** *adj* marqué, sensible. **marking** *n* correction *f*; *(of animal)*
marque *f*.

mark[2] [mɑːk] *n* *(currency)* mark *m*.

market ['mɑːkit] *n* marché *m*. **market day**
jour de marché *m*. **market gardening** culture maraîchère *f*. **market place** place du
marché *f*. **market research** étude de
marché *f*. **market value** valeur marchande *f*. *v* vendre. **marketing** *n* com-
mercialisation *f*.

marmalade ['mɑːməleid] *n* confiture
d'orange *f*.

maroon[1] [məˈruːn] *adj* bordeaux *invar*.

maroon[2] [məˈruːn] *v* abandonner.

marquee [mɑːˈkiː] *n* grande tente *f*; *(circus)* chapiteau *m*.

marquess *or* **marquis** ['mɑːkwis] *n* marquis *m*.

marquetry ['mɑːkətri] *n* marqueterie *f*.

marriage ['mɑːridʒ] *n* mariage *m*. **by marriage** par alliance. **marriage certificate**
extrait d'acte de mariage *m*. **marriage
guidance counsellor** conseiller conjugal,
conseillère conjugale *m*, *f*. **marriage
licence** dispense de bans *f*.

marrow ['mɑːrou] *n* *(of bone)* moelle *f*;
(vegetable) courge *f*.

marry ['mɑːri] *v* se marier; *(husband, wife)*
épouser; *(priest, vicar)* marier. **married**
adj marié; conjugal. **get married** se
marier. **married name** nom de femme
mariée *m*.

Mars [mɑːz] *n* Mars *f*. **Martian** *n* Martien, -enne; *adj* martien.

marsh [mɑːʃ] *n* marais *m*. **marshland** *n*
marécage *m*. **marshmallow** *n* guimauve *f*.
marshy *adj* marécageux.

marshal ['mɑːʃəl] *n* *(mil)* maréchal *m*;
(sports, etc.) membre du service d'ordre
m. *v* rassembler.

martial ['mɑːʃəl] *adj* martial.

martin ['mɑːtin] *n* martinet *m*.

martyr ['mɑːtə] *n* martyr, -e *m*, *f*. *v*
martyriser. **martyrdom** *n* martyre *m*.

marvel ['mɑːvəl] *n* merveille *f*. *v* s'étonner
(de).

marvellous ['mɑːvələs] *adj* merveilleux.

marzipan [mɑːziˈpan] *n* pâte d'amandes *f*.

mascara [maˈskɑːrə] *n* mascara *m*.

mascot ['mɑːskət] *n* mascotte *f*.

masculine ['mɑːskjulin] *nm*, *adj* masculin.
masculinity *n* masculinité *f*.

mash [mɑːʃ] *v* écraser; *(potatoes)* faire en
purée. **mashed potatoes** purée *f sing*. *n*
(animal feed) pâtée *f*; purée *f*.

mask [mɑːsk] *n* masque *m*. *v* masquer.
masking tape papier-cache adhésif *m*.

masochist ['mɑːsəkist] *n* masochiste *m*, *f*.
masochism *n* masochisme *m*. **masochistic**
adj masochiste.

mason ['meisn] *n* maçon *m*. **masonry** *n*
maçonnerie *f*.

masquerade [mɑːskəˈreid] *n* *(pretence)*
mascarade *f*. *v* **masquerade as** se faire
passer pour.

mass[1] [mas] *n* masse *f*. **mass hysteria** hystérie collective *f*. **mass media** media *m pl*.
mass-produce *v* fabriquer en série. **mass
production** fabrication en série *f*. *v* (se)
masser.

mass[2] [mas] *n* *(rel)* messe *f*.

massacre ['masəkə] *n* massacre *m*. *v* massacrer.

massage ['masɑːʒ] *n* massage *m*. *v* masser.
masseur *n* masseur *m*. **masseuse** *n* masseuse *f*.

massive ['masiv] *adj* massif, énorme.

mast [mɑːst] *n* *(naut)* mât *m*; *(radio, etc.)*
pylône *m*.

master ['mɑːstə] *n* maître *m*; *(teacher)*
professeur *m*. **master copy** original *m*.
master key passe-partout *m invar*. **mas-**

terpiece *n* chef-d'œuvre *m*. **master plan** stratégie d'ensemble *f*. *v* maîtriser; surmonter; (*learn, understand*) posséder à fond. **masterly** *adj* magistral. **mastery** *n* maîtrise *f*, domination *f*; (*skill*) virtuosité *f*.

mastermind ['mɑːstəˌmaɪnd] *n* cerveau *m*. *v* diriger.

masturbate ['mæstəbeɪt] *v* se masturber. **masturbation** *n* masturbàtion *f*.

mat [mæt] *n* (*floor*) tapis *m*; (*door*) paillasson *m*; (*table*) dessous-de-plat *m invar*; (*cloth*) napperon *m*. **matted** *adj* (*hair*) emmêle; (*cloth*) feutré.

match[1] [mætʃ] *n* allumette *f*. **matchbox** *n* boîte à allumettes *f*.

match[2] [mætʃ] *n* (*sport*) match *m*, partie *f*; (*equal*) égal, -e *m, f*. *v* égaler; (*clothes*) s'assortir à, aller bien ensemble; (*pair*) s'apparier. **matchless** *adj* sans égal.

mate [meɪt] *n* mâle, femelle *m, f*; camarade *m, f*; aide *f*; (*coll: friend*) copain, -ine *m, f*. *v* (s')accoupler.

material [mə'tɪərɪəl] *n* (*fabric*) tissu *m*; (*substance*) matière *f*; (*for book, etc.*) matériaux *m pl*. **materials** *n pl* fournitures *f pl*. *adj* matériel. **materialist** *n* matérialiste *m, f*. **materialistic** *adj* matérialiste. **materialize** *v* se matérialiser.

maternal [mə'tɜːnl] *adj* maternel.

maternity [mə'tɜːnəti] *n* maternité *f*. **maternity clothes** vêtements de grossesse *m pl*. **maternity hospital** maternité *f*.

mathematics [mæθə'mætiks] *n* mathématiques *f pl*. **mathematical** *adj* mathématique. **mathematician** *n* mathématicien, -enne *m, f*. **maths** *n* (*coll*) maths *f pl*.

matinee ['mætɪneɪ] *n* matinée *f*. **matinée coat** veste de bébé *f*.

matins ['mætɪnz] *n* matines *f pl*.

matriarch ['meɪtrɪɑːk] *n* matrone *f*. **matriarchal** *adj* matriarcal.

matrimony ['mætrɪmənɪ] *n* mariage *m*. **matrimonial** *adj* matrimonial.

matrix ['meɪtrɪks] *n* matrice *f*.

matron ['meɪtrən] *n* matrone *f*; (*hospital*) infirmière en chef *f*; (*school*) infirmière *f*; (*home*) directrice *f*.

matt [mæt] *adj* mat.

matter ['mætə] *n* (*substance*) matière *f*; affaire *f*; contenu *m*. **as a matter of fact** à vrai dire. **matter-of-fact** *adj* (*tone*) neutre; (*person*) terre à terre. **what's the matter?** qu'est-ce qu'il y a? *v* importer. **it doesn't matter** ça ne fait rien.

mattress ['mætrɪs] *n* matelas *m*.

mature [mə'tjʊə] *adj* mûr. *v* mûrir. **maturity** *n* maturité *f*.

maudlin ['mɔːdlɪn] *adj* larmoyant.

maul [mɔːl] *v* mutiler, malmener.

mausoleum [mɔːsə'lɪəm] *n* mausolée *m*.

mauve [mouv] *nm, adj* mauve.

maxim ['mæksɪm] *n* maxime *f*.

maximum ['mæksɪməm] *nm, adj* maximum.

*may [meɪ] *v* pouvoir.

May [meɪ] *n* mai *m*. **May Day** le Premier mai.

maybe ['meɪbiː] *adv* peut-être.

mayday ['meɪdeɪ] *n* mayday *m*.

mayonnaise [ˌmeɪə'neɪz] *n* mayonnaise *f*.

mayor [meə] *n* maire *m*.

maze [meɪz] *n* labyrinthe *m*.

me [miː] *pron* moi; (*direct object*) me.

mead [miːd] *n* (*drink*) hydromel *m*.

meadow ['medou] *n* pré *m*.

meagre ['miːgə] *adj* maigre.

meal[1] [miːl] *n* (*food*) repas *m*. **make a meal of** (*labour*) faire tout un plat de.

meal[2] [miːl] *n* (*flour*) farine *f*.

*mean[1] [miːn] *v* (*signify*) vouloir dire; avoir l'intention (de); destiner.

mean[2] [miːn] *n* (*not generous*) avare; (*unkind*) mesquin; (*poor*) minable. **meanness** *n* avarice *f*; mesquinerie *f*.

mean[3] [miːn] *n* milieu *m*; (*math*) moyenne *f*. *adj* moyen.

meander [mi'ændə] *v* (*river*) serpenter; (*person*) errer. *n* méandre *m*.

meaning ['miːnɪŋ] *n* sens *m*, signification *f*. **meaningful** *adj* significatif. **meaningless** *adj* dénué de sens; (*senseless*) insensé.

means [miːnz] *n* (*way*) moyen *m*; (*wealth*) moyens *m pl*. **by all means** certainement. **by means of** au moyen de. **by no means** pas du tout. **means test** enquête sur les ressources *f*.

meant [ment] *V* **mean**[1].

meanwhile ['miːnwaɪl] *adv* en attendant.

measles ['miːzlz] *n* rougeole *f*.

measure ['meʒə] *n* mesure *f*. **made to measure** fait sur mesure. *v* mesurer. **measurement** *n* mesure *f*.

meat [miːt] *n* viande *f*. **meatball** *n* boulette de viande *f*. **meat pie** pâté en croûte *m*.

mechanic [mi'kanɪk] *n* mécanicien *m*. **mechanical** *adj* mécanique. **mechanics** *pl n* mécanisme *m sing*; (*sing: science*)

mécanique f. mechanism n mécanisme m.
mechanize v mécaniser.
medal ['medl] n médaille f. medallist n médaillé, -e m, f.
meddle ['medl] v (interfere) se mêler (de); toucher (à). meddlesome adj indiscret, -ète.
media ['miːdiə] pl n media m pl.
mediate ['miːdieit] v s'entremettre; servir de médiateur. mediation n médiation f. mediator n médiateur, -trice m, f.
medical ['medikəl] adj médical. medical officer médecin du travail m. medical school école de médecine f. n visite médicale f, examen médical m. medicate v médicamenter. medicated adj (shampoo, etc.) médical.
medicine ['medsən] n (science) médecine f; (drug) médicament m. medicine chest pharmacie f. medicinal adj médicinal.
medieval [medi'iːvəl] adj médiéval.
mediocre [miːdi'oukə] adj médiocre. mediocrity n médiocrité f.
meditate ['mediteit] v méditer. meditation n méditation f. meditative adj méditatif.
Mediterranean [meditə'reiniən] adj méditerranéen. n Méditerranée f.
medium ['miːdiəm] n milieu m; (means) moyen m; (spirits) médium m. happy medium juste milieu m. adj moyen. medium-dry adj (wine) demi-sec. medium wave (radio) onde moyenne f.
medley ['medli] n mélange m; (music) pot-pourri m.
meek [miːk] adj doux, douce. meekness n douceur f.
*meet [miːt] v (se) rencontrer; (by arrangement) (se) retrouver; (gather) se réunir; (expenses, etc.) faire face à. meeting n réunion f, assemblée f; (appointment) rendez-vous m.
megaphone ['megəfoun] n porte-voix m invar.
melancholy ['melənkəli] n mélancolie f. adj also melancholic mélancolique.
mellow ['melou] adj moelleux, velouté; (matured) mûr. v mûrir; se velouter; (person) s'adoucir.
melodrama ['melədraːmə] n mélodrame m. melodramatic adj mélodramatique. melodramatically adv d'un air mélodramatique.
melody ['melədi] n mélodie f. melodious adj mélodieux.

melon ['melən] n melon m.
melt [melt] v (se) fondre. melting n fusion f.
member ['membə] n membre m. membership n adhésion f. membership card carte d'adhérent f. membership fee cotisation f.
membrane ['membrein] n membrane f. membranous adj membraneux.
memento [mə'mentou] n souvenir m.
memo ['memou] n (coll) note f.
memoirs ['memwaːz] pl n mémoires m pl.
memorable ['memərəbl] adj mémorable.
memorandum [memə'randəm] n mémorandum m, note f.
memorial [mi'moːriəl] n monument m, mémorial m. adj commémoratif.
memory ['meməri] n (faculty) mémoire f; (thing remembered) souvenir m. memorize v apprendre par cœur.
men [men] V man.
menace ['menis] n menace f. v menacer.
menagerie [mi'nadʒəri] n ménagerie f.
mend [mend] v raccommoder, réparer. n raccommodage m. be on the mend s'améliorer. mending n raccommodage m.
menial ['miːniəl] adj (task) de domestique; (person) servile.
meningitis [menin'dʒaitis] n méningite f.
menopause ['menəpoːz] n ménopause f.
menstrual ['menstruəl] adj menstruel. menstruate v avoir ses règles. menstruation n menstruation f.
mental ['mentl] adj mental; (coll: mad) timbré. mental arithmetic calcul mental m. mental home or hospital clinique psychiatrique f. mentality n mentalité f. mentally adv mentalement.
menthol ['menθəl] n menthol m.
mention ['menʃən] v mentionner. don't mention it! il n'y a pas de quoi! not to mention sans compter. n mention f.
menu ['menjuː] n menu m.
mercantile ['məːkəntail] adj marchand; commercial.
mercenary ['məːsinəri] nm, adj mercenaire.
merchandise ['məːtʃəndaiz] n marchandises f pl. merchandizing n techniques marchandes f pl.
merchant ['məːtʃənt] n négociant m, commerçant m. merchant navy marine marchande f.

mercury ['mɜɪkjuri] *n* mercure *m*.
mercy ['mɜɪsi] *n* pitié *f*, merci *f*; (*rel*) miséricorde *f*. **at the mercy of** à la merci de. **merciful** *adj* miséricordieux. **merciless** *adj* impitoyable.
mere [miə] *adj* simple. **it's a mere formality** ce n'est qu'une formalité.
merge [mɜɪdʒ] *v* se mêler; (*comm*) fusionner; unifier. **merger** *n* fusion *f*.
meridian [mə'ridiən] *nm*, *adj* méridien.
meringue [mə'raŋ] *n* meringue *f*.
merit ['merit] *n* mérite *m*. *v* mériter.
mermaid ['mɜɪmeid] *n* sirène *f*.
merry ['meri] *adj* gai, joyeux; (*coll*: *drunk*) éméché. **merry-go-round** *n* manège *m*. **merriment** *n* gaieté *f*; hilarité *f*.
mesh [meʃ] *n* maille *f*; (*network*) réseau *m*; (*gears*) engrenage *m*.
mesmerize ['mezməraiz] *v* hypnotiser.
mess [mes] *n* désordre *m*, gâchis *m*; (*dirt*) saleté *f*; (*mil*) mess *m*. **make a mess of** gâcher. *v* **mess up** salir; gâcher, mettre en désordre. **messy** *adj* en désordre; sale.
message ['mesidʒ] *n* message *m*; (*errand*) course *f*. **messenger** *n* messager, -ère *m*, *f*.
met [met] *V* meet.
metabolism [mi'tabəlizm] *n* métabolisme *m*.
metal ['metl] *n* métal *m*. **metallic** *adj* métallique. **metallurgist** *n* métallurgiste *m*. **metallurgy** *n* métallurgie *f*.
metamorphosis [metə'mɔɪfəsis] *n* métamorphose *f*.
metaphor ['metəfə] *n* métaphore *f*. **metaphorical** *adj* métaphorique.
metaphysics [metə'fiziks] *n* métaphysique *f*. **metaphysical** *adj* métaphysique.
meteor ['miɪtiə] *n* météore *m*. **meteoric** *adj* météorique; (*rapid*) fulgurant. **meteorite** *n* météorite *n*.
meteorology [miɪtiə'rolədʒi] *n* météorologie *f*. **meteorological** *adj* météorologique. **meteorologist** *n* météorologue *m*, *f*.
meter ['miɪtə] *n* compteur *m*.
methane ['miɪθein] *n* méthane *m*.
method ['meθəd] *n* méthode *f*. **methodical** *adj* méthodique.
Methodist ['meθədist] *n* méthodiste *m*, *f*. **Methodism** *n* méthodisme *m*.
methylated spirits ['meθileitid] *n* alcool à brûler *m*.

meticulous [mi'tikjuləs] *adj* méticuleux.
metre ['miɪtə] *n* mètre *m*. **metric** *adj* métrique.
metronome ['metrənoum] *n* métronome *m*.
metropolis [mə'tropəlis] *n* métropole *m*. **metropolitan** *adj* métropolitain.
mew [mjuɪ] *v* miauler. *n* miaulement *m*.
mice [mais] *V* mouse.
microbe ['maikroub] *n* microbe *m*.
microfilm ['maikrəfilm] *n* microfilm *m*.
microphone ['maikrəfoun] *n* microphone *m*.
microscope ['maikrəskoup] *n* microscope *m*. **microscopic** *adj* microscopique.
microwave ['maikrəweiv] *n* micro-onde *f*.
mid [mid] *adj* du milieu. **mid-June, July, etc.** mi-juin, juillet, etc.
mid-air [mid'eə] *n* **in mid-air** en plein ciel.
midday [mid'dei] *n* midi *m*.
middle ['midl] *n* milieu *m*. **in the middle** au milieu. *adj* du milieu. **middle-aged** *adj* d'un certain âge. **the Middle Ages** le moyen âge *m sing*. **middle-class** *adj* bourgeois. **Middle East** Moyen-Orient *m*. **middleman** *n* intermédiaire *m*. **middle-of-the-road** *adj* modéré. **middle-sized** *adj* de grandeur moyenne. **middling** *adj* comme ci comme ça.
midge [midʒ] *n* moucheron *m*.
midget ['midʒit] *n* nain, -e *m*, *f*.
midnight ['midnait] *n* minuit *m*.
midriff ['midrif] *n* diaphragme *m*; (*waist*) taille *f*.
midst [midst] *n* milieu *m*. **in our midst** parmi nous. **in the midst of** au milieu de.
midstream [mid'striɪm] *n* **in midstream** au milieu du courant.
midsummer ['midsʌmə] *n* cœur de l'été *m*. **Midsummer Day** la Saint-Jean *f*.
midway [mid'wei] *adv*, *adj* à mi-chemin.
midweek [mid'wiɪk] *n* milieu de la semaine *m*.
midwife ['midwaif] *n* sage-femme *f*. **midwifery** *n* obstétrique *f*.
midwinter [mid'wintə] *n* milieu de l'hiver *m*.
might[1] [mait] *V* may.
might[2] [mait] *n* puissance *f*.
mighty ['maiti] *adj* puissant; vaste. *adv* (*coll*) rudement.
migraine ['miɪgrein] *n* migraine *f*.

migrate [mai'greit] *v* émigrer. **migration** *n* migration *f*.

mike [maik] *n* (*coll: microphone*) micro *m*.

mild [maild] *adj* doux, douce. **mildness** *n* douceur *f*.

mildew ['mildjuː] *n* (*vine*) mildiou *m*; (*plants*) rouille *f*; (*cloth*) moisissure *f*.

mile [mail] *n* mille *m*. **mileage** *n* distance en milles *f*; (*petrol*) consommation aux cent *f*. **mileometer** *n* compteur de milles *m*. **milestone** *n* borne *f*; (*of life, etc.*) jalon *m*.

militant ['militənt] *n, adj* militant, -e.

military ['militəri] *adj* militaire.

milk [milk] *n* lait *m*. **milk chocolate** chocolat au lait *m*. **milkman** *n* laitier *m*. **milk shake** lait parfumé fouetté *m*. *v* traire. **milking** *n* traite *f*. **milky** *adj* laiteux.

mill [mil] *n* moulin *m*; (*larger*) minoterie *f*; (*factory*) usine *f*. **like a millpond** comme un lac. **millstone** *n* meule *f*; (*burden*) boulet *m*. *v* moudre. **mill round** grouiller autour de. **miller** *n* meunier *m*.

millennium [mi'leniəm] *n* millénaire *m*. **the millennium** le millénium *m*.

millet ['milit] *n* millet *m*.

milligram ['mili,gram] *n* milligramme *m*.

millilitre ['mili,liːtə] *n* millilitre *m*.

millimetre ['mili,miːtə] *n* millimètre *m*.

milliner ['milinə] *n* modiste *f*. **millinery** *n* modes *f pl*.

million ['miljən] *n* million *m*. **millionaire** *n* millionnaire *m*. **millions of** des milliers de. **millionth** *n*(*m+f*), *adj* millionième.

mime [maim] *n* mime *m*. *v* mimer.

mimic ['mimik] *n* imitateur, -trice *m, f*. *v* imiter. **mimicry** *n* imitation *f*; (*zool*) mimétisme *m*.

minaret [minə'ret] *n* minaret *m*.

mince [mins] *n* (*meat*) hachis *m*. **mincemeat** *n* hachis de fruit secs, de pommes et de graisse *m*. **mince pie** tarte anglaise au mincemeat *f*. *v* hacher; (*walk*) marcher à petits pas maniérés. **mince words** mâcher ses mots. **mincer** *n* hachoir *m*. **mincing** *adj* affecté.

mind [maind] *n* esprit *m*. **bear in mind** tenir compte de. **go out of one's mind** perdre la tête. **have a good mind to** avoir bien envie de. **in mind** dans l'idée. **make up one's mind** décider. **read someone's mind** lire la pensée de quelqu'un. **to my mind** à mon avis. *v* (*look out*) faire attention (à), prendre garde (à); (*look after*)

garder. **do you mind?** cela ne vous fait rien? **I don't mind** ça m'est égal. **never mind** ça ne fait rien.

mine[1] [main] *pron* le mien, la mienne.

mine[2] [main] *n* mine *f*. **minefield** *n* champ de mines *m*. **mineshaft** *n* puits de mine *m*. **minesweeper** dragueur de mines. *m. v* extraire; (*mil*) miner. **miner** *n* mineur *m*. **mining** *n* exploitation minière *f*. **mining town** ville minière *f*.

mineral ['minərəl] *nm, adj* minéral. **minerals** *pl n* (*drinks*) boissons gazeuses *f pl*.

mingle ['miŋgl] *v* (se) mêler (à).

miniature ['minitʃə] *n* miniature *f*; (*bottle*) mini-bouteille *f*. *adj* miniature; minuscule.

minim ['minim] *n* blanche *f*.

minimum ['miniməm] *nm, adj* minimum. **minimal** *adj* minime. **minimize** *v* minimiser.

minister ['ministə] *n* ministre *m*. **ministerial** *adj* ministériel. **ministry** *n* ministère *m*.

mink [miŋk] *n* vison *m*.

minor ['mainə] *adj* mineur, -e; (*unimportant*) petit, secondaire. *n* mineur, -e *m, f*.

minority [mai'noriti] *n* minorité *f*. **in the minority** en minorité. *adj* minoritaire.

minstrel ['minstrəl] *n* ménestrel *m*.

mint[1] [mint] *n* (*bot*) menthe *f*.

mint[2] [mint] *n* Monnaie *f*. **in mint condition** à l'état neuf. *v* battre.

minuet [minju'et] *n* menuet *m*.

minus ['mainəs] *prep* moins. **minus quantity** quantité négative *f*. **minus sign** moins *m*.

minute[1] ['minit] *n* minute *f*. **minutes** *pl n* compte rendu *m sing*. *v* (*meeting*) rédiger le compte rendu de.

minute[2] [mai'njuːt] *adj* (*tiny*) minuscule; (*detailed*) minutieux.

miracle ['mirəkl] *n* miracle *m*. **miraculous** *adj* miraculeux.

mirage ['miraːʒ] *n* mirage *m*.

mirror ['mirə] *n* miroir *m*, glace *f*; (*mot*) rétroviseur *m*. **mirror image** image invertie *f*. *v* refléter.

mirth [məːθ] *n* hilarité *f*.

misadventure [misəd'ventʃə] *n* mésaventure *f*. **death by misadventure** mort accidentelle *f*.

misanthropist [miz'anθrəpist] *n* misanthrope *m, f*. **misanthropic** *adj* misanthrope. **misanthropy** *n* misanthropie *f*.

misapprehension [misapri'henʃən] *n* malentendu *m*.

misbehave [misbi'heiv] *v* se conduire mal.

miscalculate [mis'kalkjuleit] *v* mal calculer; se tromper.

miscarriage [mis'karidʒ] *n* (*med*) fausse couche *f*; (*plans, etc.*) insuccès *m*. **miscarriage of justice** erreur judiciaire *f*.

miscellaneous [misə'leiniəs] *adj* divers.

mischief ['mistʃif] *n* malice *f*; (*of child*) sottises *f pl*; (*damage*) mal *m*. **get into mischief** faire des sottises. **make mischief** semer la discorde. **mischievous** *adj* espiègle, malicieux.

misconception [miskən'sepʃən] *n* idée fausse *f*.

misconduct [mis'kondʌkt] *n* inconduite *f*.

misconstrue [miskən'struː] *v* mal interpréter.

misdeed [mis'diːd] *n* méfait *m*.

misdemeanour [misdi'miːnə] *n* incartade *f*; (*law*) infraction *f*.

miser ['maizə] *n* avare *m, f*. **miserly** *adj* avare.

miserable ['mizərəbl] *adj* (*sad*) malheureux; pitoyable; (*wretched*) misérable; dérisoire.

misery ['mizəri] *n* (*sadness*) tristesse *f*; (*wretchedness*) misère *f*; (*coll: person*) grincheux, -euse *m, f*.

misfire [mis'faiə] *v* rater; (*mot*) avoir des ratés.

misfit ['misfit] *n* inadapté, -e *m, f*.

misfortune [mis'foːtʃən] *n* malheur *m*.

misgiving [mis'givin] *n* doute *m*, appréhension *f*.

misguided [mis'gaidid] *adj* malencontreux.

mishap ['mishap] *n* mésaventure *f*.

misinterpret [misin'təːprit] *v* mal interpréter. **misinterpretation** *n* interprétation erronée *f*.

misjudge [mis'dʒʌdʒ] *v* mal évaluer; (*person*) méjuger.

*****mislay** [mis'lei] *v* égarer.

*****mislead** [mis'liːd] *v* tromper. **misleading** *adj* trompeur, -euse.

misnomer [mis'noumə] *n* nom mal approprié *m*.

misogynist [mi'sodʒənist] *n* misogyne *m, f*. **misogyny** *n* misogynie *f*.

misplace [mis'pleis] *v* mal placer; (*lose*) égarer.

misprint ['misprint] *n* coquille *f*.

miss¹ [mis] *v* manquer; (*long for*) regret-

ter. **miss out** sauter; omettre. *n* coup manqué *m*. **missing** *adj* absent, manquant.

miss² [mis] *n* mademoiselle *f*; (*abbrev*) Mlle.

misshapen [miʃ'ʃeipən] *adj* difforme.

missile ['misail] *n* projectile *m*; (*mil*) missile *m*.

mission ['miʃən] *n* mission *f*. **missionary** *n* missionnaire *m, f*.

mist [mist] *n* (*weather*) brume *f*; (*on glass*) buée *f*. *v* **mist over** *or* **up** (s')embuer. **misty** *adj* brumeux; embué.

*****mistake** [mi'steik] *n* erreur *f*, faute *f*. **by mistake** par erreur. **make a mistake** faire une faute, se tromper. *v* mal interpréter; ne pas reconnaître; confondre. **mistaken** *adj* erroné. **be mistaken** se tromper, faire erreur.

mistletoe ['misltou] *n* gui *m*.

mistress ['mistris] *n* maîtresse *f*; (*teacher*) professeur *m*.

mistrust [mis'trʌst] *n* méfiance *f*. *v* se méfier de.

*****misunderstand** [misʌndə'stand] *v* mal comprendre. **misunderstanding** *n* méprise *f*.

misuse [mis'juːs; *v* mis'juːz] *n* abus *m*; usage impropre *m*. *v* abuser de; employer improprement.

mitigate ['mitigeit] *v* atténuer.

mitre ['maitə] *n* (*rel*) mitre *f*; (*carpentry*) onglet *m*. *v* tailler à onglet.

mitten ['mitn] *n* moufle *f*.

mix [miks] *v* (se) mélanger; (*cookery*) préparer; (*salad*) remuer. **mix up** mélanger; confondre; (*person*) embrouiller. **mix-up** *n* confusion *f*. **mixed** *adj* mixte; assorti. **mixed feelings** sentiments contraires *m pl*. **mixed grill** assortiment de grillades *m*. **mixer** *n* (*cookery*) mixer *m*; (*cement*) malaxeur *m*. **mixture** *n* mélange *m*.

moan [moun] *v* gémir; (*coll: complain*) rouspéter. *n* gémissement *m*; (*complaint*) plainte *f*.

moat [mout] *n* douves *f pl*.

mob [mob] *n* cohue *f*.

mobile ['moubail] *nm, adj* mobile. **mobility** *n* mobilité *f*. **mobilize** *v* mobiliser.

moccasin ['mokəsin] *n* mocassin *m*.

mock [mok] *v* se moquer (de); ridiculiser. *adj* faux, fausse; simulé. **mockery** *n* moquerie *f*; travestissement *m*. **mocking** *adj* moqueur, -euse.

mode [moud] *n* mode *m*.

model ['modl] *n* modèle *m*; (*fashion*) mannequin *m*. *adj* modèle; en miniature. *v* modeler; être mannequin; poser.

moderate ['modərət; *v* 'modəreit] *n, adj* modéré, -e. *v* (se) modérer. **moderately** *adv* modérément; (*fairly*) plus ou moins. **moderation** *n* modération *f*. **in moderation** modérément.

modern ['modən] *adj* moderne. **modern languages** langues vivantes *f pl*. **modernization** *n* modernisation *f*. **modernize** *v* moderniser.

modest ['modist] *adj* modeste. **modesty** *n* modestie *f*.

modify ['modifai] *v* modifier; modérer. **modification** *n* modification *f*.

modulate ['modjuleit] *v* moduler. **modulation** *n* modulation *f*.

module ['modju:l] *n* module *m*.

mohair ['mouheə] *n* mohair *m*.

moist [moist] *adj* moite, humide. **moisten** *v* humecter. **moisture** *n* humidité *f*. **moisturize** *v* humidifier; (*skin*) hydrater.

molasses [mə'lasiz] *n* mélasse *f*.

mold (*US*) *V* **mould**.

mole[1] [moul] *n* (*on skin*) grain de beauté *m*.

mole[2] [moul] *n* (zool) taupe *f*. **molehill** *n* taupinière *f*.

molecule ['molikju:l] *n* molécule *f*. **molecular** *adj* moléculaire.

molest [mə'lest] *v* molester; (*law*) attenter à la pudeur de.

mollusc ['moləsk] *n* mollusque *m*.

molt (*US*) *V* **moult**.

molten ['moultən] *adj* en fusion.

moment ['moumənt] *n* moment *m*, instant *m*. **at the moment** en ce moment. **momentary** *adj* momentané. **momentous** *adj* considérable.

Monaco ['monə,kou] *n* Monaco *f*.

monarch ['monək] *n* monarque *m*. **monarchist** *n* monarchiste *m, f*. **monarchy** *n* monarchie *f*.

monastery ['monəstəri] *n* monastère *m*. **monastic** *adj* monastique.

Monday ['mʌndi] *n* lundi *m*.

money ['mʌni] *n* argent *m*, monnaie *f*. **get one's money back** être remboursé. **get one's money's worth** en avoir pour son argent. **money-box** *n* tirelire *f*. **moneylender** *n* prêteur sur gages *m*. **moneymaking** *adj* lucratif.

mongol ['mongəl] *n, adj* (*med*) mongolien, -enne. **mongolism** *n* mongolisme *m*.

mongrel ['mʌngrəl] *n* (*dog*) chien bâtard *m*.

monitor ['monitə] *n* (*device*) moniteur *m*. *v* contrôler.

monk [mʌnk] *n* moine *m*.

monkey ['mʌnki] *n* singe *m*. *v* **monkey around** perdre son temps; faire l'idiot.

monogamy [mə'nogəmi] *n* monogamie *f*. **monogamous** *adj* monogame.

monogram ['monəgram] *n* monogramme *m*.

monologue ['monəlog] *n* monologue *m*.

monopolize [mə'nopəlaiz] *v* monopoliser. **monopoly** *n* monopole *m*.

monosyllable ['monəsiləbl] *n* monosyllabe *m*. **monosyllabic** *adj* (*word*) monosyllabe; (*reply*) monosyllabique.

monotone ['monətoun] *n* ton monocorde *m*. **monotonous** *adj* monotone. **monotony** *n* monotonie *f*.

monsoon [mon'su:n] *n* mousson *f*.

monster ['monstə] *n* monstre *m*. **monstrosity** *n* monstruosité *f*. **monstrous** *adj* monstrueux; colossal.

month [mʌnθ] *n* mois *m*.

monthly ['mʌnθli] *adj* mensuel. *adv* mensuellement, tous les mois.

monument ['monjument] *n* monument *m*. **monumental** *adj* monumental.

mood[1] [mu:d] *n* humeur *f*. **be in the mood for** avoir envie de, être d'humeur à. **moody** *adj* maussade.

mood[2] [mu:d] *n* (*gramm*) mode *m*.

moon [mu:n] *n* lune *f*. **moonbeam** *n* rayon de lune *m*. **moonlight** *n* clair de lune *m*. **moonlighting** *n* (*coll*) travail noir *m*.

moor[1] [muə] *n* lande *f*. **moorhen** *n* poule d'eau *f*.

moor[2] [muə] *v* amarrer, mouiller.

mop [mop] *n* (*floor*) balai laveur *m*; (*dishes*) lavette *f*. **mop of hair** tignasse *f*. *v* essuyer. **mop up** éponger.

mope [moup] *v* se morfondre.

moped ['mouped] *n* cyclomoteur *m*.

moral ['morəl] *adj* moral. **moral support** soutien moral *m*. *n* (*fable*) morale *f*. **morals** *pl n* moralité *f sing*. **moralist** *n* moraliste *m, f*. **morality** *n* moralité *f*. **moralize** *v* moraliser.

morale [mə'ra:l] *n* moral *m*.

morbid ['mo:bid] *adj* morbide.

more [mo:] *adj* (*larger number*) plus de; (*in addition*) encore de. *pron, adv* plus, davantage; encore. **all the more** d'autant plus. **and what's more** et qui plus est. **even more** encore plus. **more and more** de plus en plus. **once more** une fois de plus.

moreover [mɔɪ'rouvə] *adv* de plus; (*besides*) d'ailleurs.

morgue [mɔɪg] *n* morgue *f.*

Mormon ['mɔɪmən] *n, adj* mormon, -e.

morning ['mɔɪnɪŋ] *n* matin *m.* matinée *f.* **morning dress** habit *m.* **morning sickness** nausées matinales *f pl.*

Morocco [mə'rokou] *n* Maroc *m.* **Moroccan** *n* Marocain, -e *m, f*; *adj* marocain.

moron ['mɔɪron] *n* crétin, -e *m, f.* **moronic** *adj* crétin.

morose [mə'rous] *adj* morose.

morphine ['mɔɪfiɪn] *n* morphine *f.*

Morse code [mɔɪs] *n* morse *m.*

morsel ['mɔɪsəl] *n* petit morceau *m.*

mortal ['mɔɪtl] *nm, adj* mortel. **mortality** *n* mortalité *f.*

mortar ['mɔɪtə] *n* mortier *m.*

mortgage ['mɔɪgidʒ] *n* (*loan*) emprunt-logement *m*; (*law*) hypothèque *f.* *v* hypothéquer.

mortify ['mɔɪtifai] *v* mortifier. **mortification** *n* mortification *f.*

mortuary ['mɔɪtʃuəri] *n* morgue *f.*

mosaic [mə'zeiik] *n* mosaïque *f.*

Moscow ['moskou] *n* Moscou.

mosque [mosk] *n* mosquée *f.*

mosquito [mə'skiɪtou] *n* moustique *m.* **mosquito net** moustiquaire *f.*

moss [mos] *n* mousse *f.* **mossy** *adj* moussu.

most [moust] *adj* le plus de; (*majority*) la plupart de. *pron* le plus; la plupart. *adv* le plus; (*very*) bien, fort. **at most** au maximum. **make the most of** profiter de; utiliser au mieux. **mostly** *adv* surtout, pour la plupart; en général.

motel [mou'tel] *n* motel *m.*

moth [moθ] *n* papillon de nuit *m.* **clothes moth** mite *f.* **mothball** *n* boule de naphtaline *f.* **moth-eaten** *adj* mité.

mother ['mʌθə] *n* mère *f.* **mother-in-law** *n* belle-mère *f.* **mother-of-pearl** *n* nacre *f.* **Mother's Day** la fête des Mères *f.* **mother-to-be** *n* future maman *f.* *v* dorloter. **motherhood** *n* maternité *f.* **motherly** *adj* maternel.

motion ['mouʃən] *n* mouvement *m*; (*proposal*) motion *f.* **set in motion** mettre en

marche. *v* faire signe. **motionless** *adj* immobile.

motivate ['moutiveit] *v* motiver; (*person*) pousser. **motivation** *n* motivation *f.*

motive ['moutiv] *n* motif *m*; (*law*) mobile *m.* *adj* moteur, -trice.

motor ['moutə] *n* moteur *m.* **motorbike** *n* (*coll*) moto *f.* **motorboat** *n* canot automobile *m.* **motorcyclist** *n* motocycliste *m, f.* **motor racing** course automobile *f.* **motorway** *n* autoroute *f.* **motorist** *n* automobiliste *m, f.* **motorize** *v* motoriser.

mottled ['motld] *adj* tacheté.

motto ['motou] *n* devise *f.*

mould[1] or US **mold** [mould] *n* (*shape*) moule *m.* *v* mouler; modeler.

mould[2] or US **mold** [mould] *n* (*fungus*) moisissure *f.* **mouldy** *adj* moisi; (*coll: nasty*) moche. **go mouldy** moisir.

moult or US **molt** [moult] *v* muer. *n* mue *f.*

mound [maund] *n* (*natural*) tertre *m*; (*artificial*) remblai *m*; (*heap*) tas *m*; (*burial*) tumulus *m.*

mount[1] [maunt] *v* monter (sur). **mount up** s'accumuler. *n* monture *f*; (*for painting*) carton de montage *m*; (*for machine*) support *m.*

mount[2] [maunt] *n* mont *m.*

mountain ['mauntən] *n* montagne *f.* **mountaineer** *n* alpiniste *m, f.* **mountaineering** *n* alpinisme *m.* **mountainous** *adj* montagneux; énorme.

mourn [mɔɪn] *v* pleurer. **mournful** *adj* (*person*) mélancolique; (*sound*) lugubre. **mourning** *n* deuil *m.*

mouse [maus] *n, pl* **mice** souris *f.* **mousetrap** *n* souricière *f.* **mousy** *adj* timide; (*hair*) châtain clair *invar.*

mousse [muɪs] *n* mousse *f.*

moustache [mə'staɪʃ] *n* moustache *f.*

mouth [mauθ] *n* bouche *f*; (*dog, cat, etc.*) gueule *f*; (*river*) embouchure *f.* **mouth organ** harmonica *m.* **mouthpiece** *n* bec *m*; (*spokesman*) porte-parole *m invar.* **mouthwash** *n* eau dentifrice *f.* **mouthwatering** *adj* appétissant. *v* dire du bout des lèvres. **mouthful** *n* bouchée *f.*

move [muɪv] *n* mouvement *m*; (*house*) déménagement *m*; (*game*) coup *m*; (*step*) pas *m.* *v* bouger, (se) déplacer, (se) mouvoir; (*emotionally*) émouvoir; proposer; déménager; (*act*) agir. **move back** reculer; (faire) retourner. **move forward** (faire) avancer. **move in** emménager.

move out déménager. move over (s')écarter; (to make room) se pousser. move up (faire) monter. movable adj mobile. movement n mouvement m. moving adj émouvant; mobile; (pavement, etc.) roulant.

movie ['muːvi] (US) n film m. go to the movies (coll) aller au ciné.

*mow [mou] v (lawn) tondre. mow down faucher.

mown [moun] V mow.

Mr ['mistə] n Monsieur m; (abbrev) M.

Mrs ['misiz] n Madame f; (abbrev) Mme.

much [mʌtʃ] adj beaucoup de. pron, adv beaucoup. as much autant (que). how much combien (de). much as bien que. so much tant (de). too much trop (de).

muck [mʌk] n (manure) fumier m; (dirt) saleté f. v muck about (coll) perdre son temps. muck in (slang) mettre la main à la pâte. muck out nettoyer. mucky adj sale.

mucus ['mjuːkəs] n mucus m. mucous adj muqueux.

mud [mʌd] n boue f. mudguard n garde-boue m invar. muddy adj boueux.

muddle ['mʌdl] n désordre m; confusion f. v brouiller; confondre.

muff [mʌf] n manchon m.

muffle ['mʌfl] v assourdir. muffle up emmitoufler. muffler n cache-nez m invar; (US: mot) silencieux m.

mug [mʌg] n chope f; (slang: fool) poire f. v agresser. mugging n agression f.

muggy ['mʌgi] adj mou, molle.

mulberry ['mʌlbəri] n (fruit) mûre f; (bush) mûrier m.

mule¹ [mjuːl] n (animal) mulet, mule m, f. mulish adj têtu.

mule² [mjuːl] n (slipper) mule f.

multicoloured [ˌmʌlti'kʌləd] adj multicolore.

multilingual [ˌmʌlti'liŋgwəl] adj polyglotte.

multiple ['mʌltipl] nm, adj multiple. multiple sclerosis sclérose en plaques f.

multiply ['mʌltiplai] v (se) multiplier. multiplication n multiplication f.

multiracial [ˌmʌlti'reiʃəl] adj multiracial.

multi-storey [ˌmʌlti'stoːri] adj à étages.

multitude ['mʌltitjuːd] n multitude f.

mumble ['mʌmbl] v marmotter. n marmottement m.

mummy¹ ['mʌmi] n (corpse) momie f.

mummification n momification f. mummify v momifier.

mummy² ['mʌmi] n (coll: mother) maman f.

mumps [mʌmps] n oreillons m pl.

munch [mʌntʃ] v mastiquer.

mundane [mʌn'dein] adj mondain, banal.

municipal [mju'nisipəl] adj municipal. municipality n municipalité f.

mural ['mjuərəl] adj mural. n peinture murale f.

murder ['məːdə] n meurtre m. v assassiner. murderer n meurtrier, -ère m, f. murderous adj meutrier.

murky ['məːki] adj sombre; (water) trouble.

murmur ['məːmə] n murmure m. v murmurer.

muscle ['mʌsl] n muscle m. muscular adj musculaire; (person) musclé.

muse [mjuːz] v méditer, songer. n muse f.

museum [mju'ziəm] n musée m.

mushroom ['mʌʃrum] n champignon m.

music ['mjuːzik] n musique f. music centre chaîne compacte stéréo f. music hall music-hall m. music stand pupitre à musique m. musical adj musical; (gifted) musicien. musical box boîte à musique f. musical (comedy) comédie musicale f. musical instrumental instrument de musique m. musician n musicien, -enne m, f.

musk [mʌsk] n musc m.

musket ['mʌskit] n mousquet m. musketeer n mousquetaire m.

Muslim ['mʌzlim] n, adj musulman, -e.

muslin ['mʌzlin] n mousseline f.

mussel ['mʌsl] n moule f.

*must [mʌst] v devoir. n (coll) chose indispensable f.

mustard ['mʌstəd] n moutarde f. mustard pot moutardier m.

muster ['mʌstə] v (se) rassembler, (se) réunir. n assemblée f. pass muster être acceptable.

musty ['mʌsti] adj de moisi. smell musty sentir le moisi.

mute [mjuːt] adj muet, -ette. n muet, -ette m, f; (music) sourdine f. v assourdir.

mutilate ['mjuːtileit] v mutiler. mutilation n mutilation f.

mutiny ['mjuːtini] n mutinerie f; révolte f. v se mutiner; se révolter. mutinous adj mutiné; rebelle.

mutter ['mʌtə] *n* marmonner. *n* marmonnement *m*.

mutton ['mʌtn] *n* mouton *m*.

mutual ['mju:tʃuəl] *adj* mutuel; commun.

muzzle ['mʌzl] *n* (*nose*) museau *m*; (*device*) muselière *f*; (*gun*) bouche *f*. *v* museler.

my [mai] *adj* mon, ma; (*pl*) mes.

myself [mai'self] *pron* me; (*emphatic*) moi-même. **by myself** tout seul.

mystery ['mistəri] *n* mystère *m*. **mysterious** *adj* mystérieux.

mystic ['mistik] *n* mystique *m, f. adj also* **mystical** mystique; occulte; surnaturel. **mysticism** *n* mysticisme *m*.

mystify ['mistifai] *v* rendre perplexe, mystifier.

mystique [mi'stiːk] *n* mystique *f*.

myth [miθ] *n* mythe *m*. **mythical** *adj* mythique. **mythological** *adj* mythologique. **mythology** *n* mythologie *f*.

N

nag [nag] *v* harceler.

nail [neil] *n* clou *m*; (*anat*) ongle *m*. **bite one's nails** se ronger les ongles. **nail-brush** *n* brosse à ongles *f*. **nail-file** *n* lime à ongles *f*. **nail polish** vernis à ongles *m*. **nail-scissors** *pl n* ciseaux à ongles *m pl*. *v* clouer.

naive [nai'iːv] *adj* naïf. **naivety** *n* naïveté *f*.

naked ['neikid] *adj* nu; dénudé. **nakedness** *n* nudité *f*.

name [neim] *n* nom *m*. **my name is . . .** je m'appelle. . . . **namesake** *n* homonyme *m*. **what's your name?** comment vous appelez-vous? *v* nommer, appeler; donner un nom à. **nameless** *adj* sans nom; anonyme; inexprimable. **namely** *adv* à savoir.

nanny ['nani] *n* bonne d'enfants *f*.

nap¹ [nap] *n* petit somme *m*. *v* sommeiller. **catch napping** prendre à l'improviste.

nap² [nap] *n* (*of cloth*) poil *m*.

nape [neip] *n* nuque *f*.

napkin ['napkin] *n* serviette *f*.

nappy ['napi] *n* couche *f*.

narcotic [naɪ'kotic] *nm, adj* narcotique.

narrate [nə'reit] *v* raconter. **narration** *n*

narration *f*. **narrator** *n* narrateur, -trice *m, f*.

narrative ['narətiv] *n* narration *f. adj* narratif.

narrow ['narou] *adj* étroit. **narrow-minded** *adj* borné. *v* (se) rétrécir. **narrow down** se ramener. **narrowly** *adv* (*only just*) de justesse; strictement.

nasal ['neizəl] *adj* nasal; (*voice*) nasillard. **nasalize** *v* nasaliser.

nasturtium [nə'stəɪʃəm] *n* capucine *f*.

nasty ['naɪsti] *adj* (*unpleasant*) mauvais, vilain; (*unkind*) méchant.

nation ['neiʃən] *n* nation *f*. **national** *n, adj* national. **national anthem** hymne national *m*. **nationalism** *n* nationalisme *m*. **nationalist** *n* nationaliste *m, f*. **nationality** *n* nationalité *f*. **nationalization** *n* nationalisation *f*. **nationalize** *v* nationaliser.

native ['neitiv] *adj* (*town*) natal; (*language*) maternel; indigène; inné. *n* autochtone *m, f*; indigène *m, f*.

nativity [nə'tivəti] *n* nativité *f*. **nativity play** miracle de la Nativité *m*.

natural ['natʃərəl] *adj* naturel. **naturalism** *n* naturalisme *m*. **naturalist** *n* naturaliste *m, f*. **naturally** *adv* naturellement; de nature.

nature ['neitʃə] *n* nature *f*. **nature study** histoire naturelle *f*. **nature trail** circuit forestier éducatif *m*.

naughty ['noɪti] *adj* méchant. **naughtiness** *n* désobéissance *f*.

nausea ['noɪziə] *n* nausée *f*. **nauseate** *v* écœurer.

nautical ['noɪtikəl] *adj* nautique.

naval ['neivəl] *adj* naval; maritime. **naval officer** officier de marine *m*.

nave [neiv] *n* nef *f*.

navel ['neivəl] *n* nombril *m*. **navel orange** navel *f*.

navigate ['navigeit] *v* naviguer; (*steer*) diriger. **navigable** *adj* navigable. **navigation** *n* navigation *f*. **navigator** *n* navigateur *m*.

navy ['neivi] *n* marine *f*. **navy blue** bleu marine.

near [niə] *adv* près, proche. *prep* près de. *adj* proche. *v* approcher (de). **draw near** s'approcher (de). **in the near future** dans un proche avenir. **nearly** *adv* presque. **not nearly** loin de.

nearby [niə'bai] *adj* proche. *adv* près.

neat [niːt] *adj* net, nette; soigné; (*drink*) sec, sèche. **neaten** *v* ajuster; (*tidy*) ranger.

neatly *adv* avec soin; (*with skill*) habilement. **neatness** *n* netteté *f.*

necessary ['nesisəri] *adj* nécessaire. **if necessary** s'il le faut. **it is necessary** il faut. **necessitate** *v* nécessiter. **necessity** *n* nécessité *f*, chose nécessaire *f.*

neck [nek] *n* cou *m*; (*of shirt, etc.*) encolure *f*; (*of bottle, vase*) col *m*. **neck and neck** à égalité. **necklace** *n* collier *m*. **neckline** *n* encolure *f. v* (*slang*) se peloter.

nectar ['nektə] *n* nectar *m.*

née [nei] *adj* née.

need [niːd] *n* besoin *m. v* avoir besoin de; demander. **needless** *adj* inutile. **needy** *nm, adj* nécessiteux.

needle ['niːdl] *n* aiguille *f.* **needlework** *n* travaux d'aiguille *m pl. v* (*coll*) asticoter.

negative ['negətiv] *adj* négatif. *n* (*gramm*) négation *f*; (*photo*) négatif *m*; (*reply*) réponse négative *f.*

neglect [ni'glekt] *v* négliger. *n* manque de soins *m.* **in a state of neglect** à l'abandon. **neglected** *adj* abandonné. **negligible** *adj* négligeable.

negligée ['negliʒei] *n* négligé *m.*

negligence ['neglidʒəns] *n* négligence *f.* **negligent** *adj* négligent.

negotiate [ni'gouʃieit] *v* négocier; (*obstacle*) franchir. **negotiable** *adj* négociable; franchissable. **negotiation** *n* négociation *f.*

Negro ['niːgrou] *nm, adj* nègre. **Negress** *n* négresse *f.*

neigh [nei] *v* hennir. *n* hennissement *m.*

neighbour ['neibə] *n* voisin, -e *m, f.* **neighbourhood** *n* voisinage *m.* **neighbouring** *adj* avoisinant. **neighbourly** *adj* (de) bon voisin.

neither ['naiðə] *adv* ni. **neither ... nor ...** ni ... ni .... *conj* ni, non plus. *adj, pron* ni l'un ni l'autre.

neon ['niːon] *n* néon *m.*

nephew ['nefjuː] *n* neveu *m.*

nepotism ['nepətizəm] *n* népotisme *m.*

nerve [nəːv] *n* nerf *m*; courage *m*; (*coll: cheek*) toupet *m.* **get on someone's nerves** taper sur les nerfs à quelqu'un. **lose one's nerve** (*coll*) se dégonfler. **nerve-racking** *adj* éprouvant. **nerves** *pl n* (*coll: before performance*) trac *m sing.* **nervous** *adj* nerveux; (*apprehensive*) inquiet, -ète. **nervous breakdown** dépression nerveuse *f.*

nest [nest] *n* nid *m.* **nest egg** pécule *m.* **nest of tables** table gigogne *f. v* nicher.

nestle ['nesl] *v* se nicher, se blottir.

net¹ [net] *n* filet *m.* **netball** *n* netball *m.* **net curtains** voilage *m sing.* **network** *n* réseau *m. v* prendre au filet.

net² [net] *adj* net.

Netherlands ['neðələndz] *pl n* **the Netherlands** les Pays-Bas *m pl.*

nettle ['netl] *n* ortie *f.* **nettle-rash** *n* urticaire *f. v* agacer.

neuralgia [nju'raldʒə] *n* névralgie *f.*

neurosis [nju'rousis] *n* névrose *f.* **neurotic** *adj* névrosé.

neuter ['njuːtə] *nm, adj* neutre. *v* châtrer.

neutral ['njuːtrəl] *adj* neutre. *n* (*mot*) point mort *m.* **in neutral** au point mort. **neutrality** *n* neutralité *f.* **neutralize** *v* neutraliser.

never ['nevə] *adj* (ne...) jamais. **never-ending** *adj* sans fin.

nevertheless [nevəðə'les] *adv* néanmoins, malgré tout.

new [njuː] *adj* nouveau, -elle; (*brand-new*) neuf; (*fresh*) frais, fraîche. **new-born** ['njuːbɔɪn] *adj* nouveau-né. **newcomer** ['njuːkʌmə] *n* nouveau venu, nouvelle venue *m, f.*

New Delhi *n* New Delhi.

new-fangled ['njuːˌfaŋgəld] *adj* nouveau genre.

new-laid [njuː'leid] *adj* (*egg*) du jour.

newly-weds ['njuːliwedz] *pl n* nouveaux mariés *m pl.*

news [njuːz] *n* nouvelles *f pl*; (*press, TV, etc.*) informations *f pl*, actualités *f pl.* **newsagent** *n* marchand, -e de journaux *m, f.* **newsletter** *n* bulletin *m.* **newspaper** *n* journal *m.* **newsreader** *n* speaker, -erine *m, f.*

newt [njuːt] *n* triton *m.*

New Testament *n* Nouveau Testament *m.*

New Year *n* nouvel an *m.* **Happy New Year!** bonne année! **New Year's Day** le jour de l'an *m.* **New Year's Eve** la Saint-Sylvestre *f.*

New Zealand [njuː'ziːlənd] *n* Nouvelle-Zélande *f.* **New Zealander** *n* Néo-Zélandais, -e *m, f.*

next [nekst] *adj* prochain, suivant; (*adjoining*) voisin. *adv* ensuite. *n* prochain, -e *m, f.* **the next day** le lendemain. **next-door** *adj* voisin, d'à

côté. **next-of-kin** n plus proche parent m.
next to à côté de.

nib [nib] n plume f.

nibble ['nibl] v grignoter, mordiller.

nice [nais] adj beau, belle; agréable;
(kind) gentil, -ille; (food) bon, bonne.
nicely adv bien.

niche [nitʃ] n niche f.

nick [nik] n (notch) encoche f; (cut)
entaille f; (slang: prison) taule f. **in the
nick of time** juste à temps. v entailler;
(slang: steal) piquer; (slang: arrest) pincer.

nickel ['nikl] n nickel m; (US: coin) pièce
de cinq cents f.

nickname ['nikneim] n surnom m. v
surnommer.

Nicosia [nikə'siə] n Nicosie.

nicotine ['nikətiːn] n nicotine f.

niece [niːs] n nièce f.

niggle ['nigl] v tatillonner. **niggling** adj
(detail) insignifiant; (doubt) insinuant;
(pain) persistant.

night [nait] n nuit f; (evening) soir m.
night after night des nuits durant. **work
nights** être de nuit.

night-club ['naitklʌb] n boîte de nuit f.

nightdress ['naitdres] n chemise de nuit f.

nightfall ['naitfɔil] n tombée du jour f.

nightie ['naiti] n (coll) nuisette f.

nightingale ['naitiŋgeil] n rossignol m.

night-life ['naitlaif] n vie nocturne f.

night-light ['naitlait] n veilleuse f.

nightly ['naitli] adj de tous les soirs. adv
tous les soirs.

nightmare ['naitmeə] n cauchemar m.

night-school ['nait,skuːl] n cours du soir
m pl.

night-time ['nait,taim] n nuit f.

night-watchman [nait'wotʃmən] n veilleur
de nuit m.

nil [nil] n rien m; (sport) zéro m.

nimble ['nimbl] adj agile; (mind) vif. **nimbleness** n agilité f.

nine [nain] nm, adj neuf. **dressed up to
the nines** sur son trente et un. **ninth**
n(m+f), adj neuvième.

nineteen [nain'tiːn] nm, adj dix-neuf.
nineteenth n(m+f), adj dix-neuvième.

ninety ['nainti] nm, adj quatre-vingt-dix.
ninetieth n(m+f), adj quatre-vingt-dixième.

nip¹ [nip] v pincer; (bite) donner un coup
de dent à; (coll: go quickly) faire un saut.

nip in the bud tuer dans l'œuf. n pinçon
m; (bite) morsure f. **nippy** adj (cold)
piquant; (quick) preste.

nip² [nip] n (drop) goutte f.

nipple ['nipl] n mamelon m; (mot) grais-
seur m.

nit [nit] n lente f; (coll) crétin, -e m, f.

nitrogen ['naitrədʒən] n azote m.

no [nou] adv non; (with comparative) ne
... pas. adj aucun, point de, pas de; (on
sign) défense de, interdit. **no-claims
bonus** bonification pour non-sinistre f.
no more or longer ne ... plus.

noble ['noubl] nm, adj noble. **nobleness or
nobility** n noblesse f.

nobody ['noubodi] pron (ne...) personne. n (insignificant person) rien du
tout m.

nocturnal [nok'təɪnəl] adj nocturne.

nod [nod] v faire un signe de tête;
(affirmative) faire signe que oui. **nod off**
s'endormir. n signe de tête m.

noise [noiz] n bruit m; (loud) tapage m.
noiseless adj silencieux. **noisy** adj
bruyant.

nomad ['noumad] n nomade m, f. **nomadic** adj nomade.

nominal ['nominl] adj nominal; (in name
only) de nom.

nominate ['nomineit] v proposer;
(appoint) nommer. **nomination** n proposition de candidat f; nomination f.

nonchalant ['nonʃələnt] adj nonchalant.
nonchalance n nonchalance f.

nonconformist [nonkən'foimist] n(m+f),
adj non-conformiste.

nondescript ['nondiskript] adj quelconque.

none [nʌn] pron aucun.

nonentity [non'entəti] n nullité f.

nonetheless [,nʌnðə'les] adv néanmoins.

non-existent [nonig'zistənt] adj non-existant.

non-fiction [non'fikʃən] n littérature non-
romanesque f.

non-resident [non'rezidənt] n (hotel) client, -e de passage m, f.

nonsense ['nonsəns] n absurdités f pl, sottises f pl. **nonsensical** adj absurde.

non-smoker [non'smoukə] n (person)
non-fumeur m; (rail) compartiment
"non-fumeurs" m.

non-stop [non'stop] adj sans arrêt; (train,
flight) direct. adv sans arrêt.

noodles ['nuːdlz] *pl n* nouilles *f pl.*

noon [nuːn] *n* midi *m.*

no-one ['nouwʌn] *pron* (ne...) personne.

noose [nuːs] *n* nœud coulant *m*; (*hangman's*) corde *f.*

nor [noː] *conj* ni.

norm [noːm] *n* norme *f.*

normal ['noːməl] *adj* normal. *n* normale *f.*

north [noːθ] *n* nord *m. adj also* **northerly, northern** nord *invar*; au *or* du nord. *adv* au nord. **northbound** *adj* nord *invar.* **north-east** *nm, adj* nord-est. **north-west** *nm, adj* nord-ouest.

Norway ['noːwei] *n* Norvège *f.* **Norwegian** *nm, adj* norvégien; *n* (*people*) Norvégien, -enne *m, f.*

nose [nouz] *n* nez *m.* **blow one's nose** se moucher. **have a nosebleed** saigner du nez. **nosebag** *n* musette mangeoire *f.* **nose-dive** *n* piqué *m.* **nose to tail** (*cars*) pare-choc contre pare-choc. *v* **nose out** flairer. **nosy** *adj* (*coll*) fouinard.

nostalgia [no'staldʒə] *n* nostalgie *f.* **nostalgic** *adj* nostalgique.

nostril ['nostrəl] *n* narine *f*; (*horse, etc.*) naseau *m.*

not [not] *adv* (ne...) pas; non. **I hope not** j'espère que non. **not at all** pas du tout; (*acknowledging thanks*) de rien.

notable ['noutəbl] *adj* notable. **notably** *adv* notamment.

notary ['noutəri] *n* notaire *m.*

notch [notʃ] *n* entaille *f*; (*belt*) cran *m*; (*wheel, saw*) dent *f. v* encocher; cranter; denteler.

note [nout] *n* note *f*; (*short letter*) mot *m*; (*money*) billet *m.* **notebook** *n* carnet *m.* **notepaper** *n* papier à lettres *m.* **noteworthy** *adj* notable. *v* noter; (*notice*) remarquer. **noted** *adj* célèbre.

nothing ['nʌθiŋ] *pron* (ne...) rien; (*with adjective*) rien de. *n* zéro *m*; (*void*) néant *m.* **nothing but** rien que.

notice ['noutis] *n* (*poster*) affiche *f*; (*in newspaper*) annonce *f*; (*warning*) préavis *m*, délai *m*; (*dismissal*) congé *m*; (*resignation*) démission *f.* **notice-board** *n* panneau d'affichage *m.* **take no notice of** ne tenir aucun compte de. *v* s'apercevoir de, remarquer. **noticeable** *adj* perceptible; évident.

notify ['noutifai] *v* (*make known*) notifier, signaler; (*inform*) aviser. **notification** *n* avis *m*, annonce *f.*

notion ['nouʃən] *n* idée *f.*

notorious [nou'toːriəs] *adj* notoire. **notoriety** *n* notoriété *f.*

notwithstanding [notwiθ'standiŋ] *prep* malgré. *adv* néanmoins.

nougat ['nuːgaɪ] *n* nougat *m.*

nought [noːt] *n* zéro *m.*

noun [naun] *n* nom *m.*

nourish ['nʌriʃ] *v* nourrir. **nourishment** *n* nourriture *f.*

novel[1] ['novəl] *n* roman *m.* **novelist** *n* romancier, -ère *m, f.*

novel[2] ['novəl] *adj* nouveau, -elle; original. **novelty** *n* nouveauté *f*; innovation *f.*

November [nə'vembə] *n* novembre *m.*

novice ['novis] *n* novice *m, f.*

now [nau] *adv* maintenant; (*immediately*) tout de suite. **from now on** à partir de maintenant. **nowadays** *adv* de nos jours. **now and then** de temps en temps. **up to now** jusqu'ici.

nowhere ['nouweə] *adv* nulle part.

noxious ['nokʃəs] *adj* nocif.

nozzle ['nozl] *n* ajutage *m.*

nuance ['njuːãs] *n* nuance *f.*

nuclear ['njuːkliə] *adj* nucléaire.

nucleus ['njuːkliəs] *n* noyau *m*; (*of cell*) nucléus *m.*

nude ['njuːd] *n, adj* nu, -e. **in the nude** nu. **nudist** *n* nudiste *m, f.* **nudity** *n* nudité *f.*

nudge [nʌdʒ] *v* pousser du coude. *n* coup de coude *m.*

nugget ['nʌgit] *n* pépite *f.*

nuisance ['njuːsns] *n* (*thing*) ennui *m*; (*person*) peste *f.* **be a nuisance** embêter. **what a nuisance!** (*coll*) quelle barbe!

null [nʌl] *adj* nul, nulle. **null and void** nul et non avenu.

numb [nʌm] *adj* engourdi; (*with fear*) transi. *v* engourdir; transir. **numbness** *n* engourdissement *m.*

number ['nʌmbə] *n* nombre *m*; (*of house, page, etc.*) numéro *m.* **number plate** plaque de police *f. v* compter; (*house, etc.*) numéroter.

numeral ['njuːmərəl] *n* chiffre *m.*

numerate ['njuːmərət] *adj* **be numerate** savoir compter. **numeracy** *n* notions de calcul *f pl.* **numerator** *n* numérateur *m.*

numerical [njuː'merikl] *adj* numérique. **in numerical order** dans l'ordre numérique.

numerous ['njuːmərəs] *adj* nombreux.

nun [nʌn] *n* religieuse *f.*

nurse [nəːs] *n* infirmier, -ère *m, f. v* (*med*) soigner; (*cradle*) bercer; (*hope*) nourrir. **nursing home** clinique *f.*

nursery ['nəisəri] *n* (*room*) nursery *f*; crèche *f*; (*trees, etc.*) pépinière *f*. **nursery rhyme** comptine *f*. **nursery school** école maternelle *f*. **nursery slopes** (*skiing*) pentes pour débutants *f pl*.

nurture ['nəit∫ə] *v* (*rear*) élever; (*feed*) nourrir.

nut [nʌt] *n* (*bot*) noix *f*; (*tech*) écrou *m*. **in a nutshell** en un mot. **nutcase** *n* (*slang*) dingue *m, f*. **nutcracker** *n* casse-noix *m invar*. **nutmeg** *n* muscade *f*.

nutrient ['njuitriənt] *n* substance nutritive *f*.

nutrition [nju'tri∫ən] *n* nutrition *f*. **nutritional** *adj* alimentaire. **nutritious** *adj* nutritif.

nuzzle ['nʌzl] *v* (*dog*) renifler; (*pig*) fouiner.

nylon ['nailon] *n* nylon *m*.

nymph [nimf] *n* nymphe *f*.

O

oak [ouk] *n* chêne *m*.

oar [ɔi] *n* rame *f*. **oarsman** *n* rameur *m*.

oasis [ou'eisis] *n* oasis *f*.

oath [ouθ] *n* (*law*) sermon *m*; (*expletive*) juron *m*. **take the oath** prêter serment.

oats [outs] *pl n* avoine *f sing*. **oatmeal** *n* flocons d'avoine *m pl*.

obedient [ə'biidiənt] *adj* obéissant. **obedience** *n* obéissance *f*.

obelisk ['obəlisk] *n* obélisque *m*.

obese [ə'biis] *adj* obèse. **obesity** *n* obésité *f*.

obey [ə'bei] *v* obéir (à).

obituary [ə'bitjuəri] *n* nécrologie *f*.

object ['obʒikt; *v* əb'ʒekt] *n* objet *m*; (*gramm*) complément *m*; (*aim*) but *m*. *v* élever une objection (contre); protester. **objection** *n* objection *f*. **objectionable** *adj* insupportable. **objective** *nm, adj* objectif.

oblige [ə'blaidʒ] *v* obliger. **be obliged to** (*have to*) être obligé de; (*be grateful*) être reconnaissant à. **obligation** *n* obligation *f*, devoir *m*. **obligatory** *adj* obligatoire.

oblique [ə'bliik] *adj* oblique; indirect.

obliterate [ə'blitəreit] *v* effacer. **obliteration** *n* effacement *m*.

oblivion [ə'bliviən] *n* oubli *m*. **oblivious** *adj* inconscient.

oblong ['oblon] *adj* oblong, -ongue. *n* rectangle *m*.

obnoxious [əb'nok∫əs] *adj* odieux, détestable.

oboe ['oubou] *n* hautbois *m*. **oboist** *n* hautboïste *m, f*.

obscene [əb'siin] *adj* obscène. **obscenity** *n* obscénité *f*.

obscure [əb'skjuə] *adj* obscur. *v* obscurcir; (*hide*) cacher. **obscurity** *n* obscurité *f*.

observe [əb'zəiv] *v* observer; remarquer. **observant** *adj* observateur, -trice. **observation** *n* observation *f*. **observatory** *n* observatoire *m*. **observer** *n* observateur, -trice *m, f*.

obsess [əb'ses] *v* obséder. **obsession** *n* obsession *f*.

obsolescent [obsə'lesnt] *adj* obsolescent. **obsolescence** *n* obsolescence *f*. **built-in obsolescence** désuétude calculée *f*.

obsolete ['obsəliit] *adj* dépassé, désuet, -ète.

obstacle ['obstəkl] *n* obstacle *m*.

obstetrics [ob'stetriks] *n* obstétrique *f*. **obstetrician** *n* obstétricien, -enne *m, f*.

obstinate ['obstinət] *adj* obstiné, têtu. **obstinacy** *n* obstination *f*.

obstruct [əb'strʌkt] *v* obstruer; (*hinder*) entraver. **obstruction** *n* obstruction *f*; obstacle *m*.

obtain [əb'tein] *v* obtenir, procurer.

obtrusive [əb'truisiv] *adj* importun. **obtrusion** *n* intrusion *f*.

obtuse [əb'tjuis] *adj* obtus.

obverse ['obvəis] *n* (*coin*) face *f*; (*statement, etc.*) contrepartie *f*. *adj* de face; correspondant.

obvious ['obviəs] *adj* évident.

occasion [ə'keiʒən] *n* occasion *f*; (*event*) événement *m*. *v* occasionner. **occasional** *adj* intermittent. **occasionally** *adv* de temps en temps.

occult ['okʌlt] *adj* occulte. *n* **the occult** le surnaturel.

occupy ['okjupai] *v* occuper. **occupant** *or* **occupier** *n* occupant, -e *m, f*. **occupation** *n* occupation *f*; profession *f*; (*trade*) métier *m*. **occupational hazard** risque du métier *m*. **occupational therapy** ergothérapie *f*.

occur [ə'kəi] *v* (*happen*) se produire, avoir lieu; (*be found*) se trouver; (*come to mind*) venir à l'esprit (de). **occurrence** *n* événement *m*.

ocean ['ouʃən] *n* océan *m*. **oceanic** *adj* océanique.

ochre ['oukə] *n* (*colour*) ocre *m*; (*substance*) ocre *f*.

o'clock [ə'klɔk] *adv* **one o'clock** une heure. **two/three/etc. o'clock** deux/trois/etc. heures.

octagon ['ɔktəgən] *n* octogone *m*. **octagonal** *adj* octogonal.

octane ['ɔktein] *n* octane *m*. **octane number** indice d'octane *m*.

octave ['ɔktiv] *n* octave *f*.

October [ɔk'toubə] *n* octobre *m*.

octopus ['ɔktəpəs] *n* pieuvre *f*.

oculist ['ɔkjulist] *n* oculiste *m*, *f*.

odd [ɔd] *adj* bizarre, étrange; (*number*) impair; (*from pair*) déparié. **odd jobs** menus travaux *m pl*. **odd man out** exception *f*. **oddity** *n* (*person*) excentrique *m*, *f*; (*thing*) curiosité *f*; (*oddness*) singularité *f*. **oddment** *n* fin de série *f*.

odds [ɔdz] *pl n* (*betting*) cote *f sing*; chances *f pl*. **be at odds with** ne pas être d'accord avec. **it makes no odds** ça ne fait rien. **odds and ends** bouts *m pl*, restes *m pl*.

ode [oud] *n* ode *f*.

odious ['oudiəs] *adj* odieux.

odour ['oudə] *n* odeur *f*. **odourless** *adj* inodore.

oesophagus [iː'sɔfəgəs] *n* œsophage *m*.

of [ɔv] *prep* de. **of it** *or* **them** en: *j'en ai deux*.

off [ɔf] *adj* absent; (*light*) éteint; (*gas, water, etc.*) coupé; (*cancelled*) annulé; (*food*) mauvais. **a day off** un jour de congé. *prep* de, sur; (*distant*) éloigné de.

offal ['ɔfəl] *n* abats *m pl*.

off chance ['ɔftʃains] *n* **on the off chance (that)** (*coll*) au cas où.

off-colour [ɔf'kʌlə] *adj* **be off-colour** ne pas être dans son assiette.

offend [ə'fend] *v* offenser, offusquer. **offence** *n* (*law*) délit *m*. **take offence** se froisser. **offender** *n* délinquant, -e *m*, *f*; contrevenant, -e *m*, *f*. **offensive** *adj* offensant; déplaisant.

offer ['ɔfə] *n* offre *f*. *v* offrir, proposer. **offering** *n* offre *f*.

offhand [ɔf'hand] *adj* (*casual*) désinvolte; brusque. *adv* à l'improviste.

office ['ɔfis] *n* (*place*) bureau *m*; (*post*) fonction *f*. **take office** entrer en fonctions. **officer** *n* officier *m*; (*police*) agent *m*.

official [ə'fiʃəl] *adj* officiel. *n* officiel *m*, fonctionnaire *m*, *f*; employé, -e *m*, *f*.

officious [ə'fiʃəs] *adj* empressé.

offing ['ɔfiŋ] *n* **in the offing** en vue; (*naut*) au large.

off-licence ['ɔflaisns] *n* magasin de vins et spiritueux *m*.

off-peak [ɔf'piːk] *adj*, *adv* aux heures creuses.

off-putting ['ɔf,putiŋ] *adj* (*coll*) peu engageant.

off-season [ɔf'siːzn] *n* morte-saison *f*. *adv*, *adj* hors-saison.

offset [ɔf'set; *n* 'ɔfset] *v* contrebalancer. *n* (*printing*) offset *m*.

offshore ['ɔfʃɔː] *adj* (*breeze*) de terre; (*waters*) côtier.

offside [ɔf'said] *n* (*mot: right*) côté droit *m*; (*mot: left*) côté gauche *m*; (*sport*) hors-jeu *m invar*.

offspring ['ɔfspriŋ] *n* progéniture *f*; résultat *m*.

offstage ['ɔfsteidʒ] *adv*, *adj* dans les coulisses.

off-the-cuff [ɔfðə'kʌf] *adv*, *adj* au pied levé.

off-white [ɔf'wait] *nm*, *adj* blanc cassé *invar*.

often ['ɔfn] *adv* souvent. **as often as not** plus souvent. **every so often** de temps en temps.

ogre ['ougə] *n* ogre *m*. **ogress** *n* ogresse *f*.

oil [ɔil] *n* huile *f*; pétrole *m*. *v* graisser. **oily** *adj* huileux; (*hands, clothes*) graisseux; (*food*) gras, grasse; (*manners*) onctueux.

oilcan ['ɔilkan] *n* burette à huile *f*; (*storage*) bidon à huile *m*.

oilfield ['ɔilfiːld] *n* gisement pétrolifère *m*.

oil-fired [ɔil'faiəd] *adj* à mazout.

oil-painting ['ɔil,peintiŋ] *n* peinture à l'huile *f*.

oil pump *n* pompe à huile *f*.

oil refinery *n* raffinerie *f*.

oil rig *n* (*at sea*) plate-forme pétrolière *f*; (*on land*) derrick *m*.

oilskin ['ɔil,skin] *n* toile cirée *f*. **oilskins** *pl n* ciré *m sing*. *adj* en toile cirée.

oil-slick ['ɔilslik] *n* nappe de pétrole *f*.

oil-tanker ['ɔil,taŋkə] *n* (*ship*) pétrolier *m*; (*lorry*) camion-citerne *m*.

oil-well ['ɔilwel] *n* puits de pétrole *m*.

ointment ['ɔintmənt] *n* onguent *m*, pommade *f*.

O.K. [ouˈkei] *interj* d'accord!
old [ould] *adj* vieux, vieille; âgé; (*former*) ancien. **he is nine years old** il a neuf ans. **how old is he?** quel âge a-t-il? **old age** vieillesse *f*. **old-age pensioner** retraité, -e *m, f*. **old-fashioned** *adj* démodé, vieux jeu *invar*. **old maid** vieille fille *f*. **old master** (*painting*) tableau de maître *m*. **Old Testament** Ancien Testament *m*. **old wives' tale** conte de bonne femme *m*.
olive [ˈoliv] *n* (*fruit*) olive *f*; (*tree*) olivier *m*. **olive green** *nm, adj* vert olive. **olive oil** huile d'olive *f*.
Olympic [əˈlimpik] *adj* olympique. **Olympic Games** Jeux olympiques *m pl*.
omelette [ˈomlit] *n* omelette *f*.
omen [ˈoumən] *n* présage *m*, augure *m*.
ominous [ˈominəs] *adj* menaçant, sinistre.
omit [ouˈmit] *v* omettre. **omission** *n* omission *f*.
omnipotent [omˈnipətənt] *adj* omnipotent.
on [on] *prep* sur, à. *adj* (*elec*) allumé; (*tap*) ouvert. **oncoming** *adj* (*traffic*) qui approche. **onlooker** *n* spectateur, -trice *m, f*. **onset** *n* début *m*; attaque *f*. **onshore** *adj* du large. **onslaught** *n* attaque *f*. **onward(s)** *adj, adv* en avant. **from now onwards** désormais.
once [wʌns] *adv* une fois; (*formerly*) jadis. *conj* une fois que. **at once** tout de suite. **once again** encore une fois. **once and for all** une fois pour toutes.
one [wʌn] *n, adj* un, -e. *pron* un; (*impersonal*) on. **be one up on** avoir l'avantage sur. **one-armed bandit** machine à sous *f*. **one by one** un à un. **one-man band** homme-orchestre *m*. **one-sided** *adj* inégal, partial. **one-way** *adj* à sens unique. **that one** celui-là, celle-là *m, f*. **this one** celui-ci, celle-ci *m, f*. **which one** lequel, laquelle *m, f*.
oneself [wʌnˈself] *pron* se; (*emphatic*) soi-même. **by oneself** tout seul.
onion [ˈʌnjən] *n* oignon *m*.
only [ˈounli] *adj* seul, unique. **only child** enfant unique *m*. *adv* seulement; (ne...) que. *conj* mais.
onus [ˈounəs] *n* responsabilité *f*.
onyx [ˈoniks] *n* onyx *m*.
ooze [uːz] *v* suinter, exsuder.
opal [ˈoupəl] *n* opale *f*.
opaque [əˈpeik] *adj* opaque; obscur. **opacity** *n* opacité *f*; obscurité *f*.
open [ˈoupən] *v* (s')ouvrir. *adj* ouvert;

(*meeting*) public, -ique; (*question*) non résolu. **open-air** *adj* de *or* en plein air. **open-minded** *adj* sans parti pris. **open-mouthed** *adj, adv* bouche bée. **open-plan** *adj* sans cloisons.
opening [ˈoupəniŋ] *n* ouverture *f*; (*door, window*) embrasure *f*; (*ceremony*) inauguration *f*; (*opportunity*) occasion *f*. *adj* inaugural; préliminaire. **opening time** l'heure d'ouverture *f*.
opera [ˈopərə] *n* opéra *m*. **opera glasses** jumelles de théâtre *f pl*. **opera house** opéra *m*. **opera singer** chanteur, -euse d'opéra *m, f*. **operatic** *adj* d'opéra. **operetta** *n* opérette *f*.
operate [ˈopəreit] *v* opérer; (*machine*) (faire) marcher. **operable** *adj* opérable. **operating theatre** salle d'opération *f*. **operation** *n* opération *f*; marche *f*, fonctionnement *m*. **in operation** en service; en application. **operational** *adj* opérationnel. **operative** *adj* en vigueur; (*med*) opératoire. **the operative word** le mot clef. **operator** *n* opérateur, -trice *m, f*; (*phone*) standardiste *m, f*.
ophthalmic [ofˈθalmik] *adj* (*nerve*) ophtalmique; (*surgeon*) ophtalmologique.
opinion [əˈpinjən] *n* opinion *f*. **in my opinion** à mon avis. **opinion poll** sondage d'opinion *m*.
opium [ˈoupiəm] *n* opium *m*.
opponent [əˈpounənt] *n* adversaire *m, f*.
opportune [opəˈtjuːn] *adj* opportun.
opportunity [opəˈtjuːnəti] *n* occasion *f*, chance *f*.
oppose [əˈpouz] *v* s'opposer à. **opposed** *adj* opposé. **as opposed to** par opposition à. **opposition** *n* opposition *f*.
opposite [ˈopəzit] *adj* opposé; d'en face. **the opposite sex** l'autre sexe *m*. *prep* en face de. *n* opposé *m*, contraire *m*.
oppress [əˈpres] *v* opprimer; (*heat, etc.*) oppresser. **oppression** *n* oppression *f*. **oppressive** *adj* tyrannique; (*tax, etc.*) oppressif; (*heat*) accablant. **oppressor** *n* oppresseur *m*.
opt [opt] *v* opter. **opt out** se retirer; choisir de ne pas participer.
optical [ˈoptikl] *adj* optique. **optical illusion** illusion d'optique *f*. **optician** *n* opticien, -enne *m, f*.
optimism [ˈoptimizəm] *n* optimisme *m*. **optimist** *n* optimiste *m, f*. **optimistic** *adj* optimiste.

optimum ['optimǝm] *nm, adj* optimum.
option ['opʃǝn] *n* option *f*, choix *m*.
optional *adj* facultatif.
opulent ['opjulǝnt] *adj* opulent;
abondant. **opulence** *n* opulence *f*;
abondance *f*.
or [ɔɪ] *conj* ou; (*negative*) ni. **or else** ou
bien; (*threat*) sinon.
oracle ['orǝkl] *n* oracle *m*.
oral ['oɪrǝl] *nm, adj* oral.
orange ['orindʒ] *n* (*fruit*) orange *f*; (*tree*)
oranger *m*; (*colour*) orange *m*. *adj* (*colour*) orange; (*flavour*) d'orange. **orangeade** *n* orangeade *f*.
orator ['orǝtǝ] *n* orateur, -trice *m, f*. **orate**
v discourir. **oration** *or* **oratory** *n* discours
m.
orbit ['oɪbit] *n* orbite *f*. *v* orbiter.
orchard ['oɪtʃǝd] *n* verger *m*.
orchestra ['oɪkǝstrǝ] *n* orchestre *m*.
orchestral *adj* orchestral. **orchestrate** *v*
orchestrer. **orchestration** *n* orchestration
f.
orchid ['oɪkid] *n* orchidée *f*.
ordain [oɪ'dein] *v* (*rel*) ordonner; (*fate*)
décréter. **ordination** *n* ordination *f*.
ordeal [oɪ'diɪl] *n* supplice *m*.
order ['oɪdǝ] *n* ordre *m*; (*comm*) commande *f*. **in order to** pour. **out of order**
en panne. *v* ordonner; commander.
orderly ['oɪdǝli] *adj* rangé; méthodique;
en ordre. *n* (*mil*) planton *m*; (*med*) garçon de salle *m*.
ordinal ['oɪdinl] *adj* ordinal.
ordinary ['oɪdǝnǝri] *adj* ordinaire, normal; (*average*) moyen. *n* ordinaire *m*. **out
of the ordinary** hors du commun,
insolite.
ore [oɪ] *n* minerai *m*.
oregano [ori'gaɪnou] *n* origan *m*.
organ ['oɪgǝn] *n* organe *m*; (*music*) orgue
m. **organist** *n* organiste *m, f*.
organic [oɪ'ganik] *adj* organique; fondamental.
organism ['oɪgǝnizǝm] *n* organisme *m*.
organize ['oɪgǝnaiz] *v* organiser. **organization** *n* organisation *f*. **organizer** *n* organisateur, -trice *m, f*.
orgasm ['oɪgazǝm] *n* orgasme *m*.
orgy ['oɪdʒi] *n* orgie *f*.
oriental [oɪri'entl] *adj* oriental, d'Orient.
orientate ['oɪriǝnteit] *v* orienter. **orientation** *n* orientation *f*.
orifice ['orifis] *n* orifice *m*.
origin ['oridʒin] *n* origine *f*. **originate** *v*

être l'auteur de. **originate from** (*person*)
être originaire de; (*thing*) provenir de;
(*idea*) émaner de. **originator** *n* auteur *m*.
original [ǝ'ridʒinl] *adj* (*first*) originel;
(*idea, play, etc.*) original. *n* original *m*.
originally *adv* originairement, à l'origine.
ornament ['oɪnǝmǝnt] *n* (*decoration*) ornement *m*; (*vase, etc.*) bibelot *m*. *v* orner,
décorer. **ornamental** *adj* ornemental,
décoratif.
ornate [oɪ'neit] *adj* très orné.
ornithology [oɪni'θolǝdʒi] *n* ornithologie
f. **ornithological** *adj* ornithologique. **ornithologist** *n* ornithologiste *m, f*.
orphan ['oɪfǝn] *n, adj* orphelin, -e. *v* rendre orphelin. **be orphaned** devenir orphelin. **orphanage** *n* orphelinat *m*.
orthodox ['oɪθǝdoks] *adj* orthodoxe.
orthopaedic [oɪθǝ'piɪdik] *adj* orthopédique.
oscillate ['osileit] *v* osciller; fluctuer.
oscillation *n* oscillation *f*.
Oslo ['ozlou] *n* Oslo.
ostensible [o'stensǝbl] *adj* prétendu.
ostensibly *adv* en apparence.
ostentatious [osten'teiʃǝs] *adj* prétentieux; exagéré. **ostentation** *n* ostentation
f.
osteopath ['ostiǝpaθ] *n* ostéopathe *m, f*.
ostracize ['ostrǝsaiz] *n* frapper
d'ostracisme.
ostrich ['ostritʃ] *n* autruche *f*.
other ['ʌðǝ] *pron, adj* autre. *adv* autrement.
otherwise ['ʌðǝwaiz] *adv, conj* autrement.
Ottawa ['otǝwǝ] *n* Ottawa.
otter ['otǝ] *n* loutre *f*.
***ought** [oɪt] *v* devoir.
our [auǝ] *pron* nous. *adj* notre; (*pl*) nos.
ours [auǝz] *pron* le nôtre, la nôtre.
ourselves [auǝ'selvz] *pron* nous; (*emphatic*) nous-mêmes. **by ourselves** tout seuls.
oust [aust] *v* évincer.
out [aut] *adj* (*flower*) en fleur; (*light, etc.*)
éteint. *adv* dehors. **out loud** tout haut.
out of en dehors de, hors de; (*through*)
par; (*from*) de, sur; (*without*) sans.
outboard ['autboɪd] *n* hors-bord *m*.
outbreak ['autbreik] *n* début *m*,
déclenchement *m*.
outbuilding ['autbildiŋ] *n* appentis *m*,
dépendance *f*.
outburst ['autbǝɪst] *n* explosion *f*, accès
m.

outcast ['autkaıst] *n* exilé, -e *m, f*; proscrit, -e *m, f*.
outcome ['autkʌm] *n* issue *f*; conséquence *f*.
outcry ['autkrai] *n* tollé *m*.
***outdo** [aut'duː] *v* surpasser.
outdoor ['autdoɪ] *adj* de *or* en plein air. **outdoors** *adv* dehors.
outer ['autə] *adj* extérieur, -e. **outer space** espace cosmique *m*.
outfit ['autfit] *n* (*clothes*) tenue *f*; équipement *m*; (*coll*) équipe *f*.
outgoing ['autgouiŋ] *adj* (*person*) ouvert; (*tide*) descendant; (*train, mail, etc.*) en partance. **outgoings** *pl n* dépenses *f pl*.
***outgrow** [aut'grou] *v* devenir trop grand pour; perdre *or* abandonner en grandissant.
outhouse ['authaus] *n* appentis *m*.
outing ['autiŋ] *n* sortie *f*, excursion *f*.
outlandish [aut'landiʃ] *adj* exotique; bizarre.
outlaw ['autloɪ] *n* hors-la-loi *m invar*. *v* proscrire.
outlay ['autlei] *n* frais *m pl*, dépenses *f pl*.
outlet ['autlit] *n* sortie *f*; (*comm*) débouché *m*; (*for emotions, etc.*) exutoire *m*.
outline ['autlain] *n* contour *m*; (*summary*) esquisse *f*. *v* délinéer; esquisser *or* exposer à grands traits.
outlive [aut'liv] *v* survivre à.
outlook ['autluk] *n* perspective *f*; attitude *f*.
outlying ['autlaiiŋ] *adj* périphérique; (*distant*) écarté.
outnumber [aut'nʌmbə] *v* surpasser en nombre.
out-of-date [autəv'deit] *adj* (*ticket, etc.*) périmé; (*clothes*) démodé.
outpatient ['autpeiʃənt] *n* malade en consultation externe *m, f*.
outpost ['autpoust] *n* avant-poste *m*.
output ['autput] *n* production *f*, rendement *m*; (*elec*) puissance fournie *f*.
outrage ['autreidʒ] *n* scandale *m*. *v* outrager.
outrageous [aut'reidʒəs] *adj* scandaleux, outrageant.
outright [aut'rait; *adj* 'autrait] *adv* complètement; catégoriquement; franchement. *adj* complet, -ète; franc, franche; (*winner*) incontesté; (*sale*) au comptant.
outset ['autset] *n* début *m*.
outside [aut'said; *adj* 'autsaid] *adv* dehors,

à l'extérieur. *prep* à l'extérieur de, hors de; (*beyond*) en dehors de. *n* extérieur *m*, dehors *m*. *adj* extérieur, -e. **outsider** *n* étranger, -ère *m, f*; (*horse*) outsider *m*.
outsize ['autsaiz] *adj* (*clothes*) grande taille *invar*; énorme.
outskirts ['autskəɪts] *pl n* (*town*) faubourgs *m pl*; (*forest*) lisière *f sing*.
outspoken [aut'spoukən] *adj* carré. **be outspoken** avoir son franc-parler. **outspokenness** *n* franc-parler *m*.
outstanding [aut'standiŋ] *adj* exceptionnel; mémorable; (*debt*) impayé.
outstrip [aut'strip] *v* devancer.
outward ['autwəd] *adj* vers l'extérieur; (*appearance*) extérieur, -e. **outward bound** en partance. **outwardly** *adv* en apparence. **outwards** *adv* vers l'extérieur.
outweigh [aut'wei] *v* l'emporter sur.
outwit [aut'wit] *v* se montrer plus malin que; (*dodge*) dépister.
oval ['ouvəl] *nm, adj* ovale.
ovary ['ouvəri] *n* ovaire *m*.
ovation [ou'veiʃən] *n* ovation *f*.
oven ['ʌvn] *n* four *m*. **oven glove** gant isolant *m*. **ovenproof** *adj* allant au four. **oven-ready** *adj* prêt à cuire.
over ['ouvə] *adv* (par-)dessus; (*remaining*) en plus. *adj* fini. *prep* sur, par-dessus; (*above*) au-dessus de; (*during*) au cours de; (*more than*) plus de. **over and over again** à maintes reprises. **over here** ici. **over there** là-bas.
overall ['ouvəroɪl] *adj* global; total. *n* blouse *f*. **overalls** *pl n* salopette *f sing*.
overbalance [ouvə'baləns] *v* basculer; perdre l'équilibre.
overbearing [ouvə'beəriŋ] *adj* autoritaire.
overboard ['ouvəboɪd] *adv* (*fall*) à la mer; (*throw*) par-dessus bord. **go overboard** (*coll*) s'emballer.
overcast [ouvə'kaɪst] *adj* couvert.
overcharge [ouvə'tʃaɪdʒ] *v* faire payer un prix excessif; (*elec*) surcharger.
overcoat ['ouvəkout] *n* pardessus *m*.
***overcome** [ouvə'kʌm] *v* surmonter, triompher de. **be overcome by** succomber à.
overcrowded [ouvə'kraudid] *adj* surpeuplé, surchargé. **overcrowding** *n* surpeuplement *m*.
***overdo** [ouvə'duː] *v* exagérer; (*overcook*) trop cuire.
overdose ['ouvədous] *n* surdose *f*.

overdraft ['ouvədraɪft] *n* découvert *m*.
***overdraw** [ouvə'drɔɪ] *v* dépasser son crédit. **overdrawn** *adj* à découvert.
overdue [ouvə'djuɪ] *adj* (*payment*) arriéré; (*train, bus*) en retard.
overestimate [ouvə'estimeit] *v* surestimer; exagérer.
overexpose [ouvəik'spouz] *v* surexposer. **overexposure** *n* surexposition *f.*
overflow [ouvə'flou; *n* 'ouvəflou] *v* déborder. *n* débordement *m*; (*of sink*) trop-plein *m*; (*excess*) excédent *m*.
overgrown [ouvə'groun] *adj* envahi, recouvert.
***overhang** [ouvə'haŋ; *n* 'ouvəhaŋ] *v* surplomber; faire saillie. *n* surplomb *m*. **overhanging** *adj* en saillie, en surplomb.
overhaul [ouvə'hɔɪl] *v* réviser. *n* révision *f.*
overhead [ouvə'hed] *adv* au-dessus; dans le ciel. *adj* aérien. **overheads** *pl n* frais généraux *m pl.*
***overhear** [ouvə'hiə] *v* surprendre, entendre par hasard.
overheat [ouvə'hiɪt] *v* surchauffer; (*mot*) chauffer.
overjoyed [ouvə'dʒɔid] *adj* ravi.
overland [ouvə'land] *adj, adv* par voie de terre.
overlap ['ouvəlap; *v* ouvə'lap] *n* chevauchement *m*. *v* se chevaucher.
***overlay** [ouvə'lei; *n* 'ouvəlei] *v* recouvrir. *n* revêtement *m.*
overleaf [ouvə'liɪf] *adv* au verso.
overload [ouvə'loud; *n* 'ouvəloud] *v* surcharger. *n* surcharge *f.*
overlook [ouvə'luk] *v* (*miss*) oublier; (*house, etc.*) donner sur; (*ignore*) laisser passer.
overnight [ouvə'nait] *adv* jusqu'au lendemain, pendant la nuit; (*suddenly*) du jour au lendemain. *adj* (*journey*) de nuit; (*stay*) d'une nuit; (*sudden*) soudain.
overpower [ouvə'pauə] *v* subjuguer; dominer. **overpowering** *adj* irrésistible; suffocant.
overrated [ouvə'reitid] *adj* surfait.
***override** [ouvə'raid] *v* passer outre à, outrepasser; annuler. **overriding** *adj* prépondérant.
overrule [ouvə'ruɪl] *v* annuler; rejeter.
***overrun** [ouvə'rʌn] *v* envahir; (*go beyond*) dépasser.
overseas [ouvə'siɪz] *adv* outre-mer. *adj* d'outre-mer; (*trade*) extérieur, -e.

overseer [ouvə'siə] *n* contremaître *m.*
overshadow [ouvə'ʃadou] *v* ombrager; (*render insignificant*) éclipser.
***overshoot** [ouvə'ʃuɪt] *v* dépasser.
oversight ['ouvəsait] *n* omission *f.* **through an oversight** par négligence.
***oversleep** [ouvə'sliɪp] *v* dormir trop longtemps, se réveiller tard.
overspill ['ouvəspil] *n* excédent de population *m.*
overt [ou'vɜɪt] *adj* déclaré. **overtly** *adv* ouvertement.
***overtake** [ouvə'teik] *v* (*pass*) doubler, dépasser; (*catch up*) rattraper.
***overthrow** [ouvə'θrou; *n* 'ouvəθrou] *v* renverser, vaincre. *n* chute *f.*
overtime ['ouvətaim] *n* heures supplémentaires *f pl.*
overtone ['ouvətoun] *n* note *f,* sous-entendu *m.*
overture ['ouvətjuə] *n* ouverture *f.*
overturn [ouvə'tɜin] *v* (se) renverser; (*car*) capoter.
overweight [ouvə'weit] *adj* trop lourd. **be overweight** peser trop.
overwhelm [ouvə'welm] *v* accabler; (*flood*) submerger; (*conquer*) écraser. **overwhelmed** *adj* bouleversé, confus, accablé. **overwhelming** *adj* accablant; irrésistible; dominant.
overwork [ouvə'wɜik] *n* surmenage *m*. *v* (se) surmener.
overwrought [ouvə'rɔit] *adj* excédé.
ovulation [ovju'leiʃn] *n* ovulation *f.*
owe [ou] *v* devoir. **owing** *adj* dû, due. **owing to** à cause de.
owl [aul] *n* hibou *m.*
own [oun] *adj* propre. **get one's own back** prendre sa revanche. **on one's own** tout seul. *v* posséder. **own up** avouer. **owner** *n* propriétaire *m, f.* **ownership** *n* possession *f.*
ox [oks] *n, pl* **oxen** bœuf *m*. **oxtail** *n* queue de bœuf *f.*
oxygen ['oksidʒən] *n* oxygène *m.*
oyster ['oistə] *n* huître *f.*

P

pace [peis] *n* pas *m*. **keep pace with** marcher de pair avec. *v* arpenter. **pace up and down** faire les cent pas.

Pacific [pə'sifik] *nm, adj* Pacifique.

pacify ['pasifai] *v* calmer, pacifier. **pacific** *adj* pacifique. **pacifism** *n* pacifisme *m*. **pacifist** *n*(*m*+*f*), *adj* pacifiste.

pack [pak] *n* (*group*) bande *f*; (*hounds*) meute *f*; (*cards*) jeu *m*; (*packet*) paquet *m*. **packhorse** *n* cheval de charge *m*. *v* emballer; (*cram*) tasser, bourrer; (*suitcase*) faire; (*for holiday*) faire ses bagages. **packed lunch** panier-repas *m*. **packing** *n* emballage *m*.

package ['pakidʒ] *n* paquet *m*. *adj* (*deal, contract*) global; (*holiday, tour*) organisé. *v* emballer.

packet ['pakit] *n* paquet *m*; (*sweets*) sachet *m*.

pact [pakt] *n* pacte *m*.

pad[1] [pad] *n* bourrelet *m*; (*writing*) bloc *m*; (*ink*) tampon encreur *m*. *v* rembourrer, capitonner. **pad out** (*speech, essay*) délayer. **padding** *n* bourre *f*; délayage *m*.

pad[2] [pad] *v* aller à pas feutrés.

paddle[1] ['padl] *n* (*canoe*) pagaie *f*; (*of waterwheel*) aube *f*. **paddle boat** *or* **steamer** bateau à aubes *m*. *v* pagayer.

paddle[2] ['padl] *v* barboter. **paddling pool** petite piscine *f*.

paddock ['padək] *n* enclos *m*; (*racing*) paddock *m*.

paddy-field ['padifiːld] *n* rizière *f*.

padlock ['padlok] *n* cadenas *m*. *v* cadenasser.

paediatric [piːdi'atrik] *adj* de pédiatrie; infantile. **paediatrician** *n* pédiatre *m, f*. **paediatrics** *n* pédiatrie *f*.

pagan ['peigən] *n, adj* païen, -enne.

page[1] [peidʒ] *n* (*book*) page *f*.

page[2] [peidʒ] *n* *also* **page-boy** (*hotel*) groom *m*; (*court*) page *m*. *v* (*person*) faire appeler.

pageant ['padʒənt] *n* spectacle historique *m*. **pageantry** *n* apparat *m*.

paid [peid] *V* pay.

pail [peil] *n* seau *m*.

pain [pein] *n* douleur *f*. **pain-killer** *n* calmant *m*. **pains** *pl n* (*trouble*) peine *f* *sing*. **painstaking** *adj* assidu, soigné. *v* peiner. **painful** *adj* douloureux; (*distressing*) pénible. **painless** *adj* sans douleur; (*easy*) inoffensif.

paint [peint] *n* peinture *f*. **paintbox** *n* boîte de couleurs *f*. **paintbrush** *n* pinceau *m*. **paints** *pl n* couleurs *f pl*. **paint-stripper** *n* décapant *m*. **paintwork** *n* peintures *f pl*. *v* peindre; (*describe*) dépeindre. **painter** *n* peintre *m*. **painting** *n* peinture *f*; (*picture*) tableau *m*.

pair [peə] *n* paire *f*; couple *m*. *v* (*socks, etc.*) appareiller; (*mate*) (s')accoupler. **pair off** (*people*) s'arranger deux par deux.

pal [pal] *n* (*coll*) copain, copine *m, f*.

palace ['paləs] *n* palais *m*. **palatial** *adj* grandiose.

palate ['palit] *n* palais *m*. **palatable** *adj* acceptable.

pale [peil] *adj* pâle; (*unnaturally*) blême. *v* pâlir; devenir blême. **paleness** *n* pâleur *f*.

palette ['palit] *n* palette *f*.

pall[1] [poːl] *v* perdre son charme (pour).

pall[2] [poːl] *n* drap mortuaire *m*; (*smoke*) voile *m*; (*snow*) manteau *m*.

pallid ['palid] *adj* blafard.

palm[1] [paːm] *n* (*of hand*) paume *f*. *v* **palm off** (*coll*) refiler (à). **palmist** *n* chiromancien, -enne *m, f*. **palmistry** *n* chiromancie *f*.

palm[2] [paːm] *n* (*tree*) palmier *m*. **Palm Sunday** dimanche des Rameaux *m*.

palpitate ['palpiteit] *v* palpiter. **palpitation** *n* palpitation *f*.

paltry ['poːltri] *adj* misérable.

pamper ['pampə] *v* dorloter, choyer.

pamphlet ['pamflit] *n* brochure *f*.

pan [pan] *n* casserole *f*.

pancake ['pankeik] *n* crêpe *f*. **Pancake Tuesday** mardi gras *m*.

pancreas ['pankriəs] *n* pancréas *m*. **pancreatic** *adj* pancréatique.

panda ['pandə] *n* panda *m*.

pandemonium [pandi'mouniəm] *n* tohubohu *m*.

pander ['pandə] *v* **pander to** se plier à.

pane [pein] *n* vitre *f*, carreau *m*.

panel ['panl] *n* panneau *m*; (*dress*) pan *m*; jury *m*; (*radio, TV*) invités *m pl*. *v* lambrisser. **panellist** *n* invité, -e *m, f*; membre d'un jury *m*. **panelling** *n* panneaux *m pl*.

pang [paŋ] *n* serrement de cœur *m*; (*conscience*) remords *m pl*; (*hunger*) tiraillement d'estomac *m*.

panic ['panik] *n* panique *f*. **panic-stricken** *adj* affolé. *v* (s')affoler.

panorama [panə'raːmə] *n* panorama *m*. **panoramic** *adj* panoramique.

pansy ['panzi] *n* pensée *f.*
pant [pant] *v* haleter. *n* halètement *m.*
panther ['panθə] *n* panthère *f.*
pantomime ['pantəmaim] *n* spectacle de Noël *m*; (*mime*) pantomime *f.*
pantry ['pantri] *n* garde-manger *m invar.*
pants [pants] *pl n* slip *m sing*; (*coll: trousers*) pantalon *m sing.*
papal ['peipl] *adj* papal, du Pape.
paper ['peipə] *n* papier *m*; (*news*) journal *m*; (*exam*) épreuve *f*; article *m.* **paperback** *n* livre de poche *m.* **paper bag** pochette *f.* **paper-boy** *n* livreur de journaux *m.* **paper-clip** *n* trombone *m.* **paper-knife** *n* coupe-papier *m invar.* **paper-mill** *n* papeterie *f.* **paper shop** (*coll*) marchand de journaux *m.* **paperweight** *n* presse-papiers *m invar.* **paperwork** *n* écritures *f pl*; (*derog*) paperasserie *f. v* (*room*) tapisser.
paprika ['paprikə] *n* paprika *m.*
par [paɪ] *n* pair *m.* **be on a par with** aller de pair avec. **feel under par** ne pas se sentir en forme.
parable ['parəbl] *n* parabole *f.*
parachute ['parəʃuɪt] *n* parachute *m. v* descendre en parachute; parachuter. **parachutist** *n* parachutiste *m, f.*
parade [pə'reid] *n* défilé *m*; (*ceremony*) parade *f. v* défiler; (*display*) faire étalage de.
paradise ['parədais] *n* paradis *m.*
paradox ['parədoks] *n* paradoxe *m.* **paradoxical** *adj* paradoxal.
paraffin ['parəfin] *n* paraffine *f*; (*fuel*) pétrole *m.*
paragraph ['parəgraɪf] *n* paragraphe *m.* **start a new paragraph** aller à la ligne.
parallel ['parəlel] *nm, adj* parallèle. **parallelogram** *n* parallélogramme *m.*
paralyse ['parəlaiz] *v* paralyser. **paralysis** *n* paralysie *f*; immobilisation *f.* **paralytic** *adj* paralytique; (*slang: drunk*) ivre mort.
paramilitary [,parə'militəri] *adj* paramilitaire.
paramount ['parəmaunt] *adj* souverain, suprême.
paranoia [,parə'nɔiə] *n* paranoïa *f.* **paranoid** *adj* paranoïde.
parapet ['parəpit] *n* parapet *m.*
paraphernalia [,parəfə'neiliə] *n* attirail *m.*
paraphrase ['parəfreiz] *n* paraphrase *f. v* paraphraser.
paraplegic [,parə'pliɪdʒik] *n(m+f), adj* paraplégique.

parasite ['parəsait] *n* parasite *m.* **parasitic** *adj* parasite.
parasol ['parəsol] *n* ombrelle *f.*
paratrooper ['parə,truɪpə] *n* parachutiste *m.*
parcel ['paɪsəl] *n* colis *m*; (*portion*) parcelle *f.* **parcel office** bureau de messageries *m.* **parcel post** service de colis postaux *m. v also* **parcel up** emballer.
parch [paɪtʃ] *v* (*land*) dessécher; (*person*) altérer. **be parched** (*coll*) mourir de soif.
parchment ['paɪtʃmənt] *n* parchemin *m.*
pardon ['paɪdn] *n* pardon *m*; (*law*) grâce *f. v* pardonner; gracier. *interj* pardon?
pare [peə] *v* réduire; (*fruit*) peler.
parent ['peərənt] *n* père, mère *m, f.* **parents** parents *m pl.* **parental** *adj* des parents. **parenthood** *n* paternité *f,* maternité *f.*
parenthesis [pə'renθəsis] *n* parenthèse *f.* **in parenthesis** entre parenthèses.
Paris ['paris] *n* Paris.
parish ['pariʃ] *n* paroisse *f*; (*civil*) commune *f.* **parish church** église paroissiale *f.* **parishioner** *n* paroissien, -enne *m, f.*
parity ['pariti] *n* parité *f.*
park [paɪk] *n* jardin public *m*; (*of mansion*) parc *m. v* (se) garer. **parking** *n* stationnement *m.* **parking lot** (*US*) parking *m.* **parking meter** parcomètre *m.* **parking ticket** procès-verbal *m.*
parliament ['paɪləmənt] *n* parlement *m.* **parliamentary** *adj* parlementaire.
parlour ['paɪlə] *n* petit salon *m.*
parochial [pə'roukiəl] *adj* paroissial; (*derog*) de clocher.
parody ['parədi] *n* parodie *f. v* parodier.
parole [pə'roul] *n* (*law*) liberté conditionnelle *f.*
paroxysm ['parəksizəm] *n* paroxysme *m*; (*anger*) accès *m*; (*joy*) transport *m.*
parrot ['parət] *n* perroquet *m.* **parrot fashion** comme un perroquet.
parsley ['paɪsli] *n* persil *m.*
parsnip ['paɪsnip] *n* panais *m.*
parson ['paɪsn] *n* pasteur *m.* **parson's nose** croupion *m.* **parsonage** *n* presbytère *m.*
part [paɪt] *n* partie *f*; (*behalf*) part *f,* parti *m*; rôle *m*; épisode *m.* **part exchange** reprise en compte *f.* **part-time** *adj, adv* à mi-temps, à temps partiel. *v* (se) séparer; se quitter. **part one's hair** se faire une raie. **part with** se défaire de. **parting** *n*

séparation *f*; (*hair*) raie *f*. **partly** *adv* partiellement.

*partake [paɪteik] *v* partake of prendre.

partial ['paɪʃəl] *adj* partiel; (*biased*) partial. **be partial to** avoir un faible pour. **partiality** *n* partialité *f*; (*liking*) prédilection *f*.

participate [paɪ'tisipeit] *v* participer. **participant** *n* participant, -e *m, f*. **participation** *n* participation *f*.

participle ['paɪtisipl] *n* participe *m*.

particle ['paɪtikl] *n* particule *f*; (*dust, etc.*) grain *m*.

particular [pə'tikjulə] *adj* particulier; méticuleux; (*choosy*) pointilleux. *n* détail *m*. **in particular** en particulier. **particularity** *n* particularité *f*.

partisan [paɪti'zan] *n* partisan *m*.

partition [paɪ'tiʃən] *n* (*in room*) cloison *f*; division *f*. partage *m*. *v* cloisonner; diviser, partager.

partner ['paɪtnə] *n* (*comm*) associé, -e *m, f*; (*sport*) partenaire *m, f*; (*dancing*) cavalier, -ère *m, f*; (*marriage*) époux, -ouse *m, f*. *v* être l'associé de; être le partenaire de; danser avec. **partnership** *n* association *f*. **go into partnership** s'associer.

partridge ['paɪtridʒ] *n* perdrix *f*; (*cookery*) perdreau *m*.

party ['paɪti] *n* (*pol*) parti *m*; (*law*) partie *f*; groupe *m*; (*celebration*) réunion *f*, fête *f*, soirée *f*. **party line** (*phone*) ligne commune à deux abonnés *f*; (*pol*) ligne du parti *f*.

pass [paɪs] *v* passer; (*go beyond*) dépasser; (*exam*) être reçu à. **pass away** *or* **on** (*die*) s'éteindre. **pass out** s'évanouir. **pass round** faire passer; distribuer. *n* (*permit*) laissez-passer *m invar*; (*exam*) moyenne *f*; (*mountain*) col *m*; (*sport*) passe *f*.

passage ['pasidʒ] *n* passage *m*; voyage *m*; (*corridor*) couloir *m*.

passenger ['pasindʒə] *n* passager, -ère *m, f*; (*train*) voyageur, -euse *m, f*.

passer-by [ˌpaɪsə'bai] *n* passant, -e *m, f*.

passion ['paʃən] *n* passion *f*. **passionate** *adj* passionné.

passive ['pasiv] *nm, adj* passif. **passiveness** *n* passivité *f*.

Passover ['paɪsouvə] *n* Pâque des Juifs *f*.

passport ['paɪspoɪt] *n* passeport *m*.

password ['paɪswoɪd] *n* mot de passe *m*.

past [paɪst] *nm, adj* passé. *prep* (*time*) plus de; (*beyond*) au delà de; (*in front of*) devant. **ten past four** quatre heures dix. *adv* devant. **go past** passer.

pasta ['pastə] *n* pâtes *f pl*.

paste [peist] *n* pâte *f*; (*meat*) pâté *m*; (*glue*) colle *f*; (*jewellery*) strass *m*. *v* coller.

pastel ['pastəl] *n* pastel *m*.

pasteurize ['pastʃəraiz] *v* pasteuriser. **pasteurization** *n* pasteurisation *f*.

pastime ['paɪstaim] *n* passe-temps *m invar*.

pastoral ['paɪstərəl] *adj* pastoral.

pastry ['peistri] *n* pâte *f*; (*cake*) pâtisserie *f*. **puff pastry** pâte feuilletée *f*. **shortcrust pastry** pâte brisée *f*.

pasture ['paɪstʃə] *n* pâture *f*, pâturage *m*. *v* paître.

pasty[1] ['peisti] *adj* pâteux; (*face*) terreux.

pasty[2] ['pasti] *n* petit pâté *m*.

pat [pat] *v* tapoter; caresser. *n* petite tape *f*; caresse *f*; (*of butter*) noix *f*.

patch [patʃ] *n* morceau *m*; (*of colour*) tache *f*; (*on clothes*) pièce *f*; (*of land*) parcelle *f*. **patchwork** *n* patchwork *m*. *v* rapiécer. **patchy** *adj* inégal.

patent ['peitənt] *adj* patent. **patent leather** cuir verni *m*. *n* brevet *m*. *v* faire breveter. **patently** *adv* manifestement.

paternal [pə'təɪnl] *adj* paternel. **paternity** *n* paternité *f*.

path [paɪθ] *n* sentier *m*; (*garden*) allée *f*; (*of river*) cours *m*; (*of missile, etc.*) trajectoire *f*.

pathetic [pə'θetik] *adj* pitoyable.

pathology [pə'θolədʒi] *n* pathologie *f*. **pathological** *adj* pathologique. **pathologist** *n* pathologiste *m, f*.

patient ['peiʃənt] *adj* patient. *n* malade *m, f*; client, -e *m, f*. **patience** *n* patience *f*; (*game*) réussite *f*.

patio ['patiou] *n* patio *m*.

patriarchal ['peitriaɪkəl] *adj* patriarcal.

patriot ['patriət] *n* patriote *m, f*. **patriotic** *adj* (*deed*) patriotique; (*person*) patriote. **patriotism** *n* patriotisme *m*.

patrol [pə'troul] *n* patrouille *f*. **patrol car** voiture de police *f*. *v* patrouiller (dans).

patron ['peitrən] *n* (*arts*) protecteur, -trice *m, f*; (*charity*) patron, -onne *m, f*; (*shop*) client, -e *m, f*. **patron saint** saint patron, sainte patronne *m, f*. **patronage** *n* patronage *m*. **patronize** *v* (*comm*) se fournir chez. **patronizing** *adj* condescendant.

patter[1] ['patə] v (*footsteps*) trottiner; (*rain*) crépiter. n petit bruit m; crépitement m.
patter[2] ['patə] n (*comedian, etc.*) bavardage m; (*salesman*) boniment m.
pattern ['patən] n dessin m, motif m; (*sewing*) patron m; modèle f. v modeler.
patterned adj à motifs.
paunch [pɔintʃ] n panse f.
pauper ['pɔipə] n indigent, -e m, f.
pause [pɔiz] n pause f; silence m. v faire une pause, s'arrêter un instant; hésiter.
pave [peiv] v paver. **pave the way** préparer le chemin. **pavement** n trottoir m; (*US*) chaussée f. **paving** n pavage m, dallage m. **paving stone** pavé m.
pavilion [pə'viljən] n pavillon m.
paw [pɔi] n patte f. v donner un coup de patte à; (*coll: person*) tripoter.
pawn[1] [pɔin] v mettre en gage. n gage m.
pawnbroker n prêteur, -euse sur gages m, f. **pawnshop** n mont-de-piété m.
pawn[2] [pɔin] n pion m.
***pay** [pei] v payer; (*attention, compliment*) faire. **pay back** rembourser. **pay in** verser. **pay off** (*debt*) régler; (*be worthwhile*) rapporter. n paie f. **pay-day** n jour de paie m. **pay rise** augmentation de salaire f. **pay-roll** n registre du personnel m. **pay-slip** n feuille de paie f. **payable** adj payable. **payee** n bénéficiaire m, f. **payment** n paiement m; récompense f.
pea [pii] n petit pois m.
peace [piis] n paix f. **peacemaker** n pacificateur, -trice m, f. **peace offering** cadeau de réconciliation m. **peaceful** adj paisible.
peach [piitʃ] n (*fruit*) pêche f; (*tree*) pêcher m.
peacock ['piikok] n paon m.
peak [piik] n pic m; sommet m; (*on cap*) visière f. **peak hours** heures d'affluence f pl, heures de pointe f pl.
peal [piil] n (*bells*) carillon m; (*thunder*) coup m; (*laughter*) éclat m. v carillonner; (*thunder*) gronder; éclater.
peanut ['piinʌt] n cacahouète f.
pear [peə] n (*fruit*) poire f; (*tree*) poirier m.
pearl [pəil] n perle f; nacre f. v perler. **pearly** adj nacré.
peasant ['peznt] n paysan, -anne m, f.
peat [piit] n tourbe f.
pebble ['pebl] n caillou m; (*on beach*) galet m. **pebbledash** n crépi moucheté m.
pebbly adj caillouteux.

peck [pek] v becqueter, picorer; donner un coup de bec à. n coup de bec m; (*coll: kiss*) bise f.
peckish ['pekiʃ] adj **feel peckish** (*coll*) avoir la dent.
peculiar [pi'kjuiljə] adj bizarre; particulier. **peculiarity** n bizarrerie f; particularité f.
pedal ['pedl] n pédale f. v pédaler.
pedantic [pi'dantik] adj pédant.
peddle ['pedl] v colporter; (*drugs*) faire le trafic de.
pedestal ['pedistl] n piédestal m.
pedestrian [pi'destriən] n piéton m. **pedestrian crossing** passage clouté m. **pedestrian precinct** zone piétonnière f. adj (*style*) prosaïque.
pedigree ['pedigrii] n pedigree m; (*of person*) ascendance f. adj de pure race.
pedlar ['pedlə] n colporteur m.
peel [piil] v (se) peler, éplucher. **peel off** (*covering, etc.*) décoller. n pelure f, épluchure f; (*orange*) écorce f; (*candied*) écorce confite f. **peeler** n éplucheur m.
peelings pl n pelures f pl, épluchures f pl.
peep [piip] n coup d'œil m. v jeter un coup d'œil, regarder furtivement. **peeping Tom** voyeur m. **peep out** se montrer.
peer[1] [piə] v regarder d'un air interrogateur. **peer at** scruter du regard.
peer[2] [piə] n pair m. **peerage** n pairie f. **peerless** adj sans pareil.
peevish ['piiviʃ] adj grincheux, maussade.
peg [peg] n cheville f; (*washing*) pince f; (*coat, hat*) patère f; (*tent*) piquet m. **off the peg** adj prêt-à-porter. v cheviller; (*prices*) stabiliser.
pejorative [pə'dʒorətiv] adj péjoratif.
Peking [pii'kiŋ] n Pékin.
pelican ['pelikən] n pélican m.
pellet ['pelit] n boulette f; (*for gun*) plomb m.
pelmet ['pelmit] n (*wood*) lambrequin m; (*fabric*) cantonnière f.
pelt[1] [pelt] v bombarder; (*coll: rain*) tomber des cordes; (*coll: run*) galoper. n **at full pelt** à toute vitesse.
pelt[2] [pelt] n peau f; fourrure f.
pelvis ['pelvis] n bassin m. **pelvic** adj pelvien.
pen[1] [pen] n plume f, stylo m. **penfriend** n correspondant, -e m, f. **penknife** n canif m. **pen-name** n pseudonyme m.

pen² [pen] *n* (*enclosure*) parc *m*. *v* parquer.

penal ['piːnl] *adj* pénal. **penal colony** colonie pénitentiaire *f*. **penalize** *v* pénaliser. **penalty** *n* pénalité *f*. peine *f*; (*sport*) pénalisation *f*.

penance ['penəns] *n* pénitence *f*.

pencil ['pensl] *n* crayon *m*. **pencil-case** *n* trousse *f*. **pencil-sharpener** *n* taille-crayon *m*. *v* crayonner.

pendant ['pendənt] *n* pendentif *m*.

pending ['pendiŋ] *adj* pendant, en suspens. *prep* en attendant; durant.

pendulum ['pendjuləm] *n* pendule *m*.

penetrate ['penitreit] *v* pénétrer. **penetrable** *adj* pénétrable. **penetration** *n* pénétration *f*.

penguin ['peŋgwin] *n* pingouin *m*.

penicillin [peni'silin] *n* pénicilline *f*.

peninsula [pə'ninsjulə] *n* péninsule *f*. **peninsular** *adj* péninsulaire.

penis ['piːnis] *n* pénis *m*.

penitent ['penitənt] *n*, *adj* pénitent, -e. **penitence** *n* pénitence *f*.

pennant ['penənt] *n* banderole *f*.

penniless ['peniləs] *adj* sans le sou.

pension ['penʃən] *n* pension *f*; (*from company*) retraite *f*. **pension book** livret de retraite *m*. **pension scheme** caisse de retraite *f*. *v* pensionner. **pension off** mettre à la retraite. **pensioner** *n* retraité, -e *m*, *f*.

pensive ['pensiv] *adj* pensif.

pentagon ['pentəgən] *n* pentagone *m*. **pentagonal** *adj* pentagonal.

penthouse ['penthaus] *n* appentis *m*. **penthouse flat** appartement de grand standing *m*.

pent-up [,pent'ʌp] *adj* refoulé.

penultimate [pi'nʌltimit] *adj* avant-dernier.

people ['piːpl] *n* peuple *m*. *pl n* gens *m pl*, *f pl*; personnes *f pl*; (*inhabitants*) peuple *m sing*; (*coll*) famille *f sing*. *v* peupler.

pepper ['pepə] *n* (*spice*) poivre *m*; (*vegetable*) poivron *m*. **peppercorn** *n* grain de poivre *m*. **peppermint** *n* (*flavour*) menthe *f*; (*sweet*) pastille de menthe *f*. **pepper-pot** *n* poivrier *m*. *v* poivrer. **peppery** *adj* poivré.

per [pəː] *prep* par. **per cent** pour cent. **percentage** *n* pourcentage *m*.

perceive [pə'siːv] *v* percevoir; (*notice*) remarquer.

perceptible [pə'septibl] *adj* perceptible. **perceptibly** *adv* sensiblement.

perception [pə'sepʃən] *n* perception *f*; sensibilité *f*; perspicacité *f*. **perceptive** *adj* percepteur, -trice; perspicace.

perch [pəːtʃ] *n* perchoir *m*. *v* (se) percher.

percolate ['pəːkəleit] *v* passer. **percolator** *n* cafetière à pression *f*.

percussion [pə'kʌʃən] *n* percussion *f*.

perennial [pə'reniəl] *adj* perpétuel; (*plant*) vivace. *n* plante vivace *f*.

perfect ['pəːfikt; *v* pə'fekt] *nm*, *adj* parfait. *v* achever, mettre au point. **perfection** *n* perfection *f*; (*perfecting*) perfectionnement *m*. **perfectionist** *n* perfectionniste *m*, *f*.

perforate ['pəːfəreit] *v* perforer. **perforation** *n* perforation *f*.

perform [pə'fɔːm] *v* accomplir, exécuter; (*theatre*) jouer, donner; (*machine*) marcher. **performance** *n* (*theatre*) représentation *f*, séance *f*; (*of individual*) interprétation *f*; (*sport*) performance *f*; (*of car*) fonctionnement *m*; exécution *f*; (*coll: fuss*) histoire *f*. **performer** *n* artiste *m*, *f*.

perfume ['pəːfjuːm] *n* parfum *m*. *v* parfumer.

perhaps [pə'haps] *adv* peut-être.

peril ['peril] *n* péril *m*. **perilous** *adj* périlleux.

perimeter [pə'rimitə] *n* périmètre *m*.

period ['piəriəd] *n* période *f*, époque *f*; (*school*) cours *m*; (*menstrual*) règles *f pl*. **periodic** *adj* périodique. **periodical** *nm*, *adj* périodique.

peripheral [pə'rifərəl] *adj* périphérique. **periphery** *n* périphérie *f*.

periscope ['periskoup] *n* périscope *m*.

perish ['periʃ] *v* périr; (*rubber, food*) se détériorer. **be perished** (*coll*) crever de froid. **perishable** *adj* périssable.

perjure ['pəːdʒə] *v* **perjure oneself** se parjurer; (*law*) faire un faux serment. **perjurer** *n* parjure *m*, *f*. **perjury** *n* parjure *m*, faux serment *m*.

perk [pəːk] *v* **perk up** (se) ragaillardir. **perky** *adj* vif, éveillé.

perm [pəːm] *n* permanente *f*. **have a perm** se faire faire une permanente.

permanent ['pəːmənənt] *adj* permanent. **permanence** *n* permanence *f*. **permanently** *adv* en permanence, à titre définitif.

permeate ['pəːmieit] *v* pénétrer; (*spread*)

se répandre (dans). **permeable** adj perméable.

permit [pə'mɪt; n 'pɜːmɪt] v permettre. n permis m; autorisation écrite f. **permissible** adj permis; acceptable. **permission** n permission f; autorisation f. **permissive** adj tolérant; laxiste.

permutation [pɜːmju'teɪʃən] n permutation f.

pernicious [pə'nɪʃəs] adj (med) pernicieux; nuisible.

perpendicular [ˌpɜːpen'dɪkjulə] nf, adj perpendiculaire.

perpetrate ['pɜːpitreit] v perpétrer. **perpetration** n perpétration f. **perpetrator** n auteur m, coupable m, f.

perpetual [pə'petʃuəl] adj perpétual.

perpetuate [pə'petʃueit] v perpétuer. **perpetuation** n perpétuation f.

perplex [pə'pleks] v rendre perplexe; compliquer. **perplexed** adj perplexe. **perplexing** adj embarrassant. **perplexity** n perplexité f; complexité f.

persecute ['pɜːsikjuːt] v persécuter; tourmenter. **persecution** n persécution f.

persevere [ˌpɜːsi'viə] v persévérer. **perseverance** n persévérance f. **persevering** adj persévérant.

persist [pə'sɪst] v persister. **persistence** n persistance f. **persistent** adj continuel; (person) persévérant, obstiné.

person ['pɜːsn] n personne f. **personal** adj personnel. **personality** n personnalité f. **personally** adv personnellement; en personne.

personify [pə'sonifai] v personnifier. **personification** n personnification f.

personnel [ˌpɜːsə'nel] n personnel m.

perspective [pə'spektiv] n perspective f.

perspire [pə'spaɪə] v transpirer. **perspiration** n transpiration f, sueur f.

persuade [pə'sweid] v persuader. **persuasion** n persuasion f. **persuasive** adj persuasif; convaincant.

pert [pɜːt] adj impertinent; (hat) coquin.

pertain [pə'tein] v se rapporter. **pertinent** adj pertinent, approprié.

perturb [pə'tɜːb] v perturber.

peruse [pə'ruːz] v lire attentivement. **perusal** n lecture attentive f.

pervade [pə'veid] v pénétrer dans, s'étendre dans.

perverse [pə'vɜːs] adj pervers; obstiné; contrariant. **perversity** n perversité f; obstination f.

pervert [pə'vɜːt; n 'pɜːvɜːt] v pervertir, dénaturer. n perverti sexuel, pervertie sexuelle m, f. **perversion** n perversion f.

pessimism ['pesimizəm] n pessimisme m. **pessimist** n pessimiste m, f. **pessimistic** adj pessimiste.

pest [pest] n animal or insecte nuisible m; (coll: person) casse-pieds m. **pesticide** n pesticide m.

pester ['pestə] v harceler.

pet [pet] n animal familier m; (coll: favourite) chouchou, -oute m, f; (as endearment) chou m. adj favori, -ite. v (coll) chouchouter; (slang: sexually) (se) peloter.

petal ['petl] n pétale m.

petition [pə'tɪʃən] n pétition f. v pétitionner, adresser une pétition à.

petrify ['petrifai] v pétrifier de peur.

petrol ['petrəl] n essence f. **petrol pump** pompe d'essence f. **petrol station** station-service f. **petrol tank** réservoir d'essence m.

petroleum [pə'trouliəm] n pétrole m.

petticoat ['petikout] n jupon m; (slip) combinaison f.

petty ['peti] adj mesquin, petit; insignifiant. **petty cash** petite monnaie f. **petty officer** second maître m. **pettiness** n mesquinerie f; insignifiance f.

petulant ['petjulənt] adj irritable. **petulance** n irritabilité f.

pew [pjuː] n banc d'église m.

pewter ['pjuːtə] n étain m.

phantom ['fantəm] n fantôme m.

pharmacy ['faːməsi] n pharmacie f. **pharmaceutical** adj pharmaceutique. **pharmacist** n pharmacien, -enne m, f.

pharynx ['fariŋks] n pharynx m. **pharyngitis** n pharyngite f.

phase [feiz] n phase f. v **phase in** introduire progressivement. **phase out** retirer progressivement.

pheasant ['feznt] n faisan m.

phenomenon [fə'nomənən] n, pl **-ena** phénomène m. **phenomenal** adj phénoménal.

phial ['faiəl] n fiole f.

philanthropy [fi'lanθrəpi] n philanthropie f. **philanthropic** adj philanthropique. **philanthropist** n philanthrope m, f.

philately [fi'latəli] n philatélie f. **philatelist** n philatéliste m, f.

philosophy [fi'losǝfi] *n* philosophie *f*. **philosopher** *n* philosophe *m, f*. **philosophical** *adj* philosophique; (*resigned*) philosophe. **philosophize** *v* philosopher.

phlegm [flem] *n* flegme *m*.

phlegmatic [fleg'matik] *adj* flegmatique.

phobia ['foubiǝ] *n* phobie *f*.

phone [foun] (*coll*) *n* téléphone *m. v* téléphoner (à).

phonetic [fǝ'netik] *adj* phonétique. **phonetics** *n* phonétique *f*.

phoney ['founi] *adj* (*coll*) faux, fausse.

phosphate ['fosfeit] *n* phosphate *m*.

phosphorescence [fosfǝ'resǝns] *n* phosphorescence *f*. **phosphorescent** *adj* phosphorescent.

phosphorus ['fosfǝrǝs] *n* phosphore *m*. **phosphorous** *adj* phosphoreux.

photo ['foutou] *n* (*coll*) photo *f*.

photocopy ['foutou,kopi] *n* photocopie *f. v* photocopier. **photocopier** *n* photocopieur *m*. **photocopying** *n* reprographie *f*.

photogenic [,foutou'dʒenik] *adj* photogénique.

photograph ['foutǝgraɪf] *n* photographie *f*. **photograph album** album de photos *m. v* photographier. **photographer** *n* photographe *m, f*. **photographic** *adj* photographique. **photography** *n* photographie *f*.

phrase [freiz] *n* expression *f*; (*gramm*) locution *f*; (*music*) phrase *f*. **phrase-book** *n* recueil d'expressions *m. v* exprimer.

physical ['fizikǝl] *adj* physique. *n* (*coll*) examen médical *m*.

physician [fi'ziʃǝn] *n* médecin *m*.

physics ['fiziks] *n* physique *f*. **physicist** *n* physicien, -enne *m, f*.

physiology [,fizi'olǝdʒi] *n* physiologie *f*. **physiological** *adj* physiologique. **physiologist** *n* physiologiste *m, f*.

physiotherapy [,fiziou'θerǝpi] *n* kinésithérapie *f*. **physiotherapist** *n* kinésithérapeute *m, f*.

physique [fi'ziːk] *n* constitution *f*; (*appearance*) physique *m*.

piano [pi'anou] *n* piano *m*. **pianist** *n* pianiste *m, f*.

piccolo ['pikǝlou] *n* piccolo *m*.

pick¹ [pik] *n* choix *m*; (*best*) meilleur, -e *m, f*. **take one's pick** faire son choix. *v* choisir; (*fruit, flowers*) cueillir; (*lock*) crocheter. **pick at** (*food*) chipoter. **pick-**me-up *n* (*coll*) remontant *m*. **pick out** choisir; distinguer; (*highlight*) rehausser. **pickpocket** *n* pick-pocket *m*. **pick up** ramasser; (*collect*) passer prendre; s'améliorer; (*learn*) apprendre; (*coll: arrest*) cueillir.

pick² [pik] *n* (*tool*) pioche *f*.

picket ['pikit] *n* piquet *m*. **picket line** cordon de piquet de grève *m. v* organiser un piquet de grève; mettre un piquet de grève.

pickle ['pikl] *v* conserver dans du vinaigre. **pickles** *pl n* pickles *m pl*.

picnic ['piknik] *n* pique-nique *m. v* piqueniquer. **picnicker** *n* pique-niqueur, -euse *m, f*.

pictorial [pik'toːriǝl] *adj* en images; illustré.

picture ['piktʃǝ] *n* image *f*; (*painting*) tableau *m*. **picture frame** cadre *m*. **picture rail** cimaise *f*. **pictures** *n* (*coll*) cinéma *m*. **picture window** fenêtre panoramique *f. v* (s')imaginer; décrire.

picturesque [,piktʃǝ'resk] *adj* pittoresque.

pidgin ['pidʒǝn] *n* pidgin *m*. **pidgin French** petit-nègre *m*.

pie [pai] *n* tourte *f*, pâté en croûte *m*.

piece [piːs] *n* morceau *m*; (*item*) pièce *f*. **piecemeal** *adv* par bribes, petit à petit. **piecework** *n* travail à la pièce *m. v* **piece together** rassembler.

pier [piǝ] *n* jetée *f*; (*landing-stage*) appontement *m*.

pierce [piǝs] *v* percer, transpercer. **piercing** *adj* perçant; glacial.

piety ['paiǝti] *n* piété *f*.

pig [pig] *n* cochon *m*. **pigheaded** *adj* entêté. **pig-iron** *n* saumon de fonte *m*. **pigskin** *n* peau de porc *f*. **pigsty** *n* porcherie *f*. **pigtail** *n* natte *f*.

pigeon ['pidʒǝn] *n* pigeon *m*. **pigeon-hole** *n* casier *m*.

pigment ['pigmǝnt] *n* pigment *m*. **pigmentation** *n* pigmentation *f*. **pigmented** *adj* pigmenté.

pike [paik] *n* (*fish*) brochet *m*.

pilchard ['piltʃǝd] *n* pilchard *m*.

pile¹ [pail] *n* (*heap*) pile *f*, tas *m*. **piles of** (*coll*) des masses de. *v* empiler, entasser. **pile up** (s')amonceler. **pile-up** *n* carambolage *m*.

pile² [pail] *n* (*post*) pieu *m*.

pile³ [pail] *n* (*of carpet, etc.*) poils *m pl*.

piles [pailz] *pl n* (*med*) hémorroïdes *f pl*.

pilfer ['pilfə] (*coll*) v chaparder. **pilfering** n chapardage m.

pilgrim ['pilgrim] n pèlerin m. **pilgrimage** n pèlerinage m.

pill [pil] n pilule f.

pillage ['pilidʒ] n pillage m. v piller.

pillar ['pilə] n pilier m. colonne f. **pillarbox** n boîte aux lettres f.

pillion ['piljən] n siège arrière m.

pillow ['pilou] n oreiller m. **pillowcase** n taie d'oreiller f.

pilot ['pailət] n pilote m. **pilot-light** n veilleuse f. **pilot scheme** projet-pilote m. v piloter.

pimento [pi'mentou] n piment m.

pimp [pimp] n souteneur m.

pimple ['pimpl] n bouton m. **pimply** adj boutonneux.

pin [pin] n épingle f; (*tech*) goupille f; (*elec: in plug*) fiche f. **have pins and needles** avoir des fourmis. **pin-ball** n flipper m. **pincushion** n pelote à épingles f. **pin money** argent de poche m. **pinpoint** v mettre le doigt sur. **pin-stripe** n rayure très fine f. v épingler. **pin down** coincer. **pin up** (*notice*) afficher. **pin-up** n pin-up f invar.

pinafore ['pinəfɔi] n (*apron*) tablier m. **pinafore dress** robe-chasuble f.

pincers ['pinsəz] pl n (*tool*) tenailles f pl; (*of crab*) pinces f pl.

pinch [pintʃ] n pincement m; (*of salt*) pincée f. **at a pinch** au besoin. v pincer; (*shoes, etc.*) serrer; (*coll: steal*) chiper.

pine¹ [pain] n pin m. **pine-cone** n pomme de pin f.

pine² [pain] v languir. **pine for** désirer ardemment.

pineapple ['painapl] n ananas m.

ping-pong ['piŋpoŋ] n ping-pong m. **ping-pong ball** balle de ping-pong f.

pinion¹ ['pinjən] n aileron m. v lier.

pinion² ['pinjən] n (*tech*) pignon m.

pink [piŋk] n (*colour*) rose m; (*flower*) œillet m. adj rose.

pinnacle ['pinəkl] n pinacle m.

pioneer [ˌpaiə'niə] n pionnier m; explorateur, -trice m, f.

pious ['paiəs] adj pieux.

pip¹ [pip] n (*seed*) pépin m.

pip² [pip] n (*phone, etc.*) top m. **the pips** le bip-bip m sing.

pipe [paip] n (*water, etc.*) tuyau m; tube m; (*for smoking*) pipe f; (*music*) pipeau m. **pipe-cleaner** n cure-pipe m. **pipeline** n pipeline m. **in the pipeline** en route. v transporter par tuyau. **pipe down** (*coll*) mettre la sourdine. **piping** n tuyauterie f; (*sewing*) passepoil m.

piquant ['piːkənt] adj piquant. **piquancy** n (*taste*) goût piquant m; (*of story*) piquant m.

pique [piːk] n dépit m. v dépiter.

pirate ['paiərət] n pirate m; (*comm*) contrefacteur m. v contrefaire. piller. **piracy** n piraterie f; contrefaçon f; pillage m.

pirouette [piru'et] n pirouette f. v pirouetter.

Pisces ['paisiːz] n Poissons m pl.

piss [pis] (*impol*) v pisser. n pisse f. **piss off!** fous-moi le camp! **pissed** adj (*drunk*) bituré. **be pissed off** en avoir marre.

pistachio [pi'staːʃiou] n pistache f.

pistol ['pistl] n pistolet m.

piston ['pistən] n piston m.

pit [pit] n fosse f; mine f; (*hole*) trou m; (*theatre*) orchestre m. v trouer. grêler. **pit one's wits against** se mesurer avec.

pitch¹ [pitʃ] n (*throw*) lancement m; degré m; (*music*) ton m; (*sport*) terrain m. v lancer; (*music*) donner le ton de; (*tent*) dresser; (*fall*) tomber. **pitchfork** n fourche à foin f.

pitch² [pitʃ] n poix f. **pitch-black** adj noir ébène invar.

pitfall ['pitfɔil] n piège m.

pith [piθ] n (*of orange*) peau blanche f; (*of plant*) moelle f; essence f. **pithy** adj concis, piquant.

pittance ['pitəns] n maigre revenu m.

pituitary [pi'tjuːitəri] adj pituitaire.

pity ['piti] n pitié f; (*shame*) dommage m. **take pity on** avoir pitié de. **what a pity!** quel dommage! v plaindre. **piteous** adj pitoyable. **pitiful** adj pitoyable; (*bad*) lamentable. **pitiless** adj sans pitié. **pitying** adj compatissant.

pivot ['pivət] n pivot m. v (faire) pivoter.

placard ['plakaid] n affiche f. v placarder.

placate [plə'keit] v calmer.

place [pleis] n endroit m, lieu m; (*seat, position*) place f. **all over the place** partout. **out of place** déplacé; (*remark*) hors de propos. **take place** avoir lieu. v placer, mettre; situer; (*order*) passer.

placenta [plə'sentə] n placenta m.

placid ['plasid] adj placide. **placidity** n placidité f.

plagiarize ['pleidʒəraiz] v plagier. **plagiarism** n plagiat m. **plagiarist** n plagiaire m, f.

plague [pleig] n peste f; (nuisance) fléau m. v harceler, tourmenter.

plaice [pleis] n carrelet m.

plaid [plad] n tissu écossais m. adj écossais.

plain [plein] adj clair; simple; (not patterned) uni; sans beauté; (utter) pur. **plain-clothes** adj en civil. n plaine f.

plaintiff ['pleintif] n demandeur, -eresse m, f.

plaintive ['pleintiv] adj plaintif.

plait [plat] n natte f, tresse f. v natter, tresser.

plan [plan] n plan m, projet m. v projeter; organiser; préparer à l'avance. **planning** n planification f; (comm) planning m. **planning permission** permis de construire m.

plane¹ [plein] n (level) plan m; (coll: aeroplane) avion m. adj plan.

plane² [plein] n (tool) rabot. v raboter.

planet ['planit] n planète f. **planetarium** n planétarium m. **planetary** adj planétaire.

plank [plaŋk] n planche f.

plankton ['plaŋktən] n plancton m.

plant [plaɪnt] n (bot) plante f; (tech) matériel m, installation f; (factory) usine f. v planter; (hide) cacher. **plantation** n plantation f.

plaque [plaɪk] n plaque f.

plasma ['plazmə] n plasma m.

plaster ['plaɪstə] n plâtre m; (for wound) sparadrap m. **plaster of Paris** plâtre de moulage m. v plâtrer; couvrir. **plasterer** n plâtrier m.

plastic ['plastik] nm, adj plastique. **plastic surgery** chirurgie esthétique f.

plate [pleit] n (dish) assiette f; (of metal) plaque f; (in book) gravure f. v plaquer; (silver) argenter; (gold) dorer. **plateful** n assiettée f.

plateau ['platou] n plateau m.

platform ['platfoɪm] n plate-forme f; (in hall) estrade f, tribune f; (rail) quai m. **platform-soled** adj (shoes) à semelles compensées. **platform ticket** billet de quai m.

platinum ['platinəm] n platine m.

platonic [plə'tonik] adj platonique.

platoon [plə'tuɪn] n (mil) section f.

plausible ['plɔɪzəbl] adj plausible; (person) convaincant. **plausibility** n plausibilité f.

play [plei] n jeu m; (theatre) pièce f. v jouer. **player** n joueur, -euse m, f. **playful** adj enjoué. **playfulness** n enjouement m, badinage m.

play-back ['pleibak] n réécoute f. **play back** v réécouter.

playboy ['pleiboi] n playboy m.

playground ['pleigraund] n cour de récréation f.

play-group ['pleigruɪp] n garderie f.

playing card n carte à jouer f.

playing field n terrain de sport m.

playmate ['pleimeit] n camarade m, f.

play-pen ['pleipen] n parc m.

plaything ['pleiθiŋ] n jouet m.

playtime ['pleitaim] n récréation f.

playwright ['pleirait] n dramaturge m.

plea [pliɪ] n appel m; (law) argument m; excuse f.

plead [pliɪd] v supplier, implorer; (law) plaider; (as excuse) alléguer.

pleasant ['pleznt] adj agréable.

please [pliɪz] v plaire (à). **please oneself** faire comme on veut. adv s'il vous plaît. **pleased** adj content. **pleasing** adj plaisant.

pleasure ['pleʒə] n plaisir m. **pleasure boat** bateau de plaisance m. **pleasurable** adj agréable.

pleat [pliɪt] n pli m. v plisser.

plectrum ['plektrəm] n plectre m.

pledge [pledʒ] n gage m; promesse f. v engager; promettre.

plenty ['plenti] n abondance f. **plenty of** bien assez de. **plentiful** adj abondant, copieux.

pleurisy ['pluərisi] n pleurésie f.

pliable ['plaiəbl] adj flexible; (person) souple. **pliability** n flexibilité f; souplesse f.

pliers ['plaiəz] pl n pinces f pl, tenailles f pl.

plight [plait] n état critique m, crise f.

plimsoll ['plimsəl] n tennis m.

plod [plod] v marcher d'un pas lourd; (coll: work) bûcher. **plod on** persévérer. **plodder** n (coll) bûcheur m.

plonk [ploŋk] n (coll) vin ordinaire m.

plop [plop] n ploc m. v faire ploc.

plot¹ [plot] n (story, etc) intrigue f; (conspiracy) complot m. v comploter; (route) déterminer.

plot² [plot] n (land) terrain m, lotissement m.

plough [plau] *n* charrue *f*. *v* labourer; (*furrow*) creuser. **ploughing** *n* labour *m*.
pluck [plʌk] *n* courage *m*. *v* (*music*) pincer; (*fruit*) cueillir; (*fowl*) plumer; (*eyebrows*) épiler. **pluck out** arracher. **pluck up courage** prendre son courage à deux mains. **plucky** *adj* courageux.
plug [plʌg] *n* (*stopper*) bouchon *m*, tampon *m*; (*sink, bath*) bonde *f*; (*elec*) fiche *f*; (*mot*) bougie *f*. *v* boucher. **plug in** (se) brancher.
plum [plʌm] *n* (*fruit*) prune *f*; (*tree*) prunier *m*. *adj* (*colour*) lie de vin *invar*. **plum pudding** pudding *m*.
plumage ['pluːmidʒ] *n* plumage *m*.
plumb [plʌm] *n* plomb *m*. **plumbline** *n* fil à plomb *m*. *adj* vertical. *adv* en plein. *v* sonder. **plumb in** faire le raccordement de. **plumber** *n* plombier *m*. **plumbing** *n* plomberie *f*.
plume [pluːm] *n* plume *f*; (*smoke*) panache *m*. *v* lisser.
plummet ['plʌmit] *n* plomb *m*. *v* plonger; (*price, etc.*) dégringoler.
plump¹ [plʌmp] *adj* grassouillet, -ette, potelé. **plumpness** *n* rondeur *f*.
plump² [plʌmp] *v* tomber lourdement. **plump for** se décider pour.
plunder ['plʌndə] *v* piller. *n* (*loot*) butin *m*. **plunderer** *n* pillard *m*. **plundering** *n* pillage *m*.
plunge [plʌndʒ] *n* plongeon *m*; (*fall*) chute *f*. **take the plunge** se jeter à l'eau. *v* plonger; (*rush*) se jeter; (*fall*) tomber.
pluperfect [pluː'pəːfikt] *n* plus-que-parfait *m*.
plural ['pluərəl] *nm*, *adj* pluriel.
plus [plʌs] *nm*, *prep* plus. *adj* positif.
plush [plʌʃ] *n* peluche *f*. *adj* pelucheux; (*coll*) rupin.
ply¹ [plai] *v* (*tool*) manier; (*trade*) exercer; (*with questions, etc.*) presser; (*ship, etc.*) faire la navette.
ply² [plai] *n* (*wood*) feuille *f*; (*wool*) fil *m*; (*rope*) brin *m*. **plywood** *n* contre-plaqué *m*.
pneumatic [njuː'matik] *adj* pneumatique. **pneumatic drill** marteau-piqueur *m*.
pneumonia [njuː'mouniə] *n* pneumonie *f*.
poach¹ [poutʃ] *v* braconner. **poacher** *n* braconnier *m*. **poaching** *n* braconnage *m*.
poach² [poutʃ] *v* (*egg*) pocher.
pocket ['pokit] *n* poche *f*. **pocket-money** *n* argent de poche *m*. *v* empocher.
pod [pod] *n* cosse *f*.

podgy ['podʒi] *adj* (*coll*) rondelet.
poem ['pouim] *n* poème *m*.
poet ['pouit] *n* poète *m*. **poetess** *n* poétesse *f*. **poetic** *adj* poétique. **poetry** *n* poésie *f*.
poignant ['poinjənt] *adj* poignant.
point [point] *n* point *m*; (*sharp end*) pointe *f*; (*decimal*) virgule *f*; (*elec: socket*) prise *f*; (*meaning*) sens *m*. **beside the point** hors de propos. **come to the point** en venir au fait. **make a point of** ne pas manquer de. **point-blank** *adv* (*shoot*) à bout portant; (*refuse*) tout net; (*demand*) de but en blanc. **what's the point?** à quoi bon? *v* indiquer; (*aim*) pointer, braquer. **point out** (*show*) montrer; (*say*) signaler. **pointed** *adj* pointu; (*remark*) lourd de sens. **pointless** *adj* inutile.
poise [poiz] *n* équilibre *m*; (*of body*) port *m*; calme *m*, assurance *f*. *v* tenir en équilibre. **be poised** être en équilibre; être suspendu.
poison ['poizən] *n* poison *m*. *v* empoisonner. **poisoning** *n* empoisonnement *m*. **poisonous** *adj* toxique; (*animal*) venimeux; (*plant*) vénéneux.
poke [pouk] *n* poussée *f*, coup *m*. *v* pousser, enfoncer; (*fire*) tisonner. **poker** *n* tisonnier *m*.
poker ['poukə] *n* (*cards*) poker *m*. **poker-faced** *adj* au visage impassible.
Poland ['poulənd] *n* Pologne *f*. **Pole** *n* Polonais, -e *m*, *f*. **Polish** *nm*, *adj* polonais.
polar ['poulə] *adj* polaire. **polar bear** ours blanc *m*. **polarize** *v* polariser.
pole¹ [poul] *n* perche *f*; (*fixed*) poteau *m*, mât *m*. **pole-vault** *n* saut à la perche *m*.
pole² [poul] *n* (*geog, elec*) pôle *m*. **pole star** étoile polaire *f*.
police [pə'liːs] *n* police *f*, gendarmerie *f*. **the police force** la police *f*, les gendarmes *m pl*. **policeman** *n* agent de police *m*, gendarme *m*. **police station** poste de police *m*, gendarmerie *f*. **policewoman** *n* femme-agent *f*.
policy¹ ['poləsi] *n* politique *f*; ligne *f*, règle *f*.
policy² ['poləsi] *n* (*insurance*) police *f*.
polio ['pouliou] *n* polio *f*.
polish ['poliʃ] *n* (*shoes*) cirage *m*; (*floor, etc.*) cire *f*; (*shine*) poli *m*. *v* polir; cirer, faire briller. **polish off** finir. **polish up** perfectionner.

polite [pə'laɪt] *adj* poli. **politeness** *n* politesse *f*.

politics ['pɒlɪtɪks] *n* politique *f*. **political** *adj* politique. **politician** *n* homme politique, femme politique *m*, *f*.

polka ['pɒlkə] *n* polka *f*.

poll [pəʊl] *n* vote *m*; élection *f*; (*survey*) sondage *m*. *v* voter. **polling booth** isoloir *m*. **polling day** jour des élections *m*. **polling station** bureau de vote *m*.

pollen ['pɒlən] *n* pollen *m*. **pollinate** *v* féconder. **pollination** *n* pollinisation *f*.

pollute [pə'luːt] *v* polluer. **pollution** *n* pollution *f*.

polo ['pəʊləʊ] *n* polo *m*. **polo-neck** *n* col roulé *m*.

polyester [,pɒli'estə] *n* polyester *m*.

polygamy [pə'lɪgəmi] *n* polygamie *f*. **polygamous** *adj* polygame.

polygon ['pɒlɪgən] *n* polygone *m*.

polystyrene [,pɒli'staɪəriːn] *n* polystyrène *m*.

polytechnic [,pɒli'teknɪk] *n* Institut Universitaire de Technologie *m*.

polythene ['pɒliθiːn] *n* polyéthylène *m*. **polythene bag** sac en plastique *m*.

pomegranate ['pɒmɪgranɪt] *n* (*fruit*) grenade *f*; (*tree*) grenadier *m*.

pomp [pɒmp] *n* pompe *f*. **pompous** *adj* pompeux.

pond [pɒnd] *n* étang *m*; (*artificial*) bassin *m*.

ponder ['pɒndə] *v* réfléchir (à), méditer.

pony ['pəʊni] *n* poney *m*. **pony-tail** *n* queue de cheval *f*. **pony-trekking** *n* randonnée équestre *f*.

poodle ['puːdl] *n* caniche *m*.

poof [puːf] *n* (*derog*) tante *f*, tapette *f*.

pool[1] [puːl] *n* (*liquid*) flaque *f*; (*swimming*) piscine *f*.

pool[2] [puːl] *n* (*money*) cagnotte *f*; (*things*) fonds commun *m*; (*ideas*) réservoir *m*; (*comm*) pool *m*. *v* mettre en commun; unir.

poor [pʊə] *adj* pauvre; médiocre; faible.

poorly ['pʊəli] *adj* malade. *adv* pauvrement; (*badly*) mal.

pop[1] [pɒp] *n* pan *m*, bruit sec *m*; (*drink*) boisson gazeuse *f*. **popcorn** *n* pop-corn *m*. *v* (*balloon*) crever; (*cork*) (faire) sauter. **pop in** entrer en passant.

pop[2] [pɒp] *nm*, *adj* (*music*, *etc.*) pop *invar*.

pope [pəʊp] *n* pape *m*.

poplar ['pɒplə] *n* peuplier *m*.

poplin ['pɒplɪn] *n* popeline *f*.

poppy ['pɒpi] *n* pavot *m*, coquelicot *m*.

popular ['pɒpjʊlə] *adj* populaire. **popularity** *n* popularité *f*. **popularize** *v* populariser.

population [,pɒpjʊ'leɪʃən] *n* population *f*. **populate** *v* peupler.

porcelain ['pɔːslɪn] *n* porcelaine *f*.

porch [pɔːtʃ] *n* porche *m*.

porcupine ['pɔːkjʊpaɪn] *n* porc-épic *m*.

pore[1] [pɔː] *n* (*anat*) pore *m*.

pore[2] [pɔː] *v* **pore over** s'absorber dans.

pork [pɔːk] *n* porc *m*.

pornography [pɔː'nɒgrəfi] *n* pornographie *f*. **pornographic** *adj* pornographique.

porous ['pɔːrəs] *adj* poreux.

porpoise ['pɔːpəs] *n* marsouin *m*.

porridge ['pɒrɪdʒ] *n* porridge *m*.

port[1] [pɔːt] *n* (*harbour*) port *m*.

port[2] [pɔːt] *n* (*naut: left*) bâbord *m*.

port[3] [pɔːt] *n* (*wine*) porto *m*.

portable ['pɔːtəbl] *adj* portatif.

portent ['pɔːtent] *n* présage *m*.

porter ['pɔːtə] *n* (*rail, etc.*) porteur *m*; (*in flats, etc.*) concierge *m*, *f*, portier *m*.

portfolio [pɔːt'fəʊliəʊ] *n* serviette *f*; (*pol*) portefeuille *f*.

porthole ['pɔːthəʊl] *n* hublot *m*.

portion ['pɔːʃən] *n* portion *f*; partie *f*.

portrait ['pɔːtrət] *n* portrait *m*.

portray [pɔː'treɪ] *v* peindre; représenter. **portrayal** *n* peinture *f*; représentation *f*.

Portugal ['pɔːtjʊgl] *n* Portugal *m*. **Portuguese** *nm*, *adj* portugais. **the Portuguese** les Portugais.

pose [pəʊz] *n* pose *f*. *v* poser. **pose as se** faire passer pour.

posh [pɒʃ] *adj* chic *invar*.

position [pə'zɪʃən] *n* position *f*, place *f*; situation *f*. *v* placer, mettre en place.

positive ['pɒzətɪv] *adj* positif; catégorique; réel; sûr, certain.

possess [pə'zes] *v* posséder. **possession** *n* possession *f*. **possessive** *nm*, *adj* possessif.

possible ['pɒsəbl] *adj* possible. **possibility** *n* possibilité *f*. **possibly** *adv* (*perhaps*) peut-être.

post[1] [pəʊst] *n* (*pole*) poteau *m*. *v* afficher.

post[2] [pəʊst] *n* (*sentry, job*) poste *m*. *v* poster; (*send*) affecter. **posting** *n* affectation *f*.

post[3] [pəʊst] *n* (*mail*) poste *f*; (*letters*) courrier *m*. **post-box** *n* boîte aux lettres *f*. **postcard** *n* carte postale *f*. **post-code** *n* code postal *m*. **postman** *n* facteur *m*.

postmark *n* cachet de la poste *m*. **post-marked** *adj* timbré. **post office** poste *f*. *v* envoyer par la poste, poster. **postage** *n* tarifs postaux *m pl*. **postage stamp** timbre-poste *m*. **postal** *adj* postal, par la poste. **postal order** mandat *m*.

poster ['pousto] *n* affiche *f*; (*as decoration*) poster *m*. **poster paint** gouache *f*.

posterior [po'stiorio] *adj* postérieur, -e. *n* (*coll*) derrière *m*.

posterity [po'steroti] *n* postérité *f*.

postgraduate [poust'gradjuit] *adj* de troisième cycle. *n* étudiant, -e de troisième cycle *m, f*.

posthumous ['postjumos] *adj* posthume.

post-mortem [poust'mottom] *n* autopsie *f*.

postpone [pous'poun] *v* remettre, ajourner. **postponement** *n* ajournement *m*.

postscript ['pousskript] *n* post-scriptum *m*.

postulate ['postjuleit; *n* 'postjulot] *v* postuler, poser comme principe. *n* postulat *m*.

posture ['postʃo] *n* posture *f*; attitude *f*.

pot [pot] *n* pot *m*; (*for cooking*) marmite *f*. **pot-roast** *n* rôti braisé *m*. **pots and pans** batterie de cuisine *f sing*. **take pot luck** manger à la fortune du pot. *v* mettre en pot.

potassium [po'tasjom] *n* potassium *m*.

potato [po'teitou] *n* pomme de terre *f*.

potent ['poutont] *adj* puissant; (*drink*) fort.

potential [po'tenʃol] *adj* potentiel; possible. *n* (*phys, elec, etc.*) potentiel *m*; (*promise*) potentialités *f pl*.

pot-hole ['pothoul] *n* (*in road*) fondrière *f*; (*underground*) caverne *f*, grotte *f*. **pot-holer** *n* spéléologue *m, f*. **pot-holing** *n* spéléologie *f*.

potion ['pouʃon] *n* potion *f*.

potter[1] ['poto] *v* (*coll*) bricoler.

potter[2] ['poto] *n* potier *m*. **potter's wheel** tour de potier.

pottery ['potori] *n* (*place, craft*) poterie *f*; (*things made*) poteries *f pl*.

potty ['poti] *n* (*coll*) pot de bébé *m*.

pouch [pautʃ] *n* petit sac *m*; (*kangaroo*) poche *f*; (*tobacco*) blague *f*.

poultice ['poultis] *n* cataplasme *m*.

poultry ['poultri] *n* volaille *f*.

pounce [pauns] *v* bondir, sauter. *n* bond *m*.

pound[1] [paund] *v* battre, piler, pilonner, marteler.

pound[2] [paund] *n* livre *f*.

pour [poɪ] *v* verser; (*flow copiously*) couler à flots, ruisseler; (*rain*) tomber à verse; (*people, etc.*) affluer.

pout [paut] *n* moue *f*. *v* faire la moue.

poverty ['povoti] *n* pauvreté *f*.

powder ['paudo] *n* poudre *f*. **powder puff** houppette *f*. **powder room** toilettes pour dames *f pl*. *v* poudrer; pulvériser. **powdery** *adj* poudreux.

power ['pauo] *n* (*authority, capacity*) pouvoir *m*; (*energy, force*) puissance *f*; faculté *f*. **power cut** coupure de courant *f*. **power station** centrale électrique *f*. *v* faire marcher. **powerful** *adj* puissant. **powerless** *adj* impuissant.

practicable ['praktikobl] *adj* praticable.

practical ['praktikol] *adj* pratique. **practical joke** farce *f*.

practice ['praktis] *n* pratique *f*; (*training*) entraînement *m*; (*medicine, etc.*) exercice *m*; clientèle *f*.

practise ['praktis] *v* pratiquer; s'entraîner (à); (*music*) travailler, s'exercer (à); (*doctor, lawyer*) exercer.

practitioner [prak'tiʃono] *n* praticien, -enne *m, f*.

pragmatic [prag'matik] *adj* pragmatique; dogmatique.

Prague [praɪg] *n* Prague.

prairie ['preori] *n* plaine *f*, prairie *f*.

praise [preiz] *n* éloge *m*. *v* louer. **praise-worthy** *adj* louable.

pram [pram] *n* voiture d'enfant *f*.

prance [prains] *v* caracoler.

prank [praŋk] *n* frasque *f*; (*joke*) farce *f*.

prattle ['pratl] *v* jaser, babiller; (*chat*) jacasser. *n* babil *m*; jacasserie *f*.

prawn [proin] *n* crevette rose *f*. **prawn cocktail** salade de crevettes *f*.

pray [prei] *v* prier. **prayer** *n* prière *f*. **prayer-book** *n* livre de messe *m*.

preach [priitʃ] *v* prêcher. **preacher** *n* prédicateur *m*. **preaching** *n* prédication *f*.

precarious [pri'keorios] *adj* précaire.

precaution [pri'koɪʃon] *n* précaution *f*. **take precautions** prendre ses précautions.

precede [pri'siid] *v* précéder. **precedence** *n* préséance *f*; priorité *f*. **precedent** *n* précédent *m*.

precinct ['priisiŋkt] *n* enceinte *f*; limite *f*; (*shopping*) zone commerciale *f*.

precious ['preʃəs] adj précieux.
precipice ['presipis] n précipice m.
precipitate [pri'sipiteit; adj pri'sipitət] v (hasten) hâter; (throw) précipiter. adj irréfléchi. **precipitation** n précipitation f.
précis ['preisi] n précis m, résumé m.
precise [pri'sais] adj précis; méticuleux. **precision** n précision f.
preclude [pri'kluːd] v écarter; prévenir; exclure.
precocious [pri'kouʃəs] adj précoce. **precocity** n précocité f.
preconceive [,priːkən'siːv] v préconcevoir. **preconception** n idée préconçue f.
precursor [,priː'kəːsə] n (person) précurseur m; (thing) annonce f.
predator ['predətə] n prédateur m. **predatory** adj rapace, de prédateur.
predecessor ['priːdisesə] n prédécesseur m.
predestine [pri'destin] v prédestiner. **predestination** n prédestination f.
predicament [pri'dikəmənt] n situation difficile f.
predicate ['predikət] n prédicat m. v affirmer.
predict [pri'dikt] v prédire. **predictable** adj prévisible. **prediction** n prédiction f.
predominate [pri'domineit] v prédominer. **predominance** n prédominance f. **predominant** adj prédominant.
pre-eminent [priː'eminənt] adj prééminent. **pre-eminence** n prééminence f.
preen [priːn] v lisser. **preen oneself** se pomponner.
prefabricate [priː'fabrikeit] v préfabriquer. **prefab** n (coll) maison préfabriquée f.
preface ['prefis] n (book) préface f; (speech) introduction f. v faire précéder.
prefect ['priːfekt] n (school) élève chargé de la discipline m.
prefer [pri'fəː] v préférer, aimer mieux. **preferable** adj préférable. **preference** n préférence f. **preferential** adj préférentiel.
prefix ['priːfiks] n préfixe m. v préfixer.
pregnant ['pregnənt] adj (woman) enceinte; (animal) pleine. **pregnancy** n (woman) grossesse f; (animal) gestation f.
prehistoric [,priːhi'storik] adj préhistorique.
prejudice ['predʒədis] n préjugé m. v prévenir; (damage) nuire à. **prejudiced** adj de parti pris.
preliminary [pri'liminəri] adj pré-

liminaire; premier. **preliminaries** pl n préliminaires m pl.
prelude ['preljuːd] n prélude m.
premarital [priː'maritl] adj avant le mariage.
premature [premə'tʃuə] adj prématuré.
premeditate [priː'mediteit] v préméditer. **premeditation** n préméditation f.
premier ['premiə] adj premier. n premier ministre m.
première ['premieə] n première f.
premise ['premis] n prémisse f. **premises** pl n lieux m pl, locaux m pl.
premium ['priːmiəm] n prime f. **premium bond** bon à lots m.
premonition [,premə'niʃən] n prémonition f.
preoccupied [priː'okjupaid] adj préoccupé. **preoccupation** n préoccupation f.
prepare [pri'peə] v (se) préparer. **preparation** n préparation. **preparations** pl n préparatifs m pl. **preparatory** adj préparatoire; préliminaire. **preparatory school** école primaire privée f.
preposition [,prepə'ziʃən] n préposition f.
preposterous [pri'postərəs] adj absurde, ridicule.
prerogative [pri'rogətiv] n prérogative f.
prescribe [pri'skraib] v prescrire. **prescription** n (med) ordonnance f; prescription f.
presence ['prezns] n présence f.
present[1] ['preznt] adj présent; actuel. n présent m. **at present** actuellement. **presently** adv tout à l'heure.
present[2] [pri'zent] v présenter; (film, play) donner; (gift) offrir; (medal) remettre. n cadeau m. **presentable** adj présentable. **presentation** n présentation f; (of gift, medal) remise f. **presenter** n présentateur, -trice m, f.
preserve [pri'zəːv] v conserver; (from harm) préserver. **preserved** adj en conserve. **preserves** pl n conserves f pl; (jam) confiture f sing. **preservation** n conservation f; préservation f. **preservative** n agent de conservation m.
preside [pri'zaid] v présider.
president ['prezidənt] n président m. **presidency** n présidence f. **presidential** adj présidentiel.
press [pres] n presse f; (wine, cider) pressoir m. **press conference** conférence de presse f. **press release** communiqué de presse m. v appuyer (sur), presser; (iron)

repasser; insister. **press for** faire pression pour. **press-gang** v faire pression sur. **press on** continuer. **press-stud** n bouton-pression m. **press-up** n traction f. **pressing** adj urgent.

pressure ['preʃə] n pression f. **pressure-cooker** n autocuiseur m. **pressure gauge** manomètre m. **pressurize** v (cabin, etc.) pressuriser; (force) contraindre.

prestige [pre'stiːʒ] n prestige m. **prestigious** adj prestigieux.

presume [pri'zjuːm] v présumer. **presumption** n présomption f. **presumptuous** adj présomptueux.

pretend [pri'tend] v faire semblant; (claim) prétendre. **pretence** n feinte f, prétexte m; (claim) prétention f. **pretension** n prétention f. **pretentious** adj prétentieux.

pretext ['priːtekst] n prétexte m.

pretty ['priti] adj joli. adv assez.

prevail [pri'veil] v prévaloir, prédominer. **prevail upon** persuader. **prevailing** adj (wind) dominant; courant, actuel. **prevalent** adj répandu.

prevent [pri'vent] v empêcher. **prevention** n prévention f. **preventive** adj préventif.

preview ['priːvjuː] n avant-première f.

previous ['priːviəs] adj précédent. **previously** adv auparavant.

prey [prei] n proie f. **be a prey to** être en proie à. v **prey on** (animal) faire sa proie de; (fear) ronger.

price [prais] n prix m. **price-list** n tarif m. v fixer le prix de; marquer le prix de. **priceless** adj inestimable.

prick [prik] n piqûre f. v piquer. **prick up one's ears** dresser l'oreille.

prickle ['prikl] n piquant m. v piquer; (sensation) picoter. **prickly** adj hérissé.

pride [praid] n orgueil m; (satisfaction) fierté f. v **pride oneself on** être fier de.

priest [priːst] n prêtre m. **priesthood** n prêtrise f.

prim [prim] adj guindé.

primary ['praiməri] adj (first) primaire, premier; principal. **primary school** école primaire f.

primate ['praimət] n (zool) primate m; (rel) primat m.

prime [praim] adj principal; excellent, de premier choix; (math) premier. **prime minister** premier ministre m. v préparer; (for painting) apprêter. **primer** n apprêt m; (book) premier livre m.

primitive ['primitiv] adj primitif.

primrose ['primrouz] n primevère f.

prince [prins] n prince m. **princely** adj princier. **princess** n princesse f.

principal ['prinsəpəl] adj principal. n (school) directeur, -trice m, f.

principle ['prinsəpəl] n principe m. **on principle** par principe.

print [print] n (mark) empreinte f; (type) caractères m pl; (art) gravure f; (phot) épreuve f. **out of print** épuisé. v imprimer; (phot) tirer. **print-out** n listage m. **printed matter** imprimés m pl. **printer** n imprimeur m. **printing** n impression f; (phot) tirage m. **printing press** presse typographique f.

prior ['praiə] adj antérieur, -e. **prior to** antérieurement à. **priority** n priorité f.

prise [praiz] v **prise off/open** enlever/ouvrir en faisant levier; forcer.

prism ['prizm] n prisme m.

prison ['prizn] n prison f. **prisoner** n prisonnier, -ère m, f.

private ['praivət] adj privé; confidentiel; (lesson, car, etc.) particulier; personnel. n simple soldat m. **privacy** n intimité f, solitude f. **privately** adv en privé; à titre personnel.

privet ['privət] n troène m.

privilege ['privəlidʒ] n privilège m. **privileged** adj privilégié.

prize [praiz] n prix m. **prizewinner** n lauréat, -e m, f. adj primé. v priser.

probable ['probabl] adj probable; (believable) vraisemblable. **probability** n probabilité f. **probably** adv probablement.

probation [prə'beiʃən] n (law) mise à l'épreuve f, liberté surveillée f. **on probation** (job) engagé à l'essai. **probationary** adj d'essai.

probe [proub] n sonde f; enquête f. v sonder, explorer.

problem ['probləm] n problème m. **problem child** enfant difficile m, f. **problem page** courrier du cœur m. **problematic** adj problématique.

proceed [prə'siːd] v aller, continuer, avancer. **proceed to** se mettre à. **proceeds** pl n produit m sing. **procedure** n procédure f. **proceedings** pl n cérémonie f sing; (law) mesures f pl.

process ['prouses] n processus m; (method) procédé m. **in the process of** en train de, au cours de. *v* traiter; (*phot*) développer; (*admin*) s'occuper de.

procession [prə'seʃən] *n* cortège *m*, défilé *m*.

proclaim [prə'kleim] *v* proclamer; démontrer. **proclamation** *n* proclamation *f*.

procreate ['proukrieit] *v* procréer. **procreation** *n* procréation *f*.

procure [prə'kjuə] *v* obtenir; (*prostitute*) procurer.

prod [prod] *n* petit coup *m*. *v* pousser doucement; (*rouse*) aiguillonner.

prodigal ['prodigəl] *adj* prodigue.

prodigy ['prodidʒi] *n* prodige *m*. **prodigious** *adj* prodigieux.

produce [prə'djuːs; *n* 'prodjuːs] *v* produire; (*theatre*) mettre en scène. *n* produits *m pl*. **producer** *n* producteur, -trice *m*, *f*; metteur en scène *m*. **product** *n* produit *m*. **production** *n* production *f*; mise en scène *f*. **productive** *adj* productif; fécond. **productivity** *n* productivité *f*.

profane [prə'fein] *adj* profane. *v* profaner. **profanity** *n* (*oath*) juron *m*.

profess [prə'fes] *v* professer, affirmer, déclarer.

profession [prə'feʃən] *n* profession *f*. **professional** *n, adj* professionnel, -elle.

professor [prə'fesə] *n* professeur *m*. **professorship** *n* chaire *f*.

proficient [prə'fiʃənt] *adj* compétent. **proficiency** *n* compétence *f*.

profile ['proufail] *n* profil *m*; (*biographical sketch*) portrait *m*.

profit ['profit] *n* profit *m*, bénéfice *m*. **profit-making** *adj* à but lucratif. *v* **profit by** *or* **from** tirer profit de. **profitable** *adj* rentable; (*useful*) fructueux.

profound [prə'faund] *adj* profond. **profoundly** *adv* profondément.

profuse [prə'fjuːs] *adj* abondant, profus. **profusely** *adv* abondamment, à profusion. **profusion** *n* abondance *f*, profusion *f*.

programme ['prougram] *n* programme *m*; (*broadcast*) émission *f*. *v* programmer. **programmer** *n* programmeur, -euse *m*, *f*. **programming** *n* programmation *f*.

progress ['prougres] *n* progrès *m*. **in progress** en cours. **make progress** faire des progrès. *v* progresser, avancer. **progression** *n* progression *f*. **progressive** *adj* progressif; (*outlook, etc.*) progressiste.

prohibit [prə'hibit] *v* interdire, défendre;

(*prevent*) empêcher. **prohibition** *n* prohibition *f*.

project ['prodʒekt; *v* prə'dʒekt] *n* projet *m*; opération *f*; (*school*) dossier *m*. *v* projeter; (*protrude*) faire saillie. **projectile** *n* projectile *m*. **projecting** *adj* saillant. **projection** *n* projection *f*; saillie *f*. **projector** *n* projecteur *m*.

proletarian [proulə'teəriən] *n* prolétaire *m*. *adj* prolétarien. **proletariat** *n* prolétariat *m*.

proliferate [prə'lifəreit] *v* proliférer. **proliferation** *n* prolifération *f*.

prolific [prə'lifik] *adj* prolifique.

prologue ['proulog] *n* prologue *m*.

prolong [prə'loŋ] *v* prolonger. **prolongation** *n* (*time*) prolongation *f*; (*space*) prolongement *m*.

promenade [promə'naːd] *n* promenade *f*.

prominent ['prominənt] *adj* proéminent; important; (*striking*) frappant. **prominence** *n* proéminence *f*; importance *f*.

promiscuous [prə'miskjuəs] *adj* léger, immoral; (*person*) de mœurs faciles. **promiscuity** *n* promiscuité *f*.

promise ['promis] *n* promesse *f*. *v* promettre. **promising** *adj* prometteur, -euse.

promontory ['promantəri] *n* promontoire *m*.

promote [prə'mout] *v* promouvoir; (*comm*) lancer. **promotion** *n* promotion *f*; lancement *m*.

prompt [prompt] *adj* rapide, prompt; ponctuel. *v* pousser, inciter; (*theatre*) souffler. **prompter** *n* souffleur, -euse *m*, *f*.

prone [proun] *adj* enclin; (*lying*) prostré.

prong [proŋ] *n* dent *f*.

pronoun ['prounaun] *n* pronom *m*.

pronounce [prə'nauns] *v* prononcer. **pronouncement** *n* déclaration *f*. **pronunciation** *n* prononciation *f*.

proof [pruːf] *n* preuve *f*; (*of book, photo, etc.*) épreuve *f*. **proof-read** *v* corriger les épreuves de. **proof-reading** *n* correction des épreuves *f*. *adj* (*resistant*) à l'épreuve de.

prop¹ [prop] *n* support *m*. *v* (*lean*) appuyer; (*support*) étayer; (*financially*) soutenir.

prop² [prop] *n* (*coll: theatre*) accessoire *m*.

propaganda [propə'gandə] *n* propagande *f*.

propagate ['propəgeit] *v* (se) propager. **propagation** *n* propagation *f*.

propel [prə'pel] *v* propulser; (*push*) pousser. **propeller** *n* hélice *f.* **propelling pencil** porte-mine *m invar.*

proper ['prɒpə] *adj* convenable, correct; (*real*) véritable. **proper noun** nom propre *m.* **properly** *adv* comme il faut.

property ['prɒpəti] *n* propriété *f*; (*possessions*) biens *m pl.*

prophecy ['prɒfəsi] *n* prophétie *f.* **prophesy** *v* prédire, prophétiser.

prophet ['prɒfit] *n* prophète *m.* **prophetic** *adj* prophétique.

proportion [prə'pɔːʃən] *n* proportion *f*; part *f.* **out of proportion** mal proportionné; hors de proportion. *v* proportionner. **proportional** *adj* proportionnel.

propose [prə'pouz] *v* proposer; (*marriage*) faire sa demande; (*intend*) se proposer (de). **proposal** *n* proposition *f*; demande en mariage *f*; projet *m.* **proposition** *n* proposition *f*; affaire *f.*

proprietor [prə'praiətə] *n* propriétaire *m, f.*

propriety [prə'praiəti] *n* bienséance *f*; (*correctness*) justesse *f.*

propulsion [prə'pʌlʃən] *n* propulsion *f.*

prose [prouz] *n* prose *f*; (*translation*) thème *m.*

prosecute ['prosikjuːt] *v* poursuivre. **prosecution** *n* poursuites judiciaires *f pl*; (*side*) partie plaignante *f.*

prospect ['prɒspekt; *v* prə'spekt] *n* perspective *f.* **prospects** *pl n* (*of job, etc.*) avenir *m sing. v* prospecter. **prospective** *adj* futur; possible.

prospectus [prə'spektəs] *n* prospectus *m.*

prosper ['prɒspə] *v* prospérer. **prosperity** *n* prospérité *f.* **prosperous** *adj* prospère.

prostitute ['prɒstitjuːt] *n* prostituée *f. v* prostituer. **prostitution** *n* prostitution *f.*

prostrate ['prɒstreit; *v* pro'streit] *adj* prosterné, prostré; (*lying*) à plat ventre. *v* (*overcome*) accabler. **prostrate oneself** se prosterner. **prostration** *n* prosternation *f*; (*exhaustion*) prostration *f.*

protagonist [prou'tagənist] *n* protagoniste *m.*

protect [prə'tekt] *v* protéger. **protection** *n* protection *f.* **protective** *adj* protecteur, -trice; de protection.

protein ['proutiːn] *n* protéine *f.*

protest ['proutest; *v* prə'test] *n* protestation *f. v* protester. **protester** *n* (*on march*) manifestant, -e *m, f.*

Protestant ['protistənt] *n, adj* protestant, -e *m, f.*

protocol ['proutəkol] *n* protocole *m.*

prototype ['proutətaip] *n* prototype *m.*

protractor [prə'traktə] *n* rapporteur *m.*

protrude [prə'truːd] *v* dépasser, avancer. **protruding** *adj* saillant, en saillie.

proud [praud] *adj* fier; orgueilleux.

prove [pruːv] *v* prouver; se révéler.

proverb ['provəːb] *n* proverbe *m.* **proverbial** *adj* proverbial.

provide [prə'vaid] *v* fournir, pourvoir. **provided that** pourvu que.

provident ['providənt] *adj* prévoyant. **providence** *n* providence *f.*

province ['provins] *n* province *f*; domaine *m.* **the provinces** la province *f sing.* **provincial** *adj* provincial.

provision [prə'viʒən] *n* (*supply*) provision *f*; (*providing*) fourniture *f*; (*of contract, law, etc.*) disposition *f.* **make provision for** pourvoir aux besoins de. **provisions** *pl n* provisions *f pl.* **provisional** *adj* provisoire.

proviso [prə'vaizou] *n* stipulation *f*, condition *f.*

provoke [prə'vouk] *v* provoquer. **provocation** *n* provocation *f.* **provocative** *adj* provocant.

prow [prau] *n* proue *f.*

prowess ['prauis] *n* prouesse *f.*

prowl [praul] *v* rôder. **prowler** *n* rôdeur, -euse *m, f.*

proximity [prok'siməti] *n* proximité *f.*

proxy ['proksi] *n* procuration *f.* **by proxy** par procuration.

prude [pruːd] *n* prude *f.* **prudish** *adj* prude.

prudent ['pruːdənt] *adj* prudent. **prudence** *n* prudence *f.*

prune[1] [pruːn] *n* (*fruit*) pruneau *m.*

prune[2] [pruːn] *v* tailler, élaguer.

pry [prai] *v* être indiscret. **pry into** fourrer son nez dans. **prying** *adj* fureteur, -euse.

psalm [saːm] *n* psaume *m.*

pseudonym ['sjuːdənim] *n* pseudonyme *m.*

psychedelic [ˌsaikə'delik] *adj* psychédélique.

psychiatry [sai'kaiətri] *n* psychiatrie *f.* **psychiatric** *adj* psychiatrique. **psychiatrist** *n* psychiatre *m, f.*

psychic ['saikik] *adj* métapsychique; (*psych*) psychique.

psychoanalysis [,saikouə'naləsis] *n* psychanalyse *f*. **psychoanalyse** *v* psychanalyser. **psychoanalyst** *n* psychanalyste *m, f*.

psychology [sai'kolədʒi] *n* psychologie *f*. **psychological** *adj* psychologique. **psychologist** *n* psychologue *m, f*.

psychopath ['saikəpaθ] *n* psychopathe *m, f*. **psychopathic** *adj* psychopathe.

psychosis [sai'kousis] *n* psychose *f*. **psychotic** *n(m+f)*, *adj* psychotique.

psychosomatic [,saikəsə'matik] *adj* psychosomatique.

psychotherapy [,saikə'θerəpi] *n* psychothérapie *f*.

pub [pʌb] *n* pub *m*. **pub-crawl** *n* tournée des bistrots *f*.

puberty ['pjuːbəti] *n* puberté *f*.

pubic ['pjuːbik] *adj* pubien.

public ['pʌblik] *adj* public, -ique. *n* public *m*.

publican ['pʌblikən] *n* patron de bistrot *m*.

publication [,pʌbli'keifən] *n* publication *f*.

public bar *n* bar *m*.

public conveniences *pl n* toilettes *f pl*.

public footpath *n* sentier public *m*.

public holiday *n* jour férié *m*.

publicity [pʌb'lisəti] *n* publicité *f*.

publicize ['pʌblisaiz] *v* rendre public; (*advertise*) faire de la publicité pour.

public library *n* bibliothèque municipale *f*.

public relations *pl n* relations publiques *f pl*. **public relations officer** *n* public-relations *m*.

public school *n* collège secondaire privé *m*.

public speaking *n* art oratoire *m*.

public-spirited *adj* **be public-spirited** faire preuve de civisme.

public transport *n* transport en commun *m*.

publish ['pʌblif] *v* publier. **publisher** *n* éditeur, -trice *m, f*. **publishing** *n* édition *f*; publication *f*. **publishing house** maison d'édition *f*.

pucker ['pʌkə] *v* (se) plisser; (*sewing*) (faire) goder. *n* (*sewing*) faux pli *m*.

pudding ['pudiŋ] *n* dessert *m*.

puddle ['pʌdl] *n* flaque d'eau *f*.

puerile ['pjuərail] *adj* puéril.

puff [pʌf] *n* bouffée *f*, souffle *m*; (*cake*) feuilleté *m*; (*for powder*) houppe *f*. **puff**
sleeves manches bouffantes *f pl*. *v* souffler. **puff out** *or* **up** (se) gonfler. **puffy** *adj* gonflé.

pull [pul] *n* traction *f*; attraction *f*; (*action*) coup *m*. *v* tirer; (*trigger*) presser; (*muscle*) se déchirer. **pull away** démarrer, s'éloigner. **pull down** baisser, descendre; démolir. **pull off** enlever; (*deal*) conclure; (*trick*) réussir. **pull out** (*car, etc.*) déboîter; (*extract*) arracher; (*mil*) retirer. **pull to pieces** démolir. **pull up** (*car, etc.*) s'arrêter; (*socks, etc.*) remonter.

pulley ['puli] *n* poulie *f*.

pullover ['pul,ouvə] *n* pull *m*.

pulp [pʌlp] *n* pulpe *f*. *v* réduire en pulpe. **pulpy** *adj* pulpeux.

pulpit ['pulpit] *n* chaire *f*.

pulsate [pʌl'seit] *v* battre, palpiter; (*music*) vibrer. **pulsation** *n* pulsation *f*, battement *m*.

pulse [pʌls] *n* (*med*) pouls *m*; (*phys, elec*) vibration. *v* battre, palpiter.

pulverize ['pʌlvəraiz] *v* pulvériser. **pulverization** *n* pulvérisation *f*.

pump [pʌmp] *n* pompe *f*. *v* pomper. **pump up** gonfler.

pumpkin ['pʌmpkin] *n* citrouille *f*.

pun [pʌn] *n* calembour *m*.

punch¹ [pʌntf] *n* coup de poing *m*. **punch line** astuce *f*. *v* donner un coup de poing à.

punch² [pʌntf] *n* (*drink*) punch *m*.

punch³ [pʌntf] *n* (*tool*) poinçonneuse *f*; perforateur *m*. *v* poinçonner; perforer.

punctual ['pʌŋktfuəl] *adj* ponctuel, à l'heure. **punctuality** *n* ponctualité *f*, exactitude *f*.

punctuate ['pʌŋktfueit] *v* ponctuer. **punctuation** *n* ponctuation *f*.

puncture ['pʌŋktfə] *n* (*tyre*) crevaison *f*; (*leather, skin*) piqûre *f*. **have a puncture** crever. *v* crever; piquer.

pungent ['pʌndʒənt] *adj* âcre, piquant; (*remark*) mordant. **pungency** *n* âcreté *f*; mordant *m*.

punish ['pʌnif] *v* punir. **punishment** *n* punition *f*.

punt¹ [pʌnt] *n* (*boat*) bachot *m*.

punt² [pʌnt] *v* (*bet*) parier; (*cards*) ponter. **punter** *n* parieur, -euse *m, f*; ponte *m*.

puny ['pjuːni] *adj* chétif.

pupil¹ ['pjuːpl] *n* élève *m, f*.

pupil² ['pjuːpl] *n* (*eye*) pupille *f*.

puppet ['pʌpit] *n* marionnette *f.*
puppy ['pʌpi] *n* chiot *m.*
purchase ['pɜːtʃəs] *n* achat *m. v* acheter.
pure ['pjuə] *adj* pur. **purify** *v* épurer, purifier. **purity** *n* pureté *f.*
purée ['pjuərei] *n* purée *f.*
purgatory ['pɜːgətəri] *n* purgatoire *m.*
purge [pɜːdʒ] *n* purge *f. v* purger. **purgative** *nm, adj* purgatif.
puritan ['pjuəritən] *n, adj* puritain, -e. **puritanical** *adj* puritain.
purl [pɜːl] *n* maille à l'envers *f. v* tricoter à l'envers.
purple ['pɜːpl] *nm, adj* pourpre, violet.
purpose ['pɜːpəs] *n* (*aim*) but *m;* (*use*) usage *m.* **on purpose** exprès. **purposeful** *adj* résolu. **purposely** *adv* exprès.
purr [pɜː] *v* ronronner. *n* ronronnement *m.*
purse [pɜːs] *n* porte-monnaie *m invar,* bourse *f. v* **purse one's lips** se pincer les lèvres.
purser ['pɜːsə] *n* commissaire du bord *m.*
pursue [pə'sjuː] *v* poursuivre; (*seek*) rechercher. **pursuer** *n* poursuivant, -e *m, f.* **pursuit** *n* poursuite *f;* recherche *f;* occupation *f.*
pus [pʌs] *n* pus *m.*
push [puʃ] *n* poussée *f.* **push-chair** *n* poussette *f. v* pousser; (*press*) appuyer (sur). **be pushed for** être à court de.
*****put** [put] *v* mettre, poser; (*say*) dire, exprimer; (*case, etc.*) présenter. **put across** faire comprendre, communiquer. **put away** ranger. **put back** remettre. **put down** déposer; noter; attribuer; (*kill*) faire piquer. **put off** retarder, renvoyer à plus tard; (*distract*) dérouter. **put on** mettre. **put out** (*fire*) éteindre; (*bother*) déranger; (*annoy*) contrarier. **put up** (*tent*) dresser; construire; augmenter; loger; (*picture*) mettre. **put-up job** (*coll*) coup monté *m.* **put up with** supporter.
putrid ['pjuːtrid] *adj* putride.
putt [pʌt] *n* putt *m. v* putter. **putting** *n* putting *m.*
putty ['pʌti] *n* mastic *m.*
puzzle ['pʌzl] *n* énigme *f;* (*game*) casse-tête *m invar. v* rendre perplexe. **puzzle out** comprendre; éclaircir. **puzzled** *adj* perplexe. **puzzling** *adj* curieux.
pyjamas [pə'dʒɑːməz] *pl n* pyjama *m sing.*
pylon ['pailən] *n* pylône *m.*
pyramid ['pirəmid] *n* pyramide *f.*
python ['paiθən] *n* python *m.*

Q

quack¹ [kwak] *n* (*duck*) coin-coin *m. v* faire coin-coin.
quack² [kwak] *n* charlatan *m.*
quadrangle ['kwodraŋgl] *n* cour *f;* (*math*) quadrilatère *m.*
quadrant ['kwodrənt] *n* quadrant *m.*
quadrilateral [kwodrə'latərəl] *nm, adj* quadrilatère.
quadruped ['kwodruped] *nm, adj* quadrupède.
quadruple [kwod'ruːpl] *nm, adj* quadruple. *v* quadrupler.
quadruplet ['kwodruːplit] *n* quadruplé, -e *m, f.*
quagmire ['kwagmaiə] *n* bourbier *m.*
quail¹ [kweil] *n* (*bird*) caille *f.*
quail² [kweil] *v* perdre courage.
quaint [kweint] *adj* au charme vieillot; bizarre; pittoresque.
quake [kweik] *v* trembler.
qualify ['kwolifai] *v* qualifier; obtenir son diplôme; (*modify*) mitiger. **qualification** *n* capacité *f;* réserve *f.* **qualifications** *pl n* titres *m pl,* diplômes *m pl.* **qualified** *adj* qualifié, diplômé; mitigé.
quality ['kwoləti] *n* qualité *f.*
qualm [kwɑːm] *n* scrupule *m;* appréhension *f;* nausée *f.*
quandary ['kwondəri] *n* embarras *m,* dilemme *m.*
quantify ['kwontifai] *v* déterminer la quantité de.
quantity ['kwontəti] *n* quantité *f.*
quarantine ['kworəntiːn] *n* quarantaine *f. v* mettre en quarantaine.
quarrel ['kworəl] *n* querelle *f. v* se disputer. **quarrelsome** *adj* querelleur, -euse.
quarry¹ ['kwori] *n* (*stone*) carrière *f. v* extraire; exploiter (une carrière).
quarry² ['kwori] *n* proie *f;* (*game*) gibier *m.*
quarter ['kwoːtə] *n* quart *m;* (*of year*) trimestre *m;* (*of town*) quartier *m.* **quarter-final** *n* quart de finale *m.* **quartermaster** *n* (*naut*) maître de manœuvre *m.* **quarter past two** deux heures et quart. **quarters** *pl n* (*mil*) quartiers *m pl.* **quarter to two** deux heures moins le quart. *v* diviser en quatre; (*mil*) caserner. **quarterly** *adj* trimestriel.

quartet [kwɔɪ'tet] *n* quatuor *m.*
quartz [kwɔɪts] *n* quartz *m.*
quash [kwɒʃ] *v* annuler; rejeter; (*riot*) étouffer.
quaver ['kweivə] *n* (*music*) croche *f;* tremblement *m. v* chevroter.
quay [kiɪ] *n* quai *m.*
queasy ['kwiɪzi] *adj* (*stomach*) délicat. **feel queasy** avoir mal au cœur. **queasiness** *n* mal au cœur *m.*
queen [kwiɪn] *n* reine *f;* (*cards*) dame *f.* **Queen Mother** reine mère *f.*
queer [kwiə] *adj* étrange; suspect; (*slang*) homosexuel. *n* (*slang*) pédé *m.*
quell [kwel] *v* réprimer.
quench [kwentʃ] *v* (*fire*) éteindre; (*hope*) réprimer. **quench one's thirst** se désaltérer.
query ['kwiəri] *n* question *f. n* mettre en doute.
quest [kwest] *n* quête *f.*
question ['kwestʃən] *n* question *f;* doute *m.* **it's out of the question** il n'en est pas question. **question mark** point d'interrogation *m. v* interroger; mettre en doute. **questionable** *adj* douteux. **questioning** *n* interrogation *f.* **questionnaire** *n* questionnaire *m.*
queue [kjuɪ] *n* queue *f,* file *f.* **queue-jumper** *n* resquilleur, -euse *m, f. v* faire la queue.
quibble ['kwibl] *n* chicane *f. v* chicaner.
quick [kwik] *adj* rapide, prompt. **quicksand** *n* sable mouvant *m.* **quickstep** *n* fox *m.* **quick-tempered** *adj* prompt à s'emporter. **quick-witted** *adj* à l'esprit vif. *n* vif *m.* **quicken** *v* (s')accélérer; stimuler. **quickly** *adv* vite, sans tarder.
quid [kwid] *n* (*coll*) livre *f.*
quiet ['kwaiət] *adj* tranquille; (*subdued*) doux, douce; (*voice*) bas, basse. *n also* **quietness** silence *m;* tranquillité *f.* **quieten** *v* calmer. **quietly** *adv* silencieusement, doucement.
quill [kwil] *n* penne *f;* (*pen*) plume d'oie *f;* (*of porcupine*) piquant *m.*
quilt [kwilt] *n* édredon piqué *m. v* ouater, ouatiner.
quince [kwins] *n* (*fruit*) coing *m;* (*tree*) cognassier *m.*
quinine [kwi'niɪn] *n* quinine *f.*
quinsy ['kwinzi] *n* amygdalite purulente *f.*
quintet [kwin'tet] *n* quintette *m.*
quintuplet [kwin'tuɪplit] *n* quintuplé, -e *m, f.*

quirk [kwəɪk] *n* bizarrerie *f.*
*quit [kwit] *v* (*leave*) quitter; (*give up*) se rendre, renoncer. **quits** *adj* quitte.
quite [kwait] *adv* complètement, tout; (*fairly*) plutôt, assez.
quiver[1] ['kwivə] *v* trembler, frémir. *n* frémissement *m,* tremblement *m.*
quiver[2] ['kwivə] *n* (*for arrows*) carquois *m.*
quiz [kwiz] *n* quiz *m,* jeu-concours *m. v* interroger.
quizzical ['kwizikl] *adj* moqueur, -euse; amusant; bizarre.
quorum ['kwɔɪrəm] *n* quorum *m.*
quota ['kwoutə] *n* quota *m;* (*share*) quote-part *f.*
quote [kwout] *v* citer; (*reference number*) rappeler; (*comm*) indiquer. **quotation** *n* citation *f;* (*comm*) devis *m.* **quotation marks** guillemets *m pl.*

R

rabbi ['rabai] *n* rabbin *m.*
rabbit ['rabit] *n* lapin *m.*
rabble ['rabl] *n* cohue *f;* (*derog*) populace *f.*
rabies ['reibiɪz] *n* rage *f.* **rabid** *adj* enragé.
race[1] [reis] *n* (*sport*) course *f.* **racecourse** *n* champ de courses *m.* **racehorse** *n* cheval de course *m. v* (*person*) faire une course avec; (*horse*) faire courir; (*rush*) courir; (*pulse*) être très rapide. **racing car** voiture de course *f.* **racing driver** coureur automobile *m.*
race[2] [reis] *n* race *f.* **racial** *adj* racial. **racialism** *or* **racism** *n* racisme *m.* **racialist** *or* **racist** *n*(*m* + *f*), *adj* raciste.
rack [rak] *n* (*bottles*) casier *m;* (*food*) râtelier *m;* (*shelves*) étagère *f;* (*torture*) chevalet *m. v* torturer. **rack one's brains** se creuser la tête.
racket[1] ['rakit] *n* (*sport*) raquette *f.*
racket[2] ['rakit] *n* (*noise*) tapage *m,* vacarme *m;* (*scheme*) combine *f,* escroquerie *f.*
radar ['reidɑɪ] *n* radar *m.* **radar trap** piège radar *m.*
radial ['reidiəl] *adj* radial. **radial tyre** pneu à carcasse radiale *m.*

radiant ['reidiǝnt] *adj* radieux, rayonnant. **radiance** *n* éclat *m*, rayonnement *m*.
radiate ['reidieit] *v* irradier, rayonner; (*heat*) émettre. **radiation** *n* (*heat*) rayonnement *m*; (*light*) irradiation *f*; (*radioactive*) radiation *f*. **radiator** *n* radiateur *m*.
radical ['radikǝl] *nm, adj* radical.
radio ['reidiou] *n* radio *f*, poste *m*. **radio contact** contact radio *m*. **radio station** poste émetteur *m*. **radio wave** onde hertzienne *f*. *v* appeler par radio; signaler par radio.
radioactive [reidiou'aktiv] *adj* radioactif. **radioactivity** *n* radioactivité *f*.
radiography [reidi'ografi] *n* radiographie *f*. **radiographer** *n* radiologue *m, f*.
radiology [reidi'olǝdʒi] *n* radiologie *f*. **radiologist** *n* radiologue *m, f*.
radiotherapy [reidiou'θerǝpi] *n* radiothérapie *f*.
radish ['radiʃ] *n* radis *m*.
radium ['reidiǝm] *n* radium *m*.
radius ['reidiǝs] *n* rayon *m*.
raffia ['rafiǝ] *n* raphia *m*.
raffle ['rafl] *n* loterie *f*. *v* mettre en loterie.
raft [raift] *n* radeau *m*.
rafter ['raiftǝ] *n* chevron *m*.
rag¹ [rag] *n* (*piece*) loque *f*; (*for cleaning*) chiffon *m*; (*derog: newspaper*) torchon *m*. **rag doll** poupée de chiffon *f*. **rag-and-bone man** chiffonnier *m*. **rags** *pl n* haillons *m pl*. **ragged** *adj* (*clothes*) en loques; (*edge*) déchiqueté.
rag² [rag] (*coll*) *v* taquiner. *n* blague *f*.
rage [reidʒ] *n* rage *f*. **be all the rage** faire fureur. *v* (*person*) être furieux; (*storm*) faire rage. **raging** *adj* (*person*) furieux; (*pain*) atroce; (*storm*) déchaîné.
raid [reid] *n* raid *m*; (*police*) descente *f*; (*bandits*) razzia *f*. *v* faire un raid dans; faire une descente dans; razzier; (*orchard*) marauder dans; (*larder*) dévaliser. **raider** *n* pillard *m*.
rail [reil] *n* (*bar*) garde-fou *m*, balustrade *f*; (*for curtains*) tringle *m*; (*for train*) rail *m*. **by rail** par train. **railway** *or US* **railroad** chemin de fer *m*; (*track*) voie ferrée *f*.
railings ['reiliŋz] *pl n* grille *f sing*.
rain [rein] *n* pluie *f*. **rainbow** *n* arc-en-ciel *m*. **raincoat** *n* imperméable *m*. **raindrop** *n* goutte de pluie *f*. **rainfall** *n* hauteur des précipitations *f*. *v* pleuvoir. **rainy** *adj* pluvieux.

raise [reiz] *v* lever; augmenter; (*build, rear*) élever; (*question*) soulever; (*money*) se procurer.
raisin ['reizǝn] *n* raisin sec *m*.
rake [reik] *n* râteau *m*. *v* (*ground*) ratisser; (*leaves*) râteler. **rake in** (*coll*) amasser.
rally ['rali] *n* rassemblement *m*; (*mot*) rallye *m*; (*tennis*) échange *m*. *v* (se) rallier; (*get better*) aller mieux. **rally round** venir en aide.
ram [ram] *n* belier *m*. *v* enfoncer; (*pack in*) tasser; (*car*) emboutir.
ramble ['rambl] *n* randonnée *f*. *v* faire une randonnée. **ramble on** discourir.
ramp [ramp] *n* rampe *f*.
rampage [ram'peidʒ] *n* **be on the rampage** se déchaîner.
rampant ['rampǝnt] *adj* (*plant*) exubérant; (*heraldry*) rampant. **be rampant** sévir.
rampart ['rampait] *n* rempart *m*.
ramshackle ['ramʃakl] *adj* délabré.
ran [ran] *V* **run**.
ranch [raintʃ] *n* ranch *m*.
rancid ['ransid] *adj* rance. **go rancid** rancir.
rancour ['raŋkǝ] *n* rancœur *f*.
random ['randǝm] *n* **at random** au hasard. *adj* fait au hasard. **random sample** échantillon prélevé au hasard *m*.
rang [raŋ] *V* **ring²**.
range [reindʒ] *n* (*scope*) portée *f*; (*mountains*) chaîne *f*; (*extent*) étendue *f*; gamme *f*; choix *m*; (*stove*) fourneau *m*; (*mil*) champ de tir *m*. *v* ranger; (*extend*) s'étendre; (*roam*) parcourir.
rank¹ [raŋk] *n* rang *m*. **the rank and file** la masse *f*; (*mil*) les hommes de troupe *m pl*. *v* compter, (se) classer.
rank² [raŋk] *adj* (*smell*) fétide; (*plants*) exubérant; flagrant.
rankle ['raŋkl] *v* rester sur le cœur.
ransack ['ransak] *v* saccager; (*search*) fouiller.
ransom ['ransǝm] *n* rançon *f*. **hold to ransom** rançonner. *v* racheter.
rap [rap] *v* frapper. *n* petit coup sec *m*.
rape [reip] *n* viol *m*. *v* violer. **rapist** *n* violeur *m*.
rapid ['rapid] *adj* rapide. **rapids** *pl n* rapides *m pl*. **rapidity** *n* rapidité *f*.
rapier ['reipiǝ] *n* rapière *f*.
rapport [ra'poi] *n* rapport *m*.
rapture ['raptʃǝ] *n* ravissement *m*, extase *f*. **go into raptures over** s'extasier sur.

rare¹ ['reə] *adj* rare. **rarity** *n* rareté *f*.
rare² ['reə] *adj* (*meat*) saignant.
rascal ['raɪskəl] *n* polisson, -onne *m*, *f*; (*rogue*) coquin *m*.
rash¹ [raʃ] *adj* imprudent. **rashness** *n* imprudence *f*.
rash² [raʃ] *n* (*med*) éruption *f*.
rasher ['raʃə] *n* mince tranche *f*.
raspberry ['raɪzbəri] *n* (*fruit*) framboise *f*; (*bush*) framboisier *m*.
rat [rat] *n* rat *m*. **rat poison** mort-aux-rats *m*. **rat race** foire d'empoigne *f*.
rate [reit] *n* taux *m*; (*speed*) train *m*. **at any rate** en tout cas. **ratepayer** *n* contribuable *m*, *f*. **rates** *pl n* impôts locaux *m pl*. *v* évaluer; considérer; se classer.
rather ['raɪðə] *adv* plutôt; (*fairly*) assez, un peu. **I would rather ...** j'aimerais mieux .... .
ratify ['ratifai] *v* ratifier. **ratification** *n* ratification *f*.
ratio ['reiʃiou] *n* proportion *f*, raison *f*.
ration ['raʃən] *n* ration *f*. *v* rationner. **rationing** *n* rationnement *m*.
rational ['raʃənl] *adj* raisonnable, rationnel, logique. **rationale** *n* raisonnement *m*. **rationalize** *v* justifier après coup; (*organize*) rationaliser.
rattle ['ratl] *n* bruit *m*, fracas *m*; (*chains, etc.*) cliquetis *m*; (*toy*) hochet *m*. *v* faire du bruit; (*objects*) (faire) s'entrechoquer; (faire) cliqueter; (*coll*) déconcerter.
raucous ['rɔɪkəs] *adj* rauque.
ravage ['ravidʒ] *n* ravage *m*. *v* ravager.
rave [reiv] *v* délirer, divaguer; s'extasier (sur). **raving** *adj* délirant; furieux.
raven ['reivən] *n* corbeau *m*.
ravenous ['ravənəs] *adj* vorace. **be ravenous** avoir un faim de loup.
ravine [rə'viɪn] *n* ravin *m*.
ravish ['raviʃ] *v* ravir.
raw [rɔɪ] *adj* cru; (*unprocessed*) brut; novice; (*sore*) à vif. **raw deal** (*coll*) sale coup *m*. **raw edge** bord coupé *m*. **raw materials** matières premières *f pl*.
ray [rei] *n* rayon *m*.
rayon ['reiɔn] *n* rayonne *f*.
razor ['reizə] *n* rasoir *m*. **razor blade** lame de rasoir *f*.
reach [riɪtʃ] *v* atteindre, arriver à; (*extend*) s'étendre. **reach out** étendre le bras. *n* portée *f*. **out of reach** hors de portée. **within reach** à portée.
react [ri'akt] *v* réagir. **reaction** *n* réaction

f. **reactionary** *n*(*m*+*f*), *adj* réactionnaire. **reactor** *n* réacteur *m*.
*****read** [riɪd] *v* lire; étudier. **reader** *n* lecteur, -trice *m*, *f*; (*anthology*) recueil de textes *m*. **reading** *n* lecture *f*.
readjust [riɪə'dʒʌst] *v* rajuster, (se) réadapter. **readjustment** *n* réadaptation *f*, rajustement *m*.
ready ['redi] *adj* prêt; prompt. **get ready** (se) préparer. **ready cash** argent liquide *m*. **ready-made** *adj* tout fait, tout prêt. **readily** *adv* volontiers. **readiness** *n* empressement *m*.
real [riəl] *adj* réel, vrai. **realism** *n* réalisme *m*. **realist** *n* réaliste *m*, *f*. **realistic** *adj* réaliste. **reality** *n* réalité *f*. **really** *adv* vraiment.
realize ['riəlaiz] *v* se rendre compte de; (*make real*) réaliser. **realization** *n* prise de conscience *f*; réalisation *f*.
realm [relm] *n* domaine *m*; (*kingdom*) royaume *m*.
reap [riɪp] *v* moissonner; (*profit*) récolter. **reaping** *n* moisson *f*. **reaping machine** moissonneuse *f*.
reappear [riɪə'piə] *v* réapparaître. **reappearance** *n* réapparition *f*.
rear¹ [riə] *nm*, *adj* arrière. **bring up the rear** fermer la marche. **rear-admiral** *n* contre-amiral *m*. **rearguard** *n* arrière-garde *f*. **rear-view mirror** rétroviseur *m*.
rear² [riə] *n* (*family*) élever; (*lift up*) dresser; (*horse, etc.*) se cabrer.
rearrange [riɪə'reindʒ] *v* réarranger. **rearrangement** *n* réarrangement *m*.
reason ['riɪzn] *n* raison *f*. *v* raisonner. **reasonable** *adj* raisonnable. **reasoning** *n* raisonnement *m*.
reassure [riə'ʃuə] *v* rassurer. **reassurance** *n* réconfort *m*. **reassuring** *adj* rassurant.
rebate ['riɪbeit] *n* (*discount*) rabais *m*; remboursement *m*.
rebel ['rebl] *n*(*m*+*f*), *adj* rebelle. *v* se rebeller. **rebellion** *n* rébellion *f*. **rebellious** *adj* rebelle; désobéissant.
rebound [ri'baund; *n* 'riɪbaund] *v* rebondir. *n* rebond *m*; ricochet *m*.
rebuff [ri'bʌf] *n* rebuffade *f*. *v* repousser.
*****rebuild** [riɪ'bild] *v* rebâtir.
rebuke [ri'bjuɪk] *n* reproche *m*. *v* réprimander.
recall [ri'kɔɪl] *v* (se) rappeler. *n* rappel *m*.
recant [ri'kant] *v* (se) rétracter; (*rel*) abjurer.

recap ['riːkap] (*coll*) *v* faire un résumé (de). *n* récapitulation *f*.

recapture [riˈkaptʃə] *v* reprendre; (*atmosphere*) recréer. *n* arrestation *f*.

recede [riˈsiːd] *v* s'éloigner; (*tide*) descendre.

receipt [rəˈsiːt] *n* (*receiving*) réception *f*; (*slip of paper*) reçu *m*, accusé de réception *m*.

receive [rəˈsiːv] *v* recevoir. **receiver** *n* (*phone*) récepteur *m*; (*law*) administrateur judiciaire *m*.

recent ['riːsnt] *adj* récent. **recently** *adv* récemment.

receptacle [rəˈseptəkl] *n* récipient *m*.

reception [rəˈsepʃən] *n* réception *f*. **receptionist** *n* réceptionniste *m, f*.

recess [riˈses] *n* renfoncement *m*, alcôve *f*; (*pol, law*) vacances *f pl*; (*of mind*) recoin *m*.

recession [rəˈseʃən] *n* (*econ*) récession *f*; recul *m*.

recharge [riːˈtʃaɪdʒ] *v* recharger.

recipe ['resəpi] *n* recette *f*.

recipient [rəˈsipiənt] *n* (*letter*) destinataire *m, f*; (*cheque*) bénéficiaire *m, f*.

reciprocate [rəˈsiprəkeit] *v* retourner; offrir en retour. **reciprocating engine** moteur alternatif *m*. **reciprocal** *nf, adj* réciproque.

recite [rəˈsait] *v* réciter. **recital** *n* (*music*) récital *m*. **recitation** *n* récitation *f*.

reckless ['rekləs] *adj* insouciant; imprudent. **recklessness** *n* inscuciance *f*; imprudence *f*.

reckon ['rekən] *v* compter, calculer; considérer, estimer; (*coll*) penser. **reckoning** *n* compte *m*, calcul *m*; estimation *f*.

reclaim [riˈkleim] *v* réclamer; (*land*) assécher, défricher; (*by-product*) récupérer. **reclamation** *n* réclamation *f*; assèchement *m*, défrichement *m*; récupération *f*.

recline [rəˈklain] *v* reposer; être allongé.

recluse [rəˈkluːs] *n* reclus, -e *m, f*.

recognize ['rekəgnaiz] *v* reconnaître. **recognition** *n* reconnaissance *f*. **recognizable** *adj* reconnaissable.

recoil [rəˈkoil; *n* 'riːkoil] *v* reculer; (*spring*) se détendre. *n* recul *m*; détente *f*; dégoût *m*.

recollect [rekəˈlekt] *v* se souvenir (de). **recollection** *n* souvenir *m*.

recommence [riːkəˈmens] *v* recommencer.

recommend [rekəˈmend] *v* recommander,

conseiller. **recommendation** *n* recommandation *f*.

recompense ['rekəmpens] *n* récompense *f*; (*law*) dédommagement *m*. *v* récompenser; dédommager.

reconcile ['rekənsail] *v* réconcilier; (*ideas*) concilier; (*argument*) arranger. **reconcile oneself to** se résigner à. **reconciliation** *n* réconciliation *f*; conciliation *f*.

reconstruct [riːkənˈstrʌkt] *v* reconstruire; (*crime*) reconstituer. **reconstruction** *n* reconstruction *f*; reconstitution *f*.

record [rəˈkoːd; *n* ˈrekoːd] *v* enregistrer. *n* disque *m*; (*sport, etc.*) record *m*; registre *m*, rapport *m*; dossier *m*. **record-player** *n* électrophone *m*. **record token** chèque-disque *m*. **recorded** *adj* enregistré. **by recorded delivery** avec avis de réception. **recorder** *n* (*music*) flûte à bec *f*. **recording** *n* enregistrement *m*.

recount [riˈkaunt] *v* raconter.

recoup [riˈkuːp] *v* récupérer.

recover [rəˈkʌvə] *v* (*get back*) retrouver, récupérer; (*get well*) se remettre, se rétablir. **recovery** *n* récupération *f*; (*from illness*) guérison *f*.

recreation [rekriˈeiʃən] *n* récréation *f*.

recruit [rəˈkruːt] *n* recrue *f*. *v* recruter. **recruitment** *n* recrutement *m*.

rectangle ['rektaŋgl] *n* rectangle *m*. **rectangular** *adj* rectangulaire.

rectify ['rektifai] *v* rectifier.

rectum ['rektəm] *n* rectum *m*.

recuperate [rəˈkjuːpəreit] *v* (*person*) se rétablir; (*get back*) récupérer. **recuperation** *n* rétablissement *m*; récupération *f*.

recur [riˈkəː] *v* se reproduire, se retrouver; (*illness*) réapparaître. **recurrence** *n* répétition *f*. **recurrent** *or* **recurring** *adj* périodique.

red [red] *n* rouge *m*. **in the red** à découvert. *adj* rouge; (*hair*) roux, rousse. **go red** rougir. **redcurrant** *n* groseille rouge *f*. **red-handed** *adv* en flagrant délit. **redhead** *n* roux, rousse *m, f*. **red-hot** *adj* chauffé au rouge. **Red Indian** *n* peau-rouge *m, f*. **red tape** paperasserie *f*.

redeem [rəˈdiːm] *v* racheter; (*from pawn*) dégager. **redemption** *n* rachat *m*; dégagement *m*; (*rel*) rédemption *f*. **beyond redemption** irréparable; irrémédiable.

redirect [riːdaiˈrekt] *v* (*letter, etc.*) faire suivre.

redress [rəˈdres] *v* redresser. *n* redressement *m*, réparation *f*.

reduce [rə'djuːs] *v* réduire; diminuer; (*lower*) abaisser. **reduction** *n* réduction *f*; (*comm*) remise *f*, rabais *m*.

redundant [rə'dʌndənt] *adj* superflu, redondant, en surnombre. **be made redundant** être licencié. **redundancy** *n* superfluité *f*; licenciement *m*.

reed [riːd] *n* (*bot*) roseau *m*; (*of wind instrument*) anche *f*.

reef [riːf] *n* récif *m*.

reek [riːk] *v* puer. *n* puanteur *f*.

reel¹ [riːl] *n* (*thread*) bobine *f*; (*film*) bande *f*. *v* **reel off** débiter.

reel² [riːl] *v* chanceler, tituber.

refectory [rə'fektəri] *n* réfectoire *m*.

refer [rə'fəː] *v* parler; faire allusion; s'appliquer; (*consult*) se reporter; (*pass*) soumettre. **reference** *n* référence *f*; allusion *f*; (*in book*) renvoi *m*. **reference book** ouvrage de référence *m*. **reference number** numéro de référence *m*.

referee [refə'riː] *n* arbitre *m*; (*job application*) répondant, -e *m*, *f*. *v* arbitrer.

referendum [refə'rendəm] *n* référendum *m*.

refill [riː'fil; *n* 'riːfil] *v* recharger. *n* recharge *f*, cartouche *f*.

refine [rə'fain] *v* affiner, raffiner. **refinement** *n* (*person*) raffinement *m*; (*refining*) raffinage *m*, affinage *m*; perfectionnement *m*. **refinery** *n* raffinerie *f*, affinerie *f*.

reflation [rə'fleiʃn] *n* (*econ*) relance *f*.

reflect [rə'flekt] *v* (*light*) refléter; (*mirror*) réfléchir; (*think*) penser; méditer. **reflection** *n* réflexion *f*; image *f*, reflet *m*. **reflector** *n* réflecteur *m*.

reflex ['riːfleks] *nm*, *adj* réflexe. **reflexive** *adj* réfléchi.

reform [rə'fɔːm] *n* réforme *f*. *v* (se) réformer. **reformation** *n* réforme *f*. **reformed** *adj* réformé; (*person*) amendé.

refract [rə'frakt] *v* réfracter. **refraction** *n* réfraction *f*.

refrain¹ [rə'frein] *v* s'abstenir.

refrain² [rə'frein] *n* refrain *m*.

refresh [rə'freʃ] *v* rafraîchir; (*rest*) reposer. **refresher course** cours de recyclage *m*. **refreshments** *pl n* rafraîchissements *m pl*.

refrigerator [rə'fridʒəreitə] *n* réfrigérateur *m*. **refrigerate** *v* réfrigérer. **refrigeration** *n* réfrigération *f*.

refuel [riː'fjuːəl] *v* (se) ravitailler.

refuge ['refjuːdʒ] *n* refuge *m*. **take refuge** se réfugier. **refugee** *n* réfugié, -e *m*, *f*.

refund [ri'fʌnd; *n* 'riːfʌnd] *v* rembourser. *n* remboursement *m*.

refuse¹ [rə'fjuːz] *v* refuser. **refusal** *n* refus *m*.

refuse² ['refjuːs] *n* détritus *m pl*, déchets *m pl*, ordures *f pl*.

refute [ri'fjuːt] *v* réfuter.

regain [ri'gein] *v* regagner; (*health*) recouvrer; (*consciousness*) reprendre.

regal ['riːgəl] *adj* royal.

regard [rə'gaːd] *v* regarder; considérer. **as regards** en ce qui concerne. *n* égard *m*, attention *f*; respect *m*, estime *f*. **regards** *pl n* (*in letter*) amitiés *f pl*. **regarding** *prep* quant à. **regardless** *adv* quand même. **regardless of** sans regarder à.

regatta [rə'gatə] *n* régate *f*.

regent ['riːdʒənt] *n* régent, -e *m*, *f*. **regency** *n* régence *f*.

regime [rei'ʒiːm] *n* régime *m*.

regiment ['redʒimənt] *n* régiment *m*. **regimental** *adj* régimentaire.

region ['riːdʒən] *n* région *f*. **regional** *adj* régional.

register ['redʒistə] *n* registre *m*. *v* (*record*) enregistrer; (*as member, etc.*) s'inscrire; (*birth, death*) déclarer; (*meter*) indiquer; (*letter*) recommander. **registrar** *n* officier de l'état civil *m*; (*med*) interne *m*, *f*. **registration** *n* enregistrement *m*, inscription *f*. **registration number** numéro d'immatriculation *m*. **registry office** bureau de l'état civil *m*.

regress [ri'gres] *v* régresser; reculer. **regression** *n* recul *m*; régression *f*.

regret [rə'gret] *v* regretter. *n* regret *m*. **regrettable** *adj* regrettable.

regular ['regjulə] *adj* régulier; habituel, normal. *n* habitué, -e *m*, *f*. **regularity** *n* régularité *f*.

regulate ['regjuleit] *v* régler.

regulation [regju'leiʃn] *n* règlement *m*. *adj* réglementaire.

rehabilitate [riːhə'biliteit] *v* réhabiliter; (*for work*) réadapter. **rehabilitation** *n* réhabilitation *f*; réadaptation *f*.

rehearse [rə'həːs] *v* répéter. **rehearsal** *n* répétition *f*.

rehouse [riː'hauz] *v* reloger.

reign [rein] *n* règne *m*. *v* régner.

reimburse [riːim'bəːs] *v* rembourser.

rein [rein] *n* rêne *f*; (*control*) bride *f*.

reincarnation [riːinkaː'neiʃn] *n* réincarnation *f*.

reindeer ['reindiǝ] *n* renne *m.*
reinforce [riɪin'foɪs] *v* renforcer. **reinforcement** *n* renforcement *m.* **reinforcements** *pl n* renforts *m pl.*
reinstate [riɪin'steit] *v* réintégrer. **reinstatement** *n* réintégration *f.*
reinvest [riɪin'vest] *v* réinvestir.
reissue [riɪ'iʃuɪ] *v* (*book*) rééditer; (*film*) ressortir. *n* réédition *f.*
reject [rǝ'dʒekt; *n* 'riɪdʒekt] *v* refuser, rejeter. *n* pièce de rebut *f. adj* de rebut. **rejection** *n* refus *m,* rejet *m.*
rejoice [rǝ'dʒois] *v* (se) réjouir. **rejoicing** *n* réjouissance *f.*
rejoin [rǝ'dʃoin] *v* rejoindre.
rejuvenate [rǝ'dʒuɪvǝneit] *v* rajeunir.
relapse [rǝ'laps] *n* rechute *f. v* rechuter.
relate [rǝ'leit] *v* raconter; (*be connected*) se rapporter; (*associate*) établir un rapport entre. **related** *adj* apparenté. **relating to** concernant.
relation [rǝ'leiʃn] *n* (*family*) parent, -e *m, f*; (*connection*) rapport *m*; (*business, etc.*) relation *f.* **relationship** *n* liens de parenté *m pl*; (*personal*) rapports *m pl,* relations *f pl.*
relative ['relǝtiv] *adj* relatif; respectif. *n* parent, -e *m, f.* **relatively** *adv* relativement; (*rather*) assez. **relativity** *n* relativité *f.*
relax [rǝ'laks] *v* (se) relâcher; (*person*) (se) détendre; (*rules*) modérer. **relaxation** *n* relâchement *m*; détente *f,* relaxation *f.* **relaxing** *adj* délassant, relaxant.
relay ['riɪlei; *v* ri'lei] *n* relais *m.* **relay race** course de relais *f. v* relayer.
release [rǝ'liɪs] *v* libérer; (*let go*) lâcher; (*record, film*) sortir. *n* libération *f*; sortie *f.*
relegate ['religeit] *v* reléguer. **relegation** *n* relégation *f.*
relent [rǝ'lent] *v* s'adoucir; revenir sur sa décision. **relentless** *adj* implacable.
relevant ['relǝvǝnt] *adj* pertinent; approprié; significatif. **relevance** *n* rapport *m*; pertinence *f.*
reliable [ri'laiǝbl] *adj* sérieux; (*machine*) solide. **reliability** *n* sérieux *m*; sûreté *f*; solidité *f.*
relic ['relik] *n* relique *f.*
relief [rǝ'liɪf] *n* soulagement *m*; (*help*) secours *m*; (*geog, art*) relief *m. adj* supplémentaire.
relieve [rǝ'liɪv] *v* soulager; (*help*) secourir;

(*take over*) relayer; (*take away*) débarrasser, décharger.
religion [rǝ'lidʒǝn] *n* religion *f.* **religious** *adj* religieux; scrupuleux.
relinquish [rǝ'liŋkwiʃ] *v* (*give up*) renoncer à, abandonner; (*let go*) lâcher.
relish ['reliʃ] *n* goût *m,* attrait *m. v* (*food, drink*) savourer; (*enjoy*) se délecter à.
relive [riɪ'liv] *v* revivre.
reluctant [rǝ'lʌktǝnt] *adj* peu disposé. **reluctance** *n* répugnance *f.* **reluctantly** *adv* à contrecœur.
rely [rǝ'lai] *v* **rely on** compter sur.
remain [rǝ'mein] *v* rester. **remainder** *n* reste *m.* **remains** *pl n* restes *m pl.*
remand [rǝ'maɪnd] *v* renvoyer. *n* renvoi *m.* **on remand** en prévention.
remark [rǝ'maɪk] *n* remarque *f*; observation *f. v* remarquer; faire une remarque. **remarkable** *adj* remarquable.
remarry [riɪ'mari] *v* se remarier. **remarriage** *n* remariage *m.*
remedial [rǝ'miɪdiǝl] *adj* réparateur, -trice; (*teaching, class*) de rattrapage.
remedy ['remǝdi] *n* remède *m. v* remédier à.
remember [ri'membǝ] *v* se souvenir (de), se rappeler. **remembrance** *n* souvenir *m.*
remind [rǝ'maind] *v* rappeler. **reminder** *n* mémento *m*; (*comm*) lettre de rappel *f.*
reminiscence [remǝ'nisens] *n* réminiscence *f.* **reminiscent of** qui rappelle.
remiss [rǝ'mis] *adj* négligent.
remission [rǝ'miʃn] *n* rémission *f*; (*law*) remise *f.*
remit [rǝ'mit] *v* (*law, rel*) remettre; (*money*) envoyer; (*lessen*) (se) relâcher. **remittance** *n* versement *m,* paiement *m.*
remnant ['remnǝnt] *n* reste *m*; (*fabric*) coupon *m.*
remorse [rǝ'moɪs] *n* remords *m.* **remorseless** *adj* sans remords; implacable.
remote [rǝ'mout] *adj* lointain; isolé; vague. **remote control** télécommande *f.*
remould ['riɪmould; *v* riɪ'mould] *n* pneu rechapé *m. v* remouler; rechaper.
remove [rǝ'muɪv] *v* enlever; (*move house*) déménager. **removal** *n* enlèvement *m*; déménagement *m.*
remunerate [rǝ'mjuɪnǝreit] *v* rémunérer. **remuneration** *n* rémunération *f.* **remunerative** *adj* rémunérateur, -trice.
renaissance [rǝ'neisǝns] *n* renaissance *f.*
rename [riɪ'neim] *v* rebaptiser.

render [rendə] *v* rendre; remettre; *(fat)* faire fondre. **rendering** *or* **rendition** *n* interprétation *f*.

rendezvous ['rondivuɪ] *n* rendez-vous *m. v* se retrouver.

renegade ['renigeid] *n* renégat, -e *m, f*.

renew [rə'njuɪ] *v* renouveler; remplacer. **renewal** renouvellement *m*; remplacement *m*; *(of subscription)* réabonnement *m*.

renounce [ri'nauns] *v* renoncer à, renier. **renunciation** *n* renonciation *f*, reniement *m*.

renovate ['renəveit] *v* rénover, remettre à neuf. **renovation** *n* rénovation *f*; remise à neuf *f*.

renown [rə'naun] *n* renommée *f*; renom *m*. **renowned** *adj* renommé.

rent [rent] *n* loyer *m. v* louer. **rental** *n* prix de location *m*.

reopen [riɪ'oupən] *v* rouvrir; *(recommence)* reprendre. **reopening** *n* réouverture *f*.

reorganize [riɪ'ɔɪgənaiz] *v* (se) réorganiser. **reorganization** *n* réorganisation *f*.

rep [rep] *n* *(coll)* représentant, -e *m, f*.

repair [ri'peə] *v* réparer. *n* réparation *f*. **beyond repair** irréparable. **in good/bad repair** en bon/mauvais état. **repairer** *n* réparateur, -trice *m, f*.

repartee [repa'tiɪ] *n* repartie *f*.

repatriate [riɪ'patrieit; *n* riɪ'patriət] *v* rapatrier. *n* rapatrié, -e *m, f*. **repatriation** *n* rapatriement *m*.

***repay** [ri'pei] *v* rembourser; récompenser; *(debt)* s'acquitter de. **repayment** *n* remboursement *m*; récompense *f*.

repeal [rə'piɪl] *v* abroger, annuler. *n* abrogation *f*, annulation *f*.

repeat [rə'piɪt] *v* répéter; réciter; *(music)* reprendre. *n* répétition *f*; *(broadcast, music)* reprise *f*.

repel [rə'pel] *v* repousser. **repellent** *adj* repoussant.

repent [rə'pent] *v* se repentir (de). **repentance** *n* repentir *m*. **repentant** *adj* repentant.

repercussion [riɪpə'kʌʃən] *n* répercussion *f*.

repertoire ['repətwaɪ] *n* répertoire *m*.

repertory ['repətəri] *n* théâtre de répertoire *m*. **repertory company** compagnie de répertoire *f*.

repetition [repə'tiʃn] *n* répétition *f*. **repeti-**

tive *adj* *(person)* rabâcheur, -euse; *(work)* monotone.

replace [rə'pleis] *v* *(substitute)* remplacer; *(put back)* replacer. **replacement** *n* remplacement *m*; *(person)* remplaçant, -e *m, f*; replacement *m*.

replay [riɪ'plei; *n* 'riɪplei] *v* rejouer. *n* match rejoué *m*.

replenish [rə'pleniʃ] *v* remplir. **replenishment** *n* remplissage *m*.

replica ['replikə] *n* *(picture)* réplique *f*; *(document)* fac-similé *m*.

reply [rə'plai] *n* réponse *f. v* répondre.

report [rə'pɔɪt] *n* rapport *m*, compte rendu *m*; *(press)* reportage *m*; bulletin scolaire *m*; détonation *f. v* rapporter; faire un reportage; *(notify)* signaler; se présenter. **reporter** *n* reporter *m*; journaliste *m, f*.

repose [rə'pouz] *n* repos *m. v* (se) reposer.

represent [reprə'zent] *v* représenter. **representation** *n* représentation *f*.

representative [reprə'zentətiv] *adj* représentatif. *n* représentant, -e *m, f*.

repress [rə'pres] *v* réprimer. **repression** *n* répression *f*. **repressive** *adj* répressif.

reprieve [rə'priɪv] *n* sursis *m*; *(law)* grâce *f. v* accorder du répit à.

reprimand ['reprimaɪnd] *n* réprimande *f. v* réprimander.

reprint [riɪ'print; *n* 'riɪprint] *v* réimprimer. *n* réimpression *f*.

reprisal [rə'praizəl] *n* représailles *f pl*.

reproach [rə'proutʃ] *n* reproche *m. v* reprocher à. **reproachful** *adj* réprobateur, -trice.

reproduce [riɪprə'djuɪs] *v* (se) reproduire. **reproduction** *n* reproduction *f*. **reproductive** *adj* reproducteur, -trice.

reprove [rə'pruɪv] *v* *(person)* blâmer; *(action)* réprouver. **reproof** *n* réprimande *m*.

reptile ['reptail] *n* reptile *m*.

republic [rə'pʌblik] *n* république *f*. **republican** *n, adj* républicain, -e.

repudiate [rə'pjuɪdieit] *v* répudier; *(person)* renier. **repudiation** *n* répudiation *f*; reniement *m*.

repugnant [rə'pʌgnənt] *adj* répugnant. **repugnance** *n* répugnance *f*.

repulsion [rə'pʌlʃn] *n* répulsion *f*. **repulsive** *adj* répulsif, repoussant.

repute [rə'pjuɪt] *n* réputation *f*. **reputable** *adj* honorable, de bonne réputation. **rep-**

utation *n* réputation *f*. **reputed** *adj* réputé, censé.

request [ri'kwest] *n* demande *f*. *v* demander. **request stop** arrêt facultatif *m*.

requiem ['rekwiəm] *n* requiem *m*.

require [rə'kwaiə] *v* (*need*) demander, avoir besoin de; (*order*) exiger. **requirement** *n* (*need*) exigence *f*; condition *f*.

requisition [,rekwi'ziʃən] *n* demande *f*; réquisition *f*. *v* réquisitionner.

*****reread** [riːˈriːd] *v* relire.

re-route [riːˈruːt] *v* dérouter.

*****rerun** [riːˈrʌn; *n* 'riːrʌn] *v* (*film*) passer de nouveau; (*race*) courir de nouveau. *n* reprise *f*.

resale [riːˈseil] *n* revente *f*.

rescue ['reskjuː] *n* sauvetage *m*; (*help*) secours *m*; (*freeing*) délivrance *f*. *v* sauver; secourir; délivrer. **rescuer** *n* sauveteur *m*.

research [ri'səːtʃ] *n* recherche *f*. *v* faire des recherches. **researcher** *n* chercheur, -euse *m*, *f*.

*****resell** [riːˈsel] *v* revendre.

resemble [rə'zembl] *v* ressembler à. **resemblance** *n* ressemblance *f*.

resent [ri'zent] *v* s'offusquer de. **resentful** *adj* rancunier. **resentment** *n* ressentiment *m*.

reserve [rə'zəːv] *v* réserver. *n* réserve *f*; (*sport*) remplaçant, -e *m*, *f*. **reservation** *n* réserve *f*; (*booking*) réservation *f*. **reserved** *adj* réservé; (*person*) renfermé.

reservoir ['rezəvwaɪ] *n* réservoir *m*.

reside [rə'zaid] *v* résider. **residence** *n* résidence *f*; (*hostel*) foyer *m*; (*stay*) séjour *m*. **resident** *n* habitant, -e *m*, *f*; (*in hotel*) pensionnaire *m*, *f*. **residential** *adj* résidentiel.

residue ['rezidjuː] *n* reste *m*; (*chem*) résidu *m*. **residual** *adj* restant; résiduaire.

resign [rə'zain] *v* (*from job*) donner sa démission (de), démissionner. **resign oneself to** se résigner à. **resignation** *n* démission *f*; résignation *f*. **resigned** *adj* résigné.

resilient [rə'ziliənt] *adj* (*rubber*, *etc*.) élastique. **be resilient** (*person*) avoir du ressort. **resilience** *n* elasticité *f*; ressort *m*.

resin ['rezin] *n* résine *f*.

resist [rə'zist] *v* résister (à). **resistance** *n* résistance *f*. **resistant** *adj* résistant.

*****resit** [riːˈsit; *n* 'riːsit] *v* (*exam*) repasser. *n* deuxième session *f*.

resolute ['rezəluɪt] *adj* résolu.

resolution [rezə'luɪʃən] *n* résolution *f*.

resolve [rə'zolv] *v* (se) résoudre. *n* résolution *f*.

resonant ['rezənənt] *adj* sonore; (*phys*) résonant. **resonance** *n* résonance *f*. **resonate** *v* résonner.

resort [rə'zoːt] *n* recours *m*, ressource *f*; (*place*) station *f*, lieu de vacances *m*. **as a last resort** en dernier ressort. *v* **resort to** avoir recours à.

resound [rə'zaund] *v* retentir, résonner. **resounding** *adj* sonore; (*victory*, *etc*.) retentissant.

resource [rə'zoɪs] *n* ressource *f*. **resourceful** *adj* ingénieux.

respect [rə'spekt] *n* respect *m*; (*aspect*) égard *m*, rapport *m*. **pay one's respects** présenter ses respects. **with respect to** en ce qui concerne. *v* respecter. **respectable** *adj* respectable; (*dress*, *behaviour*) convenable. **respectful** *adj* respectueux. **respective** *adj* respectif.

respiration [respə'reiʃn] *n* respiration *f*.

respite ['respait] *n* répit *m*.

respond [rə'spond] *v* répondre. **response** *n* réponse *f*. **be responsive** réagir bien.

responsible [rə'sponsəbl] *adj* responsable; digne de confiance. **responsibility** *n* responsabilité *f*.

rest[1] [rest] *n* repos *m*; (*music*) silence *m*; support *m*. *v* (se) reposer; (*lean*) (s')appuyer; (*land*, *put*) (se) poser. **restful** *adj* reposant. **restive** *adj* agité; impatient. **restless** *adj* agité.

rest[2] [rest] *n* **the rest** (*remaining part*) le reste *m*; (*remaining ones*) les autres *m pl*. *v* rester.

restaurant ['restront] *n* restaurant *m*. **restaurant car** (*on train*) wagon-restaurant *m*.

restore [rə'stoɪ] *v* rendre; (*order*, *rights*, *etc*.) rétablir; (*building*, *etc*.) restaurer. **restoration** *n* rétablissement *m*; restauration *f*.

restrain [rə'strein] *v* retenir; (*temper*, *etc*.) contenir. **restraint** *n* contrainte *f*; (*moderation*) retenue *f*.

restrict [rə'strikt] *v* restreindre. **restricted** *adj* restreint; confidentiel; (*narrow*) étroit. **restriction** *n* restriction *f*; limitation *f*. **restrictive** *adj* restrictif.

result [rə'zʌlt] *n* résultat *m*; conséquence *f*. *v* résulter. **result in** aboutir à. **resultant** *adj* résultant.

resume [rə'zjuːm] v reprendre. **resumption** n reprise f.

résumé ['reizumei] n résumé m.

resurgence [rɪ'sɜɪdʒəns] n réapparition f.

resurrect [rezə'rekt] v ressusciter; (coll) remettre en service. **resurrection** n résurrection f.

resuscitate [rə'sʌsəteit] v ranimer.

retail ['riːteil] n détail m. v (se) vendre au détail. **retailer** n détaillant, -e m, f.

retain [rə'tein] v (keep) garder; (hold) retenir.

retaliate [rə'talieit] v se venger. **retaliation** n revanche f. in **retaliation** par représailles.

retard [rə'taɪd] v retarder. **retarded** adj retardé; (mentally) arriéré.

reticent ['retisənt] adj réticent. **reticence** n réticence f.

retina ['retinə] n rétine f.

retinue ['retinjuː] n suite f.

retire [rə'taiə] v se retirer; (from work) prendre sa retraite; (go to bed) se coucher. **retired** adj retraité. **retirement** n retraite f.

retort[1] [rə'tɔɪt] v rétorquer. n réplique f.

retort[2] [rə'tɔɪt] n (chem) cornue f.

retrace [rɪ'treis] v reconstituer, retracer. **retrace one's steps** rebrousser chemin.

retract [rə'trakt] v (se) rétracter.

retreat [rə'triːt] n retraite f; (place) asile m. v se retirer; (mil) battre en retraite.

retrial [riː'traiəl] n nouveau procès m.

retrieve [rə'triːv] v récupérer; sauver. **retrieval** n récupération f. **retriever** n (dog) retriever m.

retrograde ['retrəgreid] adj rétrograde.

retrospect ['retrəspekt] n in **retrospect** rétrospectivement. **retrospective** adj rétrospectif.

return [rə'tɜɪn] v retourner; (come back) revenir; (give back) rendre; (pol) élire. n retour m; (ticket) aller et retour m; (from investments, etc.) rapport m; (tax) déclaration f. in **return** en revanche. in **return for** en récompense de.

reunite [riːjuː'nait] v (se) réunir. **reunion** n réunion f.

rev [rev] (mot) n tour m. v **rev up** emballer.

reveal [rə'viːl] v révéler; laisser voir. **revealing** adj révélateur, -trice. **revelation** n révélation f.

revel ['revl] v se délecter (à). **revelry** n festivités f pl.

revenge [rə'vendʒ] n vengeance f. v venger.

revenue ['revinjuː] n revenu m.

reverberate [rə'vɜɪbəreit] v (sound) retentir, (se) répercuter; (heat, light) (se) réverbérer. **reverberation** n répercussion f; réverbération f.

reverence ['revərəns] n vénération f. **revere** v révérer. **reverent** adj respectueux.

reverse [rə'vɜɪs] adj contraire, opposé. n contraire m, opposé m; (coin) revers m; (page) verso m; (mot) marche arrière f. v renverser, retourner; (order) inverser; (mot) faire marche arrière. **reverse the charges** (phone) téléphoner en P.C.V. **reversal** n renversement m. **reversible** adj réversible.

revert [rə'vɜɪt] v revenir, retourner.

review [rə'vjuː] n revue f; révision f; critique f. v passer en revue; réconsidérer; faire la critique de. **reviewer** n critique m.

revise [rə'vaiz] v réviser; corriger. **revision** n révision f.

revive [rə'vaiv] v ranimer; reprendre connaissance; (custom) rétablir; (trade) reprendre. **revival** n reprise f.

revoke [rə'vouk] v révoquer, revenir sur; (withdraw) retirer.

revolt [rə'voult] n révolte f. v (se) révolter. **revolting** adj dégoûtant.

revolution [revə'luːʃən] n révolution f. **revolutionary** n(m+f), adj révolutionnaire. **revolutionize** v révolutionner.

revolve [rə'volv] v (faire) tourner. **revolver** n revolver m. **revolving door** tambour m.

revue [rə'vjuː] n revue f.

revulsion [rə'vʌlʃən] n dégoût m.

reward [rə'wɔːd] n récompense f. v récompenser.

*rewind [riː'waind] v (film, tape) réembobiner. **rewinding** n réembobinage m.

*rewrite [riː'rait] v récrire; recopier.

Reykjavik ['reikjəviːk] n Reykjavik.

rhesus ['riːsəs] n rhésus m. **rhesus negative/positive** rhésus négatif/positif.

rhetoric ['retərik] n rhétorique f. **rhetorical** adj rhétorique. **rhetorical question** question pour la forme f.

rheumatism ['ruːmətizəm] n rhumatisme m. **rheumatic** adj rhumatismal.

rhinoceros [rai'nosərəs] n rhinocéros m.

rhododendron [roudə'dendrən] n rhododendron m.

rhubarb ['ruːbaɪb] n rhubarbe f.

rhyme [raim] n rime f; (poetry) vers m pl. v (faire) rimer.

rhythm ['riðəm] n rythme m. **rhythmic** adj rythmique; (music) rythmé.

rib [rib] n côte f.

ribbon ['ribən] n ruban m. **in ribbons** en lambeaux.

rice [rais] n riz m. **rice paper** papier de riz m. **rice pudding** riz au lait m.

rich [ritʃ] adj riche. **riches** pl n richesses f pl. **richness** n richesse f.

rickety ['rikəti] adj branlant.

***rid** [rid] v débarrasser. **get rid of** se débarrasser de. **riddance** n débarras m.

ridden ['ridn] V ride.

riddle¹ ['ridl] n énigme f.

riddle² ['ridl] v cribler.

***ride** [raid] v monter; (horse) monter à cheval. n promenade f, tour m; (journey) trajet m. **rider** n (horse) cavalier, -ère m, f; (addition) annexe f. **riding** n équitation f. **riding school** manège m.

ridge [ridʒ] n (hills) faîte m; (roof) arête f; (on surface) strie f.

ridicule ['ridikjuːl] n ridicule m. v ridiculiser. **ridiculous** adj ridicule.

rife [raif] adj répandu.

rifle¹ ['raifl] n fusil m. **rifle range** champ de tir m.

rifle² ['raifl] v piller; (house, drawer) dévaliser.

rift [rift] n fissure f; division f.

rig [rig] n (naut) gréement m. **rig-out** n (coll) tenue f. v gréer; (falsify) truquer. **rigging** n gréement m; truquage m.

right [rait] adj (not left) droit; juste; approprié; (correct) bon, bonne. **be right** avoir raison. adv à droite; (straight) droit; (completely) tout à fait; (well) bien. n droite f; (entitlement) droit m; (good) bien m. v redresser. **right angle** angle droit m. **right-handed** adj droitier m. **right-of-way** n (public) droit de passage m; (mot) priorité f. **right-wing** adj (pol) de droite.

righteous ['raitʃəs] adj vertueux; juste.

rightful ['raitfəl] adj légitime.

rigid ['ridʒid] adj rigide; strict. **rigidity** n rigidité f.

rigmarole ['rigməroul] n (coll) comédie f; (speech) galimatias m.

rigour ['rigə] n rigueur f. **rigorous** adj rigoureux.

rim [rim] n bord m; (wheel) jante f.

rind [raind] n (fruit) peau f; (cheese) croûte f; (bacon) couenne f.

ring¹ [riŋ] n anneau m; (with gem) bague f; cercle m, rond m; (circus) piste f; (boxing) ring m. v entourer d'un cercle. **ringleader** n meneur m. **ring road** route de ceinture f.

***ring²** [riŋ] v (bell) sonner; téléphoner (à); résonner. **ring off** (phone) raccrocher. **ring up** (coll: phone) donner un coup de fil à. n sonnerie f; (coll: phone) coup de fil m.

rink [riŋk] n patinoire f.

rinse [rins] v rincer. n rinçage m.

riot ['raiət] n émeute f. v faire une émeute.

rip [rip] v (se) déchirer. **rip off** or **out** arracher. n déchirure f.

ripe [raip] adj mûr. **ripen** v mûrir. **ripeness** n maturité f.

ripple ['ripl] n ondulation f, ride f; (laughter) cascade f. v (se) rider, (faire) onduler.

***rise** [raiz] n (sun, etc.) lever m; (increase) hausse f; (in salary) augmentation f; (in importance) essor m. **give rise to** engendrer. v se lever, s'élever; augmenter, être en hausse; (rebel) se soulever. **rising** adj levant; en hausse; (anger) croissant.

risen ['rizn] V rise.

risk [risk] n risque m. **at risk** en danger. v risquer. **risky** adj risqué.

rissole ['risoul] n croquette f.

rite [rait] n rite m.

ritual ['ritʃuəl] nm, adj rituel.

rival ['raivəl] n, adj rival, -e. v rivaliser avec. **rivalry** n rivalité f.

river ['rivə] n rivière f; (larger) fleuve m. **riverside** n bord de l'eau m.

rivet ['rivit] n rivet m. v (tech) riveter; fixer, clouer. **riveting** adj fascinant.

Riviera [rivi'eərə] n **the Riviera** (French) la Côte d'Azur f; (Italian) la Riviera f.

road [roud] n route f; (to success, etc.) voie f, chemin m. **road-block** n barrage routier m. **road safety** sécurité routière f. **roadside** n bord de la route m. **road sign** panneau de signalisation m. **road-works** pl n travaux m pl.

roam [roum] v parcourir, errer.

roar [roi] v (lion) rugir; (crowd) hurler; (bull, wind) mugir; (engine) vrombir;

(*thunder*) gronder. **roar with laughter**
éclater de rire. *n* rugissement *m*; hurlement *m*; mugissement *m*; vrombissement
m; grondement *m*.
roast [roust] *v* (*meat*) rôtir; (*coffee,
chestnuts*) griller. *nm, adj* rôti.
rob [rob] *v* voler, dévaliser. **robber** *n*
voleur *m*. **robbery** *n* vol *m*.
robe [roub] *n* robe *f*. *v* revêtir.
robin ['robin] *n* rouge-gorge *m*.
robot ['roubot] *n* robot *m*.
robust [rə'bʌst] *adj* robuste, vigoureux,
solide.
rock[1] [rok] *n* (*stone*) roche *f*; (*hard*) roc
m; (*boulder*) rocher *m*. **rock bun** *or* **cake**
rocher *m*. **rock-climbing** *n* varappe *f*.
rock-plant *n* plante alpestre *f*. **rockery** *n*
rocaille *f*. **rocky** *adj* rocheux, rocailleux.
rock[2] [rok] *v* (*sway*) bercer, (se) balancer;
(*shake*) ébranler. *n* (*music*) rock *m*. **rock-
ing-chair** *n* fauteuil à bascule *m*. **rocking-
horse** *n* cheval à bascule *m*.
rocket ['rokit] *n* fusée *f*. *v* (*prices*) monter
en flèche.
rod [rod] *n* (*wood*) baguette *f*; (*metal*)
tringle *f*; (*fishing*) canne *f*.
rode [roud] *V* **ride**.
rodent ['roudənt] *n* rongeur *m*.
roe [rou] n (*hard*) œufs de poisson *m pl*;
(*soft*) laitance *f*.
rogue [roug] *n* coquin, -e *m, f*. **roguish** *adj*
espiègle.
role [roul] *n* rôle *m*.
roll [roul] *n* rouleau *m*; (*bread*) petit pain
m; (*drums*) roulement *m*; (*register*) liste
f. **roll-call** *n* appel *m*. *v* rouler. **roll in**
(*coll*) affluer; (*coll: person*) s'amener. **roll
over** (se) retourner. **roll up** rouler;
(*sleeves*) retrousser. **roller** *n* rouleau *m*.
roller-coaster *n* montagnes russes *f pl*.
roller-skate *n* patin à roulettes *m*. **rolling-
pin** *n* rouleau *m*.
romance [rou'mans] *n* (*love*) idylle *f*,
amour *m*; (*story*) roman à l'eau de rose
m. **Romance** *adj* (*language*) roman.
romantic *n*(*m*+*f*), *adj* romantique.
Romania [ruː'meinjə] *n* Roumanie *f*.
Romanian *nm, adj* roumain; *n* (*people*)
Roumain, -e *m, f*.
Rome [roum] *n* Rome. **Roman** *n* Romain,
-e *m, f*; *adj* romain. **Roman Catholic**
n(*m*+*f*), *adj* catholique. **Roman numeral**
chiffre romain *m*.
romp [romp] *n* ébats *m pl*. *v* s'ébattre.
rompers *pl n* barboteuse *f sing*.

roof [ruːf] *n, pl* **roofs** toit *m*. **roof of the
mouth** voûte du palais *f*. **roof-rack** *n*
galerie *f*.
rook [ruk] *n* (*bird*) corneille *f*. *v* (*slang*)
rouler.
room [ruːm] *n* pièce *f*; (*larger*) salle *f*;
(*hotel*) chambre *f*; (*space*) place *f*. **at
room temperature** (*wine*) chambré. **room-
mate** *n* camarade de chambre *m, f*. **room
service** service des chambres *m*. **roomy**
adj spacieux.
roost [ruːst] *n* perchoir *m*. *v* (se) jucher.
rooster *n* coq *m*.
root[1] [ruːt] *n* racine *f*; origine *f*. *v*
(s')enraciner.
root[2] [ruːt] *v* fouiller. **root for** (*slang*)
encourager. **root out** (*find*) dénicher.
rope [roup] *n* corde *f*. **know the ropes** être
au courant. **rope-ladder** *n* échelle de
corde *f*. *v* corder, lier. **rope in** (*coll*)
embringuer. **ropy** *adj* (*coll*) pas fameux.
rosary ['rouzəri] *n* chapelet *m*.
rose[1] [rouz] *V* **rise**.
rose[2] [rouz] *n* rose *f*. **rose-bush** *n* rosier *m*.
rose garden roseraie *f*. **rosewood** *n* bois
de rose *m*. **rosy** *adj* rose.
rosemary ['rouzməri] *n* romarin *m*.
rosette [rou'zet] *n* rosette *f*; (*prize*)
cocarde *f*.
rot [rot] *n* pourriture *f*, carie *f*; (*coll: rubbish*) bêtises *f pl*. *v* pourrir. **rotten** *adj*
pourri; (*coll: bad*) moche, sale; (*coll: ill*)
mal fichu.
rota ['routə] *n* liste *f*.
rotate [rou'teit] *v* (faire) tourner, (faire)
pivoter; (*crops*) alterner. **rotary** *adj* rotatif. **rotation** *n* rotation *f*.
rotor ['routə] *n* rotor *m*.
rouge [ruːʒ] *n* rouge *m*.
rough [rʌf] *adj* (*surface*) rugueux; (*coarse*)
rude; brutal, dur; (*draft*) ébauché;
approximatif. **rough-and-ready** *adj* rudimentaire. **rough copy** *or* **draft** brouillon
m. *v* **rough it** (*coll*) vivre à la dure. **roughly** *adv* à peu près. **roughness** *n* rugosité *f*;
rudesse *f*; brutalité *f*.
roulette [ruː'let] *n* roulette *f*.
round [raund] *adj* rond. *prep* autour de. *n*
rond *m*; (*of bread*) tranche *f*; (*drinks,
postman, etc.*) tournée *f*; (*game, competition*) partie *f*. **round-necked** *adj* (*pullover*)
ras du cou. **round-shouldered** *adj* voûté. *v*
arrondir. **round off** terminer. **round up**
rassembler; (*figure*) arrondir.

roundabout ['raundəbaut] *n* (*mot*) rond-point *m*; (*fair*) manège *m*. *adj* détourné, indirect.

rouse [rauz] *v* éveiller; stimuler.

route [ruːt] *n* itinéraire *m*.

routine [ruːˈtiːn] *n* routine *f*; (*theatre*) numéro *m*. *adj* d'usage; ordinaire.

rove [rouv] *v* errer (dans), vagabonder.

row[1] [rou] *n* (*side by side*) rang *m*; (*queue*) file *f*; (*trees, figures*) rangée *f*.

row[2] [rou] *v* (*boat*) ramer. *n* promenade en canot *f*. **rowing** *n* (*sport*) aviron *m*; (*for fun*) canotage *m*. **rowing boat** canot *m*.

row[3] [rau] *n* querelle *f*; (*noise*) tapage *m*. *v* se quereller.

rowdy ['raudi] *adj* chahuteur, -euse. **rowdiness** *n* tapage *m*.

royal ['roiəl] *adj* royal. **royal blue** bleu roi *invar*. **royalist** *n*(*m*+*f*), *adj* royaliste. **royalties** *pl n* droits d'auteur *m pl*. **royalty** *n* royauté *f*.

rub [rʌb] *n* frottement *m*; (*with duster*) coup de chiffon *m*. *v* frotter. **rub in** faire pénétrer; insister sur. **rub out** (s')effacer. **rub up the wrong way** prendre à rebrousse-poil. **rubbing** *n* (*brass, etc.*) frottis *m*.

rubber ['rʌbə] *n* caoutchouc *m*; (*eraser*) gomme *f*. **rubber band** élastique *m*. **rubber stamp** tampon *m*. **rubber tree** arbre à gomme *m*. **rubbery** *adj* caoutchouteux.

rubbish ['rʌbiʃ] *n* détritus *m pl*, ordures *f pl*; (*derog*) camelote *f*; (*nonsense*) bêtises *f pl*.

rubble ['rʌbl] *n* décombres *m pl*.

ruby ['ruːbi] *n* rubis *m*.

rucksack ['rʌksak] *n* sac à dos *m*.

rudder ['rʌdə] *n* gouvernail *m*.

rude [ruːd] *adj* impoli, grossier; (*sudden*) brusque; primitif. **rudeness** *n* impolitesse *f*, grossièreté *f*.

rudiment ['ruːdimənt] *n* rudiment *m*. **rudimentary** *adj* rudimentaire.

rueful ['ruːfəl] *adj* triste. **ruefully** *adv* avec regret.

ruff [rʌf] *n* (*dress*) fraise *f*; (*bird*) collier *m*.

ruffian ['rʌfiən] *n* voyou *m*.

ruffle ['rʌfl] *v* (*hair*) ébouriffer; (*surface*) agiter; (*clothes*) froisser; (*worry*) troubler.

rug [rʌg] *n* carpette *f*, petit tapis *m*; (*blanket*) couverture *f*.

rugby ['rʌgbi] *n* rugby *m*.

rugged ['rʌgid] *adj* (*cliff*) déchiqueté; (*landscape*) accidenté; (*person*) rude; (*determination*) acharné.

ruin ['ruːin] *n* ruine *f*. *v* ruiner.

rule [ruːl] *n* règle *f*; autorité *f*. **as a rule** normalement. *v* gouverner; régner; dominer; (*lines*) régler. **rule out** exclure.
ruler *n* souverain, -e *m, f*; (*measuring*) règle *f*. **ruling** *n* décision *f*.

rum [rʌm] *n* rhum *m*.

rumble ['rʌmbl] *n* grondement *m*; (*stomach*) gargouillement *m*. *v* gronder; gargouiller.

rummage ['rʌmidʒ] *n* fouiller. *n* **rummage sale** vente de charité *f*.

rumour ['ruːmə] *n* rumeur *f*, bruit *m*.

rump [rʌmp] *n* (*animal*) croupe *f*; (*beef*) culotte *f*. **rump steak** romsteck *m*.

*****run** [rʌn] *n* course *f*; (*outing*) tour *m*; (*track*) piste *f*; séquence *f*, série *f*; (*demand*) ruée *f*. **in the long run** à la longue. *v* courir; (*flow*) couler; (*colour*) s'étaler; (*function*) marcher; (*organize*) diriger; passer. **run away** *v* se sauver. **runaway** *n, adj* fugitif, -ive. **run down** *v* (*car, etc.*) renverser; (*coll*) dénigrer. **rundown** *adj* (*coll*) à plat, surmené. **run in** (*mot*) roder. **run out** expirer, s'épuiser. **run over** (*car, etc.*) écraser. **runway** *n* piste *f*. **runner** *n* coureur *m*. **runner bean** haricot à rames *m*. **runner-up** *n* second, -e *m, f*. **running** *adj* (*water, etc.*) courant; (*in succession*) de suite. **running commentary** commentaire suivi *m*. **running costs** frais d'exploitation *m pl*.

rung[1] [rʌŋ] *V* **ring**[2].

rung[2] [rʌŋ] *n* barreau *m*.

rupture ['rʌptʃə] *n* rupture *f*. *v* (se) rompre.

rural ['ruərəl] *adj* rural; de la campagne.

ruse [ruːz] *n* ruse *f*.

rush[1] [rʌʃ] *n* ruée *f*; hâte *f*. *v* se précipiter; (*do quickly*) dépêcher. **rush hour** heure de pointe *f*.

rush[2] [rʌʃ] *n* (*bot*) jonc *m*.

rusk [rʌsk] *n* biscotte *f*.

Russia ['rʌʃə] *n* Russie *f*. **Russian** *nm, adj* russe; *n* (*people*) Russe *m, f*.

rust [rʌst] *n* rouille *f*. *v* (se) rouiller. **rusty** *adj* rouillé.

rustic ['rʌstik] *adj* rustique.

rustle ['rʌsl] *v* (*leaves*) (faire) bruire; (*paper*) froisser. *n* bruissement *m*; froissement *m*.

rut [rʌt] *n* ornière *f.* **be in a rut** suivre l'ornière.

ruthless ['ruːθlis] *adj* impitoyable, sans pitié.

rye [rai] *n* seigle *m.*

S

sabbath ['sabəθ] *n* sabbat *m.*

sabbatical [sə'batikəl] *adj* sabbatique. *n* année sabbatique *f.*

sable ['seibl] *n* zibeline *f.*

sabotage ['sabətaːʒ] *n* sabotage *m.* *v* saboter. **saboteur** *n* saboteur, -euse *m, f.*

sabre ['seibə] *n* sabre *m.*

saccharin ['sakərin] *n* saccharine *f.*

sachet ['saʃei] *n* sachet *m.*

sack [sak] *n* sac *m.* **get the sack** (*coll*) être sacqué. *v* (*coll*) sacquer.

sacrament ['sakrəmənt] *n* sacrement *m.*

sacred ['seikrid] *adj* sacré.

sacrifice ['sakrifais] *n* sacrifice *m.* *v* sacrifier.

sacrilege ['sakrəlidʒ] *n* sacrilège *m.* **sacrilegious** *adj* sacrilège.

sad [sad] *adj* triste. **sadden** *v* attrister. **sadly** *adv* tristement; (*very*) bien, fort; (*unfortunately*) fâcheusement. **sadness** *n* tristesse *f.*

saddle ['sadl] *n* selle *f.* **saddle-bag** *n* (*horse*) sacoche de selle *f*; (*bicycle*) sacoche de bicyclette *f.* *v* seller. **saddle with** (*coll*) coller à. **saddler** *n* sellier *m.* **saddlery** *n* sellerie *f.*

sadism ['seidizəm] *n* sadisme *m.* **sadist** *n* sadique *m, f.* **sadistic** *adj* sadique.

safari [sə'faːri] *n* safari *m.* **safari park** réserve *f.*

safe [seif] *adj* (*person*) en sécurité; (*toy, etc.*) sans danger; sûr; solide. **safe and sound** sain et sauf. **safe keeping** bonne garde *f.* **to be on the safe side** par précaution. *n* coffre-fort *m.* **safely** *adv* sans danger; en sûreté. **safety** *n* sécurité *f*; solidité *f.* **safety-belt** *n* ceinture de sécurité *f.* **safety first** la sécurité d'abord. **safety-pin** *n* épingle de sûreté *f.*

safeguard ['seifgaːd] *n* sauvegarde *f.* *v* sauvegarder.

saffron ['safrən] *n* safran *m.*

sag [sag] *v* s'affaisser, fléchir. *n* affaissement *m*, fléchissement *m.*

saga ['saːgə] *n* saga *f.*

sage[1] [seidʒ] *nm, adj* (*wise*) sage.

sage[2] [seidʒ] *n* (*herb*) sauge *f.*

Sagittarius [sadʒi'teəriəs] *n* Sagittaire *m.*

sago ['seigou] *n* sagou *m*; (*pudding*) sagou au lait *m.*

said [sed] *V* say.

sail [seil] *n* voile *f*; (*trip*) tour en bateau *m*; (*windmill*) aile *f.* **sailcloth** *n* toile à voile *f.* **set sail** partir. *v* (*leave*) partir; (*cross*) traverser; (*boat*) piloter. **sail through** (*coll*) réussir haut la main. **sailing** *n* navigation *f*; (*sport, hobby*) voile *f.* **sailing boat** bateau à voiles *m.* **sailor** *n* marin *m.*

saint [seint] *n* saint, -e *m, f.*

sake [seik] *n* **for the sake of** pour l'amour de, par égard pour; pour le plaisir de.

salad ['saləd] *n* salade *f.* **salad cream** mayonnaise *f.* **salad dressing** vinaigrette *f.*

salami [sə'laːmi] *n* salami *m.*

salary ['saləri] *n* traitement *m*, salaire *m.* **salary scale** échelle des traitements *f.*

sale [seil] *n* vente *f*; (*reductions*) soldes *m pl.* **for sale** à vendre. **on sale** en vente. **sale-room** *n* salle des ventes *f.* **sales department** service des ventes *m.* **salesman** *n* (*shop*) vendeur *m*; représentant *m.* **salesmanship** *n* art de la vente *m.*

saline ['seilain] *adj* salin. **salinity** *n* salinité *f.*

saliva [sə'laivə] *n* salive *f.* **salivary** *adj* salivaire. **salivate** *v* saliver.

sallow ['salou] *adj* jaunâtre.

salmon ['samən] *n* saumon *m.*

salon ['salon] *n* salon *m.*

saloon [sə'luːn] *n* salle *f*, salon *m.* **saloon bar** bar *m.* **saloon car** conduite intérieure *f.*

salt [soːlt] *n* sel *m.* **salt-cellar** *n* salière *f.* *v* saler. **salty** *adj* salé.

salute [sə'luːt] *n* salut *m*; (*guns*) salve *f.* *v* saluer.

salvage ['salvidʒ] *n* sauvetage *m*; récupération *f.* *v* sauver; récupérer.

salvation [sal'veiʃən] *n* salut *m.* **Salvation Army** Armée du Salut *f.*

same [seim] *adj, pron* même. **all the same** quand même. **at the same time** en même temps.

sample ['saːmpl] *n* échantillon *m*; (*blood*) prélèvement *m.* *v* goûter.

sanatorium [sanǝ'tɔːriǝm] *n* sanatorium *m.*

sanctify ['saŋktifai] *v* sanctifier. **sanctification** *n* sanctification *f.*

sanctimonious [saŋkti'mouniǝs] *adj* moralisateur, -trice.

sanction ['saŋkʃǝn] *n* sanction *f. v* sanctionner.

sanctity ['saŋktǝti] *n* sainteté *f;* inviolabilité *f.*

sanctuary ['saŋktʃuǝri] *n* sanctuaire *m;* (*refuge*) asile *m;* (*birds, etc.*) réserve *f.*

sand [sand] *n* sable *m.* **sandbank** *n* banc de sable *m.* **sand-castle** *n* château de sable *m.* **sandpaper** *n* papier de verre *m.* **sandstone** *n* grès *m. v* sabler; (*with sandpaper*) frotter au papier de verre. **sandy** *adj* sablonneux; (*beach*) de sable; (*hair*) couleur sable.

sandal ['sandl] *n* sandale *f.*

sandwich ['sanwidʒ] *n* sandwich *m.* **sandwich board** panneau publicitaire *m.* **sandwich course** cours de formation professionnelle *m.*

sane [sein] *adj* sain d'esprit; raisonnable. **sanity** *n* santé mentale *f.*

sang [saŋ] *V* **sing.**

sanitary ['sanitǝri] *adj* sanitaire; hygiénique. **sanitary towel** serviette hygiénique *f.*

sank [saŋk] *V* **sink.**

sap [sap] *n* sève *f.*

sapphire ['safaiǝ] *n* saphir *m.*

sarcasm ['sɑːkazǝm] *n* sarcasme *m.* **sarcastic** *adj* sarcastique.

sardine [sɑː'diːn] *n* sardine *f.*

Sardinia [sɑː'dinjǝ] *n* Sardaigne *f.* **Sardinian** *nm, adj* sarde; *n* (*people*) Sarde *m, f.*

sardonic [sɑː'donik] *adj* sardonique.

sash¹ [saʃ] *n* (*uniform*) écharpe *f;* (*dress*) large ceinture *f.*

sash² [saʃ] *n* (*frame*) chassis à guillotine *m.* **sash-window** *n* fenêtre à guillotine *f.*

sat [sat] *V* **sit.**

Satan ['seitǝn] *n* Satan *m.* **satanic** *adj* satanique.

satchel ['satʃǝl] *n* cartable *m.*

satellite ['satǝlait] *n* satellite *m.*

satin ['satin] *n* satin *m.*

satire ['sataiǝ] *n* satire *f.* **satirical** *adj* satirique. **satirize** *v* faire la satire de.

satisfy ['satisfai] *v* satisfaire; convaincre. **satisfaction** *n* satisfaction *f.* **satisfactory** *adj* satisfaisant.

saturate ['satʃǝreit] *v* saturer; (*soak*) trem-

per. **saturation** *n* saturation *f.* **reach saturation point** arriver à saturation.

Saturday ['satǝdi] *n* samedi *m.*

sauce [sɔːs] *n* sauce *f;* (*slang*) toupet *m.* **saucy** *adj* impertinent; coquin.

saucepan ['sɔːspǝn] *n* casserole *f.*

saucer ['sɔːsǝ] *n* soucoupe *f.*

sauerkraut ['sauǝkraut] *n* choucroute *f.*

sauna ['sɔːnǝ] *n* sauna *m.*

saunter [sɔːntǝ] *v* flâner, se balader. *n* flânerie *f,* balade *f.*

sausage ['sɔsidʒ] *n* saucisse *f.* **sausagemeat** *n* chair à saucisse *f.* **sausage roll** friand *m.*

savage ['savidʒ] *adj* féroce, brutal; primitif, sauvage. *n* sauvage *m, f. v* attaquer férocement. **savagery** *n* sauvagerie *f.*

save¹ [seiv] *v* sauver; (*put aside*) mettre de côté, garder; économiser, épargner. **savings** *pl n* économies *f pl.* **savings bank** caisse d'épargne *f.*

save² [seiv] *prep* sauf.

saviour ['seivjǝ] *n* sauveur *m.*

savour ['seivǝ] *v* savourer. *n* saveur *f.* **savoury** *adj* savoureux, appétissant; (*not sweet*) salé.

saw¹ [sɔː] *V* **see¹.**

*saw² [sɔː] *n* scie *f.* **sawdust** *n* sciure *f.* **sawmill** *n* scierie *f. v* scier.

sawn [sɔːn] *V* **saw².**

saxophone ['saksǝfoun] *n* saxophone *m.*

*say [sei] *v* dire. **saying** *n* dicton *m,* proverbe *m.*

scab [skab] *n* croûte *f;* (*derog: non-striker*) jaune *m. v* se cicatriser; (*derog*) faire le jaune.

scaffold ['skafǝld] *n* échafaud *m.* **scaffolding** *n* échafaudage *m.*

scald [skɔːld] *v* échauder, ébouillanter. *n* brûlure *f.* **scalding** *adj* brûlant.

scale¹ [skeil] *n* (*fish, etc.*) écaille *f;* (*deposit*) tartre *m.* **scaly** *adj* écailleux; entartré.

scale² [skeil] *n* échelle *f;* (*music*) gamme *f.* **scale drawing** dessin à l'échelle *m. v* escalader. **scale down** réduire (proportionnellement).

scales [skeilz] *pl n* balance *f sing.*

scallop ['skalǝp] *n* coquille Saint-Jacques *f;* (*sewing*) feston *m.* **scallop shell** coquille *f. v* festonner.

scalp [skalp] *n* cuir chevelu *m. v* scalper.

scalpel ['skalpǝl] *n* bistouri *m.*

scamper ['skampǝ] *v* (*child*) galoper; (*mouse*) trottiner.

scampi ['skampi] *n* langoustines *f pl.*

scan [skan] *v* scruter; (*glance over*) parcourir des yeux; (*poetry*) (se) scander.

scandal ['skandl] *n* scandale *m*; (*gossip*) cancans *m pl.* **scandalize** *v* scandaliser. **scandalous** *adj* scandaleux.

Scandinavia [ˌskandi'neivjə] *n* Scandinavie *f.* **Scandinavian** *n* Scandinave *m, f*; *adj* scandinave.

scant [skant] *or* **scanty** *adj* insuffisant.

scapegoat ['skeipgout] *n* bouc émissaire *m.*

scar [skaɪ] *n* cicatrice *f*; (*from knife*) balafre *f. v* marquer d'une cicatrice; balafrer.

scarce [skeəs] *adj* peu abondant; rare. **scarcely** *adv* à peine. **scarcity** *n* manque *m*; rareté *f.*

scare [skeə] *n* peur *f*; alarme *f. v* effrayer. **be scared** avoir peur. **scarecrow** *n* épouvantail *m.*

scarf [skaɪf] *n* écharpe *f*; (*square*) foulard *m.*

scarlet ['skaɪlit] *nf, adj* écarlate. **scarlet fever** scarlatine *f.*

scathing ['skeiðiŋ] *adj* acerbe, cinglant.

scatter ['skatə] *v* éparpiller, répandre; (se) disperser. **scatterbrained** *adj* écervelé.

scavenge ['skavindʒ] *v* fouiller. **scavenger** *n* éboueur *m*; insecte *or* animal nécrophage *m.*

scene [siɪn] *n* scène *f*; (*place*) lieu *m*; spectacle *m*, vue *f.*

scenery ['siɪnəri] *n* paysage *m*; (*theatre*) décor *m.*

scent [sent] *n* parfum *m*; (*track*) piste *f. v* parfumer; (*smell*) flairer.

sceptic ['skeptik] *n* sceptique *m, f.* **sceptical** *adj* sceptique. **scepticism** *n* scepticisme *m.*

sceptre ['septə] *n* sceptre *m.*

schedule ['ʃedjuɪl] *n* programme *m*; (*timetable*) horaire *m. v* prévoir.

scheme [skiɪm] *n* plan *m*, projet *m*; (*plot*) complot *m*; arrangement *m. v* combiner, comploter.

schizophrenia [ˌskitsə'friɪniə] *n* schizophrénie *f.* **schizophrenic** *n(m+f)*, *adj* schizophrène.

scholar ['skolə] *n* érudit, -e *m, f*; (*pupil*) écolier, -ère *m, f.* **scholarly** *adj* érudit. **scholarship** *n* (*award*) bourse *f*; érudition *f.*

scholastic [skə'lastik] *adj* scolaire; scolastique.

school¹ [skuɪl] *n* école *f*; (*secondary*) collège *m*, lycée *m.* **schoolboy** *n* élève *m*, écolier *m.* **school-days** *pl n* années d'école *f pl.* **schoolgirl** *n* élève *f*, écolière *f.* **school-leaving age** âge de fin de scolarité *m.* **school year** année scolaire *f. v* dresser. **schooling** *n* scolarité *f*; instruction *f*; dressage *m.*

school² [skuɪl] *n* (*of fish*) banc *m.*

schooner ['skuɪnə] *n* schooner *m.*

sciatica [sai'atikə] *n* sciatique *f.* **sciatic** *adj* sciatique.

science ['saiəns] *n* science *f.* **science fiction** *n* science-fiction *f.* **scientific** *adj* scientifique. **scientist** *n* scientifique *m, f.*

scintillating ['sintileitiŋ] *adj* scintillant; (*remark, etc.*) brillant.

scissors ['sizəz] *pl n* ciseaux *m pl.*

scoff¹ [skof] *v* se moquer.

scoff² [skof] *v* (*coll*) bouffer.

scold [skould] *v* attraper, gronder. **scolding** *n* gronderie *f.*

scone [skon] *n* petit pain au lait *m.*

scoop [skuɪp] *n* pelle *f*, cuiller *f*; (*press*) scoop *m. v* (*pick up*) ramasser; (*water*) écoper; (*hole*) creuser.

scooter ['skuɪtə] *n* scooter *m*; (*child's*) trottinette *f.*

scope [skoup] *n* (*range*) étendue *f*; (*opportunity*) possibilité *f.*

scorch [skoɪtʃ] *n* brûlure légère *f. v* roussir, brûler.

score [skoɪ] *n* (*sport*) score *m*; (*game*) marque *f*; (*subject*) titre *m*; (*music*) partition *f*; (*twenty*) vingtaine *f*; (*cut*) rayure *f. v* marquer; rayer, strier. **scorer** *n* marqueur *m.*

scorn [skoɪn] *n* mépris *m*, dédain *m. v* mépriser, dédaigner. **scornful** *adj* méprisant, dédaigneux.

Scorpio ['skoɪpiou] *n* Scorpion *m.*

scorpion ['skoɪpiən] *n* scorpion *m.*

Scotland ['skotlənd] *n* Ecosse *f.* **Scot** *n* Ecossais, -e *m, f.* **Scotch** *n* whisky *m*, scotch *m.* **Scottish** *or* **Scots** *adj* écossais.

scoundrel ['skaundrəl] *n* vaurien *m.*

scour¹ [skauə] *v* (*clean*) récurer. **scourer** *n* (*powder*) poudre à récurer *f*; (*pad*) tampon abrasif *m.*

scour² [skauə] *v* (*search*) parcourir.

scourge [skəɪdʒ] *n* fléau *m.*

scout [skaut] *n* scout *m*, éclaireur *m.* **scoutmaster** *n* chef scout *m.* **scouting** *n* scoutisme *m.*

scowl [skaul] *v* se renfrogner. *n* mine renfrognée *f.*

scramble ['skrambl] *v* avancer avec difficulté; (*rush*) se bousculer; (*eggs, phone*) brouiller. *n* bousculade *f.*

scrap [skrap] *n* bout *m*, fragment *m*; (*metal*) ferraille *f.* **scrap-book** *n* album *m.* **scrap-merchant** *n* ferrailleur *m.* **scrap paper** brouillon *m.* **scraps** *pl n* restes *m pl.* *v* mettre au rebut; abandonner.

scrape [skreip] *n* (*noise*) grattement *m*; (*graze*) éraflure *f.* *v* gratter, racler; érafler. **scrape through** (*exam*) réussir de justesse.

scratch [skratʃ] *v* (*for itch*) (se) gratter; (*with claw*) griffer; (*graze*) érafler; (*glass, record, etc.*) rayer. *n* grattement *m*; éraflure *f*; rayure *f*; zéro *m.*

scrawl [skrɔːl] *v* gribouiller. *n* gribouillage *m.*

scream [skriːm] *n* cri aigu *m*, hurlement *m.* *v* crier, hurler.

screech [skriːtʃ] *n* cri strident *m*, hurlement *m*; (*brakes*) grincement *m.* *v* crier, hurler; grincer.

screen [skriːn] *n* (*TV, film*) écran *m*; (*hospital, room*) paravent *m*; masque *m.* **screen-play** *n* scénario *m.* **screen test** essai filmé *m.* *v* masquer, cacher; (*film*) projeter; protéger.

screw [skruː] *n* vis *m.* **screwdriver** *n* tournevis *m.* *v* visser. **screw up** (*paper*) chiffonner.

scribble ['skribl] *v* gribouiller, griffonner. **scribble out** raturer. *n* gribouillage *m*, griffonage *m.*

script [skript] *n* (*play*) texte *m*; (*film*) scénario *m*; (*writing*) script *m.*

scripture ['skriptʃə] *n* (*school*) instruction religieuse *f*; (*holy*) écriture sainte *f.*

scroll [skroul] *n* rouleau *m*; manuscrit *m*; (*arch*) volute *f.*

scrounge [skraundʒ] (*coll*) *v* chiper, taper. **scrounger** *n* parasite *m.*

scrub[1] [skrʌb] *n* nettoyage *m.* *v* nettoyer à la brosse, frotter; (*coll: cancel*) annuler. **scrubbing brush** brosse dure *f.*

scrub[2] [skrʌb] *n* broussailles *f pl.*

scruff [skrʌf] *n* **by the scruff of the neck** par la peau du cou.

scruffy ['skrʌfi] *adj* négligé, débraillé. **scruffiness** *n* débraillé *m.*

scrum [skrʌm] *n* mêlée *f.*

scruple ['skruːpl] *n* scrupule *m.* **scrupulous** *adj* scrupuleux.

scrutiny ['skruːtəni] *n* examen minutieux *m.* **scrutinize** *v* scruter.

scuffle ['skʌfl] *n* bagarre *f.* *v* se bagarrer.

scull [skʌl] *n* aviron *m*, godille *f.* *v* ramer, godiller.

scullery ['skʌləri] *n* arrière-cuisine *f.*

sculpt [skʌlpt] *v* sculpter. **sculptor** *n* sculpteur *m.* **sculpture** *n* sculpture *f.*

scum [skʌm] *n* écume *f*; (*derog*) rebut *m.*

scurf [skəːf] *n* pellicules *f pl.*

scurvy ['skəːvi] *n* scorbut *m.*

scuttle[1] ['skʌtl] *n* (*coal*) seau à charbon *m.*

scuttle[2] ['skʌtl] *v* (*naut*) saborder.

scuttle[3] ['skʌtl] *v* courir précipitamment.

scythe [saið] *n* faux *f.* *v* faucher.

sea [siː] *n* mer *f.*

sea bed *n* fond de la mer *m.*

seafaring ['siːˌfeəriŋ] *adj* marin.

seafood ['siːfuːd] *n* fruits de mer *m pl.*

sea front *n* bord de mer *m.*

seagull ['siːgʌl] *n* mouette *f.*

seahorse ['siːhɔːs] *n* hippocampe *m.*

seal[1] [siːl] *n* sceau *m*, cachet *m.* *v* sceller; (*stick down*) coller; (*fate*) décider. **sealing wax** cire à cacheter *f.*

seal[2] [siːl] *n* (*zool*) phoque *m.* **sealskin** *n* peau de phoque *f.*

sea-level *n* niveau de la mer *m.*

sea-lion *n* otarie *f.*

seam [siːm] *n* couture *f*; joint *m*; (*coal*) veine *f.*

seaman ['siːmən] *n* marin *m.*

séance ['seiãs] *n* séance de spiritisme *f.*

sear [siə] *v* flétrir; (*burn*) brûler. **searing** *adj* (*pain*) aigu, -guë.

search [səːtʃ] *n* recherche *f*; (*of house, etc.*) fouille *f.* **searchlight** *n* projecteur *m.* **search-party** *n* équipe de secours *f.* **search-warrant** *n* mandat de perquisition *m.* *v* fouiller, chercher. **searching** *adj* (*look*) pénétrant; (*examination*) rigoureux.

sea shell *n* coquillage *m.*

seashore ['siːʃɔː] *n* rivage *m*, plage *f.*

seasick ['siːsik] *adj* **be seasick** avoir le mal de mer. **seasickness** *n* mal de mer *m.*

seaside ['siːsaid] *n* bord de la mer *m.* **seaside resort** station balnéaire *f.*

season ['siːzn] *n* saison *f.* **season ticket** carte d'abonnement *f.* *v* (*food*) assaisonner; (*wood*) faire sécher. **seasonal** *adj* saisonnier. **seasoning** *n* assaisonnement *m.*

seat [siːt] *n* siège *m*; place *f*. **seat-belt** *n* ceinture de sécurité *f*. *v* (faire) asseoir; placer.

seaweed ['siːwiːd] *n* algue *f*.

seaworthy ['siːwɔːði] *adj* en état de naviguer.

secluded [si'kluːdid] *adj* à l'écart, retiré. **seclusion** *n* solitude *f*.

second[1] ['sekənd] *n* (*time*) seconde *f*. **second hand** trotteuse *f*.

second[2] ['sekənd] *n* deuxième *m*, *f*, second, -e *m*, *f*; (*comm*) article de second choix *m*. *adj, adv* deuxième, second. **on second thoughts** réflexion faite. **second-class** *adj* de deuxième classe; (*mail*) tarif réduit. **second-hand** *adj, adv* d'occasion. **second-rate** *adj* médiocre. **second to none** sans pareil. *v* appuyer (la motion de). **secondly** *adv* deuxièment, en second lieu.

secondary ['sekəndəri] *adj* secondaire.

secret ['siːkrit] *n* secret *m*. *adj* secret, -ète. **secrecy** *n* secret *m*. **secretive** *adj* réservé, dissimulé. **secretly** *adv* en secret.

secretary ['sekrətəri] *n* secrétaire *m*, *f*. **secretarial** *adj* de secrétariat, de secrétaire.

secrete [si'kriːt] *v* sécréter; (*hide*) cacher. **secretion** *n* sécrétion *f*.

sect [sekt] *n* secte *f*. **sectarian** *adj* sectaire.

section ['sekʃən] *n* section *f*, partie *f*.

sector ['sektə] *n* secteur *m*.

secular ['sekjulə] *adj* séculier, laïque.

secure [si'kjuə] *adj* solide; sûr, assuré; tranquille. *v* fixer; se procurer; garantir; assurer. **security** sécurité *f*; (*for loan*) caution *f*.

sedate [si'deit] *adj* posé, calme. **sedation** *n* sédation *f*. **sedative** *nm, adj* calmant.

sediment ['sedimənt] *n* (*geol*) sédiment *m*; (*wine, etc.*) dépôt *m*.

seduce [si'djuːs] *v* séduire. **seduction** *n* séduction *f*. **seductive** *adj* séduisant.

*****see**[1] [siː] *v* voir. **see to** s'occuper de. **see you later!** à tout à l'heure!

see[2] [siː] *n* évêché *m*.

seed [siːd] *n* graine *f*; (*source*) germe *m*. **seedless** *adj* sans pépins. **seedling** *n* semis *m*. **seedy** *adj* miteux; (*coll: ill*) mal fichu.

*****seek** [siːk] *v* chercher, rechercher; demander.

seem [siːm] *v* sembler, paraître. **seeming** *adj* apparent. **seemingly** *adv* apparemment; à ce qu'il paraît.

seen [siːn] *V* **see**[1].

seep [siːp] *v* suinter, filtrer. **seepage** *n* suintement *m*; (*leak*) fuite *f*.

seesaw ['siːsɔː] *n* bascule *f*. *v* osciller.

seethe [siːð] *v* bouillir, bouillonner. **seething** *adj* (*coll*) furibond.

segment ['segmənt] *n* segment *m*; (*orange, etc.*) quartier *m*.

segregate ['segrigeit] *v* séparer, isoler. **segregation** *n* ségrégation *f*.

seize [siːz] *v* saisir; (*with force*) s'emparer de. **seize up** (*tech*) se gripper; (*med*) s'ankyloser. **seizure** *n* saisie *f*; capture *f*; (*med*) crise *f*.

seldom ['seldəm] *adv* rarement.

select [sə'lekt] *v* selectionner, choisir. *adj* choisi; (*club, etc.*) fermé. **selection** *n* sélection *f*. **selective** *adj* sélectif.

self [self] *n* moi *m*.

self-adhesive *adj* auto-adhésif.

self-assured *adj* plein d'assurance. **self-assurance** *n* assurance *f*.

self-centred *adj* égocentrique.

self-coloured *adj* uni.

self-confident *adj* sûr de soi. **self-confidence** *n* confiance en soi *f*.

self-conscious *adj* gêné. **self-consciousness** *n* gêne *f*.

self-contained *adj* indépendant.

self-control *n* maîtrise de soi *f*. **self-controlled** *adj* maître de soi, maîtresse de soi.

self-defence *n* légitime défense *f*.

self-discipline *n* discipline personelle *f*.

self-employed *adj* **be self-employed** travailler à son compte.

self-evident *adj* qui va de soi.

self-explanatory *adj* évident en soi.

self-expression *n* expression libre *f*.

self-important *adj* suffisant. **self-importance** *n* suffisance *f*.

self-interest *n* intérêt personnel *m*.

selfish ['selfiʃ] *adj* égoïste. **selfishness** *n* égoïsme *m*.

selfless ['selflis] *adj* désintéressé.

self-opinionated *adj* opiniâtre.

self-pity *n* apitoiement sur soi-même *m*.

self-portrait *n* autoportrait *m*.

self-possessed *adj* assuré. **self-possession** *n* sang-froid *m*.

self-raising flour *n* farine à levure *f*.

self-respect *n* respect de soi *m*.

self-righteous *adj* pharisaïque. **self-righteousness** *n* pharisaïsme *m*.

self-sacrifice *n* abnégation *f*.

selfsame ['selfseim] *adj* même.
self-satisfied *adj* content de soi.
self-service *n* libre-service *m*.
self-sufficient *adj* indépendant. **self-sufficiency** *n* indépendance *f*.
self-taught *adj* autodidacte.
self-willed *adj* entêté.
*sell [sel] *v* (se) vendre; (*coll*) faire accepter. **sell off** solder, liquider. **seller** *n* vendeur, -euse *m*, *f*; marchand, -e *m*, *f*.
sellotape ® ['seləteip] *n* scotch ® *m*. *v* scotcher.
semantic [sə'mantik] *adj* sémantique. **semantics** *n* sémantique *f*.
semaphore ['seməfɔɪ] *n* signaux à bras *m pl*; (*rail*) sémaphore *m*.
semblance ['sembləns] *n* semblant *m*.
semen ['siːmən] *n* sperme *m*, semence *f*.
semibreve ['semibriːv] *n* ronde *f*.
semicircle ['semisəɪkl] *n* demi-cercle *m*. **semicircular** *adj* demi-circulaire.
semicolon [,semi'koulən] *n* point-virgule *m*.
semi-conscious *adj* à demi conscient.
semi-detached house *n* maison jumelée *f*.
semifinal [semi'fainl] *n* demi-finale *f*.
seminar ['seminaɪ] *n* séminaire *m*.
semi-precious *adj* semi-précieux.
semiquaver ['semikweivə] *n* double croche *f*.
semitone ['semitoun] *n* demi-ton *m*.
semolina [,semə'liːnə] *n* semoule *f*; (*pudding*) semoule au lait *f*.
senate ['senit] *n* sénat *m*. **senator** *n* sénateur *m*.
*send [send] *v* envoyer; rendre. **send back** renvoyer. **send for** faire venir; (*mailorder*) se faire envoyer.
senile ['siːnail] *adj* sénile. **senility** *n* sénilité *f*.
senior ['siːnjə] *adj* (*age*) aîné; (*rank*) supérieur, -e. *n* aîné, -e *m*, *f*; (*school*) grand, -e *m*, *f*. **seniority** *n* (*rank*) supériorité *f*; (*service*) ancienneté *f*; priorité d'âge *f*.
sensation [sen'seiʃən] *n* sensation *f*. **sensational** *adj* sensationnel; (*newspaper*) à sensation.
sense [sens] *n* sens *m*; sensation *f*; (*feeling*) sentiment *m*; (*wisdom*) bon sens *m*. **senses** *pl n* raison *f sing*. *v* sentir. **senseless** *adj* insensé; (*unconscious*) sans connaissance.

sensible ['sensəbl] *adj* sensé, raisonnable; (*clothes*) pratique.
sensitive ['sensitiv] *adj* sensible; susceptible; délicat. **sensitivity** *n* sensibilité *f*; susceptibilité *f*; délicatesse *f*.
sensual ['sensjuəl] *adj* sensuel. **sensuality** *n* sensualité *f*.
sensuous ['sensjuəs] *adj* sensuel.
sent [sent] *V* **send**.
sentence ['sentəns] *n* (*gramm*) phrase *f*; (*law*) condamnation *f*. *v* condamner.
sentiment ['sentimənt] *n* sentiment *m*; opinion *f*; sentimentalité *f*. **sentimental** *adj* sentimental.
sentry ['sentri] *n* sentinelle *f*.
separate ['sepərət; *v* 'sepəreit] *adj* séparé; indépendant; différent. *v* (se) séparer; diviser. **separation** *n* séparation *f*.
September [sep'tembə] *n* septembre *m*.
septic ['septik] *adj* septique; (*wound*) infecté. **go septic** s'infecter.
sequel ['siːkwəl] *n* suite *f*, conséquence *f*.
sequence ['siːkwəns] ordre *m*; (*cards, music*) séquence *f*; (*series*) suite *f*.
sequin ['siːkwin] *n* paillette *f*.
serenade [serə'neid] *n* sérénade *f*.
serene [sə'riːn] *adj* serein. **serenity** *n* sérénité *f*.
serf [səɪf] *n* serf, serve *m*, *f*.
sergeant ['saɪdʒənt] *n* (*mil*) sergent *m*; (*police*) brigadier *m*. **sergeant-major** *n* sergent-major *m*.
serial ['siəriəl] *n* feuilleton *m*. *adj* de série. **serialize** *v* adapter en feuilleton; publier en feuilleton.
series ['siərizz] *n* série *f*.
serious ['siəriəs] *adj* sérieux, grave. **seriousness** *n* sérieux *m*, gravité *f*.
sermon ['səɪmən] *n* sermon *m*.
serpent ['səɪpənt] *n* serpent *m*.
serrated [sə'reitid] *adj* dentelé.
servant ['səɪvənt] *n* domestique *m*, *f*.
serve [səɪv] *v* servir. **it serves you right** c'est bien fait pour toi.
service ['səɪvis] *n* service *m*; (*mot*) révision *f*. **service area** (*mot*) aire de services *f*. **service charge** service *m*. **serviceman** *n* militaire *m*. **service station** (*mot*) station-service *f*. *v* réviser. **serviceable** *adj* pratique, commode.
serviette [,səɪvi'et] *n* serviette *f*. **serviette ring** rond de serviette *m*.
servile ['səɪvail] *adj* servile. **servility** *n* servilité *f*.

session ['seʃən] *n* séance *f*, session *f*.
***set** [set] *n* jeu *m*, série *f*; collection *f*;
(*people*) groupe *m*; (*TV*) poste *m*; (*cinema*) plateau *m*; (*hair*) mise en plis *f*;
(*tennis*) set *m*. *adj* fixe. *v* (*put*) mettre;
(*clock*) régler; fixer; (*mount*) moırter; (*jelly, etc.*) prendre; (*sun*) se coucher; (*type*)
composer. **set about** se mettre à. **setback**
n contretemps *m*, revers *m*. **set off** (*leave*)
partir; faire exploser; (*enhance*) mettre
en valeur. **set out** partir; exposer. **set up**
dresser; établir; s'installer. **setting** *n* cadre *m*; (*gem*) monture *f*; (*sun*) coucher *m*.
settee [se'tiː] *n* canapé *m*.
settle ['setl] *v* (*problem, account, etc.*)
régler; calmer; (*bird*) se poser; (*person*)
s'installer. **settle down** se calmer;
s'installer. **settle up** (*bill*) régler. **settlement** *n* règlement *m*; accord *m*; colonie
f.
seven ['sevn] *nm, adj* sept. **seventh**
n(*m*+*f*), *adj* septième.
seventeen [sevn'tiːn] *nm, adj* dix-sept.
seventeenth *n*(*m*+*f*), *adj* dix-septième.
seventy ['sevnti] *nm, adj* soixante-dix.
seventieth *n*(*m*+*f*), *adj* soixante-dixième.
sever ['sevə] *v* (*cease*) rompre, cesser;
(*cut*) couper.
several ['sevrəl] *adj, pron* plusieurs.
severe [sə'viə] *adj* sévère; (*hard*) dur; (*illness*) grave. **severity** *n* sévérité *f*; intensité *f*.
***sew** [sou] *v* coudre. **sewing** *n* couture *f*.
sewing machine machine à coudre *f*.
sewage ['sjuidʒ] *n* vidanges *f pl*. **sewage
farm** champ d'épandage *m*.
sewer ['sjuə] *n* égout *m*.
sewn [soun] *V* sew.
sex [seks] *n* sexe *m*. **sexual** *adj* sexuel.
sexual intercourse rapports sexuels *m pl*.
sexuality *n* sexualité *f*.
sextet [seks'tet] *n* sextuor *m*.
shabby ['ʃabi] *adj* râpé, minable; (*behaviour*) mesquin.
shack [ʃak] *n* cabane *f*.
shade [ʃeid] *n* ombre *f*; nuance *f*; (*lamp*)
abat-jour *m invar*. *v* ombrager; (*painting*)
ombrer; (*drawing*) hachurer. **shady** *adj*
ombragé; (*dishonest*) louche.
shadow ['ʃadou] *n* ombre *f*. **shadow cabinet** cabinet fantôme *m*. *v* (*follow*) filer.
shadowy *adj* ombragé; indistinct.
shaft [ʃaːft] *n* (*tool*) manche *m*; (*light*)
trait *m*; (*lift*) cage *f*; (*mine, ventilation*)
puits *m*; (*spear*) hampe *f*.

shaggy ['ʃagi] *adj* hirsute.
***shake** [ʃeik] *n* secousse *f*; tremblement
m. *v* secouer; (*bottle*) agiter; trembler;
(*weaken*) ébranler. **shake hands** serrer la
main. **shake off** se débarrasser de. **shaky**
adj tremblant; (*weak, unsure*) chancelant.
shaken ['ʃeikn] *V* shake.
shall [ʃal] *aux translated by future tense.*
shallot [ʃə'lot] *n* échalote *f*.
shallow ['ʃalou] *adj* peu profond;
superficiel.
sham [ʃam] *n* imitation *f*; comédie *f*. *adj*
faux, fausse; feint, simulé. *v* feindre,
simuler; jouer la comédie.
shame [ʃeim] *n* honte *f*; (*pity*) dommage
m. *v* faire honte à. **shamefaced** *adj*
honteux; timide. **shameful** *adj* honteux.
shameless *adj* éhonté; impudique.
shampoo [ʃam'puː] *n* shampooing *m*. *v*
faire un shampooing à.
shamrock ['ʃamrok] *n* trèfle *m*.
shandy ['ʃandi] *n* panaché *m*.
shanty[1] ['ʃanti] *n* (*hut*) baraque *f*. **shanty
town** bidonville *m*.
shanty[2] ['ʃanti] *n* chanson de marins *f*.
shape [ʃeip] *n* forme *f*. *v* façonner; prendre forme. **shapeless** *adj* informe. **shapely**
adj bien fait, bien proportionné.
share [ʃeə] *n* part *f*; (*comm*) action *f*.
shareholder *n* actionnaire *m, f*. *v*
partager.
shark [ʃaːk] *n* requin *m*.
sharp [ʃaːp] *adj* aigu, -guë; (*point*) pointu;
(*edge*) tranchant; (*sudden*) brusque; (*outline*) net, nette; (*pain, wind*) vif. *n* (*music*)
dièse *m*. **sharpen** *v* aiguiser; (*pencil*) tailler; (*outline*) rendre plus net. **sharpness** *n*
tranchant *m*; netteté *f*.
shatter ['ʃatə] *v* (se) fracasser; briser,
ruiner. **shattered** *adj* bouleversé; (*tired*)
éreinté. **shattering** *adj* bouleversant.
shave [ʃeiv] *v* (se) raser. **shaving** *n* (*of
wood, metal*) copeau *m*. **shaving brush**
blaireau *m*. **shaving cream** crème à raser
f.
shawl [ʃɔːl] *n* châle *m*.
she [ʃiː] *pron* elle. **she who** celle qui. *n*
(*coll*) femelle *f*.
sheaf [ʃiːf] *n* (*corn*) gerbe *f*; (*papers*) liasse
f; (*arrows*) faisceau *m*.
***shear** [ʃiə] *v* tondre. **shears** *pl n* cisailles
f pl.

sheath [ʃiːθ] *n* gaine *f*; (*sword*) fourreau *m*; (*scissors*) étui *m*. **sheathe** *v* rengainer; recouvrir.

shed[1] [ʃed] *v* (*drop*) perdre; (*radiate*) répandre.

shed[2] [ʃed] *n* remise *f*, hutte *f*.

sheen [ʃiːn] *n* lustre *m*, éclat *m*.

sheep [ʃiːp] *n* mouton *m*. **sheep-dog** *n* chien de berger *m*. **sheepskin** *n* peau de mouton *f*. **sheepish** *adj* penaud.

sheer[1] [ʃiə] *adj* pur, absolu; (*cliff*) à pic; (*stockings*) extrêmement fin.

sheer[2] [ʃiə] *v* (*naut*) faire une embardée.

sheet [ʃiːt] *n* (*bed*) drap *m*; (*paper*) feuille *f*; (*ice, metal*) plaque *f*. **sheet lightning** éclair en nappe *m*. **sheet music** partitions *f pl*.

sheikh [ʃeik] *n* cheik *m*.

shelf [ʃelf] *n* rayon *m*, étagère *f*.

shell [ʃel] *n* coquille *f*; (*tortoise, crab*) carapace *f*; (*from beach*) coquillage *m*; (*mil*) obus *m*. **shellfish** *n* coquillage *m*; (*pl: as food*) fruits de mer *m pl*. *v* (*nut, shrimp*) décortiquer; (*peas*) écosser; (*mil*) bombarder.

shelter ['ʃeltə] *n* abri *m*. *v* (s')abriter; protéger; (*lodge*) recueillir.

shelve [ʃelv] *v* (*project*) mettre en sommeil. **shelving** *n* rayonnage *m*.

shepherd ['ʃepəd] *n* berger *m*. **shepherd's pie** hachis Parmentier *m*.

sheriff ['ʃerif] *n* shérif *m*.

sherry ['ʃeri] *n* xérès *m*.

shield [ʃiːld] *n* bouclier; (*screen*) écran *m*. *v* protéger.

shift [ʃift] *n* changement *m*; (*work*) poste *m*. **shift key** touche de majuscule *f*. **shift work** travail en équipe *m*. *v* déplacer, bouger; changer (de place). **shifty** *adj* louche.

shimmer ['ʃimə] *v* miroiter, chatoyer. *n* miroitement *m*, chatoiement *m*.

shin [ʃin] *n* tibia *m*.

***shine** [ʃain] *n* éclat *m*, brillant *m*. *v* briller. **shiny** *adj* brillant, reluisant.

shingle ['ʃingl] *n* galets *m pl*.

ship [ʃip] *n* bateau *m*; (*larger*) navire *m*. **shipbuilding** *n* construction navale *f*. **shipshape** *adj* bien rangé. **shipwreck** *n* naufrage *m*. **be shipwrecked** faire naufrage. **shipyard** *n* chantier naval *m*. *v* transporter; (*send*) expédier; (*take on*) embarquer. **shipment** *n* cargaison *m*. **shipping** *n* navigation *f*.

shirk [ʃəːk] *v* esquiver. **shirker** *n* (*coll*) tire-au-flanc *m invar*.

shirt [ʃəːt] *n* chemise *f*. **in one's shirt sleeves** en bras de chemise. **shirtwaister** *n* robe chemisier *f*.

shit [ʃit] *nf, interj* (*vulgar*) merde.

shiver ['ʃivə] *v* frissonner. *n* frisson *m*. **shivery** *adj* frissonnant; fiévreux.

shoal [ʃoul] *n* (*fish*) banc *m*.

shock [ʃok] *n* choc *m*; (*elec*) décharge *f*. **shock absorber** amortisseur *m*. **shockproof** *adj* anti-choc *invar*. **shock treatment** électrochoc *m*. *v* secouer, bouleverser; dégoûter; (*scandalize*) choquer. **shocking** *adj* affreux, atroce; scandaleux.

shod [ʃod] *V* shoe.

shoddy ['ʃodi] *adj* de mauvaise qualité. **shoddiness** *n* mauvaise qualité *f*.

***shoe** [ʃuː] *n* chaussure *f*, soulier *m*. **shoehorn** *n* chausse-pied *m*. **shoe-lace** *n* lacet de soulier *m*. **shoemaker** *n* cordonnier *m*. **shoe repairer's** cordonnerie *f*. *v* (*horse*) ferrer.

shone [ʃon] *V* shine.

shook [ʃuk] *V* shake.

***shoot** [ʃuːt] *v* (*fire*) tirer, lancer; (*kill*) abattre; (*hit*) atteindre d'un coup de fusil; (*goal*) shooter; (*film*) tourner; (*quickly*) aller en flèche. *n* (*bot*) pousse *f*. **shooting** *n* fusillade *f*; (*hunting*) chasse *f*.

shop [ʃop] *n* magasin *m*; (*smaller*) boutique *f*; (*in factory*) atelier *m*. **shop assistant** vendeur, -euse *m, f*. **shop-floor** *n* ouvriers *m pl*. **shopkeeper** *n* marchand, -e. **shoplifting** *n* vol à l'étalage *m*. **shop-soiled** *adj* défraîchi. **shop-steward** *n* délégué syndical *m*. **shop-window** *n* vitrine *f*. *v* faire ses courses. **shopping** *n* achats *m pl*. **go shopping** faire des courses. **shopping bag** sac à provisions *m*. **shopping centre** centre commercial *m*.

shore [ʃoː] *n* (*beach*) plage *f*; (*of sea*) rivage *m*; (*coast*) littoral *m*.

shorn [ʃoːn] *V* shear.

short [ʃoːt] *adj* court; bref, brève; insuffisant; brusque. **in short** en bref. **shortage** *n* manque *m*, pénurie *f*. **shorten** *v* raccourcir. **shortly** *adv* bientôt.

shortbread ['ʃoːtbred] *n* sablé *m*.

short-circuit *n* court-circuit *m*. *v* court-circuiter.

shortcoming ['ʃoːtkʌmiŋ] *n* défaut *m*.

short cut *n* raccourci *m*.

shorthand ['ʃɔːthand] *n* sténographie *f*.
shorthand typist sténodactylo *m*, *f*.
short list *n* liste de candidats sélectionnés *f*.
short-lived [ʃɔːt'livd] *adj* de courte durée.
shorts [ʃɔːts] *pl n* short *m sing*.
short-sighted *adj* myope.
short story nouvelle *f*.
short-tempered *adj* coléreux.
short-term *adj* à court terme.
short wave *n* ondes courtes *f pl*. *adj* à or sur ondes courtes.
shot[1] [ʃot] *V* **shoot**.
shot[2] [ʃot] *n* coup *m*; (*lead*) plomb *m*; (*try*) essai *m*; photo *f*. **shotgun** *n* fusil de chasse *m*.
should[1] [ʃud] *aux translated by conditional tense*.
should[2] [ʃud] *aux translated by conditional tense of* devoir.
shoulder ['ʃouldə] *n* épaule *f*; (*road*) accotement *m*. **shoulder-bag** *n* sac à bandoulière *m*. **shoulder-blade** *n* omoplate *f*. *v* endosser.
shout [ʃaut] *n* cri *m*. *v* crier.
shove [ʃʌv] *n* poussée *f*. *v* pousser.
shovel ['ʃʌvl] *n* pelle *f*. *v* pelleter.
*show [ʃou] *n* démonstration *f*; (*flowers, etc.*) exposition *f*; (*theatre*) spectacle *m*; apparence *f*; (*ostentation*) parade *f*. **show business** le monde du spectacle *m*. **showcase** *n* vitrine *f*. **show-down** *n* épreuve de force *f*. **show-jumping** *n* concours hippique *m*. **show-room** *n* salle d'exposition *f*. *v* montrer; (*be visible*) se voir. **show in** faire entrer. **show off** (*coll*) crâner. **show up** être visible; (*coll: arrive*) se pointer; (*embarrass*) faire honte à.
shower ['ʃauə] *n* (*rain*) averse *f*; (*bath*) douche *f*. **shower-proof** *adj* imperméable. *v* combler, accabler. **showery** *adj* pluvieux.
shown [ʃoun] *V* **show**.
shrank [ʃraŋk] *V* **shrink**.
shred [ʃred] *n* lambeau *m*; (*small amount*) grain *m*. *v* déchiqueter.
shrew [ʃruː] *n* (*zool*) musaraigne *f*; (*woman*) mégère *f*.
shrewd [ʃruːd] *adj* perspicace, astucieux.
shriek [ʃriːk] *n* hurlement *m*, cri perçant *m*. *v* hurler, crier.
shrill [ʃril] *adj* perçant; (*whistle*) strident.
shrimp [ʃrimp] *n* crevette *f*.
shrine [ʃrain] *n* châsse *f*; lieu saint *m*.

*shrink [ʃriŋk] *v* rétrécir; reculer.
shrinkage *n* rétrécissement *m*.
shrivel ['ʃrivl] *v* se ratatiner, se flétrir.
shroud [ʃraud] *n* linceul *m*; (*mist*) voile *m*. *v* ensevelir.
Shrove Tuesday [ʃrouv] *n* mardi gras *m*.
shrub [ʃrʌb] *n* arbrisseau *m*, arbuste *m*.
shrubbery *n* massif d'arbustes *m*.
shrug [ʃrʌg] *v* hausser (les épaules). *n* haussement d'épaules *m*.
shrunk [ʃrʌŋk] *V* **shrink**.
shudder ['ʃʌdə] *n* frisson *m*; (*engine*) vibration *f*. *v* frissonner, frémir; vibrer.
shuffle ['ʃʌfl] *v* traîner les pieds; (*cards*) battre. *n* battage *m*; réorganisation *f*.
shun [ʃʌn] *v* fuir, éviter.
shunt [ʃʌnt] *v* (*rail*) aiguiller, manœuvrer.
*shut [ʃʌt] *v* fermer. **shut in** enfermer, entourer. **shut up** (*coll*) se taire, faire taire.
shutter ['ʃʌtə] *n* (*window*) volet *m*; (*phot*) obturateur *m*.
shuttle ['ʃʌtl] *n* navette *f*. **shuttlecock** *n* volant *m*. **shuttle service** service de navette *m*.
shy [ʃai] *adj* timide. *v* (*horse*) se cabrer.
shyness *n* timidité *f*.
Siamese [ˌsaiə'miːz] *adj* (*cat, twin*) siamois.
sick [sik] *adj* malade; (*mind, humour*) malsain. **be sick** vomir. **be sick of** (*coll*) avoir marre de. **feel sick** avoir mal au cœur. **sick bay** infirmerie *f*. **sicken** *v* écœurer. **sicken for** couver. **sickening** *adj* écœurant; (*coll*) agaçant. **sickly** *adj* (*person*) maladif; pâle; (*cake*) écœurant. **sickness** *n* maladie *f*; vomissements *m pl*.
sickle ['sikl] *n* faucille *f*.
side [said] *n* côté *m*; (*hill, animal*) flanc *m*; (*edge*) bord *m*; (*team*) équipe *f*; (*argument, etc.*) camp *m*. *v* **side with** prendre parti pour.
sideboard ['saidbɔːd] *n* buffet *m*.
side-effect *n* effet secondaire *m*.
sidelight ['saidlait] *n* (*mot*) lanterne *f*.
sideline ['saidlain] *n* activité secondaire *f*; (*sport*) touche *f*.
sidelong ['saidloŋ] *adj, adv* de côté.
side-show *n* attraction *f*.
side-step *v* éviter.
side-street *n* petite rue *f*.
side-track *v* faire dévier.
sidewalk ['saidwɔːk] *n* (*US*) trottoir *m*.
sideways ['saidweiz] *adj* oblique. *adv* de côté; (*walk*) en crabe.

siding ['saidiŋ] n (rail) voie de garage f.
sidle ['saidl] v marcher de côté; avancer furtivement. **sidle up to** se glisser vers.
siege [siːdʒ] n siège m.
sieve [siv] n tamis m; (coal) crible m. v tamiser; cribler.
sift [sift] v (food) tamiser; (coal) cribler; (evidence) passer au crible. **sift out** dégager. **sifter** n (flour) saupoudreuse f.
sigh [sai] n soupir m. v soupirer.
sight [sait] n vue f; spectacle m; (on gun) mire f. **sight-read** v déchiffrer. **sightseeing** n tourisme m. v apercevoir.
sign [sain] n signe m; (notice) panneau m. **signpost** n poteau indicateur m. v signer.
signal ['signəl] n signal m. v faire signe (à); faire des signaux.
signature ['signətʃə] n signature f. **signature tune** indicatif musical m.
signify ['signifai] v signifier. **significance** n signification f. **significant** adj significatif; considérable.
silence ['sailəns] n silence m. v réduire au silence, faire taire. **silencer** n silencieux m. **silent** adj silencieux.
silhouette [silu'et] n silhouette f. v **be silhouetted against** se découper contre.
silk [silk] n soie f. **silkworm** n ver à soie m. **silky** adj soyeux.
sill [sil] n rebord m; (mot) bas de marche m.
silly ['sili] adj bête, idiot. **silliness** n sottise f.
silt [silt] n vase f. v **silt up** envaser.
silver ['silvə] n argent m; (cutlery, etc.) argenterie f; (change) monnaie f. adj d'argent; en argent. **silver birch** bouleau argenté m. **silver paper** papier d'argent m. **silversmith** n orfèvre m, f. v argenter. **silvery** adj argenté.
similar ['similə] adj semblable. **similarity** n ressemblance f.
simile ['siməli] n comparaison f.
simmer ['simə] v (faire) cuire à feu doux, mijoter; (anger) couver. **simmer down** (coll) se calmer.
simple ['simpl] adj simple. **simpleton** n nigaud, -e m, f. **simplicity** n simplicité f. **simplify** v simplifier. **simply** adv simplement; absolument.
simulate ['simjuleit] v simuler. **simulation** n simulation f.
simultaneous [,siməl'teinjəs] adj simultané.
sin [sin] n péché m. v pécher. **sinful** adj

coupable; scandaleux. **sinner** n pécheur, -eresse m, f.
since [sins] prep, adv depuis. conj depuis que; (because) puisque.
sincere [sin'siə] adj sincère. **sincerity** n sincérité f.
sinew ['sinjuː] n tendon m.
***sing** [siŋ] v chanter. **singer** n chanteur, -euse m, f. **singing** n chant m.
singe [sindʒ] v brûler légèrement, roussir. n légère brûlure f.
single ['siŋgl] adj seul; (not double) simple; célibataire. **single bed** lit d'une personne m. **single file** file indienne f. **single-handed** adv tout seul; (sail) en solitaire. **single-minded** adj résolu. **single ticket** aller simple m. **single room** chambre à un lit f. n (ticket) aller simple m; (record) 45 tours m. **singles** n (sport) simple m. v **single out** distinguer; choisir.
singular ['siŋgjulə] nm, adj singulier.
sinister ['sinistə] adj sinistre.
***sink** [siŋk] v (go under) couler; (collapse) s'affaisser; (go down) baisser; (mine) creuser. **sink in** (idea, etc.) rentrer, pénétrer. n évier m. **sink unit** bloc-évier m.
sinuous ['sinjuəs] adj sinueux.
sinus ['sainəs] n sinus m invar. **sinusitis** n sinusite f.
sip [sip] n petite gorgée f. v boire à petites gorgées.
siphon ['saifən] n siphon m. v siphonner.
sir [sə] n monsieur m; (knight) sir m.
siren ['saiərən] n sirène f.
sirloin ['sə̃loin] n aloyau m.
sister ['sistə] n sœur f; religieuse f; (hospital) infirmière en chef f. **sister-in-law** n belle-sœur f.
***sit** [sit] n (s')asseoir; (clothes) tomber; (committee) être en séance; (exam) passer. **sit down** s'asseoir. **sit-in** n sit-in m invar. **sit up** se redresser; (stay up) ne pas se coucher. **sitting** n séance f; (meal) service m. **sitting room** salon m. **sitting tenant** locataire en place m, f.
site [sait] n emplacement m; (building) chantier m; camping m. v placer.
situation [sitju'eifən] n situation f; emploi m. **situate** v placer, situer.
six [siks] nm, adj six. **sixth** n(m+f), adj sixième. **sixth form** classes de première et terminale f pl.
sixteen [siks'tiːn] nm, adj seize. **sixteenth** n(m+f), adj seizième.

sixty ['sɪksti] *nm, adj* soixante. **sixtieth** *n(m+f), adj* soixantième.

size [saiz] *n* taille *f*; grandeur *f*, dimensions *f pl*; (*shoes*) pointure *f*. *v* size up mesurer, juger. **sizeable** *adj* assez grand.

sizzle ['sizl] *v* grésiller. *n* grésillement *m*.

skate[1] [skeit] *n* patin *m*. **skateboard** *n* planche à roulettes *f*. *v* patiner. **skater** *n* patineur, -euse *m, f*. **skating** *n* patinage *m*.

skate[2] [skeit] *n* (*fish*) raie *f*.

skeleton ['skelitn] *n* squelette *m*. *adj* (*staff, etc.*) squelettique. **skeleton key** passe-partout *m invar*.

sketch [sketʃ] *n* croquis *m*; (*rough*) ébauche *f*; (*theatre*) sketch *m*. *v* esquisser. **sketchy** *adj* incomplet, -ète.

skewer ['skjuə] *n* brochette *f*. *v* embrocher.

ski [skiː] *n* ski *m*. **ski-lift** *n* remonte-pente *m*, remontée mécanique *f*. *v* faire du ski. **skier** *n* skieur, -euse *m, f*. **skiing** *n* ski *m*.

skid [skid] *n* dérapage *m*. *v* déraper.

skill [skil] *n* habileté *f*; technique *f*. **skilful** *adj* habile. **skilled** *adj* habile, adroit; (*worker*) qualifié.

skim [skim] *v* (*milk*) écrémer; (*surface*) raser; (*reading*) parcourir.

skimp [skimp] *v* lésiner (sur), économiser. **skimpy** *adj* insuffisant, maigre.

skin [skin] *n* peau *f*. **skin-diving** *n* plongée sous-marine *f*. **skin-tight** *adj* collant. *v* (*animal*) dépouiller; (*fruit, vegetable*) éplucher. **skinny** *adj* maigrelet.

skip [skip] *n* petit saut *m*. *v* gambader; sauter à la corde; (*miss*) sauter. **skipping** *n* saut à la corde *m*. **skipping rope** corde à sauter *f*.

skipper ['skipə] *n* capitaine *m*.

skirmish ['skəmiʃ] *n* escarmouche *f*.

skirt [skət] *n* jupe *f*. *v* contourner. **skirting board** plinthe *f*.

skittle ['skitl] *n* quille *f*. **skittles** *n* jeu de quilles *m*.

skull [skʌl] *n* crâne *m*. **skull and crossbones** tête de mort *f*.

skunk [skʌŋk] *n* mouffette *f*.

sky [skai] *n* ciel *m*. **sky-blue** *nm, adj* bleu ciel. **skylark** *n* alouette *f*. **skylight** *n* lucarne *f*. **skyline** *n* ligne d'horizon *f*. **skyscraper** *n* gratte-ciel *m invar*.

slab [slab] *m* bloc *m*, plaque *f*; (*paving*) dalle *f*; (*butcher's*) étal *m*.

slack [slak] *adj* (*loose*) lâche; (*trade*) faible; (*person*) négligent, peu sérieux. *n*

mou *m*. **slacken** *v* (se) relâcher; diminuer. **slacker** *n* (*coll*) flemmard, -e *m, f*.

slacks [slaks] *pl n* pantalon *m sing*.

slag [slag] *n* scories *f pl*. **slag heap** (*mining*) terril *m*.

slalom ['slɑɪləm] *n* slalom *m*.

slam [slam] *n* claquement *m*. *v* claquer. **slam on the brakes** freiner à mort.

slander ['slɑɪndə] *n* calomnie *f*; (*law*) diffamation *f*. *v* calomnier; diffamer. **slanderous** *adj* calomnieux; diffamatoire.

slang [slaŋ] *n* argot *m*.

slant [slɑɪnt] *n* inclinaison *f*; angle *m*. *v* (faire) pencher. **slanting** *adj* incliné, penché.

slap [slap] *n* claque *f*; (*on face*) gifle *f*. *v* donner une claque à; gifler; (*coll: put*) flanquer. **slapdash** *adj* (*person*) négligent; (*work*) bâclé. **slapstick** *n* grosse farce *f*. **slap-up meal** (*coll*) repas fameux *m*.

slash [slaʃ] *n* entaille *f*. *v* entailler, taillader; (*coll: prices*) casser.

slat [slat] *n* lame *f*; (*of blind*) lamelle *f*.

slate [sleit] *n* ardoise *f*. *v* ardoiser; (*coll: criticize*) éreinter.

slaughter ['slɔːtə] *n* abattage *m*; (*people*) carnage *m*. **slaughterhouse** *n* abattoir *m*. *v* abattre; massacrer.

slave [sleiv] *n* esclave *m, f*. **slave-driver** *n* négrier, -ère *m, f*. *v* trimer. **slavery** *n* esclavage *m*.

sledge [sledʒ] *n* luge *f*; (*drawn by animal*) traîneau *m*.

sledgehammer ['sledʒhamə] *n* marteau de forgeron *m*.

sleek [sliːk] *adj* lisse, brillant.

***sleep** [sliːp] *n* sommeil *m*. **go to sleep** s'endormir. **sleepwalker** *n* somnambule *m, f*. *v* dormir; (*spend the night*) coucher. **sleep in** faire la grasse matinée. **sleeper** *n* train-couchettes *m*; (*wooden beam*) traverse *f*. **sleeping-bag** *n* sac de couchage *m*. **sleeping-pill** *n* somnifère *m*. **sleepless night** nuit blanche *f*. **sleepy** *adj* endormi, somnolent.

sleet [sliːt] *n* neige fondue *f*.

sleeve [sliːv] *n* manche *f*; (*record*) pochette *f*. **sleeveless** *adj* sans manches.

sleigh [slei] *n* traîneau *m*.

slender ['slendə] *adj* svelte; fin; faible; maigre.

slept [slept] *V* **sleep**.

slice [slais] *n* tranche *f*; partie *f*. *v* couper en tranches.

slick [slik] *adj* (*derog*) facile, superficiel.
slid [slid] *V* **slide.**
*slide [slaid] *n* glissade *f*; (*chute*) toboggan *m*; (*microscope*) porte-objet *m*; (*phot*) diapositive *f*; (*hair*) barrette *f*. **slide-rule** *n* règle à calcul *f*. *v* (se) glisser.
sliding *adj* glissant; (*door, etc.*) coulissant.
slight [slait] *adj* petit, faible; (*person*) mince. *v* offenser. *n* offense *f*. **slightest** *adj* moindre. **slightly** *adv* un peu.
slim [slim] *adj* mince; faible. *v* (faire) maigrir. **slimming** *adj* (*diet, etc.*) amaigrissant.
slime [slaim] *n* vase *f*, limon *m*. **slimy** *adj* visqueux.
*sling [slin] *n* (*med*) écharpe *f*; (*weapon*) fronde *f*. *v* lancer; suspendre.
*slink [slink] *v* **slink away** s'en aller furtivement.
slip [slip] *n* erreur *f*; (*of paper*) bout *m*, fiche *f*; (*underskirt*) combinaison *f*. **slip of the tongue** *or* **pen** lapsus *m*. *v* (se) glisser. **slip-knot** *n* nœud coulant *m*. **slip-road** *n* bretelle d'accès *f*. **slipshod** *adj* négligé, négligent. **slipway** *n* cale *f*.
slipper ['slipə] *n* pantoufle *f*.
slippery ['slipəri] *adj* glissant.
*slit [slit] *n* fente *f*, incision *f*. *v* fendre, inciser.
slither ['sliðə] *v* glisser, déraper.
slobber ['slobə] *v* baver. *n* bave *f*.
sloe [slou] *n* prunelle *f*.
slog [slog] *n* gros effort *m*. *v* travailler très dur; (*ball*) donner un grand coup à.
slogan ['slougən] *n* slogan *m*.
slop [slop] *v* (*spill*) répandre; (*overflow*) déborder.
slope [sloup] *n* inclinaison *f*; (*hill*) côte *f*. *v* être incliné. **sloping** *adj* en pente, incliné.
sloppy ['slopi] *adj* (*food*) liquide; (*dress*) négligé; (*garment*) mal ajusté; (*coll: work*) bâclé.
slot [slot] *n* fente *f*. **slot-machine** *n* (*vending*) distributeur automatique *m*; (*gambling*) machine à sous *f*. *v* (s')emboîter; (s')insérer.
slouch [slautʃ] *v* se tenir mal.
slovenly ['slʌvnli] *adj* négligé.
slow [slou] *adj* lent. *adv* lentement. **in slow motion** au ralenti. **slowcoach** *n* (*coll*) lambin, -e *m, f*. *v* **slow down** ralentir.
slug [slʌg] *n* (*zool*) limace *f*; (*bullet*) balle *f*.

sluggish ['slʌgiʃ] *adj* lent, paresseux.
sluice [sluis] *n* écluse *f*. *v* laver à grande eau.
slum [slʌm] *n* taudis *m*. **slums** *pl n* quartiers pauvres *m pl*.
slumber ['slʌmbə] *n* sommeil paisible *m*. *v* dormir paisiblement.
slump [slʌmp] *n* baisse soudaine *f*; récession *f*, crise *f*. *v* s'effondrer.
slung [slʌŋ] *V* **sling.**
slunk [slʌŋk] *V* **slink.**
slur [sləi] *n* tache *f*; insulte *f*; (*music*) liaison *f*. *v* mal articuler; (*music*) lier.
slush [slʌʃ] *n* neige fondante *f*.
slut [slʌt] *n* souillon *f*.
sly [slai] *adj* rusé, sournois.
smack¹ [smak] *n* tape *f*, claque *f*; (*sound*) claquement *m*. *v* donner une tape *or* claque à.
smack² [smak] *v* **smack of** sentir. *n* léger goût *m*.
small [smoil] *adj* petit; peu nombreux. **feel small** se sentir honteux. **small change** petite monnaie *f*. **smallholding** *n* petite ferme *f*. **smallpox** *n* variole *f*. **small talk** papotage *m*. *n* **small of the back** creux des reins *m*.
smart [smait] *adj* chic *invar*, élégant; intelligent, astucieux; rapide, vif. *v* brûler, piquer. **smarten up** devenir plus élégant; rendre plus élégant. **smartness** *n* élégance *f*; intelligence *f*.
smash [smaʃ] *n* (*sound*) fracas *m*; accident *m*, collision *f*; (*blow*) coup violent *m*. *v* (se) briser (en mille morceaux), (se) fracasser. **smashing** *adj* (*slang*) formidable.
smear [smiə] *n* tache *f*. *v* (se) salir, barbouiller.
*smell [smel] *n* odeur *f*; (*sense*) odorat *m*. *v* sentir; (*sniff*) flairer. **smelly** *adj* malodorant.
smelt [smelt] *V* **smell.**
smile [smail] *n* sourire *m*. *v* sourire.
smirk [sməik] *n* petit sourire satisfait *m*. *v* sourire d'un air satisfait.
smock [smok] *n* blouse *f*. **smocking** *n* smocks *m pl*.
smog [smog] *n* brouillard enfumé *m*.
smoke [smouk] *n* fumée *f*. **smoke-screen** *n* paravent *m*. *v* fumer. **smoker** *n* fumeur, -euse *m, f*. **no smoking** défense de fumer. **smoky** *adj* enfumé.

smooth [smuːð] *adj* lisse; régulier; (*person*) doucereux. *v* lisser. **smooth out** faire disparaître. **smoothly** *adv* facilement, doucement; (*move*) sans secousses; sans incident.

smother ['smʌðə] *v* étouffer.

smoulder ['smouldə] *v* couver.

smudge [smʌdʒ] *n* tache *f.* *v* (s')étaler, (se) maculer.

smug [smʌg] *adj* suffisant.

smuggle ['smʌgl] *v* passer en contrabande; passer clandestinement. **smuggler** *n* contrebandier, -ère *m, f.* **smuggling** *n* contrebande *f.*

snack [snak] *n* casse-croûte *m invar.* **snack-bar** *n* snack-bar *m.*

snag [snag] *n* inconvénient *m*, obstacle caché *m*; (*in cloth*) accroc *m.* *v* accrocher.

snail [sneil] *n* escargot *m.*

snake [sneik] *n* serpent *m.* *v* serpenter.

snap [snap] *n* bruit sec *m*, claquement *m*, craquement *m*; photo *f.* *adj* subit, irréfléchi. **snapdragon** *n* gueule-de-loup *f.* **snapshot** *n* photo *f.* *v* (se) casser net; (faire) claquer, (*dog*) essayer de mordre; (*person*) parler d'un ton brusque.

snare [sneə] *n* piège *m.* *v* attraper.

snarl [snaɪl] *n* grondement *m.* *v* gronder.

snatch [snatʃ] *n* fragment *m*; (*theft*) vol *m.* *v* saisir, arracher (à).

sneak [sniːk] *v* se faufiler; (*slang: school*) moucharder. **sneak in/out** entrer/sortir furtivement. *n* (*coll*) mouchard, -e *m, f.*

sneer [sniə] *v* ricaner. *n* ricanement *m.* **sneering** *adj* ricaneur, -euse.

sneeze [sniːz] *n* éternuement *m.* *v* éternuer.

sniff [snif] *n* reniflement *m.* *v* renifler; (*air, aroma*) humer.

snigger ['snigə] *n* petit rire moqueur *m.* *v* pouffer de rire.

snip [snip] *v* couper à petits coups.

snipe [snaip] *n* bécassine *f.* *v* canarder. **sniper** *n* canardeur *m.*

snivel ['snivl] *v* pleurnicher. **snivelling** *adj* pleurnicheur, -euse.

snob [snob] *n* snob *m, f.* **snobbish** *adj* snob *invar.*

snooker ['snuːkə] *n* jeu de billard *m.*

snoop [snuːp] *v* (*coll*) fureter, fourrer son nez.

snooty ['snuːti] *adj* (*coll*) hautain.

snooze [snuːz] *n* roupillon *m.* *v* piquer un roupillon.

snore [snoɪ] *n* ronflement *m.* *v* ronfler. **snoring** *n* ronflements *m pl.*

snorkel ['snoɪkəl] *n* (*swimmer*) tuba *m*; (*submarine*) schnorchel *m.*

snort [snoɪt] *n* (*person*) grognement *m*; (*animal*) ébrouement *m.* *v* grogner; s'ébrouer.

snout [snaut] *n* museau *m.*

snow [snou] *n* neige *f.* **snow-drift** *n* congère *f.* **snowdrop** *n* perce-neige *m.* **snowflake** *n* flocon de neige *m.* **snowman** *n* bonhomme de neige *m.* **snow-plough** *n* chasse-neige *m invar.* **snow-shoe** *n* raquette *f.* **snowstorm** *n* tempête de neige *f.* *v* neiger. **be snowed under with** être submergé de. **snowy** *adj* neigeux; de neige.

snowball ['snoubɔɪl] *n* boule de neige *f.* *v* (*increase*) faire boule de neige.

snub [snʌb] *n* rebuffade *f.* *v* (*person*) snober; repousser.

snuff [snʌf] *n* tabac à priser. **snuffbox** *n* tabatière *f.* **take snuff** priser.

snug [snʌg] *adj* douillet, -ette, confortable.

snuggle ['snʌgl] *v* se blottir, se pelotonner.

so [sou] *adv* si, tellement, aussi; (*thus*) ainsi. *conj* donc. **and so on** et ainsi de suite. **if so** si oui. **is that so?** vraiment? **... or so** à peu près ... . **so as to** afin de. **so-called** *adj* soi-disant *invar.* **so much** *or* **many** tant (de). **so-so** *adj* (*coll*) comme ci comme ça. **so that** pour (que). **so what?** et alors?

soak [souk] *v* (faire) tremper. **soak in** pénétrer. **soak up** absorber. **soaking** *n* trempage *m.* **soaking wet** trempé.

soap [soup] *n* savon *m.* **soap-box** *n* tribune improvisée *f.* **soap-dish** *n* porte-savon *m.* **soap opera** (*coll*) mélo à épisodes *m.* **soap powder** lessive *f.* *v* savonner. **soapy** *adj* savonneux.

soar [soɪ] *v* monter en flèche; (*hope*) grandir.

sob [sob] *n* sanglot *m.* *v* sangloter.

sober ['soubə] *n* sérieux; modéré; (*not drunk*) pas ivre. *v* **sober up** désenivrer.

soccer ['sokə] *n* football *m.*

sociable ['souʃəbl] *adj* sociable.

social ['souʃəl] *adj* social; (*life, etc.*) mondain. **social club** association amicale *f.* **social science** sciences humaines *f pl.* **social security** aide sociale *f.* **social work** assistance sociale *f.* **socialism** *n* social-

isme *m*. **socialist** *n*(*m*+*f*), *adj* socialiste.
socialize *v* fréquenter des gens.
society [sə'saiəti] *n* société *f*.
sociology [sousi'olədʒi] *n* sociologie *f*.
sociological *adj* sociologique. **sociologist**
n sociologue *m*, *f*.
sock [sok] *n* chaussette *f*.
socket ['sokit] *n* cavité *f*; (*elec*) prise de
courant *f*.
soda ['soudə] *n* (*chem*) soude *f*; (*water*)
eau de Seltz *f*.
sodden ['sodn] *adj* détrempé.
sofa ['soufə] *n* sofa *m*.
Sofia ['soufjə] *n* Sofia.
soft [soft] *adj* doux, douce; (*butter*, *clay*,
etc.) mou, molle; (*coll*) stupide. **soft-
boiled** *adj* (*egg*) à la coque. **soft drink**
boisson non alcoolisée *f*. **soft toy** jouet
de peluche *m*. **soften** *v* (s')adoucir; (se)
ramollir. **softness** *n* douceur *f*; mollesse
f.
soggy ['sogi] *adj* détrempé.
soil[1] [soil] *n* sol *m*, terre *f*.
soil[2] [soil] *v* salir.
solar ['soulə] *adj* solaire, du soleil.
sold [sould] *V* **sell**.
solder ['soldə] *n* soudure *f*. *v* souder. **soldering iron** fer à souder *m*.
soldier ['souldʒə] *n* soldat *m*. *v* **soldier on**
persévérer.
sole[1] [soul] *adj* seul, unique; exclusif.
sole[2] [soul] *n* (*of shoe*) semelle *f*; (*of foot*)
plante *f*. *v* ressemeler.
sole[3] [soul] *n* (*fish*) sole *f*.
solemn ['soləm] *adj* solennel. **solemnity** *n*
solennité *f*.
solicitor [sə'lisitə] *n* avocat *m*.
solicitude [sə'lisitjuːd] *n* sollicitude *f*.
solid ['solid] *adj* solide; (*not hollow*) plein;
(*line*) continu. *n* solide *m*. **solids** *pl n*
(*food*) aliments solides *m pl*. **solidarity** *n*
solidarité *f*. **solidify** *v* (se) solidifier; (se)
congeler.
solitary ['solitəri] *adj* solitaire; seul,
unique.
solitude ['solitjuːd] *n* solitude *f*.
solo ['soulou] *n* solo *m*. *adj* solo *invar*;
(*flight*) en solitaire. **soloist** *n* soliste *m*, *f*.
solstice ['solstis] *n* solstice *m*.
soluble ['soljubl] *adj* soluble.
solution [sə'luːʃən] *n* solution *f*.
solve [solv] *v* résoudre, trouver la solution de.
solvent ['solvənt] *adj* (*finance*) solvable. *n*

(*chem*) solvant *m*. **solvency** *n* solvabilité
f.
sombre ['sombə] *adj* sombre, morne.
some [sʌm] *adj* du, de la; (*pl*) des;
certains; (*unspecified*) quelque. *pron*
quelques-uns; (*before verb*) en. *adv* environ. **somebody** *or* **someone** *pron*
quelqu'un. **somehow** *adv* d'une façon ou
d'une autre. **something** *pron* quelque
chose. **sometime** *adv* un de ces jours.
sometimes *adv* quelquefois. **somewhat**
adv quelque peu. **somewhere** *adv* quelque
part. **somewhere else** ailleurs.
somersault ['sʌməsoːlt] *n* culbute *f*. *v*
faire la culbute.
son [sʌn] *n* fils *m*. **son-in-law** *n* gendre *m*.
sonata [sə'naːtə] *n* sonate *f*.
song [soŋ] *n* chanson *f*; (*birds*) chant *m*.
sonic ['sonik] *adj* sonique. **sonic boom**
détonation supersonique *f*.
sonnet ['sonit] *n* sonnet *m*.
soon [suːn] *adv* bientôt; (*early*) tôt. **as
soon as** dès que. **sooner or later** tôt ou
tard.
soot [sut] *n* suie *f*.
soothe [suːð] *v* calmer, apaiser. **soothing**
adj apaisant; (*ointment*) lénitif.
sophisticated [sə'fistikeitid] *adj* raffiné,
élégant; (*machinery*) sophistiqué.
sopping ['sopiŋ] *adj* trempé.
soprano [sə'praːnou] *n* soprano *m*, *f*.
sordid ['soːdid] *adj* sordide.
sore [soː] *adj* douloureux. **sore point**
point délicat *m*. *n* plaie *f*. **sorely** *adv* (*bit-
terly*) amèrement; (*greatly*) fortement.
soreness *n* endolorissement *m*.
sorrow ['sorou] *n* peine *f*, chagrin *m*. *v* se
lamenter. **sorrowful** *adj* triste, affligé.
sorry ['sori] *adj* désolé; (*plight*) triste. **feel
sorry for** plaindre. *interj* pardon!
sort [soːt] *n* sorte *f*, genre *m*; (*brand*)
marque *f*. *v* trier, classer. **sort out** ranger;
(*problem*) régler; arranger. **sorting office**
bureau de tri *m*.
soufflé ['suːflei] *n* soufflé *m*.
sought [soːt] *V* **seek**.
soul [soul] *n* âme *f*. **soul-destroying** *adj*
démoralisant. **soulful** *adj* expressif.
sound[1] [saund] *n* (*noise*) son *m*, bruit *m*.
sound barrier mur du son *m*. **sound
effects** bruitage *m sing*. **soundproof** *adj*
insonorisé. **sound-track** *n* piste sonore *f*.
v sonner, retentir; (*seem*) sembler.
sound[2] [saund] *adj* sain, solide; (*advice*,

etc.) sensé; (*sleep*) profond. **be sound asleep** être profondément endormi.
sound³ [saund] *v* (*depth*) sonder.
soup [suːp] *n* soupe *f*, potage *m*. **soup-plate** *n* assiette creuse *f*.
sour [sauə] *adj* aigre, acide; (*person*) acerbe, revêche. *v* (s')aigrir.
source [soːs] *n* source *f*.
south [sauθ] *n* sud *m*. *adj also* **southerly, southern** sud *invar*; au *or* du sud. *adv* au sud; vers le sud. **southbound** *adj* sud *invar*. **south-east** *nm*, *adj* sud-est. **south-west** *nm*, *adj* sud-ouest.
souvenir [suːvə'niə] *n* souvenir *m*.
sovereign ['sovrin] *n*, *adj* souverain, -e.
*sow¹ [sou] *v* semer, ensemencer.
sow² [sau] *n* truie *f*.
sown [soun] *V* **sow¹**.
soya ['soiə] *n* soja *m*. **soya bean** graine de soja *f*. **soy sauce** sauce au soja *f*.
spa [spaː] *n* station thermale *f*.
space [speis] *n* espace *m*, place *f*. **spaceman** *n* astronaute *m*. **spaceship** *n* engin spatial *m*. *v* espacer. **spacious** *adj* spacieux.
spade¹ [speid] *n* bêche *f*, pelle *f*.
spade² [speid] *n* (*cards*) pique *m*.
spaghetti [spə'geti] *n* spaghetti *m pl*.
Spain [spein] *n* Espagne *f*. **Spaniard** *n* Espagnol, -e *m*, *f*. **Spanish** *nm*, *adj* espagnol.
span [span] *n* envergure *f*, portée *f*; (*bridge*) travée *f*; (*time*) espace *m*, durée *f*. *v* enjamber.
spaniel ['spanjəl] *n* épagneul *m*.
spank [spaŋk] *v* donner une fessée à. **spanking** *n* fessée *f*.
spanner ['spanə] *n* clef (à écrous) *f*.
spare [speə] *adj* de réserve, de trop. **spare part** (*mot*) pièce détachée *f*. **spare-rib** *n* (*cookery*) côtelette dans l'échine *f*. **spare room** chambre d'ami *f*. **spare time** temps libre *m*. **spare tyre** pneu de rechange *m*; (*coll*) bourrelet *m*. **spare wheel** roue de secours *f*. *v* se passer de; (*save*) épargner. **sparing** *adj* limité, modéré.
spark [spaːk] *n* étincelle *f*. **spark-plug** *n* bougie *f*. *v* jeter des étincelles. **spark off** provoquer.
sparkle ['spaːkl] *n* scintillement *m*; (*in eye*) étincelle *f*. *v* étinceler, scintiller. **sparkling** *adj* (*drink*) pétillant.
sparrow ['sparou] *n* moineau *m*.
sparse [spaːs] *adj* clairsemé. **sparsely** *adv* peu.

spasm ['spazəm] *n* spasme *m*; (*fit*) accès *m*. **spasmodic** *adj* (*med*) spasmodique; irrégulier.
spastic ['spastik] *n*, *adj* handicapé, -e moteur.
spat [spat] *V* **spit¹**.
spatial ['speiʃl] *adj* spatial.
spatula ['spatjulə] *n* spatule *f*.
spawn [spoin] *n* frai *m*. *v* frayer.
*speak [spiːk] *v* parler. **speak up** parler fort. **speaker** *n* orateur *m*; (*loudspeaker*) haut-parleur *m*.
spear [spiə] *n* lance *f*; (*asparagus*) pointe *f*.
special ['speʃəl] *adj* spécial, particulier; extraordinaire. **specialist** *n* spécialiste *m*, *f*. **speciality** *n* spécialité *f*. **specialize** *v* se spécialiser.
species ['spiːʃiːz] *n* espèce *f*.
specify ['spesifai] *v* spécifier. **specific** *adj* précis; (*science*) spécifique. **specification** *n* spécification *f*; stipulation *f*.
specimen ['spesimin] *n* spécimen *m*; (*urine*) échantillon *m*; (*blood*) prélèvement *m*.
speck [spek] *n* grain *m*; petite tache *f*. **speckle** *v* tacheter.
spectacle ['spektəkl] *n* spectacle *m*. **spectacles** *pl n* lunettes *f pl*. **spectacular** *adj* spectaculaire.
spectator [spek'teitə] *n* spectateur, -trice *m*, *f*.
spectrum ['spektrəm] *n* spectre *m*; (*range*) gamme *f*.
speculate ['spekjuleit] *v* spéculer; s'interroger. **speculation** *n* spéculation *f*; conjecture *f*. **speculative** *adj* spéculatif.
sped [sped] *V* **speed**.
speech [spiːtʃ] *n* (*faculty*) parole *f*; articulation *f*; (*address*) discours *m*. **speech day** distribution des prix *f*. **speech impediment** défaut d'élocution *m*. **speech therapy** orthophonie *f*. **speechless** *adj* muet.
*speed [spiːd] *n* vitesse *f*; rapidité *f*. **speedboat** *n* vedette *f*. **speed limit** limitation de vitesse *f*. **speedometer** *n* compteur de vitesse *m*. *v* (*mot*) conduire trop vite. **speed along** aller à toute vitesse. **speed up** aller plus vite; accélérer. **speeding** *n* excès de vitesse *m*. **speedy** *adj* rapide.
*spell¹ [spel] *v* épeler; (*write*) écrire; signifier. **spelling** *n* orthographe *f*.

spell² [spel] *n* (*magic*) charme *m*, formule magique *f*. **spellbound** *adj* subjugué, envoûté.

spell³ [spel] *n* période *f*; (*turn*) tour *m*.

spelt [spelt] *V* **spell¹**.

*spend [spend] *v* (*money*) dépenser; (*time*) passer. **spendthrift** *n* dépensier, -ère *m, f*. **spending** *n* dépenses *f pl*. **spending money** argent de poche *m*.

spent [spent] *V* **spend**.

sperm [spəɪm] *n* sperme *m*.

spew [spjuː] *v* vomir.

sphere [sfiə] *n* sphère *f*; domaine *m*. **spherical** *adj* sphérique.

spice [spais] *n* épice *f*. *v* épicer. **spicy** *adj* épicé.

spider ['spaidə] *n* araignée *f*.

spike [spaik] *n* pointe *f*.

*spill [spil] *v* renverser, (se) répandre.

spilt [spilt] *V* **spill**.

*spin [spin] *n* tournoiement *m*; (*drying*) essorage *m*; (*coll: ride*) balade *f*. *v* (*wool, etc.*) filer; (*turn*) (faire) tourner, tournoyer. **spin-dry** *v* essorer. **spin-dryer** *n* essoreuse *f*. **spin out** faire durer. **spinning** *n* filage *m*. **spinning top** toupie *f*. **spinning wheel** rouet *m*.

spinach ['spinidʒ] *n* (*bot*) épinard *m*; (*cookery*) épinards *m pl*.

spindle ['spindl] *n* (*spinning*) fuseau *m*, broche *f*; (*tech*) axe *m*, tige *f*. **spindly** *adj* grêle.

spine [spain] *n* (*anat*) colonne vertébrale; épine *f*; (*book*) dos *m*. **spinal** *adj* spinal, vertébral. **spiny** *adj* épineux.

spinster ['spinstə] *n* célibataire *f*.

spiral ['spaiərəl] *adj* en spirale. **spiral staircase** escalier tournant *m*. *n* spirale *f*.

spire ['spaiə] *n* flèche *f*.

spirit ['spirit] *n* esprit *m*; courage *m*; alcool *m*. **spirit-level** *n* niveau à bulle *m*. **spirited** *adj* fougueux. **spiritual** *adj* spirituel. **spiritualism** *n* spiritisme *m*. **spiritualist** *n* spirite *m, f*.

*spit¹ [spit] *n* crachat *m*; salive *f*. *v* cracher.

spit² [spit] *n* (*cookery*) broche *f*; (*geog*) pointe *f*.

spite [spait] *n* rancune *f*. **in spite of** malgré. *v* vexer. **spiteful** *adj* malveillant.

splash [splaʃ] *n* éclaboussement *m*; (*sound*) plouf *m*; (*mark*) éclaboussure *f*, tache *f*. *v* éclabousser.

spleen [spliːn] *n* (*anat*) rate *f*; mauvaise humeur *f*.

splendid ['splendid] *adj* splendide; excellent. **splendour** *n* splendeur *f*.

splice [splais] *v* épisser.

splint [splint] *n* éclisse *f*.

splinter ['splintə] *n* éclat *m*; (*in finger*) écharde *f*. *v* (se) fendre en éclats, (se) briser en éclats.

*split [split] *n* fente *f*, fissure *f*. *v* (se) fendre; (se) diviser; (*share*) (se) partager. **split second** fraction de seconde *f*.

splutter ['splʌtə] *v* (*person*) bredouiller; (*engine*) bafouiller; (*fire, fat, etc.*) crépiter. *n* bredouillement *m*; bafouillage *m*; crépitement *m*.

*spoil [spoil] *v* gâter; (*damage*) (s')abîmer. **spoil-sport** *n* trouble-fête *m, f*. **spoils** *pl n* butin *m sing*.

spoke¹ [spouk] *V* **speak**.

spoke² [spouk] *n* rayon *m*.

spoken ['spoukn] *V* **speak**.

spokesman ['spouksmən] *n* porte-parole *m invar*.

sponge [spʌndʒ] *n* éponge *f*; (*cake*) gâteau de Savoie *m*. **sponge bag** sac de toilette *m*. *v* éponger. **sponge on** vivre au crochets de. **spongy** *adj* spongieux.

sponsor ['sponsə] *n* personne (*f*) or organisme (*m*) qui assure le patronage; (*for loan*) répondant, -e *m, f*; (*fund-raising*) donateur, -trice *m, f*. *v* patronner. **sponsorship** *n* patronage *m*.

spontaneous [spon'teinjəs] *adj* spontané. **spontaneity** *n* spontanéité *f*.

spool [spuːl] *n* bobine *f*.

spoon [spuːn] *n* cuiller *f*. **spoonful** *n* cuillerée *f*.

sporadic [spə'radik] *adj* sporadique.

sport [spoɪt] *n* sport *m*. **sports car** voiture de sport *f*. **sports jacket** veste sport *f*. **sportsman** *n* sportif *m*. **sportswoman** *n* sportive *f*. *v* exhiber. **sporting** *adj* sportif. **sportive** *adj* folâtre.

spot [spot] *n* (*mark*) tache *f*; (*pimple*) bouton *m*; (*polka dot*) pois *m*; (*place*) endroit *m*; (*small amount*) goutte *f*, grain *m*. **on the spot** sur le champ. **spot check** *n* contrôle intermittent *m*. **spotlight** *n* (rayon de) projecteur *m*. *v* tacher; (*see*) apercevoir. **spotless** *adj* immaculé. **spotted** *adj* tacheté; à pois. **spotty** *adj* boutonneux.

spouse [spaus] *n* (*law*) conjoint, -e *m, f*.

spout [spaut] *n* bec *m*; jet *m*. *v* (faire) jaillir; (*coll: recite*) débiter.

sprain [sprein] *n* entorse *f*. *v* fouler.

sprang [spraŋ] *V* **spring**.

sprawl [sprɔil] *v* s'étaler, être affalé.

spray[1] [sprei] *n* gouttelettes *f pl*; (*from aerosol*) pulvérisation *f*; bombe *f*, aérosol *m*. *v* (*water*) asperger; vaporiser, pulvériser.

spray[2] [sprei] *n* (*flowers*) gerbe *f*; branche *f*.

*****spread** [spred] *n* propagation *f*, diffusion *f*; (*span*) envergure *f*; (*paste*) pâte *f*; (*coll: meal*) festin *m*. *v* (s')étaler, (s')étendre; (se) propager, (se) communiquer. **spread-eagled** *adj* vautré. **spread out** (s')étaler; se disperser.

spree [sprii] *n* fête *f*.

sprig [sprig] *n* brin *m*.

sprightly ['spraitli] *adj* alerte.

*****spring** [spriŋ] *n* (*leap*) bond *m*; (*coil*) ressort *m*; (*water*) source *f*; (*season*) printemps *m*. **spring-board** *n* tremplin *m*. **spring-cleaning** *n* grand nettoyage *m*. **spring onion** ciboule *f*. *v* bondir. **spring up** surgir, jaillir. **springy** *adj* souple.

sprinkle ['spriŋkl] *v* asperger; (*sugar, etc.*) saupoudrer. **sprinkler** *n* (*garden*) arroseur *m*; (*fire*) diffuseur *m*. **sprinkling** *n* aspersion *f*; légère couche *f*.

sprint [sprint] *n* sprint *m*. *v* (*sport*) sprinter; foncer un sprint.

sprout [spraut] *n* pousse *f*, germe *m*. **Brussels sprouts** choux de Bruxelles *m pl*. *v* pousser, germer.

spruce [spruis] *v* **spruce up** faire beau *or* belle.

sprung [sprʌŋ] *V* **spring**.

spun [spʌn] *V* **spin**.

spur [spəi] *n* éperon *m*. **on the spur of the moment** sous l'impulsion du moment. *v* éperonner.

spurious ['spjuəriəs] *adj* faux, fausse.

spurn [spəin] *v* repousser.

spurt [spəit] *n* (*water*) jet *m*; (*energy*) sursaut *m*; effort soudain *m*. *v* jaillir.

spy [spai] *n* espion, -onne *m, f*. *v* espionner; (*see*) apercevoir. **spying** *n* espionnage *m*.

squabble ['skwobl] *n* chamaillerie *f*. *v* se chamailler.

squad [skwod] *n* escouade *f*, groupe *m*.

squadron ['skwodrən] *n* (*mil*) escadron *m*; (*naut*) escadrille *f*.

squalid ['skwolid] *adj* misérable, sordide; (*dirty*) sale.

squall [skwɔil] *n* rafale *f*.

squander ['skwondə] *v* gaspiller.

square [skweə] *n* carré *m*; (*on chessboard, grid*) case *f*; (*in town*) place *f*. *adj* carré; en ordre. *v* carrer; (*settle*) régler.

squash [skwoʃ] *n* (*sport*) squash *m*; (*drink*) sirop *m*; (*crush*) cohue *f*. *v* (s')écraser; (*together*) (se) serrer.

squat [skwot] *adj* ramassé, courtaud. *v* s'accroupir; (*in house*) faire du squattage. **squatter** *n* squatter *m*.

squawk [skwoik] *v* pousser des gloussements. *n* gloussement *m*, cri rauque *m*.

squeak [skwiik] *n* grincement *m*; (*mouse, etc.*) petit cri aigu *m*. *v* grincer; (*mouse*) vagir.

squeal [skwiil] *n* cri aigu *m*; (*brakes*) grincement *m*. *v* pousser un cri aigu; grincer.

squeamish ['skwiimiʃ] *adj* délicat, facilement dégoûté.

squeeze [skwiiz] *n* pression *f*. *v* presser, serrer; (*extract*) exprimer.

squid [skwid] *n* calmar *m*.

squiggle ['skwigl] *n* gribouillis *m*. *v* gribouiller.

squint [skwint] *n* (*med*) strabisme *m*; (*glance*) coup d'œil *m*. *v* loucher.

squirm [skwəim] *v* se tortiller; (*person*) avoir un haut-le-corps.

squirrel ['skwirəl] *n* écureuil *m*.

squirt [skwəit] *n* jet *m*. *v* (faire) jaillir; asperger.

stab [stab] *n* coup de couteau *m*. *v* poignarder; donner un coup de couteau à.

stabilize ['steibilaiz] *v* stabiliser. **stabilizer** *n* stabilisateur *m*.

stable[1] ['steibl] *n* écurie *f*.

stable[2] ['steibl] *adj* stable; solide; constant. **stability** *n* stabilité *f*; solidité *f*.

staccato [stə'kaitou] *adv* staccato. *adj* (*voice, sounds, etc.*) saccadé.

stack [stak] *n* (*pile*) tas *m*; (*hay, etc.*) meule *f*; (*chimneys*) souche de cheminée *f*. **stacks of** (*coll*) un tas de. *v* empiler, entasser.

stadium ['steidiəm] *n* stade *m*.

staff [staif] *n* personnel *m*; bâton *m*. **staff-room** *n* (*school*) salle des professeurs *f*.

stag [stag] *n* cerf *m*. **stag party** (*coll*) réunion entre hommes *f*.

stage [steidʒ] *n* (*theatre*) scène *f*; (*platform*) estrade *f*; (*point*) étape *f*. **stage fright** trac *m*. **stage-manager** *n* régisseur *m.* **stage name** nom de théâtre *m.* **stage whisper** aparté *m. v* monter; organiser. **stagger** ['stagə] *v* chanceler; (*amaze*) stupéfier; (*payments, etc.*) échelonner. **staggering** *adj* renversant.

stagnant ['stagnənt] *adj* stagnant. **stagnate** *v* croupir, stagner. **stagnation** *n* stagnation *f.*

staid [steid] *adj* (*person*) posé; (*opinion*) pondéré.

stain [stein] *n* tache *f*; colorant *m.* **stain remover** détachant *m. v* tacher; (*wood*) teinter. **stained glass** verre coloré *m*; (*windows*) vitraux *m pl.* **stainless steel** acier inoxydable *m.*

stair [steə] *n* marche *f.* **staircase** *n* escalier *m.* **stairs** *pl n* escalier *m sing.*

stake¹ [steik] *n* (*post*) pieu *m*; (*for execution*) bûcher *m. v* jalonner.

stake² [steik] *n* (*betting*) enjeu *m*; intérêt *m.* **at stake** en jeu. *v* jouer.

stale [steil] *adj* (*bread*) rassis; (*air*) confiné; (*joke*) rebattu. **staleness** *n* manque de fraîcheur *m.*

stalemate ['steilmeit] *n* (*chess*) pat *m*; impasse *f.*

stalk¹ [stɔik] *n* (*plant*) tige *f*; (*fruit*) queue *f.*

stalk² [stɔik] *v* traquer. **stalk in/out** entrer/sortir avec raideur.

stall¹ [stɔil] *n* (*market*) éventaire *m*; kiosque *m*; (*theatre*) fauteuil d'orchestre *m*; (*cowshed*) stalle *f.* **stalls** *pl n* orchestre *m sing. v* (*car, etc.*) caler.

stall² [stɔil] *v* (*delay*) atermoyer. **stall off** tenir à distance.

stallion ['staljən] *n* étalon *m.*

stamina ['staminə] *n* vigueur *f*, résistance *f.*

stammer ['stamə] *n* bégaiement *m. v* bégayer.

stamp [stamp] *n* timbre *m*; (*mark*) cachet *m*; (*with foot*) trépignement *m.* **stamp-collecting** *n* philatélie *f. v* timbrer, tamponner; (*with foot*) taper du pied, trépigner.

stampede [stam'piid] *n* débandade *f*; (*rush*) ruée *f. v* fuir à la débandade; se ruer.

*****stand** [stand] *n* position *f*; support *m*; (*comm*) étalage *m*; (*at exhibition*) stand *m. v* être debout; (*get up*) se lever; (*put*) mettre; (*tolerate*) supporter; (*be based*) reposer. **stand for** représenter; tolérer.

stand out ressortir. **standstill** *n* arrêt *m.* **come to a standstill** s'immobiliser, s'arrêter. **stand up for** défendre.

standard ['standəd] *n* norme *f*, critère *m*, niveau (voulu) *m*; (*flag*) étendard *m. adj* normal, ordinaire; (*comm*) standard *invar*; (*measure*) étalon *invar*; correct. **standard lamp** lampadaire *m.* **standardize** *v* standardiser.

standing ['standiŋ] *adj* debout; fixe; permanent. **standing order** (*bank*) virement automatique *m. n* importance *f*, standing *m*; durée *f.*

stank [staŋk] *V* **stink.**

stanza ['stanzə] *n* strophe *f.*

staple¹ [steipl] *n* (*papers*) agrafe *f*; (*tech*) crampon *m. v* agrafer; cramponner.

staple² [steipl] *adj* principal; de base.

star [stɑi] *n* étoile *f*; astérisque *m*; (*cinema, etc.*) vedette *f.* **starfish** *n* étoile de mer *f. v* étoiler; (*film*) avoir pour vedette; (*person*) être la vedette. **stardom** *n* célébrité *f.* **starry** *adj* étoilé.

starboard ['stɑibəd] *n* tribord *m.*

starch [stɑitʃ] *n* amidon *m. v* amidonner. **starchy** *adj* (*food*) féculent; (*person*) guindé.

stare [steə] *n* regard fixe *m. v* dévisager, regarder fixement.

stark [stɑik] *adj* désolé, austère; (*stiff*) raide; (*utter*) pur. **stark naked** complètement nu.

starling ['stɑiliŋ] *n* étourneau *m.*

start [stɑit] *n* commencement *m*, départ *m*; (*jump*) sursaut *m. v* commencer; (*clock, etc.*) mettre en marche; (*leave*) partir; (*car*) démarrer; sursauter. **starter** *n* (*sport*) starter *m*; (*mot*) démarreur *m*; (*meal*) hors-d'œuvre *m.*

startle ['stɑitl] *v* faire sursauter. **startling** *adj* surprenant.

starve [stɑiv] *v* manquer de nourriture; (*to death*) (faire) mourir de faim; (*deliberately*) affamer; (*deprive*) priver. **starvation** *n* inanition *f*, famine *f.* **starving** *adj* affamé. **be starving** (*coll*) avoir une faim de loup.

state [steit] *n* état *m*; pompe *f.* **statesman** *n* homme d'État *m. v* déclarer; formuler; fixer. **stately** *adj* majestueux. **statement** *n* déclaration; (*law*) déposition *f*; (*bank*) relevé *m.*

static ['statik] *adj* statique. *n* (*elec, radio, etc.*) parasites *m pl.*

station ['steɪʃən] *n* (*rail*) gare *f*; (*radio, underground*) station *f*; (*position*) poste *m*; (*in life*) rang *m*. *v* poster, placer.

stationary ['steɪʃənəri] *adj* stationnaire.

stationer ['steɪʃənə] *n* papetier, -ère *m, f*. **stationer's** *n* papeterie *f*. **stationery** *n* articles de bureau *m pl*; papier à lettres *m*.

statistics [stə'tistiks] *n* (*science*) statistique *f*. *pl n* statistiques *f pl*. **statistical** *adj* statistique.

statue ['statjuː] *n* statue *f*.

stature ['statʃə] *n* stature *f*; importance *f*, envergure *f*.

status ['steɪtəs] *n* situation *f*; prestige *m*.

statute ['statjuːt] *n* loi *f*. **statutory** *adj* statutaire; légal.

staunch [stɔːntʃ] *adj* loyal, dévoué.

stay [steɪ] *n* séjour *m*. *v* rester; loger.

steadfast ['stedfaːst] *adj* ferme; constant.

steady ['stedi] *adj* stable, solide; constant, régulier. *v* maintenir; (*person*) reprendre son aplomb; (se) calmer. **steadily** *adv* fermement; progressivement; sans arrêt. **steadiness** *n* stabilité *f*; constance *f*.

steak [steik] *n* bifteck *m*; (*of pork, fish*) tranche *f*.

*****steal** [stiːl] *v* voler. **stealing** *n* vol *m*.

stealthy ['stelθi] *adj* furtif.

steam [stiːm] *n* vapeur *f*. **steam-roller** *n* rouleau compresseur *m*. *v* fumer; (*cookery*) cuire à la vapeur. **steam up** se couvrir de buée.

steel [stiːl] *n* acier *m*. **steel wool** paille de fer *f*. **steelworks** *n* aciérie *f*. **steely** *adj* dur, d'acier.

steep¹ [stiːp] *adj* raide.

steep² [stiːp] *v* tremper.

steeple ['stiːpl] *n* clocher *m*. **steeplechase** *n* steeple *m*.

steer [stiə] *v* (*ship*) gouverner; (*car*) conduire; (*person*) guider. **steering** *n* conduite *f*. **steering-wheel** *n* volant *m*.

stem¹ [stem] *n* tige *f*; (*glass*) pied *m*. *v* **stem from** provenir de.

stem² [stem] *v* (*stop*) contenir, endiguer.

stench [stentʃ] *n* puanteur *f*.

stencil ['stensl] *n* pochoir *m*; (*typing*) stencil *m*.

step [step] *n* pas *m*; mesure *f*; (*stair*) marche *f*. **step-ladder** *n* escabeau *m*. *v* faire un pas; marcher. **step up** augmenter, intensifier.

stepbrother ['stepbrʌðə] *n* demi-frère *m*.

stepdaughter ['stepdɔːtə] *n* belle-fille *f*.

stepfather ['stepfaːðə] *n* beau-père *m*.

stepmother ['stepmʌðə] *n* belle-mère *f*.

stepsister ['stepsistə] *n* demi-sœur *f*.

stepson ['stepsʌn] *n* beau-fils *m*.

stereo ['steriou] *nf, adj* stéréo. **stereophonic** *adj* stéréophonique.

stereotype ['steriətaip] *n* stéréotype *m*; (*printing*) cliché *m*. *v* stéréotyper; clicher.

sterile ['sterail] *adj* stérile. **sterility** *n* stérilité *f*. **sterilization** *n* stérilisation *f*. **sterilize** *v* stériliser.

sterling ['stɜːliŋ] *n* livres sterling *f pl. adj* (*silver*) fin; (*character*) solide.

stern¹ [stɜːn] *adj* sévère.

stern² [stɜːn] *n* arrière *m*.

stethoscope ['steθəskoup] *n* stéthoscope *m*.

stew [stjuː] *n* ragoût *m*. *v* (*meat*) cuire en ragoût; (*fruit*) faire cuire.

steward ['stjuəd] *n* intendant *m*; (*plane, ship*) steward *m*. **stewardess** *n* hôtesse *f*.

stick¹ [stik] *n* bâton *m*; petite branche *f*; (*walking*) canne *f*.

*****stick²** [stik] *v* (*stab*) planter, enfoncer; (*glue*) coller (*put*) mettre; (*get jammed*) être bloqué; (*slang: put up with*) supporter; (*stay*) rester. **stick out** sortir, (faire) dépasser. **stick up for** défendre. **sticky** *adj* poisseux, gluant.

stickler ['stiklə] *n* **be a stickler for** insister sur; être pointilleux sur.

stiff [stif] *adj* raide, rigide; (*hard to move*) dur; (*exam*) difficile; (*cool*) froid. **stiff neck** torticolis *m*. **stiffen** *v* (se) raidir; renforcer. **stiffness** *n* raideur *f*.

stifle ['staifl] *v* étouffer; (*smile, etc.*) réprimer. **stifling** *adj* suffocant.

stigma ['stigmə] *n* stigmate *m*.

stile [stail] *n* échalier *m*.

still¹ [stil] *adv* encore; (*anyway*) quand même; (*sit, stand*) sans bouger. *adj* calme, tranquille. **stillborn** *adj* mort-né. **still life** nature morte. *n* (*cinema*) photo *f*.

still² [stil] *n* alambic *m*; distillerie *f*.

stilt [stilt] *n* échasse *f*. **stilted** *adj* guindé.

stimulus ['stimjuləs] *n, pl* -**li** stimulus (*pl* -li) *m*; impulsion *f*, stimulant *m*. **stimulant** *nm, adj* stimulant. **stimulate** *v* stimuler. **stimulation** *n* stimulation *f*.

*****sting** [stiŋ] *n* (*insect*) dard *m*; (*wound*) piqûre *f*; (*iodine*) brûlure. *v* piquer; brûler; (*whip*) cingler.

*stink [stiŋk] *n* puanteur *f*. *v* puer, empester.

stint [stint] *n* ration de travail *f*. *v* lésiner sur.

stipulate ['stipjuleit] *v* stipuler. **stipulation** *n* stipulation *f*.

stir [stəɪ] *n* agitation *f*, sensation *f*. *v* (*tea, etc.*) tourner; (*move*) agiter, remuer; exciter.

stirrup ['stirəp] *n* étrier *m*.

stitch [stitʃ] *n* (*sewing*) point *m*; (*knitting*) maille *f*; (*med*) point de suture *m*; (*pain*) point de côté *m*. *v* coudre; (*med*) suturer.

stoat [stout] *n* hermine *f*.

stock [stok] *n* réserve *f*; (*farm*) cheptel *m*; (*cookery*) bouillon *m*; (*lineage*) souche *f*. **stockbroker** *n* agent de change *m*. **Stock Exchange** Bourse *f*. **stockpile** *v* stocker. **stocks and shares** valeurs *f pl*. **stocktaking** *n* inventaire *m*. *v* approvisionner.

Stockholm ['stokhoum] *n* Stockholm.

stocking ['stokiŋ] *n* bas *m*. **in one's stocking feet** sans chaussures.

stocky ['stoki] *adj* trapu.

stodge [stodʒ] (*coll*) *n* aliment bourratif *m*. **stodgy** *adj* bourratif.

stoical ['stouikl] *adj* stoïque.

stoke [stouk] *v* (*fire*) garnir; (*furnace*) alimenter; (*boiler*) chauffer.

stole[1] [stoul] *V* **steal**.

stole[2] [stoul] *n* étole *f*.

stolen ['stoulən] *V* **steal**.

stomach ['stʌmək] *n* estomac *m*; (*abdomen*) ventre *m*. **stomach-ache** *n* mal à l'estomac *m*. *v* supporter.

stone [stoun] *n* pierre *f*; (*of fruit*) noyau *m*; (*med*) calcul *m*. **stone-cold** *adj* complètement froid. *v* lapider; dénoyauter. **stony** *adj* pierreux; dur.

stood [stud] *V* **stand**.

stool [stuɪl] *n* tabouret *m*.

stoop [stuɪp] *v* se pencher, se courber; avoir le dos voûté; (*descend*) s'abaisser (jusqu'à).

stop [stop] *n* arrêt *m*. *v* (s')arrêter; cesser; (*block*) boucher; (*prevent*) empêcher. **stop-press** *n* dernière heure *f*. **stop thief!** au voleur! **stop-watch** *n* chronomètre *m*. **stoppage** *n* arrêt *m*; obstruction *f*; (*strike*) grève *f*. **stopper** *n* bouchon *m*.

store [stoɪ] *n* provision *f*; (*depot*) entrepôt *m*; (*shop*) magasin *m*. *v* mettre en réserve; emmagasiner. **storage** *n* entreposage *m*. **storage space** espace de rangement *m*.

storey ['stoɪri] *n* étage *m*.

stork [stoɪk] *n* cicogne *f*.

storm [stoɪm] *n* tempête *f*; (*thunder*) orage *m*. *v* (*mil*) prendre d'assaut; (*wind, rain*) faire rage; (*person*) fulminer. **stormy** *adj* orageux.

story ['stoɪri] *n* histoire *f*.

stout [staut] *adj* gros, grosse; solide; intrépide. *n* stout *m*.

stove [stouv] *n* (*cooker*) fourneau *m*; (*heater*) poêle *m*.

stow [stou] *v* ranger. **stow away** voyager clandestinement. **stowaway** *n* passager clandestin, passagère clandestine *m*, *f*.

straddle ['stradl] *v* enfourcher, enjamber, être à califourchon (sur).

straggle ['stragl] *v* (*plant*) pousser au hasard; (*hair*) être en désordre; (*village*) s'étendre en longueur. **straggler** *n* traînard, -e *m*, *f*.

straight [streit] *adj* droit; en ordre; franc, franche. *adv* droit; (*directly*) tout droit. **straight ahead** tout droit. **straight away** tout de suite. **straightforward** *adj* simple; honnête. **straighten** *v* redresser; mettre en ordre.

strain[1] [strein] *n* tension *f*, effort *m*; (*med*) entorse *f*. *v* forcer, tendre fortement; (*med*) froisser, filtrer; s'efforcer, peiner. **strainer** *n* passoire *f*.

strain[2] [strein] *n* race *f*; tendance *f*.

strait [streit] *n* détroit *m*.

strand[1] [strand] *n* brin *m*, fibre *f*, fil *m*.

strand[2] [strand] *v* laisser en rade; (*ship*) échouer.

strange [streindʒ] *adj* étrange; (*unfamiliar*) inconnu. **stranger** *n* inconnu, -e *m*, *f*.

strangle ['straŋgl] *v* étrangler.

strap [strap] *n* lanière *f*, sangle *f*; (*on garment*) bretelle *f*. *v* attacher avec une sangle. **strapping** *adj* costaud.

strategy ['stratədʒi] *n* stratégie *f*. **strategic** *adj* stratégique.

stratum ['straitəm] *n*, *pl* -ta strate *f*, couche *f*.

straw [stroɪ] *n* paille *f*. **it's the last straw!** c'est le comble!

strawberry ['stroɪbəri] *n* (*fruit*) fraise *f*; (*plant*) fraisier *m*.

stray [strei] *n* animal errant *m*. *adj* errant, perdu; isolé. *v* s'égarer, errer.

streak [striɪk] *n* raie *f*; tendance *f*. *v* zébrer, strier.

stream [striːm] *n* ruisseau *m*; courant *m*; flot *m*, torrent *m*. **streamlined** *adj* (*aero*) fuselé; (*mot*) aérodynamique; (*efficient*) rationalisé. *v* ruisseler; (*school*) répartir par niveau. **streamer** *n* serpentin *m*.

street [striːt] *n* rue *f*.

strength [streŋθ] *n* force *f*. **strengthen** *v* fortifier; consolider; augmenter.

strenuous ['strenjuəs] *adj* ardu; vigoureux, acharné.

stress [stres] *n* pression *f*; accent *m*; tension *f*; insistance *f*; (*tech*) travail *m*. *v* insister sur; accentuer.

stretch [stretʃ] *n* (*action*) étirement *m*; (*distance*) étendue *f*; période *f*. *v* (s')étirer, (se) tendre; (*reach*) s'étendre. **stretcher** *n* brancard *m*.

stricken ['strikən] *adj* affligé.

strict [strikt] *adj* strict; exact. **strictly** *adv* strictement. **strictly speaking** à proprement parler. **strictness** *n* sévérité *f*; exactitude *f*.

*****stride** [straid] *n* grand pas *m*, enjambée *f*. *v* marcher à grands pas.

strident ['straidənt] *adj* strident.

strife [straif] *n* conflit *m*; querelles *f pl*.

*****strike** [straik] *n* (*industry*) grève *f*; (*hit*) coup *m*; (*oil, etc.*) découverte *f*. *v* (*hit*) frapper, heurter; faire grève; (*clock*) sonner; découvrir; (*match*) allumer, frotter. **striker** *n* gréviste *m, f*. **striking** *adj* frappant; en grève.

*****string** [striŋ] *n* ficelle *f*; (*violin, racket, etc.*) corde *f*. **string bag** filet à provisions *m*. **string quartet** quatuor à cordes *m*. **string vest** gilet de coton à grosses mailles *m*. *v* (*beads*) enfiler; (*hang*) suspendre. **stringy** *adj* filandreux.

stringent ['strindʒənt] *adj* rigoureux.

strip[1] [strip] *v* dépouiller; (*undress*) (se) déshabiller; (*bed*) défaire. **strip off** enlever. **strip-tease** *n* strip-tease *m*. **stripper** *n* strip-teaseuse *f*; (*paint*) décapant *m*.

strip[2] [strip] *n* bande *f*. **strip cartoon** bande dessinée *f*.

stripe [straip] *n* raie *f*, rayure *f*. **striped** *adj* rayé.

*****strive** [straiv] *v* s'efforcer (de).

strode [stroud] *V* **stride**.

stroke[1] [strouk] *n* coup *m*; (*swimming*) nage *f*; (*mark*) trait *m*; (*med*) attaque d'apoplexie *f*.

stroke[2] [strouk] *v* caresser. *n* caresse *f*.

stroll [stroul] *n* petite promenade *f*, tour *m*. *v* se promener nonchalamment, flâner.

strong [stroŋ] *adj, adv* fort; solide. **stronghold** *n* bastion *m*; (*mil*) forteresse *f*. **strong-minded** *adj* résolu. **strong-room** *n* chambre forte.

strove [strouv] *V* **strive**.

struck [strʌk] *V* **strike**.

structure ['strʌktʃə] *n* structure *f*; construction *f*. **structural** *adj* structural; de construction.

struggle ['strʌgl] *n* lutte *f*. *v* lutter; (*to escape*) se débattre. **struggle in/out** entrer/sortir avec peine.

strum [strʌm] *v* (*guitar*) racler; (*piano*) tapoter (de).

strung [strʌŋ] *V* **string**.

strut[1] [strʌt] *v* se pavaner.

strut[2] [strʌt] *n* étai *m*, support *m*.

stub [stʌb] *n* bout *m*; (*tree*) souche *f*; (*cheque*) talon *m*. *v* (*toe, etc.*) cogner. **stub out** écraser.

stubble ['stʌbl] *n* chaume *m*.

stubborn ['stʌbən] *adj* obstiné, opiniâtre. **stubbornness** *n* obstination *f*, opiniâtreté *f*.

stuck [stʌk] *V* **stick**[2].

stud[1] [stʌd] *n* clou (à grosse tête) *m*. *v* clouter. **studded with** parsemé de.

stud[2] [stʌd] *n* écurie *f*; (*farm*) haras *m*. **be at stud** étalonner.

student ['stjuːdənt] *n* étudiant, -e *m, f*; (*trainee*) stagiaire *m, f*.

studio ['stjuːdiou] *n* studio *m*.

study ['stʌdi] *n* étude *f*; (*room*) bureau *m*. *v* étudier, faire des études. **studious** *adj* studieux.

stuff [stʌf] *n* choses *f pl*; substance *f*; (*fabric*) étoffe *f*. *v* rembourrer; (*cram*) bourrer; (*thrust*) fourrer; (*cookery*) farcir; (*animal*) empailler. **stuffing** *n* bourre *f*, farce *f*; paille *f*. **stuffy** *adj* mal ventilé; (*person*) collet monté *invar*.

stumble ['stʌmbl] *v* trébucher.

stump [stʌmp] *n* (*tree*) souche *f*; (*limb*) moignon *m*; (*pencil, etc.*) bout *m*; (*cricket*) piquet *m*. *v* (*sport*) mettre hors jeu; (*coll*) coller, faire sécher.

stun [stʌn] *v* étourdir; (*amaze*) abasourdir. **stunning** *adj* stupéfiant; (*coll*) sensationnel.

stung [stʌŋ] *V* **sting**.

stunk [stʌŋk] *V* **stink**.

stunt¹ [stʌnt] v retarder (la croissance de).
stunted adj rabougri.
stunt² [stʌnt] n tour de force m; (aero) acrobatie f; (trick, publicity) truc m. **stunt man** cascadeur m.
stupid ['stjuːpid] adj stupide. **stupidity** n .stupidité f.
stupor ['stjuːpə] n stupeur f.
sturdy ['stəːdi] adj robuste, vigoureux. **sturdiness** n robustesse f, vigueur f.
sturgeon ['stəːdʒən] n esturgeon m.
stutter ['stʌtə] n bégaiement m. v bégayer.
sty [stai] n porcherie f.
style [stail] n style m; (dress) mode f; (hair) coiffure f; (type) genre m. v créer; (call) appeler. **stylish** adj élégant, chic invar.
stylus ['stailəs] n (tool) style m; (record player) pointe de lecture f.
suave [swaːv] adj doucereux.
subconscious [sʌb'konʃəs] nm, adj subconscient.
subcontract [sʌbkən'trakt] v sous-traiter. **subcontractor** n sous-traitant m.
subdivide [sʌbdi'vaid] v (se) subdiviser. **subdivision** n subdivision f.
subdue [səb'djuː] v (riot) subjuguer; (feelings) contenir; (light) adoucir. **subdued** adj contenu; faible; (voice) bas, basse; (lighting) tamisé.
subject ['sʌbdʒikt; v səb'dʒekt] n sujet m; (school) matière f; (people) sujet, -ette m, f. adj, adv **subject to** sujet à; à condition de; exposé à. v soumettre; exposer. **subjection** n sujétion f. **subjective** adj subjectif.
subjunctive [səb'dʒʌŋktiv] nm, adj subjonctif.
sublet [sʌb'let] v sous-louer.
sublime [sə'blaim] nm, adj sublime.
submarine ['sʌbməriːn] n sous-marin m.
submerge [səb'məːdʒ] v submerger. **submersion** n submersion f.
submit [səb'mit] v (se) soumettre. **submission** n soumission f. **submissive** adj soumis.
subnormal [sʌb'noːməl] adj au-dessous de la normale; (person) arriéré.
subordinate [sə'boːdinət] adj subalterne; (gramm) subordonné. n subalterne m, f; subordonné, -e m, f. v subordonner. **subordination** n subordination f.
subscribe [səb'skraib] v **subscribe to** souscrire à; (newspaper) s'abonner à. **subscriber** n souscripteur, -trice m, f;

abonné, -e m, f. **subscription** n souscription f; (club) cotisation f; abonnement m.
subsequent ['sʌbsikwənt] adj ultérieur, -e, suivant; résultant.
subservient [səb'səːviənt] adj subalterne; (derog) obséquieux.
subside [səb'said] v (land) s'affaisser; (flood) baisser; (wind) se calmer. **subsidence** n affaissement m.
subsidiary [səb'sidiəri] adj subsidiaire, accessoire. n (comm) filiale f.
subsidize ['sʌbsidaiz] v subventionner. **subsidy** n subvention f.
subsist [səb'sist] v subsister. **subsistence** n subsistance f.
substance ['sʌbstəns] n substance f. **substantial** adj important, substantiel.
substandard [sʌb'standəd] adj de qualité inférieure.
substitute ['sʌbstitjuːt] n (person) remplaçant, -e m, f; (thing) succédané m. v substituer, remplacer. **substitution** n substitution f.
subtitle ['sʌbtaitl] n sous-titre m. v sous-titrer.
subtle ['sʌtl] adj subtil. **subtlety** n subtilité f.
subtract [səb'trakt] v soustraire. **subtraction** n soustraction f.
suburb ['sʌbəːb] n faubourg m. **suburbs** pl n banlieue f sing. **suburban** adj suburbain.
subvert [səb'vəːt] v bouleverser; corrompre. **subversion** n subversion f. **subversive** adj subversif.
subway ['sʌbwei] n passage souterrain m; (US) métro m.
succeed [sək'siːd] v réussir; (follow) succéder à. **succeeding** adj suivant; à venir. **success** n succès m, réussite f. **successful** adj couronné de succès, qui a réussi. **successfully** adv avec succès. **succession** n succession f. **successive** adj successif, consécutif. **successor** n successeur m.
succinct [sək'siŋkt] adj succinct.
succulent ['sʌkjulənt] adj succulent.
succumb [sə'kʌm] v succomber.
such [sʌtʃ] adj tel, pareil; (so much) tant (de). **such as** tel que. adv si, tellement; (as) aussi. pron (those) ceux, celles; tel, telle.
suck [sʌk] v sucer; (baby) téter. **suck up to** (slang) faire de la lèche à.

sucker ['sʌkə] *n* (*bot*) surgeon *m*; (*device*) ventouse *f*; (*slang: person*) poire *f*.

suction ['sʌkʃən] *n* succion *f*.

sudden ['sʌdən] *adj* soudain, subit; imprévu. **all of a sudden** tout à coup.

suds [sʌdz] *pl n* mousse de savon *f sing*.

sue [suɪ] *v* poursuivre en justice.

suede [sweid] *n* daim *m*.

suet ['suɪit] *n* graisse de rognon *f*.

suffer ['sʌfə] *v* souffrir; (*undergo*) subir, éprouver; tolérer. **suffering** *n* souffrance *f*.

sufficient [sə'fiʃənt] *adj* assez de, suffisant. **suffice** *v* suffire (à). **sufficiently** *adv* suffisamment.

suffix ['sʌfiks] *n* suffixe *m*.

suffocate ['sʌfəkeit] *v* suffoquer, étouffer. **suffocation** *n* suffocation *f*; (*med*) asphyxie *f*.

sugar ['ʃugə] *n* sucre *m*. **sugar-basin** *n* sucrier *m*. **sugar-beet** *n* betterave sucrière *f*. **sugar-cane** *n* canne à sucre *f*. **sugar-lump** *n* morceau de sucre *m*. *v* sucrer. **sugared almond** dragée *f*. **sugary** *adj* sucré.

suggest [sə'dʒest] *v* suggérer. **suggestion** *n* suggestion *f*; soupçon *m*. **suggestive** *adj* suggestif.

suicide ['suɪisaid] *n* suicide *m*; (*person*) suicidé, -e *m, f*. **commit suicide** se suicider. **suicidal** *adj* suicidaire.

suit [suɪt] *n* (*man's*) costume *m*; (*woman's*) tailleur *m*; (*law*) procès *m*; (*cards*) couleur *f*. **suitcase** *n* valise *f*. *v* convenir à, aller à. **suitable** *adj* qui convient; approprié.

suite [swiɪt] *n* suite *f*; (*furniture*) mobilier *m*.

sulk [sʌlk] *v* bouder. *n* bouderie *f*. **sulky** *adj* bouder, -euse.

sullen ['sʌlən] *adj* maussade, renfrogné. **sullenness** *n* maussaderie *f*.

sulphur ['sʌlfə] *n* soufre *m*. **sulphuric** *adj* sulfurique.

sultan ['sʌltən] *n* sultan *m*.

sultana [sʌl'taɪnə] *n* raisin sec de Smyrne *m*.

sultry ['sʌltri] *adj* étouffant, lourd; sensuel.

sum [sʌm] *n* somme *f*; (*math*) calcul *m*. *v* **sum up** résumer, récapituler; (*person*) jauger.

summarize ['sʌməraiz] *v* résumer, récapituler. **summary** *n* résumé *m*.

summer ['sʌmə] *n* été *m*. **summer holidays** grandes vacances *f pl*. **summer-house** *n* pavillon *m*.

summit ['sʌmit] *n* sommet *m*.

summon ['sʌmən] *v* faire venir, convoquer, mander. **summon up** rassembler, faire appel à.

summons ['sʌmənz] *n* sommation *f*; (*law*) assignation *f*. *v* assigner.

sump [sʌmp] *n* (*mot*) carter *m*.

sumptuous ['sʌmptʃuəs] *adj* somptueux.

sun [sʌn] *n* soleil *m*. *v* **sun oneself** se chauffer au soleil. **sunny** *adj* ensoleillé.

sunbathe ['sʌnbeið] *v* prendre un bain de soleil. **sunbathing** *n* bains de soleil *m pl*.

sunbeam ['sʌnbiɪm] *n* rayon de soleil *m*.

sunburn ['sʌnbəɪn] *n* (*tan*) bronzage *m*; (*pain*) coup de soleil *m*. **sunburnt** *adj* bronzé; brûlé.

Sunday ['sʌndi] *n* dimanche *m*.

sundial ['sʌndaiəl] *n* cadran solaire *m*.

sundry ['sʌndri] *adj* divers. **all and sundry** n'importe qui. **sundries** *pl n* articles divers *m pl*.

sunflower ['sʌnˌflauə] *n* tournesol *m*.

sung [sʌŋ] *V* **sing**.

sun-glasses ['sʌnglaɪsiz] *pl n* lunettes de soleil *f pl*.

sunk [sʌŋk] *V* **sink**.

sunlight ['sʌnlait] *n* soleil *m*.

sunrise ['sʌnraiz] *n* lever du soleil *m*.

sunset ['sʌnset] *n* coucher du soleil *m*.

sunshine ['sʌnʃain] *n* soleil *m*. **sunshine roof** (*mot*) toit ouvrant *m*.

sunstroke ['sʌnstrouk] *n* insolation *f*.

sun-tan ['sʌntan] *n* bronzage *m*. **sun-tan lotion/oil** lotion/huile solaire *f*.

super ['suɪpə] *adj* (*coll*) formidable.

superannuation [ˌsuɪpər021nju'eiʃən] *n* retraite *f*; (*payments*) versements pour la pension *m pl*.

superb [suɪ'pəɪb] *adj* superbe.

supercilious [ˌsuɪpə'siliəs] *adj* hautain.

superficial [ˌsuɪpə'fiʃəl] *adj* superficiel.

superfluous [suɪ'pəɪfluəs] *adj* superflu.

superhuman [suɪpə'hjuɪmən] *adj* surhumain.

superimpose [ˌsuɪpərim'pouz] *v* superposer. **superimposed** *adj* (*phot, etc.*) en surimpression.

superintendent [ˌsuɪpərin'tendənt] *n* directeur, -trice *m, f*; (*police*) commissaire *m*.

superior [suɪ'piəriə] *n, adj* supérieur, -e. **superiority** *n* supériorité *f*.

superlative [suː'pəːlətiv] *adj* suprême, sans pareil; (*gramm*) superlatif. *n* superlatif *m*.

supermarket ['suːpə‚maːkit] *n* supermarché *m*.

supernatural [‚suːpə'natʃərəl] *nm, adj* surnaturel.

supersede [‚suːpə'siːd] *v* remplacer, supplanter.

supersonic [‚suːpə'sonik] *adj* supersonique.

superstition [suːpə'stiʃən] *n* superstition *f*. **superstitious** *adj* superstitieux.

supervise ['suːpəvaiz] *v* surveiller, diriger. **supervision** *n* surveillance *f*, direction *f*. **supervisor** *n* surveillant, -e *m, f*; (*comm*) chef de rayon *m*.

supper ['sʌpə] *n* souper *m*; (*evening meal*) dîner *m*.

supple ['sʌpl] *adj* souple. **suppleness** *n* souplesse *f*.

supplement ['sʌpləmənt] *n* supplément *m*. *v* augmenter, ajouter à. **supplementary** *adj* supplémentaire.

supply [sə'plai] *n* (*stock*) provision *f*; (*fuel, etc.*) alimentation *f*. **supplies** *pl n* provisions *f pl*; matériel *m sing*. *v* fournir; alimenter.

support [sə'poːt] *n* appui *m*, soutien *m*. *v* supporter, soutenir; (*financially*) subvenir aux besoins de. **supporter** *n* partisan, -e *m, f*; (*sport*) supporter *m*.

suppose [sə'pouz] *v* supposer. **supposed** *adj* prétendu; présumé. **be supposed to** être censé, devoir. **supposedly** *adv* soidisant. **supposing** *conj* si, à supposer que. **supposition** *n* supposition *f*.

suppress [sə'pres] *v* supprimer, réprimer; (*yawn, etc.*) étouffer. **suppression** *n* suppression *f*, répression *f*; étouffement *m*.

supreme [su'priːm] *adj* suprême. **supremacy** *n* suprématie *f*.

surcharge ['səːtʃaːdʒ] *n* surcharge *f*, surtaxe *f*.

sure [ʃuə] *adj* sûr, certain. **make sure** s'assurer; (*check*) vérifier. **sure enough** effectivement, en effet. **sure-footed** *adj* au pied sûr. **surely** *adv* sûrement.

surety ['ʃuərəti] *n* caution *f*.

surf [səːf] *n* ressac *m*; (*foam*) écume *f*. **surf-board** *n* planche de surf *f*. **surfboarder** *n* surfeur, -euse *m, f*. **surf-boarding** *or* **surfing** *n* surf *m*. *v* surfer.

surface ['səːfis] *n* surface *f*. **on the surface** en apparence. *v* (*road*) revêtir; (*swimmer, etc.*) revenir à la surface, faire surface.

surfeit ['səːfit] *n* excès *m*.

surge [səːdʒ] *n* vague *f*, montée *f*. *v* déferler.

surgeon ['səːdʒən] *n* chirurgien *m*. **surgery** *n* (*skill*) chirurgie *f*; (*place*) cabinet *m*; (*time*) consultation *f*. **surgical** *adj* chirurgical.

surly ['səːli] *adj* revêche.

surmount [sə'maunt] *v* surmonter.

surname ['səːneim] *n* nom de famille *m*.

surpass [sə'paːs] *v* surpasser, dépasser.

surplus ['səːpləs] *n* surplus *m*, excédent *m*. *adj* en surplus.

surprise [sə'praiz] *n* surprise *f*. *adj* inattendu. *v* surprendre, étonner.

surrealism [sə'riəlizəm] *n* surréalisme *m*. **surrealist** *n*(*m+f*), *adj* surréaliste. **surrealistic** *adj* surréaliste.

surrender [sə'rendə] *v* (se) rendre; (*documents*) remettre; renoncer à, abandonner. *n* reddition *f*; remise *f*; renonciation *f*.

surreptitious [‚sʌrəp'tiʃəs] *adj* subreptice, furtif.

surround [sə'raund] *v* entourer, encercler. *n* bordure *f*. **surrounding** *adj* environnant. **surroundings** *pl n* alentours *m pl*; (*setting*) cadre *m sing*.

survey ['səːvei; *v* sə'vei] *n* vue générale *f*; enquête *f*; (*land*) levé *m*; (*house*) inspection *f*. *v* passer en revue; inspecter; (*land*) arpenter. **surveying** *n* arpentage *m*. **surveyor** *n* (*land*) géomètre *m*; (*house*) expert *m*.

survive [sə'vaiv] *v* survivre (à). **survival** *n* survie *f*; (*relic*) survivance *f*. **survivor** *n* survivant, -e *m, f*.

susceptible [sə'septəbl] *adj* sensible.

suspect ['sʌspekt; *v* sə'spekt] *n, adj* suspect, -e. *v* soupçonner.

suspend [sə'spend] *v* suspendre. **suspender** *n* jarretelle *f*. **suspender belt** portejarretelles *m invar*. **suspenders** *pl n* (*US*) bretelles *f pl*. **suspense** *n* incertitude *f*; (*book, film*) suspense *m*. **in suspense** en suspens. **suspension** *n* suspension *f*. **suspension bridge** pont suspendu *m*.

suspicion [sə'spiʃən] *n* soupçon *m*. **suspicious** *adj* soupçonneux; suspect.

sustain [sə'stein] *v* soutenir; (*suffer*) subir.

swab [swob] *n* (*mop*) serpillière *f*; (*med: sample*) prélèvement *m*; (*med: pad*) tampon *m*. *v* nettoyer.

swagger ['swagə] *n* air important *m. v* plastronner; (*boast*) se vanter.

swallow[1] ['swolou] *v* avaler. **swallow up** engloutir. *n* avalement *m*; (*amount*) gorgée *f*.

swallow[2] ['swolou] *n* (*bird*) hirondelle *f*.

swam [swam] *V* **swim**.

swamp [swomp] *n* marais *m. v* inonder, submerger. **swampy** *adj* marécageux.

swan [swon] *n* cygne *m*.

swank [swaŋk] (*coll*) *n* esbroufe *f. v* faire de l'esbroufe. **swank about** se vanter de.

swap or **swop** [swop] *n* troc *m*; double *m. v* échanger.

swarm [swoɪm] *n* essaim *m*; (*ants*) fourmillement *m. v* essaimer; fourmiller. **swarm in/out** entrer/sortir en masse.

swarthy ['swoɪði] *adj* basané.

swat [swot] *v* écraser.

sway [swei] *n* balancement *m*, oscillation *f. v* (se) balancer, osciller; influencer.

swear ['sweə] *v* jurer. **swear in** assermenter. **swear-word** *n* juron *m*.

sweat [swet] *n* sueur *f. v* suer. **sweater** *n* tricot *m*.

swede [swiɪd] *n* rutabaga *m*.

Sweden ['swiɪdn] *n* Suède *f*. **Swede** *n* Suédois, -e *m, f*. **Swedish** *nm, adj* suédois.

sweep [swiɪp] *n* (*chimney*) ramoneur *m*; coup de balai *m*; grand geste *m*; (*curve*) grande courbe *f. v* balayer; ramoner. **sweep in/out** entrer/sortir rapidement *or* majestueusement. **sweeping** *adj* large; radical. **sweeping statement** généralisation hâtive *f*.

sweet [swiɪt] *adj* doux, douce; (*taste*) sucré; (*kind*) gentil, -ille; (*attractive*) mignon, -onne. *n* bonbon *m*; dessert *m*. **sweetbread** *n* ris de veau *m*. **sweet corn** maïs sucré *m*. **sweetheart** *n* bien-aimé, -e *m, f*. **sweet pea** pois de senteur *m*. **sweetshop** *n* confiserie *f*. **sweeten** *v* sucrer.

sweetly *adj* (*sing*) mélodieusement; (*smile*) gentiment. **sweetness** *n* goût sucré *m*; douceur *f*.

swell [swel] *n* (*sea*) houle *f. v* (se) gonfler, (s')enfler, grossir. **swelling** *n* enflure *f*.

swelter ['sweltə] *v* étouffer de chaleur. **sweltering** *adj* étouffant.

swept [swept] *V* **sweep**.

swerve [swɔɪv] *v* dévier; (*car, ship*) faire une embardée. *n* embardée *f*.

swift [swift] *adj* prompt, rapide. *n* (*bird*) martinet *m*. **swiftness** *n* rapidité *f*.

swill [swil] *v* laver à grande eau, rincer. *n* (*for pigs*) pâtée *f*.

swim [swim] *v* nager; (*cross*) traverser à la nage. *n* baignade *f*. **swimmer** *n* nageur, -euse *m, f*. **swimming** *n* nage *f*, natation *f*. **swimming baths** or **pool** piscine *f*. **swimming costume** maillot de bain *m*.

swindle ['swindl] *n* escroquerie *f. v* escroquer. **swindler** *n* escroc *m*.

swine [swain] *n* pourceau; (*impol*) salaud *m*.

swing [swiŋ] *n* balancement *m*; (*pol*) revirement *m*; rythme *m*; (*in playground*) balançoire *f*. **be in full swing** battre son plein. **swing-door** *n* porte battante *f. v* (se) balancer, (faire) osciller; (*turn*) virer; influencer.

swipe [swaip] (*coll*) *n* grand coup *m. v* (*hit*) frapper à toute volée; (*take*) calotter.

swirl [swɔɪl] *n* tourbillon *m*, volute *f. v* tourbillonner.

swish [swiʃ] *n* bruissement *m*, sifflement *m. v* bruire, siffler.

Swiss [swis] *adj* suisse. **Swiss roll** gâteau roulé *m*. **the Swiss** les Suisses.

switch [switʃ] *n* bouton électrique *m*, interrupteur *m*; changement *m*; (*stick*) baguette *f*. **switchboard** *n* standard *m. v* changer, échanger; (*rail*) aiguiller. **switch off** éteindre. **switch on** allumer.

Switzerland ['switsələnd] *n* Suisse *f*.

swivel ['swivl] *v* (faire) pivoter. *n* pivot *m*.

swollen ['swoulən] *V* **swell**.

swoop [swuɪp] *n* descente (en piqué) *f*. **at one fell swoop** d'un seul coup. *v* fondre, piquer.

swop *V* **swap**.

sword [soɪd] *n* épée *f*. **swordfish** *n* espadon *m*.

swore [swoɪ] *V* **swear**.

sworn [swoɪn] *V* **swear**.

swot [swot] (*coll*) *n* bûcheur, -euse *m, f. v* bûcher, potasser. **swotting** *n* bachotage *m*.

swum [swʌm] *V* **swim**.

swung [swʌŋ] *V* **swing**.

sycamore ['sikəmoɪ] *n* sycomore *m*.

syllable ['siləbl] *n* syllabe *f*. **syllabic** *adj* syllabique.

syllabus ['siləbəs] *n* programme *m*.

symbol ['simbl] *n* symbole *m*. **symbolic**

adj symbolique. **symbolism** *n* symbolisme *m*. **symbolize** *v* symboliser.

symmetry ['simitri] *n* symétrie *f*. **symmetrical** *adj* symétrique.

sympathy ['simpəθi] *n* compassion *f*; solidarité *f*. **sympathetic** *adj* compatissant, bien disposé. **sympathize with** *v* compatir à, plaindre.

symphony ['simfəni] *n* symphonie *f*. **symphonic** *adj* symphonique.

symposium [sim'pouziəm] *n* symposium *m*.

symptom ['simptəm] *n* symptôme *m*. **symptomatic** *adj* symptomatique.

synagogue ['sinəgog] *n* synagogue *f*.

synchromesh ['siŋkroumeʃ] *n* synchronisation *f*.

synchronize ['siŋkrənaiz] *v* synchroniser. **synchronization** *n* synchronisation *f*.

syncopate ['siŋkəpeit] *v* syncoper. **syncopation** *n* syncope *f*.

syndicate ['sindikit] *n* syndicat *m*.

syndrome ['sindroum] *n* syndrome *m*.

synonym ['sinənim] *n* synonyme *m*. **synonymous** *adj* synonyme.

synopsis [si'nopsis] *n*, *pl* **-ses** résumé *m*.

syntax ['sintaks] *n* syntaxe *f*.

synthesis ['sinθisis] *n*, *pl* **-ses** synthèse *f*. **synthesize** *v* synthétiser. **synthetic** *adj* synthétique.

syphilis ['sifilis] *n* syphilis *f*.

syringe [si'rindʒ] *n* seringue *f*. *v* seringuer.

syrup ['sirəp] *n* sirop *m*; (*golden*) mélasse raffinée *f*. **syrupy** *adj* sirupeux.

system ['sistəm] *n* système *m*; méthode *f*. **systematic** *adj* systématique.

T

tab [tab] *n* étiquette *f*, patte *f*. **keep tabs on** (*coll*) avoir à l'œil.

tabby ['tabi] *n* chat tigré *m*.

table ['teibl] *n* table *f*. **table-cloth** *n* nappe *f*. **table-mat** *n* dessous-de-plat *m invar*. **table salt** sel fin *m*. **tablespoon** *n* cuiller de service *f*. **tablespoonful** *n* cuillerée à soupe *f*. **table tennis** ping-pong *m*.

table d'hôte [taɪblə'dout] *adj* à prix fixe.

tablet ['tablit] *n* (*pill*) comprimé *m*; (*stone*) plaque *f*; (*soap*) pain *m*.

taboo [ta'buː] *nm*, *adj* tabou. *v* proscrire.

tabulate ['tabjuleit] *v* mettre sous forme de table, classifier.

tacit ['tasit] *adj* tacite.

taciturn ['tasitəɪn] *adj* taciturne.

tack [tak] *n* (*nail*) broquette *f*; (*sewing*) point de bâti *m*; (*naut*) bord *m*. *v* clouer; bâtir; faire un bord. **tacking** *n* bâtissage *m*.

tackle ['takl] *n* (*lifting*) appareil de levage *m*; équipement *m*; (*sport*) plaquage *m*. *v* s'attaquer à; plaquer.

tact [takt] *n* tact *m*. **tactful** *adj* plein de tact, discret, -ète. **tactless** *adj* peu délicat, indiscret, -ète.

tactics ['taktiks] *pl n* tactique *f sing*. **tactical** *adj* tactique.

tadpole ['tadpoul] *n* têtard *m*.

taffeta ['tafitə] *n* taffetas *m*.

tag [tag] *n* étiquette *f*, patte *f*; (*shoelace*) ferret *m*. *v* **tag along** (*coll*) suivre; traîner derrière.

tail [teil] *n* queue *f*; (*shirt*) pan *m*. **tail-end** *n* bout *m*, fin *f*. **tails** *pl n* (*coin*) pile *f sing*. *v* (*coll*) suivre.

tailor ['teilə] *n* tailleur *m*. *v* façonner; adapter.

taint [teint] *v* infecter, polluer. *n* infection *f*; corruption *f*; (*moral*) tache *f*.

*****take** [teik] *v* prendre; (*exam*) passer; accepter; contenir; (*accompany*) emmener. **take after** ressembler à. **take away** emporter; soustraire. **take-away** *adj* (*food*) à emporter. **take in** prendre; (*dress*) reprendre; (*understand*) saisir; inclure, couvrir; (*coll: deceive*) rouler. **take off** (*aero*) décoller; (*clothes, etc.*) enlever. **take-off** *n* décollage *m*; pastiche *m*. **take out** sortir; (*insurance*) prendre. **take-over** *n* rachat *m*.

taken ['teikn] *V* **take**.

talcum powder ['talkəm] *n* talc *m*.

tale [teil] *n* conte *m*, histoire *f*. **tell tales** (*coll*) cafarder.

talent ['talənt] *n* talent *m*. **talented** *adj* talentueux, doué.

talk [toɪk] *n* propos *m pl*; conversation *f*; (*lecture*) exposé *m*. *v* parler; (*chat*) causer. **talk about** parler de. **talk into** persuader de. **talk over** discuter. **talkative** *adj* bavard.

tall [toɪl] *adj* grand; (*high*) haut. **tallboy** *n* commode *f*. **tallness** *n* grande taille *f*; hauteur *f*.

tally ['tali] *n* compte *m*. *v* s'accorder.

talon ['talən] *n* serre *f*.

tambourine [tambə'riɪn] *n* tambourin *m*.

tame [teim] *adj* apprivoisé; (*not exciting*) insipide. *v* apprivoiser; (*lion*) dompter.

tamper ['tampə] *v* **tamper with** toucher à; falsifier.

tampon ['tampon] *n* tampon *m*.

tan [tan] *n* bronzage *m*. *adj* ocre. *v* (*hide*) tanner; (*sun*) bronzer, hâler.

tandem ['tandəm] *n* tandem *m*.

tangent ['tandʒənt] *n* tangente *f*. **go off at a tangent** partir dans une digression.

tangerine [tandʒə'riɪn] *nf, adj* mandarine.

tangible ['tandʒəbl] *adj* tangible.

tangle ['taŋgl] *n* enchevêtrement *m*, confusion *f*. *v* (s')enchevêtrer, (s')embrouiller.

tank [taŋk] *n* réservoir *m*; (*mil*) char *m*. **tanker** *n* (*lorry*) camion-citerne *m*; (*ship*) pétrolier *m*.

tankard ['taŋkəd] *n* chope *f*.

tantalize ['tantəlaiz] *v* tourmenter. **tantalizing** *adj* terriblement tentant.

tantamount ['tantəmaunt] *adj* **tantamount to** équivalent à.

tantrum ['tantrəm] *n* crise de colère *f*. **throw a tantrum** piquer une colère.

tap[1] [tap] *n* petit coup *m*. **tap-dance** *n* claquettes *f pl*. **tap-dancer** *n* danseur, -euse de claquettes *m, f*. *v* frapper légèrement, tapoter.

tap[2] [tap] *n* robinet *m*. *v* (*barrel*) percer; (*tree*) inciser; (*phone*) mettre sur écoute; exploiter.

tape [teip] *n* ruban *m*, bande *f*; (*recording*) bande magnétique *f*. **tape-measure** *n* mètre à ruban *m*. **tape-recorder** *n* magnétophone *m*. **tapeworm** *n* ténia *m*. *v* (*record*) enregistrer; attacher.

taper ['teipə] *n* bougie fine *f*. *v* (s')effiler. **tapered** *adj* fuselé.

tapestry ['tapəstri] *n* tapisserie *f*.

tapioca [tapi'oukə] *n* tapioca *m*.

tar [taɪ] *n* goudron *m*. *v* goudronner.

tarantula [tə'rantjulə] *n* tarentule *f*.

target ['taɪgit] *n* cible *f*; objectif *m*.

tariff ['tarif] *n* tarif *m*.

tarmac ® ['taɪmak] *n* macadam goudronné *m*.

tarnish ['taɪniʃ] *v* (se) ternir. *n* ternissure *f*.

tarpaulin [taɪ'poɪlin] *n* bâche *f*, prélart *m*.

tarragon ['tarəgən] *n* estragon *m*.

tart[1] [taɪt] *adj* aigrelet, acerbe.

tart[2] [taɪt] *n* tarte *f*; (*small*) tartelette *f*; (*slang*) poule *f*.

tartan ['taɪtən] *n* tartan *m*. *adj* écossais.

tartar ['taɪtə] *n* tartre *m*.

task [taɪsk] *n* tâche *f*.

tassel ['tasəl] *n* gland *m*.

taste [teist] *n* goût *m*. *v* goûter; (*wine*) déguster. **taste of** avoir un goût de. **tasteful** *adj* de bon goût. **tasteless** *adj* (*flavourless*) sans saveur; insipide; (*in bad taste*) de mauvais goût. **tasty** *adj* savoureux.

tattered ['tatəd] *adj* en lambeaux.

tattoo[1] [tə'tuɪ] *v* tatouer. *n* tatouage *m*.

tattoo[2] [tə'tuɪ] *n* parade militaire *f*; (*drumming*) battements *m pl*.

tatty ['tati] *adj* (*coll*) fatigué, défraîchi.

taught [toɪt] *V* **teach**.

taunt [toɪnt] *n* raillerie *f*. *v* railler. **taunting** *adj* railleur, -euse.

Taurus ['toɪrəs] *n* Taureau *m*.

taut [toɪt] *adj* tendu. **tautness** *n* tension *f*.

tawny ['toɪni] *adj* fauve.

tax [taks] *n* impôt *m*, taxe *f*. **tax-free** *adj* exempt d'impôts. **tax haven** refuge fiscal *m*. **taxpayer** *n* contribuable *m, f*. **tax return** déclaration de revenus *f*. *v* imposer, taxer; (*patience*) mettre à l'épreuve. **taxable** *adj* imposable. **taxation** *n* taxation *f*; (*taxes*) impôts *m pl*.

taxi ['taksi] *n* taxi *m*. **taxi-driver** *n* chauffeur de taxi *m*. **taxi rank** station de taxis *f*. *v* (*aero*) rouler lentement.

tea [tiɪ] *n* thé *m*; (*snack*) goûter *m*.

tea-bag ['tiɪbag] *n* sachet de thé *m*.

teacake ['tiɪkeik] *n* petit pain brioché *m*.

tea-cosy ['tiɪkouzi] *n* couvre-théière *m*.

tea-leaf ['tiɪliɪf] *n* feuille de thé *f*.

teapot ['tiɪpot] *n* théière *f*.

tea-room ['tiɪruɪm] *n* salon de thé *m*.

tea-set ['tiɪset] *n* service à thé *m*.

teaspoon ['tiɪspuɪn] *n* petite cuiller *f*. **teaspoonful** *n* cuillerée à café *f*.

tea-towel ['tiɪtauəl] *n* torchon *m*.

tea-urn ['tiɪəɪn] *n* fontaine à thé *f*.

✝teach [tiɪtʃ] *v* apprendre, enseigner. **teacher** professeur *m*; (*primary school*) instituteur, -trice *m, f*. **teaching** *n* enseignement *m*.

teak [tiɪk] *n* teck *m*.

team [tiɪm] *n* équipe *f*; (*horses*) attelage *m*. **team-member** *n* équipier, -ère *m, f*. **team spirit** esprit d'équipe *m*. **team-work** *n* collaboration *f*.

*tear¹ [teə] *n* déchirure *f.* *v* (se) déchirer; (*snatch*) arracher. **tear along/out** filer/sortir à toute allure.

tear² [tiə] *n* larme *f.* **burst into tears** fondre en larmes. **tear-gas** *n* gaz lacrymogène *m.* **tearful** *adj* larmoyant.

tease [tiːz] *v* taquiner. **teasing** *n* taquineries *f pl.*

teat [tiːt] *n* tétine *f.*

technique [tek'niːk] *n* technique *f.* **technical** *adj* technique. **technicality** *n* détail technique *m.* **technician** *n* technicien, -enne *m, f.* **technological** *adj* technologique. **technology** *n* technologie *f.*

teddy bear ['tedi͵beə] *n* nounours *m.*

tedious ['tiːdiəs] *adj* ennuyeux.

tee [tiː] *n* tee *m.* *v* **tee off** partir du tee.

teem [tiːm] *v* (*swarm*) grouiller; (*rain*) pleuvoir à verse.

teenage ['tiːneidʒ] *adj* adolescent. **teenager** *n* adolescent, -e *m, f.* **teens** *pl n* adolescence *f sing.*

teeth [tiːθ] *V* **tooth**.

teethe [tiːð] *v* faire ses dents. **teething** *n* dentition *f.* **teething troubles** difficultés de croissance *f pl.*

teetotaller [tiː'toutələ] *n* personne qui ne boit jamais d'alcool *f.*

telecommunications [͵telikəmjuːni-'keiʃənz] *pl n* télécommunications *f pl.*

telegram ['teligram] *n* télégramme *m.*

telegraph ['teligraːf] *n* télégraphe *m.* **telegraph pole** poteau télégraphique *m.* *v* télégraphier. **telegraphic** *adj* télégraphique.

telepathy [tə'lepəθi] *n* télépathie *f.* **telepathic** *adj* télépathique.

telephone ['telifoun] *n* téléphone *m.* **telephone box** cabine téléphonique *f.* **telephone call** coup de téléphone *m.* **telephone directory** annuaire *m.* **telephone number** numéro de téléphone *m.* *v* téléphoner. **telephonist** *n* téléphoniste *m, f.*

telescope ['teliskoup] *n* télescope *m.* **telescopic** *adj* télescopique.

television ['teliviʒən] *n* télévision *f.* **televise** *v* téléviser.

telex ['teleks] *n* télex *m.*

*tell [tel] *v* dire; (*story*) raconter; (*know*) savoir. **tell off** (*coll*) gronder.

temper ['tempə] *n* tempérament *m,* humeur *f;* (*anger*) colère *f.* **lose one's temper** se mettre en colère. *v* tempérer.

temperament ['tempərəmənt] *n* tempérament *m.* **temperamental** *adj* capricieux.

temperate ['tempərət] *adj* tempéré.

temperature ['temprətʃə] *n* température *f.*

tempestuous [tem'pestjuəs] *adj* orageux.

template ['templət] *n* patron *m.*

temple¹ ['templ] *n* (*rel*) temple *m.*

temple² ['templ] *n* (*anat*) tempe *f.*

tempo ['tempou] *n* tempo *m.*

temporary ['tempərəri] *adj* temporaire; provisoire; (*secretary*) intérimaire.

tempt [tempt] *v* tenter. **temptation** *n* tentation *f.*

ten [ten] *nm, adj* dix. **tenth** *n*(*m+f*), *adj* dixième.

tenacious [tə'neiʃəs] *adj* tenace. **tenacity** *n* ténacité *f.*

tenant ['tenənt] *n* locataire *m, f.* **tenancy** *n* location *f.*

tend¹ [tend] *v* avoir tendance, incliner. **tendency** *n* tendance *f.*

tend² [tend] *v* (*look after*) garder, soigner.

tender¹ ['tendə] *adj* tendre; délicat; (*heart, bruise*) sensible. **tenderize** *v* attendrir. **tenderness** *n* tendresse *f;* (*meat*) tendreté *f.*

tender² ['tendə] *v* offrir; (*comm*) faire une soumission. *n* soumission *f.* **legal tender** cours légal *m.*

tendon ['tendən] *n* tendon *m.*

tendril ['tendril] *n* vrille *f.*

tenement ['tenəmənt] *n* logement *m.* **tenement block** bâtiment *m.*

tennis ['tenis] *n* tennis *m.* **tennis-court** *n* court de tennis *m.*

tenor ['tenə] *n* (*music*) ténor *m;* sens *m;* (*wording*) teneur *f.*

tense¹ [tens] *adj* tendu, crispé. *v* tendre. **tension** *n* tension *f.*

tense² [tens] *n* temps *m.*

tent [tent] *n* tente *f.*

tentacle ['tentəkl] *n* tentacule *m.*

tentative ['tentətiv] *adj* hésitant; expérimental; provisoire.

tenterhooks ['tentəhuks] *pl n* **be on tenterhooks** être sur des charbons ardents.

tenuous ['tenjuəs] *adj* ténu.

tepid ['tepid] *adj* tiède. **tepidness** *n* tiédeur *f.*

term [təːm] *n* terme *m;* (*school*) trimestre *m.* **terms** *pl n* (*comm*) conditions *f pl.* **come to terms with** faire face à. **on good/bad terms** en bons/mauvais termes. *v* appeler.

terminal ['tɜːminəl] *adj* terminal. *n* terminus *m invar*; (*elec*) borne *f*.

terminate ['tɜːmineit] *v* (se) terminer. **termination** *n* fin *f*.

terminology [tɜːmi'nolədʒi] *n* terminologie *f*.

terminus ['tɜːminəs] *n* terminus *m invar*.

terrace ['terəs] *n* terrasse *f*; (*houses*) rangée de maisons *f*.

terrain [tə'rein] *n* terrain *m*.

terrestrial [tə'restriəl] *adj* terrestre.

terrible ['terəbl] *adj* terrible; atroce; abominable. **terribly** *adv* (*coll: very*) drôlement.

terrier ['teriə] *n* terrier *m*.

terrify ['terifai] *v* terrifier. **terrific** *adj* (*coll: excellent*) formidable; (*coll: extreme*) énorme, terrible.

territory ['teritəri] *n* territoire *m*. **territorial** *adj* territorial.

terror ['terə] *n* terreur *f*. **terrorism** *n* terrorisme *m*. **terrorist** *n*(*m+f*), *adj* terroriste. **terrorize** *v* terroriser.

terse [tɜːs] *adj* laconique.

test [test] *n* essai *m*; (*physical, mental*) épreuve *f*; analyse *f*; (*school*) interrogation *f*. **test card** (*TV*) mire *f*. **test case** (*law*) conflit-test *m*. **test drive** *n* essai de route *m*. **test flight** vol d'essai *m*. **test-tube** *n* éprouvette *f*. *v* essayer, mettre à l'essai; mettre à l'épreuve; analyser; mesurer.

testament ['testəmənt] *n* testament *m*.

testicle ['testikl] *n* testicule *m*.

testify ['testifai] *v* témoigner, porter témoignage.

testimony ['testiməni] *n* témoignage *m*; déclaration *f*. **testimonial** *n* recommandation *f*.

tetanus ['tetənəs] *n* tétanos *m*.

tether ['teðə] *n* longe *f*. *v* attacher.

text [tekst] *n* texte *m*. **textbook** *n* manuel *m*. **textual** *adj* textuel.

textile ['tekstail] *nm*, *adj* textile.

texture ['tekstjuə] *n* contexture *f*; (*wood, paper, etc.*) grain *m*.

Thames [temz] *n* the **Thames** la Tamise *f*.

than [ðən] *conj* que, de.

thank [θaŋk] *v* remercier. **thank you** merci. **thanks** *pl n* remerciements *m pl*. **thanksgiving** *n* action de grâce *f*. **thanks to** grâce à. **thankful** *adj* reconnaissant. **thankless** *adj* ingrat.

that [ðat] *adj* ce, cette; (*emphatic*) ce ... -là, cette ... -là: *ce livre-là*. *pron* cela, ça; ce; (*that one*) celui-là, celle-là; (*who, which*) qui, que, lequel, laquelle; (*when*) où. **that is** c'est-à-dire. *conj* que.

thatch [θatʃ] *n* chaume *m*. **thatched cottage** chaumière *f*.

thaw [θɔː] *v* (faire) dégeler, (faire) fondre. *n* dégel *m*.

the [ðə] *art* le, la; (*pl*) les.

theatre ['θiətə] *n* théâtre *m*. **theatrical** *adj* théâtral.

theft [θeft] *n* vol *m*.

their [ðeə] *adj* leur.

theirs [ðeəz] *pron* le leur, la leur.

them [ðem] *pron* eux, elles; (*direct object*) les; (*indirect object*) leur.

theme [θiːm] *n* thème *m*. **thematic** *adj* thématique.

themselves [ðəm'selvz] *pron* se; (*emphatic*) eux-mêmes, elles-mêmes. **by themselves** tout seuls.

then [ðen] *adv* alors; (*next*) ensuite, puis; (*in that case*) en ce cas. *n* (*that time*) ce moment-là, cette époque-là.

theology [θi'olədʒi] *n* théologie *f*. **theologian** *n* théologien, -enne *m, f*. **theological** *adj* théologique.

theorem ['θiərəm] *n* théorème *m*.

theory ['θiəri] *n* théorie *f*. **theoretical** *adj* théorique.

therapy ['θerəpi] *n* thérapie *f*, thérapeutique *f*. **therapeutic** *adj* thérapeutique. **therapist** *n* thérapeute *m, f*.

there [ðeə] *adv* y, là. **thereabouts** *adv* environ; (*place*) par là. **thereby** *adv* de cette façon. **there is** *or* **are** il y a; (*showing*) voilà. **thereupon** *adv* sur ce.

therefore ['ðeəfɔː] *adv* donc.

thermal ['θɜːməl] *adj* thermal; (*phys*) thermique. *n* courant ascendant *m*.

thermodynamics [θɜːmoudai'namiks] *n* thermodynamique *f*.

thermometer [θə'momitə] *n* thermomètre *m*.

thermonuclear [θɜːmou'njukliə] *adj* thermonucléaire.

thermos ® ['θɜːməs] *n* thermos ® *m*.

thermostat ['θɜːməstat] *n* thermostat *m*. **thermostatic** *adj* thermostatique.

these [ðiːz] *adj* ces; (*emphatic*) ces ... -ci: *ces robes-ci*. *pron* ce; ceux-ci, celles-ci.

thesis ['θiːsis] *n, pl* **-ses** thèse *f*.

they [ðei] *pron* ils, elles; (*emphatic*) eux, elles; (*impersonal*) on.

thick [θik] *adj* épais, -aisse; (*stupid*) bête. **thick-skinned** *adj* peu sensible. **thicken** *v* (s')épaissir. **thickness** *n* épaisseur *f*.

thief [θiːf] *n* voleur, -euse *m, f*.

thigh [θai] *n* cuisse *f*.

thimble ['θimbl] *n* dé à coudre *m*.

thin [θin] *adj* mince, fin; (*person*) maigre; (*liquid*) peu épais, -aisse; (*hair*) clairsemé. *v* (s')éclaircir; (*dilute*) délayer. **thinness** *n* minceur *f*; maigreur *f*.

thing [θiŋ] *n* chose *f*. **things** *pl n* affaires *f pl*. **thingumajig** *n* (*coll*) machin *m*.

*think [θiŋk] *v* penser; imaginer. **I think so** je pense que oui. **think about** penser à. **think over** réfléchir à.

third [θəːd] *adj* troisième. *n* troisième *m, f*; (*fraction*) tiers *m*; (*musique*) tierce *f*. **third party** (*law*) tiers *m*. **third-party insurance** assurance au tiers *f*. **third-rate** *adj* de qualité très inférieure. **Third World** Tiers-Monde *m*.

thirst [θəːst] *n* soif. *v* avoir soif. **be thirsty** avoir soif.

thirteen [θəː'tiːn] *nm, adj* treize. **thirteenth** *n(m+f)*, *adj* treizième.

thirty ['θəːti] *nm, adj* trente. **thirtieth** *n(m+f)*, *adj* trentième.

this [ðis] *adj* ce,. cette; (*emphatic*) ce ... -ci, cette ... -ci: *cette maison-ci*. *pron* ceci, ce; (*this one*) celui-ci, celle-ci.

thistle ['θisl] *n* chardon *m*.

thong [θoŋ] *n* lanière *f*.

thorn [θɔːn] *n* épine *f*.

thorough ['θʌrə] *adj* profond; minutieux. **thoroughbred** *n* (*horse*) pur-sang *m invar*; bête de race *f*. **thoroughfare** *n* voie publique *f*. **thoroughly** *adv* à fond; (*completely*) tout à fait. **thoroughness** *n* minutie *f*.

those [ðouz] *adj* ces; (*emphatic*) ces ... -là: *ces chaises-là*. *pron* ce; ceux-là, celles-là.

though [ðou] *conj* bien que. *adv* pourtant. **as though** comme si.

thought [θɔːt] *V* think. *n* pensée *f*; idée *f*; opinion *f*; considération *f*. **thoughtful** *adj* pensif; sérieux; (*considerate*) prévenant, gentil, -ille. **thoughtless** *adj* étourdi; irréfléchi.

thousand ['θauzənd] *nm, adj* mille. **thousandth** *n(m+f)*, *adj* millième.

thrash [θraʃ] *v* rosser, battre violemment; (*sport, etc.*) battre à plates coutures. **thrash about** se débattre. **thrash out** (*problem, etc.*) débattre de. **thrashing** *n* correction *f*.

thread [θred] *n* fil *m*; (*screw*) pas *m*. *v* enfiler; faire passer. **threadbare** *adj* usé, râpé.

threat [θret] *n* menace *f*. **threaten** *v* menacer.

three [θriː] *nm, adj* trois. **three-dimensional** *adj* à trois dimensions. **three-point turn** demi-tour en trois manœuvres *m*.

thresh [θreʃ] *v* battre. **threshing machine** batteuse *f*.

threshold ['θreʃould] *n* seuil *m*.

threw [θruː] *V* throw.

thrift [θrift] *n* économie *f*. **thrifty** *adj* économe.

thrill [θril] *n* frisson *m*. *v* transporter. **thriller** *n* roman *or* film à suspense *m*. **thrilling** *adj* palpitant.

thrive [θraiv] *v* se développer bien, pousser bien; prospérer. **thriving** *adj* robuste; prospère.

throat [θrout] *n* gorge *f*. **clear one's throat** s'éclaircir la voix. **throaty** *adj* guttural.

throb [θrob] *n* (*heart*) pulsation *f*; (*engine*) vibration *f*. *v* palpiter; vibrer; (*pain*) lanciner.

thrombosis [θrom'bousis] *n* thrombose *f*.

throne [θroun] *n* trône *m*.

throng [θroŋ] *n* foule *f*, multitude *f*. *v* affluer, se presser.

throttle ['θrotl] *v* étrangler. *n* (*tech*) papillon des gaz *m*; (*mot*) accélérateur *m*.

through [θruː] *prep* par; (*place*) à travers; (*time*) pendant. *adv* à travers. *adj* direct. **no through road** impasse *f*. **throughout** *prep* (*place*) partout dans; (*time*) pendant.

*throw [θrou] *n* jet *m*. *v* jeter, lancer; (*hurl*) projeter. **throw away** jeter; (*waste*) gâcher, gaspiller. **throw out** rejeter; expulser. **throw up** vomir.

thrown [θroun] *V* throw.

thrush [θrʌʃ] *n* grive *f*.

*thrust [θrʌst] *n* poussée *f*; coup *m*. *v* pousser brusquement, enfoncer; imposer.

thud [θʌd] *n* bruit sourd *m*. *v* faire un bruit sourd.

thumb [θʌm] *n* pouce *m*. *v* *also* **thumb through** feuilleter. **thumb a lift** (*coll*) faire du stop.

thump [θʌmp] *n* bruit lourd *m*; (*blow*) grand coup *m*. *v* cogner (à *or* sur); (*heart*) battre fort; (*person*) assener un coup à.

thunder [ˈθʌndə] *n* tonnerre *m*; (*noise*) fracas *m*. **thunderstorm** *n* orage *m*. **thunderstruck** *adj* abasourdi. *v* tonner. **thundery** *adj* orageux.

Thursday [ˈθəɪzdɪ] *n* jeudi *m*.

thus [ðʌs] *adv* ainsi.

thwart [θwɔɪt] *v* contrecarrer, contrarier.

thyme [taɪm] *n* thym *m*.

thyroid [ˈθaɪrɔɪd] *nf, adj* thyroïde.

tiara [tɪˈɑɪrə] *n* diadème *m*.

tick¹ [tɪk] *n* (*mark*) coche *f*; (*sound*) tic-tac *m*; (*coll*) instant *m*. *v* cocher; faire tic-tac. **tick off** (*coll: scold*) attraper. **tick over** (*mot*) tourner au ralenti.

tick² [tɪk] *n* (*insect*) tique *f*.

ticket [ˈtɪkɪt] *n* billet *m*; (*bus*) ticket *m*; (*library*) carte *f*; (*label*) étiquette *f*. **ticket collector** contrôleur *m*. **ticket office** guichet *m*.

tickle [ˈtɪkl] *v* chatouiller. *n* chatouillement *m*. **ticklish** *adj* chatouilleux.

tide [taɪd] *n* marée *f*. **tide-mark** *n* ligne de marée haute *f*; (*of dirt*) ligne de crasse *f*. *v* **tide over** dépanner.

tidy [ˈtaɪdɪ] *adj* en ordre, bien rangé; (*writing, appearance*) net, nette. *v* ranger. **tidily** *adv* soigneusement. **tidiness** *n* propreté *f*.

tie [taɪ] *n* attache *f*; (*neck*) cravate *f*; (*link*) lien *m*; (*draw*) égalité *f*, match nul *m*. *v* attacher; lier; (*ribbon, etc.*) nouer; faire match nul.

tier [tɪə] *n* étage *m*; (*seating*) gradin *m*.

tiger [ˈtaɪgə] *n* tigre *m*.

tight [taɪt] *adj* raide, serré, étroit; (*seal*) étanche; (*coll: drunk*) soûl; (*coll: mean*) radin. **tight-fisted** *adj* avare. **tightrope** *n* corde raide *f*. **tightrope walker** funambule *m, f*. *adv* also **tightly** bien; hermétiquement. **tighten** *v* (se) resserrer; (*rope*) (se) tendre; (*control*) renforcer. **tights** *pl n* collant *m sing*.

tile [taɪl] *n* (*roof*) tuile *f*; (*wall, floor*) carreau *m*. *v* couvrir de tuiles; carreler.

till¹ [tɪl] *v* until.

till² [tɪl] *n* caisse *f*.

till³ [tɪl] *v* labourer.

tiller [ˈtɪlə] *n* (*naut*) barre du gouvernail *f*.

tilt [tɪlt] *n* inclinaison *f*. *v* pencher, incliner.

timber [ˈtɪmbə] *n* bois d'œuvre *m*. **timbered** *adj* (*house*) en bois.

time [taɪm] *n* temps *m*; (*clock*) heure *f*; (*occasion*) fois *f*; époque *f*; moment *m*; (*music*) mesure *f*. **a long time** longtemps.

a short time peu de temps. **at the same time** à la fois. **from time to time** de temps en temps. **in time** à temps; (*music*) en mesure. **on time** à l'heure. **time bomb** bombe à retardement *f*. **time-sheet** *n* feuille de présence *f*. **time-switch** *n* minuteur *m*. **timetable** *n* (*rail*) horaire *m*; (*school*) emploi du temps *m*. **time zone** fuseau horaire *m*. *v* fixer; (*runner, etc.*) chronométrer; (*programme, etc.*) minuter. **timeless** *adj* éternel. **timely** *adj* à propos. **timer** *n* (*cooking*) compte-minutes *m invar*.

timid [ˈtɪmɪd] *adj* timide, craintif. **timidity** *n* timidité *f*.

timpani [ˈtɪmpənɪ] *pl n* timbales *f pl*.

tin [tɪn] *n* étain *m*; (*can*) boîte *f*; (*baking*) moule *m*; (*roasting*) plat *m*. **tin foil** papier d'étain *m*. **tin-opener** *n* ouvre-boîtes *m*. **tin soldier** soldat de plomb *m*. *v* mettre en boîte. **tinny** *adj* métallique.

tinge [tɪndʒ] *n* teinte *f*. *v* teinter.

tingle [ˈtɪŋgl] *v* picoter. *n* picotement *m*.

tinker [ˈtɪŋkə] *n* romanichel, -elle *m, f*. *v* bricoler.

tinkle [ˈtɪŋkl] *v* (faire) tinter. *n* tintement *m*.

tinsel [ˈtɪnsəl] *n* clinquant *m*.

tint [tɪnt] *n* teinte *f*; (*hair*) shampooing colorant *m*. *v* teinter.

tiny [ˈtaɪnɪ] *adj* tout petit, minuscule.

tip¹ [tɪp] *n* (*end*) bout *m*, pointe *f*. **on tiptoe** sur la pointe des pieds. *v* mettre un embout à.

tip² [tɪp] *v* (se) pencher, incliner; (*overturn*) (se) renverser; (*pour*) verser, déverser. *n* (*rubbish*) dépotoir *m*.

tip³ [tɪp] *n* (*hint*) suggestion *f*, conseil *m*; (*money*) pourboire *m*. *v* donner un pourboire (à). **tip off** (*warn*) prévenir. **tip-off** *n* (*coll*) tuyau *m*.

tipsy [ˈtɪpsɪ] *adj* (*coll*) éméché.

Tirana [tɪˈrɑɪnə] *n* Tirana.

tire¹ [ˈtaɪə] *v* (se) fatiguer. **tire out** épuiser. **tired** *adj* fatigué; las, lasse. **be tired of** en avoir assez de. **tiredness** *n* fatigue *f*. **tiresome** *adj* ennuyeux.

tire² (*US*) *v* tyre.

tissue [ˈtɪʃuɪ] *n* tissu *m*; (*handkerchief*) mouchoir en papier *m*. **tissue paper** papier de soie *m*.

title [ˈtaɪtl] *n* titre *m*; (*law*) droit *m*. **title-deed** *n* titre de propriété *m*. **title-page** *n* page de titre *f*. *v* intituler. **titled** *adj* titré.

titter ['titə] *n* gloussement *m. v* glousser.
to [tu] *prep* à; *(home, shop)* chez; *(in order to)* pour. **ten to four** quatre heures moins dix. **to-do** *n (coll)* histoire *f.*
toad [toud] *n* crapaud *m.* **toadstool** *n* champignon vénéneux *m.*
toast [toust] *n* pain grillé *m*; *(speech)* toast *m.* **toast-rack** *n* porte-toast *m. v* griller; porter un toast à. **toaster** *n* grille-pain *m invar.*
tobacco [tə'bakou] *n* tabac *m.* **tobacconist's** *n* tabac *m.*
toboggan [tə'bogən] *n* toboggan *m.*
today [tə'dei] *nm, adv* aujourd'hui.
toddler ['todlə] *n* petit, -e qui commence à marcher *m, f.*
toe [tou] *n* orteil *m.* **toe-nail** *n* ongle du pied *m. v* **toe the line** obéir, se plier.
toffee ['tofi] *n* caramel *m.* **toffee-apple** *n* pomme caramélisée *f.*
together [tə'geðə] *adv* ensemble; *(simultaneously)* à la fois.
toil [toil] *n* dur travail *m. v* travailler dur.
toilet ['toilit] *n* toilettes *f pl,* cabinets *m pl.* **toilet-paper** *n* papier hygiénique *m.* **toilet water** eau de toilette *f.*
token ['toukən] *n* marque *f*; *(disc)* jeton *m*; *(voucher)* bon *m.* **as a token of** en gage de. *adj* symbolique.
Tokyo ['toukiou] *n* Tokio.
told [tould] *V* tell.
tolerate ['toləreit] *v* tolérer, supporter. **tolerable** *adj* tolérable; passable. **tolerance** *or* **toleration** *n* tolérance *f.* **tolerant** *adj* tolérant.
toll[1] [toul] *n* péage *m.* **toll-gate** *n* barrière de péage *f.*
toll[2] [toul] *v* sonner.
tomato [tə'maitou] *n* tomate *f.*
tomb [tuim] *n* tombeau *m.* **tombstone** *n* pierre tombale *f.*
tomorrow [tə'morou] *nm, adv* demain. **the day after tomorrow** après-demain.
ton [tʌn] *n* tonne *f.*
tone [toun] *n* ton *m*; *(phone)* tonalité *f*; classe *f*; sonorité *f. v (colour)* s'harmoniser. **tone down** baisser, adoucir.
tongs [toŋz] *pl n* pinces *f pl,* pincettes *f pl.*
tongue [tʌŋ] *n* langue *f.* **tongue-tied** *adj* muet, -ette.
tonic ['tonik] *adj* tonique. *n (med)* tonique *m*; *(music)* tonique *f.*
tonight [tə'nait] *n, adv* cette nuit; *(evening)* ce soir.

tonsil ['tonsil] *n* amygdale *f.* **tonsillitis** *n* amygdalite *f.*
too [tuı] *adv* trop; *(also)* aussi; *(moreover)* en plus.
took [tuk] *V* take.
tool [tuıl] *n* outil *m.* **tool-shed** *n* cabane à outils *f.*
tooth [tuıθ] *n, pl* **teeth** dent *f.* **toothache** *n* mal de dents *m.* **have toothache** avoir mal aux dents. **tooth-brush** *n* brosse à dents *f.* **toothpaste** *n* dentifrice *m.* **toothpick** *n* cure-dent *m.* **toothless** *adj* édenté.
top[1] [top] *n* haut *m*; sommet *m*; *(lid)* couvercle *m*; surface *f,* dessus *m*; *(list)* tête *f.* **at the top of one's voice** à tue-tête. *adj* du haut; *(first)* premier; *(last)* dernier. **top hat** haut-de-forme *m.* **top-heavy** *adj* trop lourd du haut. **top secret** ultra-secret, -ète. **topside** *n (meat)* gîte *m.* **topsoil** *n* couche arable *f. v* surmonter; *(exceed)* dépasser. **top up** remplir, rajouter.
top[2] [top] *n (toy)* toupie *f.*
topaz ['toupaz] *n* topaze *f.*
topic ['topik] *n* sujet *m.* **topical** *adj* d'actualité.
topography [tə'pogrəfi] *n* topographie *f.* **topographical** *adj* topographique.
topple ['topl] *v* (faire) basculer, (faire) tomber.
topsy-turvy [topsi'təivi] *adj, adv* sens dessus dessous.
torch [toitʃ] *n (electric)* lampe de poche *f*; *(burning)* torche *f.*
tore [toi] *V* tear[1].
torment ['toiment; *v* toi'ment] *n* supplice *m. v* tourmenter.
torn [toin] *V* tear[1].
tornado [toi'neidou] *n* tornade *f.*
torpedo [toi'piidou] *n* torpille *f. v* torpiller.
torrent ['torənt] *n* torrent *m.* **torrential** *adj* torrentiel.
torso ['toisou] *n* torse *m*; *(sculpture)* buste *m.*
tortoise ['toitəs] *n* tortue *f.* **tortoise-shell** *n* écaille *f.*
tortuous ['toitʃuəs] *adj* tortueux.
torture ['toitʃə] *n* torture *f. v* torturer. **torturer** *n* tortionnaire *m.*
toss [tos] *n* lancement *m*; *(coin)* coup de pile ou face *m. v* lancer; *(pancake)* faire sauter; (s')agiter; *(coin)* jouer à pile ou face.

tot¹ [tot] *n* (*child*) petit enfant *m*; (*drink*) goutte *f*.

tot² [tot] *v* **tot up** additionner.

total ['toutəl] *nm, adj* total. *v* (*add up*) totaliser; (*add up to*) s'élever à. **totalitarian** *n*(*m*+*f*), *adj* totalitaire.

totter ['totə] *v* chanceler.

touch [tʌtʃ] *n* toucher *m*; contact *m*; (*artist's*) touche *f*. *v* toucher (à), se toucher. **touchy** *adj* susceptible; délicat.

tough [tʌf] *adj* dur; (*strong*) résistant; (*struggle*) acharné. **toughen** *v* rendre plus solide; (*person*) (s')endurcir. **toughness** *n* dureté *f*; résistance *f*.

toupee ['tuːpei] *n* postiche *m*.

tour [tuə] *n* voyage *m*; (*of town, museum, etc.*) visite *f*; (*by musicians, etc.*) tournée *f*. *v* visiter. **touring** *or* **tourism** *n* tourisme *m*. **tourist** *n* touriste *m, f*. **tourist's guide** guide touristique *f*.

tournament ['tuənəmənt] *n* tournoi *m*.

tousled ['tauzld] *adj* échevelé.

tow [tou] *n* remorque *f*. *v* remorquer; (*trailer*) tirer. **tow-path** *n* chemin de halage *m*. **tow-rope** *n* remorque *f*.

towards [tə'wɔidz] *prep* vers; (*attitude*) envers.

towel ['tauəl] *n* serviette *f*; (*for hands*) essuie-mains *m*. **towel-rail** *n* porte-serviettes *m invar*. **towelling** *n* tissu éponge *m*.

tower ['tauə] *n* tour *f*. **tower block** immeuble-tour *m*. *v* **tower over** dominer. **towering** *adj* imposant.

town [taun] *n* ville *f*. **town centre** centre de la ville *m*. **town hall** hôtel de ville *m*. **town planning** urbanisme *m*.

toxic ['toksik] *adj* toxique.

toy [toi] *n* jouet *m*. *adj* petit, miniature; d'enfant. *v* **toy with** jouer avec; (*idea*) caresser.

trace [treis] *n* trace *f*. *v* tracer; (*find*) retrouver; (*through paper*) décalquer. **tracing** *n* calque *m*. **tracing paper** papier-calque *m invar*.

track [trak] *n* (*marks*) trace *f*; (*path*) chemin *m*; (*sport*) piste *f*; (*rail*) voie *f*. **track suit** survêtement *m*. *v* suivre la trace de. **track down** traquer. **tracker** *n* traqueur *m*.

tract¹ [trakt] *n* (*region*) étendue *f*; (*anat*) système *m*.

tract² [trakt] *n* (*treatise*) tract *m*.

tractor ['traktə] *n* tracteur *m*.

trade [treid] *n* commerce *m*; (*job*) métier *m*. **trademark** *n* marque *f*. **tradesman** *n* commerçant *m*. **trade union** syndicat *m*. **trade-unionist** *n* syndicaliste *m, f*. *v* faire le commerce (de); commercer (avec); échanger. **trade in** faire reprendre. **trader** *n* commerçant, -e *m, f*; négociant, -e *m, f*.

tradition [trə'diʃən] *n* tradition *f*. **traditional** *adj* traditionnel.

traffic ['trafik] *n* (*mot*) circulation *f*; (*aero, naut, etc.*) trafic *m*; commerce *m*. **traffic jam** embouteillage *m*. **traffic-light** *n* feu *m*. **traffic warden** contractuel, -elle *m, f*.

tragedy ['tradʒədi] *n* tragédie *f*. **tragic** *adj* tragique.

trail [treil] *n* traînée *f*; (*tracks*) trace *f*; (*path*) sentier *m*. *v* (*drag*) traîner; (*follow*) suivre la piste de. **trailer** *n* (*mot*) remorque *f*; film publicitaire *m*.

train [trein] *n* train *m*; (*series*) suite *f*; (*of dress*) traîne *f*. *v* (*teach*) former; (*learn*) recevoir sa formation; (*sport*) (s')entraîner; (*animal*) dresser. **trainee** *n* stagiaire *m, f*. **trainer** *n* (*sport*) entraîneur, -euse *m, f*; (*animal*) dresseur, -euse *m, f*; (*shoe*) chaussure de sport *f*. **training** *n* formation *f*; entraînement *m*; dressage *m*.

trait [treit] *n* trait *m*.

traitor ['treitə] *n* traître, -esse *m, f*.

tram [tram] *n* tram *m*.

tramp [tramp] *n* (*person*) clochard, -e *m, f*; (*hike*) randonnée *f*; (*sound*) martèlement des pas *m*. *v* marcher d'un pas lourd.

trample ['trampl] *v* piétiner, fouler aux pieds.

trampoline ['trampəliin] *n* tremplin *m*.

trance [trains] *n* transe *f*.

tranquil ['traŋkwil] *adj* tranquille. **tranquillity** *n* tranquillité *f*. **tranquillize** *v* tranquilliser. **tranquillizer** *n* tranquillisant *m*.

transact [tran'zakt] *v* traiter, régler. **transaction** *n* (*econ*) transaction *f*; (*comm*) opération *f*.

transcend [tran'send] *v* transcender; surpasser. **transcendental** *adj* transcendantal.

transcribe [tran'skraib] *v* transcrire. **transcription** *n* transcription *f*.

transept ['transept] *n* transept *m*.

transfer [trans'fəi; *n* 'transfəi] *v* transférer, être transféré. *n* transfert *m*; (*picture*) décalcomanie *f*. **not transferable** personnel.

transfixed [trans'fikst] *adj* cloué sur place.
transform [trans'fɔːm] *v* transformer. **transformation** *n* transformation *f*. **transformer** *n* (*elec*) transformateur *m*.
transfuse [trans'fjuːz] *v* transfuser. **transfusion** *n* transfusion *f*.
transient ['tranzıənt] *adj* transitoire.
transistor [tran'zıstə] *n* transistor *m*. **transistorize** *v* transistoriser.
transit ['transit] *n* transit *m*. **in transit** en transit.
transition [tran'zıʃən] *n* transition *f*. **transitional** *adj* de transition.
transitive ['transitiv] *adj* transitif.
transitory ['transitəri] *adj* transitoire.
translate [trans'leit] *v* traduire. **translation** *n* traduction *f*; (*school*) version *f*. **translator** *n* traducteur, -trice *m*, *f*.
translucent [trans'luːsnt] *adj* translucide. **translucence** *n* translucidité *f*.
transmit [tranz'mit] *v* transmettre; (*broadcast*) émettre. **transmission** *n* transmission *f*. **transmitter** *n* transmetteur *m*; émetteur *m*.
transparent [trans'peərənt] *adj* transparent. **transparency** (*phot*) diapositive *f*; transparence *f*.
transplant [trans'plaint; *n* 'transplaint] *v* transplanter. *n* transplantation *f*.
transport ['transpɔːt; *v* trans'pɔːt] *n* transport *m*. *v* transporter. **transportation** *n* transport *m*.
transpose [trans'pouz] *v* transposer. **transposition** *n* transposition *f*.
transverse ['tranzvɔːs] *adj* transversal.
transvestite [tranz'vestait] *n* travesti, -e *m*, *f*.
trap [trap] *n* piège *m*. **trapdoor** *n* trappe *f*. *v* prendre au piège; bloquer.
trapeze [trə'piːz] *n* trapèze *m*. **trapeze artist** trapéziste *m*, *f*.
trash [traʃ] *n* (*worthless*) camelote *f*; (*waste*) ordures *f pl*. **trash can** (*US*) poubelle *f*.
trauma ['trɔːmə] *n* traumatisme *m*; (*med*) trauma *m*. **traumatic** *adj* traumatisant; (*med*) traumatique.
travel ['travl] *v* voyager; (*go*) aller; (*cover*) parcourir. *n* voyage *m*. **travel agency** agence de voyages *f*. **travel brochure** dépliant touristique *m*. **travel-sickness** *n* mal de la route. **traveller** *n* voyageur, -euse *m*, *f*; (*comm*) représentant *m*. **traveller's cheque** chèque de voyage *m*.

travesty ['travəsti] *n* simulacre *m*, parodie *f*.
trawler ['trɔːlə] *n* chalutier *m*. **trawling** *n* chalutage *m*.
tray [trei] *n* plateau *m*. **tray-cloth** *n* napperon *m*.
treachery ['tretʃəri] *n* traîtrise *f*. **treacherous** *adj* traître, -esse.
treacle ['triːkl] *n* mélasse *f*.
*tread [tred] *n* (bruit de) pas *m*; (*tyre*) chape *f*. *v* marcher. **tread on** mettre le pied sur; (*crush*) écraser du pied.
treason ['triːzn] *n* trahison *f*.
treasure ['treʒə] *n* trésor *m*. *v* tenir beaucoup à; garder précieusement. **treasurer** *n* trésorier, -ère *m*, *f*. **treasury** *n* trésorerie *f*.
treat [triːt] *v* traiter; (*med*) soigner. *n* plaisir *m*. **treatment** *n* traitement *m*.
treatise ['triːtiz] *n* traité *m*.
treaty ['triːti] *n* traité *m*.
treble ['trebl] *adj* triple; de soprano. *n* soprano *m*. *v* tripler. *adv* trois fois plus.
tree [triː] *n* arbre *m*.
trek [trek] *v* cheminer. *n* randonnée *f*.
trellis ['trelis] *n* treillis *m*, treillage *m*. *v* treillisser.
tremble ['trembl] *v* trembler, frémir. *n* tremblement *m*, frémissement *m*.
tremendous [trə'mendəs] *adj* énorme; (*terrible*) épouvantable; (*coll: excellent*) formidable.
tremor ['tremə] *n* tremblement *m*.
trench [trentʃ] *n* tranchée *f*.
trend [trend] *n* tendance *f*; mode *f*; direction *f*. **trendy** *adj* (*coll*) à la mode, dans le vent.
trespass ['trespəs] *v* s'introduire sans permission. *n* entrée non autorisée *f*. **trespasser** *n* intrus, -e *m*, *f*. **trespassers will be prosecuted** défense d'entrer sous peine de poursuites.
trestle ['tresl] *n* tréteau *m*. **trestle table** table à tréteaux *f*.
trial ['traiəl] *n* (*law*) procès *m*; (*test*) essai *m*; (*trouble*) épreuve *f*. **by trial and error** par tâtonnements. *adj* d'essai.
triangle ['traiaŋgl] *n* triangle *m*. **triangular** *adj* triangulaire.
tribe [traib] *n* tribu *f*. **tribal** *adj* tribal. **tribesman** *n* membre d'une tribu *m*.
tribunal [trai'bjuːnl] *n* tribunal *m*.
tributary ['tribjutəri] *n* affluent *m*. *adj* tributaire.

tribute ['tribjuːt] *n* tribut *m*.
trick [trik] *n* tour *m*; ruse *f*; (*cards*) levée *f*. **do the trick** (*coll*) faire l'affaire. **trick photograph** photographie truquée *f*. **trick question** question-piège *f*. *v* attraper. **trickery** *n* ruse *f*. **tricky** *adj* délicat, difficile.
trickle ['trikl] *n* filet *m*. *v* couler, dégouliner.
tricycle ['traisikl] *n* tricycle *m*.
trifle ['traifl] *n* bagatelle *f*; (*sweet*) diplomate *m*. *v* **trifle with** traiter à la légère. **trifling** *adj* insignifiant.
trigger ['trigə] *n* détente *f*, gâchette *f*. *v* déclencher, provoquer.
trigonometry [trigə'nomətri] *n* trigonométrie *f*.
trill [tril] *n* trille *m*. *v* triller.
trim [trim] *adj* net, nette; (*tidy*) bien tenu. **in trim** en forme. *v* tailler légèrement; (*hair*) rafraîchir; (*decorate*) garnir. **trimmings** *pl n* garnitures *f pl*; accessoires *m pl*.
trinket ['triŋkit] *n* bibelot *m*.
trio ['triːou] *n* trio *m*.
trip [trip] *n* voyage *m*; (*stumble*) faux pas *m*; (*slang: drugs*) trip *m*. *v* trébucher. **trip up** (faire) trébucher; (*on purpose*) faire un croche-pied à.
tripe [traip] *n* tripes *f pl*; (*coll*) bêtises *f pl*.
triple ['tripl] *nm, adj* triple. *v* tripler. *adv* trois fois plus.
triplet ['triplit] *n* (*music*) triolet *m*; (*poetry*) tercet *m*; (*person*) triplé, -e *m, f*.
tripod ['traipod] *n* trépied *m*.
trite [trait] *adj* banal. **triteness** *n* banalité *f*.
triumph ['traiʌmf] *n* triomphe *m*. *v* triompher. **triumphant** *adj* triomphant. **triumphantly** *adv* triomphalement.
trivial ['triviəl] *adj* insignifiant; banal. **trivia** *or* **trivialities** *pl n* bagatelles *f pl*.
trod [trod] *V* **tread**.
trodden ['trodn] *V* **tread**.
trolley ['troli] *n* chariot *m*; (*shopping*) poussette *f*; (*tea*) table roulante *f*.
trombone [trom'boun] *n* trombone *m*.
troop [truːp] *n* bande *f*, troupe *f*. **troops** *pl n* (*mil*) troupes *f pl*. *v* **troop in/out** entrer/sortir en bande. **trooping the colour** le salut au drapeau.
trophy ['troufi] *n* trophée *m*.
tropic ['tropik] *n* tropique *m*. **tropical** *adj* tropical.

trot [trot] *n* trot *m*. **on the trot** (*coll*) de suite. *v* trotter. **trotter** *n* pied de porc *m*.
trouble ['trʌbl] *n* ennui *m*; (*bother*) peine *f*; difficulté *f*. **be in trouble** avoir des ennuis. **that's the trouble!** c'est ça l'ennui! **troublemaker** *n* fauteur, -trice de troubles *m, f*. **troublesome** *adj* fatigant, gênant. *v* (*bother*) (se) déranger; (*upset*) affliger, gêner; (*worry*) inquiéter.
trough [trof] *n* (*drinking*) abreuvoir *m*; (*food*) auge *f*; dépression *f*, creux *m*.
trousers ['trauzəz] *pl n* pantalon *m sing*; (*short*) culottes *f pl*. **trouser-suit** *n* tailleur-pantalon *m*.
trout [traut] *n* truite *f*.
trowel ['trauəl] *n* truelle *f*; (*gardening*) déplantoir *m*.
truant ['truːənt] *n* **play truant** faire l'école buissonnière. **truancy** *n* absence non autorisée *f*.
truce [truːs] *n* trêve *f*. **call a truce** faire trêve.
truck [trʌk] *n* camion *m*; (*rail*) wagon *m*. **truck-driver** *n* camionneur *m*.
trudge [trʌdʒ] *v* se traîner, marcher péniblement.
true [truː] *adj* vrai; exact; (*accurate*) fidèle; réel; (*straight*) droit; (*note*) juste. **truly** *adv* vraiment. **well and truly** bel et bien.
truffle ['trʌfl] *n* truffe *f*.
trump [trʌmp] *n* atout *m*. **turn up trumps** (*coll*) faire des merveilles. *v* couper.
trumpet ['trʌmpit] *n* trompette *f*. *v* (*elephant*) barrir. **trumpeter** *n* trompettiste *m, f*.
truncate [trʌŋ'keit] *v* tronquer.
truncheon ['trʌntʃən] *n* matraque *f*; (*police*) bâton *m*.
trunk [trʌŋk] *n* tronc *m*; (*elephant*) trompe *f*; (*case*) malle *f*. (*mot*) coffre *m*. **trunk call** communication interurbaine *f*. **trunk road** route nationale *f*. **trunks** *pl n* slip de bain *m sing*.
truss [trʌs] *n* (*hay*) botte *f*; (*fruit*) grappe *f*; (*med*) bandage herniaire *m*. *v* trousser.
trust [trʌst] *n* confiance *f*; charge *f*; (*comm*) trust *m*; (*law*) fidéicommis *m*. **trustworthy** *adj* digne de confiance. *v* avoir confiance en, se fier à; (*hope*) espérer. **trustee** *n* (*law*) fidéicommissaire *m*; (*of school*) administrateur, -trice *m, f*. **trusting** *adj* confiant. **trusty** *adj* fidèle.

truth [truːθ] *n* verité *f*. **truthful** *adj* véridique. **truthfulness** *n* véracité *f*.

try [trai] *n* essai *m*. *v* essayer; juger; (*strain*) mettre à l'épreuve; tester. **try on** essayer. **trying** *adj* pénible.

tsar [zaɪ] *n* tsar *m*.

T-shirt ['tiːʃəɪt] *n* T-shirt *m*.

tub [tʌb] *n* cuve *f*, baquet *m*; (*bath*) tub *m*.

tuba ['tjuːbə] *n* tuba *m*.

tube [tjuːb] *n* tube *m*; (*rail*) métro *m*. **tubeless** *adj* (*tyre*) sans chambre à air.

tuber ['tjuːbə] *n* tubercule *m*.

tuberculosis [tjubəɪkju'lousis] *n* tuberculose *f*.

tuck [tʌk] *n* (*sewing*) rempli *m*. **tuck-shop** *n* (*school*) boutique à provisions *f*. *v* mettre. **tuck in** (*flap*) rentrer; (*bedclothes*) border; (*coll: eat*) boulotter. **tuck up** (*in bed*) border; (*skirt*) remonter.

Tuesday ['tjuːzdi] *n* mardi *m*.

tuft [tʌft] *n* touffe *f*; (*feathers*) huppe *f*.

tug [tʌg] *n* saccade *f*; (*boat*) remorqueur *m*. **tug-of-war** *n* lutte à la corde *f*. *v* tirer; remorquer.

tuition [tju'iʃən] *n* cours *m pl*.

tulip ['tjuːlip] *n* tulipe *f*.

tumble ['tʌmbl] *n* chute *f*, culbute *f*. *v* culbuter, dégringoler; (*knock over*) faire tomber, renverser. **tumbledown** *adj* en ruines. **tumble-dryer** *n* séchoir à air chaud *m*. **tumble out** tomber en vrac. **tumbler** *n* verre droit *m*.

tummy ['tʌmi] *n* (*coll*) ventre *m*.

tumour ['tjuːmə] *n* tumeur *f*.

tumult ['tjuːmʌlt] *n* tumulte *m*. **tumultuous** *adj* tumultueux.

tuna ['tjuːnə] *n also* **tunny** thon *m*.

tune [tjuːn] *n* air *m*. **in tune** accordé; (*sing*) juste. **out of tune** désaccordé; (*sing*) faux. *v* régler; (*music*) accorder. **tuneful** *adj* mélodieux. **tuner** *n* (*person*) accordeur *m*; (*radio*) radio-préamplificateur *m*. **tuning** *n* réglage *m*; accord *m*. **tuning fork** diapason *m*.

tunic ['tjuːnik] *n* tunique *f*.

tunnel ['tʌnl] *n* tunnel *m*. *v* percer un tunnel.

turban ['təɪbən] *n* turban *m*.

turbine ['təɪbain] *n* turbine *f*.

turbot ['təɪbət] *n* turbot *m*.

turbulent ['təɪbjulənt] *adj* turbulent. **turbulence** *n* turbulence *f*.

tureen [tə'riɪn] *n* soupière *f*.

turf [təɪf] *n* gazon *m*; (*sport*) turf *m*. **turf accountant** bookmaker *m*. *v* gazonner. **turf out** (*coll: thing*) bazarder; (*coll: person*) flanquer à la porte.

turkey ['təɪki] *n* dindon *m*; (*cookery*) dinde *f*.

Turkey ['təɪki] *n* Turquie *f*. **Turk** *n* Turc, Turque *m*, *f*. **Turkish** *nm*, *adj* turc, turque. **Turkish bath** bain turc *m*. **Turkish delight** loukoum *m*.

turmeric ['təɪmərik] *n* curcuma *m*.

turmoil ['təɪmoil] *n* agitation *f*, trouble *m*.

turn [təɪn] *n* tour *m*; (*in road*) tournant *m*, virage *m*; (*med*) crise *f*; (*theatre*) numéro *m*. **do a good turn** rendre un service (à). *v* (faire) tourner; (se) retourner; changer. **turn away** (se) détourner; refuser, rejeter. **turn down** rejeter; (*lower*) baisser. **turn off** fermer, éteindre. **turn on** allumer, brancher; attaquer. **turn out** (*end up*) s'avérer; (*light*) éteindre; (*empty*) vider; (*expel*) mettre à la porte. **turnover** *n* (*comm*) roulement *m*; (*cookery*) chausson *m*. **turnstile** *n* tourniquet *m*. **turntable** *n* (*record-player*) platine *f*; (*trains, etc.*) plaque tournante *f*. **turn up** arriver; (*be found*) être trouvé; (*raise*) mettre plus fort, monter. **turning** *n* (*side road*) route latérale *f*; (*bend*) coude *m*. **turning point** tournant *m*, moment décisif *m*.

turnip ['təɪnip] *n* navet *m*.

turpentine ['təɪpəntain] *n* térébenthine *f*.

turquoise ['təɪkwoiz] *n* (*stone*) turquoise *f*; (*colour*) turquoise *m*. *adj* (*colour*) turquoise *invar*.

turret ['tʌrit] *n* tourelle *f*.

turtle ['təɪtl] *n* tortue marine *f*. **turn turtle** chavirer. **turtle-neck** *n* (*jumper*) col montant *m*.

tusk [tʌsk] *n* défense *f*.

tussle ['tʌsl] *n* lutte *f*. *v* se battre.

tutor ['tjuːtə] *n* (*private*) précepteur, -trice *m*, *f*; (*university*) directeur, -trice d'études *m*, *f*. *v* donner des cours particuliers (à).

tuxedo [tʌk'siɪdou] *n* smoking *m*.

tweed [twiːd] *n* tweed *m*.

tweezers ['twiɪzəz] *pl n* pinces fines *f pl*.

twelve [twelv] *nm*, *adj* douze. **twelfth** *n(m+f)*, *adj* douzième. **Twelfth Night** la fête des Rois *f*.

twenty ['twenti] *nm*, *adj* vingt. **twentieth** *n(m+f)*, *adj* vingtième.

twice [twais] *adv* deux fois.
twiddle ['twidl] *v* tripoter. **twiddle one's thumbs** se tourner les pouces.
twig [twig] *n* brindille *f.*
twilight ['twailait] *n* crépuscule *m.*
twin [twin] *n, adj* jumeau, -elle. **twin beds** lits jumeaux *m pl.* **twin town** ville jumelée *f. v* jumeler.
twine [twain] *n* ficelle *f. v* (*weave*) tresser; (s')enrouler; serpenter.
twinge [twindʒ] *n* (*pain*) élancement *m*; (*sadness*) pincement *m*; remords *m.*
twinkle ['twiŋkl] *v* scintiller, briller. *n* scintillement *m*; (*eyes*) pétillement *m.*
twirl [twɜːl] *v* (faire) tournoyer. *n* tournoiement *m.*
twist [twist] *n* torsion *f*; (*med*) entorse *f*; (*in wire, etc.*) tortillon *m*; (*in road*) tournant *m*; (*story*) coup de théâtre *m. v* (s')entortiller, tordre; (*turn*) tourner; (*road*) serpenter.
twit [twit] *n* (*slang*) idiot, -e *m, f.*
twitch [twitʃ] *n* tic *m*; (*pull*) coup sec *m. v* se convulser; avoir un tic; tirer d'un coup sec.
twitter ['twitə] *v* gazouiller. *n* gazouillement *m.*
two [tuː] *nm, adj* deux. **two-faced** *adj* hypocrite. **two-legged** *adj* bipède. **two-time** *v* (*coll*) doubler.
tycoon [tai'kuːn] *n* magnat *m.*
type [taip] *n* type *m*; (*sort*) genre *m.* **typesetting** *n* composition *f.* **typewriter** *n* machine à écrire *f. v* taper (à la machine). **typical** *adj* typique. **typing** *n* dactylo *f.* **typist** *n* dactylo *m, f.*
typhoid ['taifoid] *n* typhoïde *f.*
typhoon [tai'fuːn] *n* typhon *m.*
tyrant ['tairənt] *n* tyran *m.* **tyrannical** *adj* tyrannique. **tyranny** *n* tyrannie *f.*
tyre *or US* **tire** ['taiə] *n* pneu *m.*

U

ubiquitous [juˈbikwitəs] *adj* omniprésent.
udder ['ʌdə] *n* pis *m*, mamelle *f.*
ugly ['ʌgli] *adj* laid, vilain; répugnant. **ugliness** *n* laideur *f.*
ulcer ['ʌlsə] *n* ulcère *m.*
ulterior [ʌl'tiəriə] *adj* ultérieur, -e. **ulterior motive** arrière-pensée *f.*

ultimate ['ʌltimət] *adj* ultime; final; suprême. **ultimately** *adv* à la fin; (*basically*) en fin de compte. **ultimatum** *n* ultimatum *m.*
ultraviolet [ʌltrə'vaiələt] *adj* ultra-violet.
umbilical [ʌm'bilikəl] *adj* ombilical.
umbrage ['ʌmbridʒ] *n* ombrage *m.* **take umbrage** prendre ombrage.
umbrella [ʌm'brelə] *n* parapluie *m.*
umpire ['ʌmpaiə] *n* arbitre *m. v* arbitrer.
umpteen [ʌmp'tiːn] (*coll*) *adj* je ne sais combien (de). **umpteenth** *adj* énième.
unable [ʌn'eibl] *adj* incapable. **be unable to** (*lack means*) ne pas pouvoir; (*lack knowledge*) ne pas savoir.
unabridged [ʌnə'bridʒd] *adj* intégral.
unacceptable [ʌnək'septəbl] *adj* inacceptable; inadmissible.
unaccompanied [ʌnə'kumpənid] *adj* non accompagné; (*music*) sans accompagnement, seul.
unadulterated [ʌnə'dʌltəreitid] *adj* pur.
unaided [ʌn'eidid] *adj* sans aide.
unanimous [ju'naniməs] *adj* unanime. **unanimity** *n* unanimité *f.*
unarmed [ʌn'aːmd] *adj* (*combat*) sans armes; (*person*) non armé.
unattached [ʌnə'tatʃt] *adj* libre; indépendant.
unattractive [ʌnə'traktiv] *adj* peu attrayant, déplaisant.
unauthorized [ʌn'oɪθəraizd] *adj* non autorisé.
unavoidable [ʌnə'voidəbl] *adj* inévitable.
unaware [ʌnə'weə] *adj* inconscient. **be unaware of** ignorer. **unawares** *adv* à l'improviste.
unbalanced [ʌn'balənst] *adj* mal équilibré; (*mentally*) déséquilibré.
unbearable [ʌn'beərəbl] *adj* insupportable.
unbelievable [ʌnbi'liːvəbl] *adj* incroyable.
***unbend** [ʌn'bend] *v* redresser; (*person*) se détendre. **unbending** *adj* inflexible.
unbiased [ʌn'baiəst] *adj* impartial.
unbreakable [ʌn'breikəbl] *adj* incassable.
unbridled [ʌn'braidld] *adj* débridé.
unbutton [ʌn'bʌtn] *v* déboutonner.
uncalled-for [ʌn'koɪldfoɪ] *adj* injustifié, déplacé.
uncanny [ʌn'kani] *adj* étrange, troublant.
uncertain [ʌn'səɪtn] *adj* incertain. **uncertainty** *n* incertitude *f.*

uncle ['ʌŋkl] *n* oncle *m*.

uncomfortable [ʌn'kʌmfətəbl] *adj* inconfortable; mal à l'aise.

uncommon [ʌn'komən] *adj* rare.

uncompromising [ʌn'komprəmaizɪŋ] *adj* intransigeant.

unconditional [ʌnkən'diʃənl] *adj* inconditionnel.

unconscious [ʌn'konʃəs] *adj* (*med*) sans connaissance; (*unaware*) inconscient.

unconventional [ʌnkən'venʃənl] *adj* peu conventionnel.

uncooked [ʌn'kukt] *adj* non cuit.

uncouth [ʌn'kuɪθ] *adj* grossier.

uncover [ʌn'kʌvə] *v* découvrir.

uncut [ʌn'kʌt] *adj* non coupé, non taillé.

undecided [ʌndi'saidid] *adj* indécis.

undeniable [ʌndi'naiəbl] *adj* indéniable, incontestable.

under ['ʌndə] *adv* au-dessous. *prep* sous; au dessous de; (*less*) moins de; (*according to*) selon.

underarm ['ʌndərɑɪm] *adj, adv* par en-dessous.

undercharge [ʌndə'tʃɑɪdʒ] *v* ne pas faire payer assez à.

underclothes ['ʌndəklouðz] *pl n* sous-vêtements *m pl*.

undercoat ['ʌndəkout] *n* couche de fond *f*.

undercover [ʌndə'kʌvə] *adj* secret, -ète.

undercut [ʌndə'kʌt] *v* vendre moins cher que.

underdeveloped [ʌndədi'veləpt] *adj* sous-développé.

underdog ['ʌndədog] *n* (*loser*) perdant *m*; (*oppressed*) opprimé *m*.

underdone [ʌndə'dʌn] *adj* (*meat*) saignant; pas assez cuit.

underestimate [ʌndə'estimeit] *v* sous-estimer. **underestimation** *n* sous-estimation *f*.

underfoot [ʌndə'fut] *adv* sous les pieds.

*****undergo** [ʌndə'gou] *v* subir, éprouver.

undergraduate [ʌndə'gradjuət] *n* étudiant, -e *m, f*.

underground [ʌndə'graund; *adj, adv* 'ʌndəgraund] *adv* sous terre; clandestinement. *adj* sous terre, souterrain; clandestin. *n* (*rail*) métro *m*.

undergrowth ['ʌndəgrouθ] *n* broussailles *f pl*.

underhand [ʌndə'hand] *adj* en sous-main, sournois.

*****underlie** [ʌndə'lai] *v* être à la base de. **underlying** *adj* sous-jacent.

underline [ʌndə'lain] *v* souligner. **underlining** ·*n* soulignage *m*.

undermine [ʌndə'main] *v* saper, miner.

underneath [ʌndə'niɪθ] *prep* sous, au-dessous de. *nm, adv* dessous. *adj* d'en dessous.

underpaid [ʌndə'peid] *adj* sous-payé.

underpants ['ʌndəpants] *pl n* caleçon *m sing*.

underpass ['ʌndəpɑɪs] *n* (*cars*) passage inférieur *m*; (*people*) passage souterrain *m*.

underprivileged [ʌndə'privilidʒd] *adj* défavorisé.

underrate [ʌndə'reit] *v* sous-estimer.

underskirt ['ʌndəskəɪt] *n* jupon *m*.

understaffed [ʌndə'stɑɪft] *adj* à court de personnel.

*****understand** [ʌndə'stand] *v* comprendre; (*imply*) sous-entendre. **understandable** *adj* compréhensible. **understanding** *n* compréhension *f*; (*agreement*) accord *m*.

understate [ʌndə'steit] *n* minimiser. **make an understatement** ne pas assez dire. **that's an understatement!** c'est peu dire!

understudy ['ʌndəstʌdi] *n* doublure *f*. *v* doubler.

*****undertake** [ʌndə'teik] *v* entreprendre, se charger de. **undertaker** *n* ordonnateur des pompes funèbres *m*. **undertaking** *n* entreprise *f*; promesse *f*.

undertone ['ʌndətoun] *n* **in an undertone** à demi-voix.

underwater [ʌndə'wɔɪtə] *adj* sous-marin. *adv* sous l'eau.

underwear ['ʌndəweə] *n* sous-vêtements *m pl*.

underweight [ʌndə'weit] *adj* (*goods*) d'un poids insuffisant; (*person*) trop maigre.

underworld ['ʌndəwəɪld] *n* (*criminal*) milieu *m*; (*hell*) enfers *m pl*.

*****underwrite** [ʌndə'rait] *v* garantir; (*insurance*) souscrire.

undesirable [ʌndi'zaiərəbl] *adj* peu souhaitable. *n* indésirable *m, f*.

*****undo** [ʌn'duɪ] *v* défaire; (*destroy*) détruire. **come undone** se défaire. **undoing** *n* ruine *f*.

undoubted [ʌn'dautid] *adj* indubitable.

undress [ʌn'dres] *v* (se) déshabiller.

undue [ʌn'djuɪ] *adj* indu. **unduly** *adv* trop.

undulate ['ʌndjuleit] *v* onduler. **undulating** *adj* onduleux. **undulation** *n* ondulation *f*.

unearth [ʌn'əɪθ] *v* déterrer. **unearthly** *adj*
surnaturel; (*coll: hour*) impossible, indu.
uneasy [ʌn'iːzi] *adj* mal à l'aise; troublé;
anxieux.
uneducated [ʌn'edjukeitid] *adj* sans éducation.
unemployed [ʌnem'ploid] *adj* en
chômage. **the unemployed** les chômeurs
m pl. **unemployment** *n* chômage *m.*
unenthusiastic [ʌnenθjuːzi'astik] *adj* peu
enthousiaste.
unequal [ʌn'iːkwəl] *adj* inégal.
uneven [ʌn'iːvn] *adj* inégal; (*number*)
impair.
uneventful [ʌni'ventfəl] *adj* peu mouvementé.
unexpected [ʌneks'pektid] *adj* inattendu.
unfailing [ʌn'feiliŋ] *adj* inépuisable;
infaillible.
unfair [ʌn'feə] *adj* injuste. **unfairness** *n*
injustice *f.*
unfaithful [ʌn'feiθfəl] *adj* infidèle. **unfaithfulness** *n* infidélité *f.*
unfamiliar [ʌnfə'miljə] *adj* peu familier,
inconnu.
unfasten [ʌn'faɪsn] *v* défaire, ouvrir.
unfavourable [ʌn'feivərəbl] *adj*
défavorable.
unfinished [ʌn'finiʃt] *adj* inachevé; à finir.
unfit [ʌn'fit] *adj* inapte, impropre; (*ill*)
souffrant.
unfold [ʌn'fould] *v* déplier; exposer;
(*story, countryside*) se dérouler.
unforeseen [ʌnfɔː'siːn] *adj* imprévu.
unforgivable [ʌnfə'givəbl] *adj* impardon-
nable.
unfortunate [ʌn'fɔːtʃənət] *adj*
malheureux, fâcheux.
unfounded [ʌn'faundid] *adj* sans fondement; injustifié.
unfriendly [ʌn'frendli] *adj* froid; hostile.
unfurnished [ʌn'fəːniʃd] *adj* non meublé.
ungainly [ʌn'geinli] *adj* gauche.
ungrateful [ʌn'greitfəl] *adj* ingrat.
unhappy [ʌn'hapi] *adj* triste, malheureux.
unhappiness *n* tristesse *f.*
unhealthy [ʌn'helθi] *adj* malsain; (*person*)
maladif.
unheard-of [ʌn'həːdov] *adj* inouï, sans
précédent.
unhurt [ʌn'həːt] *adj* indemne, sain et sauf.
unhygienic [ʌnhai'dʒiːnik] *adj* non
hygiénique.
unicorn ['juːnikɔːn] *n* licorne *f.*

unidentified [ʌnai'dentifaid] *adj* non
identifié. **unidentified flying object
(UFO)** objet volant non identifié
(OVNI) *m.*
uniform ['juːnifɔːm] *nm, adj* uniforme.
uniformity *n* uniformité *f.*
unify ['juːnifai] *v* unifier. **unification** *n* unification *f.*
unilateral [juːni'latərəl] *adj* unilatéral.
unimaginative [ʌni'madʒinətiv] *adj* peu
imaginatif.
unimportant [ʌnim'pɔːtnt] *adj* peu important.
uninhabited [ʌnin'habitid] *adj* inhabité.
uninhibited [ʌnin'hibitid] *adj* sans inhibi-
tions.
unintentional [ʌnin'tenʃənl] *adj*
involontaire.
uninterested [ʌn'intristid] *adj* indifférent.
uninteresting *adj* inintéressant.
union ['juːnjən] *n* union *f;* (*trade*) syndicat *m.*
unique [juː'niːk] *adj* unique.
unisex ['juːniˌseks] *adj* (*coll*) unisexe.
unison ['juːnisn] *n* unisson *m.* **in unison**
en chœur.
unit ['juːnit] *n* unité *f;* bloc *m,* groupe *m.*
unite [juː'nait] *v* (s')unir, unifier. **united**
adj uni. **United Kingdom** Royaume-Uni
m. **United Nations** Nations Unies *f pl.*
United States of America Etats-Unis *m
pl.*
unity ['juːniti] *n* unité *f.*
universe ('juːnivəːs] *n* univers *m.* **universal**
adj universel.
university [juːni'vəːsəti] *n* université *f. adj*
universitaire.
unjust [ʌn'dʒʌst] *adj* injuste.
unkempt [ʌn'kempt] *adj* débraillé; (*hair*)
mal peigné.
unkind [ʌn'kaind] *adj* peu aimable,
méchant, cruel. **unkindness** *n* méchanceté
f.
unknown [ʌn'noun] *nm, adj* inconnu.
unlawful [ʌn'lɔːfəl] *adj* illégal, illégitime.
unless [ʌn'les] *conj* à moins que.
unlike [ʌn'laik] *adj* dissemblable, différent. *prep* à la différence de.
unlikely [ʌn'laikli] *adj* peu probable;
(*story*) invraisemblable.
unlimited [ʌn'limitid] *adj* illimité.
unload [ʌn'loud] *v* décharger; (*get rid of*)
se défaire de.
unlock [ʌn'lok] *v* ouvrir.

unlucky [ʌn'lʌki] *adj* malchanceux, malheureux; (*number, etc.*) qui porte malheur.

unmarried [ʌn'marid] *adj* célibataire.

unnatural [ʌn'natʃərəl] *adj* anormal; contre nature.

unnecessary [ʌn'nesəsəri] *adj* inutile; superflu.

unnerving [ʌn'nərviŋ] *adj* déconcertant.

unnoticed [ʌn'noutist] *adj* inaperçu. **go unnoticed** passer inaperçu.

unobtainable [ʌnəb'teinəbl] *adj* impossible à obtenir.

unobtrusive [ʌnəb'truːsiv] *adj* discret, -ète.

unoccupied [ʌn'okjupaid] *adj* inoccupé, (*seat*) libre.

unofficial [ʌnə'fiʃəl] *adj* officieux, non officiel.

unorthodox [ʌn'oɪθədoks] *adj* peu orthodoxe.

unpack [ʌn'pak] *v* (*case*) défaire (sa valise); (*contents*) déballer (ses affaires).

unpaid [ʌn'peid] *adj* impayé, non acquitté; (*worker*) non retribué.

unpleasant [ʌn'pleznt] *adj* désagréable, déplaisant.

unpopular [ʌn'popjulə] *adj* impopulaire.

unprecedented [ʌn'presidentid] *adj* sans précédent.

unpredictable [ʌnprə'diktəbl] *adj* imprévisible; incertain.

unqualified [ʌn'kwolifaid] *adj* non qualifié, non diplômé; (*absolute*) sans réserve.

unravel [ʌn'ravəl] *v* (s')effiler; (*mystery*) débrouiller.

unreal [ʌn'riəl] *adj* irréel.

unreasonable [ʌn'riːzənəbl] *adj* déraisonnable; excessif.

unrelenting [ʌnri'lentiŋ] *adj* implacable.

unreliable [ʌnri'laiəbl] *adj* sur qui on ne peut compter; (*machine*) peu fiable; (*source*) douteux.

unrest [ʌn'rest] *n* agitation *f.*

unruly [ʌn'ruːli] *adj* indiscipliné.

unsafe [ʌn'seif] *adj* dangereux.

unsatisfactory [ʌnsatis'faktəri] *adj* peu satisfaisant.

unscrew [ʌn'skruː] *v* (se) dévisser.

unscrupulous [ʌn'skruːpjuləs] *adj* sans scrupules, malhonnête.

unselfish [ʌn'selfiʃ] *adj* non égoïste, désintéressé.

unsettle [ʌn'setl] *v* perturber. **unsettled** *adj* perturbé; incertain; instable.

unsightly [ʌn'saitli] *adj* disgracieux.

unskilled [ʌn'skild] *adj* inexpérimenté. **unskilled worker** manœuvre *m.*

unsound [ʌn'saund] *adj* peu solide; (*health*) précaire; (*reasoning*) mal fondé.

unspeakable [ʌn'spiːkəbl] *adj* indescriptible.

unspecified [ʌn'spesifaid] *adj* non spécifié.

unstable [ʌn'steibl] *adj* instable.

unsteady [ʌn'stedi] *adj* instable, mal assuré.

unstuck [ʌn'stʌk] *adj* **come unstuck** se décoller.

unsuccessful [ʌnsək'sesfəl] *adj* infructueux; (*candidate*) réfusé; (*marriage*) malheureux. **unsuccessfully** *adv* sans succès.

unsuitable [ʌn'suːtəbl] *adj* qui ne convient pas; inopportun; peu appropié.

unsure [ʌn'ʃuə] *adj* incertain.

untangle [ʌn'taŋgl] *v* démêler.

untidy [ʌn'taidi] *adj* négligé, débraillé; (*writing*) brouillon; (*room*) en désordre. **untidiness** *n* débraillé *m*; désordre *m.*

untie [ʌn'tai] *v* défaire.

until [ən'til] *prep* jusqu'à; (*before*) avant. *conj* jusqu'à ce que.

untoward [ʌntə'woɪd] *adj* fâcheux.

untrue [ʌn'truː] *adj* faux, fausse; inexact.

unusual [ʌn'juːʒuəl] *adj* insolite; bizarre; exceptionnel.

unwanted [ʌn'wontid] *adj* superflu; non désiré.

unwell [ʌn'wel] *adj* indisposé, souffrant.

unwilling [ʌn'wiliŋ] *adj* peu disposé. **unwillingly** *adv* à contrecœur.

***unwind** [ʌn'waind] *v* (se) dérouler; (*relax*) se détendre.

unwise [ʌn'waiz] *adj* imprudent.

unworthy [ʌn'wəɪði] *adj* indigne.

unwrap [ʌn'rap] *v* défaire.

up [ʌp] *adv* en haut, en l'air; (*standing*) debout; (*out of bed*) levé; terminé. **up there** là-haut. **up to** jusqu'à. *prep* dans, sur. **go up** monter. *n* **ups and downs** hauts et bas *m pl.*

upbringing ['ʌpbriŋiŋ] *n* éducation *f.*

update [ʌp'deit] *v* mettre à jour.

upheaval [ʌp'hiːvl] *n* bouleversement *m*; (*domestic*) branle-bas *m*; (*pol*) perturbation *f.*

uphill [ʌp'hil] *adj* qui monte; (*struggle*) pénible. *adv* go uphill monter.

***uphold** [ʌp'hould] *v* soutenir, maintenir.

upholster [ʌp'houlstə] *v* rembourrer. **upholstery** *n* tapisserie *f*; (*material*) rembourrage *m*; (*in car*) garniture *f*.

upkeep ['ʌpkiːp] *n* entretien *m*.

uplift [ʌp'lift] *v* élever.

upon [ə'pon] *prep* sur.

upper ['ʌpə] *adj* supérieur, -e, du dessus. **upper-class** *adj* aristocratique. **uppermost** *adj* le plus haut; en dessus.

upright ['ʌprait] *adj*, *adv* droit. *n* montant *m*.

uprising ['ʌpraiziŋ] *n* soulèvement *m*.

uproar ['ʌprɔː] *n* tumulte *m*, vacarme *m*. **uproarious** *adj* tumultueux; hilarant.

uproot [ʌp'ruːt] *v* déraciner.

***upset** [ʌp'set; *n* 'ʌpset] *v* (*knock over*) renverser; (*plans, etc.*) déranger; (*person*) faire de la peine à, contrarier. *adj* (*angry*) fâché; (*sad*) peiné; (*stomach*) dérangé. *n* désordre *m*; dérangement *m*; chagrin *m*.

upshot ['ʌpʃot] *n* résultat *m*.

upside down [ʌpsai'daun] *adv*, *adj* sens dessus dessous, à l'envers.

upstairs [ʌp'steəz] *adv* en haut. **go upstairs** monter (l'escalier). *adj* du dessus, d'en haut.

upstream [ʌp'striːm; *adj* 'ʌpstriːm] *adv* vers l'amont, en amont; (*swim*) contre le courant. *adj* d'amont.

uptight ['ʌptait] *adj* (*coll*) crispé.

up-to-date [ʌptə'deit] *adj* moderne.

upward ['ʌpwəd] *adj* ascendant. **upwards** *adv* vers le haut, en montant.

uranium [ju'reiniəm] *n* uranium *m*.

urban ['ɜːbən] *adj* urbain.

urchin ['ɜːtʃin] *n* polisson, -onne *m*, *f*.

urge [ɜːdʒ] *n* désir ardent *m*, forte envie *f*. *v* pousser, conseiller vivement.

urgent ['ɜːdʒənt] *adj* urgent; insistant. **urgency** *n* urgence *f*; insistance *f*. **urgently** *adv* d'urgence.

urine ['juːrin] *n* urine *f*. **urinate** *v* uriner.

urn [ɜːn] *n* urne *f*.

us [ʌs] *pron* nous.

usage ['juːzidʒ] *n* usage *m*.

use [juːs; *v* juːz] *n* usage *m*, emploi *m*. **it's no use** ça ne sert à rien. *v* se servir de, employer. **use up** user, consommer, épuiser. **used** *adj* (*car*) d'occasion. **be used to** être habitué à. **get used to** s'habituer à. **useful** *adj* utile. **useless** *adj* inutile. **user** *n* usager *m*.

usher ['ʌʃə] *n* (*law*) huissier *m*; (*church*) placeur *m*. *v* **usher in** introduire; inaugurer. **usherette** *n* ouvreuse *f*.

usual ['juːzuəl] *adj* habituel. **as usual** comme d'habitude. **usually** *adv* d'habitude, généralement.

usurp [ju'zɜːp] *v* usurper.

utensil [ju'tensl] *n* ustensile *m*.

uterus ['juːtərəs] *n* utérus *m*.

utility [ju'tiləti] *n* utilité *f*. *adj* utilitaire.

utilize ['juːtilaiz] *v* utiliser.

utmost ['ʌtmoust] *adj* le plus grand; suprême; extrême. *n* plus haut point. **do one's utmost** faire tout son possible.

utter[1] ['ʌtə] *v* proférer; (*cry*) pousser.

utter[2] ['ʌtə] *adj* complet, -ète; pur; (*fool*) fini.

U-turn ['juːtɜːn] *n* demi-tour *m*.

V

vacant ['veikənt] *adj* vacant, libre; (*stare*) vague. **vacancy** *n* (*room*) chambre à louer *f*; (*job*) vacance *f*. **no vacancies** complet.

vacate [vei'keit] *v* quitter.

vacation [vei'keiʃn] *n* vacances *f pl*.

vaccine ['vaksiːn] *n* vaccin *m*. **vaccinate** *v* vacciner. **vaccination** *n* vaccination *f*.

vacillate ['vasileit] *v* vaciller. **vacillation** *n* indécision *f*, vacillation *f*.

vacuum ['vakjum] *n* vide *m*; (*phys*) vacuum *m*. **vacuum cleaner** aspirateur *m*. **vacuum flask** bouteille thermos ® *f*. **vacuum-packed** *adj* emballé sous vide. *v* passer à l'aspirateur.

vagina [və'dʒainə] *n* vagin *m*. **vaginal** *adj* vaginal.

vagrant ['veigrənt] *n*, *adj* vagabond, -e. **vagrancy** *n* vagabondage *m*.

vague [veig] *adj* vague, flou, imprécis.

vain [vein] *adj* vain, inutile, futile; (*conceited*) vaniteux. **in vain** en vain.

valiant ['valiənt] *adj* courageux.

valid ['valid] *adj* valide, valable. **validity** *n* validité *f*; force *f*.

Valletta [və'letə] *n* La Valette.

valley ['vali] *n* vallée *f*; (*smaller*) vallon *m*.

value ['valjuː] *n* valeur *f*. *v* évaluer; apprécier, tenir à. **valuable** *adj* de valeur, précieux. **valuables** *pl n* objets de valeur *m pl*. **valuation** *n* évaluation *f*, expertise *f*.

valve [valv] *n* soupape *f*, valve *f*.

vampire ['vampiə] *n* vampire *m*.

van [van] *n* camionnette *f*; (*rail*) fourgon *m*.

vandal ['vandl] *n* vandale *m*, *f*. **vandalism** *n* vandalisme *m*. **vandalize** *v* saccager.

vanilla [və'nilə] *n* vanille *f*.

vanish ['vaniʃ] *v* disparaître.

vanity ['vanəti] *n* vanité *f*. **vanity case** sac de toilette *m*.

vapour ['veipə] *n* vapeur *f*. **vaporize** *v* vaporiser.

varicose veins ['varikous] *pl n* varices *f pl*.

variety [və'raiəti] *n* variété *f*; quantité *f*. **variety show** spectacle de variétés *m*.

various ['veəriəs] *adj* divers.

varnish ['vainiʃ] *n* vernis *m*. *v* vernir.

vary ['veəri] *v* varier, changer. **vary from** différer de. **variable** *nf*, *adj* variable. **variant** *n* variante *f*. **variation** *n* variation *f*.

vase [vaiz] *n* vase *m*.

vasectomy [və'sektəmi] *n* vasectomie *f*.

vast [vaist] *adj* vaste. **vastness** *n* immensité *f*.

vat [vat] *n* cuve *f*.

Vatican ['vatikən] *n* Vatican *m*. **Vatican City** la Cité du Vatican *f*.

vault[1] [voilt] *n* (*cellar*) cave *f*; (*tomb*) caveau *m*; (*bank*) coffre-fort *m*; (*arch*) voûte *f*.

vault[2] [voilt] *v* sauter. *n* saut *m*. **vaulting horse** cheval d'arçons *m*.

veal [viil] *n* veau *m*.

veer [viə] *v* tourner, virer.

vegetable ['vedʒtəbl] *n* légume *m*. *adj* végétal. **vegetable garden** potager *m*. **vegetarian** *n*, *adj* végétarien, -enne. **vegetation** *n* végétation *f*.

vehement ['viiəmənt] *adj* ardent; violent. **vehemence** *n* ardeur *f*; violence *f*. **vehemently** *adv* avec passion; avec violence.

vehicle ['viəkl] *n* véhicule *m*.

veil [veil] *n* voile *m*. *v* voiler.

vein [vein] *n* veine *f*.

velocity [və'losəti] *n* vélocité *f*.

velvet ['velvit] *n* velours *m*. **velvety** *adj* velouteux, velouté.

vending machine ['vendiŋ] *n* distributeur automatique *m*.

veneer [və'niə] *n* placage *m*; (*superficiality*) vernis *m*. *v* plaquer.

venerate ['venəreit] *v* vénérer. **venerable** *adj* vénérable. **veneration** *n* vénération *f*.

venereal disease [və'niəriəl] *n* maladie vénérienne *f*.

Venetian blind [və'niiʃən] *n* store vénitien *m*.

vengeance ['vendʒəns] *n* vengeance *f*. **with a vengeance** (*coll*) pour de bon.

venison ['venisn] *n* venaison *f*.

venom ['venəm] *n* venin *m*. **venomous** *adj* venimeux.

vent [vent] *n* orifice *m*, trou *m*. **give vent to** donner libre cours à. *v* décharger.

ventilate ['ventileit] *v* ventiler, aérer. **ventilation** *n* aération *f*, ventilation *f*.

ventriloquist [ven'triləkwist] *n* ventriloque *m*, *f*.

venture ['ventʃə] *n* aventure *f*; entreprise (risquée) *f*. *v* (se) risquer, (se) hasarder.

venue ['venjui] *n* lieu de rendez-vous *m*.

veranda [və'randə] *n* véranda *f*.

verb [vəib] *n* verbe *m*. **verbal** *adj* verbal.

verdict ['vəidikt] *n* verdict *m*.

verge [vəidʒ] *n* bord *m*. **on the verge of** sur le point de; à deux doigts de. *v* **verge on** approcher de, frôler.

verify ['verifai] *v* vérifier. **verification** *n* vérification *f*.

vermin ['vəimin] *n* animaux nuisibles *m pl*; (*insects, people*) vermine *f*.

vermouth ['vəimə θ] *n* vermouth *m*.

vernacular [və'nakjulə] *adj* vernaculaire. *n* langue vernaculaire *f*.

versatile ['vəisətail] *adj* aux talents variés; (*mind*) souple. **versatility** *n* variété de talents *f*; souplesse *f*.

verse [vəis] *n* (*stanza*) strophe *f*; (*poetry*) vers *m pl*; (*bible*) verset *m*.

version ['vəiʃən] *n* version *f*.

versus ['vəisəs] *prep* contre.

vertebra ['vəitibrə] *n*, *pl* -brae vertèbre *f*. **vertebral** *adj* vertébral. **vertebrate** *nm*, *adj* vertébré.

vertical ['vəitikl] *adj* vertical. *n* verticale *f*.

vertigo ['vəitigou] *n* vertige *m*.

very ['veri] *adv* très, fort, bien; (*absolutely*) tout. **very much** beaucoup. *adj* (*exact*) même; (*extreme*) tout; (*mere*) seul.

vessel ['vesl] *n* vaisseau *m*.

vest [vest] *n* tricot de corps *m*; (*US*) gilet *m*.

vestibule ['vestibjuil] *n* vestibule *m*.

vestige ['vestidʒ] *n* vestige *m*; grain *m*.

vestry ['vestri] *n* sacristie *f*.

vet [vet] *n* (*coll*) vétérinaire *m*, *f*. *v* examiner de près.

veteran ['vetərən] *n* vétéran *m*. **veteran car** voiture d'époque *f*. **war veteran** ancien combattant *m*.

veterinary ['vetərinəri] *adj* vétérinaire. **veterinary surgeon** vétérinaire *m, f*.

veto ['viːtou] *n* veto *m. v* mettre son veto à.

vex [veks] *v* contrarier, fâcher. **vexation** *n* ennui *m*.

via [vaiə] *prep* par, via.

viable ['vaiəbl] *adj* viable. **viability** *n* viabilité *f*.

viaduct ['vaiədʌkt] *n* viaduc *m*.

vibrate [vai'breit] *v* vibrer. **vibration** *n* vibration *f*.

vicar ['vikə] *n* pasteur *m*. **vicarage** *n* presbytère *m*.

vicarious [vi'keəriəs] *adj* délégué; indirect.

vice[1] [vais] *n* (*evil*) vice *m*; (*fault*) défaut *m*.

vice[2] [vais] *n* (*tool*) étau *m*.

vice-chancellor [vais'tʃɑːnsələ] *n* vice-chancelier *m*; (*university*) recteur *m*.

vice-consul [vais'konsl] *n* vice-consul *m*.

vice-president [vais'prezidənt] *n* vice-president, -e *m, f*.

vice versa [vaisi'vəːsə] *adv* vice versa.

vicinity [vi'sinəti] *n* environs *m pl*, alentours *m pl*.

vicious ['viʃəs] *adj* (*remark*) méchant; (*attack*) brutal; (*animal*) vicieux. **vicious circle** cercle vicieux *m*. **viciousness** *n* méchanceté *f*; brutalité *f*.

victim ['viktim] *n* victime *f*. **victimize** *v* prendre pour victime.

victory ['viktəri] *n* victoire *f*. **victorious** *adj* victorieux.

video-tape ['vidiouteip] *n* bande de magnétoscope *f. v* enregistrer sur magnétoscope.

vie [vai] *v* lutter, rivaliser.

Vienna [vi'enə] *n* Vienne.

view [vjuː] *n* vue *f*. **in view of** étant donné, vu. **viewfinder** *n* viseur *m*. **viewpoint** *n* point de vue *m*. **with a view to** dans l'intention de, afin de. *v* visiter; considérer; regarder. **viewer** *n* (*TV*) téléspectateur, -trice *m, f*; (*slides*) visionneuse *f*.

vigil ['vidʒil] *n* veille *f*. **vigilance** *n* vigilance *f*. **vigilant** *adj* vigilant.

vigour ['vigə] *n* vigueur *f*. **vigorous** *adj* vigoureux.

vile [vail] *adj* vil; abominable.

villa ['vilə] *n* villa *f*; (*country*) maison de campagne *f*.

village ['vilidʒ] *n* village *m*. **villager** *n* villageois, -e *m, f*.

villain ['vilən] *n* scélérat *m*. **villainy** *n* infamie *f*.

vindictive [vin'diktiv] *adj* vindicatif.

vine [vain] *n* vigne *f*. **vineyard** *n* vignoble *m*.

vinegar ['vinigə] *n* vinaigre *m*.

vintage ['vintidʒ] *n* (*year*) année *f*; (*harvest*) vendange *f*. **vintage car** voiture d'époque *f*. **vintage wine** grand vin *m*.

vinyl ['vainil] *n* vinyle *m*.

viola [vi'oulə] *n* alto *m*.

violate ['vaiəleit] *v* violer. **violation** *n* violation *f*.

violence ['vaiələns] *n* violence *f*. **violent** *adj* violent.

violet ['vaiəlit] *n* (*flower*) violette *f*; (*colour*) violet *m*. *adj* violet, -ette.

violin [vaiə'lin] *n* violon *m*. **violinist** *n* violoniste *m, f*.

viper ['vaipə] *n* vipère *f*.

virgin ['vəːdʒin] *nf, adj* vierge. **virginity** *n* virginité *f*.

Virgo ['vəːgou] *n* Vierge *f*.

virile ['virail] *adj* viril. **virility** *n* virilité *f*.

virtually ['vəːtʃuəli] *adv* en fait, pratiquement.

virtue ['vəːtʃuː] *n* vertu *f*; mérite *m*. **by virtue of** en vertu de. **virtuous** *adj* vertueux.

virus ['vaiərəs] *n* virus *m*.

visa ['viːzə] *n* visa *m*.

viscount ['vaikaunt] *n* vicomte *m*. **viscountess** *n* vicomtesse *f*.

visible ['vizəbl] *adj* visible. **visibility** *n* visibilité *f*.

vision ['viʒən] *n* vision *f*. **visionary** *n(m+f)*, *adj* visionnaire.

visit ['vizit] *n* visite *f*; (*stay*) séjour *m*. *v* (*call on*) aller voir, rendre visite à; (*stay with*) faire un séjour chez; (*place*) aller à; (*go round*) visiter. **visitor** *n* visiteur, -euse *m, f*.

visor ['vaizə] *n* visière *f*.

visual ['viʒuəl] *adj* visuel. **visualize** *v* se représenter.

vital ['vaitl] *adj* vital. **vitality** *n* vitalité *f*. **vitally** *adv* absolument.

vitamin ['vitəmin] *n* vitamine *f*.

vivacious [vi'veiʃəs] *adj* vif, enjoué. **vivacity** *n* vivacité *f*.

vivid ['vivid] *adj* vif, éclatant; (*description*) vivant. **vividness** *n* vivacité *f*, éclat *m*, clarté *f*.

vivisection [vivi'sekʃən] *n* vivisection *f*.
vixen ['viksn] *n* renarde *f*.
vocabulary [və'kabjuləri] *n* vocabulaire *m*; glossaire *m*.
vocal ['voukəl] *adj* vocal. **vocalist** *n* chanteur, -euse *m*, *f*.
vocation [vou'keiʃən] *n* vocation *f*. **vocational** *adj* professionnel.
vociferous [və'sifərəs] *adj* bruyant.
vodka ['vodkə] *n* vodka *f*.
voice [vois] *n* voix *f*. *v* exprimer.
void [void] *n* vide *m*. *adj* vide; (*law*) nul, nulle. *v* évacuer.
volatile ['volətail] *adj* (*chem*) volatil; (*person*) versatile; (*situation*) explosif.
volcano [vol'keinou] *n* volcan *m*. **volcanic** *adj* volcanique.
volley ['voli] *n* volée *f*; torrent *m*. **volleyball** *n* volley *m*. *v* (*sport*) renvoyer une volée.
volt [voult] *n* volt *m*. **voltage** *n* voltage *m*, tension *f*.
volume ['voljum] *n* volume *m*.
volunteer [volən'tiə] *n* volontaire *m*, *f*. *v* s'offrir; offrir *or* fournir spontanément. **voluntary** *adj* volontaire; (*unpaid*) bénévole.
voluptuous [və'lʌptʃuəs] *adj* voluptueux. **voluptuousness** *n* volupté *f*.
vomit ['vomit] *n* vomissement *m*. *v* vomir.
voodoo ['vuːduː] *nm*, *adj* vaudou.
voracious [və'reiʃəs] *adj* vorace; avide. **voracity** *n* voracité *f*.
vote [vout] *n* vote *m*, voix *f*. **vote of thanks** discours de remerciement *m*. *v* voter; élire. **voter** *n* électeur, -trice *m*, *f*.
vouch [vautʃ] *v* **vouch for** se porter garant de, garantir.
voucher ['vautʃə] *n* bon *m*; (*receipt*) reçu *m*.
vow [vau] *n* vœu *m*. *v* jurer, vouer.
vowel ['vauəl] *n* voyelle *f*.
voyage ['voiidʒ] *n* voyage (par mer) *m*. *v* traverser, voyager (par mer).
vulgar ['vʌlgə] *adj* vulgaire, grossier. **vulgarity** *n* vulgarité *f*, grossièreté *f*.
vulnerable ['vʌlnərəbl] *adj* vulnérable.
vulture ['vʌltʃə] *n* vautour *m*.

W

wad [wod] *n* tampon *m*; (*papers*) liasse *f*.
wadding *n* bourre *f*, rembourrage *m*, ouate *f*.
waddle ['wodl] *v* se dandiner. *n* dandinement *m*.
wade [weid] *v* avancer dans l'eau.
wafer ['weifə] *n* gaufrette *f*. **wafer-thin** *adj* mince comme du papier à cigarette.
waft [woft] *n* (*carry*) porter; (*float*) flotter. *n* bouffée *f*.
wag [wag] *v* agiter, remuer. *n* remuement *m*.
wage [weidʒ] *n* salaire *m*. *v* **wage war** faire la guerre.
wager ['weidʒə] *n* pari *m*. *v* parier.
waggle ['wagl] *v* agiter, frétiller.
wagon ['wagən] *n* chariot *m*; (*rail*) wagon *m*.
waif [weif] *n* enfant abandonné *m*.
wail [weil] *n* gémissement *m*, vagissement *m*. *v* gémir, vagir.
waist [weist] *n* taille *f*, ceinture *f*. **waistband** *n* ceinture *f*. **waistcoat** *n* gilet *m*. **waistline** *n* taille *f*.
wait [weit] *n* attente *f*. **lie in wait for** guetter. *v* attendre; servir. **waiter** *n* garçon *m*. **waiting** *n* attente *f*. **waiting-list** *n* liste d'attente *f*. **waiting-room** *n* salle d'attente *f*. **waitress** *n* serveuse *f*.
waive [weiv] *v* renoncer à, abandonner.
wake[1] [weik] *n* sillage *m*.
*wake[2] [weik] *v* *also* **wake up** (se) réveiller.
Wales [weilz] *n* pays de Galles *m*.
walk [woːk] *n* promenade *f*; (*gait*) démarche *f*. *v* (*faire*) marcher; (*go on foot*) aller à pied; (*for pleasure*) se promener; (*distance*) faire à pied. **walkout** *n* grève surprise *f*. **walkover** *n* walkover *m*, victoire facile *f*. **walker** *n* promeneur, -euse *m*, *f*. **walking** *n* marche à pied *f*. **walking-stick** *n* canne *f*.
wall [woːl] *n* mur *m*, muraille *f*. *v* entourer d'un mur.
wallet ['wolit] *n* portefeuille *m*.
wallflower ['woːlflauə] *n* giroflée *f*. **be a wallflower** faire tapisserie.
wallop ['woləp] (*coll*) *n* coup *m*, beigne *f*. *v* cogner, rosser. **walloping** *adj* sacré.
wallow ['wolou] *v* se vautrer.
wallpaper ['woːlpeipə] *n* papier peint *m*. *v* tapisser.
walnut ['woːlnʌt] *n* (*nut*) noix *f*; (*tree, wood*) noyer *m*.

walrus ['wɔːlrəs] *n* morse *m*.

waltz [wɔːlts] *n* valse *f*. *v* valser.

wan [wɒn] *adj* pâle.

wand [wɒnd] *n* baguette *f*.

wander ['wɒndə] *v* errer; (*stray*) s'égarer. *n* tour *m*.

wane [weɪn] *v* décroître; diminuer.

wangle ['wæŋgl] (*coll*) *n* combine *f*. *v* resquiller, se débrouiller pour avoir.

want [wɒnt] *n* (*lack*) manque *m*; (*need*) besoin *m*. **for want of** faute de. *v* vouloir, désirer; (*ask for*) demander; (*need*) avoir besoin de. **wanted** *adj* (*police*) recherché.

wanton ['wɒntən] *adj* (*woman*) dévergondé; (*cruelty, etc.*) gratuit. **wantonness** *n* dévergondage *m*; gratuité *f*.

war [wɔː] *n* guerre *f*. **be on the war-path** chercher la bagarre. **war-dance** *n* danse guerrière *f*. **warfare** *n* guerre *f*. **war memorial** monument aux morts *m*. **warship** *n* navire de guerre *m*. **wartime** *n* temps de guerre *m*.

warble ['wɔːbl] *n* gazouillis *m*. *v* gazouiller. **warbler** *n* oiseau chanteur *m*.

ward [wɔːd] *n* (*hospital*) salle *f*; section électorale *f*; (*law*) pupille *m, f*. *v* **ward off** parer.

warden ['wɔːdn] *n* directeur, -trice *m, f*; gardien, -enne *m, f*.

warder ['wɔːdə] *n* gardien de prison *m*. **wardress** *n* gardienne de prison *f*.

wardrobe ['wɔːdroub] *n* garde-robe *f*; (*theatre*) costumes *m pl*.

warehouse ['weəhaus] *n* entrepôt *m*. *v* entreposer.

warm [wɔːm] *adj* chaud; (*welcome, etc.*) chaleureux. *v* (se) chauffer. **warm up** s'échauffer. **warming-pan** *n* bassinoire *f*. **warmth** *n* chaleur *f*; cordialité *f*.

warn [wɔːn] *v* prévenir, avertir. **warning** *n* avertissement *m*; (*written*) avis *m*. **warning light** voyant avertisseur *m*.

warp [wɔːp] *v* (se) voiler, gauchir; pervertir; débaucher. *n* voilure *f*; (*cloth*) chaîne *f*.

warrant ['wɒrənt] *n* (*police*) mandat *m*; justification *f*; (*voucher*) bon *m*. *v* justifier; garantir. **warranty** *n* garantie *f*.

warren ['wɒrən] *n* garenne *f*.

warrior ['wɒriə] *n* guerrier, -ère *m, f*.

Warsaw ['wɔːsɔː] *n* Varsovie.

wart [wɔːt] *n* verrue *f*.

wary ['weəri] *adj* prudent, précautionneux.

was [wɒz] *V* **be**.

wash [wɒʃ] *n* (*clothes*) lavage *m*; (*face, etc.*) toilette *f*; (*paint*) badigeon *m*, lavis *m*. *v* (se) laver. **wash-basin** *n* lavabo *m*. **wash off** *or* **out** (faire) partir au lavage. **wash-out** *n* (*slang*) fiasco *m*. **wash-room** *n* toilettes *f pl*. **wash up** faire la vaisselle. **washable** *adj* lavable. **washing** *n* lessive *f*. **washing-machine** *n* machine à laver *f*. **washing-powder** *n* lessive *f*. **washing-up** *n* vaisselle *f*.

washer ['wɒʃə] *n* rondelle *f*.

Washington ['wɒʃɪŋtən] *n* Washington.

wasp [wɒsp] *n* guêpe *f*.

waste [weist] *n* gaspillage *m*; (*time*) perte *f*; (*scrap*) déchets *m pl*; désert *m*. *adj* de rebut; (*lost*) perdu; (*extra*) superflu. **waste disposal unit** broyeur d'ordures *m*. **waste land** terrain vague *m*. **waste paper** vieux papiers *m pl*. **waste-paper basket** corbeille *f*. *v* gaspiller; perdre. **waste away** dépérir. **wasteful** *adj* gaspilleur, -euse; peu économique.

watch [wɒtʃ] *n* (*time*) montre *f*; garde *f*; surveillance *f*; (*naut*) quart *m*. **keep watch** faire le guet. **watch-dog** *n* chien de garde *m*. **watch-strap** *n* bracelet de montre *m*. *v* regarder; surveiller; faire attention (à); guetter. **watchful** *adj* vigilant.

water ['wɔːtə] *n* eau *f*. *v* (*plant, etc.*) arroser; (*eyes*) larmoyer. **water down** couper d'eau. **watery** *adj* aqueux; (*tea, etc.*) trop faible; pâle; insipide.

water-biscuit *n* craquelin *m*.

water-closet *n* cabinets *m pl*.

water-colour *n* aquarelle *f*.

watercress ['wɔːtəkres] *n* cresson *m*.

waterfall ['wɔːtəfɔːl] *n* chute d'eau *f*.

water-ice *n* sorbet *m*.

watering-can *n* arrosoir *m*.

water-lily *n* nénuphar *m*.

waterlogged ['wɔːtəlogd] *adj* (*land*) détrempé; (*wood*) imprégné d'eau.

water-main *n* conduite principale d'eau *f*.

watermark ['wɔːtəmaːk] *n* (*paper*) filigrane *m*; (*tide*) laisse de haute mer *f*.

water-melon *n* melon d'eau *m*.

water-pistol *n* pistolet à eau *m*.

waterproof ['wɔːtəpruːf] *nm, adj* imperméable. *v* imperméabiliser.

water-rate *n* taxe sur l'eau *f*.

watershed ['wɔːtəʃed] *n* moment critique *m*; (*geog*) ligne de partage des eaux *f*.

water-ski *v* faire du ski nautique. *n* ski nautique *m*. **water-skiing** *n* ski nautique *m*.

watertight ['wɔɪtətait] *adj* étanche; (*excuse, etc.*) inattaquable.

water-way *n* voie navigable *f.*

waterworks ['wɔɪtəwɔɪks] *n* système hydraulique *m.*

watt [wot] *n* watt *m.*

wave [weiv] *n* (*sea*) vague *f*; (*hair*) ondulation *f*; (*phys, radio, etc.*) onde *f*; geste de la main *m.* **waveband** *n* bande de fréquences *f.* **wavelength** *n* longueur d'ondes *f. v* agiter, brandir; faire signe de la main; onduler. **wavy** *adj* (*hair*) ondulé; (*line*) onduleux.

waver ['weivə] *v* vaciller; trembler; (*weaken*) lâcher pied.

wax[1] [waks] *n* cire *f.* **waxwork** *n* personnage en cire *m.* **waxworks** *n* musée de cire *m. v* cirer. **waxy** *adj* cireux.

wax[2] [waks] *v* croître.

way [wei] *n* (*path*) chemin *m*, voie *f*; (*manner*) façon *f*, manière *f*; passage *m*; distance *f*; direction *f*, sens *m.* **be in the way** gêner. **by the way** à propos. **give way** céder; laisser la priorité. **on the way** en route. **this way** par ici. **under way** en cours, en marche. **way in** entrée *f.* **way out** sortie *f.*

*****waylay** [wei'lei] *v* arrêter au passage.

wayside ['weisaid] *n* bord de la route. *adj* au bord de la route.

wayward ['weiwəd] *adj* capricieux, rebelle.

we [wiɪ] *pron* nous.

weak [wiɪk] *adj* faible. **weaken** *v* faiblir, (s')affaiblir. **weakling** *n* gringalet *m.* **weakness** *n* faiblesse *f*; point faible *m*; (*liking*) faible *m.*

wealth [welθ] *n* richesse *f*; abondance *f.* **wealthy** *adj* riche.

wean [wiɪn] *v* (*baby*) sevrer. **wean off** détourner de.

weapon ['wepən] *n* arme *f.*

*****wear** [weə] *n* usage *m*; (*deterioration*) usure *f*; (*clothes*) vêtements *m pl.* **wear and tear** usure *f. v* porter; (s')user. **wear off** passer, se dissiper. **wear out** épuiser.

weary ['wiəri] *adj* las, lasse. *v* (se) lasser. **wearily** *adv* avec lassitude. **weariness** *n* lassitude *f.*

weasel ['wiɪzl] *n* belette *f.*

weather ['weðə] *n* temps *m.* **weather-beaten** *adj* hâlé. **weathercock** *n* girouette *f.* **weather forecast** prévisions météorologiques *f pl. v* (*survive*) réchapper à.

*****weave** [wiɪv] *v* tisser; entrelacer;

(*through traffic, etc.*) se faufiler. *n also* **weaving** tissage *m.*

web [web] *n* (*spider*) toile *f*; (*on feet*) palmure *f*; (*cloth*) tissu *m.* **web-footed** *adj* palmipède.

wedding ['wediŋ] *n* mariage *m*; noces *f pl.* **wedding-dress** *n* robe de mariée *f.* **wedding-ring** *n* alliance *f.*

wedge [wedʒ] *n* cale *f*, coin *m. v* caler; (*push in*) enfoncer; (*jam*) coincer.

Wednesday ['wenzdi] *n* mercredi *m.*

weed [wiɪd] *n* mauvaise herbe *f.* **weedkiller** *n* désherbant *m. v* désherber. **weeding** *n* désherbage *m.*

week [wiɪk] *n* semaine *f.* **a week today/tomorrow** aujourd'hui/demain en huit. **weekday** *n* jour de semaine *m.* **weekend** *n* week-end *m.*

weekly ['wiɪkli] *adv* chaque semaine, tous les huit jours. *nm, adj* hebdomadaire.

*****weep** [wiɪp] *v* pleurer. **weeping willow** saule pleureur *m.*

weigh [wei] *v* peser. **weighbridge** *n* pont-bascule *m.* **weight** *n* poids *m.* **lose weight** maigrir. **put on weight** grossir. **weightlifting** *n* haltérophilie *f.* **weighting** *n* indemnité *f.* **weightlessness** *n* appesanteur *f.*

weir [wiə] *n* barrage *m.*

weird [wiəd] *adj* surnaturel; bizarre. **weirdness** *n* étrangeté *f.*

welcome ['welkəm] *adj* opportun. **be welcome** être le bienvenu. **you're welcome!** (*acknowledging thanks*) il n'y a pas de quoi! *n* accueil *m. v* accueillir; souhaiter la bienvenue à; (*news, etc.*) se réjouir de.

weld [weld] *v* souder. *n* soudure *f.* **welder** *n* soudeur *m.* **welding** *n* soudage *m.*

welfare ['welfeə] *n* bien *m.* **Welfare State** Etat-providence *m.* **welfare work** travail social *m.*

well[1] [wel] *n* puits *m. v* **well up** monter.

well[2] [wel] *adj, adv* bien. **as well** aussi.

well-behaved *adj* sage, obéissant.

well-being *n* bien-être *m.*

well-bred *adj* bien élevé.

well-built *adj* solide.

well-informed *adj* bien informé; instruit.

wellington ['weliŋtən] *n* botte de caoutchouc *f.*

well-known *adj* célèbre.

well-meaning *adj* bien intentionné.

well-nigh *adv* presque.

well-off *adj* riche, aisé.

well-paid adj bien payé.

well-spent adj (time) bien employé.

well-spoken adj poli. **be well-spoken** avoir une élocution soignée.

well-timed adj opportun.

well-to-do adj aisé, riche.

well-trodden adj battu.

well-worn adj usagé.

Welsh [welʃ] nm, adj gallois. **the Welsh** les Gallois m pl.

went [went] V go.

wept [wept] V weep.

were [wəɪ] V be.

west [west] n ouest m. **the West** l'Occident m. adj also **westerly** occidental; ouest invar; à or de l'ouest. adv à l'ouest, vers l'ouest. **westbound** adj ouest invar.

western ['westən] adj ouest invar; de l'ouest; occidental. n (film) western m.

wet [wet] adj mouillé; (damp) humide; (soaked) trempé; (weather) pluvieux. **wet blanket** rabat-joie m invar. **wet suit** combinaison de plongée f. n pluie f. v mouiller.

whack [wak] (coll) n grand coup m. v donner un grand coup à.

whale [weil] n baleine f.

wharf [wɔɪf] n quai m.

what [wot] pron (subject) (qu'est-ce) qui; (object) (qu'est-ce) que; (after prep) quoi; (relative) ce qui, ce que. adj quel, quelle. interj quoi!

whatever [wot'evə] pron tout ce que, quoi que. adj, adv quel que soit. **none whatever** pas le moindre.

wheat [wiɪt] n blé m, froment m.

wheel [wiɪl] n roue f. **wheelbarrow** n brouette f. **wheelchair** n fauteuil roulant m. v pousser, rouler; (turn) tournoyer.

wheeze [wiɪz] n respiration bruyante f. v respirer bruyamment. **wheezy** adj poussif, asthmatique.

whelk [welk] n buccin m.

when [wen] adv quand. conj quand, lorsque; (relative) où, que. **whenever** conj chaque fois que.

where [weə] adv où. conj (là) où. **whereabouts** adv où. **whereas** conj alors que. **whereupon** adv sur quoi. **wherever** conj où que; (anywhere) là où; (everywhere) partout où.

whether ['weðə] conj si.

which [witʃ] pron lequel, laquelle; (the one that) celui qui or que, celle qui or que; (relative) (ce) qui, (ce) que. adj quel, quelle.

whichever [witʃ'evə] pron (quel que soit) celui qui or que, (quelle que soit) celle qui or que. adj n'importe quel; quel que soit . . . que.

whiff [wif] n bouffée f, odeur f.

while [wail] conj pendant que; (as long as) tant que. n quelque temps. v **while away** passer.

whim [wim] n caprice m.

whimper ['wimpə] n faible geignement m. v pleurnicher, geindre faiblement.

whimsical ['wimzikl] adj capricieux; étrange.

whine [wain] n gémissement m; (siren, etc.) plainte f. v gémir; (complain) se lamenter.

whip [wip] n fouet m. **whip-round** n (coll) collecte f. v fouetter. **whip away/out** enlever/sortir brusquement. **whipping** n correction f.

whippet ['wipit] n whippet m.

whirl [wəɪl] n tourbillon m. v (faire) tourbillonner. **whirlpool** n tourbillon m. **whirlwind** n tornade f, trombe f.

whirr [wəɪ] n (wings) bruissement m; (machinery) vrombissement m. v bruire; vrombir.

whisk [wisk] n (cookery) fouet m. v fouetter; (snatch) enlever brusquement.

whisker ['wiskə] n poil m. **whiskers** pl n moustaches f pl.

whisky ['wiski] n whisky m.

whisper ['wispə] v chuchoter. n chuchotement m.

whist [wist] n whist m. **whist drive** tournoi de whist m.

whistle ['wisl] n sifflet m; (sound) sifflement m. v siffler.

Whit [wit] n also **Whitsun** la Pentecôte f. adj de Pentecôte.

white [wait] adj blanc, blanche. **white elephant** objet superflu m. n blanc m; (person) Blanc, Blanche m, f. **whiten** v blanchir. **whiteness** n blancheur f.

whitewash ['waitwoʃ] n blanc de chaux m. v blanchir à la chaux; (cover up) justifier, blanchir.

whiting ['waitiŋ] n merlan m.

whittle ['witl] v tailler au couteau. **whittle down** (expenses, etc.) rogner.

whizz [wiz] n sifflement m. **whizz-kid** (coll) petit prodige m. v aller comme une flèche.

who [huː] *pron* (qui est-ce) qui. **whoever** *pron* quiconque; qui que ce soit qui *or* que.

whole [houl] *n* totalité *f*; tout *m*. **on the whole** dans l'ensemble. *adj* entier; intact. **wholehearted** *adj* sans réserve. **wholeheartedly** *adv* de tout cœur. **wholemeal** *adj* (*flour*) brut; (*bread*) complet, -ète. **wholesome** *adj* sain.

wholesale ['houlseil] *n* vente en gros *f*. *adj* de gros; en masse, en bloc. *adv* en gros; en masse.

whom [huːm] *pron* qui; (*relative*) que, lequel, laquelle. **of whom** dont.

whooping cough ['huːpiŋ] *n* coqueluche *f*.

whore [hoː] *n* (*derog*) putain *f*.

whose [huːz] *pron* à qui. *adj* à qui, de qui; (*relative*) dont.

why [wai] *adv, conj* pourquoi. *interj* tiens!

wick [wik] *n* mèche *f*.

wicked ['wikid] *adj* mauvais, méchant, vilain. **wickedness** *n* méchanceté *f*.

wicker ['wikə] *n* osier *m*.

wicket ['wikit] *n* (*cricket*) guichet *m*.

wide [waid] *adj* large; grand; vaste. *adv* loin du but. **wide awake** bien éveillé. **widespread** *adj* répandu. **widely** *adv* largement; (*much*) beaucoup; généralement; radicalement. **widen** *v* (s')élargir.

widow ['widou] *n* veuve *f*. **be widowed** devenir veuf *or* veuve. **widower** *n* veuf *m*.

width [widθ] *n* largeur *f*.

wield [wiːld] *v* manier; brandir; exercer.

wife [waif] *n* femme *f*, épouse *f*.

wig [wig] *n* perruque *f*.

wiggle ['wigl] *v* tortiller; agiter, remuer. **wiggly** *adj* (*line*) ondulé.

wild [waild] *adj* sauvage; violent; (*unrestrained*) fou, folle. **like wildfire** comme une traînée de poudre. **wildlife** *n* faune *f*. **wildly** *adv* violemment; fiévreusement; follement.

wilderness ['wildənəs] *n* désert *m*; région sauvage *f*.

wilful ['wilfəl] *adj* (*stubborn*) entêté; volontaire; prémédité.

will¹ [wil] *aux translated by future tense.*

will² [wil] *v* vouloir; léguer. *n* volonté *f*; testament *m*. **against one's will** à contre-cœur. **willpower** *n* volonté *f*.

willing ['wiliŋ] *adj* de bonne volonté. **be willing to** être disposé à, vouloir bien. **willingly** *adv* volontiers. **willingness** *n* bonne volonté *f*, empressement *m*.

willow ['wilou] *n* saule *m*. **willow-pattern** *n* motif chinois *m*. **willowy** *adj* svelte.

wilt [wilt] *v* (se) faner, (se) dessécher; (*person*) s'affaiblir.

wily ['waili] *adj* rusé, malin, -igne.

***win** [win] *n* victoire *f*. *v* gagner. **winner** *n* gagnant, -e *m, f*. **winning** *adj* gagnant; (*smile, etc.*) charmeur, -euse. **winnings** *pl n* gains *m pl*.

wince [wins] *v* tressaillir; grimacer. *n* tressaillement *m*; grimace *f*.

winch [wintʃ] *n* treuil *m*. *v* **winch up/down** monter/descendre au treuil.

wind¹ [wind] *n* vent *m*; (*breath*) souffle *m*; (*med*) vents *m pl*. *v* couper le souffle à. **windy** *adj* (*place*) battu par les vents; (*day*) de vent.

***wind²** [waind] *v* enrouler; (*clock, etc.*) remonter; serpenter. **wind up** (se) terminer; (*comm*) liquider; (*clock, etc.*) remonter. **winder** *n* remontoir *m*. **winding** *adj* sinueux.

wind-break *n* pare-vent *m invar*.

windfall ['windfoːl] *n* fruit abattu par le vent *m*; (*surprise*) aubaine *f*.

wind instrument *n* instrument à vent *m*.

windlass ['windləs] *n* guindeau *m*.

windmill ['wind,mil] *n* moulin à vent *m*.

window ['windou] *n* fenêtre *f*; (*car*) vitre *f*; (*shop*) vitrine *f*; (*cashier's*) guichet *m*. **window-box** *n* jardinière *f*. **window-cleaner** *n* laveur, -euse de vitres *m, f*. **window-dresser** *n* étalagiste *m, f*. **window-shopping** *n* lèche-vitrine *m*. **window-sill** *n* (*inside*) appui de fenêtre *m*; (*outside*) rebord de fenêtre *m*.

windpipe ['windpaip] *n* (*anat*) trachée *f*.

windshield ['windʃiːld] *n* pare-brise *m invar*. **windshield wiper** essuie-glace *m invar*.

wind-sock *n* manche à air *f*.

windswept ['windswept] *adj* venteux, balayé par le vent.

wind tunnel *n* tunnel aérodynamique *m*.

wine [wain] *n* vin *m*. **wineglass** *n* verre à vin *m*. **wine list** carte des vins *f*. **wine-tasting** *n* dégustation *f*. **wine waiter** sommelier *m*.

wing [wiŋ] *n* aile *f*. **wing commander** lieutenant-colonel *m*. **wing-mirror** *n* rétroviseur de côté *m*. **wings** *pl n* (*theatre*) coulisses *f pl*. **wingspan** *n* envergure *f*.

wink [wiŋk] *n* clin d'œil. *v* faire un clin d'œil; (*light*) clignoter.

winkle ['wiŋkl] n bigorneau m. v **winkle out** extirper.

winter ['wintə] n hiver m. v hiverner. **wintry** adj d'hiver.

wipe [waip] n coup de torchon m. v essuyer. **wipe out** effacer; anéantir.

wire [waiə] n fil m; télégramme m. **wirebrush** n brosse métallique f. **wire-cutters** pl n cisaille f sing. **wireless** n T.S.F. f. **wire netting** treillis métallique m. v télégraphier. **wiring** n installation électrique f. **wiry** adj (hair) dru; (person) noueux.

wisdom ['wizdəm] n sagesse f; prudence f. **wisdom tooth** dent de sagesse f.

wise [waiz] adj sage; prudent; (learned) savant.

wish [wiʃ] v souhaiter, désirer. n souhait m, vœu m; désir m. **wishbone** n bréchet m.

wisp [wisp] n brin m; (hair) fine mèche f; (smoke) mince volute f. **wispy** adj fin.

wistful ['wistfəl] adj nostalgique, mélancolique. **wistfully** adv avec nostalgie or mélancolie.

wit [wit] n esprit m, intelligence f; (person) homme d'esprit, femme d'esprit m, f. **be at one's wits' end** ne plus savoir que faire.

witch [witʃ] n sorcière f. **witchcraft** n sorcellerie f. **witch-doctor** n sorcier m. **witch-hunt** n chasse aux sorcières f.

with [wið] prep avec; (having) à; (because of) de; (despite) malgré.

***withdraw** [wið'drɔ] v (se) retirer. **withdrawal** n retrait m, retraction f; (med) manque m. **withdrawn** adj renfermé.

wither ['wiðə] v (se) flétrir, (se) faner. **withered** adj flétri; desséché; (limb) atrophié. **withering** adj (look) méprisant; (remark) cinglant.

***withhold** [wið'hould] v (keep back) retenir; (put off) remettre; refuser; (hide) cacher.

within [wi'ðin] adv dedans, à l'intérieur. prep à l'intérieur de; dans; (less than) (à) moins de.

without [wi'ðaut] prep sans. adv à l'extérieur.

***withstand** [wið'stand] v résister à.

witness ['witnis] n (person) témoin m; (evidence) témoignage m. v (accident, etc.) être le témoin de; (document) attester l'authenticité de. **witness to** témoigner de.

witty ['witi] adj spirituel. **witticism** n mot d'esprit m.

wizard ['wizəd] n magicien m.

wobble ['wobl] v (faire) trembler, (faire) osciller, (faire) branler. **wobbly** adj bancal.

woke [wouk] V **wake²**.

woken ['woukn] V **wake²**.

wolf [wulf] n loup m. **wolfhound** n chien-loup m. **wolf-whistle** n sifflement admiratif m. v **wolf down** engloutir.

woman ['wumən] n, pl **women** femme f. **Women's Lib** (coll) M.L.F. m. **womanhood** n féminité f. **womanly** adj féminin.

womb [wuːm] n utérus m.

won [wʌn] V **win**.

wonder ['wʌndə] n émerveillement m; miracle m, merveille f. **no wonder** (ce n'est) pas étonnant. v se demander; (muse) songer; (marvel) s'émerveiller. **wonderful** adj merveilleux.

wood [wud] n bois m. **wooden** adj de or en bois; (stiff) raide. **woody** adj boisé; (stem) ligneux.

woodcock ['wudkok] n bécasse f.

woodcut ['wudkʌt] n gravure sur bois f.

woodland ['wudlənd] n région boisée f.

wood-louse n, pl **-lice** cloporte m.

woodpecker ['wudpekə] n pic m.

wood-pigeon n ramier m.

wood-shed n bûcher m.

wood-wind n (music) bois m pl.

woodwork ['wudwɔk] n menuiserie f.

woodworm ['wudwɔm] n vers du bois m.

wool [wul] n laine f. **woollen** adj de or en laine. **woolly** adj laineux; (ideas) confus.

word [wɔd] n mot m, parole f. **be word-perfect in** savoir sur le bout des doigts. **in other words** autrement dit. v formuler, rédiger. **wording** n termes m pl. **wordy** adj verbeux.

wore [wɔ] V **wear**.

work [wɔk] n travail m, œuvre f, ouvrage m. **out of work** en chômage. **work-force** n main d'œuvre f. **workman** n ouvrier m. **workmanship** n maîtrise f. **work permit** permis de travail m. **works** n usine f. **workshop** n atelier m. **work-to-rule** n grève du zèle f. v travailler; (machine, etc.) (faire) marcher; exploiter. **work out** résoudre; (plan) élaborer; calculer. **worker** n travailleur, -euse m, f. **working-class** adj ouvrier. **workings** pl n mécanisme m.

world [wəɪld] *n* monde *m*. **First/Second World War** Première/Deuxième guerre mondiale *f*. **world-wide** *adj* mondial. **worldly** *adj* terrestre; matérialiste.

worm [wəɪm] *n* ver *m*.

worn [woɪn] *V* **wear**.

worry ['wʌri] *n* souci *m*. *v* (s')inquiéter; (*sheep*) harceler. **don't worry!** ne vous en faites pas! **worried** *adj* inquiet, -ète.

worse [wəɪs] *adj* pire, plus mauvais. *adv* plus mal. **get worse** empirer, se détériorer. **to make matters worse** pour comble de malheur. *n* pire *m*. **worsen** *v* empirer, se détériorer.

worship ['wəɪʃip] *n* adoration *f*; culte *m*. *v* adorer, vénérer; faire ses dévotions.

worst [wəɪst] *adj* le pire, la pire, le plus mauvais, la plus mauvaise. *adv* le plus mal. *n* pire *m*. **at worst** au pis aller.

worsted ['wustid] *n* worsted *m*.

worth [wəɪθ] *n* valeur *f*. *adj* **be worth** valoir. **be worth it** valoir la peine. **worthwhile** *adj* qui en vaut la peine; utile; notable. **worthless** *adj* qui ne vaut rien. **worthy** *adj* digne; (*effort, cause*) louable.

would [wud] *aux translated by conditional or imperfect tense.*

wound¹ [waund] *V* **wind**².

wound² [wuɪnd] *n* blessure *f*. *v* blesser.

wove [wouv] *V* **weave**.

woven ['wouvn] *V* **weave**.

wrangle ['raŋgl] *n* dispute *f*. *v* se disputer.

wrap [rap] *v* envelopper; (*parcel*) emballer. **wrapper** *n* papier *m*. **wrapping** *n* emballage *m*. **wrapping paper** papier d'emballage *m*; (*fancy*) papier cadeau *m*.

wreath [riːθ] *n* guirlande *f*, couronne *f*.

wreck [rek] *n* (*ship*) naufrage *m*; (*car*) voiture accidentée *f*; (*person*) épave *f*. *v* démolir, détruire; (*hopes, etc.*) ruiner, briser. **wreckage** *n* débris *m pl*.

wren [ren] *n* roitelet *m*.

wrench [rentʃ] *n* (*tool*) clef à écrous *f*; mouvement de torsion *m*; (*emotional*) déchirement *m*. *v* tirer violemment, arracher; (*med*) tordre.

wrestle ['resl] *v* lutter. **wrestle with** (*problem*) se débattre avec. **wrestler** *n* lutteur, -euse *m, f*; catcheur, -euse *m, f*. **wrestling** *n* lutte *f*, catch *m*.

wretch [retʃ] *n* malheureux, -euse *m, f*; misérable *m, f*. **wretched** *adj* misérable; (*coll: annoying*) maudit.

wriggle ['rigl] *v* (se) tortiller, remuer; (*fish*) frétiller.

*wring [riŋ] *v* tordre; (*wet clothes*) essorer. **wringer** *n* essoreuse *f*. **wringing wet** trempé.

wrinkle ['riŋkl] *n* ride *f*; (*in cloth*) pli *m*. *v* rider; (se) plisser.

wrist [rist] *n* poignet *m*. **wrist-watch** *n* montre-bracelet *f*.

writ [rit] *n* acte judiciaire *m*. **issue a writ against** assigner.

*write [rait] *v* écrire. **writer** *n* auteur *m*, écrivain *m*. **writing** *n* écriture *f*. **in writing** par écrit. **writing-case** *n* correspondancier *m*. **writing-pad** *n* bloc-notes *m*. **writing-paper** *n* papier à lettres *m*.

writhe [raið] *v* se tordre, frémir.

written ['ritn] *V* **write**.

wrong [roŋ] *adj* (*bad*) mal; erroné; incorrect, faux, fausse; (*end, side, etc.*) mauvais. **be wrong** avoir tort, se tromper; (*amiss*) ne pas aller. *adv* mal. *n* mal *m*, tort *m*; injustice *f*. **wrongful** *adj* injustifié.

wrought iron [ˌroɪt'aiən] *n* fer forgé *m*.

wrote [rout] *V* **write**.

wrung [rʌŋ] *V* **wring**.

wry [rai] *adj* désabusé.

X

xenophobia [ˌzenə'foubiə] *n* xénophobie *f*. **xenophobic** *adj* xénophobe.

Xerox ® ['ziəroks] *n* (*machine*) photocopieuse *f*; (*copy*) photocopie *f*. *v* photocopier.

Xmas ['krisməs] *V* **Christmas**.

X-ray ['eksrei] *n* (*photo*) radio *f*; (*ray*) rayon X *m*. **have an X-ray** se faire radiographier. *v* radiographier.

xylophone ['zailəfoun] *n* xylophone *m*.

Y

yacht [jot] *n* yacht *m*. **yachting** *n* yachting *m*.

yank [jaŋk] *n* coup sec *m*. *v* tirer d'un coup sec.
yap [jap] *v* japper. *n* jappement *m*.
yard [jɑɪd] *n* cour *f*; (*site*) chantier *m*.
yarn [jɑɪn] *n* fil *m*; (*tale*) histoire *f*.
yawn [jɔɪn] *v* bâiller; (*hole*) s'ouvrir. *n* bâillement *m*.
year [jiə] *n* an *m*, année *f*. **yearly** *adj* annuel.
yearn [jəɪn] *v* languir (après), aspirer (à). **yearning** *n* désir ardent *m*, envie *f*.
yeast [jiɪst] *n* levure *f*.
yell [jel] *n* hurlement *m*. *v* hurler.
yellow ['jelou] *nm*, *adj* jaune. *v* jaunir.
yelp [jelp] *v* glapir, japper. *n* glapissement *m*, jappement *m*.
yes [jes] *adv* oui; (*after negative*) si. *n* oui *m invar*.
yesterday ['jestədi] *nm*, *adv* hier. **the day before yesterday** avant-hier *m*.
yet [jət] *adv* encore; (*already*) déjà. *conj* cependant, toutefois.
yew [juɪ] *n* if *m*.
yield [jiɪld] *v* produire, rapporter; céder. *n* production *f*, rapport *m*.
yodel ['joudl] *v* jodler. *n* tyrolienne *f*.
yoga ['jougə] *n* yoga *m*.
yoghurt ['yogət] *n* yaourt *m*.
yoke [jouk] *n* joug *m*; (*dress*) empièce-ment *m*. *v* accoupler.
yolk [jouk] *n* jaune *m*.
yonder ['jondə] *adv* là-bas.
you [juɪ] *pron* (*subject*: *fam*) tu; (*subject*: *pl or fml*) vous; (*after prep*) toi, vous; (*before verb*) te, vous; (*impersonal*) on.
young [jʌŋ] *adj* jeune. *pl n* (*people*) jeunes *m pl*; (*animals*) petits *m pl*. **youngster** *n* jeune *m*.
your [jɔɪ] *adj* (*fam*) ton, ta, (*pl*) tes; (*pl or fml*) votre, (*pl*) vos; (*impersonal*) son, sa, (*pl*) ses. **yours** *pron* (*fam*) le tien, la tienne; (*pl or fml*) le vôtre, la vôtre.
yourself [jə'self] *pron* (*fam*) te; (*pl or fml*) vous; (*impersonal*) se; (*emphatic*) toi-même, vous-même, soi-même. **by yourself** tout seul.
youth [juɪθ] *n* jeunesse *f*; (*boy*) jeune homme *m*. **youth hostel** auberge de la jeunesse *f*.
yo-yo ['joujou] *n* yo-yo *m*.
Yugoslavia [juɪgou'slɑɪviə] *n* Yougoslavie *f*. **Yugoslav** *adj* yougoslave; *n* Yougos-lave *m*, *f*. **Yugoslavian** *adj* yougoslave.

Z

Zaire [zɑɪ'iɪə] *n* Zaïre *m*.
zany ['zeini] *adj* (*coll*) toqué.
zeal [ziɪl] *n* zèle *m*. **zealous** *adj* zélé; dévoué.
zebra ['zebrə] *n* zèbre *m*. **zebra crossing** passage pour piétons *m*.
zero ['ziərou] *n* zéro *m*.
zest [zest] *n* entrain *m*; saveur *f*.
zigzag ['zigzag] *n* zigzag *m*. *v* zigzaguer.
zinc [ziŋk] *n* zinc *m*.
zip [zip] *n* fermeture éclair *f*. **zip code** (*US*) code postal *m*. *v* **zip up** (se) fermer avec une fermeture éclair.
zodiac ['zoudiak] *n* zodiaque *m*.
zone [zoun] *n* zone *f*. *v* diviser en zones.
zoo [zuɪ] *n* zoo *m*.
zoology [zou'olədʒi] *n* zoologie *f*. **zoologi-cal** *adj* zoologique. **zoologist** *n* zoologiste *m*, *f*.
zoom [zuɪm] *n* vrombissement *m*. **zoom lens** zoom *m*. *v* vrombir. **zoom past/through** (*coll*) passer/traverser en trombe.

French–Anglais

A

à [a] *prep* (*vers*) to; (*position*) at; (*ville*) in; (*d'après*) according to; (*transport*) by; (*pour*) for.

abaisser [abese] *v* lower. **s'abaisser** *v* fall; (*personne*) humble oneself. **abaissement** *nm* fall; (*personne*) subservience; degradation.

abandon [abɑ̃dɔ̃] *nm* desertion; renunciation, giving up; neglect. **à l'abandon** in a state of neglect. **avec abandon** without constraint.

abandonner [abɑ̃dɔne] *v* abandon, give up. **s'abandonner à** give way to, indulge in.

abasourdir [abazurdir] *v* stun. **abasourdissement** *nm* stupefaction.

abat-jour *nm invar* lampshade.

abats [aba] *nm pl* offal *sing*; (*volaille*) giblets *pl*.

abattoir [abatwar] *nm* abattoir.

***abattre** [abatrə] *v* pull *or* knock down; (*arbre*) fell; (*tuer*) kill; (*affaiblir*) weaken. **s'abattre** fall, collapse. **abattement** *nm* depression, low spirits *pl*; (*fatigue*) exhaustion; (*rabais*) reduction. **abattu** *adj* exhausted; feeble; depressed.

abbaye [abei] *nf* abbey.

abbé [abe] *nm* abbot. **abbesse** *nf* abbess.

abcès [apsɛ] *nm* abscess.

abdiquer [abdike] *v* abdicate. **abdication** *nf* abdication.

abdomen [abdɔmɛn] *nm* abdomen. **abdominal** *adj* abdominal.

abeille [abɛj] *nf* bee.

abhorrer [abɔre] *v* abhor.

abîme [abim] *nm* abyss, gulf.

abîmer [abime] *v* spoil, damage.

abject [abʒɛkt] *adj* despicable, abject.

abnégation [abnegɑsjɔ̃] *nf* self-denial.

aboiement [abwamɑ̃] *nm* bark.

abois [abwa] *nm pl* **aux abois** at bay.

abolir [abɔlir] *v* abolish. **abolition** *nf* abolition.

abominable [abɔminablə] *adj* abominable. **abomination** *nf* abomination. **avoir en abomination** loathe.

abonder [abɔ̃de] *v* abound, be plentiful. **abondance** *nf* abundance; (*richesse*) wealth. **abondant** *adj* plentiful, profuse; (*cheveux*) thick; (*repas*) copious.

s'abonner [abɔne] *v* subscribe. **abonné, -e** *nm, nf* subscriber; (*gaz, etc.*) consumer. **abonnement** *nm* subscription; (*rail, sport, etc.*) season ticket.

abord [abɔr] *nm* manner; access. **abords** *nm pl* surroundings *pl*. **au premier abord** at first sight. **d'abord** *adv* (at) first.

aborder [abɔrde] *v* approach; (*arriver à*) reach; (*problème, etc.*) tackle. **abordable** *adj* reasonable; approachable; accessible.

aborigène [abɔriʒɛn] *n(m+f)* aborigine. *adj* aboriginal.

aboutir [abutir] *v* succeed. **aboutir à** end up in *or* at, come to. **aboutissement** *nm* result; success.

aboyer [abwaje] *v* bark.

abrasif [abrazif] *nm, adj* abrasive. **abrasion** *nf* abrasion.

abréger [abreʒe] *v* shorten; (*texte*) abridge. **abrégé** *nm* summary.

abreuver [abrœve] *v* (*animal*) water; (*tremper*) soak; (*inonder*) shower, swamp. **s'abreuver** *v* quench one's thirst.

abréviation [abrevjɑsjɔ̃] *nf* abbreviation.

abri [abri] *nm* shelter; protection. **à l'abri** sheltered, safe.

abricot [abriko] *nm* apricot. **abricotier** *nm* apricot (tree).

abriter [abrite] *v* shelter; (*du soleil*) shade. **s'abriter** *v* take cover.

abroger [abrɔʒe] v repeal. **abrogation** nf repeal.

abrutir [abrytir] v exhaust, daze, stupefy.

absent [apsɑ̃], **-e** nm, nf absentee. adj absent; (qui manque) missing. **absence** nf absence.

abside [apsid] nf apse.

absinthe [apsɛ̃t] nf absinthe.

absolu [apsɔly] nm, adj absolute.

absorber [apsɔrbe] v absorb; (temps, etc.) occupy, take up. **absorbant** adj absorbing; (matière) absorbent. **absorption** nf absorption.

*****absoudre** [apsudrə] v absolve. **absolution** nf absolution.

*****s'abstenir** [apstənir] v abstain, refrain. **abstention** nf abstention. **abstinence** nf abstinence.

abstrait [apstrɛ] adj abstract. nm abstract; abstract art; abstract artist. **abstraction** nf abstraction; abstract idea. **faire abstraction de** disregard.

absurde [apsyrd] nm, adj absurd. **absurdité** nf absurdity.

abus [aby] nm abuse; over-use, over-indulgence. **abuser de** v abuse, misuse; exploit; over-use, over-indulge. **abusif** adj excessive; improper.

académie [akademi] nf academy; school. **académique** adj academic.

acajou [akaʒu] nm mahogany.

acariâtre [akarjɑtrə] adj sour-tempered.

accabler [akable] v overwhelm, overcome; (questions, injures) shower. **accablant** adj overwhelming; (chaleur, travail) exhausting. **accablement** nm exhaustion; depression.

accaparer [akapare] v monopolize; (absorber) take up completely.

accéder [aksede] v **accéder à** (lieu) reach, get to; attain; (désirs) comply with.

accélérer [akselere] v accelerate, speed up. **accélérateur** nm accelerator. **accélération** nf acceleration.

accent [aksɑ̃] nm accent; emphasis, stress; tone.

accentuer [aksɑ̃tɥe] v accent; emphasize, accentuate; intensify.

accepter [aksɛpte] v accept; (être d'accord) agree. **acceptable** adj acceptable; satisfactory. **acceptation** nf acceptance.

accès [aksɛ] nm access, approach; (crise) fit, bout. **accessible** adj accessible; (personne) approachable.

accessoire [akseswar] adj secondary; additional. nm accessory.

accident [aksidɑ̃] nm accident, mishap. **accidenté** adj (terrain) uneven. **accidentel** adj accidental.

acclamer [aklame] v acclaim, cheer. **acclamations** nf pl cheers pl.

acclimater [aklimate] v acclimatize. **s'acclimater** v adapt (oneself), become acclimatized.

accommoder [akɔmɔde] v adapt; (cuisine) prepare. **s'accommoder de** put up with.

accompagner [akɔ̃paɲe] v accompany. **accompagnement** nm accompaniment.

accomplir [akɔ̃plir] v accomplish, carry out, achieve; complete. **accomplissement** nm accomplishment, fulfilment; completion.

accord [akɔr] nm agreement; harmony; (musique) chord. **d'accord** (fam) O.K. **être d'accord** agree.

accordéon [akɔrdeɔ̃] nm accordion.

accorder [akɔrde] v grant, give; (musique) tune. **s'accorder** v agree; match, be in harmony.

accotement [akɔtmɑ̃] nm (auto) shoulder, verge. **accotement stabilisé** hard shoulder.

accoucher [akuʃe] v give birth. **accouchement** nm childbirth, delivery. **accoucheuse** nf midwife.

accouder [akude] v **s'accouder à** or **sur** lean one's elbows on.

*****accourir** [akurir] v rush up, hurry.

accoutumer [akutyme] v accustom. **s'accoutumer à** get used to.

accroc [akro] nm tear; (tache) blot; (anicroche) hitch.

accrocher [akrɔʃe] v catch; (tableau, etc.) hang; (voiture) bump into. **s'accrocher à** cling to. **accrocheur, -euse** adj persistent; (affiche, etc.) eye-catching, catchy.

*****accroître** [akrwatrə] v increase. **accroissement** nm increase.

s'accroupir [akrupir] v squat, crouch.

*****accueillir** [akœjir] v (aller chercher) welcome; receive; meet; (loger) accommodate. **accueil** nm reception, welcome.

accumuler [akymyle] v accumulate. **accumulateur** nm accumulator. **accumulation** nf accumulation.

accuser [akyze] v accuse, blame; accentuate; (montrer) show. **accuser réception de** acknowledge receipt of. **accusation** nf accusation. **accusé, -e** *nm*, *nf* accused, defendant.

acerbe [asɛrb] *adj* caustic.

acharner [aʃarne] *v* **s'acharner à** *or* **sur** try desperately to, work furiously at. **s'acharner contre** hound, set oneself against. **acharné** *adj* relentless; determined, set; (*combat*) fierce. **acharnement** *nm* relentlessness; determination; fierceness.

achat [aʃa] *nm* purchase. **faire des achats** go shopping.

acheminer [aʃmine] *v* forward, dispatch; transport. **s'acheminer vers** head for.

acheter [aʃte] *v* buy. **acheteur, -euse** *nm*, *nf* buyer.

achever [aʃve] *v* finish. **s'achever** end. **achevé** *adj* downright; accomplished. **achèvement** *nm* completion.

acide [asid] *nm*, *adj* acid. **acidité** *nf* acidity.

acier [asje] *nm* steel. **acier inoxydable** stainless steel. **aciérie** *nf* steelworks.

acné [akne] *nf* acne.

acompte [akɔ̃t] *nm* (*arrhes*) deposit, down payment; (*versement partiel*) instalment.

acoustique [akustik] *adj* acoustic. *nf* acoustics *pl*.

*acquérir [akerir] *v* acquire; (*gagner*) win, gain. **acquéreur** *nm* purchaser.

acquiescer [akjese] *v* acquiesce, assent; approve. **acquiescement** *nm* acquiescence; approval.

acquis [aki] *adj* acquired; established. *nm* experience.

acquisition [akizisjɔ̃] *nf* acquisition.

acquit [aki] *nm* receipt.

acquitter [akite] *v* acquit; pay. **s'acquitter de** (*dette*) discharge; (*promesse, tâche*) fulfil. **acquittement** *nm* acquittal; payment; discharge; fulfilment.

âcre [akrə] *adj* acrid. **âcreté** *nf* acridity.

acrimonie [akrimɔni] *nf* acrimonie. **acrimonieux** *adj* acrimonious.

acrobate [akrɔbat] *n(m+f)* acrobat. **acrobatie** *nf* acrobatics. **acrobatique** *adj* acrobatic.

acrylique [akrilik] *adj* acrylic.

acte[1] [akt] *nm* action, act; (*jur*) deed, certificate. **acte de décès/mariage/naissance** death/marriage/birth certificate.

acte[2] [akt] *nm* (*théâtre*) act.

acteur [aktœr] *nm* actor. **actrice** *nf* actress.

actif [aktif] *adj* active. *nm* credit.

action [aksjɔ̃] *nf* action, act, deed; (*comm*) share. **actionnaire** *n(m+f)* shareholder.

activer [aktive] *v* speed up; (*chim*) activate. **activiste** *n(m+f)* activist. **activité** *nf* activity. **être en activité** function, be in operation.

actuaire [aktɥɛr] *n(m+f)* actuary.

actualité [aktɥalite] *nf* topicality; current events *pl*. **les actualités** the news *sing*.

actuel [aktɥɛl] *adj* current, present; (*livre*, *etc.*) topical. **actuellement** *adv* at the moment.

acupuncture [akypɔ̃ktyr] *nf* acupuncture.

adapter [adapte] *v* adapt, fit. **adaptable** *adj* adaptable. **adaptateur** *nm* adapter. **adaptation** *nf* adaptation.

addenda [adɛ̃da] *nm* addenda.

additif [aditif] *nm* additive; (*clause*) rider.

additionner [adisjɔne] *v* add (up). **addition** *nf* addition; (*facture*) bill. **additionnel** *adj* additional.

adénoïde [adenɔid] *adj* adenoidal. **végétations adénoïdes** *nf pl* adenoids *pl*.

adhérer [adere] *v* adhere, stick. **adhérer à** (*pneu, etc.*) grip; support; (*parti*) join, be a member of. **adhérence** *nf* adhesion; grip. **adhérent, -e** *nm*, *nf* adherent, member. **adhésif** *nm*, *adj* adhesive. **adhésion** *nf* support; membership.

adieu [adjø] *nm* farewell. *interj* goodbye! **faire ses adieux** say goodbye.

adjacent [adʒasɑ̃] *adj* adjacent.

adjectif [adʒɛktif] *nm* adjective. *adj* adjectival.

adjoint [adʒwɛ̃], **-e** *nm*, *nf* assistant.

adjudication [adʒydikasjɔ̃] *nf* sale by auction. **offrir par adjudication** put up for tender.

adjuger [adʒyʒe] *v* auction; (*contrat, etc.*) award. **une fois, deux fois, trois fois, adjugé!** going, going, gone!

*admettre [admɛtrə] *v* admit; receive; (*candidat*) pass; accept; suppose.

administrer [administre] *v* administer; (*gérer*) manage, run. **administrateur, -trice** *nm*, *nf* administrator; director. **administratif** *adj* administrative. **administration** *nf* administration; management, government.

admirer [admire] *v* admire. **admirable** *adj* admirable. **admirateur, -trice** *nm*, *nf* admirer. **admiration** *nf* admiration.

admission [admisjɔ̃] *nf* admission, admittance; entry; acceptance. **admissible** *adj* admissible; acceptable; (*candidat*) eligible.

adolescence [adɔlesɑ̃s] *nf* adolescence. **adolescent, -e** *n, adj* adolescent.

adonner [adɔne] *v* **s'adonner à** devote oneself to; (*boisson, etc.*) take to.

adopter [adɔpte] *v* adopt. **adoptif** *adj* (*enfant*) adopted; (*parent*) adoptive. **adoption** *nf* adoption.

adorer [adɔre] *v* adore; (*rel*) worship. **adorable** *adj* adorable; delightful. **adorateur, -trice** *nm, nf* worshipper. **adoration** *nf* adoration; worship.

adosser [adose] *v* **adosser à** *or* **contre** lean *or* stand against.

adoucir [adusir] *v* soften; sweeten; ease, soothe.

adrénaline [adrenalin] *nf* adrenalin.

adresse[1] [adrɛs] *nf* skill, dexterity.

adresse[2] [adrɛs] *nf* address. **adresser** *v* address, direct. **s'adresser à** apply to; (*parler*) speak to.

adroit [adrwa] *adj* skilful, deft, clever.

adulation [adylɑsjɔ̃] *nf* adulation.

adulte [adylt] *n(m+f), adj* adult.

adultère [adyltɛr] *adj* adulterous. *nm* adultery.

*advenir [advənir] *v* happen. **advenir de** become of.

adverbe [advɛrb] *nm* adverb. **adverbial** *adj* adverbial.

adverse [advɛrs] *adj* opposing, adverse. **adversité** *nf* adversity.

aérer [aere] *v* air; (*terre*) aerate. **aérateur** *nm* ventilator. **aération** *nf* airing; ventilation; aeration.

aérien [aerjɛ̃] *adj* aerial, air. *nm* aerial.

aérodynamique [aerɔdinamik] *adj* aerodynamic, streamlined. *nf* aerodynamics.

aéroglisseur [aerɔglisœr] *nm* hovercraft.

aéronautique [aerɔnotik] *adj* aeronautical. *nf* aeronautics.

aéroport [aerɔpɔr] *nm* airport.

aéroporté [aerɔpɔrte] *adj* airborne.

aérosol [aerɔsɔl] *nm* aerosol.

affable [afablə] *adj* affable. **affabilité** *nf* affability.

affaiblir [afeblir] *v* weaken. **s'affaiblir** grow weaker; (*son*) fade; (*tempête*) die down. **affaiblissement** *nm* weakening.

affaire [afɛr] *nf* affair, matter, business; transaction, deal. **affaires** *nf pl* (*commerce*) business *sing*; (*effets personnels*) things *pl*, belongings *pl*. **avoir affaire à** have to deal with. **faire l'affaire** do nicely, come in handy. **occupe-toi de tes affaires!** mind your own business! **affairé** *adj* busy.

s'affaisser [afese] *v* sink, subside; (*personne*) collapse. **affaissement** *nm* subsidence.

affamer [afame] *v* starve. **affamé** *adj* starving, ravenous.

affecter[1] [afɛkte] *v* feign; (*adopter*) take on, assume. **affectation** *nf* affectation.

affecter[2] [afɛkte] *v* allocate, assign; (*nommer*) appoint. **affectation** *nf* allocation; appointment.

affecter[3] [afɛkte] *v* affect, touch, move.

affection [afɛksjɔ̃] *nf* affection; (*méd*) ailment. **affectionner** *v* be fond of. **affectueux** *adj* affectionate.

affiche [afiʃ] *nf* poster, bill. **afficher** *v* stick up; (*péj*) flaunt, display.

affilier [afilje] *v* affiliate. **affiliation** *nf* affiliation.

affiner [afine] *v* refine.

affinité [afinite] *nf* affinity.

affirmer [afirme] *v* assert, affirm. **affirmatif** *adj* affirmative; positive. **affirmation** *nf* assertion. **affirmative** *nf* affirmative.

affliction [afliksjɔ̃] *nf* affliction.

affliger [afliʒe] *v* distress. **être affligé de** be afflicted with.

affluence [aflyɑ̃s] *nf* crowd.

affoler [afɔle] *v* throw into a panic, terrify. **s'affoler** panic. **affolant** *adj* alarming. **affolé** *adj* panic-stricken. **affolement** *nm* panic.

affranchir [afrɑ̃ʃir] *v* (*lettre*) stamp; (*timbre*) frank; (*libérer*) free, emancipate.

affréter [afrete] *v* charter, hire.

affreux [afrø] *adj* dreadful, horrible, ghastly.

affronter [afrɔ̃te] *v* confront, face, brave.

afin [afɛ̃] *prep* **afin de** so as to, in order to. **afin que** so that, in order that.

Afrique [afrik] *nf* Africa. **africain** *adj* African. **Africain, -e** *nm, nf* African.

agacer [agase] *v* irritate, annoy. **agacement** *nm* irritation, annoyance.

âge [ɑʒ] *nm* age. **quel âge avez-vous?** how old are you? **âgé** *adj* old, elderly. **âgé de quatre ans** four years old.

agence [aʒɑ̃s] *nf* agency, office, bureau.

agenda [aʒɛ̃da] *nm* diary.

s'agenouiller [aʒnuje] *v* kneel (down).

agent [aʒɑ̃] *nm* agent; policeman; officer. **agent de change** stockbroker. **agent immobilier** estate agent.

agglomération [aglɔmerɑsjɔ̃] *nf* built-up area, town; conglomeration.

aggraver [agrave] *v* aggravate, worsen; (*redoubler*) increase. **aggravation** *nf* aggravation, worsening; increase.

agile [aʒil] *adj* agile, nimble. **agilité** *nf* agility.

agir [aʒir] *v* act. **s'agir de** be a matter *or* question of, be about.

agiter [aʒite] *v* shake, wave, flap; trouble; debate, discuss. **s'agiter** fidget, get restless. **agitation** *nf* agitation; restlessness. **agité** *adj* troubled; restless; (*mer*) rough.

agneau [aɲo] *nm* lamb.

agnostique [agnɔstik] *n(m+f)*, *adj* agnostic.

agoniser [agɔnize] *v* be dying. **agonie** *nf* mortal agony; (*déclin*) death throes *pl*. **à l'agonie** at death's door.

agrafe [agraf] *nf* hook; (*papiers*) staple. **agrafer** *v* hook, fasten; staple. **agrafeuse** *nf* stapler.

agrandir [agrɑ̃dir] *v* enlarge; (*développer*) expand, extend. **agrandissement** *nm* (*phot*) enlargement; expansion, extension.

agréable [agreablə] *adj* pleasant.

agréer [agree] *v* accept. **agréer à** please. **agrément** *nm* charm, pleasantness.

agression [agrɛsjɔ̃] *nf* aggression; attack. **agressif** *adj* aggressive.

agricole [agrikɔl] *adj* agricultural.

agriculture [agrikyltyr] *nf* agriculture.

agrumes [agrym] *nm pl* citrus fruits *pl*.

aguets [agɛ] *nm pl* **aux aguets** on the look-out.

ahurir [ayrir] *v* astound. **ahurissement** *nm* stupefaction.

aide [ɛd] *nf* help, aid, assistance. *n(m+f)* assistant. **à l'aide!** help! **à l'aide de** with the help of. **venir en aide à** come to the assistance of.

aider [ede] *v* help, aid, assist.

aïeux [ajø] *nm pl* forefathers *pl*.

aigle [ɛglə] *nm* eagle.

aiglefin [egləfɛ̃] *nm* haddock.

aigre [ɛgrə] *adj* sour; (*son*) shrill; (*froid*) bitter. **aigre-doux**, **-douce** *adj* bittersweet; (*cuisine*) sweet and sour. **aigreur** *nf* sourness.

aigrir [egrir] *v* embitter, sour.

aigu, **-uë** [egy] *adj* acute, sharp; (*son*) high-pitched.

aiguille [egɥij] *nf* needle; (*horloge*) hand. **travail à l'aiguille** *nm* needlework.

aiguillon [egɥijɔ̃] *nm* (*insecte*) sting; (*plante*) thorn; stimulus. **aiguillonner** *v* spur on.

aiguiser [egize] *v* sharpen; stimulate.

ail [aj] *nm*, *pl* **aulx** garlic.

aile [ɛl] *nf* wing; (*moulin*) sail. **ailé** *adj* winged.

ailleurs [ajœr] *adv* elsewhere. **d'ailleurs** *adv* besides. **par ailleurs** otherwise.

aimable [ɛmablə] *adj* kind, nice.

aimant [ɛmɑ̃] *nm* magnet. **aimanter** *v* magnetize.

aimer [eme] *v* like; (*d'amour*) love. **aimer mieux** prefer.

aine [ɛn] *nf* groin.

aîné [ene], **-e** *adj* elder, eldest. *nm*, *nf* eldest child; senior.

ainsi [ɛ̃si] *adv* in this way, thus, so. **ainsi que** just as, as well as. **et ainsi de suite** and so on. **pour ainsi dire** as it were.

air[1] [ɛr] *nm* air; atmosphere.

air[2] [ɛr] *nm* (*apparence*) air, look. **avoir l'air de** look *or* seem like.

air[3] [ɛr] *nm* (*musique*) tune, air; (*opéra*) aria.

aire [ɛr] *nf* area.

aise [ɛz] *nf* pleasure, joy. **à l'aise** at ease, comfortable. **mal à l'aise** ill at ease, uncomfortable. *adj* glad. **aisance** *nf* ease; (*richesse*) affluence. **aisé** *adj* easy.

aisselle [ɛsɛl] *nf* armpit.

ajonc [aʒɔ̃] *nm* gorse.

ajourner [aʒurne] *v* adjourn, postpone. **ajournement** *nm* adjournment, postponement.

ajouter [aʒute] *v* add. **s'ajouter à** add to.

ajuster [aʒyste] *v* adjust, fit; adapt.

alarme [alarm] *nf* alarm. **alarmer** *v* alarm. **alarmiste** *n(m+f)*, *adj* alarmist.

Albanie [albani] *nf* Albania. **albanais** *nm*, *adj* Albanian. **Albanais**, **-e** *nm*, *nf* Albanian.

albatros [albatros] *nm* albatross.

album [albɔm] *nm* album. **album à colorier** colouring book.

alcali [alkali] *nm* alkali. **alcalin** *adj* alkaline.

alchimie [alʃimi] *nf* alchemy. **alchimiste** *nm* alchemist.

alcool [alkɔl] *nm* alcohol. **alcool à brûler** methylated spirits. **alcoolique** *n(m+f)*, *adj* alcoholic. **alcoolisme** *nm* alcoholism.

alcôve [alkov] *nf* alcove.

aléatoire [aleatwar] *adj* uncertain, chancy.

alentour [alɑ̃tur] *adv* around. **alentours** *nm pl* surroundings *pl*, neighbourhood *sing*.

alerte [alɛrt] *adj* agile, alert, brisk. *nf* alert, alarm, warning. **alerter** *v* alert, notify, warn.

algèbre [alʒɛbrə] *nf* algebra. **algèbrique** *adj* algebraic.

Alger [alʒe] *n* Algiers.

Algérie [alʒeri] *nf* Algeria. **algérien** *adj* Algerian. **Algérien, -enne** *nm*, *nf* Algerian.

algue [alg] *nf* seaweed.

alias [aljɑs] *adv* alias.

alibi [alibi] *nm* alibi.

aliéner [aljene] *v* alienate; (*droits, etc.*) give up. **aliénation** *nf* alienation; (*méd*) derangement. **aliéné, -e** *nm*, *nf* insane person.

aligner [aliɲe] *v* align, line up. **alignement** *nm* alignment.

aliment [alimɑ̃] *nm* food. **alimentation** *nf* feeding; (*comm*) foodstuffs *pl*. **alimenter** *v* feed, supply.

alinéa [alinea] *nm* paragraph.

aliter [alite] *v* confine to bed. **alité** *adj* bedridden.

allaiter [alete] *v* (*femme*) (breast-)feed; (*animal*) suckle. **allaitement** *nm* (breast-) feeding; suckling.

allée [ale] *nf* path.

alléger [aleʒe] *v* alleviate; (*poids*) lighten, make lighter. **allégement** *nm* alleviation.

allégorie [alegori] *nf* allegory. **allégorique** *adj* allegorical.

allègre [alɛgrə] *adj* cheerful, lively. **allégresse** *nf* elation.

alléguer [alege] *v* allege; (*excuse*) put forward. **allégation** *nf* allegation.

alléluia [aleluja] *nm*, *interj* hallelujah.

Allemagne [almaɲ] *nf* Germany. **allemand** *nm*, *adj* German. **Allemand, -e** *nm*, *nf* German.

*aller [ale] *v* go; (*futur*) be going to. **aller à** (*style*) suit; (*mesure*) fit. **aller chercher** fetch. **aller de soi** be obvious. **allez-y!** go on! **allons!** come on! **allons-y!** let's go! **ça va** all right. **comment allez-vous?** how are you? **s'en aller** go away. *nm* (*trajet*) outward journey; (*billet*) single. **aller-retour** *nm* return.

allergie [alɛrʒi] *nf* allergy. **allergique** *adj* allergic.

allier [alje] *v* ally; unite, combine. **alliage** *nm* alloy. **alliance** *nf* alliance; union; (*bague*) wedding ring; combination. **allié, -e** *nm*, *nf* ally.

alligator [aligatɔr] *nm* alligator.

allitération [aliterasjɔ̃] *nf* alliteration.

allô [alo] *interj* hello!

allocation [alɔkasjɔ̃] *nf* allocation; (*somme*) allowance. **allocation de chômage** unemployment benefit. **allocations familiales** family allowance *sing*.

allocution [alɔkysjɔ̃] *nf* short speech.

allonger [alɔ̃ʒe] *v* lengthen; (*étendre*) stretch out; (*cuisine*) thin. **allonger le cou** crane one's neck.

allouer [alwe] *v* allocate, allot.

allumer [alyme] *v* light; (*lampe, etc.*) turn on. **allumage** *nm* lighting; (*auto*) ignition. **allumette** *nf* match.

allure [alyr] *nf* (*vitesse*) speed, pace; (*démarche*) walk, bearing; air, appearance. **à toute allure** at full speed.

allusion [alyzjɔ̃] *nf* allusion. **faire allusion à** allude to.

almanach [almana] *nm* almanac.

aloi [alwa] *nm* **de bon aloi** respectable, worthy. **de mauvais aloi** of doubtful reputation *or* quality.

alors [alɔr] *adv* then; so; in that case. **alors même que** even if *or* though. **alors que** while.

alouette [alwɛt] *nf* lark.

alourdir [alurdir] *v* make heavy, weigh down.

aloyau [alwajo] *nm* sirloin.

alphabet [alfabɛ] *nm* alphabet. **alphabétique** *adj* alphabetical.

alpinisme [alpinismə] *nm* mountaineering. **alpiniste** *n(m+f)* mountaineer.

altercation [altɛrkasjɔ̃] *nf* altercation.

altérer [altere] *v* (*donner soif*) make thirsty; falsify; (*abîmer*) spoil, debase. **altération** *nf* deterioration; falsification.

alterner [altɛrne] *v* alternate. **alternance** *nf* alternation. **alternatif** *adj* alternate; (*élec*) alternating. **alternative** *nf* alternative.

Altesse [altɛs] *nf* Highness.

altier [altje] *adj* haughty.

altitude [altityd] *nf* altitude, height.
alto [alto] *nm* viola.
aluminium [alyminjɔm] *nm* aluminium.
amabilité [amabilite] *nf* kindness.
amadouer [amadwe] *v* coax, cajole.
amaigrir [amegrir] *v* make thin *or* thinner. **amaigrissant** *adj* (*régime*) slimming. **amaigrissement** *nm* thinness; slimming.
amalgamer [amalgame] *v* combine; (*métal*) amalgamate.
amande [amɑ̃d] *nf* almond. **amandier** *nm* almond (tree).
amant [amɑ̃] *nm* lover.
amarrer [amare] *v* (*naut*) moor; (*fixer*) make fast. **amarrage** *nm* mooring.
amas [amɑ] *nm* heap, mass. **amasser** *v* amass, accumulate.
amateur [amatœr] *nm* (*non-professionnel*) amateur; enthusiast. **d'amateur** *adj* amateurish.
ambassade [ɑ̃basad] *nf* embassy; mission. **ambassadeur, -drice** *nm, nf* ambassador.
ambiance [ɑ̃bjɑ̃s] *nf* atmosphere.
ambidextre [ɑ̃bidɛkstrə] *adj* ambidextrous.
ambigu, -uë [ɑ̃bigy] *adj* ambiguous. **ambiguïté** *nf* ambiguity.
ambition [ɑ̃bisjɔ̃] *nf* ambition. **ambitieux** *adj* ambitious.
ambivalent [ɑ̃bivalɑ̃] *adj* ambivalent. **ambivalence** *nf* ambivalence.
ambre [ɑ̃brə] *nm* amber.
ambulance [ɑ̃bylɑ̃s] *nf* ambulance. **ambulancier** *nm* ambulance man.
ambulant [ɑ̃bylɑ̃] *adj* itinerant, travelling.
âme [ɑm] *nf* soul.
améliorer [ameljɔre] *v* improve. **amélioration** *nf* improvement.
aménager [amenaʒe] *v* fit out *or* up; (*parc*) lay out; develop. **aménagement** *nm* fitting-out; development.
amender [amɑ̃de] *v* amend. **amende** *nf* fine.
amener [amne] *v* bring; cause.
amer [amɛr] *adj* bitter. **amertume** *nf* bitterness.
Amérique [amerik] *nf* America. **américain** *adj* American. **Américain, -e** *nm, nf* American.
améthyste [ametist] *nf, adj* amethyst.
ameublement [amœblǝmɑ̃] *nm* furnishing; (*meubles*) furniture.
ami [ami], **-e** *nm, nf* friend. *adj* friendly.
amiable [amjablǝ] *adj* amicable.

amiante [amjɑ̃t] *nm* asbestos.
amibe [amib] *nf* amoeba.
amical [amikal] *adj* friendly. **amicale** *nf* association.
amidon [amidɔ̃] *nm* starch. **amidonner** *v* starch.
amiral [amiral] *nm* admiral.
amitié [amitje] *nf* friendship. **amitiés** *nf pl* best wishes *pl*. **prendre en amitié** befriend.
ammoniaque [amɔnjak] *nf* ammonia.
amnésie [amnezi] *nf* amnesia.
amnistie [amnisti] *nf* amnesty.
amoindrir [amwɛ̃drir] *v* reduce, weaken diminish.
amollir [amɔlir] *v* soften, weaken.
amonceler [amɔ̃sle] *v* pile up, accumulate. **amoncellement** *nm* heap; accumulation.
amont [amɔ̃] *nm* **d'amont** *adj* (*eau*) upstream; (*pente*) uphill. **en amont** *ad* upstream; uphill.
amoral [amɔral] *adj* amoral.
amorcer [amɔrse] *v* bait; (*commencer*) begin. **amorce** *nf* bait; beginning.
amorphe [amɔrf] *adj* (*roche*) amorphous (*personne*) passive, lifeless.
amortir [amɔrtir] *v* absorb, cushion deaden; (*dette*) pay off. **amortisseur** *nn* shock absorber.
amour [amur] *nm* love. **amour-propre** *nn* pride, self-esteem. **amoureux** *adj* (*personne*) in love; (*tendre*) loving.
ampère [ɑ̃pɛr] *nm* amp.
amphétamine [ɑ̃fetamin] *nf* amphetamine.
amphibie [ɑ̃fibi] *adj* amphibious. *nm* amphibian.
amphithéâtre [ɑ̃fiteatrə] *nm* amphitheatre; (*université*) lecture theatre.
ample [ɑ̃plə] *adj* ample, full. **ampleur** *nf* (*importance*) scale, extent; fullness.
amplifier [ɑ̃plifje] *v* develop, expand; (*son*) amplify. **amplificateur** *nm* amplifier.
ampoule [ɑ̃pul] *nf* (*élec*) bulb; (*méd*) blister.
amputer [ɑ̃pyte] *v* amputate; (*texte, etc.*) reduce drastically.
Amsterdam [amstɛrdam] *n* Amsterdam.
amuser [amyze] *v* amuse. **s'amuser** enjoy oneself, have fun. **amusement** *nm* entertainment, amusement; pastime.
amygdale [amidal] *nf* tonsil. **amygdalite** *nf* tonsillitis.

an [ɑ̃] *nm* year. **avoir 15 ans** be 15 years old.

anachronisme [anakrɔnismə] *nm* anachronism.

anagramme [anagram] *nf* anagram.

anal [anal] *adj* anal.

analogie [analɔʒi] *nf* analogy.

analphabète [analfabɛt] *adj* illiterate. **analphabétisme** *nm* illiteracy.

analyser [analize] *v* analyse; (*méd*) test. **analyse** *nf* analysis; test. **analytique** *adj* analytical.

ananas [anana] *nm* pineapple.

anarchie [anarʃi] *nf* anarchy. **anarchiste** *n*(*m*+*f*) anarchist.

anatomie [anatɔmi] *nf* anatomy.

ancêtre [ɑ̃sɛtrə] *n*(*m*+*f*) ancestor.

anchois [ɑ̃ʃwa] *nm* anchovy.

ancien [ɑ̃sjɛ̃], **-enne** *adj* (*vieux*) ancient; (*d'autrefois*) former. *nm*, *nf* elder; (*élève*) old boy, old girl. **ancienneté** *nf* seniority; great age.

ancre [ɑ̃krə] *nf* anchor. **ancrer** *v* anchor.

Andorre [ɑ̃dɔr] *nm* Andorra.

âne [ɑn] *nm* donkey, ass.

anéantir [aneɑ̃tir] *v* annihilate; destroy; (*accabler*) overwhelm. **anéanti** *adj* (*fatigué*) exhausted; overwhelmed. **anéantissement** *nm* annihilation; destruction; exhaustion.

anecdote [anɛkdɔt] *nf* anecdote.

anémie [anemi] *nf* anaemia. **anémique** *adj* anaemic.

anémone [anemɔn] *nf* anemone.

anesthésier [anɛstezje] *v* anaesthetize. **anesthésique** *nm*, *adj* anaesthetic. **anesthésiste** *n*(*m*+*f*) anaesthetist.

ange [ɑ̃ʒ] *nm* angel.

angélique¹ [ɑ̃ʒelik] *adj* angelic.

angélique² [ɑ̃ʒelik] *nf* angelica.

angine [ɑ̃ʒin] *nf* sore throat. **angine de poitrine** angina.

angle [ɑ̃glə] *nm* angle; (*coin*) corner. **angle droit** right angle.

Angleterre [ɑ̃glətɛr] *nf* England. **anglais** *nm*, *adj* English. **les Anglais** the English.

anglican [ɑ̃glikɑ̃], **-e** *n*, *adj* Anglican.

angoisse [ɑ̃gwas] *nf* anguish, distress; (*peur*) dread. **angoissant** *adj* harrowing. **angoissé** *adj* anguished, distressed.

anguille [ɑ̃gij] *nf* eel.

anguleux [ɑ̃gylø] *adj* angular, bony.

anicroche [anikrɔʃ] *nf* (*fam*) hitch, snag.

animal¹ [animal] *nm* animal.

animal² [animal] *adj* animal.

animer [anime] *v* animate; (*discussion, etc.*) lead; (*pousser*) drive, impel; (*soirée, etc.*) liven up. **s'animer** come to life, liven up. **animateur, -trice** *nm*, *nf* compère; (*cinéma*) animator. **animation** *nf* animation; liveliness. **animé** *adj* busy, lively.

animosité [animozite] *nf* animosity.

anis [ani] *nm* aniseed.

annales [anal] *nf pl* annals *pl*.

anneau [ano] *nm* ring; (*chaîne*) link.

année [ane] *nf* year. **année bissextile** leap year. **année-lumière** *nf* light year.

annexer [anɛkse] *v* annex. **annexe** *nf* annexe.

annihiler [aniile] *v* destroy, ruin, annihilate. **annihilation** *nf* annihilation, destruction, ruin.

anniversaire [anivɛrsɛr] *nm* (*naissance*) birthday; (*événement*) anniversary. **anniversaire de mariage** (wedding) anniversary.

annoncer [anɔ̃se] *v* announce; (*prédire*) forecast, foreshadow; indicate. **s'annoncer** approach. **s'annoncer bien** look promising. **annonce** *nf* announcement; sign, indication; (*publicité*) advertisement.

annoter [anɔte] *v* annotate. **annotation** *nf* annotation.

annuaire [anɥɛr] *nm* annual, yearbook; telephone directory.

annuel [anɥɛl] *adj* annual.

annuler [anyle] *v* (*rendre nul*) nullify; (*mariage*) annul; (*commande, etc.*) cancel. **annulation** *nf* nullification; annulment; cancellation.

anode [anɔd] *nf* anode.

anodin [anɔdɛ̃] *adj* insignificant, trivial; (*sans danger*) harmless.

anomalie [anɔmali] *nf* anomaly.

anonyme [anɔnim] *adj* anonymous; impersonal. **anonymat** *nm* anonymity.

anormal [anɔrmal] *adj* abnormal.

anse [ɑ̃s] *nf* handle; (*géog*) cove.

antagonist [ɑ̃tagɔnist] *n*(*m*+*f*) antagonist. *adj* antagonistic. **antagonisme** *nm* antagonism.

antarctique [ɑ̃tarktik] *adj* antarctic. **l'Antarctique** *nm* the Antarctic.

antenne [ɑ̃tɛn] *nf* antenna; (*TV, radio*) aerial. **sur** *or* **à l'antenne** on the air.

antérieur, -e [ɑ̃terjœr] *adj* previous; (*patte, membre*) front, fore. **antérieur à** prior to.

anthologie [ɑ̃tɔlɔʒi] *nf* anthology.
anthropologie [ɑ̃trɔpɔlɔʒi] *nf* anthropology. **anthropologique** *adj* anthropological. **anthropologiste** *n(m+f)* anthropologist.
antiaérien [ɑ̃tiaerjɛ̃] *adj* anti-aircraft; *(abri)* air-raid.
antialcoolique [ɑ̃tialkɔlik] *adj* against alcohol *or* alcoholism. **ligue antialcoolique** *nf* temperance league.
antibiotique [ɑ̃tibjɔtik] *nm*, *adj* antibiotic.
antichoc [ɑ̃tiʃɔk] *adj* shockproof.
anticiper [ɑ̃tisipe] *v* anticipate. **anticipation** *nf* anticipation. **par anticipation** in advance.
anticonceptionnel [ɑ̃tikɔ̃sɛpsjɔnɛl] *adj* contraceptive.
anticorps [ɑ̃tikɔr] *nm* antibody.
anticyclone [ɑ̃tisiklon] *nm* anticyclone.
antidater [ɑ̃tidate] *v* backdate.
antidote [ɑ̃tidɔt] *nm* antidote.
antigel [ɑ̃tiʒɛl] *nm* antifreeze.
antihistaminique [ɑ̃tiistaminik] *nm*, *adj* antihistamine.
antilope [ɑ̃tilɔp] *nf* antelope.
antipathique [ɑ̃tipatik] *adj* unpleasant.
antique [ɑ̃tik] *adj* antique, ancient. **antiquaire** *n(m+f)* antique dealer. **antiquité** *nf* antiquity. **antiquités** *nf pl (meubles, etc.)* antiques *pl*.
antisémite [ɑ̃tisemit] *adj* anti-Semitic. *n(m+f)* anti-Semite. **antisémitisme** *nm* anti-Semitism.
antiseptique [ɑ̃tisɛptik] *nm*, *adj* antiseptic.
antisocial [ɑ̃tisɔsjal] *adj* antisocial.
antithèse [ɑ̃titɛz] *nf* antithesis. **antithétique** *adj* antithetical.
antonyme [ɑ̃tɔnim] *nm* antonym.
antre [ɑ̃trə] *nm* den.
anus [anys] *nm* anus.
anxiété [ɑ̃ksjete] *nf* anxiety. **anxieux** *adj* anxious.
août [u] *nm* August.
apaiser [apeze] *v* calm, soothe; *(soif)* quench. **s'apaiser** die down; calm down; be satisfied.
aparté [aparte] *nm* aside.
apathie [apati] *nf* apathy. **apathique** *adj* apathetic.
*apercevoir [apɛrsəvwar] *v* see; *(brièvement)* catch sight of. **s'apercevoir de** notice. **aperçu** *nm* outline; *(coup d'œil)* glimpse.
apéritif [aperitif] *nm* aperitif.

aphrodisiaque [afrɔdizjak] *nm*, *adj* aphrodisiac.
aplanir [aplanir] *v* level; *(problèmes)* smooth away, iron out.
aplatir [aplatir] *v* flatten. **s'aplatir devant** grovel to. **aplati** *adj* flat.
aplomb [aplɔ̃] *nm* self-assurance; balance, equilibrium. **d'aplomb** *adv (stable)* steady; *(vertical)* straight down.
apogée [apɔʒe] *nm* peak, apogee.
apologie [apɔlɔʒi] *nf* apologia, defence.
apostrophe [apɔstrɔf] *nf* apostrophe; *(interpellation)* rude remark.
apôtre [apotrə] *nm* apostle.
*apparaître [aparɛtrə] *v* appear; seem.
apparat [apara] *nm* pomp. **d'apparat** *adj* ceremonial.
appareil [aparɛj] *nm* device, apparatus, appliance; *(TV, radio)* set; *(fam)* phone; *(dents)* brace; *(fracture)* splint; *(anat)* system. **à l'appareil** *(téléphone)* speaking. **appareil photo** *nm* camera. **appareil à sous** slot machine.
apparence [aparɑ̃s] *nf* appearance; semblance. **en apparence** apparently. **apparent** *adj* obvious; visible.
apparenter [aparɑ̃te] *v* **s'apparenter à** ally oneself with; marry into; *(ressembler)* be similar to.
apparition [aparisjɔ̃] *nf* appearance; vision, apparition.
appartement [apartəmɑ̃] *nm* flat; *(hôtel)* suite.
*appartenir [apartənir] *v* **appartenir à** belong to; *(impersonnel)* be up to.
appât [apɑ] *nm (pêche)* bait; lure. **appâter** *v* lure; *(piège)* bait.
appeler [aple] *v* call; summon, send for; telephone. **en appeler à/de** appeal to/against. **s'appeler** be called. **comment vous appelez-vous?** what is your name? **appel** *nm* appeal; *(cri)* call; *(école)* register. **faire appel** appeal.
appendice [apɛ̃dis] *nm* appendix. **appendicite** *nf* appendicitis.
appentis [apɑ̃ti] *nm* lean-to; *(toit)* sloping. roof.
appétit [apeti] *nm* appetite. **appétissant** *adj* appetizing.
applaudir [aplodir] *v* applaud. **s'applaudir** congratulate oneself. **applaudissements** *nm pl* applause *sing*.
appliquer [aplike] *v* apply. **applicable** *adj* applicable. **application** *nf* application. **appliqué** *adj* industrious.

appointements [apwɛtmɑ̃] *nm pl* salary *sing*.

apporter [apɔrte] *v* bring.

apposer [apoze] *v* affix.

apprécier [apresje] *v* appreciate; value, assess. appréciable *adj* appreciable. appréciation *nf* assessment.

appréhender [apreɑ̃de] *v* apprehend; (*craindre*) dread. appréhensif *adj* apprehensive. appréhension *nf* apprehension.

*apprendre [aprɑ̃drə] *v* learn; (*enseigner*) teach; (*aviser*) inform (of).

apprenti [aprɑ̃ti], -e *nm*, *nf* apprentice; (*débutant*) beginner. apprentissage *nm* apprenticeship.

apprivoiser [aprivwaze] *v* tame. apprivoisé *adj* tame.

approbation [aprɔbasjɔ̃] *nf* approval. approbateur, -trice *adj* approving.

approcher [aprɔʃe] *v* approach, draw *or* go near; (*objet*) move near. s'approcher de come *or* go near to, approach. approche *nf* approach.

approfondir [aprɔfɔ̃dir] *v* deepen; (*étudier*) go into. approfondi *adj* thorough.

approprier [aprɔprije] *v* suit, adapt. s'approprier appropriate. s'approprier à be appropriate to, suit. approprié *adj* appropriate.

approuver [apruve] *v* approve (of).

approvisionner [aprɔvizjɔne] *v* supply.

approximatif [aprɔksimatif] *adj* approximate. approximation *nf* approximation.

appui [apчi] *nm* support. appui-bras *nm* armrest.

appuyer [apчije] *v* press; support; (*poser*) lean, rest. appuyer sur press; rest on; stress, accentuate. s'appuyer sur rely on.

âpre [ɑprə] *adj* pungent, acrid; (*cruel*) bitter; (*dur*) grim; (*rude*) harsh.

après [aprɛ] *prep* after. *adv* afterwards. après-demain *adv* the day after tomorrow. après-midi *nm* afternoon. après-rasage *nm* after-shave. d'après (*selon*) according to; (*suivant*) next, following.

à-propos [apropo] *nm* aptness.

apte [aptə] *adj* apte à capable of, fit for. aptitude *nf* aptitude, ability.

aquarelle [akwarɛl] *nf* watercolour.

aquarium [akwarjɔm] *nm* aquarium.

aquatique [akwatik] *adj* aquatic.

aqueduc [akdyk] *nm* aqueduct.

aqueux [akø] *adj* aqueous.

arable [arablə] *adj* arable.

arachide [araʃid] *nf* peanut.

araignée [areɲe] *nf* spider.

arbitrer [arbitre] *v* arbitrate; (*sport*) referee, umpire. arbitrage *nm* arbitration. arbitraire *adj* arbitrary. arbitre *nm* judge; (*sport*) referee, umpire.

arbre [arbrə] *nm* tree; (*tech*) shaft. arbre à cames camshaft. arbre de Noël Christmas tree. arbre généalogique family tree.

arbrisseau [arbriso] *nm* shrub.

arbuste [arbyst] *nm* bush.

arc [ark] *nm* arc; (*arme*) bow; arch. arc-en-ciel *nm* rainbow.

arcade [arkad] *nf* archway. arcades *nf pl* arcade *sing*, arches *pl*.

archaïque [arkaik] *adj* archaic.

arche[1] [arʃ] *nf* arch.

arche[2] [arʃ] *nf* (*rel*) ark.

archéologie [arkeɔlɔʒi] *nf* archaeology. archéologique *adj* archaeological. archéologue *n(m + f)* archaeologist.

archet [arʃɛ] *nm* bow.

archevêque [arʃəvɛk] *nm* archbishop.

archi- [arʃi] *prefix* tremendously, utterly. archiplein *adj* (*fam*) chock-a-block.

archiduc [arʃidyk] *nm* archduke.

archipel [arʃipɛl] *nm* archipelago.

architecte [arʃitɛkt] *nm* architect. architectural *adj* architectural. architecture *nf* architecture.

archives [arʃiv] *nf pl* archives *pl*.

arctique [arktik] *adj* arctic. l'arctique *nm* the Arctic.

ardent [ardɑ̃] *adj* burning; passionate; ardent.

ardeur [ardœr] *nf* ardour; passion.

ardoise [ardwaz] *nf* slate.

ardu [ardy] *adj* arduous.

arène [arɛn] *nf* arena.

arête [arɛt] *nf* fishbone; (*bord*) ridge; (*cube*) edge.

argent [arʒɑ̃] *nm* money; (*métal*) silver. argent comptant cash. argent de poche pocket money. argent liquide ready money. argenté *adj* silvery, silvered. argenterie *nf* silverware.

argile [arʒil] *nf* clay.

argot [argo] *nm* slang. argotique *adj* slang.

argument [argymɑ̃] *nm* argument. argumenter *v* argue, reason.

aride [arid] *adj* arid, dry. aridité *nf* aridity.

aristocratie [aristɔkrasi] *nf* aristocracy. **aristocrate** *n(m+f)* aristocrat. **aristocratique** *adj* aristocratic.

arithmétique [aritmetik] *nf* arithmetic. *adj* arithmetical.

arme [arm] *nf* weapon, arm. **armes** *nf pl* coat of arms *sing*.

armée [arme] *nf* army. **armée de l'air** air force. **Armée du Salut** Salvation Army.

armer [arme] *v* arm; equip; reinforce; *(fusil)* cock.

armoire [armwar] *nf* cupboard.

armure [armyr] *nf* armour.

arôme [arom] *nm* aroma; fragrance.

arpenter [arpɑ̃te] *v* *(terrain)* measure; pace up and down. **arpentage** *nm* surveying.

arquer [arke] *v* curve; arch. **arqué** *adj* curved; arched. **avoir les jambes arquées** be bow-legged.

arracher [araʃe] *v* snatch; *(extraire)* pull up *or* out; *(déchirer)* tear off *or* out. **d'arrache-pied** *adv* relentlessly.

arranger [arɑ̃ʒe] *v* arrange; *(régler)* settle; be convenient; *(réparer)* fix. **s'arranger** manage; *(se mettre d'accord)* come to an agreement; *(situation)* work out. **arrangement** *nm* arrangement; agreement.

arrérages [areraʒ] *nm pl* arrears *pl*.

arrestation [arɛstasjɔ̃] *nf* arrest.

arrêt [arɛ] *nm* stop; stopping; judgment. **arrêt d'autobus** bus stop. **arrêt du cœur** cardiac arrest. **arrêt de mort** death sentence.

arrêté [arete] *adj* firm, fixed. *nm* order, decree.

arrêter [arete] *v* stop; *(abandonner)* give up; *(police)* arrest; fix, decide on. **s'arrêter (de)** stop.

arrhes [ar] *nf pl* deposit *sing*.

arrière [arjɛr] *nm* rear, back; *(naut)* stern. **en arrière** backwards; *(derrière)* behind. *adj* rear, back. **arrière-goût** *nm* aftertaste. **arrière-pensée** *nf* ulterior motive. **arrière-plan** *nm* background. **arriéré** *adj* *(comm)* overdue, in arrears; *(personne, pays)* backward.

arriver [arive] *v* arrive; *(se passer)* happen. **arriver à** reach; *(réussir à)* manage. **j'arrive!** I'm coming! **arrivée** *nf* arrival.

arrogance [arɔgɑ̃s] *nf* arrogance. **arrogant** *adj* arrogant.

arrondir [arɔ̃dir] *v* round (off), make rounded. **arrondi** *adj* round.

arrondissement [arɔ̃dismɑ̃] *nm* district.

arroser [aroze] *v* water, spray; *(fam: repas)* wash down. **arrosoir** *nm* watering-can.

arsenal [arsənal] *nm* arsenal.

arsenic [arsənik] *nm* arsenic.

art [ar] *nm* art; *(adresse)* skill. **arts ménagers** domestic science *sing*.

artère [artɛr] *nf* artery. **artériel** *adj* arterial.

arthrite [artrit] *nf* arthritis. **arthritique** *adj* arthritic.

artichaut [artiʃo] *nm* globe artichoke.

article [artiklə] *nm* article, item. **article réclame** special offer. **articles de Paris** fancy goods *pl*. **articles de toilette** toiletries *pl*.

articuler [artikyle] *v* articulate. **articulation** *nf* *(anat)* joint; articulation. **articulation du doigt** knuckle. **articulé** *adj* articulate; jointed.

artifice [artifis] *nm* device, trick, artifice.

artificiel [artifisjɛl] *adj* artificial.

artillerie [artijri] *nf* artillery.

artisan [artizɑ̃] *nm* craftsman, artisan.

artiste [artist] *n(m+f)* artist; *(théâtre)* performer. **artistique** *adj* artistic.

as [as] *nm* ace.

asbeste [asbɛst] *nm* asbestos.

ascendant [asɑ̃dɑ̃] *adj* upward, rising. *nm* influence, ascendancy. **ascendance** *nf* ancestry.

ascenseur [asɑ̃sœr] *nm* elevator.

ascension [asɑ̃sjɔ̃] *nf* ascent.

Asie [azi] *nf* Asia. **asiatique** *adj* Asian. **Asiatique** *n(m+f)* Asian.

asile [azil] *nm* refuge, asylum, sanctuary; *(vieillards)* home.

aspect [aspɛ] *nm* aspect; appearance, look.

asperge [aspɛrʒ] *nf* asparagus.

asperger [aspɛrʒe] *v* spray, sprinkle.

asphalte [asfalt] *nm* asphalt.

asphyxie [asfiksi] *nf* suffocation, asphyxia.

aspirer [aspire] *v* inhale; *(liquide)* suck up. **aspirer à** aspire to, long for. **aspirant, -e** *nm, nf* candidate. **aspirateur** *nm* vacuum cleaner. **aspiration** *nf* aspiration.

aspirine [aspirin] *nf* aspirin.

*assaillir [asajir] *v* assail, attack.

assainir [asenir] *v* clean up; purify.

assaisonner [asɛzɔne] *v* season. **assaisonnement** *nm* seasoning.

assassiner [asasine] v murder; (pol) assassinate. **assassin, -e** nm, nf murderer; assassin. **assassinat** nm murder; assassination.

assaut [aso] nm assault, attack. **prendre d'assaut** take by storm.

assembler [asɑ̃ble] v assemble. **assemblage** nm assembling, assembly. **assemblée** nf assembly, meeting.

assentiment [asɑ̃timɑ̃] nm assent.

***asseoir** [aswar] v sit; establish. **s'asseoir** (chaise, etc.) sit down; (lit) sit up.

assez [ase] adv enough; (plutôt) rather, fairly. **en avoir assez de** be fed up with.

assidu [asidy] adj assiduous; regular.

assiéger [asjeʒe] v besiege, beset.

assiette [asjɛt] nf plate; (cavalier) seat. **assiette creuse** soup dish. **assiette plate** dinner plate. **ne pas être dans son assiette** be off-colour.

assigner [asiɲe] v assign, allot, allocate; (jur) summons. **assignation** nf assignation; summons.

assimiler [asimile] v assimilate, absorb. **assimiler à** liken to. **assimilation** nf assimilation.

assis [asi] adj sitting, seated.

assises [asiz] nf pl assizes pl.

assister [asiste] v assist. **assister à** attend, witness. **assistance** nf (aide) assistance; (assemblée) audience, attendance. **assistant, -e** nm, nf assistant.

associer [asɔsje] v associate, combine. **s'associer** join together; (comm) form a partnership. **association** nf association; partnership. **associé, -e** nm, nf associate; partner.

assombrir [asɔ̃brir] v darken; (personne) make gloomy. **assombri** adj gloomy, sombre.

assommer [asɔme] v knock out; (fam) bore stiff.

assortir [asɔrtir] v (couleurs, etc.) match; accompany; (comm) supply. **assorti** adj assorted; matched. **assortiment** nm assortment; arrangement; (vaisselle, etc.) set.

assoupir [asupir] v numb, dull, deaden. **s'assoupir** (s'endormir) doze off. **assoupissement** nm drowsiness.

assourdir [asurdir] v deafen; (amortir) muffle.

assujettir [asyʒetir] v subject, subjugate; (fixer) secure.

assumer [asyme] v assume, take on.

assuré [asyre], **-e** adj assured; certain, sure. nm, nf insured person, policyholder.

assurer [asyre] v assure; (maison, etc.) insure; maintain, provide; (rendre sûr) secure, ensure. **s'assurer** make sure, check; insure oneself. **assurance** nf assurance; self-confidence; (contrat) insurance.

astérisque [asterisk] nm asterisk.

asthme [asmə] nm asthma. **asthmatique** adj asthmatic.

astre [astrə] nm star.

***astreindre** [astrɛ̃drə] v force, compel.

astringent [astrɛ̃ʒɑ̃] nm, adj astringent.

astrologie [astrɔlɔʒi] nf astrology. **astrologique** adj astrological. **astrologue** nm astrologer.

astronaute [astrɔnot] n(m+f) astronaut.

astronomie [astrɔnɔmi] nf astronomy. **astronome** nm astronomer. **astronomique** adj astronomical.

astucieux [astysjø] adj shrewd. **astuce** nf shrewdness; (truc) trick.

asymétrique [asimetrik] adj asymmetric.

atelier [atəlje] nm workshop; (art) studio.

athée [ate] adj atheistic. n(m+f) atheist. **athéisme** nm atheism.

Athènes [atɛn] n Athens. **athénien** adj Athenian. **Athénien, -enne** nm, nf Athenian.

athlète [atlɛt] n(m+f) athlete. **athlétique** adj athletic. **athlétisme** nm athletics.

atlantique [atlɑ̃tik] adj Atlantic. **l'Atlantique** nm the Atlantic (Ocean).

atlas [atlɑs] nm atlas.

atmosphère [atmɔsfɛr] nf atmosphere. **atmosphérique** adj atmospheric.

atome [atom] nm atom. **atomique** adj atomic.

atout [atu] nm trump; (avantage) asset, trump card.

âtre [ɑtrə] nm hearth.

atroce [atrɔs] adj atrocious, dreadful. **atrocité** nf atrocity.

s'attabler [atable] v sit (down) at table.

attacher [ataʃe] v attach; (lier) tie up, fasten. **s'attacher** (fermeture) fasten, do up. **attachant** adj engaging. **attache** nf fastener, string; (lien) tie. **à l'attache** tied up. **attaché** nm attached.

attaquer [atake] v attack; (problème) tackle; (travail) set about. **s'attaquer à** attack. **attaque** nf attack.

attarder [atarde] v make late. **s'attarder** v linger.

*atteindre [atɛ̃drə] v reach; (balle, etc.) hit; (maladie) affect. **être atteint de** be suffering from. **atteinte** nf attack.

atteler [atle] v harness. **s'atteler à** get down to.

attenant [atnɑ̃] adj adjoining.

attendre [atɑ̃drə] v wait (for); (compter sur) expect. **faire attendre** keep waiting. **s'attendre à** expect. **en attendant** meanwhile.

attendrir [atɑ̃drir] v (personne) move; (viande) tenderize. **s'attendrir sur** feel sorry for. **attendrissant** adj touching, moving. **attendrissement** nm emotion; pity. **attendrisseur** nm tenderizer.

attendu [atɑ̃dy] adj long-awaited; expected. prep considering. **attendu que** seeing that.

attentat [atɑ̃ta] nm murder attempt; attack; (jur) violation; offence.

attente [atɑ̃t] nf wait, waiting; expectation.

attention [atɑ̃sjɔ̃] nf attention, care. **avec attention** carefully. **faire attention** take care. **faire attention à** pay attention to. interj watch out! careful! **attentif** adj attentive; (scrupuleux) careful; (prévenant) thoughtful.

atténuer [atenɥe] v tone down, lighten; (douleur) alleviate; (faute) mitigate. **s'atténuer** die down, subside.

atterrer [atere] v appal.

atterrir [aterir] v land. **atterrissage** nm landing.

attester [atɛste] v testify to, attest.

attirail [atiraj] nm (fam) gear.

attirer [atire] v attract; (appâter) lure, entice; cause. **attirance** nf attraction; lure. **attirant** adj attractive.

attiser [atize] v poke, stir up.

attitré [atitre] adj accredited; regular.

attitude [atityd] nf attitude.

attraction [atraksjɔ̃] nf attraction.

attrait [atrɛ] nm appeal, attraction.

attraper [atrape] v catch, get; (tromper) take in; (gronder) tell off. **attrape** nf trick.

attrayant [atrɛjɑ̃] adj appealing, attractive.

attribuer [atribɥe] v attribute; allocate, accord, award. **s'attribuer** claim. **attribut** nm attribute.

attrister [atriste] v sadden.

s'attrouper [atrupe] v flock together.

au [o] contraction of **à le**.

aubaine [obɛn] nf godsend, windfall.

aube[1] [ob] nf (du jour) dawn.

aube[2] [ob] nf (bateau) paddle; (moulin) vane.

aubépine [obepin] nf hawthorn.

auberge [obɛrʒ] nf inn. **auberge de la jeunesse** youth hostel. **aubergiste** nm innkeeper, landlord.

aubergine [obɛrʒin] nf aubergine.

aucun [okœ̃] adj, pron any. **ne ... aucun** not any, no, none. **aucunement** adv in no way, not in the least.

audace [odas] nf audacity, daring. **audacieux** adj daring, bold, audacious.

au-delà [odla] nm, adv beyond.

au-dessous [odəsu] adv below, underneath.

au-dessus [odəsy] adv above, over.

au-devant [odəvɑ̃] adv ahead. **aller au-devant de** anticipate; (personne) go and meet.

audible [odiblə] adj audible.

audience [odjɑ̃s] nf audience, hearing.

auditeur [oditœr], **-trice** nm, nf listener.

audition [odisjɔ̃] nf (essai) audition; recital; (ouïe) hearing.

auditoire [oditwar] nm audience.

auge [oʒ] nf trough.

augmenter [ɔgmɑ̃te] v increase. **augmentation** nf increase, rise.

aujourd'hui [oʒurdɥi] adv today. **aujourd'hui en huit** a week today.

aulx [o] V **ail**.

aumône [omon] nf alms; charity. **aumônier** nm chaplain.

auparavant [oparavɑ̃] adv before, previously.

auprès [oprɛ] prep **auprès de** next to, close to; compared with; in the opinion of.

auquel [okɛl] contraction of **à lequel**.

aura [ɔra] nf aura.

auréole [ɔreɔl] nf halo.

Aurigny [ɔriɲi] nf Alderney.

aurore [ɔrɔr] nf dawn, daybreak.

aussi [osi] adv too, also; (comparaison) as; (si) so. **aussi bien** just as well. conj therefore.

aussitôt [osito] adv straight away. **aussitôt que** as soon as.

austère [ɔstɛr] adj austere. **austérité** nf austerity.

Australie [ɔstrali] *nf* Australia. **australien** *adj* Australian. **Australien, -enne** *nm, nf* Australian.

autant [otɑ̃] *adv* as much, so much. **autant de** as much, as many; (*tant*) so much, so many. **autant que** as much as. **autant que possible** as far as possible. **d'autant plus** all the more.

autel [ɔtɛl] *nm* altar.

auteur [otœr] *nm* author, writer; (*musique*) composer.

authentique [ɔtɑ̃tik] *adj* authentic, genuine. **authenticité** *nf* authenticity.

autistique [ɔtistik] *adj* autistic.

auto [oto] *nf* car. **auto-école** *nf* driving school. **auto-stop** *nm* hitch-hiking. **faire de l'auto-stop** hitch-hike. **auto-stoppeur, -euse** *nm, nf* hitch-hiker.

autobiographie [ɔtɔbjɔɡrafi] *nf* autobiography. **autobiographique** *adj* autobiographical.

autobus [ɔtɔbys] *nm* bus.

autocar [ɔtɔkar] *nm* coach.

autodidacte [ɔtɔdidakt] *adj* self-taught.

autographe [ɔtɔɡraf] *nm* autograph.

automatique [ɔtɔmatik] *adj* automatic. **automation** *or* **automatisation** *nf* automation. **automatiser** *v* automate.

automne [ɔtɔn] *nm* autumn. **automnal** *adj* autumnal.

automobile [ɔtɔmɔbil] *nf* motor car. **l'automobile** *nf* the motor industry; (*sport*) motoring. **automobiliste** *n(m+f)* motorist.

autonome [ɔtɔnɔm] *adj* autonomous. **autonomie** *nf* autonomy.

autopont [ɔtɔpɔ̃] *nm* flyover.

autopsie [ɔtɔpsi] *nf* post-mortem.

autoriser [ɔtɔrize] *v* authorize, give permission. **autorisation** *nf* authorization, permission. **autorisé** *adj* authorized; official.

autorité [ɔtɔrite] *nf* authority. **autoritaire** *n(m+f)*, *adj* authoritarian.

autoroute [ɔtɔrut] *nf* motorway.

autour [otur] *adv* around. *prep* **autour de** around.

autre [otrə] *adj* other; different. **autre chose** something else. **autre part** somewhere else. **d'autre part** on the other hand. *pron* another. **d'autres** others. **rien/personne d'autre** nothing/nobody else.

autrefois [otrəfwa] *adv* in the past. **d'autrefois** of the past.

autrement [otrəmɑ̃] *adv* differently, in another way; (*sinon*) otherwise. **autrement dit** in other words, that is.

Autriche [otriʃ] *nf* Austria. **autrichien** *adj* Austrian. **Autrichien, -enne** *nm, nf* Austrian.

autruche [otryʃ] *nf* ostrich.

autrui [otrɥi] *pron* others.

auvent [ovɑ̃] *nm* awning, canopy.

aux [o] *contraction of* **à les**.

auxiliaire [ɔksiljɛr] *adj* auxiliary, secondary. *n(m+f)* assistant, auxiliary.

auxquels, auxquelles [okɛl] *contractions of* **à lesquels, à lesquelles**.

aval [aval] *nm* **d'aval** *adj* (*eau*) downstream; (*pente*) downhill. **en aval** *adv* downstream; downhill.

avalanche [avalɑ̃ʃ] *nf* avalanche; torrent, flood.

avaler [avale] *v* swallow.

avancer [avɑ̃se] *v* advance; move *or* bring forward; (*accélérer*) speed up; make progress; (*montre*) gain. **avance** *nf* advance; lead. **à l'avance** in advance, beforehand. **d'avance** in advance. **en avance** (*heure*) early; ahead. **avancement** *nm* promotion; progress.

avant [avɑ̃] *prep* before. *adv* before; (*mouvement*) forward. *nm* front; (*naut*) bow. **avant tout** above all. **d'avant** *adj* previous. **en avant** (*mouvement*) forward; (*position*) ahead.

avantage [avɑ̃taʒ] *nm* advantage. **avantageux** *adj* worthwhile.

avant-bras *nm invar* forearm.

avant-coureur *nm* forerunner.

avant-dernier, -ère *n, adj* last but one.

avant-garde *nf* avant-garde. **d'avant-garde** *adj* avant-garde.

avant-goût *nm* foretaste.

avant-hier *adv* the day before yesterday.

avant-poste *nm* outpost.

avant-première *nf* preview.

avant-propos *nm invar* foreword.

avant-veille *nf* two days before.

avare [avar] *adj* miserly. *n(m+f)* miser. **avarice** *nf* avarice.

avarie [avari] *nf* damage. **avarié** *adj* rotting, damaged.

avec [avɛk] *prep* with.

avènement [avɛnmɑ̃] *nm* advent; (*roi*) accession.

avenir [avnir] *nm* future. **à l'avenir** from now on.

Avent [avã] *nm* Advent.
aventure [avãtyr] *nf* adventure; (*entreprise*) venture. **à l'aventure** at random, aimlessly. **s'aventurer** *v* venture. **aventureux** *adj* adventurous; risky. **aventurier** *nm* adventurer.
avenue [avny] *nf* avenue.
s'avérer [avere] *v* prove to be, turn out to be.
averse [avɛrs] *nf* shower.
aversion [avɛrsjɔ̃] *nf* aversion, loathing. **avoir en aversion** loathe.
avertir [avɛrtir] *v* warn; (*renseigner*) inform. **avertissement** *nm* warning; notice.
aveu [avø] *nm* confession, admission.
aveugle [avœglə] *adj* blind. *n*(*m*+*f*) blind person. **aveugler** *v* blind; (*éblouir*) dazzle. **s'aveugler sur** shut one's eyes to. **à l'aveuglette** blindly.
aviateur [avjatœr] *nm* airman. **aviation** *nf* aviation, flying; (*mil*) air force.
avide [avid] *adj* eager, avid; (*cupide*) greedy. **avidité** *nf* eagerness; greed.
avilir [avilir] *v* degrade, debase.
avion [avjɔ̃] *nm* aeroplane. **par avion** by airmail.
aviron [avirɔ̃] *nm* oar; (*sport*) rowing. **faire de l'aviron** row.
avis [avi] *nm* opinion; (*conseil*) advice; notice. **à mon avis** in my opinion. **avis au lecteur** foreword.
aviser [avize] *v* inform, notify; (*apercevoir*) notice. **aviser à** see to. **s'aviser de** realize suddenly; (*oser*) dare to. **avisé** *adj* sensible.
avocat¹ [avɔka], **-e** *nm*, *nf* (*jur*) barrister; advocate.
avocat² [avɔka] *nm* avocado (pear). **avocatier** *nm* avocado (tree).
avoine [avwan] *nf* oats *pl*.
***avoir¹** [avwar] *v* have; (*obtenir*) get; (*être*) be. **il y a** there is *or* are; (*temps écoulé*) ago. **il n'y a pas de quoi** don't mention it. **qu'est-ce qu'il y a?** what's the matter?
avoir² [avwar] *nm* assets *pl*; (*comm*) credit.
avoisiner [avwazine] *v* border on, be close to. **avoisinant** *adj* neighbouring, nearby.
avorter [avɔrte] *v* abort; (*projet*) fail. **se faire avorter** have an abortion. **avortement** *nm* abortion. **avorteur, -euse** *nm*, *nf* abortionist.

avouer [avwe] *v* confess, admit. **avoué** *nm* solicitor.
avril [avril] *nm* April.
axe [aks] *nm* axis; (*tech*) axle.
azalée [azale] *nf* azalea.
azote [azɔt] *nf* nitrogen.

B

babiller [babije] *v* (*personne*) chatter; (*ruisseau*) babble; (*oiseau*) twitter. **babillage** *nm* chatter; babble; twitter. **babillard, -e** *nm*, *nf* chatterbox.
babines [babin] *nf pl* lips *pl*, chops *pl*.
bâbord [babɔr] *nm* (*naut*) port (side).
babouin [babwɛ̃] *nm* baboon.
bac [bak] *nm* ferry-boat; (*récipient*) tub, tray, sink.
baccalauréat [bakalɔrea] *nm* examination equivalent to A-levels.
bâche [baʃ] *nf* canvas cover. **bâche goudronnée** tarpaulin.
bâcler [bakle] *v* hurry through; (*travail*) botch. **bâclé** *adj* slapdash.
bactérie [bakteri] *nf* bacterium (*pl* -ria).
badigeonner [badiʒɔne] *v* (*mur*) distemper, whitewash; (*méd*) paint. **badigeon** *nm* distemper, whitewash.
badiner [badine] *v* banter; (*avec négatif*) treat lightly, trifle with. **badinage** *nm* banter.
bafouiller [bafuje] *v* splutter; (*bredouiller*) stammer.
bagage [bagaʒ] *nm* bag, piece of luggage. **bagages** *nm pl* luggage *sing*. **bagages à main** hand baggage *sing*.
bagarre [bagar] *nf* fight. **(se) bagarrer** *v* (*fam*) fight, scrap.
bagatelle [bagatɛl] *nf* trifle; (*objet*) trinket.
bagne [baɲ] *nm* hard labour.
bagnole [baɲɔl] *nf* (*fam*) old banger.
bague [bag] *nf* ring.
baguette [bagɛt] *nf* stick; (*musique*) baton; (*pour manger*) chopstick; (*pain*) thin French loaf; (*magique*) wand.
bahut [bay] *nm* chest; (*argot*) school.
bai [bɛ] *adj* bay.
baie¹ [bɛ] *nf* (*géog*) bay.

baie² [bɛ] *nf* (*bot*) berry.
baigner [beɲe] *v* bathe; (*bébé*) bath; (*tremper*) soak. **se baigner** (*mer*, *piscine*) go swimming; (*se laver*) have a bath. **baignade** *nf* bathe, bathing. **baigneur, -euse** *nm, nf* bather. **baignoire** *nf* bath.
bail [baj] *nm, pl* **baux** lease.
bâiller [bɑje] *v* yawn; (*couture, col, etc.*) gape; (*porte*) be ajar. **bâillement** *nm* yawn.
bâillonner [bɑjɔne] *v* gag. **bâillon** *nm* gag.
bain [bɛ̃] *nm* (*baignoire*) bath; (*piscine, mer*) swim, bathe. **bain de foule** walkabout. **bain de mousse** bubble bath. **prendre un bain de soleil** sunbathe.
baïonnette [bajɔnɛt] *nf* bayonet.
baiser [beze] *nm* kiss. *v* (*embrasser*) kiss; (*vulgaire*) screw.
baisser [bese] *v* (*mettre plus bas*) lower; (*décliner*) fall, drop. **se baisser** bend down. **baisse** *nf* fall, drop.
bal [bal] *nm, pl* **bals** dance, ball; (*lieu*) dance hall. **bal costumé** fancy-dress ball.
balader [balade] (*fam*) *v* trail round. **se balader** go for a walk; (*en voiture*) go for a drive. **balade** *nf* walk; drive.
balafrer [balafre] *v* gash. **balafre** *nf* gash; (*cicatrice*) scar. **balafré** *adj* scarred.
balai [balɛ] *nm* broom, brush. **balai mécanique** carpet sweeper.
balance [balɑ̃s] *nf* scales *pl*; (*comm*) balance. **Balance** *nf* Libra.
balancer [balɑ̃se] *v* swing, rock; (*compte*) balance; (*argot*) chuck (out). **se balancer** sway, swing. **balancier** *nm* pendulum. **balançoire** *nf* swing; (*bascule*) seesaw.
balayer [baleje] *v* sweep.
balbutier [balbysje] *v* stammer, mumble.
balcon [balkɔ̃] *nm* balcony; (*théâtre*) dress circle.
baldaquin [baldakɛ̃] *nm* canopy.
baleine [balɛn] *nf* whale.
balise [baliz] *nf* beacon; (*flottante*) buoy.
balistique [balistik] *adj* ballistic. *nf* ballistics.
balivernes [balivɛrn] *nf pl* nonsense *sing*.
ballade [balad] *nf* ballad.
ballant [balɑ̃] *adj* dangling.
balle [bal] *nf* (*projectile*) bullet; (*sport*) ball.
ballet [balɛ] *nm* ballet. **ballerine** *nf* ballerina.
ballon [balɔ̃] *nm* balloon; (*sport*) ball.
ballotter [balɔte] *v* jolt, toss *or* shake about.

balnéaire [balneɛr] *adj* bathing. **station balnéaire** *nf* seaside resort.
balustrade [balystrad] *nf* handrail.
bambou [bɑ̃bu] *nm* bamboo.
banal [banal] *adj* banal, commonplace. **banalité** *nf* banality; (*propos*) platitude.
banane [banan] *nf* banana. **bananier** *nm* banana (tree).
banc [bɑ̃] *nm* bench, seat; (*géol*) layer, bed. **banc d'église** pew. **banc de sable** sandbank. **banc des accusés** dock.
bancal [bɑ̃kal] *adj* wobbly, shaky; (*personne*) bandy-legged.
bandage [bɑ̃daʒ] *nm* bandage.
bande¹ [bɑ̃d] *nf* strip, band; (*magnétophone*) tape; (*méd*) bandage. **bande dessinée** comic strip. **bande sonore** sound-track.
bande² [bɑ̃d] *nf* band, group, gang.
bandeau [bɑ̃do] *nm* (*ruban*) headband; (*yeux*) blindfold.
bander [bɑ̃de] *v* bandage; (*tendre*) stretch. **bander les yeux à** blindfold.
bandit [bɑ̃di] *nm* bandit, thief; (*escroc*) crook.
banlieue [bɑ̃ljø] *nf* suburbs *pl*.
banne [ban] *nf* (*magasin*) awning; (*manne*) hamper.
bannière [banjɛr] *nf* banner.
bannir [banir] *v* banish. **banni, -e** *nm, nf* exile. **bannissement** *nm* banishment.
banque [bɑ̃k] *nf* bank; (*métier*) banking. **banquier** *nm* banker.
banqueroute [bɑ̃krut] *nf* bankruptcy. **faire banqueroute** go bankrupt. **banqueroutier, -ère** *nm, nf* bankrupt.
banquet [bɑ̃kɛ] *nm* banquet.
banquette [bɑ̃kɛt] *nf* seat.
baptême [batɛm] *nm* baptism, christening.
baptiser [batize] *v* baptize, christen.
bar [bar] *nm* bar.
baragouiner [baragwine] *v* (*fam*) gabble; talk gibberish. **baragouin** *nm* gibberish.
baraque [barak] *nf* stand, stall; (*abri*) shed; (*fam: maison*) place.
baratte [barat] *nf* churn. **baratter** *v* churn.
barbare [barbar] *adj* barbarous, barbaric. *nm* barbarian. **barbarie** *nf* barbarity.
barbe [barb] *nf* beard. **barbe à papa** candy floss. **quelle barbe!** (*fam*) what a drag!
barbecue [barbəkju] *nm* barbecue.

barbelé [barbəle] *adj* **fil de fer barbelé** barbed wire.

barbier [barbje] *nm* barber.

barbiturique [barbityrik] *nm* barbiturate.

barboter [barbɔte] *v* paddle, splash about; (*fam*) pinch. **barboteuse** *nf* rompers *pl*.

barbouiller [barbuje] *v* smear, daub; (*écrire*) scribble. **barbouillis** *nm* daub; scribble.

barbu [barby] *adj* bearded. *nm* bearded man.

barème [barɛm] *nm* list, scale, table.

bariolé [barjɔle] *adj* gaudy, multicoloured.

baromètre [barɔmɛtrə] *nm* barometer.

baron [barɔ̃] *nm* baron. **baronne** *nf* baroness. **baronnet** *nm* baronet.

baroque [barɔk] *adj* weird, strange; (*arch*) baroque. *nm* baroque.

barque [bark] *nf* small boat.

barrage [baraʒ] *nm* (*rivière*) dam; barrier; barricade.

barre [bar] *nf* bar, rod; (*trait*) stroke; (*naut*) helm, tiller.

barreau [baro] *nm* (*échelle*) rung; (*cage, jur*) bar.

barrer [bare] *v* bar, obstruct; (*rayer*) cross (out); (*naut*) steer.

barrette [barɛt] *nf* hair-slide.

barricade [barikad] *nf* barricade. **barricader** *v* barricade.

barrière [barjɛr] *nf* (*porte*) gate; (*clôture*) fence; (*obstacle*) barrier.

baryton [baritɔ̃] *nm, adj* baritone.

bas¹, basse [ba, bas] *adj* low. *adv* low; (*parler*) in a low voice. *nm* bottom. **en bas** down below; (*maison*) downstairs. **basse** *nf* bass.

bas² [ba] *nm* stocking.

basculer [baskyle] *v* fall over, topple; (*renverser*) tip up *or* out. **bascule** *nf* (*jeu*) see-saw. **cheval/fauteuil à bascule** *nm* rocking-horse/chair.

base [baz] *nf* base; (*fondement*) basis. **de base** basic.

base-ball [bɛzbol] *nm* baseball.

baser [baze] *v* base.

basilic [bazilik] *nm* basil.

basket-ball [baskɛtbol] *nm* basketball.

bassin [basɛ̃] *nm* pond, pool; (*géog*) basin; (*anat*) pelvis; (*naut*) dock.

basson [basɔ̃] *nm* bassoon.

bastille [bastij] *nf* fortress.

bataclan [bataklɑ̃] *nm* (*fam*) junk.

bataille [bataj] *nf* battle, fight. **bataillon** *nm* battalion.

bâtard [batar], **-e** *n, adj* bastard.

bateau [bato] *nm* boat. **bateau à voiles** sailing boat. **bateau de sauvetage** lifeboat.

bâtiment [batimɑ̃] *nm* building; (*naut*) ship.

bâtir [batir] *v* build; (*couture*) tack. **bâti** *nm* frame; tacking.

bâton [batɔ̃] *nm* stick.

battant [batɑ̃] *nm* flap; (*porte*) door; (*cloche*) clapper.

batte [bat] *nf* (*sport*) bat.

battement [batmɑ̃] *nm* beat, beating; interval, pause. **battement de paupières** blink.

batterie [batri] *nf* battery; (*musique*) percussion, drums.

*battre [batrə] *v* beat; (*parcourir*) scour; (*cartes*) shuffle. **battre des mains** clap. **battre son plein** be at its height. **se battre** fight.

baux [bo] *V* **bail**.

bavard [bavar], **-e** *adj* talkative. *nm, nf* (*fam*) chatterbox.

bavarder [bavarde] *v* chatter; (*papoter*) gossip. **bavardage** *nm* chatter; gossip.

baver [bave] *v* dribble, slobber. **bave** *nf* dribble, slobber. **bavette** *nf* bib.

béant [beɑ̃] *adj* gaping, wide open.

béat [bea] *adj* smug; (*sourire*) blissful.

beau [bo], **belle** *adj* beautiful, fine, lovely. **bel et bien** well and truly. **de plus belle** all the more. **beauté** *nf* beauty.

beaucoup [boku] *adv* (very) much, a great deal, a lot; (*personnes*) many. **de beaucoup** by far.

beau-fils *nm* son-in-law; (*remariage*) stepson.

beau-frère *nm* brother-in-law.

beau-père *nm* father-in-law; (*remariage*) stepfather.

beaux-arts [bozar] *nm pl* fine arts *pl*.

bébé [bebe] *nm* baby.

bec [bɛk] *nm* beak; (*plume*) nib; (*carafe*) lip; (*théière*) spout.

bécane [bekan] *nf* (*fam*) bike.

bécasse [bekas] *nf* woodcock. **bécassine** *nf* snipe.

bêcher [beʃe] *v* dig. **bêche** *nf* spade.

becqueter [bɛkte] *v* peck.

bedaine [bədɛn] *nf* (*fam*) paunch.

bée [be] *adj* **bouche bée** open-mouthed.
beffroi [befrwa] *nm* belfry.
bégayer [begeje] *v* stammer, stutter.
bégueule [begœl] *nf* prude. *adj* prudish.
béguin [begɛ̃] *nm* bonnet. **avoir le béguin pour** (*fam*) have a crush on, take a fancy to.
beige [bɛʒ] *nm, adj* beige.
beignet [beɲɛ] *nm* fritter; (*soufflé*) doughnut.
bel [bɛl] *form of* **beau** *used before vowel or mute h.*
bêler [bele] *v* bleat.
belette [bəlɛt] *nf* weasel.
Belgique [bɛlʒik] *nf* Belgium. **belge** *adj* Belgian. **belge** *n(m + f)* Belgian.
Belgrade [bɛlgrad] *n* Belgrade.
bélier [belje] *nm* ram. **Bélier** *nm* Aries.
belle [bɛl] *V* **beau.**
belle-fille *nf* daughter-in-law; (*remariage*) stepdaughter.
belle-mère *nf* mother-in-law; (*remariage*) stepmother.
belle-sœur *nf* sister-in-law.
bémol [bemɔl] *nm* flat.
bénédicité [benedisite] *nm* grace.
bénédiction [benediksjɔ̃] *nf* blessing.
bénéfice [benefis] *nm* (*comm*) profit; advantage, benefit. **bénéficiaire** *n(m + f)* beneficiary; (*chèque*) payee. **bénéficier de** *v* benefit from; (*jouir de*) enjoy; (*obtenir*) get.
bénévole [benevɔl] *adj* voluntary, unpaid.
benin, -igne [benɛ̃, -iɲ] *adj* mild, slight; (*tumeur*) benign.
bénir [benir] *v* bless. **bénit** *adj* consecrated, holy.
béquille [bekij] *nf* crutch.
bercer [bɛrse] *v* rock; (*apaiser*) lull. **se bercer** delude oneself. **berceau** *nm* cradle. **berceuse** *nf* lullaby.
berger [bɛrʒe] *nm* shepherd; (*chien*) sheepdog. **berger allemand** alsatian. **bergère** *nf* shepherdess.
Berlin [bɛrlɛ̃] *n* Berlin.
Berne [bɛrn] *n* Bern.
besogne [bəzɔɲ] *nf* work.
besoin [bəzwɛ̃] *nm* need. **au besoin** if necessary. **avoir besoin de** need.
bétail [betaj] *nm* livestock; (*bovins*) cattle.
bête [bɛt] *nf* animal, creature, beast. **bête à bon dieu** ladybird. **bête noire** pet hate. **faire la bête** act stupid. *adj* stupid. **bêtise** *nf* stupidity; (*erreur*) blunder; (*action*) silly thing. **dire des bêtises** talk nonsense.

béton [betɔ̃] *nm* concrete. **bétonner** *v* concrete.
betterave [bɛtrav] *nf* beet. **betterave rouge** beetroot. **betterave sucrière** sugar beet.
beugler [bøgle] *v* bellow; (*radio*) blare; (*vache*) low.
beurre [bœr] *nm* butter. **beurrer** *v* butter.
bévue [bevy] *nf* blunder.
biais [bjɛ] *nm* (*détour*) expedient, device; (*aspect*) angle; (*couture*) bias; (*oblique*) slant. **de biais** at an angle; indirectly. **en biais** diagonally, at an angle.
bibelot [biblo] *nm* trinket, knick-knack.
biberon [bibrɔ̃] *nm* feeding bottle. **élevé au biberon** bottle-fed.
Bible [biblə] *nf* Bible. **biblique** *adj* biblical.
bibliographie [biblijɔgrafi] *nf* bibliography.
bibliothécaire [biblijɔtekɛr] *n(m + f)* librarian.
bibliothèque [biblijɔtɛk] *nf* library; (*meuble*) bookcase.
biceps [bisɛps] *nm* biceps.
biche [biʃ] *nf* doe.
bicyclette [bisiklɛt] *nf* bicycle; (*sport*) cycling. **aller à bicyclette** cycle.
bidon [bidɔ̃] *nm* can, tin.
bien [bjɛ̃] *adv* well; (*très*) very; (*beaucoup*) very much; (*plutôt*) rather; certainly, indeed; (*tout à fait*) properly, carefully. *adj* good; (*beau*) nice. *nm* good; possession. **bien de** much. **bien que** although. **biens** *nm pl* goods *pl*; property *sing*.
bien-aimé [bjɛ̃neme], **-e** *n, adj* beloved.
bien-être [bjɛ̃nɛtrə] *nm* well-being.
bienfaisant [bjɛ̃fəzɑ̃] *adj* beneficial; (*personne*) kind. **bienfaisance** *nf* charity.
bienfaiteur [bjɛ̃fɛtœr] *nm* benefactor. **bienfaitrice** *nf* benefactress.
bienheureux [bjɛ̃nœrø] *adj* (*rel*) blessed; happy.
biennal [bjenal] *adj* biennial.
bienséance [bjɛ̃seɑ̃s] *nf* propriety. **bienséant** *adj* proper, seemly.
bientôt [bjɛ̃to] *adv* soon. **à bientôt!** see you!
bienveillance [bjɛ̃vejɑ̃s] *nf* kindness, benevolence. **bienveillant** *adj* benevolent, kindly.
bienvenu [bjɛ̃vny], **-e** *adj* well-chosen. *nm, nf* welcome person *or* thing. **être le bienvenu** be welcome. **bienvenue** *nf* welcome.

bière¹ [bjɛr] *nf (boisson)* beer. **bière (à la) pression** draught beer. **bière blonde** lager.

bière² [bjɛr] *nf* coffin.

biffer [bife] *v* cross out.

bifocal [bifɔkal] *adj* bifocal. **lunettes bifocales** *nf pl* bifocals *pl.*

bifteck [biftɛk] *nm* steak.

bifurcation [bifyrkasjɔ̃] *nf* fork, branching off. **bifurquer** *v* fork, branch off.

bigame [bigam] *adj* bigamous. *n(m+f)* bigamist. **bigamie** *nf* bigamy.

bigorneau [bigɔrno] *nm* winkle.

bigot [bigo], **-e** *adj* bigoted. *nm, nf* bigot.

bigoudi [bigudi] *nm* curler, roller.

bijou [biʒu] *nm, pl* **-oux** jewel. **bijouterie** *nf* jewellery; *(boutique)* jeweller's. **bijoutier, -ère** *nm, nf* jeweller.

bikini [bikini] *nm* bikini.

bilan [bilɑ̃] *nm* assessment; consequence; *(comm)* balance sheet. **bilan de santé** check-up.

bile [bil] *nf* bile. **se faire de la bile** get worried.

bilingue [bilɛ̃g] *adj* bilingual.

billard [bijar] *nm* billiards; billiard table.

bille [bij] *nf* marble; billiard ball.

billet [bijɛ] *nm* ticket; note. **billet de banque** banknote.

billot [bijo] *nm* block.

binaire [binɛr] *adj* binary.

biner [bine] *v* hoe. **binette** *nf* hoe.

biographie [bjɔgrafi] *nf* biography. **biographe** *n(m+f)* biographer. **biographique** *adj* biographical.

biologie [bjɔlɔʒi] *nf* biology. **biologique** *adj* biological. **biologiste** *n(m+f)* biologist.

bis [bis] *nm, interj* encore. *adv (musique)* repeat.

bisannuel [bizanɥɛl] *adj* biennial.

biscornu [biskɔrny] *adj* irregular; *(bizarre)* peculiar.

biscotte [biskɔt] *nf* rusk.

biscuit [biskɥi] *nm* biscuit; *(gâteau)* sponge cake.

bise¹ [biz] *nf (vent)* north wind.

bise² [biz] *nf* kiss.

bistouri [bisturi] *nm* scalpel.

bistro [bistro] *nm* pub, café.

bizarre [bizar] *adj* strange, odd. **bizarrerie** *nf* strangeness, oddness.

blafard [blafar] *adj* pale, wan.

blague [blag] *nf* joke; *(farce)* trick. **sans blague?** really? **blaguer** *(fam) v (taquiner)* tease; *(plaisanter)* be joking.

blaireau [blɛro] *nm* badger; *(brosse)* shaving brush.

blâmer [blame] *v* blame; reprimand. **blâme** *nm* blame, reprimand.

blanc, blanche [blɑ̃, blɑ̃ʃ] *nm, adj (couleur)* white; *(page, etc.)* blank. **blanc cassé** off-white. **blancheur** *nf* whiteness.

blanchir [blɑ̃ʃir] *v* whiten; *(mur)* whitewash; *(toile)* bleach; *(linge)* launder; *(devenir blanc)* go *or* turn white. **blanchisserie** *nf* laundry.

blasé [blaze] *adj* blasé. **être blasé de** be bored with.

blason [blazɔ̃] *nm* coat of arms; heraldry.

blasphémer [blasfeme] *v* blaspheme. **blasphématoire** *adj* blasphemous. **blasphème** *nm* blasphemy.

blatte [blat] *nf* cockroach.

blé [ble] *nm* wheat, corn.

blêmir [blemir] *v* turn *or* go pale. **blême** *adj* pallid, wan.

blessé [blese], **-e** *adj* wounded. *nm, nf* casualty.

blesser [blese] *v* hurt, injure, wound. **blessure** *nf* wound.

blet, blette [blɛ, blɛt] *adj* overripe.

bleu [blø] *adj* blue. *nm* blue; *(meurtrissure)* bruise; *(vêtement)* overalls *pl*; *(débutant)* beginner. **bleu marine** navy blue. **bleu roi** royal blue.

bleuet [bløɛ] *nm* cornflower.

blindé [blɛ̃de] *adj* armoured, reinforced.

bloc [blɔk] *nm (pierre, bois)* block; *(papier)* pad; group; *(d'éléments)* unit. **à bloc** fully, properly. **en bloc** outright.

blocage [blɔkaʒ] *nm (prix, etc.)* freeze; *(blocaille)* rubble.

blocus [blɔkys] *nm* blockade. **faire le blocus de** blockade.

blond [blɔ̃] *adj* fair, blond; *(sable)* golden. **blonde** *nf* blonde.

bloquer [blɔke] *v* block, jam, wedge; group together; *(salaires, etc.)* freeze.

se blottir [blɔtir] *v* snuggle up.

blouse [bluz] *nf* overall; *(chemisier)* blouse.

blue-jean [bludʒin] *nm* jeans *pl.*

bluff [blœf] *nm (fam)* bluff. **bluffer** *v* bluff.

bobine [bɔbin] *nf* spool, reel, bobbin; *(élec)* coil. **bobiner** *v* wind.

bocage [bɔkaʒ] *nm* grove; *(géog)* bocage.

bocal [bɔkal] *nm* jar; *(poissons)* bowl.

bock [bɔk] *nm* glass of beer.

bœuf [bœf] *nm* (*animal*) bullock, ox; (*viande*) beef.

bohème [bɔɛm] *n*(*m+f*), *adj* bohemian.

*boire [bwar] *v* drink; absorb.

bois [bwa] *nm* wood; (*cerf*) antler; (*musique*) wood-wind instrument. **bois de chauffage** firewood. **de** *or* **en bois** wooden. **boisé** *adj* wooded, woody. **boiserie** *nf* panelling.

boisson [bwasɔ̃] *nf* drink. **boisson alcoolisée** alcoholic drink.

boîte [bwat] *nf* box; (*métal*) tin, can. **boîte à lettres** pillar-box. **boîte à ordures** dustbin. **boîte de nuit** night-club. **boîte de vitesses** gearbox.

boiter [bwate] *v* limp. **boiteux** *adj* lame; (*meuble*) wobbly; (*projet*) shaky.

bol [bɔl] *nm* bowl.

bombarder [bɔ̃barde] *v* bombard; bomb. **bombardier** *nm* (*avion*) bomber.

bombe [bɔ̃b] *nf* bomb; aerosol, spray. **bombe atomique** atom bomb.

bomber [bɔ̃be] *v* bulge, stick out; (*route*) camber. **bombé** *adj* rounded, bulging. **bombement** *nm* bulge; camber.

bon [bɔ̃], **bonne** *adj* good; (*agréable*) nice; (*gentil*) kind; (*valable*) valid; (*correct*) right. **à quoi bon?** what's the use? **bon à** *or* **pour** fit for. **de bonne heure** early. **pour de bon** for good. *nm* good person; good part. *interj* right!

bon² [bɔ̃] *nm* form; coupon, voucher; (*titre*) bond.

bon anniversaire *interj* happy birthday!

bonasse [bɔnas] *adj* meek.

bonbon [bɔ̃bɔ̃] *nm* sweet. **bonbon à la menthe** mint.

bond [bɔ̃] *nm* leap, bound; (*balle*) bounce.

bonde [bɔ̃d] *nf* plug, stopper.

bondé [bɔ̃de] *adj* packed, crammed.

bondir [bɔ̃dir] *v* leap (up), jump (up); (*balle*) bounce; (*sursauter*) start.

bon enfant *adj invar* good-natured.

bonheur [bɔnœr] *nm* happiness; joy; (*chance*) luck. **au petit bonheur** haphazardly. **par bonheur** fortunately.

bonhomie [bɔnɔmi] *nf* good nature.

bonhomme [bɔnɔm] *nm* (*fam*) chap, bloke. **bonhomme de neige** (*fam*) snowman. *adj invar* good-natured.

boni [bɔni] *nm* profit.

bonjour [bɔ̃ʒur] *nm, interj* hello; (*matin*) good morning; (*après-midi*) good afternoon.

bon marché *adj invar* cheap.

Bonn [bɔn] *n* Bonn.

bonne [bɔn] *V* **bon¹**. *nf* maid.

bonne année *interj* happy New Year!

bonne-maman *nf* (*fam*) granny, grandma.

bonnet [bɔnɛ] *nm* hat, bonnet; (*soutien-gorge*) cup. **bonnet d'âne** dunce's cap. **bonnet de bain** bathing cap. **bonneterie** *nf* hosiery.

bon-papa *nm* (*fam*) grand-dad, grandpa.

bon sens *nm* common sense.

bonsoir [bɔ̃swar] *nm, interj* good evening; (*en se couchant*) goodnight.

bonté [bɔ̃te] *nf* kindness, goodness.

bord [bɔr] *nm* edge, side; (*verre*) rim. **à bord** on board, aboard. **à ras bord** to the brim. **au bord de** (*lac, etc.*) by, alongside; (*larmes, ruine*) on the verge *or* brink of. **au bord de la mer** at the seaside. **bord du trottoir** kerb. **bordure** *nf* edge, border.

bordeaux [bɔrdo] *nm* Bordeaux. **bordeaux rouge** claret. *adj invar* maroon.

bordel [bɔrdɛl] *nm* brothel.

border [bɔrde] *v* edge; (*rue*) line; (*lit*) tuck in.

bordereau [bɔrdəro] *nm* note, slip; (*relevé*) statement.

borgne [bɔrɲə] *adj* one-eyed; (*louche*) shady.

borner [bɔrne] *v* limit; (*terrain*) mark out. **se borner à** content oneself with, confine oneself to. **borne** *nf* limit; (*kilométrique*) milestone. **sans bornes** limitless. **borné** *adj* narrow-minded; limited.

bosquet [bɔskɛ] *nm* copse.

bosse [bɔs] *nf* bump, lump; (*bossu*) hump. **avoir la bosse de** (*fam*) be good at, have a flair for.

bosseler [bɔsle] *v* emboss; (*déformer*) dent. **bosselé** *adj* dented, battered; (*sol*) bumpy. **bosselure** *nf* dent.

bossu [bɔsy], **-e** *adj* hunchbacked. *nm, nf* hunchback.

bot [bo] *adj* **pied bot** club foot.

botanique [bɔtanik] *adj* botanical. *nf* botany. **botaniste** *n*(*m+f*) botanist.

botte¹ [bɔt] *nf* boot. **botte de caoutchouc** wellington, gumboot. **bottillon** *nm* bootee.

botte² [bɔt] *nf* bunch, bundle.

botte³ [bɔt] *nf* (*escrime*) thrust.

botter [bɔte] *v* put boots on; (*fam, sport*) kick.

Bottin ® [bɔtɛ̃] *nm* directory.
bouc [buk] *nm* goat. **bouc émissaire** scapegoat.
boucaner [bukane] *v* (*viande*) cure; (*peau*) tan.
bouche [buʃ] *nf* mouth. **bouche à bouche** *nm invar* kiss of life. **bouchée** *nf* mouthful.
boucher[1] [buʃe] *v* block; (*bouteille*) cork; (*trou*) plug, fill up. **boucher le passage** be in the way. **bouché** *adj* (*temps*) cloudy; (*argot*) stupid, thick.
boucher[2] [buʃe] *nm* butcher. **boucherie** *nf* butcher's.
bouchon [buʃɔ̃] *nm* stopper, top; (*liège*) cork; (*évier*) plug; (*auto*) traffic jam.
boucler [bukle] *v* (*fermer*) buckle, fasten up; complete; (*cheveux*) curl. **boucler la boucle** (*aéro*) loop the loop; come full circle; complete. **boucle** *nf* buckle; curl; (*ruban, etc.*) loop. **boucle d'oreille** earring. **bouclé** *adj* curly.
bouclier [buklije] *nm* shield.
bouddhisme [budismə] *nm* Buddhism. **bouddhiste** *n*(*m*+*f*), *adj* Buddhist.
bouder [bude] *v* sulk. **boudeur, -euse** *adj* sulky.
boudin [budɛ̃] *nm* black pudding.
boue [bu] *nf* mud.
bouée [bwe] *nf* buoy. **bouée de sauvetage** lifebuoy.
boueux [bwø] *adj* muddy. *nm* dustman.
bouffer [bufe] *v* puff out; (*fam*) eat. **bouffant** *adj* (*manche*) full; (*pantalon, etc.*) baggy. **bouffe** *nf* (*argot*) grub. **bouffée** *nf* puff; (*vent*) gust; (*parfum*) whiff.
bouffir [bufir] *v* puff up. **bouffi** *adj* bloated, swollen; (*yeux*) puffy. **bouffissure** *nf* puffiness.
bouffon, -onne [bufɔ̃, -ɔn] *adj* comical. *nm* buffoon, clown. **bouffonnerie** *nf* clowning.
bouger [buʒe] *v* move, stir.
bougie [buʒi] *nf* candle; (*auto*) spark plug. **bougeoir** *nm* candlestick.
***bouillir** [bujir] *v* boil. **bouilloire** *nf* kettle.
bouillon [bujɔ̃] *nm* broth, stock; (*bulle*) bubble. **bouillon cube** stock cube.
bouillonner [bujɔne] *v* bubble, foam, seethe.
bouillotte [bujɔt] *nf* hot-water bottle.
boulanger [bulɑ̃ʒe] *nm* baker. **boulangerie** *nf* baker's, bakery.
boule [bul] *nf* ball. **boule de neige** snowball. **boules** *nf pl* (*jeu*) bowls *sing*.

bouleau [bulo] *nm* birch.
bouledogue [buldɔg] *nm* bulldog.
boulet [bulɛ] *nm* cannon-ball.
boulette [bulɛt] *nf* pellet.
boulevard [bulvar] *nm* boulevard.
bouleverser [bulvɛrse] *v* (*renverser*) turn upside down; disrupt, change completely; (*personne*) overwhelm, distress deeply. **bouleversement** *nm* upheaval.
boulon [bulɔ̃] *nm* bolt. **boulonner** *v* bolt.
boulot[1], **-otte** [bulo, -ɔt] *adj* plump.
boulot[2] [bulo] *nm* (*fam*) work.
boulotter [bulɔte] *v* (*fam*) eat.
bouquet[1] [bukɛ] *nm* bouquet, bunch; (*arbres*) clump. **c'est le bouquet!** that's the last straw!
bouquet[2] [bukɛ] *nm* (*crevette*) prawn.
bouquin [bukɛ̃] *nm* (*fam*) book. **bouquiniste** *nm* second-hand bookseller.
bourbe [burb] *nf* mire, mud. **bourbeux** *adj* miry, muddy.
bourdon [burdɔ̃] *nm* bumble-bee; (*musique*) drone.
bourdonner [burdɔne] *v* hum, buzz. **bourdonnement** *nm* buzz, hum.
bourg [bur] *nm* market town.
bourgeois [burʒwa], **-e** *adj* middle-class; (*péj*) bourgeois, conventional. *nm, nf* middle-class person. **bourgeoisie** *nf* middle class.
bourgeon [burʒɔ̃] *nm* bud. **bourgeonner** *v* bud.
bourgogne [burgɔɲ] *nm* burgundy.
bourrade [burad] *nf* thump, prod.
bourrage [buraʒ] *nm* stuffing, filling.
bourrasque [burask] *nf* gust of wind.
bourre [bur] *nf* stuffing, wadding.
bourreau [buro] *nm* torturer; executioner.
bourrelet [burlɛ] *nm* (*porte, etc.*) draught excluder; (*chair*) roll.
bourrer [bure] *v* stuff, cram.
bourriche [buriʃ] *nf* hamper.
bourru [bury] *adj* surly, gruff.
bourse [burs] *nf* purse; (*d'étudiant*) grant. **la Bourse** the Stock Exchange.
boursoufler [bursufle] *v* puff up. **se boursoufler** (*peinture*) blister. **boursouflé** *adj* puffy, swollen; blistered; (*style*) turgid. **boursouflure** *nf* puffiness; blister; turgidity.
bousculer [buskyle] *v* jostle; (*heurter*) bump into; (*renverser*) knock over. **bousculade** *nf* hustle, crush; (*hâte*) rush.

bousiller [buzije] (*fam*) *v* (*travail*) botch; (*abîmer*) wreck.

boussole [busɔl] *nf* compass.

bout [bu] *nm* end, tip; (*morceau*) piece, bit. **à bout** at the end of one's tether. **à bout de souffle** out of breath. **à bout portant** point-blank. **au bout de** at the end of; (*après*) after. **au bout du compte** all things considered. **de bout en bout** from start to finish. **jusqu'au bout** to the (bitter) end.

bouteille [butɛj] *nf* bottle. **en bouteille** bottled.

boutique [butik] *nf* shop. **boutiquier, -ère** *nm, nf* shopkeeper.

bouton [butɔ̃] *nm* button; (*élec*) switch; (*porte*) handle; (*fleur*) bud; (*méd*) pimple. **bouton de col** collar stud. **bouton de manchette** cuff-link. **bouton d'or** buttercup. **bouton-pression** *nm* press stud. **boutonner** *v* button. **boutonneux** *adj* pimply. **boutonnière** *nf* buttonhole.

bouture [butyr] *nf* cutting. **faire des boutures** take cuttings.

bouvier [buvje] *nm* herdsman.

bovin [bɔvɛ̃] *adj* bovine. **bovins** *nm pl* cattle *pl*.

boxer [bɔkse] *v* box. **boxe** *nf* boxing. **boxeur** *nm* boxer.

boyau [bwajo] *nm* gut; passageway. **boyaux** *nm pl* entrails *pl*.

boycotter [bɔjkɔte] *v* boycott. **boycottage** *nm* boycott.

bracelet [braslɛ] *nm* bracelet; (*montre*) strap. **bracelet-montre** *nm* wristwatch.

braconner [brakɔne] *v* poach. **braconnage** *nm* poaching. **braconnier** *nm* poacher.

braguette [bragɛt] *nf* (*pantalon*) fly.

braille [braj] *nm* braille.

brailler [braje] *v* bawl, yell.

***braire** [brɛr] *v* bray.

braise [brɛz] *nf* embers *pl*.

braiser [breze] *v* braise.

brancard [brɑ̃kar] *nm* stretcher; (*bras*) shaft.

branche [brɑ̃ʃ] *nf* branch.

brancher [brɑ̃ʃe] *v* plug in, connect up.

brandir [brɑ̃dir] *v* brandish.

branle-bas [brɑ̃lba] *nm invar* bustle, commotion.

branler [brɑ̃le] *v* be shaky *or* unsteady; (*dent*) be loose. **branle** *nm* swing. **mettre en branle** set in motion, get moving.

braquer [brake] *v* aim, point; (*auto*) turn (the wheel).

bras [bra] *nm* arm; (*tech*) handle; (*travailleur*) worker. **bras dessus, bras dessous** arm in arm. **en bras de chemise** in shirt sleeves.

brasero [brazero] *nm* brazier.

brasier [brazje] *nm* inferno.

brasse [bras] *nf* breast-stroke. **brasse papillon** butterfly.

brassée [brase] *nf* armful.

brasser [brase] *v* stir, mix; (*bière*) brew. **brasserie** *nf* brewery; (*café*) brasserie.

brave [brav] *adj* good, nice; brave, courageous.

braver [brave] *v* brave, defy, stand up to.

bravoure [bravur] *nf* bravery.

break [brɛk] *nm* estate car.

brebis [brəbi] *nf* ewe, sheep. **brebis galeuse** black sheep.

brèche [brɛʃ] *nf* breach, gap.

bredouiller [brəduje] *v* stammer, mumble. **bredouille** *adj* empty-handed.

bref, brève [brɛf, brɛv] *adj* brief, short. **(en) bref** in short.

breloque [brələk] *nf* charm.

Bretagne [brətaɲ] *nf* Brittany.

bretelle [brətɛl] *nf* strap. **bretelles** *nf pl* braces *pl*.

breuvage [brœvaʒ] *nm* drink, beverage.

brevet [brəvɛ] *nm* certificate, diploma; (*d'invention*) patent. **breveter** *v* patent.

bribe [brib] *nf* scrap, snatch, bit.

bricoler [brikɔle] *v* potter about, do odd jobs; (*réparer*) mend. **bricolage** *nm* do-it-yourself; makeshift repair. **bricoleur** *nm* handyman.

brider [bride] *v* bridle, restrain. **bride** *nf* bridle, rein; (*bonnet*) string, strap. **à bride abattue** (*fam*) flat out. **tenir en bride** keep a tight rein on.

bridge [bridʒ] *nm* bridge.

brièvement [brijɛvmɑ̃] *adv* briefly. **brièveté** *nf* brevity.

brigade [brigad] *nf* brigade; (*police*) squad; (*équipe*) team.

brigand [brigɑ̃] *nm* (*péj*) crook; (*enfant*) rascal. **brigandage** *nm* (armed) robbery.

brigue [brig] *nf* intrigue. **briguer** *v* covet, crave; solicit.

brillant [brijɑ̃] *adj* brilliant; (*luisant*) shiny, bright; outstanding, excellent. *nm* brilliance; shine, brightness.

briller [brije] *v* shine, sparkle.

brin [brɛ̃] *nm* sprig; (*herbe*) blade; (*fil*) strand. **un brin de** a bit of.

brindille [brɛ̃dij] *nf* twig.

brioche [brijɔʃ] *nf* bun.

brique [brik] *nf* brick.

briquet [brikɛ] *nm* cigarette lighter.

brise [briz] *nf* breeze.

briser [brize] *v* break, smash; (*espérance, rebelle*) crush. **brise-lames** *nm invar* breakwater.

britannique [britanik] *adj* British. **les Britanniques** the British.

broc [bro] *nm* pitcher.

brocanter [brɔkɑ̃te] *v* deal in second-hand goods. **brocante** *nf* second-hand goods *pl*; (*commerce*) second-hand trade. **brocanteur, -euse** *nm, nf* second-hand dealer.

broche [brɔʃ] *nf* (*bijou*) brooch; (*cuisine*) spit; (*tech*) pin.

broché [brɔʃe] *adj* **livre broché** paperback book.

brochet [brɔʃɛ] *nm* pike.

brochette [brɔʃɛt] *nf* (*broche*) skewer; (*plat*) kebab.

brochure [brɔʃyr] *nf* brochure, booklet.

brocoli [brɔkɔli] *nm* broccoli.

broder [brɔde] *v* embroider. **broder sur** elaborate on. **broderie** *nf* embroidery.

broncher [brɔ̃ʃe] *v* (*cheval*) stumble. **sans broncher** (*sans peur*) without flinching; (*sans faute*) without faltering.

bronchite [brɔ̃ʃit] *nf* bronchitis.

bronzer [brɔ̃ze] *v* tan; (*métal*) bronze. **bronzage** *nm* suntan. **bronze** *nm* bronze.

brosser [brɔse] *v* brush. **brosse** *nf* brush; (*cheveux*) crew-cut. **brosse à cheveux/dents/ongles** hair/tooth/nailbrush.

brouette [bruɛt] *nf* wheelbarrow.

brouhaha [bruaa] *nm* hubbub.

brouillard [brujar] *nm* fog. **il fait du brouillard** it's foggy.

brouiller [bruje] *v* (*troubler*) blur; (*mêler*) mix *or* muddle up. **se brouiller** become confused; (*se fâcher*) fall out. **brouille** *nf* quarrel.

brouillon, -onne [brujɔ̃, -ɔn] *adj* untidy; unsystematic. *nm* rough copy.

broussailles [brusɑj] *nf pl* undergrowth *sing*, scrub *sing*. **broussailleux** *adj* bushy.

brouter [brute] *v* graze.

broyer [brwaje] *v* grind, crush.

bru [bry] *nf* daughter-in-law.

bruiner [brɥine] *v* drizzle. **bruine** *nf* drizzle.

bruire [brɥir] *v* rustle; (*eau*) murmur. **bruissement** *nm* rustle; murmur.

bruit [brɥi] *nm* noise; rumour; (*histoires*) fuss. **bruitage** *nm* sound effects *pl*.

brûler [bryle] *v* burn. **brûlant** *adj* burning, scorching; (*objet*) red hot; (*liquid*) boiling hot. **brûlure** *nf* burn.

brume [brym] *nf* mist. **brumeux** *adj* misty.

brun [brœ̃] *adj* brown, dark. *nm* brown. **brune** *nf* brown ale; (*femme*) brunette.

brunir [brynir] *v* darken; (*peau*) tan, get sunburnt.

brusque [brysk] *adj* brusque, abrupt. **brusquerie** *nf* brusqueness, abruptness.

brut [bryt] *adj* crude, raw, rough; (*comm*) gross. **brute** *nf* brute.

brutal [brytal] *adj* rough, brutal; (*franc*) blunt, plain. **brutalité** *nf* brutality.

brutaliser [brytalize] *v* bully, ill-treat.

Bruxelles [brysɛl] *n* Brussels.

bruyant [brɥijɑ̃] *adj* noisy.

bruyère [bryjɛr] *nf* heather.

Bucarest [bykarɛst] *n* Bucharest.

buccin [byksɛ̃] *nm* whelk.

bûche [byʃ] *nf* log; (*fam*) blockhead.

bûcher[1] [byʃe] *nm* (*remise*) woodshed; (*supplice*) stake.

bûcher[2] [byʃe] *v* (*fam*) swot.

bucheron [byʃrɔ̃] *nm* woodcutter, lumberjack.

Budapest [bydapɛst] *n* Budapest.

budget [bydʒɛ] *nm* budget.

buée [bɥe] *nf* steam, condensation. **couvert de buée** misted up.

buffet [byfɛ] *nm* buffet; (*meuble*) sideboard. **buffet de cuisine** dresser.

buffle [byflə] *nm* buffalo.

buisson [bɥisɔ̃] *nm* bush.

bulbe [bylbə] *nm* bulb. **bulbeux** *adj* bulbous.

Bulgarie [bylgari] *nf* Bulgaria. **bulgare** *nm, adj* Bulgarian. **Bulgare** *nm, nf* Bulgarian.

bulle [byl] *nf* bubble; (*méd*) blister.

bulletin [byltɛ̃] *nm* bulletin; ticket; certificate; (*école*) report. **bulletin de vote** ballot paper. **bulletin météorologique** weather report.

bungalow [bœ̃galo] *nm* bungalow; (*motel*) chalet.

bureau [byro] *nm* (*meuble*) desk; (*cabinet*) study; (*lieu*) office; (*section*) department. **bureau de location** booking office. **bureau**

de poste post office. **bureau de vote** polling station.

bureaucratie [byrokrasi] *nf* bureaucracy. **bureaucrate** *n(m+f)* bureaucrat. **bureaucratique** *adj* bureaucratic.

buriner [byrine] *v* engrave.

burlesque [byrlɛsk] *adj* comical, ludicrous.

buste [byst] *nm* bust, chest.

but [by] *nm* goal, aim. **de but en blanc** point-blank, suddenly.

buter [byte] *v* stumble; (*sport*) score a goal; (*mur*) prop up. **se buter à** bump into. **buté** *adj* stubborn.

butin [bytɛ̃] *nm* booty, spoils.

butoir [bytwar] *nm* buffer.

butte [byt] *nf* mound. **être en butte à** be exposed to.

buvard [byvar] *nm* blotting paper.

buvette [byvɛt] *nf* refreshment bar.

buveur [byvœr], **-euse** *nm*, *nf* drinker.

byzantin [bizɑ̃tɛ̃] *adj* Byzantine.

C

c' [s] *V* ce².

ça [sa] *informal contraction of* **cela**.

çà [sa] *adv* **çà et là** here and there.

cabale [kabal] *nf* cabal.

cabane [kaban] *nf* hut, shed, cabin. **cabane à outils** toolshed. **cabane en rondins** log cabin.

cabaret [kabarɛ] *nm* night-club, cabaret.

cabillaud [kabijo] *nm* fresh cod.

cabine [kabin] *nf* cabin; (*réduit*) cubicle, booth. **cabine de bain** beach hut. **cabine téléphonique** telephone box.

cabinet [kabinɛ] *nm* (*bureau*) office; (*médecin, dentiste*) surgery; (*meuble, pol*) cabinet. **cabinet de débarras** box-room. **cabinet de toilette** toilet. **cabinet de travail** study.

câble [kablə] *nm* cable. **câbler** *v* cable.

cabosser [kabɔse] *v* dent.

se cabrer [kabre] *v* rear up; rebel.

cabriole [kabrijɔl] *nf* caper; (*danse*) cabriole; (*culbute*) somersault. **cabrioler** *v* caper about.

cacahouette [kakawɛt] *nf* peanut.

cacao [kakao] *nm* cocoa.

cachemire [kaʃmir] *nm* cashmere.

cacher [kaʃe] *v* hide, conceal. **cache-cache** *nm invar* hide-and-seek. **cache-col** *or* **cache-nez** *nm invar* scarf. **se cacher de** hide from.

cachet [kaʃɛ] *nm* seal, stamp; (*comprimé*) tablet; style. **cachet de la poste** postmark. **cacheter** *v* seal.

cachette [kaʃɛt] *nf* hiding-place. **en cachette** on the quiet, secretly.

cachot [kaʃo] *nm* dungeon.

cactus [kaktys] *nm invar* cactus (*pl* -ti).

cadavre [kadavrə] *nm* corpse; (*animal*) carcass. **cadavéreux** *or* **cadavérique** *adj* deathly.

cadeau [kado] *nm* present, gift.

cadenas [kadna] *nm* padlock. **cadenasser** *v* padlock.

cadence [kadɑ̃s] *nf* rhythm; (*musique*) cadence; (*vitesse*) rate. **cadencé** *adj* rhythmic.

cadet, -ette [kade, -ɛt] *adj* younger, youngest. *nm*, *nf* (*famille*) youngest child; junior.

cadran [kadrɑ̃] *nm* dial, face. **cadran solaire** sundial.

cadre [kadrə] *nm* frame; (*milieu*) setting; (*formulaire*) space; scope, limits *pl*; context; (*responsable*) executive. **les cadres** management *sing*.

cadrer [kadre] *v* tally, conform; (*phot*) centre.

caduc, -uque [kadyk] *adj* (*feuilles*) deciduous; (*jur*) null and void; (*périmé*) outmoded.

cafard [kafar] *nm* (*insecte*) cockroach; (*tristesse*) depression; (*mouchard*) sneak. **avoir le cafard** be down in the dumps. **cafarder** *v* sneak, tell tales.

café [kafe] *nm* coffee; (*lieu*) café. **café au lait** white coffee. **café noir** *or* **nature** black coffee. **café soluble** instant coffee.

caféine [kafein] *nf* caffeine.

cafetière [kaftjɛr] *nf* coffee-pot.

cage [kaʒ] *nf* cage; (*tech*) casing. **cage à poules** hen-coop.

cagneux [kaɲø] *adj* knock-kneed.

cagnotte [kaɲɔt] *nf* kitty.

cagoule [kagul] *nf* hood.

cahier [kaje] *nm* notebook, exercise book.

cahin-caha [kaɛ̃kaa] *adv* (*fam*) so-so.

cahot [kao] *nm* jolt, bump. **cahotant** *or* **cahoteux** *adj* bumpy. **cahoter** *v* jolt.

caille [kaj] *nf* quail.

cailler [kɑje] v (*lait*) curdle; (*sang*) clot. **caillé** nm curds pl. **caillot** nm clot.
caillou [kɑju] nm, pl -**oux** stone, pebble. **caillouteux** adj stony, pebbly.
caisse [kɛs] nf box, case; (*argent*) cashbox, till; (*guichet*) cash-desk; (*tambour*) drum. **caisse d'épargne** savings bank. **caissier, -ère** nm, nf cashier.
cajoler [kaʒɔle] v coax, cajole; (*câliner*) make a fuss of.
cake [kɛk] nm fruit cake.
calamité [kalamite] nf calamity, disaster.
calcaire [kalkɛr] adj chalky; (*eau*) hard. nm limestone.
calcium [kalsjɔm] nm calcium.
calculer [kalkyle] v calculate, work out. **calcul** nm calculation, sum; arithmetic.
cale¹ [kal] nf (*naut*) hold; (*plan incliné*) slipway. **cale sèche** dry dock.
cale² [kal] nf wedge.
caleçon [kalsɔ̃] nm underpants pl. **caleçon de bain** bathing trunks pl.
calembour [kalɑ̃bur] nm pun.
calendrier [kalɑ̃drije] nm calendar; (*programme*) timetable, schedule.
calepin [kalpɛ̃] nm notebook.
caler [kale] v wedge; prop up, support; (*moteur*) stall; (*fam*) give up.
calfeutrer [kalføtre] v stop up; (*pièce*) draughtproof.
calibre [kalibrə] nm calibre; (*qualité*) grade; (*grosseur*) size; (*instrument*) gauge. **calibrer** v gauge; grade.
califourchon [kalifurʃɔ̃] nm **à califourchon** astride.
câlin [kɑlɛ̃] adj cuddly; tender. nm cuddle. **câliner** v fondle, cuddle. **câlinerie** nf tenderness; caress.
calleux [kalø] adj callous.
calmant [kalmɑ̃] adj soothing. nm tranquillizer; (*analgésique*) pain-killer.
calmar [kalmar] nm squid.
calme [kalmə] adj quiet, calm, peaceful. nm stillness, peace, calmness.
calmer [kalme] v calm, soothe. **se calmer** calm down; (*diminuer*) ease, subside.
calomnier [kalɔmnje] v slander; (*par écrit*) libel. **calomnie** nf slander; libel. **calomnieux** adj slanderous; libellous.
calorie [kalɔri] nf calorie.
calorifuger [kalɔrifyʒe] v lag, insulate. **calorifugeage** nm lagging, insulation.
calquer [kalke] v trace; copy exactly. **calque** nm tracing; exact copy. **papier-calque** nm tracing paper.

calvitie [kalvisi] nf baldness.
camarade [kamarad] n(m + f) companion, friend. **camarade de jeu** playmate.
cambrer [kɑ̃bre] v arch, bend. **se cambrer** arch one's back. **cambrure** nf curve, arch.
cambrioler [kɑ̃brijɔle] v break into, burgle. **cambriolage** nm burglary. **cambrioleur** nm burglar.
camée [kame] nm cameo.
caméléon [kameleɔ̃] nm chameleon.
camelote [kamlɔt] nf (*fam*) junk.
caméra [kamera] nf cine-camera.
Cameroun [kamrun] nm Cameroon.
camion [kamjɔ̃] nm truck. **camion-citerne** nm tanker. **camionnette** nf van. **camionneur** nm truck driver.
camoufler [kamufle] v camouflage; (*cacher*) conceal; disguise. **camouflage** nm camouflage.
camp [kɑ̃] nm camp; (*parti*) side. **camp de concentration** concentration camp.
campagne [kɑ̃paɲ] nf country, countryside; (*pol, mil, etc.*) campaign. **campagnard, -e** n, adj rustic.
camper [kɑ̃pe] v camp. **se camper** plant oneself. **campeur, -euse** nm, nf camper.
camping nm camping; (*lieu*) campsite.
campus [kɑ̃pys] nm campus.
Canada [kanada] nm Canada. **canadien** adj Canadian. **Canadien, -enne** nm, nf Canadian.
canaille [kanɑj] adj coarse. nf scoundrel, rogue.
canal [kanal] nm channel; (*artificiel, anat*) canal. **canaliser** v channel.
canapé [kanape] nm sofa, settee; (*cuisine*) canapé.
canard [kanar] nm duck; false report; (*musique*) false note. **canardeau** nm duckling. **canardière** nf duck-pond.
canari [kanari] nm canary.
cancan [kɑ̃kɑ̃] nm gossip. **cancaner** v gossip. **cancanier, -ère** nm, nf gossip, scandalmonger.
cancer [kɑ̃ser] nm cancer. **Cancer** nm Cancer. **cancérigène** adj carcinogenic.
cancre [kɑ̃krə] nm (*fam*) dunce.
candeur [kɑ̃dœr] nf naivety.
candidat [kɑ̃dida], -**e** nm, nf candidate, applicant.
candide [kɑ̃did] adj naive, ingenuous.
cane [kan] nf (female) duck. **caneton** nm duckling.

canevas [kanva] *nm* (*toile*) canvas; (*ébauche*) framework.

caniche [kaniʃ] *nm* poodle.

canif [kanif] *nm* penknife.

canin [kanɛ̃] *adj* canine.

caniveau [kanivo] *nm* gutter.

canne [kan] *nf* cane; walking stick. **canne à pêche** fishing rod. **canne à sucre** sugar cane.

canneler [kanle] *v* flute. **cannelure** *nf* groove.

cannelle [kanɛl] *nf* cinnamon.

canoë [kanɔe] *nm* canoe. **faire du canoë** go canoeing.

canon[1] [kanɔ̃] *nm* gun, cannon; (*tube*) barrel.

canon[2] [kanɔ̃] *nm* canon; model.

cañon [kaɲɔ̃] *nm* canyon.

canoniser [kanɔnize] *v* canonize.

canot [kano] *nm* boat, dinghy. **canot automobile** motor boat. **canot de sauvetage** lifeboat. **canot pneumatique** rubber dinghy. **canotage** *nm* boating, rowing. **faire du canotage** go boating *or* rowing. **canotier** *nm* boater.

cantatrice [kɑ̃tatris] *nf* singer.

cantine [kɑ̃tin] *nf* canteen.

canton [kɑ̃tɔ̃] *nm* canton, district; section.

cantonnier [kɑ̃tɔnje] *nm* road-mender.

canular [kanylar] *nm* hoax. **faire un canular à** hoax, play a hoax on.

caoutchouc [kautʃu] *nm* rubber. **caoutchouc mousse** foam rubber. **caoutchouteux** *adj* rubbery.

cap [kap] *nm* cape; headland.

capable [kapablə] *adj* capable, able.

capacité [kapasite] *nf* capacity; ability.

cape [kap] *nf* cape, cloak.

capitaine [kapitɛn] *nm* captain.

capital [kapital] *adj* major, chief; fundamental. *nm* capital; fund. **capitale** *nf* capital (letter); capital (city). **capitaliser** *v* amass, accumulate. **capitalisme** *nm* capitalism. **capitaliste** *n(m+f)*, *adj* capitalist.

capiteux [kapitø] *adj* heady; (*femme*) alluring.

capitonner [kapitɔne] *v* pad. **capitonnage** *nm* padding. **capitonné de** lined with.

caporal [kapɔral] *nm* corporal.

capot [kapo] *nm* (*auto*) bonnet *or* US hood.

capote [kapɔt] *nf* (*auto*) hood; (*manteau*) greatcoat.

câpre [kɑprə] *nf* caper.

caprice [kapris] *nm* whim, caprice. **capricieux** *adj* capricious, temperamental.

Capricorne [kaprikɔrn] *nm* Capricorn.

capsule [kapsyl] *nf* capsule; (*pistolet*) cap.

capter [kapte] *v* win, gain; (*émission*) pick up.

captieux [kapsjø] *adj* specious.

captif [kaptif], **-ive** *n*, *adj* captive. **captivité** *nf* captivity.

captiver [kaptive] *v* captivate, fascinate.

capuchon [kapyʃɔ̃] *nm* hood; (*stylo*) cap.

capucine [kapysin] *nf* nasturtium.

caquet [kakɛ] *nm* cackle. **caqueter** *v* cackle.

car[1] [kar] *nm* coach.

car[2] [kar] *conj* because, for.

carabine [karabin] *nf* rifle.

caractère [karaktɛr] *nm* character, nature. **caractériser** *v* characterize. **caractéristique** *nf*, *adj* characteristic.

carafe [karaf] *nf* carafe, decanter.

caramboler [karɑ̃bɔle] *v* collide with. **carambolage** *nm* pile-up.

caramel [karamɛl] *nm* caramel; (*dur*) toffee.

carapace [karapas] *nf* shell.

carat [kara] *nm* carat.

caravane [karavan] *nf* caravan.

carbone [karbɔn] *nm* carbon.

carboniser [karbɔnize] *v* (*forêt*) burn to the ground; (*cuisine*) burn to a cinder. **carbonisé** *adj* charred.

carburant [karbyrɑ̃] *nm* fuel.

carburateur [karbyratœr] *nm* carburettor.

carcasse [karkas] *nf* carcass; (*charpente*) frame.

cardiaque [kardjak] *adj* cardiac. **être cardiaque** have heart trouble, suffer from heart disease.

cardinal [kardinal] *nm*, *adj* cardinal.

carême [karɛm] *nm* fast. **Carême** *nm* Lent.

carence [karɑ̃s] *nf* deficiency.

carène [karɛn] *nf* hull.

caresser [karese] *v* caress, stroke; (*projet*) toy with. **caresse** *nf* caress.

cargaison [kargɛzɔ̃] *nf* cargo.

caricaturer [karikatyre] *v* caricature. **caricature** *nf* caricature.

carier [karje] *v* decay. **carie** *nf* tooth decay.

carillon [karijɔ̃] *nm* chime. **carillonner** *v* chime, ring. **carillonneur** *nm* bell-ringer.

carnage [karnaʒ] *nm* carnage.

carnassier [karnasje] *adj* carnivorous. *nm* carnivore.

carnaval [karnaval] *nm* carnival.

carnet [karnɛ] *nm* notebook. **carnet de chèques** chequebook. **carnet de billets/timbres** book of tickets/stamps.

carnivore [karnivɔr] *adj* carnivorous. *nm* carnivore.

carotte [karɔt] *nf* carrot.

carpette [karpɛt] *nf* rug.

carquois [karkwa] *nm* quiver.

carré [kare] *adj* square; (*franc*) straight, forthright. *nm* square. **carrément** *adv* bluntly, straight.

carreau [karo] *nm* (*mur, sol*) tile; (*vitre*) pane; (*tissu*) check; (*papier*) square; (*cartes*) diamond.

carrefour [karfur] *nm* crossroads.

carreler [karle] *v* tile; (*papier*) square. **carrelage** *nm* tiling.

carrelet [karlɛ] *nm* plaice.

carrer [kare] *v* square. **se carrer** ensconce oneself.

carrière¹ [karjɛr] *nf* (*pierre*) quarry.

carrière² [karjɛr] *nf* (*profession*) career.

carrosse [karɔs] *nm* coach. **carrosserie** *nf* (*auto*) body, bodywork.

carrure [karyr] *nf* build; stature.

cartable [kartablə] *nm* schoolbag, satchel.

carte [kart] *nf* card; (*géog*) map; menu. **carte à jouer** playing card. **carte de crédit** credit card. **carte des vins** wine list. **carte d'identité** identity card. **carte postale** postcard.

cartilage [kartilaʒ] *nm* cartilage; (*viande*) gristle. **cartilagineux** *adj* cartilaginous; gristly.

carton [kartɔ̃] *nm* cardboard; (*boîte*) box. **cartouche** [kartuʃ] *nf* cartridge; (*cigarettes*) carton.

carvi [karvi] *nm* caraway.

cas [ka] *nm* case; situation. **au cas où** in case. **cas limite** borderline case. **cas urgent** emergency. **en aucun cas** under no circumstances. **en tout cas** in any case. **faire cas de** attach importance to.

cascade [kaskad] *nf* waterfall; torrent. **cascadeur** *nm* stuntman.

case [kaz] *nf* (*papier, échiquier*) square; compartment; hut.

caser [kaze] *v* find a place for; fix up;

(*fam*) put. **se caser** settle down; find a job.

caserne [kazɛrn] *nf* barracks. **caserne de pompiers** fire station.

casier [kazje] *nm* compartment; (*courrier*) pigeon-hole; (*fermant à clef*) locker; (*bouteilles*) rack. **casier judiciaire** police record.

casino [kazino] *nm* casino.

casque [kask] *nm* helmet; (*à écouteurs*) headphones *pl*.

casquette [kaskɛt] *nf* cap.

casse [kas] *nf* breakage, damage. **mettre à la casse** scrap.

casser [kase] *v* break; (*jur*) annul, quash. **casse-cou** *nm invar* (*fam*) reckless person. **casse-croûte** *nm invar* snack. **casse-noisettes** *nm invar* nutcracker. **casse-pieds** *n(m+f) invar* (*fam*) nuisance. **cassable** *adj* breakable. **cassant** *adj* brittle; brusque, abrupt. **cassure** *nf* break.

casserole [kasrɔl] *nf* saucepan.

cassette [kasɛt] *nf* casket; (*magnétophone*) cassette.

cassis [kasis] *nm* blackcurrant.

cassonade [kasɔnad] *nf* brown sugar.

caste [kast] *nf* caste.

castor [kastɔr] *nm* beaver.

cataloguer [katalɔge] *v* catalogue, list. **catalogue** *nm* catalogue, list.

catalyseur [katalizœr] *nm* catalyst.

catamaran [katamarɑ̃] *nm* catamaran.

cataphote [katafɔt] *nm* reflector; (*route*) cat's-eye.

cataplasme [kataplasmə] *nm* poultice.

cataracte [katarakt] *nf* cataract.

catarrhe [katar] *nm* catarrh.

catastrophe [katastrɔf] *nf* disaster, catastrophe.

catch [katʃ] *nm* wrestling. **catcheur, -euse** *nm, nf* wrestler.

catéchisme [kateʃismə] *nm* catechism. **aller au catéchisme** go to Sunday school.

catégoriser [kategɔrize] *v* categorize. **catégorie** *nf* category. **catégorique** *adj* categorical.

cathédrale [katedral] *nf* cathedral.

cathode [katɔd] *nf* cathode.

catholique [katɔlik] *n(m+f), adj* Catholic. **catholicism** *nm* Catholicism.

cauchemar [koʃmar] *nm* nightmare. **cauchemardesque** *adj* nightmarish.

cause [koz] *nf* cause; (*jur*) case, brief. **à cause de** because of. **en cause** in question. **pour cause de** on account of.

causer[1] [koze] v (*occasionner*) cause.
causer[2] [koze] v (*bavarder*) chat, talk.
causant adj (*fam*) talkative. **causerie** nf chat, talk.
caustique [kostik] adj caustic.
cauteleux [kotlø] adj wily.
caution [kosjɔ̃] nf guarantee; (*jur*) bail; support. **sous caution** on bail.
cautionnement [kosjɔnmɑ̃] nm guarantee.
cavalerie [kavalri] nf cavalry.
cavalier [kavalje], **-ère** adj offhand. nm, nf (*cheval*) rider; (*bal*) partner. nm escort; (*échecs*) knight.
cave[1] [kav] nf cellar.
cave[2] [kav] adj hollow, sunken.
caveau [kavo] nm vault.
caverne [kavɛrn] nf cave. **caverneux** adj cavernous.
caviar [kavjar] nm caviar.
cavité [kavite] nf cavity.
ce[1] [sə], **cette** adj (*ci*) this; (*là*) that.
ce[2] [sə], **c'** pron it; (*homme*) he; (*femme*) she. **ce que** or **qui** what, which.
ceci [səsi] pron this.
cécité [sesite] nf blindness.
céder [sede] v give up or in; (*fléchir, succomber*) give way.
cédille [sedij] nf cedilla.
cèdre [sɛdrə] nm cedar.
*ceindre [sɛ̃drə] v encircle; (*mettre*) put on.
ceinture [sɛ̃tyr] nf belt; (*gaine*) girdle; (*écharpe*) sash; (*anat*) waist. **ceinture de sécurité** seat or safety belt.
cela [səla] pron that; it. **cela** or **ça ne fait rien** it doesn't matter.
célèbre [selɛbrə] adj famous. **célébrité** nf celebrity.
célébrer [selebre] v celebrate. **célébration** nf celebration.
celer [sle] v conceal.
céleri [sɛlri] nm celery.
céleste [selɛst] adj celestial, heavenly.
célibataire [selibatɛr] adj single. nm bachelor, single man. nf single girl or woman. **célibat** nm celibacy.
cellule [selyl] nf cell.
celte [sɛlt] adj also **celtique** Celtic. **Celte** n(m+f) Celt.
celui, celle [səlɥi, sɛl] pron the one. **celui-ci, celle-ci** this one; (*dernier*) the latter. **celui-là, celle-là** that one; (*premier*) the former.
cendre [sɑ̃drə] nf ash. **cendrier** nm ashtray.

cène [sɛn] nf (*rel*) Communion. **la Cène** the Last Supper.
censé [sɑ̃se] adj supposed.
censeur [sɑ̃sœr] nm censor; critic; (*lycée*) deputy head.
censurer [sɑ̃syre] v (*film, etc.*) censor; (*critiquer*) censure. **censure** nf censorship; censure.
cent [sɑ̃] nm, adj a hundred. **faire les cent pas** pace up and down. **pour cent** per cent. **une centaine (de)** about a hundred. **centième** n(m+f), adj hundredth.
centenaire [sɑ̃tnɛr] adj hundred-year-old. n(m+f) centenarian. nm centenary.
centigrade [sɑ̃tigrad] adj centigrade.
centime [sɑ̃tim] nm centime.
centimètre [sɑ̃timetrə] nm centimetre; (*ruban*) tape measure.
central [sɑ̃tral] adj central. nm telephone exchange. **centrale** nf power station.
centraliser [sɑ̃tralize] v centralize. **centralisation** nf centralization.
centre [sɑ̃trə] nm centre. **centre commercial** shopping centre. **centre-ville** nm town centre.
cep [sɛp] nm stock.
cependant [səpɑ̃dɑ̃] conj however, nevertheless.
céramique [seramik] nf, adj ceramic. **la céramique** ceramics.
cerceau [sɛrso] nm hoop.
cercle [sɛrklə] nm circle; club; (*étendue*) range. **cercle vicieux** vicious circle.
cercueil [sɛrkœj] nm coffin.
céréale [sereal] nf cereal.
cérébral [serebral] adj cerebral; mental.
cérémonie [seremɔni] nf ceremony. **faire des cérémonies** stand on ceremony; (*fam*) make a fuss. **sans cérémonie** informal, informally. **cérémonieux** adj ceremonious, formal.
cerf [sɛr] nm stag. **cerf-volant** nm kite.
cerise [səriz] nf cherry. **cerisier** nm cherry (tree).
cerner [sɛrne] v encircle, surround. **avoir les yeux cernés** have rings under one's eyes.
certain [sɛrtɛ̃] adj certain; definite. **certains** pron, adj some, certain. **certainement** adv certainly; most probably.
certes [sɛrt] adv indeed, most certainly; admittedly.
certifier [sɛrtifje] v certify; (*signature*) witness; assure. **certificat** nm certificate.

certitude [sɛrtityd] *nf* certainty.
cerveau [sɛrvo] *nm* brain; (*intelligence*) mind; (*personne*) mastermind.
cervelle [sɛrvɛl] *nf* brains *pl*.
Cervin [sɛrvɛ̃] *nm* Matterhorn.
ces [se] *adj* (*ci*) these; (*là*) those.
cesse [sɛs] *nf* **sans cesse** continually; incessantly.
cesser [sese] *v* stop, cease. **faire cesser** put a stop to.
cet [sɛt] *form of* **ce¹** *used before vowel or mute h.*
cette [sɛt] *V* **ce¹**.
ceux, celles [sø, sɛl] *pron* the ones, those. **ceux-ci, celles-ci** these; (*derniers*) the latter. **ceux-là, celles-là** those; (*premiers*) the former.
chacal [ʃakal] *nm, pl* **-als** jackal.
chacun [ʃakœ̃] *pron* each; (*tout le monde*) everyone.
chagrin [ʃagrɛ̃] *adj* despondent; morose. *nm* sorrow, grief.
chagriner [ʃagrine] *v* distress, worry.
chahut [ʃay] *nm* rumpus. **chahuteur, -euse** *n, adj* rowdy.
chaîne [ʃɛn] *nf* chain; (*montagnes*) range; (*usine*) production line; (*TV*) channel.
chair [ʃɛr] *nf* flesh. **chair à saucisse** sausage-meat. **chair de poule** goose-flesh.
chaire [ʃɛr] *nf* (*rel*) pulpit; (*université*) chair.
chaise [ʃɛz] *nf* chair.
chaland [ʃalɑ̃] *nm* barge.
châle [ʃal] *nm* shawl.
chalet [ʃalɛ] *nm* chalet.
chaleur [ʃalœr] *nf* heat, warmth; fervour. **chaleureux** *adj* warm.
chaloupe [ʃalup] *nf* launch. **chaloupe de sauvetage** lifeboat.
chalumeau [ʃalymo] *nm* (*tech*) blowlamp; (*musique*) pipe.
chalut [ʃaly] *nm* trawl. **pêcher au chalut** trawl. **chalutier** *nm* trawler.
se chamailler [ʃamaje] *v* (*fam*) squabble. **chamailleur, -euse** *adj* quarrelsome.
chambellan [ʃɑ̃belɑ̃] *nm* chamberlain.
chambranle [ʃɑ̃brɑ̃l] *nm* frame; (*cheminée*) mantelpiece.
chambre [ʃɑ̃brə] *nf* room; (*à coucher*) bedroom; (*tech, admin*) chamber; (*pol*) house. **chambre d'ami** spare room. **chambre d'enfants** nursery. **chambre noire** dark-room. **chambrer** *v* (*vin*) bring to room temperature; (*personne*) corner.
chameau [ʃamo] *nm* camel.

chamois [ʃamwa] *nm* chamois. *adj invar* buff.
champ [ʃɑ̃] *nm* field. **champ d'aviation** airfield. **champ de courses** racecourse. **champ de foire** fairground.
champagne [ʃɑ̃paɲ] *nm* champagne.
champêtre [ʃɑ̃pɛtrə] *adj* rural.
champignon [ʃɑ̃piɲɔ̃] *nm* mushroom; (*vénéneux*) toadstool; (*terme générique*) fungus; (*fam*) accelerator.
champion, -onne [ʃɑ̃pjɔ̃, -ɔn] *nm, nf* champion. *adj* (*fam*) first-rate. **championnat** *nm* championship.
chance [ʃɑ̃s] *nf* luck; (*possibilité*) chance. **avoir de la chance** be lucky. **pas de chance!** hard luck! **chanceux** *adj* lucky.
chanceler [ʃɑ̃sle] *v* totter, falter. **chancelant** *adj* unsteady, shaky.
chancelier [ʃɑ̃səlje] *nm* chancellor.
chandail [ʃɑ̃daj] *nm* sweater.
chandelle [ʃɑ̃dɛl] *nf* candle. **chandelier** *nm* candlestick.
changer [ʃɑ̃ʒe] *v* change; exchange; (*modifier*) alter. **change** *nm* exchange; (*taux*) exchange rate. **changeant** *adj* changeable. **changement** *nm* change; alteration.
chanoine [ʃanwan] *nm* canon.
chanson [ʃɑ̃sɔ̃] *nf* song.
chant [ʃɑ̃] *nm* singing; (*chanson*) song. **chant de Noël** Christmas carol.
chanter [ʃɑ̃te] *v* sing. **faire chanter** blackmail. **chantage** *nm* blackmail. **chanteur, -euse** *nm, nf* singer.
chantier [ʃɑ̃tje] *nm* yard, site; (*route*) roadworks *pl*. **chantier naval** shipyard.
chantonner [ʃɑ̃tone] *v* hum, croon.
chanvre [ʃɑ̃vrə] *nm* hemp.
chaos [kao] *nm* chaos.
chape [ʃap] *nf* (*pneu*) tread; (*rel*) cope.
chapeau [ʃapo] *nm* hat. **chapeau melon** bowler hat.
chapelain [ʃaplɛ̃] *nm* chaplain.
chapelet [ʃaplɛ] *nm* rosary.
chapelle [ʃapɛl] *nf* chapel.
chapelure [ʃaplyr] *nf* breadcrumbs *pl*.
chaperon [ʃaprɔ̃] *nm* chaperon. **chaperonner** *v* chaperon.
chapitre [ʃapitrə] *nm* chapter; subject.
chaque [ʃak] *adj* every, each.
char [ʃar] *nm* (*mil*) tank; (*carnaval*) float.
charabia [ʃarabja] *nm* (*fam*) gibberish.
charbon [ʃarbɔ̃] *nm* coal. **charbon de bois** charcoal. **charbonnage** *nm* coal-mining. **charbonnier** *nm* coalman.

charcuterie [ʃarkytri] *nf* (*magasin*) pork butcher's, delicatessen; (*viande*) cooked pork meats. **charcutier, -ère** *nm, nf* pork butcher.

chardon [ʃardɔ̃] *nm* thistle.

chardonneret [ʃardɔnrɛ] *nm* goldfinch.

charger [ʃarʒe] *v* load; (*mil, élec*) charge. **charger de** ask to, put in charge of. **se charger de** see to, take care of. **charge** *nf* load; charge; responsibility; (*frais*) expense. **à charge de** on condition that. **chargé** *adj* loaded, laden; (*rempli, occupé*) full, heavy. **chargement** *nm* loading.

chariot [ʃarjo] *nm* trolley; (*charrette*) wagon; (*tech*) carriage.

charité [ʃarite] *nf* charity; (*gentillesse*) kindness.

charivari [ʃarivari] *nm* hullabaloo.

charlatan [ʃarlatɑ̃] *nm* charlatan; (*médecin*) quack.

charmer [ʃarme] *v* charm, enchant. **charmant** *adj* charming, delightful. **charme** *nm* charm; (*magique*) spell.

charnel [ʃarnɛl] *adj* carnal.

charnière [ʃarnjɛr] *nf* hinge.

charnu [ʃarny] *adj* fleshy.

charpente [ʃarpɑ̃t] *nf* framework, structure; (*carrure*) build. **charpenté** *adj* built.

charrette [ʃarɛt] *nf* cart.

charrue [ʃary] *nf* plough.

charte [ʃart] *nf* charter.

chasse [ʃas] *nf* hunting, hunt; (*au fusil*) shooting; (*poursuite*) chase; (*d'eau*) flush. **tirer la chasse** pull the chain.

châsse [ʃas] *nf* shrine.

chasser [ʃase] *v* hunt; (*au fusil*) shoot; (*faire partir*) drive out, chase away; (*dissiper*) dispel. **chasse-neige** *nm invar* snowplough. **chasseur** *nm* hunter; (*hôtel*) page.

châssis [ʃasi] *nm* frame; (*auto*) chassis.

chaste [ʃast] *adj* chaste. **chasteté** *nf* chastity.

chat, chatte [ʃa, ʃat] *nm, nf* cat. **chaton** *nm* (*zool*) kitten; (*bot*) catkin.

châtaigne [ʃatɛɲ] *nf* chestnut. **châtaignier** *nm* chestnut (tree).

châtain [ʃatɛ̃] *adj* chestnut, auburn.

château [ʃato] *nm* castle; (*manoir*) mansion.

châtier [ʃatje] *v* punish; refine. **châtiment** *nm* punishment.

chatouiller [ʃatuje] *v* tickle. **chatouille-ment** *nm* tickle. **chatouilleux** *adj* ticklish; (*irritable*) touchy, sensitive.

chatoyer [ʃatwaje] *v* glisten, shimmer, sparkle. **chatoiement** *nm* glistening, shimmer, sparkle.

châtrer [ʃatre] *v* castrate.

chaud [ʃo] *adj* warm, hot. *nm* heat, warmth. **avoir chaud** be warm *or* hot. **chaudière** *nf* boiler.

chauffer [ʃofe] *v* warm (up), heat (up); (*moteur*) overheat. **chauffe-eau** *nm invar* water-heater. **chauffe-plats** *nm invar* hot-plate. **chauffage** *nm* heating. **chauffage central** central heating.

chauffeur [ʃofœr] *nm* driver; (*privé*) chauffeur.

chaume [ʃom] *nm* stubble; (*toit*) thatch. **chaumière** *nf* thatched cottage.

chaussée [ʃose] *nf* road; causeway.

chausser [ʃose] *v* (*mettre*) put (shoes) on; (*marchand*) supply with shoes; (*chaussure*) fit. **chausse-pied** *nm* shoehorn. **chaussette** *nf* sock. **chausson** *nm* slipper. **chaussure** *nf* shoe, boot; footwear.

chauve [ʃov] *adj* bald. **chauve-souris** *nf* bat.

chauvin [ʃovɛ̃], **-e** *nm, nf* chauvinist. *adj* chauvinistic. **chauvinisme** *nm* chauvinism.

chaux [ʃo] *nf* lime. **blanchir à la chaux** whitewash.

chavirer [ʃavire] *v* capsize, overturn.

chef [ʃɛf] *nm* head; (*patron*) boss; (*tribu*) chief; (*révolte, etc.*) leader; (*cuisine*) chef. **chef d'équipe** foreman; (*sport*) captain. **chef de gare** station-master. **chef de train** guard. **chef-d'œuvre** *nm* masterpiece. **chef d'orchestre** conductor. **chef-lieu** *nm* county town.

cheik [ʃɛk] *nm* sheik.

chelem [ʃlɛm] *nm* (*cartes*) slam.

chemin [ʃəmɛ̃] *nm* way, path; (*campagne*) lane. **chemin de fer** railway. **chemin faisant** on the way. **se mettre en chemin** set off.

chemineau [ʃəmino] *nm* tramp.

cheminée [ʃəmine] *nf* chimney; (*foyer*) fireplace; (*encadrement*) mantelpiece; (*paquebot*) funnel.

cheminer [ʃəmine] *v* walk; (*péniblement*) trudge along; (*eau, sentier*) make its way.

chemise [ʃəmiz] *nf* shirt; (*dossier*) folder; (*tech*) lining, jacket. **chemise de nuit** nightdress. **chemisier** *nm* blouse.

chenal [ʃənal] *nm* channel; canal.
chêne [ʃɛn] *nm* oak.
chenille [ʃənij] *nf* caterpillar.
chèque [ʃɛk] *nm* check. **chèque-cadeau** *nm* gift token. **chèque de voyage** traveller's check. **chèque en blanc** blank check. **chéquier** *nm* check book.
cher [ʃɛr] *adj* dear; (*coûteux*) expensive. *adv* dearly. **coûter/payer cher** cost/pay a lot. **cherté** *nf* high price *or* cost.
chercher [ʃɛrʃe] *v* look for, seek. **chercher à** try to. **chercheur, -euse** *nm, nf* researcher.
chéri [ʃeri] *-e adj* beloved. *nm, nf* darling.
chérir [ʃerir] *v* cherish.
chérubin [ʃerybɛ̃] *nm* cherub.
chétif [ʃetif] *adj* (*enfant, etc.*) puny; (*repas, etc.*) meagre.
cheval [ʃəval] *nm* horse; (*auto*) horsepower. **à cheval** on horseback; (*chaise, etc.*) astride, straddling. **cheval à bascule** rocking horse. **cheval de course** racehorse.
chevalerie [ʃəvalri] *nf* chivalry. **chevaleresque** *adj* chivalrous.
chevalet [ʃəvalɛ] *nm* (*peinture*) easel; (*menuiserie*) trestle; (*violon*) bridge.
chevalier [ʃəvalje] *nm* knight. **chevalière** *nf* signet ring.
chevaucher [ʃəvoʃe] *v* be astride, straddle; (*tuile, pan*) overlap.
chevelu [ʃəvly] *adj* long-haired, hairy. **chevelure** *nf* (head of) hair.
chevet [ʃəvɛ] *nm* bedside.
cheveu [ʃəvø] *nm* hair. **cheveux** *nm pl* hair *sing*. **tiré par les cheveux** far-fetched.
cheville [ʃəvij] *nf* ankle; (*fiche*) peg, pin.
chèvre [ʃɛvrə] *nf* goat. **chevreau** *nm* kid.
chèvrefeuille [ʃɛvrəfœj] *nm* honeysuckle.
chevron [ʃəvrɔ̃] *nm* rafter; (*motif*) chevron.
chevroter [ʃəvrɔte] *v* quaver.
chez [ʃe] *prep* at *or* to the house of; (*avec*) with, in, among; (*docteur, etc.*) at, to; (*adresse*) care of, c/o. **chez soi** at home. **faites comme chez vous!** make yourself at home!
chic [ʃik] *nm* style. **avoir le chic pour** have the knack of. *adj invar* smart; (*fam*) nice, decent. *interj* great! terrific!
chicaner [ʃikane] *v* quibble. **chicanerie** *nf* quibbling.
chiche [ʃiʃ] *adj* niggardly, paltry, mean.
chicorée [ʃikɔre] *nf* (*salade*) endive; (*café*) chicory.

chien [ʃjɛ̃] *nm* dog. **chien d'aveugle** guide dog. **chien de berger** sheepdog. **chien de garde** guard dog. **entre chien et loup** in the twilight. **temps de chien** *nm* filthy weather. **chienne** *nf* bitch.
chiffon [ʃifɔ̃] *nm* rag; (*de papier*) scrap; (*à poussière*) duster.
chiffonner [ʃifɔne] *v* crumple, crease; (*fam*) bother, worry.
chiffre [ʃifrə] *nm* figure; total; code. **chiffre d'affaires** turnover.
chiffrer [ʃifre] *v* code; (*évaluer*) assess; (*pages*) number. **se chiffrer à** add up to.
chignon [ʃiɲɔ̃] *nm* bun.
chimère [ʃimɛr] *nf* dream, fancy. **chimérique** *adj* fanciful; imaginary.
chimie [ʃimi] *nf* chemistry. **chimique** *adj* chemical. **chimiste** *n(m+f)* chemist.
chimpanzé [ʃɛ̃pɑ̃ze] *nm* chimpanzee.
Chine [ʃin] *nf* China. **chinois** *nm, adj* Chinese. **les Chinois** the Chinese.
chiot [ʃjo] *nm* puppy.
chiper [ʃipe] *v* (*fam*) pinch.
chipoter [ʃipɔte] (*fam*) *v* haggle, quibble; (*manger*) pick at.
chips [ʃip] *nm pl* potato chips *pl.*
chiquenaude [ʃiknod] *nf* flick, flip.
chiromancie [kirɔmɑ̃si] *nf* palmistry. **chiromancien, -enne** *nm, nf* palmist.
chirurgie [ʃiryrʒi] *nf* surgery. **chirurgical** *adj* surgical. **chirurgien** *nm* surgeon.
chlore [klɔr] *nm* chlorine. **chlorer** *v* chlorinate.
chloroforme [klɔrɔfɔrm] *nm* chloroform. **chloroformer** *v* chloroform.
chlorophylle [klɔrɔfil] *nf* chlorophyll.
choc [ʃɔk] *nm* shock; impact, crash; (*conflit*) clash.
chocolat [ʃɔkɔla] *nm* chocolate. **chocolat à croquer** plain chocolate. **chocolat au lait** milk chocolate. **chocolat en poudre** drinking chocolate. *adj invar* chocolate-coloured.
chœur [kœr] *nm* chorus; (*chanteurs*) choir. **en chœur** in chorus.
*choir [ʃwar] *v* fall.
choisir [ʃwazir] *v* choose, select. **choisi** *adj* chosen; (*raffiné*) select.
choix [ʃwa] *nm* choice, selection. **de choix** choice.
choléra [kɔlera] *nm* cholera.
cholestérol [kɔlɛsterɔl] *nm* cholesterol.
chômer [ʃome] *v* be idle; (*travailleur*) be unemployed; (*usine, etc.*) be at a standstill. **chômage** *nm* unemployment. **au**

chômage unemployed. **mettre au chômage** make redundant. **chômeur, -euse** *nm, nf* unemployed person.

chope [ʃɔp] *nf* tankard.

choquer [ʃɔke] *v* shock, appal; (*offusquer*) offend; (*commotionner*) shake up; (*heurter*) knock, clink. **se choquer** be shocked.

choral [kɔral] *adj* choral. *nm* chorale. **chorale** *nf* choral society, choir.

chorégraphie [kɔregrafi] *nf* choreography. **chorégraphe** *n(m + f)* choreographer.

chose [ʃoz] *nf* thing. *nm* (*fam*) thingumajig. **être tout chose** (*fam*) feel peculiar.

chou [ʃu] *nm, pl* **choux** cabbage; (*ruban*) rosette; (*cuisine*) puff. **chou de Bruxelles** Brussels sprout. **chou-fleur** *nm* cauliflower.

choucas [ʃuka] *nm* jackdaw.

chouchou, -oute [ʃuʃu, -ut] *nm, nf* (*fam*) pet.

choucroute [ʃukrut] *nf* sauerkraut.

chouette[1] [ʃwɛt] *adj, interj* (*fam*) smashing, great.

chouette[2] [ʃwɛt] *nf* owl.

choyer [ʃwaje] *v* pamper; cherish.

chrétien [kretjɛ̃] *adj* Christian. **Chrétien, -enne** *nm, nf* Christian.

christianisme [kristjanismə] *nm* Christianity.

chromatique [krɔmatik] *adj* chromatic.

chrome [krom] *nm* chromium, chrome. **chromé** *adj* chromium-plated.

chromosome [krɔmozom] *nm* chromosome.

chronique[1] [krɔnik] *adj* chronic.

chronique[2] [krɔnik] *nf* chronicle; (*journal*) column.

chronologique [krɔnɔlɔʒik] *adj* chronological.

chronométrer [krɔnɔmetre] *v* time. **chronomètre** *nm* stopwatch.

chrysalide [krizalid] *nf* chrysalis.

chrysanthème [krizɑ̃tɛm] *nm* chrysanthemum.

chuchoter [ʃyʃɔte] *v* whisper. **chuchotement** *nm* whisper.

chuinter [ʃɥɛ̃te] *v* hiss softly; (*chouette*) hoot.

chut [ʃyt] *interj* hush!

chute [ʃyt] *nf* fall; (*ruine*) collapse, downfall. **chute d'eau** waterfall.

Chypre [ʃiprə] *n* Cyprus.

ci [si] *adv* this; here. **ci-après** *adv* below. **ci-contre** *adv* opposite. **ci-dessous** below.

ci-dessus *adv* above. **ci-devant** *adv* formerly. **ci-inclus** *adj* enclosed. **ci-joint** *adj* enclosed, attached.

cible [siblə] *nf* target.

ciboule [sibul] *nf* spring onion. **ciboulette** *nf* chive.

cicatrice [sikatris] *nf* scar.

cidre [sidrə] *nm* cider.

ciel [sjɛl] *nm, pl* **ciels** or **cieux** sky; (*rel*) heaven.

cierge [sjɛrʒ] *nm* candle.

cigale [sigal] *nf* cicada.

cigare [sigar] *nm* cigar. **cigarette** *nf* cigarette.

cigogne [sigɔɲ] *nf* stork.

cil [sil] *nm* eyelash.

cime [sim] *nf* peak; (*montagne*) summit; (*arbre*) top.

ciment [simɑ̃] *nm* cement. **cimenter** *v* cement.

cimetière [simtjɛr] *nm* cemetery, graveyard.

cinéaste [sineast] *n(m + f)* film-maker.

cinéma [sinema] *nm* cinema.

cinétique [sinetik] *adj* kinetic. *nf* kinetics.

cingler [sɛ̃gle] *v* lash, whip. **cinglant** *adj* biting; (*pluie*) driving. **cinglé** *adj* (*fam*) mad, crazy.

cinq [sɛ̃k] *nm, adj* five. **cinquième** *n(m + f), adj* fifth.

cinquante [sɛ̃kɑ̃t] *nm, adj* fifty. **cinquantième** *n(m + f), adj* fiftieth.

cintrer [sɛ̃tre] *v* arch; bend. **cintre** *nm* arch; (*vêtements*) coat-hanger.

cirage [siraʒ] *nm* shoe polish.

*circoncire [sirkɔ̃sir] *v* circumcize. **circoncision** *nf* circumcision.

circonférence [sirkɔ̃ferɑ̃s] *nf* circumference.

circonflexe [sirkɔ̃flɛks] *adj* circumflex.

circonscription [sirkɔ̃skripsjɔ̃] *nf* district; (*électorale*) constituency.

*circonscrire [sirkɔ̃skrir] *v* confine; (*math*) circumscribe.

circonspect [sirkɔ̃spɛkt] *adj* circumspect, cautious.

circonstance [sirkɔ̃stɑ̃s] *nf* circumstance; occasion. **de circonstance** appropriate.

circuit [sirkɥi] *nm* circuit; (*excursion*) tour.

circuler [sirkyle] *v* circulate; (*voiture, piéton*) go, move along. **circulaire** *nf, adj* circular. **circulation** *nf* circulation; (*auto*) traffic.

cirer [sire] v polish. **cire** nf wax; (meubles) polish. **ciré** nm oilskin. **cireux** adj waxy.

cirque [sirk] nm circus.

cisaille [sizɑj] nf shears pl.

ciseau [sizo] nm chisel. **ciseaux** nm pl scissors pl.

ciseler [sizle] v chisel, carve.

cité [site] nf city, town. **cité universitaire** halls of residence pl.

citer [site] v quote, cite; (jur) summon. **citation** nf quotation; summons.

citerne [sitɛrn] nf tank.

cithare [sitar] nf zither.

citoyen [sitwajɛ̃] **-enne** nm, nf citizen.

citron [sitrɔ̃] nm, adj lemon. **citron pressé** lemon juice. **citronnade** nf lemon squash. **citronnier** nm lemon tree.

citrouille [sitruj] nf pumpkin.

civette [sivɛt] nf chive.

civière [sivjɛr] nf stretcher.

civil [sivil] adj civil; civilian. nm civilian. **en civil** in plain clothes.

civiliser [sivilize] v civilize. **civilisation** nf civilization.

civique [sivik] adj civic.

clair [klɛr] adj clear; (lumineux) light, bright; (sauce, tissu) thin; (couleur) pale; (evident) plain. adv clearly. nm light. **clair de lune** moonlight.

clairière [klɛrjɛr] nf clearing.

clairon [klɛrɔ̃] nm bugle.

clairsemé [klɛrsəme] adj scattered, sparse.

clairvoyant [klɛrvwajɑ̃] adj perceptive, clear-sighted.

clameur [klamœr] nf clamour.

clan [klɑ̃] nm clan.

clandestin [klɑ̃dɛstɛ̃] adj secret, clandestine, underground.

clapier [klapje] nm hutch.

clapoter [klapote] v lap. **clapotement** or **clapotis** nm lapping.

claquemurer [klakmyre] v coop up, shut away.

claquer [klake] v (son) bang, snap, crack; (gifler) slap; (fam: fatiguer) tire out; (fam: mourir) die. **claque** nf slap. **claquement** nm bang, snap, crack.

clarifier [klarifje] v clarify. **clarification** nf clarification.

clarinette [klarinɛt] nf clarinet.

clarté [klarte] nf brightness, clearness; (lumière) light; (netteté) clarity.

classe [klɑs] nf class; (salle) classroom;

(école) school. **aller en classe** go to school. **faire la classe** teach. **sans classe** classless.

classer [klɑse] v class, classify; (ranger) file; (élève, fruits) grade. **classement** nm classification; filing; grading. **classeur** nm file; (meuble) filing cabinet.

classifier [klasifje] v classify. **classification** nf classification.

classique [klasik] adj classic; (art, musique, etc.) classical; (habituel) usual. nm (ouvrage) classic; (auteur) classicist.

claustrophobie [klostrofobi] nf claustrophobia.

clavecin [klavsɛ̃] nm harpsichord.

clavicule [klavikyl] nf collarbone.

clavier [klavje] nm keyboard.

clef or **clé** [kle] nf key; (tech) spanner; (musique) clef. **clef de contact** ignition key. **sous clef** under lock and key.

clémence [klemɑ̃s] nf clemency; (temps) mildness. **clément** adj lenient; mild.

clerc [klɛr] nm clerk.

clergé [klɛrʒe] nm clergy.

clérical [klerikal] adj clerical.

cliché [kliʃe] nm cliché; (phot) negative.

client [klijɑ̃] **-e** nm, nf customer, client; (hôtel) guest; (médecin) patient. **clientèle** nf clientèle; (magasin) customers pl; (médecin) practice; (comm) custom.

cligner [kliɲe] v **cligner les yeux** blink; (fermer à demi) screw up one's eyes. **clignement** nm blink.

clignoter [kliɲote] v (yeux) blink; (étoile) twinkle; (vaciller) flicker; (signal) flash. **clignotant** nm (auto) indicator.

climat [klima] nm climate. **climatique** adj climatic.

climatiser [klimatize] v air-condition. **climatisation** nf air-conditioning. **climatiseur** nm air-conditioner.

clin [klɛ̃] nm **clin d'œil** wink.

clinique [klinik] adj clinical. nf nursing home.

clinquant [klɛ̃kɑ̃] adj flashy. nm tinsel.

cliqueter [klikte] v rattle, clatter; (métal) clink, jingle. **cliquetis** nm clatter; clink, jingle.

clitoris [klitoris] nm clitoris.

clochard [klɔʃar] **-e** nm, nf (fam) tramp.

cloche [klɔʃ] nf bell; cover.

clocher¹ [klɔʃe] nm church tower, steeple.

clocher² [klɔʃe] v (fam) be wrong.

cloison [klwazɔ̃] nf partition; barrier.

cloître [klwatrə] *nm* cloister.
clopiner [klɔpine] *v* hobble along. **clopin-clopant** *adv* hobbling. **entrer/sortir clopin-clopant** hobble in/out.
cloporte [klɔpɔrt] *nm* wood-louse (*pl* -lice).
***clore** [klɔr] *v* close, end, conclude.
clos [klo] *adj* closed, enclosed. *nm* enclosed field; vineyard.
clôture [klotyr] *nf* (*fermeture*) closure, closing; (*enceinte*) fence.
clou [klu] *nm* nail; (*chaussée*) stud; (*méd*) boil; (*théâtre*) star turn. **clou de girofle** clove.
clouer [klue] *v* nail down, pin down. **cloué au lit** confined to bed. **cloué sur place** rooted to the spot.
clouter [klute] *v* stud.
clovisse [klɔvis] *nf* clam.
clown [klun] *nm* clown.
club [klœb] *nm* club.
coaguler [kɔagyle] *v* congeal; (*sang*) coagulate; (*lait*) curdle.
coalition [kɔalisjɔ̃] *nf* coalition.
coasser [kɔase] *v* croak. **coassement** *nm* croak.
cobaye [kɔbaj] *nm* guinea-pig.
cobra [kɔbra] *nm* cobra.
cocarde [kɔkard] *nf* rosette.
cocasse [kɔkas] *adj* comical.
coccinelle [kɔksinɛl] *nf* ladybird.
cocher¹ [kɔʃe] *v* (*crayon*) tick; (*entaille*) notch.
cocher² [kɔʃe] *nm* coachman.
cochon, -onne [kɔʃɔ̃, -ɔn] *nm* pig. **cochon d'Inde** guinea-pig. *adj* (*argot*) dirty. **cochonnerie** (*fam*) *nf* rubbish; (*saleté*) filth; (*tour*) dirty trick.
cocktail [kɔktɛl] *nm* cocktail; cocktail party.
cocon [kɔkɔ̃] *nm* cocoon.
cocotier [kɔkɔtje] *nm* coconut palm.
cocotte¹ [kɔkɔt] *nf* (*poule*) hen; (*péj: femme*) tart.
cocotte² [kɔkɔt] *nf* casserole.
code [kɔd] *nm* code. **code de la route** highway code. **se mettre en code** (*auto*) dip one's headlights.
cœur [kœr] *nm* heart; courage; (*fruit*) core. **avoir mal au cœur** feel sick. **de bon cœur** willingly. **parler à cœur ouvert** have a heart-to-heart.
coexister [kɔɛgziste] *v* coexist. **coexistence** *nf* coexistence.

coffre [kɔfrə] *nm* chest; (*auto*) trunk. **coffre-fort** *nm* safe.
cognac [kɔɲak] *nm* cognac.
cogner [kɔɲe] *v* hit, knock; (*plus fort*) hammer, bang.
cohabiter [kɔabite] *v* live together.
cohérent [kɔerɑ̃] *adj* coherent, consistent. **cohérence** *nf* coherence, consistency.
cohue [kɔy] *nf* crowd.
coiffer [kwafe] *v* (*mettre*) put (a hat) on; cover. **coiffer quelqu'un** do someone's hair. **se coiffer** do one's hair. **se coiffer** put on; (*péj*) become infatuated with. **coiffeur** *nm* hairdresser; (*hommes*) barber. **coiffeuse** *nf* hairdresser; (*meuble*) dressing table. **coiffure** *nf* hair-style; (*métier*) hairdressing.
coin [kwɛ̃] *nm* corner; (*lieu*) spot, area. **au coin du feu** by the fireside. **du coin** local.
coincer [kwɛ̃se] *v* wedge, jam.
coïncider [kɔɛ̃side] *v* coincide. **coïncidence** *nf* coincidence.
coin-coin [kwɛ̃kwɛ̃] *nm, interj* quack.
coing [kwɛ̃] *nm* quince.
col [kɔl] *nm* (*vêtement*) collar; (*géog*) pass; (*vase*) neck. **col roulé** polo-neck.
coléoptère [kɔleɔptɛr] *nm* beetle.
colère [kɔlɛr] *nf* anger, rage. **en colère** angry. **coléreux** *adj* quick-tempered.
colimaçon [kɔlimasɔ̃] *nm* snail. **en colimaçon** spiral.
colin [kɔlɛ̃] *nm* hake.
colique [kɔlik] *nf* stomach-ache; colic; diarrhoea.
colis [kɔli] *nm* parcel. **par colis postal** by parcel post.
collaborer [kɔlabɔre] *v* collaborate. **collaborateur, -trice** *nm, nf* collaborator; (*journal*) contributor. **collaboration** *nf* collaboration; contribution.
collant [kɔlɑ̃] *nm* (*bas*) tights *pl*; (*acrobate*) leotard. *adj* sticky; (*vêtement*) close-fitting, clinging.
colle [kɔl] *nf* glue, paste; (*fam: question*) poser.
collectif [kɔlɛktif] *adj* collective; (*hystérie*) mass; (*billet*) group. **collectivité** *nf* group; community.
collection [kɔlɛksjɔ̃] *nf* collection.
collectionner [kɔlɛksjɔne] *v* collect. **collectionneur, -euse** *nm, nf* collector.
collège [kɔlɛʒ] *nm* secondary school; college. **collégien** *nm* schoolboy. **collégienne** *nf* schoolgirl.

collègue [kɔlɛg] *n(m + f)* colleague.

coller [kɔle] *v* stick, cling.

collet [kɔlɛ] *nm* (*piège*) snare; (*tech*) collar, neck. **collet monté** prim, strait-laced.

collier [kɔlje] *nm* (*femme*) necklace; (*animal*) collar.

colline [kɔlin] *nf* hill.

collision [kɔlizjɔ̃] *nf* collision; (*conflit*) clash.

colombe [kɔlɔ̃b] *nf* dove. **colombier** *nm* dovecote.

colonel [kɔlɔnɛl] *nm* colonel.

colonie [kɔlɔni] *nf* colony. **colonie de vacances** holiday camp for children. **colonial** *nm*, *adj* colonial. **coloniser** *v* colonize.

colonne [kɔlɔn] *nf* column; (*arch*) pillar. **colonne vertébrale** spine.

colorer [kɔlɔre] *v* colour; (*tissu*) dye; (*bois*) stain. **coloration** *nf* colouring. **coloré** *adj* colourful; (*teint*) ruddy. **colorier** *v* colour in.

coloris [kɔlɔri] *nm* colour, colouring.

colosse [kɔlɔs] *nm* giant, colossus. **colossal** *adj* colossal.

colporter [kɔlpɔrte] *v* peddle. **colporteur, -euse** *nm*, *nf* pedlar.

coma [kɔma] *nm* coma.

combat [kɔ̃ba] *nm* fight, combat; (*sport*) match.

***combattre** [kɔ̃batrə] *v* fight, combat.

combien [kɔ̃bjɛ̃] *adv* (*quantité*) how much; (*nombre*) how many. **combien de temps** how long. **le combien sommes-nous?** what date is it?

combinaison [kɔ̃binɛzɔ̃] *nf* combination; (*sous-vêtement*) slip; (*astuce*) device, scheme.

combiner [kɔ̃bine] *v* combine; (*élaborer*) devise, plan. **combine** *nf* (*truc*) trick; (*péj*) scheme. **combiné** *nm* (*chim*) compound; (*téléphone*) receiver.

comble[1] [kɔ̃blə] *nm* height, climax, peak; (*toit*) roof timbers *pl*. **c'est le comble!** that's the last straw! **pour comble** to cap it all.

comble[2] [kɔ̃blə] *adj* packed.

combler [kɔ̃ble] *v* fill; (*déficit*) make good; (*désir*) fulfil.

combustible [kɔ̃bystiblə] *adj* combustible. *nm* fuel. **combustion** *nf* combustion.

comédie [kɔmedi] *nf* comedy, play; (*fam*) fuss. **comédie musicale** musical. **jouer la comédie** put on an act. **comédien** *nm*

comedian; actor; comedy actor. **comédienne** *nf* comedienne; actress; comedy actress.

comestible [kɔmɛstiblə] *adj* edible. **comestibles** *nm pl* food *sing*.

comète [kɔmɛt] *nf* comet.

comique [kɔmik] *adj* comic; (*drôle*) comical. *nm* comedy; (*artiste*) comic.

comité [kɔmite] *nm* committee, board.

commander [kɔmɑ̃de] *v* order; command; control. **commandant** *nm* commander; (*mil*) major; (*naut*) captain. **commande** *nf* order; control. **de commande** affected, forced. **fait sur commande** made to order. **commandement** *nm* command; (*rel*) commandment.

commanditer [kɔmɑ̃dite] *v* finance.

comme [kɔm] *conj* as; (*tel que*) like, such as. *adv* how. **comme ça** like that. **comme ci comme ça** so-so. **comme si** as if, as though. **comme il faut** properly. ... **comme tout** as ... as can be.

commémorer [kɔmemɔre] *v* commemorate. **commémoratif** *adj* commemorative, memorial. **commémoration** *nf* commemoration.

commencer [kɔmɑ̃se] *v* begin, start. **commencement** *nm* beginning, start.

comment [kɔmɑ̃] *adv* how. **comment allez-vous?** how are you? **comment s'appelle-t-il?** what's his name? *interj* what.

commenter [kɔmɑ̃te] *v* comment on; (*sport*) give a commentary on. **commentaire** *nm* comment; (*exposé*) commentary. **commentateur, -trice** *nm*, *nf* (*sport*) commentator; (*journal*) correspondent.

commérage [kɔmeraʒ] *nm* gossip.

commerçant [kɔmɛrsɑ̃], **-e** *adj* commercial; (*rue*) shopping. *nm*, *nf* shopkeeper, tradesman.

commerce [kɔmɛrs] *nm* trade, commerce, business. **commercial** *adj* commercial. **commerciale** *nf* van.

***commettre** [kɔmɛtrə] *v* commit.

commis [kɔmi] *nm* assistant; (*bureau*) clerk.

commissaire [kɔmisɛr] *nm* commissioner; (*surveillant*) steward. **commissaire de police** police superintendant. **commissaire-priseur** *nm* auctioneer.

commissariat [kɔmisarja] *nm* police station.

commission [kɔmisjɔ̃] *nf* commission; message; (*course*) errand; committee. **commissions** *nf pl* shopping.
commissionnaire [kɔmisjɔnɛr] *nm* messenger; (*livreur*) delivery man; (*hôtel*) commissionnaire; (*comm*) agent.
commode [kɔmɔd] *adj* handy, convenient; (*facile*) easy; (*personne*) easygoing. *nf* chest of drawers. **commodité** *nf* convenience.
commotion [kɔmosjɔ̃] *nf* shock. **commotion cérébrale** concussion. **commotionner** *v* shock, shake.
commun [kɔmœ̃] *adj* common; (*partagé*) shared, communal. **hors du commun** out of the ordinary. **peu commun** uncommon.
communauté [kɔmynote] *nf* community; (*cohabitation*) commune.
commune [kɔmyn] *nf* district, borough; parish. **communal** *adj* local; council.
communiant [kɔmynjɑ̃], **-e** *nm*, *nf* communicant.
communication [kɔmynikasjɔ̃] *nf* communication; message; telephone call. **communication interurbaine/en PCV/avec préavis** trunk/reverse-charge/personal call.
communion [kɔmynjɔ̃] *nf* communion.
communiquer [kɔmynike] *v* communicate; pass on; transmit. **se communiquer** spread; (*personne*) be communicative.
communisme [kɔmynismə] *nm* communism. **communiste** *n(m+f)*, *adj* communist.
compact [kɔ̃pakt] *adj* compact; dense.
compagnie [kɔ̃paɲi] *nf* company. **compagnon, compagne** *nm*, *nf* companion.
comparer [kɔ̃pare] *v* compare. **comparable** *adj* comparable. **comparaison** *nf* comparison. **comparatif** *nm*, *adj* comparative.
compartiment [kɔ̃partimɑ̃] *nm* compartment.
compas [kɔ̃pa] *nm* compass; (*math*) pair of compasses.
compassion [kɔ̃pasjɔ̃] *nf* compassion, sympathy.
compatible [kɔ̃patiblə] *adj* compatible. **compatibilité** *nf* compatibility.
compatir [kɔ̃patir] *v* sympathize. **compatissant** *adj* compassionate, sympathetic.
compenser [kɔ̃pɑ̃se] *v* compensate (for). **compensation** *nf* compensation.

compère [kɔ̃pɛr] *nm* accomplice.
compétent [kɔ̃petɑ̃] *adj* competent. **compétence** *nf* competence.
compétition [kɔ̃petisjɔ̃] *nf* competition; event, race. **compétiteur, -trice** *nm*, *nf* competitor. **compétitif** *adj* competitive.
compiler [kɔ̃pile] *v* compile. **compilation** *nf* compilation.
complaisance [kɔ̃plɛzɑ̃s] *nf* kindness; servility; indulgence; self-satisfaction. **complaisant** *adj* kind; servile; indulgent; self-satisfied.
complément [kɔ̃plemɑ̃] *nm* complement. **complémentaire** *adj* complementary; additional.
complet, -ète [kɔ̃plɛ, -ɛt] *adj* complete; (*plein*) full. *nm* suit.
compléter [kɔ̃plete] *v* complete; (*augmenter*) supplement, add to.
complexe [kɔ̃plɛks] *nm*, *adj* complex. **complexité** *nf* complexity.
complication [kɔ̃plikasjɔ̃] *nf* complication.
complice [kɔ̃plis] *n(m+f)* accomplice. *adj* knowing. **être complice de** be a party to. **complicité** *nf* complicity.
compliment [kɔ̃plimɑ̃] *nm* compliment. **compliments** *nm pl* congratulations *pl*. **complimenter** *v* compliment; congratulate.
compliquer [kɔ̃plike] *v* complicate. **se compliquer** get complicated.
complot [kɔ̃plo] *nm* plot. **comploter** *v* plot.
comporter [kɔ̃pɔrte] *v* consist of; (*impliquer*) entail; include. **se comporter** behave, perform. **comportement** *nm* behaviour, performance.
composer [kɔ̃poze] *v* compose, make up; (*numéro*) dial. **composer avec** come to terms with. **se composer de** consist of. **composé** *nm*, *adj* compound. **compositeur, -trice** *nm*, *nf* composer. **composition** *nf* composition.
compote [kɔ̃pɔt] *nf* stewed fruit.
compréhensif [kɔ̃preɑ̃sif] *adj* understanding. **comprehension** *nf* understanding, comprehension.
*****comprendre** [kɔ̃prɑ̃drə] *v* understand; consist of, comprise; include. **se faire comprendre** make oneself understood. **compris** *adj* included. **tout compris** all inclusive. **y compris** including.

compresse [kɔ̃prɛs] *nf* compress.

compression [kɔ̃presjɔ̃] *nf* compression; (*réduction*) cut-back.

comprimer [kɔ̃prime] *v* compress; (*réduire*) cut back; (*contenir*) hold back.

***compromettre** [kɔ̃prɔmɛtrə] *v* compromise; (*santé, etc.*) jeopardize. **compromis** *nm* compromise.

comptable [kɔ̃tablə] *adj* accounts; (*responsable*) accountable.

compte [kɔ̃t] *nm* account; number; (*calcul*) count. **compte à rebours** countdown. **compte rendu** report, review. **tenir compte de** take into account.

compter [kɔ̃te] *v* count; (*escompter*) reckon; pay; (*facturer*) charge for. **comptant** *nm, adv* cash.

compteur [kɔ̃tœr] *nm* meter. **compteur de vitesse** speedometer. **compteur kilométrique** milometer.

comptine [kɔ̃tin] *nf* nursery rhyme.

comptoir [kɔ̃twar] *nm* counter; bar.

comte [kɔ̃t] *nm* count. **comtesse** *nf* countess.

comté [kɔ̃te] *nm* county.

concave [kɔ̃kav] *adj* concave.

concéder [kɔ̃sede] *v* concede, grant.

concentrer [kɔ̃sɑ̃tre] *v* concentrate. **concentration** *nf* concentration. **concentré** *nm* concentrate, extract.

concentrique [kɔ̃sɑ̃trik] *adj* concentric.

concept [kɔ̃sɛpt] *nm* concept.

conception [kɔ̃sɛpsjɔ̃] *nf* conception; idea.

concerner [kɔ̃sɛrne] *v* concern.

concert [kɔ̃sɛr] *nm* concert. **de concert** together, in unison.

concerté [kɔ̃sɛrte] *adj* concerted.

concertina [kɔ̃sɛrtina] *nm* concertina.

concerto [kɔ̃sɛrto] *nm* concerto.

concession [kɔ̃sesjɔ̃] *nf* concession.

***concevoir** [kɔ̃səvwar] *v* conceive; (*comprendre*) understand; (*rédiger*) express.

concierge [kɔ̃sjɛrʒ] *n(m+f)* caretaker. **conciergerie** *nf* caretaker's lodge.

concilier [kɔ̃silje] *v* reconcile; (*attirer*) win, gain.

concis [kɔ̃si] *adj* concise.

***conclure** [kɔ̃klyr] *v* conclude. **concluant** *adj* conclusive. **conclusion** *nf* conclusion.

concombre [kɔ̃kɔ̃brə] *nm* cucumber.

concorder [kɔ̃kɔrde] *v* agree, tally. **concordance** *nf* agreement. **concorde** *nf* concord.

***concourir** [kɔ̃kurir] *v* compete; converge.

concours [kɔ̃kur] *nm* competition; (*examen*) competitive examination; aid.

concret, -ète [kɔ̃krɛ, -ɛt] *adj* concrete.

concurrence [kɔ̃kyrɑ̃s] *nf* competition. **faire concurrence à** compete with. **concurrent, -e** *nm, nf* competitor; (*examen*) candidate. **concurrentiel** *adj* competitive.

condamner [kɔ̃dɑne] *v* condemn; (*jur*) sentence; (*porte, etc.*) block up. **condamnation** *nf* condemnation; sentence.

condenser [kɔ̃dɑ̃se] *v* condense. **condensation** *nf* condensation.

condescendre [kɔ̃desɑ̃drə] *v* condescend. **condescendance** *nf* condescension.

condition [kɔ̃disjɔ̃] *nf* condition; (*comm*) term; (*rang*) station. **à condition** on approval. **à condition de** provided that. **conditionnel** *nm, adj* conditional.

conditionner [kɔ̃disjone] *v* condition; (*emballer*) package. **conditionnement** *nm* conditioning; packaging.

condoléances [kɔ̃dɔleɑ̃s] *nf pl* condolences *pl*.

conducteur [kɔ̃dyktœr], **-trice** *nm, nf* driver; (*chef*) leader. *nm* (*élec*) conductor. **conduction** *nf* conduction.

***conduire** [kɔ̃dᵁir] *v* (*véhicule*) drive; (*emmener*) take; (*guider*) lead; (*élec*) conduct; (*diriger*) run. **se conduire** behave. **conduit** *nm* duct, pipe. **conduite** *nf* driving; running; behaviour. conduct; pipe. **conduite d'eau/de gaz** water/gas main. **conduite intérieure** saloon car.

cône [kon] *nm* core.

confectionner [kɔ̃fɛksjone] *v* make. **confection** *nf* making; clothing industry. **de confection** ready-made, off-the-peg.

confédéré [kɔ̃federe] *adj* confederate. **confédération** *nf* confederation.

conférer [kɔ̃fere] *v* confer; compare. **conférence** *nf* conference; (*exposé*) lecture. **conférencier, -ère** *nm, nf* lecturer.

confesser [kɔ̃fese] *v* confess. **confession** *nf* confession.

confetti [kɔ̃feti] *nm* confetti.

confiance [kɔ̃fjɑ̃s] *nf* confidence, trust. **avec confiance** confidently. **avoir confiance en** trust. **confiance en soi** self-confidence. **de confiance** trustworthy. **confiant** *adj* confident.

confidence [kɔ̃fidɑ̃s] *nf* confidence, personal secret. **confidentiel** *adj* confidential.

confier [kɔ̃fje] v confide. **se confier à** (*se livrer*) confide in; (*se fier*) put one's trust in.

confiner [kɔ̃fine] v confine. **confiner à** border on. **confins** nm pl borders pl.

***confire** [kɔ̃fir] v preserve.

confirmer [kɔ̃firme] v confirm. **confirmation** nf confirmation.

confiserie [kɔ̃fizri] nf confectionery; (*magasin*) confectioner's, sweet-shop. **confiseur, -euse** nm, nf confectioner.

confisquer [kɔ̃fiske] v confiscate. **confiscation** nf confiscation.

confit [kɔ̃fi] adj candied.

confiture [kɔ̃fityr] nf jam. **confiture d'oranges** marmalade.

conflit [kɔ̃fli] nm conflict, clash.

confluer [kɔ̃flye] v join, converge. **confluence** nf mingling. **confluent** nm confluence.

confondre [kɔ̃fɔ̃drə] v mix up, confuse; (*ennemi*) confound; (*étonner*) astound; join, meet. **se confondre** merge. **se confondre en excuses/remerciements** apologize/thank profusely. **confondu** adj overwhelmed.

conforme [kɔ̃fɔrm] adj **conforme à** true to; in accordance with; in keeping with. **conformément à** in accordance with.

conformer [kɔ̃fɔrme] v model. **se conformer à** conform to. **conformité** nf conformity; similarity.

confort [kɔ̃fɔr] nm comfort. **confortable** adj comfortable.

confrère [kɔ̃frɛr] nm colleague.

confronter [kɔ̃frɔ̃te] v confront; compare. **confrontation** nf confrontation; comparison.

confus [kɔ̃fy] adj confused; (*honteux*) ashamed. **confusion** nf confusion; (*honte*) embarrassment.

congé [kɔ̃ʒe] nm holiday, leave; (*renvoi*) notice. **prendre congé** take one's leave.

congédier [kɔ̃ʒedje] v dismiss.

congeler [kɔ̃ʒle] v freeze. **congélateur** nm freezer.

congestion [kɔ̃ʒɛstjɔ̃] nf congestion. **congestionné** adj congested; (*visage*) flushed.

congrès [kɔ̃grɛ] nm congress.

conifère [kɔnifɛr] nm conifer.

conique [kɔnik] adj conical.

conjoint [kɔ̃ʒwɛ̃], **-e** nm, nf spouse. adj joint.

conjonction [kɔ̃ʒɔ̃ksjɔ̃] nf conjunction.

conjugal [kɔ̃ʒygal] adj conjugal.

conjuguer [kɔ̃ʒyge] v conjugate; combine. **conjugaison** nf conjugation.

connaissance [kɔnɛsɑ̃s] nf knowledge; (*personne*) acquaintance; (*conscience*) consciousness. **sans connaissance** unconscious.

connaisseur [kɔnɛsœr], **-euse** adj expert. nm, nf connoisseur.

***connaître** [kɔnɛtrə] v know; be acquainted or familiar with; (*éprouver*) experience. **faire connaître** make known.

connu [kɔny] adj known; (*répandu, fameux*) well-known.

***conquérir** [kɔ̃kerir] v conquer.

conquête [kɔ̃kɛt] nf conquest.

consacrer [kɔ̃sakre] v consecrate; (*dédier*) devote, dedicate. **consacré** adj consecrated, hallowed; accepted, established. **consécration** nf consecration.

conscience [kɔ̃sjɑ̃s] nf consciousness; (*morale*) conscience. **avoir conscience de** be aware of. **consciencieux** adj conscientious. **conscient** adj conscious.

conscription [kɔ̃skripsjɔ̃] nf conscription.

conscrit [kɔ̃skri] nm conscript.

consécutif [kɔ̃sekytif] adj consecutive.

conseil [kɔ̃sɛj] nm advice; (*organisme*) board, council. **conseil d'administration** board of directors. **conseil de guerre** court-martial. **conseiller, -ère** nm, nf adviser; councillor.

conseiller [kɔ̃seje] v recommend; advise.

***consentir** [kɔ̃sɑ̃tir] v consent, agree. **consentement** nm consent.

conséquence [kɔ̃sekɑ̃s] nf consequence, result. **conséquent** adj logical; consistent. **par conséquent** consequently.

conservateur [kɔ̃sɛrvatœr], **-trice** adj conservative. nm, nf (*musée*) curator; (*pol*) Conservative.

conservatoire [kɔ̃sɛrvatwar] nm academy, school.

conserve [kɔ̃sɛrv] nf **en conserve** tinned, canned. **mettre en conserve** can.

conserver [kɔ̃sɛrve] v keep, retain, conserve; (*aliments, etc.*) preserve. **conservation** nf preservation.

considérer [kɔ̃sidere] v consider; regard; respect. **considérable** adj considerable. **considération** nf consideration; reflection; respect.

consigner [kɔ̃siɲe] v (*par écrit*) record; (*en dépôt*) deposit; (*soldat*) confine to barracks. **consignation** nf deposit; (*comm*) consignment. **consigne** nf orders

pl; (bagages) left-luggage office; (comm) deposit. **consigné** adj (bouteille, etc.) returnable.
consister [kɔ̃siste] v consist. **consister en** consist of. **consistance** nf consistency. **consistant** adj solid.
consoler [kɔ̃sɔle] v console. **consolation** nf consolation.
consolider [kɔ̃sɔlide] v strengthen, consolidate. **consolidation** nf strengthening, consolidation.
consommer [kɔ̃sɔme] v consume; use; (manger) eat; (mariage) consummate. **consommateur, -trice** nm, nf consumer; (café) customer. **consommation** nf consumption; (café) drink; consummation. **consommé** nm consommé.
consonne [kɔ̃sɔn] nf consonant.
conspirer [kɔ̃spire] v conspire. **conspirateur, -trice** nm, nf conspirator. **conspiration** nf conspiracy.
conspuer [kɔ̃spᶣe] v shout down.
constant [kɔ̃stɑ̃] adj constant. **constamment** adv constantly. **constance** nf constancy.
constater [kɔ̃state] v note, notice; (consigner) record, certify. **constatation** nf observation.
constellation [kɔ̃stelasjɔ̃] nf constellation.
consterner [kɔ̃stɛrne] v dismay. **consternation** nf consternation, dismay.
constipation [kɔ̃stipasjɔ̃] nf constipation. **constipé** adj constipated.
constituer [kɔ̃stitᶣe] v constitute; (fonder) put together, set up; (jur) appoint. **constituant** adj constituent. **constitution** nf constitution; composition.
construction [kɔ̃stryksjɔ̃] nf construction; (bâtiment) building. **constructif** adj constructive.
***construire** [kɔ̃strᶣir] v construct; build.
consul [kɔ̃syl] nm consul. **consulat** nm consulate.
consulter [kɔ̃sylte] v consult. **consultation** nf consultation.
consumer [kɔ̃syme] v consume; destroy.
contact [kɔ̃takt] nm contact; (auto) ignition.
contagieux [kɔ̃taʒjø] adj contagious, infectious. **contagion** nf contagion.
contaminer [kɔ̃tamine] v contaminate. **contamination** nf contamination.
conte [kɔ̃t] nm tale, story. **conte de fée** fairy tale.
contempler [kɔ̃tɑ̃ple] v contemplate. **con-**

templatif adj contemplative. **contemplation** nf contemplation.
contemporain [kɔ̃tɑ̃pɔrɛ̃], **-e** n, adj contemporary.
contenance [kɔ̃tnɑ̃s] nf capacity; attitude. **faire bonne contenance** put on a brave face.
***contenir** [kɔ̃tnir] v contain; (récipient) hold.
content [kɔ̃tɑ̃] adj pleased, happy; satisfied, content.
contenter [kɔ̃tɑ̃te] v satisfy. **se contenter de** content oneself with. **contentement** nm contentment, satisfaction.
contenu [kɔ̃tny] adj restrained. nm content; (récipient) contents pl.
conter [kɔ̃te] v recount, relate. **conteur, -euse** nm, nf storyteller.
contester [kɔ̃tɛste] v contest, dispute; protest. **contestable** adj questionable. **contestation** nf dispute.
contexte [kɔ̃tɛkst] nm context.
contigu, -uë [kɔ̃tigy] adj adjacent, adjoining.
continent [kɔ̃tinɑ̃] nm continent. **continental** adj continental.
contingent [kɔ̃tɛ̃ʒɑ̃] nm contingent; quota; (part) share.
continuer [kɔ̃tinᶣe] v continue. **continu** adj continuous. **continuel** adj continual; continuous. **continuité** nf continuity; continuation.
contourner [kɔ̃turne] v skirt round, bypass; (façonner) shape; (déformer) twist.
contraception [kɔ̃trasɛpsjɔ̃] nf contraception. **contraceptif** nm, adj contraceptive.
contracter¹ [kɔ̃trakte] v (raidir) tense, contract. **contraction** nf contraction.
contracter² [kɔ̃trakte] v contract; (dette) incur; (alliance) enter into.
contractuel [kɔ̃traktᶣɛl], **-elle** adj contractual. nm, nf traffic warden.
contradiction [kɔ̃tradiksjɔ̃] nf contradiction; debate, argument. **contradictoire** adj contradictory.
***contraindre** [kɔ̃trɛ̃drə] v force, compel. **contrainte** nf constraint.
contraire [kɔ̃trɛr] adj contrary; opposite; conflicting. nm opposite. **au contraire** on the contrary.
contrarier [kɔ̃trarje] v (irriter) annoy; (gêner) thwart. **contrariant** adj tiresome; (personne) contrary.

contraster [kɔ̃traste] *v* contrast. **contraste** *nm* contrast.

contrat [kɔ̃tra] *nm* contract, agreement.

contravention [kɔ̃travɑ̃sjɔ̃] *nf* (*amende*) fine; (*procès-verbal*) parking ticket; (*jur*) contravention.

contre [kɔ̃trə] *prep* against; (*protection*) from; (*échange*) for; (*rapport*) to. **par contre** on the other hand.

contre-amiral *nm* rear admiral.

contre-attaque *nf* counter-attack. **contre-attaquer** *v* counter-attack.

contre-avion *adj* anti-aircraft.

contrebande [kɔ̃trəbɑ̃d] *nf* contraband; (*activité*) smuggling. **faire la contrebande de** smuggle. **contrebandier, -ère** *nm, nf* smuggler.

contrebasse [kɔ̃trəbas] *nf* double bass.

contre-boutant *nm* buttress.

contrecarrer [kɔ̃trəkare] *v* thwart.

contrecœur [kɔ̃trəkœr] *adv* **à contrecœur** grudgingly.

contrecoup [kɔ̃trəku] *nm* repercussions *pl*.

*contredire [kɔ̃trədir] *v* contradict.

contrée [kɔ̃tre] *nf* region.

contrefaçon [kɔ̃trəfasɔ̃] *nf* forgery, counterfeit, imitation.

*contrefaire [kɔ̃trəfɛr] *v* counterfeit, forge; disguise; imitate. **contrefait** *adj* deformed.

contre-interrogatoire *nm* cross-examination.

contremaître [kɔ̃trəmɛtrə] *nm* foreman.

contremander [kɔ̃trəmɑ̃de] *v* cancel.

contre-manifestation *nf* counter-demonstration.

contre-pied *nm* opposite.

contre-plaqué *nm* plywood.

contrepoids [kɔ̃trəpwa] *nm* counterbalance.

contre-poil *adv* **à contre-poil** the wrong way.

contrepoison [kɔ̃trəpwazɔ̃] *nm* antidote.

contresens [kɔ̃trəsɑ̃s] *nm* misinterpretation. **à contresens** the wrong way. **à contresens de** against.

contretemps [kɔ̃trətɑ̃] *nm* hitch. **à contretemps** at an inconvenient time.

contre-torpilleur *nm* destroyer.

*contrevenir [kɔ̃trəvnir] *v* contravene.

contrevent [kɔ̃trəvɑ̃] *nm* shutter.

contre-voie *adv* **à contre-voie** (*rail*) on the wrong side.

contribuer [kɔ̃tribɥe] *v* contribute. **contribuable** *n(m+f)* taxpayer. **contribution** *nf* contribution. **contributions** *nf pl* (*à l'état*) taxes *pl*; (*à la commune*) rates *pl*; (*bureau*) tax office *sing*.

contrôler [kɔ̃trole] *v* control; (*vérifier*) check; (*argent, or*) hallmark. **contrôle** *nm* control; check, inspection; list; hallmark. **contrôleur** *nm* inspector; bus conductor; ticket collector.

controverse [kɔ̃trɔvɛrs] *nf* controversy.

contusion [kɔ̃tyzjɔ̃] *nf* bruise. **contusionner** *v* bruise.

*convaincre [kɔ̃vɛ̃krə] *v* convince, persuade; (*jur*) convict.

convalescence [kɔ̃valesɑ̃s] *nf* convalescence. **convalescent, -e** *nm, nf* convalescent.

*convenir [kɔ̃vnir] *v* suit; (*être utile*) be convenient; (*être approprié*) be suitable; (*avouer*) acknowledge; admit; (*s'accorder*) agree on. **convenable** *adj* fitting, suitable, appropriate; decent, acceptable, proper. **convenance** *nf* convenience; preference. **les convenances** propriety *sing*. **convenu** *adj* agreed.

convention [kɔ̃vɑ̃sjɔ̃] *nf* convention; (*accord*) understanding; (*pacte*) agreement. **conventionnel** *adj* conventional.

converger [kɔ̃vɛrze] *v* converge.

convers [kɔ̃vɛr] *adj* lay.

conversation [kɔ̃vɛrsasjɔ̃] *nf* conversation.

conversion [kɔ̃vɛrsjɔ̃] *nf* conversion.

convertir [kɔ̃vɛrtir] *v* convert. **converti, -e** *nm, nf* convert. **convertible** *adj* convertible.

convexe [kɔ̃vɛks] *adj* convex.

conviction [kɔ̃viksjɔ̃] *nf* conviction.

convier [kɔ̃vje] *v* invite, urge.

convive [kɔ̃viv] *n(m+f)* guest.

convocation [kɔ̃vɔkasjɔ̃] *nf* summons.

convoi [kɔ̃vwa] *nm* convoy.

convoiter [kɔ̃vwate] *v* covet. **convoitise** *nf* lust.

convoquer [kɔ̃vɔke] *v* (*assemblée*) convene; (*personne*) summon.

convulsion [kɔ̃vylsjɔ̃] *nf* convulsion. **convulsif** *adj* convulsive.

coopérer [kɔɔpere] *v* cooperate. **coopératif** *adj* cooperative. **coopération** *nf* cooperation. **coopérative** *nf* cooperative.

coordination [kɔɔrdinasjɔ̃] *nf* coordination.

coordonner [kɔɔrdɔne] *v* coordinate.

copain, copine [kɔpɛ̃, kɔpin] *nm, nf (fam)* pal, mate.
Copenhague [kɔpənag] *n* Copenhagen.
copier [kɔpje] *v* copy. **copie** *nf* copy; *(examen)* paper.
copieux [kɔpjø] *adj* copious.
copuler [kɔpyle] *v* copulate. **copulation** *nf* copulation.
coq [kɔk] *rm* cock.
coque [kɔk] *nf* shell; *(mollusque)* cockle; *(bateau)* hull.
coquelicot [kɔkliko] *nm* poppy.
coqueluche [kɔklyʃ] *nf* whooping cough.
coquet, -ette [kɔke, -ɛt] *adj* flirtatious; clothes-conscious; charming; *(fam: somme)* tidy.
coquetier [kɔktje] *nm* egg-cup.
coquille [kɔkij] *nf* shell; *(récipient)* scallop; *(erreur)* misprint. **coquille Saint-Jacques** scallop. **coquillage** *nm* shellfish.
coquin [kɔkɛ̃], **-e** *adj* mischievous, naughty. *nm, nf* rascal.
cor [kɔr] *nm (musique)* horn; *(méd)* corn. **cor anglais** cor anglais. **cor d'harmonie** French horn.
corail [kɔraj] *nm, pl* **-aux** coral.
corbeau [kɔrbo] *nm* crow.
corbeille [kɔrbɛj] *nf* basket. **corbeille à papier** wastepaper basket.
corbillard [kɔrbijar] *nm* hearse.
cordages [kɔrdaʒ] *nm pl* ropes *pl*, rigging *sing*.
corde [kɔrd] *nf* rope; *(musique, raquette)* string; *(tissu)* thread. **corde à linge** clothes-line. **corde à sauter** skipping-rope. **corde raide** tightrope. **cordes vocales** vocal cords *pl*.
corder [kɔrde] *v* twist; *(raquette)* string.
cordon [kɔrdɔ̃] *nm* cord, string; *(soldats, police)* cordon. **cordonnier** *nm* cobbler.
coriace [kɔrjas] *adj* tough.
corne [kɔrn] *nf* horn. **corne de brume** foghorn.
corneille [kɔrnɛj] *nf* crow.
cornemuse [kɔrnəmyz] *nf* bagpipes *pl*.
cornet [kɔrnɛ] *nm (papier, glace)* cone, cornet. **cornet à pistons** cornet.
cornichon [kɔrniʃɔ̃] *nm* gherkin.
Cornouailles [kɔrnwaj] *nf* Cornwall.
cornu [kɔrny] *adj* horned.
corporation [kɔrpɔrasjɔ̃] *nf* guild, corporate body.
corporel [kɔrpɔrɛl] *adj* corporal.
corps [kɔr] *nm* body; *(mil)* corps; *(cadavre)* corpse. **corps à corps** *adv* hand-to-hand. **le corps enseignant/médical** the teaching/medical profession.
corpulent [kɔrpylɑ̃] *adj* stout, corpulent.
corpuscule [kɔrpyskyl] *nm* corpuscle.
correct [kɔrɛkt] *adj* correct, accurate, right. **correction** *nf* correction; *(châtiment)* thrashing; accuracy.
correspondant [kɔrɛspɔ̃dɑ̃], **-e** *adj* corresponding. *nm, nf* correspondent. **correspondance** *nf* correspondence; *(transport)* connection.
correspondre [kɔrɛspɔ̃drə] *v* correspond; connect. **correspondre à** fit, agree with, suit.
corrida [kɔrida] *nf* bullfight.
corridor [kɔridɔr] *nm* corridor.
corriger [kɔriʒe] *v* correct; *(punir)* thrash.
corroborer [kɔrɔbɔre] *v* corroborate. **corroboration** *nf* corroboration.
corroder [kɔrɔde] *v* corrode. **corrodant** *adj* corrosive.
corrompre [kɔrɔ̃prə] *v* corrupt; *(eau, aliments)* taint; *(soudoyer)* bribe. **corrompu** *adj* corrupt.
corruption [kɔrypsjɔ̃] *nf* corruption; bribery; decomposition.
corsage [kɔrsaʒ] *nm* bodice.
corrosion [kɔrozjɔ̃] *nf* corrosion. **corrosif** *adj* corrosive; *(ironie, etc.)* scathing.
Corse [kɔrs] *nf* Corsica. *n(m+f)* Corsican. **corse** *nm, adj* Corsican.
corset [kɔrsɛ] *nm* corset.
cortège [kɔrtɛʒ] *nm* procession.
corvée [kɔrve] *nf* chore; *(mil)* fatigue.
cosmétique [kɔsmetik] *adj* cosmetic.
cosmique [kɔsmik] *adj* cosmic.
cosmopolite [kɔsmɔpɔlit] *adj* cosmopolitan.
cosmos [kɔsmɔs] *nm* cosmos.
cosse [kɔs] *nf* pod, hull.
cossu [kɔsy] *adj* well-off, opulent.
costaud [kɔsto] *adj* strong, sturdy.
costume [kɔstym] *nm* costume, dress; *(complet)* suit.
cote [kɔt] *nf* rating, popularity; *(comm)* quotation; *(courses)* odds *pl*; mark.
côte [kot] *nf (anat, tricot)* rib; *(pente)* slope, hill; *(littoral)* coast, coastline.
côté [kote] *nm* side; way, direction. **à côté** *(maison, pièce)* next door; *(près)* nearby. **à côté de** beside; compared to. **de côté** sideways; aside.
coteau [kɔto] *nm* hill, slope.

côtelette [kotlɛt] *nf* chop, cutlet.

coter [kɔte] *v* rate, mark; *(comm)* quote.

côtier [kotje] *adj* coastal, inshore.

se cotiser [kɔtize] *v* subscribe; *(groupe)* club together. **cotisant, -e** *nm, nf* (*club*) subscriber; *(pension)* contributor. **cotisation** *nf* subscription; contribution; collection.

coton [kɔtɔ̃] *nm* cotton. **coton à broder/repriser** embroidery/darning thread.

côtoyer [kotwaje] *v* skirt, run alongside; *(frôler)* be close to, be verging on.

cou [ku] *nm* neck. **cou-de-pied** *nm* instep.

couchant [kuʃɑ̃] *adj* setting. *nm* west; sunset.

couche [kuʃ] *nf* layer; *(peinture)* coat; *(bébé)* nappy. **couches** *nf pl* (*méd*) confinement *sing*.

coucher [kuʃe] *v* lay down; *(loger)* put up; *(séjourner)* sleep; *(mettre au lit)* put to bed. **se coucher** go to bed; *(s'étendre)* lie down; *(soleil)* set. *nm* **coucher du soleil** sunset. **couché** *adj* lying down; in bed; *(penché)* sloping. **couchette** *nf* couchette, berth.

coucou [kuku] *nm* cuckoo.

coude [kud] *nm* elbow; *(rivière, tuyau)* bend.

*coudre [kudr] *v* sew, stitch.

coudrier [kudrije] *nm* hazel tree.

couenne [kwan] *nf* rind.

couic [kwik] *interj* squeak!

couler [kule] *v* run, flow; *(fuir)* leak; *(bateau)* sink; *(verser)* pour. **se couler** slip. **coulant** *adj* smooth, flowing. **coulé** *nm* (*musique*) slur. **coulée** *nf* casting.

couleur [kulœr] *nf* colour; *(cartes)* suit; *(peinture)* paint.

couleuvre [kulœvrə] *nf* grass snake.

coulisse [kulis] *nf* runner, slide. **coulisses** *nf pl* wings *pl*. **dans les coulisses** behind the scenes. **porte à coulisse** *nf* sliding door.

couloir [kulwar] *nm* corridor; *(voie)* lane; *(pol)* lobby.

coup [ku] *nm* blow, knock; *(pinceau, plume)* stroke; *(bruit)* sound; *(essai)* try; *(tour)* trick. **à coup sûr** definitely. **après coup** afterwards. **du coup** suddenly. **du premier coup** first time. **tout à coup** suddenly.

coupable [kupablə] *adj* guilty. *n(m+f)* culprit.

coup de bec *nm* peck.

coup de coude *nm* nudge.

coup de feu *nm* shot.

coup de fil *nm* (*fam*) phone call.

coup de froid *nm* chill.

coup de main *nm* (helping) hand.

coup d'envoi *nm* kick-off.

coup de pied *nm* kick.

coup de poing *nm* punch.

coup de soleil *nm* sunburn.

coup de sonnette *nm* ring.

coup de téléphone *nm* telephone call.

coup de vent *nm* gust.

coup d'œil *nm* glance.

coupe¹ [kup] *nf* (*dessert*) dish; *(boire)* goblet; *(sport)* cup.

coupe² [kup] *nf* cut, cutting. **coupe transversale** cross section.

couper [kupe] *v* cut; *(eau, élec, etc.)* cut off; *(traverser)* cross; *(voyage)* break; *(vin)* dilute, blend. **coupe-papier** *nm* paper knife. **coupant** *adj* sharp. **coupure** *nf* cut; *(journal)* cutting; *(courant)* power cut.

couple [kuplə] *nm* couple, pair. **coupler** *v* couple.

couplet [kuplɛ] *nm* verse.

coupon [kupɔ̃] *nm* coupon; *(reste)* remnant.

cour [kur] *nf* court; *(bâtiment)* yard, courtyard; *(école)* playground; *(gare)* forecourt; *(femme)* courtship. **cour de ferme** farmyard. **faire la cour (à)** court.

courage [kuraʒ] *nm* courage; spirit, will. **perdre courage** lose heart. **courageux** *adj* brave, courageous.

couramment [kuramɑ̃] *adv* fluently; commonly.

courant [kurɑ̃] *adj* (*normal*) ordinary, standard; *(fréquent)* common; *(actuel)* current. *nm* current; movement; course. **au courant** well-informed, up to date. **courant d'air** draught.

courbature [kurbatyr] *nf* ache. **courbaturé** *adj* aching, stiff.

courbe [kurb] *adj* curved. *nf* curve.

courber [kurbe] *v* bend, curve. **se courber** bend down; *(saluer)* bow.

courge [kurʒ] *nf* marrow. **courgette** *nf* courgette.

*courir [kurir] *v* run; *(sport)* race; *(aller vite)* rush, speed; *(chasser)* hunt; *(parcourir)* roam. **coureur, -euse** *nm, nf* runner; *(sport)* competitor. **coureur automobile** racing driver.

couronner [kurɔne] *v* crown; (*ceindre*) encircle; award a prize to. **couronne** *nf* crown; (*fleurs*) wreath. **couronnement** *nm* coronation.

courrier [kurje] *nm* mail, letters *pl*; (*journal*) column, page.

courroie [kurwa] *nf* belt, strap. **courroie de ventilateur** fan belt.

courroux [kuru] *nm* wrath.

cours [kur] *nm* course; (*monnaie*) currency; (*leçon*) class. **au cours de** during. **avoir cours** be current. **cours du change** exchange rate. **en cours** in progress.

course [kurs] *nf* run, running; (*épreuve*) race; (*achat*) shopping, errand; (*voyage*) journey. **faire des courses** go shopping.

court[1] [kur] *adj, adv* short. **à court de** short of. **court-circuit** *nm* short-circuit.

court[2] [kur] *nm* tennis court.

courtier [kurtje], **-ère** *nm, nf* broker.

courtisan [kurtizɑ̃] *nm* courtier; (*flatteur*) sycophant.

courtois [kurtwa] *adj* courteous.

cousin[1] [kuzɛ̃], **-e** *nm, nf* cousin. **cousin germain** first cousin.

cousin[2] [kuzɛ̃] *nm* gnat.

coussin [kusɛ̃] *nm* cushion. **coussinet** *nm* pad; (*tech*) bearing.

cousu [kuzy] *adj* sewn, stitched.

coût [ku] *nm* cost.

couteau [kuto] *nm* knife. **couteau à découper** carving knife. **couteau de poche** pocket knife. **couteau-éplucheur** *nm* peeler.

coutellerie [kutɛlri] *nf* cutlery.

coûter [kute] *v* cost. **coûte que coûte** at all costs. **coûter cher** be expensive. **coûteux** *adj* expensive.

coutume [kutym] *nf* custom. **coutumier** *adj* customary.

couture [kutyr] *nf* sewing; (*confection*) dressmaking; (*suite de points*) seam. **couturier** *nm* fashion designer. **couturière** *nf* dressmaker.

couvent [kuvɑ̃] *nm* convent.

couver [kuve] *v* (*feu, haine*) smoulder; (*émeute*) brew; (*poule*) brood, sit on; (*œufs*) hatch. **couvée** *nf* brood, clutch. **couveuse** *nf* incubator.

couvercle [kuvɛrklə] *nm* lid, cover, top.

couvert [kuvɛr] *adj* covered; (*ciel*) overcast. *nm* place setting; (*restaurant*) cover charge; (*abri*) cover, shelter. **mettre le couvert** lay the table.

couverture [kuvɛrtyr] *nf* cover; (*lit*) blanket. **couverture chauffante** electric blanket.

***couvrir** [kuvrir] *v* cover; (*cacher*) conceal. **se couvrir** (*vêtements*) wrap up; (*chapeau*) put on one's hat; (*ciel*) cloud over. **couvre-feu** *nm* curfew. **couvre-lit** *nm* bedspread.

crabe [krab] *nm* crab.

crac [krak] *interj* crack!

cracher [kraʃe] *v* spit (out). **crachat** *nm* spit, spittle. **crachement** *nm* spitting.

crachiner [kraʃine] *v* drizzle. **crachin** *nm* drizzle.

craie [krɛ] *nf* chalk.

***craindre** [krɛdrə] *v* fear, be afraid (of).

crainte [krɛt] *nf* fear. **craintif** *adj* timid.

cramoisi [kramwazi] *adj* crimson.

crampe [krɑ̃p] *nf* cramp.

cramponner [krɑ̃pɔne] *v* clamp; (*fam*) cling to. **se cramponner à** clutch, cling to. **crampon** *nm* clamp; (*chaussure*) stud.

cran [krɑ̃] *nm* notch; (*fusil*) catch; (*cheveux*) wave; (*fam*) guts *pl*.

crâne [kran] *nm* skull, head.

crâner [krane] (*fam*) *v* show off. **crâneur, -euse** *nm, nf* show-off.

crapaud [krapo] *nm* toad.

crapuleux [krapylø] *adj* (*vie*) dissolute; (*action*) villainous.

craquer [krake] *v* crack; (*neige*) crunch; (*parquet*) creak; (*bas, pantalon*) rip. **craquement** *nm* crack, creak.

crasse [kras] *nf* grime, filth. **crasseux** *adj* grimy, filthy.

cratère [kratɛr] *nm* crater.

cravate [kravat] *nf* tie.

crawl [krol] *nm* crawl. **dos crawlé** *nm* backstroke.

crayon [krɛjɔ̃] *nm* pencil; (*dessin*) pencil sketch. **crayon de couleur** crayon.

crayonner [krɛjɔne] *v* jot down, scribble; (*dessin*) sketch.

créance [kreɑ̃s] *nf* debt, claim. **créancier, -ère** *nm, nf* creditor.

créateur [kreatœr] **-trice** *adj* creative. *nm, nf* creator.

création [kreasjɔ̃] *nf* creation.

créature [kreatyr] *nf* creature.

crèche [krɛʃ] *nf* crèche; (*rel*) crib.

crédit [kredi] *nm* credit; bank; trust. **créditer** *v* credit. **créditeur, -trice** *adj* credit.

crédule [kredyl] *adj* gullible. **crédulité** *nf* gullibility.

créer [kree] v create.
crémaillère [kremajɛr] nf (tech) rack. **pendre la crémaillère** have a house-warming party.
crématoire [krematwar] nm crematorium. **crémation** nf cremation.
crème [krɛm] nf, adj cream. **crème anglaise** custard. **crème à raser** shaving cream. **crème patissière** confectioner's custard. **crémerie** nf dairy. **crémeux** adj creamy.
crénelé [krɛnle] adj notched; (bordure) scalloped; (mur) crenellated.
crêpe¹ [krɛp] nf (cuisine) pancake. **crêperie** nf pancake shop or café.
crêpe² [krɛp] nm (tissu) crepe.
crépiter [krepite] v crackle.
crépuscule [krepyskyl] nm twilight.
cresson [kresɔ̃] nm cress.
crête [krɛt] nf ridge, crest; (coq) comb; (mur) top.
creuser [krøze] v dig (out), hollow (out); (problème) go into thoroughly.
creux [krø] adj hollow; (vide) empty; (visage) gaunt; (jours) slack. **heures creuses** off-peak periods pl. nm hollow; slack period. **creux des reins** small of the back.
crevaison [krəvɛzɔ̃] nf puncture.
crevasser [krəvase] v crack; (mains) chap. **crevasse** nf crack, crevice.
crever [krəve] v burst; (pneu) puncture; (fam: fatiguer) wear out; (fam: mourir) die.
crevette [krəvɛt] nf shrimp; (rose) prawn.
cri [kri] nm cry, shout.
criailler [kriɑje] v squawk, screech; (bébé) bawl; (rouspéter) grumble.
criard [krijar] adj yelling, squawking; (couleur) garish; (son) piercing.
cribler [krible] v sift; (percer) riddle. **crible** nm sieve, riddle. **passer au crible** examine closely. **criblé de** riddled with; covered with; (dettes) crippled with.
cric [krik] nm jack. **soulever au cric** jack up.
cricket [krikɛt] nm cricket.
cri-cri [krikri] nm (grillon) cricket.
criée [krije] nf auction.
crier [krije] v shout, cry, scream; (oiseau) call; (grincer) squeak, squeal.
crime [krim] nm crime. **criminel, -elle** n, adj criminal.
crin [krɛ̃] nm hair, horsehair. **crinière** nf mane; (personne) mop of hair.
crique [krik] nf creek.

criquet [krikɛ] nm locust.
crise [kriz] nf crisis; (accès) attack, fit; (pénurie) shortage. **crise cardiaque** heart attack. **crise de foie** bilious attack. **piquer une crise** (fam) fly off the handle.
crisper [krispe] v tense, clench; (plisser) shrivel up. **se crisper** become tense, clench. **crispation** nf contraction; (nervosité) tension; (spasme) twitch. **crispé** adj nervous, tense, on edge.
crisser [krise] v (gravier) crunch; (freins) screech; (soie) rustle. **crisser des dents** grind one's teeth.
cristal [kristal] nm crystal. **cristal taillé** cut glass. **cristallin** adj crystalline; (son) crystal-clear.
cristalliser [kristalize] v crystallize. **cristallisation** nf crystallization.
critère [kritɛr] nm criterion.
critique [kritik] adj critical; crucial. nf criticism; (analyse) critique, review. n(m+f) critic. **critiquer** v criticize.
croasser [krɔase] v caw. **croassement** nm caw.
croc [kro] nm fang, tooth; (grappin) hook. **faire un croc-en-jambe à** trip up.
croche [krɔʃ] nf quaver.
crochet [krɔʃɛ] nm hook; (technique) crochet; detour; (véhicule) swerve. **crochets** nm pl square brackets pl. **faire du crochet** crochet. **vivre aux crochets de** sponge on, live off.
crochu [krɔʃy] adj hooked.
crocodile [krɔkɔdil] nm crocodile.
crocus [krɔkys] nm crocus.
***croire** [krwar] v believe, think. **croire à** or **en** believe in.
croisade [krwazad] nf crusade.
croiser [krwaze] v cross; pass; (naut) cruise. **croisé** adj double-breasted. **croisement** nm crossing; (carrefour) crossroads. **croisière** nf cruise.
croissance [krwasɑ̃s] nf growth, development.
croissant [krwasɑ̃] nm crescent; (pain) croissant. adj growing, increasing, rising.
***croître** [krwatrə] v grow, increase; (rivière, vent) rise.
croix [krwa] nf cross. **croix gammée** swastika.
croquer [krɔke] v crunch, munch; (salade, fruit) be crisp; (dessiner) sketch. **croquant** adj crisp, crunchy. **croque-monsieur** nm invar toasted cheese and ham sandwich.

croquet [krɔkɛ] *nm* croquet.

croquis [krɔki] *nm* sketch.

crosse [krɔs] *nf* (*sport*) club, stick; (*fusil*) butt; (*rel*) crook.

crotter [krɔte] *v* dirty, make muddy, soil. **crotte** *nf* droppings *pl*, dung.

crouler [krule] *v* collapse; (*délabré*) be tumbledown; (*empire, etc.*) totter. **croulant** *adj* crumbling, tumbledown.

croupe [krup] *nf* rump, hindquarters *pl*; (*colline*) hilltop. **monter en croupe** ride pillion.

croupir [krupir] *v* stagnate; (*personne*) wallow. **croupi** *adj* stagnant.

croustiller [krustije] *v* be crisp *or* crunchy; (*pain*) be crusty. **croustillant** *adj* crisp, crunchy; crusty; (*grivois*) spicy.

croûte [krut] *nf* (*pain*) crust; (*fromage*) rind; (*plaie*) scab. **croûton** *nm* crust; (*cuisine*) crouton.

croyable [krwajablə] *adj* credible.

croyance [krwajɑ̃s] *nf* belief. **croyant, -e** *nm, nf* believer.

cru¹ [kry] *adj* raw, crude; (*lumière*) harsh; (*franc*) blunt.

cru² [kry] *nm* (*vignoble*) vineyard; (*vin*) vintage, wine.

cruauté [kryote] *nf* cruelty.

cruche [kryʃ] *nf* jug, pitcher.

crucifier [krysifje] *v* crucify. **crucifixion** *nf* crucifixion.

crucifix [krysifi] *nm* crucifix.

crudité [krydite] *nf* crudeness; harshness. **crudités** *nf pl* coarse remarks *pl*; (*cuisine*) salads *pl*.

crue [kry] *nf* swelling, rising.

cruel [kryɛl] *adj* cruel.

crûment [krymɑ̃] *adv* bluntly.

crustacé [krystase] *nm* shellfish. **crustacés** *nm pl* (*cuisine*) seafood *sing*.

crypte [kript] *nf* crypt.

cube [kyb] *nm* cube; (*d'enfant*) block, brick. *adj* cubic. **cubique** *adj* cubic.

*cueillir [kœjir] *v* pick, gather; (*attraper*) catch.

cuiller [kɥijɛr] *nf* spoon. **cuiller à café** teaspoon. **cuiller de service** tablespoon. **cuillerée** *nf* spoonful. **cuillerée à soupe** tablespoonful.

cuir [kɥir] *nm* leather; (*avant tannage*) hide. **cuir chevelu** scalp. **cuir suédé** suede. **cuir verni** patent leather.

cuirasse [kɥiras] *nf* armour; (*chevalier*) breastplate.

cuirassé [kɥirase] *adj* armoured. *nm* battleship.

*cuire [kɥir] *v* cook; (*pain*) bake; (*porcelaine*) fire; (*brûler*) smart. **à cuire** *adj* cooking. **cuire à feu doux** simmer. **cuire à l'eau** boil. **cuire au four** (*viande*) roast; (*pain*) bake.

cuisant [kɥizɑ̃] *adj* burning, stinging; (*regret*) bitter.

cuisine [kɥizin] *nf* (*pièce*) kitchen; (*art*) cookery, cooking. **faire la cuisine** cook. **cuisinier** *nm* cook. **cuisinière** *nf* (*personne*) cook; (*fourneau*) cooker.

cuisse [kɥis] *nf* thigh; (*cuisine*) leg.

cuit [kɥi] *adj* cooked, ready. **cuit à point** done to a turn.

cuivre [kɥivrə] *nm* copper. **cuivre jaune** brass.

cul [ky] *nm* bottom; (*vulgaire*) arse.

culasse [kylas] *nf* cylinder head.

culbuter [kylbyte] *v* somersault; (*tomber*) tumble, topple; (*renverser*) knock over. **culbute** *nf* somersault; tumble, fall; (*fam: banque, etc.*) collapse.

culinaire [kyliner] *adj* culinary.

culminer [kylmine] *v* culminate, reach its highest point.

culot [kylo] *nm* cap, base; (*fam*) cheek.

culotte [kylɔt] *nf* short trousers *pl*; (*slip*) pants *pl*.

culpabilité [kylpabilite] *nf* guilt.

culte [kylt] *nm* cult, worship.

cultiver [kyltive] *v* cultivate. **cultivateur, -trice** *nm, nf* farmer. **cultivé** *adj* cultured.

culture [kyltyr] *nf* (*champ, etc.*) cultivation; (*esprit*) culture. **culturel** *adj* cultural.

cupide [kypid] *adj* greedy. **cupidité** *nf* greed.

cure [kyr] *nf* cure; course of treatment.

curé [kyre] *nm* parish priest.

curer [kyre] *v* clean out; (*nez*) pick. **cure-dent** *nm* toothpick. **cure-pipe** *nm* pipe cleaner.

curieux, -euse *adj* curious; interested, keen; (*indiscret*) inquisitive. *nm* strange thing. *nm, nf* inquisitive person.

curiosité [kyrjozite] *nf* curiosity; inquisitiveness; (*d'une ville, etc.*) strange sight *or* feature; (*bibelot*) curio.

curry [kyri] *nm* curry. **au curry** curried.

cuver [kyve] *v* ferment. **cuve** *nf* vat, tank. **cuvée** *nf* vintage. **cuvette** *nf* basin.

cycle¹ [siklə] *nm* (*révolution*) cycle.

cycle² [siklə] *nm* (*bicyclette*) cycle. **cyclisme** *nm* cycling. **cycliste** *n*(*m+f*) cyclist.
cyclomoteur [siklɔmɔtœr] *nm* moped.
cyclone [siklon] *nm* cyclone.
cygne [siɲ] *nm* swan.
cylindre [silɛ̃drə] *nm* cylinder; roller. **cylindrique** *adj* cylindrical.
cymbale [sɛ̃bal] *nf* cymbal.
cynique [sinik] *adj* cynical. *nm* cynic.
cyprès [siprɛ] *nm* cypress.
cypriote [siprijɔt] *adj* Cypriot. **Cypriote** *n*(*m+f*) Cypriot.

D

d' [d] *V* de.
dactylographier [daktilɔgrafje] *v* type. **dactylo** *nf* typist. **dactylographie** *nf* typing.
dague [dag] *nm* dagger.
daigner [deɲe] *v* condescend, deign.
daim [dɛ̃] *nm* (*animal*) deer; (*cuir*) suede.
dais [dɛ] *nm* canopy.
daller [dale] *v* pave. **dallage** *nm* paving. **dalle** *nf* (*pierre*) slab; (*trottoir*) paving stone.
daltonien [daltɔnjɛ̃] *adj* colour-blind. **daltonisme** *nm* colour-blindness.
damas [dama] *nm* damask. **prune de Damas** *nf* damson.
dame [dam] *nf* lady; (*cartes*) queen. **dames** *nf pl* (*jeu*) draughts *sing*.
damier [damje] *nm* draughtboard.
damner [dɑne] *v* damn. **damnation** *nf* damnation. **damné** *adj* (*fam*) confounded.
se dandiner [dɑ̃dine] *v* waddle. **dandinement** *nm* waddle.
Danemark [danmark] *nm* Denmark.
danger [dɑ̃ʒe] *nm* danger. **mettre en danger** endanger. **sans danger** *adv* safely. **dangereux** *adj* dangerous.
danois [danwa] *nm, adj* Danish. **Danois, -e** *nm, nf* Dane.
dans [dɑ̃] *prep* in; into.
danser [dɑ̃se] *v* dance. **danse** *nf* dance; (*art*) dancing. **danseur, -euse** *nm, nf* dancer.
dard [dar] *nm* sting.
darder [darde] *v* (*lancer*) shoot; (*dresser*) point.

dater [date] *v* date. **date** *nf* date. **date limite** deadline.
datte [dat] *nf* date. **dattier** *nm* date palm.
daube [dob] *nf* stew, casserole.
dauphin [dofɛ̃] *nm* dolphin.
davantage [davɑ̃taʒ] *adv* (*plus*) more, any more; (*plus longtemps*) longer, any longer.
de [də], **d'** *prep* of; from. **de/du/de la/des** some, any.
dé [de] *nm* dice. **couper en dés** dice. **dé à coudre** thimble.
débâcle [debɑklə] *nf* collapse; (*mil*) rout; (*glace*) breaking up.
déballer [debale] *v* unpack. **déballage** *nm* unpacking.
se débander [debɑ̃de] *v* disperse, scatter. **débandade** *nf* scattering. **à la débandade** in disorder.
débarbouiller [debarbuje] *v* wash. **se débarbouiller** wash one's face.
débarcadère [debarkadɛr] *nm* landing stage.
débardeur [debardœr] *nm* docker.
débarquer [debarke] *v* land; (*navire*) disembark; (*décharger*) unload. **débarquement** *nm* landing; unloading.
débarras [debara] *nm* lumber room. **bon débarras!** good riddance!
débarrasser [debarase] *v* rid; (*table*) clear. **se débarrasser de** get rid of.
débat [deba] *nm* debate; discussion.
*débattre [debatrə] *v* debate; discuss. **se débattre** struggle.
débaucher [deboʃe] *v* lead astray; (*ouvriers*) lay off, make redundant. **débauche** *nf* debauchery. **debauché** *adj* debauched.
débile [debil] *adj* weak, feeble.
débit¹ [debi] *nm* (*comm*) turnover; (*fluide*) flow, output; (*élocution*) delivery. **débit de boissons** bar. **débit de tabac** tobacconist's.
débit² [debi] *nm* debit.
débiter¹ [debite] *v* (*comm*) retail; (*fluide*) produce; recite; (*couper*) cut up.
débiter² [debite] *v* debit.
déblai [deblɛ] *nm* clearing. **déblais** *nm pl* rubble *sing*, debris *sing*.
déblayer [debleje] *v* clear.
déboîter [debwate] *v* (*méd*) dislocate; (*séparer*) disconnect; (*auto*) pull out. **déboîtement** *nm* dislocation.

débonnaire [debɔner] *adj* easy-going.
déborder [debɔrde] *v* (*liquide*) overflow; (*dépasser*) go beyond, jut out; (*drap*) untuck. **débordant** *adj* exuberant, unbounded. **débordé de** (*fam*) snowed under with. **débordement** *nm* overflowing; outburst.
déboucher¹ [debuʃe] *v* (*tuyau*) unblock; (*bouteille*) uncork.
déboucher² [debuʃe] *v* emerge. **débouché** *nm* opening; (*comm*) outlet.
débourser [deburse] *v* pay out. **débours** *nm* outlay.
debout [dəbu] *adv, adj* standing. **être debout** stand. **se mettre debout** stand up.
déboutonner [debutɔne] *v* unbutton.
débraillé [debrɑje] *adj* slovenly, untidy. *nm* slovenliness.
débrancher [debrɑ̃ʃe] *v* disconnect; (*appareil électrique*) unplug.
débrayer [debreje] *v* (*auto*) let out the clutch; (*fam*) knock off work.
débris [debri] *nm pl* fragments *pl*; (*restes*) remains *pl*; debris *sing*.
débrouiller [debruje] *v* sort out; (*fils*) disentangle. **se débrouiller** manage, cope.
début [deby] *nm* beginning. **au début** at first. **débuts** *nm pl* début *sing*. **débutant, -e** *nm, nf* beginner. **débuter** *v* start.
deçà [dəsa] *adv* **en deçà de** on this side of.
décade [dekad] *nf* decade.
décadent [dekadɑ̃] *adj* decadent. **décadence** *nf* decadence.
décaler [dekale] *v* shift; (*avancer*) bring forward; (*reculer*) put back. **décalage** *nm* gap; (*temps*) interval; (*concepts*) discrepancy; (*horaire, etc.*) change.
décamper [dekɑ̃pe] *v* (*fam*) clear off.
décanter [dekɑ̃te] *v* (*liquide*) allow to settle; (*verser*) decant. **se décanter** settle; (*idées*) become clear. **décanteur** *nm* decanter.
décapotable [dekapɔtablə] *adj* (*voiture*) convertible.
décéder [desede] *v* die. **décédé, -e** *n, adj* deceased.
déceler [desle] *v* detect; reveal.
décembre [desɑ̃brə] *nm* December.
décent [desɑ̃] *adj* decent; (*acceptable*) proper. **décence** *nf* decency.
déception [desɛpsjɔ̃] *nf* disappointment.
décerner [deserne] *v* award.
décès [desɛ] *nm* decease.

*décevoir [desvwar] *v* disappoint.
déchaîner [deʃene] *v* (*colère, etc.*) unleash; (*enthousiasme*) rouse. **se déchaîner** (*personne*) rage; (*tempête*) break out. **déchaînement** *nm* fury.
décharger [deʃarʒe] *v* discharge; (*bagages*) unload; (*tirer*) fire. **décharger de** relieve of, release from. **décharge** *nf* discharge; (*arme*) volley of shots; (*ordures*) rubbish tip.
décharné [deʃarne] *adj* bony, emaciated.
se déchausser [deʃose] *v* take one's shoes off. **déchaussé** *adj* barefooted.
déchéance [deʃeɑ̃s] *nf* decline; degeneration; (*pol*) deposition.
déchet [deʃɛ] *nm* (*reste*) scrap; (*comm*) waste. **déchets** *nm pl* rubbish, waste.
déchiffrer [deʃifre] *v* decipher, decode; (*musique*) sight-read.
déchiqueter [deʃikte] *v* tear to pieces, shred. **déchiqueté** *adj* jagged.
déchirer [deʃire] *v* tear. **déchirant** *adj* heartrending. **déchirure** *nf* tear.
*déchoir [deʃwar] *v* (*se dégrader*) demean oneself; decline.
décibel [desibɛl] *nm* decibel.
décider [deside] *v* decide; persuade; determine. **se décider** (*personne*) make up one's mind; (*question*) be settled. **décidé** *adj* determined; settled. **décidément** *adv* undoubtedly.
décimal [desimal] *adj* decimal. **décimale** *nf* decimal.
décisif [desizif] *adj* decisive.
décision [desizjɔ̃] *nf* decision.
déclarer [deklare] *v* declare, announce; (*naissance*) register. **déclaration** *nf* declaration; (*discours*) statement; (*aveu*) admission; registration.
déclencher [deklɑ̃ʃe] *v* (*mécanisme*) release, activate; (*attaque*) launch; (*entraîner*) trigger off.
déclin [deklɛ̃] *nm* decline; (*jour*) close; (*lune*) wane.
décliner [dekline] *v* decline. **déclinaison** *nf* declension.
décoiffé [dekwafe] *adj* dishevelled.
décoller [dekɔle] *v* unstick; (*avion*) take off. **se décoller** come unstuck. **décollage** *nm* take-off.
décolorer [dekɔlɔre] *v* fade; (*cheveux*) bleach.
décombres [dekɔ̃brə] *nm pl* rubble *sing*.
décommander [dekɔmɑ̃de] *v* cancel.

décomposer [dekɔ̃poze] v split up; (visage) distort. **se décomposer** decompose.
décomposition nf decomposition.
décompte [dekɔ̃t] nf deduction; (compte) breakdown. **décompter** v deduct.
déconcerter [dekɔ̃sɛrte] v disconcert.
décongeler [dekɔ̃ʒle] v thaw out.
déconseiller [dekɔ̃seje] v advise against. **déconseillé** adj inadvisable.
décontracter [dekɔ̃trakte] v relax. **décontraction** nf relaxation.
déconvenue [dekɔ̃vny] nf disappointment.
décor [dekɔr] nm scenery; (maison) décor; (cadre) setting.
décorer [dekɔre] v decorate. **décorateur, -trice** nm, nf decorator. **décoratif** adj decorative. **décoration** nf decoration.
découper [dekupe] v cut out or up. **se découper** stand out.
décourager [dekuraʒe] v discourage. **découragement** nm discouragement.
décousu [dekuzy] adj disjointed; (couture) undone.
découvert [dekuvɛr] adj uncovered; (terrain) exposed, open. nm overdraft, deficit. **découverte** nf discovery.
*découvrir [dekuvrir] v (trouver) discover, find out; (exposer) uncover.
décrasser [dekrase] v clean.
décret [dekrɛ] nm decree. **décréter** v decree, order.
*décrire [dekrir] v describe.
décrocher [dekrɔʃe] v take down; (téléphone) pick up (the receiver).
*décroître [dekrwatrə] v decrease, decline, (lune) wane. **décroissance** nf decrease, decline.
dédaigner [dedɛɲe] v despise, scorn. **dédaigneux** adj scornful, contemptuous.
dédain [dedɛ̃] nm contempt, scorn.
dédale [dedal] nm maze.
dedans [dədɑ̃] adv inside, indoors. nm inside.
dédicace [dedikas] nf dedication. **dédicacer** v sign, autograph.
dédier [dedje] v dedicate.
se *dédire [dedir] v go back on (one's word); retract.
dédit [dedi] nm forfeit; retraction.
dédommager [dedɔmaʒe] v compensate. **dédommagement** nm compensation.
déduction [dedyksjɔ̃] nf deduction; conclusion.

*déduire [dedɥir] v (comm) deduct; (conclure) deduce.
déesse [deɛs] nf goddess.
*défaillir [defajir] v weaken, fail; (s'évanouir) faint. **défaillance** nf (faiblesse) weakness; (incapacité) failure; faint.
*défaire [defɛr] v (couture, nœud) undo; (valise) unpack; (construction) dismantle. **se défaire** come undone or apart. **se défaire de** get rid of.
défaite [defɛt] nf defeat.
défalquer [defalke] v deduct.
défaut [defo] nm fault, flaw, defect; (manque) lack. **faire défaut** be lacking; (jur) default.
défection [defɛksjɔ̃] nf desertion, defection.
défectueux [defɛktɥø] adj defective, faulty.
défendre [defɑ̃drə] v (protéger) defend; (interdire) forbid.
défense [defɑ̃s] nf defence. **défense de fumer/stationner** no smoking/parking. **défense d'entrer** keep out.
déférer [defere] v defer; (jur) hand over. **déférence** nf deference. **déférent** adj deferential.
défi [defi] nm challenge; (bravade) defiance.
déficeler [defisle] v untie.
déficit [defisit] nm deficit.
défier [defje] v defy, challenge. **se défier de** distrust. **défiance** nf distrust. **défiant** adj distrustful.
défigurer [defigyre] v disfigure, spoil; (verité) distort; (monument) deface. **défiguration** nf distortion; disfigurement.
défilé [defile] nm procession; (géog) gorge, pass.
définir [definir] v define. **défini** adj definite. **définitif** adj final, definitive. **définition** nf definition; (mots croisés) clue.
défoncer [defɔ̃se] v smash in, break up.
déformer [deforme] v deform, distort; (métal, etc.) bend or put out of shape. **déformation** nf deformation, distortion.
défraîchi [defreʃi] adj faded.
défricher [defriʃe] v clear. **défricher le terrain** prepare the ground.
défunt [defɛ̃], **-e** n, adj deceased.
dégager [degaʒe] v clear; (libérer) free; (exhaler) give off. **dégagé** adj clear; (allure) casual.

dégarnir [degarnir] v strip, clear, empty. **dégarni** adj bare.

dégât [dega] nm damage.

dégel [deʒɛl] nm thaw. **dégeler** v thaw (out).

dégénérer [deʒenere] v degenerate. **dégénéré** adj degenerate. **dégénérescence** nf degeneration, degeneracy.

dégivrer [deʒivre] v defrost, de-ice. **dégivreur** nm defroster, de-icer.

dégonfler [degɔ̃fle] v deflate. **se dégonfler** go down; (fam) back out. **dégonflé** adj (pneu) flat; (fam) chicken.

dégorger [degɔrʒe] v discharge, pour out; (déboucher) clear out.

dégouliner [deguline] v trickle, drip. **dégoulinade** nf trickle.

dégourdir [degurdir] v warm up. **se dégourdir** stretch one's legs. **dégourdi** adj (fam) smart, bright.

dégoûter [degute] v disgust. **dégoût** nm disgust.

dégoutter [degute] v drip.

dégrader [degrade] v degrade, debase; (mur, monument) deface, damage. **se dégrader** debase oneself; deteriorate. **dégradation** nf degradation.

dégrafer [degrafe] v unfasten.

dégraisser [degrese] v remove the fat or grease from. **dégraissage** nm cleaning.

degré [dəgre] nm degree; stage.

dégringoler [degrɛ̃gɔle] v tumble (down). **dégringolade** nf tumble.

dégriser [degrize] v sober up.

déguenillé [dɛgnije] adj ragged.

déguerpir [degɛrpir] v (fam) clear off.

dégueulasse [degœlas] adj (argot) lousy, rotten, revolting.

déguiser [degize] v disguise. **se déguiser** (en) dress up (as). **déguisé** adj in disguise; (travesti) in fancy dress. **déguisement** nm disguise; fancy dress.

déguster [degyste] v taste, sample; savour, enjoy. **dégustation** nf wine-tasting.

dehors [dəɔr] adv outside, outdoors. **en dehors de** outside; (sauf) apart from. nm outside; appearance.

déjà [deʒa] adv already; (encore) yet.

déjeuner [deʒœne] v have lunch. nm lunch.

delà [dəla] adv **au delà** beyond. **en delà** beyond, outside. **par delà** beyond. prep **au delà de** beyond, over.

délabré [delabre] adj dilapidated, falling down; (vêtements) ragged.

délai [delɛ] nm delay; time limit, deadline. **à bref délai** at short notice; (bientôt) very soon.

délaisser [delese] v abandon; neglect; (jur) relinquish. **délaissement** nm desertion; neglect.

délasser [delase] v refresh, relax. **délassement** nm relaxation.

délavé [delave] adj faded, washed-out.

délayer [deleje] v mix; dilute, thin down; (péj) spin out.

déléguer [delege] v delegate. **délégation** nf delegation. **délégué, -e** nm, nf delegate.

délibérer [delibere] v deliberate, confer, consider. **délibération** nf deliberation; resolution. **délibéré** adj deliberate; resolute.

délicat [delika] adj delicate; refined; scrupulous; sensitive; (difficile) fussy. **délicatesse** nf delicacy; tact; refinement.

délice [delis] nm delight. **délicieux** adj delightful; (goût) delicious.

délier [delje] v untie, loosen. **délié** adj agile; fine, slender.

délinquant [delɛ̃kɑ̃], **-e** n, adj delinquent. **délinquance** nf delinquency.

délire [delir] nm delirium; frenzy. **avoir le délire** be delirious. **délirer** v be delirious.

délit [deli] nm offence.

délivrer [delivre] v (libérer) free; (débarrasser) relieve; (livrer) issue. **délivrance** nf release; relief; issue.

déloyal [delwajal] adj disloyal; (procédé) unfair. **déloyauté** nf disloyalty; unfairness.

delta [dɛlta] nm delta.

déluge [delyʒ] nm deluge, flood; (pluie) downpour.

déluré [delyre] adj smart, resourceful.

se démailler [demaje] v (bas) ladder; (tricot) unravel.

demain [dəmɛ̃] adv tomorrow. **à demain!** see you tomorrow! **demain en huit** a week tomorrow.

demander [dəmɑ̃de] v ask for; enquire, ask; (médecin, etc.) send for; (avoir besoin de) require, need. **se demander** wonder. **demande** nf request; (emploi) application; (remboursement) claim; (comm) demand. **demandé** adj in demand.

démanger [demɑ̃ʒe] v itch. **démangeaison** nf itch.

démaquiller [demakije] *v* remove make-up from. **démaquillant** *nm* make-up remover.

démarche [demarʃ] *nf* gait; procedure, step; approach.

démarrer [demare] *v* (*auto*) start; (*partir*) move off. **bien démarrer** get off to a good start. **démarreur** *nm* (*auto*) starter.

démêler [demele] *v* untangle. **démêlé** *nm* dispute.

démembrer [demãbre] *v* dismember, carve up.

déménager [demenaʒe] *v* move (house). **déménagement** *nm* removal, move. **déménageur** *nm* removal man.

démence [demãs] *nf* madness.

se démener [dɛmne] *v* struggle; make an effort.

***démentir** [demãtir] *v* refute, deny, contradict. **démenti** *nm* denial.

démesuré [deməzyre] *adj* immoderate; enormous.

***démettre** [demɛtrə] *v* dislocate; (*renvoyer*) dismiss. **se démettre** resign.

demeurer [dəmœre] *v* (*rester*) remain; (*habiter*) live. **au demeurant** for all that. **demeure** *nf* residence. **à demeure** permanent.

demi [dəmi], **-e** *n*, *adj* half. **à demi** *adv* half.

demi-bouteille *nf* half-bottle.

demi-cercle *nm* semicircle. **en demi-cercle** semicircular.

demi-douzaine *nf* half-dozen. **une demi-douzaine** half-a-dozen.

demi-finale *nf* semifinal. **demi-finaliste** *n*(*m* + *f*) semifinalist.

demi-frère *nm* half-brother.

demi-heure *nf* half-hour. **une demi-heure** half an hour.

demi-pension *nf* half-board.

demi-sœur *nf* half-sister.

démission [demisjɔ̃] *nf* resignation; abdication. **donner sa démission** hand in one's notice. **démissionner** *v* resign.

demi-tarif *nm* half-price; (*transport*) half-fare.

demi-teinte *nf* half-tone.

demi-tour *nm* about-turn; (*auto*) U-turn.

démocratie [demɔkrasi] *nf* democracy. **démocrate** *n*(*m* + *f*) democrat. **démocratique** *adj* democratic.

démodé [demɔde] *adj* old-fashioned.

demoiselle [dəmwazɛl] *nf* young lady. **demoiselle d'honneur** bridesmaid.

démolir [demɔlir] *v* demolish; destroy. **démolition** *nf* demolition.

démon [demɔ̃] *nm* demon.

démonter [demɔ̃te] *v* dismantle, take apart; disconcert.

démontrer [demɔ̃tre] *v* demonstrate. **démonstratif** *adj* demonstrative. **démonstration** *nf* demonstration.

démoraliser [demɔralize] *v* demoralize. **se démoraliser** lose heart. **démoralisation** *nf* demoralization.

démordre [demɔrdrə] *v* give up. **ne pas démordre de** stick to.

démunir [demynir] *v* deprive, divest. **démuni de** without.

dénaturer [denatyre] *v* distort. **dénaturé** *adj* unnatural.

dénégation [denegasjɔ̃] *nf* denial.

dénicher [deniʃe] (*fam*) *v* discover; (*personne*) track down; (*objet*) unearth.

dénigrer [denigre] *v* denigrate, run down.

dénivellation [denivɛlasjɔ̃] *nf* unevenness; (*pente*) slope; (*auto*) ramp.

dénombrer [denɔ̃bre] *v* count; enumerate.

dénominateur [denɔminatœr] *nm* denominator.

dénommer [denɔme] *v* name.

dénoncer [denɔ̃se] *v* denounce; (*coupable*) give away; (*révéler*) expose.

dénoter [denɔte] *v* denote, indicate.

dénouer [denwe] *v* (*nœud*) undo; (*intrigue*) untangle, resolve. **se dénouer** come undone; be resolved. **dénouement** *nm* outcome; (*théâtre*) dénouement.

denrée [dãre] *nf* foodstuff.

dense [dãs] *adj* dense; compact.

densité [dãsite] *nf* density.

dent [dã] *nf* tooth (*pl* teeth); (*fourche*) prong; (*roue*) cog. **avoir la dent** (*fam*) be peckish. **avoir une dent contre** have a grudge against. **du bout des dents** half-heartedly. **en dents de scie** serrated. **faire ses dents** teethe. **dentaire** *adj* dental.

denteler [dãtle] *v* indent. **dentelé** *adj* jagged.

dentelle [dãtɛl] *nf* lace.

dentier [dãtje] *nm* denture.

dentifrice [dãtifris] *nm* toothpaste.

dentiste [dãtist] *n*(*m* + *f*) dentist.

dénuder [denyde] *v* strip, bare. **dénudé** *adj* bare; (*crâne*) bald.

dénué [denɥe] *adj* **dénué de** devoid of, lacking in.

déodorant [deɔdɔrɑ̃] *nm, adj* deodorant.

dépanner [depane] *v* fix, repair. **dépannage** *nm* repairing. **service de dépannage** *nm* breakdown service. **dépanneuse** *nf* breakdown lorry.

dépaqueter [depakte] *v* unpack.

dépareillé [depareje] *adj* (*objet*) odd; (*collection*) incomplete.

départ [depar] *nm* departure; (*début*) start.

département [departəmɑ̃] *nm* department.

départir [departir] *v* assign. **se départir de** abandon, depart from.

dépasser [depɑse] *v* pass; (*auto*) overtake; exceed, go beyond; (*clou, rocher, etc.*) stick out. **dépassé** *adj* outmoded; (*fam*) out of one's depth. **dépassement** *nm* overtaking.

dépaysé [depeize] *adj* disorientated. **sentir dépaysé** not feel at home.

dépêcher [depeʃe] *v* dispatch. **se dépêcher** hurry. **dépêche** *nf* dispatch; telegram.

***dépeindre** [depɛ̃drə] *v* depict.

dépendance [depɑ̃dɑ̃s] *nf* dependence, dependency; subordination; (*bâtiment*) outbuilding. **dépendant de** (*employé*) answerable to; dependent on.

dépendre¹ [depɑ̃drə] *v* **dépendre de** depend on, be dependent on; (*employé*) be answerable to; (*appartenir*) belong to.

dépendre² [depɑ̃drə] *v* take down.

dépens [depɑ̃] *nm pl* costs *pl*. **aux dépens de** at the expense of.

dépenser [depɑ̃se] *v* (*argent*) spend; (*consumer*) use (up). **se dépenser** exert oneself. **dépense** *nf* expenditure, expense; consumption. **dépensier** *adj* extravagant. **être dépensier** be a spendthrift.

dépérir [deperir] *v* decline; (*personne*) waste away; (*plante*) wither.

dépêtrer [depetre] *v* extricate, free.

dépister [depiste] *v* (*découvrir*) detect, track down; (*détourner*) throw off the scent.

dépit [depi] *nm* vexation, resentment. **en dépit de** in spite of.

déplacer [deplase] *v* move, shift; (*air, eau, etc.*) displace. **se déplacer** move (around); (*voyager*) travel. **déplacé** *adj* uncalled-for; out of place. **déplacement** *nm* displacement; moving, movement; travel.

***déplaire** [deplɛr] *v* **déplaire à** be disliked by, displease. **se déplaire** be unhappy, dislike it. **déplaisant** *adj* unpleasant. **déplaisir** *nm* displeasure.

déplantoir [deplɑ̃twar] *nm* trowel.

déplier [deplije] *v* unfold, open out. **dépliant** *nm* leaflet, folder.

déplorer [deplɔre] *v* regret, deplore. **déplorable** *adj* deplorable.

déployer [deplwaje] *v* spread out; (*troupes*) deploy; (*étaler*) display.

se déplumer [deplyme] *v* moult.

déporter [depɔrte] *v* deport. **déportation** *nf* deportation.

déposer¹ [depoze] *v* set *or* put down; (*argent, sédiment*) deposit; (*admin*) file, register; (*roi*) depose. **déposant, -e** *nm, nf* depositor. **déposition** *nf* deposition.

dépositaire [depozitɛr] *n(m+f)* guardian; agent.

dépôt [depo] *nm* deposit; (*train, autobus*) depot; (*entrepôt*) warehouse; (*garde*) trust.

dépouiller [depuje] *v* strip; (*examiner*) peruse, study. **se dépouiller de** shed. **dépouille** *nf* skin, hide. **dépouillé** *adj* bare.

dépourvu [depurvy] *adj* **dépourvu de** devoid of, lacking in, without. **nm au dépourvu** unprepared.

dépraver [deprave] *v* deprave. **dépravation** *nf* depravity.

déprécier [depresje] *v* depreciate; (*dénigrer*) belittle. **dépréciation** *nf* depreciation.

dépression [depresjɔ̃] *nf* depression.

déprimer [deprime] *v* depress.

depuis [dəpɥi] *prep* since, from. *adv* ever since.

députation [depytɑsjɔ̃] *nf* deputation.

député [depyte] *nm* member of parliament; (*envoyé*) delegate.

déraciner [derasine] *v* (*détruire*) eradicate; (*arbre*) uproot. **déracinement** *nm* eradication.

dérailler [deraje] *v* be derailed. **déraillement** *nm* derailment.

déraisonnable [derɛzɔnablə] *adj* unreasonable.

déranger [derɑ̃ʒe] *v* disturb; (*coiffure*) ruffle; (*gêner*) trouble; (*routine*) upset. **se déranger** put oneself out; move aside. **dérangement** *nm* trouble; disorder.

déraper [derape] *v* skid. **dérapage** *nm* skid.

derechef [dərəʃɛf] *adv* once more.

dérégler [deregle] *v* disturb, unsettle, upset. **se dérégler** go wrong. **déréglé** *adj* out of order; (*mœurs*) dissolute; upset. **dérèglement** *nm* disturbance; dissoluteness.

dérision [derizjɔ̃] *nf* derision, mockery. **dérisoire** *adj* derisory.

dériver[1] [derive] *v* derive; (*rivière*) divert. **dérivation** *nf* derivation; diversion. **dérivé** *nm* derivative, by-product.

dériver[2] [derive] *v* drift. **dérive** *nf* drift. **à la dérive** adrift.

dernier [dɛrnje], **-ère** *adj* last; (*plus récent*) latest; (*extrême*) utmost; (*pire*) bottom; (*ultime*) top. *nm*, *nf* last. **ce dernier, cette dernière** the latter. **dernièrement** *adv* recently.

dérober [derɔbe] *v* (*cacher*) hide; (*voler*) steal. **se dérober** shy away; (*échapper*) slip away; (*s'effondrer*) give way. **dérobé** *adj* secret. **à la dérobée** secretly.

déroger [derɔʒe] *v* **déroger à** (*jur*) go against; (*s'abaisser*) lower oneself.

dérouler [derule] *v* unroll, unwind. **se dérouler** (*fil*) unwind, unroll; develop, progress; (*se passer*) take place.

dérouter [derute] *v* (*avion*) divert; disconcert. **déroute** *nf* rout. **déroutement** *nm* diversion.

derrière [dɛrjɛr] *prep* behind. *adv* behind, at the back. *nm* back, rear; (*fam*) behind.

des [de] *contraction of* **de les**.

dès [dɛ] *prep* from, since. **dès lors** from then on, from that moment. **dès que** as soon as.

désabuser [dezabyze] *v* disillusion. **désabusé** *adj* disenchanted. **désabusement** *nm* disillusionment.

désaccord [dezakɔr] *nm* discord; conflict, disagreement; (*contradiction*) discrepancy.

désaffecter [dezafɛkte] *v* close down. **désaffecté** *adj* disused.

désagréable [dezagreablə] *adj* unpleasant.

désagréger [dezagreʒe] *v* disintegrate, break up. **désagrégation** *nf* disintegration.

désagrément [dezagremã] *nm* annoyance, trouble.

se désaltérer [dezaltere] *v* quench one's thirst. **désaltérant** *adj* thirst-quenching.

désappointer [dezapwɛte] *v* disappoint.

désapprobation [dezaprɔbasjɔ̃] *nf* disapproval. **désapprobateur, -trice** *adj* disapproving.

désapprouver [dezapruve] *v* disapprove of.

désarmer [dezarme] *v* disarm.

désarroi [dezarwa] *nm* confusion.

désassorti [dezasɔrti] *adj* unmatching.

désastre [dezastrə] *nm* disaster. **désastreux** *adj* disastrous.

désavantage [dezavɑ̃taʒ] *nm* disadvantage, handicap.

désaveu [dezavø] *nm* disavowal, repudiation; retraction.

désavouer [dezavwe] *v* disown, repudiate. **se désavouer** retract.

désaxé [dezakse] *adj* unbalanced.

descendant [desɑ̃dɑ̃], **-e** *adj* downward, descending. *nm*, *nf* descendant.

descendre [desɑ̃drə] *v* go down, come down; (*transport*) get out *or* off; (*tomber*) fall; (*baisser*) lower; (*porter*) take down. **descendre de** be descended from.

descente [desɑ̃t] *nf* descent; raid; (*pente*) downward slope. **descente de lit** bedside rug.

description [dɛskripsjɔ̃] *nf* description. **descriptif** *adj* descriptive.

désemparer [dezɑ̃pare] *v* (*naut*) disable. **sans désemparer** without stopping. **désemparé** *adj* bewildered; (*navire, avion*) crippled.

désencombrer [dezɑ̃kɔ̃bre] *v* clear.

désenfler [dezɑ̃fle] *v* go down, become less swollen.

désengager [dezɑ̃gaʒe] *v* free, release; (*mil*) disengage.

désenivrer [dezɑ̃nivre] *v* sober up.

déséquilibré [dezekilibre] *adj* unbalanced.

désert [dezɛr] *adj* deserted. *nm* desert.

déserter [dezɛrte] *v* desert. **déserteur** *nm* deserter. **désertion** *nf* desertion.

désespérer [dezɛspere] *v* despair, lose hope; (*désoler*) drive to despair. **désespérant** *adj* maddening. **désespéré** *adj* desperate.

désespoir [dezɛspwar] *nm* despair.

déshabiller [dezabije] *v* undress. **déshabillé** *nm* negligee.

désherber [dezɛrbe] *v* weed. **désherbage** *nm* weeding. **désherbant** *nm* weed-killer.

déshériter [dezerite] *v* disinherit; (*désavantager*) deprive.

déshonneur [dezɔnœr] *nm* disgrace, dishonour.

déshonorer [dezɔnɔre] *v* disgrace, dishonour.

déshydrater [dezidrate] *v* dehydrate. **déshydratation** *nf* dehydration.

désigner [deziɲe] *v* designate; (*montrer*) point out; (*nommer*) name, appoint. **désignation** *nf* designation; appointment.

désillusionner [dezilyzjɔne] *v* disillusion. **désillusion** *nf* disillusionment.

désinfecter [dezɛ̃fɛkte] *v* disinfect. **désinfectant** *nm, adj* disinfectant. **désinfection** *nf* disinfection.

désintégrer [dezɛ̃tegre] *v* split *or* break up. **se désintégrer** disintegrate. **désintégration** *nf* disintegration.

désintéressé [dezɛ̃terese] *adj* disinterested, unselfish. **désintéressement** *nm* unselfishness.

désinvolte [dezɛ̃vɔlt] *adj* casual. **avec désinvolture** casually.

désirer [dezire] *v* desire, want. **désir** *nm* desire, wish. **désirable** *adj* desirable. **désireux de** anxious to.

désobéir [dezɔbeir] *v* disobey. **désobéissance** *nf* disobedience. **désobéissant** *adj* disobedient.

désodorisant [dezɔdɔrizɑ̃] *nm, adj* deodorant.

désœuvré [dezœvre] *adj* idle. **désœuvrement** *nm* idleness.

désoler [dezɔle] *v* distress, upset; devastate. **désolation** *nf* distress, grief; devastation. **désolé** sorry, distressed; (*endroit*) desolate.

désopilant [dezɔpilɑ̃] *adj* hilarious.

désordonné [dezɔrdɔne] *adj* disorderly, untidy, muddled.

désordre [dezɔrdrə] *nm* disorder, untidiness; confusion. **désordres** *nm pl* disturbances *pl*.

désorganiser [dezɔrganize] *v* disorganize, disrupt. **désorganisation** *nf* disorganization.

désorienter [dezɔrjɑ̃te] *v* disorientate, bewilder.

désormais [dezɔrmɛ] *adv* in future, from now on.

désosser [dezɔse] *v* bone.

desquels, desquelles [dekɛl] *contractions of* de lesquels, de lesquelles.

dessécher [deseʃe] *v* dry out, parch; (*feuille*) wither; (*aliments*) dehydrate; (*amaigrir*) emaciate.

dessein [desɛ̃] *nm* intention, plan. **à dessein** intentionally. **avoir des desseins sur** have designs on.

desserrer [desere] *v* loosen, release. **desserrer les dents** open one's mouth, speak. **desserré** *adj* loose.

dessert [desɛr] *nm* dessert, sweet.

*desservir[1] [desɛrvir] *v* clear the table; (*nuire*) harm, do a disservice to.

*desservir[2] [desɛrvir] *v* (*transport*) serve; (*porte*) lead into.

dessin [desɛ̃] *nm* drawing; (*motif*) pattern; (*contour*) outline. **dessin animé** cartoon (film). **dessin humoristique** cartoon. **dessinateur, -trice** *nm, nf* draughtsman; designer; cartoonist.

dessiner [desine] *v* draw; design. **se dessiner** stand out; become apparent.

dessous [dəsu] *adv* under, below. *nm* bottom, underside. **avoir le dessous** get the worst of it. **dessous de plat** table mat. **dessous de verre** coaster.

dessus [dəsy] *adv* above, over, on top. *nm* top. **avoir le dessus** have the upper hand. **dessus de lit** bedspread.

destin [dɛstɛ̃] *nm* fate, destiny.

destination [dɛstinasjɔ̃] *nf* destination. **à destination de** bound for.

destiner [dɛstine] *v* destine; intend. **destinée** *nf* fate, destiny.

destituer [dɛstitɥe] *v* dismiss. **destitution** *nf* dismissal, discharge.

destruction [dɛstryksjɔ̃] *nf* destruction. **destructif** *adj* destructive.

désuet, -ète [desɥɛ, -ɛt] *adj* outdated. **désuétude** *nf* disuse. **tomber en désuétude** become obsolete.

désunir [dezynir] *v* divide, disunite.

détacher[1] [detaʃe] *v* (*dénouer*) untie, undo; (*ôter*) remove; separate. **se détacher** come undone; come off *or* away; (*ressortir*) stand out. **se détacher de** renounce. **détachable** *adj* detachable. **détachement** *nm* detachment.

détacher[2] [detaʃe] *v* clean, remove stains from. **détachant** *nm* stain remover.

détail [detaj] *nm* detail; (*facture*) breakdown; (*comm*) retail.

détailler [detaje] *v* explain in detail; (*articles*) sell separately; (*comm*) retail. **détaillant, -e** *nm, nf* retailer. **détaillé** *adj* detailed.

détective [detɛktiv] *nm* détective privé private detective.

*déteindre [detɛ̃drə] *v* (*au soleil*) fade; (*au lavage*) run.

détendre [detɑ̃drə] *v* release, loosen. **se détendre** relax.
***détenir** [detnir] *v* have, hold; (*prisonnier*) detain. **détenteur, -trice** *nm, nf* holder. **détenu, -e** *nm, nf* prisoner.
détente [detɑ̃t] *nf* relaxation; (*élan*) spring; (*gâchette*) trigger.
détergent [detɛrʒɑ̃] *nm, adj* detergent.
détériorer [deterjɔre] *v* damage. **se détériorer** deteriorate. **détérioration** *nf* damage; deterioration.
déterminer [detɛrmine] *v* determine; fix; decide. **se déterminer** make up one's mind. **détermination** *nf* determination; resolution. **déterminé** *adj* determined; specific.
déterrer [detere] *v* dig up, unearth.
détester [detɛste] *v* hate, detest. **détestable** *adj* loathsome.
détoner [detɔne] *v* detonate. **détonant** *nm, adj* explosive. **détonateur** *nm* detonator.
détonner [detɔne] *v* clash, be out of place; (*musique*) go out of tune.
détour [detur] *nm* detour; (*courbe*) bend. **sans détours** straight out.
détourner [deturne] *v* divert; (*regard*) turn away; (*avion*) hijack; (*argent*) embezzle. **détourné** *adj* indirect, roundabout. **détournement** *nm* diversion; hijacking; embezzlement.
détraqué [detrake] *adj* broken down, out of order; (*temps*) unsettled; (*fam: personne*) crazy.
détremper [detrɑ̃pe] *v* soak; dilute, mix with water.
détresse [detrɛs] *nf* distress.
détritus [detritys] *nm pl* rubbish *sing*, refuse *sing*.
***détruire** [detrɥir] *v* destroy; ruin.
dette [dɛt] *nf* debt.
deuil [dœj] *nm* mourning; (*perte*) bereavement.
deux [dø] *adj* two; (*quelques*) a couple of; (*épelant*) double. *nm* two. **deux-points** *nm invar* colon. **(tous) les deux** both. **tous les deux jours** every other day. **deuxième** *n(m+f), adj* second.
dévaler [devale] *v* rush *or* hurtle down.
dévaliser [devalize] *v* burgle, rob.
dévaluer [devalɥe] *v* devalue. **dévaluation** *nf* devaluation.
devancer [dəvɑ̃se] *v* forestall; (*question, etc.*) anticipate; (*coureur*) get ahead of, leave behind. **devancier, -ère** *nm, nf* precursor.
devant [dəvɑ̃] *prep* in front of, before. *adv* in front, ahead. *nm* front. **aller au-devant de** anticipate.
devanture [dəvɑ̃tyr] *nf* (*étalage*) window, display; (*façade*) shop front. **à la devanture** in the window.
dévaster [devaste] *v* devastate. **dévastation** *nf* devastation.
développer [devlɔpe] *v* develop; (*industrie, etc.*) expand. **se développer** develop, spread. **développement** *nm* development; expansion.
***devenir** [dəvnir] *v* become.
dévergondé [devɛrgɔ̃de] *adj* shameless; licentious.
déverser [devɛrse] *v* pour out. **déversoir** *nm* overflow.
dévêtir [devetir] *v* undress.
dévier [devje] *v* deviate, veer off course; divert. **déviation** *nf* deviation; diversion.
deviner [dəvine] *v* guess; (*énigme*) solve. **devinette** *nf* riddle.
devis [dəvi] *nm* estimate.
dévisager [devizaʒe] *v* stare at.
devise [dəviz] *nf* motto; (*comm*) slogan. **devises** *nf pl* currency *sing*.
dévisser [devise] *v* unscrew.
dévoiler [devwale] *v* unveil; reveal, disclose.
***devoir** [dəvwar] *v* have to, must; (*argent, etc.*) owe. *nm* duty; (*école*) homework.
dévorer [devɔre] *v* devour; consume.
dévot [devo], **-e** *adj* devout, pious. *nm, nf* pious person. **dévotion** *nf* devoutness.
se dévouer [devwe] *v* devote oneself; sacrifice oneself. **dévouement** *nm* devotion.
dextérité [dɛksterite] *nf* skill, dexterity.
diabète [djabɛt] *nm* diabetes. **diabétique** *n(m+f), adj* diabetic.
diable [djɑblə] *nm* devil. **diablerie** *nf* mischief. **diabolique** *adj* diabolical.
diablotin [djɑblɔtɛ̃] *nm* (*enfant*) imp; (*pétard*) cracker.
diadème [djadɛm] *nm* diadem; (*bijou*) tiara.
diagnostiquer [djagnɔstike] *v* diagnose. **diagnostic** *nm* diagnosis.
diagonal [djagɔnal] *adj* diagonal. **diagonale** *nf* diagonal.
dialecte [djalɛkt] *nm* dialect.
dialogue [djalɔg] *nm* dialogue, conversation.
diamant [djamɑ̃] *nm* diamond.

diamètre [djamɛtrə] *nm* diameter. **diamétralement opposé** diametrically opposed.
diaphragme [djafragmə] *nm* diaphragm.
diapositive [djapozitiv] *nf* slide, transparency.
diapré [djapre] *adj* mottled.
diarrhée [djare] *nf* diarrhoea.
dictateur [diktatœr] *nm* dictator. **dictature** *nf* dictatorship.
dicter [dikte] *v* dictate. **dictée** *nf* dictation.
dictionnaire [diksjɔnɛr] *nm* dictionary.
dicton [diktɔ̃] *nm* saying.
dièse [djɛz] *nm*, *adj* sharp.
diesel [djezɛl] *nm* diesel.
diète [djɛt] *nf* diet.
dieu [djø] *nm* god.
diffamer [difame] *v* slander; (*par écrit*) libel. **diffamation** *nf* slander; libel. **diffamatoire** *adj* slanderous; libellous.
différence [diferɑ̃s] *nf* difference. **à la différence de** unlike. **différent** *adj* different.
différencier [diferɑ̃sje] *v* differentiate. **différenciation** *nf* differentiation.
différend [diferɑ̃] *nm* disagreement, difference of opinion.
différentiel [diferɑ̃sjɛl], **-elle** *n*, *adj* differential.
différer [difere] *v* differ; (*renvoyer*) defer, postpone.
difficile [difisil] *adj* difficult. **difficulté** *nf* difficulty.
difforme [difɔrm] *adj* deformed. **difformité** *nf* deformity.
diffuser [difyze] *v* diffuse, spread; (*émission*) broadcast.
digérer [diʒere] *v* digest.
digestion [diʒɛstjɔ̃] *nf* digestion.
digitale [diʒital] *nf* **digitale pourprée** foxglove.
digne [diɲ] *adj* worthy; (*grave*) dignified.
dignité [diɲite] *nf* dignity.
dique [dig] *nf* dyke.
dilapider [dilapide] *v* squander; (*détourner*) embezzle.
dilater [dilate] *v* dilate, distend. **se dilater** swell, expand. **dilatation** *nf* dilation.
dilemme [dilɛm] *nm* dilemma.
diluer [dilɥe] *v* dilute. **dilution** *nf* dilution.
dimanche [dimɑ̃ʃ] *nm* Sunday. **dimanche des Rameaux** Palm Sunday.
dimension [dimɑ̃sjɔ̃] *nf* dimension, size, measurement.
diminuer [diminɥe] *v* diminish, reduce,

decrease. **diminutif** *nm*, *adj* diminutive. **diminution** *nf* reduction, decrease.
dinde [dɛ̃d] *nf* turkey. **dindon** *nm* turkey.
dîner [dine] *v* have dinner, dine. *nm* dinner. **dîneur, -euse** *nm*, *nf* diner.
dingue [dɛ̃g] (*fam*) *adj* barmy, crazy. *n(m + f)* nutcase.
dinosaure [dinozɔr] *nm* dinosaur.
diocèse [djɔsɛz] *nm* diocese.
diphtongue [diftɔ̃g] *nf* diphthong.
diplomate [diplɔmat] *adj* diplomatic. *n(m + f)* diplomat. *nm* (*cuisine*) trifle. **diplomatie** *nf* diplomacy. **diplomatique** *adj* diplomatic.
diplôme [diplom] *nm* diploma; examination.
diplômé [diplome], **-e** *adj* qualified. *nm*, *nf* holder of a diploma.
***dire** [dir] *v* say, tell. **c'est-à-dire** that is. **vouloir dire** mean.
direct [dirɛkt] *adj* direct, straight, immediate. *nm* fast train, express. **directement** *adv* directly, straight, immediately.
directeur [dirɛktœr] *nm* director; (*responsable*) manager; (*école*) headmaster. **directeur général** managing director. **directrice** *nf* director; manageress; headmistress.
direction [dirɛksjɔ̃] *nf* direction; (*gestion*) management; (*auto*) steering.
diriger [diriʒe] *v* direct; (*gérer*) run, manage; (*arme*) point, aim; steer. **se diriger** find one's way. **se diriger vers** head for.
discerner [disɛrne] *v* discern; distinguish.
disciple [disiplə] *nm* disciple.
discipline [disiplin] *nf* discipline. **disciplinaire** *adj* disciplinary. **discipliner** *v* discipline, control.
discontinu [diskɔ̃tiny] *adj* discontinuous; intermittent.
discorde [diskɔrd] *nf* discord, dissension. **discordant** *adj* discordant.
discothèque [diskɔtɛk] *nf* record collection; (*club*) discotheque.
discours [diskur] *nm* speech.
discréditer [diskredite] *v* discredit. **discrédit** *nm* discredit.
discret, -ète [diskrɛ, -ɛt] *adj* discreet; quiet, sober; (*quantité*) discrete. **discrétion** *nf* discretion. **avec discrétion** discreetly. **discrétionnaire** *adj* discretionary.
discrimination [diskriminasjɔ̃] *nf* discrimination.
discussion [diskysjɔ̃] *nf* discussion; (*querelle*) argument.

discuter [diskyte] *v* discuss; question, dispute; (*protester*) argue. **discutable** *adj* debatable; questionable.

disette [dizɛt] *nf* scarcity, shortage.

disgrâce [disgrɑs] *nf* disgrace. **disgracié** *adj* in disgrace.

disgracieux [disgrasjø] *adj* inelegant; (*laid*) unsightly.

disloquer [dislɔke] *v* (*méd*) dislocate; (*désunir*) dismantle; (*briser*) break up; (*dissoudre*) disperse. **dislocation** *nf* dislocation.

*disparaître [disparɛtrə] *v* disappear, vanish. **faire disparaître** get rid of, remove. **disparition** *nf* disappearance.

disparate [disparat] *adj* disparate, ill-assorted. **disparité** *nf* disparity.

disparu [dispary], **-e** *adj* vanished; (*époque*) bygone; (*mort*) dead; (*mil, etc.*) missing. *nm, nf* dead person; missing person.

dispendieux [dispɑ̃djø] *adj* extravagant, expensive.

dispenser [dispɑ̃se] *v* dispense; exempt. **se dispenser de** avoid, get out of. **dispense** *nf* exemption.

disperser [dispɛrse] *v* disperse, scatter.

disponible [dispɔniblə] *adj* available, free. **disponibilité** *nf* availability.

dispos [dispo] *adj* alert, in good form.

disposer [dispoze] *v* arrange, lay out; (*engager*) dispose, incline. **disposer de** have at one's disposal. **se disposer à** be about to, prepare to. **disposition** *nf* arrangement; disposal; (*humeur*) mood; tendancy; aptitude; (*jur*) clause.

dispositif [dispozitif] *nm* device; plan of action.

disputer [dispyte] *v* fight, contest; (*fam*) tell off. **se disputer** quarrel; fight over. **dispute** *nf* quarrel.

disqualifier [diskalifje] *v* disqualify; (*discréditer*) dishonour. **disqualification** *nf* disqualification.

disque [disk] *nm* disc; (*musique*) record.

dissemblable [disɑ̃blablə] *adj* dissimilar, different. **dissemblance** *nf* dissimilarity.

disséminer [disemine] *v* scatter.

dissentiment [disɑ̃timɑ̃] *nm* disagreement.

disséquer [diseke] *v* dissect.

dissident [disidɑ̃], **-e** *n*, *adj* dissident. **dissidence** *nf* dissidence, rebellion.

dissimuler [disimyle] *v* conceal; disguise. **dissimulation** *nf* dissimulation.

dissiper [disipe] *v* dispel, disperse; (*gaspiller*) waste, squander. **dissipation** *nf* dissipation; dispersal.

dissocier [disɔsje] *v* dissociate. **dissociation** *nf* dissociation.

*dissoudre [disudrə] *v* dissolve.

dissuader [disɥade] *v* dissuade. **dissuasion** *nf* dissuasion.

distance [distɑ̃s] *nf* distance. **distant** *adj* distant.

distiller [distile] *v* distil. **distillerie** *nf* distillery.

distinct [distɛ̃] *adj* distinct. **distinctif** *adj* distinctive. **distinction** *nf* distinction.

distinguer [distɛ̃ge] *v* distinguish; honour. **distingué** *adj* distinguished; eminent.

distraction [distraksjɔ̃] *nf* absent-mindedness, lack of attention; (*détente*) recreation, entertainment.

*distraire [distrɛr] *v* distract; (*divertir*) entertain. **se distraire** amuse oneself. **distrait** *adj* absent-minded.

distribuer [distribɥe] *v* distribute; arrange; (*cartes*) deal; (*courrier*) deliver. **distributeur** *nm* distributor. **distributeur automatique** slot machine. **distribution** *nf* distribution; arrangement; delivery; (*acteurs*) cast.

divaguer [divage] *v* ramble.

divan [divɑ̃] *nm* divan.

diverger [divɛrʒe] *v* diverge. **divergence** *nf* divergence.

divers [divɛr] *adj* diverse; different; (*plusieurs*) various, several. **diversité** *nf* diversity, variety.

divertir [divɛrtir] *v* amuse, entertain. **divertissement** *nm* amusement, entertainment.

dividende [dividɑ̃d] *nm* dividend.

divin [divɛ̃] *adj* divine. **divinité** *nf* divinity.

diviser [divize] *v* divide. **divisible** *adj* divisible. **division** *nf* division; discord.

divorcer [divɔrse] *v* get divorced. **divorce** *nm* divorce. **divorcé, -e** *nm, nf* divorcee.

divulguer [divylge] *v* divulge, disclose.

dix [dis] *nm, adj* ten. **dixième** *n(m + f)*, *adj* tenth.

dix-huit [dizɥit] *nm, adj* eighteen. **dix-huitième** *n(m + f)*, *adj* eighteenth.

dix-neuf [diznœf] *nm, adj* nineteen. **dix-neuvième** *n(m + f)*, *adj* nineteenth.

dix-sept [disɛt] *nm, adj* seventeen. **dix-septième** *n(m + f)*, *adj* seventeenth.

dizaine [dizɛn] *nf* **une dizaine (de)** about ten.

docile [dɔsil] *adj* docile.

docte [dɔktə] *adj* learned.

docteur [dɔktœr] *nm* doctor.

doctrine [dɔktrin] *nf* doctrine.

document [dɔkymɑ̃] *nm* document. **documentaire** *nm*, *adj* documentary. **documentation** *nf* documentation, information, research. **documenter** *v* document, research.

dodu [dɔdy] *adj* (*fam*) plump, chubby.

dogmatique [dɔgmatik] *adj* dogmatic.

dogme [dɔgmə] *nm* dogma.

doigt [dwa] *nm* finger. **doigt de pied** toe. **doigté** *nm* (*musique*) fingering; tact.

doit [dwa] *nm* debit.

doléances [dɔleɑ̃s] *nf pl* complaints *pl*.

dollar [dɔlar] *nm* dollar.

domaine [dɔmɛn] *nm* domain; property, estate; sphere, field.

dôme [dom] *nm* dome.

domestique [dɔmɛstik] *n(m+f)* servant. *adj* domestic.

domestiquer [dɔmɛstike] *v* domesticate. **domestication** *nf* domestication.

domicile [dɔmisil] *nm* home, place of residence; address.

dominer [dɔmine] *v* dominate; surpass; (*contrôler*) master; prevail; (*donner sur*) overlook. **dominant** *adj* dominant, main. **dominateur, -trice** *adj* domineering. **domination** *nf* domination.

dominion [dɔminjɔn] *nm* dominion.

domino [dɔmino] *nm* domino.

dommage [dɔmaʒ] *nm* harm, damage. **dommages-intérêts** *nm pl* damages *pl*. **quel dommage!** what a pity!

dompter [dɔ̃te] *v* tame; subdue; master. **dompteur, -euse** *nm*, *nf* tamer.

don [dɔ̃] *nm* gift; talent; (*argent*) donation. **faire don de** donate. **donateur, -trice** *nm*, *nf* donor.

donc [dɔk] *conj* so, then, thus. **dis donc** I say; tell me. **tais-toi donc!** do be quiet!

donner [dɔne] *v* give; (*cartes*) deal; produce. **donner dans** fall into. **donner pour** present as, make out to be. **donner sur** overlook, open onto. **se donner à** devote oneself to. **donne** *nf* (*cartes*) deal. **donné** *adj* given. **étant donné que** seeing that. **données** *nf pl* data *pl*, facts *pl*. **donneur, -euse** *nm*, *nf* dealer; (*méd*) donor.

dont [dɔ̃] *pron* whose; (*objet*) of which; (*personne*) of whom.

dorénavant [dɔrenavɑ̃] *adv* from now on.

dorer [dɔre] *v* gild; (*cuisine*) brown; (*peau*) tan. **doré** *adj* gilt; (*blé*, *etc*.) golden.

dorloter [dɔrlɔte] *v* pamper, cosset.

***dormir** [dɔrmir] *v* sleep, be asleep. **dormir à poings fermés** sleep soundly.

dortoir [dɔrtwar] *nm* dormitory.

dorure [dɔryr] *nf* gilt, gilding.

dos [do] *nm* back; (*livre*) spine.

dose [doz] *nf* dose, dosage.

dossier [dɔsje] *nm* file; (*siège*) back.

dot [dɔt] *nf* dowry.

doter [dɔte] *v* endow; equip.

douane [dwan] *nf* customs *pl*. **exempté de douane** duty-free. **douanier, -ère** *nm*, *nf* customs officer.

double [dublə] *adj*, *adv* double. *nm* double; copy; duplicate.

doubler [duble] *v* double; (*école*) repeat; (*film*) dub; (*acteur*) stand in for; (*revêtir*) line; (*auto*) overtake. **doubler le pas** speed up. **doublage** *nm* dubbing; lining. **doublure** *nf* lining; (*acteur*) stand-in, understudy.

douceur [dusœr] *nf* softness; (*clémence*) mildness; (*goût*, *son*, *etc*.) sweetness; (*personne*) gentleness.

douche [duʃ] *nf* shower.

douer [dwe] *v* endow. **doué** *adj* gifted, talented.

douille [duj] *v* socket; cartridge case.

douillet, -ette [duje, -ɛt] *adj* cosy, soft.

douleur [dulœr] *nf* pain; (*chagrin*) sorrow, distress. **douloureux** *adj* painful; distressing.

douter [dute] *v* **douter de** doubt. **se douter de** suspect. **doute** *nm* doubt. **mettre en doute** question. **sans doute** doubtless. **douteux** *adj* doubtful; uncertain; (*péj*) dubious.

douve [duv] *nf* moat, ditch.

Douvres [duvrə] *n* Dover.

doux, douce [du, dus] *adj* soft; (*clément*, *pas fort*) mild; (*agréable*, *sucré*) sweet; (*personne*, *pente*) gentle.

douze [duz] *nm*, *adj* twelve. **douzaine** *nf* dozen. **douzième** *n(m+f)*, *adj* twelfth.

doyen [dwajɛ̃], **-enne** *nm*, *nf* dean; senior member.

drachme [drakmə] *nf* drachma.

dragée [draʒe] *nf* sugared almond.

dragon [dragɔ̃] *nm* dragon.

draguer [drage] *v* dredge, drag.
dramatiser [dramatize] *v* dramatize. **dramatique** *adj* dramatic.
dramaturge [dramatyrʒ] *nm, nf* dramatist, playwright.
drame [dram] *nm* drama.
drap [dra] *nm* sheet.
drapeau [drapo] *nm* flag.
draper [drape] *v* drape. **draperie** *nf* drapery. **drapier** *nm* draper.
dresser [drese] *v* put up, erect; (*liste, plan*) draw up; (*lever*) raise; (*animal*) train. **dresser l'oreille** prick up one's ears. **se dresser** stand (up); rise (up). **dressage** *nm* training. **dressoir** *nm* dresser.
drogue [drɔg] *nf* drug. **drogué, -e** *nm, nf* drug addict. **se droguer** take drugs.
droit¹ [drwa] *adj* (*côté*) right; (*ligne*) straight; (*vertical*) upright; honest. *adv* straight. **droitier** *adj* right-handed.
droit² [drwa] *nm* right; (*taxe*) duty; (*d'entrée, etc.*) fee, charge; (*jur*) law. **droits d'auteur** royalties *pl*. **droit de passage** right of way.
droite [drwat] *nf* right, right-hand side.
drôle [drol] *adj* funny. **drôlement** *adv* (*fam*) terribly, awfully.
dromadaire [drɔmadɛr] *nm* dromedary.
dru [dry] *adj* thick, dense. *adv* thick and fast; (*pluie*) heavily.
du [dy] *contraction of* **de le**.
dû, due [dy] *adj* owing, due. *nm* due.
duc [dyk] *nm* duke. **duchesse** *nf* duchess.
duel [dɥɛl] *nm* duel.
dûment [dymã] *adv* duly.
dune [dyn] *nf* dune.
Dunkerque [dœkɛrk] *n* Dunkirk.
duo [dɥo] *nm* duet.
duper [dype] *v* dupe, deceive.
duquel [dykɛl] *contraction of* **de lequel**.
dur [dyr] *adj* hard, stiff, tough; (*pénible*) harsh. *adv* (*fam*) hard. **à la dure** rough. **durcir** *v* harden. **dureté** *nf* hardness.
durer [dyre] *v* last. **durable** *adj* lasting. **durant** *prep* during, for. **durée** *nf* duration, length; (*ampoule, pile, etc.*) life.
duvet [dyvɛ] *nm* down; sleeping-bag.
dynamique [dinamik] *adj* dynamic. *nf* dynamics. **dynamisme** *nm* dynamism.
dynamite [dinamit] *nf* dynamite.
dynamo [dinamo] *nf* dynamo.
dynastie [dinasti] *nf* dynasty.
dysenterie [disãtri] *nf* dysentery.

dyslexie [dislɛksi] *nf* dyslexia. **dyslexique** *n(m+f)*, *adj* dyslexic.
dyspepsie [dispɛpsi] *nf* dyspepsia.

E

eau [o] *nf* water. **eau de Javel** bleach. **eau de vie** brandy. **eau douce** fresh water. **eau gazeuse** soda water. **eau minérale** mineral water. **eau potable** drinking water. **eau salée** salt water. **faire eau** leak. **prendre l'eau** leak.
ébahir [ebair] *v* astound. **ébahi** *adj* flabbergasted, dumbfounded. **ébahissement** *nm* astonishment.
ébats [eba] *nm pl* frolics *pl*.
ébaucher [ebofe] *v* sketch out, outline. **s'ébaucher** take shape. **ébauche** *nf* outline, rough draft.
ébène [ebɛn] *nf* ebony.
éberlué [ebɛrlɥe] *adj* astounded, flabbergasted.
éblouir [ebluir] *v* dazzle. **éblouissement** *nm* dazzle; (*méd*) dizzy turn.
éboulement [ebulmã] *nm* landslide.
ébouriffer [eburife] *v* tousle, ruffle; (*fam*) amaze.
ébranler [ebrãle] *v* shake; (*affaiblir*) weaken. **s'ébranler** move off. **ébranlement** *nm* (*choc*) shock; weakening.
ébrécher [ebrefe] *v* chip, nick; (*fortune*) break into. **ébréchure** *nf* chip, nick.
ébrouer [ebrue] *v* snort; (*s'agiter*) shake oneself. **ébrouement** *nm* snort.
ébullition [ebylisjɔ̃] *nf* boiling point; (*agitation*) turmoil. **en ébullition** boiling; (*ville, personne*) seething.
écailler [ekaje] *v* scale. **s'écailler** flake, peel. **écaille** *nf* scale; (*peinture*) flake; (*de tortue*) tortoise-shell. **écailleux** *adj* scaly, flaky.
écaler [ekale] *v* shell. **écale** *nf* shell.
écarlate [ekarlat] *nf, adj* scarlet.
écarquiller [ekarkije] *v* open wide.
écart [ekar] *nm* gap; difference; (*contradiction*) discrepancy; (*faute*) lapse. **à l'écart** on one side; (*isolé*) out of the way; (*distant*) aloof. **à l'écart de** well away from. **faire le grand écart** do the splits. **faire un écart** (*cheval*) shy; (*auto*) swerve.

écarter [ekarte] *v* separate, open; (*exclure*) dismiss; (*éloigner*) push aside, lead away from. **s'écarter** (*séparer*) part; (*s'éloigner*) move away; deviate, wander. **écarté** *adj* remote.

ecclésiastique [eklezjastik] *adj* ecclesiastical. *nm* ecclesiastic.

écervelé [esɛrvəle], **-e** *adj* scatterbrained. *nm, nf* scatterbrain.

échafaud [eʃafo] *nm* scaffold. **échafaudage** *nm* scaffolding.

échalier [eʃalje] *nm* stile.

échalote [eʃalɔt] *nf* shallot.

échancré [eʃɑ̃kre] *adj* (*robe*) V-necked, with a scooped neckline; (*côte*) indented; (*feuille*) serrated.

échanger [eʃɑ̃ʒe] *v* exchange. **échange** *nm* exchange. **échangeable** *adj* exchangeable.

échantillon [eʃɑ̃tijɔ̃] *nm* sample.

échapper [eʃape] *v* escape. **échapper à** escape (from). **laisser échapper** let out, let slip. **échappatoire** *nf* loophole, way out. **échappement** *nm* (*auto*) exhaust.

écharde [eʃard] *nf* splinter.

écharpe [eʃarp] *nf* scarf; (*méd*) sling; (*maire*) sash.

échasse [eʃas] *nf* stilt.

échauder [eʃode] *v* scald; (*laver*) wash in hot water; (*théière*) warm.

échauffer [eʃofe] *v* make hot; (*moteur*) overheat; excite. **s'échauffer** (*sport*) warm up; (*s'animer*) become heated. **échauffement** *nm* overheating; warm-up.

échéance [eʃeɑ̃s] *nf* expiry date; date of payment; term. **échéant** *adj* due, payable. **le cas échéant** if the case arises.

échec [eʃɛk] *nm* failure; (*revers*) setback; (*jeu*) check. **échec et mat** checkmate. **échecs** *nm pl* (*jeu*) chess *sing*.

échelle [eʃɛl] *nf* ladder; (*carte, etc.*) scale.

échelon [eʃlɔ̃] *nm* rung; step, grade; (*niveau*) level.

échelonner [eʃlɔne] *v* space *or* spread out; (*vacances, etc.*) stagger.

échevelé [eʃəvle] *adj* dishevelled; (*effréné*) wild.

échine [eʃin] *nf* spine.

échiquier [eʃikje] *nm* chessboard.

écho [eko] *nm* echo.

***échoir** [eʃwar] *v* fall due; expire.

échouer [eʃwe] *v* fail; (*naut*) run aground; (*aboutir*) end up. **faire échouer** foil, thwart.

éclabousser [eklabuse] *v* splash. **éclaboussure** *nf* splash; (*tache*) stain, smear.

éclair [eklɛr] *nm* flash; (*temps*) lightning; (*cuisine*) eclair.

éclaircir [eklɛrsir] *v* lighten; (*soupe, plantes*) thin; (*question, mystère*) explain, clarify. **s'éclaircir** (*temps*) clear up; thin out, become thin. **éclaircie** *nf* bright interval, break. **éclaircissement** *nm* clarification.

éclairer [eklere] *v* light up; (*problème, texte*) throw light on; (*personne*) enlighten. **s'éclairer** light up; (*rue, maison, etc.*) be lit. **éclairage** *nm* lighting. **éclaireur** *nm* scout. **éclaireuse** *nf* guide.

éclat [ekla] *nm* brightness; splendour, glamour; fragment, splinter; (*rire, colère*) burst; (*scandale*) fuss.

éclater [eklate] *v* (*pneu*) burst; (*bombe*) explode; (*briser*) break up, shatter; (*guerre*) break out. **éclater de rire** burst out laughing. **faire éclater** blow up. **éclatant** *adj* bright; (*fort*) loud; (*victoire*) resounding.

éclipse [eklips] *nf* eclipse. **éclipser** *v* eclipse.

éclisse [eklis] *nf* splint.

éclopé [eklɔpe] *adj* lame.

***éclore** [eklɔr] *v* hatch; (*fleur*) open out. **éclosion** *nf* hatching; (*apparition*) birth, dawn.

écluse [eklyz] *nf* lock.

écœurer [ekœre] *v* nauseate, sicken; disgust. **écœurant** *adj* disgusting; (*gâteau*) sickly. **écœurement** *nm* nausea; disgust; discouragement.

école [ekɔl] *nf* school. **école de secrétariat** secretarial college. **école maternelle** nursery school. **école normale** college of education. **faire l'école buissonnière** play truant. **écolier** *nm* schoolboy. **écolière** *nf* schoolgirl.

écologie [ekɔlɔʒi] *nf* ecology. **écologique** *adj* ecological.

***éconduire** [ekɔ̃dɥir] *v* dismiss; reject.

économe [ekɔnɔm] *adj* thrifty. **économie** *nf* economy; (*science*) economics; (*épargne*) saving. **faire des économies** save. **économique** *adj* economic.

économiser [ekɔnɔmize] *v* economize, save. **économiste** *n(m + f)* economist.

écoper [ekɔpe] *v* bale out.

écorcer [ekɔrse] *v* peel; (*arbre*) bark. **écorce** *nf* peel; bark.

écorcher [ekɔrʃe] *v* (*animal*) skin; (*égratigner*) graze, scratch; (*frotter*) chafe;

(*fam: estamper*) fleece. **écorchure** *nf* graze, scratch.

écorné [ekɔrne] *adj* (*livre*) dog-eared.

Écosse [ekɔs] *nf* Scotland. **écossais** *adj* Scottish, Scots; (*whisky*) Scotch; (*tissu*) tartan. **Écossais, -e** *nm, nf* Scot.

écot [eko] *nm* share.

écouler [ekule] *v* get rid of; (*comm*) move, sell. **s'écouler** (*liquide*) flow, ooze; pass; sell. **écoulement** *nm* flow; (*méd*) discharge; passing.

écourter [ekurte] *v* shorten.

écouter [ekute] *v* listen (to). **écouter aux portes** eavesdrop.

écouteur, -euse [ekutœr, -øz] *nm, nf* listener; eavesdropper. *nm* (*telephone*) receiver. **écouteurs** *nm pl* headphones *pl*.

écran [ekrɑ̃] *nm* screen.

écraser [ekrɑze] *v* crush; (*voiture*) run over; (*accabler*) overcome. **s'écraser** (*voiture, avion*) crash. **se faire écraser** get run over. **écrasant** *adj* overwhelming; (*poids*) crushing; (*travail*) gruelling.

écrémer [ekreme] *v* cream, skim.

écrevisse [ekrəvis] *nf* crayfish.

s'écrier [ekrije] *v* exclaim.

écrin [ekrɛ̃] *nm* jewel case.

***écrire** [ekrir] *v* write. **écrit** *nm* writing; (*examen*) written paper. **par écrit** in writing. **écriteau** *nm* notice. **écritoire** *nf* writing case. **écriture** *nf* writing; (*comm*) entry.

écrivain [ekrivɛ̃] *nm* writer.

écrou [ekru] *nm* nut.

s'écrouler [ekrule] *v* collapse, crumble, fall (down). **écroulement** *nm* collapse, fall.

écru [ekry] *adj* raw; (*toile*) unbleached.

écu [eky] *nm* shield.

écueil [ekœj] *nm* reef; (*piège*) pitfall.

écuelle [ekɥɛl] *nf* bowl.

écumer [ekyme] *v* skim; (*mousser*) foam, froth; pillage, scour. **écume** *nf* foam, froth; (*crasse*) scum. **écumeux** *adj* frothy.

écureuil [ekyrœj] *nm* squirrel.

écurie [ekyri] *nf* stable.

écuyer [ekɥije], **-ère** *nm* rider.

eczéma [ɛgzema] *nm* eczema.

édenté [edɑ̃te] *adj* toothless.

édifice [edifis] *nm* building; structure.

édifier [edifje] *v* edify; construct, build.

Edimbourg [edɛ̃bur] *n* Edinburgh.

édit [edi] *nm* edict.

éditer [edite] *v* publish; (*annoter*) edit. **éditeur, -trice** *nm, nf* publisher; editor.

édition *nf* publishing; edition. **éditorial** *nm* leading article.

édredon [edrədɔ̃] *nm* eiderdown.

éducation [edykɑsjɔ̃] *nf* education; (*familiale*) upbringing. **éducatif** *adj* educational.

éduquer [edyke] *v* educate; (*élever*) bring up.

effacer [efase] *v* erase, obliterate. **s'effacer** fade, wear away; (*s'écarter*) step aside. **effacé** *adj* faded; (*personne*) retiring.

effarer [efare] *v* alarm. **effarement** *nm* alarm.

effaroucher [efaruʃe] *v* scare; shock. **s'effaroucher** take fright; be shocked.

effectif [efɛktif] *adj* effective, actual, real. *nm* size, strength.

effectuer [efɛktɥe] *v* carry out, make, execute.

efféminé [efemine] *adj* effeminate.

effervescence [efɛrvesɑ̃s] *nf* effervescence; agitation, turmoil.

effet [efɛ] *nm* effect; impression; (*comm*) bill. **effets** *nm pl* things *pl*, clothes *pl*. **en effet** indeed.

s'effeuiller [efœje] *v* shed its leaves.

efficace [efikas] *adj* effective; (*personne*) efficient. **efficacité** *nf* effectiveness; efficiency.

effigie [efiʒi] *nf* effigy.

effiler [efile] *v* (*amincir*) taper; (*forme*) streamline; (*étoffe*) fray.

effleurer [eflœre] *v* touch lightly.

s'effondrer [efɔ̃dre] *v* collapse, cave in. **effondrement** *nm* collapse.

s'efforcer [efɔrse] *v* try hard, do one's best.

effort [efɔr] *nm* effort; (*tech*) stress.

effrayer [efreje] *v* frighten.

effréné [efrene] *adj* wild, frantic.

effriter [efrite] *v* crumble.

effroi [efrwa] *nm* terror. **effroyable** *adj* appalling.

effronté [efrɔ̃te] *adj* insolent, cheeky; (*ehonté*) brazen. **effronterie** *nf* insolence.

égal [egal], **-e** *adj* equal; (*constant*) even. **ça m'est égal** I don't mind. *nm, nf* equal. **également** *adv* equally; (*aussi*) also. **égaler** *v* equal, match. **égalité** *nf* equality; evenness.

égaliser [egalize] *v* equalize; (*sol*) level out.

égard [egar] *nm* respect, consideration. **à l'égard de** (*envers*) towards; concerning. **avoir égard à** take into account.

égarer [egare] v lead astray; (perdre) mislay. **s'égarer** get lost. **égaré** adj lost; (animal) stray; (isolé) remote; (éperdu) distraught.

égayer [egeje] v brighten up; (divertir) amuse.

église [egliz] nf church.

égocentrique [egɔsɑ̃trik] adj self-centred.

égoïste [egɔist] adj selfish. **égoïsme** nm selfishness.

égorger [egɔrʒe] v cut the throat of.

égout [egu] nm sewer, drain.

égoutter [egute] v drain; (linge) drip. **égouttoir** nm draining board.

égratigner [egratiɲe] v scratch, scrape. **égratignure** nf scratch.

égrener [egrəne] v (écosser) shell; (raisins) pick off; (chapelet) say.

éhonté [eɔ̃te] adj shameless, brazen.

éjaculer [eʒakyle] v ejaculate. **éjaculation** nf ejaculation.

éjecter [eʒɛkte] v eject.

élaborer [elabɔre] v work out, elaborate.

élaguer [elage] v prune. **élagage** nm pruning.

élan [elɑ̃] nm rush, surge; (vitesse) momentum; vigour, spirit.

s'élancer [elɑ̃se] v rush, dash. **élancé** adj slender. **élancement** nm sharp pain.

élargir [elarʒir] v widen, stretch; (jur) release.

élastique [elastik] adj elastic; flexible. nm elastic; rubber band.

élection [elɛksjɔ̃] nf election; choice. **élection partielle** by-election.

électoral [elɛktɔral] adj electoral. **électorat** nm electorate.

électricité [elɛktrisite] nf electricity. **électricien** nm electrician.

électrique [elɛktrik] adj electric.

électriser [elɛktrize] v electrify.

électrocuter [elɛktrɔkyte] v electrocute. **électrocution** nf electrocution.

électrode [elɛktrɔd] nf electrode.

électronique [elɛktrɔnik] adj electronic. nf electronics.

électrophone [elɛktrɔfɔn] nm record player.

élégant [elegɑ̃] adj elegant. **élégance** nf elegance.

élégie [eleʒi] nf elegy.

élément [elemɑ̃] nm element; fact; (préfabriqué) unit. **éléments** nm pl rudiments pl. **élémentaire** adj elementary, basic.

éléphant [elefɑ̃] nm elephant.

élevage [ɛlvaʒ] nm breeding, rearing; farm. **faire l'élevage de** breed, rear.

élévation [elevasjɔ̃] nf elevation; (action) raising; erection.

élève [elɛv] n(m+f) pupil, student.

élever [ɛlve] v raise; (enfant) bring up; (animal) rear, breed; erect. **s'élever** rise, go up. **s'élever à** add up to. **élevé** adj high, lofty. **bien/mal élevé** well-/ill-mannered.

elfe [ɛlf] nm elf.

éligible [eliʒiblə] adj eligible.

éliminer [elimine] v eliminate. **élimination** nf elimination.

***élire** [elir] v elect.

élite [elit] nf elite.

elle [ɛl] pron (sujet: personne) she; (objet: personne) her; (chose, animal) it. **elle-même** pron herself; itself. **elles** pron (sujet) they; (objet) them. **elles-mêmes** pron themselves.

ellipse [elips] nf ellipse. **elliptique** adj elliptical.

élocution [elɔkysjɔ̃] nf elocution, diction. **défaut d'élocution** nm speech impediment.

éloge [elɔʒ] nm praise. **faire l'éloge de** praise.

éloigner [elwaɲe] v remove; move or take away; (ajourner) postpone. **s'éloigner** go away. **éloigné** adj distant, far. **éloignement** nm distance; removal; absence; postponement.

éloquent [elɔkɑ̃] adj eloquent. **éloquence** nf eloquence.

élu [ely], -e adj elected, chosen. nm, nf elected member or representative.

éluder [elyde] v evade, elude.

émaciation [emasjasjɔ̃] nf emaciation. **émacié** adj emaciated.

émail [emaj] nm, pl -aux enamel. **émailler** v enamel; (parsemer) dot.

émanciper [emɑ̃sipe] v emancipate, liberate. **émancipation** nf emancipation, liberation.

emballer [ɑ̃bale] v pack, wrap; (fam) thrill. **s'emballer** (moteur) race; (cheval) bolt; (fam) get worked up. **emballage** nm packing, wrapping; (comm) package.

embarcadère [ɑ̃barkadɛr] nm landing stage, pier.

embardée [ɑ̃barde] nf swerve. **faire une embardée** swerve.

embargo [ɑ̃bargo] *nm* embargo.

embarquer [ɑ̃barke] *v* embark, board; (*cargaison*) load. **s'embarquer dans** (*fam*) get involved in. **embarquement** *nm* boarding; loading.

embarras [ɑ̃bara] *nm* obstacle; (*gêne*) embarrassment; (*situation difficile*) predicament; dilemma. **faire des embarras** make a fuss.

embarrasser [ɑ̃barase] *v* hinder, hamper; put in a predicament. **s'embarrasser** be troubled; (*s'emmêler*) get tangled up. **embarrassant** *adj* awkward. **embarrassé** *adj* embarrassed, ill-at-ease; confused.

embaucher [ɑ̃boʃe] *v* take on, hire.

embaumer [ɑ̃bome] *v* embalm; perfume; (*sentir bon*) be fragrant.

embellir [ɑ̃belir] *v* make attractive; embellish. **embellissement** *nm* embellishment.

embêter [ɑ̃bete] (*fam*) *v* bother, annoy. **s'embêter** be fed up. **embêtement** *nm* nuisance, annoyance.

emblée [ɑ̃ble] *adv* **d'emblée** straight away.

emblème [ɑ̃blɛm] *nm* emblem.

emboîter [ɑ̃bwate] *v* fit together.

embouchure [ɑ̃buʃyr] *nf* (*fleuve*) mouth; (*musique*) mouthpiece.

embouteiller [ɑ̃buteje] *v* block. **embouteillage** *nm* traffic jam.

emboutir [ɑ̃butir] *v* crash intó.

embrancher [ɑ̃brɑ̃ʃe] *v* join up. **embranchement** *nm* branch; junction.

embraser [ɑ̃braze] *v* set ablaze. **s'embraser** blaze up, flare up. **embrasement** *nm* blaze.

embrasser [ɑ̃brase] *v* embrace; (*donner un baiser*) kiss.

embrayer [ɑ̃breje] *v* (*auto*) let in the clutch. **embrayage** *nm* clutch.

embrouiller [ɑ̃bruje] *v* muddle (up); (*ficelle*) tangle (up).

embryon [ɑ̃brijɔ̃] *nm* embryo.

embuscade [ɑ̃byskad] *nf* ambush.

éméché [emeʃe] *adj* tipsy.

émeraude [ɛmrod] *nf, adj* emerald.

émerger [emɛrʒe] *v* emerge.

émerveiller [emɛrveje] *v* fill with wonder. **s'émerveiller de** marvel at. **émerveillement** *nm* wonder.

*émettre [emɛtrə] *v* give out, emit; (*TV, radio*) transmit, broadcast; (*monnaie, etc.*) issue. **émetteur** *nm* transmitter.

émeu [emø] *nm* emu.

émeute [emøt] *nf* riot.

émietter [emjete] *v* crumble; split up, disperse.

émigrer [emigre] *v* emigrate; (*oiseau*) migrate. **émigrant, -e** *nm, nf* emigrant. **émigration** *nf* emigration.

éminent [eminɑ̃] *adj* eminent.

émission [emisjɔ̃] *nf* (*radio, TV*) programme, broadcast; emission; issue.

emmagasiner [ɑ̃magazine] *v* store (up). **emmagasinage** *nm* storage.

emmancher [ɑ̃mɑ̃ʃe] *v* put a handle on; (*fam*) make a start (on). **emmanchure** [ɑ̃mɑ̃ʃyr] *nf* armhole.

emmêler [ɑ̃mele] *v* tangle; confuse, muddle.

emménager [ɑ̃menaʒe] *v* move in.

emmener [ɑ̃mne] *v* take (away), (*équipe*) lead.

emmitoufler [ɑ̃mitufle] *v* muffle up.

émoi [emwa] *nm* agitation, commotion.

émonder [emɔ̃de] *v* prune.

émotion [emosjɔ̃] *nf* emotion; (*peur*) fright. **émotif** or **émotionnel** *adj* emotional.

*émouvoir [emuvwar] *v* move, affect; (*indigner*) rouse; (*troubler*) upset. **émouvant** *adj* (*compassion*) moving, touching; (*admiration*) stirring.

empailler [ɑ̃paje] *v* stuff.

empaqueter [ɑ̃pakte] *v* pack, wrap up. **empaquetage** *nm* packing.

emparer [ɑ̃pare] *v* **s'emparer de** seize, take possession of.

empâter [ɑ̃pate] *v* thicken, fatten.

empêcher [ɑ̃peʃe] *v* prevent, stop. **n'empêche (que)** all the same.

empereur [ɑ̃prœr] *nm* emperor.

empeser [ɑ̃pəze] *v* starch.

empester [ɑ̃pɛste] *v* stink.

s'empêtrer [ɑ̃petre] *v* get entangled *or* involved.

empiéter [ɑ̃pjete] *v* encroach.

s'empiffrer [ɑ̃pifre] *v* (*fam*) stuff oneself.

empiler [ɑ̃pile] *v* pile, stack.

empire [ɑ̃pir] *nm* empire; influence.

empirer [ɑ̃pire] *v* worsen.

empirique [ɑ̃pirik] *adj* empirical.

emplacement [ɑ̃plasmɑ̃] *nm* site.

emplâtre [ɑ̃platrə] *nm* plaster.

emplette [ɑ̃plɛt] *nf* purchase. **faire des emplettes** do some shopping.

emplir [ɑ̃plir] v fill.

emploi [ɑ̃plwa] nm use; (poste) job, employment. **emploi du temps** timetable, schedule.

employer [ɑ̃plwaje] v use; (ouvrier) employ. **s'employer à** apply oneself to. **employé, -e** nm, nf employee; (bureau) clerk. **employeur, -euse** nm, nf employer.

empoigner [ɑ̃pwaɲe] v grasp, grab; (lecture, etc.) grip.

empoisonner [ɑ̃pwazɔne] v poison; (empester) stink; (fam) annoy, aggravate. **empoisonnement** nm poisoning; (fam) bother.

emporter [ɑ̃pɔrte] v take (away); (entraîner) carry away or along; (gagner) win. **l'emporter sur** get the better of. **s'emporter** lose one's temper. **emporté** adj angry; (personne) quick-tempered. **emportement** nm anger.

s'empourprer [ɑ̃purpre] v flush, turn crimson.

***empreindre** [ɑ̃prɛ̃drə] v imprint; (marquer) stamp, tinge.

empreinte [ɑ̃prɛ̃t] nf impression; mark, stamp; (animal) track. **empreinte de pas** footprint. **empreinte digitale** fingerprint.

s'empresser [ɑ̃prese] v (se hâter) hurry; (s'affairer) bustle around. **empressé** adj attentive; (péj) over-zealous. **empressement** nm attentiveness; (hâte) eagerness.

emprisonner [ɑ̃prizɔne] v imprison. **emprisonnement** nm imprisonment.

emprunter [ɑ̃prœ̃te] v borrow; derive. **emprunt** nm loan. **d'emprunt** (nom) assumed. **emprunté** adj ill-at-ease, awkward.

ému [emy] adj moved, touched; excited; emotional.

emulsion [emylsjɔ̃] nf emulsion.

en[1] [ɑ̃] prep in; (à) to; (transport) by; (comme) as; (composition) made of; (durée) while, when.

en[2] [ɑ̃] pron of it or them; (lieu) from there; (cause) about it; (des) some, any.

encadrer [ɑ̃kadre] v frame; (entourer) surround; (instruire) train. **encadrement** nm frame; training.

encaisser [ɑ̃kese] v collect; (chèque) cash. **encaisse** nf cash in hand.

enceinte[1] [ɑ̃sɛ̃t] adj pregnant.

enceinte[2] [ɑ̃sɛ̃t] nf enclosure; (mur) surrounding wall; (palissade) fence.

encens [ɑ̃sɑ̃] nm incense.

encercler [ɑ̃sɛrkle] v surround, encircle.

enchaîner [ɑ̃ʃene] v chain up; (lier) link together; continue, carry on. **enchaînement** nm series, chain.

enchanter [ɑ̃ʃɑ̃te] v enchant; (ravir) delight. **enchanté** adj delighted; (salutation) pleased to meet you. **enchantement** nm enchantment; magic; delight.

enchère [ɑ̃ʃɛr] nf bid. **enchères** nf pl auction sing.

enchérir [ɑ̃ʃerir] v **enchérir sur** (comm) bid higher than; (dépasser) go further than. **enchérisseur, -euse** nm, nf bidder.

enchevêtrer [ɑ̃ʃəvetre] v entangle; confuse, muddle.

enclin [ɑ̃klɛ̃] adj inclined, prone.

***enclore** [ɑ̃klɔr] v enclose, shut in.

enclos [ɑ̃klo] nm enclosure; (chevaux) paddock.

enclume [ɑ̃klym] nf anvil.

encoche [ɑ̃kɔʃ] nf notch.

encoignure [ɑ̃kɔɲyr] nf corner.

encolure [ɑ̃kɔlyr] nf neck; (comm) collar size.

encombrer [ɑ̃kɔ̃bre] v clutter, obstruct; (ligne téléphonique) block. **s'encombrer de** load oneself with. **encombrant** adj cumbersome. **sans encombre** without mishap. **encombrement** nm congestion; clutter.

encontre [ɑ̃kɔ̃trə] prep **à l'encontre de** against, counter to; contrary to.

encore [ɑ̃kɔr] adv (toujours) still; (de nouveau) again; (en plus) more; (aussi) also; (même) even. **pas encore** not yet.

encorner [ɑ̃kɔrne] v gore.

encourager [ɑ̃kuraʒe] v encourage. **encouragement** nm encouragement.

***encourir** [ɑ̃kurir] v incur.

encrasser [ɑ̃krase] v clog (up); (salir) dirty.

encre [ɑ̃krə] nf ink.

encroûter [ɑ̃krute] v encrust. **s'encroûter** (fam) get into a rut.

encyclopédie [ɑ̃siklɔpedi] nf encyclopedia.

endémique [ɑ̃demik] adj endemic.

s'endetter [ɑ̃dete] v get into debt. **endetté** adj in debt.

endiablé [ɑ̃djable] adj boisterous, wild.

s'endimancher [ɑ̃dimɑ̃ʃe] v put on one's Sunday best.

endive [ɑ̃div] nf endive; chicory.

endoctriner [ɑ̃dɔktrine] v indoctrinate. **endoctrination** nf indoctrination.

endolori [ãdɔlɔri] *adj* painful.
endommager [ãdɔmaʒe] *v* damage.
endommagement *nm* damage.
*endormir [ãdɔrmir] *v* send to sleep;
(*douleur*) deaden. **s'endormir** *v* fall
asleep. **endormi** *adj* asleep.
endosser [ãdose] *v* (*vêtement*) put on;
(*chèque, etc.*) endorse. **endossement** *nm*
endorsement.
endroit [ãdrwa] *nm* place; (*roman, film,
etc.*) point, part. **à l'endroit** (*vêtement*)
the right side out; (*objet*) the right way
round.
*enduire [ãdɥir] *v* coat. **enduit** *nm* coating.
endurcir [ãdyrsir] *v* harden.
endurer [ãdyre] *v* endure. **endurance** *nf*
endurance.
énergie [enerʒi] *nf* energy; (*fermeté*) spirit, force. **énergique** *adj* energetic; forceful.
énerver [ãnɛrve] *v* irritate. **s'énerver** get
excited.
enfant [ãfã] *n(m+f)* child (*pl* children).
enfant unique only child. **enfance** *nf*
childhood; (*bébé*) infancy. **enfantin** *adj*
childlike; (*puéril*) childish.
enfanter [ãfãte] *v* give birth (to).
enfer [ãfɛr] *nm* hell.
enfermer [ãfɛrme] *v* shut up *or* in; (*sous
clef*) lock up.
enfiler [ãfile] *v* thread; (*fam: vêtement*)
slip on; (*rue, etc.*) take.
enfin [ãfɛ̃] *adv* at last, finally; (*bref*) in
short; (*après tout*) after all.
enflammer [ãflame] *v* (*allumer*) set fire
to; (*irriter*) inflame. **s'enflammer** catch
fire; (*colère, désir*) flare up. **enflammé** *adj*
blazing; inflamed.
enfler [ãfle] *v* swell. **enflé** *adj* swollen.
enflure *nf* swelling.
enfoncer [ãfɔ̃se] *v* (*clou, etc.*) drive in;
(*porte*) break down. **s'enfoncer** sink,
plunge.
enfouir [ãfwir] *v* bury.
*enfreindre [ãfrɛ̃drə] *v* infringe.
*s'enfuir [ãfɥir] *v* run away.
engager [ãgaʒe] *v* engage; (*lier*) bind;
(*entraîner*) involve; (*clef, etc.*) insert.
s'engager (*promettre*) commit oneself,
undertake; (*mil*) enlist. **engagement** *nm*
(*promesse*) agreement; enlistment;
(*acteur*) engagement.
engelure [ãʒlyr] *nf* chilblain.
engendrer [ãʒãdre] *v* generate, create.

engin [ãʒɛ̃] *nm* machine; (*outil*) tool.
englober [ãglɔbe] *v* include.
engloutir [ãglutir] *v* (*navire*) swallow up;
(*manger*) gulp down.
engorger [ãgɔrʒe] *v* block.
engouffrer [ãgufre] *v* engulf; (*fam: manger*) wolf down. **s'engouffrer** rush.
engourdir [ãgurdir] *v* numb; (*esprit*) dull.
engourdi *adj* numb. **engourdissement** *nm*
numbness.
engrais [ãgrɛ] *nm* fertilizer; (*organique*)
manure.
engraisser [ãgrese] *v* (*animal*) fatten up;
(*terre*) fertilize.
engrenage [ãgrənaʒ] *nm* (*tech*) gearing;
(*enchaînement*) chain.
engueuler [ãgœle] (*fam*) *v* shout at.
s'engueuler have a row. **engueulade** *nf*
shouting at; (*dispute*) row.
enhardir [ãardir] *v* embolden. **s'enhardir**
become bolder.
énigme [enigmə] *nf* (*mystère*) enigma;
(*devinette*) riddle, puzzle. **énigmatique** *adj*
enigmatic.
enivrer [ãnivre] *v* intoxicate. **s'enivrer** get
drunk. **enivrement** *nm* intoxication.
enjamber [ãʒãbe] *v* step over; (*pont*)
straddle. **enjambée** *nf* stride.
enjeu [ãʒø] *nm* stake.
enjôler [ãʒole] *v* coax.
enjoliveur [ãʒɔlivœr] *nm* (*auto*) hub cap.
enjoué [ãʒwe] *adj* jolly, playful. **enjouement** *nm* jollity, playfulness.
enlacer [ãlase] *v* entwine. **s'enlacer** (*fils*)
intertwine; (*amants*) embrace.
enlaidir [ãledir] *v* (*déparer*) make ugly;
(*personne*) become ugly.
enlever [ãlve] *v* remove, take off *or* away;
kidnap. **s'enlever** come off. **enlèvement**
nm kidnapping; removal.
enliser [ãlize] *v* get stuck. **s'enliser** sink.
ennemi [ɛnmi], **-e** *nm, nf* enemy. *adj* hostile. **être ennemi de** be opposed to.
ennui [ãnɥi] *nm* boredom; (*difficulté*)
trouble.
ennuyer [ãnɥije] *v* (*lasser*) bore;
(*inquiéter*) worry; (*importuner*) bother;
(*agacer*) annoy. **s'ennuyer** be bored.
ennuyeux *adj* boring, annoying.
énoncer [enɔ̃se] *v* state.
enorgueillir [ãnɔrgœjir] *v* make proud.
s'enorgueillir de boast about.
énorme [enɔrm] *adj* enormous. **énormément** *adv* tremendously. **énormément de**
a tremendous amount of.

s'enquérir [ãkerir] *v* inquire. **s'enquérir de** ask after.

enquête [ãkɛt] *nf* inquiry; (*police*) investigation; (*sondage*) survey; (*mort*) inquest. **enquêter** *v* investigate.

enraciné [ãrasine] *adj* deep-rooted, entrenched.

enragé [ãraʒe], **-e** *nm, nf* (*fam*) fanatic. *adj* furious; (*fam*) mad keen. **enrager** *v* be furious.

enrayer [ãreje] *v* (*maladie*) check; (*machine*) jam. **s'enrayer** jam.

enregistrer [ãrʒistre] *v* register; (*son*) record. **enregistrement** *nm* registration; recording.

s'enrhumer [ãryme] *v* catch a cold. **être enrhumé** have a cold.

enrichir [ãriʃir] *v* enrich. **enrichissement** *nm* enrichment.

enrôler [ãrole] *v* enrol; (*mil*) enlist. **enrôlé** *nm* recruit. **enrôlement** *nm* enrolment; enlistment.

enroué [ãrwe] *adj* hoarse.

enseigne [ãsɛɲ] *nf* sign; (*mil, naut*) ensign.

enseigner [ãseɲe] *v* teach. **enseignant, -e** *nm, nf* teacher. **enseignement** *nm* education; teaching.

ensemble [ãsãblə] *adv* together. *nm* whole; unity; (*groupe*) set; (*vêtements*) outfit. **dans l'ensemble** on the whole. **d'ensemble** overall.

ensemencer [ãsmãse] *v* sow.

ensevelir [ãsəvlir] *v* bury; (*cacher*) shroud, hide.

ensoleillé [ãsɔleje] *adj* sunny.

ensorceler [ãsɔrsəle] *v* bewitch, cast a spell on.

ensuite [ãsɥit] *adv* then, next; afterwards.

*s'ensuivre [ãsɥivrə] *v* follow.

entaille [ãtaj] *nf* cut, gash, notch. **entailler** *v* cut, gash, notch.

entamer [ãtame] *v* start (on), open; (*couper*) cut into.

entasser [ãtase] *v* pile up; amass; (*serrer*) cram.

entendre [ãtãdrə] *v* hear; (*écouter*) listen to; (*comprendre*) understand; intend, mean. **entendre parler de** hear of. **s'entendre** agree; (*s'accorder*) get on. **entendu** *adj* agreed; understood. **bien entendu** of course.

entente [ãtãt] *nf* understanding; (*accord*) agreement; harmony.

enterrer [ãtere] *v* bury. **enterrement** *nm* burial; (*cérémonie*) funeral.

en-tête *nm* heading. **papier à lettres à en-tête** *nm* headed notepaper.

entêté [ãtete] *adj* stubborn. **entêtement** *nm* stubbornness.

enthousiaste [ãtuzjast] *n(m+f)* enthusiast. *adj* enthusiastic. **enthousiasme** *nm* enthusiasm. **s'enthousiasmer** *v* be enthusiastic.

enticher [ãtiʃe] *v* **s'enticher de** become infatuated with.

entier [ãtje] *adj* entire, whole; intact; absolute. **en entier** totally. **tout entier** entirely, completely.

entité [ãtite] *nf* entity.

entonnoir [ãtɔnwar] *nm* funnel.

entorse [ãtɔrs] *nf* sprain, twist.

entortiller [ãtɔrtije] *v* twist, wind; (*fam: enjôler*) get round. **s'entortiller** twist; get entangled.

entourer [ãture] *v* surround. **entourage** *nm* circle, entourage; (*bordure*) surround.

entracte [ãtrakt] *nm* interval, interlude.

entrailles [ãtraj] *nf pl* entrails *pl*.

entrain [ãtrɛ̃] *nm* spirit, gusto.

entraîner [ãtrene] *v* carry along; (*causer*) bring about; (*athlète*) train; (*influencer*) lead. **entraînement** *nm* training; force, impetus. **entraîneur, -euse** *nm, nf* trainer, coach.

entraver [ãtrave] *v* hinder; (*animal*) shackle. **entrave** *nf* hindrance; shackle.

entre [ãtrə] *prep* between; (*parmi*) among; (*dans*) in.

entrebâillé [ãtrəbaje] *adj* ajar.

s'entrechoquer [ãtrəʃɔke] *v* knock together; (*verres*) clink.

entrecouper [ãtrəkupe] *v* interrupt, intersperse. **s'entrecouper** intersect.

s'entrecroiser [ãtrəkrwaze] *v* (*fils*) intertwine; (*lignes*) intersect.

entrée [ãtre] *nf* entry, entrance; (*accès*) admission; (*début*) outset; (*cuisine*) first course, entrée.

entrefaites [ãtrəfɛt] *nf pl* **sur ces entrefaites** at that moment.

entrefilet [ãtrəfilɛ] *nm* paragraph; (*journal*) item.

entremets [ãtrəmɛ] *nm* dessert.

*s'entremettre [ãtrəmɛtrə] *v* intervene. **entremise** *nf* intervention.

entrepôt [ãtrəpo] *nm* warehouse.

*entreprendre [ãtrəprãdrə] *v* undertake;

(*commencer*) begin, embark upon.
entreprenant *adj* enterprising.
entrepreneur, -euse [ɑ̃trəprənœr, -øz] *nm*, *nf* contractor. **entrepreneur de pompes funèbres** undertaker.
entreprise [ɑ̃trəpriz] *nf* firm; enterprise, venture.
entrer [ɑ̃tre] *v* enter, go *or* come in. **faire entrer** (*personne*) show in; (*objet*) put in. **laisser entrer** let in.
entre-temps *adv* meanwhile.
***entretenir** [ɑ̃trətnir] *v* maintain; (*famille*) support; (*sentiment*) keep alive. **s'entretenir** converse; support oneself. **entretien** *nm* maintenance, upkeep; (*subsistance*) keep; discussion, conversation; interview.
***entrevoir** [ɑ̃trəvwar] *v* make out, glimpse.
entrevue [ɑ̃trəvy] *nf* meeting; interview.
entrouvert [ɑ̃truvɛr] *adj* half-open.
envahir [ɑ̃vair] *v* invade; (*occuper*) overrun. **envahissement** *nm* invasion. **envahisseur, -euse** *nm*, *nf* invader.
envelopper [ɑ̃vlɔpe] *v* wrap; (*entourer*) envelop, shroud. **enveloppe** *nf* envelope; (*emballage*) wrapping, covering.
envenimer [ɑ̃vnime] *v* poison; aggravate. **s'envenimer** fester.
envergure [ɑ̃vɛrgyr] *nf* scope, range; (*ailes*) wingspan; calibre.
envers[1] [ɑ̃vɛr] *prep* towards, to.
envers[2] [ɑ̃vɛr] *nm* wrong side; (*médaille*) reverse. **à l'envers** (*vêtement*) inside out; (*dessus dessous*) upside down; (*devant derrière*) back to front.
envier [ɑ̃vje] *v* envy. **enviable** *adj* enviable. **envie** *nf* desire; envy; (*anat*) birthmark. **avoir envie de** want, fancy. **envieux** *adj* envious.
environ [ɑ̃virɔ̃] *adv* about. **environs** *nm pl* surroundings *pl*, vicinity *sing*.
environnement [ɑ̃virɔnmɑ̃] *nm* environment.
envisager [ɑ̃vizaʒe] *v* envisage; consider.
envoi [ɑ̃vwa] *nm* sending; (*colis*) parcel, consignment.
s'envoler [ɑ̃vɔle] *v* fly away; (*avion*) take off; disappear, vanish.
***envoyer** [ɑ̃vwaje] *v* send. **envoyer chercher** send for. **envoyé, -e** *nm*, *nf* messenger; (*pol*) envoy; (*journal*) correspondent.
enzyme [ɑ̃zim] *nm* enzyme.

épagneul [epaɲœl] *nm* spaniel.
épais, -aisse [epɛ, -ɛs] *adj* thick. **épaisseur** *nf* thickness; (*neige, nuit*) depth. **épaissir** *v* thicken.
épancher [epɑ̃ʃe] *v* (*sentiments*) pour out; (*colère*) vent.
épandre [epɑ̃drə] *v* spread.
s'épanouir [epanwir] *v* blossom, open out; (*visage*) light up. **épanoui** *adj* (*fleur*) in full bloom; (*sourire*) radiant.
épargner [eparɲe] *v* save, spare. **épargne** *nf* saving.
éparpiller [eparpije] *v* scatter, disperse.
épars [epar] *adj* scattered.
épater [epate] (*fam*) *v* amaze, stagger. **épatement** *nm* amazement.
épaule [epol] *nf* shoulder.
épave [epav] *nf* wreck, ruin; (*débris*) wreckage.
épée [epe] *nf* sword.
épeler [ɛple] *v* spell.
éperdu [epɛrdy] *adj* distraught, frantic; passionate.
éperon [eprɔ̃] *nm* spur. **éperonner** *v* spur on.
éphémère [efemɛr] *adj* ephemeral, short-lived.
épi [epi] *nm* (*blé*) ear; (*cheveux*) tuft.
épice [epis] *nf* spice.
épicier [episje], **-ère** *nm*, *nf* grocer. **épicerie** *nf* grocer's; (*aliments*) groceries *pl*.
épidémie [epidemi] *nf* epidemic. **épidémique** *adj* epidemic; contagious.
épier [epje] *v* spy on; (*guetter*) watch for.
épilepsie [epilɛpsi] *nf* epilepsy. **épileptique** *n(m+f)*, *adj* epileptic.
épiler [epile] *v* remove hair from; (*sourcils*) pluck.
épilogue [epilɔg] *nm* epilogue; conclusion.
épinards [epinar] *nm pl* spinach *sing*.
épine [epin] *nf* (*plante*) thorn; (*animal*) spine, quill. **épine dorsale** backbone. **épineux** *adj* thorny; (*situation*) tricky.
épingle [epɛ̃glə] *nf* pin. **épingle à cheveux** hairpin. **épingle de nourrice** *or* **sûreté** safety-pin. **épingler** *v* pin.
Épiphanie [epifani] *nf* Twelfth Night, Epiphany.
épique [epik] *adj* epic.
épiscopal [episkɔpal] *adj* episcopal.
épisode [epizɔd] *nm* episode. **épisodique** *adj* episodic, occasional; secondary, minor.

épitaphe [epitaf] *nf* epitaph.

éploré [eplɔre] *adj* tearful, in tears.

éplucher [eplyʃe] *v* (*légumes*) peel; (*salade*) clean; (*texte*) examine closely. **éplucheur** *nm* peeler. **épluchures** *nf pl* peelings *pl*.

épointé [epwɛte] *adj* blunt.

éponger [epɔ̃ʒe] *v* mop (up). **éponge** *nf* sponge.

épopée [epɔpe] *nf* epic.

époque [epɔk] *nf* time; (*passé*) age, era; (*géol*) period.

épouser [epuze] *v* marry. **épouse** *nf* wife.

épousseter [epuste] *v* dust. **époussetage** *nm* dusting.

épouvanter [epuvɑ̃te] *v* terrify, appal. **épouvantable** *adj* dreadful, terrible. **épouvantail** *nm* scarecrow. **épouvante** *nf* terror, dread. **film d'épouvante** *nm* horror film.

époux [epu] *nm* husband.

****éprendre** [eprɑ̃drə] *v* **s'éprendre de** fall in love with.

épreuve [eprœv] *nf* test; (*peine*) ordeal; (*sport*) event; (*texte*) proof; (*phot*) print.

éprouver [epruve] *v* feel, experience; (*subir*) suffer; test. **éprouvette** *nf* test tube.

épuiser [epɥize] *v* exhaust; use up. **épuisé** *adj* worn out; (*comm*) sold out. **épuisement** *nm* exhaustion.

épurer [epyre] *v* purify, refine. **épuration** *nf* purification, refinement.

équateur [ekwatœr] *nm* equator. **équatorial** *adj* equatorial.

équation [ekwasjɔ̃] *nf* equation.

équerre [ekɛr] *nf* set square. **en équerre** at right angles.

équestre [ekɛstrə] *adj* equestrian.

équilatéral [ekɥilateral] *adj* equilateral.

équilibre [ekilibrə] *nm* balance; (*mental, tech*) equilibrium; harmony. **en équilibre** balanced. **équilibré** *adj* well-balanced. **équilibrer** *v* balance; counterbalance.

équinoxe [ekinɔks] *nm* equinox.

équiper [ekipe] *v* equip, fit out. **équipage** *nm* crew; equipment. **équipe** *nf* team; (*usine*) shift. **équipement** *nm* equipment.

équitable [ekitablə] *adj* fair.

équitation [ekitasjɔ̃] *nf* riding.

équité [ekite] *nf* equity.

équivalent [ekivalɑ̃] *nm, adj* equivalent.

****équivaloir** [ekivalwar] *v* be equivalent.

équivoque [ekivɔk] *adj* ambiguous; (*louche*) dubious. *nf* ambiguity; doubt.

érable [erablə] *nm* maple.

érafler [erɑfle] *v* scratch, graze. **éraflure** *nf* scratch, graze.

éraillé [erɑje] *adj* scratched; (*voix*) hoarse, rasping.

ère [ɛr] *nf* era.

érection [erɛksjɔ̃] *nf* erection.

éreinter [erɛ̃te] *v* exhaust; (*fam: critiquer*) slate.

ergoter [ergɔte] *v* quibble.

ériger [eriʒe] *v* establish, set up; (*monument*) erect.

ermite [ɛrmit] *nm* hermit.

éroder [erɔde] *v* erode. **érosif** *adj* erosive. **érosion** *nf* erosion.

érotique [erɔtik] *adj* erotic.

errer [ɛre] *v* wander, stray.

erreur [ɛrœr] *nf* mistake, error.

éruption [erypsjɔ̃] *nf* eruption. **entrer en éruption** erupt.

ès [ɛs] *prep* in the. **licencié ès lettres/sciences** *nm* Bachelor of Arts/Science.

escabeau [ɛskabo] *nm* stool; (*échelle*) step-ladder.

escadron [ɛskadrɔ̃] *nm* squadron.

escalader [ɛskalade] *v* climb, scale. **escalade** *nf* climbing.

escale [ɛskal] *nf* stop; (*naut*) port of call.

escalier [ɛskalje] *nm* staircase, stairs. **escalier de secours** fire escape. **escalier roulant** escalator. **escalier tournant** spiral staircase.

escalope [ɛskalɔp] *nf* escalope.

escamoter [ɛskamɔte] *v* (*esquiver*) dodge, evade; (*carte, etc.*) make disappear; (*fam*) pinch. **escamoteur, -euse** *nm, nf* conjuror.

escarbille [ɛskarbij] *nf* smut.

escargot [ɛskargo] *nm* snail.

escarmouche [ɛskarmuʃ] *nf* skirmish.

escarpé [ɛskarpe] *adj* steep.

escient [esjɑ̃] *nm* **à bon escient** advisedly. **à mauvais escient** ill-advisedly.

esclandre [ɛsklɑ̃drə] *nm* scene.

esclave [ɛsklav] *nm* slave. **esclavage** *nm* slavery.

escompter [ɛskɔ̃te] *v* discount; (*attendre*) expect, count on. **escompte** *nm* discount.

escorte [ɛskɔrt] *nf* escort. **escorter** *v* escort.

escrime [ɛskrim] *nf* fencing. **faire de l'escrime** fence.

escroc [εskro] *nm* swindler.
escroquer [εskrɔke] *v* swindle. **escroquerie** *nf* swindle, fraud.
espace [εspas] *nm* space. **espacer** *v* space out.
espadon [εspadɔ̃] *nm* swordfish.
Espagne [εspaɲ] *nf* Spain. **espagnol** *nm*, *adj* Spanish. **Espagnol, -e** *nm*, *nf* Spaniard.
espèce [εspεs] *nf* sort, kind; (*bot*, *zool*) species. **espèces** *nf pl* cash *sing*.
espérer [εspere] *v* hope (for). **espérer en** trust in. **espérance** *nf* hope, expectation.
espiègle [εspjεglə] *adj* mischievous. **espièglerie** *nf* mischief.
espion, -onne [εspjɔ̃, -ɔn] *nm*, *nf* spy. **espionnage** *nm* espionage. **espionner** *v* spy on.
esplanade [εsplanad] *nf* esplanade.
espoir [εspwar] *nm* hope.
esprit [εspri] *nm* spirit; (*pensée*) mind; (*humour*) wit. **avoir l'esprit large/étroit** be broad-/narrow-minded.
esquimau, -aude [εskimo, -od] *nm*, *adj* Eskimo. **Esquimau, -aude** *nm*, *nf* Eskimo.
esquisser [εskise] *v* sketch, outline. **esquisse** *nf* sketch, outline.
esquiver [εskive] *v* dodge, evade. **s'esquiver** slip away.
essai [εsε] *nm* try, attempt; (*produit*, *voiture*) trial, test; (*littéraire*) essay. **à l'essai** on trial.
essaim [εsε̃] *nm* swarm. **essaimer** *v* swarm; (*se disperser*) scatter, spread.
essayer [εseje] *v* try; test; (*vêtement*) try on.
essence [εsɑ̃s] *nf* (*carburant*) gasoline; (*extrait*) oil, essence.
essentiel [εsɑ̃sjεl] *adj* essential. *nm* main thing, essentials *pl*. **l'essentiel de** the best part of.
essieu [εsjø] *nm* axle.
essor [εsɔr] *nm* development, expansion; (*oiseau*) flight.
essorer [εsɔre] *v* wring (out); (*machine*) spin-dry. **essoreuse** *nf* spin-dryer; (*à rouleaux*) mangle.
essoufflé [εsufle] *adj* breathless, out of breath.
essuyer [εsɥije] *v* wipe; (*sécher*) dry; (*subir*) suffer. **essuie-glace** *nm* windscreen wiper. **essuie-mains** *nm* hand towel. **essuie-pieds** doormat.
est [εst] *nm* east. *adj invar* east; (*région*) eastern; (*direction*) eastward.

estaminet [εstaminε] *nm* tavern.
estamper [εstɑ̃pe] *v* stamp; (*fam*) diddle. **estampe** *nf* engraving, print.
estampille [εstɑ̃pij] *nf* stamp.
esthétique [εstetik] *adj* aesthetic. **esthéticien, -enne** *nm*, *nf* beautician.
estimer [εstime] *v* estimate; value; respect, esteem; consider. **estime** *nf* esteem, respect.
estivant [εstivɑ̃], **-e** *nm*, *nf* holiday-maker.
estomac [εstɔma] *nm* stomach.
estomper [εstɔ̃pe] *v* blur.
estrade [εstrad] *nf* platform.
estragon [εstragɔ̃] *nm* tarragon.
estropier [εstrɔpje] *v* cripple. **estropié, -e** *nm*, *nf* cripple.
estuaire [εstɥεr] *nm* estuary.
esturgeon [εstyrʒɔ̃] *nm* sturgeon.
et [e] *conj* and.
étable [etablə] *nf* cowshed.
établir [etablir] *v* establish, set up; (*liste*, *plan*) draw up. **s'établir** become established; (*s'installer*) settle. **établissement** *nm* establishment.
étage [etaʒ] *nm* floor, storey; (*gâteau*) tier. **étagère** *nf* shelf; (*meuble*) set of shelves.
étai [etε] *nm* stay, prop.
étain [etε̃] *nm* tin; (*alliage*) pewter.
étaler [etale] *v* spread (out); (*comm*) display; parade, flaunt. **s'étaler** stretch out. **étalage** *nm* display; (*vitrine*) shop window. **étalagiste** *n(m+f)* window-dresser.
étalon[1] [etalɔ̃] *nm* (*cheval*) stallion.
étalon[2] [etalɔ̃] *nm* standard.
étancher [etɑ̃ʃe] *v* stem, staunch; make watertight. **étanche** *adj* watertight. **étanche à l'air** airtight.
étang [etɑ̃] *nm* pond.
étape [etap] *nf* stage; (*arrêt*) stop.
état [eta] *nm* state; condition; (*comm*) statement. **état-major** *nm* (*mil*) staff; (*comm*) senior management.
États-Unis [etazyni] *nm pl* United States *sing*.
étau [eto] *nm* (*tech*) vice.
étayer [eteje] *v* support, prop up.
été [ete] *nm* summer.
***éteindre** [etε̃drə] *v* extinguish; (*lampe*, *radio*, *etc.*) switch *or* turn off; (*calmer*) quench. **s'éteindre** (*feu*, *etc.*) go out; (*mourir*) die out. **éteint** *adj* dull, faded; feeble; (*disparu*) extinct.

étendard [etɑ̃dar] *nm* standard.
étendre [etɑ̃drə] *v* extend, expand; (*étaler*) spread (out), stretch out; dilute. **étendu** *adj* vast, extensive. **étendue** *nf* (*terre*) expanse, area; (*pouvoir*) scope, extent.
éternel [etɛrnɛl] *adj* eternal; perpetual. **éternité** [etɛrnite] *nf* eternity.
éternuer [etɛrnɥe] *v* sneeze. **éternuement** *nm* sneeze.
éther [etɛr] *nm* ether.
éthique [etik] *adj* ethical. *nf* ethics *pl.*
ethnique [etnik] *adj* ethnic.
étinceler [etɛ̃sle] *v* sparkle, glitter. **étincelle** *nf* spark. **étincellement** *nm* sparkle, gleam.
étiquette [etikɛt] *nf* label; (*protocole*) etiquette. **étiqueter** *v* label.
étirer [etire] *v* stretch.
étoffe [etɔf] *nf* material. **avoir l'étoffe de** have the makings of.
étoile [etwal] *nf* star. **étoile de mer** starfish.
étole [etɔl] *nf* stole.
étonner [etɔne] *v* surprise, amaze. **étonnement** *nm* surprise, amazement.
étouffer [etufe] *v* stifle, suffocate; (*bruit*) muffle; (*sentiments*, *révolte*) suppress. **étouffement** *nm* suffocation; suppression.
étourdir [eturdir] *v* stun, daze; (*altitude*, *etc.*) make dizzy; (*douleur*) deaden; (*bruit*) deafen. **étourderie** *nf* thoughtlessness. **étourdi** *adj* scatterbrained, thoughtless. **étourdissement** *nm* dizzy spell.
étourneau [eturno] *nm* starling.
étrange [etrɑ̃ʒ] *adj* strange.
étranger [etrɑ̃ʒe], **-ère** *adj* foreign; (*inconnu*) strange, unfamiliar. *nm* foreign country. **à l'étranger** abroad. *nm, nf* foreigner; stranger.
étrangler [etrɑ̃gle] *v* strangle, choke. **étranglement** *nm* strangulation.
étrave [etrav] *nf* stem.
***être** [ɛtrə] *v* be. **être à** belong to. *nm* being; (*âme*) soul. **être humain** *nm* human being.
***étreindre** [etrɛ̃drə] *v* embrace; (*serrer*) grasp, grip. **étreinte** *nf* embrace; grasp, grip.
étrenne [etrɛn] *nf* New Year's gift.
étrier [etrije] *nm* stirrup.
étriqué [etrike] *adj* narrow, cramped, tight.
étroit [etrwa] *adj* narrow; (*vêtement*)

tight; (*intime*) close; strict. **étroitesse** *nf* narrowness; tightness.
étude [etyd] *nf* study.
étudier [etydje] *v* study; examine. **étudiant, -e** *nm, nf* student.
étui [etɥi] *nm* case.
étymologie [etimɔlɔʒi] *nf* etymology. **étymologique** *adj* etymological.
eucalyptus [økaliptys] *nm* eucalyptus.
Eucharistie [økaristi] *nf* Eucharist.
eunuque [ønyk] *nm* eunuch.
euphémisme [øfemismə] *nm* euphemism. **euphémique** *adj* euphemistic.
euphorie [øfɔri] *nf* euphoria. **euphorique** *adj* euphoric.
Europe [ørɔp] *nf* Europe. **européen** *adj* European. **Européen, -enne** *nm, nf* European.
euthanasie [øtanazi] *nf* euthanasia.
eux [ø] *pron* (*sujet*) they; (*objet*) them. **eux-mêmes** *pron* themselves.
évacuer [evakɥe] *v* evacuate. **évacuation** *nf* evacuation. **évacué -e** *nm, nf* evacuee.
s'évader [evade] *v* escape.
évaluer [evalɥe] *v* (*bijou*) value; (*dégâts*) assess; estimate.
évangélique [evɑ̃ʒelik] *adj* evangelical. **évangéliste** *nm* evangelist.
évangile [evɑ̃ʒil] *nm* gospel.
s'évanouir [evanwir] *v* (*personne*) faint; (*disparaître*) vanish. **évanouissement** *nm* loss of consciousness; disappearance.
évaporer [evapɔre] *v* evaporate. **évaporation** *nf* evaporation.
évasé [evɑze] *adj* flared.
évasion [evazjɔ̃] *nf* escape. **évasif** *adj* evasive.
éveiller [eveje] *v* arouse, awaken. **éveil** *nm* alert, alarm. **en éveil** on the alert. **éveillé** *adj* alert; awake.
événement [evɛnmɑ̃] *nm* event.
éventail [evɑ̃taj] *nm* fan.
éventer [evɑ̃te] *v* fan, air; discover. **s'éventer** go flat *or* stale. **éventé** *adj* stale, flat.
éventrer [evɑ̃tre] *v* tear open; (*taureau*) gore.
éventuel [evɑ̃tɥɛl] *adj* possible. **éventualité** *nf* possibility, eventuality.
évêque [evɛk] *nm* bishop.
s'évertuer [evɛrtɥe] *v* strive, do one's utmost.
évidence [evidɑ̃s] *nf* evidence; (*fait*) obvious fact. **en évidence** conspicuous.

évidemment *adv* obviously, of course.
évident *adj* obvious, evident.
évider [evide] *v* hollow out.
évier [evje] *nm* sink.
évincer [evɛ̃se] *v* oust.
éviter [evite] *v* avoid. **évitable** *adj* avoidable.
évocateur, -trice [evɔkatœr, -tris] *adj* evocative.
évoluer [evɔlɥe] *v* evolve, develop; move about, manoeuvre. **évolution** *nf* evolution, development; movement, manoeuvre.
évoquer [evɔke] *v* evoke, recall.
exacerber [ɛgzasɛrbe] *v* exacerbate.
exact [ɛgzakt] *adj* exact; correct; (*vrai*) true; precise, accurate; punctual. **exactitude** *nf* exactness; precision; accuracy; punctuality.
exagérer [ɛgzaʒere] *v* exaggerate; (*abuser*) go too far. **exagération** *nf* exaggeration.
exalter [ɛgzalte] *v* excite; (*glorifier*) exalt. **exaltation** *nf* great excitement. **exalté** *adj* excited, elated; (*imagination*) vivid; fanatical.
examen [ɛgzamɛ̃] *nm* examination; test.
examiner [ɛgzamine] *v* examine.
exaspérer [ɛgzaspere] *v* exasperate, aggravate. **exaspération** *nf* exasperation.
exaucer [ɛgzose] *v* grant.
excaver [ɛkskave] *v* excavate. **excavation** *nf* excavation.
excéder [ɛksede] *v* exceed; exasperate. **excédent** *nm* surplus, excess.
excellent [ɛksɛlɑ̃] *adj* excellent. **excellence** *nf* excellence. **Excellence** *nf* Excellency.
exceller [ɛksele] *v* excel.
excentrique [ɛksɑ̃trik] *n(m+f)*, *adj* eccentric. **excentricité** *nf* eccentricity.
excepter [ɛksɛpte] *v* exclude. **excepté** *prep* except. **exception** *nf* exception. **exceptionnel** *adj* exceptional.
excès [ɛksɛ] *nm* excess; surplus. **excès de vitesse** (*auto*) speeding. **excessif** *adj* excessive.
exciter [ɛksite] *v* excite; (*provoquer*) arouse; stimulate; (*encourager*) urge. **s'exciter** (*fam*) get worked up. **excitation** *nf* excitement; stimulation.
s'exclamer [ɛksklame] *v* exclaim. **exclamation** *nf* exclamation.
⁺exclure [ɛksklyr] *v* exclude; (*chasser*) expel. **exclusif** *adj* exclusive; sole. **exclusion** *nf* exclusion; expulsion.

excommunier [ɛkskɔmynje] *v* excommunicate. **excommunication** *nf* excommunication.
excréter [ɛkskrete] *v* excrete. **excrément** *nm* excrement. **excrétion** *nf* excretion.
excursion [ɛkskyrsjɔ̃] *nf* excursion, trip.
excuser [ɛkskyze] *v* excuse; pardon, forgive. **excusez-moi** I'm sorry. **s'excuser** apologize. **excuse** *nf* excuse. **excuses** *nf pl* apology *sing*.
exécrer [ɛgzekre] *v* loathe. **exécrable** *adj* atrocious.
exécuter [ɛgzekyte] *v* execute, perform, carry out. **exécutif** *adj* executive. **exécution** *nf* execution.
exemplaire [ɛgzɑ̃plɛr] *adj* exemplary. *nm* copy; specimen.
exemple [ɛgzɑ̃plə] *nm* example. **par exemple** for example; (*surprise*) indeed, really.
exempt [ɛgzɑ̃] *adj* exempt, free. **exempter** *v* exempt. **exemption** *nf* exemption.
exercer [ɛgzɛrse] *v* exercise; practise; (*force*) exert; (*entraîner*) train. **s'exercer** practise.
exercice [ɛgzɛrsis] *nm* exercise; practice; (*mil*) drill.
exhaler [ɛgzale] *v* exhale; (*odeur*) give off; (*soupir*) utter.
exhiber [ɛgzibe] *v* exhibit, show, display. **exhibition** *nf* exhibition; show. **exhibitionniste** *n(m+f)*, *adj* exhibitionist.
exiger [ɛgziʒe] *v* demand, insist; (*nécessiter*) need, require. **exigences** *nf pl* demands *pl*, requirements *pl*.
exigu, -uë [ɛgzigy] *adj* cramped.
exiler [ɛgzile] *v* exile, banish. **exil** *nm* exile.
exister [ɛgziste] *v* exist; (*être*) be. **existence** *nf* existence. **existentialisme** *nm* existentialism.
exorbitant [ɛgzɔrbitɑ̃] *adj* exorbitant.
exorciser [ɛgzɔrsize] *v* exorcize. **exorcisme** *nm* exorcism. **exorciste** *nm* exorcist.
exotique [ɛgzɔtik] *adj* exotic.
expansion [ɛkspɑ̃sjɔ̃] *nf* expansion. **expansif** *adj* expansive.
expatrier [ɛkspatrije] *v* expatriate. **expatrié, -e** *n*, *adj* expatriate.
expédier [ɛkspedje] *v* send, dispatch; (*fam*) dispose of. **expédient** *nm*, *adj* expedient. **expéditeur, -trice** *nm*, *nf* sender. **expédition** *nf* dispatch; (*paquet*) consignment; (*voyage*) expedition.

expérience [ɛksperjɑ̃s] *nf* experience; (*scientifique*) experiment.

expérimenter [ɛksperimɑ̃te] *v* experiment; test, try out. **expérimental** *adj* experimental. **expérimenté** *adj* experienced.

expert [ɛksper] *nm, adj* expert. **expert-comptable** *nm* chartered accountant.

expier [ɛkspje] *v* atone for. **expiation** *nf* atonement.

expirer [ɛkspire] *v* expire; (*air*) breathe out. **expiration** *nf* expiry.

explication [ɛksplikasjɔ̃] *nf* explanation; (*texte*) analysis, commentary. **explicatif** *adj* explanatory.

explicite [ɛksplisit] *adj* explicit.

expliquer [ɛksplike] *v* explain; (*texte*) analyse.

exploit [ɛksplwa] *nm* exploit.

exploiter [ɛksplwate] *v* exploit; operate, run.

explorer [ɛksplɔre] *v* explore; examine. **explorateur, -trice** *nm, nf* explorer. **exploration** *nf* exploration.

exploser [ɛksploze] *v* explode. **explosif** *nm, adj* explosive. **explosion** *nf* explosion.

exporter [ɛksporte] *v* export. **exportation** *nf* export.

exposer [ɛkspoze] *v* expose; exhibit, display; (*expliquer*) explain. **exposant, -e** *nm, nf* exhibitor. **exposé** *nm* talk, account. **exposition** *nf* exhibition; (*à l'air, etc.*) exposure; (*maison*) aspect.

exprès [ɛkspre] *adj invar* express. *adv* on purpose; specially.

express [ɛkspres] *nm* fast train.

expression [ɛkspresjɔ̃] *nf* expression. **expressif** *adj* expressive.

exprimer [ɛksprime] *v* express.

expulser [ɛkspylse] *v* expel; (*locataire*) evict. **expulsion** *nf* expulsion; eviction.

exquis [ɛkski] *adj* exquisite, delightful.

extase [ɛkstaz] *nf* ecstasy. **extasié** *adj* ecstatic.

extension [ɛkstɑ̃sjɔ̃] *nf* extension, expansion.

exténuer [ɛkstenɥe] *v* exhaust.

extérieur, -e [ɛksterjœr] *adj* outer, external, outside; (*étranger*) foreign. *nm* exterior, outside. **à l'extérieur** outside. **en extérieur** on location.

exterminer [ɛkstermine] *v* exterminate. **extermination** *nf* extermination.

externe [ɛkstern] *adj* external. **pour l'usage externe** for external use only. *n(m+f)* day pupil. **externat** *nm* day school.

extinction [ɛkstɛ̃ksjɔ̃] *nf* extinction. **extincteur** *nm* extinguisher.

extirper [ɛkstirpe] *v* eradicate; (*arracher*) pull out.

extorquer [ɛkstɔrke] *v* extort. **extorsion** *nf* extortion.

extra [ɛkstra] *adj invar* first-rate, top-quality; (*fam*) fantastic. *adv* extra.

extraction [ɛkstraksjɔ̃] *nf* extraction.

extrader [ɛkstrade] *v* extradite. **extradition** *nf* extradition.

*****extraire** [ɛkstrɛr] *v* extract; (*charbon*) mine; (*pierre*) quarry. **extrait** *nm* extract.

extraordinaire [ɛkstraɔrdinɛr] *adj* extraordinary; exceptional.

extravagant [ɛkstravagɑ̃] *adj* extravagant; (*prix*) excessive; (*idée*) crazy. **extravagance** *nf* extravagance.

extraverti [ɛkstravɛrti], **-e** *n, adj* extrovert.

extrême [ɛkstrɛm] *nm* extreme. *adj* extreme; (*loin*) far; intense; (*suprême*) utmost. **Extrême-Orient** *nm* Far East. **extrémiste** *n(m+f)*, *adj* extremist. **extrémité** *nf* end, tip; limit. **extrémités** *nf pl* (*anat*) extremities *pl.*

exubérant [ɛgzyberɑ̃] *adj* exuberant. **exubérance** *nf* exuberance.

F

fable [fablə] *nf* fable.

fabricant [fabrikɑ̃] *nm* manufacturer. **fabrication** *nf* manufacture.

fabriquer [fabrike] *v* manufacture, make; (*mensonge*) fabricate. **fabrique** *nf* factory.

fabuleux [fabylø] *adj* fabulous.

fac [fak] *nf* (*argot*) university, college.

façade [fasad] *nf* façade, front.

face [fas] *nf* face; (*côté*) side. **de face** frontal. **en face (de)** opposite. **face à** facing. **faire face à** face.

facétie [fasesi] *nf* joke, trick. **facétieux** *adj* mischievous; humorous.

facette [fasɛt] *nf* facet.

fâcher [faʃe] *v* make angry. **se fâcher** get angry; (*se brouiller*) fall out. **fâché** *adj* angry; (*désolé*) sorry. **fâcheux** *adj* unfortunate; (*ennuyeux*) annoying.

facile [fasil] *adj* easy; (*spontané*) ready.

faciliter [fasilite] *v* facilitate, make easier.

facilité *nf* ease, easiness; aptitude; tendency. **facilités** *nf pl* facilities *pl*.

façon [fasɔ̃] *nf* way, manner; (*robe*) cut. **de façon à** so as to. **de toute façon** anyway. **façons** *nf pl* (*conduite*) behaviour *sing*; (*chichis*) fuss *sing*.

façonner [fasɔne] *v* shape, form; (*fabriquer*) manufacture, make.

fac-similé [faksimile] *nm* facsimile.

facteur [faktœr] *nm* factor; postman.

factice [faktis] *adj* artificial, false.

faction [faksjɔ̃] *nf* faction; guard, sentry.

facture [faktyr] *nf* bill; (*comm*) invoice. **facturer** *v* invoice; (*compter*) charge for.

facultatif [fakyltatif] *adj* optional; (*arrêt*) request.

faculté [fakylte] *nf* faculty; (*pouvoir*) power; (*droit*) right; (*argot*) university, college.

fadaises [fadɛz] *nf pl* nonsense *sing*.

fade [fad] *adj* insipid, dull.

fagot [fago] *nm* bundle of sticks.

fagoter [fagɔte] *v* (*péj*) rig out.

faible [fɛblə] *adj* weak, feeble; (*petit*) low, small, slight. *nm* (*personne*) weakling; (*penchant*) weakness. **faiblesse** *nf* weakness.

faiblir [feblir] *v* weaken, fail.

faïence [fajɑ̃s] *nf* earthenware.

faillible [fajiblə] *adj* fallible. **faillibilité** *nf* fallibility.

*faillir [fajir] *v* fail. **faillir faire** almost do, narrowly miss doing. **failli, -e** *n, adj* bankrupt. **faillite** *nf* bankruptcy; (*chute*) collapse. **faire faillite** go bankrupt.

faim [fɛ̃] *nf* hunger. **avoir faim** be hungry.

fainéant [fɛneɑ̃], **-e** *adj* lazy, idle. *nm, nf* idler. **fainéantise** *nf* idleness.

*faire [fɛr] *v* make; do; (*mesurer, temps*) be; (*sport, théâtre*) play; (*paraître*) look; (*dire*) say. **ça ne fait rien** it doesn't matter. **faire faire** have done. **faire-part** *nm invar* announcement. **faire voir** show. **se faire à** get used to.

faisable [fəzablə] *adj* feasible.

faisan [fəzɑ̃] *nm* pheasant.

faisceau [fɛso] *nm* bundle; (*rayon*) beam.

fait¹ [fɛ] *nm* fact; event; act. **au fait** (*à propos*) by the way; (*au courant*) informed. **en fait** in fact. **fait divers** news item.

fait² [fɛ] *adj* made; done; (*mûr*) ripe. **c'est bien fait pour toi!** it serves you right!

faîte [fɛt] *nm* summit, top.

faix [fɛ] *nm* burden.

falaise [falɛz] *nf* cliff.

*falloir [falwar] *v* be necessary. **il faut le faire** it must be done. **s'en falloir (de)** be lacking.

falsifier [falsifje] *v* falsify, alter. **falsification** *nf* falsification.

famé [fame] *adj* **mal famé** disreputable.

fameux [famø] *adj* famous; first-rate, excellent; (*rude*) real. **pas fameux** not so good.

familial [familjal] *adj* family, domestic.

familiariser [familjarize] *v* familiarize. **familiarité** *nf* familiarity.

familier [familje] *adj* familiar; (*amical*) informal; (*mot*) colloquial. *nm* regular visitor.

famille [famij] *nf* family.

famine [famin] *nf* famine.

fanal [fanal] *nm* lantern.

fanatique [fanatik] *adj* fanatical. *n(m + f)* fanatic.

faner [fane] *v* make hay. **se faner** fade, wither.

fanfare [fɑ̃far] *nf* fanfare, flourish; (*orchestre*) brass band.

fanfaron, -onne [fɑ̃farɔ̃, -ɔn] *adj* boastful.

fange [fɑ̃ʒ] *nf* mire.

fantaisie [fɑ̃tezi] *nf* fantasy, fancy; (*caprice*) whim; extravagance; imagination.

fantastique [fɑ̃tastik] *adj* fantastic; (*bizarre*) weird, uncanny.

fantoche [fɑ̃tɔʃ] *nm* puppet.

fantôme [fɑ̃tom] *nm* ghost, phantom. **cabinet fantôme** *nm* shadow cabinet.

faon [fɑ̃] *nm* fawn.

farce¹ [fars] *nf* joke, prank; (*théâtre*) farce. **farceur, -euse** *nm, nf* practical joker.

farce² [fars] *nf* stuffing.

farcir [farsir] *v* stuff.

fard [far] *nm* make-up.

fardeau [fardo] *nm* burden.

farder [farde] *v* make up; disguise.

farfouiller [farfuje] *v* (*fam*) rummage about.

farine [farin] *nf* flour. **farine d'avoine** oatmeal. **farine de maïs** cornflour. **farineux** *adj* floury.

farouche [faruʃ] *adj* fierce; timid; savage, wild; unsociable.

fart [far] *nm* wax. **farter** *v* wax.

fascicule [fasikyl] *nm* volume; part, instalment.

fasciner [fasine] *v* fascinate. **fascination** *nf* fascination.

fascisme [fasismə] *nm* fascism. **fasciste** *n(m+f)*, *adj* fascist.

faste [fast] *nm* splendour.

fastidieux [fastidjø] *adj* tedious.

fastueux [fastɥø] *adj* sumptuous, luxurious.

fatal [fatal] *adj* fatal; inevitable. **fatalité** *nf* fate.

fatiguer [fatige] *v* tire, strain; *(agacer)* annoy. **se fatiguer** get tired. **fatigant** *adj* tiring; *(agaçant)* tiresome. **fatigue** *nf* fatigue, tiredness.

fatras [fatra] *nm* jumble.

faubourg [fobur] *nm* suburb.

faucher [foʃe] *v* mow, cut; *(fam)* pinch, nick. **fauché** *adj* *(fam)* broke, hard up.

faucon [fokɔ̃] *nm* falcon; hawk.

faufiler [fofile] *v* tack. **se faufiler** thread or edge one's way.

faune [fon] *nm* fauna.

fausser [fose] *v* distort, alter; *(courber)* bend, buckle. **fausser compagnie à** slip away from.

fausset [fosɛ] *nm* falsetto.

faute [fot] *nf* fault; mistake, error; *(jur)* offence. **faute de** for lack of. **fautif** *adj* at fault, guilty; incorrect.

fauteuil [fotœj] *nm* armchair; *(théâtre)* seat. **fauteuil à bascule** rocking chair. **fauteuil roulant** wheelchair.

fauve [fov] *adj* tawny, fawn. *nm* wild animal; *(couleur)* fawn.

faux¹, fausse [fo, fos] *adj* false; *(incorrect)* wrong; *(argent, etc.)* fake, forged. **fausse alerte** false alarm. **fausse couche** miscarriage. **faux-filet** *nm* sirloin. **faux pli** crease. *adv* out of tune. *nm* falsehood; forgery. **à faux** wrongly. **fausseté** *nf* falseness, falsity.

faux² [fo] *nf* scythe.

faveur [favœr] *nf* favour. **billet de faveur** *nm* complimentary ticket. **en faveur de** on behalf of. **favorable** *adj* favourable.

favori, -ite [favɔri, -it] *n*, *adj* favourite. **favoriser** *v* favour.

fébrile [febril] *adj* feverish. **fébrilité** *nf* feverishness.

fécond [fekɔ̃] *adj* fertile; prolific. **fécondité** *nf* fertility.

fécule [fekyl] *nf* starch. **féculent** *adj* starchy.

fédérer [federe] *v* federate. **fédéral** *adj* federal. **fédération** *nf* federation.

fée [fe] *nf* fairy. **féerique** *adj* magical.

*feindre [fɛ̃drə] *v* feign. **feindre de** pretend.

fêler [fele] *v* crack. **fêlure** *nf* crack.

féliciter [felisite] *v* congratulate. **félicitations** *nf pl* congratulations *pl*.

félin [felɛ̃] *adj* feline.

femelle [fəmɛl] *nf*, *adj* female.

féminin [feminɛ̃] *adj* feminine, female. *nm* feminine. **féminisme** *nm* feminism. **féministe** *n(m+f)*, *adj* feminist. **féminité** *nf* femininity.

femme [fam] *nf* woman; *(épouse)* wife. **femme de chambre** chambermaid. **femme de ménage** cleaner.

fémur [femyr] *nm* femur.

fendre [fɑ̃drə] *v* split, crack.

fenêtre [fənɛtrə] *nf* window. **fenêtre à guillotine** sash window. **fenêtre en saillie** bay window.

fenouil [fənuj] *nm* fennel.

fente [fɑ̃t] *nf* crack, fissure; *(interstice)* slit; slot.

féodal [feɔdal] *adj* feudal.

fer [fɛr] *nm* iron. **fer à cheval** horseshoe. **fer à repasser** iron. **fer-blanc** *nm* tin. **fer forgé** wrought iron.

férié [ferje] *adj* **jour férié** *nm* public holiday.

ferme¹ [fɛrm] *adj* firm; *(solide)* steady. *adv* hard. **fermeté** *nf* firmness; steadiness.

ferme² [fɛrm] *nf* farm; *(maison)* farmhouse. **fermier** *nm* farmer. **fermière** *nf* farmer's wife.

fermenter [fɛrmɑ̃te] *v* ferment. **ferment** *nm* ferment. **fermentation** *nf* fermentation.

fermer [fɛrme] *v* close, shut; *(boucher)* block; *(gaz, eau, etc.)* turn off. **fermer à clef** lock. **fermeture** *nf* *(vêtement, sac, etc.)* fastener, catch; *(action)* closing. **fermeture à glissière** zip.

féroce [ferɔs] *adj* ferocious, fierce. **férocité** *nf* ferocity.

ferraille [fɛraj] *nf* scrap iron.

ferré [fɛre] *adj* *(canne)* steel-tipped; *(soulier)* hobnailed. **voie ferrée** *nf* railway track or line.

ferroviaire [fɛrɔvjɛr] *adj* railway.
fertile [fɛrtil] *adj* fertile. **fertilisation** *nf* fertilization. **fertiliser** *v* fertilize. **fertilité** *nf* fertility.
fervent [fɛrvã] *adj* fervent. **ferveur** *nm* fervour.
fesser [fese] *v* spank. **fesse** *nf* buttock. **fesses** *nf pl* bottom *sing*. **fessée** *nf* spanking.
festin [fɛstɛ̃] *nm* feast.
festival [fɛstival] *nm* festival.
feston [fɛstɔ̃] *nm* festoon; (*couture*) scallop. **festonner** *v* festoon; scallop.
fête [fɛt] *nf* festival; (*congé*) holiday; (*rel*) feast day; (*foire*) fair; celebration. **fête des Mères** Mothers' Day. **fête foraine** funfair.
fêter [fete] *v* celebrate.
fétiche [fetiʃ] *nm* fetish; mascot.
fétide [fetid] *adj* fetid.
feu¹ [fø] *nm* fire; (*lumière, lampe*) light; (*cuisine*) ring, burner; (*chaleur*) heat. **feu d'artifice** firework. **feu de joie** bonfire. **feu de position** sidelight. **feux** *nm pl* (*auto*) traffic lights *pl*.
feu² [fø] *adj* late, deceased.
feuille [fœj] *nf* leaf; (*papier, etc.*) sheet; form; (*bulletin*) slip. **feuillage** *nm* foliage. **feuillet** *nm* (*livre*) leaf, page.
feuilleter [fœjte] *v* leaf *or* skim through. **pâte feuilletée** *nf* puff pastry.
feuilleton [fœjtɔ̃] *nm* serial.
feutre [føtrə] *nm* felt; (*stylo*) felt-tip pen. **feutré** *adj* muffled.
fève [fɛv] *nf* broad bean.
février [fevrije] *nm* February.
fiacre [fjakrə] *nm* cab.
fiancé [fjãse] *adj* engaged. *nm* fiancé. **fiancée** *nf* fiancée.
se fiancer [fjãse] *v* get engaged. **fiançailles** *nf pl* engagement *sing*.
fiasco [fjasko] *nm* fiasco.
fibre [fibrə] *nf* fibre.
ficeler [fisle] *v* tie up. **ficelle** *nf* string.
ficher¹ [fiʃe] *v* (*enfoncer*) stick, drive in; (*mettre en fiche*) file. **fiche** *nf* (*cheville*) peg; (*élec*) pin; index card; form, slip. **fichier** *nm* file.
ficher² [fiʃe] (*fam*) *v* do, be up to; (*donner*) give; (*mettre*) put. **ficher le camp** clear off. **se ficher de** (*se moquer*) make fun of; (*être indifférent*) not care about.
fichu *adj* (*mauvais*) rotten; (*perdu*) done for; capable, likely.

fiction [fiksjɔ̃] *nf* fiction. **fictif** *adj* fictitious; false; imaginary.
fidèle [fidɛl] *adj* faithful; loyal; (*habituel*) regular. *n(m+f)* (*rel*) believer; regular. **fidélité** *nf* faithfulness; loyalty; (*conjugale*) fidelity.
fiel [fjɛl] *nm* gall.
fiente [fjãt] *nm* droppings *pl*.
fier¹ [fjɛr] *adj* proud. **fierté** *nf* pride.
fier² [fje] *v* **se fier à** trust.
fièvre [fjɛvrə] *nf* fever. **fievreux** *adj* feverish.
figer [fiʒe] *v* congeal, clot, coagulate; (*paralyser*) freeze, stiffen.
figue [fig] *nf* fig. **figuier** *nm* fig tree.
figure [figyr] *nf* figure; (*visage*) face; (*image*) picture.
figurer [figyre] *v* represent; appear. **se figurer** imagine. **figurant, -e** *nm, nf* (*cinéma*) extra; (*théâtre*) walk-on; (*pantin*) puppet. **figuré** *adj* figurative.
fil [fil] *nm* thread; (*élec*) wire; (*linge, pêche*) line; (*bois*) grain; (*tranchant*) edge; current. **fil à plomb** plumbline. **fil de fer** wire.
filament [filamã] *nm* filament; (*fil*) thread.
file [fil] *nf* line; (*auto*) lane; (*d'attente*) queue. **à la file** in single file; one after the other.
filer [file] *v* spin; prolong, draw out; (*liquide, sable*) flow, run; (*bas*) ladder; (*fam: courir*) fly, dash; (*fam: s'en aller*) slip away.
filet¹ [filɛ] *nm* streak; (*eau*) trickle; (*fumée*) wisp.
filet² [filɛ] *nm* (*viande, etc.*) fillet.
filet³ [filɛ] *nm* (*sport, pêche*) net; (*bagages*) rack. **filet à provisions** string bag.
filial [filjal] *adj* filial. **filiale** *nf* subsidiary company.
filigrane [filigran] *nm* (*papier*) watermark; (*argent, verre, etc.*) filigree.
fille [fij] *nf* girl; (*opposé à fils*) daughter. **fillette** *nf* little girl.
filleul [fijœl] *nm* (*garçon*) godson; (*enfant*) godchild. **filleule** *nf* goddaughter.
film [film] *nm* film. **film fixe** filmstrip. **filmer** *v* film.
filou [filu] *nm* rogue.
filouter [filute] (*fam*) *v* diddle; (*tricher*) cheat; (*voler*) filch.
fils [fis] *nm* son; (*après nom*) junior.

filtrer [filtre] *v* filter. **filtre** *nm* filter; (*cigarette*) filter-tip.

fin¹ [fɛ̃] *adj* fine; (*mince*) thin; (*vue*) sharp; (*personne*) shrewd, astute; (*aliments*) choice; (*habile*) expert. **fines herbes** *nf pl* mixed herbs *pl*.

fin² [fɛ̃] *nf* end; (*but*) purpose. **en fin de compte** in the end. **fin de série** oddment.

final [final] *adj* final. **finale** *nf* (*sport*) final. **finalement** *adv* in the end, finally. **finaliste** *n(m+f)* finalist.

finance [finɑ̃s] *nf* finance. **financer** *v* finance.

financier [finɑ̃sje] *adj* financial. *nm* financier.

finaud [fino] *adj* wily.

finesse [finɛs] *nf* fineness; (*vue*) sharpness; (*broderie*) delicacy; subtlety.

finir [finir] *v* finish, end; (*arrêter*) stop. **fini** *adj* finished; (*terminé*) over; (*complet*) utter.

Finlande [fɛ̃lɑ̃d] *nf* Finland. **finlandais** *adj* Finnish. **Finlandais, -e** *nm*, *nf* Finn. **finnois** *nm*, *adj* Finnish. **Finnois, -e** *nm*, *nf* Finn, Finnish speaker.

fioriture [fjorityr] *nf* flourish.

firme [firm] *nf* firm.

fisc [fisk] *nm* Inland Revenue. **fiscal** *adj* tax, fiscal.

fission [fisjɔ̃] *nf* fission.

fissure [fisyr] *nf* crack, fissure.

fixer [fikse] *v* fix; decide, settle; arrange, set. **fixation** *nf* fixation; (*attache*) fastening; (*ski*) binding. **fixe** *adj* fixed, set.

flacon [flakɔ̃] *nm* bottle.

flageller [flaʒele] *v* flog. **flagellation** *nf* flogging.

flagrant [flagrɑ̃] *adj* blatant, glaring. **prendre en flagrant délit** catch red-handed.

flairer [flere] *v* smell, sniff (at); (*discerner*) sense, scent. **flair** *nm* sense of smell; intuition.

flamand [flamɑ̃] *nm*, *adj* Flemish. **les Flamands** the Flemish.

flamant [flamɑ̃] *nm* flamingo.

flambeau [flɑ̃bo] *nm* torch; candlestick.

flamber [flɑ̃be] *v* blaze; (*cheveux*) singe. **flambée** *nf* blaze; (*colère, etc.*) outburst.

flamboyant [flɑ̃bwajɑ̃] *adj* blazing, fiery.

flamme [flam] *nf* flame; (*ardeur, éclat*) fire. **flammèche** *nf* spark.

flan [flɑ̃] *nm* (*cuisine*) egg custard; (*tech*) mould.

flanc [flɑ̃] *nm* side, flank.

flanelle [flanɛl] *nf* flannel.

flâner [flane] *v* stroll; (*péj*) dawdle.

flanquer [flɑ̃ke] *v* flank; (*fam*) fling, chuck.

flaque [flak] *nf* pool. **flaque d'eau** puddle.

flasque [flask] *adj* flaccid, flabby, limp; (*personne*) spineless.

flatter [flate] *v* flatter; encourage; (*caresser*) stroke. **se flatter** delude oneself. **se flatter de** pride oneself on. **flatterie** *nf* flattery. **flatteur, -euse** *adj* flattering.

flatulence [flatylɑ̃s] *nf* flatulence.

fléau [fleo] *nm* scourge; (*fam*) plague.

flèche [flɛʃ] *nf* arrow; (*église*) spire. **monter en flèche** soar, rocket. **fléchette** *nf* dart.

fléchir [fleʃir] *v* bend, sag; (*personne*) yield.

flegme [flɛgmə] *nm* composure. **flegmatique** *adj* phlegmatic.

flet [flɛ] *nm* flounder.

flétan [fletɑ̃] *nm* halibut.

flétrir¹ [fletrir] *v* (*faner*) wither, fade.

flétrir² [fletrir] *v* condemn; (*marquer*) brand. **flétrissure** *nf* (*tache*) stain, blemish; brand.

fleur [flœr] *nf* flower; (*arbre*) blossom; (*meilleur*) prime. **à fleur de** just above, on the surface of. **fleuriste** *n(m+f)* florist.

fleurir [flœrir] *v* flower, bloom; blossom; flourish, prosper; decorate with flowers. **fleuri** *adj* flowery; (*plante*) in flower; (*teint*) florid.

fleuve [flœv] *nm* river.

flexible [flɛksiblə] *adj* flexible.

flibustier [flibystje] *nm* buccaneer, pirate.

flic [flik] *nm* (*fam*) copper, policeman.

flirter [flœrte] *v* flirt. **flirteur, -euse** *nm*, *nf* flirt.

flocon [flɔkɔ̃] *nm* flake.

floral [flɔral] *adj* floral.

flore [flɔr] *nf* flora.

florissant [flɔrisɑ̃] *adj* flourishing; (*santé*) blooming.

flot [flo] *nm* flood, stream. **à flot** afloat. **à flots** in torrents.

flotter [flɔte] *v* float; (*brume*) drift; (*parfum*) waft; (*drapeau*) flutter, fly; hesitate. **flottabilité** *nf* buoyancy. **flottable** *adj* buoyant. **flottant** *adj* floating; (*vêtement*) loose; irresolute. **flotte** *nf* fleet. **flotteur** *nm* float.

flou [flu] *adj* blurred; vague.

fluctuer [flyktЧe] v fluctuate. **fluctuation** nf fluctuation.

fluet, -ette [flyɛ, -ɛt] adj slender.

fluide [flЧid] nm, adj fluid. **fluidité** nf fluidity, flow.

fluorescent [flyɔresɑ̃] adj fluorescent. **fluorescence** nf fluorescence.

flûte [flyt] nf flute; (pain) long thin loaf. **flûte à bec** recorder. **flûtiste** n(m+f) flautist.

flux [fly] nm flood; (méd) flow; (phys) flux.

fluxion [flyksjɔ̃] nf inflammation, swelling. **fluxion dentaire** gumboil. **fluxion de poitrine** pneumonia.

focal [fɔkal] adj focal.

fœtus [fetys] nm fœtus. **fœtal** adj foetal.

foi [fwa] nf faith; (parole) word.

foie [fwa] nm liver.

foin [fwɛ̃] nm hay.

foire [fwar] nf fair.

fois [fwa] nf time. **à la fois** at once. **des fois** (fam) sometimes. **deux fois** twice. **une fois** once.

foisonner [fwazɔne] v abound. **à foison** in abundance.

fol [fɔl] form of **fou** used before vowel or mute h.

folâtre [fɔlɑtrə] adj playful, lively.

folie [fɔli] nf (méd) madness; (bêtise) folly; (dépense) extravagance.

folklore [fɔlklɔr] nm folklore. **folklorique** adj folk; (fam) weird, outlandish.

folle [fɔl] V **fou**.

follet, -ette [fɔlɛ, -ɛt] adj scatter-brained.

follicule [fɔlikyl] nm follicle.

foncer [fɔ̃se] v charge, rush; (fam) tear along; (puits) sink; (couleur) go darker. **foncé** adj dark.

foncier [fɔ̃sje] adj land; fundamental.

fonction [fɔ̃ksjɔ̃] nf function; post, office. **faire fonction de** act as. **fonctionnaire** n(m+f) civil servant. **fonctionnel** adj functional.

fonctionner [fɔ̃ksjɔne] v function, work, operate.

fond [fɔ̃] nm bottom; (pièce) back; (tableau) background; (essentiel) heart, core; (profondeur) depth; (lie) sediment. **à fond** thoroughly. **au fond** deep down, basically. **de fond** basic.

fondamental [fɔ̃damɑ̃tal] adj fundamental, basic.

fondant [fɔ̃dɑ̃] adj melting. nm fondant.

fonder [fɔ̃de] v found; base; (foyer) start, set up; justify. **se fonder sur** (idée) be based on; (personne) go on. **fondateur, -trice** nm, nf founder. **fondation** nf foundation. **fondement** nm foundation, base, grounds pl.

fonderie [fɔ̃dri] nf foundry.

fondre [fɔ̃drə] v melt; (dans l'eau) dissolve; (statue, etc.) cast; (couleur) merge. **fondre sur** swoop down on.

fondrière [fɔ̃drijɛr] nf pothole, rut.

fonds [fɔ̃] nm fund, collection; (comm) business. nm pl funds pl.

fontaine [fɔ̃tɛn] nf fountain.

fonts [fɔ̃] nm pl **fonts baptismaux** font sing.

football [futbol] nm football. **footballeur** nm footballer.

footing [futiŋ] nm jogging. **faire du footing** go jogging.

for [fɔr] nm **dans son for intérieur** in one's heart of hearts.

forain [fɔrɛ̃] nm (marchand) stallholder; fairground entertainer.

forçat [fɔrsa] nm convict.

force [fɔrs] nf force, strength. **à force de** by dint of.

forcené [fɔrsəne], **-e** adj (fou) deranged; (acharné) frenzied. nm, nf fanatic, maniac.

forceps [fɔrsɛps] nm forceps pl.

forcer [fɔrse] v force; (claquer) strain, overdo. **forcé** adj forced; inevitable. **forcément** adv inevitably, of course. **pas forcément** not necessarily.

forer [fɔre] v drill, bore. **foreuse** nf drill.

forêt [fɔre] nf forest. **forestier** nm forester.

forfait[1] [fɔrfɛ] nm (sport) withdrawal; serious crime. **déclarer forfait** withdraw.

forfait[2] [fɔrfɛ] nm fixed price; contract. **forfaitaire** adj inclusive.

forger [fɔrʒe] v forge; create, form; (mot) coin; (inventer) contrive, concoct. **forge** nf forge. **forgeron** nm blacksmith.

se formaliser [fɔrmalize] v take offence.

format [fɔrma] nm format, size.

former [fɔrme] v form; make up; (éduquer) train; develop. **formalité** nf formality. **formation** nf formation; training. **forme** nf form; (contour) shape. **être en forme** be fit. **formel** adj formal; definite.

formidable [fɔrmidablə] adj tremendous; (fam) incredible, fantastic.

formuler [fɔrmyle] v formulate; (sentiment) express; (ordonnance) draw up.

formulaire nm form. **formule** nf formula; expression; system, method; form.

fort [fɔr] adj strong; (gros) large; (bruit) loud; (grand) great; (violent) hard; (doué) good, able. adv loudly; hard; (très) very, most; (beaucoup) greatly, very much. nm strong point, forte; (forteresse) fort; (milieu) height, depths pl.

forteresse [fɔrtərɛs] nf fortress, stronghold.

fortifier [fɔrtifje] v fortify, strengthen. **fortification** nf fortification.

fortuit [fɔrtɥi] adj fortuitous, chance.

fortune [fɔrtyn] nf fortune; (chance) luck. **de fortune** makeshift. **fortuné** adj (riche) wealthy; (heureux) fortunate.

fosse [fos] nf pit; (tombe) grave. **fossé** nm ditch; (écart) gulf. **fossette** nf dimple. **fossoyeur** nm gravedigger.

fossile [fosil] nm fossil. adj fossilized.

fou [fu], **folle** adj mad; (fam) terrific, tremendous. **avoir le fou rire** have the giggles. nm, nf lunatic.

foudre [fudrə] nf lightning. **coup de foudre** love at first sight.

foudroyer [fudrwaje] v strike (down). **foudroyant** adj (vitesse, attaque) lightning; violent; (succès) thundering.

fouet [fwɛ] nm whip; (cuisine) whisk. **fouetter** v whip.

fougère [fuʒɛr] nf fern.

fougue [fug] nf ardour, spirit. **fougueux** adj fiery, spirited.

fouiller [fuje] v search; (creuser) dig, excavate. **fouiller dans** rummage in, go through. **fouille** nf excavation; search.

fouillis [fuji] nm jumble, muddle.

fouir [fwir] v dig, burrow.

foulard [fular] nm scarf.

foule [ful] nf crowd, mob.

fouler [fule] v trample, tread; (méd) sprain. **foulure** nf sprain.

four [fur] nm oven; (usine) furnace; (poterie) kiln.

fourbe [furb] adj deceitful, treacherous. **fourberie** nf deceit, treachery.

fourche [furʃ] nf fork; (foin) pitchfork; (anat) crotch. **fourcher** v split. **fourchette** nf fork. **fourchu** adj forked; (pied) cloven.

fourgon [furgɔ̃] nm coach, wagon, van.

fourmi [furmi] nf ant. **avoir des fourmis** have pins and needles. **fourmilier** nm anteater. **fourmilière** nf ant-hill.

fourmiller [furmije] v swarm.

fourneau [furno] nm furnace; (cuisine) stove.

fournir [furnir] v supply, provide. **fourni** adj bushy, thick. **fournisseur** nm tradesman, stockist; (comm) supplier. **fournitures** nf pl supplies pl.

fourrer [fure] v (cuisine) stuff, fill; (vêtement) line with fur; (fam) shove, stick. **fourreau** nm sheath. **fourre-tout** nm invar (pièce) lumber room; (sac) holdall. **fourreur** nm furrier. **fourrure** nf fur.

*****foutre** [futrə] (impol) v do. **fous-moi le camp!** bugger off! **se foutre de** not give a damn about. **va te faire foutre!** fuck off! **foutaise** nf rubbish.

foyer [fwaje] nm home; (âtre) hearth; (jeunes) hostel; (théâtre) foyer; (phys) focus; (infection, etc.) seat, centre.

fracas [fraka] nm crash, din.

fracasser [frakase] v smash, shatter.

fraction [fraksjɔ̃] nf fraction.

fracturer [fraktyre] v fracture, break. **fracture** nf fracture.

fragile [fraʒil] adj fragile, delicate, frail. **fragilité** nf fragility, frailty.

fragment [fragmɑ̃] nm fragment, bit.

frai [frɛ] nm spawn.

frais¹, **fraîche** [frɛ, frɛʃ] adj fresh; (froid) cool; (nouveau) new. **fraîcheur** nf freshness; coolness.

frais² [frɛ] nm pl costs pl, expenses pl.

fraise¹ [frɛz] nf (fruit) strawberry. **fraisier** nm strawberry plant.

fraise² [frɛz] nf (col) ruff; (dentiste) drill.

framboise [frɑ̃bwaz] nf raspberry. **framboisier** nm raspberry bush.

franc¹ [frɑ̃] nm franc.

franc², **franche** [frɑ̃, frɑ̃ʃ] adj frank, candid; (libre) free; (péj) utter, downright; (net) clear. **franc-parler** nm invar outspokenness.

France [frɑ̃s] nf France. **français** nm, adj French. **les Français** the French.

franchir [frɑ̃ʃir] v (obstacle) clear, get over; (traverser) cross; pass.

franchise [frɑ̃ʃiz] nf frankness; exemption; (bagages) allowance.

franco [frɑ̃ko] adv post-free, carriage-paid.

frange [frɑ̃ʒ] nf fringe.

frapper [frape] v hit, strike; (glacer) chill, ice; (porte) knock.

fraternel [fratɛrnɛl] adj brotherly, fraternal. **fraternité** nf brotherhood, fraternity.

fraterniser [fratɛrnize] v fraternize.
fraude [frod] nf fraud, cheating. **passer en fraude** smuggle in. **frauder** v defraud, cheat. **frauduleux** adj fraudulent.
frayer [freje] v clear, open up; (poisson) spawn. **frayer avec** mix or associate with.
fredaine [frɔdɛn] nf mischief.
fredonner [frɔdɔne] v hum.
frein [frɛ̃] nm brake; (cheval) bit. **frein à main** handbrake. **mettre le frein à** curb, check. **freiner** v slow down; (auto) brake; (contrarier) check.
frêle [frɛl] adj frail, flimsy.
frelon [frɔlɔ̃] nm hornet.
frémir [fremir] v shudder, tremble; (de froid) shiver. **frémissement** nm shudder, shiver.
frêne [frɛn] nm ash.
frénésie [frenezi] nf frenzy. **frénétique** adj frenzied, frenetic.
fréquence [frekɑ̃s] nf frequency. **fréquent** adj frequent.
fréquenter [frekɑ̃te] v frequent; (amis, etc.) go around with, see often.
frère [frɛr] nm brother; (moine) friar.
fresque [frɛsk] nf fresco.
fret [frɛ] nm freight.
fréter [frete] v charter.
frétiller [fretije] v wriggle; (queue) wag.
friable [frijablɔ] adj crumbly.
friand [frijɑ̃] adj **friand de** fond of, partial to. **friandise** nf sweet, delicacy.
fricoter [frikɔte] v (fam) cook up.
friction [friksjɔ̃] nf friction. **frictionner** v rub.
frigide [friʒid] adj frigid. **frigidité** nf frigidity.
frigo [frigo] nm (fam) fridge.
frileux [frilø] adj sensitive to cold, chilly.
friper [fripe] v crumple.
fripon, -onne [fripɔ̃, -ɔn] adj cheeky, mischievous. nm, nf (fam) rascal.
*frire [frir] v fry.
frise [friz] nf frieze.
friser [frize] v curl; (frôler) skim; (approcher) verge on. **frisé** adj curly.
frisquet, -ette, [friskɛ, -ɛt] adj chilly.
frissonner [frisɔne] v tremble, shudder; (de froid) shiver; (feuillage) rustle. **frisson** nm shiver.
frit [fri] adj fried. **frites** nf pl chips pl. **friteuse** nf chip pan, deep-fryer. **friture** nf frying; fried food.
frivole [frivɔl] adj frivolous. **frivolité** nf frivolity.

froid [frwa] adj cold. nm cold. **avoid froid** be cold. **froideur** nf coldness.
froisser [frwase] v crumple, crease; (personne) offend. **se froisser** take offence.
frôler [frole] v brush against, skim.
fromage [frɔmaʒ] nm cheese. **fromage blanc** cream cheese. **fromage maigre** cottage cheese.
froment [frɔmɑ̃] nm wheat.
froncer [frɔ̃se] v gather. **froncer les sourcils** frown. **fronce** nm gather. **froncement de sourcils** nm frown.
fronde [frɔ̃d] nf sling.
front [frɔ̃] nm front; (anat) forehead. **de front** head-on; (côte à côte) abreast. **faire front à** face up to. **frontal** adj frontal.
frontière [frɔ̃tjɛr] nf frontier, border.
frotter [frɔte] v rub; (nettoyer) scrub; (allumette) strike.
fructueux [fryktɥø] adj fruitful, profitable.
frugal [frygal] adj frugal. **frugalité** nf frugality.
fruit [frɥi] nm fruit. **fruits de mer** seafood sing. **fruits secs** dried fruit sing.
fruste [fryst] adj unpolished, crude.
frustrer [frystre] v frustrate. **frustration** nf frustration.
fugace [fygas] adj fleeting.
fugitif [fyʒitif], **-ive** nm, nf fugitive. adj runaway; (fugace) fleeting.
*fuir [fɥir] v run away, escape; (éviter) shun, avoid; (gaz, liquide) leak. **fuite** nf escape, flight; leak.
fumer [fyme] v smoke; (vapeur) steam. **fumée** nf smoke; steam. **fumeur, -euse** nm, nf smoker.
fumier [fymje] nf dung, manure.
funambule [fynɑ̃byl] n(m + f) tightrope walker.
funèbre [fynɛbrɔ] adj funeral; (lugubre) mournful, gloomy.
funérailles [fyneraj] nf pl funeral sing.
funeste [fynɛst] adj disastrous; fatal, deadly.
fur [fyr] nm **au fur et à mesure** as, as soon as, as fast as.
furet [fyrɛ] nm ferret.
fureter [fyrte] v ferret about; (fouiller) rummage.
fureur [fyrœr] nf fury, rage; passion, mania. **furibond** adj furious, mad. **furie** nf fury; mania. **furieux** adj furious.

furoncle [fyrɔ̃klə] *nm* boil.

furtif [fyrtif] *adj* furtive.

fusée [fyze] *nf* rocket; (*mine*) fuse; (*tech*) spindle.

fusil [fyzi] *nm* gun, rifle. **fusil de chasse** shotgun. **fusiller** *v* shoot.

fusion [fyzjɔ̃] *nf* fusion; (*métal, glace*) melting.

fusionner [fyzjɔne] *v* merge, amalgamate.

fustiger [fystiʒe] *v* censure.

fût [fy] *nm* (*arbre*) bole; (*tonneau*) barrel; (*colonne*) shaft.

futaie [fytɛ] *nf* forest, plantation of timber trees.

futaille [fytɑj] *nf* barrel.

futile [fytil] *adj* futile; (*frivole*) trivial. **futilité** *nf* futility; triviality.

futur [fytyr] *adj* future, prospective. **future maman** *nf* mother-to-be. **futur mari** *nm* husband-to-be. *nm* future.

fuyant [fЧijɑ̃] *adj* elusive; (*menton, etc.*) receding.

G

gâcher [gɑʃe] *v* (*gaspiller*) waste; (*gâter*) spoil; (*travail*) botch. **gâchis** *nm* mess; waste.

gâchette [gɑʃɛt] *nf* trigger.

gaffe [gaf] *nf* (*impair*) blunder; (*naut*) boat-hook.

gage [gaʒ] *nm* guarantee, security; (*preuve*) proof, evidence; (*jeu*) forfeit. **gages** *nm pl* wages *pl*. **gager** *v* wager; guarantee.

gagner [gaɲe] *v* (*toucher, mériter*) earn; (*être vainqueur*) win; (*obtenir*) gain; (*arriver à*) reach. **gagnant, -e** *nm, nf* winner.

gai [ge] *adj* cheerful, gay, merry. **gaieté** *nf* gaiety, cheerfulness.

gaillard [gajar] *adj* strong; (*alerte*) lively, sprightly; (*grivois*) ribald. *nm* strapping fellow. **gaillardise** *nf* ribald remark.

gain [gɛ̃] *nm* gain; (*salaire*) earnings *pl*. **gains** *nm pl* profits *pl*; (*jeu*) winnings *pl*.

gaine [gɛn] *nf* sheath; (*vêtement*) girdle. **gainer** *v* sheathe, cover.

galant [galɑ̃] *adj* gallant; courteous; romantic. **galanterie** *nf* gallantry.

galaxie [galaksi] *nf* galaxy.

galbe [galbə] *nm* curve.

gale [gal] *nf* mange, scabies. **galeux** *adj* mangy; (*sordide*) squalid, seedy.

galère [galɛr] *nf* galley.

galerie [galri] *nf* gallery; (*auto*) roof rack.

galet [galɛ] *nm* pebble. **galets** *nm pl* shingle *sing*.

galette [galɛt] *nf* (*crêpe*) pancake; biscuit; (*gâteau*) cake.

galion [galjɔ̃] *nm* galleon.

Galles [gal] *nf pl* **pays de Galles** *nm* Wales. **gallois** *nm, adj* Welsh. **les Gallois** the Welsh.

gallon [galɔ̃] *nm* gallon.

galon [galɔ̃] *nm* braid; (*mil*) stripe.

galop [galo] *nm* gallop. **petit galop** canter. **galoper** *v* gallop.

galvaniser [galvanize] *v* galvanize.

gambader [gɑ̃bade] *v* gambol, leap about. **gambade** *nf* leap, caper.

gamin [gamɛ̃], **-e** *adj* playful; (*puéril*) childish. *nm, nf* (*fam*) kid.

gamme [gam] *nf* scale; (*série*) range.

gangrène [gɑ̃grɛn] *nf* gangrene.

gangster [gɑ̃gstɛr] *nm* gangster.

gant [gɑ̃] *nm* glove. **gant de toilette** facecloth, flannel.

garage [garaʒ] *nm* garage. **garagiste** *nm* garage owner; garage mechanic.

garant [garɑ̃], **-e** *nm, nf* (*personne*) guarantor; (*chose*) guarantee. **se porter garant de** stand bail for.

garantir [garɑ̃tir] *v* guarantee; assure; protect. **garantie** *nf* guarantee.

garce [gars] *nf* (*impol*) bitch.

garçon [garsɔ̃] *nm* boy; (*magasin*) assistant; (*restaurant*) waiter; (*célibataire*) bachelor. **garçon d'honneur** best man.

garde [gard] *nf* guard; (*jur*) custody; (*surveillance*) care. **garde-à-vous!** (*mil*) attention! **prendre garde** be careful, take care. *nm* guard; (*château*) warden. **garde du corps** bodyguard.

garder [garde] *v* (*surveiller*) look after, guard; (*conserver, retenir*) keep. **garde-boue** *nm invar* fender. **garde-chasse** *nm* gamekeeper. **garde-feu** *nm invar* fireguard. **garde-fou** *nm* railing, parapet. **garde-manger** *nm invar* pantry, larder. **garde-nappe** *nm* tablemat. **garde-robe** *nf* wardrobe. **se garder de** beware of, be careful not to. **garderie** *nf* crèche, day nursery.

gardien [gardjɛ̃], **-enne** *nm, nf* guard; (*prison*) warder; (*château*) warden; (*zoo*) keeper; (*musée*) attendant; (*défenseur*) guardian. **gardien de but** goalkeeper. **gardien de nuit** night watchman.

gare¹ [gar] *nf* station. **gare routière** bus station.

gare² [gar] *interj* look out! beware!

garenne [garɛn] *nf* rabbit warren.

garer [gare] *v* (*voiture*) park: (*bateau*) dock. **se garer** park; (*piéton*) move aside. **se garer de** avoid.

se gargariser [gargarize] *v* gargle. **gargarisme** *nm* gargle.

gargouiller [garguje] *v* gurgle; (*intestin*) rumble. **gargouille** *nf* gargoyle.

garnir [garnir] *v* (*remplir*) fill, stock; (*équiper*) fit; (*doubler*) line; cover; decorate; (*cuisine*) garnish. **garnison** *nm* garrison. **garniture** *nf* fittings *pl*; (*cuisine*) garnish, trimmings *pl*; (*légumes*) vegetables *pl*; lining.

gars [ga] *nm* (*fam*) lad.

gaspiller [gaspije] *v* waste. **gaspillage** *nm* waste. **gaspilleur, -euse** *adj* wasteful.

gastrique [gastrik] *adj* gastric.

gastronomie [gastrɔnɔmi] *nf* gastronomy. **gastronomique** *adj* gastronomic.

gâteau [gato] *nm* cake; (*dessert*) gâteau. **petit gâteau** (**sec**) biscuit.

gâter [gate] *v* spoil, ruin. **se gâter** go bad *or* off; take a turn for the worse.

gauche [goʃ] *adj* left; (*maladroit*) awkward, clumsy. *nf* left, left-hand side. **gaucher** *adj* left-handed. **gaucherie** *nf* awkwardness, clumsiness.

gauchir [goʃir] *v* warp; (*fausser*) distort.

gaz [gaz] *nm invar* gas. **gazeux** *adj* gaseous; (*boisson*) fizzy.

gaze [gaz] *nf* gauze.

gazéifier [gazeifje] *v* aerate.

gazelle [gazɛl] *nf* gazelle.

gazon [gazɔ̃] *nm* lawn; (*motte*) turf.

gazouiller [gazuje] *v* (*oiseau*) chirp; (*bébé*) gurgle; (*ruisseau*) babble.

géant [ʒeã] *adj* gigantic, giant. *nm* giant.

***geindre** [ʒɛ̃drə] *v* groan, moan, whine.

gel [ʒɛl] *nm* frost.

gélatine [ʒelatin] *nf* gelatine.

geler [ʒəle] *v* freeze, be frozen. **gelé** *adj* frozen; (*membre*) frostbitten. **gelée** *nf* frost; (*cuisine*) jelly. **gelure** *nf* frostbite.

gélignite [ʒelignit] *nf* gelignite.

Gémeaux [ʒemo] *nm pl* Gemini *sing*.

gémir [ʒemir] *v* groan, moan, whine; (*grincer*) creak. **gémissement** *nm* groan, moan.

gemme [ʒɛm] *nf* gem.

gencive [ʒãsiv] *nf* gum.

gendarme [ʒãdarm] *nm* policeman.

gendre [ʒãdrə] *nm* son-in-law.

gène [ʒɛn] *nm* gene.

gêne [ʒɛn] *nf* trouble, bother; embarrassment; (*physique*) discomfort; financial difficulties *pl*.

généalogie [ʒenealɔʒi] *nf* genealogy. **généalogique** *adj* genealogical.

gêner [ʒene] *v* bother, embarrass; (*obstacle*) hamper; inconvenience. **se gêner** put oneself out. **gênant** *adj* embarrassing, awkward. **gêné** *adj* embarrassed, uncomfortable; short of money.

général [ʒeneral] *nm, adj* general. **en général** in general, usually. **général de brigade** brigadier. **généralisation** *nf* generalization. **généraliser** *v* generalize. **généraliste** *nm* general practitioner.

génération [ʒenerasjɔ̃] *nf* generation.

génératrice [ʒeneratris] *nf* generator.

généreux [ʒenerø] *adj* generous. **générosité** *nf* generosity.

générique [ʒenerik] *adj* generic. *nm* (*cinéma*) credits *pl*.

génétique [ʒenetik] *adj* genetic. *nf* genetics.

génie [ʒeni] *nm* genius; spirit. **le génie** (*mil*) the Engineers. **génial** *adj* brilliant, inspired.

genièvre [ʒənjɛvrə] *nm* (*arbre*) juniper; (*fruit*) juniper berry; (*boisson*) gin.

génital [ʒenital] *adj* genital. **organes génitaux** *nm pl* genitals *pl*.

genou [ʒənu] *nm, pl* **-oux** knee. **à genoux** kneeling.

genre [ʒãr] *nm* kind, sort; (*gramm*) gender; (*art, etc.*) genre; family, genus. **le genre humain** mankind.

gens [ʒã] *nm pl* people *pl*.

gentiane [ʒãsjan] *nf* gentian.

gentil, -ille [ʒãti, -ij] *adj* nice; (*personne*) kind; (*sage*) good. **gentillesse** *nf* kindness; favour. **gentiment** *adv* nicely; kindly.

génuflexion [ʒenyflɛksjɔ̃] *nf* genuflexion.

géographie [ʒeɔgrafi] *nf* geography. **géographe** *n(m+f)* geographer. **géographique** *adj* geographical.

geôle [ʒol] *nf* jail. **geôlier, -ère** *nm, nf* jailer.

géologie [ʒeɔlɔʒi] *nf* geology. **géologique** *adj* geological. **géologue** *n(m+f)* geologist.

géométrie [ʒeɔmetri] *nf* geometry. **géomètre** *nm* surveyor. **géométrique** *adj* geometrical.

géranium [ʒeranjɔm] *nm* geranium.

gerbe [ʒɛrb] *nf* sheaf, bundle; (*fleurs*) spray; (*eau, étincelles*) shower.

gercer [ʒɛrse] *v* chap, crack. **gerçure** *nf* crack.

gérer [ʒere] *v* manage. **gérance** *nf* management. **gérant** *nm* manager. **gérante** *nf* manageress.

gériatrie [ʒerjatri] *nf* geriatrics. **gériatrique** *adj* geriatric.

germanique [ʒɛrmanik] *adj* Germanic.

germer [ʒɛrme] *v* germinate; (*plante*) sprout, shoot. **germe** *nm* germ; (*source*) seed. **germination** *nf* germination.

gérondif [ʒerɔ̃dif] *nm* gerund, gerundive.

*gésir [ʒezir] *v* lie, be lying.

geste [ʒɛst] *nm* gesture; act, deed.

gesticuler [ʒɛstikyle] *v* gesticulate. **gesticulation** *nf* gesticulation.

gestion [ʒɛstjɔ̃] *nf* management, administration.

geyser [ʒɛzɛr] *nm* geyser.

ghetto [gɛto] *nm* ghetto.

gibet [ʒibɛ] *nm* gallows.

gibier [ʒibje] *nm* game.

giboulée [ʒibule] *nf* shower.

gicler [ʒikle] *v* spurt, squirt. **giclée** *nf* spurt, squirt.

gifler [ʒifle] *v* slap in the face. **gifle** *nf* slap in the face.

gigantesque [ʒigɑ̃tɛsk] *adj* gigantic, immense.

gigot [ʒigo] *nm* leg of lamb.

gigue [ʒig] *nf* jig.

gilet [ʒilɛ] *nm* waistcoat; cardigan. **gilet de sauvetage** life-jacket.

gin [dʒin] *nm* gin.

gingembre [ʒɛ̃ʒɑ̃brə] *nm* ginger.

girafe [ʒiraf] *nf* giraffe.

girofle [ʒirɔflə] *nm* clove.

giron [ʒirɔ̃] *nm* lap.

girouette [ʒirwɛt] *nf* weathercock.

gisement [ʒizmɑ̃] *nm* deposit.

gitan [ʒitɑ̃] *adj* gipsy. **Gitan, -e** *nm, nf* gipsy.

gîte [ʒit] *nm* shelter.

givre [ʒivrə] *nm* hoar-frost. **givrer** *v* ice up.

glabre [glabrə] *adj* hairless; (*rasé*) clean-shaven.

glacer [glase] *v* freeze; (*boissons, etc.*) chill; (*cuisine*) glaze; (*gâteau*) ice. **glaçage** *nm* icing. **glace** *nf* ice; (*crème*) ice cream; mirror; (*vitre*) window; (*verre*) glass. **glacé** *adj* frozen, icy; (*boisson*) iced. **glacial** *adj* icy, frosty. **glacière** *nf* icebox. **glaçon** *nm* icicle; (*boisson*) ice cube.

glacier [glasje] *nm* glacier. **glaciation** *nf* glaciation.

glaise [glɛz] *nf* clay.

gland [glɑ̃] *nm* acorn; (*ornement*) tassel.

glande [glɑ̃d] *nf* gland. **glandulaire** *adj* glandular.

glaner [glane] *v* glean.

glapir [glapir] *v* yelp, squeal.

glisser [glise] *v* slide, slip; (*voilier, patineur*) glide; (*véhicule*) skid. **se glisser** slip, creep. **glissade** *nf* slide, slip; skid. **glissant** *adj* slippery. **glissière** *nf* groove, channel. **à glissière** sliding. **glissoire** *nf* slide.

globe [glɔb] *nm* globe. **globe oculaire** eyeball. **global** *adj* global, overall, total.

gloire [glwar] *nf* glory; (*renommée*) fame; distinction, credit. **glorieux** *adj* glorious. **glorifier** [glɔrifje] *v* glorify. **se glorifier de** glory in. **glorification** *nf* glorification.

glossaire [glɔsɛr] *nm* glossary.

glouglouter [gluglute] *v* (*eau*) gurgle; (*dindon*) gobble. **glouglou** *nm* gurgling; gobbling.

glousser [gluse] *v* (*poule*) cluck; (*personne*) chuckle. **gloussement** *nm* cluck; chuckle.

glouton, -onne [glutɔ̃, -ɔn] *adj* greedy. *nm, nf* glutton. **gloutonnerie** *nf* gluttony, greed.

gluant [glyɑ̃] *adj* sticky.

glucose [glykoz] *nm* glucose.

glycine [glisin] *nf* wisteria.

gnome [gnom] *nm* gnome.

go [go] *adv* (*fam*) **tout de go** straight; (*dire*) straight out.

gobelet [gɔblɛ] *nm* beaker; (*verre*) tumbler; (*papier*) cup.

gober [gɔbe] *v* swallow whole; (*mensonge*) swallow, believe. **se gober** fancy oneself.

godasse [gɔdas] *nf* (*fam*) shoe.

godet [gɔde] *nm* pot, jar.

godiche [gɔdiʃ] *adj* awkward, oafish.

goéland [gɔelɑ̃] *nm* seagull.

goélette [gɔelɛt] *nf* schooner.

gogo [gɔgo] *adv* **à gogo** (*fam*) galore.

golf [gɔlf] *nm* golf; (*terrain*) golf course. **golfeur, -euse** *nm, nf* golfer.

golfe [gɔlf] *nm* gulf, bay.

gommer [gɔme] *v* (*effacer*) erase, rub out; (*coller*) gum. **gomme** *nf* eraser, rubber; gum. **gommeux** *adj* sticky.

gond [gɔ̃] *nm* hinge.

gondole [gɔ̃dɔl] *nf* gondola. **gondolier, -ère** *nm, nf* gondolier.

gonfler [gɔ̃fle] *v* swell; (*d'air*) inflate. **gonflé** *adj* swollen; (*yeux*) puffy; (*ventre*) bloated. **gonflement** *nm* swelling; inflation.

gong [gɔ̃] *nm* gong.

gorge [gɔrʒ] *nf* (*gosier*) throat; (*poitrine*) breast; (*défilé*) gorge; (*rainure*) groove. **gorgée** *nf* mouthful. **petite gorgée** sip. **se gorger** *v* gorge.

gorille [gɔrij] *nm* gorilla.

gosier [gozje] *nm* throat.

gosse [gɔs] *n(m + f)* (*fam*) kid.

gothique [gɔtik] *nm* Gothic.

goudron [gudrɔ̃] *nm* tar. **goudronner** *v* tar.

gouffre [gufrə] *nm* abyss.

goulot [gulo] *nm* neck.

goulu [guly] *adj* greedy.

gourde [gurd] *nf* gourd; (*bidon*) flask; (*fam*) clot.

gourmand [gurmɑ̃] *adj* greedy. **gourmandise** *nf* greed.

gourmet [gurmɛ] *nm* gourmet.

gousse [gus] *nf* pod. **gousse d'ail** clove of garlic.

goût [gu] *nm* taste; (*penchant*) liking; style. **de bon/mauvais goût** in good/bad taste.

goûter [gute] *v* taste; savour, enjoy. **goûter à** taste, sample. *nm* afternoon tea.

goutte [gut] *nf* drop; (*méd*) gout. **goutte-à-goutte** *nm invar* (*méd*) drip. **tomber goutte à goutte** drip. **gouttière** *nf* gutter.

gouvernail [guvɛrnaj] *nm* rudder; (*barre*) helm.

gouverner [guvɛrne] *v* govern, rule; control; (*naut*) steer. **gouvernante** *nf* housekeeper; (*des enfants*) governess. **gouvernement** *nm* government. **gouverneur** *nm* governor.

grâce [grɑs] *nf* grace; favour; charm; pardon, mercy. **de bonne grâce** willingly. **grâce à** thanks to. **gracieux** *adj* graceful; amiable, kindly.

gracile [grasil] *adj* slender.

grade [grad] *nm* grade; (*échelon*) rank; (*titre*) degree.

gradin [gradɛ̃] *nm* terrace, step; (*théâtre*) tier.

graduer [gradɥe] *v* increase gradually; (*exercices*) grade; (*règle, etc.*) graduate. **graduel** *adj* gradual; progressive.

graffiti [grafiti] *nm pl* graffiti *pl.*

grain [grɛ̃] *nm* grain; (*café*) bean; (*collier*) bead. **grain de beauté** mole. **grain de poivre** peppercorn. **grain de raisin** grape. **graine** [grɛn] *nf* seed.

graisser [grese] *v* grease. **graisse** *nf* fat, grease. **graisse de rognon** suet. **graisse de viande** dripping. **graisseux** *adj* greasy, fatty.

grammaire [gramɛr] *nf* grammar. **grammatical** *adj* grammatical.

gramme [gram] *nm* gram.

grand [grɑ̃], **-e** *adj* large, big; (*personne*) tall; (*intense, important*) great; (*principal*) main; (*réception, etc.*) grand. *nm, nf* senior *or* older pupil. **grandeur** *nf* greatness; (*dimension*) size.

grand-chose *n(m + f)* *invar* much.

Grande-Bretagne *nf* Great Britain.

grande ligne *nf* (*rail*) main line.

grandes vacances *nf pl* summer holidays *pl.*

grandiose [grɑ̃djoz] *adj* grand, imposing.

grandir [grɑ̃dir] *v* grow; (*augmenter*) increase; exaggerate; (*grossir*) magnify; (*hausser*) make taller.

grand magasin *nm* department store.

grand-mère *nf* grandmother.

grand ouvert *adj* wide open.

grand-parent *nm* grandparent.

grand-père *nm* grandfather.

grand-route *nf* main road.

grand-voile *nf* mainsail.

grange [grɑ̃ʒ] *nf* barn.

granit [granit] *nm* granite.

graphique [grafik] *adj* graphic. *nm* graph.

grappe [grap] *nf* cluster. **grappe de raisin** bunch of grapes.

gras, grasse [grɑ, grɑs] *adj* fat; (*graisseux*) greasy; (*épais*) thick; rich. **faire la grasse matinée** have a lie-in. *nm* fat. **grassouillet, -ette** *adj* (*fam*) plump, podgy.

gratifier [gratifje] *v* present, give, favour. **gratification** *nf* bonus.

gratin [gratɛ̃] *nm* **au gratin** topped with breadcrumbs or grated cheese.

gratitude [gratityd] *nf* gratitude.
gratter [grate] *v* scratch, scrape. **gratte-ciel** *nm invar* skyscraper.
gratuit [gratɥi] *adj* free; (*injustifié*) gratuitous.
grave [grav] *adj* serious, grave; (*digne*) solemn; (*son*) deep, low. **gravité** *nf* gravity, seriousness.
graver [grave] *v* engrave; (*disque*) cut. **graver à l'eau-forte** etch. **graveur** *nm* engraver. **gravure** *nf* engraving; (*illustration*) plate; (*réproduction*) print.
gravier [gravje] *nm* gravel.
gravir [gravir] *v* climb.
gré [gre] *nm* (*volonté*) will; (*goût*) taste, liking.
Grèce [grɛs] *nf* Greece. **grec, grecque** *nm*, *adj* Greek. **Grec, Grecque** *nm*, *nf* Greek.
gréer [gree] *v* rig. **gréement** *nm* rigging.
greffer [grefe] *v* graft; (*organe*) transplant. **greffe** *nf* graft; transplant.
greffier [grefje] *nm* clerk of the court.
grégaire [gregɛr] *adj* gregarious.
grêle[1] [grɛl] *adj* spindly, lanky; (*son*) shrill.
grêle[2] [grɛl] *nf* hail. **grêler** *v* hail. **grêlon** *nm* hailstone.
grelotter [grəlɔte] *v* shiver; (*tinter*) jingle.
grenade[1] [grənad] *nf* (*fruit*) pomegranate. **grenadier** *nm* pomegranate tree.
grenade[2] [grənad] *nf* grenade. **grenade à main** hand grenade. **grenadier** *nm* grenadier.
grenier [grənje] *nm* attic, loft.
grenouille [grənuj] *nf* frog.
grès [grɛ] *nm* sandstone.
grésiller [grezije] *v* sizzle; (*phone, radio*) crackle.
grève[1] [grɛv] *nf* (*rivière*) bank; (*mer*) shore.
grève[2] [grɛv] *nf* strike. **faire grève** be on strike. **grève de la faim** hunger strike. **grève du zèle** work-to-rule. **grève perlée** go-slow. **se mettre en grève** strike, go on strike. **gréviste** *n(m+f)* striker.
grever [grəve] *v* burden, put a strain on.
gribouiller [gribuje] *v* scribble; (*dessiner*) doodle. **gribouillage** *nm* scribble; doodle.
grief [grijɛf] *nm* grievance. **grièvement blessé** seriously injured.
griffer [grife] *v* scratch. **griffe** *nf* claw; signature.
griffonner [grifɔne] *v* scribble. **griffonnage** *nm* scribble.

grignoter [griɲɔte] *v* nibble (at).
gril [gril] *nm* grill pan.
grille [grij] *nf* grid; (*claire-voie*) grille; (*prison*) bars *pl*; (*clôture*) gate; (*égout*) grating.
griller [grije] *v* grill; (*pain*) toast; (*brûler*) burn, scorch. **grille-pain** *nm invar* toaster. **grillade** *nm* grill.
grillon [grijɔ̃] *nm* cricket.
grimacer [grimase] *v* grimace, pull a face; (*sourire*) grin. **grimace** *nf* grimace.
grimer [grime] *v* (*théâtre*) make up. **grimage** *nm* make-up.
grimper [grɛ̃pe] *v* climb (up).
grincer [grɛ̃se] *v* (*métal*) grate; (*bois*) creak. **grincer des dents** gnash one's teeth.
grincheux [grɛ̃ʃø] *adj* grumpy.
grippe [grip] *nf* flu, influenza. **prendre en grippe** take a sudden dislike to.
gris [gri] *adj* grey; (*morne*) dull; (*ivre*) drunk. *nm* grey. **griser** *v* intoxicate. **se griser** get drunk. **grisonner** *v* go grey.
grive [griv] *nf* thrush.
grivois [grivwa] *adj* saucy.
Groënland [grɔɛnlɑ̃d] *nm* Greenland. **Groënlandais, -e** *nm*, *nf* Greenlander.
grogner [grɔɲe] *v* (*chien*) growl; (*cochon*) grunt; (*grommeler*) grumble. **grognement** *nm* growl, grunt.
groin [grwɛ̃] *nm* snout.
grommeler [grɔmle] *v* mutter, grumble.
gronder [grɔ̃de] *v* (*enfant*) scold; (*train, orage*) rumble; (*chien*) growl.
gros, grosse [gro, gros] *adj* big, large; (*personne*) fat; (*épais*) thick, heavy; (*important*) great; (*rude*) coarse. **gros lot** *nm* jackpot. **gros plan** *nm* close-up. **gros titre** *nm* headline. *nm* fat man; (*principal*) main part, bulk; (*comm*) wholesale. **en gros** wholesale; broadly, roughly. **grosse** *nf* fat woman; (*comm*) gross.
groseille [grozɛj] *nf* (*rouge*) red currant; (*blanche*) white currant. **groseille à maquereau** gooseberry. **groseillier** *nm* currant bush.
grossier [grosje] *adj* coarse, rough, crude. **grossièreté** *nf* coarseness, crudeness.
grossir [grosir] *v* swell, grow; (*personne*) put on weight; (*augmenter*) increase; exaggerate; (*agrandir*) enlarge, magnify.
grotesque [grɔtɛsk] *adj* grotesque; (*risible*) ludicrous. *nm* grotesque.
grotte [grɔt] *nf* cave; (*artificielle*) grotto.

grouiller [gruje] v mill about. **grouiller de** be swarming or crawling with.

grouper [grupe] v group, put together. **groupe** nm group.

grue [gry] nf crane.

grumeau [grymo] nm lump.

se grumeler [grymle] v go lumpy; (lait) curdle. **grumeleux** adj lumpy.

gué [ge] nm ford. **passer à gué** ford.

guenille [gənij] nf rag.

guépard [gepar] nm cheetah.

guêpe [gɛp] nf wasp. **guêpier** nm wasp's nest; (piège) trap.

guère [gɛr] adv hardly, scarcely; not much.

guérilla [gerija] nf guerrilla warfare. **guérillero** nm guerilla.

guérir [gerir] v (maladie) cure; (blessure) heal; (malade) get better. **guérison** nf recovery.

Guernesey [gɛrnəzɛ] nf Guernsey.

guerre [gɛr] nf war; (stratégie) warfare. **en guerre** at war. **guerre mondiale** world war. **guerrier, -ère** nm, nf warrior.

guerroyer [gɛrwaje] v wage war.

guet [gɛ] nm watch. **faire le guet** be on the look-out. **guet-apens** nm ambush, trap.

guetter [gete] v watch (for); (menace) lie in wait for.

gueuler [gœle] v (argot) bawl, yell. **gueule** nf mouth; (fam: figure) face. **gueule de bois** (fam) hangover. **gueule-de-loup** nf snapdragon.

gueux [gø], **gueuse** nm, nf beggar.

gui [gi] nm mistletoe.

guichet [giʃɛ] nm window, counter; (théâtre) box office; (gare) ticket office; (porte) hatch, grille.

guide [gid] nm guide; (livre) guidebook. nf rein; (jeune fille) girl guide. **guider** v guide.

guidon [gidɔ̃] nm handlebars pl.

guigne [giɲ] nf (fam) bad luck.

guillemets [gijmɛ] nm pl inverted commas pl, quotation marks pl. **entre guillemets** in inverted commas.

guilleret, -ette [gijrɛ, -ɛt] adj perky, lively; (propos) saucy.

guillotine [gijɔtin] nf guillotine. **guillotiner** v guillotine.

guimauve [gimov] nf marshmallow.

guindé [gɛ̃de] v (air) stiff; (style) stilted.

Guinée [gine] nf Guinea.

guingois [gɛ̃gwa] adv **de guingois** (fam) askew, lop-sided.

guirlande [girlɑ̃d] nf garland. **guirlande de Noël** tinsel. **guirlande électrique** or **lumineuse** fairy lights pl.

guise [giz] nf **à sa guise** as one pleases. **en guise de** by way of.

guitare [gitar] nf guitar. **guitariste** n(m+f) guitarist.

gymnase [ʒimnaz] nm gymnasium. **gymnaste** n(m+f) gymnast. **gymnastique** nf (sport) gymnastics; exercises pl.

gynécologie [ʒinekɔlɔʒi] nf gynaecology. **gynécologique** adj gynaecological. **gynécologue** n(m+f) gynaecologist.

gypse [ʒips] nm gypsum.

gyroscope [ʒirɔskɔp] nm gyroscope.

H

habile [abil] adj skilful, clever; (malin) cunning. **habileté** nf skill, cleverness.

habiller [abije] v dress, clothe; cover. **s'habiller** get dressed. **s'habiller en** dress up as. **habillement** nm clothing; outfit.

habit [abi] nm (costume) dress, outfit; (soirée) formal dress; (rel) habit. **habits** nm pl clothes pl.

habiter [abite] v live (in). **habitable** adj habitable. **habitant, -e** nm, nf inhabitant; (maison) occupant. **habitat** nm habitat. **habitation** nf residence, home; (logement) housing.

habitude [abityd] nf habit; custom. **avoir l'habitude de** be used to. **comme d'habitude** as usual. **d'habitude** usually.

habituer [abitɥe] v accustom. **s'habituer à** get used to. **habitué** nm regular. **habituel** adj usual, habitual.

hâbleur, -euse ['ablœr, -øz] adj boastful. nm, nf braggart. **hablerie** nf bragging, boasting.

hacher ['aʃe] v chop; (menu) mince. **hache** nf axe. **haché** adj minced; (phrases) jerky. **hachette** nf hatchet. **hachis** nm mince. **hachis Parmentier** cottage pie. **hachoir** nm chopper; mincer.

hagard ['agar] adj wild, distraught.

haie ['ɛ] nf hedge; (sport) hurdle, fence; (rangée) line.

haillon ['ɑjɔ̃] nm rag.
haine ['ɛn] nf hatred.
*haïr ['air] v detest, hate.
Haïti [aiti] nf Haiti.
halage ['alaʒ] nm towing. chemin de halage nm towpath.
hâle ['ɑl] nm sunburn, tan. hâlé adj sunburnt, tanned.
haleine [alɛn] nf breath. hors d'haleine out of breath. reprendre haleine get one's breath back.
haler ['ale] v tow; (ancre) haul in.
haleter ['alte] v pant, gasp for breath. haletant adj panting, breathless.
hall ['ol] nm hall.
halle ['al] nf covered market.
hallucination [alysinɑsjɔ̃] nf hallucination.
halte ['alt] nf stop, pause; (rail) halt. faire halte stop, halt. interj stop! halt!
haltérophilie [alterɔfili] nf weight-lifting.
hamac ['amak] nm hammock.
hameau ['amo] nm hamlet.
hameçon [amsɔ̃] nm hook.
hampe ['ɑp] nf pole, shaft.
hamster ['amstɛr] nm hamster.
hanche ['ɑ̃ʃ] nf hip; (cheval) haunch.
handicaper ['ɑ̃dikape] v handicap. handicap nm handicap. handicapé, -e nm, nf handicapped person. handicapé moteur spastic.
hangar ['ɑ̃gar] nm shed; (aéro) hangar.
hanter ['ɑ̃te] v haunt. hantise nf obsession.
happer ['ape] v snatch, grab.
haras ['arɑ] nm stud farm.
harassé ['arase] adj exhausted.
harceler ['arsəle] v harass, pester.
harde ['ard] nf herd.
hardes ['ard] nf pl old clothes pl.
hardi ['ardi] adj bold, daring. hardiesse nf boldness; effrontery, audacity.
hareng ['arɑ̃] nm herring. hareng fumé kipper.
hargneux ['arɲø] adj aggressive.
haricot ['ariko] nm bean. haricot à rames runner bean. haricot beurre/blanc/rouge/vert butter/haricot/kidney/French bean.
harmonica [armɔnika] nm harmonica.
harmonie [armɔni] nf harmony. harmonieux adj harmonious. harmonique nm, adj harmonic. harmoniser v harmonize.

harnacher ['arnaʃe] v harness.
harnais ['arnɛ] nm harness.
harpe ['arp] nf harp. harpiste n(m+f) harpist.
harpon ['arpɔ̃] nm harpoon.
hasard ['azar] nm chance, luck; risk, hazard; coincidence. au hasard at random. par hasard by accident. hasarder v risk. hasardeux adj risky, dangerous.
haschich ['aʃiʃ] nm hashish.
hâter ['ɑte] v hasten, hurry. hâte nf haste, hurry; impatience. à la hâte hurriedly. hâtif adj hasty, hurried; precocious, early.
hausser ['ose] v raise. hausser les épaules shrug one's shoulders. hausse nf rise, increase.
haut ['o] adj high; (arbre, édifice) tall; noble. adv high; (fort) loudly. nm top. à haute voix aloud. de haut en bas downwards; (regarder) up and down. en haut at the top; (dessus) above; (maison) upstairs. haut-de-forme nm top hat. haut fourneau blast furnace. haut-parleur nm loudspeaker.
hautain ['otɛ̃] adj haughty.
hautbois ['obwa] nm oboe. hautboïste n(m+f) oboist.
hauteur ['otœr] nf height; (son) pitch; nobility; (arrogance) haughtiness. à la hauteur de level with; equal to.
hâve ['av] adj haggard, gaunt.
havre ['avrə] nm haven.
havresac ['avrəsak] nm haversack.
Haye ['ɛ] nf La Haye the Hague.
hebdomadaire [ɛbdɔmadɛr] nm, adj weekly.
héberger [ebɛrʒe] v lodge, take in.
hébéter [ebete] v daze, numb. hébétement nm stupor.
hébraïque [ebraik] adj Hebrew.
hébreu [ebrø] nm, adj Hebrew. Hebreu nm Hebrew.
hectare [ɛktar] nm hectare.
hein ['ɛ̃] interj (fam) eh?
hélas ['elɑs] interj alas!
héler ['ele] v hail.
hélice [elis] nf propeller.
hélicoptère [elikɔptɛr] nm helicopter.
hémisphère [emisfɛr] nm hemisphere.
hémorragie [emɔraʒi] nf haemorrhage.
hémorroïdes [emɔrɔid] nf pl haemorrhoids pl.
henné ['ene] nm henna.

hennir ['enir] v neigh. **hennissement** nm neigh.

héraldique [eraldik] adj heraldic. nf heraldry.

héraut ['ero] nm herald.

herbe [ɛrb] nf grass; (cuisine) herb. **en herbe** (plante) unripe; (personne) budding. **herbeux** or **herbu** adj grassy. **herbicide** nm weed-killer.

hérédité [eredite] nf heredity. **héréditaire** adj hereditary.

hérésie [erezi] nf heresy.

hérétique [eretik] adj heretical. n(m+f) heretic.

hérisser ['erise] v bristle, spike; (personne) ruffle. **se hérisser** stand on end, bristle up. **hérissé** adj bristly, prickly.

hérisson ['erisɔ̃] nm hedgehog.

hériter [erite] v inherit. **héritage** nm inheritance; (civilisation) heritage. **héritier** nm heir. **héritière** nf heiress.

hermétique [ɛrmetik] adj sealed; (étanche) watertight; (à l'air) airtight; impenetrable.

hermine [ɛrmin] nf ermine; (animal) stoat.

hernie ['ɛrni] nf hernia. **hernie discale** slipped disc.

héroïne¹ [erɔin] nf (femme) heroine.

héroïne² [erɔin] nf (drogue) heroin.

héroïsme [erɔismə] nm heroism. **héroïque** adj heroic.

héron ['erɔ̃] nm heron.

héros ['ero] nm hero.

hésiter [ezite] v hesitate. **hésitant** adj hesitant. **hésitation** nf hesitation.

hétéroclite [eterɔklit] adj sundry, assorted; (personne) eccentric.

hétérosexual [eterɔsɛksɥɛl] adj heterosexual.

hêtre ['ɛtrə] nm beech.

heure [œr] nf time; (mesure) hour. **à l'heure** on time. **deux/trois etc. heures** two/three etc. o'clock. **heure d'affluence** rush hour. **heures creuses** off-peak periods pl. **heures supplémentaires** overtime sing. **tout à l'heure** (passé) just now; (futur) shortly.

heureux [œrø] adj happy; fortunate, lucky.

heurter ['œrte] v strike, hit; (sentiments, idées) conflict with, go against. **se heurter** collide; (s'opposer) clash. **heurt** nm collision; clash. **sans heurts** smoothly. **heurtoir** nm door-knocker.

hexagone [ɛgzagɔn] nm hexagon. **hexagonal** adj hexagonal.

hiberner [ibɛrne] v hibernate. **hibernation** nf hibernation.

hibou ['ibu] nm, pl -oux nm owl.

hideux ['idø] adj hideous.

hier [jɛr] adv yesterday. **hier soir** yesterday evening, last night.

hiérarchie ['jerarʃi] nf hierarchy. **hiérarchique** adj hierarchical.

hilare [ilar] adj merry, mirthful. **hilarité** nf hilarity.

hindou [ɛ̃du] adj Hindu. **Hindou, -e** nm, nf Hindu. **hindouisme** nm Hinduism.

hippique [ipik] adj horse, equestrian. **concours hippique** nm show-jumping. **hippisme** nm (courses) horse-racing; (équitation) horse-riding.

hippocampe [ipɔkɑ̃p] nm sea-horse.

hippodrome [ipɔdrom] nm racecourse.

hippopotame [ipɔpɔtam] nm hippopotamus.

hirondelle [irɔ̃dɛl] nf swallow.

hisser ['ise] v hoist. **se hisser** heave or haul oneself up.

histoire [istwar] nf history; (conte) story; (fam: affaire) business. **histoires** nf pl (fam) fuss sing, trouble sing. **historien, -enne** nm, nf historian. **historique** adj historical; (événement) historic.

hiver [ivɛr] nm winter. **hivernal** adj winter; (temps) wintry.

hocher ['ɔʃe] v **hocher la tête** (oui) nod; (non) shake one's head. **hochement de tête** nm nod; shake of the head.

hochet ['ɔʃɛ] nm rattle.

hockey ['ɔkɛ] nm hockey.

Hollande ['ɔlɑ̃d] nf Holland. **hollandais** nm, adj Dutch. **les Hollandais** the Dutch.

homard ['ɔmar] nm lobster.

homicide [ɔmisid] nm murder. **homicide involontaire** manslaughter.

hommage [ɔmaʒ] nm homage, tribute; (témoignage) token. **hommages** nm pl respects pl.

homme [ɔm] nm man (pl men); (espèce) mankind. **homme à tout faire** odd-job man. **homme d'affaires** businessman. **homme de loi** lawyer. **homme d'État** statesman. **homme-grenouille** nm frogman. **homme politique** politician.

homogène [ɔmɔʒɛn] adj homogeneous.

homonyme [ɔmɔnim] nm homonym; (personne) namesake.

homosexuel [ɔmɔsɛksɥɛl], **-elle** n, adj homosexual. **homosexualité** nf homosexuality.

Hongrie ['ɔ̃gri] nf Hungary. **hongrois** nm, adj Hungarian. **Hongrois, -e** nm, nf Hungarian.

honnête [ɔnɛt] adj honest; decent; (juste) fair, reasonable. **honnêteté** nf honesty; decency; fairness.

honneur [ɔnœr] nm honour; (mérite) credit.

honorer [ɔnɔre] v honour; do credit to; respect. **honorable** adj honourable, worthy. **honoraire** adj honorary.

honte ['ɔ̃t] nf shame; (déshonneur) disgrace. **avoir honte** be ashamed. **faire honte à** put to shame. **honteux** adj (penaud) ashamed; (scandaleux) shameful, disgraceful.

hôpital [ɔpital] nm hospital.

hoquet ['ɔke] nm hiccup. **avoir le hoquet** have hiccups. **hoqueter** v hiccup.

horaire [ɔrɛr] adj hourly. nm timetable.

horde ['ɔrd] nf horde.

horizon [ɔrizɔ̃] nm horizon; (paysage) landscape, view.

horizontal [ɔrizɔ̃tal] adj horizontal. **horizontale** nf horizontal.

horloge [ɔrlɔʒ] nf clock.

hormis ['ɔrmi] prep but, save.

hormone [ɔrmɔn] nf hormone.

horoscope [ɔrɔskɔp] nm horoscope.

horreur [ɔrœr] nf horror. **avoir horreur de** loathe, detest. **faire horreur à** disgust.

horrible [ɔriblə] adj horrible, dreadful.

horrifier [ɔrifje] v horrify.

hors ['ɔr] prep except, apart from. **horsbord** nm invar speedboat. **hors de** out of; (dehors) outside; (loin de) away from. **être hors de soi** be beside oneself. **hors d'œuvre** nm invar hors d'oeuvre, starter. **hors-jeu** nm, adj invar offside. **hors-la-loi** nm invar outlaw. **hors-taxe** adv, adj invar duty-free.

horticulture [ɔrtikyltyr] nf horticulture. **horticole** adj horticultural.

hospice [ɔspis] nm home.

hospitalier [ɔspitalje] adj (service) hospital; (accueillant) hospitable. **hospitalité** nf hospitality.

hostile [ɔstil] adj hostile.

hôte [ot] nm host. n(m+f) (invité) guest. **hôtesse** nf hostess. **hôtesse de l'air** air hostess.

hôtel [otɛl] nm hotel; (particulier) mansion. **hôtel de ville** town hall. **hôtel-Dieu** nm general hospital. **hôtelier, -ère** nm, nf hotelier.

houblon ['ublɔ̃] nm hop.

houe ['u] nf hoe.

houille ['uj] nf coal. **houille blanche** hydro-electric power. **houillère** nf coalmine.

houle ['ul] nf swell. **houleux** adj turbulent, stormy.

houppe ['up] nf tuft, tassel. **houppette** nf powder puff.

houspiller ['uspije] v scold, tell off.

housse ['us] nf cover.

houx ['u] nm holly.

hublot ['yblo] nm porthole.

huer ['ɥe] v boo; (chouette) hoot. **huées** nf pl boos pl.

huile [ɥil] nf oil. **huile de coude** (fam) elbow grease. **huile de ricin** castor oil. **huile solaire** suntan oil. **huiler** v oil. **huileux** adj oily.

huis [ɥi] nm **à huis clos** in camera.

huissier [ɥisje] nm usher; (jur) bailiff.

huit ['ɥit] nm, adj eight. **huit jours a** week. **... en huit** a week on .... **huitaine** nf about eight; about a week. **huitième** n(m+f), adj eighth.

huître [ɥitrə] nf oyster.

humain [ymɛ̃] adj human; (compatissant) humane. nm human. **humanitaire** adj humanitarian. **humanité** nf humanity.

humble [œ̃blə] adj humble.

humecter [ymɛkte] v dampen, moisten.

humer ['yme] v smell; (air) inhale.

humeur [ymœr] nf mood, humour; temperament, temper; (colère) bad temper. **d'humeur égale** even-tempered.

humide [ymid] adj damp, moist; (climat) humid. **humidité** nf humidity; dampness, damp.

humilier [ymilje] v humiliate. **humiliation** nf humiliation. **humilité** nf humility, humbleness.

humour [ymur] nm humour; sense of humour. **humoriste** n(m+f) humorist. **humoristique** adj humorous.

huppe ['yp] nf crest.

hurler ['yrle] v yell, roar; (chien) howl. **hurlement** nm yell, roar; howl.

hussard ['ysar] nm hussar.

hutte ['yt] nf hut.

hybride [ibrid] nm, adj hybrid.

hydrate [idrat] *nm* **hydrate de carbone** carbohydrate.

hydraulique [idrolik] *adj* hydraulic.

hydro-électrique [idrɔelɛktrik] *adj* hydroelectric.

hydrofoil [idrɔfɔjl] *nm* hydrofoil.

hydrogène [idrɔʒɛn] *nm* hydrogen.

hydromel [idrɔmɛl] *nm* mead.

hydrophile [idrɔfil] *adj* absorbent.

hyène [jɛn] *nf* hyena.

hygiène [iʒɛn] *nf* hygiene. **hygiénique** *adj* hygienic.

hymne [imnə] *nm* hymn. **hymne national** national anthem.

hypermétropie [ipɛrmetrɔpi] *nf* long-sightedness. **hypermétrope** *adj* long-sighted.

hypertension [ipɛrtɑ̃sjɔ̃] *nf* high blood pressure.

hypnose [ipnoz] *nf* hypnosis. **hypnotique** *adj* hypnotic. **hypnotiser** *v* hypnotize. **hypnotiseur** *nm* hypnotist. **hypnotisme** *nm* hypnotism.

hypocondrie [ipɔkɔ̃dri] *nf* hypochondria. **hypocondriaque** *n(m+f)*, *adj* hypochondriac.

hypocrite [ipɔkrit] *adj* hypocritical. *n(m+f)* hypocrite. **hypocrisie** *nf* hypocrisy.

hypodermique [ipɔdɛrmik] *adj* hypodermic.

hypotension [ipɔtɑ̃sjɔ̃] *nf* low blood pressure.

hypothéquer [ipɔteke] *v* mortgage. **hypothèque** *nf* mortgage.

hypothèse [ipɔtɛz] *nf* hypothesis. **hypothétique** *adj* hypothetical.

hystérectomie [isterɛktɔmi] *nf* hysterectomy.

hystérie [isteri] *nf* hysteria. **hystérique** *adj* hysterical.

I

iceberg [ajsbɛrg] *nm* iceberg.

ici [isi] *adv* (*lieu*) here; (*temps*) now. **d'ici là** before then. **d'ici peu** before long. **par ici** this way.

icône [ikon] *nf* icon.

idéal [ideal] *nm*, *adj* ideal.

idéaliste [idealist] *adj* idealistic. *n(m+f)* idealist.

idée [ide] *nf* idea; (*esprit*) mind. **idée fixe** obsession. **idée lumineuse** brainwave.

identifier [idɑ̃tifje] *v* identify. **identification** *nf* identification.

identique [idɑ̃tik] *adj* identical. **identité** *nf* identity.

idéologie [ideɔlɔʒi] *nf* ideology.

idiome [idjom] *nm* idiom. **idiomatique** *adj* idiomatic.

idiosyncrasie [idjɔsɛ̃krazi] *nf* idiosyncrasy.

idiot [idjo], **-e** *adj* idiotic. *nm*, *nf* idiot. **idiotie** *nf* idiocy, stupidity; (*action, propos*) idiotic or stupid thing.

idiotisme [idjɔtismə] *nm* idiom.

idolâtrer [idɔlatre] *v* idolize. **idolâtrie** *nf* idolatry.

idole [idɔl] *nf* idol.

idyllique [idilik] *adj* idyllic.

if [if] *nm* yew.

igloo [iglu] *nm* igloo.

ignifuger [ignifyʒe] *v* fireproof. **ignifuge** *adj* fireproof.

ignorer [iɲɔre] *v* not know, be unaware of. **ignorance** *nf* ignorance. **ignorant** *adj* ignorant. **ignorant de** unaware of. **ignoré** *adj* unknown.

il [il] *pron* it; (*personne*) he. **il y a** (*sing*) there is; (*pl*) there are.

île [il] *nf* island. **les îles anglo-normandes** the Channel Islands.

illégal [ilegal] *adj* illegal. **illégalité** *nf* illegality.

illégitime [ileʒitim] *adj* illegitimate. **illégitimité** *nf* illegitimacy.

illettré [iletre], **-e** *n*, *adj* illiterate.

illicite [ilisit] *adj* illicit.

illimité [ilimite] *adj* unlimited, boundless.

illisible [iliziblə] *adj* (*écriture*) illegible; (*livre*) unreadable.

illogique [ilɔʒik] *adj* illogical.

illuminer [ilymine] *v* light up, illuminate. **illumination** *nf* illumination, lighting.

illusion [ilyzjɔ̃] *nf* illusion. **illusion d'optique** optical illusion.

illustre [ilystrə] *adj* illustrious.

illustrer [ilystre] *v* illustrate. **illustrateur, -trice** *nm*, *nf* illustrator. **illustration** *nf* illustration.

ils [il] *pron* they.

image [imaʒ] *nf* image; (*dessin*) picture; reflection.

imaginer [imaʒine] *v* imagine; (*inventer*) think up. **s'imaginer** imagine; (*croire*) think. **imaginaire** *adj* imaginary. **imaginatif** *adj* imaginative. **imagination** *nf* imagination.

imbécile [ɛbesil] *adj* stupid. *n(m+f)* imbecile.

imbiber [ɛbibe] *v* saturate, impregnate, soak. **s'imbiber** absorb.

imbu [ɛby] *adj* **imbu de** full of, steeped in.

imiter [imite] *v* imitate; copy; (*signature*) forge; (*ressembler*) look like; (*célébrité*) impersonate. **imitation** *nf* imitation; forgery; impersonation.

immaculé [imakyle] *adj* immaculate, spotless.

immanquable [ɛmɑ̃kablə] *adj* inevitable; infallible.

immatriculer [imatrikyle] *v* register. **immatriculation** *nf* registration.

immédiat [imedja] *adj* immediate.

immense [imɑ̃s] *adj* vast, immense; (*espace*) boundless.

immerger [imɛrʒe] *v* immerse, submerge. **immersion** *nf* immersion, submersion.

immeuble [imœblə] *nm* building; (*appartements*) block of flats; (*bureaux*) office block.

immigrer [imigre] *v* immigrate. **immigrant, -e** *nm, nf* immigrant. **immigration** *nf* immigration.

imminent [iminɑ̃] *adj* imminent, impending.

immiscer [imise] *v* **s'immiscer dans** interfere with.

immobile [imɔbil] *adj* immobile, motionless, still. **immobilier** *adj* property. **immobiliser** *v* immobilize. **s'immobiliser** come to a standstill.

immonde [imɔ̃d] *adj* vile, foul; (*rel*) unclean. **immondices** *nf pl* refuse *sing*.

immoral [imɔral] *adj* immoral. **immoralité** *nf* immorality.

immortel [imɔrtɛl] *adj* immortal. **immortaliser** *v* immortalize. **immortalité** *nf* immortality.

immuniser [imynize] *v* immunize. **immunisation** *nf* immunization. **immunisé** *adj* immune. **immunité** *nf* immunity.

impact [ɛpakt] *nm* impact.

impair [ɛpɛr] *adj* odd, uneven. *nm* blunder.

imparfait [ɛparfɛ] *nm, adj* imperfect.

impartial [ɛparsjal] *adj* impartial, unbiased. **impartialité** *nf* impartiality.

impasse [ɛpɑs] *nf* dead end, no through road; (*situation*) impasse, deadlock.

impassible [ɛpasiblə] *adj* impassive.

impatience [ɛpasjɑ̃s] *nf* impatience. **impatient** *adj* impatient; (*avide*) eager.

impatienter [ɛpasjɑ̃te] *v* irritate. **s'impatienter** lose one's patience.

impeccable [ɛpekablə] *adj* perfect, impeccable.

imper [ɛpɛr] *nm* (*fam*) mac.

impératif [ɛperatif] *nm, adj* imperative.

impératrice [ɛperatris] *nf* empress.

impérial [ɛperjal] *adj* imperial. **impériale** *nf* (*autobus*) top deck. **autobus à impériale** double-decker.

imperméable [ɛpɛrmeablə] *adj* waterproof; (*roches*) impervious. *nm* raincoat. **imperméabiliser** *v* waterproof.

impersonnel [ɛpersɔnɛl] *adj* impersonal.

impertinent [ɛpɛrtinɑ̃] *adj* impertinent. **impertinence** *nf* impertinence.

impétueux [ɛpetɥø] *adj* impetuous.

impitoyable [ɛpitwajablə] *adj* merciless, ruthless.

implicite [ɛplisit] *adj* implicit.

impliquer [ɛplike] *v* imply; (*mêler*) involve.

implorer [ɛplɔre] *v* implore.

impoli [ɛpɔli] *adj* impolite.

impopulaire [ɛpɔpylɛr] *adj* unpopular. **impopularité** *nf* unpopularity.

importer[1] [ɛpɔrte] *v* (*comm*) import. **importation** *nf* import.

***importer**[2] [ɛpɔrte] *v* matter. **n'importe** never mind, it doesn't matter. **n'importe comment/où/quand/quel/qui/quoi** anyhow/anywhere/anytime/any/anybody/ anything. **importance** *nf* importance; (*grandeur*) size, extent. **important** *adj* important; considerable.

importuner [ɛpɔrtyne] *v* bother, trouble.

imposer [ɛpoze] *v* impose; (*prescrire*) set; tax. **imposable** *adj* taxable. **imposant** *adj* imposing, impressive.

impossible [ɛpɔsiblə] *adj* impossible.

imposteur [ɛpɔstœr] *nm* impostor.

impôt [ɛpo] *nm* tax; taxation.

impotent [ɛpɔtɑ̃, -e] *adj* disabled, crippled. *nm, nf* disabled person. **impotence** *nf* disability.

imprécis [ɛpresi] *adj* imprecise.

imprégner [ɛpreɲe] *v* impregnate; (*air*) pervade. **s'imprégner de** absorb, soak up.

impression [ɛ̃presjɔ̃] *nf* impression; (*imprimerie*) printing. **impressionable** *adj* impressionable. **impressionnant** *adj* impressive. **impressionner** *v* impress; (*bouleverser*) upset.
imprévu [ɛ̃prevy] *adj* unexpected, unforeseen.
imprimer [ɛ̃prime] *v* print; (*cachet*) stamp; (*marquer*) imprint; publish. **imprimé** *nm* (*poste*) printed matter; (*tissu*) print. **imprimerie** *nf* printing; printing house *or* works. **imprimeur** *nm* printer.
improbable [ɛ̃prɔbablə] *adj* improbable, unlikely.
impromptu [ɛ̃prɔ̃pty] *adj*, *adv* impromptu.
improviser [ɛ̃prɔvize] *v* improvise. **improvisation** *nf* improvisation.
improviste [ɛ̃prɔvist] *nm* à l'**improviste** without warning, unexpectedly.
imprudent [ɛ̃prydɑ̃] *adj* unwise, foolish, careless. **imprudence** *nf* foolishness, carelessness.
impudent [ɛ̃pydɑ̃] *adj* impudent. **impudence** *nf* impudence.
impuissant [ɛ̃pɥisɑ̃] *adj* powerless; (*effort*) ineffectual; (*sexuellement*) impotent. **impuissance** *nf* impotence.
impulsion [ɛ̃pylsjɔ̃] *nf* impulse; impetus. **impulsif** *adj* impulsive.
impur [ɛ̃pyr] *adj* impure. **impureté** *nf* impurity.
imputer [ɛ̃pyte] *v* impute, attribute; (*frais*) charge.
inaccessible [inaksesiblə] *adj* inaccessible.
inactif [inaktif] *adj* inactive, idle.
inadapté [inadapte], -e *nm*, *nf* misfit. *adj* (*psychol*) maladjusted.
inadvertance [inadvɛrtɑ̃s] *nf* oversight. **par inadvertance** inadvertently.
inanimé [inanime] *adj* inanimate; (*personne*) unconscious.
inaperçu [inapersy] *adj* unnoticed. **passer inaperçu** go unnoticed.
inappréciable [inapresjablə] *adj* invaluable; imperceptible.
inapte [inapt] *adj* incapable, unfit.
inarticulé [inartikyle] *adj* inarticulate.
inattendu [inatɑ̃dy] *adj* unexpected.
inaudible [inodiblə] *adj* inaudible.
inaugurer [inogyre] *v* inaugurate; (*plaque*) unveil; (*exposition*) open. **inaugural** *adj* inaugural; (*voyage*) maiden. **inauguration** *nf* inauguration; unveiling; opening.

incapable [ɛ̃kapablə] *adj* incapable, unable.
incapacité [ɛ̃kapasite] *nf* incapacity; incompetence; inability; (*invalidité*) disability.
incendier [ɛ̃sɑ̃dje] *v* set fire to, burn. **incendiaire** *adj* incendiary. **incendie** *nm* fire. **incendie volontaire** arson.
incertain [ɛ̃sɛrtɛ̃] *adj* uncertain. **incertitude** *nf* uncertainty.
incessant [ɛ̃sɛsɑ̃] *adj* incessant. **incessamment** *adv* very soon.
inceste [ɛ̃sɛst] *nm* incest. **incestueux** *adj* incestuous.
incident [ɛ̃sidɑ̃] *adj* incidental. *nm* incident; (*anicroche*) setback, hitch. **incidemment** *adv* incidentally.
incinérer [ɛ̃sinere] *v* (*ordures*) incinerate; (*cadavre*) cremate. **incinérateur** *nm* incinerator. **incinération** *nf* incineration; cremation.
inciter [ɛ̃site] *v* incite, encourage.
incliner [ɛ̃kline] *v* slope, tilt; tend, be inclined. **s'incliner** bow. **inclinaison** *nm* slope, incline. **inclination** *nf* inclination.
*****inclure** [ɛ̃klyr] *v* include; (*joindre*) enclose; insert. **inclus** *adj* enclosed; included, inclusive. **inclusion** *nf* inclusion; insertion. **inclusivement** *adv* inclusively.
incognito [ɛ̃kɔɲito] *adv* incognito.
incohérent [ɛ̃kɔerɑ̃] *adj* incoherent.
incolore [ɛ̃kɔlɔr] *adj* colourless.
incommoder [ɛ̃kɔmɔde] *v* disturb, bother. **incommode** *adj* inconvenient, awkward; (*siège*) uncomfortable. **incommodité** *nf* inconvenience.
incompatible [ɛ̃kɔ̃patiblə] *adj* incompatible. **incompatibilité** *nf* incompatibility.
incompétent [ɛ̃kɔ̃petɑ̃] *adj* incompetent. **incompétence** *nf* incompetence; (*ignorance*) lack of knowledge.
incomplet, -ète [ɛ̃kɔ̃plɛ, -ɛt] *adj* incomplete.
inconcevable [ɛ̃kɔ̃svablə] *adj* inconceivable.
inconfort [ɛ̃kɔ̃fɔr] *nm* discomfort. **inconfortable** *adj* uncomfortable.
inconnu [ɛ̃kɔny], -e *adj* unknown; strange. *nm*, *nf* stranger. **l'inconnu** the unknown.
inconscience [ɛ̃kɔ̃sjɑ̃s] *nf* unconsciousness; (*folie*) thoughtlessness, rashness. **inconscient** *adj* unconscious; thoughtless, rash.

inconséquent [ɛ̃kɔ̃sekɑ̃] adj inconsistent; (irréfléchi) thoughtless.

inconstant [ɛ̃kɔ̃stɑ̃] adj fickle.

incontestable [ɛ̃kɔ̃tɛstablə] adj unquestionable, undeniable.

inconvenant [ɛ̃kɔ̃vnɑ̃] adj improper, unseemly.

inconvénient [ɛ̃kɔ̃venjɑ̃] nm disadvantage, drawback; risk.

incorporer [ɛ̃kɔrpɔre] v incorporate; mix.

incorrect [ɛ̃kɔrɛkt] adj incorrect; impolite.

incrédule [ɛ̃kredyl] adj incredulous. n(m+f) (rel) unbeliever. incrédulité nf incredulity.

incriminer [ɛ̃krimine] v incriminate.

incroyable [ɛ̃krwajablə] adj incredible.

incuber [ɛ̃kybe] v incubate, hatch. incubation nf incubation.

inculper [ɛ̃kylpe] v charge. inculpation nf charge.

inculte [ɛ̃kylt] adj uncultivated; (négligé) unkempt.

incurable [ɛ̃kyrablə] adj incurable.

Inde [ɛ̃d] nf India.

indécent [ɛ̃desɑ̃] adj indecent. indécence nf indecency.

indécis [ɛ̃desi] adj (irrésolu) indecisive; (hésitant) undecided; (douteux) unsettled; vague.

indéfini [ɛ̃defini] adj indefinite.

indemne [ɛ̃dɛmnə] adj unharmed, unhurt.

indemniser [ɛ̃dɛmnize] v compensate, reimburse. indemnité nf compensation, indemnity; (frais) allowance.

indépendant [ɛ̃depɑ̃dɑ̃] adj independent; (appartement) self-contained; (journaliste, etc.) freelance. indépendance nf independence.

index [ɛ̃dɛks] nm index; (aiguille) needle, pointer; (doigt) index finger.

indicatif [ɛ̃dikatif] adj indicative. nm (musical) signature tune; (téléphonique) dialling code; (gramm) indicative.

indication [ɛ̃dikasjɔ̃] nf indication; (renseignement) information; instruction, direction. indicateur nm indicator; (horaire) timetable; guide; gauge.

indice [ɛ̃dis] nm indication, sign; (clef) clue; index, rating.

indien [ɛ̃djɛ̃] adj Indian. Indien, -enne nm, nf Indian.

indifférent [ɛ̃diferɑ̃] adj indifferent; (sans importance) immaterial. indifférence nf indifference.

indigence [ɛ̃diʒɑ̃s] nf poverty. indigent adj poor, destitute.

indigène [ɛ̃diʒɛn] n(m+f), adj native.

indigestion [ɛ̃diʒɛstjɔ̃] nf indigestion.

indigne [ɛ̃diɲ] adj unworthy.

indigner [ɛ̃diɲe] v make indignant. s'indigner be indignant. indignation nf indignation. indigné adj indignant.

indiquer [ɛ̃dike] v indicate, show, point out.

indirect [ɛ̃dirɛkt] adj indirect.

indiscipliné [ɛ̃disipline] adj unruly.

indiscret, -ète [ɛ̃diskrɛ, -ɛt] adj indiscreet. indiscrétion nf indiscretion.

indispensable [ɛ̃dispɑ̃sablə] adj essential.

indisposé [ɛ̃dispoze] adj unwell.

individu [ɛ̃dividy] nm individual. individualité nf individuality. individuel adj individual; personal, private.

indolent [ɛ̃dɔlɑ̃] adj idle, indolent. indolence nf idleness, indolence.

indolore [ɛ̃dɔlɔr] adj painless.

*induire [ɛ̃dɥir] v infer. induire en erreur mislead.

indulgence [ɛ̃dylʒɑ̃s] nf indulgence, leniency. indulgent adj indulgent, lenient.

industrie [ɛ̃dystri] nf industry. industrialiser v industrialize. industriel adj industrial.

inébranlable [inebrɑ̃lablə] adj steadfast, solid.

inefficace [inefikas] adj (mesure) ineffective; (employé) inefficient.

inégal [inegal] adj (irrégulier) uneven; (différent) unequal. inégalité nf inequality; unevenness; difference.

inepte [inɛpt] adj inept.

inerte [inɛrt] adj inert, lifeless; passive, apathetic. inertie nf inertia; apathy.

inestimable [inɛstimablə] adj invaluable.

inévitable [inevitablə] adj inevitable; (accident) unavoidable.

inexact [inɛgzakt] adj inaccurate; unpunctual. inexactitude nf inaccuracy; unpunctuality.

inexpérimenté [inɛksperimɑ̃te] adj (personne) inexperienced; (produit) untested.

infaillible [ɛ̃fajiblə] adj infallible.

infâme [ɛ̃fɑm] adj infamous; (odieux) vile, despicable. infamie nf infamy.

infanterie [ɛ̃fɑ̃tri] nf infantry.

infarctus [ɛ̃farktys] nm infarctus du myocarde coronary thrombosis.

infatué [ɛ̃fatᶣe] *adj* conceited, vain.
infécond [ɛ̃fekɔ̃] *adj* sterile, infertile.
infécondité *nf* sterility, infertility.
infect [ɛ̃fɛkt] *adj* vile, revolting.
infecter [ɛ̃fɛkte] *v* infect, contaminate.
s'infecter turn septic. **infectieux** *adj*
infectious. **infection** *nf* infection;
(*puanteur*) stench.
inférieur, -e [ɛ̃ferjœr] *adj* (*plus bas*) lower; (*qualité*) inferior; (*quantité*) smaller.
nm, nf inferior. **infériorité** *nf* inferiority.
infester [ɛ̃fɛste] *v* infest. **infestation** *nf*
infestation.
infidèle [ɛ̃fidɛl] *adj* unfaithful; (*inexact*)
inaccurate. **infidélité** *nf* unfaithfulness;
(*mari, femme*) infidelity; inaccuracy.
s'infiltrer [ɛ̃filtre] *v* infiltrate; (*liquide*)
percolate; (*lumière*) filter through. **infil-**
tration *nf* infiltration.
infime [ɛ̃fim] *adj* tiny, minute.
infini [ɛ̃fini] *adj* infinite; interminable. *nm*
infinity. **infinité** *nf* infinity; infinite
number. **infinitif** *nm, adj* infinitive.
infirme [ɛ̃firm] *adj* crippled, disabled;
(*vieillards*) infirm. *nm, nf* cripple, disabled person. **infirmerie** *nf* (*école*) sick
bay. **infirmier, -ère** *nm, nf* nurse.
infirmité *nf* disability; infirmity.
inflammable [ɛ̃flamablə] *adj* inflammable.
inflammation *nf* inflammation.
inflation [ɛ̃flasjɔ̃] *nf* inflation.
inflexion [ɛ̃flɛksjɔ̃] *nf* inflection; (*courbe*)
bend.
infliger [ɛ̃fliʒe] *v* inflict; impose.
influencer [ɛ̃flyɑ̃se] *v* influence. **influence**
nf influence. **influent** *adj* influential.
influer [ɛ̃flye] *v* **influer sur** have an influence on.
informe [ɛ̃fɔrm] *adj* shapeless.
informer [ɛ̃fɔrme] *v* inform. **s'informer**
inquire, find out. **information** *nf* information; (*jur*) inquiry. **informations** *nf pl*
news *sing*.
infortune [ɛ̃fɔrtyn] *nf* misfortune. **infor-**
tuné *adj* ill-fated, wretched.
infraction [ɛ̃fraksjɔ̃] *nf* offence; (*loi*)
infringement, breach.
infroissable [ɛ̃frwasablə] *adj* crease-resistant.
infuser [ɛ̃fyze] *v* (*thé*) brew, infuse.
ingénieur [ɛ̃ʒenjœr] *nm* engineer.
ingénieux [ɛ̃ʒenjø] *adj* ingenious. **ingéni-**
osité *nf* ingenuity.
ingénu [ɛ̃ʒeny] *adj* naïve, ingenuous.

s'ingérer [ɛ̃ʒere] *v* interfere, meddle.
ingérence *nf* interference.
ingrat [ɛ̃gra] *adj* ungrateful; (*tâche*)
thankless; (*déplaisant*) unattractive.
ingratitude *nf* ingratitude.
ingrédient [ɛ̃gredjɑ̃] *nm* ingredient.
inhabile [inabil] *adj* clumsy, inept.
inhabité [inabite] *adj* uninhabited, unoccupied.
inhaler [inale] *v* inhale.
inhérent [inerɑ̃] *adj* inherent.
inhiber [inibe] *v* inhibit. **inhibition** *nf*
inhibition.
inhumain [inymɛ̃] *adj* inhuman.
inimitié [inimitje] *nf* enmity.
initial [inisjal] *adj* initial. **initiale** *nf* initial.
initiative [inisjativ] *nf* initiative.
initier [inisje] *v* initiate. **initiation** *nf* initiation.
injecter [ɛ̃ʒɛkte] *v* inject. **injection** *nf*
injection.
injurier [ɛ̃ʒyrje] *v* abuse, insult. **injure** *nf*
abuse, insult. **injurieux** *adj* abusive,
insulting.
injuste [ɛ̃ʒyst] *adj* unjust, unfair. **injustice**
nf injustice, unfairness.
inné [ine] *adj* innate.
innocent [inɔsɑ̃], **-e** *adj* innocent. *nm, nf*
innocent (person); idiot, simpleton.
innocence *nf* innocence.
innovation [inɔvasjɔ̃] *nf* innovation.
inoccupé [inɔkype] *adj* unoccupied.
inoculer [inɔkyle] *v* inoculate. **inoculation**
nf inoculation.
inonder [inɔ̃de] *v* flood; (*tremper*) soak.
inondation *nf* flood.
inopiné [inɔpine] *adj* unexpected.
inouï [inwi] *adj* incredible, unheard-of.
inoxydable [inɔksidablə] *adj* stainless;
(*couteau, etc.*) stainless steel.
inquiéter [ɛ̃kjete] *v* worry, bother. **inquiet,**
-ète *adj* worried, anxious. **inquiétude** *nf*
worry, anxiety.
inquisition [ɛ̃kizisjɔ̃] *nf* inquisition.
inscription [ɛ̃skripsjɔ̃] *nf* inscription;
(*club, cours, etc.*) enrolment, registration.
***inscrire** [ɛ̃skrir] *v* write down, enrol, reg-
ister; (*graver*) inscribe.
insecte [ɛ̃sɛkt] *nm* insect. **insecticide** *nm*
insecticide.
insécurité [ɛ̃sekyrite] *nf* insecurity.
inséminer [ɛ̃semine] *v* inseminate. **insémi-**
nation *nf* insemination.

insensé [ɛ̃sɑ̃se] *adj* insane, crazy.

insensible [ɛ̃sɑ̃siblə] *adj* insensitive; imperceptible. **insensibilité** *nf* insensitivity.

insérer [ɛ̃sere] *v* insert. **s'insérer dans** fit into. **insertion** *nf* insertion.

insidieux [ɛ̃sidjø] *adj* insidious.

insigne [ɛ̃siɲ] *adj* distinguished, notable. *nm* badge, insignia.

insignifiant [ɛ̃siɲifjɑ̃] *adj* insignificant. **insignifiance** *nf* insignificance.

insinuer [ɛ̃sinɥe] *v* insinuate, imply. **s'insinuer dans** worm one's way into. **insinuation** *nf* insinuation.

insipide [ɛ̃sipid] *adj* insipid.

insister [ɛ̃siste] *v* insist. **insister sur** stress. **insistance** *nf* insistence. **insistant** *adj* insistent.

insolation [ɛ̃sɔlasjɔ̃] *nf* (*méd*) sunstroke; (*temps*) sunshine.

insolent [ɛ̃sɔlɑ̃] *adj* insolent. **insolence** *nf* insolence.

insolite [ɛ̃sɔlit] *adj* strange, unusual.

insomnie [ɛ̃sɔmni] *nf* insomnia. **insomniaque** *n(m+f)*, *adj* insomniac.

insonore [ɛ̃sɔnɔr] *adj* soundproof. **insonoriser** *v* soundproof.

insouciant [ɛ̃susjɑ̃] *adj* carefree, happy-go-lucky.

inspecter [ɛ̃spɛkte] *v* inspect. **inspecteur, -trice** *nm, nf* inspector. **inspection** *nf* inspection.

inspirer [ɛ̃spire] *v* inspire; (*respirer*) breathe in. **inspiration** *nf* inspiration.

instable [ɛ̃stablə] *adj* unstable. **instabilité** *nf* instability.

installer [ɛ̃stale] *v* install; (*pièce*) fit out. **s'installer** settle in (*or* down); (*emménager*) move in, set up home. **installation** *nf* installation. **installations** *nf pl* fittings *pl*, facilities *pl*; (*usine*) plant *sing*.

instant [ɛ̃stɑ̃] *nm* moment, instant. **à l'instant** at this moment; (*passé*) a moment ago. **par instants** at times. **pour l'instant** for the time being. **instantané** *adj* instantaneous; (*café*) instant.

instar [ɛ̃star] *nm* **à l'instar de** after the fashion of.

instigation [ɛ̃stigasjɔ̃] *nf* instigation. **instigateur, -trice** *nm, nf* instigator.

instinct [ɛ̃stɛ̃] *nm* instinct. **instinctif** *adj* instinctive.

instituer [ɛ̃stitɥe] *v* institute. **institut** *nm* institute. **instituteur, -trice** *nm, nf* pri-

mary school teacher. **institution** *nf* institution; (*école*) private school.

instruction [ɛ̃stryksjɔ̃] *nf* education. **instructions** *nf pl* instructions *pl*. **instructif** *adj* instructive.

*****instruire** [ɛ̃strɥir] *v* teach, instruct; educate; inform.

instrument [ɛ̃strymɑ̃] *nm* instrument; (*outil*) tool. **instrumental** *adj* instrumental.

insu [ɛ̃sy] *nm* **à l'insu de** unknown to. **à mon insu** without my knowing it.

insubordonné [ɛ̃sybɔrdɔne] *adj* insubordinate. **insubordination** *nf* insubordination.

insuccès [ɛ̃syksɛ] *nm* failure.

insuffisant [ɛ̃syfizɑ̃] *adj* inadequate; (*quantité*) insufficient. **insuffisance** *nf* inadequacy; insufficiency.

insulaire [ɛ̃sylɛr] *adj* insular. *n(m+f)* islander.

insuline [ɛ̃sylin] *nf* insulin.

insulter [ɛ̃sylte] *v* insult. **insulte** *nf* insult.

insupportable [ɛ̃sypɔrtablə] *adj* unbearable, intolerable.

s'insurger [ɛ̃syrʒe] *v* rebel. **insurgé, -e** *nm, nf* rebel. **insurrection** *nf* revolt.

intact [ɛ̃takt] *adj* intact.

intègre [ɛ̃tɛgrə] *adj* honest. **intégrité** *nf* integrity.

intégrer [ɛ̃tegre] *v* integrate. **intégral** *adj* complete, full; (*texte*) unabridged. **intégration** *nf* integration.

intellect [ɛ̃telɛkt] *nm* intellect. **intellectuel, -elle** *n*, *adj* intellectual.

intelligence [ɛ̃teliʒɑ̃s] *nf* intelligence; (*compréhension*) understanding. **intelligent** *adj* intelligent, clever.

intelligible [ɛ̃teliʒiblə] *adj* intelligible.

intendant [ɛ̃tɑ̃dɑ̃] *nm* (*école*) bursar; (*maison*) steward; (*mil*) quartermaster.

intense [ɛ̃tɑ̃s] *adj* intense. **intensif** *adj* intensive. **intensifier** *v* intensify. **intensité** *nf* intensity.

intention [ɛ̃tɑ̃sjɔ̃] *nf* intention. **à l'intention de** for the benefit of, for. **avoir l'intention de** intend to. **intentionnel** *adj* intentional.

intercéder [ɛ̃tɛrsede] *v* intercede.

intercepter [ɛ̃tɛrsɛpte] *v* intercept; (*boucher*) block, cut off. **interception** *nf* interception.

*****interdire** [ɛ̃tɛrdir] *v* forbid, ban. **interdiction** *nf* ban. **interdit** *adj* prohibited.

intéresser [ɛ̃terese] *v* interest; concern. **s'intéresser à** be interested in. **intéressant** *adj* interesting; (*offre, prix*) attractive.

intérêt [ɛ̃terɛ] *nm* interest; importance.

intérieur, -e [ɛ̃terjœr] *adj* inner, internal, inside; (*pol*) domestic, home. *nm* interior, inside. **à l'intérieur** inside.

intérim [ɛ̃terim] *nm* interim. **intérimaire** *adj* temporary.

interjection [ɛ̃terʒɛksjɔ̃] *nf* interjection.

interloquer [ɛ̃terlɔke] *v* dumbfound, take aback.

intermède [ɛ̃termɛd] *nm* interlude.

intermédiaire [ɛ̃termedjɛr] *adj* intermediate. *n(m+f)* go-between; (*comm*) middleman. **sans intermédiaire** directly.

interminable [ɛ̃terminablə] *adj* endless, interminable.

intermittent [ɛ̃termitɑ̃] *adj* intermittent.

internat [ɛ̃terna] *nm* boarding school.

international [ɛ̃ternasjɔnal] *adj* international.

interne [ɛ̃tern] *adj* internal. *n(m+f)* boarder; (*méd*) houseman, intern. **internement** *nm* internment. **interner** *v* intern.

interpeller [ɛ̃terpele] *v* (*appeler*) call out to; (*apostropher*) shout at; question.

interphone [ɛ̃terfɔn] *nm* intercom.

interposer [ɛ̃terpoze] *v* interpose. **s'interposer** intervene.

interpréter [ɛ̃terprete] *v* interpret; (*théâtre, musique*) perform. **interprétation** *nf* interpretation. **interprète** *n(m+f)* interpreter; performer.

interroger [ɛ̃terɔʒe] *v* question; examine; (*police, etc.*) interrogate. **interrogatif** *nm, adj* interrogative. **interrogation** *nf* questioning, interrogation; question; (*école*) test. **interrogatoire** *nm* questioning; (*jur*) cross-examination.

*interrompre [ɛ̃terɔ̃prə] *v* interrupt; (*arrêter*) break off.

interruption [ɛ̃terypsjɔ̃] *nf* interruption. **interrupteur** *nm* switch.

interurbain [ɛ̃teryrbɛ̃] *adj* (*téléphone*) long-distance.

intervalle [ɛ̃terval] *nm* interval; space. **dans l'intervalle** in the meantime.

*intervenir [ɛ̃tervənir] *v* intervene; (*survenir*) take place, occur. **intervention** *nf* intervention.

intervertir [ɛ̃tervertir] *v* invert, reverse.

interview [ɛ̃tervju] *nf* interview.

intestin [ɛ̃testɛ̃] *nm* intestine. **intestins** *nm pl* bowels *pl. adj* internal. **intestinal** *adj* intestinal.

intime [ɛ̃tim] *adj* intimate; private, personal; (*ami*) close. *n(m+f)* close friend. **intimité** *nf* intimacy; privacy.

intimider [ɛ̃timide] *v* intimidate. **intimidation** *nf* intimidation.

intituler [ɛ̃tityle] *v* entitle, call. **intitulé** *nm* title.

intolérable [ɛ̃tɔlerablə] *adj* intolerable. **intolérance** *nf* intolerance. **intolérant** *adj* intolerant.

intonation [ɛ̃tɔnasjɔ̃] *nf* intonation.

intoxiquer [ɛ̃tɔksike] *v* poison. **intoxication** *nf* poisoning. **intoxiqué, -e** *nm, nf* addict.

intransitif [ɛ̃trɑ̃zitif] *nm, adj* intransitive.

intraveineux [ɛ̃travɛnø] *adj* intravenous.

intrépide [ɛ̃trepid] *adj* intrepid, bold.

intriguer [ɛ̃trige] *v* intrigue; (*comploter*) scheme. **intrigue** *nf* scheme; (*film, livre, etc.*) plot.

intrinsèque [ɛ̃trɛ̃sɛk] *adj* intrinsic.

*introduire [ɛ̃trɔdⁿir] *v* introduce; insert; (*faire entrer*) show in. **s'introduire** get in. **introduction** *nf* introduction; insertion; admission.

introverti [ɛ̃trɔverti], **-e** *adj* introverted. *nm, nf* introvert.

intrus [ɛ̃try], **-e** *nm, nf* intruder. *adj* intrusive. **intrusion** *nf* intrusion.

intuition [ɛ̃tⁿisjɔ̃] *nf* intuition. **intuitif** *adj* intuitive.

inutile [inytil] *adj* useless; (*effort*) pointless; (*superflu*) needless.

invaincu [ɛ̃vɛ̃ky] *adj* unbeaten.

invalide [ɛ̃valid] *n(m+f)* disabled person. *adj* disabled. **invalidité** *nf* disability.

invariable [ɛ̃varjablə] *adj* invariable.

invasion [ɛ̃vazjɔ̃] *nf* invasion.

inventaire [ɛ̃vɑ̃tɛr] *nm* inventory; (*comm*) stocktaking.

inventer [ɛ̃vɑ̃te] *v* invent; (*forger*) make up; (*imaginer*) think up. **inventeur, -trice** *nm, nf* inventor. **invention** *nf* invention.

inverse [ɛ̃vers] *nm, adj* opposite, reverse. **inversement** *adv* conversely. **inverser** reverse, invert. **inversion** *nf* inversion.

invertébré [ɛ̃vertebre] *nm, adj* invertebrate.

investigation [ɛ̃vestigasjɔ̃] *nf* investigation.

investir [ɛ̃vestir] *v* invest. **investissement** *nm* investment.

invisible [ɛ̃viziblə] *adj* invisible.
inviter [ɛ̃vite] *v* invite, ask. **invitation** *nf* invitation. **invité, -e** *nm, nf* guest.
involontaire [ɛ̃vɔlɔ̃tɛr] *adj* involuntary; unintentional.
invoquer [ɛ̃vɔke] *v* call upon; (*excuse*) put forward.
invraisemblable [ɛ̃vrɛsɑ̃blablə] *adj* unlikely, improbable; incredible.
iode [jɔd] *nm* iodine.
ion [jɔ̃] *nm* ion.
iris [iris] *nm* iris.
Irlande [irlɑ̃d] *nf* Ireland. **irlandais** *nm, adj* Irish. **les Irlandais** the Irish.
ironie [irɔni] *nf* irony. **ironique** *adj* ironic.
irrationnel [irasjɔnɛl] *adj* irrational.
irréel [irɛɛl] *adj* unreal.
irréfléchi [ireflefi] *adj* thoughtless, hasty.
irrégulier [iregylje] *adj* irregular. **irrégularité** *nf* irregularity.
irrésistible [irezistiblə] *adj* irresistible.
irrespect [irɛspɛ] *nm* disrespect. **irrespectueux** *adj* disrespectful.
irrévocable [irevɔkablə] *adj* irrevocable.
irriguer [irige] *v* irrigate. **irrigation** *nf* irrigation.
irriter [irite] *v* irritate; annoy. **irritable** *adj* irritable. **irritation** *nf* irritation.
irruption [irypsjɔ̃] *nf* **faire irruption** burst in.
Islam [islam] *nm* Islam. **islamique** *adj* Islamic.
Islande [islɑ̃d] *nf* Iceland. **islandais** *nm, adj* Icelandic. **Islandais, -e** *nm, nf* Icelander.
isoler [izɔle] *v* isolate; (*élec*) insulate. **isolation** *nf* insulation. **isolé** *adj* isolated, lonely, remote. **isolement** *nm* isolation. **isoloir** *nm* polling booth.
issu [isy] *adj* **issu de** descended from.
issue [isy] *nf* (*sortie*) exit; solution; (*fin*) outcome; (*eau*) outlet.
isthme [ismə] *nm* isthmus.
Italie [itali] *nf* Italy. **italien** *nm, adj* Italian. **Italien, -enne** *nm, nf* Italian.
italique [italik] *nm* italics *pl. adj* italic.
itinéraire [itinɛrɛr] *nm* itinerary, route.
ivoire [ivwar] *nm* ivory. **Côte d'Ivoire** *nf* Ivory Coast.
ivre [ivrə] *adj* drunk. **ivresse** *nf* drunkenness; ecstasy, exhilaration. **ivrogne** *n(m+f)* drunkard.

J

j' [ʒ] *V* **je.**
jabot [ʒabo] *nm* (*chemise*) jabot; (*zool*) crop.
jacasser [ʒakase] *v* chatter. **jacasse** *nf* magpie. **jacassement** *nm* chatter.
jachère [ʒaʃɛr] *nf* fallow.
jacinthe [ʒasɛ̃t] *nf* hyacinth. **jacinthe des bois** bluebell.
jade [ʒad] *nm* jade.
jadis [ʒadis] *adv* formerly, long ago.
jaguar [ʒagwar] *nm* jaguar.
jaillir [ʒajir] *v* gush forth, spurt out; (*rires, etc.*) burst out; (*surgir*) spring up. **jaillissement** *nm* spurt, gush.
jais [ʒɛ] *nm* jet.
jalonner [ʒalɔne] *v* mark out; (*border*) line.
jaloux, -ouse [ʒalu, -uz] *adj* jealous. **jalousie** *nf* jealousy; (*store*) blind.
jamais [ʒamɛ] *adv* ever; (*négatif*) never. **à tout jamais** for ever and ever. **ne ... jamais** never.
jambe [ʒɑ̃b] *nf* leg.
jambon [ʒɑ̃bɔ̃] *nm* ham.
jante [ʒɑ̃t] *nf* rim.
janvier [ʒɑ̃vje] *nm* January.
Japon [ʒapɔ̃] *nm* Japan. **japonais** *nm, adj* Japanese. **les Japonais** the Japanese.
japper [ʒape] *v* yap. **jappement** *nm* yap.
jaquette [ʒakɛt] *nf* jacket; (*homme*) morning coat.
jardin [ʒardɛ̃] *nm* garden. **jardin d'enfants** nursery school. **jardin maraîcher** market garden. **jardin public** park.
jardiner [ʒardine] *v* garden. **jardinage** *nm* gardening. **jardinier** *nm* gardener. **jardinière** *nf* gardener; (*caisse*) window box.
jargon [ʒargɔ̃] *nm* jargon.
jarret [ʒarɛ] *nm* (*anat*) back of the knee; (*zool*) hock; (*cuisine*) knuckle.
jarretelle [ʒartɛl] *nf* suspender *or US* garter.
jarretière [ʒartjɛr] *nf* garter.
jars [ʒar] *nm* gander.
jaser [ʒaze] *v* chatter; (*médire*) gossip; (*ruisseau*) babble.
jasmin [ʒasmɛ̃] *nm* jasmine.
jatte [ʒat] *nf* bowl.
jauger [ʒoʒe] *v* measure, gauge; (*personne*) size up. **jauge** *nf* gauge; capacity.

jauge d'essence petrol gauge. **jauge d'huile** dipstick.

jaune [ʒon] *adj* yellow. *nm* yellow; (*œuf*) yolk; (*péj*) blackleg. **jaunir** *v* turn yellow. **jaunisse** *nf* jaundice.

javelot [ʒavlo] *nm* javelin.

jazz [dʒaz] *nm* jazz.

je [ʒə], **j'** *pron* I.

jean [dʒin] *nm* jeans *pl*.

jeep [ʒip] *nf* jeep.

jersey [ʒɛrzɛ] *nm* jersey, jumper.

Jersey [ʒɛrzɛ] *nf* Jersey.

jet¹ [ʒɛ] *nm* (*liquide*) jet, spurt, stream; (*lumière*) beam; (*pierre*) throw; (*fam: coup*) go.

jet² [dʒɛt] *nm* (*aéro*) jet.

jetée [ʒəte] *nf* jetty; pier.

jeter [ʒəte] *v* throw.

jeton [ʒətɔ̃] *nm* token; (*jeu*) counter.

jeu [ʒø] *nm* play; game; (*série*) set; (*casino*) gambling. **jeu de cartes** (*ensemble*) pack of cards; (*partie*) card game. **jeu de mots** pun.

jeudi [ʒødi] *nm* Thursday. **jeudi saint** Maundy Thursday.

jeun [ʒœ̃] *adv* **à jeun** on an empty stomach.

jeune [ʒœn] *adj* young; (*cadet*) junior, younger. *n(m+f)* young person. **jeunesse** *nf* youth; (*personnes*) young people *pl*.

jeûner [ʒøne] *v* go without food; (*rel*) fast. **jeûne** *nm* fast.

joaillier [ʒɔaje], **-ère** *nm, nf* jeweller. **joaillerie** *nf* jewellery; (*magasin*) jeweller's.

jockey [ʒɔkɛ] *nm* jockey.

jodler [ʒɔdle] *v* yodel.

joie [ʒwa] *nf* joy, delight.

***joindre** [ʒwɛ̃drə] *v* join; (*unir*) combine; (*inclure*) attach, enclose; (*personne*) contact.

joint [ʒwɛ̃] *nm* joint; (*auto*) gasket; (*robinet*) washer. *adj* joint. **jointure** *nf* joint.

joli [ʒɔli] *adj* pretty, nice. **joliment** *adv* nicely; (*fam*) pretty, jolly.

jonc [ʒɔ̃] *nm* (*plante*) rush; cane; (*bracelet*) bangle; (*baque*) ring.

joncher [ʒɔ̃ʃe] *v* strew, litter.

jonction [ʒɔ̃ksjɔ̃] *nf* junction.

jongler [ʒɔ̃gle] *v* juggle. **jonglerie** *nf* juggling, jugglery. **jongleur, -euse** *nm, nf* juggler.

jonquille [ʒɔ̃kij] *nf* daffodil.

joue [ʒu] *nf* cheek.

jouer [ʒwe] *v* play; (*théâtre*) act; (*clef, etc.*) be loose; (*casino*) gamble; (*argent*) stake. **jouer de** use, make use of. **se jouer de** (*tromper*) deceive; (*moquer*) scoff at. **jouet** *nm* toy. **joueur, -euse** *nm, nf* player; gambler.

joufflu [ʒufly] *adj* chubby-cheeked.

joug [ʒu] *nm* yoke.

jouir [ʒwir] *v* **jouir de** enjoy. **jouissance** *nf* pleasure, delight; (*jur*) use.

jour [ʒur] *nm* day; (*lumière*) light; (*ouverture*) gap. **de nos jours** nowadays. **jour de congé** day off. **jour férié** bank holiday. **jour ouvrable** weekday. **le jour de l'An** New Year's day. **quinze jours** a fortnight. **vivre au jour le jour** live from hand to mouth. **journée** *nf* day.

journal [ʒurnal] *nm* newspaper; magazine, journal; (*intime*) diary. **journalier** *adj* daily; (*banal*) everyday. **journalisme** *nm* journalism. **journaliste** *n(m+f)* journalist.

jovial [ʒɔvjal] *adj* jovial, jolly. **jovialité** *nf* joviality, jollity.

joyau [ʒwajo] *nm* jewel, gem.

joyeux [ʒwajø] *adj* joyful, merry.

jubilé [ʒybile] *nm* jubilee.

jubiler [ʒybile] *v* (*fam*) be jubilant. **jubilation** *nf* jubilation.

jucher [ʒyʃe] *v* perch.

judaïsme [ʒydaismə] *nm* Judaism.

judiciaire [ʒydisjɛr] *adj* judicial.

judicieux [ʒydisjø] *adj* judicious.

judo [ʒydo] *nm* judo.

juger [ʒyʒe] *v* judge; (*jur*) try; consider; decide. **au jugé** by guesswork. **juge** *nm* judge. **juge de paix** Justice of the Peace. **jugement** *nm* judgment; (*jur*) sentence.

juif [ʒɥif] *adj* Jewish. **Juif, Juive** *nm, nf* Jew.

juillet [ʒɥijɛ] *nm* July.

juin [ʒɥɛ̃] *nm* June.

jumeau, -elle [ʒymo, -ɛl] *adj* twin; (*maisons*) semi-detached. *nm, nf* twin. **vrais jumeaux, vraies jumelles** identical twins. **jumelles** *nf pl* binoculars *pl*.

jumeler [ʒymle] *v* twin; join. **jumelé** *adj* double; twin.

jument [ʒymɑ̃] *nf* mare.

jungle [ʒɔ̃glə] *nf* jungle.

junte [ʒœ̃t] *nf* junta.

jupe [ʒyp] *nf* skirt. **jupon** *nm* waist slip.

jurer [ʒyre] *v* swear, vow; (*couleurs*) clash. **juré, -e** *nm, nf* juror.

juridique [ʒyridik] *adj* legal. **juridiction** *nf* jurisdiction.

juron [ʒyrɔ̃] *nm* oath, curse.

jury [ʒyri] *nm* jury.

jus [ʒy] *nm* juice. **jus de viande** gravy.

jusant [ʒyzɑ̃] *nm* ebb.

jusque [ʒyskə] *prep* up to. **jusqu'à** up to; (*lieu*) as far as; (*temps*) until; (*même*) even. **jusqu'à ce que** until. **jusqu'au bout** to the bitter end. **jusqu'ici** so far; (*lieu*) up to here; (*temps*) until now. **jusqu'où?** how far?

juste [ʒyst] *adj* just, fair; exact, accurate, right; (*pertinent*) sound; (*musique*) in tune; (*trop petit*) tight, barely enough. *adv* just; exactly; accurately; in tune. **au juste** exactly. **tout juste** only just, barely; exactly. **justesse** *nf* accuracy; soundness.

justice [ʒystis] *nf* justice, fairness; (*pol*) law.

justifier [ʒystifje] *v* justify; prove. **justifiable** *adj* justifiable. **justification** *nf* justification; proof.

jute [ʒyt] *nm* jute.

juteux [ʒytø] *adj* juicy.

juvénile [ʒyvenil] *adj* young, youthful.

juxtaposer [ʒykstapoze] *v* juxtapose. **juxtaposition** *nf* juxtaposition.

K

kaki [kaki] *nm, adj* khaki.

kaléidoscope [kaleidɔskɔp] *nm* kaleidoscope.

kangourou [kɑ̃guru] *nm* kangaroo.

karaté [karate] *nm* karate.

kayak [kajak] *nm* kayak.

kermesse [kɛrmɛs] *nf* fair, bazaar.

kidnapper [kidnape] *v* kidnap. **kidnappeur, -euse** *nm, nf* kidnapper.

kilo [kilo] *nm* kilo.

kilogramme [kilɔgram] *nm* kilogram.

kilomètre [kilɔmɛtrə] *nm* kilometre. **kilométrage** *nm* mileage.

kilowatt [kilɔwat] *nm* kilowatt.

kimono [kimɔno] *nm* kimono.

kinésithérapie [kineziterapi] *nf* physiotherapy. **kinésithérapeute** *n(m+f)* physiotherapist.

kiosque [kjɔsk] *nm* kiosk; (*jardin*) summer-house.

kiwi [kiwi] *nm* kiwi.

klaxon ® [klaksɔn] *nm* horn. **klaxonner** *v* sound one's horn, hoot.

kleptomanie [klɛptɔmani] *nf* kleptomania. **kleptomane** *n(m+f)*, *adj* kleptomaniac.

kyste [kist] *nm* cyst.

L

l' [l] *V* **la, le.**

la [la], **l'** *art* the. *pron* (*personne*) her; (*animal, chose*) it.

là [la] *adv* there; (*ici*) here; (*temps*) then; (*cela*) that. **là-bas** *adv* over there. **là-dedans** *adv* inside, in it. **là-dessous** *adv* underneath. **là-dessus** *adv* on that; (*à ce sujet*) about that; (*alors*) at that point. **là-haut** up there.

laboratoire [labɔratwar] *nm* laboratory.

laborieux [labɔrjø] *adj* (*pénible*) laborious; (*diligent*) hard-working.

labourer [labure] *v* plough. **laboureur** *nm* ploughman.

labyrinthe [labirɛ̃t] *nm* labyrinth, maze.

lac [lak] *nm* lake.

lacer [lase] *v* lace (up). **lacet** *nm* lace; (*route*) sharp bend; (*piège*) snare. **en lacet** winding.

lacérer [lasere] *v* tear up; (*corps*) lacerate. **lacération** *nf* laceration.

lâche [lɑʃ] *adj* loose; (*personne*) cowardly. *n(m+f)* coward. **lâcheté** *nf* cowardice.

lâcher [lɑʃe] *v* release, let go (of); (*ceinture*) loosen; (*fam: abandonner*) give up, drop. **lâcher pied** give way. **lâcher prise** let go.

lacrymogène [lakrimɔʒɛn] *adj* **gaz lacrymogène** *nm* tear-gas.

lacté [lakte] *adj* milky.

lacune [lakyn] *nf* gap.

ladre [lɑdrə] *adj* mean. *n(m+f)* miser.

lagune [lagyn] *nf* lagoon.

laid [lɛ] *adj* ugly. **laideur** *nf* ugliness.

laine [lɛn] *nf* wool. **de laine** woollen. **laineux** *adj* woolly.

laïque [laik] *adj* lay, secular. *nm* layman. **laïques** *nm pl* laity *sing*.

laisse [lɛs] *nf* lead, leash.

laisser [lese] v leave; let. laisser-aller nm invar carelessness. laissez-passer nm invar pass.

lait [lɛ] nm milk. lait caillé curds pl. lait concentré evaporated milk. laiterie nf dairy. laiteux adj milky. laitier nm milk-man.

laiton [lɛtɔ̃] nm brass.

laitue [lety] nf lettuce.

lama [lama] nm llama.

lambeau [lãbo] nm scrap, shred.

lambrequin [lãbrəkɛ̃] nm pelmet.

lame [lam] nf (bande) strip; (tranchant) blade; (vague) wave.

se lamenter [lamãte] v lament, moan. lamentable adj lamentable, awful; (cri) pitiful. lamentation nf lament.

lampadaire [lãpadɛr] nm standard lamp.

lampe [lãp] nf lamp, light. lampe de poche torch.

lamper [lãpe] (fam) v swig. lampée nf swig.

lance [lãs] nf spear.

lancer [lãse] v throw, hurl; (émettre) send out; (mettre en mouvement) launch. lance-pierres nm invar catapult. se lancer (sauter) leap; (se précipiter) dash. se lancer dans embark on.

lanciner [lãsine] v throb; obsess, torment.

landau [lãdo] nm pram.

lande [lãd] nf moor.

langage [lãgaʒ] nm language.

langouste [lãgust] nf crayfish. langoustines nf pl scampi pl.

langue [lãg] nf (anat) tongue; language.

languir [lãgir] v languish; (conversation) flag; (désirer) pine, long. languissant adj (personne) listless; (récit) dull.

lanière [lanjɛr] nf strap, thong.

lanterne [lãtɛrn] nf lantern; lamp, light; (auto) sidelight.

Laos [laɔs] nm Laos.

laper [lape] v lap (up).

lapin [lapɛ̃] nm rabbit.

Laponie [laponi] nf Lapland. lapon nm, adj Lapp. Lapon, -e nm, nf Lapp.

lapsus [lapsys] nm (parlé) slip of the tongue; (écrit) slip of the pen.

laque [lak] nf lacquer. laquer v lacquer.

laquelle [lakɛl] V lequel.

larcin [larsɛ̃] nm (vol) theft.

lard [lar] nm bacon; (gras) fat.

large [larʒ] adj wide, broad; generous. nm width; (place) space, room; (naut) open

sea. largement adv widely; generously; (de loin) greatly; (au moins) at least, easily. largesse nf generosity. largeur nf width, breadth.

larme [larm] nf tear.

larmoyer [larmwaje] v whimper; (yeux) water. larmoyant adj tearful.

larve [larv] nf larva, grub.

larynx [larɛ̃ks] nm larynx. laryngite nf laryngitis.

las, lasse [lɑ, lɑs] adj weary.

lascif [lasif] adj lascivious.

laser [lazɛr] nm laser.

lasser [lɑse] v weary. se lasser de grow tired of.

lasso [laso] nm lasso. prendre au lasso lasso.

latent [latã] adj latent.

latéral [lateral] adj lateral.

latin [latɛ̃] nm, adj Latin.

latitude [latityd] nf latitude.

laurier [lɔrje] nm laurel; (cuisine) bay leaves pl.

lavable [lavablə] adj washable.

lavabo [lavabo] nm washbasin. lavabos nm pl toilets pl.

lavage [lavaʒ] nm wash, washing. lavage de cerveau brainwashing.

lavande [lavãd] nf lavender.

lave [lav] nf lava.

laver [lave] v wash; (plaie) bathe. lave-vaisselle nm invar dishwasher. se laver have a wash. laverie automatique nf launderette. lavette nf dishcloth. laveur de vitres nm window-cleaner.

laxatif [laksatif] nm, adj laxative.

le [lə], l' art the. pron (personne) him; (animal, chose) it.

lécher [leʃe] v lick. faire du lèche-vitrines go window-shopping.

leçon [ləsɔ̃] nf lesson.

lecteur, -trice [lɛktœr, -tris] nm, nf reader. lecture nf reading.

ledit, ladite [lədi, ladit] adj, pl lesdits, lesdites the aforementioned or aforesaid.

légal [legal] adj legal; official. légaliser v legalize. légalité nf legality.

légende [leʒãd] nf legend; (illustration) caption. légendaire adj legendary.

léger [leʒe] adj light; (petit) slight; agile; (licencieux) ribald. à la légère thoughtlessly; not seriously. légèreté nf lightness.

légiférer [leʒifere] v legislate.

légion [leʒjɔ̃] *nf* legion; vast number. **être légion** be numberless.

législation [leʒislɑsjɔ̃] *nf* legislation.

légitime [leʒitim] *adj* legitimate, lawful.

legs [lɛg] *nm* legacy.

léguer [lege] *v* bequeath.

légume [legym] *nm* vegetable.

Léman [lemɑ̃] *nm* **lac Léman** *nm* Lake Geneva.

lendemain [lɑ̃dmɛ̃] *nm* day after, next day; future. **le lendemain matin/soir** the next morning/evening.

lent [lɑ̃] *adj* slow. **lenteur** *nf* slowness.

lentille [lɑ̃tij] *nf* lentil; (*optique*) lens.

léopard [leɔpar] *nm* leopard.

lépreux [leprø], **-euse** *adj* leprous. *nm, nf* leper. **lèpre** *nf* leprosy.

lequel [ləkɛl], **laquelle** *pron, pl* **lesquels, lesquelles** which; (*personne*) who, whom.

les [le] *art* the. *pron* them.

lesbienne [lɛsbjɛn] *nf* lesbian.

léser [leze] *v* wrong; injure.

lésiner [lezine] *v* skimp.

lessive [lesiv] *nf* washing; (*substance*) washing powder.

lest [lɛst] *nm* ballast.

leste [lɛst] *adj* nimble, sprightly; risqué; (*cavalier*) offhand.

léthargie [letarʒi] *nf* lethargy. **léthargique** *adj* lethargic.

lettre [lɛtrə] *nf* letter. **au pied de la lettre** literally. **lettres** *nf pl* (*université*) arts *pl*; literature *sing*. **lettres de créance** credentials *pl*.

leu [lø] *nm* **à la queue leu leu** in single file.

leucémie [løsemi] *nf* leukaemia.

leur [lœr] *pron* them, to them. *adj* their. **le** *or* **la leur** theirs.

leurrer [lœre] *v* deceive, delude. **leurre** *nm* delusion; (*appât*) lure; (*piège*) trap.

levé [ləve] *nm* survey. *adj* raised.

lever [ləve] *v* raise, lift; (*impôts*) levy; (*séance*) close; (*cuisine*) rise. **se lever** rise, get up. *nm* rising. **lever du soleil** sunrise.

levée *nf* raising; closing; (*poste*) collection; (*cartes*) trick.

levier [ləvje] *nm* lever. **levier de vitesse** gear lever.

lèvre [lɛvrə] *nf* lip.

lévrier [levrije] *nm* greyhound.

levure [ləvyr] *nf* yeast.

lézard [lezar] *nm* lizard. **lézarde** *nf* crack.

lézarder *v* crack; (*au soleil*) bask in the sun.

liaison [ljɛzɔ̃] *nf* (*d'affaires*) relationship; contact; (*rapport*) connection, link; (*amoureuse*) affair.

liasse [ljas] *nf* bundle, wad.

libelle [libɛl] *nm* libel; (*satire*) lampoon.

libellule [libelyl] *nf* dragonfly.

libéral [liberal], **-e** *adj* liberal; (*pol*) Liberal. *nm, nf* Liberal.

libérer [libere] *v* release, free, liberate. **libération** *nf* release, liberation.

liberté [libɛrte] *nf* freedom, liberty. **liberté conditionnelle** parole. **liberté sous caution** bail. **liberté surveillée** probation.

librairie [libreri] *nf* bookshop. **libraire** *n(m+f)* bookseller.

libre [librə] *adj* free. **libre-service** *nm* self-service shop *or* restaurant.

licence [lisɑ̃s] *nf* (*université*) degree; (*comm*) licence; permit. **licencié, -e** *nm, nf* graduate. **licencié ès lettres/sciences** Bachelor of Arts/Science.

licorne [likɔrn] *nf* unicorn.

licou [liku] *nm* halter.

lie [li] *nf* dregs *pl*.

Liechtenstein [liʃtɛnʃtajn] *nm* Liechtenstein.

liège [ljɛʒ] *nm* cork.

lien [ljɛ̃] *nm* (*attache*) bond; (*liaison*) link; (*de famille, etc.*) tie.

lier [lje] *v* tie up, bind; (*relier*) link up; unite; (*cuisine*) thicken.

lierre [ljɛr] *nm* ivy.

lieu [ljø] *nm* place. **au lieu de** instead of. **avoir lieu** take place. **avoir lieu de** have good reason to. **donner lieu à** give rise to. **sur les lieux** at the scene, on the spot. **tenir lieu de** take the place of.

lieutenant [ljøtnɑ̃] *nm* lieutenant. **lieutenant-colonel** *nm* wing commander.

lièvre [ljɛvrə] *nm* hare.

ligament [ligamɑ̃] *nm* ligament.

ligne [liɲ] *nf* line; (*rangée*) row; (*silhouette*) figure. **à la ligne** new paragraph. **hors ligne** outstanding. **ligne d'horizon** skyline.

ligoter [ligɔte] *v* tie, bind.

ligue [lig] *nf* league.

lilas [lila] *nm, adj invar* lilac.

limace [limas] *nf* slug. **limaçon** *nm* snail.

limaille [limɑj] *nf* filings *pl*.

limbe [lɛ̃b] *nm* **les limbes** limbo *sing*. **dans les limbes** (*rel*) in limbo; (*projet*) in the air.

limer [lime] v file. **lime** nf file. **lime à ongles** nail-file.

limier [limje] nm bloodhound; (policier) sleuth.

limite [limit] nf limit; (pays) boundary. adj maximum. **cas limite** nm borderline case. **date limite** nf deadline.

limiter [limite] v limit, restrict; (frontière) border. **limitation** nf limitation, restriction.

limon [limɔ̃] nm silt.

limonade [limɔnad] nf lemonade.

lin [lɛ̃] nm flax.

linceul [lɛ̃sœl] nm shroud.

linéaire [lineɛr] adj linear.

linge [lɛ̃ʒ] nm linen; (lessive) washing; (sous-vêtements) underwear; (torchon) cloth. **lingerie** nf lingerie.

lingot [lɛ̃go] nm ingot.

linguistique [lɛ̃gɥistik] nf linguistics. adj linguistic. **linguiste** n(m+f) linguist.

linoléum [linɔleɔm] nm linoleum. **lino** nm (fam) lino.

lion [ljɔ̃] nm lion. **Lion** nm Leo. **lionceau** nm lion cub. **lionne** nf lioness.

liqueur [likœr] nf liqueur.

liquide [likid] nm, adj liquid. **liquidation** nf liquidation; (règlement) settlement. **liquider** v liquidate; settle.

*__lire__¹ [lir] v read.

lire² [lir] nf lira.

lis [lis] nm lily.

Lisbonne [lisbɔn] n Lisbon.

lisible [lizibl] adj (écriture) legible; (livre) readable. **lisibilité** nf legibility.

lisière [lizjɛr] nf edge; (tissu) selvage.

lisse [lis] adj smooth. **lisser** v smooth.

liste [list] nf list.

lit [li] nm bed; (couche) layer. **lit de camp** camp-bed. **lit d'enfant** cot. **lit d'une personne** single bed. **literie** nf bedding.

litanie [litani] nf litany.

litée [lite] nf litter.

litre [litrə] nm litre.

littéraire [literɛr] adj literary.

littéral [literal] adj literal.

littérature [literatyr] nf literature.

littoral [litɔral] adj coastal. nm coast.

livide [livid] adj pallid, livid.

livraison [livrɛzɔ̃] nm delivery; (revue) part, issue.

livre¹ [livrə] nm book. **livre à succès** best-seller. **livre de bord** logbook. **livre de poche** paperback. **livre d'images** picture book. **livre d'or** visitors' book.

livre² [livrə] nf pound.

livrer [livre] v deliver; (abandonner) hand over, give up. **se livrer** confide. **se livrer à** (s'adonner) indulge in; (se consacrer) devote oneself to.

livret [livrɛ] nm (musique) libretto; (carnet) booklet, record book.

lobe [lɔb] nm lobe.

local [lɔkal] adj local. nm premises pl. **localiser** v localize; (déterminer) locate; (limiter) confine. **localité** nf locality.

locataire [lɔkatɛr] n(m+f) tenant.

location [lɔkasjɔ̃] nf (maison) renting; (voiture, bateau) hiring. **bureau de location** nm booking office.

locomotive [lɔkɔmɔtiv] nf locomotive, engine.

locuste [lɔkyst] nf locust.

locution [lɔkysjɔ̃] nf phrase.

logarithme [lɔgaritmə] nm logarithm.

loger [lɔʒe] v lodge; accommodate, put up; (habiter) live. **se loger** find accommodation; (se coincer) get stuck. **loge** nf lodge; (artiste) dressing room; (spectateur) box. **logement** nm housing; accommodation, lodgings pl. **logeur** nm landlord. **logeuse** nf landlady.

logique [lɔʒik] nf logic. adj logical.

logis [lɔʒi] nm dwelling.

loi [lwa] nf law.

loin [lwɛ̃] adv far. **au loin** in the distance. **de loin** from a distance; (de beaucoup) by far. **plus loin** further.

lointain [lwɛ̃tɛ̃] adj distant, remote. nm (tableau) background. **au lointain** in the distance.

loir [lwar] nm dormouse.

loisir [lwazir] nm leisure, spare time.

lombric [lɔ̃brik] nm earthworm.

Londres [lɔ̃drə] n London.

long, longue [lɔ̃, lɔ̃g] adj long. **à long terme** long-term. **à longue portée** long-range. **de longue date** long-standing. **longue-vue** nf telescope. adv **en savoir/dire long** know/say a lot. nm length. **de long en large** back and forth. **le long de** along. nf **à la longue** at last, in the end. **longueur** nf length. **longueur d'onde** wavelength.

longer [lɔ̃ʒe] v border; (sentier, etc.) run alongside; (personne) walk along.

longévité [lɔ̃ʒevite] nf longevity.

longitude [lɔ̃ʒityd] nf longitude.

longtemps [lɔ̃tɑ̃] *adv* (for) a long time, (for) long.
loque [lɔk] *nf* rag.
loquet [lɔkɛ] *nm* latch.
lorgner [lɔrɲe] *v* (*fam*) peer at, eye up.
lors [lɔr] *adv* **dès lors** from then on. **lors de** at the time of. **lors même que** even if.
lorsque [lɔrskə] *conj* when.
losange [lɔzɑ̃ʒ] *nm* diamond.
lot [lo] *nm* (*assortiment*) set, batch; (*portion*) share; (*prix*) prize.
loterie [lɔtri] *nf* lottery, raffle.
lotion [losjɔ̃] *nf* lotion.
lotus [lɔtys] *nm* lotus.
louange [lwɑ̃ʒ] *nf* praise.
louche¹ [luʃ] *adj* dubious, shady. **loucher** *v* have a squint.
louche² [luʃ] *nf* ladle.
louer¹ [lwe] *v* (*exalter*) praise. **louable** *adj* praiseworthy.
louer² [lwe] *v* rent, hire.
loufoque [lufɔk] *adj* (*fam*) crazy.
loup [lu] *nm* wolf. **loup-cervier** *nm* lynx. **loup-garou** *nm* werewolf.
loupe [lup] *nf* magnifying glass.
louper [lupe] (*fam*) *v* bungle, make a mess of; (*occasion*) miss; (*examen*) fail.
lourd [lur] *adj* heavy; (*temps*) close; (*important*) serious; (*gauche*) clumsy. **lourdeur** *nf* heaviness.
loutre [lutrə] *nf* otter.
louveteau [luvto] *nm* wolf cub; cub scout.
loyal [lwajal] *adj* loyal; (*honnête*) fair. **loyauté** *nf* loyalty; fairness.
loyer [lwaje] *nm* rent.
lubie [lybi] *nf* whim, fad.
lubrifier [lybrifje] *v* lubricate. **lubrifiant** *nm* lubricant. **lubrification** *nf* lubrication.
lucarne [lykarn] *nf* skylight, dormer window.
lucide [lysid] *adj* lucid. **lucidité** *nf* lucidity.
lucratif [lykratif] *adj* lucrative, profitable.
lueur [lɥœr] *nf* glimmer, glow.
luge [lyʒ] *nf* sledge, toboggan.
lugubre [lygybrə] *adj* gloomy, dismal.
lui [lɥi] *pron* (*homme*) him, to him; (*femme*) her, to her; (*chose, animal*) it, to it; (*sujet*) he. **lui-même** *pron* himself; itself.
*luire [lɥir] *v* gleam, shine. **luisant** *nm* sheen, gloss.
lumbago [lɔ̃bago] *nm* lumbago.
lumière [lymjɛr] *nf* light.

lumineux [lyminø] *adj* luminous.
lundi [lœ̃di] *nm* Monday.
lune [lyn] *nf* moon. **lune de miel** honeymoon. **lunaire** *adj* lunar.
lunette [lynɛt] *nf* telescope. **lunettes** *nf pl* glasses *pl*. **lunettes de soleil** sunglasses *pl*. **lunettes protectrices** goggles *pl*.
lurette [lyrɛt] *nf* **il y a belle lurette** ages ago.
lustrer [lystre] *v* polish; make shiny. **lustre** *nm* lustre; (*appareil d'éclairage*) chandelier. **lustré** *adj* shiny.
luth [lyt] *nm* lute.
lutin [lytɛ̃] *nm* imp. *adj* impish, mischievous.
lutrin [lytrɛ̃] *nm* lectern.
lutter [lyte] *v* struggle, fight. **lutte** *nf* struggle, fight; (*sport*) wrestling. **lutteur, -euse** *nm, nf* fighter; wrestler.
luxe [lyks] *nm* luxury. **luxueux** *adj* luxurious.
Luxembourg [lyksɑ̃bur] *nm* Luxembourg.
luxure [lyksyr] *nf* lust. **luxurieux** *adj* lascivious.
lycée [lise] *nm* secondary school. **lycéen, -enne** *nm, nf* secondary school pupil.
lyncher [lɛ̃ʃe] *v* lynch.
lynx [lɛ̃ks] *nm* lynx.
lyre [lir] *nf* lyre.
lyrique [lirik] *adj* lyrical.

M

m' [m] *V* me.
ma [ma] *V* mon.
macabre [makɑbrə] *adj* macabre.
macaroni [makarɔni] *nm* macaroni.
macédoine [masedwan] *nf* (*fam*) jumble. **macédoine de fruits** fruit salad. **macédoine de légumes** mixed vegetables *pl*.
mâcher [mɑʃe] *v* chew, munch. **mâchoire** *nf* jaw.
machin [maʃɛ̃] (*fam*) *nm* thing, contraption; whatsit. **Machin** *nm* what's-his-name.
machine [maʃin] *nf* machine; (*rail, naut*) engine. **machine à coudre/laver** sewing/washing machine. **machine à écrire** typewriter. **machine à sous** slot machine. **machinal** *adj* mechanical, automatic. **machinerie** *nf* machinery.

macis [masi] *nm* mace.

maçon [masɔ̃] *nm* (*pierre*) mason; (*construction*) builder; (*briques*) bricklayer. **maçonner** *v* build. **maçonnerie** *nf* masonry; building.

maculer [makyle] *v* stain. **macule** *nf* smudge.

madame [madam] *nf, pl* **mesdames** madam. **Madame** *nf* (*suivi du nom de famille*) Mrs.

mademoiselle [madmwazɛl] *nf, pl* **mesdemoiselles** miss, young lady. **Mademoiselle** *nf* (*suivi du nom de famille*) Miss.

madère [madɛr] *nm* (*vin*) Madeira. **Madère** *nf* (*île*) Madeira.

Madrid [madrid] *n* Madrid.

madrier [madrije] *nm* beam.

magasin [magazɛ̃] *nm* shop; (*entrepôt*) warehouse; (*fusil*) magazine. **magasin à succursales multiples** chain store.

magazine [magazin] *nm* magazine.

magie [maʒi] *nf* magic. **magicien, -enne** *nm, nf* magician. **magique** *adj* magic, magical.

magistral [maʒistral] *adj* masterly, brilliant; authoritative.

magistrat [maʒistra] *nm* magistrate.

magnanime [maɲanim] *adj* magnanimous. **magnanimité** *nf* magnanimity.

magnat [magna] *nm* tycoon, magnate.

magnétiser [maɲetize] *v* magnetize. **magnétique** *adj* magnetic. **magnétisme** *nm* magnetism.

magnétophone [maɲetɔfɔn] *nm* taperecorder.

magnifique [maɲifik] *adj* magnificent.

mai [mɛ] *nm* May.

maigre [mɛgrə] *adj* thin; (*viande*) lean; (*petit*) meagre, slight; (*médiocre*) poor. *nm* lean meat. **maigreur** *nf* thinness. **maigrir** *v* lose weight; (*exprès*) slim.

maille [mɑj] *nf* stitch; (*armure*) link; (*filet*) mesh. **maille filée** ladder.

maillet [majɛ] *nm* mallet.

maillot [majo] *nm* vest; (*sport*) jersey; (*danse*) leotard. **maillot de bain** (*homme*) swimming trunks *pl*; (*femme*) bathing costume.

main [mɛ̃] *nf* hand. **à la main** by hand. **en venir aux mains** come to blows. **fait main** handmade. **main-d'œuvre** *nf* labour, manpower. **sous la main** to or at hand.

maint [mɛ̃] *adj* many (a). **maintes fois** time and again.

maintenant [mɛ̃tnɑ̃] *adv* now.

*maintenir [mɛ̃tnir] *v* maintain; support; (*garder*) keep. **se maintenir** hold one's own, keep up; continue, persist. **maintien** *nm* maintenance, upholding; (*posture*) deportment.

maire [mɛr] *nm* mayor. **mairie** *nf* town hall.

mais [mɛ] *conj* but. *nm* objection.

maïs [mais] *nm* maize *or US* corn.

maison [mɛzɔ̃] *nf* house; (*foyer*) home; firm, company; (*domestiques*) household. *adj invar* home-made. **maison de repos** convalescent home. **maison de retraite** old people's home. **maison de santé** nursing home.

maître, -esse [mɛtrə, -ɛs] *adj* main, major. *nm* master. **être maître de** be in control of. **maître chanteur** blackmailer. **maître de chapelle** choirmaster. **maître d'hôtel** (*maison*) butler; (*hôtel*) head waiter. *nf* mistress.

maîtriser [mɛtrize] *v* control, master, overcome. **maîtrise** *nf* mastery; control. **maîtrise de soi** self-control.

majesté [maʒɛste] *nf* majesty. **majestueux** *adj* majestic.

majeur, -e [maʒœr] *adj* major; (*principal*) main; (*jur*) of age.

majorité [maʒɔrite] *nf.* majority. **être majoritaire** be in the majority.

majuscule [maʒyskyl] *nf, adj* capital.

mal [mal] *adv* badly; ill; (*incorrectement*) wrongly; with difficulty. **mal acquis** ill-gotten. **mal à l'aise** ill-at-ease. **mal comprendre** misunderstand. **mal élevé** ill-mannered. **mal interpréter** misinterpret. **pas mal** rather well, not badly. **pas mal de** (*fam*) quite a lot of. *adj invar* bad, wrong; (*malade*) ill; (*mal à l'aise*) uncomfortable. *nm* evil; (*douleur*) pain; (*maladie*) sickness; (*tristesse*) sorrow; difficulty, trouble; (*dommage*) harm. **avoir mal** be in pain, ache. **avoir mal à** have a pain in. **avoir mal aux dents/oreilles** have toothache/earache. **faire du mal à** hurt, harm. **mal de l'air** airsickness. **mal de mer** seasickness. **mal de tête** headache. **mal du pays** homesickness. **se faire mal** hurt oneself.

malade [malad] *adj* ill, sick. *n(m+f)* invalid, sick person; (*d'un médecin*) patient. **maladie** *nf* illness, disease. **maladif** *adj* sickly.

maladresse [maladrɛs] *nf* clumsiness, awkwardness; (*gaffe*) blunder.

maladroit [maladrwa] *adj* clumsy; (*indélicat*) tactless.

malaise [malɛz] *nm* discomfort; (*trouble*) uneasiness.

malappris [malapri] *adj* ill-mannered.

malaria [malarja] *nf* malaria.

malavisé [malavize] *adj* unwise, ill-advised.

malchance [malʃɑ̃s] *nf* misfortune, bad luck. **malchanceux** *adj* unlucky.

malcommode [malkɔmɔd] *adj* inconvenient; (*peu pratique*) unsuitable.

mâle [mɑl] *adj* male; virile. *nm* male.

malédiction [malediksjɔ̃] *nf* curse.

malentendu [malɑ̃tɑ̃dy] *nm* misunderstanding.

malfaisant [malfəzɑ̃] *adj* evil, harmful.

malgré [malgre] *prep* despite, in spite of.

malheur [malœr] *nm* misfortune; (*épreuve*) hardship; (*accident*) mishap. **malheureux** *adj* unfortunate; miserable.

malhonnête [malɔnɛt] *adj* dishonest; (*impoli*) rude. **malhonnêteté** *nf* dishonesty; rudeness.

Mali [mali] *nm* Mali.

malice [malis] *nf* mischief; (*malignité*) malice. **malicieux** *adj* mischievous.

malin, -igne [malɛ̃, -iɲ] *adj* cunning, shrewd; (*fam*) difficult; (*mauvais*) malicious; (*méd*) malignant.

malingre [malɛ̃grə] *adj* sickly, puny.

malle [mal] *nf* trunk; (*auto*) boot.

malmener [malmǝne] *v* manhandle.

malotru [malɔtry], **-e** *nm, nf* uncouth person, lout.

malpropre [malprɔprə] *adj* dirty; (*travail*) slovenly; (*indélicat*) unsavoury. **malpropreté** *nf* dirtiness; (*propos*) unsavoury remark; (*acte*) low trick.

malsain [malsɛ̃] *adj* unhealthy.

malséant [malseɑ̃] *adj* unseemly.

malt [malt] *nm* malt.

Malte [malt] *nf* Malta. **maltais** *nm, adj* Maltese. **les Maltais** the Maltese.

maltraiter [maltrete] *v* ill-treat, manhandle; misuse.

malveillant [malvejɑ̃, -ɑ̃t] *adj* malevolent, malicious. **malveillance** *nf* malevolence.

maman [mamɑ̃] *nf* (*fam*) mummy, mum.

mamelle [mamɛl] *nf* (*femme*) breast; (*animal*) teat; (*pis*) udder. **mamelon** *nm* nipple.

mammifère [mamifɛr] *nm* mammal.

mammouth [mamut] *nm* mammoth.

manche¹ [mɑ̃ʃ] *nf* sleeve. **à manches courtes/longues** short-/long-sleeved. **la Manche** the English Channel. **manchette** *nf* cuff; (*journal*) headline. **manchon** *nm* muff.

manche² [mɑ̃ʃ] *nf* handle. **manche à balai** broomstick; (*aéro*) joystick.

manchot [mɑ̃ʃo] *adj* one-armed; (*sans bras*) armless. *nm* penguin.

mandarine [mɑ̃darin] *nf* mandarin, tangerine.

mandat [mɑ̃da] *nm* mandate; (*police*) warrant. **mandat-poste** *nm* postal order. **mandater** *v* commission; elect.

mandoline [mɑ̃dɔlin] *nf* mandolin.

manège [manɛʒ] *nm* (*fête foraine*) roundabout; (*équitation*) riding school; (*jeu*) game.

manette [manɛt] *nf* lever.

manger [mɑ̃ʒe] *v* eat; (*fortune*) squander. *nm* food. **mangeable** *adj* edible.

mangue [mɑ̃g] *nf* mango. **manguier** *nm* mango tree.

maniaque [manjak] *adj* fussy, fanatical. *n(m + f)* fanatic.

manie [mani] *nf* odd habit; (*obsession*) mania.

manier [manje] *v* handle. **maniable** *adj* manageable; easily influenced; (*accommodant*) amenable. **maniement** *nm* handling.

manière [manjɛr] *nf* way, manner; style. **de manière à** so as to. **d'une manière ou d'une autre** somehow or other. **manières** *nf pl* manners *pl*, behaviour *sing*. **maniéré** *adj* affected.

manifeste [manifɛst] *adj* obvious, evident. *nm* manifesto.

manifester [manifɛste] *v* show, indicate; (*pol*) demonstrate. **manifestant, -e** *nm, nf* demonstrator. **manifestation** *nf* demonstration; expression; appearance.

manipuler [manipyle] *v* manipulate; (*objet*) handle. **manipulation** *nf* manipulation; handling.

manivelle [manivɛl] *nf* crank.

manne [man] *nf* hamper.

mannequin [manikɛ̃] *nm* (*personne*) model; (*objet*) dummy.

manœuvre [manœvrə] *nf* manœuvre, operation; (*intrigue*) scheme. *nm* labourer. **manœuvrer** *v* manoeuvre; (*machine*) operate.

manoir [manwar] *nm* manor house.

manquer [mɑ̃ke] *v* miss; (*rater*) make a mess of, botch; (*faire défaut*) be lacking; be absent; (*échouer*) fail. **manquer à** be missed by. **manquer de** lack. **manquer de faire** almost do. **ne pas manquer de** be sure to. **manque** *nm* lack, shortage; (*lacune*) gap; (*méd*) withdrawal.

mansarde [mɑ̃sard] *nf* attic.

manteau [mɑ̃to] *nm* coat.

manuel [manɥɛl] *nm, adj* manual.

manuscrit [manyskri] *adj* handwritten. *nm* manuscript.

manutention [manytɑ̃sjɔ̃] *nf* handling.

maquereau[1] [makro] *nm* (*poisson*) mackerel.

maquereau[2] [makro] *nm* (*argot*) pimp.

maquette [makɛt] *nf* model.

maquiller [makije] *v* make up; (*document, etc.*) fake. **maquillage** *nm* make-up.

maquis [maki] *nm* scrub, bush.

maraîcher [mareʃe], **-ère** *nm, nf* market gardener.

marais [marɛ] *nm* marsh.

marathon [maratɔ̃] *nm* marathon.

marbre [marbrə] *nm* marble.

marchand [marʃɑ̃], **-e** *nm, nf* (*boutiquier*) shopkeeper, tradesman; dealer, merchant. **marchand de journaux** newsagent. **marchand de légumes** greengrocer. **marchand de poissons** fishmonger. *adj* (*valeur*) market; (*navire*) merchant.

marchander [marʃɑ̃de] *v* haggle (over), bargain.

marchandise [marʃɑ̃diz] *nf* merchandise, goods *pl*.

marche [marʃ] *nf* walk, walking; (*mil, etc.*) march; (*machine, véhicule*) running; progress; (*escalier*) step. **marche arrière** reverse. **mettre en marche** start, set going.

marché [marʃe] *nm* market; (*contrat*) bargain, deal. **Marché commun** Common Market. **marché noir** black market.

marcher [marʃe] *v* walk; (*mil*) march; (*mettre le pied*) step, tread; (*fonctionner*) work.

mardi [mardi] *nm* Tuesday. **Mardi gras** Shrove Tuesday.

mare [mar] *nf* (*étang*) pond; (*flaque*) pool.

marécage [mareka3] *nm* marsh, bog. **marécageux** *adj* marshy.

maréchal [mareʃal] *nm* marshal, field marshal. **maréchal-ferrant** *nm* blacksmith.

marée [mare] *nf* tide. **marée noire** oil slick.

margarine [margarin] *nf* margarine.

marge [mar3] *nf* margin. **marginal** *adj* marginal.

marguerite [margərit] *nf* daisy.

mari [mari] *nm* husband.

mariage [marja3] *nm* marriage; (*cérémonie*) wedding.

marié [marje], **-e** *adj* married. *nm* bridegroom. *nf* bride.

marier [marje] *v* marry; (*couleurs, etc.*) blend. **se marier** get married.

marihuana [mariɥana] *nf* marijuana.

marin [marɛ̃] *adj* sea, marine. *nm* sailor.

marina [marina] *nf* marina.

marine [marin] *nf, adj invar* navy. **marine marchande** merchant navy.

mariner [marine] *v* marinade. **marinade** *nf* marinade.

marionnette [marjɔnɛt] *nf* puppet.

marital [marital] *adj* marital.

maritime [maritim] *adj* maritime; (*ville*) coastal; (*commerce, etc.*) shipping.

marjolaine [marʒɔlɛn] *nf* marjoram.

mark [mark] *nm* mark.

marmite [marmit] *nf* pot.

marmonner [marmɔne] *v* mumble, mutter.

marmot [marmo] *nm* (*fam*) kid, brat.

marmotter [marmɔte] *v* mumble, mutter.

Maroc [marɔk] *nm* Morocco. **marocain** *adj* Moroccan. **Marocain, -e** *nm, nf* Moroccan.

marotte [marɔt] *nf* hobby, craze.

marquer [marke] *v* mark; indicate, show; (*écrire*) write *or* note down; (*événement*) stand out. **marque** *nf* mark; (*comm*) brand, make; (*sport*) score. **de marque** (*produit*) high-class; (*personne*) distinguished, important. **marque de fabrique** trademark.

marqueterie [markətri] *nf* marquetry.

marquis [marki] *nm* marquis *or* marquess. **marquise** *nf* marchioness.

marraine [marɛn] *nf* godmother.

marre [mar] (*fam*) *adv* **en avoir marre** be fed up. **marrant** *adj* funny. **se marrer** *v* laugh.

marron [marɔ̃] *nm* chestnut; (*couleur*) brown. **marron d'Inde** horse-chestnut. *adj invar* brown. **marronnier** *nm* chestnut tree.

mars [mars] *nm* March.
Mars [mars] *nm* Mars. **martien, -enne** *n*, *adj* Martian.
marsouin [marswɛ̃] *nm* porpoise.
marsupial [marsypjal] *nm*, *adj* marsupial.
marteau [marto] *nm* hammer; (*porte*) knocker. **marteau-piqueur** *nm* pneumatic drill.
marteler [martəle] *v* hammer, pound.
martial [marsjal] *adj* martial, warlike.
martinet [martinɛ] *nm* swift.
martin-pêcheur [martɛ̃pɛʃœr] *nm* kingfisher.
martre [martrə] *nf* marten. **martre zibeline** sable.
martyr [martir], **-e** *nm*, *nf* martyr. **martyre** *nm* martyrdom; (*souffrance*) agony. **martyriser** *v* (*rel*) martyr; torture; (*bébé*) batter.
mascara [maskara] *nm* mascara.
mascarade [maskarad] *nf* masquerade.
mascotte [maskɔt] *nf* mascot.
masculin [maskylɛ̃] *nm*, *adj* masculine. **masculinité** *nf* masculinity.
masochiste [mazɔʃist] *n(m+f)* masochist. *adj* masochistic. **masochisme** *nm* masochism.
masquer [maske] *v* hide, mask. **masque** *nm* mask; air, façade. **masque de beauté** face-pack.
massacrer [masakre] *v* massacre; (*animaux*) slaughter; (*fam*) make a mess of. **massacre** *nm* massacre; slaughter.
masse¹ [mas] *nf* mass; (*élec*) earth.
masse² [mas] *nf* (*maillet*) sledge-hammer; (*bâton*) mace.
massepain [maspɛ̃] *nm* marzipan.
masser¹ [mase] *v* assemble, gather together.
masser² [mase] *v* massage. **massage** *nm* massage. **masseur** *nm* masseur. **masseuse** *nf* masseuse.
massif [masif] *adj* massive; solid, heavy. *nm* clump; (*géog*) massif.
massue [masy] *nf* club.
mastic [mastik] *nm* putty.
mastiquer¹ [mastike] *v* (*mâcher*) chew.
mastiquer² [mastike] *v* apply putty to.
mastodonte [mastɔdɔ̃t] *nm* (*camion*) juggernaut; (*personne*) colossus.
se masturber [mastyrbe] *v* masturbate. **masturbation** *nf* masturbation.
mat¹ [mat] *nm* checkmate. *adj invar* checkmated. **faire mât** checkmate.

mat² [mat] *adj* matt, dull.
mât [mɑ] *nm* (*naut*) mast; (*poteau*) pole.
match [matʃ] *nm* match. **match nul** draw.
matelas [matla] *nm* mattress. **matelas pneumatique** air-bed. **matelasser** *v* pad.
matelot [matlo] *nm* sailor.
se matérialiser [materjalize] *v* materialize.
matérialiste [materjalist] *adj* materialistic. *n(m+f)* materialist.
matériaux [materjo] *nm pl* material(s).
matériel [materjɛl] *adj* material. *nm* equipment, materials *pl*; (*tech*) plant.
maternel [matɛrnɛl] *adj* maternal; (*soin, geste*) motherly. **école maternelle** *nf* nursery school. **maternité** *nf* maternity, motherhood; maternity hospital.
mathématique [matematik] *adj* mathematical. **mathématiques** *nf pl* mathematics *sing*. **mathématicien, -enne** *nm*, *nf* mathematician. **maths** *nf pl* (*fam*) maths *sing*.
matière [matjɛr] *nf* matter; subject; material. **matière grasse** fat. **matières premières** raw materials *pl*.
matin [matɛ̃] *nm* morning. **de bon matin** early in the morning. **matinal** *adj* morning, early. **matinée** *nf* morning; (*théâtre*) afternoon performance, matinée.
matois [matwa] *adj* wily, sly.
matraque [matrak] *nf* truncheon, cosh.
matriarcal [matrijarkal] *adj* matriarchal.
matrice [matris] *nf* matrix; (*utérus*) womb.
matrimonial [matrimɔnjal] *adj* matrimonial.
maturité [matyrite] *nf* maturity.
maudire [modir] *v* curse.
mausolée [mozɔle] *nm* mausoleum.
maussade [mosad] *adj* sullen, morose; (*triste*) gloomy.
mauvais [mɔvɛ] *adj* bad; (*erroné*) wrong; (*vilain*) wicked, evil; (*désagréable*) nasty, unpleasant. **mauvaise herbe** *nf* weed.
mauve [mov] *nm*, *adj* mauve.
maxime [maksim] *nf* maxim.
maximum [maksimɔm] *nm*, *adj* maximum.
mayonnaise [majɔnɛz] *nf* mayonnaise.
mazout [mazut] *nm* oil.
me [mə], **m'** *pron* me, to me; (*réfléchi*) myself.
méandre [meɑ̃drə] *nm* meander.
mec [mɛk] *nm* (*argot*) bloke.

mécanique [mekanik] *adj* mechanical. *nf* mechanics. **mécanicien, -enne** *nm, nf* mechanic; (*naut, aéro*) engineer. **mécaniser** *v* mechanize. **mécanisme** *nm* mechanism; mechanics *pl*.

méchant [meʃɑ̃] *adj* nasty; (*malveillant*) spiteful; (*enfant*) naughty; (*vilain*) wicked. **méchanceté** *nf* nastiness; (*propos*) spiteful remark.

mèche [mɛʃ] *nf* (*bougie*) wick; (*bombe*) fuse; (*cheveux*) lock; (*tech*) bit. **être de mèche avec** be in league with.

mécompte [mekɔ̃t] *nm* (*déception*) disappointment; (*erreur*) miscalculation.

mécontent [mekɔ̃tɑ̃] *adj* discontented, dissatisfied; (*contrarié*) annoyed. **mécontentement** *nm* dissatisfaction. **mécontenter** *v* displease, annoy.

médaille [medaj] *nf* medal.

médecin [medsɛ̃] *nm* doctor. **médecine** *nf* medicine.

media [medja] *nm pl* mass media *pl*.

médiation [medjɑsjɔ̃] *nf* mediation. **médiateur, -trice** *nm, nf* mediator.

médical [medikal] *adj* medical.

médicament [medikamɑ̃] *nm* medicine.

médication [medikasjɔ̃] *nf* treatment, medication.

médicinal [medisinal] *adj* medicinal.

médiéval [medjeval] *adj* medieval.

médiocre [medjɔkrə] *adj* mediocre, poor. **médiocrité** *nf* mediocrity.

*médire [medir] *v* speak ill, malign. **médisance** *nf* scandal, gossip.

méditer [medite] *v* meditate, contemplate. **Méditerrané** [mediterane] *nf* Mediterranean (Sea). **méditerranéen** *adj* Mediterranean.

méduse [medyz] *nf* jellyfish.

méfait [mefɛ] *nm* misdemeanour. **méfaits** *nm pl* ravages *pl*, damage *sing*.

se méfier [mefje] *v* be careful, look out. **se méfier de** mistrust, be suspicious of; beware of. **méfiance** *nf* distrust. **méfiant** *adj* suspicious.

mégarde [megard] *nf* **par mégarde** accidentally, inadvertently.

mégère [meʒɛr] *nf* shrew.

mégot [mego] *nm* (*fam*) fag end.

meilleur, -e [mejœr] *adj, adv* better. **le meilleur, la meilleure** (the) best.

mélancolie [melɑ̃kɔli] *nf* melancholy. **mélancolique** *adj* melancholy, melancholic.

mélanger [melɑ̃ʒe] *v* mix (up); (*couleurs, etc.*) blend. **mélange** *nm* mixture; blend.

mélasse [melas] *nf* treacle.

mêler [mele] *v* mix, mingle; (*cartes*) shuffle; (*impliquer*) involve. **se mêler à** join, mingle with; get involved in. **se mêler de** meddle with, interfere in. **mêle-toi de tes affaires!** mind your own business! **mêlée** *nf* fray, mêlée; (*rugby*) scrum. **mêlée générale** free-for-all.

mélèze [melɛz] *nm* larch.

mélodie [melɔdi] *nf* melody. **mélodieux** *adj* melodious. **mélodique** *adj* melodic.

mélodrame [melɔdram] *nm* melodrama. **mélodramatique** *adj* melodramatic.

melon [məlɔ̃] *nm* melon; (*chapeau*) bowler.

membrane [mɑ̃bran] *nf* membrane.

membre [mɑ̃brə] *nm* (*anat*) limb; (*société*) member.

même [mɛm] *adj* (*semblable*) same; very. *pron* same. *adv* even. **de même** likewise. **quand même** all the same.

mémé [meme] *nf* (*fam*) granny, grandma.

mémento [memɛ̃to] *nm* (*agenda*) engagement diary; note.

mémoire[1] [memwar] *nf* memory.

mémoire[2] [memwar] *nm* memorandum; report; (*comm*) bill; (*exposé*) paper. **mémoires** *nm pl* memoirs *pl*.

mémorable [memorablə] *adj* memorable.

mémorandum [memorɑ̃dɔm] *nm* memorandum.

menacer [mənase] *v* threaten. **menaçant** *adj* menacing, threatening. **menace** *nf* threat.

ménage [menaʒ] *nm* (*entretien*) housekeeping, housework; married couple; (*communauté*) household. **ménager** *adj* household, domestic. **ménagère** *nf* (*femme*) housewife; (*couverts*) canteen of cutlery.

ménager [menaʒe] *v* spare; (*personne*) show consideration for; (*argent, etc.*) use sparingly *or* carefully; (*amener*) bring about; arrange. **ménagement** *nm* care, consideration.

mendier [mɑ̃dje] *v* beg (for). **mendiant, -e** *nm, nf* beggar. **mendicité** *nf* begging.

mener [məne] *v* lead; (*emmener*) take; (*enquête, conversation*) conduct; (*affaires, entreprise*) manage, run. **menées** *nf pl* intrigues *pl*. **meneur, -euse** *nm, nf* leader.

ménestrel [menɛstrɛl] *nm* minstrel.

méningite [menɛ̃ʒit] *nf* meningitis.

ménopause [menɔpoz] *nf* menopause.

menottes [mənɔt] *nf pl* handcuffs *pl*.

mensonge [mɑ̃sɔ̃ʒ] *nm* lie. **mensonger** *adj* false.

menstruel [mɑ̃stryɛl] *adj* menstrual. **menstruation** *nf* menstruation.

mensuel [mɑ̃sЧɛl] *adj* monthly. **mensuellement** *adv* monthly.

mensuration [mɑ̃syrɑsjɔ̃] *nf* measurement.

mental [mɑ̃tal] *adj* mental. **mentalité** *nf* mentality.

menteur, -euse [mɑ̃tœr, -øz] *adj* false; illusory; (*personne*) untruthful. *nm, nf* liar.

menthe [mɑ̃t] *nf* mint.

menthol [mɛ̃tɔl] *nm* menthol.

mention [mɑ̃sjɔ̃] *nf* mention; note; (*examen*) grade, class. **avec mention très bien** with distinction. **mentionner** *v* mention.

*****mentir** [mɑ̃tir] *v* lie.

menton [mɑ̃tɔ̃] *nm* chin.

menu [məny] *adj* (*fin*) small, slight; (*peu important*) petty, minor. *adv* finely, small. *nm* menu.

menuisier [mənЧizje] *nm* joiner, carpenter. **menuiserie** *nf* joinery, carpentry, woodwork.

se *méprendre [meprɑ̃drə] *v* make a mistake.

mépris [mepri] *nm* contempt, scorn.

méprise [mepriz] *nf* mistake.

mépriser [meprize] *v* scorn, despise. **méprisable** *adj* contemptible. **méprisant** *adj* contemptuous.

mer [mɛr] *nf* sea; (*marée*) tide. **en mer** at sea.

mercenaire [mɛrsənɛr] *nm, adj* mercenary.

mercerie [mɛrsəri] *nf* haberdashery.

merci [mɛrsi] *interj* thank you; (*refus*) no thank you. **merci beaucoup** *or* **bien** thank you very much. *nm* thank-you, thanks *pl*. *nf* mercy.

mercier [mɛrsje] **, -ère** *nm, nf* haberdasher.

mercredi [mɛrkrədi] *nm* Wednesday. **mercredi des Cendres** Ash Wednesday.

mercure [mɛrkyr] *nm* mercury.

merde [mɛrd] (*vulgaire*) *nf* shit. *interj* hell! shit!

mère [mɛr] *nf* mother.

méridien [meridjɛ̃] *nm, adj* meridian.

méridional [meridjɔnal] *adj* southern; from the south of France. **Méridional, -e** *nm, nf* Southerner.

meringue [mərɛ̃g] *nf* meringue.

mériter [merite] *v* deserve, merit; (*exiger*) require; (*valoir*) be worth. **mérite** *nm* merit; (*respect*) credit; quality.

merlan [mɛrlɑ̃] *nm* whiting.

merle [mɛrl] *nm* blackbird.

merveille [mɛrvɛj] *nf* wonder, marvel. **à merveille** perfectly, marvellously. **merveilleux** *adj* wonderful, marvellous.

mes [me] *V* **mon**.

mésaventure [mezavɑ̃tyr] *nf* misadventure, misfortune.

mesquin [mɛskɛ̃] *adj* mean, stingy; (*étroit*) petty. **mesquinerie** *nf* meanness; pettiness.

message [mesaʒ] *nm* message. **messager, -ère** *nm, nf* messenger. **messageries** *nf pl* parcels service *sing*. **bureau de messageries** *nm* parcel office.

messe [mɛs] *nf* mass.

mesurer [məzyre] *v* measure; (*évaluer*) assess; limit, ration. **mesure** *nf* measure; measurement; (*musique*) bar; (*cadence*) time; moderation. **à mesure que** as. **fait sur mesure** made-to-measure. **mesuré** *adj* measured; moderate; (*ton*) steady.

métabolisme [metabɔlismə] *nm* metabolism.

métal [metal] *nm* metal. **métallique** *adj* metallic. **métallurgie** *nf* metallurgy. **métallurgiste** *nm* metallurgist; (*ouvrier*) metal-worker.

métamorphose [metamɔrfoz] *nf* metamorphosis.

métaphore [metafɔr] *nf* metaphor. **métaphorique** *adj* metaphorical.

métaphysique [metafizik] *adj* metaphysical. *nf* metaphysics.

météore [meteɔr] *nm* meteor. **météorique** *adj* meteoric. **météorite** *nm* meteorite.

météorologie [meteɔrɔlɔʒi] *nf* meteorology. **météorologique** *adj* meteorological, weather. **météorologue** *n(m + f)* meteorologist.

méthane [metan] *nm* methane.

méthode [metɔd] *nf* method. **méthodique** *adj* methodical.

méthodiste [metɔdist] *n(m + f), adj* Methodist. **méthodisme** *nm* Methodism.

méticuleux [metikylø] *adj* meticulous.

métier [metje] *nm* job, trade, profession; technique, experience; (*machine*) loom.

métis, -isse [metis] *n, adj* half-caste, half-breed. **métisser** *v* cross.

métrage [metraʒ] *nm* length; measurement.

mètre [mɛtrə] *nm* metre; (*règle*) rule. **mètre à ruban** tape measure. **métrique** *adj* metric.

metro [metro] *nm* subway, tube.

métronome [metrɔnɔm] *nm* metronome.

métropole [metrɔpɔl] *nf* metropolis. **métropolitain** *adj* metropolitan.

mets [mɛ] *nm* dish.

*mettre [mɛtrə] *v* put; (*vêtements*) put on, wear; (*temps*) take, spend; suppose. **se mettre à** start. **metteur en scène** *nm* (*théâtre*) producer; (*cinéma*) director.

meubler [mœble] *v* furnish; (*remplir*) fill (out). **meuble** *nm* piece of furniture. **meubles** *nm pl* furniture *sing*.

meugler [møgle] *v* moo, low. **meuglement** *nm* lowing.

meule[1] [møl] *nf* (*moudre*) millstone; (*aiguiser*) grindstone.

meule[2] [møl] *nf* stack, rick. **meule de foin** haystack.

meunier [mønje] *nm* miller.

meurtre [mœrtrə] *nm* murder.

meurtrier [mœrtrije], **-ère** *nm, nf* murderer. *adj* murderous, lethal.

meurtrir [mœrtrir] *v* bruise. **meurtrissure** *nf* bruise.

meute [møt] *nf* pack.

mi- [mi] *prefix* half-, mid-. **à mi-chemin** halfway. **à mi-corps** to the waist. **à mi-côte** halfway up *or* down. **à mi-temps** part-time. **à mi-voix** in an undertone. **mi-janvier, mi-février, etc.** mid-January, mid-February, etc.

miche [miʃ] *nf* round loaf.

micro [mikro] *nm* (*fam*) mike.

microbe [mikrɔb] *nm* germ, microbe.

microfilm [mikrɔfilm] *nm* microfilm.

microphone [mikrɔfɔn] *nm* microphone.

microscope [mikrɔskɔp] *nm* microscope. **microscopique** *adj* microscopic.

microsillon [mikrɔsijɔ̃] *nm* long-playing record.

midi [midi] *nm* midday, noon; lunchtime; (*géog*) south. **le Midi** the South of France.

mie [mi] *nf* soft part of bread.

miel [mjɛl] *nm* honey. **mielleux** *adj* (*péj*) sugary, smooth.

mien [mjɛ̃], **mienne** *pron* **le mien, la mienne** mine.

miette [mjɛt] *nf* crumb.

mieux [mjø] *adj, adv* better. **le** *or* **la mieux** (the) best.

mièvre [mjɛvrə] *adj* mawkish, affected.

mignon, -onne [miɲɔ̃, -ɔn] *adj* sweet, dainty. *nm, nf* darling.

migraine [migrɛn] *nf* headache; (*méd*) migraine.

migration [migrasjɔ̃] *nf* migration.

mijoter [miʒɔte] *v* simmer; (*fam*) plot, cook up.

mildiou [mildju] *nm* mildew.

milieu [miljø] *nm* middle; environment; (*social*) circle, background. **au milieu de** in the middle of. **juste milieu** happy medium.

militaire [militɛr] *adj* military. *nm* soldier.

militant [militɑ̃], **-e** *n, adj* militant.

mille[1] [mil] *nm, adj invar* (a) thousand. **mille-pattes** *nm invar* centipede. **milliard** *nm* thousand million. **millième** *n(m + f), adj* thousandth. **millier** *nm* thousand or so. **des milliers de** thousands *or* millions of.

mille[2] [mil] *nm* mile.

millénaire [milenɛr] *nm* millennium, thousand years. *adj* thousand-year-old, ancient.

milligramme [miligram] *nm* milligram.

millilitre [mililitrə] *nm* millilitre.

millimètre [milimɛtrə] *nm* millimetre.

million [miljɔ̃] *nm* million. **millionnaire** *n(m + f)* millionnaire. **millionième** *n(m + f), adj* millionth.

mimer [mime] *v* mime; (*imiter*) mimic. **mime** *nm* mime; mimic.

minable [minablə] *adj* (*lieu*) seedy, shabby; miserable, wretched; (*fam: piètre*) pathetic, hopeless.

minauder [minode] *v* mince, simper.

mince [mɛ̃s] *adj* thin; (*svelte*) slim, slender; (*insignifiant*) slight, small. *adv* thinly. *interj* blast! drat! **minceur** *nf* thinness.

mine[1] [min] *nf* expression; look, appearance. **avoir bonne/mauvaise mine** look well/unwell. **faire mine de** pretend to, make as if to.

mine[2] [min] *nf* mine; (*crayon*) lead. **miner** *v* (*mil*) mine; (*saper*) undermine. **mineur** *nm* miner. **minier** *adj* mining.

minerai [minrɛ] *nm* ore.

minéral [mineral] *nm, adj* mineral.

mineur, -e [minœr] *n, adj* minor.

miniature [minjatyr] *nf, adj* miniature.

minime [minim] *adj* minimal; (*insignifiant*) trivial; (*piètre*) paltry. **minimiser** *v* minimize. **minimum** *nm, adj* minimum.

ministère [minister] *nm* ministry; government. **ministériel** *adj* ministerial. **ministre** *nm* minister.

minorité [minɔrite] *nf* minority. **minoritaire** *adj* minority.

minuit [minᶣi] *nm* midnight.

minuscule [minyskyl] *adj* minute, tiny; (*lettre*) small. *nf* small letter.

minute [minyt] *nf* minute; moment, instant.

minutieux [minysjø] *adj* meticulous, minute. **minutie** *nf* meticulousness; (*ouvrage*) minute detail.

mioche [mjɔʃ] *n(m+f)* (*fam*) kid, brat.

miracle [mirɑklə] *nm* miracle. **miraculeux** *adj* miraculous.

mirage [miraʒ] *nm* mirage.

mirer [mire] *v* mirror. **se mirer** be reflected.

miroir [mirwar] *nm* mirror.

miroiter [mirwate] *v* sparkle, gleam.

misanthrope [mizɑ̃trɔp] *n(m+f)* misanthropist. *adj* misanthropic. **misanthropie** *nf* misanthropy.

mise [miz] *nf* putting; (*enjeu*) stake; (*vêtements*) clothing. **être de mise** be acceptable. **mise en plis** set. **mise en scène** production. **miser** *v* stake, bet.

misérable [mizerablə] *adj* miserable; (*pitoyable*) wretched; (*pauvre*) destitute; (*minable*) paltry. *n(m+f)* wretch.

misère [mizɛr] *nf* (*malheur*) misery, misfortune; poverty. **faire des misères à** (*fam*) be nasty to.

miséricorde [mizerikɔrd] *nf* mercy. **miséricordieux** *adj* merciful.

misogyne [mizɔʒin] *n(m+f)* misogynist. **misogynie** *nf* misogyny.

missile [misil] *nm* missile.

mission [misjɔ̃] *nf* mission. **missionnaire** *n(m+f)* missionary.

mite [mit] *nf* clothes moth. **mité** *adj* moth-eaten. **miteux** *adj* seedy, shabby.

mitoyen [mitwajɛ̃] *adj* dividing, common. **mur mitoyen** *nm* party wall.

mitrailleuse [mitrɑjøz] *nf* machine gun.

mitre [mitrə] *nf* mitre.

mixte [mikst] *adj* mixed; (*école*) coeducational.

mobile [mɔbil] *adj* mobile, moving, movable. *nm* motive; (*art*) mobile. **mobiliser** *v* mobilize. **mobilité** *nf* mobility.

mobilier [mɔbilje] *adj* (*jur*) personal, movable. *nm* furniture.

mocassin [mɔkasɛ̃] *nm* moccasin.

moche [mɔʃ] (*fam*) *adj* (*mauvais*) rotten; (*laid*) ugly.

mode¹ [mɔd] *nf* fashion; style. **à la mode** fashionable.

mode² [mɔd] *nm* mode; method; (*gramm*) mood. **mode d'emploi** directions for use.

modeler [mɔdle] *v* model, shape, mould. **modèle** *nm, adj* model.

modérer [mɔdere] *v* moderate, restrain. **se modérer** control oneself. **modération** *nf* moderation; reduction. **modéré** *adj* moderate.

moderne [mɔdɛrn] *adj* modern. **modernisation** *nf* modernization. **moderniser** *v* modernize.

modeste [mɔdɛst] *adj* modest. **modestie** *nf* modesty.

modifier [mɔdifje] *v* modify. **modification** *nf* modification.

modique [mɔdik] *adj* modest, small.

module [mɔdyl] *nm* module.

moduler [mɔdyle] *v* modulate. **modulation** *nf* modulation.

moelle [mwal] *nf* (*anat*) marrow; pith. **moelle épinière** spinal cord. **moelleux** *adj* soft, smooth, mellow.

mœurs [mœr] *nf pl* morals *pl*; customs *pl*; habits *pl*; manners *pl*.

mohair [mɔɛr] *nm* mohair.

moi [mwa] *pron* me; (*sujet*) I. *nm* self, ego. **moi-même** *pron* myself.

moignon [mwaɲɔ̃] *nm* stump.

moindre [mwɛ̃drə] *adj* less; (*plus bas*) lower; (*inférieur*) poorer. **le** *or* **la moindre** the least, the slightest.

moine [mwan] *nm* monk.

moineau [mwano] *nm* sparrow.

moins [mwɛ̃] *nm, adv* less. **à moins de** barring, unless. **à moins que** unless. **au moins** at least. **du moins** at least. **le** *or* **la moins** (the) least. **moins de** less (than); (*heure*) before. *prep* minus. **six heures moins dix** ten to six.

mois [mwa] *nm* month. **au mois** by the month, monthly.

moisir [mwazir] *v* go mouldy. **moisi** *adj* mouldy. **sentir le moisi** smell musty. **moisissure** *nf* mould.

moisson [mwasɔ̃] *nf* harvest, crop. **mois-**

sonner v harvest, reap. **moissonneuse-batteuse** nf combine harvester.
moite [mwat] adj moist, clammy.
moitié [mwatje] nf half. **à moitié** half. **moitié moitié** half-and-half.
mol [mɔl] form of **mou** used before a vowel or mute h.
molécule [mɔlekyl] nf molecule. **moléculaire** adj molecular.
molester [mɔlɛste] v manhandle, maul.
mollasse [mɔlas] (fam) adj lethargic; (flasque) flabby.
molle [mɔl] V **mou**.
mollesse [mɔlɛs] nf softness; (manque de fermeté) limpness; lethargy, lifelessness.
mollet, -ette [mɔlɛ, -ɛt] adj soft; (œuf) soft-boiled. nm (anat) calf.
mollir [mɔlir] v soften; (vent) abate; (fléchir) yield; give way.
mollusque [mɔlysk] nm mollusc.
môme [mom] n(m+f) (fam) kid, brat.
moment [mɔmɑ̃] nm moment; time. **en ce moment** at the moment. **momentané** adj momentary, brief.
momie [mɔmi] nf mummy. **momification** nf mummification. **momifier** v mummify.
mon [mɔ̃], **ma** adj, pl **mes** my.
Monaco [mɔnako] nm Monaco.
monarque [mɔnark] nm monarch. **monarchie** nf monarchy. **monarchiste** n(m+f) monarchist.
monastère [mɔnastɛr] nm monastery. **monastique** adj monastic.
monceau [mɔ̃so] nm heap, pile.
monde [mɔ̃d] nm world; (gens) people; society, circle. **tout le monde** everybody. **mondain** adj fashionable; society; refined; (rel) worldly. **mondial** adj worldwide.
monétaire [mɔnetɛr] adj monetary.
mongolien [mɔ̃gɔljɛ̃], **-enne** n, adj mongol. **mongolisme** nm mongolism.
moniteur, -trice [mɔnitœr, -tris] nm, nf (sport) instructor; (surveillant) supervisor.
monnaie [mɔnɛ] nf (devises) currency; (pièce) coin; (appoint) change. **monnayer** v mint; (tirer profit de) capitalize on.
monogamie [mɔnɔgami] nf monogamy. **monogame** adj monogamous.
monogramme [mɔnɔgram] nm monogram.
monologue [mɔnɔlɔg] nm monologue.
monopole [mɔnɔpɔl] nm monopoly. **monopoliser** v monopolize.

monosyllabe [mɔnɔsilab] nm monosyllable. **monosyllabique** adj monosyllabic.
monotone [mɔnɔtɔn] adj monotonous. **monotonie** nf monotony.
monseigneur [mɔ̃sɛɲœr] nm Your or His Grace, Your or His Lordship.
monsieur [məsjø] nm, pl **messieurs** gentleman; (titre) sir. **Monsieur** nm (suivi du nom de famille) Mr.
monstre [mɔ̃strə] nm monster. adj (fam) colossal. **monstrueux** adj monstrous. **monstruosité** nf monstrosity.
mont [mɔ̃] nm mount. **mont-de-piété** nm pawnshop.
montagne [mɔ̃taɲ] nf mountain. **montagnes russes** big dipper sing. **montagneux** adj mountainous.
montant [mɔ̃tɑ̃] adj upward, rising; (col, corsage) high. nm (portant) upright; (somme) total.
monter [mɔ̃te] v mount; go up, rise; ascend, climb; (porter) take up; (cheval) ride; (théâtre) put on, produce; assemble; equip. **monter à cheval/bicyclette** ride a horse/bicycle. **monter dans** or **en** get on or into. **se monter à** amount to. **montage** nm assembly; (cinéma) editing. **montée** nf ascent, climb; rise; (côte) hill. **monture** nf frame, setting, mount.
montre [mɔ̃trə] nf watch. **faire montre de** show, display. **montre-bracelet** nf wristwatch.
montrer [mɔ̃tre] v show. **se montrer** appear; prove to be.
monument [mɔnymɑ̃] nm monument. **monumental** adj monumental.
moquer [mɔke] v **se moquer de** make fun of; (mépriser) not care about. **moquerie** nf mockery.
moral [mɔral] adj moral. nm morale. **morale** or **moralité** nf morality; (mœurs) morals pl; (fable) moral. **moraliser** v moralize. **moraliste** n(m+f) moralist.
morbide [mɔrbid] adj morbid.
morceau [mɔrso] nm piece; (bout) bit; extract, passage.
mordre [mɔrdrə] v bite. **mordant** adj biting; (acerbe) scathing, cutting. **mordu** adj (fam) mad keen.
se morfondre [mɔrfɔ̃drə] v mope.
morgue[1] [mɔrg] nf morgue, mortuary.
morgue[2] [mɔrg] nf (arrogance) pride, haughtiness.

moribond [mɔribɔ̃] *adj* dying.

mormon [mɔrmɔ̃], **-e** *n, adj* Mormon.

morne [mɔrn] *adj* gloomy, dismal.

morose [mɔroz] *adj* sullen, morose.

morphine [mɔrfin] *nf* morphine.

mors [mɔr] *nm* bit.

morse¹ [mɔrs] *nm* (*zool*) walrus.

morse² [mɔrs] *nm* Morse code.

morsure [mɔrsyr] *nf* bite.

mort¹ [mɔr], **-e** *adj* dead. *nm, nf* dead person. **morte-saison** *nf* off season. **mort-né** *adj* stillborn.

mort² [mɔr] *nf* death. **mort-aux-rats** *nf* rat poison.

mortalité [mɔrtalite] *nf* mortality; (*taux*) death rate.

mortel [mɔrtɛl] *adj* mortal; fatal; (*poison, etc.*) lethal, deadly.

mortier [mɔrtje] *nm* mortar.

mortifier [mɔrtifje] *v* mortify. **mortification** *nf* mortification.

mortuaire [mɔrtⁿɛr] *adj* mortuary. **dépôt mortuaire** *nm* funeral parlour.

morue [mɔry] *nf* cod.

morveux [mɔrvø], **-euse** *nm, nf* (*argot*) kid, brat.

mosaïque [mɔzaik] *nf* mosaic.

Moscou [mɔsku] *n* Moscow.

mosquée [mɔske] *nf* mosque.

mot [mo] *nm* word; note; (*expression*) saying. **mot de passe** password. **mots croisés** crossword *sing*.

motel [mɔtɛl] *nm* motel.

moteur, -trice [mɔtœr, -tris] *nm* motor, engine. **moteur à explosion** internal combustion engine. **moteur à réaction** jet engine. *adj* (*anat*) motor; (*tech*) driving.

motif [mɔtif] *nm* motive, grounds *pl*; (*ornement, musique*) motif.

motion [mosjɔ̃] *nf* motion.

motiver [mɔtive] *v* motivate; justify; (*expliquer*) account for. **motivation** *nf* motivation.

moto [mɔto] *nf* (*fam*) motorbike. **motocycliste** *n*(*m+f*) motorcyclist.

motte [mɔt] *nf* lump; (*terre*) clod; (*gazon*) turf.

mou [mu], **molle** *adj* soft; (*sans fermeté*) limp; (*flasque*) flabby; feeble, weak; lethargic; (*temps*) muggy. *nm* softness. **avoir du mou** be slack.

mouche [muʃ] *nf* fly. **prendre la mouche** (*fam*) get in a huff. **moucheron** *nm* midge.

moucher [muʃe] *v* (*fam*) snub; (*chandelle*) snuff. **se moucher** blow one's nose.

moucheter [muʃte] *v* speckle. **moucheture** *nf* speck, spot.

mouchoir [muʃwar] *nm* handkerchief. **mouchoir en papier** tissue.

***moudre** [mudrə] *v* grind.

moue [mu] *nf* pout. **faire la moue** pout, pull a face.

mouette [mwɛt] *nf* sea-gull.

mouffette [mufɛt] *nf* skunk.

moufle [muflə] *nf* mitten.

mouiller [muje] *v* wet; (*naut*) moor, anchor. **mouillage** *nm* mooring, anchorage. **mouillé** *adj* wet.

moule¹ [mul] *nm* mould.

moule² [mul] *nf* (*zool, cuisine*) mussel.

mouler [mule] *v* mould, cast; (*vêtements*) hug, fit closely.

moulin [mulɛ̃] *nm* mill. **moulin à café** coffee-mill. **moulin à paroles** (*fam*) chatterbox. **moulin à vent** windmill. **moulinet** *nm* (*pêche*) reel.

moulu [muly] *adj* ground.

***mourir** [murir] *v* die.

mousquet [muskɛ] *nm* musket. **mousquetaire** *nm* musketeer.

mousse¹ [mus] *nf* (*bot*) moss; (*écume*) froth, foam; (*savon*) lather; (*cuisine*) mousse. **mousser** *v* froth, foam; lather; (*vin*) sparkle. **mousseux** *adj* frothy; sparkling. **moussu** *adj* mossy.

mousse² [mus] *nm* cabin boy.

mousseline [muslin] *nf* muslin.

mousson [musɔ̃] *nf* monsoon.

moustache [mustaʃ] *nf* moustache. **moustaches** *nf pl* (*animal*) whiskers *pl*.

moustique [mustik] *nm* mosquito.

moutarde [mutard] *nf* mustard.

mouton [mutɔ̃] *nm* sheep; (*cuisine*) mutton.

***mouvoir** [muvwar] *v* drive, move. **se mouvoir** move. **mouvant** *adj* changing, shifting. **mouvement** *nm* movement; activity; impulse. **mouvementé** *adj* lively, eventful.

moyen [mwajɛ̃], **-enne** *adj* medium, average; middle. **moyen âge** *nm* Middle Ages *pl*. **Moyen-Orient** *nm* Middle East. *nm* means, way. **au moyen de** by means of. **moyens** *nm pl* means *pl*. *nf* average.

moyennant [mwajɛnɑ̃] *prep* (in return) for.

moyeu [mwajø] *nm* hub.

muer [mɥe] v moult; (voix) break.
muet, -ette [mɥɛ, -ɛt] adj silent; (infirme) dumb. nm, nf mute, dumb person.
mufle [myflə] nm muzzle; (argot) lout.
mugir [myʒir] v bellow, roar; (vache) moo.
muguet [mygɛ] nm lily of the valley.
mule [myl] nf mule.
mulet [mylɛ] nm mule.
multicolore [myltikɔlɔr] adj multicoloured.
multiple [myltiplə] adj multiple, numerous, many. nm multiple.
multiplier [myltiplije] v multiply; (augmenter) increase. **multiplication** nf multiplication.
multitude [myltityd] nf multitude, vast number.
municipal [mynisipal] adj municipal; (conseil) local; (piscine, etc.) public. **municipalité** nf municipality; town council.
munir [mynir] v munir de provide with, equip with. **munitions** nf pl ammunition sing.
mur [myr] nm wall; barrier. **muraille** nf high wall.
mûr [myr] adj (fruit) ripe; (personne) mature.
mural [myral] adj mural. **peinture murale** nf mural.
mûre [myr] nf (ronce) blackberry; (mûrier) mulberry. **mûrier** nm mulberry bush; blackberry bush.
mûrir [myrir] v ripen; mature.
murmurer [myrmyre] v murmur. **murmure** nm murmur.
musc [mysk] nm musk.
muscade [myskad] nf nutmeg.
muscle [mysklə] nm muscle. **musclé** adj muscular.
museau [myzo] nm muzzle; (porc) snout.
musée [myze] nm museum; (d'art) art gallery.
museler [myzle] v muzzle. **muselière** nf muzzle.
muséum [myzeɔm] nm natural history museum.
musicien [myzisjɛ̃], -enne nm, nf musician. adj musical.
musique [myzik] nf music; (mil) band. **musical** adj musical.
musulman [myzylmɑ̃], -e n, adj Muslim.
mutiler [mytile] v mutilate; (personne)

maim. **mutilation** nf mutilation. **mutilé, -e** nm, nf disabled person.
mutin [mytɛ̃] adj mischievous. nm rebel.
se mutiner [mytine] v mutiny; rebel. **mutiné** adj mutinous. **mutinerie** nf mutiny; rebellion.
mutisme [mytismə] nm silence; (méd) dumbness.
mutuel [mytɥɛl] adj mutual.
myope [mjɔp] adj short-sighted. **myopie** nf short-sightedness.
myrtille [mirtij] nf bilberry.
mystère [mistɛr] nm mystery. **mystérieux** adj mysterious.
mystifier [mistifje] v fool, take in.
mystique [mistik] n(m+f) mystic. adj mystical, mystic. **mysticisme** nm mysticism.
mythe [mit] nm myth. **mythique** adj mythical. **mythologie** nf mythology. **mythologique** adj mythological.

N

n' [n] V ne.
nabot [nabo], -e adj tiny. nm, nf dwarf.
nacre [nakrə] nf mother-of-pearl. **nacré** adj pearly.
nager [naʒe] v swim; float; (naut) row. **nage** nf (action) swimming; (manière) stroke. **nage libre** freestyle. **nageoire** nf (poisson) fin; (phoque) flipper. **nageur, -euse** nm, nf swimmer.
naguère [nagɛr] adv not long ago; (autrefois) formerly.
naïf [naif], -ive adj naive. nm, nf gullible fool. **naïveté** nf naivety.
nain [nɛ̃], -e n, adj dwarf.
naissance [nɛsɑ̃s] nf birth; source.
***naître** [nɛtrə] v be born; (surgir) arise, spring up. **faire naître** arouse; create.
nappe [nap] nf tablecloth; (eau) sheet; (brouillard) blanket. **nappe de pétrole** oil slick. **napperon** nm mat.
narcotique [narkɔtik] nm, adj narcotic.
narine [narin] nf nostril.
narquois [narkwa] adj mocking, derisive.
narrer [nare] v narrate. **narrateur, -trice** nm, nf narrator. **narratif** adj narrative. **narration** nf narration; (récit) narrative.

nasal [nazal] *adj* nasal. **nasaliser** *v* nasalize. **naseau** *nm* nostril. **nasillard** *adj* nasal.

natal [natal] *adj* native. **natalité** *nf* birth rate.

natation [natasjɔ̃] *nf* swimming.

natif [natif] **-ive** *n, adj* native.

nation [nɑsjɔ̃] *nf* nation. **national, -e** *n, adj* national. **nationalisation** *nf* nationalization. **nationaliser** *v* nationalize. **nationalisme** *nm* nationalism. **nationaliste** *n(m+f)* nationalist. **nationalité** *nf* nationality.

nativité [nativite] *nf* nativity.

natter [nate] *v* plait. **natte** *nf* (*cheveux*) plait; (*paille, etc.*) mat.

naturalisme [natyralismə] *nm* naturalism. **naturaliste** *n(m+f)* naturalist.

nature [natyr] *nf* nature. **en nature** in kind. **nature morte** still life. *adj invar* plain, neat.

naturel [natyrɛl] *adj* natural. *nm* disposition.

naufrage [nofraʒ] *nm* shipwreck; ruin. **naufragé** *adj* shipwrecked.

nausée [noze] *nf* nausea. **avoir la nausée** feel sick. **nauséabond** *adj* nauseating.

nautique [notik] *adj* nautical.

naval [naval] *adj* naval.

navet [navɛ] *nm* turnip; (*fam*) rubbish.

navette [navɛt] *nf* shuttle (service). **faire la navette** commute; go backwards and forwards.

naviguer [navige] *v* (*bateau*) sail; (*avion*) fly; (*piloter*) navigate. **navigateur** *nm* navigator. **navigation** *nf* navigation; traffic.

navire [navir] *nm* ship.

navrer [navre] *v* distress; (*irriter*) annoy. **navré** *adj* sorry; distressed.

ne [nə], **n'** *adv* not. **ne ... guère** scarcely. **ne ... jamais** never. **ne ... pas** not. **ne ... personne** nobody. **ne ... plus** no longer. **ne ... que** only. **ne ... rien** nothing.

né [ne] *adj* born.

néanmoins [neɑ̃mwɛ̃] *adv* nevertheless, yet.

néant [neɑ̃] *nm* nothing, void.

nébuleux [nebylø] *adj* nebulous, vague; (*ciel*) cloudy.

nécessaire [nesesɛr] *adj* necessary; indispensable. *nm* essentials *pl*. **le nécessaire** what is needed. **nécessité** *nf* necessity. **nécessiter** *v* necessitate.

nécrologie [nekrɔlɔʒi] *nf* (*notice*) obituary; (*liste*) obituary column.

nectar [nɛktar] *nm* nectar.

néerlandais [neɛrlɑ̃dɛ] *nm, adj* Dutch. **les Néerlandais** the Dutch.

nef [nɛf] *nf* nave.

néfaste [nefast] *adj* (*nuisible*) harmful; (*funeste*) unlucky.

négatif [negatif] *nm, adj* negative.

négligé [negliʒe] *adj* neglected; (*tenue*) slovenly; (*travail*) careless. *nm* slovenliness; (*vêtement*) négligée.

négliger [negliʒe] *v* neglect; (*occasion*) miss. **négligeable** *adj* negligible. **négligence** *nf* negligence, carelessness. **négligent** *adj* negligent, careless.

négocier [negɔsje] *v* negotiate. **négoce** *nm* trade. **négociable** *adj* negotiable. **négociant, -e** *nm, nf* merchant. **négociation** *nf* negotiation.

nègre [nɛgrə] *nm, adj* Negro. **petit nègre** pidgin French. **négresse** *nf* Negress. **négrier** *nm* (*péj*) slave-driver.

neige [nɛʒ] *nf* snow. **neige fondue** sleet. **neiger** *v* snow. **neigeux** *adj* snowy.

nénuphar [nenyfar] *nm* water-lily.

néon [neɔ̃] *nm* neon.

néo-zélandais [neozelɑ̃dɛ] *adj* New Zealand. **Néo-Zélandais, -e** *nm, nf* New Zealander.

nerf [nɛr] *nm* nerve; spirit, energy. **nerveux** *adj* nervous; energetic, vigorous; (*musclé*) sinewy. **nervosité** *nf* nervousness; tension; irritability.

net, nette [nɛt] *adj* neat; (*propre*) clean; (*comm*) net; (*clair*) clear; distinct. *adv* net; frankly; (*sur le coup*) outright; (*s'arrêter*) dead. **netteté** *nf* neatness; clearness.

nettoyer [nɛtwaje] *v* clean. **nettoyer à sec** dry-clean. **nettoyage** *nm* cleaning.

neuf¹ [nœf] *nm, adj* nine. **neuvième** *n(m+f), adj* ninth.

neuf² [nœf] *adj* new. **à neuf** as good as new.

neutre [nøtrə] *nm, adj* neutral; (*genre*) neuter. **neutraliser** *v* neutralize. **neutralité** *nf* neutrality.

neveu [nəvø] *nm* nephew.

névralgie [nevralʒi] *nf* neuralgia.

névrose [nevroz] *nf* neurosis. **névrosé** *adj* neurotic.

nez [ne] *nm* nose; flair; (*figure*) face.

ni [ni] *conj* nor, or. **ni ... ni ...** neither ... nor ....

niais [njɛ], **-e** *adj* simple, silly. *nm, nf* simpleton. **niaiserie** *nf* silliness; *(propos)* foolish talk.

nicher [niʃe] *v* nest. **niche** *nf* niche; *(chien)* kennel. **nichée** *nf* brood.

nickel [nikɛl] *nm* nickel.

Nicosie [nikɔsi] *n* Nicosia.

nicotine [nikɔtin] *nf* nicotine.

nid [ni] *nm* nest. **nid de poule** pot-hole.

nièce [njɛs] *nf* niece.

nier [nje] *v* deny.

nigaud [nigo], **-e** *adj* silly, simple. *nm, nf* simpleton.

nimbe [nɛ̃b] *nm* halo.

nitouche [nituʃ] *nf* **sainte nitouche** hypocrite. **faire la sainte nitouche** look as if butter wouldn't melt in one's mouth.

niveau [nivo] *nm* level; *(degré)* standard. **niveau à bulle** spirit level. **niveau de vie** standard of living.

niveler [nivle] *v* level, even out.

noble [nɔblə] *nm, adj* noble. **noblesse** *nf* nobleness, nobility.

noce [nɔs] *nf* wedding. **faire la noce** *(fam)* live it up.

nocif [nɔsif] *adj* noxious, harmful.

nocturne [nɔktyrn] *adj* nocturnal.

Noël [nɔɛl] *nm* Christmas.

nœud [nø] *nm* knot; *(de ruban)* bow; *(lien)* bond; *(rail, route)* junction. **nœud coulant** slip-knot. **nœud papillon** bow tie.

noir [nwar] *adj* black; *(obscur)* dark; *(profond)* deep. *nm* black; darkness. **Noir** *nm* black man. **noire** *nf* crotchet. **Noire** *nf* black woman. **noircir** *v* blacken; darken.

noisette [nwazɛt] *nf* hazelnut. *adj invar* hazel. **noisetier** *nm* hazel tree.

noix [nwa] *nf* walnut. **noix de beurre** knob of butter. **noix de coco** coconut.

nom [nɔ̃] *nm* name; *(gramm)* noun. **nom de baptême** Christian name. **nom de famille** surname. **nom de jeune fille** maiden name. **nom d'emprunt** assumed name. **nom de théâtre** stage name. **nom propre** proper noun.

nomade [nɔmad] *adj* nomadic. *n(m+f)* nomad.

nombre [nɔ̃brə] *nm* number. **nombreux** *adj* numerous.

nombril [nɔ̃bri] *nm* navel.

nominal [nɔminal] *adj* nominal.

nomination [nɔminasjɔ̃] *nf* appointment, nomination.

nommer [nɔme] *v* name; *(désigner)* appoint.

non [nɔ̃] *adv* no; *(pas)* not. **non plus** neither. *nm invar* no.

nonchalant [nɔ̃ʃalɑ̃] *adj* nonchalant. **nonchalance** *nf* nonchalance.

non-conformiste [nɔ̃kɔ̃fɔrmist] *n(m+f)*, *adj* nonconformist.

non-existant [nɔnɛgzistɑ̃] *adj* non-existent.

nonobstant [nɔnɔpstɑ̃] *prep, adv* notwithstanding.

nord [nɔr] *nm* north. *adj invar* north; *(région)* northern; *(direction)* northward. **nord-est** *nm, adj invar* north-east. **nord-ouest** *nm, adj invar* north-west.

normal [nɔrmal] *adj* normal. **normale** *nf* norm, normal.

norme [nɔrm] *nf* norm; standard.

Norvège [nɔrvɛʒ] *nf* Norway. **norvégien** *nm, adj* Norwegian. **Norvégien, -enne** *nm, nf* Norwegian.

nos [no] *V* notre.

nostalgie [nɔstalʒi] *nf* nostalgia. **nostalgique** *adj* nostalgic.

notable [nɔtablə] *adj* notable.

notaire [nɔtɛr] *nm* notary.

notamment [nɔtamɑ̃] *adv* notably, in particular.

notation [nɔtasjɔ̃] *nf* notation; *(devoir)* marking.

noter [nɔte] *v* *(écrire)* note down; *(remarquer)* notice, note; *(devoir)* mark. **note** *nf* note; mark; *(compte)* bill.

notice [nɔtis] *nf* note; instructions *pl*.

notifier [nɔtifje] *v* notify. **notification** *nf* notification.

notion [nosjɔ̃] *nf* notion.

notoire [nɔtwar] *adj* well-known; *(criminal)* notorious. **notoriété** *nf* fame; notoriety. **notoriété publique** common knowledge.

notre [nɔtrə] *adj, pl* **nos** our.

nôtre [notrə] *pron* **le** or **la nôtre** ours.

nouer [nwe] *v* tie, knot; *(amitié, etc.)* strike up; *(intrigue)* build up. **noueux** *adj* knotty, gnarled.

nouilles [nuj] *nf pl* noodles *pl*.

nounou [nunu] *nf* *(fam)* nanny.

nounours [nunurs] *nm* *(fam)* teddy.

nourrice [nuris] *nf* nurse. **nourricier** *adj* nutritive.

nourrir [nurir] *v* feed, nourish; *(espoir, etc.)* nurse, harbour. **nourrisson** *nm* infant. **nourriture** *nf* food, nourishment.

nous [nu] *pron* (*sujet*) we; (*objet*) us, to us; (*réfléchi*) ourselves, each other. **nous-mêmes** *pron* ourselves.

nouveau, -elle [nuvo, -ɛl] *adj* new; fresh. **à nouveau** afresh. **de nouveau** again. **nouveau-né** *adj* newborn. **Nouveau Testament** *nm* New Testament. **nouveau venu, nouvelle venue** *nm, nf* newcomer. **nouveaux-mariés** *nm pl* newly-weds *pl*. **nouvel an** *nm* New Year. **Nouvelle-Zélande** *nf* New Zealand. *nf* piece of news; (*récit*) short story. **nouvelles** *nf pl* news *sing*. **nouveauté** *nf* novelty; change; (*mode*) fashion.

nouvel [nuvɛl] *form of* **nouveau** *used before a vowel or mute h.*

novateur, -trice [nɔvatœr, -tris] *adj* innovative. *nm, nf* innovator.

novembre [nɔvɑ̃brə] *nm* November.

novice [nɔvis] *adj* inexperienced. *n(m+f)* novice.

noyau [nwajo] *nm* (*fruit*) stone; nucleus; (*tech*) core; small group.

noyer[1] [nwaje] *nm* (*arbre, bois*) walnut.

noyer[2] [nwaje] *v* drown; (*auto*) flood; (*submerger*) swamp. **noyade** *nf* drowning.

nu [ny] *adj* bare; (*sans vêtements*) naked; (*style*) plain. *nm* nude. **mettre à nu** expose, lay bare. **nu-pieds** *adv* barefoot.

nuage [nɥaʒ] *nm* cloud. **nuageux** *adj* cloudy.

nuance [nɥɑ̃s] *nf* nuance; (*couleur*) shade; slight difference. **nuancer** *v* shade.

nucléaire [nykleɛr] *adj* nuclear.

nudité [nydite] *nf* nudity; (*dénuement*) bareness. **nudiste** *n(m+f)* nudist.

nue [ny] *nf* **porter aux nues** praise to the skies. **tomber des nues** be flabbergasted.

nuée [nɥe] *nf* cloud; (*multitude*) horde.

***nuire** [nɥir] *v* **nuire à** harm. **nuisible** *adj* harmful. **animal** or **insecte nuisible** *nm* pest.

nuit [nɥi] *nf* night; (*obscurité*) darkness. **cette nuit** (*passé*) last night; (*futur*) tonight. **nuit blanche** sleepless night.

nul, nulle [nyl] *adj* (*aucun*) no; (*résultat*) nil; (*personne*) useless. **nul et non avenu** null and void. **nulle part** nowhere. *pron* no-one. **nullement** *adv* not at all.

numéral [nymeral] *nm* numeral.

numérique [nymerik] *adj* numerical.

numéro [nymero] *nm* number; (*journal*) issue. **numéro minéralogique** (*auto*) registration number.

numéroter [nymerɔte] *v* number.

nuptial [nypsjal] *adj* bridal, nuptial.

nuque [nyk] *nf* nape of the neck.

nutrition [nytrisjɔ̃] *nf* nutrition. **nutritif** *adj* nutritious, nourishing.

nylon [nilɔ̃] *nm* nylon.

nymphe [nɛ̃f] *nf* nymph.

O

oasis [ɔazis] *nf* oasis.

obéir [ɔbeir] *v* **obéir à** obey. **obéissance** *nf* obedience. **obéissant** *adj* obedient.

obélisque [ɔbelisk] *nm* obelisk.

obèse [ɔbɛz] *adj* obese. **obésité** *nf* obesity.

objecter [ɔbʒɛkte] *v* object; (*raison*) put forward; (*prétexter*) plead. **objection** *nf* objection.

objectif [ɔbʒɛktif] *adj* objective. *nm* objective; (*appareil-photo*) lens.

objet [ɔbʒɛ] *nm* object; (*but*) purpose; subject. **objets trouvés** lost property *sing*.

obliger [ɔbliʒe] *v* oblige; force, compel. **obligation** *nf* obligation; (*devoir*) duty. **obligatoire** *adj* compulsory; (*fam*) inevitable.

oblique [ɔblik] *adj* oblique. **regard oblique** *nm* sidelong glance.

oblitérer [ɔblitere] *v* cancel.

oblong, -ongue [ɔblɔ̃, -ɔ̃g] *adj* oblong.

obscène [ɔpsɛn] *adj* obscene. **obscénité** *nf* obscenity.

obscur [ɔpskyr] *adj* obscure; (*sombre*) dark; humble. **obscurité** *nf* obscurity; darkness.

obscurcir [ɔpskyrsir] *v* obscure; darken.

obséder [ɔpsede] *v* obsess, haunt. **obsédant** *adj* obsessive, haunting. **obsédé, -e** *nm, nf* (*fam*) fanatic.

obsèques [ɔpsɛk] *nf pl* funeral *sing*.

observateur, -trice [ɔpsɛrvatœr, -tris] *nm, nf* observer. *adj* observant.

observer [ɔpsɛrve] *v* observe; (*regarder*) watch; (*remarquer*) notice. **observation** *nf* observation; remark. **observatoire** *nm* observatory.

obsession [ɔpsesjɔ̃] *nf* obsession.

obstacle [ɔpstaklə] *nm* obstacle; (*hippisme*) fence.

obstétrique [ɔpstetrik] *nf* obstetrics.

s'obstiner [ɔpstine] *v* insist. **s'obstiner à** persist obstinately in. **obstination** *nf* obstinacy. **obstiné** *adj* obstinate.

obstruer [ɔpstrye] *v* obstruct, block. **obstruction** *nf* obstruction.

***obtenir** [ɔptənir] *v* obtain, get; (*atteindre*) achieve.

obturateur [ɔptyratœr] *nm* (*phot*) shutter.

obtus [ɔbty] *adj* obtuse.

obus [ɔby] *nm* shell.

occasion [ɔkazjɔ̃] *nf* opportunity, chance; (*circonstance*) occasion; cause; (*comm*) bargain; (*marché*) second-hand market. **d'occasion** second-hand. **occasionnel** *adj* casual; (*fortuit*) chance. **occasionner** *v* cause.

occident [ɔksidɑ̃] *nm* west. **occidental** *adj* western.

occulte [ɔkylt] *adj* occult; secret, hidden.

occuper [ɔkype] *v* occupy. **s'occuper de** attend to, take care of. **occupant, -e** *nm, nf* occupant, occupier. **occupation** *nf* occupation. **occupé** *adj* busy; (*téléphone, toilettes*) engaged; (*mil*) occupied.

océan [ɔseɑ̃] *nm* ocean. **océanique** *adj* oceanic.

ocre [ɔkrə] *nf* ochre. *nm* (*couleur*) ochre.

octane [ɔktan] *nm* octane.

octave [ɔktav] *nf* octave.

octobre [ɔktɔbrə] *nm* October.

octogone [ɔktɔgɔn] *nm* octagon. **octogonal** *adj* octagonal.

octroyer [ɔktrwaje] *v* grant.

oculiste [ɔkylist] *n(m+f)* oculist.

ode [ɔd] *nf* ode.

odeur [ɔdœr] *nf* odour, smell; (*agréable*) fragrance, scent. **odorant** *adj* sweet-smelling. **odorat** *nm* sense of smell.

odieux [ɔdjø] *adj* obnoxious, odious.

œil [œj] *nm, pl* **yeux** eye; (*expression*) look. **œil poché** black eye. **œillade** *nf* wink. **œillères** *nf pl* blinkers *pl*. **œillet** *nm* carnation; (*trou*) eyelet.

œsophage [ezɔfaʒ] *nm* oesophagus.

œuf [œf] *nm* egg. **œuf à la coque** boiled egg. **œuf du jour** new-laid egg. **œuf dur** hard-boiled egg. **œuf mollet** soft-boiled egg. **œuf poché** poached egg. **œufs brouillés** scrambled eggs *pl*. **œuf sur le plat** fried egg.

œuvre [œvrə] *nf* work; (*tâche*) task; charity. **œuvre d'art** work of art.

offenser [ɔfɑ̃se] *v* offend. **s'offenser** take offence. **offensant** *adj* offensive. **offense** *nf* insult; (*rel*) trespass. **offensive** *nm* (*mil*) offensive.

office [ɔfis] *nm* office; bureau, agency; (*rel*) service. **faire office de** act as. **officiel, -elle** *n*, *adj* official. **officier** *nm* officer. **officieux** *adj* unofficial.

officine [ɔfisin] *nf* dispensary.

***offrir** [ɔfrir] *v* offer; present; (*cadeau*) give. **s'offrir** treat oneself to. **offrande** *nf* offering. **offre** *nf* offer; (*enchères*) bid; (*comm*) tender.

offusquer [ɔfyske] *v* offend.

ogre [ɔgrə] *nm* ogre. **ogresse** *nf* ogress.

oie [wa] *nf* goose.

oignon [ɔɲɔ̃] *nm* (*légume*) onion; (*bot*) bulb.

***oindre** [wɛ̃drə] *v* anoint.

oiseau [wazo] *nm* bird.

oisif [wazif] *adj* idle. **oisiveté** *nf* idleness.

oison [wazɔ̃] *nm* gosling.

olive [ɔliv] *nf* olive. **olivier** *nm* olive tree.

olympique [ɔlɛ̃pik] *adj* Olympic.

ombrage [ɔ̃braʒ] *nm* shade. **prendre ombrage** take umbrage. **ombrager** *v* shade. **ombrageux** *adj* touchy.

ombre [ɔ̃brə] *nf* shadow; (*ombrage*) shade; obscurity, dark. **ombrer** *v* shade.

omelette [ɔmlɛt] *nf* omelette.

***omettre** [ɔmɛtrə] *v* omit. **omission** *nf* omission.

omnibus [ɔmnibys] *nm* slow train.

omnipotent [ɔmnipɔtɑ̃] *adj* omnipotent.

omoplate [ɔmɔplat] *nf* shoulder blade.

on [ɔ̃] *pron* one, (*les gens*) they, people; (*tu, vous*) you; (*nous*) we; (*quelqu'un*) someone. **on demande ...** ... wanted. **on-dit** *nm invar* rumour, hearsay.

oncle [ɔ̃klə] *nm* uncle.

onde [ɔ̃d] *nf* wave. **grandes ondes** long wave(s). **ondes courtes/moyennes** short/medium wave(s). **sur les ondes** on the air.

ondoyer [ɔ̃dwaje] *v* ripple, wave. **ondoyant** *adj* undulating; (*flamme*) wavering; (*forme*) supple.

onduler [ɔ̃dyle] *v* undulate; (*cheveux*) be wavy. **ondulant** *adj* undulating; (*pouls*) uneven. **ondulation** *nf* undulation. **ondulé** *adj* (*cheveux*) wavy. **onduleux** *adj* wavy; (*movement*) sinuous.

ongle [ɔ̃glə] *nm* nail; (*animal*) claw.

onguent [ɔ̃gɑ̃] *nm* ointment.

onyx [ɔniks] *nm* onyx.

onze [ɔ̃z] *nm*, *adj* eleven. **onzième** *n(m+f)*, *adj* eleventh.

opale [ɔpal] *nf* opal.

opaque [ɔpak] *adj* opaque. **opacité** *nf* opacity.

opéra [ɔpera] *nm* opera; (*édifice*) opera house. **opérette** *nf* operetta.

opérer [ɔpere] *v* operate; (*accomplir*) carry out; (*effectuer*) bring about; (*faire*) make; (*agir*) act, work. **se faire opérer** have an operation. **opérateur, -trice** *nm, nf* operator. **opération** *nf* operation; (*comm*) deal; (*tech*) process. **salle d'opération** *nf* operating theatre.

ophtalmique [ɔftalmik] *adj* ophthalmic.

s'opiniâtrer [ɔpinjatre] *v* persist stubbornly. **opiniâtre** *adj* stubborn, obstinate; persistent. **opiniâtreté** *nf* stubbornness, obstinacy.

opinion [ɔpinjɔ̃] *nf* opinion.

opium [ɔpjɔm] *nm* opium.

opportun [ɔpɔrtœ̃] *adj* opportune; appropriate. **opportunité** *nf* timeliness.

opposé [ɔpoze] *adj* opposite; conflicting, opposing; contrasting. **opposé à** opposed to. *nm* opposite.

opposer [ɔpoze] *v* place opposite; contrast. **s'opposer à** oppose. **opposition** *nf* opposition; conflict; contrast. **par opposition à** as opposed to.

opprimer [ɔprime] *v* oppress.

opprobre [ɔprɔbrə] *nm* disgrace.

opter [ɔpte] *v* opt, choose. **option** *nf* option.

opticien [ɔptisjɛ̃], **-enne** *nm, nf* optician.

optimiste [ɔptimist] *n(m+f)* optimist. *adj* optimistic. **optimisme** *nm* optimism.

optimum [ɔptimɔm] *nm, adj* optimum.

optique [ɔptik] *adj* optical, optic. *nf* optics.

opulent [ɔpylɑ̃] *adj* wealthy, rich, opulent. **opulence** *nf* richness, opulence.

or[1] [ɔr] *nm* gold. **d'or** golden.

or[2] [ɔr] *conj* now.

oracle [ɔraklə] *nm* oracle.

orage [ɔraʒ] *nm* storm. **orageux** *adj* stormy.

oraison [ɔrezɔ̃] *nf* prayer.

oral [ɔral] *nm, adj* oral.

orange [ɔrɑ̃ʒ] *nf* orange. *nm, adj invar* (*couleur*) orange. **oranger** *nm* orange tree.

orateur, -trice [ɔratœr, -tris] *nm, nf* orator, speaker.

orbite [ɔrbit] *nf* orbit. **orbiter** *v* orbit.

orchestre [ɔrkɛstrə] *nm* orchestra; (*danse, jazz*) band; (*théâtre*) stalls *pl*. **orchestral**

adj orchestral. **orchestration** *nf* orchestration. **orchestrer** *v* orchestrate.

orchidée [ɔrkide] *nf* orchid.

ordinaire [ɔrdinɛr] *adj* ordinary; common; (*habituel*) usual. *nm* ordinary.

ordinal [ɔrdinal] *adj* ordinal.

ordinateur [ɔrdinatœr] *nm* computer.

ordonner [ɔrdɔne] *v* order; arrange, organize; (*méd*) prescribe; (*rel*) ordain. **ordonnance** *nf* order; prescription; organization. **ordonné** *adj* orderly, tidy.

ordre [ɔrdrə] *nm* order. **de premier/deuxième ordre** first-/second-rate. **en ordre** tidy. **ordre du jour** agenda.

ordure [ɔrdyr] *nf* dirt, filth. **ordures** *nf pl* rubbish *sing*, refuse *sing*; obscenities *pl*.

oreille [ɔrɛj] *nf* ear; (*ouïe*) hearing. **oreiller** *nm* pillow. **oreillons** *nm pl* mumps *sing*.

ores [ɔr] *adv* **d'ores et déjà** already, here and now.

orfèvre [ɔrfɛvrə] *nm* (*argent*) silversmith; (*or*) goldsmith.

organe [ɔrgan] *nm* organ; instrument; (*porte-parole*) spokesman, mouthpiece.

organique [ɔrganik] *adj* organic.

organiser [ɔrganize] *v* organize. **organisateur, -trice** *nm, nf* organizer. **organisation** *nf* organization. **organisme** *nm* organism; (*institution*) body.

organiste [ɔrganist] *n(m+f)* organist.

orgasme [ɔrgasmə] *nm* orgasm.

orge [ɔrʒ] *nf* barley.

orgie [ɔrʒi] *nf* orgy; (*excès*) profusion.

orgue [ɔrg] *nm* organ.

orgueil [ɔrgœj] *nm* pride, arrogance. **orgueilleux** *adj* proud, arrogant.

orient [ɔrjɑ̃] *nm* east. **oriental** *adj* eastern, oriental.

orienter [ɔrjɑ̃te] *v* orientate; direct; (*disposer*) position, adjust. **orienter vers** turn towards. **s'orienter** find one's bearings. **orientation** *nf* orientation; direction; positioning; (*maison, jardin*) aspect. **orientation professionnelle** careers guidance.

origan [ɔrigɑ̃] *nm* oregano.

origine [ɔriʒin] *nf* origin. **à l'origine** originally. **originaire** *adj* original; native. **original** *nm, adj* original; (*péj*) eccentric. **originalité** *nf* originality; eccentricity. **originel** *adj* original.

orme [ɔrm] *nm* elm.

ornement [ɔrnəmɑ̃] *nm* ornament. **orne-**

mental *adj* ornamental. **ornementation** *nf* ornamentation.

orner [ɔrne] *v* decorate; embellish. **orné** *adj* ornate.

ornière [ɔrnjɛr] *nf* rut.

ornithologie [ɔrnitɔlɔʒi] *nf* ornithology. **ornithologique** *adj* ornithological. **ornithologiste** *n(m + f)* ornithologist.

orphelin [ɔrfəlɛ̃], -e *n, adj* orphan. **orphelinat** *nm* orphanage.

orteil [ɔrtɛj] *nm* toe.

orthodoxe [ɔrtɔdɔks] *adj* orthodox.

orthographe [ɔrtɔgraf] *nf* spelling. **orthographier** *v* spell.

orthopédique [ɔrtɔpedik] *adj* orthopaedic.

orthophonie [ɔrtɔfɔni] *nf* (*méd*) speech therapy. **orthophoniste** *n(m + f)* speech therapist.

ortie [ɔrti] *nf* nettle.

os [ɔs] *nm* bone. **os à moelle** marrowbone. **trempé jusqu'aux os** soaked to the skin.

osciller [ɔsile] *v* oscillate; (*se balancer*) rock, swing; (*hésiter*) waver; (*prix, etc.*) fluctuate. **oscillation** *nf* oscillation; fluctuation.

oser [oze] *v* dare. **osé** *adj* bold, daring.

osier [ozje] *nm* wicker. **en osier** wickerwork.

ossature [ɔsatyr] *nf* (*corps*) frame; framework; (*visage*) bone structure.

osseux [ɔsø] *adj* bony.

ostentation [ɔstɑ̃tasjɔ̃] *nf* ostentation.

ostraciser [ɔstrasize] *v* ostracize. **ostracisme** *nm* ostracism.

otage [ɔtaʒ] *nm* hostage.

otarie [ɔtari] *nf* sea-lion.

ôter [ote] *v* take away *or* off, remove.

ou [u] *conj* or. **ou bien** or else. **ou ... ou ...** either ... or ... .

où [u] *adv* where; (*temps*) when.

ouate [wat] *nf* cotton wool; (*rembourrage*) wadding. **ouater** *v* quilt.

oublier [ublije] *v* forget. **oubli** *nm* oblivion; lapse of memory; omission, oversight.

ouest [wɛst] *nm* west. *adj invar* west; (*région*) western; (*direction*) westward.

oui [wi] *adv, nm invar* yes.

*ouïr [wir] *v* hear. **ouï-dire** *nm invar* hearsay. **ouïe** *nf* hearing.

ouragan [uragɑ̃] *nm* hurricane.

ourdir [urdir] *v* (*complot*) hatch.

ourler [urle] *v* hem. **ourlet** *nm* hem.

ours [urs] *nm* bear. **ours blanc** polar bear.

outil [uti] *nm* tool, implement. **outillage** *nm* set of tools; equipment. **outiller** *v* provide with tools; equip.

outrager [utraʒe] *v* outrage; insult. **outrage** *nm* insult. **outrage à la pudeur** indecent behaviour. **outrage à magistrat** contempt of court.

outrance [utrɑ̃s] *nf* excess.

outre [utrə] *prep* as well as. **en outre** moreover, besides. **outre-mer** *adv* overseas.

outrer [utre] *v* outrage; exaggerate. **outré** *adj* excessive, overdone; outraged.

ouvert [uvɛr] *adj* open. **ouvertement** *adv* openly, overtly. **ouverture** *nf* opening; (*musique, avance*) overture.

ouvrable [uvrablə] *adj* **jour ouvrable** weekday.

ouvrage [uvraʒ] *nm* work, piece of work.

ouvreuse [uvrøz] *nf* usherette.

ouvrier [uvrije], **-ère** *adj* labour, industrial; working-class. *nm, nf* worker.

*ouvrir [uvrir] *v* open; (*gaz, robinet, etc.*) turn on. **ouvre-boîte** *nm invar* tin-opener. **ouvre-bouteille** *nm invar* bottle-opener.

ovaire [ɔvɛr] *nf* ovary.

ovale [ɔval] *nm, adj* oval.

ovation [ɔvasjɔ̃] *nf* ovation.

ovulation [ɔvylasjɔ̃] *nf* ovulation.

oxygène [ɔksiʒɛn] *nm* oxygen.

P

pacage [pakaʒ] *nm* pasture.

pacifier [pasifje] *v* pacify. **pacifique** *adj* peaceful, peaceable. **pacifisme** *nm* pacifism. **pacifiste** *n(m + f), adj* pacifist.

Pacifique [pasifik] *nm, adj* Pacific.

pacte [paktə] *nm* pact, treaty.

pagaie [pagɛ] *nf* paddle. **pagayer** *v* paddle.

pagaïe [pagaj] *nf* mess; (*cohue*) chaos.

page¹ [paʒ] *nf* (*livre*) page. **à la page** up-to-date.

page² [paʒ] *nm* (*garçon*) page.

pagode [pagɔd] *nf* pagoda.

paie [pɛ] *nf* pay. **paiement** *nm* payment.

païen [pajɛ̃], **-enne** *n, adj* pagan, heathen.

paillasson [pɑjasɔ̃] *nm* doormat.

paille [paj] *nf* straw; (*défaut*) flaw. **paille de fer** steel wool. **paillette** *nf* speck; (*savon*) flake; (*ornement*) sequin; flaw.

pain [pɛ̃] *nm* bread; (*miche*) loaf; (*savon*) bar. **pain bis/complet** brown/wholemeal bread. **pain de mie** sandwich loaf. **pain d'épice** gingerbread. **pain grillé** toast. **petit pain** roll.

pair¹ [pɛr] *nm* peer. **au pair** *adj* au pair. **pairie** *nf* peerage.

pair² [pɛr] *adj* even.

paire [pɛr] *nf* pair.

paisible [peziblə] *adj* peaceful, quiet.

*paître [pɛtrə] *v* graze.

paix [pɛ] *nf* peace.

palace [palas] *nm* luxury hotel.

palais¹ [palɛ] *nm* palace. **palais de justice** law courts *pl*.

palais² [palɛ] *nm* (*anat*) palate.

pâle [pal] *adj* pale; (*faible*) faint, weak. **paleur** *nf* paleness.

palefrenier [palfrənje] *nm* groom.

palette [palɛt] *nf* palette; (*aube*) paddle.

palier [palje] *nm* landing; (*étape*) stage.

pâlir [palir] *v* turn pale; (*couleur, etc.*) fade; (*lumière*) grow dim.

palissade [palisad] *nf* fence.

palmarès [palmarɛs] *nm* prize list.

palme [palmə] *nf* palm leaf; (*nageur*) flipper. **palmé** *adj* (*patte*) webbed. **palmier** *nm* palm tree. **palmipède** *adj* web-footed.

palombe [palɔ̃b] *nf* wood-pigeon.

palourde [palurd] *nf* clam.

palper [palpe] *v* feel, finger.

palpiter [palpite] *v* (*cœur*) beat; (*violemment*) pound, throb; (*frémir*) quiver. **palpitant** *adj* thrilling. **palpitation** *nf* palpitation.

paludisme [palydismə] *nm* malaria.

pâmer [pame] *v* **se pâmer de** be overcome with.

pamphlet [pɑ̃flɛ] *nm* lampoon.

pamplemousse [pɑ̃pləmus] *nm* grapefruit.

pan [pɑ̃] *nm* piece; (*côté*) side. **pan de chemise** shirt-tail.

panache [panaʃ] *nm* plume; gallantry.

panaché [panaʃe] *adj* multicoloured; mixed, motley. *nm* shandy. **panacher** *v* vary; (*mélanger*) blend.

panais [panɛ] *nm* parsnip.

pancarte [pɑ̃kart] *nf* sign; (*manifestation*) placard.

pancréas [pɑ̃kreas] *nm* pancreas. **pancréatique** *adj* pancreatic.

panda [pɑ̃da] *nm* panda.

paner [pane] *v* coat with breadcrumbs.

panier [panje] *nm* basket. **panier à salade** salad shaker; (*fam*) police van, Black Maria. **panier-repas** *nm* packed lunch.

panique [panik] *nf* panic.

panne [pan] *nf* breakdown, failure. **être en panne** break down. **être en panne de** run out of.

panneau [pano] *nm* panel; (*écriteau*) sign. **panneau d'affichage** notice-board. **panneau de signalisation** road sign. **panneau-réclame** *nm* hoarding.

panoplie [panɔpli] *nf* outfit.

panorama [panɔrama] *nm* panorama. **panoramique** *adj* panoramic.

panse [pɑ̃s] *nf* paunch.

panser [pɑ̃se] *v* (*plaie*) dress; bandage; (*cheval*) groom. **pansement** *nm* dressing; bandage; (*sparadrap*) plaster.

pantalon [pɑ̃talɔ̃] *nm* trousers *pl*; pair of trousers.

pantelant [pɑ̃tlɑ̃] *adj* panting; (*cœur*) throbbing.

panthère [pɑ̃tɛr] *nf* panther.

pantomime [pɑ̃tɔmim] *nf* mime.

pantoufle [pɑ̃tuflə] *nf* slipper.

paon [pɑ̃] *nm* peacock.

papa [papa] *nm* (*fam*) dad, daddy.

pape [pap] *nm* pope. **papal** *adj* papal. **papauté** *nf* papacy.

papeterie [papetri] *nf* stationery; (*magasin*) stationer's; (*fabrique*) paper mill. **papetier, -ère** *nm*, *nf* stationer.

papier [papje] *nm* paper.

papier à lettres *nm* notepaper.

papier à musique *nm* manuscript paper.

papier buvard *nm* blotting paper.

papier calque *nm* tracing paper.

papier d'aluminium *nm* kitchen foil.

papier de soie *nm* tissue paper.

papier de verre *nm* sandpaper.

papier hygiénique *nm* toilet paper.

papier millimétré *nm* graph paper.

papier peint *nm* wallpaper.

papillon [papijɔ̃] *nm* butterfly; (*police*) parking ticket. **papillon de nuit** moth.

paprika [paprika] *nm* paprika.

paquebot [pakbo] *nm* liner.

pâquerette [pakrɛt] *nf* daisy.

Pâques [pak] *nm* Easter.

paquet [pakɛ] *nm* packet, pack; (*colis*) parcel; (*tas*) pile, mass. **mettre en paquet** parcel up.

par [par] *prep* by; through; (*distribution*) per. **par-ci par-là** here and there; (*temps*) now and then. **par-dessous** *prep, adv* under. **par-dessus** *prep, adv* over. **par ici/là** this/that way.

parabole [parabɔl] *nf* (*rel*) parable; (*math*) parabola.

parachute [paraʃyt] *nm* parachute. **parachuter** *v* parachute. **parachutiste** *n(m+f)* parachutist; (*mil*) paratrooper.

parade [parad] *nf* parade; (*ostentation*) show. **faire parade de** show off, brag about.

paradis [paradi] *nm* paradise, heaven.

paradoxe [paradɔks] *nm* paradox. **paradoxal** *adj* paradoxical.

paraffine [parafin] *nf* paraffin (wax).

parages [paraʒ] *nm pl* vicinity *sing*. **dans les parages** round about, in the area.

paragraphe [paragraf] *nm* paragraph.

*paraître [parɛtrə] *v* appear; (*sembler*) seem; be visible, show; be published.

parallèle [paralɛl] *nm, adj* parallel. *nf* parallel line. **parallélogramme** *nm* parallelogram.

paralyser [paralize] *v* paralyse. **paralysie** *nf* paralysis. **paralytique** *adj* paralytic.

paramilitaire [paramilitɛr] *adj* paramilitary.

paranoïa [paranɔja] *nf* paranoia. **paranoïde** *adj* paranoid.

parapet [parapɛ] *nm* parapet.

paraphraser [parafraze] *v* paraphrase. **paraphrase** *nf* paraphrase.

paraplégique [parapleʒik] *n(m+f), adj* paraplegic.

parapluie [paraplɥi] *nm* umbrella.

parasite [parazit] *nm* parasite. **parasites** *nm pl* (*radio*) interference *sing*. *adj* parasitic.

paratonnerre [paratɔnɛr] *nm* lightning conductor.

parc [park] *nm* park; (*château*) grounds *pl*; (*animal*) pen; (*bébé*) play-pen.

parcelle [parsɛl] *nf* fragment, bit. **parcelle de terre** plot of land.

parce que [parskə] *conj* because.

parchemin [parʃəmɛ̃] *nm* parchment. **parcheminé** *adj* wrinkled.

parcomètre [parkɔmɛtrə] *nm* parking meter.

*parcourir [parkurir] *v* travel through, cover; (*livre*) glance through.

parcours [parkur] *nm* distance; (*trajet*) journey; course; (*itinéraire*) route.

pardessus [pardəsy] *nm* overcoat.

pardon [pardɔ̃] *nm* forgiveness, pardon. **demander pardon** apologize. *interj* (*comment*) pardon; (*désolé*) sorry, excuse me. **pardonner** *v* forgive, pardon; excuse.

pareil, -eille [parɛj] *adj* the same, alike; (*tel*) such. *nm, nf* equal, peer.

parement [parmɑ̃] *nm* facing.

parent [parɑ̃], **-e** *nm, nf* relation. **parents** *nm pl* (*père, mère*) parents *pl*. **parenté** *nf* relationship.

parenthèse [parɑ̃tɛz] *nf* parenthesis; digression; (*signe*) bracket. **entre parenthèses** in brackets; incidentally.

parer¹ [pare] *v* (*orner*) adorn; (*robe*) trim; (*préparer*) dress.

parer² [pare] *v* ward off. **pare-balles** *adj invar* bulletproof. **pare-brise** *nm invar* windshield. **pare-chocs** *nm invar* bumper. **pare-étincelles** *nm invar* fireguard. **parer à** deal with; prepare for.

paresseux [paresø] *adj* lazy. **paresse** *nf* laziness.

parfait [parfɛ] *adj* perfect; complete; absolute.

parfois [parfwa] *adv* sometimes; occasionally.

parfum [parfœ̃] *nm* perfume, scent; (*glace*) flavour. **parfumer** *v* perfume; flavour.

pari [pari] *nm* bet. **parier** *v* bet.

Paris [pari] *n* Paris.

parité [parite] *nf* parity.

parjure [parʒyr] *adj* false. *nm* perjury, false witness. *n(m+f)* perjurer. **se parjurer** *v* perjure oneself, bear false witness.

parking [parkiŋ] *nm* car park.

parlement [parləmɑ̃] *nm* parliament. **parlementaire** *adj* parliamentary.

parler [parle] *v* talk, speak. **sans parler de** not to mention. **tu parles!** (*fam*) you're telling me! *nm* speech.

parmi [parmi] *prep* among.

parodie [parɔdi] *nf* parody. **parodier** *v* parodier.

paroi [parwa] *nf* wall; (*cloison*) partition; rock face; (*récipient*) inside surface.

paroisse [parwas] *nf* parish. **paroissial** *adj* parish. **salle paroissiale** *nf* church hall. **paroissien, -enne** *nm, nf* parishioner.

parole [parɔl] *nf* word; (*faculté*) speech; remark. **parolier, -ère** *nm, nf* lyricist.

paroxysme [parɔksismə] *nm* height, climax.

parquer [parke] *v* (*auto*) park; (*enfermer*) pen in; (*entasser*) pack in.

parquet [parkɛ] *nm* floor.

parrain [parɛ̃] *nm* godfather.

parsemer [parsəme] *v* scatter, sprinkle.

part [par] *nf* part; portion, share. **à part** (*de côté*) aside; separately; except for, apart from. **d'autre part** moreover. **de la part de** on behalf of. **faire part de** announce.

partager [partaʒe] *v* share; divide. **partage** *nm* share, portion; (*distribution*) sharing out; division.

partance [partɑ̃s] *nf* **en partance** outbound. **en partance pour** (bound) for.

partenaire [partənɛr] *n*(*m*+*f*) partner.

parterre [partɛr] *nm* border, flower-bed; (*théâtre*) stalls *pl*.

parti [parti] *nm* party, side; decision; (*mariage*) match. **parti pris** prejudice, bias. **prendre le parti de** stand up for. **prendre parti pour** side with. **tirer parti de** take advantage of, put to good use.

partial [parsjal] *adj* partial, biased. **partialité** *nf* partiality, bias.

participe [partisip] *nm* participle.

participer [partisipe] *v* **participer à** participate in, take part in; (*frais*) contribute to; (*profits, etc.*) share in. **participant, -e** *nm, nf* participant; (*concours*) entrant.

participation *nf* participation; (*comm*) interest.

particularité [partikylarite] *nf* particularity, characteristic.

particule [partikyl] *nf* particle.

particulier [partikylje] *adj* particular; special, exceptional; (*étrange*) peculiar; private. *nm* person, individual.

partie [parti] *nf* part; (*sport, etc.*) game; (*droit, divertissement*) party. **faire partie de** belong to.

partiel [parsjɛl] *adj* partial.

***partir** [partir] *v* leave, go; (*fusil*) go off; (*commencer*) start. **à partir de** from.

partisan [partizɑ̃], **-e** *nm, nf* supporter, advocate. **être partisan de** be in favour of.

partition [partisjɔ̃] *nf* (*musique*) score.

partout [partu] *adv* everywhere. **partout où** wherever.

parure [paryr] *nf* finery; (*bijoux*) jewels *pl*; (*ensemble*) set; (*ornement*) trimming.

***parvenir** [parvənir] *v* **parvenir à** reach, get to; (*réussir*) manage to, succeed in.

parvenu, -e *nm, nf* (*péj*) upstart.

pas¹ [pɑ] *nm* step; (*vitesse*) pace; (*trace*) footprint; (*géog*) pass. **à pas de loup** stealthily. **pas de la porte** doorstep.

pas² [pɑ] *adv* not. **ne ... pas** not. **pas du tout** not at all. **pas mal de** (*fam*) quite a lot of.

passage [pasaʒ] *nm* passage; change, transition; (*traversée*) crossing. **passage à niveau** level crossing. **passage clouté** pedestrian crossing. **passage interdit** no thoroughfare. **passage souterrain** subway.

passager [pasaʒe], **-ère** *adj* passing, brief; (*oiseau*) migratory; (*rue*) busy. *nm, nf* passenger. **passager clandestin** stowaway.

passant [pasɑ̃], **-e** *nm, nf* passer-by.

passe [pɑs] *nf* pass. **en passe de** on the way to.

passé [pase] *adj* past; (*dernier*) last. *nm* past. *prep* after.

passe-partout *nm invar* skeleton key.

passeport [paspɔr] *nm* passport.

passer [pase] *v* pass; go past; (*aller*) go; (*franchir*) get through *or* over; (*examen*) sit, take; (*temps*) spend; (*film*) show; (*cuisine*) strain; (*traverser*) cross. **passer par** go through. **passer prendre** pick up, call for. **passer voir** call on. **se passer** happen, take place; (*finir*) be over. **se passer de** do without.

passerelle [pasrɛl] *nf* (*pont*) foot-bridge; (*naut*) gangway.

passe-temps *nm invar* pastime.

passif [pasif] *nm, adj* passive. **passivité** *nf* passiveness.

passion [pasjɔ̃] *nf* passion.

passionné [pasjone], **-e** *adj* passionate. *nm, nf* fanatic.

passionner [pasjone] *v* fascinate. **se passionner pour** be mad keen on.

passoire [paswar] *nf* sieve; (*plus grande*) colander.

pastel [pastɛl] *nm, adj invar* pastel.

pastèque [pastɛk] *nf* water-melon.

pasteuriser [pastœrize] *v* pasteurize. **pasteurisation** *nf* pasteurization.

pastille [pastij] *nf* pastille.

pastis [pastis] *nm* (*boisson*) pastis; (*argot*) jam, fix.

pastoral [pastɔral] *adj* pastoral.

pat [pat] *nm* stalemate.

pataud [pato] *adj* clumsy.

patauger [patoʒe] *v* wade, splash; (*se perdre*) flounder.

pâte [pɑt] *nf* paste; cream; (*tarte*) pastry; (*à frire*) batter; (*gâteau*) mixture; (*pain*) dough. **pâte à modeler** plasticine ®. **pâte brisée** shortcrust pastry. **pâte dentifrice** toothpaste. **pâte feuilletée** puff pastry. **pâtes** *nf pl* pasta *sing*.

pâté [pɑte] *nm* (*cuisine*) pâté; (*encre*) blot; (*maisons*) block; (*sable*) sand-castle. **pâté en croûte** pie.

patelin [patlɛ̃] *nm* (*fam*) village.

patelle [patɛl] *nf* limpet.

patent [patɑ̃] *adj* patent, obvious.

patenté [patɑ̃te] *adj* licensed.

patère [patɛr] *nf* peg.

paternel [patɛrnɛl] *adj* paternal; (*bienveillant*) fatherly. **paternité** *nf* paternity.

pâteux [pɑtø] *adj* pasty; (*langue*) furred; (*voix*) husky.

pathétique [patetik] *adj* pathetic. *nm* pathos.

pathologie [patɔlɔʒi] *nf* pathology. **pathologique** *adj* pathological. **pathologiste** *n(m + f)* pathologist.

patient [pasjɑ̃], **-e** *n, adj* patient. **patience** *nf* patience. **patienter** *v* wait.

patin [patɛ̃] *nm* skate; (*luge*) runner. **patin à glace** ice-skate. **patin à roulettes** rollerskate. **patinage** *nm* skating. **patiner** *v* skate; (*auto*) spin. **patineur, -euse** *nm, nf* skater. **patinoire** *nf* ice rink.

patio [patjo] *nm* patio.

pâtir [pɑtir] *v* suffer.

pâtisserie [pɑtisri] *nf* (*magasin*) cake shop; (*gâteau*) pastry, cake; (*métier*) confectionery. **pâtissier, -ère** *nm, nf* confectioner.

patois [patwa] *nm* patois, dialect.

patrie [patri] *nf* homeland.

patrimoine [patrimwan] *nm* inheritance, heritage.

patriote [patrijɔt] *n(m + f)* patriot. *adj* patriotic. **patriotique** *adj* patriotic. **patriotisme** *nm* patriotism.

patron, -onne [patrɔ̃, -ɔn] *nm, nf* proprietor; employer; (*fam*) boss; (*protecteur*) patron; (*naut*) skipper. *nm* pattern. **patronage** *nm* patronage. **patronat** *nm* management. **patronner** *v* support, sponsor.

patrouille [patruj] *nf* patrol. **patrouiller** *v* patrol.

patte [pat] *nf* (*jambe*) leg; (*pied*) paw, foot; (*languette*) flap, tongue. **patte de derrière** hind leg. **patte de devant** foreleg. **patte de mouche** scrawl.

pâture [pɑtyr] *nf* pasture; (*nourriture*) food. **pâturage** *nm* pasture.

paume [pom] *nf* palm.

paupière [popjɛr] *nf* eyelid.

pause [poz] *nf* break, pause. **pause-café** *nf* coffee break.

pauvre [povrə] *adj* poor; (*piètre*) weak. *n(m + f)* poor person. **pauvreté** *nf* poverty; poorness; weakness.

se pavaner [pavane] *v* strut about.

paver [pave] *v* pave; (*chaussée*) cobble. **pavé** *nm* paving stone; (*rond*) cobblestone.

pavillon [pavijɔ̃] *nm* pavilion; lodge; (*villa*) house; (*drapeau*) flag.

pavot [pavo] *nm* poppy.

payer [peje] *v* pay (for). **se payer** (*fam*) treat oneself to. **payable** *adj* payable.

pays [pei] *nm* country, land; region. **du pays** local. **les Pays-Bas** the Netherlands *pl*. **pays de Galles** Wales. **paysage** *nm* landscape; scenery. **paysan, -anne** *nm, nf* peasant.

péage [peaʒ] *nm* toll.

peau [po] *nf* skin; (*cuir*) hide; (*fruit*) peel. **peau de chamois** chamois leather. **peau de mouton** sheepskin. **Peau-Rouge** *n(m + f)* Red Indian.

pêche[1] [pɛʃ] *nf* (*fruit*) peach. **pêcher** *nm* peach tree.

pêche[2] [pɛʃ] *nf* fishing. **aller à la pêche** go fishing.

pécher [peʃe] *v* sin. **péché** *nm* sin. **pécheur, -eresse** *nm, nf* sinner.

pêcher [peʃe] *v* fish (for); (*attraper*) catch. **pêcheur** *nm* fisherman.

pédagogique [pedagɔʒik] *adj* educational.

pédaler [pedale] *v* pedal. **pédale** *nf* pedal.

pédant [pedɑ̃] *adj* pedantic.

pédéraste [pederast] *nm* homosexual. **pédé** *nm* (*argot*) queer. **pédérastie** *nf* homosexuality.

pédiatre [pedjatrə] *n(m + f)* paediatrician. **pédiatrie** *nf* paediatrics.

pédicure [pedikyr] *n(m + f)* chiropodist.

pedigree [pedigri] *nm* pedigree.

peigner [peɲe] *v* comb. **se peigner** comb one's hair. **mal peigné** dishevelled. **peigne** *nm* comb. **peignoir** *nm* dressing-gown.

*peindre [pɛ̃drə] *v* paint; (*décrire*) depict, portray.

peine [pɛn] *nf* effort, trouble; (*tristesse*) sorrow; difficulty; punishment. **à peine** scarcely, hardly.

peiner [pene] *v* (*s'efforcer*) labour, struggle; (*affliger*) grieve, distress.

peintre [pɛtrə] *n*(*m*+*f*) painter. **peinture** *nf* painting; (*surface*) paintwork; (*matière*) paint.

péjoratif [peʒɔratif] *adj* derogatory.

Pékin [pekɛ̃] *n* Peking.

pelage [pəlaʒ] *nm* coat, fur.

pêle-mêle [pɛlmɛl] *adv* pell-mell, any old how. *nm invar* jumble.

peler [pəle] *v* peel.

pèlerin [pɛlrɛ̃] *nm* pilgrim. **pèlerinage** *nm* pilgrimage. **pèlerine** *nf* cape.

pélican [pelikɑ̃] *nm* pelican.

pelle [pɛl] *nf* shovel; (*d'enfant*) spade. **pelle à ordures** dustpan. **pelleter** *v* shovel (up).

pelletier [pɛltje], **-ère** *nm, nf* furrier.

pellicule [pelikyl] *nf* film. **pellicules** *nf pl* dandruff *sing.*

pelote [pəlɔt] *nf* ball; (*à épingles*) pincushion.

se peloter [pəlɔte] *v* (*fam*) pet, neck.

peloton [pəlɔtɔ̃] *nm* small ball; group, squad.

pelotonner [pəlɔtɔne] *v* (*laine*) wind into a ball. **se pelotonner** curl up, snuggle up.

pelouse [pəluz] *nf* lawn.

peluche [pəlyʃ] *nf* plush, fur fabric; (*poil, flocon*) bit of fluff. **en peluche** fluffy. **pelucheux** *adj* fluffy.

pelure [pəlyr] *nf* peel, peeling.

pénal [penal] *adj* penal. **pénaliser** *v* penalize. **pénalité** *nf* penalty.

penaud [pəno] *adj* sheepish, contrite.

pencher [pɑ̃ʃe] *v* tilt, lean (over), slant. **se pencher** lean (over); (*se baisser*) bend (down). **penchant** *nm* tendency; (*goût*) liking. **penché** *adj* sloping.

pendant[1] [pɑ̃dɑ̃] *adj* hanging, drooping; (*affaire*) pending. *nm* counterpart, match.

pendant[2] [pɑ̃dɑ̃] *prep* during, for. **pendant que** *conj* while.

pendentif [pɑ̃dɑ̃tif] *nm* pendant.

pendiller [pɑ̃dije] *v* flap about.

pendre [pɑ̃drə] *v* hang; (*s'affaisser*) sag; (*bras, jambes*) dangle. **pendaison** *nf* hanging.

pendule [pɑ̃dyl] *nf* clock. *nm* pendulum.

pêne [pɛn] *nm* bolt.

pénétrer [penetre] *v* penetrate. **pénétrer dans** enter. **pénétrable** *adj* penetrable.

pénétrant *adj* piercing, penetrating;

(*pluie*) drenching; (*esprit, personne*) shrewd. **pénétration** *nf* penetration.

pénible [peniblə] *adj* hard, difficult; (*fatigant*) tiresome; (*douloureux*) painful.

péniche [peniʃ] *nf* barge.

pénicilline [penisilin] *nf* penicillin.

péninsule [penɛ̃syl] *nf* peninsula. **péninsulaire** *adj* peninsular.

pénis [penis] *nm* penis.

pénitent [penitɑ̃], **-e** *n, adj* penitent. **pénitence** *nf* penitence; (*peine*) penance; punishment.

penser [pɑ̃se] *v* think. **penser à** think of or about; (*réfléchir*) think over. **penser de** think of. **penser faire** be thinking of doing, expect to do. **pensée** *nf* thought; (*bot*) pansy. **pensif** *adj* pensive.

pension [pɑ̃sjɔ̃] *nf* (*allocation*) pension; (*hôtel*) guest house; (*école*) boarding school; (*hébergement*) board and lodging. **pension complète** full board. **pension de famille** boarding house. **pensionnaire** *n*(*m*+*f*) (*école*) boarder; (*maison*) lodger; (*hôtel*) resident. **pensionnat** *nm* boarding school.

pentagone [pɛ̃tagɔn] *nm* pentagon. **pentagonal** *adj* pentagonal.

pente [pɑ̃t] *nf* slope. **en pente** sloping, on a slope.

Pentecôte [pɑ̃tkot] *nf* Whitsun. **lundi de Pentecôte** *nm* Whit Monday.

pénurie [penyri] *nf* shortage.

pépé [pepe] *nm* (*fam*) grandad, grandpa.

pépier [pepje] *v* chirp, tweet. **pépiement** *nm* chirping.

pépin [pepɛ̃] *nm* pip; (*fam*) snag, hitch. **pépinière** *nf* nursery.

pépite [pepit] *nf* nugget.

percepteur, -trice [pɛrsɛptœr, -tris] *adj* perceptive. *nm* tax collector.

perception [pɛrsɛpsjɔ̃] *nf* perception; (*impôt, etc*) collection; (*bureau*) tax office. **perceptible** *adj* perceptible; payable. **perceptif** *adj* perceptive.

percer [pɛrse] *v* pierce; (*avec perceuse*) drill, bore; penetrate; (*abcès*) burst; (*mil, soleil*) break through. **perce-neige** *nm invar* snowdrop. **perce-oreille** *nm* earwig. **percer des dents** cut one's teeth, be teething. **percée** *nf* opening, gap. **perceuse** *nf* drill.

***percevoir** [pɛrsəvwar] *v* perceive; (*impôt*) collect.

perche[1] [pɛrʃ] *nf* (*poisson*) perch.

perche² [pɛrʃ] *nf* pole.
percher [pɛrʃe] *v* perch. **perchoir** *nm* perch.
perclus [pɛrkly] *adj* paralysed.
percussion [pɛrkysjɔ̃] *nf* percussion.
perdre [pɛrdrə] *v* lose; (*gaspiller*) waste; (*manquer*) miss; (*réservoir, etc.*) leak; ruin. **se perdre** get lost; disappear; go to waste. **perdant, -e** *nm, nf* loser. **perdu** *adj* lost, wasted; missed; ruined; isolated.
perdrix [pɛrdri] *nf* partridge.
père [pɛr] *nm* father. **le père Noël** Father Christmas.
perfection [pɛrfɛksjɔ̃] *nf* perfection. **perfectionner** *v* improve, perfect. **perfectionniste** *n(m+f)* perfectionist.
perfide [pɛrfid] *adj* treacherous, false. **perfidie** *nf* perfidy.
perforer [pɛrfɔre] *v* perforate; (*poinçonner*) punch. **perforation** *nf* perforation.
péril [peril] *nm* peril. **périlleux** *adj* perilous.
périmé [perime] *adj* out-of-date.
périmètre [perimɛtrə] *nm* perimeter; (*zone*) area.
période [perjɔd] *nf* period.
périodique [perjɔdik] *adj* periodic, periodical; (*math, méd*) recurring. *nm* periodical.
péripétie [peripesi] *nf* event, episode.
périphérique [periferik] *adj* peripheral. *nm* ring road. **périphérie** *nf* periphery; (*ville*) outskirts *pl*.
périr [perir] *v* perish, die. **périssable** *adj* perishable.
périscope [periskɔp] *nm* periscope.
périssoire [periswar] *nf* canoe.
perle [pɛrl] *nf* pearl; (*grain*) bead; (*goutte*) drop; (*erreur*) howler.
permanence [pɛrmanɑ̃s] *nf* permanence; (*bureau*) office. **en permanence** permanently; continuously. **être de permanence** be on duty. **permanent** *adj* permanent; continuous. **permanente** *nf* perm.
perméable [pɛrmeablə] *adj* permeable, pervious.
*permettre [pɛrmɛtrə] *v* allow, permit; (*rendre possible*) enable.
permis [pɛrmi] *adj* permitted. *nm* permit, licence. **permis de conduire** driving licence. **permis de construire** planning permission. **permis de séjour/travail** residence/work permit.

permission [pɛrmisjɔ̃] *nf* permission; (*mil*) leave.
permutation [pɛrmytasjɔ̃] *nf* permutation.
pernicieux [pɛrnisjø] *adj* pernicious; (*nuisible*) harmful.
pérorer [perɔre] *v* hold forth.
peroxyde [perɔksid] *nm* peroxide.
perpendiculaire [pɛrpɑ̃dikylɛr] *nf, adj* perpendicular.
perpétrer [pɛrpetre] *v* perpetrate. **perpétration** *nf* perpetration.
perpétuer [pɛrpetɥe] *v* perpetuate, carry on. **se perpétuer** survive. **perpétuel** *adj* perpetual; constant; permanent. **perpétuité** *nf* perpetuity. **à perpétuité** for ever; (*jur*) for life.
perplexe [pɛrplɛks] *adj* perplexed, puzzled. **perplexité** *nf* perplexity, confusion.
perquisition [pɛrkizisjɔ̃] *nf* search. **perquisitionner** *v* search.
perron [pɛrɔ̃] *nm* steps *pl*.
perroquet [pɛrɔke] *nm* parrot.
perruche [peryʃ] *nf* budgerigar.
perruque [peryk] *nf* wig.
persécuter [pɛrsekyte] *v* persecute; harass. **persécution** *nf* persecution.
persévérer [pɛrsevere] *v* persevere. **persévérance** *nf* perseverance. **persévérant** *adj* persevering.
persienne [pɛrsjɛn] *nf* shutter.
persifler [pɛrsifle] *v* mock. **persiflage** *nm* mockery.
persil [pɛrsi] *nm* parsley.
persister [pɛrsiste] *v* persist. **persister à** persist in. **persistance** *nf* persistence. **persistant** *adj* persistent. **à feuilles persistantes** (*arbre, plante*) evergreen.
personne [pɛrsɔn] *nf* person. *pron* anyone. **ne ... personne** nobody. **personnage** *nm* character; individual; celebrity, important person. **personnalité** *nf* personality.
personnel [pɛrsɔnɛl] *adj* personal. *nm* staff, personnel.
personnifier [pɛrsɔnifje] *v* personify. **personnification** *nf* personification, embodiment.
perspective [pɛrspɛktiv] *nf* perspective; view, angle; (*éventualité*) prospect.
perspicace [pɛrspikas] *adj* shrewd. **perspicacité** *nf* shrewdness, insight.
persuader [pɛrsɥade] *v* persuade; convince. **persuasif** *adj* persuasive. **persuasion** *nf* persuasion; (*croyance*) belief.

perte [pɛrt] *nf* loss; ruin; (*gaspillage*) waste. **à perte de vue** as far as the eye can see.

pertinent [pɛrtinɑ̃] *adj* pertinent, relevant; (*juste*) apt. **pertinence** *nf* pertinence, relevance; aptness.

perturbateur, -trice [pɛrtyrbatœr, -tris] *adj* disruptive. *nm, nf* troublemaker.

perturber [pɛrtyrbe] *v* disturb, disrupt; (*personne*) perturb. **perturbation** *nf* disturbance, disruption.

pervers [pɛrvɛr] *adj* perverse; depraved, perverted. **perversion** *nf* perversion. **perversité** *nf* perversity; depravity.

pervertir [pɛrvɛrtir] *v* pervert, corrupt. **perverti, -e** *nm, nf* pervert.

peser [pəze] *v.* weigh; (*appuyer*) press. **pesant** *adj* heavy. **pesanteur** *nf* heaviness; (*phys*) gravity; (*poids*) weight.

pessimiste [pesimist] *adj* pessimistic. *n(m+f)* pessimist. **pessimisme** *nm* pessimism.

peste [pɛst] *nf* plague; (*personne*) nuisance, pest.

pet [pɛ] *nm* (*vulgaire*) fart.

pétale [petal] *nm* petal.

pétarader [petarade] *v* backfire.

pétard [petar] *nm* banger, firecracker; (*mil*) explosive charge; (*fam: tapage*) row, din.

péter [pete] *v* (*vulgaire*) fart; (*fam: casser*) bust; (*fam: exploser*) burst, go off.

pétiller [petije] *v* sparkle; (*champagne*) bubble; (*feu*) crackle. **pétillant** *adj* sparkling; bubbly.

petit [pəti], **-e** *adj* small, little; (*mince*) slim, thin; (*jeune*) young; (*court*) short; (*faible*) faint, slight; (*mesquin*) petty. **petit ami** *nm* boyfriend. **petit déjeuner** *nm* breakfast. **petite amie** *nf* girlfriend. **petite-fille** *nf* granddaughter. **petit-enfant** *nm* grandchild. **petit-fils** *nm* grandson. **petit gâteau** *nm* biscuit. **petit-pois** *nm* pea. *adv* **petit à petit** little by little. *nm, nf* young child; small person; (*animal*) young. **petitesse** *nf* smallness; pettiness.

pétrin [petrɛ̃] *nm* mess, fix.

pétrir [petrir] *v* knead; mould.

pétrole [petrɔl] *nm* oil, petroleum. **pétrole lampant** paraffin. **pétrolifère** *adj* oil-bearing. **gisement pétrolifère** *nm* oilfield.

pétrolier [petrɔlje] *adj* oil. *nm* tanker.

pétulant [petylɑ̃] *adj* vivacious. **pétulance** *nf* vivacity.

peu [pø] *nm* little. *adv* little; (*quantité*) not much; (*nombre*) few; (*pas très*) not very. **à peu près** about; (*presque*) almost. **peu à peu** little by little.

peupler [pœple] *v* populate, fill. **peuple** *nm* people; nation; (*foule*) crowd.

peuplier [pøplije] *nm* poplar.

peur [pœr] *nf* fear; fright. **avoir peur** be frightened *or* afraid. **faire peur à** frighten, scare. **peureux** *adj* fearful, timorous.

peut-être [pøtɛtrə] *adv* perhaps, maybe.

phallus [falys] *nm* phallus. **phallique** *adj* phallic. **phallocrate** *nm* (*fam*) male chauvinist pig.

phare [far] *nm* lighthouse; (*balise*) beacon; (*auto*) headlight. **phare antibrouillard** fog lamp.

pharmacie [farmasi] *nf* pharmacy; (*magasin*) chemist's; (*armoire*) medicine chest. **pharmaceutique** *adj* pharmaceutical. **pharmacien, -enne** *nm, nf* chemist, pharmacist.

pharynx [farɛ̃ks] *nm* pharynx. **pharyngite** *nf* pharyngitis.

phase [faz] *nf* phase; stage.

phénix [feniks] *nm* phoenix.

phénomène [fenɔmɛn] *nm* phenomenon (*pl* -ena); (*personne*) freak. **phénoménal** *adj* phenomenal.

philanthropie [filɑ̃trɔpi] *nf* philanthropy. **philanthrope** *n(m+f)* philanthropist. **philanthropique** *adj* philanthropic.

philatélie [filateli] *nf* philately. **philatéliste** *n(m+f)* philatelist.

philosophe [filɔzɔf] *adj* philosophical. *n(m+f)* philosopher. **philosophie** *nf* philosophy. **philosophique** *adj* philosophical.

phobie [fɔbi] *nf* phobia.

phonétique [fɔnetik] *adj* phonetic. *nf* phonetics.

phonographe [fɔnɔgraf] *nm* gramophone.

phoque [fɔk] *nm* seal.

phosphate [fɔsfat] *nm* phosphate.

phosphore [fɔsfɔr] *nm* phosphorus. **phosphoreux** *adj* phosphorous.

phosphorescence [fɔsfɔresɑ̃s] *nf* phosphorescence. **phosphorescent** *adj* phosphorescent, luminous.

photo [fɔto] *nf* photo.

photocopier [fɔtɔkɔpje] *v* photocopy. **photocopie** *nf* photocopy. **photocopieur** *nm* photocopier.

photogénique [fɔtɔʒenik] *adj* photogenic.

photographie [fɔtɔgrafi] *nf* (*image*) photograph; (*art*) photography. **photographe** *n(m+f)* photographer. **photographier** *v*

photograph, take a picture of.
photographique *adj* photographic.
phrase [fraz] *nf* phrase; (*gramm*) sentence.
physiologie [fizjɔlɔʒi] *nf* physiology.
physiologique *adj* physiological. **physiologiste** *n(m + f)* physiologist.
physique¹ [fizik] *adj* physical. *nm* physique.
physique² [fizik] *nf* physics. **physicien, -enne** *nm, nf* physicist.
piaffer [pjafe] *v* stamp, paw the ground.
piailler [pjɑje] *v* (*fam*) squawk, screech.
piano [pjano] *nm* piano. **piano à queue** grand piano. **pianiste** *n(m + f)* pianist.
piauler [pjole] *v* whine; (*enfant*) whimper; (*oiseau*) cheep.
pic¹ [pik] *nm* (*oiseau*) woodpecker; (*instrument*) pick.
pic² [pik] *nm* (*cime*) peak. **à pic** sheer; (*arriver, tomber*) just at the right time.
piccolo [pikɔlo] *nm* piccolo.
picorer [pikɔre] *v* peck (at).
picoter [pikɔte] *v* (*yeux*) smart, sting; (*gorge*) tickle; (*peau*) prickle; (*picorer*) peck.
pie [pi] *nf* magpie.
pièce [pjɛs] *nf* piece; (*machine*) part; document; (*maison*) room; (*théâtre*) play; (*monnaie*) coin; (*couture*) patch. **à la pièce** separately. **pièce détachée** spare part.
pied [pje] foot; (*table*) leg; base; (*verre*) stem. **à pied** on foot. **au pied de la lettre** literally. **en pied** full-length. **être sur pied** be under way. **mettre les pieds dans le plat** put one's foot in it. **mettre sur pied** set up. **perdre pied** get out of one's depth. **pied bot** *adj* club-footed.
piédestal [pjedɛstal] *nm* pedestal.
piège [pjɛʒ] *nm* trap. **piéger** *v* trap; (*engin, etc.*) booby-trap. **lettre/voiture piégée** *nf* letter/car bomb.
pierre [pjɛr] *nf* stone. **pierre à briquet** flint. **pierre à chaux** limestone. **pierre d'achoppement** stumbling block. **pierre de gué** stepping stone. **pierre ponce** pumice stone. **pierre tombale** tombstone. **pierreux** *adj* stony.
piété [pjete] *nf* piety; devotion.
piétiner [pjetine] *v* (*fouler*) trample (on); (*trépigner*) stamp; make no progress.
piéton [pjetɔ̃] *nm* pedestrian.
piètre [pjɛtrə] *adj* paltry, very poor.
pieu [pjø] *nm* post; (*pointu*) stake.

pieuvre [pjœvrə] *nf* octopus.
pieux [pjø] *adj* pious, devout.
pigeon [piʒɔ̃] *nm* pigeon.
piger [piʒe] (*argot*) *v* cotton on, twig. **tu piges?** do you get it?
pigment [pigmɑ̃] *nm* pigment. **pigmentation** *nf* pigmentation.
pignon [piɲɔ̃] *nm* (*arch*) gable; (*tech*) pinion.
pile¹ [pil] *nf* (*tas*) pile; support; (*élec*) battery.
pile² [pil] *nf* (*pièce*) tails *pl*. **côté pile** reverse side. **pile ou face?** heads or tails? **tirer à pile ou face** toss up. *adv* (*fam*) dead, exactly.
piler [pile] *v* crush, pound.
pilier [pilje] *nm* pillar.
piller [pije] *v* pillage, plunder. **pillage** *nm* pillage, looting.
pilote [pilɔt] *nm* pilot; (*auto*) driver; guide. *adj* experimental. **piloter** *v* pilot; (*avion*) fly; drive; (*personne*) show round.
pilule [pilyl] *nf* pill.
piment [pimɑ̃] *nm* pimento; piquancy, spice. **piment doux** capsicum. **piment rouge** chilli. **pimenté** *adj* (*plat*) hot; (*récit*) spicy.
pimpant [pɛ̃pɑ̃] *adj* trim, smart.
pin [pɛ̃] *nm* pine.
pinacle [pinaklə] *nm* pinnacle.
pince [pɛ̃s] *nf* pliers *pl*; (*charbon, sucre*) tongs *pl*; (*levier*) crowbar; (*couture*) dart; (*crabe*) pincer, claw. **pince à épiler** eyebrow tweezers *pl*. **pince à linge** clothes peg. **pincé** *adj* stiff; (*sourire*) tight-lipped.
pincée *nf* pinch. **pincer** *v* pinch, nip; (*serrer*) grip; (*musique*) pluck; (*fam*) catch.
pinceau [pɛ̃so] *nm* paintbrush.
pingouin [pɛ̃gwɛ̃] *nm* penguin.
ping-pong [piŋpɔ̃g] *nm* table tennis.
pinson [pɛ̃sɔ̃] *nm* chaffinch.
piocher [pjɔʃe] *v* dig with a pick; (*fam*) swot; (*cartes, etc.*) pick up. **pioche** *nf* pick, pickaxe.
pion [pjɔ̃] *nm* (*jeu*) piece; (*échecs*) pawn; student supervising schoolchildren.
pionnier [pjɔnje] *nm* pioneer.
pipe [pip] *nf* pipe.
piquant [pikɑ̃] *adj* (*tige*) prickly; (*goût*) hot, pungent; (*vin*) tart; (*mordant*) biting; (*sauce, détail*) piquant. *nm* prickle; (*hérisson*) spine; piquancy.
pique¹ [pik] *nf* (*arme*) pike. *nm* (*cartes*) spade.

pique² [pik] *nf* cutting remark.
pique-nique [piknik] *nm* picnic. **pique-niquer** *v* picnic. **pique-niqueur, -euse** *nm, nf* picnicker.
piquer [pike] *v* prick; sting; *(insecte, serpent)* bite; *(aiguille, etc.)* jab, stick; excite, arouse; *(fam: voler)* pinch; *(moutarde, etc.)* be hot *or* pungent; *(avion, oiseau)* swoop down. **piquer une colère** fly into a rage. **piquer une crise** throw a fit. **se faire piquer** have an injection. **se piquer** get stung; give oneself an injection; take offence. **piqué** *adj (couture)* quilted; *(marqué)* dotted, pitted; *(fam)* barmy. **piqûre** *nf* prick; sting; bite; injection; *(couture)* stitch; *(trou)* hole.
piquet [pikɛ] *nm* post, stake; *(tente)* peg; *(de grève)* picket.
pirate [pirat] *nm, adj* pirate. **pirate de l'air** hijacker. **piraterie** nf piracy.
pire [pir] *adj* worse. **le** *or* **la pire** (the) worst.
pirouette [pirwɛt] *nf* pirouette. **pirouetter** *v* pirouette.
pis¹ [pi] *nm* udder.
pis² [pi] *adj, adv* worse. **de pis en pis** worse and worse. *nm* worst. **au pis aller** if the worst comes to the worst. **pis-aller** *nm invar* makeshift.
piscine [pisin] *nf* swimming pool; *(publique)* baths *pl*.
pissenlit [pisɑ̃li] *nm* dandelion.
pisser [pise] *(vulgaire)* *v* piss. **pisse** *nf* piss.
pistache [pistaʃ] *nf* pistachio.
piste [pist] *nf* track; *(traces)* trail; *(aéro)* runway; *(ski)* run; *(police)* lead. **piste cavalière** bridle-path. **piste sonore** soundtrack.
pistolet [pistɔlɛ] *nm* pistol, gun.
piston [pistɔ̃] *nm* piston; *(musique)* valve. **avoir du piston** *(fam)* have friends in the right places.
pitié [pitje] *nf* pity. **avoir pitié de** take pity on; *(compâtir)* feel sorry for. **piteux** *adj* pitiful, sorry; *(honteux)* shamefaced. **pitoyable** *adj* pitiful.
pitre [pitrə] *nm* clown.
pittoresque [pitɔrɛsk] *adj* picturesque.
pivot [pivo] *nm* pivot. **pivoter** *v* pivot, revolve, swivel round.
placage [plakaʒ] *nm (bois)* veneer; *(pierre)* facing.
placard [plakar] *nm (armoire)* cupboard;

(affiche) notice, placard. **placarder** *v* *(affiche)* stick up; *(mur)* placard.
place [plas] *nf* place; space; *(siège)* seat; *(prix)* fare; *(ville)* square; *(emploi)* job. **à la place de** instead of; *(personne)* on behalf of. **à ta** *or* **votre place** if I were you. **faire place à** give way to. **sur place** on the spot.
placenta [plasɛ̃ta] *nm* placenta.
placer [plase] *v* place, put; *(argent)* invest; *(vendre)* sell. **se placer** *(debout)* stand; *(assis)* sit; *(avoir lieu)* take place; find a job. **placement** *nm* investment. **placeur** *nm* usher.
placide [plasid] *adj* placid. **placidité** *nf* placidity.
plafond [plafɔ̃] *nm* ceiling.
plage [plaʒ] *nf* beach; *(ville)* seaside resort; *(disque)* track.
plagier [plaʒje] *v* plagiarize. **plagiaire** *n(m+f)* plagiarist. **plagiat** *nm* plagiarism.
plaider [plede] *v* plead.
plaie [plɛ] *nf* wound; *(fam)* nuisance.
***plaindre** [plɛ̃drə] *v* pity, feel sorry for. **se plaindre** moan, complain, grumble.
plaine [plɛn] *nf* plain.
plain-pied [plɛ̃pje] *adv* **de plain-pied avec** on the same level as.
plainte [plɛ̃t] *nf* complaint; *(gémissement)* moan. **plaintif** *adj* plaintive.
***plaire** [plɛr] *v* **plaire à** please; *(convenir à)* suit. **se plaire** be happy, enjoy oneself. **se plaire à** like, delight in. **s'il te** *or* **vous plaît** please.
plaisance [plɛzɑ̃s] *nf* **maison de plaisance** *nf* country house. **navigation de plaisance** *nf* boating; yachting.
plaisant [plɛzɑ̃] *adj* pleasant; amusing.
plaisanter [plɛzɑ̃te] *v* joke; *(taquiner)* tease. **plaisanterie** *nf* joke.
plaisir [plezir] *nm* pleasure. **faire plaisir à** please, make happy.
plan¹ [plɑ̃] *adj* flat, level, plane. *nm* plane, level; *(cinéma)* shot. **premier plan** foreground.
plan² [plɑ̃] *nm* plan; *(carte)* map.
planche [plɑ̃ʃ] *nf* board, plank; *(rayon)* shelf. **faire la planche** float on one's back. **planche à dessin/repasser** drawing/ironing board. **planche à pain** breadboard.
plancher [plɑ̃ʃe] *nm* floor.
plancton [plɑ̃ktɔ̃] *nm* plankton.
planer [plane] *v* glide, hover; *(monter)* soar. **planer sur** *(danger)* hang over;

(*regard*) look down over. **planeur** *nm* glider.

planète [planɛt] *nf* planet. **planétaire** *adj* planetary. **planétarium** *nm* planetarium.

plant [plɑ̃] *nm* seedling, young plant; (*arbres*) plantation; (*légumes, fleurs*) bed.

plantation [plɑ̃tɑsjɔ̃] *nf* plantation; (*action*) planting.

plante¹ [plɑ̃t] *nf* (*bot*) plant. **plante grimpante** creeper.

plante² [plɑ̃t] *nf* (*anat*) sole of the foot.

planter [plɑ̃te] *v* plant; (*enfoncer*) drive *or* stick in; (*mettre*) put, stick; (*installer*) put *or* set up. **planter là** (*fam*) dump, ditch.

planton [plɑ̃tɔ̃] *nm* orderly.

plantureux [plɑ̃tyrø] *adj* copious, lavish.

plaque [plak] *nf* plate, sheet; (*pierre, chocolat*) slab; (*tache*) patch, blotch; (*commémorative*) plaque; (*insigne*) badge. **plaque chauffante** hotplate. **plaque minéralogique** *or* **d'immatriculation** number plate.

plaquer [plake] *v* (*bois*) veneer; (*métal*) plate; (*fam*) ditch, chuck; (*aplatir*) plaster down, flatten; (*sport*) tackle.

plasma [plasma] *nm* plasma.

plastique [plastik] *nm, adj* plastic.

plat [pla] *adj* flat; (*fade*) dull; (*cheveux*) straight. **à plat** flat. **plate-bande** *nf* flowerbed. **plate-forme** *nf* platform. *nm* flat part; (*cuisine*) dish; (*partie d'un repas*) course.

plateau [plato] *nm* tray; (*géog*) plateau; (*théâtre*) stage. **plateau à** *or* **de fromages** cheeseboard.

platine [platin] *nm* platinum.

platonique [platɔnik] *adj* (*amour*) platonic; vain, futile.

plâtrer [platre] *v* plaster; (*méd*) set in plaster. **plâtre** *nm* plaster; (*méd, art*) plaster cast. **plâtrier** *nm* plasterer.

plausible [plozibl(ə)] *adj* plausible. **plausibilité** *nf* plausibility.

plectre [plɛktr(ə)] *nm* plectrum.

plein [plɛ̃] *adj* full; complete; solid; (*animal*) pregnant. **en plein …** at the height of …, in the middle of …. **en plein jour** in broad daylight. **plein air** *nm* open air. **pleine mer** *nf* open sea; (*marée*) high tide. *adv* full. *nm* **faire le plein** fill up.

pleurer [plœre] *v* cry; (*yeux*) water; lament, bemoan; (*mort*) mourn. **pleureur, -euse** *adj* tearful; (*enfant*) whining.

pleurnicher [plœrniʃe] *v* snivel, whine.

*pleuvoir [pløvwar] *v* rain.

pli [pli] *nm* fold; (*faux*) crease; (*couture*) pleat; (*genou*) bend; envelope; (*forme*) shape; habit.

plier [plije] *v* fold; (*courber*) bend; (*céder*) yield, give way. **se plier à** submit to. **pliant** *adj* collapsible, folding.

plinthe [plɛ̃t] *nf* skirting board.

plisser [plise] *v* (*jupe, etc.*) pleat; (*rider*) pucker, crease.

plomb [plɔ̃] *nm* lead; (*chasse*) shot; (*élec*) fuse. **à plomb** straight down. **de plomb** leaden; (*sommeil*) heavy. **plombage** *nm* filling. **plomber** *v* weight; (*dent*) fill. **plomberie** *nf* plumbing. **plombier** *nm* plumber.

plonger [plɔ̃ʒe] *v* plunge, dive. **plonge** *nf* washing-up. **plongé dans** *adj* immersed in, buried in. **plongée** *nf* diving. **plongée sous-marine** skin-diving. **plongeoir** *nm* diving board. **plongeon** *nm* dive. **plongeur, -euse** *nm, nf* diver; (*restaurant*) washer-up.

plouf [pluf] *nm, interj* splash.

ployer [plwaje] *v* bend; (*plancher*) sag; (*céder*) give way.

pluie [plɥi] *nf* rain; (*averse*) shower.

plume [plym] *nf* (*oiseau*) feather; (*écrire*) pen; (*bec*) nib. **plumage** *nm* plumage. **plumer** *v* pluck; (*argot*) fleece.

plupart [plypar] *nf* **la plupart** most, the majority. **pour la plupart** mostly.

pluriel [plyrjɛl] *nm, adj* plural.

plus [ply] *adv* more. **de** *or* **en plus** on top, extra, in addition, besides. **de plus en plus** more and more. **le** *or* **la plus** the most. **ne … plus** no more; (*temps*) no longer. **plus de** more than, over. **plus-que-parfait** *nm* pluperfect. *conj* plus.

plusieurs [plyzjœr] *adj* several.

plutôt [plyto] *adv* rather.

pluvieux [plyvjø] *adj* rainy, wet.

pneu [pnø] *nm* tyre. **pneu réchapé** remould.

pneumatique [pnømatik] *adj* pneumatic; (*canot, matelas*) inflatable.

pneumonie [pnømɔni] *nf* pneumonia.

pochard [pɔʃar], **-e** *nm, nf* (*argot*) drunk.

poche [pɔʃ] *nf* pocket; (*sac*) bag; (*zool*) pouch. **de poche** pocket; (*livre*) paperback. **pochette** *nf* pocket handkerchief; envelope, case.

pocher [pɔʃe] *v* poach. **pocher un œil à** give a black eye to. **pochade** *nf* quick sketch. **pochoir** *nm* stencil.

poêle[1] [pwɑl] *nf* frying pan.

poêle[2] [pwɑl] *nm* stove.

poème [pɔɛm] *nm* poem. **poésie** *nf* poetry. **poète** *nm* poet. **poétesse** *nf* poetess. **poétique** *adj* poetic.

poids [pwa] *nm* weight. **poids lourd** heavyweight; (*camion*) lorry. **prendre du poids** put on weight.

poignant [pwaɲɑ̃] *adj* poignant, harrowing.

poignard [pwaɲar] *nm* dagger. **poignarder** *v* stab, knife.

poigne [pwaɲ] *nf* grip; (*main*) hand. **poignée** *nf* (*valise, porte, etc.*) handle; (*quantité*) handful. **poignée de main** handshake. **poignet** *nm* wrist; (*vêtement*) cuff.

poil [pwal] *nm* hair; (*brosse*) bristle; (*tapis, tissu*) pile. **à poil** (*fam*) naked. **poilu** *adj* hairy.

poinçon [pwɛ̃sɔ̃] *nm* awl; (*or, etc.*) die, stamp; (*marque*) hallmark. **poinçonner** *v* stamp; hallmark; (*billet*) punch.

*****poindre** [pwɛ̃drə] *v* (*jour*) dawn; (*aube*) break; (*plante*) come up.

poing [pwɛ̃] *nm* fist.

point[1] [pwɛ̃] *nm* point; (*marque*) dot; (*tache*) spot; (*ponctuation*) full stop; (*couture, tricot*) stitch. **à point** just right; (*bifteck*) medium. **au point** (*phot*) in focus; perfect. **être sur le point de** be just about to. **mettre au point** perfect; (*phot*) focus; finalize. **point de côté** stitch. **point de mire** focal point. **point de suture** (*méd*) stitch. **point d'exclamation** exclamation mark. **point d'interrogation** question mark. **point du jour** daybreak. **point mort** (*auto*) neutral. **point noir** (*visage*) blackhead; (*auto*) black spot. **point virgule** semicolon.

point[2] [pwɛ̃] *adv* not. **ne … point** not at all.

pointe [pwɛ̃t] *nf* point; (*bout*) tip; (*maximum*) peak; (*soupçon*) touch, dash. **sur la pointe des pieds** on tiptoe.

pointer[1] [pwɛ̃te] *v* (*cocher*) tick off; (*braquer*) aim, point; (*employé*) clock in *or* out. **pointeur** *nm* timekeeper.

pointer[2] [pwɛ̃te] *v* (*piquer*) stick; appear; (*dresser*) soar up.

pointillé [pwɛ̃tije] *adj* dotted. *nm* dotted line. **pointiller** *v* (*art*) stipple.

pointilleux [pwɛ̃tijø] *adj* particular.

pointu [pwɛ̃ty] *adj* pointed; (*aigu*) sharp; (*péj*) touchy, peevish.

pointure [pwɛ̃tyr] *nf* size.

poire [pwar] *nf* pear; (*fam*) mug. **poirier** *nm* pear tree.

poireau [pwaro] *nm* leek.

pois [pwa] *nm* pea; (*point*) dot, spot. **pois cassés** split peas *pl*. **pois chiche** chickpea. **pois de senteur** sweet pea.

poison [pwazɔ̃] *nm* poison.

poisseux [pwasø] *adj* sticky.

poisson [pwasɔ̃] *nm* fish. **poisson d'avril** April fool. **poisson rouge** goldfish. **Poissons** *nm pl* Pisces *sing*. **poissonnerie** *nm* fish shop. **poissonnier, -ère** *nm, nf* fishmonger.

poitrine [pwatrin] *nf* chest; (*seins*) bust; (*cuisine*) breast.

poivre [pwavrə] *nm* pepper. **poivre de Cayenne** Cayenne pepper. **poivré** *adj* peppery; (*récit*) spicy. **poivrer** *v* pepper. **poivrier** *nm* pepper-pot. **poivron** *nm* pepper.

poix [pwa] *nf* pitch.

polaire [pɔlɛr] *adj* polar.

polariser [pɔlarize] *v* polarize; attract; (*concentrer*) focus. **se polariser sur** be centred on.

pôle [pol] *nm* pole.

polémique [pɔlemik] *adj* controversial. *nf* controversy, argument.

poli[1] [pɔli] *adj* polite.

poli[2] [pɔli] *adj* polished. *nm* shine.

police[1] [pɔlis] *nf* police. **faire la police** keep order.

police[2] [pɔlis] *nf* (*assurance*) policy.

policier [pɔlisje] *nm* policeman; (*roman*) detective novel. *adj* police; detective.

polio [pɔljo] *nf* polio.

polir [pɔlir] *v* polish.

polisson, -onne [pɔlisɔ̃, -ɔn] *nm, nf* rascal. *adj* (*enfant*) naughty; (*grivois*) saucy. **polissonnerie** *nf* naughty trick; saucy remark *or* action.

politesse [pɔlitɛs] *nf* politeness, courtesy; polite remark *or* gesture.

politique [pɔlitik] *adj* political. *nf* (*science*) politics; (*ligne de conduite*) policy. **politicien, -enne** *nm, nf* politician.

polka [pɔlka] *nf* polka.

pollen [pɔlɛn] *nm* pollen. **pollinisation** *nf* pollination.

polluer [pɔlɥe] *v* pollute. **pollution** *nf* pollution.

Pologne [pɔlɔɲ] *nf* Poland. **polonais** *nm*, *adj* Polish. **Polonais, -e** *nm*, *nf* Pole.

poltron, -onne [pɔltrɔ̃, -ɔn] *nm*, *nf* coward. *adj* cowardly. **poltronnerie** *nf* cowardice.

polycopier [pɔlikɔpje] *v* duplicate, stencil.

polyester [pɔliɛstɛr] *nm* polyester.

polyéthylène [pɔlietilɛn] *nm* polythene.

polygame [pɔligam] *adj* polygamous. *nm* polygamist. **polygamie** *nf* polygamy.

polyglotte [pɔliglɔt] *adj* multilingual. *n(m+f)* polyglot.

polygone [pɔligɔn] *nm* polygon.

pommade [pɔmad] *nf* ointment.

pomme [pɔm] *nf* apple; (*laitue, chou*) heart; (*arrosoir*) rose. **pomme à couteau/cuire** eating/cooking apple. **pomme d'Adam** Adam's apple. **pomme de pin** pine cone. **pomme de terre** potato. **pommes frites** chips *pl*. **pommier** *nm* apple tree.

pommelé [pɔmle] *adj* (*cheval*) dappled.

pommette [pɔmɛt] *nf* cheekbone.

pompe¹ [pɔ̃p] *nf* pump. **pompe à incendie** fire engine. **pomper** *v* pump. **pompier** *nm* fireman. **pompiste** *n(m+f)* petrol pump attendant.

pompe² [pɔ̃p] *nf* pomp. **pompeux** *adj* pompous.

poncer [pɔ̃se] *v* rub down, sandpaper.

ponctuel [pɔ̃ktɥɛl] *adj* punctual; (*assidu*) meticulous. **ponctualité** *nf* punctuality; meticulousness.

ponctuer [pɔ̃ktɥe] *v* punctuate. **ponctuation** *nf* punctuation.

pondérer [pɔ̃dere] *v* balance. **pondéré** *adj* level-headed.

pondre [pɔ̃drə] *v* lay; (*œuvre*) produce.

poney [pɔnɛ] *nm* pony.

pont [pɔ̃] *nm* bridge; (*naut*) deck. **pont aérien** airlift. **pont-levis** *nm* drawbridge. **pont suspendu** suspension bridge. **pont tournant** swing bridge.

popeline [pɔplin] *nf* poplin.

populace [pɔpylas] *nf* rabble.

populaire [pɔpylɛr] *adj* popular; (*république, etc.*) people's, of the people. **populariser** *v* popularize. **popularité** *nf* popularity.

population [pɔpylasjɔ̃] *nf* population.

porc [pɔr] *nm* pig; (*viande*) pork. **porc-épic** *nm* porcupine.

porcelaine [pɔrsəlɛn] *nf* porcelain, china.

porche [pɔrʃ] *nm* porch.

porcherie [pɔrʃəri] *nf* pigsty.

pore [pɔr] *nm* pore. **poreux** *adj* porous.

pornographie [pɔrnɔgrafi] *nf* pornography. **pornographique** *adj* pornographic.

port¹ [pɔr] *nm* port; (*bassin*) harbour.

port² [pɔr] *nm* carriage; postage; (*comportement*) bearing; (*casque, barbe, etc.*) wearing.

porte [pɔrt] *nf* door; (*aéro, jardin, écluse*) gate; (*embrasure*) doorway. **mettre à la porte** throw out; (*licencier*) sack.

porte-avions *nm invar* aircraft carrier.

porte-bagages *nm invar* luggage rack.

porte-bébé *nm* carrycot.

porte-bonheur *nm invar* lucky charm.

porte-clefs *nm invar* key ring.

porte d'entrée *nf* front door.

porte-fenêtre *nf* French window.

portefeuille [pɔrtəfœj] *nm* wallet; (*pol*) portfolio.

portemanteau [pɔrtmɑ̃to] *nm* coat rack.

porte-mine *nm* propelling pencil.

porte-monnaie *nm invar* purse.

porte-parole *nm invar* spokesman.

porter [pɔrte] *v* carry; bear; (*vêtement*) wear; (*amener*) take; direct, turn; (*comm*) put down, enter; (*ressentir*) feel; (*inciter*) prompt, induce; (*coup*) strike home. **se porter bien/mal** be well/ill. **portable** *adj* wearable. **portatif** *adj* portable. **porté** *adj* inclined, prone. **portée** *nf* range, reach; (*effet*) significance, consequences *pl*; (*animal*) litter; (*musique*) stave. **porteur, -euse** *nm*, *nf* bearer; (*valises*) porter; messenger.

porte-serviettes *nm invar* towel rail.

porte-voix *nm invar* megaphone.

portière [pɔrtjɛr] *nf* door.

portion [pɔrsjɔ̃] *nf* portion; part.

porto [pɔrto] *nm* port.

portrait [pɔrtrɛ] *nm* portrait.

Portugal [pɔrtygal] *nm* Portugal. **portugais** *nm*, *adj* Portuguese. **les Portugais** the Portuguese.

poser [poze] *v* put, lay; set down; (*question*) ask; (*tableau, étagères*) put up; (*art*) pose. **se poser** alight, come down; (*regard*) rest; (*question*) crop up, arise. **se poser en** pose as. **pose** *nf* pose; (*phot*) exposure; affectation; laying; (*chauffage, etc.*) installation. **posé** *adj* sedate, staid; (*allure*) steady.

positif [pozitif] *adj* positive; real; definite.

position [pozisjɔ̃] *nf* position.

posséder [posede] *v* possess, have. **possessif** *nm*, *adj* possessive. **possession** *nf* possession.

possible [posiblə] *adj* possible; feasible; potential. **possibilité** *nf* possibility.

poste[1] [post] *nf* post; (*bureau*) post office. **mettre à la poste** post. **poste aérienne** air mail. **postal** *adj* postal.

poste[2] [post] *nm* post; (*emploi*) job; (*TV, radio*) set; (*téléphone*) extension. **poste de police** police station. **poste d'essence** petrol station.

poster [poste] *v* post.

postérieur, -e [posterjœr] *adj* (*temps*) later; (*espace*) back; (*pattes, etc.*) hind. *nm* (*fam*) behind.

postérité [posterite] *nf* posterity.

posthume [postym] *adj* posthumous.

postiche [postiʃ] *adj* false. *nm* hairpiece.

postscolaire [postskɔlɛr] *adj* **enseignement postscolaire** *nm* further education.

post-scriptum [postskriptɔm] *nm invar* postscript.

postuler [postyle] *v* (*emploi*) apply for; (*poser*) postulate. **postulant, -e** *nm, nf* applicant. **postulat** *nm* postulate.

posture [postyr] *nf* posture, position.

pot [po] *nm* pot; (*verre*) jar; (*lait*) jug; carton; (*fam: chance*) luck. **pot à bière** tankard. **pot-au-feu** *nm invar* stew. **pot-de-vin** *nm* bribe.

potable [potablə] *adj* drinkable; (*fam*) reasonable, decent.

potage [potaʒ] *nm* soup.

potager [potaʒe] *adj* vegetable; (*plante*) edible. *nm* vegetable garden.

potassium [potasjɔm] *nm* potassium.

poteau [poto] *nm* post. **poteau indicateur** signpost. **poteau télégraphique** telegraph pole.

potelé [potle] *adj* plump, chubby.

potence [potɑ̃s] *nf* (*gibet*) gallows; (*support*) bracket.

potentiel [potɑ̃sjɛl] *nm, adj* potential.

poterie [potri] *nf* pottery. **potier** *nm* potter.

potin [potɛ̃] *nm* din, racket. **potins** *nm pl* gossip *sing*. **potiner** *v* gossip.

potion [posjɔ̃] *nf* potion.

potiron [potirɔ̃] *nm* pumpkin.

pou [pu] *nm, pl* **poux** louse (*pl* lice).

poubelle [pubɛl] *nf* bin.

pouce [pus] *nm* thumb; (*orteil*) big toe; (*mesure*) inch.

poudre [pudrə] *nf* powder. **poudre à canon** gunpowder. **poudre de riz** face powder. **poudrer** *v* powder. **poudreux** *adj* dusty. **poudrier** *nm* powder compact.

pouffer [pufe] *v* snigger.

poulain [pulɛ̃] *nm* foal.

poule [pul] *nf* hen; (*cuisine*) fowl. **poulailler** *nm* henhouse. **poulet** *nm* chicken.

pouliche [puliʃ] *nf* filly.

poulie [puli] *nf* pulley.

poulpe [pulp] *nm* octopus.

pouls [pu] *nm* pulse.

poumon [pumɔ̃] *nm* lung.

poupe [pup] *nf* stern.

poupée [pupe] *nf* doll.

pour [pur] *prep* for; (*comme*) as; (*but*) to. **pour cent** per cent. **pour que** so that.

pourboire [purbwar] *nm* tip.

pourceau [purso] *nm* (*péj*) swine.

pourcentage [pursɑ̃taʒ] *nm* percentage.

pourchasser [purʃase] *v* pursue.

pourpre [purprə] *nm, adj* crimson, purple.

pourquoi [purkwa] *conj, adv* why.

pourrir [purir] *v* rot, decay; (*fruit*) go rotten *or* bad; (*gâter*) spoil. **pourri** *adj* rotten, bad. **pourriture** *nf* rot.

***poursuivre** [pursɥivrə] *v* pursue; (*harceler*) hound; (*jur*) prosecute; continue, carry on. **poursuite** *nf* pursuit, chase. **poursuites** *nf pl* legal proceedings *pl*. **poursuivant, -e** *nm, nf* pursuer.

pourtant [purtɑ̃] *adv* yet, nevertheless.

pourtour [purtur] *nm* circumference; perimeter.

***pourvoir** [purvwar] *v* provide, equip, supply. **pourvoir à** provide for, cater for. **pourvoyeur, -euse** *nm, nf* supplier.

pourvu [purvy] *adj* **être pourvu de** (*personne*) be endowed with; (*chose*) be fitted *or* equipped with. **pourvu que** *conj* provided that, as long as.

pousser [puse] *v* push; (*stimuler, inciter*) drive, urge; continue, pursue; (*cri*) utter, let out; (*grandir*) grow. **pousser du coude** nudge. **pousse** *nf* growth; (*bot*) shoot. **poussé** *adj* advanced; elaborate; (*enquête*) exhaustive. **poussée** *nf* push, thrust; (*prix, pol*) upsurge. **poussette** *nf* push-chair.

poussière [pusjɛr] *nf* dust. **poussiéreux** *adj* dusty.

poussin [pusɛ̃] *nm* chick.

poutre [putrə] *nf* beam; (*métal*) girder.

***pouvoir** [puvwar] *v* can; (*permission*) may, be allowed to; (*capacité*) be able to; (*possibilité*) might, could. **n'en plus pouvoir** be tired out. **n'y rien pouvoir** be unable to do anything about it. **se pouvoir** be possible. *nm* power; (*capacité*) ability; influence.

pragmatique [pragmatik] *adj* pragmatic.

Prague [prag] *n* Prague.

prairie [preri] *nf* meadow, grassland; (*Amérique*) prairie.

praticable [pratikablə] *adj* practicable; feasible; (*chemin*) passable.

praticien [pratisjɛ̃], **-enne** *nm, nf* practitioner.

pratique¹ [pratik] *adj* practical; (*commode*) handy, convenient.

pratique² [pratik] *nf* practice.

pratiquer [pratike] *v* practise; (*faire*) make; (*employer*) use; (*rel*) go to church.

pré [pre] *nm* meadow.

préalable [prealablə] *adj* preliminary, prior. *nm* **au préalable** first.

préavis [preavi] *nm* (advance) notice.

précaire [prekɛr] *adj* precarious.

précaution [prekosjɔ̃] *nf* precaution; (*prudence*) care, caution.

précédent [presedɑ̃] *adj* previous. *nm* precedent.

précéder [presede] *v* precede.

précepteur [preseptœr] *nm* tutor. **préceptrice** *nf* governess.

prêcher [preʃe] *v* preach. **prêche** *nm* sermon.

précieux [presjø] *adj* precious; affected.

précipice [presipis] *nm* precipice, chasm.

précipiter [presipite] *v* precipitate; (*lancer*) throw, hurl; (*hâter*) hasten, speed up. **se précipiter** rush. **précipitamment** *adv* hurriedly, hastily. **précipitation** *nf* precipitation; haste. **précipité** *adj* hurried, rapid; (*décision*) hasty; (*fuite*) headlong.

précis [presi] *adj* precise. *nm* précis, summary; (*manuel*) handbook. **précisément** *adv* precisely; exactly; just. **préciser** *v* specify, make clear; be more precise (about). **se préciser** become clear, take shape. **précision** *nf* precision; detail, point.

précoce [prekɔs] *adj* precocious; (*fruit, etc.*) early; (*sénilité*) premature. **précocité** *nf* precocity; earliness.

préconçu [prekɔ̃sy] *adj* preconceived.

préconiser [prekɔnize] *v* recommend; advocate.

précurseur [prekyrsœr] *nm* precursor.

prédateur, -trice [predatœr, -tris] *nm* predator. *adj* predatory.

prédécesseur [predesesœr] *nm* predecessor.

prédestiner [predɛstine] *v* predestine. **prédestination** *nf* predestination.

prédicat [predika] *nm* predicate.

prédicateur [predikatœr] *nm* preacher.

***prédire** [predir] *v* predict, foretell. **prédiction** *nf* prediction.

prédominer [predɔmine] *v* predominate, prevail. **prédominance** *nf* predominance. **prédominant** *adj* predominant, prevailing.

prééminent [preeminɑ̃] *adj* pre-eminent. **prééminence** *nf* pre-eminence.

préfabriqué [prefabrike] *adj* prefabricated.

préface [prefas] *nf* preface.

préfecture [prefɛktyr] *nf* prefecture. **préfecture de police** Paris police headquarters.

préférer [prefere] *v* prefer. **préférable** *adj* preferable. **préféré, -e** *n, adj* favourite. **préférence** *nf* preference. **préférentiel** *adj* preferential.

préfet [prefɛ] *nm* prefect, chief administrative officer of a French department. **préfet de police** chief of Paris police.

préfixe [prefiks] *nm* prefix. **préfixer** *v* prefix.

préhistorique [preistɔrik] *adj* prehistoric.

préjudice [preʒydis] *nm* harm, wrong; (*matériel*) loss. **au préjudice de** at the expense of. **préjudiciable** *adj* detrimental.

préjugé [preʒyʒe] *nm* prejudice.

prélever [prɛlve] *v* take; (*argent*) deduct. **prélèvement** *nm* taking; deduction. **faire un prélèvement de sang** take a blood sample.

préliminaire [preliminɛr] *adj* preliminary. **préliminaires** *nm pl* preliminaries *pl*.

prélude [prelyd] *nm* prelude.

prématuré [prematyre] *adj* premature.

préméditer [premedite] *v* premeditate. **préméditation** *nf* premeditation.

premier [prəmje], **-ère** *adj* first; (*le plus bas*) bottom; (*le plus haut*) top; (*le plus important*) greatest, foremost; (*fondamental*) basic; original. **premier ministre** *nm* prime minister. **premiers secours** *nm pl* first aid *sing. nm* first; (*étage*) first

floor. *nf* first; (*cinéma*) première; (*transport*) first class; (*lycée*) lower sixth form.
prémisse [premis] *nf* premise.
prémonition [premɔnisjɔ̃] *nf* premonition.
prenant [prɔnɑ̃] *adj* absorbing, fascinating.
***prendre** [prɑ̃drɔ] *v* take; (*aller chercher*) fetch, pick up; (*attraper*) catch; (*repas*) have; (*acheter*) buy; (*air*) assume, put on; (*manier*) handle; (*durcir*) set. **s'en prendre à** take it out on; blame; attack. **s'y prendre** set about it.
prénom [prenɔ̃] *nm* Christian name.
prénuptial [prenypsjal] *adj* premarital.
préoccuper [preɔkype] *v* (*absorber*) preoccupy; (*inquiéter*) worry. **se préoccuper de** be concerned with *or* about. **préoccupation** *nf* preoccupation; worry.
préparer [prepare] *v* prepare; (*faire*) make; (*apprêter*) get ready; (*réserver*) have in store. **préparatifs** *nm pl* preparations *pl*. **préparation** *nf* preparation. **préparatoire** *adj* preparatory.
préposé [prepoze], **-e** *nm*, *nf* employer, official; (*vestiaire*) attendant.
préposition [prepozisjɔ̃] *nf* preposition.
prérogative [prerɔgativ] *nf* prerogative.
près [prɛ] *adv* near, close. **à cela près** apart from that. **de près** closely. **près de** close to; (*presque*) almost.
présager [prezaʒe] *v* be an omen of; (*prédire*) predict. **présage** *nm* omen.
presbyte [prɛsbit] *adj* long-sighted. **presbytie** *nf* long-sightedness.
***prescrire** [prɛskrir] *v* prescribe; order; stipulate. **prescription** *nf* prescription; order.
préséance [preseɑ̃s] *nf* precedence.
présence [prezɑ̃s] *nf* presence; (*bureau, école*) attendance.
présent[1] [prezɑ̃] *nm*, *adj* present. **à présent** now. **d'à présent** of today, present-day.
présent[2] [prezɑ̃] *nm* present, gift.
présenter [prezɑ̃te] *v* present; introduce; (*exposer*) set out; turn. **se présenter** appear; (*occasion*) arise; (*élection*) stand; (*concours*) go in for; (*examen*) take. **présentable** *adj* presentable. **présentateur, -trice** *nm*, *nf* presenter. **présentation** *nf* presentation; introduction.
préserver [prezɛrve] *v* protect; save. **préservatif** *nm* condom. **préservation** *nf* preservation, protection.
président [prezidɑ̃] *nm* president;

(*comité*) chairman. **présidence** *nf* presidency. **présidentiel** *adj* presidential.
présider [prezide] *v* preside (over); (*débat*) chair.
présomption [prezɔ̃psjɔ̃] *nf* presumption. **présomptueux** *adj* presumptuous.
presque [prɛskɔ] *adv* almost, nearly; (*guère*) scarcely, hardly.
presqu'île [prɛskil] *nf* peninsula.
presser [prese] *v* press; (*serrer*) squeeze; (*hâter*) speed up, hurry; be urgent. **presse-papiers** *nm invar* paperweight. **se presser** hurry; squeeze up, crowd together. **pressant** *adj* urgent. **presse** *nf* press. **pressé** *adj* hurried, in a hurry; urgent. **pression** *nf* pressure. **à la pression** on draught. **pressoir** *nm* press. **pressuriser** *v* pressurize.
preste [prɛst] *adj* nimble.
prestidigitateur, -trice [prɛstidiʒitatœr, -tris] *nm*, *nf* conjuror. **prestidigitation** *nf* conjuring.
prestige [prɛstiʒ] *nm* prestige. **prestigieux** *adj* prestigious.
présumer [prezyme] *v* presume.
prêt[1] [prɛ] *adj* ready. **prêt-à-porter** *nm* ready-to-wear clothes *pl*.
prêt[2] [prɛ] *nm* loan; advance; (*action*) lending.
prétendre [pretɑ̃drɔ] *v* claim; intend, mean. **prétendant, -e** *nm*, *nf* candidate. **prétendu** *adj* so-called, alleged. **prétention** *nf* claim, pretension; (*vanité*) pretentiousness. **prétentieux** *adj* pretentious.
prêter [prete] *v* lend; attribute; (*offrir*) give; (*tissu*) stretch. **prête-nom** *nm* figurehead. **prêter attention à** pay attention to. **prêter serment** take an oath. **prêteur, -euse** *nm*, *nf* lender. **prêteur sur gages** pawnbroker.
prétexte [pretɛkst] *nm* pretext, excuse.
prêtre [prɛtrɔ] *nm* priest. **prêtrise** *nf* priesthood.
preuve [prœv] *nf* proof, evidence.
***prévaloir** [prevalwar] *v* prevail. **se prévaloir de** (*profiter*) take advantage of; (*se flatter*) pride oneself on.
***prévenir** [prevnir] *v* (*avertir*) warn; inform; anticipate; (*éviter*) avert; (*influencer*) prejudice. **prévenance** *nf* kindness, consideration. **prévenant** *adj* kind, considerate. **prévenu, -e** *n*, *adj* accused.
préventif [prevɑ̃tif] *adj* preventive. **prévention** *nf* prevention; (*jur*) custody; (*préjugé*) prejudice.

prévision [previzjɔ̃] *nf* prediction, forecast. **prévisions météorologiques** weather forecast *sing*. **prévisible** *adj* foreseeable.

***prévoir** [prevwar] *v* anticipate; (*temps*) forecast; (*projeter*) plan; (*envisager*) allow; (*jur*) provide for. **prévoyance** *nf* foresight.

prier [prije] *v* pray; invite, ask; (*implorer*) beg. **je vous en prie** (*de rien*) don't mention it; (*faites donc*) please do. **prière** *nf* prayer; (*demande*) request, plea.

prieuré [prijœre] *nm* priory.

primaire [primɛr] *adj* primary.

prime¹ [prim] *nf* premium; bonus; (*cadeau*) free gift.

prime² [prim] *adj* first, earliest.

primer¹ [prime] *v* prevail over, outdo.

primer² [prime] *v* award a prize to.

primesautier [primsotje] *adj* impulsive.

primeurs [primœr] *nf pl* early fruit and vegetables *pl*.

primevère [primvɛr] *nf* primrose.

primitif [primitif] *adj* primitive; original.

primordial [primɔrdjal] *adj* primordial, essential.

prince [prɛ̃s] *nm* prince. **princesse** *nf* princess. **princier** *adj* princely.

principal [prɛ̃sipal] *adj* main, principal; (*employé*) chief, head. *nm* principal; main point.

principe [prɛ̃sip] *nm* principle. **par principe** on principle.

printanier [prɛ̃tanje] *adj* spring, spring-like.

printemps [prɛ̃tɑ̃] *nm* spring, springtime.

priorité [prijɔrite] *nf* priority; (*auto*) right of way.

pris [pri] *adj* (*place*) taken, occupied; (*mains*) full; (*personne*) busy, engaged.

prise [priz] *nf* hold, grip; capture; (*élec: à fiches*) plug; (*élec: à douilles*) socket. **en prise** (*auto*) in gear. **prise multiple** adapter.

priser [prize] *v* prize.

prisme [prismə] *nm* prism.

prison [prizɔ̃] *nf* prison, jail; imprisonment. **prisonnier, -ère** *nm, nf* prisoner.

privé [prive] *adj* private.

priver [prive] *v* deprive. **se priver** deny oneself. **se priver de** do without. **privation** *nf* deprivation.

privilège [privilɛʒ] *nm* privilege. **privilégié** *adj* privileged.

prix [pri] *nm* price, cost; (*récompense*) prize. **à tout prix** at all costs. **prix fixe** set price.

probable [prɔbablə] *adj* probable, likely. **probabilité** *nf* probability, likelihood.

probe [prɔb] *adj* honest. **probité** *nf* integrity.

problème [prɔblɛm] *nm* problem. **problématique** *adj* problematic.

procéder [prɔsede] *v* proceed. **procédé** *nm* process; conduct, behaviour. **procédure** *nf* procedure.

procès [prɔsɛ] *nm* (*jur*) trial; (*poursuite*) proceedings *pl*, lawsuit; (*affaire*) case. **procès-verbal** *nm* minutes *pl*, report.

procession [prɔsesjɔ̃] *nf* procession.

processus [prɔsesys] *nm* process.

prochain [prɔʃɛ̃] *adj* next; (*départ, etc.*) imminent; (*proche*) near, nearby. **prochainement** *adv* soon.

proche [prɔʃ] *adj* near, close; (*village, rue, etc.*) nearby. **proches** *nm pl* close relations *pl*.

proclamer [prɔklame] *v* proclaim, declare; announce. **proclamation** *nf* proclamation.

procréer [prɔkree] *v* procreate. **procréation** *nf* procreation.

procurer [prɔkyre] *v* (*fournir*) provide; (*donner*) give; (*apporter*) bring. **se procurer** get, obtain. **procuration** *nf* proxy; power of attorney. **procureur** *nm* public prosecutor, attorney.

prodige [prɔdiʒ] *nm* wonder, marvel; (*personne*) prodigy. **prodigieux** *adj* fantastic, prodigious, phenomenal.

prodigue [prɔdig] *adj* prodigal, extravagant; generous, lavish. **prodigalité** *nf* extravagance.

***produire** [prɔdɥir] *v* produce. **se produire** happen. **producteur, -trice** *nm, nf* producer. **productif** *adj* productive. **production** *nf* production; (*produit*) product. **productivité** *nf* productivity. **produit** *nm* product. **produits** *nm pl* (*légumes, etc.*) produce *sing*; (*comm*) goods *pl*. **produits chimiques** chemicals *pl*. **produits de beauté** cosmetics *pl*.

proéminence [prɔeminɑ̃s] *nf* prominence. **proéminent** *adj* prominent.

profane [prɔfan] *adj* secular, profane. *n(m+f)* layman. **profaner** *v* desecrate, profane, debase.

professer [prɔfese] *v* profess, declare; (*enseigner*) teach.

professeur [prɔfɛsœr] *nm* teacher; (*université*) professor.

profession [prɔfɛsjɔ̃] *nf* profession; occupation.

professionnel [prɔfɛsjɔnɛl], **-elle** *adj* professional; (*formation*) vocational. *nm, nf* professional; (*ouvrier*) skilled worker.

profil [prɔfil] *nm* profile; contour, outline.

profit [prɔfi] *nm* profit; advantage, benefit. **tirer profit de** profit from. **profitable** *adj* beneficial.

profiter [prɔfite] *v* **profiter à** benefit, be beneficial to. **profiter de** take advantage of.

profond [prɔfɔ̃] *adj* deep; (*sentiment, remarque*) profound. **peu profond** shallow. **profondément** *adv* deeply; profoundly. **profondeur** *nf* depth.

profus [prɔfy] *adj* profuse. **profusion** *nf* profusion.

progéniture [prɔʒenityr] *nf* offspring.

programme [prɔgram] *nm* programme; (*scolaire*) curriculum, syllabus; (*ordinateur*) program. **programmation** *nf* programming. **programmer** *v* programme. **programmeur, -euse** *nm, nf* computer programmer.

progrès [prɔgrɛ] *nm* progress; advance, improvement.

progresser [prɔgrese] *v* progress; advance; make progress. **progressif** *adj* progressive. **progression** *nf* progression; progress. **progressiste** *n(m+f), adj* progressive.

prohiber [prɔibe] *v* prohibit. **prohibition** *nf* prohibition.

proie [prwa] *nf* prey. **être en proie à** be a prey to; be a victim of.

projecteur [prɔʒɛktœr] *nm* projector; (*théâtre*) spotlight; (*monument, sport*) floodlight; (*pour chercher*) searchlight.

projectile [prɔʒɛktil] *nm* missile, projectile.

projection [prɔʒɛksjɔ̃] *nf* projection.

projet [prɔʒɛ] *nm* plan; (*ébauche*) draft. **projeter** *v* project; plan.

prolétariat [prɔletarja] *nm* proletariat. **prolétaire** *nm* proletarian. **prolétarien** *adj* proletarian.

proliférer [prɔlifere] *v* proliferate. **prolifération** *nf* proliferation.

prolifique [prɔlifik] *adj* prolific.

prologue [prɔlɔg] *nm* prologue.

prolonger [prɔlɔ̃ʒe] *v* prolong, extend. **se prolonger** go on, persist. **prolongation** *nf* prolongation. **prolongement** *nm* extension.

promener [prɔmne] *v* take for a walk. **se promener** go for a walk; (*errer*) wander. **promenade** *nf* walk, stroll; (*en voiture*) drive; (*à cheval*) ride.

promesse [prɔmɛs] *nf* promise.

***promettre** [prɔmɛtrə] *v* promise. **prometteur, -euse** *adj* promising.

promotion [prɔmosjɔ̃] *nf* promotion.

***promouvoir** [prɔmuvwar] *v* promote.

prompt [prɔ̃] *adj* swift, prompt, quick. **promptitude** *nf* swiftness, promptness.

prône [pron] *nm* sermon.

pronom [prɔnɔ̃] *nm* pronoun.

prononcer [prɔnɔ̃se] *v* pronounce; (*dire*) utter;· (*discours*) deliver. **se prononcer** come to a decision; give an opinion. **prononciation** *nf* pronunciation.

propagande [prɔpagɑ̃d] *nf* propaganda.

propager [prɔpaʒe] *v* propagate, spread. **propagation** *nf* propagation.

prophète [prɔfɛt] *nm* prophet. **prophétie** *nf* prophecy. **prophétique** *adj* prophetic. **prophétiser** *v* prophesy.

propice [prɔpis] *adj* favourable.

proportion [prɔpɔrsjɔ̃] *nf* proportion. **proportionnel** *adj* proportional. **proportionner** *v* proportion, make proportional.

propos [prɔpo] *nm* purpose, intention; subject. *nm pl* talk *sing*; remarks *pl*. **à propos** by the way; (*arriver*) at the right time; (*remarque*) apt. **à propos de** concerning, about.

proposer [prɔpoze] *v* propose; suggest; offer. **se proposer de** intend to. **proposition** *nf* proposal, proposition; suggestion; (*gramm*) clause.

propre [prɔprə] *adj* (*pas sale*) clean; (*net*) neat; (*chien, chat*) house-trained; honest; (*possessif*) own; appropriate, suitable. **propre à** suitable for; (*coutume, etc.*) peculiar to. **proprement** *adv* cleanly; neatly; (*comme il faut*) properly; strictly. **à proprement parler** strictly speaking. **propreté** *nf* cleanness; neatness.

propriétaire [prɔprijetɛr] *nm* owner; (*hôtel*) proprietor; (*location*) landlord. *nf* owner; proprietress; landlady. **propriété** *nf* property; (*droit*) ownership; correctness, suitability.

propulser [prɔpylse] *v* propel. **propulseur** *nm* propeller. **propulsion** *nf* propulsion.

*proscrire [prɔskrir] *v* ban, prohibit; (*personne*) banish, exile. **proscrit, -e** *nm, nf* outlaw; exile.

prose [proz] *nf* prose.

prospectus [prɔspɛktys] *nm* leaflet, brochure.

prospérer [prɔspere] *v* thrive, flourish; (*personne*) prosper. **prospère** *adj* thriving, flourishing; prosperous. **prospérité** *nf* prosperity.

se prosterner [prɔstɛrne] *v* bow down, prostrate oneself; (*s'humilier*) grovel. **prosternation** *nf* prostration. **prosterné** *adj* prostrate.

prostituer [prɔstitɥe] *v* prostitute. **prostituée** *nf* prostitute. **prostitution** *nf* prostitution.

protagoniste [prɔtagɔnist] *nm* protagonist.

protecteur, -trice [prɔtɛktœr, -tris] *adj* protective. *nm, nf* protector; (*art*) patron. **protection** *nf* protection; patronage.

protéger [prɔteʒe] *v* protect; patronize, be a patron of.

protéine [prɔtein] *nf* protein.

protester [prɔtɛste] *v* protest; declare. **protestant, -e** *n, adj* Protestant. **protestation** *nf* protest.

protocole [prɔtɔkɔl] *nm* protocol; etiquette.

prototype [prɔtɔtip] *nm* prototype.

proue [pru] *nf* bow, prow.

prouesse [pruɛs] *nf* prowess; (*acte*) feat.

prouver [pruve] *v* prove.

*provenir [prɔvnir] *v* **provenir de** come from; be the result of. **provenance** *nf* origin, source. **en provenance de** (coming) from.

proverbe [prɔvɛrb] *nm* proverb. **proverbial** *adj* proverbial.

providence [prɔvidãs] *nf* providence.

province [prɔvɛ̃s] *nf* province. **provincial** *adj* provincial.

proviseur [prɔvizœr] *nm* headmaster.

provision [prɔvizjɔ̃] *nf* stock, supply. **provisions** *nf pl* provisions *pl*, food *sing*.

provisoire [prɔvizwar] *adj* provisional, temporary.

provoquer [prɔvɔke] *v* provoke; cause; incite; (*duel*) challenge; (*colère, curiosité*) arouse. **provocant** *adj* provocative. **provocation** *nf* provocation.

proximité [prɔksimite] *nf* proximity.

prude [pryd] *nf* prude. *adj* prudish.

prudent [prydã] *adj* prudent; (*circonspect*) careful, cautious; (*sage*) sensible. **prudence** *nf* prudence; care, caution.

prune [pryn] *nf* plum. **pruneau** *nm* prune. **prunelle** *nf* (*bot*) sloe; (*anat*) pupil. **prunier** *nm* plum tree.

psaume [psom] *nm* psalm.

pseudonyme [psødɔnim] *nm* pseudonym.

psychanalyse [psikanaliz] *nf* psychoanalysis. **psychanalyser** *v* psychoanalyse. **psychanalyste** *n(m + f)* psychoanalyst.

psychédélique [psikedelik] *adj* psychedelic.

psychiatrie [psikjatri] *nf* psychiatry. **psychiatre** *n(m + f)* psychiatrist. **psychiatrique** *adj* psychiatric.

psychique [psiʃik] *adj* psychic.

psychologie [psikɔlɔʒi] *nf* psychology. **psychologique** *adj* psychological. **psychologue** *n(m + f)* psychologist.

psychopathe [psikɔpat] *n(m + f)* psychopath.

psychose [psikoz] *nf* psychosis. **psychotique** *n(m + f), adj* psychotic.

psychosomatique [psikɔsɔmatik] *adj* psychosomatic.

psychothérapie [psikɔterapi] *nf* psychotherapy.

puanteur [pɥãtœr] *nf* stink.

puberté [pybɛrte] *nf* puberty.

pubien [pybjɛ̃] *nf* puberty.

public, -ique [pyblik] *adj* public. *nm* public; audience. **le grand public** the general public.

publicité [pyblisite] *nf* publicity; (*comm*) advertising; (*annonce*) advertisement. **publicitaire** *adj* advertising.

publier [pyblije] *v* publish. **publication** *nf* publication; publishing.

puce [pys] *nf* flea. **jeu de puce** *nm* tiddlywinks. **puceron** *nm* greenfly.

pucelle [pysɛl] *nf* virgin.

pudeur [pydœr] *nf* modesty, decency.

pudique [pydik] *adj* modest; discreet.

puer [pɥe] *v* stink.

puéril [pɥeril] *adj* childish.

puis [pɥi] *adv* then.

puiser [pɥize] *v* draw. **puiser dans** dip into.

puisque [pɥiskə] *conj* since, seeing that, as.

puissance [pɥisãs] *nf* power; (*jur*) authority. **en puissance** potentially. **puissant** *adj* powerful.

puits [pᴴi] *nm* well; (*mine*) shaft.

pull [pyl] *nm* (*fam*) jumper.

pulluler [pylyle] *v* swarm, teem. **pullulation** *nf* swarm, multitude.

pulpe [pylp] *nf* pulp. **pulpeux** *adj* pulpy.

pulsation [pylsɑsjɔ̃] *nf* beat, pulsation. **pulsation du cœur** heartbeat.

pulvériser [pylverize] *v* pulverize; (*liquide*) spray; demolish. **pulvérisateur** *nm* spray. **pulvérisation** *nf* pulverization; spraying; demolition.

punaise [pynɛz] *nf* (*zool*) bug; (*clou*) drawing-pin.

punch [pɔ̃ʃ] *nm* punch.

punir [pynir] *v* punish. **punition** *nf* punishment.

pupille¹ [pypij] *nf* (*anat*) pupil.

pupille² [pypij] *n(m+f)* ward.

pupitre [pypitrə] *nm* desk; (*rel*) lectern; music stand.

pur [pyr] *adj* pure; (*boisson*) neat; honest; (*absolu*) sheer. **pur-sang** *nm* thoroughbred. **pureté** *nf* purity.

purée [pyre] *nf* (*tomates, etc.*) purée; (*pommes de terre*) mashed potato.

purgatoire [pyrgatwar] *nm* purgatory.

purger [pyrʒe] *v* purge; (*tech*) flush out, drain. **purgatif** *nm, adj* purgative. **purge** *nf* purge.

purifier [pyrifje] *v* purify, cleanse. **purification** *nf* purification.

puritain [pyritɛ̃], **-e** *adj* puritanical. *nm, nf* puritan.

pus [py] *nm* pus.

pusillanime [pyzilanim] *adj* faint-hearted.

putain [pytɛ̃] *nf* (*argot*) whore.

putride [pytrid] *adj* putrid.

puzzle [pœzlə] *nm* jigsaw.

pygmée [pigme] *nm* pygmy.

pyjama [piʒama] *nm* pyjamas *pl*.

pylône [pilon] *nm* pylon.

pyramide [piramid] *nf* pyramid.

python [pitɔ̃] *nm* python.

Q

qu' [k] *V* **que**.

quadrant [kadrɑ̃] *nm* quadrant.

quadrilatère [kadrilatɛr] *nm* quadrilateral.

quadrillé [kadrije] *adj* squared.

quadrupède [kadrypɛd] *nm, adj* quadruped.

quadrupler [kadryple] *v* quadruple. **quadruple** *nm, adj* quadruple. **quadruplé, -e** *nm, nf* quadruplet.

quai [ke] *nm* quay; (*gare*) platform; (*rivière*) embankment.

qualifier [kalifje] *v* qualify; describe, call. **qualification** *nf* qualification; description, label.

qualité [kalite] *nf* quality; (*don*) skill; (*fonction*) position, capacity.

quand [kɑ̃] *conj, adv* when. **quand même** all the same, nevertheless.

quant [kɑ̃] *adv* **quant à** as for; regarding.

quantité [kɑ̃tite] *nf* quantity, amount; great number, great deal.

quarantaine [karɑ̃tɛn] *nf* quarantine. **mettre en quarantaine** quarantine.

quarante [karɑ̃t] *nm, adj* forty. **quarantième** *n(m+f), adj* fortieth.

quart [kar] *nm* quarter; (*naut*) watch. ... **et quart** quarter past ... . **moins le quart** quarter to ... . **quart de finale** quarter-final. **quart d'heure** quarter of an hour.

quartier [kartje] *nm* quarter; (*ville*) district, area; (*portion*) piece. **du quartier** local. **quartier général** headquarters.

quartz [kwarts] *nm* quartz.

quasi [kazi] *adv* almost.

quatorze [katɔrz] *nm, adj* fourteen. **quatorzième** *n(m+f), adj* fourteenth.

quatre [katrə] *nm, adj* four. **à quatre pattes** on all fours. **quatrième** *n(m+f), adj* fourth.

quatre-vingt-dix *nm, adj* ninety. **quatre-vingt-dixième** *n(m+f), adj* ninetieth.

quatre-vingts *nm, adj* eighty. **quatre-vingtième** *n(m+f), adj* eightieth.

quatuor [kwatᴴɔr] *nm* quartet.

que¹ [kə] *conj* that; (*but*) so that; (*comparaison*) than; (*aussi*) as. **ne ... que** only. **que ... que ...** whether ... or ...

que² [kə] *adv* how.

que³ [kə] *pron* that, which; (*temps*) when; (*personne*) that, whom; (*interrogatif*) what. **qu'est-ce que** *or* **qui** what.

quel [kɛl], **quelle** *pron, adj* what, which. **quel que** whatever; (*personne*) whoever.

quelconque [kɛlkɔ̃k] *adj* any, some; (*médiocre*) poor; ordinary.

quelque [kɛlkə] *adj, adv* some. **quelque chose** something. **quelquefois** *adv* sometimes. **quelque part** somewhere. **quelque peu** somewhat. **quelques** *adj* some, a few; (*peu de*) few. **quelques-uns, -unes** *pron* some, a few. **quelqu'un** *pron* somebody.

quémander [kemɑ̃de] *v* beg. for.

querelle [kərɛl] *nf* quarrel. **se quereller** *v* quarrel. **querelleur, -euse** *adj* quarrelsome.

question [kɛstjɔ̃] *nf* question. **il n'en est pas question** it's out of the question. **questionnaire** *nm* questionnaire. **questionner** *v* question, interrogate.

quêter [kete] *v* collect money; (*chercher*) seek. **quête** *nf* collection; (*recherche*) quest, search. **en quête de** in search of. **faire la quête** collect for charity; (*rel*) take the collection.

queue [kø] *nf* tail; (*file*) queue; (*bout, fin*) end; (*liste*) bottom; (*fleur, fruit*) stalk; (*train*) rear; (*billard*) cue. **faire la queue** queue.

qui [ki] *pron* who; (*objet*) whom; (*chose*) which, that; (*quiconque*) whoever, anyone who. **à** *or* **de qui** (*possessif*) whose.

quiche [kiʃ] *nf* quiche.

quiconque [kikɔ̃k] *pron* whoever; (*personne*) anyone.

quignon [kiɲɔ̃] *nm* hunk of bread; (*croûton*) crust.

quille¹ [kij] *nf* (*jeu*) skittle; (*fam: jambe*) pin, leg. **jeu de quilles** skittles.

quille² [kij] *nf* (*naut*) keel.

quincaillerie [kɛ̃kɑjri] *nf* hardware; (*magasin*) hardware shop. **quincaillier, -ère** *nm, nf* ironmonger.

quinine [kinin] *nf* quinine.

quinte [kɛ̃t] *nf* coughing fit; (*musique*) fifth.

quintessence [kɛ̃tesɑ̃s] *nf* quintessence.

quintette [kɛ̃tɛt] *nm* quintet.

quintuplé [kɛ̃typle], **-e** *nm, nf* quintuplet.

quinze [kɛ̃z] *nm, adj* fifteen. **demain en quinze** a fortnight tomorrow. **quinze jours** a fortnight. **quinzaine** *nf* fortnight. **quinzième** *n(m+f), adj* fifteenth.

quiproquo [kiprɔko] *nm* mistake; (*malentendu*) misunderstanding.

quittance [kitɑ̃s] *nf* receipt.

quitter [kite] *v* leave; (*espoir*) give up. **ne quittez pas** (*téléphone*) hold the line. **se quitter** part. **quitte** *adj* quits, even; (*débarrassé*) clear, rid.

quoi [kwa] *pron* what. **à quoi bon?** what's the use? **avoir de quoi** have (the) means. **il n'y a pas de quoi** don't mention it. **quoi que** whatever.

quoique [kwakə] *conj* although.

quorum [kɔrɔm] *nm* quorum.

quote-part [kɔtpar] *nf* share, quota.

quotidien [kɔtidjɛ̃] *adj* daily; (*banal*) everyday. *nm* daily newspaper.

R

rabâcher [rabɑʃe] *v* harp on, keep repeating.

rabais [rabɛ] *nm* reduction, discount.

rabaisser [rabese] *v* belittle, disparage; reduce.

rabat [raba] *nm* flap.

*rabattre [rabatrə] *v* (*fermer*) close; (*faire retomber*) pull *or* turn down; (*drap*) fold back; reduce; deduct. **rabat-joie** *nm invar* spoilsport. **se rabattre** close; (*voiture*) cut in.

rabbin [rabɛ̃] *nm* rabbi.

rabot [rabo] *nm* plane. **raboter** *v* plane; (*fam*) scrape. **raboteux** *adj* uneven, rough.

rabougri [rabugri] *adj* stunted; (*ratatiné*) shrivelled.

racaille [rakaj] *nf* rabble.

raccommoder [rakɔmɔde] *v* mend; (*fam*) reconcile. **se raccommoder** (*fam*) make it up. **raccommodage** *nm* (*action*) mending; (*endroit*) mend. **raccommodement** *nm* (*fam*) reconciliation.

raccorder [rakɔrde] *v* join, link up, connect. **raccord** *nm* join, link.

raccourcir [rakursir] *v* shorten; get shorter. **raccourci** *nm* (*résumé*) summary; (*chemin*) short cut. **en raccourci** in miniature.

raccrocher [rakrɔʃe] *v* (*téléphone*) hang up, ring off; (*attraper*) grab, get hold of; (*tableau, etc.*) hang up again. **se raccrocher à** cling to; (*relier*) link with.

race [ras] *nf* race; (*animal*) breed; (*famille*) stock, blood. **de race** pedigree, thoroughbred. **racial** *adj* racial. **racisme** *nm* racialism, racism. **raciste** *n(m+f), adj* racialist, racist.

racheter [raʃte] v buy back; (dette) redeem; (otage) ransom; (péché) atone for; (faute) make up for. **rachat** nm redemption; ransom; atonement.

racine [rasin] nf root.

racler [rɑkle] v scrape. **se racler la gorge** clear one's throat. **raclée** nf (fam) thrashing.

racoler [rakɔle] v (prostituée) solicit; (vendeur) tout for.

raconter [rakɔ̃te] v tell, relate. **racontar** nm story, piece of gossip. **raconteur, -euse** nm, nf story-teller, narrator.

se racornir [rakɔrnir] v shrivel up; (durcir) become hard or tough.

radar [radar] nm radar.

rade [rad] nf harbour. **laisser en rade** leave stranded, abandon.

radeau [rado] nm raft.

radial [radjal] adj radial.

radiateur [radjatœr] nm radiator; (à gaz) heater. **radiateur électrique** electric fire. **radiateur soufflant** fan heater.

radiation [radjasjɔ̃] nf radiation.

radical [radikal] nm, adj radical.

radier [radje] v cross or strike off.

radieux [radjø] adj radiant.

radin [radɛ̃], -e (fam) adj stingy. nm, nf skinflint.

radio [radjo] nf radio; (méd) X-ray.

radioactif [radjɔaktif] adj radioactive. **radioactivité** nf radioactivity.

radiodiffuser [radjɔdifyze] v broadcast. **radiodiffusion** nf broadcasting.

radiographie [radjɔgrafi] nf radiography. **radiographier** v X-ray.

radiologie [radjɔlɔʒi] nf radiology.

radiothérapie [radjɔterapi] nf radiotherapy.

radis [radi] nm radish.

radium [radjɔm] nm radium.

radoter [radɔte] v (péj) ramble on. **radotage** nm drivel.

radoucir [radusir] v soften. **se radoucir** (personne) calm down; (temps, voix) become milder.

rafale [rafal] nf gust, blast.

raffermir [rafɛrmir] v strengthen; (durcir) harden; (voix) steady. **se raffermir** grow stronger; harden; become steady.

raffiner [rafine] v refine. **raffinage** nm refining. **raffinement** nm refinement. **raffinerie** nf refinery.

raffoler [rafɔle] v **raffoler de** be very fond of.

raffut [rafy] nm (fam) row, racket.

rafistoler [rafistɔle] v patch up.

rafle [rɑflə] nf police raid. **rafler** v (fam) swipe.

rafraîchir [rafreʃir] v refresh; (visage) freshen up; (refroidir) cool; (vêtement, appartement, etc.) brighten up; (cheveux) trim. **rafraîchissements** nm pl refreshments pl.

rage [raʒ] nf rage; mania; (méd) rabies. **rage de dents** raging toothache. **rager** v fume, be furious. **rageur, -euse** adj hot-tempered.

ragots [rago] nm pl (fam) gossip sing.

ragoût [ragu] nm stew.

raide [rɛd] adj stiff; (cheveux) straight; (corde) tight; (pente) steep; (fam: histoire) far-fetched; (osé) daring. adv steeply. **raideur** nf stiffness; straightness; tightness; steepness. **raidir** v stiffen.

raie¹ [rɛ] nf line; (bande) stripe; (cheveux) parting; (éraflure) scratch.

raie² [rɛ] nf (poisson) skate, ray.

raifort [rɛfɔr] nm horse-radish.

rail [rɑj] nm rail.

railler [rɑje] v scoff at. **raillerie** nf mockery. **railleur, -euse** adj mocking.

rainure [renyr] nf groove; (plus courte) slot.

raisin [rɛzɛ̃] nm grape. **raisin de Corinthe** currant. **raisin de Smyrne** sultana. **raisin sec** raisin.

raison [rɛzɔ̃] nf reason; (math) ratio. **avoir raison** be right. **raisonnable** adj reasonable; (sensé) sensible. **raisonnement** nm reasoning; argument. **raisonner** v reason; (convaincre) reason with; argue.

rajeunir [raʒœnir] v rejuvenate; modernize; (rafraîchir) brighten up; (personne) look or feel younger.

rajuster [raʒyste] v readjust; rearrange, tidy.

ralenti [ralɑ̃ti] adj slow. nm (cinéma) slow motion; (auto) tick-over. **au ralenti** in slow motion. **tourner au ralenti** tick over, idle.

ralentir [ralɑ̃tir] v slow down.

rallier [ralje] v rally; unite; (gagner) win over. **se rallier à** join, side with.

rallonger [ralɔ̃ʒe] v lengthen, extend. **rallonge** nf extension; (table) leaf. **à rallonges** (fam: nom) double-barrelled.

ramasser [ramɑse] v pick up; collect; (récolter) gather. **ramassé** adj crouched, huddled up; (trapu) squat, compact.

rame¹ [ram] *nf* (*aviron*) oar. **ramer** *v* row. **rameur** *nm* oarsman.

rame² [ram] *nf* train; (*papier*) ream.

rame³ [ram] *nf* (*branche*) stick, stake.

rameau [ramo] *nm* branch.

ramener [ramne] *v* bring back; (*tirer*) draw, pull.

ramier [ramje] *nm* wood-pigeon.

se ramifier [ramifje] *v* branch out.

ramollir [ramɔlir] *v* soften; (*courage, etc.*) weaken. **ramolli** *adj* soft.

ramoner [ramɔne] *v* sweep. **ramoneur** *nm* chimney-sweep.

ramper [rãpe] *v* crawl, creep. **rampe** *nf* ramp; (*côte*) slope; (*balustrade*) handrail; (*escalier*) banister; (*théâtre*) footlights *pl*.

rancart [rãkar] *nm* **mettre au rancart** (*argot*) scrap, chuck out.

rance [rãs] *adj* rancid.

rançon [rãsɔ̃] *nf* ransom. **rançonner** *v* hold to ransom.

rancune [rãkyn] *nf* spite; grudge.

randonnée [rãdɔne] *nf* (*voiture*) drive; (*bicyclette*) ride; (*pied*) walk, hike.

rang [rã] *nm* (*rangée*) row; (*place*) rank.

ranger [rãʒe] *v* arrange; (*à sa place*) put away; (*en ordre*) tidy up; (*compter*) rank. **se ranger** (*s'écarter*) step aside; (*voiture*) pull over; (*soldats, etc.*) line up; (*fam*) settle down. **se ranger à** go along with, fall in with. **rangé** *adj* orderly; settled. **rangée** *nf* row.

ranimer [ranime] *v* revive; (*feu, amour*) rekindle.

rapace [rapas] *adj* (*avide*) rapacious; (*oiseau*) predatory.

rapatrier [rapatrije] *v* repatriate. **rapatrié, -e** *nm, nf* repatriate. **rapatriement** *nm* repatriation.

râper [rɑpe] *v* (*cuisine*) grate; (*bois*) rasp. **râpe** *nf* grater; rasp. **râpé** *adj* grated; (*usé*) threadbare. **râpeux** *adj* rough.

rapetisser [raptise] *v* shorten; (*vêtement*) take up *or* in; look smaller; (*vieillard*) shrink; (*dénigrer*) belittle.

raphia [rafja] *nm* raffia.

rapide [rapid] *adj* fast, rapid, quick. *nm* express train. **rapides** *nm pl* rapids *pl*. **rapidité** *nf* speed, rapidity.

rapiécer [rapjese] *v* patch, mend.

rappeler [raple] *v* call back; (*faire souvenir*) remind, recall. **se rappeler** remember. **rappel** *nm* recall; reminder.

rapport [rapɔr] *nm* connection; relation-

ship; (*exposé*) report; revenue, yield; (*math*) ratio. **être en rapport avec** (*s'accorder*) be in keeping with; (*comm, etc.*) have dealings with. **par rapport à** in relation to; (*envers*) with regard to.

rapporter [rapɔrte] *v* bring back; (*revenu*) yield, bring in; report; (*argot*) tell tales, sneak. **se rapporter à** relate to, refer to. **s'en rapporter à** rely on. **rapporteur** *nm* (*fam*) sneak; (*géom*) protractor. **rapporteuse** *nf* (*fam*) sneak.

rapprocher [raprɔʃe] *v* bring together; (*approcher*) bring nearer; compare. **se rapprocher** come together; get closer, approach; be reconciled. **rapprochement** *nm* comparison; reconciliation; (*lien*) link, parallel.

raquette [rakɛt] *nf* racket.

rare [rar] *adj* rare; (*peu*) few; (*peu abondant*) scarce, sparse; exceptional. **rareté** *nf* rarity.

ras [rɑ] *adj* short; (*cheveux*) close-cropped. **à ras bords** to the brim. **au ras de** level with. **en avoir ras le bol** (*fam*) be fed up with.

raser [rɑze] *v* shave; (*effleurer*) skim, scrape; (*fam*) bore. **se raser** have a shave; (*fam*) be bored. **rasage** *nm* shaving. **raseur, -euse** *nm, nf* (*fam*) bore. **rasoir** *nm* razor; (*fam*) bore.

rassasier [rasazje] *v* satisfy. **se rassasier** eat one's fill. **se rassasier de** tire of.

rassembler [rasãble] *v* collect, assemble, gather (together); (*remonter*) reassemble.

rassis [rasi] *adj* stale; (*personne*) composed, calm.

rassurer [rasyre] *v* reassure. **se rassurer** put one's mind at ease.

rat [ra] *nm* rat.

ratatiner [ratatine] *v* wrinkle, shrivel up.

râteau [rɑto] *nm* rake.

râtelier [rɑtəlje] *nm* rack; (*fam*) set of false teeth.

rater [rate] *v* (*fusil*) misfire; (*affaire*) go wrong; (*fam: manquer*) miss; (*fam: gâcher*) mess up; (*fam: échouer*) fail.

ratifier [ratifje] *v* ratify. **ratification** *nf* ratification.

ration [rɑsjɔ̃] *nf* ration.

rationaliser [rasjɔnalize] *v* rationalize. **rationnel** *adj* rational.

rationner [rasjɔne] *v* ration. **rationnement** *nm* rationing.

ratisser [ratise] *v* rake (up).

rattacher [ratafe] v fasten again; join; (*relier*) link, relate.

rattraper [ratrape] v catch again; (*regagner, réparer*) make up for; (*rejoindre*) catch up with.

rature [ratyr] nf deletion, erasure.

rauque [rok] adj hoarse; (*cri*) raucous.

ravager [ravaʒe] v ravage, devastate. **ravages** nm pl ravages pl, devastation sing.

ravaler [ravale] v swallow; (*colère, larmes*) hold back; (*mur*) restore.

ravauder [ravode] v mend.

ravin [ravɛ̃] nm ravine, gully.

ravir [ravir] v delight; (*enlever*) carry off. **ravissant** adj delightful, beautiful. **ravissement** nm rapture.

se raviser [ravize] v change one's mind.

ravitailler [ravitaje] v (*carburant*) refuel; (*vivres, etc.*) provide with fresh supplies.

rayer [reje] v (*marquer*) line; (*érafler*) scratch; (*biffer*) cross out. **rayé** adj (*papier*) ruled, lined; (*tissu*) striped; scratched.

rayon¹ [rejɔ̃] nm ray, beam; (*roue*) spoke; (*cercle*) radius. **rayon X** X-ray.

rayon² [rejɔ̃] nm (*planche*) shelf; (*comm*) department; (*comptoir*) counter; (*miel*) honeycomb.

rayon³ [rejɔ̃] nm row, drill.

rayonne [rejɔn] nf rayon.

rayonner [rejɔne] v radiate; (*briller*) shine (forth), be radiant. **rayonnant** adj radiant. **rayonnement** nm radiance; radiation; influence.

rayure [rejyr] nf (*bande*) stripe; (*éraflure*) scratch.

razzia [razja] nf raid.

réaction [reaksjɔ̃] nf reaction. **moteur à réaction** jet engine. **réacteur** nm reactor. **réactionnaire** n(m+f), adj reactionary.

réadapter [readapte] v readjust; (*méd*) rehabilitate. **réadaptation** nf readjustment; rehabilitation.

réagir [reaʒir] v react.

réaliser [realize] v realize; (*ambition*) fulfil; (*projet*) carry out; (*cinéma*) produce. **réalisateur, -trice** nm, nf director. **réalisation** nf realization; fulfilment; production.

réaliste [realist] adj realistic. n(m+f) realist. **réalisme** nm realism.

réalité [realite] nf reality.

*réapparaître [reaparɛtrə] v reappear. **réapparition** nf reappearance.

réarranger [rearɑ̃ʒe] v rearrange. **réarrangement** nm rearrangement.

rébarbatif [rebarbatif] adj forbidding, daunting.

rebattu [rəbaty] adj hackneyed.

rebelle [rəbɛl] adj rebellious; (*cheveux*) unruly; (*virus*) resistant. n(m+f) rebel. **se rebeller** v rebel. **rébellion** nf rebellion.

rebondir [rəbɔ̃dir] v bounce, rebound. **rebond** nm bounce, rebound. **rebondi** adj (*personne*) plump, portly; (*forme*) rounded.

rebord [rəbɔr] nm edge; (*plat, assiette*) rim; (*vêtement*) hem. **rebord de fenêtre** window ledge *or* sill.

rebours [rəbur] nm à rebours the wrong way; (*compter*) backwards. à rebours de against.

rebrousser [rəbruse] v brush up *or* back. à rebrousse-poil the wrong way. prendre à rebrousse-poil rub up the wrong way. **rebrousser chemin** turn back, retrace one's steps.

rebuffade [rəbyfad] nf rebuff.

rebut [rəby] nm scrap. mettre au rebut throw out, discard.

rebuter [rəbyte] v discourage, put off; (*répugner*) repel.

receler [rəsəle] v (*secret*) conceal; (*malfaiteur*) harbour; (*objet volé*) receive.

recensement [rəsɑ̃smɑ̃] nm census.

récent [resɑ̃] adj recent; (*nouveau*) new. **récemment** adv recently.

récépissé [resepise] nm receipt.

récepteur, -trice [reseptœr, -tris] adj receiving. nm receiver.

réception [resɛpsjɔ̃] nf reception; (*d'une lettre, etc.*) receipt. **réceptionniste** n(m+f) receptionist.

récession [resesjɔ̃] nf recession.

recette [rəsɛt] nf (*cuisine*) recipe; (*comm*) takings pl. **recettes** nf pl receipts pl, revenue sing.

*recevoir [rəsvwar] v receive; (*invité*) entertain; (*contenir*) take, hold. être reçu (à) (*examen*) pass. **receveur, -euse** nm, nf tax collector; bus conductor.

rechange [rəfɑ̃ʒ] nm de rechange spare; alternative. **rechange de vêtements** change of clothes.

réchapper [refape] v réchapper de come through.

recharger [rəfarʒe] v (*stylo, etc.*) refill; (*fusil, etc.*) reload; (*batterie*) recharge. **recharge** nf refill.

réchaud [refo] *nm* stove.

réchauffer [refofe] *v* warm up; (*cuisine*) reheat.

rêche [rɛʃ] *adj* rough, harsh.

rechercher [rəfɛrfe] *v* seek; (*chercher*) search for; (*viser*) strive for, pursue; (*s'informer*) inquire into. **recherche** *nf* search; pursuit; investigation; (*université*) research. **à la recherche de** in search of. **recherché** *adj* in demand; (*soigné*) meticulous; (*péj*) affected.

rechute [rəfyt] *nf* relapse.

récif [resif] *nm* reef.

récipient [resipjɑ̃] *nm* container, receptacle.

réciproque [resiprɔk] *adj* reciprocal, mutual.

réciter [resite] *v* recite. **récit** *nm* story, account. **récital** *nm* recital. **récitation** *nf* recitation.

réclamer [reklame] *v* (*demander*) ask for, call for; (*protester*) complain; (*droit, etc.*) claim. **réclamation** *nf* complaint. **réclame** *nf* (*annonce*) advertisement; (*publicité*) advertising. **en réclame** on offer. **faire de la réclame** advertise.

reclus [rəkly], **-e** *nm, nf* recluse. *adj* cloistered.

recoin [rəkwɛ̃] *nm* nook, recess.

récolter [rekɔlte] *v* harvest; collect. **récolte** *nf* harvest, crop; collection.

recommander [rəkɔmɑ̃de] *v* recommend; (*conseiller*) advise; (*poste*) register. **recommandation** *nf* recommendation. **recommandé** *adj* recommended; advisable; registered. **en recommandé** by registered post; (*avec avis de réception*) recorded delivery.

recommencer [rəkɔmɑ̃se] *v* start again.

récompenser [rekɔ̃pɑ̃se] *v* reward. **récompense** *nf* reward.

réconcilier [rekɔ̃silje] *v* reconcile. **réconciliation** *nf* reconciliation.

*reconduire [rəkɔ̃dɥir] *v* (*raccompagner*) take back; (*renouveler*) renew.

réconforter [rekɔ̃fɔrte] *v* comfort; (*remonter*) fortify. **réconfort** *nm* comfort.

*reconnaître [rəkɔnɛtrə] *v* recognize; (*avouer*) admit, acknowledge; (*mil*) reconnoitre. **reconnaissable** *adj* recognizable. **reconnaissance** *nf* recognition; acknowledgement; (*mil*) reconnaissance; gratitude. **reconnaissant** *adj* grateful.

reconstituer [rəkɔ̃stitɥe] *v* (*crime*) reconstruct; (*édifice*) restore. **reconstitution** *nf* reconstruction; restoration.

*reconstruire [rəkɔ̃strɥir] *v* rebuild, reconstruct. **reconstruction** *nf* reconstruction.

record [rəkɔr] *nm* record.

recours [rəkur] *nm* recourse, resort. **avoir recours à** resort to.

*recouvrir [rəkuvrir] *v* cover.

récréation [rekreasjɔ̃] *nf* recreation; (*école*) break.

recrue [rəkry] *nf* recruit.

recruter [rəkryte] *v* recruit. **recrutement** *nm* recruitment.

rectangle [rɛktɑ̃glə] *nm* rectangle, oblong. *adj* right-angled. **rectangulaire** *adj* rectangular, oblong.

rectifier [rɛktifje] *v* rectify, correct; adjust; (*rendre droit*) straighten.

rectitude [rɛktityd] *nf* rectitude.

rectum [rɛktɔm] *nm* rectum.

reçu [rəsy] *adj* accepted; (*candidat*) successful. *nm* receipt.

recueil [rəkœj] *nm* collection; (*poèmes*) anthology. **recueil d'expressions** phrasebook.

*recueillir [rəkœjir] *v* collect, gather; (*réfugié*) take in; (*enregistrer*) record, take down. **se recueillir** collect one's thoughts. **recueillement** *nm* meditation. **recueilli** *adj* meditative.

reculer [rəkyle] *v* move back; (*fusil*) recoil; (*mil*) retreat; (*diminuer*) decline, subside; (*date, décision*) postpone. **reculer devant** (*hésiter*) shrink from. **recul** *nm* retreat; recoil; decline; postponement; distance. **reculé** *adj* remote. **à reculons** backwards.

récupérer [rekypere] *v* recover; (*ferraille, etc.*) salvage, retrieve; (*heures*) make up. **récupération** *nf* recovery; salvage.

récurer [rekyre] *v* scour.

rédacteur, -trice [redaktœr, -tris] *nm, nf* editor; (*article*) writer. **rédaction** *nf* (*contrat*) drafting; writing; editing; (*personnel*) editorial staff; (*école*) essay.

rédiger [rediʒe] *v* write; (*contrat*) draft, draw up.

*redire [rədir] *v* repeat. **trouver à redire à** find fault with.

redondant [rədɔ̃dɑ̃] *adj* redundant, superfluous.

redoubler [rəduble] *v* increase, intensify; (*école*) repeat a year.

redouter [rədute] *v* dread, fear.
redoutable *adj* formidable.
redresser [rədrese] *v* straighten (up); (*relever*) right, set upright; rectify. **se redresser** stand up straight.
***réduire** [redɥir] *v* reduce. **se réduire à** amount to; limit oneself to. **se réduire en** be reduced to. **réduction** *nf* reduction.
réduit [redɥi] *adj* small-scale, miniature; (*prix*) reduced. *nm* tiny room; (*recoin*) recess.
réel [reɛl] *adj* real. *nm* reality.
***refaire** [rəfɛr] *v* do *or* make again; (*pièce*, *meuble*) do up, renovate. **se refaire** recover.
réfectoire [refɛktwar] *nm* canteen, refectory.
référence [referɑ̃s] *nf* reference. **faire référence à** refer to.
référendum [referɛ̃dɔm] *nm* referendum.
référer [refere] *v* **se référer à** refer to; consult.
réfléchir [refleʃir] *v* reflect; (*penser*) think. **réfléchir à** think over *or* about. **réfléchi** *adj* (*personne*) thoughtful; (*action*) well thought out; (*gramm*) reflexive.
réflecteur [reflɛktœr] *nm* reflector.
reflet [rəflɛ] *nm* reflection; (*lumière*) light, glint.
refléter [rəflete] *v* reflect, mirror.
réflexe [reflɛks] *nm*, *adj* reflex.
réflexion [reflɛksjɔ̃] *nf* reflection; (*pensée*) thought; remark. **réflexion faite** on second thoughts.
reflux [rəfly] *nm* ebb.
réformer [reforme] *v* reform; (*mil*) discharge. **réforme** *nf* reform; (*rel*) reformation; discharge.
refouler [rəfule] *v* force back, repress.
réfracter [refrakte] *v* refract. **réfraction** *nf* refraction.
refrain [rəfrɛ̃] *nm* refrain.
réfrigérer [refriʒere] *v* refrigerate. **réfrigérateur** *nm* refrigerator. **réfrigération** *nf* refrigeration.
refroidir [rəfrwadir] *v* cool (down). **refroidissement** *nm* cooling; (*méd*) chill.
refuge [rəfyʒ] *nm* refuge; (*pour piétons*) traffic island.
se réfugier [refyʒje] *v* take refuge. **réfugié**, **-e** *nm*, *nf* refugee.
refuser [rəfyze] *v* refuse; (*client*) turn away. **être refusé** (**à**) (*examen*) fail. **refus** *nm* refusal.
réfuter [refyte] *v* refute.

regagner [rəgaɲe] *v* regain; (*argent, etc.*) win back; (*temps*) make up; (*lieu*) get back to.
regain [rəgɛ̃] *nm* renewal, revival.
régal [regal] *nm*, *pl* **-als** delight, treat. **régaler** *v* treat.
regarder [rəgarde] *v* look at; (*action*) watch; concern, regard. **regarder fixement** stare at, gaze at. **regard** *nm* look, glance; expression; (*égout*) manhole. **regard fixe** gaze, stare. **regard furieux** glare.
régate [regat] *nf* regatta.
régent [reʒɑ̃], **-e** *nm*, *nf* regent. **régence** *nf* regency.
régie [reʒi] *nf* state control.
régime [reʒim] *nm* regime; system; government; (*méd*) diet.
régiment [reʒimɑ̃] *nm* regiment. **régimentaire** *adj* regimental.
région [reʒjɔ̃] *nf* region, area. **régional** *adj* regional.
régir [reʒir] *v* govern. **régisseur** *nm* (*théâtre*) stage manager; (*gérant*) steward.
registre [rəʒistrə] *nm* register.
régler [regle] *v* settle; adjust, regulate; (*papier*) rule. **réglage** *nm* adjustment; (*moteur, TV, etc.*) tuning. **règle** *nf* rule; (*instrument*) ruler. **en règle** (*papiers*) in order. **règle à calcul** slide rule. **règles** *nf pl* (*méd*) period *sing*. **réglé** *adj* regular; (*papier*) lined. **règlement** *nm* settlement; (*règle*) rule. **réglementaire** *adj* regulation; statutory.
réglisse [reglis] *nf* liquorice.
régner [reɲe] *v* reign. **règne** *nm* reign; (*bot, zool*) kingdom.
regret [rəgrɛ] *nm* regret. **regrettable** *adj* regrettable. **regretter** *v* regret; (*personne*) miss; (*pays, etc.*) miss; (*être désolé*) be sorry; deplore.
régulier [regylje] *adj* regular; (*constant*) steady; (*égal*) even. **régularité** *nf* regularity; steadiness; evenness.
réhabiliter [reabilite] *v* rehabilitate; restore to favour. **réhabilitation** *nf* rehabilitation.
rehausser [rəose] *v* (*relever*) raise, make higher; (*beauté, goût, etc.*) enhance, bring out.
rein [rɛ̃] *nm* kidney. **reins** *nm pl* back *sing*.
réincarnation [reɛ̃karnɑsjɔ̃] *nf* reincarnation.

reine [rɛn] *nf* queen. **reine-claude** *nf* greengage.

réintégrer [reɛ̃tegre] *v* reinstate; return to. **réintégration** *nf* reinstatement; return.

rejeter [rəʒte] *v* reject; (*relancer*) throw back; (*lave, déchets, etc.*) throw out; (*expulser*) cast out, expel. **se rejeter sur** fall back on. **rejet** *nm* rejection; expulsion; (*bot*) shoot.

*rejoindre [rəʒwɛ̃drə] *v* rejoin; join; (*rattraper*) catch up with. **se rejoindre** meet.

réjouir [reʒwir] *v* delight, thrill. **se réjouir** be delighted; rejoice. **réjouissance** *nf* rejoicing. **réjouissant** *adj* amusing; (*nouvelle*) cheerful.

relâcher [rəlɑʃe] *v* relax; (*desserrer*) loosen; (*libérer*) release. **relâche** *nf* rest, respite; (*théâtre*) closure; (*naut*) port of call. **relâché** *adj* loose; (*discipline*) lax.

relais [rəlɛ] *nm* relay; (*usine*) shift.

relatif [rəlatif] *adj* relative. **relativité** *nf* relativity.

relation [rəlɑsjɔ̃] *nf* relationship; (*connaissance*) acquaintance, connection; (*récit*) account. **relations** *nf pl* relations *pl*.

relayer [rəleje] *v* (*remplacer*) relieve, take over from; (*TV, radio*) relay. **se relayer** take turns.

reléguer [rəlege] *v* relegate. **relégation** *nf* relegation.

relevé [rəlve] *adj* raised, elevated; (*manches*) rolled-up; (*col*) turned-up; (*cuisine*) highly-seasoned. *nm* summary, statement; list; (*facture*) bill. **relevé de compte** bank statement.

relever [rəlve] *v* (*redresser*) pick up, stand up; (*remonter*) raise; (*manche*) roll up; (*chaussette*) pull up; (*col*) turn up; (*cuisine*) season; (*relayer*) relieve; (*faute*) find; (*notes*) take down. **relever de** be a matter for, be the concern of. **relève** *nf* relief. **relève de la garde** changing of the guard.

relief [rəljɛf] *nm* relief. **en relief** in relief; (*en-tête*) embossed; (*phot*) three-dimensional. **mettre en relief** bring out, accentuate.

relier [rəlje] *v* link, connect, (*livre*) bind.

religieux [rəliʒjø] *adj* religious. *nm* monk. **religieuse** *nf* nun.

religion [rəliʒjɔ̃] *nf* religion; (*foi*) faith.

relique [rəlik] *nf* relic.

*relire [rəlir] *v* re-read.

*reluire [rəlɥir] *v* shine, gleam. **reluisant** *adj* shiny.

remanier [rəmanje] *v* revise, modify.

se remarier [rəmarje] *v* remarry. **remariage** *nm* remarriage.

remarquer [rəmarke] *v* notice; (*faire une remarque*) remark. **faire remarquer** point out. **remarquable** *adj* remarkable. **remarque** *nf* remark, comment.

remblai [rɑ̃blɛ] *nm* embankment.

rembourrer [rɑ̃bure] *v* stuff, pad. **rembourrage** *nm* stuffing, padding.

rembourser [rɑ̃burse] *v* repay; (*dépenses*) refund, reimburse. **remboursement** *nm* repayment; refund, reimbursement.

remède [rəmɛd] *nm* remedy, cure. **remédier à** *v* remedy.

remercier [rəmɛrsje] *v* thank. **remerciement** *nm* thanks *pl*.

*remettre [rəmɛtrə] *v* put back; (*donner*) hand over; (*ajourner*) postpone; (*dette, péché*) remit. **se remettre** recover, get better.

réminiscence [reminisɑ̃s] *nf* reminiscence.

remise [rəmiz] *nf* (*rabais*) discount; (*livraison*) delivery; (*grâce*) remission; (*resserre*) shed; (*ajournement*) postponement.

rémission [remisjɔ̃] *nf* remission.

remonter [rəmɔ̃te] *v* go up (again); return, go back; (*cheval*) remount; (*relever*) raise; (*montre*) wind up; (*moral*) cheer up; (*machine, etc.*) reassemble. **remontant** *nm* tonic. **remontée** *nf* ascent, rise.

remords [rəmɔr] *nm* remorse.

remorquer [rəmɔrke] *v* tow. **remorque** *nf* towing; (*câble*) tow-rope; (*véhicule*) trailer. **en remorque** on tow. **remorqueur** *nm* tugboat.

remous [rəmu] *nm* (*eau*) wash, swirl; (*air*) eddy; (*foule*) bustle; (*agitation*) stir.

rempart [rɑ̃par] *nm* rampart.

remplacer [rɑ̃plase] *v* replace; (*acteur, etc.*) stand in for; be a substitute for. **remplaçant, -e** *nm, nf* replacement; substitute; (*sport*) reserve; (*théâtre*) understudy. **remplacement** *nm* replacement; substitution.

rempli [rɑ̃pli] *adj* full. *nm* (*vêtement*) tuck.

remplir [rɑ̃plir] *v* fill; (*à nouveau*) refill; (*devoir*) fulfil; (*travail*) carry out.

remporter [rɑ̃pɔrte] *v* take away; (*victoire*) win; (*prix*) carry off.

remuer [rəmɥe] *v* move; (*tourner*) stir. **remue-ménage** *nm invar* commotion.

rémunérer [remynere] *v* remunerate, pay. **rémunérateur, -trice** *adj* remunerative, lucrative. **rémunération** *nf* remuneration.

renâcler [rənɑkle] *v* (*animal*) snort; (*personne*) grumble.

renaissance [rənɛsɑ̃s] *nf* rebirth.

renard [rənar] *nm* fox.

renchérir [rɑ̃ʃerir] *v* (*prix*) get more expensive; (*ajouter*) add, go further; (*péj*) go one better.

rencontrer [rɑ̃kɔ̃tre] *v* meet; (*trouver*) come across; (*obstacle*) come up against, encounter. **rencontre** *nf* meeting, encounter.

rendez-vous [rɑ̃devu] *nm invar* appointment; (*lieu*) meeting place. **donner rendez-vous à** make an appointment with.

se ***rendormir** [rɑ̃dɔrmir] *v* go back to sleep.

rendre [rɑ̃drə] *v* return, give back; (*achat*) take *or* send back; render; (*faire*) make; (*mil*) surrender; (*terre*) yield. **se rendre** surrender. **se rendre à** go to. **se rendre compte de** realize. **rendement** *nm* yield, output.

rêne [rɛn] *nf* rein.

renégat [rənega], **-e** *nm, nf* renegade.

renfermer [rɑ̃fɛrme] *v* contain. **renfermé** *adj* withdrawn. **sentir le renfermé** smell stuffy.

renforcer [rɑ̃fɔrse] *v* reinforce, strengthen; intensify. **renforcement** *nm* reinforcement, strengthening; intensification.

renfort [rɑ̃fɔr] *nm* reinforcement. **de** *or* **en renfort** extra, additional. **renforts** *nm pl* supplies *pl*.

se **renfrogner** [rɑ̃frɔɲe] *v* scowl. **renfrogné** *adj* sullen, sulky.

rengaine [rɑ̃gɛn] *nf* hackneyed expression.

renier [rənje] *v* renounce, deny; repudiate, disown; (*promesse*) go back on. **reniement** *nm* renunciation, denial; repudiation.

renifler [rənifle] *v* sniff. **reniflement** *nm* sniff.

renne [rɛn] *nm* reindeer.

renom [rənɔ̃] *nm* renown, fame. **renommé** *adj* renowned, famous. **renommée** *nf* renown, fame.

renoncer [rənɔ̃se] *v* **renoncer à** give up, renounce, abandon. **renonciation** *nf* renunciation.

renoncule [rənɔ̃kyl] *nf* buttercup.

renouer [rənwe] *v* tie again; (*conversation, etc.*) renew, resume.

renouveler [rənuvle] *v* renew. **se renouveler** recur. **renouvellement** *nm* renewal; recurrence.

rénover [renɔve] *v* renovate; (*méthodes, etc.*) reform. **rénovation** *nf* renovation; restoration.

renseigner [rɑ̃seɲe] *v* inform, give information to. **se renseigner** find out, make inquiries. **renseignements** *nm pl* information *sing*; inquiries *pl*; (*mil*) intelligence *sing*.

rente [rɑ̃t] *nf* pension, allowance. **rentes** *nf pl* private income *sing*. **rentable** *adj* profitable.

rentrer [rɑ̃tre] *v* return, go *or* come back; (*chez soi*) go home; (*entrer*) go in; (*à nouveau*) go back in; (*amener*) bring *or* take in. **rentrer dans** go into; (*voiture*) crash into; be included in. **rentrée** *nf* return; reopening; beginning of school term; (*acteur*) comeback.

renverser [rɑ̃vɛrse] *v* (*faire tomber*) knock over; (*mettre à l'envers*) turn upside down; (*gouvernement*) overthrow; (*inverser*) invert, reverse; (*fam*) stagger, astound. **se renverser** overturn. **renversé** *adj* upside down; inverted. **renversement** *nm* inversion, reversal; overthrow.

***renvoyer** [rɑ̃vwaje] *v* send back; (*employé*) dismiss; (*élève*) expel; (*soldat*) discharge; refer; (*ajourner*) postpone; echo. **renvoi** *nm* dismissal; expulsion; discharge; cross-reference; postponement; (*rot*) belch.

réorganiser [reɔrganize] *v* reorganize. **réorganisation** *nf* reorganization.

repaire [rəpɛr] *nm* den.

répandre [repɑ̃drə] *v* (*renverser*) spill; (*disperser*) scatter; (*étendre*) spread; (*odeur, chaleur, etc.*) give off. **répandu** *adj* widespread.

***reparaître** [rəparɛtrə] *v* reappear.

réparer [repare] *v* mend, repair; correct; (*compenser*) make up for. **réparation** *nf* repair; correction; compensation.

repartie [rəparti] *nf* repartee; (*riposte*) retort.

répartir [repartir] v share out, divide up; distribute; (*étaler*) spread. **répartition** *nf* distribution; allocation.

repas [rəpɑ] *nm* meal. **repas léger** snack.

repasser [rəpɑse] v (*frontière*) go back across; (*souvenir, trait*) go (back) over; (*examen*) resit; (*film, émission*) show again; (*au fer*) iron; (*couteau*) sharpen. **repassage** *nm* ironing; sharpening.

se *repentir [rəpɑ̃tir] v repent. **se repentir de** regret, be sorry for. *nm* repentance. **repentant** *adj* repentant.

répercussion [repɛrkysjɔ̃] *nf* repercussion.

répercuter [repɛrkyte] v echo; reflect. **se répercuter** reverberate.

repérer [rəpere] v locate; (*fam*) spot, discover. **repère** *nm* mark, marker; (*monument, etc.*) landmark.

répertoire [repɛrtwar] *nm* index, list; (*carnet*) notebook; (*théâtre*) repertory; (*chanteur*) repertoire.

répéter [repete] v repeat; (*théâtre*) rehearse. **répétiteur, -trice** *nm, nf* tutor. **répétition** *nf* repetition; rehearsal. **répétition générale** dress rehearsal.

répit [repi] *nm* respite.

replacer [rəplase] v replace, put back; (*employé*) find a new job for.

replier [rəplije] v fold up; (*mil*) withdraw. **se replier** curl up; (*se renfermer*) withdraw. **repli** *nm* fold; withdrawal.

réplique [replik] *nf* reply, retort; counterattack; (*théâtre*) line, cue; (*art*) replica. **répliquer** v reply, retort; (*se venger*) retaliate.

répondre [repɔ̃drə] v answer, reply; (*réagir*) respond. **répondre de** answer for.

réponse [repɔ̃s] *nf* answer, reply; (*réaction*) response.

reporter[1] [rəpɔrte] v (*ramener*) take back; (*différer*) put off, postpone; transfer; copy out. **se reporter à** refer to; (*penser*) think back to.

reporter[2] [rəpɔrtɛr] *nm* reporter. **reportage** *nm* report; (*sport*) commentary.

repos [rəpo] *nm* rest; pause; (*tranquillité*) peace.

reposer[1] [rəpoze] v rest; (*être étendu*) lie. **se reposer** rest; (*compter*) rely. **reposant** *adj* restful.

reposer[2] [rəpoze] v put back; (*question*) repeat, raise again.

repousser [rəpuse] v repulse, repel; (*écarter*) push away; reject; (*différer*) put off, postpone; (*cheveux, etc.*) grow again. **repoussant** *adj* repulsive.

*reprendre [rəprɑ̃drə] v take back; (*récupérer*) recover, get back; (*recommencer*) resume; (*attraper*) recapture; reprimand. **se reprendre** correct onself; (*se ressaisir*) pull oneself together.

représailles [rəprezɑj] *nf pl* reprisals *pl*, retaliation *sing*.

représenter [rəprezɑ̃te] v represent; (*art*) depict, portray; (*théâtre*) perform. **se représenter** imagine; (*survenir*) occur or arise again; (*à un examen*) resit. **représentant, -e** *nm, nf* representative. **représentatif** *adj* representative. **représentation** *nf* representation; performance.

répressif [represif] *adj* repressive. **répression** *nf* repression.

réprimande [reprimɑ̃d] *nf* reprimand. **réprimander** v reprimand.

réprimer [reprime] v repress, suppress.

reprise [rəpriz] *nf* (*recommencement*) resumption, renewal; (*film, émission*) repeat; (*affaires, etc.*) recovery; (*chaussette*) darn; (*fois*) occasion, time. · **à maintes reprises** many times. **repriser** v darn.

reprocher [rəprɔʃe] v reproach; criticize. **reproche** *nm* reproach.

reproduction [rəprɔdyksjɔ̃] *nf* reproduction.

*reproduire [rəprɔdɥir] v reproduce. **se reproduire** recur.

réprouver [repruve] v reprove, condemn.

reptile [rɛptil] *nm* reptile.

républicain [repyblikɛ̃], **-e** *n, adj* republican.

république [repyblik] *nf* republic.

répudier [repydje] v repudiate, renounce. **répudiation** *nf* repudiation.

répugnant [repyɲɑ̃] *adj* repugnant, revolting. **répugnance** *nf* repugnance, loathing.

répulsif [repylsif] *adj* repulsive. **répulsion** *nf* repulsion.

réputation [repytasjɔ̃] *nf* reputation, repute. **réputé** *adj* reputable, renowned; (*prétendu*) reputed.

*requérir [rəkerir] v require, call for; (*solliciter*) request.

requête [rəkɛt] *nf* request, petition.

requiem [rekɥijɛm] *nm invar* requiem.

requin [rəkɛ̃] *nm* shark.

requis [rəki] *adj* required, requisite.

réquisition [rekizisjɔ̃] *nf* requisition.
réquisitionner *v* requisition.
rescapé [rɛskape], **-e** *nm, nf* survivor.
réseau [rezo] *nm* network.
réserver [rezɛrve] *v* reserve; (*mettre de côté*) keep, save; (*destiner*) have in store. **réservation** *nf* reservation. **réserve** *nf* reserve; (*restriction*) reservation; (*provision*) stock; (*entrepôt*) storeroom.
réservoir [rezɛrvwar] *nm* tank; (*étang*) reservoir; (*poissons*) fishpond.
résider [rezide] *v* reside. **résidence** *nf* residence. **résidentiel** *adj* residential.
résidu [rezidy] *nm* residue.
se résigner [reziɲe] *v* resign oneself. **résignation** *nf* resignation.
résilier [rezilje] *v* terminate, cancel.
résille [rezij] *nf* net; (*coiffure*) hairnet.
résine [rezin] *nf* resin.
résister [reziste] *v* **résister à** resist, withstand. **résistance** *nf* resistance. **résistant** *adj* strong, robust.
résolu [rezɔly] *adj* resolute, determined. **résolution** *nf* resolution; solution.
résonner [rezɔne] *v* resonate, resound. **resonance** *nf* resonance.
*****résoudre** [rezudrə] *v* resolve; (*problème*) solve.
respect [rɛspɛ] *nm* respect. **respect de soi** self-respect. **respectable** *adj* respectable. **respecter** *v* respect. **respectif** *adj* respective. **respectueux** *adj* respectful.
respirer [rɛspire] *v* breathe. **respiration** *nf* breathing. **respiration artificielle** artificial respiration.
resplendir [rɛsplɑ̃dir] *v* beam, shine, gleam. **resplendissant** *adj* radiant.
responsable [rɛspɔ̃sablə] *adj* responsible. *n(m+f)* (*coupable*) culprit; (*dirigeant*) official. **responsabilité** *nf* responsibility.
resquiller [rɛskije] *v* get in without paying; jump the queue; (*carotter*) wangle.
se ressaisir [rəsezir] *v* pull oneself together.
ressembler [rəsɑ̃blə] *v* **ressembler à** resemble, be like. **se ressembler** be alike. **ressemblance** *nf* resemblance; similarity.
*****ressentir** [rəsɑ̃tir] *v* feel. **se ressentir de** (*personne*) feel the effects of; (*travail*) show the effects of. **ressentiment** *nm* resentment.
resserrer [rəsere] *v* tighten.
ressort¹ [rəsɔr] *nm* spring.
ressort² [rəsɔr] *nm* scope, province.

*****ressortir** [rəsɔrtir] *v* go *or* come out again; (*retirer*) bring *or* take out again; (*se détacher*) stand out. **ressortir de** be the result of.
ressource [rəsurs] *nf* resource; possibility; (*recours*) resort.
ressusciter [resysite] *v* revive; (*rel, péj*) resurrect.
restant [rɛstɑ̃] *adj* remaining. *nm* rest, remainder.
restaurant [rɛstɔrɑ̃] *nm* restaurant.
restaurer [rɛstɔre] *v* restore. **restauration** *nf* restoration.
rester [rɛste] *v* stay, remain; (*subsister*) be left; (*durer*) last. **en rester à** go no further than. **reste** *nm* rest, remainder; (*morceau*) piece left over. **du reste** moreover. **restes** *nm pl* remains *pl*; (*nourriture*) left-overs *pl*.
restituer [rɛstitɥe] *v* restore; (*rendre*) return.
*****restreindre** [rɛstrɛ̃drə] *v* restrict, limit.
restriction [rɛstriksjɔ̃] *nf* restriction. **restrictif** *adj* restrictive.
résulter [rezylte] *v* result. **résultat** *nm* result.
résumer [rezyme] *v* summarize, sum up. **résumé** *nm* summary, résumé.
résurrection [rezyrɛksjɔ̃] *nf* resurrection.
rétablir [retablir] *v* restore; (*réintégrer*) reinstate. **se rétablir** (*malade*) recover. **rétablissement** *nm* recovery; restoration.
retard [rətar] *nm* delay; (*personne*) lateness; (*peuple, enfant*) backwardness. **en retard** late. **retardé** *adj* backward. **retarder** *v* delay; (*remettre*) put back; (*montre*) be slow.
*****retenir** [rətnir] *v* hold back; (*garder*) keep, retain; (*retarder*) detain; (*réserver*) book; (*contenir*) restrain.
retentir [rətɑ̃tir] *v* ring, resound, echo. **retentissement** *nm* repercussion; effect.
retenue [rətny] *nf* restraint, reserve; (*prélèvement*) deduction; (*école*) detention.
réticent [retisɑ̃] *adj* reticent; hesitant. **réticence** *nf* reservation.
rétif [retif] *adj* restive.
rétine [retin] *nf* retina.
retirer [rətire] *v* remove, withdraw. **se retirer** retire, withdraw.
retomber [rətɔ̃be] *v* fall (again); (*fusée, etc.*) land, come down; (*pendre*) hang down.

rétorquer [retɔrke] v retort.

retors [rətɔr] adj sly, wily.

retoucher [rətuʃe] v touch up; (vêtement) alter. **retouche** nf alteration.

retour [rətur] nm return. **être de retour** be back.

retourner [rəturne] v return; (renverser) turn over; (sens opposé) turn round.

rétracter [retrakte] v retract.

retrait [rətrɛ] nm withdrawal. **en retrait** set back.

retraite [rətrɛt] nf retreat; (vieux travailleur) retirement; pension. **prendre sa retraite** retire.

retraité [rətrete], **-e** adj retired. nm, nf pensioner.

retrancher [rətrɑ̃ʃe] v deduct, take away; (couper) cut out or off. **se retrancher** (mil) entrench oneself; take refuge.

rétrécir [retresir] v (tissu) shrink; (rue) narrow; (pupille) contract. **rétrécissement** nm shrinkage; contraction.

rétribuer [retribɥe] v pay. **rétribution** nf payment.

rétrograder [retrɔgrade] v regress, go backward; (officier) demote. **rétrogradation** nf regression; demotion. **rétrograde** adj retrograde, backward.

rétrospectif [retrɔspɛktif] adj retrospective. **rétrospectivement** adv in retrospect.

retrousser [rətruse] v (manche) roll up; (lèvre) curl up; (jupe, etc.) hitch up; (nez) turn up.

retrouver [rətruve] v find (again); (personne) meet, join; (santé) regain. **se retrouver** meet up, get together.

rétroviseur [retrɔvizœr] nm driving mirror.

réunir [reynir] v collect, gather (together); join; (ennemis, anciens amis) reunite. **se réunir** unite; (amis) get together. **réunion** nf (séance) meeting; reunion; collection.

réussir [reysir] v succeed. **réussir à** succeed in; (examen) pass; (air, nourriture) agree with. **réussi** adj successful. **réussite** nf success; (cartes) patience.

revanche [rəvɑ̃ʃ] nf revenge. **en revanche** (au contraire) on the other hand; (en retour) in return.

rêvasser [rɛvase] v daydream.

rêve [rɛv] nm dream.

revêche [rəvɛʃ] adj surly.

réveiller [reveje] v wake (up); (raviver) rouse, reawaken, revive. **se réveiller** wake

up, awake. **réveil** nm waking; (à la réalité) awakening; (pendule) alarm clock. **réveillé** adj awake.

révéler [revele] v reveal. **révélateur, -trice** adj revealing. **révélation** nf revelation.

revendiquer [rəvɑ̃dike] v claim, demand. **revendication** nf claim, demand.

*__revenir__ [rəvnir] v come back, return. **revenir à** come to, amount to. **revenir à soi** come round. **revenir de** get over. **revenir sur** (promesse) go back on; (passé) go back over. **revenant, -e** nm, nf ghost. **revenu** nm income, revenue.

rêver [reve] v dream. **rêverie** nf daydream. **rêveur, -euse** adj dreamy.

réverbérer [reverbere] v reverberate, reflect. **réverbération** nf reverberation. **réverbère** nm street lamp.

révérence [reverɑ̃s] nf (homme) bow; (femme) curtsy; (respect) reverence. **faire une révérence** bow; curtsy.

revers [rəver] nm back; (monnaie) reverse; (tissu) wrong side; (veste) lapel; (manche) cuff. **réversible** adj reversible.

*__revêtir__ [rəvetir] v assume, take on; (habiller) clothe; cover, coat. **revêtement** nm covering, coating; surface.

revirement [rəvirmɑ̃] nm sudden change, reversal.

réviser [revize] v revise; (examiner) review; (voiture, machine) service, overhaul. **révision** nf revision; review; service.

*__revivre__ [rəvivrə] v relive. **faire revivre** revive.

*__revoir__ [rəvwar] v see again; revise. **au revoir!** goodbye!

révolter [revɔlte] v revolt, outrage. **se révolter** revolt, rebel. **révolte** nf revolt, rebellion.

révolution [revɔlysjɔ̃] nf revolution. **révolutionnaire** n(m+f), adj revolutionary. **révolutionner** v revolutionize.

revolver [revɔlver] nm gun, revolver.

révoquer [revɔke] v revoke; (destituer) dismiss.

revue [rəvy] nf review; (spectacle) revue; magazine; (mil) inspection.

rez-de-chaussée [redʃose] nm invar ground floor.

rhésus [rezys] nm rhesus. **rhésus négatif/positif** rhesus negative/positive.

rhétorique [retɔrik] nf rhetoric. adj rhetorical.

rhinocéros [rinɔserɔs] *nm* rhinoceros.
rhododendron [rɔdɔdɛ̃dr5] *nm* rhododendron.
rhubarbe [rybarb] *nf* rhubarb.
rhum [rɔm] *nm* rum.
rhumatisme [rymatismə] *nm* rheumatism.
rhumatismal *adj* rheumatic.
rhume [rym] *nm* cold. **rhume des foins** hay fever.
riant [rjɑ̃] *adj* cheerful, smiling.
ricaner [rikane] *v* snigger, sneer. **ricanement** *nm* snigger, sneer.
riche [riʃ] *adj* rich. *n(m+f)* rich person. **richesse** *nf* richness; (*argent*) wealth; abundance. **richesses** *nf pl* riches *pl.*
ride [rid] *nf* (*peau*) wrinkle; (*eau*) ripple. **rider** *v* wrinkle; ripple.
rideau [rido] *nm* curtain; (*écran*) screen. **rideau de fer** Iron Curtain.
ridicule [ridikyl] *adj* ridiculous. *nm* ridicule; absurdity. **ridiculiser** *v* ridicule.
rien [rjɛ̃] *pron* nothing; (*quelque chose*) anything. **ça ne fait rien** (*fam*) it doesn't matter. **de rien** (*fam*) not at all, you're welcome. **ne ... rien** nothing. *nm* nothing; (*bagatelle*) trivial thing; (*goutte*) touch, hint.
rigide [riʒid] *adj* rigid, stiff; strict. **rigidité** *nf* rigidity, stiffness; strictness.
rigole [rigɔl] *nf* channel; (*d'écoulement*) drain; (*sillon*) furrow.
rigoler [rigɔle] (*fam*) *v* (*plaisanter*) joke; (*rire*) laugh; (*s'amuser*) have fun. **rigolo, -ote** *adj* funny, comical.
rigoureux [rigurø] *adj* rigorous, (*sévère*) harsh; strict.
rigueur [rigœr] *nf* rigour; (*sévérité*) harshness; strictness; precision. **à la rigueur** if need be; possibly. **de rigueur** compulsory; (*étiquette*) the done thing.
rime [rim] *nf* rhyme. **rimer** *v* rhyme.
rincer [rɛ̃se] *v* rinse. **rinçage** *nm* rinse.
riposter [ripɔste] *v* retort; (*contre-attaquer*) retaliate. **riposte** *nf* retort.
***rire** [rir] *v* laugh; (*plaisanter*) joke; (*s'amuser*) have fun. **se rire de** laugh at. *nm* laugh; (*éclat*) laughter. **petit rire** chuckle. **petit rire nerveux** giggle.
ris [ri] *nm* **ris de veau** sweetbread.
risée [rize] *nf* ridicule; (*personne*) laughing stock.
risquer [riske] *v* risk. **risquer de** may well. **risque-tout** *n(m+f) invar* daredevil. **se risquer** venture. **risque** *nm* risk. **risqué** *adj* risky; (*licencieux*) risqué.

ristourne [risturn] *nf* rebate, refund.
rite [rit] *nm* rite.
rituel [ritɥɛl] *nm, adj* ritual.
rival [rival], **-e** *n, adj* rival.
rivaliser [rivalize] *v* **rivaliser avec** rival, vie with. **rivalité** *nf* rivalry.
rive [riv] *nf* (*mer*) shore; (*rivière*) bank. **rivage** *nm* shore.
river [rive] *v* rivet; (*lier*) bind. **rivet** *nm* rivet.
rivière [rivjɛr] *nf* river.
rixe [riks] *nf* brawl.
riz [ri] *nm* rice. **riz au lait** rice pudding.
robe [rɔb] *nf* dress; (*magistrat*) robe; (*professeur*) gown; (*peau*) skin. **robe-chasuble** *nf* pinafore dress. **robe de chambre** dressing-gown. **robe de grossesse** maternity dress, smock. **robe de mariée** wedding dress. **robe du soir** evening dress.
robinet [rɔbinɛ] *nm* tap.
robot [rɔbo] *nm* robot.
robuste [rɔbyst] *adj* robust.
roc [rɔk] *nm* rock. **rocaille** *nf* (*jardin*) rockery.
roche [rɔʃ] *nf* rock. **rocher** *nm* rock; (*gros bloc*) boulder.
roder [rɔde] *v* (*auto*) run in. **en rodage** running in.
rôder [rode] *v* (*en maraude*) prowl; (*au hasard*) roam. **rôdeur, -euse** *nm, nf* prowler.
rogner [rɔɲe] *v* trim, clip; (*dépense*) whittle down.
rognon [rɔɲ3] *nm* kidney.
rogue [rɔg] *adj* haughty, arrogant.
roi [rwa] *nm* king. **la fête des Rois** Twelfth Night.
roitelet [rwatlɛ] *nm* wren.
rôle [rol] *nm* role, part; (*liste*) roll.
romain [rɔmɛ̃] *adj* Roman. **Romain, -e** *nm, nf* Roman.
roman¹ [rɔmɑ̃] *nm* novel; (*récit*) story. **roman-feuilleton** *nm* serial. **roman policier** detective story. **romans** *nm pl* fiction *sing.* **romancier, -ère** *nm, nf* novelist.
roman² [rɔmɑ̃] *adj* (*langue*) Romance; (*arch*) Romanesque.
romanesque [rɔmanɛsk] *adj* (*personne*) romantic; (*récit*) fantastic; (*amour*) storybook.
romantique [rɔmɑ̃tik] *n(m+f), adj* romantic.

romarin [rɔmarɛ̃] *nm* rosemary.

Rome [rɔm] *n* Rome.

rompre [rɔ̃prə] *v* break. **rompu** *adj* broken; (*fatigué*) exhausted. **rompu à** experienced in.

romsteck [rɔmstɛk] *nm* rump steak.

ronce [rɔs] *nf* bramble; (*mûrier*) blackberry bush.

rond [rɔ̃] *adj* round; (*gras*) chubby, plump; (*fam*) drunk. **rond-de-cuir** *nm* clerk. **rond-point** *nm* roundabout. *nm* ring; (*tranche*) slice. **en rond** in a circle. **ronde** *nf* patrol, rounds *pl*; (*musique*) semibreve. **rondelle** *nf* washer; disc. **rondement** *adv* (*promptement*) briskly; frankly. **rondeur** *nf* roundness; plumpness. **rondin** *nm* log.

ronfler [rɔ̃fle] *v* snore; (*rugir*) roar; (*vrombir*) hum. **ronflement** *nm* snore; roar; hum.

ronger [rɔ̃ʒe] *v* gnaw at, eat into; (*malade*) sap. **se ronger les ongles** bite one's nails. **rongeur** *nm* rodent.

ronronner [rɔ̃rɔne] *v* purr. **ronron** *or* **ronronnement** *nm* purr.

roquet [rɔkɛ] *nm* ill-tempered little dog.

roquette [rɔkɛt] *nf* rocket.

rosaire [rozɛr] *nm* rosary.

rosbif [rɔsbif] *nm* roast beef.

rose [roz] *nf* rose. *nm* pink. *adj* pink; (*joues*) rosy. **roseraie** *nf* rose garden. **rosier** *nm* rose-bush.

roseau [rozo] *nm* reed.

rosée [roze] *nf* dew.

rosette [rozɛt] *nf* rosette; (*nœud*) bow.

rosser [rɔse] *v* thrash. **rossée** *nf* (*fam*) thrashing, hiding.

rossignol [rɔsiɲɔl] *nm* nightingale; (*fam*) piece of junk.

rot [ro] (*fam*) *nm* burp. **roter** *v* burp.

rotatif [rɔtatif] *adj* rotary.

rôtir [rotir] *v* roast. **rôti** *nm* joint, roast. **rôtisserie** *nf* steak-house.

rotor [rɔtɔr] *nm* rotor.

rotule [rɔtyl] *nf* kneecap.

rouage [rwaʒ] *nm* cog; part. **rouages** *nm pl* works *pl*.

roublard [rublar] *adj* (*fam*) crafty, wily.

roucouler [rukule] *v* coo. **roucoulement** *nm* coo.

roue [ru] *nf* wheel. **faire la roue** (*se pavaner*) strut about; (*gymnaste*) do a cart-wheel. **roue de secours** spare wheel.

roué [rwe] *adj* cunning.

rouge [ruʒ] *adj* red. **rouge-gorge** *nm* robin. *nm* red; (*fard*) rouge. **rouge à lèvres** lipstick. **rougeur** *nf* redness; (*visage*) flush, flushing; (*de gêne, honte*) blush, blushing.

rougeole [ruʒɔl] *nf* measles.

rougir [ruʒir] *v* go *or* turn red, redden; (*visage*) flush; (*de gêne, honte*) blush.

rouiller [ruje] *v* rust, go rusty. **rouille** *nf* rust. **rouillé** *adj* rusty.

rouleau [rulo] *nm* roller; (*papier, pellicule, tabac, etc.*) roll; (*parchemin*) scroll. **rouleau à pâtisserie** rolling pin. **rouleau compresseur** steam-roller. **rouleau de papier hygiénique** toilet roll.

rouler [rule] *v* roll; (*enrouler*) roll up; (*pousser*) wheel; (*aller*) go, run; (*conduire*) drive; (*fam: duper*) con, diddle. **roulant** *adj* moving; (*meuble*) on wheels; (*argot*) hilarious. **roulement** *nm* roll; movement; (*bruit*) rumble. **roulement à billes** ball bearings *pl*. **roulette** *nf* castor; (*jeu*) roulette.

roulotte [rulɔt] *nf* caravan.

Roumanie [rumani] *nf* Romania. **roumain** *nm*, *adj* Romanian. **Roumain, -e** *nm*, *nf* Romanian.

roupiller [rupije] (*fam*) *v* snooze. **roupillon** *nm* snooze.

rouquin [rukɛ̃], **-e** (*fam*) *nm*, *nf* redhead. *adj* red-haired.

rouspéter [ruspete] *v* (*fam*) moan, grumble.

roussir [rusir] *v* (*brûler*) scorch, singe; (*feuilles*) go brown. **rousseur** *nf* redness.

route [rut] *nf* road; (*chemin*) way; (*ligne*) route. **en route** on the way. **en route pour** bound for. **se mettre en route** set off. **routier** *adj* road.

routine [rutin] *nf* routine. **routinier** *adj* humdrum, routine.

*rouvrir [ruvrir] *v* reopen.

roux, rousse [ru, rus] *adj* reddish-brown; (*cheveux*) red, auburn, ginger. *nm*, *nf* redhead.

royal [rwajal] *adj* royal; majestic, regal. **royaliste** *n(m+f)*, *adj* royalist. **royauté** *nf* royalty; monarchy.

royaume [rwajom] *nm* kingdom, realm. **Royaume-Uni** *nm* United Kingdom.

ruban [rybã] *nm* ribbon; band, tape.

rubéole [rybeɔl] *nf* German measles.

rubis [rybi] *nm* ruby.

rubrique [rybrik] *nf* (*article*) column; (*titre*) heading.

ruche [ryʃ] *nf* hive.
rude [ryd] *adj* (*pénible, dur*) hard, harsh; (*surface*) rough; (*grossier*) crude. **rudement** *adv* harshly; roughly; (*fam*) terribly, awfully. **rudesse** *nf* harshness; roughness; crudeness.
rudiment [rydimã] *nm* rudiment. **rudimentaire** *adj* rudimentary.
rudoyer [rydwaje] *v* treat roughly.
rue [ry] *nf* street. **rue à sens unique** one-way street. **ruelle** *nf* alley.
ruer [rɥe] *v* kick out. **se ruer** dash, rush, hurl oneself. **se ruer sur** pounce on. **ruée** *nf* rush, stampede.
rugby [rygbi] *nm* rugby.
rugir [ryʒir] *v* roar. **rugissement** *nm* roar.
rugueux [rygø] *adj* rough. **rugosité** *nf* roughness.
ruine [rɥin] *nf* ruin. **ruiner** *v* ruin.
ruisseau [rɥiso] *nm* stream; (*caniveau*) gutter.
ruisseler [rɥisle] *v* stream.
rumeur [rymœr] *nf* (*nouvelle*) rumour; (*son*) murmur, hum, hubbub.
rupture [ryptyr] *nf* rupture, break. **rupture de contrat** breach of contract.
rural [ryral] *adj* rural, country.
ruse [ryz] *nf* (*procédé*) trick, ruse; (*art*) cunning, guile. **ruses de guerre** tactics *pl*. **rusé** *adj* sly, cunning.
Russie [rysi] *nf* Russia. **russe** *nm, adj* Russian. **Russe** *n(m+f)* Russian.
rustique [rystik] *adj* rustic.
rustre [rystrə] *nm* lout.
rutabaga [rytabaga] *nm* swede.
rythme [ritmə] *nm* rhythm; (*vitesse*) rate. **rythmé** *or* **rythmique** *adj* rhythmic.

S

s' [s] *V* **se, si**[1].
sa [sa] *V* **son**[1].
sabbat [saba] *nm* sabbath.
sable[1] [sablə] *nm* sand. **sables mouvants** quicksands *pl*. **sabler** *v* sand. **sableux** *or* **sablonneux** *adj* sandy. **sablier** *nm* hourglass.
sable[2] [sablə] *nm* sable.
sablé [sable] *nm* shortbread.
saborder [saborde] *v* scuttle.

sabot [sabo] *nm* (*chaussure*) clog; (*animal*) hoof.
saboter [sabote] *v* sabotage. **sabotage** *nm* sabotage. **saboteur, -euse** *nm, nf* saboteur.
sabre [sabrə] *nm* sabre.
sac [sak] *nm* bag; (*à charbon, etc.*) sack. **sac à dos** rucksack. **sac à main** handbag. **sac à provisions** shopping bag. **sac de couchage** sleeping bag.
saccade [sakad] *nf* jerk. **par saccades** jerkily, in fits and starts. **saccadé** *adj* jerky.
saccager [sakaʒe] *v* wreck, devastate; (*piller*) ransack. **saccage** *nm* havoc.
saccharine [sakarin] *nf* saccharin.
sacerdoce [saserdos] *nm* priesthood.
sachet [saʃɛ] *nm* sachet; (*bonbons*) bag. **sachet de thé** tea-bag.
sacoche [sakɔʃ] *nf* bag; (*cycliste*) saddlebag; (*écolier*) satchel.
sacquer [sake] (*fam*) *v* sack; (*recaler*) fail.
sacrement [sakrəmã] *nm* sacrament.
sacrer [sakre] *v* consecrate; (*roi*) crown; (*fam*) swear. **sacre** *nm* consecration; (*roi*) coronation. **sacré** *adj* sacred; (*fam*) blasted, damned.
sacrifier [sakrifje] *v* sacrifice. **sacrifice** *nm* sacrifice.
sacrilège [sakrilɛʒ] *nm* sacrilege. *adj* sacrilegious.
sacristie [sakristi] *nf* vestry.
sadique [sadik] *adj* sadistic. *n(m+f)* sadist. **sadisme** *nm* sadism.
safari [safari] *nm* safari.
safran [safrã] *nm* saffron.
saga [saga] *nf* saga.
sagace [sagas] *adj* shrewd. **sagacité** *nf* shrewdness.
sage [saʒ] *adj* wise, sensible; (*enfant*) good; moderate. **sage-femme** *nf* midwife. **sois sage!** be good! behave yourself! *nm* wise man, sage. **sagesse** *nf* wisdom; good behaviour; moderation.
Sagittaire [saʒitɛr] *nm* Sagittarius.
sagou [sagu] *nm* sago.
saigner [seɲe] *v* bleed. **saignant** *adj* bleeding; (*viande*) rare, underdone.
saillir [sajir] *v* jut out, protrude. **saillant** *adj* prominent, protruding; (*frappant*) outstanding. **saillie** *nf* projection; (*boutade*) witticism. **en saillie** overhanging.
sain [sɛ̃] *adj* healthy; (*d'esprit*) sane;

(*robuste*) sound. **sain et sauf** safe and sound.

saindoux [sɛ̃du] *nm* lard.

saint [sɛ̃], **-e** *adj* holy; pious, saintly. *nm, nf* saint. **Saint-Esprit** *nm* Holy Spirit. **Saint-Jean** *nm* Midsummer Day. **saint patron** patron saint. **Saint-Sylvestre** *nf* New Year's Eve. **sainteté** *nf* holiness, sanctity; saintliness.

saisir [sezir] *v* seize, take hold of; (*comprendre*) grasp; (*serrer*) grip. **saisie** *nf* seizure; capture. **saisissant** *adj* (*spectacle*) gripping; (*frappant*) striking; (*froid*) biting. **saisissement** *nm* (*frisson*) shiver; rush of emotion.

saison [sczɔ̃] *nf* season. **hors de saison** out of season; (*prix*) low-season. **saisonnier** *adj* seasonal.

salade [salad] *nf* salad; (*laitue*) lettuce; (*fam*) muddle.

salaire [salɛr] *nm* pay; (*à la semaine*) wages *pl*; (*au mois*) salary; (*récompense*) reward.

salami [salami] *nm* salami.

salaud [salo] *nm* (*impol*) bastard, sod.

sale [sal] *adj* dirty; (*fam*) nasty, lousy. **saleté** *nf* dirt; obscenity; (*sale tour*) dirty trick; (*fam: camelote*) rubbish.

saler [sale] *v* salt; (*fam*) do, overcharge. **salé** *adj* salty; salted; (*fam: grivois*) spicy; (*fam: sévère*) stiff, steep. **salière** *nf* salt-cellar.

salin [salɛ̃] *adj* saline. **salinité** *nf* salinity.

salir [salir] *v* dirty, soil; corrupt, sully. **se salir** get dirty; tarnish one's reputation.

salive [saliv] *nf* saliva. **salivaire** *adj* salivary. **saliver** *v* salivate.

salle [sal] *nf* room; hall; auditorium; (*hôpital*) ward. **salle à manger** dining room. **salle d'attente** waiting room. **salle de bain** bathroom. **salle de bal** ballroom. **salle de classe** classroom. **salle de séjour** living room. **salle des professeurs** staffroom. **salle d'opération** operating theatre.

saloperie [salɔpri] (*argot*) *nf* (*camelote*) rubbish; (*ordure*) muck; (*sale tour*) dirty trick.

salopette [salɔpɛt] *nf* (*ouvrier*) overalls *pl*; (*enfant, femme*) dungarees *pl*; (*ski*) salopette.

saltimbanque [saltɛ̃bɑ̃k] *n(m+f)* acrobat, member of travelling circus.

salubre [salybrə] *adj* healthy.

saluer [salɥe] *v* greet; (*mil*) salute; (*acteur*) bow; (*acclamer*) hail.

salut [saly] *nm* (*mil*) salute; (*salutation*) greeting; (*révérence*) bow; (*sécurité*) safety; (*rel*) salvation. *interj* (*fam: bonjour*) hi! (*fam: au revoir*) bye! **salutation** *nf* greeting.

salutaire [salytɛr] *adj* salutary, beneficial; profitable; (*sain*) healthy.

samedi [samdi] *nm* Saturday.

sanatorium [sanatɔrjɔm] *nm* sanatorium.

sanctifier [sɑ̃ktifje] *v* hallow, sanctify. **sanctification** *nf* sanctification.

sanction [sɑ̃ksjɔ̃] *nf* sanction; (*peine*) punishment, penalty. **sanctionner** *v* sanction; punish.

sanctuaire [sɑ̃ktɥɛr] *nm* sanctuary.

sandale [sɑ̃dal] *nf* sandal.

sandwich [sɑ̃dwitʃ] *nm* sandwich.

sang [sɑ̃] *nm* blood. **à sang chaud/froid** warm-/cold-blooded. **sang-froid** *nm invar* calmness, coolness. **sang-mêlé** *n(m+f) invar* half-caste.

sanglant [sɑ̃glɑ̃] *adj* bloody; (*visage, habit, etc.*) covered in blood; cruel.

sangle [sɑ̃glə] *nf* strap; (*selle*) girth. **sangler** *v* strap up.

sanglier [sɑ̃glije] *nm* boar.

sanglot [sɑ̃glo] *nm* sob. **sangloter** *v* sob.

sangsue [sɑ̃sy] *nf* leech.

sanguin [sɑ̃gɛ̃] *adj* blood; (*visage*) ruddy; (*tempérament*) fiery. **sanguinaire** *adj* bloodthirsty.

sanitaire [sanitɛr] *adj* sanitary.

sans [sɑ̃] *prep* without; but for. **sans-abri** *n(m+f) invar* homeless person. **sans ça** or else. **sans faute** without fail. **sans-gêne** *adj invar* offhand. **sans quoi** otherwise. **sans-souci** *adj invar* carefree.

sansonnet [sɑ̃sɔnɛ] *nm* starling.

santé [sɑ̃te] *nf* health. **à votre santé!** cheers!

saper [sape] *v* undermine, sap.

sapeur [sapœr] *nm* (*mil*) sapper. **sapeur-pompier** *nm* fireman.

saphir [safir] *nm* sapphire.

sapin [sapɛ̃] *nm* fir.

sarcasme [sarkasmə] *nm* sarcasm. **sarcastique** *adj* sarcastic.

sarcler [sarkle] *v* weed. **sarclage** *nm* weeding.

Sardaigne [sardɛɲ] *nf* Sardinia. **sarde** *nm, adj* Sardinian. **Sarde** *n(m+f)* Sardinian.

sardine [sardin] *nf* sardine.

sardonique [sardɔnik] *adj* sardonic.

Satan [satɑ̃] *nm* Satan. **satanique** *adj* satanic.

satellite [satelit] *nm* satellite.

satin [satɛ̃] *nm* satin.

satire [satir] *nf* satire. **faire la satire de** satirize. **satirique** *adj* satirical.

satisfaction [satisfaksjɔ̃] *nf* satisfaction.

*satisfaire [satisfɛr] *v* satisfy. **satisfaire à** satisfy; (*condition*) fulfil. **satisfaisant** *adj* satisfactory. **satisfait** *adj* satisfied.

saturer [satyre] *v* saturate. **saturation** *nf* saturation.

sauce [sos] *nf* sauce; (*jus de viande*) gravy.

saucée [sose] *nf* (*fam*) downpour.

saucisse [sosis] *nf* sausage. **saucisson** *nm* large sausage.

sauf [sof] *adj* unharmed; intact. *prep* except, but; (*à moins de*) unless.

sauge [soʒ] *nf* sage.

saugrenu [sogrəny] *adj* ludicrous.

saule [sol] *nm* willow.

saumon [somɔ̃] *nm* salmon.

saumure [somyr] *nf* brine.

sauna [sona] *nm* sauna.

saupoudrer [sopudre] *v* sprinkle. **saupoudreuse** *nf* dredger.

saut [so] *nm* jump, leap. **saut à la corde** skipping. **saut-de-lit** *nm invar* housecoat. **saut-de-mouton** *nm* flyover. **saut en hauteur/longueur** high/long jump. **saut périlleux** somersault.

sauter [sote] *v* jump, leap; explode; (*fusible*) blow; (*omettre*) skip. **faire sauter** (*mine, etc.*) blow up; (*crêpe*) toss. **saute-mouton** *nm* leapfrog. **saute** *nf* sudden change. **sauté** *adj* sauté. **sauterelle** *nf* grasshopper. **sauterie** *nf* party.

sautiller [sotije] *v* hop; (*enfant*) skip.

sauvage [sovaʒ] *adj* wild; (*brutal, primitif*) savage; unsociable. *n(m+f)* savage; recluse. **sauvagerie** *nf* savagery.

sauvegarder [sovgarde] *v* safeguard. **sauvegarde** *nf* safeguard.

sauver [sove] *v* save, rescue; (*récupérer*) salvage. **sauve-qui-peut** *nm invar* stampede. **se sauver** run away. **sauvetage** *nm* rescue; (*technique*) life-saving; salvage. **sauveur** *nm* saviour.

savant [savɑ̃] *adj* learned, scholarly; (*habile*) skilful; (*chien*) performing. *nm* scholar; scientist.

savate [savat] (*fam*) *nf* old shoe *or* slipper; (*maladroit*) clumsy oaf.

saveur [savœr] *nf* (*goût*) flavour; (*piment*) savour.

*savoir [savwar] *v* know; (*être capable de*) know how to. **à savoir** namely, that is. **faire savoir à** inform. **sans le savoir** unknowingly. *nm* learning, knowledge.

savon [savɔ̃] *nm* soap. **savonner** *v* soap, lather. **savonneux** *adj* soapy.

savourer [savure] *v* savour. **savoureux** *adj* tasty; (*histoire*) spicy.

saxophone [saksɔfɔn] *nm* saxophone.

scabreux [skabrø] *adj* indecent, shocking; risky.

scandale [skɑ̃dal] *nm* scandal; scene, fuss. **scandaleux** *adj* scandalous. **scandaliser** *v* scandalize, shock.

Scandinavie [skɑ̃dinavi] *nf* Scandinavia. **scandinave** *adj* Scandinavian. **Scandinave** *n(m+f)* Scandinavian.

scaphandrier [skafɑ̃drije] *nm* diver.

scarlatine [skarlatin] *nf* scarlet fever.

sceau [so] *nm* seal; (*marque*) stamp.

scélérat [selera], **-e** *nm, nf* villain. *adj* wicked.

sceller [sele] *v* seal.

scénario [senarjo] *nm* scenario; (*dialogue, etc.*) screenplay.

scène [sɛn] *nf* scene; (*estrade, profession*) stage. **mettre en scène** present; (*pièce*) stage; (*film*) direct. **scénique** *adj* theatrical.

sceptique [sɛptik] *adj* sceptical. *n(m+f)* sceptic. **scepticisme** *nm* scepticism.

sceptre [sɛptrə] *nm* sceptre.

schéma [ʃema] *nm* diagram; (*résumé*) outline.

schizophrénie [skizɔfreni] *nf* schizophrenia. **schizophrène** *n(m+f)*, *adj* schizophrenic.

sciatique [sjatik] *nf* sciatica. *adj* sciatic.

scie [si] *nf* saw; (*péj: personne*) bore. **scie à découper** fretsaw. **scie à métaux** hacksaw.

sciemment [sjamɑ̃] *adv* knowingly.

science [sjɑ̃s] *nf* science; (*savoir*) knowledge. **science-fiction** *nf* science fiction.

scientifique [sjɑ̃tifik] *adj* scientific. *n(m+f)* scientist.

scintiller [sɛ̃tije] *v* sparkle, glitter; (*esprit*) scintillate.

scolaire [skɔlɛr] *adj* school, scholastic. **scolarité** *nf* schooling.

scooter [skutɛr] *nm* scooter.

scorpion [skɔrpjɔ̃] *nm* scorpion. **Scorpion** *nm* Scorpio.

scotch¹ [skɔtʃ] *nm* (*boisson*) Scotch.
scotch² ® [skɔtʃ] *nm* sellotape ®
scrupule [skrypyl] *nm* scruple. **sans scrupules** *adj* unscrupulous. **scrupuleux** *adj* scrupulous.
scruter [skryte] *v* scrutinize, examine.
scrutin [skrytɛ̃] *nm* (*vote*) ballot; (*élection*) poll.
sculpter [skylte] *v* sculpt. **sculpteur** *nm* sculptor. **sculpture** *nf* sculpture.
se [sə], **s'** *pron* (*réfléchi*) oneself; (*homme*) himself; (*femme*) herself; (*chose, animal*) itself; (*au pluriel*) themselves; (*réciproque*) each other.
séance [seɑ̃s] *nf* session; (*réunion*) meeting; (*théâtre*) performance.
séant [seɑ̃] *nm* (*fam*) behind, posterior. *adj* seemly.
seau [so] *nm* bucket.
sec, sèche [sɛk, sɛʃ] *adj* dry; (*raisin, etc.*) dried; (*maigre*) lean; (*dur*) hard, cold; (*bref*) curt; (*alcool*) neat. *nm* **à sec** dried-up; (*fam*) broke. **au sec** in a dry place. *nf* (*argot*) fag. *adv* hard. **sécheresse** *nf* dryness; hardness; coldness; curtness.
sécher [seʃe] *v* dry. **sèche-cheveux** *nm invar* hair-drier. **séchoir** *nm* drier. **séchoir à linge** clothes-horse.
second [səgɔ̃] *adj* second. *nm* second; (*étage*) second floor. **seconde** *nf* second; (*transport*) second class. **secondaire** *adj* secondary.
secouer [səkwe] *v* shake.
***secourir** [səkurir] *v* help.
secours [səkur] *nm* help, aid; (*mil*) relief. **au secours!** help! **de secours** (*de rechange*) spare; (*d'urgence*) emergency.
secousse [səkus] *nf* jolt, bump; shock; (*saccade*) jerk. **par secousses** jerkily.
secret, -ète [səkrɛ, -ɛt] *adj* secret; (*caché*) hidden. *nm* secret; (*silence, discrétion*) secrecy. **en secret** secretly, in secret.
secrétaire [səkretɛr] *n(m+f)* secretary. *nm* (*meuble*) writing desk.
sécréter [sekrete] *v* secrete. **sécrétion** *nf* secretion.
secte [sɛkt] *nf* sect. **sectaire** *adj* sectarian.
secteur [sɛktœr] *nm* sector; (*zone*) area; (*élec*) mains (supply).
section [sɛksjɔ̃] *nf* section; (*autobus*) fare stage.
séculaire [sekylɛr] *adj* a hundred years old; (*très vieux*) age-old; (*jeux, fête, etc.*) occurring once a century.
séculier [sekylje] *adj* secular.

sécurité [sekyrite] *nf* security; (*sûreté*) safety.
sédatif [sedatif] *nm, adj* sedative. **sédation** *nf* sedation.
sédiment [sedimɑ̃] *nm* sediment.
***séduire** [sedɥir] *v* seduce; (*attirer*) charm; (*plaire*) appeal to. **séduction** *nf* seduction; charm; appeal. **séduisant** *adj* seductive; appealing, attractive.
segment [sɛgmɑ̃] *nm* segment.
ségrégation [segregasjɔ̃] *nf* segregation.
seigle [sɛglə] *nm* rye.
seigneur [sɛɲœr] *nm* lord.
sein [sɛ̃] *nm* breast; (*milieu*) bosom.
séisme [seismə] *nm* earthquake; (*bouleversement*) upheaval.
seize [sɛz] *nm, adj* sixteen. **seizième** *n(m+f)*, *adj* sixteenth.
séjour [seʒur] *nm* stay; (*demeure*) abode. **séjourner** *v* stay.
sel [sɛl] *nm* salt; (*esprit*) wit; (*piquant*) spice. **sel de cuisine/table** cooking/table salt.
sélection [seleksjɔ̃] *nf* selection. **sélectif** *adj* selective.
sélectionner [seleksjɔne] *v* select.
selle [sɛl] *nf* saddle. **seller** *v* saddle. **sellerie** *nf* saddlery; (*lieu*) harness room. **sellier** *nm* saddler.
selon [səlɔ̃] *prep* according to.
Seltz [sɛls] *nf* **eau de Seltz** soda water.
semaine [səmɛn] *nf* week.
sémantique [semɑ̃tik] *adj* semantic. *nf* semantics.
sémaphore [semafɔr] *nm* semaphore.
sembler [sɑ̃ble] *v* seem. **semblable** *adj* similar; (*tel*) such. **semblable à** like. **semblant** *nm* semblance. **faire semblant de** pretend.
semelle [səmɛl] *nf* sole. **semelle intérieure** insole. **semelles compensées** platform soles *pl*.
semence [səmɑ̃s] *nf* seed.
semer [səme] *v* sow; (*en dispersant*) scatter; (*parsemer*) sprinkle, dot.
semestre [səmɛstrə] *nm* half-year. **semestriel** *adj* half-yearly.
séminaire [seminɛr] *nm* (*université*) seminar; (*rel*) seminary.
semi-précieux *adj* semi-precious.
semoule [səmul] *nf* semolina.
sempiternel [sɛpitɛrnɛl] *adj* never-ending.
sénat [sena] *nm* senate. **sénateur** *nm* senator.

sénile [senil] *adj* senile. **sénilité** *nf* senility.

sens [sɑ̃s] *nm* sense; direction; (*signification*) meaning. **à sens unique** (*rue*) one-way. **bon sens** common sense. **dans le sens des aiguilles d'une montre** clockwise. **sens dessus dessous** upside down. **sens devant derrière** back to front. **sens interdit** no entry.

sensation [sɑ̃sɑsjɔ̃] *nf* sensation; (*impression*) feeling. **sensationnel** *adj* sensational; (*fam*) fantastic, terrific.

sensé [sɑ̃se] *adj* sensible.

sensible [sɑ̃siblə] *adj* sensitive; perceptible, noticeable; (*cœur*) tender; (*impressionnable*) susceptible. **sensibilité** *nf* sensitivity.

sensuel [sɑ̃sɥɛl] *adj* (*charnel*) sensual; (*esthétique*) sensuous. **sensualité** *nf* sensuality; sensuousness.

sentence [sɑ̃tɑ̃s] *nf* (*jur*) sentence; maxim.

sentier [sɑ̃tje] *nm* path.

sentiment [sɑ̃timɑ̃] *nm* feeling; (*péj*) sentiment. **sentimental** *adj* sentimental.

sentinelle [sɑ̃tinɛl] *nf* sentry.

*****sentir** [sɑ̃tir] *v* feel; (*odeur*) smell; (*goût*) taste; (*pressentir*) sense; (*être conscient de*) be aware of.

*****seoir** [swar] *v* be fitting. **seoir à** become.

séparer [separe] *v* separate; (*diviser*) part, split. **séparation** *nf* separation; parting; division. **séparé** *adj* separated; (*éloigné*) apart.

sept [sɛt] *nm, adj* seven. **septième** *n(m+f), adj* seventh.

septembre [sɛptɑ̃brə] *nm* September.

septentrional [sɛptɑ̃trijɔnal] *adj* northern.

septique [sɛptik] *adj* septic.

séquence [sekɑ̃s] *nf* sequence.

serein [sərɛ̃] *adj* serene, calm.

sérénade [serenad] *nf* serenade.

serf [sɛrf], **serve** *nm, nf* serf.

sergent [sɛrʒɑ̃] *nm* sergeant.

série [seri] *nf* series; (*ensemble*) set. **de série** standard. **fait en série** mass-produced. **hors série** (*machine*) custom-built; (*qualité*) outstanding.

sérieux [serjø] *adj* serious; (*sage*) responsible; (*sûr*) reliable; (*grand*) considerable. *nm* seriousness. **prendre au sérieux** take seriously.

serin [sərɛ̃] *nm* canary.

seringue [sərɛ̃g] *nf* syringe.

serment [sɛrmɑ̃] *nm* oath.

sermon [sɛrmɔ̃] *nm* sermon.

serpent [sɛrpɑ̃] *nm* snake, serpent. **serpent à sonnettes** rattlesnake.

serpenter [sɛrpɑ̃te] *v* snake, wind.

serre [sɛr] *nf* greenhouse; (*contiguë à une maison*) conservatory; (*griffe*) talon. **serre chaude** hothouse.

serrer [sere] *v* grip; (*dents, poings*) clench; (*vêtement*) be tight; (*nœud, écrou*) tighten; (*rester près de*) keep close to; (*rapprocher*) close up. **serrer la main à** shake hands with. **se serrer** squeeze up, crowd together. **serré** *adj* tight; (*personnes*) packed, crowded; dense.

serrure [seryr] *nf* lock. **serrurier** *nm* locksmith.

servante [sɛrvɑ̃t] *nf* servant, maid.

serveur [sɛrvœr] *nm* (*restaurant*) waiter; (*bar*) barman. **serveuse** *nf* waitress; barmaid.

service [sɛrvis] *nm* service; (*travail*) duty; department; (*ensemble*) set. **être de service** be on duty. **service à thé** tea-set.

serviette [sɛrvjɛt] *nf* (*de toilette*) towel; (*de table*) serviette; (*cartable*) briefcase. **serviette hygiénique** sanitary towel.

servile [sɛrvil] *adj* servile. **servilité** *nf* servility.

*****servir** [sɛrvir] *v* serve; (*dîneur, patron*) wait on; (*client*) attend to; aid. **servir à** be used for; (*être utile*) be useful for. **servir de** act as. **se servir** help oneself. **se servir de** use.

serviteur [sɛrvitœr] *nm* servant.

ses [se] *V* **son¹**.

session [sesjɔ̃] *nf* session.

seuil [sœj] *nm* threshold; (*porte*) doorway; (*dalle*) doorstep.

seul [sœl] *adj* only; (*sans compagnie*) alone; (*isolé*) lonely; (*unique*) single, sole. *adv* by oneself. **seulement** *adv* only.

sève [sɛv] *nf* sap.

sévère [sevɛr] *adj* severe. **sévérité** *nf* severity.

sévir [sevir] *v* act ruthlessly; punish severely; (*régime, fléau*) rage.

sexe [sɛks] *nm* sex. **sexualité** *nf* sexuality. **sexuel** *adj* sexual, sex.

sextuor [sɛkstɥɔr] *nm* sextet.

shampooing [ʃɑ̃pwɛ̃] *nm* shampoo.

shérif [ʃerif] *nm* sheriff.

short [ʃɔrt] *nm* shorts *pl*.

si¹ [si], **s'** *conj* if.

si² [si] *adv* so; (*aussi*) as; (*oui*) yes. **si bien que** so that. **si ... que** however.

siamois [sjamwa] *adj* Siamese.

sidérer [sidere] *v* (*fam*) stagger, shatter.

siècle [sjɛklə] *nm* century; (*époque*) age.

siège [sjɛʒ] *nm* seat; (*organisation*) headquarters; (*épiscopal*) see; (*mil*) siege. **siège éjectable** ejector seat.

siéger [sjeʒe] *v* be located; (*tenir séance*) sit.

sien [sjɛ̃], **sienne** *pron* **le sien, la sienne** (*homme*) his; (*femme*) hers; (*chose, animal*) its own; (*réfléchi*) one's own.

sieste [sjɛst] *nf* siesta; (*petit somme*) nap.

siffler [sifle] *v* whistle; (*serpent, gaz*) hiss. **sifflement** *nm* whistle, hiss. **sifflet** *nm* whistle.

signal [siɲal] *nm* signal.

signaler [siɲale] *v* indicate; (*faire un signe*) signal; (*faire un exposé*) report. **se signaler** stand out, distinguish oneself. **signalement** *nm* description.

signature [siɲatyr] *nf* signature; (*action*) signing.

signe [siɲ] *nm* sign; mark. **faire signe à** beckon. **signet** *nm* bookmark.

signer [siɲe] *v* sign.

signifier [siɲifje] *v* mean, signify. **significatif** *adj* significant. **signification** *nf* significance, meaning.

silence [silɑ̃s] *nm* silence; pause; (*musique*) rest.

silencieux [silɑ̃sjø] *adj* silent. *nm* silencer.

silex [silɛks] *nm* flint.

silhouette [silwɛt] *nf* silhouette, outline; figure.

sillage [sijaʒ] *nm* wake.

sillon [sijɔ̃] *nm* furrow; (*disque*) groove. **sillonner** *v* furrow; (*traverser*) cross.

simagrée [simagre] *nf* pretence. **simagrées** *nf pl* fuss *sing*, play-acting *sing*.

simple [sɛ̃plə] *adj* simple; (*billet*) single. **simplement** *adv* simply; (*seulement*) merely, just. **simplicité** *nf* simplicity. **simplifier** *v* simplify.

simulacre [simylakrə] *nm* pretence, show.

simuler [simyle] *v* simulate; feign. **simulation** *nf* simulation. **simulé** *adj* simulated; feigned, sham.

simultané [simyltane] *adj* simultaneous.

sincère [sɛ̃sɛr] *adj* sincere; (*authentique*) genuine, true. **sincérité** *nf* sincerity.

singe [sɛ̃ʒ] *nm* monkey, ape.

singer [sɛ̃ʒe] *v* mimic, ape. **singeries** *nf pl* antics *pl*, clowning *sing*.

singulier [sɛ̃gylje] *adj* (*gramm*) singular; remarkable; uncommon. *nm* singular. **singularité** *nf* peculiarity. **singulièrement** *adv* remarkably; strangely; particularly.

sinistre [sinistrə] *adj* sinister. *nm* disaster; (*assurances*) damage, loss.

sinon [sinɔ̃] *conj* if not; (*autrement*) otherwise; (*sauf*) except, other than.

sinueux [sinɥø] *adj* winding; (*ligne*) sinuous.

sinus [sinys] *nm invar* (*anat*) sinus. **sinusite** *nf* sinusitis.

siphon [sifɔ̃] *nm* siphon. **siphonner** *v* siphon.

sirène [sirɛn] *nf* siren; (*mythologie*) mermaid.

sirop [siro] *nm* syrup; (*boisson*) squash, cordial. **sirupeux** *adj* syrupy.

siroter [sirɔte] *v* sip.

site [sit] *nm* site; (*environnement*) setting; (*tourisme*) beauty spot, place of interest.

sitôt [sito] *adv* immediately, no sooner. **sitôt que** as soon as.

situer [sitɥe] *v* situate, locate; (*par la pensée*) place. **situation** *nf* situation; position; (*emploi*) job.

six [sis] *nm, adj* six. **sixième** *n(m+f), adj* sixth.

ski [ski] *nm* ski; (*sport*) skiing. **faire du ski** ski, go skiing. **ski nautique** water-skiing. **skieur, -euse** *nm, nf* skier.

slalom [slalɔm] *nm* slalom.

slip [slip] *nm* briefs *pl*, pants *pl*. **slip de bain** (*homme*) trunks *pl*.

slogan [slɔgɑ̃] *nm* slogan.

smoking [smɔkiŋ] *nm* dinner jacket.

snob [snɔb] *n(m+f)* snob. *adj* snobbish.

sobre [sɔbrə] *adj* temperate, abstemious; (*repas*) frugal; (*style*) sober. **sobriété** *nf* temperance; frugality; (*modération*) restraint; sobriety.

sobriquet [sɔbrikɛ] *nm* nickname.

sociable [sɔsjablə] *adj* sociable.

social [sɔsjal] *adj* social. **socialisme** *nm* socialism. **socialiste** *n(m+f), adj* socialist.

société [sɔsjete] *nf* society; club; company. **société anonyme** limited company. **sociétaire** *n(m+f)* member.

sociologie [sɔsjɔlɔʒi] *nf* sociology. **sociologique** *adj* sociological. **sociologue** *n(m+f)* sociologist.

socle [sɔklə] *nm* base; pedestal.

socquette [sɔkɛt] *nf* ankle sock.
sœur [sœr] *nf* sister; (*rel*) nun.
sofa [sɔfa] *nm* sofa.
soi [swa] *pron* one, oneself. **aller de soi** be obvious, stand to reason. **soi-même** *pron* oneself.
soi-disant *adj invar* so-called. *adv* supposedly.
soie [swa] *nf* silk; (*poil*) bristle.
soif [swaf] *nf* thirst. **avoir soif** be thirsty.
soigner [swaɲe] *v* look after, take care of; (*malade*) treat. **soigné** *adj* neat, tidy; (*consciencieux*) carefully done. **soigneux** *adj* careful; (*soigné*) neat, tidy.
soin [swɛ̃] *nm* care.
soir [swar] *nm* evening. **ce soir** this evening, tonight. **soirée** *nf* evening; party; (*théâtre*) evening performance.
soit [swa] *adv* very well, so be it. *conj* whether; (*à savoir*) that is to say. **soit que** whether. **soit ,... soit ...** either ... or

soixante [swasɑ̃t] *nm, adj* sixty. **soixantième** *n(m+f)*, *adj* sixtieth.
soixante-dix *nm, adj* seventy. **soixante-dixième** *n(m+f)*, *adj* seventieth.
soja [sɔʒa] *nm* soya.
sol [sɔl] *nm* ground; (*plancher*) floor; (*territoire*) soil.
solaire [sɔlɛr] *adj* solar; (*crème, etc.*) suntan.
soldat [sɔlda] *nm* soldier.
solde[1] [sɔld] *nf* pay.
solde[2] [sɔld] *nm* (*compte*) balance; (*vente*) sale; (*marchandises*) sale goods *pl*.
sole [sɔl] *nf* sole.
soleil [sɔlɛj] *nm* sun; (*lumière*) sunshine. **il fait du soleil** it's sunny.
solennel [sɔlanɛl] *adj* solemn; ceremonial. **solennité** *nf* solemnity; grand occasion.
solide [sɔlid] *adj* solid; (*sérieux, durable*) sound; robust, sturdy. *nm* solid. **solidarité** *nf* solidarity. **solidement** *adv* solidly; firmly. **solidifier** *v* solidify.
soliste [sɔlist] *n(m+f)* soloist.
solitaire [sɔlitɛr] *adj* solitary; deserted; (*seul, sans compagnie*) lonely. *n(m+f)* recluse. **solitairement** *adv* alone.
solitude [sɔlityd] *nf* solitude; loneliness.
solive [sɔliv] *nf* joist.
solliciter [sɔlisite] *v* appeal to; (*demander*) seek, request.
solo [sɔlo] *nm, adj invar* solo.
soluble [sɔlyblə] *adj* soluble.
solution [sɔlysjɔ̃] *nf* solution.

solvable [sɔlvablə] *adj* solvent. **solvabilité** *nf* solvency.
sombre [sɔ̃brə] *adj* dark; (*morne*) sombre, gloomy.
sombrer [sɔ̃bre] *v* sink, founder.
sommaire [sɔmɛr] *adj* brief, basic. *nm* summary.
sommation [sɔmasjɔ̃] *nf* (*jur*) summons; demand.
somme[1] [sɔm] *nf* **bête de somme** *nf* beast of burden.
somme[2] [sɔm] *nm* nap, snooze. **faire un petit somme** have a nap.
somme[3] [sɔm] *nf* sum, amount. **en somme** all in all; (*en résumé*) in short. **faire la somme de** add up. **somme toute** when all is said and done.
sommeil [sɔmɛj] *nm* sleep; (*envie de dormir*) sleepiness. **avoir sommeil** feel sleepy.
sommeiller [sɔmeje] *v* doze.
sommelier [sɔmǝlje] *nm* wine waiter.
sommer [sɔme] *v* (*jur*) summon.
sommet [sɔmɛ] *nm* summit, top.
somnambule [sɔmnɑ̃byl] *n(m+f)* sleepwalker. **somnambulisme** *nm* sleep-walking.
somnifère [sɔmnifɛr] *nm* sleeping-pill.
somnoler [sɔmnɔle] *v* doze. **somnolent** *adj* sleepy, drowsy.
son[1] [sɔ̃], **sa** *adj, pl* **ses** (*homme*) his, (*femme*) her; (*chose, animal*) its; (*indéfini*) one's.
son[2] [sɔ̃] *nm* (*bruit*) sound.
son[3] [sɔ̃] *nm* bran.
sonate [sɔnat] *nf* sonata.
sonder [sɔ̃de] *v* (*fouiller*) probe; (*naut*) sound; (*personne*) sound out; (*tech*) bore, drill. **sondage** *nm* probe; sounding; drilling; (*d'opinion*) poll. **sonde** *nf* probe; drill.
songer [sɔ̃ʒe] *v* (*rêver*) dream; reflect. **songer à** consider, think of. **songe** *nm* dream.
songeur, -euse [sɔ̃ʒœr, -øz] *adj* pensive. *nm, nf* dreamer.
sonique [sɔnik] *adj* sonic.
sonner [sɔne] *v* (*cloche, etc.*) ring; (*trompette, etc.*) sound; (*heure*) strike. **sonnerie** *nf* ringing; (*sonnette*) bell; (*pendule*) chimes *pl*. **sonnette** *nf* bell.
sonnet [sɔnɛ] *nm* sonnet.
sonore [sɔnɔr] *adj* resonant; (*rire, gifle, etc.*) resounding; (*film, onde, effet*) sound.

soprano [sɔprano] *n(m+f)* soprano.
sorcier [sɔrsje] *nm* sorcerer, wizard.
sorcière *nf* witch. **sorcellerie** *nf* witchcraft, sorcery.
sordide [sɔrdid] *adj* sordid.
sort [sɔr] *nm* fate; (*condition*) lot; (*charme*) spell. **tirer au sort** draw lots.
sorte [sɔrt] *nf* sort, kind. **de la sorte** in that way. **de sorte que** so that. **en quelque sorte** in a way.
*****sortir** [sɔrtir] *v* go out; come out; (*quitter, partir*) leave; (*retirer*) take *or* bring out; (*film, disque*) release. **sortie** *nf* (*endroit, porte*) way out, exit; (*promenade*) outing; (*emportement*) outburst; publication; release. **sortie de secours** emergency exit.
sot, sotte [so, sɔt] *adj* silly, foolish. *nm, nf* fool. **sottise** *nf* silliness; silly thing.
sou [su] *nm* penny. **sans le sou** penniless.
soubresaut [subrəso] *nm* jolt, start.
souche [suʃ] *nf* (*arbre*) stump; (*talon*) stub; (*famille*) founder.
souci[1] [susi] *nm* (*bot*) marigold.
souci[2] [susi] *nm* (*tracas*) worry; (*préoccupation*) concern.
se soucier [susje] *v* **se soucier de** care about. **soucieux** *adj* concerned.
soucoupe [sukup] *nf* saucer.
soudain [sudɛ̃] *adj* sudden. *adv* suddenly.
soude [sud] *nf* soda.
souder [sude] *v* (*autogène*) weld; (*avec fil à souder*) solder; unite. **se souder** (*os*) knit together. **soudeur** *nm* welder; solderer. **soudure** *nf* welding; soldering; (*substance*) solder; (*endroit*) weld.
soudoyer [sudwaje] *v* bribe.
souffler [sufle] *v* blow; (*bougie*) blow out; (*se reposer*) get one's breath back; (*haleter*) puff, pant; (*dire*) whisper; (*théâtre*) prompt; (*fam: voler*) pinch; (*fam: étonner*) stagger. **souffle** *nm* blow, puff; (*respiration*) breathing; (*haleine*) breath; inspiration. **être à bout de souffle** be out of breath.
soufflet[1] [suflɛ] *nm* bellows *pl*; (*couture*) gusset.
soufflet[2] [suflɛ] *nm* (*gifle*) slap (in the face). **souffleter** *v* slap (in the face).
*****souffrir** [sufrir] *v* suffer; (*avoir mal*) be in pain; (*supporter*) endure, bear; (*permettre*) allow. **souffrance** *nf* suffering. **en souffrance** pending. **souffrant** *adj* suffering; (*malade*) unwell.

soufre [sufrə] *nm* sulphur.
souhait [swɛ] *nm* wish. **à souhait** to perfection, as well as one could wish. **souhaiter** *v* wish; (*espérer*) hope.
souiller [suje] *v* soil, dirty; (*réputation*) tarnish; (*profaner*) defile. **souillon** *nm* slut. **souillure** *nf* stain.
soûl [su] *adj* drunk. **tout son soûl** to one's heart's content. **soûlard, -e** *nm, nf* (*argot*) drunkard. **soûler** *v* intoxicate. **se soûler** get drunk.
soulager [sulaʒe] *v* relieve; (*conscience*) ease. **soulagement** *nm* relief.
soulever [sulve] *v* raise; (*lever*) lift; (*provoquer*) arouse, stir up. **soulèvement** *nm* uprising.
soulier [sulje] *nm* shoe.
souligner [suliɲe] *v* underline; accentuate, emphasize.
*****soumettre** [sumɛtrə] *v* (*dompter*) subject; (*présenter*) submit. **se soumettre** submit. **soumis** *adj* submissive. **soumission** *nf* submission; (*comm*) tender.
soupape [supap] *nf* valve.
soupçon [supsɔ̃] *nm* suspicion; (*ombre*) touch, hint; (*goutte*) drop. **soupçonner** *v* suspect. **soupçonneux** *adj* suspicious.
soupe [sup] *nf* soup.
soupente [supɑ̃t] *nf* cupboard (under the stairs).
souper [supe] *nm* supper. *v* have supper.
soupir [supir] *nm* sigh. **soupirer** *v* sigh.
soupirail [supiraj] *nm, pl* **-aux** basement window.
souple [suplə] *adj* supple; flexible; (*gracieux*) lithe. **souplesse** *nf* suppleness; flexibility; litheness.
source [surs] *nf* source; (*point d'eau*) spring.
sourcil [sursi] *nm* eyebrow.
sourd [sur], **-e** *adj* deaf; (*son, couleur*) muted; (*douleur*) dull; (*caché*) hidden. *nm, nf* deaf person.
sourd-muet, sourde-muette *adj* deaf and dumb. *nm, nf* deaf mute.
sourdine [surdin] *nf* mute.
souricière [surisjɛr] *nf* mousetrap.
*****sourire** [surir] *nm* smile. *v* smile.
souris [suri] *nf* mouse.
sournois [surnwa] *adj* underhand, deceitful; (*air*) shifty.
sous [su] *prep* under; (*temps*) within; (*pluie, soleil, etc.*) in.
sous-alimentation *nf* malnutrition.

*souscrire [suskrir] *v* subscribe; sign. **souscripteur, -trice** *nm, nf* subscriber. **souscription** *nf* subscription.
sous-développé *adj* underdeveloped.
sous-entendre *v* imply, infer.
sous-entendu *adj* understood. *nm* innuendo.
sous-estimer *v* underestimate, underrate. **sous-estimation** *nf* underestimation.
sous-jacent *adj* underlying.
sous-louer *v* sublet.
sous-marin *adj* underwater. *nm* submarine.
sous-payé *adj* underpaid.
sous-sol *nm* (*maison*) basement; (*terre*) subsoil.
sous-titre *nm* subtitle. **sous-titrer** *v* subtitle.
*soustraire [sustrer] *v* take away; (*math*) subtract; (*cacher*) shield. **se soustraire à** shirk, escape. **soustraction** *nf* subtraction.
sous-traiter *v* subcontract. **sous-traitant** *nm* subcontractor.
sous-vêtements *nm pl* underwear *sing.*
soutane [sutan] *nf* cassock.
*soutenir [sutnir] *v* support; (*faire durer*) sustain, keep up; (*résister à*) withstand; (*affirmer*) uphold. **soutenu** *adj* sustained; elevated.
souterrain [suterɛ̃] *adj* underground. *nm* underground passage.
soutien [sutjɛ̃] *nm* support. **soutien de famille** breadwinner. **soutien-gorge** *nm* bra.
*souvenir [suvnir] *nm* memory; (*souvenance*) recollection; (*objet*) memento; (*pour touristes*) souvenir. *v* **se souvenir (de)** remember.
souvent [suvɑ̃] *adv* often. **peu souvent** seldom.
souverain [suvrɛ̃], **-e** *adj* supreme, sovereign. *nm, nf* sovereign.
soyeux [swajø] *adj* silky.
spacieux [spasjø] *adj* spacious.
spaghetti [spageti] *nm pl* spaghetti.
sparadrap [sparadra] *nm* sticking plaster.
spasme [spasmə] *nm* spasm. **spasmodique** *adj* spasmodic.
spatial [spasjal] *adj* spatial; (*voyage, engin, etc.*) space.
spatule [spatyl] *nf* spatula.
speaker, speakerine [spikœr, spikrin] *nm, nf* announcer.
spécial [spesjal] *adj* special; (*bizarre*)

peculiar. **spécialement** *adv* particularly, especially; (*exprès*) specially. **se spécialiser** *v* specialize. **spécialiste** *n(m+f)* specialist. **spécialité** *nf* speciality.
spécieux [spesjø] *adj* specious.
spécifier [spesifje] *v* specify, state. **spécification** *nf* specification. **spécifique** *adj* specific.
spécimen [spesimɛn] *nm* specimen; (*exemplaire*) sample copy.
spectacle [spektaklə] *nm* sight, spectacle; (*représentation*) show. **spectaculaire** *adj* spectacular.
spectateur, -trice [spektatœr, -tris] *nm, nf* onlooker; (*sport*) spectator. **spectateurs** *nm pl* (*théâtre*) audience *sing.*
spectre [spektrə] *nm* (*fantôme*) spectre; (*phys*) spectrum.
spéculer [spekyle] *v* speculate. **spéculatif** *adj* speculative. **spéculation** *nf* speculation.
spéléologie [speleɔlɔʒi] *nf* pot-holing. **spéléologue** *n(m+f)* pot-holer.
sperme [spermə] *nm* sperm.
sphère [sfɛr] *nf* sphere. **sphérique** *adj* spherical.
spinal [spinal] *adj* spinal.
spiral [spiral] *adj* spiral. **spirale** *nf* spiral.
spirite [spirit] *n(m+f)* spiritualist. **spiritisme** *nm* spiritualism.
spirituel [spiritɥɛl] *adj* spiritual; (*fin*) witty.
spiritueux [spiritɥø] *nm* (*liqueur*) spirit.
splendeur [splɑ̃dœr] *nf* splendour; glory. **splendide** *adj* splendid, magnificent.
spongieux [spɔ̃ʒjø] *adj* spongy.
spontané [spɔ̃tane] *adj* spontaneous. **spontanéité** *nf* spontaneity.
sporadique [spɔradik] *adj* sporadic.
sport [spɔr] *nm* sport. **de sport** sports.
sportif [spɔrtif] *adj* sports; competitive; (*personne*) athletic; (*attitude*) sporting. *nm* sportsman. **sportive** *nf* sportswoman.
square [skwar] *nm* square with public garden.
squelette [skɔlɛt] *nm* skeleton. **squelettique** *adj* skeletal; (*très maigre*) scrawny; (*exposé*) sketchy.
stabiliser [stabilize] *v* stabilize. **stabilisateur** *nm* stabilizer.
stable [stablə] *adj* stable. **stabilité** *nf* stability.
stade [stad] *nm* (*étape*) stage; (*sport*) stadium.

stage [staʒ] *nm* training period; training course. **stagiaire** *n(m+f)*, *adj* trainee, student.

stagnant [stagnã] *adj* stagnant. **stagnation** *nf* stagnation. **stagner** *v* stagnate.

stalle [stal] *nf* stall.

standard [stãdar] *nm* switchboard. *adj* standard. **standardiser** *v* standardize. **standardiste** *n(m+f)* switchboard operator.

starter [startɛr] *nm* (*auto*) choke; (*sport*) starter.

station [stɑsjɔ̃] *nf* station; (*halte*) stop; site; (*de vacances*) resort; posture. **station balnéaire** seaside resort. **station de taxis** taxi rank. **station-service** *nf* petrol station.

stationner [stasjɔne] *v* park. **stationnaire** *adj* stationary. **stationnement** *nm* parking.

statique [statik] *adj* static.

statistique [statistik] *nf* statistic; (*science*) statistics. *adj* statistical.

statue [staty] *nf* statue.

stature [statyr] *nf* stature.

statut [staty] *nm* status. **statuts** *nm pl* statutes *pl*, rules *pl*. **statutaire** *adj* statutory.

steeple [stiplə] *nm* steeplechase.

stencil [stɛnsil] *nm* stencil.

sténodactylo [stenɔdaktilo] *nf* (*personne*) shorthand typist; (*emploi*) shorthand typing.

sténographie [stenɔgrafi] *nf* shorthand.

stéréo [stereo] *nf*, *adj* stereo. **stéréophonique** *adj* stereophonic.

stéréotype [stereɔtip] *nm* stereotype.

stérile [steril] *adj* sterile; (*terre*) barren; (*effort*) fruitless. **stérilet** *nm* (*méd*) coil. **stérilisation** *nf* sterilization. **stériliser** *v* sterilize. **stérilité** *nf* sterility; barrenness; fruitlessness.

stéthoscope [stetɔskɔp] *nm* stethoscope.

stigmate [stigmat] *nm* stigma; mark.

stimulant [stimylã] *adj* stimulating. *nm* stimulant; stimulus (*pl* -li).

stimuler [stimyle] *v* stimulate. **stimulation** *nf* stimulation.

stimulus [stimylys] *nm*, *pl* -li stimulus (*pl* -li).

stipuler [stipyle] *v* stipulate, specify. **stipulation** *nf* stipulation.

stock [stɔk] *nm* stock. **stocker** *v* stock; (*amasser*) stockpile.

Stockholm [stɔkɔlm] *n* Stockholm.

stoïque [stɔik] *adj* stoical. **stoïcisme** *nm* stoicism.

stop [stɔp] *interj* stop! *nm* (*panneau*) stop sign; (*feu*) brake light; (*fam*) hitch-hiking. **faire du stop** hitch-hike.

store [stɔr] *nm* blind; (*magasin*) awning.

strabisme [strabismə] *nm* squint.

strapontin [strapɔ̃tɛ̃] *nm* folding seat.

strate [strat] *nf* stratum (*pl* -ta).

stratégie [strateʒi] *nf* strategy. **stratégique** *adj* strategic.

strict [strikt] *adj* strict; (*tenue*) plain.

strident [stridã] *adj* strident, shrill.

strié [strije] *adj* streaked; (*en relief*) ridged.

strophe [strɔf] *nf* verse, stanza.

structure [stryktyr] *nf* structure. **structural** *adj* structural.

studieux [stydjø] *adj* studious.

studio [stydjo] *nm* studio; (*logement*) flatlet.

stupéfiant [stypefjã] *adj* astounding. *nm* drug, narcotic.

stupéfier [stypefje] *v* stun, astound. **stupéfaction** *nf* amazement. **stupéfait** *adj* astounded, dumbfounded.

stupeur [stypœr] *nf* amazement; (*méd*) stupor.

stupide [stypid] *adj* stupid, silly. **stupidité** *nf* stupidity.

style [stil] *nm* style.

stylo [stilo] *nm* pen. **stylo à bille** ballpoint pen.

suaire [sɥɛr] *nm* shroud.

suant [sɥã] *adj* sweaty.

suave [sɥav] *adj* smooth; (*musique, etc.*) sweet. **suavité** *nf* smoothness; sweetness.

subalterne [sybaltɛrn] *n(m+f)*, *adj* subordinate.

subconscient [sypkɔ̃sjã] *nm*, *adj* subconscious.

subdiviser [sybdivize] *v* subdivide. **subdivision** *nf* subdivision.

subir [sybir] *v* undergo; endure; suffer.

subit [sybi] *adj* sudden. **subitement** *adv* suddenly. **subito** *adv* (*fam*) suddenly, at once.

subjectif [sybʒɛktif] *adj* subjective.

subjonctif [sybʒɔ̃ktif] *nm*, *adj* subjunctive.

subjuguer [sybʒyge] *v* captivate.

sublime [syblim] *nm*, *adj* sublime.

submerger [sybmɛrʒe] *v* submerge; (*ennemi, émotion*) overwhelm; (*travail, etc.*) swamp. **submersion** *nf* submersion.

subordonner [sybɔrdɔne] *v* subordinate.
subordination *nf* subordination.
subordonné, -e *n, adj* subordinate.
subreptice [sybrɛptis] *adj* surreptitious.
subsidiaire [sypsidjɛr] *adj* subsidiary.
subsister [sybziste] *v* survive, live; (*rester*) remain, subsist. **subsistance** *nf* subsistence, maintenance.
substance [sypstɑ̃s] *nf* substance. **substantiel** *adj* substantial.
substituer [sypstitɥe] *v* substitute. **substitution** *nf* substitution.
subtil [syptil] *adj* subtle. **subtilité** *nf* subtlety.
suburbain [sybyrbɛ̃] *adj* suburban.
*subvenir [sybvənir] *v* **subvenir à** meet, provide for.
subvention [sybvɑ̃sjɔ̃] *nf* grant, subsidy. **subventionner** *v* subsidize.
subversion [sybvɛrsjɔ̃] *nf* subversion. **subversif** *adj* subversive.
suc [syk] *nm* juice; essence, pith.
succédané [syksedane] *nm* substitute.
succéder [syksede] *v* **succéder à** succeed; (*suivre*) follow. **succès** *nm* success. **à succès** successful. **avec succès** successfully.
successeur *nm* successor. **successif** *adj* successive. **succession** *nf* succession.
succinct [syksɛ̃] *adj* succinct.
succion [syksjɔ̃] *nf* suction.
succomber [sykɔ̃be] *v* succumb, yield; (*mourir*) die.
succulent [sykylɑ̃] *adj* succulent, delicious.
succursale [sykyrsal] *nf* branch.
sucer [syse] *v* suck. **sucette** *nf* lollipop; (*tétine*) dummy.
sucre [sykrə] *nm* sugar. **sucre d'orge** barley sugar. **sucre en poudre** caster sugar. **sucre glace** icing sugar. **sucre semoule** granulated sugar. **sucré** *adj* sweet. **sucrer** *v* sweeten; (*thé, café, etc.*) put sugar in. **sucrier** *nm* sugar-basin.
sud [syd] *nm* south. *adj invar* south; (*région*) southern; (*direction*) southward. **sud-est** *nm, adj invar* south-east. **sud-ouest** *nm, adj invar* south-west.
suède [sɥɛd] *nm* suede.
Suède [sɥɛd] *nf* Sweden. **suédois** *nm, adj* Swedish. **Suédois, -e** *nm, nf* Swede.
suer [sɥe] *v* sweat. **sueur** *nf* sweat.
*suffire [syfir] *v* suffice, be enough *or* sufficient. **ça suffit** that will do, that's enough. **suffisant** *adj* sufficient; (*résultat*) satisfactory; (*personne*) self-important.

suffixe [syfiks] *nm* suffix.
suffoquer [syfɔke] *v* suffocate, choke. **suffocation** *nf* suffocation.
suffrage [syfraʒ] *nm* suffrage; (*voix*) vote; approbation, approval.
suggérer [sygʒere] *v* suggest. **suggestif** *adj* suggestive. **suggestion** *nf* suggestion.
se suicider [sɥiside] *v* commit suicide. **suicidaire** *adj* suicidal. **suicide** *nm* suicide. **suicidé, -e** *nm, nf* suicide.
suie [sɥi] *nf* soot.
suif [sɥif] *nm* tallow.
suinter [sɥɛ̃te] *v* ooze.
Suisse [sɥis] *nf* Switzerland. **les Suisses** the Swiss. **suisse** *adj* Swiss.
suite [sɥit] *nf* result, effect; succession, series; (*musique, appartement*) suite; (*feuilleton*) next episode, continuation; (*roman, film*) sequel; coherence, consistency. **de suite** in succession. **faire suite à** follow. **par la suite** afterwards, subsequently. **par suite** consequently. **suite à** (*comm*) further to. **tout de suite** at once, immediately.
suivant [sɥivɑ̃], **-e** *adj* next, following. *nm, nf* next (one). *prep* according to.
*suivre [sɥivrə] *v* follow; (*cours*) attend; (*en classe*) keep up (with). **faire suivre** forward. **suivi** *adj* consistent; regular; coherent.
sujet, -ette [syʒɛ, -ɛt] *adj* subject, liable, prone. *nm* subject; (*d'examen*) question. **au sujet de** about, concerning. **sujet de** cause for. *nm, nf* (*personne*) subject. **sujétion** *nf* subjection.
sultan [syltɑ̃] *nm* sultan.
superbe [sypɛrb] *adj* superb, magnificent.
supercherie [sypɛrʃəri] *nf* trick.
superficie [sypɛrfisi] *nf* surface area.
superficiel [sypɛrfisjɛl] *adj* superficial.
superflu [sypɛrfly] *adj* superfluous.
supérieur, -e [sypɛrjœr] *adj* upper; (*hautain, meilleur*) superior; (*plus grand*) greater; (*plus haut*) higher. *nm, nf* superior. **supériorité** *nf* superiority.
superlatif [sypɛrlatif] *nm, adj* superlative.
supermarché [sypɛrmarʃe] *nm* supermarket.
supersonique [sypɛrsɔnik] *adj* supersonic.
superstition [sypɛrstisjɔ̃] *nf* superstition. **superstitieux** *adj* superstitious.
suppléant [sypleɑ̃], **-e** *adj* temporary. *nm, nf* deputy; (*professeur*) supply teacher; (*médecin*) locum.

suppléer [syplee] v supply, provide; (*lacune*) fill in; (*manque*) make up (for); replace. **suppléer à** (*remédier*) make up for; (*remplacer*) substitute for.

supplément [syplemɑ̃] nm supplement; (*tarif*) extra charge; (*transport*) excess fare. **en supplément** extra. **supplémentaire** adj additional, extra, supplementary.

supplice [syplis] nm torture; torment. **dernier supplice** execution.

supplier [syplije] v implore, entreat.

support [sypɔr] nm support; (*moyen*) medium.

supporter [sypɔrte] v support; endure, bear; tolerate, put up with; (*résister à*) withstand. **supportable** adj bearable; tolerable.

supposer [sypoze] v suppose; imply. **supposition** nf supposition.

supprimer [syprime] v suppress; (*enlever*) remove; (*mot*) delete; abolish, do away with; (*train, etc.*) cancel. **suppression** nf suppression; removal; deletion; abolition; cancellation.

suprême [syprɛm] adj supreme. **suprématie** nf supremacy.

sur [syr] prep on; (*par-dessus*) over; (*au-dessus*) above; (*sujet*) about; (*proportion*) out of; (*mesure*) by; (*après*) after. **sur-le-champ** adv immediately.

sûr [syr] adj sure, certain; (*sans danger*) safe; (*sérieux*) reliable. **à coup sûr** definitely.

surabondance [syrabɔ̃dɑ̃s] nf overabundance. **surabondant** adj overabundant.

suranné [syrane] adj outdated, outmoded.

surcharger [syrʃarʒe] v overload. **surcharge** nf extra or excess load; (*surabondance*) surfeit; (*impôt*) surcharge.

surchauffer [syrʃofe] v overheat.

surcroît [syrkrwa] nm excess; (*augmentation*) increase. **par surcroît** in addition.

surdité [syrdite] nf deafness.

surdose [syrdoz] nf overdose.

sureau [syro] nm elder. **baie du sureau** elderberry

surélever [syrɛlve] v raise, heighten.

surenchère [syrɑ̃ʃɛr] nf higher bid.

surestimer [syrɛstime] v overestimate.

sûreté [syrte] nf (*sécurité*) safety; (*précision*) reliability; guarantee.

surexposer [syrɛkspoze] v overexpose. **surexposition** nf overexposure.

surface [syrfas] nf surface; (*aire*) surface area. **faire surface** surface.

surfait [syrfɛ] adj overrated.

surgeler [syrʒəle] v deep-freeze.

surgir [syrʒir] v appear suddenly; (*jaillir*) spring up; (*problème, etc.*) arise.

surhumain [syrymɛ̃] adj superhuman.

surimpression [syrɛ̃presjɔ̃] nf superimposition. **en surimpression** superimposed.

surlendemain [syrlɑ̃dmɛ̃] nm next day but one. **le surlendemain** two days later.

surmener [syrməne] v overwork. **surmenage** nm overwork.

surmonter [syrmɔ̃te] v surmount; (*vaincre*) overcome; (*dôme, etc.*) top.

surnaturel [syrnatyrɛl] nm, adj supernatural.

surnom [syrnɔ̃] nm nickname. **surnommer** v nickname.

surnombre [syrnɔ̃brə] nm **en surnombre** too many.

surpasser [syrpase] v surpass.

surpeuplé [syrpœple] adj overpopulated, overcrowded. **surpeuplement** nm overpopulation, overcrowding.

surplomb [syrplɔ̃] nm overhang. **surplomber** v overhang.

surplus [syrply] nm surplus. **au surplus** moreover.

*****surprendre** [syrprɑ̃drə] v surprise; discover, detect; (*prendre*) catch (out). **surpris** adj surprised. **surprise** nf surprise.

surréaliste [syrrealist] adj surrealistic. n(m+f) surrealist. **surréalisme** nm surrealism.

sursaut [syrso] nm start, jump. **sursauter** v start, jump.

*****surseoir** [syrswar] v **surseoir à** defer, postpone. **sursis** nm reprieve.

surtaxer [syrtakse] v surcharge. **surtaxe** nf surcharge.

surtout [syrtu] adv above all; especially, particularly.

surveiller [syrveje] v (*garder, épier*) watch; (*contrôler*) supervise. **surveillance** nf watch; supervision. **surveillant, -e** nm, nf supervisor; (*prison*) warder; (*école*) person in charge of discipline.

*****survenir** [syrvənir] v occur, take place; (*problème*) arise; (*personne*) arrive unexpectedly.

survêtement [syrvɛtmɑ̃] nm tracksuit.

*****survivre** [syrvivrə] v survive. **survivre à** outlive. **survivance** nf survival. **survivant, -e** nm, nf survivor.

sus [sy] *adv* en sus in addition.

susceptible [syseptiblə] *adj* sensitive, touchy. **susceptible à** (*possible*) likely to; capable of.

susciter [sysite] *v* arouse; (*obstacles, etc.*) create.

susdit [sysdi] *adj* aforesaid.

suspect [syspɛkt], **-e** *adj* suspicious; (*douteux*) suspect. **suspect de** suspected of. *nm, nf* suspect.

suspendre [syspɑ̃drə] *v* suspend; (*fixer, accrocher*) hang (up). **suspendu** *adj* suspended; hanging.

suspens [syspɑ̃] *nm* en suspens (*projet, etc.*) in abeyance; in suspense; in suspension. **suspense** *nm* suspense.

suspension [syspɑ̃sjɔ̃] *nf* suspension.

susurrer [sysyre] *v* murmur.

suture [sytyr] *nf* suture. **suturer** *v* (*méd*) stitch (up).

svelte [svɛlt] *adj* slender.

sycomore [sikɔmɔr] *nm* sycamore.

syllabe [silab] *nf* syllable. **syllabique** *adj* syllabic.

sylvestre [silvɛstrə] *adj* forest, woodland. **sylviculture** *nf* forestry.

symbole [sɛ̃bɔl] *nm* symbol. **symbolique** *adj* symbolic; (*donation, contribution*) nominal. **symboliser** *v* symbolize. **symbolisme** *nm* symbolism.

symétrie [simetri] *nf* symmetry. **symétrique** *adj* symmetrical.

sympathie [sɛ̃pati] *nf* liking; affinity. **sympathique** *adj* nice, pleasant; (*personne*) likeable, friendly.

symphonie [sɛ̃fɔni] *nf* symphony. **symphonique** *adj* symphonic.

symposium [sɛ̃pozjɔm] *nm* symposium.

symptôme [sɛ̃ptom] *nm* symptom; sign. **symptomatique** *adj* symptomatic.

synagogue [sinagɔg] *nf* synagogue.

synchroniser [sɛ̃krɔnize] *v* synchronize. **synchronisation** *nf* synchronization.

syncoper [sɛ̃kɔpe] *v* (*musique*) syncopate. **syncope** *nf* syncopation; (*méd*) black-out, fainting fit.

syndicat [sɛ̃dika] *nm* syndicate; (*ouvrier*) union; association. **syndicat d'initiative** tourist information bureau. **syndical** *adj* union. **syndicaliste** *n*(*m*+*f*) trade unionist. **syndiqué, -e** *nm, nf* union member.

syndrome [sɛ̃drom] *nm* syndrome.

synonyme [sinɔnim] *nm* synonym. *adj* synonymous.

syntaxe [sɛ̃taks] *nf* syntax.

synthèse [sɛ̃tɛz] *nf* synthesis (*pl* -ses). **synthétique** *adj* synthetic. **synthétiser** *v* synthesize.

syphilis [sifilis] *nf* syphilis.

système [sistɛm] *nm* system. **systématique** *adj* systematic.

T

t' [t] *V* te.

ta [ta] *V* ton[1].

tabac [taba] *nm* tobacco; (*magasin*) tobacconist's. **tabac à priser** snuff. **tabatière** *nf* snuffbox.

table [tablə] *nf* table; tablet. **faire table rase** make a clean sweep. **table basse** coffee table. **table des matières** table of contents. **table gigogne** nest of tables. **table roulante** trolley.

tableau [tablo] *nm* picture; (*peinture*) painting; scene; (*support, panneau*) board; list; (*graphique*) table, chart. **tableau de bord** dashboard. **tableau noir** blackboard.

tablette [tablɛt] *nf* tablet; (*rayon*) shelf; (*chocolat*) bar.

tablier [tablije] *nm* apron.

tabou [tabu] *nm, adj* taboo.

tabouret [taburɛ] *nm* stool.

tache [taʃ] *nf* mark, spot; (*sang, vin, etc.*) stain; (*pâté*) blot. **tache de rousseur** *or* **son** freckle. **tacher** *v* mark; stain.

tâche [taʃ] *nf* task, work. **tâcher** *v* try, endeavour.

tacheté [taʃte] *adj* speckled, spotted.

tacite [tasit] *adj* tacit.

taciturne [tasityrn] *adj* taciturn.

tact [takt] *nm* tact. **avoir du tact** be tactful.

tactique [taktik] *nf* tactics *pl. adj* tactical.

taffetas [tafta] *nm* taffeta.

taie [tɛ] *nf* **taie d'oreiller** pillowcase.

taillade [tɑjad] *nf* slash, gash. **taillader** *v* slash, gash.

taille [tɑj] *nf* size; (*hauteur*) height; (*corps, vêtement*) waist; (*coupe*) cutting, cut; (*tranchant*) edge. **à la taille de** in keeping with. **être de taille à** be up to.

tailler [tɑje] *v* cut; (*bois*) carve; (*barbe, haie, etc.*) trim; (*crayon*) sharpen. **taille-**

crayon nm invar pencil sharpener. **tailleur** nm (personne) tailor; (costume) suit.
taillis [taji] nm copse.
***taire** [tɛr] v conceal, hush up. **faire taire** silence. **se taire** be quiet.
talc [talk] nm talcum powder.
talent [talɑ̃] nm talent. **talentueux** adj talented.
talon [talɔ̃] nm heel; (chèque) stub; (pain) crust.
talonner [talɔne] v (suivre) follow closely; (harceler) hound; (cheval) spur on.
talus [taly] nm embankment.
tambour [tɑ̃bur] nm drum; (joueur) drummer. **tambourin** nm tambourine. **tambouriner** v drum.
tamis [tami] nm sieve. **tamiser** v sieve, sift; filter.
Tamise [tamiz] nf **la Tamise** the Thames.
tampon [tɑ̃pɔ̃] nm pad, wad; (pour boucher) plug; (pour · règles) tampon; (timbre) stamp; (rail) buffer. **tamponner** v dab, mop; stamp; plug; (heurter) crash into.
tancer [tɑ̃se] v scold, reprimand.
tandem [tɑ̃dɛm] nm tandem; (couple) pair.
tandis [tɑ̃di] conj **tandis que** while; (contraste) whereas.
tangente [tɑ̃ʒɑ̃t] nf tangent.
tangible [tɑ̃ʒiblə] adj tangible.
tanguer [tɑ̃ge] v pitch, reel.
tanière [tanjɛr] nf den, lair.
tanner [tane] v tan; (fam) pester, annoy.
tan-sad [tɑ̃sad] nm pillion.
tant [tɑ̃] adv so much, so. **en tant que** as. **tant de** (quantité) so much; (nombre) so many; (qualité) such. **tant mieux** so much the better. **tant pis** too bad. **tant que** as long as, while. **tant s'en faut** far from it.
tante [tɑ̃t] nf aunt.
tantôt [tɑ̃to] adv this afternoon. **tantôt . . . tantôt . . .** sometimes . . . sometimes . . . .
taon [tɑ̃] nm horse-fly.
tapage [tapaʒ] nm (vacarme) uproar, din; (scandale) fuss. **tapageur, -euse** adj rowdy; (criard) showy, flashy.
taper [tape] v knock, hit; (battre) beat; (à la machine) type. **taper sur les nerfs de quelqu'un** get on someone's nerves. **tape** nf slap.
tapioca [tapjɔka] nm tapioca.
se tapir [tapir] v crouch; (se cacher) hide away.

tapis [tapi] nm carpet; (carpette) rug; (natte) mat; (table) cloth, covering. **tapis de sol** groundsheet. **tapis roulant** conveyor belt.
tapisser [tapise] v cover; (sol) carpet; (mur) paper. **tapisserie** nf tapestry; (papier peint) wallpaper. **tapissier** nm upholsterer; (maison) interior decorator.
tapoter [tapɔte] v pat, tap.
taquin [takɛ̃] adj teasing. **taquiner** v tease; (inquiéter) bother, worry. **taquinerie** nf teasing.
tard [tar] adv late.
tarder [tarde] v (différer) delay, put off; (être lent) take a long time, be long. **tardif** adj late; (remords, etc.) belated.
tarif [tarif] nm tariff, rate; (tableau) price list; (transport) fare.
tarir [tarir] v run dry, dry up.
tarte [tart] nf tart. **tartelette** nf tart. **tartine** nf slice of bread (and butter). **tartiner** v spread.
tartre [tartrə] nm tartar; (bouilloire) fur.
tas [tɑ] nm pile, heap; (fam: foule) crowd. **un tas de** (fam) loads of, lots of.
tasse [tɑs] nf cup. **tasse à thé/café** tea/coffee cup.
tasser [tɑse] v pack (down), cram. **se tasser** (se serrer) squeeze up; (s'affaisser) settle; (corps) shrink.
tâter [tate] v (palper) feel; (opinion, etc.) sound out; (essayer) try out.
tâtonner [tatɔne] v grop along or around, feel one's way. **par tâtonnements** by trial and error.
tâtons [tatɔ̃] adv **avancer à tâtons** feel one's way along. **chercher à tâtons** feel around for.
tatouer [tatwe] v tattoo. **tatouage** nm tattoo.
taudis [todi] nm slum.
taule [tol] nf (argot: prison) nick.
taupe [top] nf mole.
taureau [tɔro] nm bull. **Taureau** nm Taurus.
taux [to] nm rate; degree, level. **taux de change** exchange rate.
taxer [takse] v tax; (comm) fix the price of; accuse. **taxation** nf taxation. **taxe** nf tax; (douane) duty; fixed price.
taxi [taksi] nm taxi.
Tchécoslovaquie [tʃekɔslɔvaki] nf Czechoslovakia. **tchécoslovaque** nm, adj Czechoslovak. **Tchécoslovaque** n(m+f) Czech-

oslovak. **tchèque** *nm, adj* Czech. **Tchèque** *n(m+f)* Czech.

te [tə], **t'** *pron* you, to you; (*réfléchi*) yourself.

technique [tɛknik] *adj* technical. *nf* technique. **technicien, -enne** *nm, nf* technician. **technologie** *nf* technology. **technologique** *adj* technological.

teck [tɛk] *nm* teak.

***teindre** [tɛ̃drə] *v* dye; colour, tinge.

teint [tɛ̃] *adj* dyed. *nm* complexion, colouring. **teinte** *nf* shade, tint; colour; (*trace*) tinge, hint.

teinter [tɛ̃te] *v* (*verre*) tint; (*bois*) stain.

teinture [tɛ̃tyr] *nf* (*substance*) dye; (*action*) dyeing. **teinturerie** *nf* cleaner's.

tel [tɛl], **telle** *adj* such (a), like, as. **tel que** such as, like. **tel quel** as it stands, as it is. *pron* one, someone.

télécommande [telekɔmɑ̃d] *nf* remote control.

télécommunications [telekɔmynikɑsjɔ̃] *nf pl* telecommunications *pl*.

télégramme [telegram] *nm* telegram.

télégraphier [telegrafje] *v* telegraph, cable. **télégraphe** *nm* telegraph. **télégraphique** *adj* telegraphic; (*poteau*) telegraph.

télépathie [telepati] *nf* telepathy. **télépathique** *adj* telepathic.

téléphérique [teleferik] *nm* cable-car.

téléphone [telefɔn] *nm* telephone, phone. **téléphoner** *v* telephone, phone. **téléphonique** *adj* telephone. **téléphoniste** *n(m+f)* telephonist.

télescope [telɛskɔp] *nm* telescope. **télescopique** *adj* telescopic.

télésiège [telesjɛʒ] *nm* chair-lift.

téléski [teleski] *nm* ski-lift.

téléviser [televize] *v* televise. **télévision** *nf* television. **téléviseur** *nm* television set.

télex [telɛks] *nm* telex.

tellement [tɛlmɑ̃] *adv* so (much). **pas tellement** not (very) much.

téméraire [temerɛr] *adj* rash, reckless. **témérité** *nf* rashness, recklessness.

témoigner [temwaɲe] *v* testify; (*montrer*) show; reveal. **témoigner de** bear witness to. **témoignage** *nm* evidence, testimony; (*récit*) account; expression; (*cadeau*) token. **témoin** *nm* witness; evidence, testimony; (*sport*) baton.

tempe [tɑ̃p] *nf* temple.

tempérament [tɑ̃peramɑ̃] *nm* temperament, disposition; constitution. **achat à tempérament** *nm* hire purchase.

température [tɑ̃peratyr] *nf* temperature.

tempérer [tɑ̃pere] *v* temper; (*douleur*) soothe. **tempéré** *adj* temperate.

tempête [tɑ̃pɛt] *nf* storm. **tempétueux** *adj* stormy, tempestuous.

temple [tɑ̃plə] *nm* temple; Protestant church.

tempo [tɛmpo] *nm* tempo.

temporaire [tɑ̃pɔrɛr] *adj* temporary.

temporel [tɑ̃pɔrɛl] *adj* temporal, worldly.

temps [tɑ̃] *nm* time; (*météorologie*) weather; (*musique*) beat; (*gramm*) tense. **à temps** in time. **de temps en temps** now and again. **quel temps fait-il?** what's the weather like?

tenace [tənas] *adj* stubborn, persistent, tenacious. **ténacité** *nf* stubbornness, persistence, tenacity.

tenailles [tənaj] *nf pl* pincers *pl*. **tenailler** *v* torture, torment.

tendance [tɑ̃dɑ̃s] *nf* tendency; (*évolution*) trend; (*opinions*) leanings *pl*. **avoir tendance à** tend to.

tendon [tɑ̃dɔ̃] *nm* tendon.

tendre[1] [tɑ̃drə] *v* (*raidir*) tighten; (*tirer sur*) stretch; (*muscle*) tense; (*poser*) set; (*tapisserie, etc.*) hang; (*présenter*) hold out. **tendre à** tend to; (*viser à*) aim at *or* to. **tendre le cou** crane one's neck. **tendre l'oreille** prick up one's ears. **tendu** *adj* taut, tight; tense; (*bras*) outstretched. **tendu de** hung with.

tendre[2] [tɑ̃drə] *adj* tender; soft, delicate. **tendresse** *nf* tenderness, affection. **tendreté** *nf* tenderness.

ténèbres [tenebrə] *nf pl* darkness *sing*, gloom *sing*. **ténébreux** *adj* dark, gloomy; obscure; mysterious.

***tenir** [tənir] *v* hold; (*garder*) keep; (*avoir*) have; (*magasin, etc.*) run; (*occuper*) take up; (*durer*) last. **se tenir** (*se conduire*) behave; (*debout*) stand. **se tenir à** hold on to. **tenir à** (*vouloir*) be anxious to, insist on; (*aimer*) be fond of; (*résulter*) stem from. **tenir compte de** take into account. **tenir de** take after. **tenir pour** regard as.

tennis [tenis] *nm* tennis; tennis court. *nf pl* plimsolls *pl*.

ténor [tenɔr] *nm* tenor.

tension [tɑ̃sjɔ̃] *nf* tension; (*méd*) blood pressure; (*élec*) voltage.

tentacule [tɑ̃takyl] *nm* tentacle.

tente [tɑ̃t] *nf* tent.

tenter [tɑ̃te] *v* (*tentation*) tempt; (*tentative*) attempt. **tentation** *nf* temptation. **tentative** *nf* attempt.

tenture [tɑ̃tyr] *nf* hanging; (*rideau*) curtain.

tenu [təny] *adj* **bien tenu** neat, well-kept. **être tenu de** be obliged to. **mal tenu** untidy, neglected. **tenue** *nf* (*habillement*) dress; (*maintien*) posture; (*conduite*) manners *pl*; (*magasin, etc.*) running; control.

ténu [teny] *adj* fine; (*subtil*) tenuous.

térébenthine [terebɑ̃tin] *nf* turpentine.

tergiverser [tɛrʒivɛrse] *v* prevaricate.

terme [tɛrm] *nm* term; (*date limite*) deadline; (*loyer*) rent. **avant terme** prematurely.

terminaison [terminɛzɔ̃] *nf* ending.

terminal [terminal] *adj* terminal. **terminale** *nf* (*classe*) upper sixth.

terminer [tɛrmine] *v* end, finish, terminate.

terminologie [terminɔlɔʒi] *nf* terminology.

terminus [tɛrminys] *nm* terminus.

ternir [tɛrnir] *v* tarnish, dull. **terne** *adj* dull, drab.

terrain [tɛrɛ̃] *nm* ground, land; (*sport*) pitch, field; (*parcelle*) plot, site. **terrain de jeu** playing field. **terrain vague** wasteland.

terrasse [teras] *nf* terrace.

terrasser [tɛrase] *v* overcome, overwhelm.

terre [tɛr] *nf* earth; (*sol*) ground; (*étendue, pays*) land. **à terre** ashore. **par terre** on the ground. **terre-à-terre** *adj invar* down-to-earth.

terrestre [tɛrɛstrə] *adj* earthly, terrestrial.

terreur [tɛrœr] *nf* terror.

terrible [tɛriblə] *adj* terrible, dreadful; (*fam*) terrific.

terrier [tɛrje] *nm* hole; (*lapin*) burrow; (*renard*) earth; (*race de chien*) terrier.

terrifier [tɛrifje] *v* terrify.

terrine [tɛrin] *nf* earthenware dish; pâté.

territoire [tɛritwar] *nm* territory. **territorial** *adj* territorial.

terroir [tɛrwar] *nm* soil.

terroriser [tɛrɔrize] *v* terrorize. **terrorisme** *nm* terrorism. **terroriste** *n(m+f)*, *adj* terrorist.

tes [te] *V* **ton**[1].

tesson [tesɔ̃] *nm* piece of broken glass.

testament [tɛstamɑ̃] *nm* testament; (*jur*) will.

testicule [tɛstikyl] *nm* testicle.

tétanos [tetanos] *nm* tetanus.

têtard [tɛtar] *nm* tadpole.

tête [tɛt] *nf* head; (*visage*) face; (*devant*) front; (*haut*) top; (*esprit*) mind. **en tête** in front; at the top. **tenir tête à** stand up to. **tête-à-tête** *nm invar* private conversation.

tétine [tetin] *nf* teat; (*vache*) udder; (*sucette*) dummy.

têtu [tety] *adj* stubborn.

texte [tɛkst] *nm* text; passage; subject. **textuel** *adj* textual.

textile [tɛkstil] *nm, adj* textile.

texture [tɛkstyr] *nf* texture.

thé [te] *nm* tea. **théière** *nf* teapot.

théâtre [teatrə] *nm* theatre; drama. **théâtral** *adj* theatrical; dramatic.

thème [tɛm] *nm* theme; (*traduction*) prose. **thématique** *adj* thematic.

théologie [teɔlɔʒi] *nf* theology. **théologien, -enne** *nm, nf* theologian. **théologique** *adj* theological.

théorème [teɔrɛm] *nm* theorem.

théorie [teɔri] *nf* theory. **théorique** *adj* theoretical.

thérapeutique [terapøtik] *adj* therapeutic. *nf* also **thérapie** therapy. **thérapeute** *n(m+f)* therapist.

thermal [tɛrmal] *adj* thermal. **station thermale** *nf* spa.

thermique [tɛrmik] *adj* thermal, heat.

thermodynamique [tɛrmɔdinamik] *nf* thermodynamics.

thermomètre [tɛrmɔmɛtrə] *nm* thermometer.

thermonucléaire [tɛrmɔnyklɛɛr] *adj* thermonuclear.

thermos ® [tɛrmos] *nm* thermos flask ®.

thermostat [tɛrmɔsta] *nm* thermostat.

thésauriser [tezɔrize] *v* hoard (money).

thèse [tɛz] *nf* thesis.

thon [tɔ̃] *nm* tuna.

thym [tɛ̃] *nm* thyme.

thyroïde [tirɔid] *nf, adj* thyroid.

tiare [tjar] *nf* tiara.

tic [tik] *nm* tic, twitch; (*manie*) mannerism.

ticket [tikɛ] *nm* ticket.

tic-tac [tiktak] *nm* tick, ticking. **faire tic-tac** tick.

tiède [tjɛd] *adj* lukewarm, tepid; (*doux*) mild.

tien [tjɛ̃], **tienne** *pron* le tien, la tienne yours.

tiens [tjɛ̃] *interj* well! (*en donnant*) here! (*en expliquant*) look!

tiers, tierce [tjɛr, tjɛrs] *adj* third. **Tiers-Monde** *nm* Third World. *nm* third; (*jur*) third party. *nf* (*musique*) third.

tige [tiʒ] *nf* stem, stalk; (*métal*) rod.

tigre [tigrə] *nm* tiger. **tigré** *adj* (*tacheté*) spotted; (*rayé*) striped. **chat tigré** *nm* tabby cat.

tilleul [tijœl] *nm* lime tree.

timbale [tɛ̃bal] *nf* kettledrum; (*gobelet*) metal tumbler. **timbales** *nf pl* timpani *pl*.

timbre [tɛ̃brə] *nm* stamp; (*son*) tone; (*sonnette*) bell. **timbrer** *v* stamp; (*d'un cachet*) postmark.

timide [timid] *adj* timid; (*mal à l'aise*) shy. **timidité** *nf* timidity; shyness.

tintamarre [tɛ̃tamar] *nm* din.

tinter [tɛ̃te] *v* ring; (*clochette*) tinkle; (*clefs, monnaie, etc.*) jingle; (*verres*) chink.

tir [tir] *nm* firing; (*feu*) fire; (*sport*) shooting. **tir à l'arc** archery.

tirailler [tiraje] *v* tug *or* pull at; (*harceler*) plague; (*douleur*) gnaw *or* stab at. **tiraillement** *nm* pulling, tugging; conflict; stabbing *or* gnawing pain.

tirelire [tirlir] *nf* money-box.

tirer [tire] *v* pull, draw; extract, get out, take from; (*fusil*) fire, shoot; (*imprimer*) print. **se tirer de** (*s'échapper*) get out of; (*se débrouiller*) handle, cope with. **tire-bouchon** *nm* corkscrew. **tirage** *nm* printing; (*journal*) circulation; edition; (*loterie*) draw.

tiroir [tirwar] *nm* drawer. **tiroir-caisse** *nm* till.

tisane [tizan] *nf* herb tea.

tisonner [tizɔne] *v* poke. **tisonnier** *nm* poker.

tisser [tise] *v* weave. **tissage** *nm* weaving.

tissu [tisy] *nm* cloth, fabric, material; (*bot, anat*) tissue.

titre [titrə] *nm* title; (*diplôme*) qualification; (*bourse*) bond, security; (*droit*) right, claim. **à ce titre** as such. **à titre de** as, in the capacity of.

tituber [titybe] *v* stagger.

toast [tost] *nm* toast.

toboggan [tɔbɔgɑ̃] *nm* toboggan; (*glissière*) slide, chute.

toi [twa] *pron* you. **toi-même** *pron* yourself.

toile [twal] *nf* cloth; (*grosse*) canvas; linen; cotton; (*araignée*) web. **toile cirée** oilskin. **toile de fond** backcloth, backdrop.

toilette [twalɛt] *nf* (*soins de propreté*) wash; (*habillement*) outfit, clothes *pl*. **toilettes** *nf pl* toilet *sing*.

toison [twazɔ̃] *nf* fleece.

toit [twa] *nm* roof.

Tokio [tɔkjo] *n* Tokyo.

tôle [tol] *nf* metal sheet. **tôle ondulée** corrugated iron.

tolérer [tɔlere] *v* tolerate; endure, stand. **tolérable** *adj* tolerable. **tolérance** *nf* tolerance, toleration. **tolérant** *adj* tolerant.

tomate [tɔmat] *nf* tomato.

tombe [tɔ̃b] *nf* grave, tomb. **tombeau** *nm* tomb.

tomber [tɔ̃be] *v* fall; (*baisser*) drop; (*pendre*) hang. **laisser tomber** drop. **tomber juste** be exactly right. **tomber sur** come across. **tombée** *nf* fall.

tome [tɔm] *nm* volume.

ton[1] [tɔ̃], **ta** *adj*, *pl* **tes** your.

ton[2] [tɔ̃] *nm* tone; (*hauteur*) pitch; (*échelle musicale*) key.

tondre [tɔ̃drə] *v* clip; (*mouton*) shear; (*pelouse*) mow. **tondeuse** *nf* shears *pl*; clippers *pl*; lawn-mower. **tondu** *adj* closely-cropped.

tonifier [tɔnifje] *v* tone up, invigorate. **tonifiant** *adj* invigorating, bracing.

tonique [tɔnik] *nm* tonic. *nf* (*musique*) tonic.

tonne [tɔn] *nf* ton.

tonneau [tɔno] *nm* barrel.

tonner [tɔne] *v* thunder. **tonnerre** *nm* thunder.

topaze [tɔpaz] *nf* topaz.

toper [tɔpe] *v* agree. **tope-là!** (*fam*) it's a deal!

topographie [tɔpɔgrafi] *nf* topography. **topographique** *adj* topographical.

torche [tɔrʃ] *nf* torch.

torcher [tɔrʃe] *v* (*fam*) wipe.

torchon [tɔrʃɔ̃] *nm* cloth; (*à vaisselle*) tea towel; (*chiffon*) duster.

tordre [tɔrdrə] *v* twist; (*linge, cou*) wring; (*déformer*) distort. **se tordre de douleur/rire** be doubled up with pain/laughter. **tordu** *adj* twisted, crooked.

tornade [tɔrnad] *nf* tornado.

torpille [tɔrpij] *nf* torpedo. **torpiller** *v* torpedo.

torréfier [tɔrefje] *v* roast.

torrent [tɔrɑ̃] *nm* torrent. **torrentiel** *adj* torrential.

tors [tɔr] *adj* twisted, crooked.

torse [tɔrs] *nm* torso; (*poitrine*) chest.

tort [tɔr] *nm* wrong; fault; (*dommage*) harm. **à tort** wrongly. **avoir tort** be wrong.

torticolis [tɔrtikɔli] *nm* stiff neck.

tortiller [tɔrtije] *v* twist; (*cheveux, doigts*) twiddle; (*hanches*) wiggle. **se tortiller** wriggle; (*fumée*) curl.

tortue [tɔrty] *nf* tortoise. **tortue de mer** turtle.

tortueux [tɔrtɥø] *adj* (*chemin, etc.*) twisting, winding; (*oblique*) tortuous.

torturer [tɔrtyre] *v* torture. **torture** *nf* torture.

tôt [to] *adv* early, soon. **tôt ou tard** sooner or later.

total [tɔtal] *adj* total; complete, absolute. *nm* total. **totaliser** *v* total. **totalitaire** *adj* totalitarian. **totalité** *nf* whole. **la totalité de** all (of).

toucher [tuʃe] *v* touch; concern, affect; (*être contigu*) adjoin; (*frapper*) hit; contact, reach; (*pension, etc.*) draw; (*chèque*) cash; (*salaire*) get. **toucher à** touch; (*modifier*) meddle with; approach. *nm* touch. **touche** *nf* touch; (*piano*) key.

touffe [tuf] *nf* tuft; (*arbres, fleurs*) clump. **touffu** *adj* bushy, thick; (*roman*) complex.

toujours [tuʒur] *adv* always; (*encore*) still; (*en tout cas*) anyway.

toupet [tupɛ] *nm* (*cheveux*) quiff; (*fam*) nerve, cheek.

toupie [tupi] *nf* spinning-top.

tour[1] [tur] *nf* tower.

tour[2] [tur] *nm* turn; (*excursion*) trip; (*tourisme*) tour; (*poitrine, taille, etc.*) measurement; (*farce, ruse*) trick; (*tech*) lathe. **à tour de rôle** in turn. **faire le tour de** go round. **tour de main** knack. **tour de piste** lap.

tourbe [turb] *nf* peat.

tourbillon [turbijɔ̃] *nm* (*vent*) whirlwind; (*eau*) whirlpool; (*vie, plaisir, etc.*) whirl. **tourbillonner** *v* whirl, swirl.

tourelle [turɛl] *nf* turret.

tourisme [turismə] *nm* (*industrie*) tourism; (*activité*) sightseeing. **touriste** *n(m+f)* tourist. **touristique** *adj* tourist.

tourment [turmɑ̃] *nm* agony, torment. **tourmenter** *v* torment. **se tourmenter** fret, worry.

tourmente [turmɑ̃t] *nf* storm; (*pol*) upheaval.

tournant [turnɑ̃] *adj* (*pivotant*) revolving, swivel; (*escalier*) spiral; (*sinueux*) winding, twisting. *nm* bend; (*moment décisif*) turning point.

tourner [turne] *v* turn; (*film*) make, shoot; (*lait*) turn sour; (*disque, etc.*) revolve, go round; (*moteur*) run. **bien/mal tourner** turn out well/badly. **tourne-disque** *nm* record player. **tournevis** *nm* screwdriver. **tournée** *nf* round; tour.

tournesol [turnəsɔl] *nm* sunflower.

tourniquet [turnikɛ] *nm* (*barrière*) turnstile; (*méd*) tourniquet.

tournoi [turnwa] *nm* tournament.

tournoyer [turnwaje] *v* whirl, swirl.

tournure [turnyr] *nf* turn; turn of phrase; (*apparence*) shape, face.

tourte [turt] *nf* pie.

tourterelle [turtərɛl] *nf* turtle-dove.

Toussaint [tusɛ̃] *nf* All Saints' Day.

tousser [tuse] *v* cough.

tout [tu], **toute** *adj*, *pl* **tous**, **toutes** all; (*chaque*) every; (*n'importe quel*) any; (*total*) utmost, full. **de toute façon** in any case. **tous les deux** both. **tous risques** (*assurance*) fully comprehensive. *pron* everything, all. *nm* whole. **du tout** at all. **pas du tout** not at all. *adv* quite, completely; (*très*) very; (*quoique*) though, however. **tout à coup** suddenly. **tout à fait** quite, entirely. **tout à l'heure** (*futur*) presently; (*passé*) just now. **tout au plus/moins** at the very most/least. **tout de même** all the same. **tout de suite** at once. **tout en ...** while ... . **tout fait** ready-made. **tout neuf** brand new. **tout-puissant** *adj* omnipotent.

toutefois [tutfwa] *adv* however.

toux [tu] *nf* cough.

toxique [tɔksik] *adj* toxic.

trac [trak] *nm* fit of nerves; (*théâtre*) stage fright.

tracas [traka] *nm* worry, bother. **tracasser** *v* worry, bother.

trace [tras] *nf* trace; mark, sign; (*chemin*) track, path; (*empreinte*) tracks *pl*, trail. **suivre à la trace** track.

tracer [trase] *v* trace, draw; (*chemin*) mark out.

tract [trakt] *nm* pamphlet.

tracteur [traktœr] *nm* tractor.

tradition [tradisjɔ̃] *nf* tradition. **traditionnel** *adj* traditional.

*****traduire** [tradᵁir] *v* translate; express, convey. **traducteur, -trice** *nm, nf* translator. **traduction** *nf* translation.

trafic [trafik] *nm* traffic; (*péj*) dealings *pl.* **trafiquer** *v* traffic, trade illicitly.

tragédie [traʒedi] *nf* tragedy. **tragique** *adj* tragic.

trahir [trair] *v* betray; (*forces, etc.*) fail; (*mal exprimer*) misrepresent. **trahison** *nf* betrayal; (*crime*) treason.

train [trɛ̃] *nm* train; (*allure*) pace; (*file*) line. **en train** under way. **être en train de** be in the middle of.

train-train *nm* daily routine.

traîner [trene] *v* drag; (*mots*) drawl; (*s'attarder*) dawdle, lag behind; (*pendre*) trail; (*s'éterniser*) drag on; (*être éparpillé*) lie around. **se traîner** drag oneself, crawl. **traîneau** *nm* sledge, sleigh. **traînée** *nf* streak; (*trace*) trail.

*****traire** [trɛr] *v* milk.

trait [trɛ] *nm* line; (*caractéristique*) trait; (*visage*) feature; (*de lumière, satire, etc.*) shaft; (*gorgée*) gulp. **d'un trait** at one go. **trait d'union** hyphen.

traiter [trete] *v* treat; (*qualifier*) call; (*s'occuper de*) deal with; (*négocier*) have dealings. **traité** *nm* (*convention*) treaty; (*livre*) treatise. **traitement** *nm* treatment; salary.

traître, -esse [trɛtrə, -ɛs] *adj* treacherous. *nm, nf* traitor. **traîtrise** *nf* treachery.

trajet [traʒɛ] *nm* (*voyage*) journey; distance.

trame [tram] *nf* (*tissu*) thread; (*vie*) texture, web. **tramer** *v* (*combiner*) plot; (*tisser*) weave.

tramway [tramwɛ] *nm* tram.

tranchant [trɑ̃ʃɑ̃] *adj* sharp; (*personne*) assertive. *nm* cutting edge.

trancher [trɑ̃ʃe] *v* cut, sever; resolve, settle; contrast sharply. **tranche** *nf* slice; section; (*bord*) edge. **tranché** *adj* clearcut, distinct. **tranchée** *nf* trench.

tranquille [trɑ̃kil] *adj* quiet; calm, peaceful; (*esprit*) easy, at rest. **laisser tranquille** leave alone. **tranquillisant** *nm* tranquilizer. **tranquilliser** *v* reassure. **tranquillité** *nf* peace, tranquillity.

transaction [trɑ̃zaksjɔ̃] *nf* transaction; compromise.

transatlantique [trɑ̃zatlɑ̃tik] *adj* transatlantic. *nm* (*chaise*) deckchair.

transcender [trɑ̃sɑ̃de] *v* transcend. **transcendantal** *adj* transcendental.

*****transcrire** [trɑ̃skrir] *v* transcribe; copy out. **transcription** *nf* transcription; copy.

transe [trɑ̃s] *nf* trance. **transes** *nf pl* agony *sing.*

transept [trɑ̃sɛpt] *nm* transept.

transférer [trɑ̃sfere] *v* transfer. **transfert** *nm* transfer.

transformer [trɑ̃sfɔrme] *v* change, alter; (*radicalement*) transform; convert. **transformateur** *nm* transformer. **transformation** *nf* change; transformation; conversion.

transfuge [trɑ̃sfyʒ] *n(m+f)* renegade.

transfuser [trɑ̃sfyze] *v* transfuse. **transfusion** *nf* transfusion.

transiger [trɑ̃ziʒe] *v* come to an agreement, compromise.

transir [trɑ̃zir] *v* numb; (*froid*) chill to the bone; (*peur*) transfix. **transi** *adj* numb with cold; transfixed with fear.

transistor [trɑ̃zistɔr] *nm* transistor. **transistoriser** *v* transistorize.

transit [trɑ̃zit] *nm* transit. **en transit** in transit.

transitif [trɑ̃zitif] *adj* transitive.

transition [trɑ̃zisjɔ̃] *nf* transition. **de transition** transitional.

transitoire [trɑ̃zitwar] *adj* transient, transitory; provisional.

translucide [trɑ̃slysid] *adj* translucent. **translucidité** *nf* translucence.

*****transmettre** [trɑ̃smɛtrə] *v* pass on; (*tech*) transmit. **transmetteur** *nm* transmitter. **transmission** *nf* transmission.

transparent [trɑ̃sparɑ̃] *adj* transparent.

transpirer [trɑ̃spire] *v* sweat, perspire; (*secret*) come to light. **transpiration** *nf* perspiration.

transplanter [trɑ̃splɑ̃te] *v* transplant. **transplantation** *nf* transplant.

transport [trɑ̃spɔr] *nm* transport; (*marchandises*) carriage, transportation. **transporter** *v* carry, convey; (*avec un véhicule*) transport; (*exalter*) carry away.

transposer [trɑ̃spoze] *v* transpose. **transposition** *nf* transposition.

transvaser [trɑ̃svɑze] *v* decant.

transversal [trɑ̃svɛrsal] *adj* transverse.
trapèze [trapɛz] *nm* (*sport*) trapeze; (*géom*) trapezium. **trapéziste** *n(m + f)* trapeze artist.
trappe [trap] *nf* trapdoor.
trapu [trapy] *adj* squat, stocky.
traquer [trake] *v* track (down), hunt (out); (*harceler*) hound. **traquenard** *nm* trap; (*embûche*) pitfall.
trauma [troma] *nm* trauma. **traumatique** *adj* traumatic. **traumatisant** *adj* traumatic. **traumatisme** *nm* trauma.
travail [travaj] *nm, pl* -aux work; (*métier, tâche*) job; (*méd, ouvriers*) labour. **travaux d'aiguille** needlework *sing*.
travailler [travaje] *v* work; (*vin*) ferment; (*exercer*) practise, work at; (*agir sur*) work on; torment, distract. **travaillé** *adj* (*style*) polished; (*ornement*) intricate; (*façonné*) wrought.
travailleur, -euse [travajœr, -øz] *adj* hard-working. *nm, nf* worker.
travailliste [travajist] *adj* Labour. *n(m + f)* member of the Labour party. **les travaillistes** *nm pl* Labour *sing*.
travers [travɛr] *nm* failing, fault. **à travers** (*milieu*) through; (*surface*) across. **au travers** through. **de travers** (*pas droit*) crooked; (*mal*) wrong. **en travers** across.
traverser [travɛrse] *v* (*surface*) cross; (*milieu*) go through. **traverse** *nf* (*rail*) sleeper; (*tech*) strut, cross-piece. **traversée** *nf* crossing.
traversin [travɛrsɛ̃] *nm* bolster.
travestir [travɛstir] *v* dress up; (*vérité*) misrepresent. **se travestir** (*bal*) put on fancy dress; (*cabaret, psych*) dress up as a woman.
travesti [travɛsti], -e *adj* disguised; (*bal*) fancy-dress. *nm* fancy dress; (*cabaret*) drag artist. *nm, nf* (*psych*) transvestite.
trébucher [trebyʃe] *v* stumble. **faire trébucher** trip up. **trébuchant** *adj* staggering; (*voix*) halting.
trèfle [trɛflə] *nm* clover; (*cartes*) club.
treillis [treji] *nm* trellis, lattice. **treillis métallique** wire netting.
treize [trɛz] *nm, adj* thirteen. **treizième** *n(m + f), adj* thirteenth.
trembler [trɑ̃ble] *v* tremble, shake; (*de froid*) shiver; (*lumière*) flicker. **tremblement** *nm* tremble, tremor; shiver. **tremblement de terre** earthquake.
se trémousser [tremuse] *v* fidget, wriggle; (*se dandiner*) wiggle.

tremper [trɑ̃pe] *v* soak; (*plonger*) dip. **faire trempette** dunk one's bread *or* sugar.
tremplin [trɑ̃plɛ̃] *nm* spring-board; (*piscine*) diving-board.
trente [trɑ̃t] *nm, adj* thirty. **trentième** *n(m + f), adj* thirtieth.
trépas [trepa] *nm* death. **trépasser** *v* die, pass away.
trépider [trepide] *v* vibrate. **trépidation** *nf* vibration; (*agitation*) flurry.
trépied [trepje] *nm* tripod.
trépigner [trepiɲe] *v* stamp.
très [trɛ] *adv* very; (*devant un participe*) highly, very much.
trésor [trezɔr] *nm* treasure; (*source*) mine, wealth; (*endroit*) treasury; (*de l'état*) exchequer. **trésorerie** *nf* treasury; finances *pl*, funds *pl*. **trésorier, -ère** *nm, nf* treasurer.
*****tressaillir** [tresajir] *v* quiver; (*de peur*) shudder; (*de douleur*) wince; (*sursauter*) start; vibrate, shake. **tressaillement** *nm* quiver; shudder; start; vibration.
tresser [trese] *v* (*cheveux*) plait; (*guirlande*) weave; (*corde*) twist. **tresse** *nf* plait; (*cordon*) braid.
tréteau [treto] *nm* trestle.
treuil [trœj] *nm* winch.
trève [trɛv] *nf* (*mil, pol*) truce; respite. **sans trève** unceasingly, relentlessly.
tri [tri] *nm* sorting; selection. **faire le tri de** sort; select. **triage** *nm* sorting, selection.
triangle [trijɑ̃glə] *nm* triangle. **triangulaire** *adj* triangular.
tribord [tribɔr] *nm* starboard.
tribu [triby] *nf* tribe.
tribunal [tribynal] *nm* court, tribunal. **tribune** *nf* (*église*) gallery; (*stade*) stand; platform; (*journal, radio, etc.*) forum.
tribut [triby] *nm* tribute.
tributaire [tribytɛr] *adj* tributary.
tricher [triʃe] *v* cheat. **tricherie** *nf* cheating. **tricheur, -euse** *nm, nf* cheat.
tricot [triko] *nm* (*technique*) knitting; (*vêtement*) jumper. **tricot de corps** vest. **tricoter** *v* knit.
trictrac [triktrak] *nm* backgammon.
tricycle [trisiklə] *nm* tricycle.
trier [trije] *v* sort (out); select. **trier sur le volet** hand-pick.
trille [trij] *nm* trill. **triller** *v* trill.

trimballer [trɛ̃bale] v (fam) cart around.

trimestre [trimɛstrə] nm quarter; (école) term. **trimestriel** adj quarterly; end-of-term.

tringle [trɛ̃glə] nf rod.

trinquer [trɛ̃ke] v clink glasses.

trio [trijo] nm trio.

triompher [trijɔ̃fe] v triumph, win. **triompher de** overcome, conquer. **triomphant** adj triumphant. **triomphe** nm triumph.

tripes [trip] nf pl (cuisine) tripe sing; (fam) guts pl.

triple [triplə] adj triple, treble. nm **le triple** three times as much. **triplé, -e** nm, nf triplet. **tripler** v triple, treble.

tripoter [tripote] v fiddle with; (fouiller) rummage about; (affaire) be involved in.

triste [trist] adj sad, miserable; (sombre) dreary, dismal. **tristesse** nf sadness, sorrow; dreariness.

triton [tritɔ̃] nm newt.

trivial [trivjal] adj (grossier) coarse; (ordinaire) mundane. **trivialité** nf coarseness; coarse remark or detail; mundane nature.

troc [trɔk] nm exchange; (système économique) barter.

trognon [trɔɲɔ̃] nm core.

trois [trwa] nm, adj three. **à trois dimensions** three-dimensional. **trois-quarts** nm pl three quarters. **troisième** n(m+f), adj third.

trombe [trɔ̃b] nf (pluie) downpour; (tornade) whirlwind.

trombone [trɔ̃bɔn] nm trombone; (agrafe) paper-clip.

trompe [trɔ̃p] nf (éléphant) trunk; (musique) horn.

tromper [trɔ̃pe] v deceive; (par accident) mislead; (poursuivant) elude; (duper) fool, trick. **se tromper** be wrong, make a mistake. **tromperie** nf deception, deceit. **trompeur, -euse** adj (apparence) deceptive, misleading; (personne) deceitful.

trompette [trɔ̃pɛt] nf trumpet. **trompettiste** n(m+f) trumpeter.

tronc [trɔ̃] nm trunk.

tronçon [trɔ̃sɔ̃] nm section.

trône [tron] nm throne.

tronquer [trɔ̃ke] v truncate; (texte) cut down; (détails) cut out.

trop [tro] adv too, too much. **de trop** (quantité) too much; (nombre) too many; (importun) in the way. **trop de** too much; too many. **trop-plein** nm overflow. nm excess.

trophée [trɔfe] nm trophy.

tropique [trɔpik] nm tropic. **tropical** adj tropical.

troquer [trɔke] v exchange, swap; (transaction commerciale) barter.

trot [tro] nm trot; (souris) scamper. **trotter** v trot. **trottinette** nf scooter.

trottoir [trɔtwar] nm pavement.

trou [tru] nm hole; (vide) gap. **trou de serrure** keyhole. **trou d'homme** manhole.

trouble¹ [trublə] adj (eau) cloudy; (vue) blurred, misty; (affaire) shady.

trouble² [trublə] nm (agitation) turmoil; discord; embarrassment; (inquiétude) distress; (méd) disorder.

troubler [truble] v disturb, trouble; (eau) make cloudy. **se troubler** (personne) get flustered; (eau) become cloudy. **trouble-fête** n(m+f) invar spoilsport.

trouer [true] v make a hole in; pierce; (parsemer) dot. **trouée** nf gap; (mil) breach.

troupe [trup] nf (mil) troop; (chanteurs, etc.) troupe; band, group. **troupeau** nm herd; (moutons) flock.

trousse [trus] nf case, kit; (sac) bag. **trousseau** nm (clefs) bunch; (mariée) trousseau. **trousser** v truss.

trouver [truve] v find. **se trouver** be; (se sentir) feel; (arriver) happen. **trouvaille** nf find.

truc [tryk] nm trick; (fam: combine) knack; (fam: chose) thing; (fam: machin) whatsit, thingummy.

truelle [tryɛl] nf trowel.

truffe [tryf] nf truffle.

truie [trɥi] nf sow.

truite [trɥit] nf trout.

truquer [tryke] v rig, fix. **truquage** nm rigging, fixing; (cinéma) trick photography, special effects pl.

tsar [dzar] nm tsar.

tu [ty] pron you.

tuba [tyba] nm tuba.

tube [tyb] nm tube; pipe; (fam: chanson, disque) hit.

tuberculose [tybɛrkyloz] nf tuberculosis.

tuer [tɥe] v kill. **à tue-tête** at the top of one's voice. **tuerie** nf slaughter. **tueur, -euse** nm, nf killer.

tuile [tɥil] nf tile; (fam) blow.

tulipe [tylip] *nf* tulip.

tumeur [tymœr] *nf* tumour.

tumulte [tymylt] *nm* tumult, commotion. **tumultueux** *adj* turbulent, stormy.

tunique [tynik] *nf* tunic.

tunnel [tynɛl] *nm* tunnel.

turban [tyrbɑ̃] *nm* turban.

turbine [tyrbin] *nf* turbine.

turbot [tyrbo] *nm* turbot.

turbulent [tyrbylɑ̃] *adj* turbulent; (*agité*) boisterous, unruly. **turbulence** *nf* turbulence.

turf [tyrf] *nm* (*hippisme*) racing; (*terrain*) racecourse.

turquoise [tyrkwaz] *nf, adj invar* turquoise.

tutelle [tytɛl] *nf* (*surveillance*) supervision; protection; (*jur*) guardianship.

tuteur, -trice [tytœr, -tris] *nm, nf* guardian. *nm* stake.

tutoyer [tytwaje] *v* address as 'tu'. **tutoiement** *nm* use of the 'tu' form.

tuyau [tᵁijo] *nm* pipe; (*d'arrosage*) hose; (*fam*) tip. **tuyau d'échappement** exhaust pipe.

tympan [tɛ̃pɑ̃] *nm* eardrum.

type [tip] *nm* type; (*représentant*) classic example; (*fam*) bloke, chap.

typhoïde [tifɔid] *nf, adj* typhoid.

typhon [tifɔ̃] *nm* typhoon.

typique [tipik] *adj* typical.

tyran [tirɑ̃] *nm* tyrant. **tyrannie** *nf* tyranny. **tyrannique** *adj* tyrannical.

U

ulcérer [ylsere] *v* (*méd*) ulcerate; (*blesser*) wound, embitter. **ulcère** *nm* ulcer.

ultérieur, -e [ylterjœr] *adj* later, subsequent.

ultimatum [yltimatɔm] *nm* ultimatum.

ultime [yltim] *adj* ultimate, final.

ultrasonique [yltrasɔnik] *adj* ultrasonic.

ultraviolet, -ette [yltravjɔlɛ, -ɛt] *adj* ultraviolet.

un [œ̃], **une** *art* a, an. *n, adj, pron* one. **les uns** some. **l'un et l'autre** both. **l'un ou l'autre** either. **unième** *adj* first.

unanime [ynanim] *adj* unanimous. **unanimité** *nf* unanimity.

uni [yni] *adj* (*tissu, couleur*) plain; (*famille*) close; (*lisse*) smooth, even.

unifier [ynifje] *v* unify. **unification** *nf* unification.

uniforme [ynifɔrm] *adj* uniform; (*surface*) even. *nm* uniform. **uniformité** *nf* uniformity.

union [ynjɔ̃] *nf* union; association; combination.

unique [ynik] *adj* (*seul*) only; (*exceptionnel*) unique. **uniquement** *adv* only.

unir [ynir] *v* unite; combine; join. **unité** *nf* (*élément*) unit; (*cohésion*) unity.

unisexe [ynisɛks] *adj invar* unisex.

unisson [ynisɔ̃] *nm* unison. **à l'unisson** in unison.

univers [ynivɛr] *nm* universe. **universel** *adj* universal; (*outil*) all-purpose.

université [ynivɛrsite] *nf* university. **universitaire** *adj* university.

urbain [yrbɛ̃] *adj* urban, town. **urbanisme** *nm* town planning. **urbaniste** *n(m + f)* town planner.

urgent [yrʒɑ̃] *adj* urgent. **urgence** *nf* urgency; (*cas urgent*) emergency.

uriner [yrine] *v* urinate. **urine** *nf* urine. **urinoir** *nm* urinal.

urne [yrn] *nf* (*vase*) urn; (*pol*) ballot-box.

usage [yzaʒ] *nm* use; custom; (*gramm*) usage; (*politesse*) breeding. **usagé** *adj* (*usé*) worn, old, (*d'occasion*) second-hand, used.

user [yze] *v* wear out; (*consommer*) use. **user de** use, make use of. **usé** *adj* worn; (*banal*) hackneyed; (*râpé*) threadbare. **usure** *nf* wear.

usine [yzin] *nf* factory, works.

ustensile [ystɑ̃sil] *nm* implement; (*de cuisine*) utensil.

usuel [yzᵁɛl] *adj* common, everyday; (*d'usage*) usual.

usurper [yzyrpe] *v* usurp. **usurpateur, -trice** *nm, nf* usurper. **usurpation** *nf* usurpation.

utérus [yterys] *nm* womb, uterus.

utile [ytil] *adj* useful. **utilité** *nf* use, usefulness.

utiliser [ytilize] *v* use, utilize. **utilisable** *adj* usable.

V

vacance [vakɑ̃s] *nf* vacancy. **vacances** *nf pl* holiday *sing*, vacation *sing*. **en vacances** on holiday. **vacant** *adj* vacant.

vacarme [vakarm] *nm* din, row.

vaccin [vaksɛ̃] *nm* vaccine. **vaccination** *nf* vaccination. **vacciner** *v* vaccinate.

vache [vaʃ] *nf* cow; (*argot*) bitch, swine. *adj* (*argot*) rotten. **vachement** *adv* (*argot*) bloody.

vaciller [vasije] *v* wobble, sway; (*flamme*) flicker; (*courage*) falter, fail. **vacillant** *adj* unsteady; flickering; (*santé*) shaky; indecisive.

va-et-vient [vaevjɛ̃] *nm invar* comings and goings *pl*; (*mécanisme*) movement to and fro.

vagabond [vagabɔ̃], **-e** *adj* (*errant*) roaming, restless; (*nomade*) wandering. *nm, nf* tramp, vagrant. **vagabondage** *nm* wandering; vagrancy. **vagabonder** *v* roam, wander.

vagin [vaʒɛ̃] *nm* vagina. **vaginal** *adj* vaginal.

vague[1] [vag] *adj* vague. *nm* vagueness. **regarder dans le vague** stare into space.

vague[2] [vag] *nf* wave; (*montée*) surge. **vague de chaleur** heat wave.

vaillant [vajɑ̃] *adj* brave, valiant; vigorous, robust.

vain [vɛ̃] *adj* vain; empty, futile. **en vain** in vain.

***vaincre** [vɛ̃krə] *v* conquer, defeat, overcome.

vainqueur [vɛ̃kœr] *nm* conqueror; (*sport*) winner. *adj* victorious.

vaisseau [vɛso] *nm* vessel; (*naut*) ship.

vaisselle [vɛsɛl] *nf* crockery, dishes *pl*; (*lavage*) washing-up. **faire la vaisselle** wash up.

val [val] *nm* valley.

valable [valablə] *adj* valid; (*notable*) worthwhile.

valet [valɛ] *nm* servant, valet; (*cartes*) jack. **valet d'écurie** groom. **valet de ferme** farm-hand.

valeur [valœr] *nf* value; (*qualité*) worth. **de valeur** valuable. **mettre en valeur** exploit; (*détail*) bring out, highlight. **objets de valeur** *nm pl* valuables *pl*. **valeurs** *nf pl* (*bourse*) securities *pl*.

valide [valid] *adj* (*billet*) valid; (*personne*) fit; able-bodied. **validité** *nf* validity.

valise [valiz] *nf* suitcase.

vallée [vale] *nf* valley.

***valoir** [valwar] *v* be worth; be valid, apply; (*équivaloir à*) be as good as; (*causer*) bring, earn. **faire valoir** exploit; (*caractéristique*) bring out, highlight. **il vaut mieux** it is better. **valoir la peine** be worth it.

valse [vals] *nf* waltz. **valser** *v* waltz.

valve [valv] *nf* valve.

vampire [vɑ̃pir] *nm* vampire.

vandale [vɑ̃dal] *n(m+f)* vandal. **vandalisme** *nm* vandalism.

vanille [vanij] *nf* vanilla.

vanité [vanite] *nf* vanity, conceit; futility. **vaniteux** *adj* vain, conceited.

vanter [vɑ̃te] *v* praise. **se vanter** boast. **se vanter de** pride oneself on. **vantard** *adj* boastful. **vantardise** *nf* boasting, boastfulness; (*propos*) boast.

vapeur [vapœr] *nf* vapour, steam. **bateau à vapeur** *nm* steamer. **cuire à la vapeur** steam. **vaporiser** *v* (*parfum*) spray; (*phys*) vaporize.

varice [varis] *nf* varicose vein.

varicelle [varisɛl] *nf* chicken-pox.

varier [varje] *v* vary. **variable** *nf, adj* variable. **variante** *nf* variant. **variation** *nf* variation. **variété** *nf* variety.

variole [varjɔl] *nf* smallpox.

Varsovie [varsɔvi] *n* Warsaw.

vase[1] [vɑz] *nm* vase.

vase[2] [vɑz] *nf* mud, sludge.

vaste [vast] *adj* vast, immense.

Vatican [vatikɑ̃] *nm* Vatican.

vau [vo] *nm* **à vau-l'eau** with the current; (*projets, etc.*) down the drain. **aller à vau-l'eau** be on the road to ruin.

vaudou [vodu] *nm, adj invar* voodoo.

vaurien [vorjɛ̃], **-enne** *nm, nf* good-for-nothing.

vautour [votur] *nm* vulture.

se vautrer [votre] *v* sprawl. **se vautrer dans** wallow in.

veau [vo] *nm* calf; (*cuisine*) veal.

vedette [vədɛt] *nf* (*cinéma, etc.*) star; (*bateau*) launch.

végétal [veʒetal] *adj* plant, vegetable.

végétation [veʒetasjɔ̃] *nf* vegetation. **végétations adénoïdes** adenoids *pl*.

véhément [veemɑ̃] *adj* vehement. **véhémence** *nf* vehemence.

véhicule [veikyl] *nm* vehicle.

veille [vɛj] *nf* (*garde*) watch, vigil; (*jour précédent*) eve, day before; (*état*) wakefulness. **veillée** *nf* evening; (*mort*) watch. **veiller** *v* (*mort*, *malade*) sit up with, watch over; (*rester éveillé*) stay awake; be vigilant. **veiller à** attend to, see to. **veiller sur** watch over. **veilleuse** *nf* (*flamme*) pilot-light; (*lampe*) night-light.

veine [vɛn] *nf* vein; (*fam*) luck.

vélo [velo] *nm* (*fam*) bike.

vélocité [velɔsite] *nf* swiftness, nimbleness; (*vitesse*) velocity.

velours [vəlur] *nm* velvet. **velours côtelé** corduroy. **velouté** *adj* velvety, smooth.

velu [vəly] *adj* hairy.

venaison [vənɛzɔ̃] *nf* venison.

vendange [vɑ̃dɑ̃ʒ] *nf* grape harvest.

vendre [vɑ̃drə] *v* sell. **vendre la mèche** (*fam*) give the game away. **vendeur, -euse** *nm, nf* seller; (*magasin*) shop assistant.

vendredi [vɑ̃drədi] *nm* Friday. **vendredi saint** Good Friday.

vénéneux [venenø] *adj* poisonous.

vénérer [venere] *v* venerate, revere. **vénérable** *adj* venerable. **vénération** *nf* veneration.

vénérien [venerjɛ̃] *adj* venereal. **maladie vénérienne** venereal disease.

venger [vɑ̃ʒe] *v* avenge. **se venger** take one's revenge. **vengeance** *nf* vengeance, revenge.

venin [vənɛ̃] *nm* venom. **venimeux** *adj* venomous.

*****venir** [vənir] *v* come. **en venir à** come to, resort to. **faire venir** send for. **venir de** come from; (*suivi d'un infinitif*) have just.

vent [vɑ̃] *nm* wind. **dans le vent** (*fam*) trendy, fashionable. **il fait du vent** it is windy. **venteux** *adj* windswept.

vente [vɑ̃t] *nf* sale. **vente aux enchères** auction. **vente de charité** bazaar, jumble sale.

ventiler [vɑ̃tile] *v* ventilate. **ventilateur** *nm* fan, ventilator. **ventilation** *nf* ventilation.

ventouse [vɑ̃tuz] *nf* sucker, suction pad.

ventre [vɑ̃trə] *nm* stomach, belly.

ventriloque [vɑ̃trilɔk] *n(m+f)* ventriloquist.

venue [vəny] *nf* coming.

ver [vɛr] *nm* worm; (*larve*) grub; (*asticot*) maggot. **ver à soie** silkworm. **ver du bois** woodworm.

véranda [verɑ̃da] *nf* veranda.

verbe [vɛrb] *nm* verb. **verbal** *adj* verbal.

verdict [vɛrdikt] *nm* verdict.

verdir [vɛrdir] *v* turn green. **verdure** *nf* greenery.

verge [vɛrʒ] *nf* rod; penis.

verger [vɛrʒe] *nm* orchard.

verglas [vɛrgla] *nm* black ice.

vergogne [vɛrgɔɲ] *nf* shame.

véridique [veridik] *adj* truthful.

vérifier [verifje] *v* check, verify; (*comptes*) audit; confirm, prove. **vérification** *nf* check, verification; auditing; confirmation.

vérité [verite] *nf* truth; (*sincérité*) truthfulness. **véritable** *adj* real, true, genuine.

vermeil, -eille [vɛrmɛj] *adj* bright red.

vermine [vɛrmin] *nf* vermin.

vermouth [vɛrmut] *nm* vermouth.

vernaculaire [vɛrnakylɛr] *adj* vernacular.

vernir [vɛrnir] *v* varnish. **verni** *adj* varnished; (*luisant*) glossy. **cuir verni** patent leather. **vernis** *nm* varnish; (*poterie*) glaze; (*éclat*) gloss; (*apparence*) veneer. **vernis à ongles** nail varnish *or* polish. **vernisser** *v* glaze.

vérole [verɔl] *nf* **petite vérole** smallpox.

verre [vɛr] *nm* glass; (*optique*) lens; (*boisson*) drink. **verres de contact** contact lenses *pl*.

verrou [vɛru] *nm* bolt.

verrouiller [vɛruje] *v* bolt.

verrue [vɛry] *nf* wart.

vers¹ [vɛr] *prep* towards, to; (*approximation*) about, around.

vers² [vɛr] *nm* line. *nm pl* verse *sing*.

versant [vɛrsɑ̃] *nm* side, slope.

verse [vɛrs] *nf* **à verse** in torrents. **il pleut à verse** it is pouring down.

Verseau [vɛrso] *nm* Aquarius.

verser [vɛrse] *v* pour; (*sang, larmes*) shed; pay; (*basculer*) overturn. **versement** *nm* payment; (*échelonné*) instalment.

version [vɛrsjɔ̃] *nf* version; (*traduction*) translation.

verso [vɛrso] *nm* back.

vert [vɛr] *adj* green; (*fruit*) unripe; (*propos*) spicy. *nm* green.

vertèbre [vɛrtɛbrə] *nf* vertebra (*pl* -brae). **vertébral** *adj* vertebral. **vertébré** *nm, adj* vertebrate.

vertical [vɛrtikal] *adj* vertical. **verticale** *nf* vertical.

vertige [vɛrtiʒ] *nm* vertigo, dizziness. **avoir le vertige** feel dizzy. **pris de vertige** dizzy, giddy. **vertigineux** *adj* breathtaking; (*hauteur*) giddy.

vertu [vɛrty] nf virtue. vertueux adj virtuous.

verve [vɛrv] nf vigour, zest; eloquence.

vessie [vesi] nf bladder.

veste [vɛst] nf jacket.

vestiaire [vɛstjɛr] nm cloakroom; (piscine, etc.) changing-room.

vestibule [vɛstibyl] nm hall, vestibule.

vestige [vɛstiʒ] nm vestige, remnant, trace.

veston [vɛstɔ̃] nm jacket.

vêtement [vɛtmɑ̃] nm garment. vêtements nm pl clothes pl, clothing sing.

vétéran [veterɑ̃] nm veteran.

vétérinaire [veterinɛr] nm vet. adj veterinary.

vétille [vetij] nf trifle.

*vêtir [vetir] v clothe, dress. vêtu de wearing.

veto [veto] nm veto. mettre son veto à veto.

vétuste [vetyst] adj ancient, decrepit. vétusté nf age, decay.

veuf [vœf] adj widowed. nm widower. veuve nf widow. veuvage nm widowhood.

veule [vøl] adj spineless, weak.

vexer [vɛkse] v upset, hurt. vexant adj hurtful; (contrariant) annoying.

via [vja] prep via.

viable [vjablə] adj viable. viabilité nf viability; (chemin) practicability.

viaduc [vjadyk] nm viaduct.

viager [vjaʒe] adj for life.

viande [vjɑ̃d] nf meat.

vibrer [vibre] v vibrate; (voix) quiver. vibration nf vibration.

vicaire [vikɛr] nm curate.

vice [vis] nm vice; fault.

vice-chancelier nm vice-chancellor.

vice-consul nm vice-consul.

vice-président, -e nm, nf (état) vice-president; (réunion) vice-chairman.

vice versa [visevɛrsa] adv vice versa.

vicier [visje] v pollute, taint; (jur) invalidate.

vicieux [visjø] adj licentious, depraved; (animal) unruly; (fautif) incorrect.

vicomte [vikɔ̃t] nm viscount. vicomtesse nf viscountess.

victime [viktim] nf victim.

victoire [viktwar] nf victory. victorieux adj victorious.

vidange [vidɑ̃ʒ] nf emptying; (auto) oil change. vidanges nf pl sewage sing. vidanger v empty, drain.

vide [vid] adj empty; (disponible) vacant. nm emptiness; (espace) void; (sans air) vacuum; (creux) gap. vider v empty; (bassin, etc.) drain; (quitter) vacate; (cuisine) gut; (fam: épuiser) wear out; (fam: expulser) throw out.

vie [vi] nf life; (moyens) living.

vieil [vjɛj] form of vieux used before a vowel or mute h.

vieillir [vjejir] v age, grow old. vieillard nm old man. vieillesse nf old age.

Vienne [vjɛn] n Vienna.

vierge [vjɛrʒ] nf virgin. Vierge nf Virgo. adj (terre, etc.) virgin; (papier) blank.

vieux, vieille [vjø, vjɛj] adj old. vieille fille spinster. vieux jeu adj invar old-fashioned. nm old man. nf old woman.

vif [vif] adj lively; brusque; (aigu) sharp, keen; intense, vivid; (fort) strong, great; (froid) biting; (éclat) bright; (allure) brisk. nm quick.

vigile [viʒil] nf vigil. vigilance nf vigilance. vigilant adj vigilant.

vigne [viɲ] nf vine. vignoble nm vineyard.

vignette [viɲɛt] nf label; (auto) tax disc.

vigoureux [vigurø] adj vigorous; robust, sturdy.

vigueur [vigœr] nf vigour; (robustesse) sturdiness; (force) strength. entrer en vigueur come into effect. en vigueur in force, current.

vil [vil] adj vile, base.

vilain [vilɛ̃] adj nasty; (laid) ugly; (méchant) mean, wicked.

vilebrequin [vilbrəkɛ̃] nm (auto) crankshaft; (tech) brace.

villa [villa] nf villa, detached house.

village [vilaʒ] nm village. villageois, -e nm, nf villager.

ville [vil] nf town; (plus grande) city. ville d'eau spa.

villégiature [vileʒatyr] nf holiday; (lieu) holiday resort.

vin [vɛ̃] nm wine. grand vin vintage wine.

vinaigre [vinɛgrə] nm vinegar. vinaigrette nf French dressing, vinaigrette.

vindicatif [vɛ̃dikatif] adj vindictive.

vingt [vɛ̃] nm, adj twenty. vingtième n(m+f), adj twentieth.

vinyle [vinil] nm vinyl.

viol [vjɔl] nm rape.

violent [vjɔlɑ̃] adj violent; (effort) strenuous; (fort) strong, intense. violence nf violence.

violer [vjɔle] v violate; (femme) rape; (loi, promesse) break. **violation** nf violation.

violet, -ette [vjɔlɛ, -ɛt] adj purple, violet. nm purple. nf violet.

violon [vjɔlɔ̃] nm violin. **violoncelle** nm cello. **violoniste** n(m+f) violinist.

vipère [vipɛr] nf adder, viper.

virage [viraʒ] nm bend, turn.

virer [vire] v turn; change; (argent) transfer. **virement** nm transfer.

virginité [virʒinite] nf virginity.

virgule [virgyl] nf comma; (math) decimal point.

viril [viril] adj virile, manly; masculine. **virilité** nf virility.

virtuel [virtɥɛl] adj potential. **virtuellement** adv potentially; (pratiquement) virtually.

virus [virys] nm virus.

vis [vis] nf screw.

visa [viza] nm (passeport) visa; (timbre) stamp; (de censure) certificate.

visage [vizaʒ] nm face.

vis-à-vis [vizavi] adv opposite, face to face. nm en vis-à-vis opposite each other. prep vis-à-vis de opposite; (comparaison) beside, next to; (envers) towards.

viser [vize] v aim (at); (remarque) be directed at. **visée** nf aim; design.

visible [viziblə] adj visible; (évident) obvious. **visibilité** nf visibility.

visière [vizjɛr] nf (casquette) peak; (armure) visor.

vision [vizjɔ̃] nf vision; (faculté) eyesight. **visionnaire** n(m+f), adj visionary.

visiter [vizite] v visit; (ville, château) go round; examine; (fouiller) search. **visite** nf visit; tour; inspection, examination. **rendre visite à** visit, call on. **visiteur, -euse** nm, nf visitor.

vison [vizɔ̃] nm mink.

visser [vise] v screw down or on.

visuel [vizɥɛl] adj visual.

vital [vital] adj vital. **vitalité** nf vitality, energy.

vitamine [vitamin] nf vitamin.

vite [vit] adv fast, quickly; (tôt) soon. interj quick! **vitesse** nf speed; (auto) gear; velocity.

vitrer [vitre] v put glass in, glaze. **vitrail** nm, pl -aux stained-glass window. **vitre** nf pane of glass; (fenêtre) window. **vitrine** nf (magasin) shop-window; (armoire) display cabinet, glass case.

vivace [vivas] adj (plante) hardy; (foi, haine) undying. **vivacité** nf vivacity, liveliness; (éclat) brightness; (mordant) sharpness; intensity.

vivant [vivɑ̃] adj alive, living; (vivace) lively. nm living person; (vie) lifetime.

vivier [vivje] nm fish-pond.

vivifier [vivifje] v invigorate.

vivisection [vivisɛksjɔ̃] nf vivisection.

*****vivre** [vivrə] v live, be alive. **vive ... !** interj long live ... ! three cheers for ... ! **vivre de** live on. nm board. **vivres** nm pl provisions pl.

vocabulaire [vɔkabylɛr] nm vocabulary.

vocal [vɔkal] adj vocal.

vocation [vɔkasjɔ̃] nf vocation, calling.

vodka [vɔdka] nf vodka.

vœu [vø] nm (souhait) wish; (promesse) vow.

vogue [vɔg] nf fashion, vogue. **en vogue** fashionable.

voguer [vɔge] v sail; (pensées, etc.) drift.

voici [vwasi] prep (sing) here is, this is; (pl) here are, these are. **voici ... que** it is ... since. **voici une heure** an hour ago.

voie [vwa] nf way, road; (rail) track, line; (autoroute, etc.) lane. **voie d'eau** leak. **voie ferrée** railway line. **voie publique** public highway. **voie sans issue** no through road.

voilà [vwala] prep (sing) there is, that is; (pl) there are, those are. **voilà ... que** it is ... since. **voilà une heure** an hour ago.

voile¹ [vwal] nf sail; (sport) sailing. **voilier** nm sailing ship or boat.

voile² [vwal] nm veil; (tissu) net.

voiler [vwale] v veil, shroud. **se voiler** mist over, grow hazy.

*****voir** [vwar] v see. **aller voir** call on, visit. **faire voir** show. **n'avoir rien à voir avec** have nothing to do with. **se voir** show, be obvious.

voire [vwar] adv indeed.

voirie [vwari] nf (voies) highways pl; (entretien) highway maintenance; (enlèvement des ordures) refuse collection; (dépotoir) refuse dump.

voisin [vwazɛ̃], **-e** adj neighbouring; (adjacent) adjoining; (ressemblant) akin. nm, nf neighbour. **voisinage** nm neighbourhood; proximity.

voiture [vwatyr] nf car; (wagon) coach, carriage. **voiture d'enfant** pram.

voix [vwa] nf voice; (pol) vote. **à voix basse/haute** in a low/loud voice. **être sans voix** be speechless.

vol¹ [vɔl] *nm* flight. **à vol d'oiseau** as the crow flies. **vol à voile** gliding. **vol libre** hang-gliding.

vol² [vɔl] *nm* theft. **vol à l'étalage** shoplifting. **vol à main armée** armed robbery.

volaille [vɔlaj] *nf* poultry, fowl.

volant [vɔlɑ̃] *nm* (*auto*) steering wheel; (*tech*) flywheel; (*sport*) shuttlecock; (*robe*) flounce. *adj* flying.

volatil [vɔlatil] *adj* volatile.

volcan [vɔlkɑ̃] *nm* volcano. **volcanique** *adj* volcanic.

voler¹ [vɔle] *v* fly. **volée** *nf* flight; (*groupe*) flock, swarm; (*coups, sport*) volley.

voler² [vɔle] *v* (*chose*) steal; (*personne*) rob. **voleur, -euse** *nm, nf* thief. **au voleur!** stop thief!

volet [vɔlɛ] *nm* shutter; (*tech*) flap.

volière [vɔljɛr] *nf* aviary.

volontaire [vɔlɔ̃tɛr] *adj* voluntary; intentional; (*décidé*) headstrong, determined. *n(m+f)* volunteer.

volonté [vɔlɔ̃te] *nf* will; (*détermination*) willpower. **bonne volonté** goodwill, willingness. **volontiers** *adv* gladly, willingly.

volt [vɔlt] *nm* volt. **voltage** *nm* voltage.

volte-face [vɔltəfas] *nf invar* about-turn.

voltiger [vɔltiʒe] *v* flutter about.

volume [vɔlym] *nm* volume.

volupté [vɔlypte] *nf* sensual delight, voluptuousness. **voluptueux** *adj* voluptuous.

vomir [vɔmir] *v* vomit. **vomissement** *nm* vomiting; (*matière*) vomit.

vorace [vɔras] *adj* voracious. **voracité** *nf* voracity.

vos [vo] *V* votre.

voter [vɔte] *v* vote; (*loi*) pass. **vote** *nm* vote.

votre [vɔtrə] *adj, pl* vos your.

vôtre [votrə] *pron* le *or* la vôtre yours.

vouer [vwe] *v* (*promettre*) vow; (*consacrer*) devote; (*condamner*) doom.

✦vouloir [vulwar] *v* want; (*essayer*) try; require, need. **en vouloir à** have a grudge against. **vouloir bien** be willing. **vouloir dire** mean. *nm* will.

vous [vu] *pron* you, to you; (*réfléchi*) yourselves, each other. **vous-mêmes** *pron* yourselves.

voûter [vute] *v* arch. **voûte** *nf* vault, arch. **voûté** *adj* arched; (*personne*) stooped.

vouvoyer [vuvwaje] *v* address as 'vous'. **vouvoiement** *nm* use of the 'vous' form.

voyage [vwajaʒ] *nm* (*course*) journey, trip; (*action*) travel, travelling; (*par mer, d'exploration*) voyage. **voyage de noces** honeymoon. **voyage organisé** package tour. **voyager** *v* travel. **voyageur, -euse** *nm, nf* traveller; passenger.

voyant [vwajɑ̃] *adj* gaudy, garish.

voyelle [vwajɛl] *nf* vowel.

voyou [vwaju] *nm* hooligan, lout.

vrai [vrɛ] *adj* true; real. *nm* truth. **à vrai dire** to tell the truth, in actual fact. **pour de vrai** (*fam*) for real. **vraiment** *adv* really.

vraisemblable [vrɛsɑ̃blablə] *adj* likely, probable; (*histoire*) convincing, plausible. **vraisemblance** *nf* likelihood, probability; plausibility.

vrille [vrij] *nf* (*bot*) tendril; (*tech*) gimlet; spiral.

vrombir [vrɔ̃bir] *v* hum. **vrombissement** *nm* humming.

vu [vy] *adj* **bien vu** highly regarded. **mal vu** poorly thought of. *prep* in view of. *conj* **vu que** seeing that. **vue** *nf* view; (*sens, spectacle*) sight; (*projet*) plan, design.

vulgaire [vylgɛr] *adj* (*grossier*) vulgar; (*banal*) common. **vulgarité** *nf* vulgarity.

vulnérable [vylnerablə] *adj* vulnerable.

W

wagon [vagɔ̃] *nm* (*marchandises*) truck, wagon; (*voyageurs*) carriage. **wagon-lit** *nm* sleeping-car. **wagon-restaurant** *nm* restaurant-car.

watt [wat] *nm* watt.

week-end [wikɛnd] *nm* weekend.

western [wɛstɛrn] *nm* western.

whisky [wiski] *nm* whisky.

whist [wist] *nm* whist.

X

xénophobe [ksenɔfɔb] *adj* xenophobic.
n(m + f) xenophobe. **xénophobie** *nf* xenophobia.
xérès [gzerɛs] *nm* sherry.
xylophone [ksilɔfɔn] *nm* xylophone.

Y

y [i] *adv* there. *pron* it, about it, to it, in
it. **n'y être pour rien** have nothing to do
with it.
yacht [jɔt] *nm* yacht.
yaourt [jaurt] *nm* yoghurt.
yeux [jø] *V* œil.
yoga [jɔga] *nm* yoga.
Yougoslavie [jugɔslavi] *nf* Yugoslavia.
yougoslave *adj* Yugoslav, Yugoslavian.
Yougoslave *n(m + f)* Yugoslav.
youyou [juju] *nm* dinghy.
yo-yo [jojo] *nm invar* yo-yo.

Z

zèbre [zɛbrə] *nm* zebra. **zébrer** *v* stripe.
zébrure *nf* stripe; (*d'un coup*) weal.
zèle [zɛl] *nm* zeal. **zélé** *adj* zealous.
zéro [zero] *nm* zero, nought.
zeste [zɛst] *nm* peel, zest.
zézayer [zezeje] *v* lisp. **zézaiement** *nm*
lisp.
zibeline [ziblin] *nf* sable.
zigzag [zigzag] *nm* zigzag. **zigzaguer** *v* zigzag.
zinc [zɛ̃g] *nm* zinc; (*fam*) bar, counter.
zodiaque [zɔdjak] *nm* zodiac.
zone [zɔn] *nf* zone, area.
zoo [zoo] *nm* zoo.
zoologie [zɔɔlɔʒi] *nf* zoology. **zoologique**
adj zoological

Dictionaries from Hippocrene Books

Catalan-English/English-Catalan   Concise Dictionary
0451 ISBN 0-7818-0099-4 $8.95 paper

French-English/English-French   Practical Dictionary
0199 ISBN 0-88254-815-8 $6.95 paper

German-English/English-German   Practical Dictionary
0200 ISBN 0-88254-813-1 $6.95 paper

Hungarian-English/English-Hungarian Concise Dictionary:
with Complete Phonetics
0254 ISBN 0-87052-891-2 $7.95 paper

Irish-English/English-Irish   Dictionary   and Phrasebook
1037 ISBN 0-87052-110-1 $7.95 paper

Italian-English/English-Italian   Practical Dictionary
0201 ISBN 0-88254-816-6 $6.95 paper

Portugese-English/English-Portugese Dictionary
0477 ISBN 0-87052-980-3 $14.95 paper

Spanish Verbs: Ser and Estar
0292 ISBN 07818-0024-2 $8.95

Spanish Grammar
0273 ISBN 0-87052-893-9 $8.95

Spanish-English/English-Spanish Practical Dictionary
0211 ISBN 0-88254-814-X $6.95 paper
2064 ISBN 0-88254-905-7 $12.95 cloth

Spanish-English/English-Spanish Dictionary of Computer Terms
0036 ISBN 0-7818-0148-6 $16.95 cloth